Homelessness and Allocations

tenth edition

Andrew Arden QC founded Arden Chambers in 1993 to provide a centre for specialist practice, primarily in the area of housing law, together with local government and property. The set has been described in Chambers and Partners as 'a trailblazer ... extremely well-regarded and strong in its niche areas of local government, property and housing' and in Legal 500 as 'a pre-eminent set for housing law'.

Andrew Arden QC has appeared in many of the leading cases in housing law over the past 30 years. He is author or editor of the principal practitioner texts on housing law, including the *Encyclopaedia of Housing Law, Housing Law Reports, Journal of Housing Law, Arden & Partington's Housing Law, Local Government Constitutional and Administrative Law* (all Sweet & Maxwell), *Manual of Housing Law* and *Quiet Enjoyment* (LAG).

Justin Bates is a barrister and member of Arden Chambers. His practice covers all aspects of housing, property and local government law. Justin is the deputy general editor of the *Encyclopaedia of Housing Law*, a contributing editor to *Arden & Partington's Housing Law* and *Local Government Constitutional and Administrative Law* (all Sweet & Maxwell) and co-author of *Leasehold Disputes* (LAG).

Toby Vanhegan is a barrister and member of Arden Chambers specialising in housing law particularly homelessness, immigration and asylum, human rights and EU law. He has a particular knowledge and expertise in issues of eligibility, especially in the context of housing. Toby has written articles for *Journal of Housing Law* and *Legal Action* concerning freedom of movement of persons within the newly expanded EU. He speaks regularly at conferences and provides legal training courses.

Available as an ebook – with additional supplementary materials – at www.lag.org.uk/ebooks

LAG eBook

The purpose of the Legal Action Group is to promote equal access to justice for all members of society who are socially, economically or otherwise disadvantaged. To this end, it seeks to improve law and practice, the administration of justice and legal services.

HOMELESSNESS AND ALLOCATIONS (10TH ED)

Errata

Please note the following changes to the Housing Act 1997 Part 7 as reproduced in appendix A.

A corrected version of Parts 6 and 7 of the Housing Act 1996 is available as a pdf on the *Homelessness and Allocations* page of the LAG website at: www.lag.org.uk.

Section 193
Subs (3A) has been repealed.
Subs (7AA): remove words 'in a restricted case'.
Subss (7A)–(7E), (7F)(b) have been repealed.
Subs (12) should read:
In subsection (10) 'the appropriate authority'–
(a) in relation to local housing authorities in England, means the Secretary of State;
(b) in relation to local housing authorities in Wales, means the Welsh Ministers.

Section 195
Subs (3A) has been repealed.
Subs (4B): remove '(3A) to'.

Section 199
Subss (2), (3)(a) and (4) have been repealed.
Subs (5): remove word 'other'.

Homelessness and Allocations

A guide to the Housing Act 1996 Parts 6 and 7

TENTH EDITION

Andrew Arden QC, Justin Bates and
Toby Vanhegan

LAG the access to justice charity

Legal Action Group
2017

arden chambers

Tenth edition published in Great Britain 2017
by LAG Education and Service Trust Limited
National Pro Bono Centre, 48 Chancery Lane, London WC2A 1JF
www.lag.org.uk

First edition 1982 as *The Homeless Persons Act* by Andrew Arden
Second edition 1986 as *Homeless Persons* by Andrew Arden
Third edition 1988 as *Homeless Persons* by Andrew Arden
Fourth edition 1992 as *Homeless Persons* by Caroline Hunter and Siobhan McGrath
Fifth edition 1997 as *Homelessness & Allocations* by Andrew Arden QC and Caroline Hunter
Sixth edition 2002 by Andrew Arden QC and Caroline Hunter
Revised sixth edition 2003 by Andrew Arden QC and Caroline Hunter
Seventh edition 2006 by Andrew Arden QC and Caroline Hunter
Eighth edition 2010 by Andrew Arden QC, Emily Orme and Toby Vanhegan
Ninth edition 2012 by Andrew Arden QC, Emily Orme and Toby Vanhegan

British Library Cataloguing in Publication Data
a CIP catalogue record for this book is available from the British Library.

print ISBN 978 1 908407 92 4
ebook ISBN 978 1 908407 93 1

Typeset by Regent Typesetting, London
Printed in Great Britain by Hobbs the Printers, Totton, Hampshire

Preface

Quiet Enjoyment: protection from rogue landlords, 8th edn; *Manual of Housing Law*, 10th edn and *Homelessness and Allocations*, 10th edn

Background

For the first time, these three books are being published contemporaneously and by the same publisher.

Historically, the first of these books started life as *Housing: security and rent control*, in 1978, originally paired with *Housing: repairs and improvements*, by Tom Hadden (1979). Both were published by Sweet & Maxwell, as have been all subsequent editions of the *Manual of Housing Law* (as it became from the second edition in 1983, expanded to include the material in *Repairs and Improvements*). The first edition of *Quiet Enjoyment, remedies for harassment and illegal eviction*, co-authored with Martin Partington, was published by LAG, also in 1978, a booklet rather than a full-length book. The first edition of *Homelessness and Allocations*, under the title *The Homeless Persons Act*, followed from LAG in 1982. Over the years, I have been joined by a number of co-authors; there was a small number of editions of the LAG books which I did not write. Here I find myself, still writing them just shy of 40 years after they were first published, the books still in use.

Until the mid-1970s, the term 'housing law' was in scant use: it was a term applied to a sub-division of planning law and on occasion merited a mention in landlord and tenant or local government. The subject covered the powers and duties of local authorities, mainly in relation to slum clearance (by area or individual unit), the provision of public housing and related matters such as improvement grants. Reflecting the growth of legal aid, the introduction of law centres and the underlying social demand for rights, housing law began to develop in the early 1970s – largely through the pages of the *LAG Bulletin* (as *Legal Action* was then called) – bringing together all the law as it affected the use of a property as a home, whether derived from private rights or from the public powers and duties conferred or imposed on local authorities, whether formally identified as housing or because it impacted on housing in practice.

At that time, LAG did not publish many full-length books; hence the observation that *Quiet Enjoyment* was initially no more than a booklet. This was one reason why the *Manual* was published by Sweet & Maxwell, one of the two leading legal publishers. Sweet & Maxwell had, however, given the subject a further boost when, in the same year as the first edition of what became the *Manual* was published, it decided to expand the coverage of the *Encyclopaedia of Housing Law and Practice* to reflect the new vision of housing law.

The topics taken into the subject through the efforts of these two publishers included the Rent Acts (governing private sector security and harassment/illegal eviction), leasehold enfranchisement and extension, matrimonial law so far as it affected the family home on domestic breakdown, environmental health (statutory nuisance and other provisions affecting housing), social security, mobile homes, judicial review (enjoying its own period of unprecedented growth, itself in part a reflection of the same rise in rights awareness), as well as some planning law, compulsory purchase, conveyancing, landlord and tenant, contract and tort. Subsequent significant developments include the mass of law directly or indirectly reflecting policies on anti-social behaviour, much of it focused on housing, enhanced long leaseholder rights, human rights and the divergence of housing law as between England and Wales.

Sweet & Maxwell continues to publish the *Encyclopaedia*, along with the *Housing Law Reports*, the *Journal of Housing Law* and *Arden & Partington's Housing Law*; but for a change of direction in relation to titles such as the *Manual*, it would have remained in its list – regardless of legalities, it would not have been right to seek to move it after the publisher had done so much for the subject, as it continues to do through these other titles; and, while I am delighted both to bring the *Manual* 'home' to LAG and to be able to publish it as part of a discrete set, it would be wrong not to mark the departure by expressing my own gratitude for its support for the title over so many years.

Books

The three books have had different aims. Since the 1970s, the *Manual of Housing Law* has sought to provide a guide to housing law as described above, for a fairly wide array of interested individuals: the practitioner starting out in housing law; the non-specialist practitioner who needs occasional but ready access to the subject; lay advisers; students both of housing and of law; housing officers in local authorities and other social housing providers; environmental health officers working in housing; and, local councillors with a remit or interest in the subject.

Without claiming to describe all the detail of the subject, the intention has remained the same: to enable the reader to understand housing law as a whole, to know where to find it and to know how to apply it, whether to the problems of individuals or to the policies and practices of landlords and local authorities. This has been the essential approach to housing law as a subject: it exists not for its theory but to be applied.

While the focus of *Quiet Enjoyment* and *Homelessness and Allocations* has been on particular – and particularly important – aspects of the subject, that approach is also at their core, although their target audiences have been somewhat different, aimed primarily at actual and emerging specialist practitioners, specialist lay advisers and specialist officers in local authorities rather than students and others: the emphasis has nonetheless throughout been on practical application of the law. Hence, each of them contains specimen documentation to help the adviser bring cases into court as quickly as they usually need (although this did not arrive in *Homelessness and Allocations* until the seventh edition, the second one following the introduction of the right of appeal on a point of law to the county court by Housing Act 1996, before which it was uncommon for judicial review applications to be prepared by anyone other than relatively experienced public law counsel).

Status

It is this central approach of practical application which generated the proposition that the fundamental starting-point in relation to any housing law problem or discussion requires identification of the *status* of the occupier, which is to say the class of occupational right both at common law and under statute which determines the body of rights, duties and remedies to which the occupation is subject, without which the occupier's entitlements are unknown and, of as much importance, without which the implications are uncertain as to how a problem or other matter should be addressed so as to achieve the greatest gain in living conditions for the occupier while averting the worst consequences, in particular eviction and rent increases.

The number of statuses has long been a problem. Even during the 1970s, there were Rent Act protected and statutory tenancies subject to full and partial exceptions, furnished tenants, tenants with resident landlords, restricted contracts, tenants and licensees exempt from any protection, Rent (Agriculture) Act 1976 tenancies and licences for tied workers in agriculture and forestry, as well as residual controlled tenancies dating from before repeal of the previous security and rent regime in 1957. Moreover, there were housing association tenancies within rent regulation but outside security and other lettings wholly outside both, primarily local authority tenancies but also those from other bodies, such as New Town Development Corporations and the Crown.

The Housing Act 1980 introduced the secure tenancy for most public sector tenants – and licensees – as well as for those in the remainder of the social rented sector, ie housing associations and trusts, together with its own schedule of exceptions, full and qualified; at the same time, it sought to revivify the private rented sector by means, first, of new protected shorthold tenancies and, secondly, a class of new-build letting called assured tenancy, modelled on the security available to business tenants under the Landlord and Tenant Act 1954 Part 2, the latter of which attracted negligible interest. In addition, the 1980 Act brought tenants of the Crown into Rent Act security and rent control if the property was under the management of the Crown Estate Commissioners.

In 1988, the modern assured tenancy was introduced for the fully private sector as well as for housing association and trust tenants, together with assured shorthold tenancies and assured agricultural occupancies, again subject to their own exceptions; the regime also replaced the short-lived new-build 1980 Act predecessor of the same name. In 1996, introductory tenancies were added to the secure tenancy regime. Subsequent developments include demoted tenancies (from both secure and assured status) and family intervention tenancies. In 2011, the dawn of putative localism brought with it the flexible tenancy – in effect, a shorthold secure tenancy albeit for somewhat longer periods than usual in the private sector. The year 2016 brought the distinction between old (existing) secure tenancies and new secure tenancies (which are not secure at all), which is, as it were, still waiting at the platform for the government to set in motion.

I should add that, obviously, this reflects wholesale disregard in England for the Law Commission's *Renting Homes: The Final Report* (2006), the proposals by Martin Partington and his team, *inter alia* to reduce the number of available forms of rental occupation of residential property to two (standard contract and secure contract) and for model contract terms. These were, however, taken up by the Welsh Government, which accepted the recommendations (revisited in *Renting Homes: a better way for Wales*, May 2013) and enacted them in the Renting Homes (Wales) Act 2016, also yet to be brought into force.

As I wrote in the Introduction to the ninth edition of the *Manual*:

> ... [H]ousing law is a subject in a state of constant evolution (if not revolution) and, if this history is anything to go by, is probably destined so to remain. ... That makes it difficult to keep up with. Furthermore, law is rarely retrospective. Accordingly, one set of rules does not replace another, so much as two (or ten) sets co-exist for a period. And, as this is about where people live, that can commonly mean decades rather than years.

Concept, complexity and consistency

Although housing law's approach is practical rather than theoretical, that does not mean that there is no underlying concept: its *purpose* was to seek a housing focus for housing cases, however they were categorised in law, to ensure that decisions reflect awareness that what is in issue is someone's home, not merely property, local authority discretion or an abstract interpretation of statute. This is not to say that the subject is one that 'belongs' exclusively to occupiers, although there was undoubtedly a significant element in its origins which was intended to redress an historical imbalance; the idea was to ensure that all those involved in housing share that purpose as a common, guiding principle, not only to enhance the rights of occupiers but to help all the subject's 'clients' or 'constituents' better to understand how housing cases are likely to be treated in the courts and housing law itself is likely to develop.

The exponential growth in the number of statuses, this most fundamental aspect of housing law and its key structural foundation, has, however, posed a continuing problem in terms both of this purpose and of these books; it has complicated the subject and made it more and more difficult to understand, to write about and to apply, especially as tenancies can and do last for a very long time indeed and tenants may remain in the same accommodation not merely for years but for decades, which means that even law which ceased to apply to new tenancies 20–30 years ago may still be applicable to some older tenants (or their successors) and may still need to be considered. Moreover, old laws may sometimes remain applicable to a new tenancy granted to an existing tenant, in the same or different premises, to prevent tenants being talked into exchanging one set of rights for another, less favourable set.

Status is, however, not the only source of complexity and obfuscation. Central governments of all parties have micro-managed housing law, using it both as an economic tool, which may be expected, and as a political football, responding to populist perceptions without regard to its purpose: this has been particularly acute in the areas of immigration and anti-social behaviour. Given that it is only rarely, and only more recently, that this involves the removal of existing rights, this piles more and more layers of law on top of one another, so that rights turn not merely on status, but increasingly on when something occurred, eg the array of rules governing discharge of duty to homeless applicants depending on when an application was made. There is also something of a ping-pong between criminal and civil law: at points in time, functions which may properly be thought to belong to the criminal law – again, in particular in relation to anti-social behaviour – have been passed to local authorities and other social housing providers, while measures to tackle unlawful immigration have been handed out not only to those landlords but to all; at other times, functions which have historically been issues of civil law – eg trespass and unlawful sub-letting – have been criminalised.

Nor is it only governments who have lost sight of any central concept of housing law: courts have increasingly been led by so-called 'merits', that most subjective of approaches, without regard to the need to preserve any kind of over-arching principle or consistency of approach. Sometimes, this has been motivated by the best of intentions – to jettison archaic rules which are unacceptable in a more modern, human rights-oriented climate. Sometimes, it has been solely motivated by consideration of cost to the public purse. Sometimes, it has been motivated by a largely uninformed assumption as to what will advance the interests of housing. Sometimes, a return to abstract interpretation has countered the positive gains that a housing focus has otherwise achieved – for example in relation to the powers of local authorities to enforce standards in the (ever-increasing and much troubled) private sector.

This is not the place to pursue an analysis of these developments. While it has always been true that the outcome of very few cases has ever been capable of certain prediction, it is now the position, more widely than at any time I have known in my career as legal practitioner and writer, that how an issue will be determined by the courts depends predominantly upon who determines it and how the merits are perceived. Even leaving aside the effects of constant legislative change, this undermines consistency and increases the complexity of housing law. Sad to say, housing is being reduced to a set of detailed rules, not dissimilar to the intricacies of social security legislation, a subject with which it is increasingly coming to have in common an absence of access to qualified advice.

Current editions

This, then, is the climate in which these new editions are published and in which they have had to be re-considered. In earlier editions, chapter 1 of the *Manual* tied classes of occupation to their security of tenure, which is their first and foremost concern: by the last edition, the growth of statuses meant that this approach had become too unwieldy and it had proved necessary to separate class of occupation from security and eviction, a problem that further developments would have exacerbated. Moreover, a substantial chunk of *Quiet Enjoyment* – a subject to which status is critical – would need to be given over to describing the numerous different ways in which people occupy rented accommodation, adding to its length, even though much of its readership is sufficiently familiar with most of them not to need more than occasional reference to the issue. Aspects of homelessness law itself also depend on status: in particular, whether someone is homeless (defined in terms of rights of occupation) and whether someone is intentionally homeless (often turning on whether there was a right to remain in accommodation). It is also central to the new assessment and initial help duties which will come in with the Homelessness Reduction Act 2017.

As the books are now all under one roof and published together, it has been possible to introduce an element of rationalisation: status in *Quiet Enjoyment* now relies exclusively on the *Manual*, affording more space for the considerable body of new law which has emerged over the last few years to reflect the resurgence in private renting and to control the abuses to which it has given rise: I no more foresaw that *Quiet Enjoyment*, newly suffixed *Protection from rogue landlords*, would come back into its own any the more than I ever expected to see the term 'rogue landlords' enshrined in statute. *Homelessness and Allocations* also relies on the *Manual* for status where appropriate, as well as for other questions, eg whether a valid section 21 notice has been served on an assured shorthold tenant.

The *Manual* provides an introduction to the new laws protecting tenants from abuse; *Quiet Enjoyment* considers them in close detail. Both have been restructured. The *Manual*, as mentioned, had already separated out classes of occupation from security of tenure and eviction; in addition, protection from rogue landlords has now been separated out from anti-social behaviour, which is more largely about the conduct of occupiers. The *Manual* includes a wholly new chapter on mobile homes and houseboats, a subject which had slipped out of coverage but that needs to be brought back in as more and more people resort to them as a permanent home for want of being able to afford either owner-occupation or even renting. Naturally, the book continues coverage of rents, other rights (such as leasehold enfranchisement and right to buy), domestic breakdown, regulation of social landlords and housing conditions, including contract and tort, housing standards, environmental health, overcrowding, multiple occupation and licensing.

Quiet Enjoyment for the first time separates out eviction and harassment, as the law on the latter grows to reflect increased awareness of the many different ways that some people set out to distress others and seeks to protect victims. Mobile homes and houseboats are also afforded treatment. There are wholly new chapters on tenancy deposits, licensing of landlords, banning orders and a range of additional duties in respect of rented property many of which impact on a landlord's rights to take advantage of reduced security but which, in turn, may in practice give rise to additional unacceptable and unlawful conduct towards tenants when they are enforced, eg duties in relation to gas, fire, electricity and smoke alarms. As before, there are separate chapters on bringing civil and criminal proceedings, and the traditional collection of case reports on awards of damages is retained and updated, albeit now to be found in an appendix.

The *Manual* also outlines homelessness and allocations law, which *Homelessness and Allocations* addresses fully. The structure of the latter has not changed: an introduction to policy, an outline of the law, detailed consideration of the key concepts – eligibility, homelessness, priority need, intentionality, local connection, protection of property – followed by chapters on enquiries and decisions (including review), discharge of homelessness duties, allocations, enforcement by way of appeal to the county court and judicial review, other provisions to which recourse may need to be had in order to secure housing by way of social and child care provisions, strategy, practice, aid and advice, and criminal offences.

The two key changes since the last edition are the separate development of homelessness in Wales under the Housing (Wales) Act 2014 Part 2, and the Homelessness Reduction Act 2017, through which England adopted some of the changes which Wales had already introduced. The new duties in England include the extension from 28 days to 56 of the period during which a person is threatened with homelessness (dating, where appropriate and as qualified, from service of a valid notice under Housing Act 1988 s21), the introduction of a new assessment duty and consideration of support to ensure that applicants have or retain suitable accommodation, including reasonable steps to be taken by authorities to help applicants secure that accommodation does not cease to be available for their occupation, as well as a new initial duty requiring authorities to take reasonable steps for 56 days to help applicants to secure accommodation, regardless of whether they are in priority need. These developments have added to the increasing complexity of the subject and result in significant changes to chapter 10, on discharge.

Otherwise, the book continues the approach taken in previous editions so far as concerns the development of the law: every detail of homelessness and allocations law is recorded, analysed and applied; nothing which has gone before, however revised by the courts, has been wholly abandoned even if relegated to footnote or analysis reduced to reflect current lack of importance; nothing is divorced from its history and evolution. Experience has shown that cases come back again and again – as true as it may well be of other areas of law, homelessness and allocations have a marked tendency to shift with the winds: nothing is ever finally overruled or permanently irrelevant.

In addition to the structural changes and coverage of new law, in both England and Wales, the opportunity has been taken to reconsider the text of each book. Too often, later editions take for granted what has been written previously, focusing instead on the need to bring books up to date: these books have been no less guilty of this than others. It is not merely that it can leave text feeling stale so much as it can cause a loss of focus or even coherence: the branches can so change the tree that it is not the same picture at all. I have therefore undertaken a line by line – and paragraph by paragraph – revision which I hope will recover some of the freshness which I strove to achieve 'back in the day'.

I extend my thanks to my co-authors, to LAG and, in particular, our publisher Esther Pilger, as well as to colleagues in Chambers and on other publications with which I am associated, and, as always, to my very long-standing writing partners – and friends – Professors Martin Partington CBE, QC (Hon) and Caroline Hunter. My wife and daughter have suffered the stresses and strains of my legal writing – including these books – for far too long for either thanks or apology to make up for what it has cost them. Finally, I should like to dedicate this set of books to the late Pat Reddin, since the early

1970s the go-to housing surveyor of choice in housing disrepair cases both for tenants and for social landlords, who died in April 2015: he is missed both as professional colleague and close friend over the whole of the time-span I have been discussing in this Preface; he remains uppermost in my thoughts and emotions.

The law is predominantly stated as at 30 April 2017, although it has been possible to add a small number of subsequent amendments during the publication process. Two key developments which were due prior to the General Election, which these books have therefore been unable to accommodate, are: the commencement of the Homelessness Reduction Act 2017 (for which no date had been set); and, the introduction of banning orders under the Housing and Planning Act 2016 ss14 and 15 (which had been expected to be implemented from 1 October 2017), although the provisions of each have been fully described so far as available.

Andrew Arden QC
Arden Chambers
London

21 May 2017

Contents

Preface v
Table of cases xix
Table of statutes lxiii
Table of statutory instruments lxxxvii
Table of international conventions ci
Table of European legislation ciii
Abbreviations cvii

1 The policy of the provisions 1
Introduction 3
National Assistance Act 1948 4
Housing (Homeless Persons) Act 1977; Housing Act 1985 Part 3 8
Re Puhlhofer 14
Housing and Planning Act 1986 17
Asylum and Immigration Appeals Act 1993 18
Ex p Awua 18
Housing Act 1996 Parts 6 and 7 19
Between Acts 25
Homelessness Act 2002 28
Changes following the Homelessness Act 2002 31
Localism Act 2011 33
Housing (Wales) Act 2014 36
Homelessness Reduction Act 2017 38

2 The provisions in outline 41
Introduction 43
Definitions 46

3 Immigration 105
Introduction 106
Immigration control 110
Eligibility – homelessness: Housing Act 1996 Part 7 and Housing (Wales) Act 2014 Part 2 152
Eligibility – allocations: Housing Act 1996 Part 6 168

4 Homelessness 173
Introduction 175
Accommodation 175
Accommodation available for occupation 178
Rights of occupation 183
Restriction on entry or use 189
Reasonable to continue to occupy 191
Threatened with homelessness 209

5 Priority need 211
Introduction 213
Immigration 215
Pregnancy 216
Dependent children 217
Vulnerability 222
Emergency 231
Other categories 232

6 Intentional homelessness 241
Introduction 243
Principal definition 244
Deliberate act or omission 249
In consequence 265
Cessation of occupation 278
Available for occupation 279
Reasonable to continue to occupy 280
Extended definition – collusive arrangements 281

7 Local connection 283
Introduction 284
What is a local connection? 286
When are the local connection provisions applicable? 295
Procedure on prospective reference 301
Resolution of disputes 305
Post-resolution procedure 310

8 Protection of property 313
Introduction 314
To whom is a duty owed? 314
When is the duty owed? 315
What is the duty? 316
The power to protect property 318
Notification of cessation of responsibility 319

9 Homelessness decisions 321
Introduction 323
Applications 325
Enquiries 338
Decisions 362
Review 368
Review procedure 372

10 Discharge of homelessness duties 385
Introduction 387
Accommodation pending decision 389
Accommodation pending review 397
Assessment and plan 400
Duties to those threatened with homelessness 404
Initial help duty 409
Other duties without priority need 415
Other duties to the intentionally homeless 419
Duties where local connection referral 425
Other duties towards the unintentionally homeless in priority need 425

11 Allocations 465
Introduction 467
Meaning of 'allocation' 469
Eligibility and qualification 472
Applications for housing 486
The allocation scheme 487
Procedure 500
Internal review and challenge 505
Allocations by private registered providers of social housing (England) and registered social landlords (Wales) 506

12 Enforcement 513
Introduction 514
Substantive law 514
Procedural law 556
Annex: Specimen documents 602

13 Other statutory provisions 637
Introduction 638
Care Act 2014/Social Services and Well-being (Wales) Act 2014 639
Immigration and Asylum Act 1999 648
Children Act 1989/Social Services and Well-being (Wales) Act 2014 653

Local Government Act 2000/Localism Act 2011 673
Other statutory provisions 676

14 Strategy, practice, aid and advice 677
Introduction 678
Homelessness strategies 678
Provision of advisory services 685
Aid to voluntary organisations 689

15 Criminal offences 691
Introduction 692
Making a false statement 692
Withholding information 693
Failure to notify changes 694

APPENDICES

A Statutes 699

B Statutory instruments 771

C Guidance 793

Index 1073

Table of cases

A (children) (abduction: interim powers), *Re, sub nom* EA v GA [2010] EWCA Civ 586, [2011] Fam 179, [2011] 2 WLR 1269	13.98
A and others v Secretary of State for the Home Department, X and another v Secretary of State for the Home Department [2004] UKHL 56, [2005] 2 AC 68	12.27
A Barrister (Wasted Costs Order), *Re* [1993] QB 293, CA	12.184
A Barrister (Wasted Costs Order) (No 1 of 1991), *Re* [1992] 3 All ER 429, CA	12.182
A Solicitor (Wasted Costs Order), *Re* [1993] 2 FLR 959, CA	12.186
AA v Southwark LBC [2014] EWHC 500 (QB)	12.216
AG Securities v Vaughan, Antoniades v Villiers [1990] AC 417, (1988) 21 HLR 79, HL	4.44
AM (Somalia) v Entry Clearance Officer [2009] EWCA Civ 634, [2009] UKHRR 1073	9.19, 11.40
Aadan v Brent LBC (2000) 32 HLR 848, CA	12.166
Abdi v Barnet LBC and First Secretary of State; Ismail v Barnet LBC and First Secretary of State [2006] EWCA Civ 383, [2006] HLR 23	3.17
Abdirahman v Secretary of State for Work and Pensions [2007] EWCA Civ 657, [2008] 1 WLR 254, [2007] 4 All ER 882	3.17
Abdullah v Westminster City Council [2007] EWCA Civ 1566, [2007] JHL D89	10.173
Abdullah v Westminster City Council [2011] EWCA Civ 1171, [2012] HLR 5	4.56
Adan v Newham LBC [2001] EWCA Civ 1916, [2002] HLR 28	12.33, 12.35
Ahmad v Secretary of State for the Home Department [2014] EWCA Civ 988, [2015] 1 WLR 593	3.41
Ahmed v Leicester City Council [2007] EWCA Civ 843, [2008] HLR 6	4.78, 10.193
Ahmed v Secretary of State for the Home Department [2013] UKUT 89 (IAC) 538, [2013] Imm AR	3.97
Ahmed v Secretary of State for the Home Department [2017] EWCA Civ 99	3.59
Ajilore v LB Hackney [2014] EWCA Civ 1273, [2014] HLR 46	5.33

Akerman-Livingstone v Aster Communities Ltd (formerly Flourish Homes Ltd) [2015] UKSC 15, [2015] HLR 20	10.18
Akhtar v Birmingham City Council [2011] EWCA Civ 383, [2011] HLR 28	9.196, 10.19
Akinbolu v Hackney LBC (1996) 29 HLR 259, CA	3.163, 3.164, 3.165
Al-ameri v Kensington and Chelsea RLBC; Osmani v Harrow LBC [2004] UKHL 4, [2004] HLR 20	1.109, 7.19, 7.33
Alarape and another (article 12, EC Reg 1612/68) Nigeria [2011] UKUT 413 (IAC)	3.86
Alarape and Tijani v Secretary of State for the Home Department and AIRE Centre, Case C-529/11 [2013] 1 WLR 2883, [2013] 3 CMLR 38	3.86
Alghile v Westminster City Council [2001] EWCA Civ 363, (2001) 33 HLR 57	9.158, 10.218, 12.112
Ali v Birmingham City Council [2010] UKSC 8, [2010] HLR 22	9.174, 12.5, 12.28, 12.36, 12.64, 12.96, 12.97, 12.98
Ali v Birmingham City Council; Ibrahim v Same; Tomlinson v Same, Case C-310/08 [2008] EWCA Civ 1228, [2009] 2 All ER 501	3.83
Ali v Newham LBC [2002] HLR 20, CA	12.219
Ali v Secretary of State for the Home Department [2006] EWCA Civ 484	3.23
Ali v United Kingdom, App No 40378/10 (2016) 63 EHRR 20, [2015] HLR 46, ECtHR	9.174, 12.28, 12.97, 12.98
Ali v Westminster City Council (1998) 31 HLR 349, CA	12.197
Ali (Mohram) v Tower Hamlets LBC [1993] QB 407, (19920 24 HLR 474, CA	12.216
Allen v Jambo Holdings Ltd [1980] 1 WLR 1252, CA	12.145
American Cyanamid v Ethicon [1975] AC 396, HL	12.144
Anisminic Ltd v Foreign Compensation Commission [1969] 2 AC 147, HL	12.19, 12.34
Arthur JS Hall & Co (a firm) v Simons [2002] 1 AC 615, HL	12.183, 12.184
Aslam v South Bedfordshire DC [2001] EWCA Civ 514, [2001] RVR 65	12.37
Associated Provincial Picture Houses Ltd v Wednesbury Corp [1948] 1 KB 223, CA	1.53, 4.34, 9.45, 9.62, 10.11, 10.138, 10.167, 11.100, 12.12, 12.13, 12.15, 12.19, 12.20, 12.21, 12.22, 12.24, 12.25, 12.26, 12.27, 12.29, 12.30, 12.32, 12.52, 12.53, 12.137, 12.234

Aston Cantlow and Wilmcote with Billisley Parochial Church Council v Wallbank [2003] UKHL 37, [2004] 1 AC 546	11.121
Attorney-General v News Group Newspapers Ltd [1987] QB 1, CA	12.201
Attorney-General, *ex rel* Tilley v Wandsworth LBC [1981] 1 WLR 854, CA	4.65
Aurelio de Brito and Lizette de Noronha v Secretary of State for the Home Department [2012] EWCA Civ 709	3.35
Avon CC v Buscott [1988] QB 656, CA	12.16
Aw-Aden v Birmingham City Council [2005] EWCA Civ 1834	6.29, 6.37, 9.176, 12.160
Azimi v Newham LBC (2000) 33 HLR 51, CA	12.193
B (a child) (looked after child), *Re* [2013] EWCA Civ 964, [2014] FLR 277	13.75
Bah v United Kingdom, App No 56328/07 (2012) 54 EHRR 21, [2012] HLR 2, ECtHR	1.110, 5.8, 12.104
Banks v Kingston Upon Thames RLBC [2008] EWCA Civ 1443, [2008] HLR 29	9.181
Barber v Croydon LBC LB [2010] EWCA Civ 51, [2010] HLR 26	10.18
Barrett v Southwark LBC [2008] EWHC 1568 (QB), [2008] JHL D107	12.167
Barry v Southwark LBC [2008] EWCA Civ 1140, [2009] HLR 30	3.34
Barty-King v Ministry of Defence [1979] 2 All ER 80, Ch D	12.151
Baumbast and R v Secretary of State for the Home Department, Case C-413/99 [2002] ECR I-7091, [2002] 3 CMLR 23	3.82, 3.83
Begum (Nipa) v Tower Hamlets LBC [2000] 1 WLR 306, (1999) 32 HLR 445, CA	4.2, 4.5, 4.18, 4.63, 4.73, 4.95, 4.102, 9.100, 12.5, 12.159, 12.204, 12.206
Begum (Rikha) v Tower Hamlets LBC [2005] EWCA Civ 340, [2005] HLR 34	9.29, 9.31, 9.32, 9.33, 9.34, 10.219, 11.49, 12.177
Begum (Runa) v Tower Hamlets LBC [2003] UKHL 5, [2003] 2 AC 430, [2003] HLR 32; [2002] EWHC 633 (Admin), [2002] JHL D58	9.65, 9.174, 10.118, 12.5, 12.28, 12.30, 12.37, 12.64, 12.96, 12.97, 12.99, 12.159
Bellouti v Wandsworth LBC [2005] EWCA Civ 602, [2005] HLR 46	5.33, 5.36, 9.7, 9.121, 9.186, 12.64
Bernard v Enfield LBC [2001] EWCA Civ 1831	4.129, 12.78

Betts, *Re* [1983] 2 AC 613, (1983) 10 HLR 97, HL	4.65, 7.11–7.15, 7.45, 12.44
Betts v Eastleigh BC [1983] 1 WLR 774, (1983) 8 HLR 28, CA	7.11–7.15
Bhatia Best Ltd v Lord Chancellor [2014] EWHC 746 (QB), [2014] 1 WLR 3487	12.5
Bigia and others v Entry Clearance Officer [2009] EWCA Civ 79	3.52
Birmingham City Council v Ali; Moran v Manchester City Council (Secretary of State for Communities and Local Government and another intervening) [2009] UKHL 36, [2009] 1 WLR 1506, [2009] HLR 41	1.112, 4.13, 4.14, 4.40, 4.69, 4.70, 4.71, 4.72, 4.132, 4.133, 6.129, 9.20, 9.21, 9.45, 9.47, 10.20, 10.107, 10.119, 10.175, 11.85, 12.234
Birmingham City Council v Aweys and others [2008] EWCA Civ 48, [2008] HLR 32	9.45
Birmingham City Council v Balog [2013] EWCA Civ 1582, [2014] HLR 14	12.41, 12.75
Birmingham City Council v Qasim [2009] EWCA Civ 1080, [2009] All ER (D) 206 (Oct), [2010] HLR 19	3.163, 11.11, 11.61
Birmingham City Council v Wilson [2016] EWCA Civ 1137, [2017] HLR 4	9.69, 9.93, 9.185
Board of Education v Rice [1911] AC 179, HL	12.64
Boddington v British Transport Police [1999] 2 AC 143, HL	12.5, 12.19
Bond v Leicester City Council [2001] EWCA Civ 1544, [2002] HLR 6	4.85, 4.86, 4.87, 4.138, 6.66, 12.234
Boreh v Ealing LBC [2008] EWCA Civ 1176, [2009] HLR 22	10.174
Bratton v Croydon LBC [2002] EWCA Civ 1494, [2002] All ER (D) 404 (Jul)	6.85
Brawley v Marczynski, Business Lines Ltd [2002] EWCA Civ 756, [2002] 1 All ER 1060	12.140
Brent LBC v Corcoran [2010] EWCA Civ 774, [2010] HLR 43	11.31
Brent LBC v Risk Management Partners Ltd [2011] UKSC 7, [2011] 2 AC 34; *Reversing on another point* [2009] EWCA Civ 490	13.88
Bristol City Council v FV [2011] UKUT 494 (AAC)	3.32
Bristol City Council v Mousah (1997) 30 HLR 32, CA	6.60, 11.31
Bristol Corp v Stockford (1973) (unreported)	1.11
British Oxygen Co Ltd v Minister of Technology [1971] AC 610, HL	4.65, 12.44

Bubb v Wandsworth LBC [2011] EWCA Civ 1285, [2012] HLR 13	12.36, 12.98, 12.136, 12.160, 12.176
Bugdaycay v Secretary of State for the Home Department [1987] AC 514, HL	12.25, 12.37
Bunning v King's Lynn and West Norfolk Council, *see* King's Lynn and West Norfolk Council v Bunning—	
Bury MBC v Gibbons [2010] EWCA Civ 327, [2010] HLR 33	9.45, 9.187
Butler v Fareham BC, May 2001 *Legal Action* 24, CA	9.167
CJ v Cardiff City Council [2011] EWCA Civ 1590, [2012] HLR 20	13.55
Camden LBC v Gilsenan (1998) 31 HLR 81, CA	11.31
Camden LBC v Mallett (2001) 33 HLR 20, CA	11.31
Cannock Chase DC v Kelly [1978] 1 WLR 1, CA	12.54, 12.137
Carthew v Exeter City Council [2012] EWCA Civ 1913, [2013] HLR 19	6.51
Chapman v United Kingdom, App No 27238/95 (2001) 33 EHRR 18, (2001) 10 BHRC 48, ECtHR	12.100
Charles Terence Estates Ltd v Cornwall CC [2012] EWCA Civ 1439, [2013] 1 WLR 466, 2013] HLR 12	12.18
Chishimba v Kensington and Chelsea RLBC [2013] EWCA Civ 786, [2013] HLR 34	4.114, 6.50
Ciliz v Netherlands [2000] 2 FLR 429	3.166
City of Gloucester v Miles (1985) 17 HLR 292, CA	4.15, 6.94, 6.106, 12.76
Clauder, *see* Proceedings Concerning Clauder—	
Cocks v Thanet DC [1983] AC 286, (1983) 6 HLR 15, HL	1.47, 12.216
Codona v Mid-Bedfordshire DC [2005] EWCA Civ 925, [2005] HLR 1	10.176
Council of Civil Service Unions v Minister for the Civil Service [1985] 1 AC 374, HL	12.22, 12.24, 12.31, 12.34, 12.93
Crake v Supplementary Benefits Commission [1982] 1 All ER 498, QBD	12.37
Cramp v Hastings BC; Phillips v Camden LBC [2005] EWCA Civ 1005, [2005] HLR 48	9.69, 9.81, 9.92, 9.93, 9.94, 9.95, 9.185, 12.172, 12.193
Crawley BC v B (2000) 32 HLR 636, CA	7.62, 9.127, 9.128, 9.183, 10.85, 12.13, 12.19, 12.151, 12.158, 12.175, 12.207, 12.208, 12.212
Crawley BC v Sawyer (1988) 20 HLR 98, CA	10.183
Crédit Suisse v Allerdale MBC; Same v Waltham Forest LBC [1997] QB 306, [1996] 4 All ER 129, CA; [1995] 1 Lloyds LR 315, Comm Ct	12.5, 12.18, 12.46, 12.48

Crédit Suisse v Waltham Forest LBC [1997] QB 362, (1996) 29 HLR 115, CA	10.122
Croke v Secretary of State for Communities and Local Government [2016] EWHC 2484 (Admin), [2017] PTSR 116, [2016] ACD 131	12.166
Crossley v Westminster City Council [2006] EWCA Civ 140, [2006] HLR 26	5.36, 5.53, 5.55, 5.73, 9.63, 9.137
Croydon LBC and Hackney LBC v R (AW, A and Y) [2007] EWCA Civ 266, [2007] 1 WLR 3168	13.21
D, In the matter of (1998) 1 CCLR 190	12.154, 12.156
Danesh v Kensington and Chelsea RLBC [2006] EWCA Civ 1404, [2007] HLR 17	4.83, 6.66, 7.43, 12.195
Dano v Jobcenter Leipzig, Case C-333/13 [2015] 1 WLR 2519, ECJ	3.13
Darlington BC v Sterling (1997) 29 HLR 309, CA	6.24, 6.60, 11.31
Dawkins v Central Bedfordshire Council [2013] EWHC 4757 (QB)	12.168
De Falco, Silvestri v Crawley BC [1980] QB 460, CA	4.5, 4.98, 6.55, 6.135, 9.79, 10.97, 10.98, 10.99, 12.41, 12.88, 12.91, 12.144, 12.145
De-Winter Heald and others v Brent LBC [2009] EWCA Civ 930, [2010] HLR 8	9.65, 12.63, 12.99
Deadman v Southwark LBC (2001) 33 HLR 75, CA	8.5
Delahaye v Oswestry BC (1980) *Times* 29 July, QBD	7.37, 7.59, 9.23, 9.27, 9.55
Demetri v Westminster City Council [2000] 1 WLR 772, (2000) 32 HLR 470, CA	9.124, 9.161, 12.165, 12.169
Dempsey v Johnstone [2003] EWCA Civ 1134, [2003] All ER (D) 515	12.183
Denton v Southwark LBC [2007] EWCA Civ 623, [2008] HLR 11	4.74, 4.78, 6.62, 6.78, 6.146
Depesme, Kerrou, Kauffmann and Lefort v Ministre de l'Enseignement superieur et de la Recherche, Cases C-401/15 to C-403/15	3.86
Dereci and others v Bundesministerium fur Inneres, Case C-256/11	3.92
Desnousse v Newham LBC, Paddington Churches Housing Association, Veni Properties Ltd [2006] EWCA Civ 547, [2006] HLR 38	4.55
Devenport v Salford City Council (1983) 8 HLR 54, CA	6.23, 6.26, 6.60, 9.109
Dharmaraj v Hounslow LBC [2011] EWCA Civ 312, [2011] HLR 18	9.162
Diatta v Land Berlin [1985] EUECJ R 267/83	3.52

Din v Wandsworth LBC [1983] 1 AC 657, (1981–82) 1 HLR 73, HL	6.51, 6.83, 6.84, 6.86, 6.102, 6.104, 6.130–6.132, 6.133, 10.25
Dragic v Wandsworth LBC [2011] JHL D59	9.162
Dyson v Kerrier DC [1980] 1 WLR 1205, CA	1.50, 4.1446.5, 6.83, 10.96
E v Secretary of State for the Home Department [2004] EWCA Civ 49, [2004] QB 1044	12.37
ECO (Dubai) v M (Ivory Coast) [2010] UKUT 277 (IAC)	3.80
Eagil Trust Co Ltd v Piggot Brown [1985] 3 All ER 119, CA	12.70
Eastleigh BC v Walsh [1985] 1 WLR 525, (1985) 17 HLR 392, HL	10.16
Echternach and Moritz v Minister van Onderwijs en Wetenschappen, Cases 389/87 and 390/87 [1989] ECR 723	3.25, 3.51
Edwin H Bradley & Sons v Secretary of State for the Environment (1984) P&CR 374, (1982) 266 EG 926, QBD	9.67
Ehiabor v Kensington and Chelsea RLBC [2008] EWCA Civ 1074	3.113, 5.8
Ekwuru v Westminster City Council [2003] EWCA Civ 1293, [2004] HLR 14	6.58, 12.211, 12.212
El-Dinnaoui v Westminster City Council [2013] EWCA Civ 231, [2013] HLR 23	12.52
El Goure v Kensington and Chelsea RLBC [2012] EWCA Civ 670, [2012] HLR 36	5.29, 9.178
Elmi v Secretary of State for Work and Pensions [2011] EWCA Civ 1403	3.35
Elrify v Westminster City Council [2007] EWCA Civ 322, [2007] HLR 36	9.139, 12.194
Enfield LBC V Najim [2015] EWCA Civ 319, [2015] HLR 19	6.84
English v Emery Reimbold & Strick Ltd [2002] EWCA Civ 605, [2002] 1 WLR 2409	12.70
Ephraim v Newham LBC (1993) 25 HLR 207, CA	10.88, 12.216
Eren v Haringey LBC [2007] EWCA Civ 409	9.140
European Commission v United Kingdom of Great Britain and Northern Ireland, Case C-308/14	3.13
F, *Re* [1994] FLR 548	3.102
F v Birmingham City Council [2006] EWCA Civ 1427, [2007] HLR 18	6.28, 6.29, 6.41, 6.143, 9.138
Fairmount Investments v Secretary of State for the Environment [1976] 1 WLR 1255, HL	12.37
Family Housing Association v Miah (1982) 5 HLR 94, CA	10.16
Farah v Hillingdon LBC [2014] EWCA Civ 359, [2014] HLR 24	9.76

Fawcett Properties Ltd v Buckingham City Council [1961] AC 636, [1960] 3 WLR 831, HL	5.20
Feld v Barnet LBC; Pour v Westminster City Council [2004] EWCA Civ 1307, [2005] HLR 9	9.65, 9.167, 9.169, 12.59, 12.62
Fellowes v Fisher [1976] QB 122, CA	12.144
Findlay, *Re* [1985] AC 318, HL	12.39
Firoozmand v Lambeth LBC [2015] EWCA Civ 952, [2015] HLR 45	10.178
Fletcher v Brent LBC [2006] EWCA Civ 960, [2007] HLR 12	4.42, 4.45
Francis v Kensington and Chelsea RLBC [2003] EWCA Civ 443, [2003] HLR 50	12.202
Frilli v Belgium, Case 1/72 [1972] ECR 457, [1973] CMLR 386, ECJ	3.29
Gallagher v Castle Vale HAT [2001] EWCA Civ 994, (2001) 33 HLR 72	11.37, 11.47
Gardiner v Haringey LBC [2009] EWHC 2699 (Admin)	9.32
Gardner v London Chatham and Dover Railway Co (No 1) (1867) LR 2 Ch App 201	12.48
Gentle v Wandsworth LBC [2005] EWCA Civ 1377	12.193
Ghaidan v Godin-Mendoza [2004] UKHL 30, [2004] HLR 46	12.103
Gilby v Westminster City Council [2007] EWCA Civ 604, [2008] HLR 7	9.67
Givaudan & Co Ltd v Minister of Housing and Local Government [1967] 1 WLR 250, QBD	12.67
Goddard v Torridge DC, January 1982 *LAG Bulletin* 9, QBD	6.67, 9.114
Goodger v Ealing LBC [2002] EWCA Civ 751, [2003] HLR 6	6.93, 9.188
Goodman v Dolphin Square Trust Ltd (1979) 38 P&CR 257, CA	14.34
Green v Croydon LBC [2007] EWCA Civ 1367, [2008] HLR 28	9.67
Griffin v Westminster City Council [2004] EWCA Civ 108, [2004] HLR 32	5.33, 12.41
Griffiths v St Helens MBC [2006] EWCA Civ 160, [2006] 1 WLR 2233, [2006] HLR 29	10.175, 10.185, 10.201
Gwynedd CC v Grunshaw (1999) 32 HLR 610, CA	12.167
HTV Ltd v Price Commission [1976] ICR 170, CA	12.37
Hackney LBC v Ekinci [2001] EWCA Civ 776, [2002] HLR 2	5.13, 12.101
Hackney LBC v Haque [2017] EWCA Civ 4, [2017] HLR 14	9.70, 10.169
Hackney LBC v Lambourne (1992) 25 HLR 172, CA	12.16, 12.216
Hackney LBC v Sareen [2003] EWCA Civ 351, [2003] HLR 54	7.46, 9.55, 9.154, 12.112

Haile v Waltham Forest LBC [2015] UKSC 34, [2015] AC 1471, [2015] HLR 24	6.84, 6.133
Hall v Wandsworth LBC; Carter v Wandsworth LBC [2004] EWCA Civ 1740, [2005] 2 All ER 192, [2005] HLR 23	5.33, 5.44, 9.121, 9.178, 9.180, 9.190, 12.85
Hallam Peel & Co v Southwark LBC [2008] EWCA Civ 1120	12.182
Handley v Lake Jackson Solicitors [2016] EWCA Civ 465, [2016] HLR 23	12.188
Hanniff v Robinson [1993] QB 419, CA	4.60
Hanton-Rhouila v Westminster City Council [2010] EWCA Civ 1334, [2011] HLR 12	9.135
Harley v McDonald [2001] 2 AC 678, PC	12.185
Harouki v Kensington and Chelsea RLBC [2007] EWCA Civ 1000, [2008] HLR 16	4.69, 4.111, 10.146
Harripaul v Lewisham LBC [2012] EWCA Civ 266, [2012] HLR 24	12.141, 12.177
Harrison (Jamaica) and AB (Morocco) v Secretary of State for the Home Department [2012] EWCA Civ 1736	3.96
Harrow LBC and Secretary of State for the Home Department v Ibrahim [2008] EWCA Civ 386, [2009] HLR 2	3.83, 3.85
Hemans & Hemans v Windsor and Maidenhead RBC [2011] EWCA Civ 374, [2011] HLR 25	4.44
Higgs v Brighton and Hove City Council [2003] EWCA Civ 895, [2004] HLR 2	4.68, 5.56, 5.60
Hijazi v Kensington and Chelsea RLBC [2003] EWCA Civ 692, [2003] HLR 73	9.104, 12.85
Hill v Bailey [2003] EWHC 2835 (Ch)	12.143
Hines v Lambeth LBC [2014] EWCA Civ 660, [2014] HLR 32	3.98
Hobbs v Sutton LBC (1993) 26 HLR 132, CA	12.86
Holmes-Moorhouse v Richmond Upon Thames LBC [2009] UKHL 7, [2009] HLR 34	1.112, 5.23, 5.25, 5.26, 5.29, 9.141, 10.53, 11.88, 12.38, 12.74, 12.75
Honig v Lewisham LBC (1958) 122 JPJ 302	12.167
Hotak v Southwark LBC; Kanu v Southwark LBC; Johnson v Solihull MBC [2015] UKSC 30, [2015] HLR 23; *Affirming* [2013] EWCA Civ 752, [2013] HLR 39	5.32, 5.35, 5.36, 5.37, 5.42, 5.55, 5.77, 12.75
Hounslow LBC v Powell; Frisby v Birmingham City Council; Hall v Leeds City Council [2011] UKSC 8, [2011] 2 AC 186, [2011] HLR 23	10.18, 12.161
Huda v Redbridge LBC [2016] EWCA Civ 709, [2016] HLR 30	6.117

Hussein v Waltham Forest LBC [2015] EWCA Civ 14, [2015] HLR 16	4.83, 5.80, 7.4, 7.43
Huzrat v Hounslow LBC [2013] EWCA Civ 1865, [2014] HLR 17	6.25, 10.42, 10.106
Ibraham v Birmingham City Council, *see* Ali v Birmingham City Council, Ibrahim v Same, Tomlinson v Same—	
Iida v Stadt Ulm, Case C-40/11 [2013] Fam 121, 2013] 2 WLR 788, ECJ	3.94
Islam, *Re*, *see* R v Hillingdon LBC ex p Islam—	
Islington LBC v Uckac [2006] EWCA Civ 340, [2006] HLR 35	12.19
J (a minor) (abduction: custody rights), *Re* [1990] 2 AC 562, [1990] 3 WLR 492, HL	3.102
Jagendorf and Trott v Secretary of State for the Environment and Krasucki [1986] JPL 771	12.37
Jany v Staatssecretaris van Justitie, Case C-268/99 [2001] ECR I-8615, ECJ	3.32,3.37
Jennings v Northavon DC, January 1982 *LAG Bulletin* 9, QBD	6.67
Jia v Migrationsverket, Case C-1/05 [2007] QB 545, [2007] 2 WLR 1005, ECJ	3.53
Jobcenter Berlin Neukolin v Alimanovic, Case C-67/14 [2016] QB 308, [2016] 2 WLR 208, ECJ	3.14
Johnson v City of Westminster [2015] EWCA Civ 554, [2015] HLR 35	7.3
Johnson v Solihull MBC, *see* Hotak v Southwark LBC; Kanu v Southwark LBC; Johnson v Solihull MBC Johnston v Westminster City Council—	
Johnson v Westminster City Council [2013] EWCA Civ 773, [2013] HLR 45	12.197
KOO Golden East Mongolia v Bank of Nova Scotia [2008] EWHC 1120 (QB)	12.182
KS v Secretary of State for Work and Pensions [2016] UKUT 269 (AAC)	3.35
Kacar v Enfield LBC (2001) 33 HLR 5, CA	9.106
Kanda v Government of the Federation of Malaya [1962] AC 362, PC	12.64
Keeves v Dean [1924] 1 KB 685, CA	4.51
Kelly v Monklands DC (1985) Ct of Session 12 July (OH), 1986 SLT 169	12.70
Kempf v Staatssecretaris van Justitie, Case 139/85 [1986] ECR 1741, [1987] 1 CMLR 764, ECJ	3.33
Kensington and Chelsea RLBC v Hayden (1984) 17 HLR 114, CA	10.16
Kensington and Chelsea RLBC v Simmonds [1996] 3 FCR 246, (1996) 29 HLR 507, CA	11.31, 11.37, 11.47
Khana v Southwark LBC [2001] EWCA Civ 999, [2002] HLR 31, (2001) 4 CCLR 267	13.22, 13.26

Khatun v Newham LBC [2004] EWCA Civ 55, [2005] QB 37, [2004] HLR 29	10.179, 10.215, 10.216, 12.41
King's Lynn and West Norfolk Council v Bunning [2016] EWCA Civ 1037, [2017] HLR 9	12.139
Knight v Vale Royal BC [2003] EWCA Civ 1258, [2004] HLR 9	6.116
Knowsley Housing Trust v McMullen (by her litigation friend) [2006] EWCA Civ 539, [2006] HLR 43	11.37
Knowsley Housing Trust v Prescott [2009] EWHC 924 (QB), [2009] L&TR 24	11.31
Konodyba v Royal Borough of Kensington and Chelsea [2012] EWCA Civ 982	3.35
Krishnan v Hillingdon LBC, January 1981 *LAG Bulletin* 137, QBD	4.111, 6.95, 6.96, 9.89
Kruja v Enfield LBC [2004] EWCA Civ 1769, [2005] HLR 13	12.12, 12.160
Kuteh v Secretary of State for Education [2014] EWCA Civ 1586	12.150
Lally v Kensington and Chelsea RLBC (1980) *Times* 27 March, QBD	9.66, 10.105, 12.10
Lambeth LBC v A; Lambeth LBC v Lindsay [2002] EWCA Civ 1084, [2002] HLR 57; *Affirming* [2001] EWHC Admin 900, (2002) JHL D1	11.65, 11.74
Lambeth LBC v Henry (2000) 32 HLR 874, CA	11.38
Lambeth LBC v Howard (2001) 33 HLR 58, CA	11.31
Lambeth LBC v Johnston [2008] EWCA Civ 690, [2009] HLR 10	9.178, 9.179
Lambeth LBC v Kay; Leeds City Council v Price [2006] UKHL 10, [2006] 2 AC 465, [2006] HLR 22	12.100
Lavender & Son v Minister of Housing and Local Government [1970] 1 WLR 1231, QBD	12.46
Lawrie-Blum v Land Baden Wurttemberg, Case 66/85 [1986] ECR 2121, ECJ	3.32, 3.33
Lee-Lawrence v Penwith DC [2006] EWCA Civ 507	6.141
Lekpo Bozua v Hackney LBC [2010] EWCA Civ 909, [2010] HLR 46	3.115, 5.9
Levin v Staatssecretaris van Justitie, Case 53/81 [1982] ECR 1035	3.33
Lewis v Havering LBC [2006] EWCA Civ 1793, [2007] HLR 20	12.202
Lewis v Lewis [1956] 1 WLR 200	3.102
Lewisham LBC v Akinsola (1999) 32 HLR 414, CA	11.31
Lismane v Hammersmith and Fulham LBC (1998) 31 HLR 427, CA	3.142
Lloyd v McMahon [1987] AC 625, [1987] 2 WLR 821, HL	12.59
Lockley v National Blood Transfusion Service [1992] 1 WLR 492, CA	12.143
Lomotey v Enfield LBC [2004] EWCA Civ 627, [2004] HLR 45	6.154, 9.187

London & Quadrant Housing Trust v Root [2005] EWCA Civ 43, [2005] HLR 28 — 11.31, 11.37
M v Secretary of State for Work and Pensions [2006] UKHL 11, [2006] 2 AC 91 — 12.103
MR (Bangladesh) and others v Secretary of State for the Home Department [2010] UKUT 449 (IAC) — 3.57
MSS v Belgium and Greece, App No 30696/09 (2011) 53 EHRR 2, [2011] INLR 553, ECtHR — 3.159
McCarthy v Secretary of State for the Home Department Case C-434/09 [2011] All ER (EC) 729, [2011] All ER (D) 156 (May) — 3.90
Magill v Porter [2001] UKHL 67, [2002] 2 AC 357 — 12.55, 12.61
Makisi v Birmingham City Council; Yosief v Birmingham City Council; Nagi v Birmingham City Council [2011] EWCA Civ 355, [2011] HLR 27 — 9.179, 9.187
Manchester City Council v Cochrane [1999] 1 WLR 809, CA — 12.16
Manchester City Council v Higgins [2005] EWCA Civ 1423, [2006] HLR 14 — 11.31, 11.37
Manchester City Council v Pinnock [2010] UKSC 45, [2011] 2 AC 104, [2011] HLR 7 — 12.161
Manydown Co Ltd v Basingstoke and Deane BC [2012] EWHC 977 (Admin), [2012] JPL 1188 — 12.37
Mario Lopes da Veiga v Staatssecretaris van Justitie, Case 9/88 — 3.25, 3.51
Marshall v South Staffordshire Tramways Co [1895] 2 Ch 36 — 12.48
Martin Hill v Bedfordshire CC [2007] EWHC 2435 (Admin), [2008] ELR 191 — 12.37
Mason v Secretary of State for the Environment and Bromsgrove DC [1984] JPL 332 — 12.37
Maswaku v Westminster City Council [2012] EWCA Civ 669, [2012] HLR 37 — 9.178, 10.185
Mazari v Italy (1999) 28 EHRR CD 175, (2000) 30 EHRR 218 — 12.100
Meade v Haringey LBC [1979] 1 WLR 1, CA — 12.43
Medcalf v Mardell [2002] UKHL 27, [2003] 1 AC 120 — 12.184, 12.185
Medicaments and Related Classes of Goods (No 2), *Re* [2001] 1 WLR 700, CA — 12.61
Mendes and another v Southwark LBC [2009] EWCA Civ 594, [2010] HLR 3 — 12.138, 12.140
Metock v Minister for Justice, Equality and Law Reform, Case C-127/08 [2009] QB 318, [2009] All ER (EC) 40 — 3.27, 3.54
Miah v Newham LBC [2001] EWCA Civ 487 — 5.21
Minister voor Vreemdelingenzaken en Integratie v RNG Eind, Case C-291/05 — 3.23
Mirga v Secretary of State for Work and Pensions; Samin v Westminster City Council [2016] UKSC 1, [2016] HLR 7; *Affirming on other grounds* [2012] EWCA Civ 1468, [2013] 2 CMLR 6, [2013] HLR 7 — 3.11, 3.35
Mitchell v Ealing LBC [1979] QB 1, QBD — 8.13

Mitu v Camden LBC [2011] EWCA Civ 1249, [2012] HLR 10	9.180
Mohamed v Hammersmith and Fulham LBC [2001] UKHL 57, [2002] 1 AC 547, [2002] HLR 7	3.110, 5.7, 5.67, 7.16, 7.19, 9.57, 9.123, 9.177, 9.181, 12.51, 12.214, 15.12
Mohamed v Manek and Royal Borough of Kensington and Chelsea (1995) 27 HLR 439, CA	4.55
Mohammed v Islington LBC [2013] EWCA Civ 739, [2013] HLR 41	9.76
Mohammed v Westminster City Council [2005] EWCA Civ 796, [2005] HLR 47	6.102, 6.106, 6.118
Mohamoud v Birmingham City Council [2014EWCA Civ 227, [2014 HLR 22	9.180
Mohamoud v Kensington and Chelsea RLBC; Saleem v Wandsworth LBC [2015] EWCA Civ 780, [2015] HLR 38	6.25, 9.69
Mountview Court Properties Ltd v Devlin (1970) 21 P&CR 689, QBD	12.67
Munting v Hammersmith and Fulham LBC [1998] JHL D91	7.27
Muse v Brent LBC [2008] EWCA Civ 1447	10.186
N v UK, App No 26565/05 (2008) 47 EHRR 39, [2008] INLR 335, ECtHR	3.159
NJ v Wandsworth LBC [2013] EWCA Civ 1373, [2014] HLR 6	7.17, 9.66
National Aids Trust v National Health Service Commissioning Board (NHS England) [2016] EWHC 2005 (Admin)	12.34
Nessa v Chief Adjudication Officer [1998] 2 All ER 728, [1999] 4 All ER 677, [1999] 1 WLR 1937, HL	3.102
New Charter HA v Ashcroft [2004] EWCA Civ 310, [2004] HLR 36	11.31
Newcastle City Council v Morrison (2000) 32 HLR 891, CA	11.31, 11.37
Ninni Orasche v Bundesminster für Wissenschaft, Verkehr und Kunst, Case C-413/01 [2003] ECR I-13187, ECJ	3.34
Nipa Begum v Tower Hamlets LBC, *see* Begum (Nipa) v Tower Hamlets LBC—	
Noble v South Hertfordshire DC (1983) 17 HLR 80, CA	5.57, 5.58, 5.59
Noel v Hillingdon LBC [2013] EWCA Civ 1602, [2014] HLR 10	6.59
Noh v Hammersmith and Fulham LBC [2001] JHL D54, CA	9.103
Norman v Mathews (1916) 23 TLR 369, CA; *Affirming* (1916) 85 LJKB 857	12.154
Norris v Checksfield (1991) 23 HLR 425, CA	4.47
Nottingham City Council v Calverton Parish Council [2015] EWHC 503 (Admin)	12.166

Nottinghamshire CC v Secretary of State for the Environment, *see* R v Secretary of State for the Environment ex p Nottinghamshire CC—	
Nzamy v Brent LBC [2011] EWCA Civ 283, [2011] HLR 20	9.150
Nzolameso v Westminster City Council [2015] UKSC 22, [2015] HLR 22	10.42, 10.106, 10.139, 10.140, 14.10
O v Wandsworth LBC [2000] 1 WLR 2539, (2001) 33 HLR 39, CA	13.16
O (a child) v Doncaster MBC [2014] EWHC 2309 (Admin)	13.75
O and S v Maahanmuuttovirasto, Cases C-356/11 and C-357/11 [2003] Fam 203, [2013] 2 WLR 1093, ECJ	3.94
Oakley v South Cambridgeshire DC [2017] EWCA Civ 71, [2017] 2 P&CR 4	12.65
Obiorah v Lewisham LBC [2013] EWCA Civ 325, [2013] HLR 35	12.94
Oboh and others v Secretary of State for the Home Department [2013] EWCA Civ 1525, [2014] 1 WLR 1680	3.57
O'Connor v Kensington and Chelsea RLBC [2004] EWCA Civ 394, [2004] HLR 37	6.27, 6.46, 6.47, 12.203
Office national d'allocations familiales pour travailleurssalaries (ONAFTS) v Ahmed, Case C 45/12	3.25, 3.48, 3.88
Okafor and others v Secretary of State for the Home Department [2011] EWCA Civ 499	3.87
Olsson v Sweden (1988) 11 EHRR 259	3.155
Omar v Birmingham City Council [2007] EWCA Civ 610, [2007] HLR 43	10.194
Omar v Westminster City Council [2008] EWCA Civ 421, [2008] HLR 36	9.159
Onuekwere v Secretary of State for the Home Department; Secretary of State for the Home Department v MG, Cases C-378/12 and C-400/12	3.44
O'Rourke v Camden LBC [1998] AC 188, HL	12.216
O'Rourke v United Kingdom, App No 39022/97, ECtHR	12.100
Ortiz v Westminster City Council (1993) 27 HLR 364, CA	5.33
Osei v Southwark LBC [2007] EWCA Civ 787, [2008] HLR 15	4.113
Osmani v Camden LBC [2004] EWCA Civ 1706, [2005] HLR 22	5.33, 5.34, 5.36, 5.42, 5.44, 9.101, 12.12, 12.70, 12.71
Osseily v Westminster City Council [2007] EWCA Civ 1108, [2008] HLR 18	10.217
Oxford City Council v Bull [2011] EWCA Civ 609, [2011] HLR 35	4.33, 5.7, 6.86

Ozbek v Ipswich BC [2006] EWCA Civ 534, [2006] HLR 41 — 7.15, 7.27, 7.33, 7.46
P v P [2015] EWCA Civ 447 — 12.188
PG and VG [2007] UKAIT 19 — 3.52
Padfield v Minister of Agriculture, Fisheries and Food [1968] AC 997, HL — 10.146, 12.43
Paposhvili v Belgium, App No 41738/10 — 3.159
Parker v Camden LBC [1986] 1 Ch 162, CA — 12.48
Parr v Wyre BC (1982) 2 HLR 71, CA — 1.57, 4.12, 10.130, 10.215
Patmalniece v Secretary of State for Work and Pensions [2011] UKSC 11, [2011] 1 WLR 783 — 3.12
Patterson v Greenwich LBC (1993) 26 HLR 159, CA — 7.48, 9.66, 12.234
Peake v Hackney LBC [2013] EWHC 2528 (QB) — 12.167
Pedro v Secretary of State for Work and Pensions [2009] EWCA Civ 1358 — 3.53
Pensionsversicherungsanstalt v Brey, Case C-140/12 [2014] 1 WLR 1080, [2014] 1 CMLR 37, ECJ — 3.14
Pepper v Hart [1993] AC 625, HL — 1.67
Persaud (Luke) v Persaud (Mohan) [2003] EWCA Civ 394, [2003] PNLR 26 — 12.183, 12.187
Pieretti v Enfield LBC [2010] EWCA Civ 1104, [2011] HLR 3 — 9.69, 9.93, 9.95, 9.185
Poorsalehy v Wandsworth LBC [2013] EWHC 3687 (QB) — 12.167
Port Swettenham Authority v TW Wu & Co [1979] AC 580, PC — 8.13
Porteous v West Dorset DC [2004] EWCA Civ 244, [2004] HLR 30 — 9.129, 12.19, 12.37
Portsmouth City Council v Bryant (2000) 32 HLR 906, CA — 11.31, 11.35
Poshteh v Kensington and Chelsea RLBC [2017] UKSC 36, [2017] 2 WLR 1417; *Affirming* [2015] EWC Civ 711, [2015] HLR 36 — 9.70, 10.169, 9.174
Powell v Hounslow LBC, *see* Hounslow LBC v Powell; Frisby v Birmingham City Council; Hall v Leeds City Council—
Poyser and Mills Arbitration, *Re* [1964] 2 QB 467, QBD — 12.67
Pritam Kaur v S Russell & Sons Ltd [1973] QB 336, CA — 12.166
Proceedings Concerning Clauder, Case E-4/11 [2012] 1 CMLR 1, EFTA — 3.49
Pryce v Southwark LBC [2013] EWCA Civ 1732, [2013] HLR 10 — 3.95
Puhlhofer, *Re*, *see* R v Hillingdon LBC ex p Puhlhofer—
Putans v Tower Hamlets LBC [2006] EWHC 1634 (Ch), [2007] HLR 10 — 3.62
R (A) v Croydon LBC [2009] UKSC 8, [2009] 1 WLR 2557, [2010] 1 All ER 469 — 12.36, 13.54

R (A) v Lambeth LBC [2003] UKHL 57, [2004] AC 208, [2004] HLR 10; *Affirming* [2001] EWCA Civ 1624, [2000] HLR 13, (2001) 4 CCLR 486	13.1, 13.43, 13.57, 13.68
R (A) v Lambeth LBC; R (Lindsay) v Lambeth LBC [2002] EWCA Civ 1084, [2002] HLR 57	11.65, 11.74, 11.79, 12.234
R (A) (FC) v Croydon LBC and (1) Secretary of State for the Home Department (2) Children's Commissioner; R (M) (FC) v Lambeth LBC and (1) Secretary of State for the Home Department (2) Children's Commissioner, *see* R (A) v Croydon LBC—	
R (AH) v Cornwall Council [2010] EWHC 3192 (Admin), [2011] PTSR D23	13.58
R (AK) v Secretary of State for the Home Department [2011] EWHC 3188 (Admin)	13.56
R (AM) v Havering LBC and Tower Hamlets LBC [2015] EWHC 1004 (Admin), [2015] PTSR 1242	13.41
R (AW) v Croydon LBC [2005] EWHC 2950 (QB), (2005) 9 CCLR 252	3.156, 13.21
R (Abdi) v Lambeth LBC [2007] EWHC 1565 (Admin), [2008] HLR 5	9.170, 9.189
R (Adow) v Newham LBC [2010] EWHC 951 (Admin), [2010] JHL D101	11.102, 12.119
R (Aguiar) v Newham LBC [2002] EWHC 1325 (Admin), [2002] JHL D92	12.112
R (Abdulrahman) v Hillingdon LBC [2016] EWHC 2647 (Admin), [2017] HLR 1	9.33
R (Abdusemed) v Lambeth LBC, HC (Administrative Court), 19 February 2016, (2016) *Housing View*, February 29, QBD (Admin Court)	10.33
R (Ahmad) v Newham LBC [2009] UKHL 14, [2009] HLR 31; *Reversing* [2008] EWCA Civ 140; *Affirming* [2007] EWHC 2332 (Admin)	1.112, 9.58, 10.195, 11.66, 11.79–11.87, 12.14, 12.234
R (Ahmed) v Waltham Forest LBC [2001] EWHC Admin 540, [2001] JHL D89	10.33
R (Alam) v Tower Hamlets LBC [2009] EWHC 44 (Admin), [2009] JHL D47	4.14, 11.62
R (Alansi) v Newham LBC [2013] EWHC 3722 (Admin), [2014] HLR 25	11.73, 12.94
R (Alconbury Developments Ltd) v Secretary of State for the Environment, Transport and the Regions [2001] UKHL 23, [2003] 2 AC 295	12.37, 12.58
R (Alemi) v Westminster City Council [2014] EWHC 3858 (Admin)	11.39, 11.75
R (Ariemuguvbe) v Islington LBC [2009] EWCA Civ 1308	3.165, 10.170

R (Association of British Civilian Internees (Far East Region)) v Secretary of State for Defence) [2003] EWCA Civ 473, [2003] QB 1397, [2003] 3 WLR 80	12.27, 12.29
R (Aweys) v Birmingham City Council [2007] EWHC 52 (Admin), [2007] HLR 27	9.45, 9.46
R (B) v Merton LBC [2003] EWHC 1689 (Admin), [2003] 4 All ER 280	13.56
R (B) v Nottingham City Council [2011] EWHC 2933 (Admin), [2012] JHL D2, QDB	13.58
R (B) v Southwark LBC [2003] EWHC 1678 (Admin), [2004] HLR 3	4.13, 4.40, 4.132
R (Babakandi) v Westminster City Council [2011] EWHC 1756 (Admin), [2011] JHL D105	11.75, 11.78
R (Bancoult) v Secretary of State for the Foreign and Commonwealth Office [2001] QB 1067, CA	12.107
R (Bantamagbari) v Westminster City Council [2003] EWHC 1350 (Admin), [2003] JHL D70	7.73, 12.112
R (Batantu) v Islington LBC (2001) 33 HLR 76, (2001) 4 CCLR 445, QBD	13.22
R (Bateman (Teresa)) v Legal Service Commission (Costs) [2001] EWHC 797 (Admin), [2002] ACD 29	12.138
R (Bates) v Barking and Dagenham LBC [2012] EWHC 4218 (Admin)	13.41, 13.44, 13.57
R (Bauer-Czarnomski) v Ealing LBC [2010] EWHC 130 (Admin), [2010] JHL D38	11.101
R (Begum) v Tower Hamlets LBC [2002] EWHC 633 (Admin), [2003] HLR 8	9.118
R (Bempoa) v Southwark LBC [2002] EWHC 153 (Admin), [2002] JHL D44, Admin Ct	12.129
R (Bhata) v Secretary of State for the Home Department [2011] EWCA Civ 895	12.140
R (Bibi) v Camden LBC [2004] EWHC 2527 (Admin), [2005] HLR 18	11.61, 11.88
R (Bibi) v Newham LBC, *see* R v Newham LBC ex p Bibi and Al-Nashed—	
R (Bidar) v London Borough of Ealing and Secretary of State for Education and Skills, Case C-209/03 [2005] ECR I-2119	3.48
R (Bilverstone) v Oxford City Council [2003] EWHC 2434 (Admin), [2004] JHL D12	9.21
R (Birara) v Hounslow LBC [2010] EWHC 2113 (Admin), [2010] 3 FCR 21, (2010) 13 CCLR 685	13.77
R (Blackburn-Smith) v Lambeth LBC [2007] EWHC 767 (Admin), (2007) 10 CCLR 352	3.156
R (Boolen) v Barking and Dagenham LBC [2009] EWHC 2196 (Admin), [2009] JHL D113	11.68, 11.103
R (Boxall) v Waltham Forest LBC (2001) 4 CCLR 258, QBD	12.139, 12.140, 12.141
R (Brooks) v Islington LBC [2015] EWHC 2657 (Admin), [2016] HLR 2	10.8

R (Burkett) v Hammersmith and Fulham LBC [2004] EWCA Civ 1342	12.143
R (Burns) v Southwark LBC [2004] EWHC 1901 (Admin), [2004] JHL D105	3.111, 10.11
R (C) v Hackney LBC [2014] EWHC 3670 (Admin), [2015] PTSR 1011	13.66
R (C) v Islington LBC [2017] EWHC 1288 (Admin)	11.40, 11.103
R (C) v Lewisham LBC [2003] EWCA Civ 927, [2004] HLR 4	9.161, 9.163, 12.112
R (C) v Nottingham City Council [2010] EWCA Civ 790, [2011] 1 FCR 127	13.79
R (C, T, M, U) v Southwark LBC [2016] EWCA Civ 707, [2016] HLR 36; *Affirming on another point* [2014] EWHC 3983 (Admin)	13.43
R (Cafun) v Bromley LBC (2000) (unreported) October 17, CO/1481/2000, QBD (unreported)	10.132, 10.137
R (Calgin) v Enfield LBC [2005] EWHC 1716 (Admin), [2006] HLR 4	10.124, 10.131, 10.138, 14.10
R (Cali and others) v Waltham Forest LBC [2006] EWHC 2950 (Admin), [2007] HLR 1	11.79
R (Carson) v Secretary of State for Work and Pensions [2005] UKHL 37, [2006] 1 AC 173, HL; *Affirming* [2003] EWCA Civ 797, [2003] 3 All ER 577	12.102, 12.103
R (Casey) v Restormel BC [2007] EWHC 2554 (Admin), [2008] JHL D27, (2008) ACD 1	12.112, 12.149
R (Clue) v Birmingham City Council [2010] EWCA Civ 460, [2011] 1 WLR 99, [2010] 2 FLR 1011, (2010) 13 CCLR 276	3.157, 3.158, 13.47, 13.48
R (Conde) v Lambeth LBC [2005] EWHC 62 (Admin), [2005] HLR 29	3.160
R (Conville) v Richmond upon Thames LBC [2006] EWCA Civ 718, [2006] HLR 45; *Reversing on another point* [2005] EWHC 1430 (Admin), [2006] HLR 1	10.87, 10.95, 10.102, 12.38
R (Cornwall CC) v Secretary of State for Health [2015] UKSC 46, [2015] HLR 32	13.10
R (Couronne and others) v (1) Crawley BC (2) Secretary of State for Work and Pensions and (3) First Secretary of State; R (Bontemps and others) v Secretary of State for Work and Pensions [2006] EWHC 1514 (Admin), [2006] JHL D106	12.102
R (Cranfield-Adams) v Richmond Upon Thames LBC [2012] EWHC 3334 (Admin), [2012] All ER (D) 114 (Jun), [2012] JHL D10	11.75
R (Cunningham) v Exeter Crown Court [2003] EWHC 184 (Admin), [2003] 2 Cr App R (S) 64	12.151
R (Daly) v Secretary of State for the Home Department [2001] UKHL 26, [2001] 2 AC 532	12.9, 12.27, 12.28

R (Darby, as administratix of the estate of Lee Rabbetts) v Richmond upon Thames LBC [2015] EWHC 909 (QB) 11.10, 12.216
R (De Almeida) v Kensington and Chelsea RLBC [2012] EWHC 1082 (Admin) 13.21
R (Demsey) v Sutton LBC [2013] EWCA Civ 863 12.142
R (Dixon) v Wandsworth LBC [2007] EWHC 3075 (Admin), [2008] JHL D21 11.32
R (E) v Governing Body of JFS [2009] UKSC 1, [2009] 1 WLR 2353 12.139
R (E) v Governing Body of JFS and the Admissions Appeal Panel of JFS and others; R (E) v Governing Body of JFS and the Admissions Appeal Panel of JFS (United Synagogue) and others, *see* R (E) v Governing Body of JFS—
R (Edwards) v Birmingham City Council [2016] EWHC 173 (Admin), [2016] HLR 11 4.71, 9.10, 9.45, 9.47, 9.49, 10.11
R (FZ) v Croydon LBC [2011] EWCA Civ 59, [2011] HLR 22 13.56
R (Faarah) v Southwark LBC [2008] EWCA Civ 807, [2009] HLR 12 11.103
R (Faizi) v Brent LBC [2015] EWHC 2449 (Admin) 10.29
R (Flash) v Southwark LBC [2004] EWHC 717 (Admin), [2004] JHL D60 10.172
R (G) v Barnet LBC; R (W) v Lambeth LBC; R (A) v Lambeth LBC [2003] UKHL 57, [2004] AC 208, [2004] HLR 10 13.41, 13..43, 13.44
R (G) v Ealing LBC (No 2) [2002] EWHC 250 (Admin), [2002] MHLR 140 12.136
R (G) v Southwark LBC [2009] UKHL 26, [2009] 1 WLR 1299 5.67, 13.44, 13.51, 13.52, 13.58
R (GE (Eritrea)) v Secretary of State for the Home Department [2014] EWCA Civ 1490, [2015] 1 WLR 4123 13.78
R (GS) v Camden LBC [2016] EWHC 1762 (Admin), [2016] HLR 43 13.7, 13.22, 13.91, 13.92
R (Gordon Binomugisha) v Southwark LBC [2006] EWHC 2254 (Admin), [2007] ACD 35 13.20
R (Grant) v Lambeth LBC [2004] EWCA Civ 1711, [2005] 1 WLR 1781, [2005] HLR 27 3.158, 13.88, 13.93
R (Griffin) v Southwark LBC [2004] EWHC 2463 (Admin), [2005] HLR 12 9.35
R (Grimshaw) v Southwark LBC [2013] EWHC 4504 (Admin) 12.138
R (HA) v Ealing LBC [2015] EWHC 2375 (Admin), [2016] PTSR 16 11.39, 11.40, 11.42
R (Halvai) v Hammersmith and Fulham LBC [2017] EWHC 802 (Admin) 10.44

R (Hammia) v Wandsworth LBC [2005] EWHC 1127 (Admin), [2005] HLR 46	12.45, 12.112
R (Hassan) v Croydon LBC [2009] JHL D56, Admin Court	10.42
R (Heaney) v Lambeth LBC [2006] EWHC 3332 (Admin), [2007] JHL D25	11.55, 11.65
R (Hertforshire CC) v Hammersmith and Fulham LBC [2011] EWCA Civ 77	13.9
R (Hooper) v Secretary of State for Work and Pensions [2005] UKHL 29, [2006] 1 All ER 487, [2005] 1 WLR 1681	13.93
R (Hoyte) v Southwark LBC [2016] EWHC 1665 (Admin), [2016] HLR 35	9.33
R (Hunt) v North Somerset Council [2015] UKSC 51, [2015] 1 WLR 3575	12.142
R (IA) v Westminster City Council [2013] EWHC 1273 (QB)	9.62
R (Iran and others) v Secretary of State for the Home Department [2005] EWCA Civ 982	12.70
R (J) v Enfield LBC [2002] EWHC 432 (Admin), [2002] HLR 38, (2002) 5 CCLR 434	3.158, 13.88, 13.92, 13.93
R (J) v Hackney LBC [2010] EWHC 3021 (Admin), [2010] JHL D20	12.140
R (J) v Waltham Forest LBC [2002] EWHC 487 (Admin), [2002] JHL D38	9.28
R (J) v Worcestershire CC [2014] EWCA Civ 1518, [2015] 1 WLR 2825	13.41
R (Jakimaviciute) v Hammersmith and Fulham LBC [2014] EWCA Civ 1438, [2015] HLR 5	1.118, 11.39, 11.42
R (Joseph) v Newham LBC [2009] EWHC 2983 (Admin), [2010] JHL D37	11.75
R (K) v Birmingham City Council [2011] EWHC 1559 (Admin)	13.56
R (K) v Lambeth LBC [2003] EWCA Civ 1150, [2004] 1 WLR 272, [2004] HLR 15	3.156
R (KA) v Essex CC [[2013] EWHC 43 (Admin), [2013] 1 WLR 1163	13.48
R (Kabashi) v Redbridge LBC [2009] EWHC 2984 (Admin), [2011] JHL D1	11.87
R (Kadri) v Birmingham City Council [2012] EWCA Civ 1432, [2013] HLR 4	13.56
R (Kathro) v Rhondda Cynon Taff CBC [2001] EWHC Admin 527, [2002] Env LR 196	12.37
R (Kelly and Mehari) v Birmingham City Council [2009] EWHC 3240 (Admin), [2009] JHL D24	10.8
R (Kensington and Chelsea RBC) v Ealing LBC [2017] EWHC 24 (Admin), [2017] HLR 13	9.44, 10.219
R (Kent CC) v Secretary of State for Health [2015] EWCA Civ 81, [2015] 1 WLR 1221	13.9

R (Keyu) v Secretary of State for Foreign and Commonwealth Affairs [2015] UKSC 69, [2015] HLR 2	2.29
R (Khan) v Newham LBC [2001] EWHC Admin 589, [2001] JHL D90	10.118, 10.148
R (Khan) v Oxfordshire CC [2004] EWCA Civ 309, [2004] HLR 41	13.88
R (Khazai and others) v Birmingham City Council [2010] EWHC 2576 (Admin), [2011] JHL D9	12.216
R (Kiana) v Secretary of State for the Home Department [2010] EWHC 1002 (Admin)	13.38
R (Kimvono) v Tower Hamlets LBC (2001) 33 HLR 78, QBD	3.165
R (Konodyba) v Kensington and Chelsea RLBC [2012] EWCA Civ 982, [2012] HLR 45; *Affirming* [2011] EWHC 2653 (Admin), [2011] JHL D10	12.149
R (L and D) v Lambeth LBC [2001] EWHC Admin 900, [2002] JHL D1	11.65, 11.74
R (Lawer) v Restormel BC [2007] EWHC 2299 (Admin), [2008] HLR 20	12.125, 12.149
R (Lichfield Securities Ltd) v Lichfield DC [2001] EWCA Civ 304, [2001] 3 PLR 33	12.121
R (Limbuela) v Secretary of State for the Home Department (Shelter intervener) [2005] UKHL 66, [2006] 1 AC 396	13.32
R (Lin) v Barnet LBC [2007] EWCA Civ 132, [2007] HLR 30; *Reversing in part* [2006] EWHC 1041 (Admin), [2006] HLR 44	11.74, 12.120
R (Lusamba) v Islington LBC [2008] EWHC 1149 (Admin), [2008] JHL D89	5.14, 12.112
R (Lynch) v Lambeth LBC [2006] EWHC 2737 (Admin), [2007] HLR 15	9.69, 9.102, 9.178, 9.185
R (M) v Croydon LBC [2012] EWCA Civ 595, [2010] 3 All ER 1237	12.142
R (M) v Hackney LBC [2009] EWHC 2255 (Admin), [2010] JHL D1	11.32
R (M) v Hammersmith and Fulham LBC [2008] UKHL 14, [2008] 1 WLR 535, [2008] 4 All ER 271, HL; *Affirming* [2006] EWCA Civ 917, [2007] HLR 6	5.66, 5.68, 9.46, 10.11
R (M) v Slough BC [2008] UKHL 52, [2008] 1 WLR 1808	13.16, 13.24
R (M and A) v Islington LBC [2016] EWHC 332 (Admin), [2016] HLR 19	13.66
R (MM) v Lewisham LBC [2009] EWHC 416 (Admin)	13.45
R (MN and KN) v Hackney LBC [2013] EWHC 1205 (Admin)	9.189, 13.46
R (MT by his father as litigation friend) v Oxford City Council [2015] EWHC 795 (Admin)	9.19
R (Maali) v Lambeth LBC [2003] EWHC 2231 (Admin), [2003] JHL D83	11.100

R (McDonagh) v Hackney LBC [2012] EWHC 373, [2012] JHL D60 11.84
R (McDonagh) v Hounslow LBC [2004] EWHC 511 (Admin), [2004] JHL D61 9.86
R (McIntyre) v Gentoo Group Ltd [2010] EWHC 5 (Admin), [2010] JHL D22, D40 11.121
R (McKenzie) v Waltham Forest LBC [2009] EWHC 1097 (Admin), [2009] JHL D94 12.119
R (Macleod) v Peabody Trust Governors [2016] EWHC 737 (Admin), [2016] HLR 27 12.7
R (Mahmood) v Secretary of State for the Home Department [2001] 1 WLR 840, CA 12.26
R (Mani) v Lambeth LBC [2003] EWCA Civ 836, (2003) 6 CCLR 376, [2004] HLR 5 13.16
R (March) v Secretary of State for Health [2010] EWHC 765 (Admin) 12.37
R (Meredith) v Merthyr Tydfil CBC [2002] EWHC 634 (Admin) 12.37
R (Mohamed) v Harrow LBC [2005] EWHC 3194 (Admin), [2006] HLR 18 3.160
R (Morris) v Newham LBC [2002] EWHC 1262 (Admin), [2002] JHL D77 12.100, 12.216
R (Morris) v Westminster City Council [2003] EWHC 2266 (Admin), [2004] HLR 18 12.126
R (Morris) v Westminster City Council (No 3) [2005] EWCA Civ 1184, [2006] 1 WLR 505, [2006] HLR 8; *Affirming* [2004] EWHC 2191 (Admin), [2005] 1 All ER 351, [2005] HLR 7 1.110, 3.113, 3.119, 5.8, 12.95, 12.102, 12.104, 13.93
R (Murphy) v Secretary of State for the Home Department [2005] EWHC 140 (Admin), [2005] 2 All ER 763, [2005] 1 WLR 3516 12.36
R (Murua) v Croydon LBC [2001] EWHC Admin 830, (2002) 5 CCLR 51, QBD 13.16
R (N) v Lambeth LBC [2006] EWHC 3427 (Admin), [2007] ACD 49 13.18
R (N) v (1) Newham LBC (2) Essex CC [2013] EWHC 2475 (Admin) 13.41
R (NM) v Islington LBC [2012] EWHC 414 (Admin) 13.14
R (NS) v First Tier Tribunal (Social Security Entitlement Chamber) and Secretary of State for the Home Department [2009] EWHC 3819 (Admin) 13.37
R (Nassery) v Brent LBC [2011] EWCA Civ 539, [2011] PTSR 1639; *Affirming* [2010] EWHC 2326, QBD 13.25
R (Naureen) v Salford City Council [2012] EWCA Civ 1795 12.142
R (O) v Barking and Dagenham LBC [2010] EWCA Civ 1101, [2011] 1 WLR 1283, [2011] 1 FLR 734, [2011] HLR 4, (2010) 13 CCLR 591 13.77

R (O) v East Riding of Yorkshire CC [2011] EWCA Civ 196, [2011] 3 All ER 137	13.58
R (O) v Hammersmith and Fulham LBC [2011] EWCA Civ 925, [2012] 1 WLR 1057	13.61
R (Okil) v Southwark LBC [2012] EWHC 1202 (Admin)	13.23
R (Omar) v Wandsworth LBC [2015] EWHC 4110 (Admin)	10.11
R (Osei) v Newham LBC Lettings Agency [2010] EWHC 368 (Admin), [2010] JHL D37	11.61, 11.75
R (P) v Ealing LBC [2013] EWCA Civ 1579, [2014] HLR 5	12.213
R (PB) v Haringey LBC and (1) Secretary of State for Health (2) Secretary of State for Communities and Local Government (interested parties) [2006] EWHC 225 (Admin), [2007] HLR 13, (2007) 10 CCLR 99	3.158, 13.19
R (PK and another) v Harrow LBC [2014] EWHC 584 (Admin)	13.51
R (Pajaziti) v Lewisham LBC and Secretary of State for the Home Department (interested party) [2007] EWCA Civ 1351	13.17
R (Patrick) v Newham LBC (2001) 4 CCLR 48, QBD	13.26
R (Paul-Coker) v Southwark LBC [2006] EWHC 497 (Admin), [2006] HLR 32	3.101, 10.38, 12.66
R (Price) v Carmarthenshire CC [2003] EWHC 42 (Admin), [2003] JHL D43	10.176
R (ProLife Alliance) v British Broadcasting Corporation [2003] UKHL 23, [2004] 1 AC 185	12.27, 12.30
R (Q) v Secretary of State for the Home Department [2003] EWCA Civ 364, [2004] QB 36	12.34
R (R) v Croydon LBC [2013] EWHC 4243 (Admin), [2012] JHL D58	13.78
R (RJM) v Secretary of State for Work and Pensions [2008] UKHL 63, [2009] 1 AC 311	12.105
R (Raw) v Lambeth LBC [2010] EWHC 507 (Admin), [2010] JHL D40	12.119
R (Richards) v West Somerset Council [2008] EWHC 3215 (Admin)	13.88
R (Rushbridger) v Attorney General [2004] 1 AC 357, HL	12.119
R (S) v Chief Constable of South Yorkshire Police [2004] UKHL 39, [2004] 1 WLR 2196	12.104
R (S) v Secretary of State for the Home Department [2007] EWCA Civ 546, [2007] Imm AR 781	12.151
R (S) v Sutton LBC [2007] EWCA Civ 790, (2007) 10 CCLR 615	5.65, 5.66, 13.58
R (SG) v Haringey LBC [2017] EWCA Civ 322; *Affirming on another point* [2015] EWHC 2579 (Admin), (2015) CCLR 444	13.22
R (SL) v Westminster City Council [2013] UKSC 27, [2013] 1 WLR 1445, [2013] HLR 30	13.16, 13.24
R (ST (Eritrea)) v Secretary of State for the Home Department [2012] UKSC 12, [2012] 2 AC 125; *Affirming* [2010] EWCA Civ 643, [2010] 1 WLR 2858	3.6

R (Sabiri) v Croydon LBC [2012] EWHC 1236 (Admin)	13.77
R (Sacupima) v Newham LBC [2001] 1 WLR 563, (2001) 33 HLR 2, CA; *Reversing in part* (2001) 33 HLR 1, [2000] COD 133, QBD	4.61, 4.120, 4.143, 10.137, 10.164, 10.173
R (Sambotin) v Brent LBC [2017] EWHC 1190 (Admin)	9.129, 12.65
R (Sandra Stewart) v Wandsworth LBC and others [2001] EWHC Admin 709, [2002] FLR 469	13.41
R (Savage) v Hillingdon LBC [2010] EWHC 88 (Admin), [2010] JHL D44	10.86, 10.99, 12.45, 12.112
R (Scott) v Hackney LBC [2009] EWCA Civ 217	12.140
R (Slaiman) v Richmond upon Thames LBC [2006] EWHC 329 (Admin), [2006] HLR 20	9.129, 9.163, 12.112
R (T) v Hertfordshire CC [2016] EWCA Civ 1108, [2017] HLR 10	13.75
R (TG) v Lambeth LBC [2011] EWCA Civ 526, [2011] HLR 33	13.78
R (Tanushi) v (1) Westminster City Council (2) Hillingdon LBC, CO/156/2016, High Court (QBD), 2 January 2016	7.7
R (Theophilus) v Lewisham LBC [2002] EWHC 1371 (Admin), [2002] 3 All ER 851	13.88, 13.93
R (Tilianu) v Secretary of State for Work and Pensions [2010] EWCA Civ 1397	3.38
R (Tout a Tout) v Haringey LBC; R (Heff) v Haringey LBC [2012] EWHC 873 (Admin), [2012] JHL D77	10.195
R (VC) v Newcastle City Council (interested party Secretary of State for the Home Department) [2011] EWHC 2673 (Admin), [2012] PTSR 546, [2012] JHL D3	13.39, 13.49
R (Van der Stolk) v Camden LBC LBC [2002] EWHC 1261 (Admin), [2002] JHL D77	12.112
R (W) v Lambeth LBC [2002] EWCA Civ 613, [2002] HLR 41, (2002) 5 CCLR 203, CA	13.43, 13.88
R (W) v Sheffield City Council [2005] EWHC 720 (Admin)	12.112, 12.113
R (Wahid) v Tower Hamlets LBC [2002] EWCA Civ 287, [2003] HLR 2; *Affirming* [2001] EWHC Admin 641, (2001) 4 CCLR 455, QBD	1.112, 11.84, 12.14, 13.22
R (Wasid) v Secretary of State for the Home Department [2016] EWCA Civ 82, [2016] 1 WLR 2793	12.132
R (Watt) v Hackney LBC [2016] EWHC 1978 (Admin), [2017] JPL 192	12.37
R (Weaver) v London & Quadrant Housing Trust [2009] EWCA Civ 587, [2010] 1 WLR 363, [2009] HLR 40, CA; *Affirming* [2008] EWHC 1377 (Admin), [2008] JHL D94, DC	11.120, 11.21, 12.7, 12.95

R (Webb) v Bristol City Council [2001] EWHC Admin 696, [2001] JHL D90 12.127
R (Wilkinson) v Broadmoor Special Hospital Authority [2001] EWCA Civ 1545, [2002] 1 WLR 419 12.36
R (Wiltshire CC) v Hertfordshire CC [2014] EWCA Civ 712, [2014] HLR 41 13.9
R (Woolfe) v Islington LBC [2016] EWHC 1907 (Admin), [2016] HLR 42 11.65, 12.213
R (X) v Tower Hamlets LBC [2013] EWHC 480 (Admin), [2013] 3 All ER 157 6.55
R (XC) v Lambeth LBC [2017] EWHC 736 (Admin), [2017] HLR 24 11.40, 11.91
R (YA) v Hammersmith and Fulham LBC [2016] EWHC 1850 (Admin), [2016] HLR 39 11.28, 11.39
R (Yazar) v Southwark LBC [2008] EWHC 515 (Admin), [2008] JHL D55 11.103
R (Yekini) v Southwark LBC [2014] EWHC 2096 (Admin) 10.15
R (Yeter) v Enfield LBC [2002] EWHC 2185 (Admin), [2003] JHL D19 5.42
R (Yumsak) v Enfield LBC [2002] EWHC 280 (Admin), [2002] JHL D38 10.131, 10.173
R (ZH and CN) v Newham LBC and Lewisham LBC [2014] UKSC 62, [2015] AC 1259, [2015] HLR 6 4.55, 10.18, 10.112, 10.222, 12.161
R (Zaher) v Westminster City Council [2003] EWHC 101 (Admin), [2003] JHL D41 9.152, 10.149
R (Zoolife International Ltd) v Secretary of State for the Environment, Food and Rural Affairs [2007] EWHC 2995 (Admin), [2008] ACD 44 12.119
R v Attorney General of Hong Kong ex p Ng Yuen Shiu [1983] 2 AC 629, PC 12.92
R v Barking and Dagenham LBC ex p Okuneye (1995) 28 HLR 174, QBD 4.36
R v Barnet LBC ex p Babalola (1995) 28 HLR 196, QBD 9.66
R v Barnet LBC ex p Grumbridge (1992) 24 HLR 433, QBD 9.68
R v Barnet LBC ex p O'Connor (1990) 22 HLR 486, QBD 6.22
R v Barnet LBC ex p Rughooputh (1993) 25 HLR 607, CA 6.49
R v Barnet LBC ex p Shah [1983] 2 AC 309, HL 7.15, 13.10
R v Basingstoke and Deane BC ex p Bassett (1983) 10 HLR 125, QBD 4.134, 6.124
R v Bath City Council ex p Sangermano (1984) 17 HLR 94, QBD 5.33, 5.47, 5.53, 9.103
R v Beverley BC ex p McPhee (1978) *Times* 26 October, QBD 9.142, 9.145
R v Birmingham City Council ex p Mohammed [1999] 1 WLR 33, (1999) 31 HLR 392, QBD 12.38
R v Blankley [1979] Crim LR 166 4.57

R v Bradford City Council ex p Parveen (1996) 28 HLR 681, QBD	4.118, 12.86
R v Braintree DC ex p Halls (2000) 32 HLR 770, CA	12.43
R v Brent LBC ex p Awua [1996] AC 55, (1995) 27 HLR 453, HL; *Affirming* (1994) 26 HLR 539, CA; *Reversing* (1993) 25 HLR 626, QBD	1.6, 1.39, 1.63, 1.66, 1.112, 4.8, 4.9, 4.11, 4.12, 4.13, 4.15, 4.95, 6.85, 6.94, 6.102, 6.103, 6.109, 6.136, 10.26, 10.56, 10.163, 12.41
R v Brent LBC ex p Bariise (1998) 31 HLR 50, CA	9.85, 12.71, 12.80, 12.234
R v Brent LBC ex p Baruwa (1997) 29 HLR 915, CA	4.129, 6.82, 9.84, 12.68, 12.78, 12.87
R v Brent LBC ex p Grossett (1994) 28 HLR 9, CA	4.129
R v Brent LBC ex p McManus (1993) 25 HLR 643, QBD	4.78, 4.135, 6.147, 9.118
R v Brent LBC ex p O'Connor (1998) 31 HLR 923, QBD	12.111, 12.167
R v Brent LBC ex p Omar (1991) 23 HLR 446, QBD	10.165, 10.166, 10.167
R v Brent LBC ex p Sadiq (2000) 33 HLR 47, QBD	9.128, 12.112
R v Brent LBC ex p Yusuf (1995) 29 HLR 48, QBD	6.132
R v Brighton and Hove Council ex p Marmont (1998) 30 HLR 1046, QBD	12.38
R v Brighton and Hove Council ex p Nacion (1999) 31 HLR 1095, CA	10.39, 10.40, 12.147, 12.202
R v Brighton BC ex p Harvey (1997) 30 HLR 670, QBD	6.127
R v Bristol City Council ex p Bradic (1995) 27 HLR 584, CA	5.59, 5.60
R v Bristol City Council ex p Browne [1979] 1 WLR 1437, DC	7.50, 10.128
R v Bristol City Council ex p Johns (1992) 25 HLR 249, QBD	11.77
R v Bristol City Council ex p Penfold (1998) 1 CCLR 315, QBD	12.38, 13.22
R v Camden LBC ex p Adair (1996) 29 HLR 236, QBD	9.68, 12.73, 12.86
R v Camden LBC ex p Aranda (1996) 28 HLR 672, QBD	4.127, 6.90
R v Camden LBC ex p Cosmo (1997) 30 HLR 817, QBD	9.111
R v Camden LBC ex p Gillan (1988) 21 HLR 114, QBD	9.45, 9.62, 9.63
R v Camden LBC ex p Hersi (2001) 33 HLR 52, CA	5.18, 6.25, 9.37
R v Camden LBC ex p Jibril (1997) 29 HLR 785, QBD	10.147
R v Camden LBC ex p Martin [1997] 1 WLR 359, QBD	12.184
R v Camden LBC ex p Mohammed (1998) 30 HLR 315, QBD	9.118, 10.33, 10.34, 10.35, 10.36, 10.38, 12.69, 12.84, 12.112, 12.147, 12.202

R v Camden LBC ex p Pereira (1998) 31 HLR 317, CA 5.33, 5.37
R v Canterbury City Council ex p Gillespie (1987) 19 HLR 7, QBD 11.77
R v Cardiff City Council ex p Barry (1989) 22 HLR 261, CA 12.146
R v Cardiff City Council ex p John (1982) 9 HLR 56, QBD 9.109, 12.86
R v Chief Constable of Sussex ex p International Trader's Ferry [1999] 2 AC 418, HL 12.24
R v Chiltern DC ex p Dyason (1990) 23 HLR 387, QBD 10.56
R v Chiltern DC ex p Roberts *et al* (1990) 23 HLR 387, QBD 4.67, 8.11, 9.45
R v Christchurch BC ex p Conway (1987) 19 HLR 238, QBD 6.35, 6.137
R v Civil Service Appeal Board ex p Cunningham [1991] 4 All ER 310, CA 12.59
R v Criminal Injuries Compensation Board ex p A [1999] 2 AC 330, HL 12.37
R v Croydon LBC ex p Easom (1992) 25 HLR 262, QBD 6.114
R v Croydon LBC ex p Graham (1993) 26 HLR 286, CA 12.70, 12.72, 12.86, 12.234
R v Croydon LBC ex p Jarvis (1993) 26 HLR 194, QBD 4.118, 9.53
R v Croydon LBC ex p Toth (1987) 20 HLR 576, CA 4.140, 6.30
R v Dacorum BC ex p Brown (1989) 21 HLR 405, QBD 9.117, 12.120, 12.167
R v Dacorum BC ex p Walsh (1991) 24 HLR 401, QBD 9.125
R v Dairy Produce Quota Tribunal ex p Caswell [2009] 2 AC 738, HL 12.121
R v Devon CC ex p Baker [1995] 1 All ER 73, CA 12.92
R v Dinefwr BC ex p Marshall (1984) 17 HLR 310, QBD 4.12, 6.106
R v Ealing LBC ex p Denny (1995) 27 HLR 424, QBD 10.215
R v Ealing LBC ex p McBain [1985] 1 WLR 1351, (1985) 18 HLR 59, CA 9.26
R v Ealing LBC ex p Parkinson (1997) 29 HLR 179, QBD 12.151
R v Ealing LBC ex p Salmons (1990) 23 HLR 272, QBD 6.22
R v Ealing LBC ex p Sidhu (1982) 2 HLR 45, QBD 4.12, 5.16, 6.14, 9.132, 10.14
R v Ealing LBC ex p Sukhija (1994) 26 HLR 726, QBD 6.33, 6.37
R v Ealing LBC ex p Surdonja (1998) 31 HLR 686, QBD 10.172
R v East Devon DC ex p Robb (1997) 30 HLR 922, QBD 7.46
R v East Hertfordshire DC ex p Bannon (1986) 18 HLR 515, QBD 6.24, 6.60
R v East Hertfordshire DC ex p Hunt (1985) 18 HLR 51, QBD 6.136, 10.26
R v East Northamptonshire DC ex p Spruce (1988) 20 HLR 508, QBD 6.21
R v East Sussex CC ex p Tandy [1998] AC 714, HL 12.38
R v East Yorkshire Borough of Beverley Housing Benefits Review Board, ex p Hare (1995) 27 HLR 637, QBD 12.109

R v Eastleigh BC ex p Beattie (No 1) (1983) 10 HLR 134, QBD 4.29, 4.111, 6.6, 6.63, 9.88
R v Eastleigh BC ex p Beattie (No 2) (1984) 17 HLR 168, QBD 4.111, 6.15, 6.30, 6.44
R v Eastleigh BC ex p Evans (1984) 17 HLR 515, QBD 4.85, 4.138
R v Exeter City Council ex p Gliddon (1984) 14 HLR 103, QBD 6.98–6.100, 10.21
R v Exeter City Council ex p Tranckle (1993) 26 HLR 244, CA 6.27, 6.50
R v Forest Heath DC ex p West and Lucas (1991) 24 HLR 85, CA 11.75
R v Gateshead MBC ex p Lauder (1997) 29 HLR 360, QBD 11.77
R v Gloucester City Council ex p RADAR (1998) 1 CCLR 476 13.14
R v Gough [1993] AC 646, HL 12.61
R v Gravesham BC ex p Winchester (1986) 18 HLR 208, QBD 4.79, 4.107, 9.66, 9.122, 12.204
R v Greenwich LBC ex p Dukic (1996) 29 HLR 87, QBD 5.46
R v Hackney LBC ex p Ajayi (1997) 30 HLR 473, QBD 6.115, 6.128
R v Hackney LBC ex p Decordova (1994) 27 HLR 108, QBD 9.118
R v Hackney LBC ex p Tonnicodi (1997) 30 HLR 916, QBD 4.37
R v Hambleton DC ex p Geoghan [1985] JPL 394, QBD 9.123
R v Hammersmith and Fulham LBC ex p Avdic (1998) 30 HLR 1, [1997] COD 122, CA; *Affirming* (1996) 28 HLR 897, QBD 7.27, 7.32
R v Hammersmith and Fulham LBC ex p Burkett [2002] UKHL 23, [2002] 1 WLR 153 12.107
R v Hammersmith and Fulham LBC ex p Duro-Rama (1983) 9 HLR 71, QBD 4.77, 4.126, 4.130
R v Hammersmith and Fulham LBC ex p Fleck (1997) 30 HLR 679, QBD 10.34
R v Hammersmith and Fulham LBC ex p Lusi (1991) 23 HLR 460, QBD 6.32, 6.37, 6.39
R v Hammersmith and Fulham LBC ex p M; R v Lambeth LBC ex p P and X; R v Westminster City Council ex p A (1998) 30 HLR 10, (1997) 1 CCLR 85 13.23
R v Hammersmith and Fulham LBC ex p O'Brian (1985) 17 HLR 471, QBD 7.61, 9.42
R v Hammersmith and Fulham LBC ex p P (1989) 22 HLR 21, QBD 6.60, 6.88, 6.146, 6.147
R v Haringey LBC ex p Karaman (1996) 29 HLR 366, QBD 10.167
R v Harrow LBC ex p Carter (1992) 26 HLR 32, QBD 7.51

R v Harrow LBC ex p Fahia [1998] 1 WLR 1396, (1998) 30 HLR 1124, HL; *Affirming* (1997) 29 HLR 974, CA — 6.121–6.125, 6.126, 9.26, 9.27, 9.28, 9.43, 10.219
R v Harrow LBC ex p Holland (1982) 4 HLR 108, CA — 9.97
R v Herstmere BC ex p Woolgar (1995) 27 HLR 703, QBD — 9.59, 9.60, 12.46
R v Higher Education Funding Council ex p Institute of Dental Surgery [1994] 1 WLR 242, DC — 12.59
R v Hillingdon LBC ex p H (1988) 20 HLR 554, QBD — 4.92, 4.140, 12.77
R v Hillingdon LBC ex p Islam, *sub nom* R v Hillingdon Homeless Families Panel ex p Islam [1983] 1 AC 688, (1981) 1 HLR 107, HL; *Reversing* [1981] 3 WLR 109, [1981] 2 All ER 1089, CA; *Affirming* (1980) *Times* 10 February, QBD — 1.41, 4.28, 4.29, 4.33, 4.130, 5.15, 6.6, 6.138, 6.139, 9.114, 9.136, 12.34, 12.90, 12.91
R v Hillingdon LBC ex p McDonagh (1999) 31 HLR 531, QBD — 12.38, 12.39
R v Hillingdon LBC ex p Puhlhofer [1986] AC 484, (1986) 18 HLR 158, HL; (1985) 17 HLR 588, CA; (1985) 17 HLR 278, QBD — 1.6, 1.46, 1.52, 1.55, 1.57, 1.112, 4.10, 4.12, 4.13, 4.15, 4.69, 4.110, 6.17, 6.94, 6.106, 10.19, 10.130, 10.145, 10.215, 12.13, 12.35, 12.37, 12.146
R v Hillingdon LBC ex p Royco Homes Ltd [1974] 1 QB 720, DC — 12.108
R v Hillingdon LBC ex p Streeting (No 2) [1980] 1 WLR 1425, [1980] 4 All ER 413, CA; *Affirming* [1980] 124 SJ 274, QBD — 1.61, 3.6, 3.164, 4.4, 7.52, 9.9, 9.12, 9.56
R v Hillingdon LBC ex p Thomas (1987) 19 HLR 196, QBD — 6.13, 12.37
R v Hillingdon LBC ex p Tinn (1988) 20 HLR 305, (1988) 152 LGR 750, [1988] Fam Law 388, QBD — 4.127, 4.128, 6.79, 12.114
R v Hillingdon LBC ex p Wilson (1983) 13 HLR 61, QBD — 6.148
R v HM Inspectorate of Pollution ex p Greenpeace Ltd (No 2) [1994] 4 All ER 329, QBD — 12.112
R v Horsham DC ex p Wenman [1995] 1 WLR 680, QBD — 12.170
R v Hounslow LBC ex p R (1997) 29 HLR 939, (1997) *Times* 25 February, QBD — 6.92, 6.93
R v Hull Prison Visitors ex p St Germain (No 2) [1979] 1 WLR 1401, QBD — 12.59

R v Immigration Appeal Tribunal ex p Antonissen, Case C-292/98 [1991] ECR I-745, ECJ	3.31
R v IRC ex p MFK Underwriting Agents Ltd [1990] 1 WLR 1545, QBD	12.93
R v IRC ex p National Federation of Self Employed and Small Businesses Ltd [1982] AC 617, HL	12.112
R v IRC ex p Preston [1985] AC 835, HL	12.37
R v Islington LBC ex p Adigun (1986) 20 HLR 600, QBD	7.14, 7.31, 7.50
R v Islington LBC ex p Aldabbagh (1994) 27 HLR 271, QBD	11.75, 11.77, 12.41
R v Islington LBC ex p B (1997) 30 HLR 706, QBD	9.20, 12.153
R v Islington LBC ex p Bashir Hassan (1995) 27 HLR 485, QBD	6.83, 10.28
R v Islington LBC ex p Bibi (1996) 29 HLR 498, QBD, (1996) *Times* 10 July	4.128, 6.81
R v Islington LBC ex p Hinds (1996) 28 HLR 302, CA; *Reversing* (1995) 27 HLR 65, QBD	6.89, 12.65, 12.73
R v Islington LBC ex p Reilly and Mannix (1998) 31 HLR 651, QBD	11.19, 11.78, 11.79, 12.234
R v Islington LBC ex p Thomas (1997) 30 HLR 111, QBD	10.178, 11.98
R v Kensington and Chelsea RLBC ex p Amarfio (1995) 27 HLR 543, CA	5.19
R v Kensington and Chelsea RLBC ex p Bayani (1990) 22 HLR 406, CA	4.79, 9.82, 9.92, 9.111
R v Kensington and Chelsea RLBC ex p Ben-El-Mabrouk (1995) 27 HLR 564, CA	4.109, 5.58
R v Kensington and Chelsea RLBC ex p Byfield (1999) 31 HLR 913, QBD	9.158, 12.112
R v Kensington and Chelsea RLBC ex p Cunha (1988) 21 HLR 16, QBD	9.99, 9.111
R v Kensington and Chelsea RLBC ex p Ghebregiogis (1994) 27 HLR 602, QBD	12.118
R v Kensington and Chelsea RLBC ex p Grillo (1995) 28 HLR 94, CA	12.59
R v Kensington and Chelsea RLBC ex p Hammell [1989] QB 518, (1988) 20 HLR 666, CA	12.146, 12.148
R v Kensington and Chelsea RLBC ex p Kassam (1993) 26 HLR 455, QBD	9.82
R v Kensington and Chelsea RLBC ex p Kujtim [1999] 4 All ER 161, (2000) 32 HLR 579, (1999) 2 CCLR 340, CA	10.27, 13.22, 13.26
R v Kensington and Chelsea RLBC ex p Minton (1988) 20 HLR 648	4.47
R v Kensington and Chelsea RLBC ex p Moncada (1996) 29 HLR 289, QBD	4.139
R v Kensington and Chelsea RLBC ex p Silchenstedt (1996) 29 HLR 728, QBD	9.78

R v Kensington and Chelsea RLBC, Hammersmith and Fulham LBC, Westminster City Council and Islington LBC ex p Kihara and others (1996) 29 HLR 147, CA 5.36, 5.50, 5.51, 5.52
R v Kerrier DC ex p Uzell (1995) 71 P&CR 566, QBD 12.38
R v Kingswood BC ex p Smith-Morse (1994) *Times* ?? December, QBD 5.25
R v Lambeth LBC ex p A (1998) 30 HLR 933, CA 10.124, 12.38
R v Lambeth LBC ex p Ashley (1996) 29 HLR 385, QBD 11.74, 11.77
R v Lambeth LBC ex p Barnes (1992) 25 HLR 140, QBD 12.216
R v Lambeth LBC ex p Bodunrin (1992) 24 HLR 647, QBD 5.14
R v Lambeth LBC ex p Campbell (1994) 26 HLR 618, QBD 10.147
R v Lambeth LBC ex p Carroll (1987) 20 HLR 142, QBD 5.33, 5.44, 9.101
R v Lambeth LBC ex p Ekpo-Wedderman (1999) 31 HLR 498, QBD 10.124, 12.94
R v Lambeth LBC ex p Ly (1986) 19 HLR 51, QBD 4.34
R v Lambeth LBC ex p Miah (1994) 27 HLR 21, QBD 9.123
R v Lambeth LBC ex p Njomo (1996) 28 HLR 737, QBD 11.75, 11.77
R v Lambeth LBC ex p Pattinson (1985) 28 HLR 214, QBD 9.20
R v Lambeth LBC ex p Trabi (1997) 30 HLR 975, QBD 12.93
R v Lambeth LBC ex p Vagliviello (1990) 22 HLR 392, CA 5.23
R v Lambeth LBC ex p Wilson (1997) 30 HLR 64, (1997) *Times* 25 March, CA 12.181
R v Lambeth LBC ex p Woodburne (1997) 29 HLR 836, QBD 10.167
R v Leeds City Council ex p Adamiec (1991) 24 HLR 138, QBD 6.82, 6.145, 9.83
R v Legal Aid Committee No 10 (East Midlands) ex p McKenna (1990) 2 Admin LR 585, [1990] COD 358, (1989) *Times* 20 December, DC 12.37
R v Lewisham LBC ex p Creppy (1991) 24 HLR 121, CA 5.14
R v Lewisham LBC ex p Dolan (1992) 25 HLR 68, QBD 10.166
R v Lincolnshire CC and Wealden DC ex p Atkinson [1995] 8 Admin LR 529, DC 12.38
R v Local Commissioner for Administration for the North etc ex p Bradford MBC [1979] QB 287, CA 12.221
R v Local Commissioner for the South etc ex p Eastleigh BC [1988] 1 QB 855, CA 12.221
R v London Residuary Board ex p ILEA (1987) *Times* 3 July, CA 12.37
R v Luton Family Proceedings Court Justices ex p R [1998] 1 FCR 605, CA 12.184
R v Macclesfield BC ex p Duddy [2001] JHL D16, QBD 11.61
R v McCall and others ex p Eastbourne BC (1981) (unreported), but referred to at (1981) 8 HLR 48, QBD 7.28, 7.78

R v Medina BC ex p Dee (1992) 24 HLR 562, QBD	4.108
R v Merton LBC ex p Ruffle (1989) 21 HLR 361, QBD	6.108–6.110, 6.112
R v Merton LBC ex p Sembi (1999) 32 HLR 439, QBD	10.117
R v Ministry of Agriculture Fisheries and Food ex p First City Trading Ltd [1997] 1 CMLR 250, QBD	12.25, 12.28
R v Ministry of Defence ex p Murray [1998] COD 134, QBD	12.59
R v Ministry of Defence ex p Smith [1996] QB 517, CA	12.25
R v Mole Valley DC ex p Burton (1988) 20 HLR 479, QBD	6.30
R v Mole Valley DC ex p Minnett (1983) 12 HLR 49, QBD	4.119
R v Newham LBC ex p Ajayi (1994) 28 HLR 25, QBD	4.97, 9.90, 9.99, 12.120
R v Newham LBC ex p Bautista, April 2001 *Legal Action* 22	10.34
R v Newham LBC ex p Begum (1999) 32 HLR 808, QBD	10.118
R v Newham LBC ex p Bibi and Al-Nashed [2001] EWCA Civ 607, (2001) 33 HLR 84	12.93, 12.94, 12.153
R v Newham LBC ex p Bones (1993) 25 HLR 357, QBD	12.41
R v Newham LBC ex p Campbell (1993) 26 HLR 183, QBD	6.83, 10.28, 11.77
R v Newham LBC ex p Dada (1995) 27 HLR 502, CA	4.30
R v Newham LBC ex p Dawson (1994) 26 HLR 747, QBD	11.77
R v Newham LBC ex p Khan and Hussain (2001) 33 HLR 29, QBD	4.34, 4.61, 4.120, 4.145, 10.56
R v Newham LBC ex p Lumley (2001) 33 HLR 11, [2000] COD 315, QBD	5.42, 5.44, 9.105, 10.37, 12.70, 12.84
R v Newham LBC ex p McIlroy (1991) 23 HLR 570, QBD	4.92, 4.140, 6.147
R v Newham LBC ex p Miah (1995) 28 HLR 279, QBD	10.114, 11.75, 11.103
R v Newham LBC ex p Ojuri (No 3) (1998) 31 HLR 452, QBD	10.164, 10.173
R v Newham LBC ex p Ojuri (No 5) (1998) 31 HLR 631, QBD	10.41
R v Newham LBC ex p Sacupima, *see* R (Sacupima) v Newham LBC—	
R v Newham LBC ex p Smith (1996) 29 HLR 213, QBD	7.50, 9.57
R v Newham LBC ex p Tower Hamlets LBC (1990) 23 HLR 62, CA	4.97, 7.46, 7.47, 7.59, 9.41
R v Newham LBC ex p Ugbo (1993) 26 HLR 263, QBD	4.116, 4.118
R v Newham LBC ex p Watkins (1993) 26 HLR 434, QBD	11.77
R v North and East Devon Health Authority ex p Coughlan [2001] QB 213, CA	12.92, 12.93

R v North Devon DC ex p Lewis [1981] 1 WLR 328, QBD	6.11, 6.14, 6.15, 6.18, 6.67, 9.23, 9.36, 9.122, 10.99
R v North Yorkshire CC ex p Hargreaves (1997) 96 LGR 39, QBD	4.65
R v Northampton BC ex p Carpenter (1992) 25 HLR 349, QBD	12.73
R v Northampton BC ex p Clarkson (1992) 24 HLR 529, QBD	4.141
R v Northavon DC ex p Palmer (1995) 27 HLR 576, CA	9.51, 12.216
R v Northavon DC ex p Smith [1994] 2 AC 402, (1994) 26 HLR 659, HL	10.67, 13.67, 13.70
R v Northumberland Compensation Appeal Tribunal ex p Shaw [1952] 1 KB 338, CA	12.12
R v Nottingham City Council ex p Caine (1995) 28 HLR 374, CA	6.13
R v Nottingham City Council ex p Costello (1989) 21 HLR 301, QBD	9.82, 9.112
R v Nottingham City Council ex p Edwards (1998) 31 HLR 33, QBD	9.82
R v Oldham BC ex p Garlick; R v Bexley BC ex p Bentum; R v Tower Hamlets LBC ex p Begum (Ferdous) [1993] AC 509, (1993) 25 HLR 319, HL	5.13, 6.25, 9.17, 9.19, 12.36
R v Oxford City Council ex p Crowder (1998) 31 HLR 485, QBD	11.99
R v Oxford City Council ex p Doyle (1997) 30 HLR 506, QBD	5.28
R v Paddington Valuation Officer ex p Peachey Property Corp Ltd [1966] 1 QB 380, CA	12.108
R v Penwith DC ex p Hughes, August 1980 *LAG Bulletin* 187, QBD	6.144
R v Penwith DC ex p Trevena (1984) 17 HLR 526, QBD	6.16
R v Peterborough City Council ex p Carr (1990) 22 HLR 207, CA	4.35
R v Poole BC ex p Cooper (1995) 27 HLR 605, QBD	9.118
R v Port Talbot BC ex p Jones [1988] 2 All ER 208, QBD	12.48
R v Port Talbot BC ex p McCarthy (1990) 23 HLR 208, CA	5.25, 5.27
R v Portsmouth City Council ex p Knight (1983) 10 HLR 115, QBD	4.115
R v Preseli DC ex p Fisher (1984) 17 HLR 147, QBD	4.12, 4.106, 9.80
R v Purbeck DC ex p Cadney (1985) 17 HLR 534, QBD	4.85, 4.86, 6.112
R v Reigate and Banstead BC ex p Paris (1984) 17 HLR 103, QBD	6.135, 9.66, 9.77, 9.79
R v Rochester City Council ex p Trotman (1983) *Times* 13 May	12.120
R v Rugby BC ex p Hunt (1992) 26 HLR 1, QBD	4.145, 9.52
R v Ryedale DC ex p Smith (1983) 16 HLR 66, QBD	1.57, 9.66

R v Secretary of State for Foreign and Commonwealth Affairs, ex p World Development Movement Ltd [1995] 1 WLR 386, QBD	12.112
R v Secretary of State for Health ex p Eastside Cheese Co [1999] 3 CMLR *123, [1999] ELR 968, CA*	12.25, 12.28, 12.42
R v Secretary of State for Social Security ex p B and Joint Council for the Welfare of Immigrants (1996) 29 HLR 129, CA	10.15
R v Secretary of State for Social Services ex p Child Poverty Action Group [1990] 2 QB 540, CA	12.112
R v Secretary of State for the Environment ex p Brent LBC [1982] QB 593, [1982] 2 WLR 693, DC	12.44
R v Secretary of State for the Environment ex p Hillingdon LBC [1986] 1 WLR 807, CA	12.48
R v Secretary of State for the Environment ex p Nottinghamshire CC [1986] 1 AC 240, HL	1.53, 12.13, 12.22
R v Secretary of State for the Environment ex p Powis [1981] 1 WLR 584, CA	12.36
R v Secretary of State for the Environment ex p Tower Hamlets LBC [1993] QB 632, (1993) 25 HLR 524, CA	9.9, 9.13, 9.16
R v Secretary of State for the Environment ex p Walters; R v Brent LBC ex p O'Malley (1997) 30 HLR 328, CA	12.153
R v Secretary of State for the Home Department ex p Begum [1995] COD 177	12.170
R v Secretary of State for the Home Department ex p Brind [1991] 1 AC 696, HL	12.12
R v Secretary of State for the Home Department ex p Bugdaycay, *see* Bugdaycay v Secretary of State for the Home Department—	
R v Secretary of State for the Home Department ex p Doody [1994] 1 AC 531, HL	12.57, 12.59
R v Secretary of State for the Home Department ex p Khawaja [1984] AC 74, HL	12.12, 12.36
R v Secretary of State for the Home Department ex p Leech [1994] QB 198, CA	12.24
R v Secretary of State for the Home Department, ex p Salem [1999] 1 AC 450, HL	12.119
R v Secretary of State for the Home Department ex p Swati [1986] 1 WLR 477, CA	12.107
R v Secretary of State for Trade and Industry ex p Lonrho plc [1989] 1 WLR 525, HL	12.12
R v Sedgemoor DC ex p McCarthy (1996) 28 HLR 608, QBD	4.80, 9.81, 12.81
R v Sefton MBC ex p Healiss (1994) 27 HLR 34, QBD	4.137
R v Sevenoaks DC ex p Reynolds (1989) 22 HLR 250, CA	9.119
R v Sheffield City Council ex p Leek (1993) 26 HLR 669, CA	5.45
R v Shrewsbury and Atcham BC ex p Griffiths (1993) 25 HLR 613, QBD	4.127, 4.135, 6.81, 9.118

R v Slough BC ex p Ealing LBC [1981] QB 801, CA	6.26, 7.1, 7.59, 7.60, 7.85, 9.38, 9.40, 9.44, 9.55
R v Slough BC ex p Khan (1995) 27 HLR 492, QBD	7.29, 7.32, 12.81
R v South Herefordshire DC ex p Miles (1983) 17 HLR 82, QBD	4.12, 4.15, 4.105, 6.106, 9.140
R v South Holland DC ex p Baxter (1998) 30 HLR 1069, QBD	10.178
R v Southampton City Council ex p Ward (1984) 14 HLR 114, QBD	6.26, 9.112, 10.22
R v Southwark LBC ex p Anderson (1998) 32 HLR 96, QBD	10.116, 10.117
R v Southwark LBC ex p Bediako (1997) 30 HLR 22, QBD	3.110
R v Southwark LBC ex p Campisi (1998) 31 HLR 560, CA	9.26
R v Southwark LBC ex p Dagou (1995) 28 HLR 72, QBD	9.126, 9.129, 12.86
R v Southwark LBC ex p Davies (1993) 26 HLR 677, QBD	12.77
R v Southwark LBC ex p Hughes (1998) 30 HLR 1082, QBD	7.22
R v Southwark LBC ex p Mason (1999) 32 HLR 88, QBD	11.113
R v Southwark LBC ex p Melak (1996) 29 HLR 223, QBD	11.77
R v Southwark LBC ex p Ryder (1995) 28 HLR 56, QBD	4.37
R v Southwark LBC ex p Solomon (1994) 26 HLR 693, QBD	10.171
R v Stratford on Avon DC ex p Jackson [1985] 1 WLR 1319, CA	12.120, 12.167
R v Surrey Heath BC ex p Li (1984) 16 HLR 79, QBD	4.115, 9.64
R v Swansea City Council ex p Evans (1990) 22 HLR 467, CA	6.111
R v Swansea City Council ex p Hearn (1990) 23 HLR 372, QBD	4.136
R v Swansea City Council ex p John (1982) 9 HLR 56, QBD	6.24, 6.60
R v Swansea City Council ex p Thomas (1983) 9 HLR 64, QBD	6.18
R v Thanet DC ex p Reeve (1981) 6 HLR 31, QBD	6.74, 6.87
R v Thurrock DC ex p Williams (1981) 1 HLR 128, QBD	6.68–6.73, 6.75, 9.111, 9.122
R v Tower Hamlets LBC ex p Abdul Subhan (1992) 24 HLR 541, QBD	10.171
R v Tower Hamlets LBC ex p Ali; R v Tower Hamlets LBC ex p Bibi (1992) 25 HLR 158, CA	7.61, 9.42, 9.43
R v Tower Hamlets LBC ex p Begum, *see* R v Oldham BC ex p Garlick; R v Bexley BC ex p Bentum; R v Tower Hamlets LBC ex p Begum (Ferdous)—	
R v Tower Hamlets LBC ex p Bibi (1991) 23 HLR 500, QBD	4.111

R v Tower Hamlets LBC ex p Byas (1992) 25 HLR 105, CA 13.66, 13.70
R v Tower Hamlets LBC ex p Camden LBC (1988) 21 HLR 197, QBD 9.40
R v Tower Hamlets LBC ex p Chetnik Developments Ltd [1988] AC 858, HL 12.43, 12.53
R v Tower Hamlets LBC ex p Jalika Begum (1990) 24 HLR 188, QBD 9.65
R v Tower Hamlets LBC ex p Kaur (1994) 26 HLR 597, QBD 10.163
R v Tower Hamlets LBC ex p Khalique (1994) 26 HLR 517, QBD 10.114, 12.43, 12.48
R v Tower Hamlets LBC ex p Khatun (1993) 27 HLR 344, (1994) 27 HLR 465, CA 6.20, 6.33, 9.65
R v Tower Hamlets LBC ex p Mohib Ali (1993) 25 HLR 218, DC 12.120
R v Tower Hamlets LBC ex p Monaf (1988) 20 HLR 529, CA 4.96, 4.97, 10.106, 12.79
R v Tower Hamlets LBC ex p Ojo (1991) 23 HLR 488, QBD 4.111
R v Tower Hamlets LBC ex p Rouf (1989) 21 HLR 294, QBD 4.31, 9.118, 12.234
R v Tower Hamlets LBC ex p Rouf (1991) 23 HLR 460, QBD 6.42
R v Tower Hamlets LBC ex p Saber (1992) 24 HLR 611, QBD 9.117
R v Tower Hamlets LBC ex p Ullah (1992) 24 HLR 680, QBD 9.84
R v Tynedale DC ex p Shield (1987) 22 HLR 144, QBD 12.69
R v Vale of White Horse DC ex p Smith and Hay (1984) 17 HLR 160, QBD 7.18, 7.21, 7.24, 7.31
R v Wandsworth LBC ex p Banbury (1986) 19 HLR 76, QBD 5.33, 5.44, 5.45
R v Wandsworth LBC ex p Dodia (1997) 30 HLR 562, QBD 9.66, 9.118, 12.73
R v Wandsworth LBC ex p Hawthorne [1994] 1 WLR 1442, (1994) 27 HLR 59, CA 6.58, 6.80, 4.41
R v Wandsworth LBC ex p Henderson (1986) 18 HLR 522, QBD 9.98
R v Wandsworth LBC ex p Lindsay (1986) 18 HLR 502, QBD 10.215
R v Wandsworth LBC ex p Mansoor. See R v Wandsworth LBC ex p Wingrove—
R v Wandsworth LBC ex p Nimako-Boateng (1984) 11 HLR 95, QBD 4.85, 4.86, 4.138
R v Wandsworth LBC ex p Onwudiwe (1994) 26 HLR 302, CA 6.43, 12.42
R v Wandsworth LBC ex p Rose (1983) 11 HLR 105, QBD 6.97, 9.116

R v Wandsworth LBC ex p Wingrove; R v Wandsworth LBC ex p Mansoor [1997] QB 953, [1996] 3 All ER 913, (1997) 29 HLR 801, CA	4.95, 10.175
R v Warrington BC ex p Bryant (2001) JHL D5, QBD	6.58
R v Warwickshire CC ex p Williams [1995] COD 182, QBD	4.65
R v Waveney DC ex p Bowers [1983] QB 238, (1982) 4 HLR 118, (1982) *Times* 25 May, CA	4.11, 4.12, 5.36, 5.44, 5.50, 12.41
R v West Dorset DC ex p Phillips (1984) 17 HLR 336, QBD	6.15, 9.62, 9.90
R v West Dorset DC, West Dorset HA ex p Gerrard (1994) 27 HLR 150, QBD	9.59, 12.46
R v Westminster City Council ex p Al-Khorshan (2001) 33 HLR 6, QBD	11.78, 11.79
R v Westminster City Council ex p Ali (1983) 11 HLR 83, QBD	4.31, 4.111
R v Westminster City Council ex p Ali and Bibi (1992) 25 HLR 109, QBD	6.39
R v Westminster City Council ex p Alouat (1989) 21 HLR 477, QBD	4.111
R v Westminster City Council ex p Augustin (1993) 25 HLR 281, CA	9.87, 12.83
R v Westminster City Council ex p Benniche (1996) 29 HLR 230, (1996) *Times* 15 April, CA	7.14, 7.31
R v Westminster City Council ex p Bishop (1993) 25 HLR 459, CA	4.81, 5.18, 5.24
R v Westminster City Council ex p Bishop (1997) 29 HLR 546, QBD	5.18, 5.24
R v Westminster City Council ex p Castelli; R v Same ex p Tristran-Garcia (1995) 27 HLR 125, (1996) 28 HLR 616, CA	1.61, 3.6, 3.111, 9.9, 9.13, 12.154
R v Westminster City Council ex p Chambers (1982) 6 HLR 24, QBD	9.23, 9.26, 10.27, 10.185, 12.90, 12.91
R v Westminster City Council ex p Ellioua (1998) 31 HLR 440, CA	9.161, 12.165
R v Westminster City Council ex p Ermakov [1996] 2 All ER 302, (1995) 28 HLR 819, CA	12.65, 12.86
R v Westminster City Council ex p Iqbal (1988) 22 HLR 215, QBD	9.80
R v Westminster City Council ex p Jaafer (1997) 30 HLR 698, QBD	9.119
R v Westminster City Council ex p Khan (1991) 23 HLR 230, QBD	6.82, 6.140
R v Westminster City Council ex p Moklis Ali (1996) 29 HLR 580, QBD	4.127, 6.82, 6.145
R v Westminster City Council ex p Moozary-Oraky (1993) 26 HLR 214, QBD	6.53

R v Westminster City Council ex p Obeid (1996) 29 HLR 389, QBD	6.29, 6.36, 6.52
R v Westminster City Council ex p Reid (1994) 26 HLR 691, QBD	6.91
R v Wigan MBC ex p Tammadge (1998) 1 CCLR 581, QBD	13.22
R v Wimborne DC ex p Curtis (1985) 18 HLR 79, QBD	4.38
R v Winchester City Council ex p Ashton (1991) 24 HLR 520, CA; *Affirming* (1991) 24 HLR 48, QBD	4.131, 6.34, 6.113, 12.40
R v Wirral MBC ex p Bell (1994) 27 HLR 234, QBD	6.61, 12.125
R v Wolverhampton MBC ex p Watters (1997) 29 HLR 931, CA	11.74
R v Woodspring DC ex p Walters (1984) 16 HLR 73, QBD	9.66, 9.75
R v Wycombe DC ex p Hazeltine (1993) 25 HLR 313, CA	9.158, 10.216
R v Wycombe DC ex p Homes (1988) 22 HLR 150, QBD	4.101
R v Wycombe DC ex p Mahsood (1988) 20 HLR 683, QBD	9.99
R v Wyre BC ex p Joyce (1983) 11 HLR 73, QBD	6.54, 9.116
RM (Zimbabwe) v Secretary of State for the Home Department [2013] EWCA Civ 775	3.46
Ravichandran v Lewisham LBC [2010] EWCA Civ 755, [2010] HLR 42	9.152, 9.157, 10.194, 10.213
Restormel DC v Buscombe (1982) 14 HLR 91, CA	10.16
Reyes v Migrationsverket, Case C 423/12	3.52
Richmond Upon Thames LBC v Kubicek [2012] EWHC 3292 (QB)	12.36, 12.160
Ridehalgh v Horsefield [1994] Ch 205, [1994] 3 All ER 848, CA	12.138, 12.183, 12.184
Ridge v Baldwin [1964] AC 40, HL	12.60
Roberts v Dorset CC (1976) 75 LGR 462	1.11
Robinson v Brent LBC (1999) 31 HLR 1015, CA	9.118, 9.187, 12.78
Robinson v Hammersmith and Fulham LBC [2006] EWCA Civ 1122, [2006] 1 WLR 3295, [2006] HLR 7	5.16, 5.67, 5.69, 9.131, 9.132, 9.133, 9.142, 9.183, 10.126, 10.133, 12.43, 12.151, 12.209, 12.214, 13.53, 14.24
Robinson v Torbay BC [1982] 1 All ER 726, QBD	6.26, 6.91
Rowley v Rugby BC [2007] EWCA Civ 483, [2007] HLR 40	9.69, 9.115
Rushcliffe BC v Watson (1991) 24 HLR 124, CA	11.31
Ryde v Enfield LBC [2005] EWCA Civ 1281	12.193
S, *Re* [1998] AC 750	3.102
SG v Tameside MBC [2010] UKUT 243	3.42

SS v Secretary of State for Work and Pensions (ESA) [2011] UKUT 8 (AAC)	3.57
St Prix v Secretary of State for Work and Pensions [2011] EWCA Civ 806, 2011] CMLR 45	3.36
St Prix v Secretary of State for Work and Pensions [2012] UKSC 49, [2013] 1 All ER 752	3.36
St Prix v Secretary of State for Work and Pensions, Case-C 507/12 [2014] PTSR 1448, [2015] 1 CMLR 5, ECJ	3.36
Samin v Westminster City Council, *see* Mirga v Secretary of State for Work and Pensions; Samin v Westminster City Council—	
Samuels v Birmingham City Council [2015] EWCA Civ 1051, [2015] HLR 47	4.121, 6.82, 10.153, 12.75, 12.86, 12.87
Sandwell MBC v Hensley [2008] HLR 22, CA	11.31
Sanneh and others v Secretary of State for Work and Pensions and others [2015] EWCA Civ 49, [2015] HLR 27	3.25, 3.48, 3.99
Sahadid v Camden LBC [2004] EWCA Civ 1485, [2005] HLR 11	11.61, 12.234
Save Britain's Heritage v Secretary of State for the Environment [1991] 1 WLR 153, HL	12.67
Schmidt v Secretary of State for Home Affairs [1969] 2 Ch 149, CA	12.92
Secretary of State for Education and Science v Tameside MBC [1977] AC 1014, [1976] 3 WLR 641, HL; *Affirming* (1976) 120 SJ 539, CA	11.98, 12.15, 12.36, 12.37, 12.38, 12.41
Secretary of State for the Home Department v CS, Case C-304/14 [2017] QB 558, [2017] 1 WLR 180, ECJ	3.94
Secretary of State for the Home Department v FB [2010] UKUT 447 (IAC)	3.35
Secretary of State for the Home Department v NA (Pakistan), Case C-115/15 [2017] QB 109, [2016] 3 WLR 1439	3.59, 3.89
Secretary of State for the Home Department v Rahman and others, Case C 83-11	3.57
Secretary of State for the Home Department v Rendon Marin, Case C-165/14	3.94
Secretary of State for Work and Pensions v AL [2010] UKUT 451 (AAC)	3.39
Secretary of State for Work and Pensions v IM [2011] UKUT 231 (AAC)	3.86
Secretary of State for Work and Pensions v JS (IS) [2010] UKUT 347 (AAC)	3.86
Secretary of State for Work and Pensions v MB (JSA) and others [2016] UKUT 372 (AAC)	3.35
Secretary of State for Work and Pensions v MP (IS) [2011] UKUT 109 (AAC)	3.86

Secretary of State for Work and Pensions v RR (IS) [2011] UKUT 451 (AAC) 3.91
Secretary of State for Work and Pensions v SFF and others [2015] UKUT 0502 (AAC) 3.36
Secretary of State for Work and Pensions v SW [2011] UKUT 508 (AAC) 3.41
Secretary of State for Work and Pensions v Czop (Case C-147/11) and Punakova (Case C-148/11) [2012] All ER (D) 65 (Sep), ECJ 3.41, 3.86
Secretary of State for Work and Pensions v Dias [2009] EWCA Civ 807, [2010] 1 CMLR 4 3.36, 3.51
Secretary of State for Work and Pensions v Lassal and Child Poverty Action Group (intervener), Case C-162/09 [2011] 1 CMLR 31, [2011] All ER (EC) 1169, ECJ 3.48, 3.87
Secretary of State for Work and Pensions v Maria Dias, Case C-325/09 [2011] 3 CMLR 40, [2011] All ER (EC) 199, ECJ 3.25, 3.48
Shah v Barnet LBC [1983] 2 AC 309, [1983] 1 All ER 226, HL 3.103
Shala v Birmingham City Council [2007] EWCA Civ 624, [2008] HLR 8 4.108, 5.39, 5.41, 9.107, 9.108, 9.190, 10.173
Sharif v Camden LBC [2013] UKSC 10, [2013] HLR 16 4.17, 10.12, 10.172
Sheffield City Council v Hopkins [2001] EWCA Civ 1023, [2002] HLR 12 11.37
Sheridan v Basildon BC [2012] EWCA Civ 335, [2012] HLR 29 10.125
Short v Birmingham City Council [2004] EWCA Crim 2112 (QB), [2005] HLR 6 12.168
Short v Poole Corporation [1926] Ch 66, CA 12.20
Shortt v Secretary of State for Communities and Local Government [2015] EWCA Civ 1192, [2016] 1 P&CR 15 5.20
Shrewsbury and Atcham BC v Evans (1997) 30 HLR 123, CA 11.31
Simms v Islington LBC [2008] EWCA Civ 1083, [2009] HLR 20 5.39
Simplex GE (Holdings) Ltd v Secretary of State for the Environment [1988] 3 PLR 25, CA 12.37
Singh and others v Minister for Justice and Equality and Immigrant Council of Ireland, Case C-218/14 [2016] QB 208, ECJ 3.59
Slater v Lewisham LBC [2006] EWCA Civ 394, [2006] HLR 37 10.168, 10.190, 10.213, 12.210
Slattery v Basildon CC [2014] EWCA Civ 30, [2014] HLR 16 10.125
Smith v Bristol City Council, December 1981 *LAG Bulletin* 287 6.23, 10.101

Smith v East Elloe Rural DC [1956] AC 736, HL	12.53
Smith v Wokingham DC, April 1980 *LAG Bulletin* 92	4.68
Sanade and others v Secretary of State for the Home Department [2012] UKUT 48 (IAC)	3.91
Solihul MBC v Khan [2014] EWCA Civ 41, [2014] HLR 33	9.196
Southwark LBC v Williams [1971] Ch 734, CA	1.11
Sternberg, Reed, Taylor and Gill, *Re* (1999) *Times* 26 July, CA	12.183
Steward v Kingston Upon Thames LBC [2007] EWCA Civ 565, [2007] HLR 42	10.177
Stewart v Lambeth LBC [2002] EWCA Civ 753, [2002] HLR 40	4.13, 6.48, 6.93, 6.119, 6.129
Street v Mountford [1985] AC 809, (1985) 17 HLR 402, HL	4.44, 10.16
Stubbs v Slough BC, January 1980 *LAG Bulletin* 16, CC	9.110
Swaddling v Adjudication Officer, Case C-90/97 [1999] All ER (EC) 217, [1999] ECR I-1090, ECJ	3.102
Szoma v Secretary of State for Work and Pensions [2005] UKHL 64, [2006] 1 AC 564, [2006] 1 All ER 1	3.17, 9.9
Szpak v Secretary of State for Work and Pensions [2013] EWCA Civ 46	3.65
Tachie v Welwyn Hatfield BC [2013] EWHC 3972 (QB), [2014] PTSR 662	9.5, 12.47
Tarakhel v Switzerland, App No 29217/12 (2015) 60 EHRR 28, [2015] Imm AR 282, ECtHR	3.159
Teixeira v Lambeth LBC and Secretary of State for the Home Department, Case C-480/08 [2008] EWCA Civ 1088, [2009] HLR 9	3.83, 3.84, 3.85
Temur v Hackney LBC [2014] EWCA Civ 877, [2014] HLR 39	9.198
Tesco Stores Ltd v Secretary of State for the Environment [1995] 1 WLR 759, HL	12.41
Tetteh v Kingston Upon Thames RLBC [2004] EWCA Civ 1775, [2005] HLR 21	5.33, 9.63, 9.120
Thomas v DPP [2009] EWHC 3906 (Admin), (2009) *Times* 25 November	10.17
Thornton v Kirklees MBC [1979] QB 626, CA	12.69, 12.216
Three Rivers DC v Bank of England (No 3) [2003] 2 AC 1, HL	12.216
Tickner v Mole Valley DC, August 1980 *LAG Bulletin* 187, CA, [1980] 2 April, CA transcript	4.98, 4.99, 9.91, 12.71
Tompkins v Wandsworth LBC [2015] EWCA Civ 846, [2015] HLR 44	10.17
Tower Hamlets LBC v Abdi (1992) 25 HLR 80, CA	12.216
Tower Hamlets LBC v Deugi [2006] EWCA Civ 159, [2006] HLR 28	12.174, 12.212

Tower Hamlets LBC v Rahanara Begum [2005] EWCA Civ 116, [2006] HLR 9 — 9.152, 10.180, 10.192, 10.194
Tower Hamlets LBC v Secretary of State for the Environment [1993] QB 632, (1993) 25 HLR 524, CA — 3.6, 3.111, 3.164, 3.165
Trojani v Centre public d'aide sociale de Bruxelles (CPAS), Case C-456/02 [2004] ECR I-7573, ECJ — 3.23, 3.25, 3.48, 3.51
Tsfayo v United Kingdom, App No 60860/00 (2009) 48 EHRR 18, [2007] HLR 19, ECtHR — 12.98
Ugiagbe v Southwark LBC [2009] EWCA Civ 31, [2009] HLR 35 — 6.28, 6.30, 6.40, 6.47, 6.143
Unichi v Southwark LBC [2013] EWHC 3681 (QB) — 12.177
Uphill v BRB (Residuary) Ltd [2005] EWCA Civ 60, [2005] 1 WLR 2070 — 12.192, 12.193
Van Aken v Camden LBC [2002] EWCA Civ 1724, [2003] 1 WLR 684, [2003] HLR 33 — 12.166
Vatsouras and Koupatantze v Arbeitgemeinschaft (ARGE) Nurnberg 900, Cases C-22/08 and C-23/08 [2009] All ER (EC) 747, [2009] All ER (D) 51 (Jun), ECJ — 3.32, 3.33, 3.34
Viackiene v Tower Hamlets LBC [2013] EWCA Civ 1764, [2014] HLR 13 — 6.59
Vilvarajah v UK (1991) 14 EHRR 248, ECtHR — 12.25
Vilvarasa v Harrow LBC [2010] EWCA Civ 1278, [2010] HLR 11 — 10.192
W (China) v Secretary of State for the Home Department [2006] EWCA Civ 1494, [2006] All ER (D) 97 (Nov) — 3.41, 3.80
Wall v Lefever [1998] 1 FCR 605, CA — 12.184
Waltham Forest LBC v Hussein, *see* Hussein v Waltham Forest LBC—
Waltham Forest LBC v Maloba [2007] EWCA Civ 1281, [2008] HLR 26 — 4.73, 4.77, 10.163, 12.179
Waltham Forest LBC v Roberts [2004] EWCA Civ 940, [2005] HLR 2 — 11.31
Wandsworth LBC v A [2000] 1 WLR 1246, CA — 12.37
Wandsworth LBC v NJ, *see* NJ v Wandsworth LBC—
Wandsworth LBC v Michalak [2002] EWCA Civ 271, [2003] 1 WLR 617 — 12.103
Wandsworth LBC v Watson [2010] EWCA Civ 1558, [2011] HLR 9 — 12.160
Wandsworth LBC v Winder [1985] AC 461, HL — 12.16
Warsame v Hounslow LBC (1999) 32 HLR 335, CA — 9.152, 9.157
Watchman v Ipswich BC [2007] EWCA Civ 348, [2007] HLR 33 — 6.51, 6.84
Webb v EMO Air Cargo (UK) Ltd, Case C-32/93 [1994] ECR I-3567, ECJ — 3.36

Weldemichael and Obular v Secretary of State for the Home Department [2015] UKUT 540 (IAC), [2016] 1 CMLR 30	3.36
West Kent HA v Davies (1998) 31 HLR 415, CA	11.31
Westminster City Council v Great Portland Estates plc [1985] 1 AC 661, HL	12.65, 12.67
Westminster City Council v National Asylum Support Service [2002] UKHL 38, [2002] 1 WLR 2958	13.16
White v Exeter City Council, December 1981 *LAG Bulletin* 287, CC	6.45
William v Wandsworth LBC; Bellamy v Hounslow LBC [2006] EWCA Civ 535, [2006] HLR 42	6.58, 6.76, 6.77, 12.71, 12.189, 12.190
Williams v Birmingham City Council [2007] EWCA Civ 691, [2008] HLR 4	9.123
Williams v Cynon Valley Council (unreported), noted at January 1980 *LAG Bulletin* 16, CC	4.12, 9.109
Williams v Exeter City Council, September 1981 *LAG Bulletin* 211, CC	7.38, 7.39, 10.52
Wincentzen v Monklands DC (1988) SLT (Court of Session) 259, September 1988 *LAG Bulletin* 13	6.31
Wiseman v Boreman [1971] AC 297, HL	12.59
Woodspring DC v Taylor (1982) 4 HLR 95	12.12
Wyness v Poole BC, July 1979 *LAG Bulletin* 166, CC	9.42, 9.43, 10.129
X v Federal Republic of Germany (1965) 8 Yearbook of the ECHR 158	12.100
Yemshaw v Hounslow LBC [2011] UKSC 3, [2011] HLR 16	4.82, 4.83, 5.80, 7.4, 7.41, 7.43
Ymeraga and others v Ministre du Travail, de l'emploi et de l'immigration, Case C-87/12 [2013] 3 CMLR 33, ECJ	3.94
Zalewska v Department for Social Development (Northern Ireland) [2008] UKHL 67, [2008] 1 WLR 2602, HL (NI)	3.62
Zambrano (Ruiz) v Office national de l'emploi (ONEm) Case C-34/09 [2012] QB 265, [2011] All ER (EC) 491	3.91, 3.91, 3.94, 3.95, 3.96, 3.97, 3.98, 3.99
Zhu and Chen v Secretary of State for the Home Department Case C-200/02 [2004] ECR I-9925, ECJ	3.23, 3.79
Ziolkowski and Szeja v Land Berlin, Cases C-424/10 and C-425/10 [2011] EUECJ C-424/10, 14 September 2011	3.50

Table of statutes

Adoption and Children Act 2002—
  s116(1) 13.43, 13.44
Air Force Act 1955—
  s223 7.18
Anti-social Behaviour, Crime and Policing Act 2014—
  s1 11.31
  s30 11.31
  s94 11.31
Armed Forces Act 2006—
  s374 7.18, 11.41, 14.32
Army Act 1955—
  s225 7.18
Asylum and Immigration (Treatment of Claimants, etc) Act 2004 13.35
  s9 3.153
  s11 1.109, 2.43, 7.33, 7.36
  s11(2) 7.36
  s11(3)(a) 7.36
  s11(3)(b) 7.36
Asylum and Immigration Act 1996 1.76, 1.77, 2.16, 2.174
  s9 3.7
  s13 3.17
Asylum and Immigration Appeals Act 1993 1.6, 1.59–1.61, 1.62, 1.65, 3.7
  s4 3.7
  s4(4) 1.61
  s5 3.7
Borders, Citizenship and Immigration Act 2009 3.21
British Nationality Act 1981 3.21, 3.22
  s1(1) 3.21
  s1(3) 3.21
  s1(4) 3.21
  s2 3.21
  s6 3.21
  s11 3.22
  s11(1) 3.21
  Sch 1 3.21
  Sch 3 3.22
Building Act 1984—
  s77 5.58
Care Act 2014 3.3, 3.4, 11.9, 13.2, 13.5, 13.7–13.26
  Pt 1 3.152, 13.7, 13.8
  s1(4) 13.8
  s8(1)(a) 13.8
  s9 13.7
  s9(1) 13.14
  s11(1) 13.14
  s11(2)(a) 13.14
  s11(3) 13.14
  s13 13.14
  s14 13.9
  s14(2)(b) 13.12
  s14(2)(c) 13.12
  s15 13.9
  s18 13.8, 13.12
  s18(1) 13.9
  s18(1)(a) 13.9
  s18(1)(b) 13.9
  s18(1)(c) 13.9
  s18(2)–(4) 13.9
  s19 13.8, 13.12
  s19(1) 13.12

Care Act 2014 *continued*
s20 13.8
ss21–23 13.12
s21(1) 13.15
s21(1)(a) 13.22
s39 13.9
s78 13.14
Care Standards Act 2000 10.162
Child Abduction and Custody Act 1985 13.97, 13.98
s1 13.98
s5 13.97, 13.98
Child Support Act 1991 4.123, 10.153
Children (Leaving Care) Act 2000 13.74
Children Act 1989 2.27, 3.3, 3.4, 4.90, 5.25, 5.66, 5.71, 6.25, 9.189, 10.42, 10.106, 12.36, 12.140, 13.1, 13.2, 13.5, 13.20, 13.40–13.86
Pt III 2.166, 13.40, 13.64, 13.70, 13.78
s1 13.61
s8 5.16, 5.28, 11.88
s11 10.42
s17 3.99, 3.152, 10.137, 11.9, 13.39, 13.41–13.49, 13.58, 13.62
s17(1) 13.41, 13.43
s17(1)(b) 13.41
s17(2) 13.43
s17(6) 9.189, 13.43, 13.44, 13.47, 13.49
s17(10) 13.43
s20 2.32, 5.65, 5.66, 11.9, 12.36, 13.44, 13.50–13.65, 13.78, 13.86
s20(1) 10.106, 13.51
s20(3) 13.51
s20(4) 13.51
s22 5.71, 5.72, 13.62, 13.63
s22(1)(a) 13.62

Children Act 1989 *continued*
s22(1)(b) 13.62
s22(3) 13.62
s22(3A) 13.62
s22A 2.40, 7.58, 13.63, 13.65
s22B 13.63
s22C 13.57, 13.63, 13.75
s22D 13.63
s22E 13.63
s22G 11.89
s23(6) 13.57
s23A 2.32, 5.65, 13.76
s23B 13.62, 13.76
s23B(1) 13.76
s23B(10) 13.76
s23C 2.40, 3.152, 7.57, 13.62, 13.77, 13.78, 13.80
s23C(1) 14.32
s23C(4) 13.77
s23CA 3.152
s24(2) 2.32
s24A 3.152, 13.64
s24B 3.152
s24B(3) 2.32, 5.71
s27 13.66, 13.69, 13.70
s28 10.42
s82(5) 14.32
s108(5) 13.1
Sch 1 para 1 11.20
Sch 2 Pt I 13.43
Sch 2 Pt II para 19B 13.75
Sch 2 Pt II para 19B(2)(b) 13.75
Sch 2 Pt II para 19C 13.75
Sch 5 Pt II 11.20
Sch 7 para 9(2) 11.20
Sch 7 para 9(3) 11.20
Sch 13 para 11 13.1
Children Act 2004 14.10
s10 13.66
s11 6.25, 9.69, 10.106
s17 13.41

Children Act 2004 *continued*
s28 10.106
s52 13.62
Children and Social Work Act 2017—
Pt 1 13.74
s2 13.74
Children and Young Persons Act 2008—
s22(6) 3.152
Civil Partnership Act 2004 4.56, 4.88, 11.20
Sch 8 2.27, 4.90
Contempt of Court Act 1981—
s2(2) 12.201
s11 12.154, 12.156
County Courts Act 1984—
s38 12.218
Courts and Legal Services Act 1990—
s4 12.181
Crime and Disorder Act 1998—
s38(4) 13.78
s39(5)(a) 13.78
s39(7) 13.78
s42(1) 13.78
Criminal Justice Act 1982—
s37 2.161, 2.203, 15.2
Criminal Justice Act 2003—
s242(2) 5.77
Deregulation and Contracting Out Act 1994—
s69(5) 9.5
s70 12.47
s70(4) 9.5
Disability Discrimination Act 1995—
s49A 9.69, 9.93, 9.185
Education Act 1962 7.15, 13.10
Education Act 1996—
Pt IV 13.58
s312 13.58
s323 13.58
s324 13.58
s324(5) 13.58
s342 13.58
Equality Act 2010 3.99, 9.69, 9.70, 10.18, 10.169
s4 11.40
s13 11.40
s13(3) 11.40
s19 11.40
Equality Act 2010 *continued*
s19(1) 11.40
s19(2) 11.40
s19(3) 11.40
s38(3) 11.40
s38(4) 11.40
s149 5.35, 9.69, 9.93, 9.95, 9.185, 10.169, 11.40
European Union (Accessions) Act 2003 3.62
European Union (Accessions) Act 2006 3.67
European Union (Croatian Accession and Irish Protocol) Act 2013—
s4 3.72
s4(11) 3.76
Family Law Act 1996—
Pt IV 4.43, 4.56
Government of Wales Act 1998 1.107
s22 1.107, 2.11
s58 1.107
s161 1.107
Sch 2 para 9 1.107, 2.11
Sch 11 para 30 1.107
Government of Wales Act 2006—
s58 2.11
s95 1.107, 2.11
s161 2.11
Sch 11 para 30 2.11
Greater London Council (General Powers) Act 1984—
s37 5.61
s38(1) 5.61
s38(2) 5.61
s39 5.58, 5.61
Homelessness Act 2002 1.1, 1.5, 1.6, 1.90, 1.92–1.106, 1.107–1.112, 1.113, 1.117, 2.1, 2.128, 2.197, 3.9, 4.92, 6.2, 9.152, 10.31, 10.80–10.83, 10.85, 10.86, 10.87, 10.111, 10.135, 10.192, 11.5, 12.167, 12.197, 13.68, 14.23
ss1–4 1.93
s1 2.129, 11.59, 14.3
s1(1) 2.128, 14.3

Homelessness Act 2002 *continued*
s1(2) 2.130, 14.4
s1(3) 2.129, 14.3
s1(4) 2.129, 14.3
s1(5) 2.130, 14.4
s1(6) 2.130, 14.4
s2 14.6
s2(1) 2.131
s2(2) 2.131
s2(3) 2.132, 14.8
s3(1) 2.133, 14.9
s3(2) 2.134, 14.12
s3(3) 2.135, 14.13
s3(4) 14.13
s3(5) 2.135, 14.14
s3(6) 2.136, 14.18
s3(7) 2.136, 14.18
s3(7A) 14.10
s3(8) 2.136, 2.137, 14.18
s3(9) 14.19
s4 14.6, 14.9, 14.13
s5 1.96, 2.86
s6 1.94
s7 1.95
s8 2.149, 9.158
s8(2) 1.99
s9 1.94
s10 1.97
s11 1.98
s13 1.101, 3.163, 11.19
s14 1.105
Sch 1 para 10 2.84
Sch 1 para 17 1.99
Homelessness etc (Scotland) Act 2003 2.2
Homelessness Reduction Act 2017 1.1, 1.5, 1.6, 1.123–1.125, 2.1, 2.6, 2.40, 2.61, 2.64, 2.71, 2.77, 2.86, 2.87, 2.115–2.117, 2.118, 2.142, 2.146, 2.148, 4.146, 7.57, 7.68, 8.3, 9.22, 9.48, 9.50, 9.143, 9.147, 9.152, 9.153, 10.10, 10.29, 10.43, 10.52, 10.58, 10.66, 10.67, 10.78, 10.79, 10.81, 10.83, 10.84, 10.85, 10.86, 10.90, 10.109, 10.123, 10.144, 10.155, 10.203, 10.210, 10.220–10.225, 13.65, 13.68, 13.70, 13.71, 13.80, 13.94, 14.2, 14.20, 14.23, 14.31–14.33
s1 1.124, 2.29, 4.146, 9.22, 9.49, 10.84
s2 2.142, 2.143, 2.144, 14.31, 14.32, 14.33
s3 1.124
s3(1) 2.61, 2.62, 2.63, 10.43, 10.44, 10.45, 10.46, 10.47, 10.48
s3(2) 2.87, 10.90
s4 1.124, 2.64, 2.65, 2.66, 2.67, 2.77, 2.78, 2.79, 2.80, 10.58, 10.59, 10.60, 10.61, 10.75, 10.83, 10.221
s4(2) 9.152, 10.10, 10.52
s4(3) 9.147
s4(4) 9.22, 10.84, 10.203
s4(5) 9.152
s4(7) 13.68, 13.70
s5 1.124, 2.73, 7.68, 10.69, 10.70, 10.75, 10.221
s5(2) 2.71, 2.72, 10.66, 10.68
s5(3) 9.143, 9.147, 10.210
s5(4) 10.10, 10.29
s5(5) 9.153, 10.85
s5(6) 2.86, 9.152, 10.81, 10.85
s5(7) 10.109
s5(8) 7.64, 7.68
s5(9) 7.64, 7.68, 7.69, 7.70, 7.71, 7.72
s5(10) 7.64
s5(12) 2.118, 8.3
s6 10.67, 10.123, 10.144

Homelessness Reduction Act 2017 *continued*
s7(1) 2.67, 2.68, 2.73, 2.80, 2.115, 2.116, 2.117, 10.61, 10.67, 10.70, 10.71, 10.72, 10.73, 10.74, 10.220, 10.221, 10.222, 10.224, 10.225
s8 2.40, 7.57, 7.58, 13.65, 13.80
s9(1) 2.148, 9.153
s9(2) 2.148, 9.153
s10 9.50, 13.71, 13.94, 13.95
s11 2.146, 14.20, 14.21, 14.22
s12 10.155
s12(5) 10.155
Housing (Consequential Provisions) Act 1985—
s5 1.22
Sch 4 para 8 1.22
Housing (Homeless Persons) Act 1977 1.1, 1.2, 1.3, 1.4, 1.5, 1.6, 1.8, 1.15, 1.16, 1.20, 1.21–1.46, 1.47, 1.51, 1.53, 2.2, 3.6, 4.4, 4.28, 5.12, 6.103, 7.1, 7.12, 7.45, 8.1, 8.18, 9.149, 10.16, 10.19, 10.20, 12.13, 12.34
s1 1.30, 1.31, 1.52
s1(2) 1.55
s2 1.19, 1.32
s2(1)(b) 5.57
s6(1) 1.44
s6(2) 1.45
s14 1.22
s16 1.41, 4.28
s17 1.41
s18 1.23
s19 1.22
s20 1.8
Sch 1.8
Housing (Scotland) Act 1986—
s21(2) 1.55
s33 7.74
s38 2.163
Housing (Scotland) Act 1987 2.2, 2.13, 7.59
s33 7.59
s34 7.59
Housing (Scotland) Act 1988 7.9
Housing (Scotland) Act 2001 2.2
Housing (Wales) Act 2014 1.5, 1.6, 1.119–1.122, 1.123, 2.1, 2.7, 2.82, 2.98, 2.105, 2.110, 2.113, 3.33, 3.151, 4.24, 5.11, 5.37, 6.2, 7.18, 7.23, 7.33, 7.36, 7.68, 9.4, 9.5, 9.135, 10.19, 10.78, 10.111, 10.184, 10.185–10.187, 10.188, 10.189, 10.194, 10.196–10.198, 10.199–10.201, 10.202–10.204, 10.205–10.207, 10.208–10.211, 10.212, 11.62, 13.22, 15.11
Pt 1 10.145
Pt 2 1.1, 1.122, 2.2, 2.3, 2.21, 2.38, 2.49, 2.50, 2.113, 2.145, 2.160, 2.164, 3.2, 3.3, 3.5, 3.15, 3.29, 3.31, 3.40, 3.43, 3.106, 3.110–3.160, 4.29, 5.1, 5.19, 5.29, 5.56, 6.149, 6.150, 7.1, 7.2, 7.5, 7.30, 7.53, 8.1, 8.2, 8.18, 9.11, 9.14, 9.17, 9.54, 9.73, 9.74, 9.170, 9.171, 10.1, 10.3, 10.4, 10.6, 10.15, 10.17, 10.18, 10.49, 10.79, 10.112, 10.135, 10.184, 11.25, 11.62, 11.98, 12.1, 12.2, 12.11, 12.12, 12.15, 12.41, 12.47, 12.58, 12.65, 12.94, 12.95, 12.100, 12.106, 12.107, 12.108, 12.110, 12.114, 12.115, 12.123, 12.143, 12.216, 15.1, 15.2, 15.4, 15.5, 15.7, 15.9
Pt 4 11.127
Pt 6 10.63
s18(1) 10.75
s20 10.160
s50 2.129, 14.5
s50(1) 2.129, 14.5
s50(2) 2.129, 14.5
s50(4) 2.130, 14.5
s51 2.131, 14.6

Housing (Wales) Act 2014 *continued*

s51(1)(b)(iii)	14.6
s51(1)(c)	14.6
s51(2)	2.132, 14.8
s52	2.133
s52(1)	14.9
s52(2)	2.134, 14.12
s52(3)	2.135, 14.13
s52(4)	2.135, 14.13
s52(5)	2.135, 14.14
s52(6)	2.134, 14.11
s52(7)	2.136, 14.18
s52(8)	2.136, 14.18
s52(9)	2.137, 14.18, 14.19
s52(10)	14.18
s52(11)	14.18
s55	2.21, 2.28, 2.29, 4.2, 6.5
s55(1)	4.2, 4.5, 4.39
s55(2)	4.2, 6.65
s55(2)(a)	4.62
s55(2)(b)	4.66
s55(3)	4.2, 4.69
s55(4)	1.122, 4.141, 4.144
s56	2.22, 2.58, 2.89, 4.3, 4.17, 4.20, 4.37, 7.43, 10.91, 10.92
s57	2.23, 4.75, 7.48
s57(1)	4.75, 4.82
s57(3)	4.75, 4.78, 4.93
s57(4)	476
s58	2.24, 2.27, 2.94, 4.83, 4.90, 5.80, 7.4
s58(1)	2.25, 2.26, 4.82, 4.92
s58(2)	4.88
s58(2)(h)	2.27, 4.90
s58(3)	4.91
s58(4)	4.91
s59	2.88, 2.104, 9.157, 10.19, 10.91, 10.145
s59(2)	4.122, 4.124, 9.67, 10.158
s59(3)	2.104, 10.151
s60	1.122, 4.145, 5.6,14.23, 14.30

Housing (Wales) Act 2014 *continued*

s60(1)	2.139
s60(2)	2.140, 14.26
s60(3)	2.140, 14.26
s60(4)	2.140, 14.26
s60(5)	2.141, 14.27
s61	2.4, 2.16
s62	1.122, 2.44, 9.48, 9.71, 10.43
s62(1)	2.49, 9.11, 9.25, 10.49
s62(2)	9.11, 9.25, 10.219
s62(3)	2.49, 10.49
s62(4)	2.49, 3.110, 10.49
s62(5)	2.49, 10.49
s62(6)	2.50, 10.49
s62(8)	2.50, 10.49
s62(9)	2.50, 10.49
s63	2.18, 9.142, 15.12
s63(1)	2.54, 10.50
s63(2)	2.54, 9.147, 10.50
s63(3)	2.54, 10.50
s63(4)	2.54, 10.50
s63(4)(a)	10.51
s63(4)(b)	10.51
s63(5)	3.117
s64	10.121, 10.126
s64(1)	2.82, 10.64
s64(2)	2.82, 10.64
s64(2)(h)	2.84, 10.89
s65(a)	2.69, 2.81, 10.63, 10.76
s65(b)–(c)	2.69, 2.81, 10.76
s66	1.122, 2.118, 2.147, 2.167, 2.189, 3.112, 3.116, 8.4, 9.152, 10.63, 10.83, 10.89, 11.62, 13.72
s66(1)	2.81, 10.62
s66(2)	2.81, 10.62
s67	2.83, 10.65
s67(2)	2.83, 10.65
s67(3)	2.83, 10.65
s67(4)	2.83, 10.65

Housing (Wales) Act 2014 *continued*
s68 2.55, 2.118, 2.147, 2.167, 3.112, 3.116, 7.3, 7.63, 7.92, 8.4, 9.46, 9.152, 10.8, 10.12, 13.72
s68(1) 4.14
s68(2) 7.63
s68(4) 2.57, 10.8
s69 2.59, 10.29
s69(10) 12.147
s69(11) 2.97, 2.150, 4.14, 10.29, 12.147
s70 1.19, 5.5, 5.63, 5.64, 9.152
s70(1)(a)–(d) 2.30
s70(1)(a) 5.12
s70(1)(b) 5.13
s70(1)(c) 5.32, 5.37, 5.38, 5.39, 5.50
s70(1)(d) 5.56
s70(1)(e)–(j) 2.33
s70(1)(e) 5.80
s70(1)(f) 5.70, 9.18
s70(1)(g) 5.81
s70(1)(h) 5.72
s70(1)(i) 5.76
s70(1)(j) 5.78
s71 2.30, 5.37
s71(2) 5.37, 9.152
s72 2.33, 5.5, 5.62
s72(3) 5.62
s73 2.69, 2.147, 2.167, 2.189, 3.112, 3.116, 7.3, 7.37, 7.61, 7.68, 7.91, 7.92, 9.152, 10.81, 10.89, 10.109, 10.110, 11.62, 13.72
s73(1) 10.75
s73(2) 7.68, 10.75
s74(2) 2.70, 2.90, 10.77, 10.91, 10.93
s74(3) 2.70, 10.77
s74(4) 2.70, 10.77

Housing (Wales) Act 2014 *continued*
s75 2.54, 2.89, 2.100, 2.118, 2.147, 2.167, 2.189, 3.112, 3.116, 7.65, 8.4, 9.147, 9.152, 10.50, 10.91, 10.92, 10.109, 10.110, 10.111–10.219, 11.62, 13.72
s74(5) 2.70, 10.77
s75(1) 10.91, 10.109, 10.110
s75(2) 10.91, 10.109
s75(3) 2.89, 2.90, 10.92, 10.93, 10.110
s75(4) 10.93
s76 2.18, 2.103, 2.110, 4.24, 5.11, 10.111, 10.121, 10.211
s76(2)–(4) 10.202
s76(2) 9.157, 10.185, 10.197, 10.204
s76(2)(a) 2.113
s76(2)(b) 2.113, 10.134
s76(3) 2.113, 10.190, 10.197, 10.203
s76(3)(a) 10.188
s76(3)(c) 2.113, 9.152
s76(4)(c) 2.113, 10.202
s76(5) 2.114, 3.117, 9.147
s76(6) 2.113, 10.183
s76(7) 2.113
s77 9.152, 10.110
s77(2) 2.34
s77(3) 2.37, 6.27
s77(4) 2.38, 6.2, 6.149
s78 1.122, 2.3, 2.37, 6.3, 10.91, 10.110
s78(3) 6.3
s79(2) 2.70, 2.83, 3.112, 10.65, 10.77, 10.182
s79(3) 2.70, 2.83, 10.65, 10.77
s79(4) 2.70, 2.83, 10.65, 10.77
s79(5) 2.70, 2.83, 10.65, 10.77
ss80–83 12.113

Housing (Wales) Act 2014 *continued*

s80	2.3, 2.14, 7.43, 7.61, 9.55
s80(1)–(3)	2.91
s80(1)	2.69, 7.40
s80(2)	7.64
s80(3)	7.4, 7.41, 9.172
s80(3)(c)	7.41
s80(4)	7.42
s80(5)	2.98, 7.7, 7.73
s80(6)	7.73
s81	2.3, 2.39, 7.9, 7.37
s81(1)	7.9
s81(2)(a)	7.17
s81(3)	2.41, 7.17
s81(4)	2.41
s81(4)(a)	2.42, 7.25
s81(4)(b)	7.17
s81(5)	7.33, 7.34
s81(6)	7.33, 7.34
s82	2.95, 2.96, 2.97, 2.118, 7.18, 8.5
s82(1)	7.3, 7.7, 7.59, 7.64, 7.68
s82(2)	2.97, 7.69, 7.86, 7.89, 9.143
s82(3)	7.70, 7.91
s82(4)	7.3, 7.59, 7.71, 7.92
s82(5)	10.32
s82(6)	7.68, 10.32
s82(7)	2.97
s83	7.92
s84	2.83, 2.90, 2.93, 2.97, 2.113, 7.62, 7.69, 7.72, 9.144, 9.146, 10.65, 10.93, 10.187, 10.203
s84(3)	2.97
s84(4)	2.97
s85	2.99, 2.147, 9.149, 9.170, 10.180, 10.219, 12.112, 12.163
s85(1)	9.151, 12.206
s85(1)(b)	9.152
s85(1)(c)	7.89, 9.152, 9.154, 9.157, 9.172

Housing (Wales) Act 2014 *continued*

s85(2)	2.151
s85(3)	2.149, 9.158
s85(4)	2.149, 9.160, 12.165
s85(5)	9.160, 9.163, 12.112
s86	2.152, 2.153, 9.164, 12.198
s86(2)(a)	9.165
s86(2)(c)	2.153
s86(3)	9.144
s86(4)	2.153, 9.198, 12.65, 12.163
s86(5)	2.153, 12.163
s86(6)	2.153
s86(7)	2.153
s88	2.99, 2.154, 2.155, 2.156, 7.90, 10.180, 12.2, 12.119, 12.188, 12.197, 12.198, 12.215
s88(1)	12.110, 12.148, 12.159, 12.164, 12.218
s88(1)(b)	12.163, 12.198
s88(2)	12.163, 12.166
s88(3)	2.156, 12.167
s88(4)	2.157, 12.203
s88(5)	2.158, 4.14, 12.148, 12.196
s89	2.158, 12.197, 12.198, 12.199
s89(1)	12.197
s89(2)	12.197
s89(4)	2.158
s89(4)(a)	12.199, 12.200
s89(4)(b)	12.200
s89(5)	2.159, 12.202
s89(6)	2.159, 12.200
s89(7)	2.159, 12.200
s90	2.105, 10.15
s91	2.106
s91(2)–(3)	10.141
s91(3)	2.107, 10.142
s91(4)	2.108
s92	10.17
s92(2)	10.17
s93	7.64, 8.18, 12.113

Housing (Wales) Act 2014 *continued*
s93(1) 2.120, 8.5, 8.10
s93(2) 2.118, 8.4
s93(3) 8.7
s93(4) 2.122, 8.12
s93(5) 2.121, 8.19
s93(6) 2.119, 8.4
s94 12.113
s94(1) 2.123, 8.10
s94(2) 8.10
s94(3) 8.10
s94(4) 2.124
s94(6) 2.125, 8.6
s94(7) 2.125, 8.8
s94(8) 2.126, 8.20
s94(9) 2.126, 8.20
s95 9.58, 10.13
s95(1) 2.164, 10.6
s95(2) 2.165, 10.7
s95(3) 2.165, 10.7
s95(4) 2.165, 10.7
s95(5) 2.165, 9.58, 10.7
s95(6) 2.165, 10.7
s95(7) 2.165, 10.7
s96 10.13
s96(1) 2.167, 13.72
s96(2) 2.169, 13.73
s96(4) 2.167, 13.73
s97 2.161, 15.1
s97(1) 2.160, 15.7, 15.9
s97(2) 2.162
s97(3) 2.162, 15.14
s97(4)–(5) 15.15
s97(4) 2.162, 15.14
s97(5) 2.162
s97(6) 2.162
s98 2.145
s98(1) 12.41
s99 2.12, 2.13, 10.17, 10.200, 10.206
Sch 2 para 1 3.8, 3.17, 14.13
Sch 2 para 1(2) 2.17
Sch 2 para 1(3) 2.16
Sch 2 para 1(5) 3.113
Sch 2 para 1(6) 3.114
Sch 2 para 2 3.8, 4.24, 5.11
Sch 2 para 3 2.19, 2.20, 3.106
Sch 2 para 3(2) 3.108
Sch 2 para 3(3) 3.108

Housing (Wales) Act 2014 *continued*
Sch 3 para 1 2.109, 10.17, 10.135
Sch 3 para 3 2.189
Sch 3 para 11 7.53, 7.73
Sch 3 para 12 7.92
Sch 3 para 13 7.92
Housing Act 1935—
s51 1.45
Housing Act 1936—
s85(2) 1.45
Housing Act 1957—
Pt V 1.13, 1.44
s1 1.13
s113(2) 1.45
Housing Act 1964 11.116
Housing Act 1974 11.116
Housing Act 1980 11.103
Pt I 1.46
s69(1) 4.55
s89 4.142
Housing Act 1985 1.21, 1.33, 1.40, 1.44, 1.57, 1.81, 2.104, 4.4, 4.42, 4.52, 4.142, 5.58, 6.2, 8.1, 8.18, 9.125, 9.146, 10.17, 10.19, 10.82, 10.145, 11.22, 11.62
Pt II 1.13, 1.44, 2.103, 2.105, 3.29, 3.33, 3.40, 3.116, 3.128, 11.1, 11.3, 11.11
Pt III 1.2, 1.6, 1.21–1.46, 1.51, 1.57, 3.6, 5.19, 6.58, 6.61, 6.103, 9.23, 9.68, 9.149, 10.79, 10.215, 11.3, 12.46
Pt IV 1.46, 2.169, 10.16, 11.11
Pt V 1.46
Pt IX 5.58
Pt X 4.109, 9.139
s1 1.13, 2.13
s9 10.124
s17 10.124
s22 1.45, 1.73, 11.2, 11.3, 11.74

Housing Act 1985 *continued*

s24	2.105, 10.15
s27B	10.17
s32	11.11
s58	1.30, 1.31, 1.52, 1.55, 4.86, 4.95
s58(1)	1.63, 6.103
s58(2A)	4.69
s58(4)	1.64
s59	1.19, 1.33, 5.23
s60	1.41, 4.95
s60(1)	1.63, 6.103
s61	1.23
s64	4.126
s65(2)	1.63, 2.189, 6.103, 7.39, 11.62, 11.98
s68(2)	2.189, 7.39, 11.62
s69(1)	1.44
s69(1)(a)	11.3
s71	1.60
s75	1.41, 4.28
s79(3)	11.12
s80	10.200, 10.202, 10.206
s80(1)	10.17
s82	4.61
s84	2.177, 11.35, 11.36
s84(2)	11.30, 11.33, 11.35
s84A	11.30
s85	11.35, 11.36
s85(2)	11.35
ss87–90	11.20
s92	11.20
s106	11.103
s107A	11.20
s195(2)	7.39
s554	11.22
s555	11.22
Sch 1 para 2	2.169
Sch 1 para 4	2.88, 2.109, 10.17, 10.135, 11.13
Sch 1 para 5	2.169, 6.34, 6.113, 11.13
Sch 1 para 10	2.169, 11.13
Sch 2 grounds 1–7	2.177, 11.30, 11.34

Housing Act 1985 *continued*

Sch 2 ground 1	11.31
Sch 2 ground 2	11.31
Sch 2 ground 2A	11.31
Sch 2 ground 3	11.31
Sch 2 ground 4	11.31
Sch 2 ground 5	11.31
Sch 2 ground 6	11.31
Sch 2 ground 7	11.31
Sch 2 ground 7A	11.31
Sch 2 ground 8	11.31
Sch 2 ground 10	11.31
Sch 2 ground 11	11.31
Sch 2 ground 12	11.31
Sch 2 ground 14	11.31

Housing Act 1988	4.42, 4.52, 4.53, 4.54, 4.142, 10.17, 10.82, 11.31
Pt 1	2.169, 4.53
s5	4.61
s21	1.124, 2.29, 2.78, 4.61, 4.117, 4.141, 4.146, 9.22, 9.49, 10.9, 10.59, 10.84, 10.203
s30	4.55
s45(1)	10.200
Sch 1	11.15
Sch 2 ground 12	11.31
Sch 2 ground 13	11.31
Sch 2 ground 14	11.31
Sch 2 ground 14A	11.31
Sch 2 ground 15	11.31
Sch 2 ground 17	11.31

Housing Act 1996 1.3, 1.5, 1.66, 1.68, 1.72, 1.94, 1.102, 1.114, 1.118, 2.11, 3.163, 5.35, 6.2, 6.38, 6.50, 9.23, 9.62, 9.180, 10.19, 10.67, 10.111, 10.114, 10.118, 11.3, 11.4, 11.117, 12.36, 12.38, 12.39, 12.70, 12.111, 12.207, 12.234, 13.22, 14.10

Housing Act 1996 *continued*
Pt 1 1.76, 2.169, 11.116, 11.118, 11.127
Pt 5 Ch I 2.169, 11.11
Pt 6 1.1, 1.2, 1.4, 1.5, 1.6, 1.66–1.79, 1.80, 1.81, 1.87, 1.100, 1.101, 1.110, 1.112, 1.113, 2.1, 2.2, 2.3, 2.7, 2.69, 2.73, 2.81, 2.102, 2.111, 2.113, 2.115, 2.117, 2.168, 2.202, 3.2, 3.3, 3.5, 3.9, 3.15, 3.17, 3.29, 3.31, 3.33, 3.40, 3.43, 3.93, 3.116, 3.128, 3.146, 3.161–3.174, 9.167, 10.29, 10.71, 10.76, 10.80, 10.81, 10.116, 10.119, 10.135, 10.188, 10.189, 10.190, 10.194, 10.195, 10.197, 10.198, 10.212, 10.220, 10.225, 11.5, 11.8, 11.10, 11.11, 1, 12.141.20, 11.21, 11.54, 11.84, 11.85, 11.88, 11.104, 11.111, 11.115, 11.130, 12.1, 12.2, 12.11, 12.12, 12.15, 12.41, 12.47, 12.51, 12.58, 12.65, 12.94, 12.95, 12.107, 12.108, 12.114, 12.115, 12.123, 12.143, 12.234, 13.1, 13.22, 14.16, 15.1, 15.2, 15.4, 15.5, 15.6, 15.7, 15.9, 15.10
Pt 7 1.1, 1.2, 1.6, 1.66–1.79, 1.80, 1.81, 1.82, 1.96, 1.109, 1.110, 1.122, 2.1, 2.2, 2.3, 2.7, 2.21, 2.38, 2.47, 2.62, 2.63, 2.91, 2.98, 2.105, 2.107, 2.111, 2.113, 2.138, 2.142, 2.145, 2.146, 2.160, 2.163, 3.2, 3.3, 3.4, 3.5, 3.8, 3.15, 3.17, 3.29, 3.31, 3.33, 3.40, 3.43, 3.83, 3.84, 3.93, 3.106, 3.110–3.160, 3.171, 4.8, 4.14, 4.22, 4.29, 4.141, 5.1, 5.9, 5.13, 5.19, 5.29, 5.35, 5.56, 6.2, 6.149, 6.150, 7.1, 7.2, 7.5, 7.18, 7.23, 7.30, 7.33, 7.53, 7.65, 7.70, 7.71, 8.1, 8.2, 8.18, 9.4, 9.10, 9.14, 9.17, 9.20, 9.25, 9.45, 9.54, 9.68, 9.69, 9.73, 9.74, 9.134, 9.135, 9.170, 10.1,

Housing Act 1996 *continued*
Pt 7 10.3, 10.4, 10.10, 10.15, 10.17, 10.18, 10.42, 10.44, 10.45, 10.46, 10.79, 10.81, 10.85, 10.106, 10.112, 10.125, 10.135, 10.179, 10.184, 11.8, 11.25, 11.49, 11.62, 11.86, 11.98, 12.1, 12.2, 12.11, 12.12, 12.15, 12.30, 12.41, 12.43, 12.45, 12.47, 12.51, 12.58, 12.65, 12.94, 12.95, 12.100, 12.102, 12.106, 12.107, 12.108, 12.110, 12.112, 12.114, 12.115, 12.123, 12.143, 12.149, 12.193, 12.216, 12.231, 12.234, 13.1, 13.6, 13.41, 13.52, 13.58, 13.68, 14.2, 14.20, 14.31, 14.34, 15.1, 15.2, 15.4, 15.5, 15.7, 15.9, 15.11
s22 11.17
s33A 11.123
s33B 11.123
s36 11.128
s50C 11.129
s50G 11.129
s50H 11.129
s50O 11.129
s93 10.84
s125 11.13, 11.20
s133 11.20
s134 11.20
s159 1.77
s159(1) 2.168
s159(1)(c) 10.189, 10.197
s159(2) 2.169, 3.161, 11.10
s159(2)(a) 11.11
s159(2)(b) 11.14
s159(2)(c) 11.15
s159(3) 2.169, 11.12, 11.13
s159(4) 2.169, 11.16, 11.18
s159(4A) 1.118, 2.171, 11.19
s159(4A)(a) 11.19
s159(4A)(b) 11.19
s159(4B) 1.118, 2.171, 2.175, 11.19, 11.27

Housing Act 1996 *continued*

s159(5)	1.118, 2.170, 3.161, 3.163, 11.19
s160	2.172,11.20
s160(2)(a)–(d)	3.162
s160(2)(e)	3.162
s160(3)	3.162
s160(4)	11.21
s160(5)	11.21
s160(7)(b)	11.50
s160(10)	11.46
s160A	2.173, 2.196, 3.167, 11.52
s160A(1)–(6)	3.9
s160A(1)	2.173, 11.23
s160A(1)(c)	2.173, 11.24
s160A(2)	2.173, 11.26
s160A(3)	2.174, 3.17
s160A(4)	2.174
s160A(5)	2.174
s160A(6)	2.175, 11.27
s160A(7)–(11)	3.1
s160A(7)	2.176, 11.28, 11.32, 11.62, 11.75
s160A(8)	2.177
s160A(8)(a)	11.30
s160A(8)(aa)	11.30
s160A(9)	2.179, 11.46, 11.110
s160A(10)	2.179, 11.46
s160A(11)	2.178, 11.47
s160ZA	1.118, 2.173
s160ZA(1)	2.173, 11.23, 11.53
s160ZA(1)(b)	2.173, 11.24
s160ZA(2)	2.174
s160ZA(3)	2.174
s160ZA(4)	2.174
s160ZA(5)	2.175, 11.27
s160ZA(6)	2.180, 11.29, 11.39
s160ZA(7)	2.180, 2.192, 11.29, 11.39, 11.62
s160ZA(8)	2.180, 11.41
s160ZA(9)	2.180, 2.196, 11.46, 11.53, 11.110, 14.25

Housing Act 1996 *continued*

s160ZA(10)	2.180, 11.46
s160ZA(11)	2.180, 11.48, 11.53
s161	1.77
s161(4)	11.5
ss162–166	11.4
s162(3)	11.4
s165	11.111
s166	14.23
s166(1)(a)	2.181, 11.56
s166(1)(b)	2.182, 11.56
s166(1A)	2.183
s166(2)	2.183
s166(3)	2.184, 11.51, 11.55, 11.80, 11.83
s166(4)	2.184, 11.58
s166A	2.171, 2.175, 11.84, 12.234, 14.10
s166A(1)	2.185, 11.59, 12.234
s166A(2)	2.188, 11.60
s166A(3)	2.189, 2.190, 11.39, 11.62, 11.64, 11.65, 11.74, 11.94, 12.234
s166A(3)(b)	11.62
s166A(3)(c)	12.234
s166A(3)(d)	12.234
s166A(4)	11.63
s166A(5)	2.191, 11.62, 11.68, 11.82
s166A(6)	2.194, 11.93
s166A(7)	10.80, 11.64
s166A(8)	2.193, 11.76
s166A(9)	2.180, 2.186, 11.111, 14.25
s166A(9)(a)	11.57
s166A(9)(a)(i)	11.106
s166A(9)(a)(ii)	11.107
s166A(9)(b)	2.195, 11.57, 11.109, 11.110
s166A(9)(c)	2.196, 11.53, 11.110
s166A(10)	2.187, 11.96
s166A(11)	2.197
s166A(12)	2.197, 11.59

Housing Act 1996 *continued*

s166A(13)	2.197, 11.73
s166A(14)	2.185, 11.61, 12.234
s167	11.3, 11.84, 12.14
s167(1)	2.185, 11.59
s167(1A)	2.188, 11.60
s167(2)	1.78, 2.189, 2.190, 11.62, 11.64, 11.65, 11.74, 11.80, 11.82, 11.83, 11.94
s167(2)(b)	11.62
s167(2A)	2.191, 11.62, 11.68, 11.82
s167(2B)–(2D)	2.192
s167(2B)	11.62, 11.70
s167(2C)	2.195, 2.196, 11.70, 11.72
s167(2E)	2.194, 11.93
s167(2ZA)	1.110, 2.189, 3.166, 11.63
s167(3)	1.81, 2.193, 10.80, 11.64
s167(4)	2.193, 11.76
s167(4A)	2.179, 11.111, 12.65
s167(4A)(a)	2.186, 11.57
s167(4A)(a)(i)	11.106
s167(4A)(a)(ii)	11.107
s167(4A)(b)	2.195, 11.57, 11.72, 11.110
s167(4A)(c)	2.195, 11.57, 11.72
s167(4A)(d)	2.196, 11.110
s167(5)	2.187, 11.96
s167(6)	2.197
s167(7)	2.197, 11.73
s167(8)	2.185, 3.163
s167A(4A)(c)	11.109
s168(1)	2.200, 11.104
s168(2)	2.200, 11.104
s168(3)	2.201, 11.53, 11.105
s169	2.198
s169(1)	12.41
s170	2.199, 11.115
s171	15.1

Housing Act 1996 *continued*

s171(1)	2.202, 15.6, 15.7, 15.10
s171(2)	2.203
s175	4.2, 10.145
s175(1)	2.21, 4.2, 4.5, 4.14, 4.39, 4.59, 12.234
s175(1)(c)	4.61
s175(2)	2.28, 4.2, 4.140, 6.65
s175(2)(a)	4.62
s175(2)(b)	4.66, 4.68
s175(3)	2.23, 4.2, 4.13, 4.69, 4.86, 12.234
s175(4)	1.64, 2.29, 4.3, 4.141, 4.146
s175(5)	2.29, 4.146
s176	2.22, 2.58, 2.88, 4.17, 4.20, 4.28, 4.37, 10.12, 10.91
s177	4.13, 4.75, 4.78, 4.86, 4.92, 4.140, 6.34, 7.48
s177(1)	2.24, 4.75, 4.82, 5.79, 12.234
s177(1A)	2.25, 2.26, 4.75, 4.82, 4.88
s177(2)	2.23, 4.75, 4.78, 4.93, 4.97, 4.98, 4.112, 4.126, 4.131
s177(3)	4.76
s178	2.27, 4.90
s178(2)	4.91
s178(2A)	4.91
s179	2.142, 3.8, 5.69, 14.23, 14.24, 14.31, 14.37
s179(1)	2.139, 2.142
s179(2)	2.143, 14.28, 14.32
s179(3)	2.144, 14.28, 14.33
s179(4)	2.144, 14.33
s179(5)	14.32
s180	2.138, 14.37
s180(1)	14.35
s180(2)	14.36, 14.37

Housing Act 1996 *continued*

s180(3)	14.6, 14.13, 14.34, 14.38
s181	2.138
s181(4)	14.39
s181(5)	14.40
s181(6)	14.40
s182	1.60, 2.145
s182(1)	12.41
s183	3.113, 3.114, 4.21, 5.8, 15.5, 15.9
s183(1)	9.10
s183(2)	3.8, 9.10
s183(3)	3.8, 10.210, 14.30
s184	2.52, 2.153, 4.145, 5.69, 9.27, 9.50, 9.53, 9.59, 9.69, 9.73, 9.93, 9.162, 9.185, 10.27, 10.29, 10.178, 10.187, 12.36, 12.141, 12.198, 13.69, 13.96, 14.24, 15.12
s184(1)	2.44, 2.47, 9.8, 9.49, 9.50, 10.187
s184(1)(a)	3.110
s184(2)	2.48, 7.46, 7.64, 9.55
s184(3)	2.51, 9.141, 9.198
s184(3A)	9.147, 10.210
s184(4)	7.64, 9.143
s184(5)	2.53, 9.145
s184(6)	2.53, 2.97, 9.146
s184(7)	3.117, 4.22, 5.4, 10.205, 11.63
s185	1.76, 2.4, 3.8, 4.24, 5.11
s185(1)	2.16
s185(2)	2.16, 3.17
s185(2A)	2.16
s185(3)	2.17
s185(4)	1.76, 1.110, 3.113, 4.21, 4.22, 5.8,12.102, 12.104

Housing Act 1996 *continued*

s185(5)	2.18
s185(7)	2.18
s186	2.17, 3.8, 3.142, 4.24, 5.11
s187	3.106
s187(1)	2.19
s187(2)	2.19, 3.108
s187(3)	2.20, 3.108
s188	2.118, 4.14, 4.59, 5.66, 7.63, 7.64, 7.68, 8.3, 10.27, 10.29, 10.97, 10.118, 12.161
s188(1)	2.55, 2.58, 4.55, 7.19, 9.46, 9.47, 10.8, 10.31
s188(1A)	2.56, 9.22, 10.9, 10.10
s188(1ZA)	10.10
s188(1ZB)	10.10
s188(2)	2.57, 2.59, 7.63, 10.8
s188(2A)	10.29
s188(3)	2.59, 2.150, 3.151, 4.55, 7.19, 9.170, 10.29, 10.31, 10.33, 10.34, 10.41, 10.42, 12.116, 12.147
s189	1.19, 5.5, 5.23
s189(1)	2.30, 5.2
s189(1)(a)	5.12
s189(1)(b)	5.13
s189(1)(c)	5.36, 5.38, 5.39, 5.50, 5.53
s189(1)(d)	5.56, 5.57
s189(2)	1.89, 2.31, 5.4, 5.62, 6.86
s189(3)	5.62
s189A	1.124, 2.61, 2.87, 10.43, 10.90
s189A(1)	2.61, 10.43
s189A(2)	2.61, 10.43
s189A(3)	2.61, 10.43
s189A(4)	2.62, 10.44
s189A(5)	2.62, 10.45
s189A(6)	2.62, 10.45

Housing Act 1996 *continued*
s189A(7) 2.62, 10.45
s189A(8) 2.62, 10.45
s189A(9) 2.63, 10.46
s189A(10) 2.63, 10.46
s189A(11) 2.63, 10.47
s189A(12) 10.48
s189B 1.124, 2.118, 7.70, 8.3, 10.155
s189B(1) 2.71, 7.64, 7.70, 9.143, 10.66
s189B(2) 2.71, 2.87, 7.64, 7.68, 9.147, 10.10, 10.29, 10.66, 10.74, 10.90, 10.109, 10.210
s189B(3) 2.71, 10.66
s189B(4) 2.72, 7.70, 10.68
s189B(5) 2.72, 10.68
s189B(6) 2.73, 10.69
s189B(7) 2.72, 7.70, 10.68
s189B(8) 10.69
s189B(9) 10.69, 10.221
ss190–193 2.147, 9.152
s190 2.118, 8.3, 9.157, 10.10, 10.118, 10.142
s190(1) 9.152
s190(2) 2.189, 4.55, 11.62, 12.112
s190(2)(a) 2.88, 8.7, 10.31, 10.91, 10.99, 10.102, 12.38
s190(2)(b) 2.84, 2.87, 10.90
s190(3) 2.84, 2.86, 9.152, 10.85
s190(4) 2.84, 2.87, 10.86, 10.90, 12.112
s190(5) 2.84, 2.87, 10.86, 10.90
s191 6.86, 9.152
s191(1) 2.34, 4.74, 6.4, 6.27, 6.47, 6.86, 6.87, 12.234
s191(2) 2.37, 6.27, 6.29, 6.41, 6.47, 9.138, 12.82
s191(3) 2.38, 6.2, 6.149
s191(4) 6.2

Housing Act 1996 *continued*
s192 2.84, 5.6, 9.152, 10.85, 10.86
s192(2) 10.85
s192(3) 2.189, 10.81, 11.62
s192(4) 10.86
s192(5) 10.86
s193 1.76, 1.95, 2.73, 2.95, 2.110, 2.115, 2.11, 5.10, 7.3, 7.18, 7.36, 7.37, 7.39, 7.61, 7.64, 7.65, 7.67, 7.91, 7.92, 8.3, 9.25, 9.29, 9.42, 9.128, 9.129, 9.145, 9.152, 9.157, 9.174, 10.9, 10.10, 10.27, 10.71, 10.84, 10.109, 10.111–10.219, 10.220, 10.222, 10.223, 12.28, 12.97, 12.100
s193(1) 10.109
s193(1A) 10.109
s193(2) 1.72, 2.3, 2.100, 2.189, 3.112, 3.114, 4.14, 4.17, 4.23, 5.10, 9.147, 10.20, 10.56, 10.57, 10.111, 10.119, 10.125, 10.174, 10.175, 10.186, 10.201, 10.206, 10.210, 10.217, 11.62, 11.75, 11.86, 12.207
s193(3)–(9) 10.56, 10.57
s193(3) 2.110, 10.111
s193(3A) 2.102
s193(3B) 3.117, 4.23, 5.10, 10.205
s193(5) 2.111, 2.113, 10.185, 10.186, 10.187, 10.188, 10.194, 10.198, 10.201, 10.215, 10.217, 10.218, 12.98
s193(6) 9.152, 9.157, 9.158, 10.26, 10.185
s193(6)(a) 2.111, 3.112, 9.134, 10.182
s193(6)(b) 2.111, 2.113, 6.136, 10.25, 10.183
s193(6)(c) 2.111, 2.113, 10.189, 10.197
s193(6)(cc) 2.111, 2.113, 10.200

Housing Act 1996 *continued*

s193(6)(d)	2.111, 2.113, 10.183
s193(7)	2.111, 2.113, 9.152, 9.157, 9.158, 10.26, 10.190, 10.191, 10.192, 10.194, 10.197, 10.198, 10.218, 12.36
s193(7)(b)	10.192
s193(7A)	2.111, 2.113, 9.152, 9.152, 10.197
s193(7AA)–(7AC)	2.113
s193(7AA)–(7AD)	10.203
s193(7AA)	2.18, 10.202, 10.207, 10.209
s193(7AB)	10.207, 10.209
s193(7AC)	2.92, 4.23, 10.134, 10.202, 10.206, 10.208
s193(7AD)	2.114, 3.117, 4.23, 5.10, 9.147, 10.57, 10.208
s193(7B)	2.111, 10.185, 10.200, 10.206
s193(7C)	2.112, 10.201
s193(7D)	2.111, 10.201, 10.200
s193(7E)	2.112, 10.201
s193(7F)	2.111, 2.112, 2.113, 4.78, 9.157, 10.155, 1.204, 10.212, 10.215, 12.36
s193(7F)(a)	10.190, 10.212
s193(7F)(ab)	10.212
s193(7F)(b)	10.200, 10.212
s193(8)	2.111, 2.113, 10.204, 10.215
s193(9)	9.25, 10.219
s193(10)–(12)	2.113
ss193A–193C	9.153
s193A	2.73, 10.67, 10.70, 10.155, 10.220

Housing Act 1996 *continued*

s193A(1)	2.115, 10.71, 10.220
s193A(2)	2.115, 10.71, 10.220
s193A(3)	2.73, 10.71, 10.109, 10.220
s193A(4)	2.73, 10.71, 10.220
s193A(5)	2.73, 10.71, 10.220
s193A(6)	2.73, 10.71, 10.220
s193A(7)	2.73, 10.71, 10.220
s193B	2.67, 2.68, 2.73, 2.80, 10.61, 10.70
s193B(1)	2.68, 2.115, 10.72
s193B(2)	2.68, 2.115, 10.72, 10.109
s193B(3)	2.68, 10.73
s193B(4)	2.68, 10.73
s193B(5)	2.68, 10.73
s193B(6)	2.68, 10.72
s193B(7)	2.68, 10.73
s193B(8)	2.68, 10.73
s193C	2.73, 2.115, 2.117, 10.70, 10.109, 10.155, 10.221–10.225
s193C(1)	10.74
s193C(2)	10.74
s193C(3)	10.61, 10.70, 10.74, 10.221, 10.222
s193C(4)	10.61, 10.70, 10.74, 10.221, 10.222
s193C(5)	2.116, 10.224
s193C(6)	2.117, 10.225
s193C(7)	2.117, 10.225
s193C(8)	2.117, 10.225
s193C(9)	2.117, 10.225
s193C(10)	2.117, 10.225
s194	1.76, 7.59
s194(6)	7.64
ss195–196	2.147, 9.152

Housing Act 1996 *continued*

s195	1.124, 2.64, 2.74, 2.118, 8.3, 9.152, 10.52, 10.58, 10.83
s195(1)	2.64, 2.77, 10.9, 10.58
s195(2)	2.65, 2.76, 2.77, 2.189, 7.38, 9.147, 10.56, 10.58, 10.74, 10.83, 10.210, 11.62
s195(3)	2.65, 2.76, 2.77, 10.56, 10.58
s195(4)	2.77, 10.46, 10.58
s195(4A)	9.147, 10.57
s195(4B)	10.57
s195(5)	2.66, 2.74, 2.78, 10.9, 10.53, 10.59
s195(5)(a)	2.84
s195(6)	2.74, 2.78, 2.86, 10.53, 10.59
s195(7)	2.67, 2.74, 2.79, 10.53, 10.60
s195(8)	2.66, 2.75, 2.78, 10.54, 10.59
s195(9)	2.75, 2.79, 10.55, 10.60
s195(10)	2.67, 2.80, 10.61, 10.221
s195A	2.113, 10.9
s195A(1)	2.85, 2.101, 5.1, 9.22, 10.84, 10.203
s195A(2)	4.61, 9.22, 10.84, 10.203
s195A(3)–(5)	10.203
s195A(3)	5.1, 9.22, 10.84, 10.203
s195A(4)	4.141, 9.22, 10.84
s195A(5)	10.84, 10.203
s195A(6)	2.56, 2.85, 2.101, 4.61, 4.141, 5.1, 9.22, 9.46, 9.49, 10.9, 10.84, 10.206
s196	9.152, 9.153

Housing Act 1996 *continued*

s196(1)	2.35, 6.5
s196(2)	2.37
s196(3)	2.38
s197	1.76, 1.94, 1.117, 6.2
s198	7.43, 7.61, 9.42
s198(A1)	7.64, 7.68
s198(1)	2.3, 2.91, 7.37, 7.40, 7.64, 9.154
s198(2)	2.91, 7.4, 7.41, 9.143
s198(2A)	2.93, 7.4, 7.42
s198(2ZA)	2.92, 7.6, 7.56
s198(3)	2.94, 7.48
s198(4)	2.91, 7.5, 7.59, 10.143
s198(4A)	7.5, 7.53
s198(5)	2.98, 2.99, 7.7, 7.73, 9.154, 9.172
s198(5A)	7.73
s198(6)	7.73
s199	1.109, 7.9, 7.18, 11.68
s199(1)	2.39, 7.9
s199(1)(a)	7.17
s199(1)(c)	7.32
s199(2)	7.18, 7.25
s199(3)	2.41, 7.17
s199(4)	5.75, 7.18
s199(5)	2.41, 2.42, 7.17, 7.25
s199(6)	2.43, 7.34
s199(7)	2.43, 7.34
s199(8)	2.40, 7.57, 13.80
s199(9)	2.40, 7.58
s199(10)	2.40, 7.58, 13.65
s199A(1)	7.64, 7.68
s199A(2)	7.68
s199A(3)	7.69, 7.70
s199A(4)	7.70
s199A(5)	7.71
s199A(6)	7.68, 7.70
s199A(7)	7.72
ss200–201	12.113
s200	2.118, 8.3, 9.145, 9.157, 10.32, 10.118, 10.142

Housing Act 1996 *continued*
s200(1) 2.96, 4.55, 7.3, 7.5, 7.19, 7.64
s200(1A) 7.64
s200(2) 2.97, 7.59, 7.86, 7.89, 10.125
s200(3) 2.95, 7.91, 9.156
s200(4) 2.95, 7.92, 9.156
s200(5) 2.95, 2.97, 7.19, 10.32
s200(6) 2.97, 7.89
s201 2.2, 2.13, 2.15, 7.9, 7.59
s201A 7.92
s202 1.79, 2.147, 9.93, 9.149, 9.167, 9.185, 10.180, 12.59, 12.62, 12.112, 12.141, 12.207, 12.234
s202(1) 2.148, 9.153, 12.206
s202(1)(a) 9.151
s202(1)(b) 9.152, 9.153
s202(1)(c) 9.154
s202(1)(d) 2.99, 7.89, 9.154, 9.172
s202(1)(e) 2.99, 9.154
s202(1)(f) 9.157
s202(1)(g) 9.157
s202(1A) 2.149, 9.158, 10.218, 12.112
s202(2) 2.149, 9.160, 9.161
s202(3) 2.151, 9.162, 9.163, 12.112
s202(4) 9.149
s203 2.152, 9.145
s203(1) 9.164
s203(2)(a) 9.165
s203(4) 2.153, 7.3, 9.144, 9.198, 12.65, 12.163, 12.234
s203(5) 2.153, 12.163
s203(6) 2.153, 12.163
s203(7) 2.153, 12.163
s203(8) 2.153

Housing Act 1996 *continued*
s204 1.47, 1.79, 1.125, 7.90, 9.174, 10.180, 12.2, 12.5, 12.87, 12.96, 12.99, 12.112, 12.119, 12.141, 12.153, 12.161, 12.178, 12.179, 2.188, 12.197, 12.198, 12.199, 12.202, 12.215, 12.234
s204(1) 2.154, 2.155, 12.110, 12.159, 12.164, 12.218
s204(1)(b) 12.163, 12.198
s204(2) 2.156, 12.165, 12.166
s204(2A) 2.156, 12.167
s204(3) 2.157, 12.203
s204(4) 2.158, 3.151, 4.14, 4.55, 4.59, 10.39, 12.196, 12.197, 12.200
s204A 2.158, 10.39, 12.148, 12.197, 12.198, 12.199, 12.202
s204A(1) 12.197
s204A(2) 12.197
s204A(4) 2.159, 12.202
s204A(4)(a) 2.158, 12.199, 12.200
s204A(4)(b) 2.158, 12.200
s204A(5) 2.159, 12.200
s204A(6)(a) 2.159
s204A(6)(b) 12.200
s205 2.88, 10.67, 10.91
s205(3) 10.123, 10.144
s206 2.88, 9.47, 10.91, 10.121, 10.122, 10.123
s206(1) 2.103, 10.13, 10.19, 10.121, 10.124
s206(1)(c) 10.126
s206(1A) 10.150
s206(2) 2.105, 10.15
s207 1.76, 10.135
s208 10.137, 10.138, 10.144, 13.41
s208(1) 2.106, 10.136
s208(1A) 10.136

Housing Act 1996 *continued*

s208(2)	2.107,10.141
s208(3)	2.107, 10.142
s208(4)	2.108, 10.141
s209	10.17, 10.112
s209(1)	10.82
s209(2)	2.88, 10.17
s210	10.145, 10.146, 10.150, 10.165
s210(1)	2.104, 10.19
s210(1A)	10.150
s210(2)	2.104, 10.151
s211	8.7, 8.18, 12.113
s211(1)	2.120, 8.5
s211(2)	2.118, 7.64, 8.3, 8.7, 8.10
s211(3)	2.121, 8.19
s211(4)	2.122, 8.12
s211(5)	2.119, 8.3
s212	12.113
s212(1)	2.123, 8.10
s212(2)	2.124
s212(3)	2.125, 8.6, 8.8
s212(4)	2.126, 8.20
s212(5)	2.126, 8.20
s213	9.58, 9.59, 9.140, 10.67, 12.113, 13.70, 13.66
s213(1)	2.163, 10.5
s213(1)(a)	2.163, 10.5
s213(2)	2.163, 9.58, 10.5
s213(2)(a)	9.60, 13.69
s213(2)(b)	13.69
s213(3)	2.163
s213(3)(a)	13.69
s213(3)(b)	13.69
s213(9)	10.219
s213A	10.106
s213A(1)	2.166, 13.68
s213A(2)	2.166
s213A(4)	13.69
s213A(5)	2.166, 13.70
s213A(6)	2.166, 13.70
s213B	9.50, 13.71, 13.94, 13.96
s213B(2)	13.95
s213B(3)	13.95
s213B(4)	13.94
s213B(5)	13.94

Housing Act 1996 *continued*

s214	15.1, 15.5, 15.9, 15.12
s214(1)	2.160, 15.5, 15.7, 15.9
s214(2)	2.162, 15.12, 15.14
s214(3)	2.162, 15.15
s214(4)	2.161, 2.162
s214A(1)	2.146, 14.20
s214A(2)	2.146, 14.20
s214A(3)	2.146, 14.20
s214A(4)–(8)	14.21
s214A(9)–(10)	14.21
s214A(11)	14.21
s214A(12)	2.146, 14.22
s215	2.91
s217	2.2, 2.12, 2.13, 2.14, 2.15, 7.9, 7.59,10.17, 10.200, 10.202, 10.206
s217(1)	10.200
s230	2.13, 4.61
Sch 1	11.117
Sch 1 Pt II para 4	11.129
Sch 1 Pt II paras 6–8	11.129
Sch 1 Pt II para 14	11.129
Sch 1 Pt II paras 15–15A	11.129
Sch 1 Pt IIIA	11.129
Sch 1 Pt IV	11.129
Sch 2	11.118
Sch 2 para 1(1)	11.118
Sch 2 para 1(2)	11.118
Sch 2 para 3	11.118
Sch 2 para 7	11.119
Sch 2 para 7(2)	11.119
Sch 2 para 7(3)	11.119
Sch 2 para 7(5)	11.119
Sch 2 paras 7A–7D	12.228
Sch 2 para 7A	12.228
Sch 2 para 7B(1)	12.229
Sch 2 para 7B(2)(a)(i)	12.229

Housing Act 1996 *continued*
Sch 2 para 7B(2)(a)(ii) 12.229
Sch 2 para 7C(1) 12.228
Sch 2 para 7D(1) 12.230
Sch 16 11.13
Sch 17 5.61, 11.13
Sch 17 para 3 2.88
Housing Act 2004 2.104, 10.145, 11.22
Pt 1 4.109, 6.106, 10.146
s54 10.155
s55 10.155
s133 10.155
s223 11.62
Housing and Planning Act 1986 1.6, 155–1.58, 1.62, 1.63, 4.8
s14 10.145
s14(2) 1.55, 4.69, 4.95
s14(3) 10.19
Housing and Regeneration Act 2008 1.110, 1.111, 11.17, 11.116, 11.117
Pt 1 Ch 4 11.117
Pt 1 Ch 6 11.117
Pt 1 Ch 7 11.117, 11.124
Pt 2 11.116
s64 11.116
s69 12.7
s81 11.116
s92K 11.122, 11.126
s94B 11.116
s193 11.117
s193(2)(a) 11.122, 11.123
s195 11.122
s197 11.123
s197(7) 11.123
s198 11.124
s198A 11.125
s198B 11.125
s253 11.117, 11.124
s297 11.22
s314 1.110, 3.114, 4.21, 5.8, 10.212
s315(a) 7.25
s321(1) 7.25
Housing and Regeneration Act 2008 *continued*
Sch 15 Pt 1 1.110, 3.114, 4.21, 5.8
Sch 15 Pt 1 para 1 10.212
Sch 15 Pt 1 para 5(1) 10.212
Sch 15 Pt 1 para 6 10.212
Sch 15 Pt 1 para 7 9.157
Sch 16 7.25
Human Rights Act 1998 11.120, 11.121, 12.7, 12.23–12.30, 12.31, 12.95–12.105, 12.234, 12.39
s3(1) 12.95
s4 12.104
s6(1) 12.95
s6(3) 12.95, 13.94
s7(1) 12.95
Immigration Act 1971 3.17, 3.20
s1(1) 3.20
s1(2) 3.113, 5.8
s2 3.21, 3.22, 3.81
s2(1)(c) 3.21, 3.22
s2(1)(d) 3.22
s2(2) 3.22
s3 3.18
s3A 3.18
s4 12.126
s7(1) 3.20
s8 3.18, 3.81
s8(1) 3.18
s8(2) 3.76, 3.81
s8(3) 3.76
s8(3A) 3.76
s8(4) 3.18
s8(6) 3.18
s14 9.9
s33(2A) 3.76
Sch 2 para 21 13.36
Immigration Act 1988—
s7(1) 3.23
Immigration Act 2016—
s77(1) 9.63

Immigration and Asylum Act 1999 3.152, 13.3, 13.5, 13.16, 13.27–13.39
- Pt VI 13.27
- s4 13.36, 13.38, 13.39, 13.49
- s4(1) 13.36
- s4(2) 13.36
- s94(1) 13.29
- s94(3) 13.35
- s94(5) 13.35
- s95 2.43, 7.34, 13.33, 13.34, 13.36, 13.38, 13.77
- s95(1) 13.29
- s95(3) 13.31
- s95(4) 13.31
- s96(1) 13.34
- s97(1) 13.34
- s97(2) 13.34
- s97(4) 13.34
- s98 13.33, 13.36
- s115 2.16, 2.174, 13.15, 13.27

Land Compensation Act 1973 4.109, 5.58
- s39 4.109, 5.58, 11.22

Landlord and Tenant Act 1954—
- Pt I 4.54

Landlord and Tenant Act 1985—
- s8 6.106

Legal Aid, Sentencing and Punishment of Offenders Act 2012—
- s85 2.161, 2.203, 15.2
- s91(4) 2.33

Limitation Act 1980 11.75

Local Authority Social Services Act 1970 13.59, 13.62, 14.4
- s1 2.15
- s7 1.10

Local Government (Contracts) Act 1997—
- s1 12.46

Local Government (Miscellaneous Provisions) Act 1982 8.18
- s41 8.14, 8.15

Local Government (Wales) Act 1994—
- s17 2.13

Local Government Act 1972 1.13, 1.16, 2.13, 12.48, 13.59
- Pt II 12.222
- s2 3.152
- s26(1) 12.222
- s101 12.48
- s111 10.122
- s112 12.46
- s193 1.13
- s195 1.16
- Sch 22 1.13
- Sch 23 1.16

Local Government Act 1974 12.228
- Pt III 12.220
- s26 12.220
- s26A 12.226
- s26B 12.225
- s26C 12.226
- s26D 12.226
- s28 12.226
- s30(1) 12.227
- s31 12.227
- s31(2) 12.227
- s31(2A) 12.227
- s31(2D) 12.227

Local Government Act 1985 13.59

Local Government Act 1988—
- Pt III 11.17

Local Government Act 2000 3.4, 3.158, 12.49, 13.4, 13.5, 13.60, 13.87–13.96
- Pt I 3.3, 3.158
- s2 3.4, 13.87, 13.88, 13.92, 13.93
- s2(2)(a) 13.88
- s2(2)(b) 13.88
- s2(3) 13.92

Local Government Act 2000 *continued*
s3(1) 13.88
s4 13.92
s9D 12.49, 12.50
s9D(2) 12.49
s9D(3) 12.49
ss9E–9EB 12.49
s9F 12.50
ss13–15 9.166
s13 12.49
s13(2) 12.49
s13(3)(b) 12.49
s13(9) 12.50
s13(10) 12.49
s13(10)(a) 12.50
ss14–16 12.49
s18 12.49
s21 12.50
s92 12.227

Local Government Act 2003—
Pt 1 1.46
s99(4) 14.3

Local Government and Housing Act 1989 1.46, 12.222
Sch 10 4.54

Local Government and Public Involvement in Health Act 2007 2.13
Pt 9 12.222
s173(2) 12.222
s236 12.49

Local Government, Planning and Land Act 1980 1.46

Localism Act 2011 1.1, 1.5, 1.6, 1.112–1.118, 2.1, 2.46, 2.110, 2.113, 2.192, 3.3, 3.4, 3.118, 3.158, 9.157, 10.84, 10.175, 10.184, 10.185–10.187, 10.188, 10.189, 10.194, 10.196–10.198, 10.199–10.201, 10.202–10.204, 10.205–10.207, 10.208–10.211, 10.213, 11.6, 11.8, 11.29, 11.75, 11.117, 11.118, 13.4, 13.5, 13.60, 13.87–13.96, 14.23
Pt 1 Ch 1 3.158
Pt 7 Ch 5 11.116
s1 3.4, 3.152, 10.122, 13.89, 13.90, 13.93

Localism Act 2011 *continued*
s2 3.4, 10.122, 13.91
s25 12.61
s48 10.84
s145 2.171, 2.180, 11.19
s145(2) 11.19
s146 11.29, 11.39, 11.41, 11.48
s146(1) 2.180
s147 10.80, 11.59, 11.69
s147(4) 14.25
s147(5)(b) 11.69
s148 2.113, 4.23, 9.157, 10.9, 10.199, 10.205, 10.212
s148(3) 2.110, 10.185, 10.188, 10.189, 10.196
s148(4) 10.197
s149 2.56, 2.85, 2.92, 2.102, 4.61, 4.141, 5.1, 9.22, 10.9, 10.84
s149(2) 2.75, 10.9, 10.55, 10.84
s149(4) 10.9, 10.84
s149(6) 7.6, 7.56
s150 2.197, 11.59, 14.10
s151 11.59
s153 14.10
s154 1.113
s158 11.20
ss180–182 12.228
ss180–183 12.220
s180 12.228, 12.229, 12.230
Sch 1 3.4
Sch 16 11.116
Sch 17 11.116

London Government Act 1963 13.59

Matrimonial and Family Proceedings Act 1984—
s24 11.20

Matrimonial Causes Act 1973—
s17 11.20

Mental Capacity Act 2005 13.9
Mental Health Act 1983 7.17
National Assistance Act 1948 1.7–1.20, 1.112, 11.84, 12.14, 13.1, 13.2, 13.7, 13.8, 13.9, 13.18, 13.22, 13.23, 13.24
  Pt III 1.6, 13.8
  s21 1.8, 10.27, 12.129, 13.1, 13.7, 13.19, 13.20, 13.22, 13.25
  s21(1) 1.7
  s21(1A) 13.15, 13.18
  s24 1.9
  s29 13.1
  s33 1.10
  s48 8.10
National Health Service (Wales) Act 2006 13.9
National Health Service Act 2006 13.9
  s275(1) 14.32
Nationality, Immigration and Asylum Act 2002 3.152
  s11 3.153
  s22 2.43, 7.34, 7.36
  s55(1) 13.32
  s55(5) 13.32
  s55(5)(a) 13.32
  Sch 3 3.4, 3.151, 3.153, 3.157
  Sch 3 para 1 13.15, 13.48
  Sch 3 para 1(1)(g) 3.152
  Sch 3 para 1(1)(j) 3.151
  Sch 3 para 1(1)(k) 3.152
  Sch 3 para 1(1)(ka) 3.152
  Sch 3 para 1(1)(l) 3.152
  Sch 3 para 1(1)(n) 3.152
Nationality, Immigration and Asylum Act 2002 *continued*
  Sch 3 para 1(1)(o) 3.152
  Sch 3 para 2(1)(a) 3.151
  Sch 3 para 2(1)(b) 3.151
  Sch 3 para 3 3.154, 13.21
  Sch 3 para 3(a) 13.17
  Sch 3 para 3(b) 13.17
  Sch 3 paras 4–7A 3.151
  Sch 3 para 4 3.153
  Sch 3 para 5 3.153
  Sch 3 para 6 3.153
  Sch 3 para 7 3.153, 13.35
  Sch 3 para 7A 3.153
Planning (Listed Buildings and Conservation Areas) Act 1990 12.234
Powers of Criminal Courts (Sentencing) Act 2000—
  s76 5.77
  s107(1)(e) 14.32
Poor Laws 1.12
Poor Law 1601 7.1
Powers of Criminal Courts (Sentencing) Act 2000—
  s76 2.33
Protection from Eviction Act 1977 4.50, 4.53, 4.57, 7.65, 10.30, 10.82, 10.94, 10.112, 10.222
  s1(1) 4.50
  s2 4.55
  s3 4.55, 4.60, 10.18, 10.112, 10.222
  s3(2B) 4.55, 4.57
  s8(2) 4.55
Public Services Ombudsman (Wales) Act 2005—
  s4 12.233
  s7 12.233
  s7(3) 12.233
  s7(4) 12.233
  s8 12.233
  s10 12.233

Public Services Ombudsman (Wales) Act 2005 *continued*
s31 12.233
Sch 3 12.233
Rehabilitation of Offenders Act 1974 11.28
Rent (Agriculture) Act 1976 4.53
Rent Act 1977 4.51, 4.53, 4.54, 4.142, 6.111, 6.144, 11.31
s19 4.55
Sch 15 case 1 11.31
Sch 15 case 2 11.31
Sch 15 case 3 11.31
Sch 15 case 4 11.31
Sch 15 case 13 6.144
Senior Courts Act 1981—
s31 12.116
s31(2A) 12.153
s31(3C) 12.234
s51 12.138, 12.170, 12.181
Sexual Offences Act 2003—
Sch 3 10.155
Social Services and Well-being (Wales) Act 2014 2.15, 3.3, 13.2, 13.5, 13.7–13.26, 13.40–13.86
Pt 3 13.14
Pt 4 3.152
Pt 6 13.86
s19(1) 13.14
s20(1) 13.14
s20(2) 13.14
s20(3) 13.14
s21(1) 13.82
s21(4)(b) 13.82, 13.84
s32 13.14, 13.82
s34(2)(a) 13.8, 13.81
s35 13.8
s35(2) 13.9
s35(3)(a) 13.9
s35(3)(b) 13.9
s35(4)(a) 13.9

Social Services and Well-being (Wales) Act 2014 *continued*
s35(4)(b) 13.9
s36 13.8
s36(1) 13.13
s36(3) 13.13
s37 13.81
s37(2) 13.83
s37(3) 13.83
s37(5) 13.83
s37(6) 13.83
s38 13.81
s38(1) 13.85
s38(3) 13.85
s40 13.8
s42 13.81
s45 13.8, 13.81
ss46–48 13.12
s46(1) 13.15
s48(a) 13.22
s59 13.9
s74 5.72
s76 5.62, 13.86
s104(2) 5.65
ss105–116 3.152
s145 13.14
s194 13.9
s197(1) 13.8, 13.81
Social Work (Scotland) Act 1968 2.15
Town and Country Planning Act 1990 12.234
Trusts of Land and Appointment of Trustees Act 1996—
s14 6.77
s15 6.77
Violence against Women, Domestic Abuse and Sexual Violence (Wales) Act 2015—
s24 4.89
Welfare Reform Act 2012 11.92
s96 10.153
Well-being of Future Generations (Wales) Act 2015 2.129, 14.5

Table of statutory instruments

Access to Justice Act 1999 (Destination of Appeals) Order 2016 SI No 917	12.188
reg 5	12.188
Accession (Immigration and Worker Authorisation) (Amendment) Regulations 2007 SI No 475—	
reg 2(1)	3.69
reg 2(2)(a)	3.69
reg 2(2)(c)	3.69
Accession (Immigration and Worker Authorisation) Regulations 2006 SI No 3317	3.67
reg 1(2)(f)	3.69
reg 1(2)(t)	3.69
reg 1(3)	3.64
reg 2(2)	3.69
reg 2(3)	3.69
reg 2(4)	3.69
reg 2(5)	3.69
reg 2(5A)	3.69
reg 2(6)	3.69
reg 2(6A)	3.69
reg 2(7)	3.69
reg 2(8)	3.69
reg 2(8A)	3.69
reg 2(9)	3.69
reg 2(10)	3.69
reg 2(10A)	3.69
reg 2(10B)	3.69
reg 2(11)	3.69
reg 2(12)(c)	3.69
reg 2(13)(a)	3.69
reg 3	3.71
reg 6(1)	3.68
reg 6(2)	3.68
reg 6(3)	3.68
reg 7(1)	3.68
reg 7(2)	3.68
reg 9(2)	3.70
reg 10(1)(a)	3.71

Accession (Immigration and Worker Authorisation) Regulations 2006 SI No 3317 *continued*

reg 10(1)(b) 3.71
Sch 1 3.69
Sch 2 para 1(1) 3.64
Sch 2 para 2(a) 3.64

Accession (Immigration and Worker Registration) (Amendment) Regulations 2009 SI No 892 3.61

Accession (Immigration and Worker Registration) (Revocation, Savings and Consequential Provisions) Regulations 2011 SI No 544 3.61

Accession (Immigration and Worker Registration) Regulations 2004 SI No 1219 3.62

reg 1(2)(k) 3.64
reg 2(1) 3.64
reg 2(2) 3.64
reg 2(3) 3.64
reg 2(4) 3.64
reg 2(5) 3.64
reg 2(5A) 3.64
reg 2(6)(a) 3.64
reg 2(6)(b) 3.64
reg 2(8) 3.64
reg 2(9)(b) 3.64
reg 4(2) 3.63
reg 4(3) 3.63
reg 5(2) 3.63
reg 5(3) 3.63
reg 5(4) 3.63
reg 5(5) 3.63
reg 7(2)(a) 3.65
reg 7(2)(b) 3.65
reg 7(2)(c) 3.65
reg 7(3) 3.65

Accession (Worker Authorisation and Worker Registration) (Amendment) Regulations 2007 SI No 3012—

reg 2(1) 3.69
reg 2(2)(a) 3.69
reg 2(2)(b) 3.69
reg 3(a) 3.64

Accession (Worker Authorisation and Worker Registration) (Amendment) Regulations 2009 SI No 2426—

reg 1 3.64, 3.69, 3.71
reg 2(2)(a) 3.69
reg 2(2)(b) 3.69
reg 2(2)(c) 3.69
reg 2(3) 3.71
reg 3(a) 3.64
reg 3(b) 3.64

Accession of Croatia (Immigration and Worker Authorisation) Regulations 2013 SI No 1460	3.72
reg 1(2)	3.75, 3.76
reg 2	3.76
reg 2(2)	3.76
reg 2(3)	3.76
reg 2(4)	3.76
reg 2(6)	3.76
reg 2(7)	3.76
reg 2(8)	3.76
reg 2(9)	3.76
reg 2(10)	3.76
reg 2(11)	3.76
reg 2(12)	3.76
reg 2(13)	3.76
reg 2(14)	3.76
reg 2(15)	3.76
reg 2(16)	3.76
reg 2(17)	3.76
reg 2(18)	3.76
reg 2(19)	3.76
reg 2(20)	3.76
reg 3	3.76
reg 4	3.74
reg 5	3.74, 3.147
reg 7	3.76
reg 8(1)	3.77
reg 8(2)	3.77
reg 8(4)	3.77
reg 9	3.77
reg 11	3.78
reg 15	3.78
reg 16	3.78
Allocation of Housing (England) Regulations 2002 SI No 3624—	
reg 3	11.22
Allocation of Housing (Procedure) Regulations 1997 SI No 483—	
reg 3	11.97
Allocation of Housing (Qualification Criteria for Armed Forces) (England) Regulations 2012 SI No 1869—	
reg 2	11.41
reg 3	11.41
Allocation of Housing (Qualification Criteria for Right to Move) (England) Regulations 2015 SI No 967	11.41
reg 4(a)	11.41
reg 4(b)	11.41
reg 4(c)	11.41
reg 5	11.41

Allocation of Housing (Reasonable and Additional Preference) Regulations 1997 SI No 1902	1.81, 11.5
Allocation of Housing (Wales) Regulations 2003 SI No 239—	
reg 3	11.22
Allocation of Housing and Homelessness (Eligibility) (England) (Amendment) Regulations 2012 SI No 2588	3.10, 3.90, 3.93, 3.171
Allocation of Housing and Homelessness (Eligibility) (England) (Amendment) Regulations 2013 SI No 435—	
reg 2(5)(c)	3.143
reg 2(6)(c)	3.147
Allocation of Housing and Homelessness (Eligibility) (England) (Amendment) Regulations 2014 SI No 1467	3.10
Allocation of Housing and Homelessness (Eligibility) (England) (Amendment) Regulations 2016 SI No 965—	
reg 2(3)(b)(i)	3.170
reg 2(3)(c)	3.170
reg 2(4)(a)	3.138
reg 2(4)(c)	3.144
Allocation of Housing and Homelessness (Eligibility) (England) Regulations 2006 SI No 1294	2.4, 2.16, 2.17, 3.10, 3.73, 3.90, 3.93
reg 3	3.120, 3.168, 3.169
reg 3(a)–(f)	3.170
reg 3(e)	3.170
reg 3(f)	3.170
reg 4	3.120, 3.168, 3.169, 3.171, 3.174
reg 4(1)	3.43
reg 4(1)(b)(ii)	3.29, 3.31
reg 4(1)(b)(iii)	3.171
reg 4(1)(b)(iv)	3.171
reg 4(1)(c)	3.171
reg 5	3.120
reg 5(1)(a)	3.122
reg 5(1)(b)	3.128
reg 5(1)(c)	3.131
reg 5(1)(d)	3.134
reg 5(1)(e)	3.138
reg 5(1)(f)	3.143
reg 5(1)(g)	3.144
reg 6	3.120
reg 6(1)	3.43, 3.146, 3.174
reg 6(1)(a)	3.146
reg 6(1)(b)(i)	3.146
reg 6(1)(b)(ii)	3.29, 3.31, 3.146
reg 6(1)(b)(iii)	3.146

Allocation of Housing and Homelessness (Eligibility) (England) Regulations 2006 SI No 1294 *continued*

reg 6(1)(b)(iv)	3.146
reg 6(1)(c)	3.146
reg 6(1)(c)(i)	3.146
reg 6(1)(c)(ii)	3.146
reg 6(2)	3.147
reg 6(2)(a)	3.147
reg 6(2)(b)	3.147
reg 6(2)(c)	3.147
reg 6(2)(d)	3.147
reg 6(2)(e)	3.147
reg 6(2)(g)	3.147
reg 15(1)(c)	3.147
reg 15(1)(d)	3.147
reg 15(1)(e)	3.147
reg 15A(1)	3.146
reg 15A(4A)	3.146
Allocation of Housing and Homelessness (Eligibility) (Wales) Regulations 2014 SI No 2603	2.4, 2.16, 2.17, 3.10, 3.148, 3.174
reg 3	3.120, 3.168, 3.172, 3.173
reg 3(e)	3.173
reg 4	3.120, 3.168, 3.172, 3.174
reg 4(1)	3.43
reg 4(1)(b)(ii)	3.29, 3.31
reg 5	3.120, 3.149
reg 6	3.120, 3.150
reg 6(1)	3.43
reg 6(1)(b)(ii)	3.29, 3.31
Allocation of Housing and Homelessness (Miscellaneous Provisions) (England) Regulations 2006 SI No 2527	2.91, 7.54
reg 2(1)	3.134
reg 2(3)	3.134
Allocation of Housing and Homelessness (Review Procedures) Regulations 1999 SI No 71	9.102, 9.164, 9.168, 9.173, 9.177, 9.180, 9.191, 9.198, 11.111
reg 1	9.172
reg 2	9.166, 9.167, 12.59
reg 6(2)(a)	9.175
reg 6(2)(b)	9.176
reg 6(3)(a)	9.175
reg 6(3)(b)	9.176
reg 7(1)	9.173
reg 7(2)	9.173
reg 7(5)	9.177
reg 8(1)	9.177

Allocation of Housing and Homelessness (Review Procedures) Regulations 1999 SI No 71 *continued*	
reg 8(1)(b)	9.178
reg 8(2)	9.178, 9.180, 9.181, 9.187
reg 8(2)(b)	9.178
reg 9(1)(a)	9.191
reg 9(1)(b)	9.192
reg 9(1)(b)	9.192
reg 9(3)	9.192
Allocation of Housing and Homelessness (Review Procedures and Amendment) Regulations 1996 SI No 3122—	
reg 8(1)	9.177
Asylum and Immigration (Treatment of Claimants, etc) Act 2004 (Commencement No 2) Order 2004 SI No 2999	3.153
Asylum Seekers (Reception Conditions) Regulations 2005 SI No 7	13.28
reg 1(2)	13.28
reg 5	13.29
Asylum Support (Amendment) Regulations 2005 SI No 11	13.28
Asylum Support Regulations 2000 SI No 704—	
reg 2(2)	13.35
reg 2(4)	13.29
reg 7	13.29
reg 12	13.34
Care Act 2014 (Transitional Provision) Order 2015 SI No 995—	
Art 2	13.8
Care and Support (Charging) (Wales) Regulations 2015 SI No 1843	13.9
Care and Support (Charging and Assessment of Resources) Regulations 2014 SI No 2672	13.9
Care and Support (Eligibility) (Wales) Regulations 2015 SI No 1578—	
reg 1(3)	13.84
reg 3	13.11
reg 3(b)	13.11
reg 4(1)(a)	13.84
reg 4(1)(b)	13.84
reg 4(1)(c)	13.84
reg 4(1)(d)	13.84
reg 4(2)(i)	13.84
Care and Support (Eligibility Criteria) Regulations 2015 SI No 313—	
reg 2(1)	13.11
reg 2(2)	13.11
Care Leavers (England) Regulations 2010 SI No 2571—	
reg 3	5.65

Care Leavers (England) Regulations 2010 SI No 2571 *continued*	
Sch 2	13.76
Sch 2 para 1	13.76
Sch 2 para 2	13.76
Care Leavers (Wales) Regulations 2015 SI No 1820	13.86
Care Planning, Placement and Case Review (England) Regulations 2010 SI No 959	13.75
Children (Leaving Care) (England) Regulations 2001 SI No 2874	13.75
Civil Procedure (Amendment No 3) Rules 2016 SI No 788	12.192
Civil Procedure Rules 1998 SI No 3132	8.2, 4.61, 12.123, 12.175, 12.189
r2.3(1)	12.123
PD 2B(9)	12.175
r3.1	12.120
r8.6(1)	12.136
r19.4A(1)	12.126
Pt 23	12.129
r23.8	12.129
Pt 25	12.129
r39.2(3)(d)	12.158
r39.2(4)	12.157
Pt 44	2.138
r44.2	12.143, 12.170
r44.2(1)–(5)	12.138
r44.2(2)(a)	12.138
r44.12	12.178
Pt 45	12.234
r45.43	12.234
r46.8	12.181
r48.7	12.138
PD 48	12.182
Pt 52	12.170, 12.171, 12.175, 12.189
r52.3(1)	12.135
r52.6	12.135
r52.7	12.189, 12.194
r52.7(2)(a)	12.191, 12.192
r52.7(2)(b)	12.191, 12.192
r52.8	12.132
r52.8(3)	12.135
r52.8(5)	12.135
r52.8(6)	12.135
r52.12	12.189
r52.13	12.173
r52.17	12.171
r52.19	12.234
PD 52A–52E	12.171
PD 52B para 4.1	12.171
PD 52B para 8.3	12.234

Civil Procedure Rules 1998 SI No 3132 *continued*
PD 52D para 24.2(1) 12.199
PD 52D para 24.2(2) 12.199
PD 52D para 28 12.234
PD 52D para 28.1 12.171
PD 52D para 28.1(4) 12.199
PD 52D para 28.1(5)(a) 12.171
PD 52D para 28.1(5)(b) 12.171
PD 52D para 28.1(5)(c) 12.171
PD 52D para 28.1(5)(d) 12.171
Pt 54 1.47, 12.116, 12.122, 13.37
r54.1 12.123
r54.3(1) 12.150
r54.3(2) 12.152
r54.5 12.120
r54.5(2) 12.120
r54.7 12.126
r54.8 12.126
r54.9 12.127
r54.12 12.132
r54.12(7) 12.127
r54.14 12.131
r54.16 12.133, 12.136
PD 54 12.116, 12.234
PD 54A para 4.1 12.120
PD 54A paras 5.6–5.9 1.123
PD 54A paras 8.5–8.6 12.130
PD 54A para 12.1 12.133
PD 54A para 15 12.132
PD 54A para 54.6 12.120
Pt 83 4.60
Civil Procedure Rules 1998, Costs PDs 12.116
Civil Procedure Rules 1998, Judicial Review Pre-action Protocol 12.116, 12.234
para 6 12.116
para 7 12.116
para 9 12.234
para 14 12.117
para 16 12.117
para 18 12.117
para 20 12.118
para 21 12.118
para 22 12.118
Annex B 12.118
Code of Practice (English Language Requirements for Public Sector Workers) Regulations 2016 SI No 1157 9.63
Discretionary Financial Assistance Regulations 2001 SI No 1167 10.44

Discretionary Housing Payments (Grants) Order 2001 SI No 2340	10.44
Electrical Equipment (Safety) Regulations 1994 SI No 3260—	
reg 5	10.155
reg 7	10.155
Energy Performance of Buildings (Certificates and Inspections) (England and Wales) Regulations 2007 SI No 991	10.155
Furniture and Furnishings (Fire) (Safety) Regulations 1988 SI No 1324	10.155
Gas Safety (Installation and Use) Regulations 1998 SI No 2451—	
reg 36	10.155
Homeless Persons (Priority Need) (Wales) Order 2001 SI No 607	1.90
Homelessness (Abolition of Priority Need Test) (Scotland) Order 2012 SI No 330	1.121, 2.2
Homelessness (Asylum-Seekers) (Interim Period) (England) Order 1999 SI No 3126	7.55, 10.136, 10.146, 10.150
Art 6	10.150
Homelessness (Decisions on Referrals) Order 1998 SI No 1578	7.2, 7.74, 9.172
Sch para 1	7.82
Sch para 2	7.82
Sch para 3	7.82
Sch para 4(1)	7.82
Sch para 4(2)	7.82
Sch para 5(2)	7.83
Sch para 5(3)	7.83
Sch para 5(4)	7.83
Sch para 6	7.86
Sch para 7(1)	7.88
Sch para 7(2)	7.84
Homelessness (Decisions on Referrals) (Scotland) Order 1998 SI No 1603	7.74
Homelessness (Intentionality) (Specified Categories) (Wales) Regulations 2015 SI No 1265	2.37, 6.3
Homelessness (Isles of Scilly) Order 1997 SI No 797	7.9
Homelessness (Priority Need for Accommodation) (England) Order 2002 SI No 2051	1.90, 2.32, 5.4, 5.5, 5.64
Art 3	5.64, 9.18
Art 4	9.18
Homelessness (Review Procedure) (Wales) Regulations 2015 SI No 1266	9.164, 9.168, 9.173, 9.180, 9.191
reg 2	9.175
reg 2(2)(b)	9.176

Homelessness (Review Procedure) (Wales) Regulations 2015 SI No 1266 *continued*	
reg 3	9.4, 9.165, 9.166, 12.59
reg 4	9.172, 9.173, 9.177
reg 5(2)	9.178
reg 6(1)(a)	9.191
reg 6(1)(b)	9.192
reg 6(1)(c)	9.192
reg 6(2)	9.193
reg 6(3)	9.192
Homelessness (Suitability of Accommodation) (England) Order 2003 SI No 3326	1.108, 2.104, 10.146, 10.156, 10.162
Art 2	10.157
Homelessness (Suitability of Accommodation) (England) Order 2012 SI No 2601	2.104, 10.131, 10.146
Art 2	10.154, 10.173
Art 3	10.146, 10.155
Homelessness (Suitability of Accommodation) Order 1996 SI No 3204	2.104, 4.122, 4.124, 6.78, 9.67, 10.146, 10.152, 10.163
Art 2(a)	4.123
Art 2(b)	4.124
Homelessness (Suitability of Accommodation) (Wales) Order 2006 SI No 650	10.146, 10.159, 10.161
Homelessness (Suitability of Accommodation) (Wales) Order 2015 SI No 1268	10.146, 10.159, 10.161, 10.173
Part 3	10.160
reg 2	10.162
Sch	10.161
Homelessness Act 2002 (Commencement) (Wales) Order 2002 SI No 1736	11.5
Art 2	2.129
Homelessness Act 2002 (Commencement No 1) (England) Order 2002 SI No 1799—	
Art 2	2.129
Homelessness Act 2002 (Commencement No 3) (England) Order 2002 SI No 3114	11.5
Housing (Homeless Persons) (Appropriate Arrangements) Order 1978 SI No 69	7.87, 7.88
Housing (Northern Ireland) Order 1988 SI No 1990 (NI 23)	2.2
Housing (Northern Ireland) Order 2003 SI No 412 (NI 2)	2.2

Housing (Wales) Act 2014 (Commencement No 3 and Transitory, Transitional and Saving Provisions) Order 2015 SI No 1272	2.2, 10.49
Art 7	2.110, 10.185, 10.189, 10.199, 10.205, 10.212
Housing (Wales) Act 2014 (Consequential Amendments) Regulations 2015 SI No 752	2.2, 9.171, 12.47
Housing Act 1996 (Additional Preference for Armed Forces) (England) Regulations 2012 SI No 2989	11.64
Housing and Regeneration Act 2008 (Commencement No 1 and Saving Provisions) Order 2009 SI No 415—	
Art 2	10.212
Housing and Regeneration Act 2008 (Commencement No 2 and Transitional, Saving and Transitory Provisions) Order 2008 SI No 3068	7.25
Housing and Regeneration Act 2008 (Commencement No 7 and Transitional and Saving Provisions) Order 2010 SI No 862—	
Art 2	11.116
Housing and Regeneration Act 2008 (Consequential Provisions) Order 2010 SI No 866—	
Sch 2	2.163, 2.169, 2.199, 10.5
Housing Benefit (General) Regulations 1987 SI No 1971	6.36
reg 7A	3.138
Housing Benefit Regulations 2006 SI No 213—	
reg B13	11.92
Housing Corporation (Dissolution) Order 2009 SI No 484	11.116
Immigration (European Economic Area) (Amendment) Regulations 2011 SI No 1247	3.55
Immigration (European Economic Area) (Amendment) Regulations 2012 SI No 1547—	
Sch 1 para 8(a)	3.87
Sch 1 para 9	3.81
Immigration (European Economic Area) (Amendment) (No 2) Regulations 2012 SI No 2560	3.90, 3.93
Immigration (European Economic Area) Regulations 2006 SI No 1003	3.55, 3.93
reg 13	3.64
reg 15	3.76
reg 15(1A)	3.87
reg 15A(4A)	3.90
Immigration (European Economic Area) Regulations 2016 SI No 1052	3.23, 3.24, 3.55, 3.80, 3.81
reg 2(1)	3.52, 3.56
reg 4(1)(b)	3.37
reg 4(1)(c)	3.40

Housing (Wales) Act 2014 (Commencement No 3 and Transitory, Transitional and Saving Provisions) Order 2015 SI No 1272 *continued*

reg 4(1)(d)	3.43
reg 5(2)	3.45
reg 5(3)	3.46
reg 6(1)	3.24, 3.31
reg 6(1)(a)–(e)	3.30
reg 6(2)	3.35, 3.61
reg 6(3)	3.35
reg 6(4)	3.38
reg 6(5)	3.35
reg 6(6)	3.35
reg 7(1)	3.52
reg 7(1)(a)	3.52
reg 7(1)(c)	3.52
reg 7(3)	3.56
reg 7A	3.61
reg 8	3.52, 3.56
reg 8(2)	3.56
reg 8(3)	3.56
reg 8(4)	3.56
reg 8(5)	3.56
reg 10	3.59
reg 10(2)	3.58
reg 10(3)	3.58
reg 10(4)	3.58
reg 10(5)	3.59
reg 11(1)	3.27
reg 11(2)	3.27
reg 13	3.28, 3.40
reg 14(2)	3.58
reg 15(1)	3.44
reg 15(1)(b)	3.44
reg 15(1)(c)	3.45
reg 15(1)(d)	3.45
reg 15(2)	3.87
reg 15A	3.81
reg 16	3.81
reg 16(7)(a)	3.86
reg 16(8)	3.81
reg 17	3.51
reg 18	3.51
reg 19	3.51
reg 20	3.51
Immigration and Asylum (Provision of Accommodation to Failed Asylum-Seekers) Regulations 2005 SI No 930	13.36
reg 3(2)	13.37

Local Authorities (Contracting Out of Allocation of Housing and Homelessness Functions) Order 1996 SI No 3205	9.5, 9.171, 12.47
Art 3	9.5
Sch 2	9.5
Local Authorities (Executive Arrangements) (Functions and Responsibilities) (Wales) Regulations 2007 SI No 399	12.49
Sch 2 para 2	12.51
Local Authorities (Functions and Responsibilities) (England) Regulations 2000 SI No 2853	9.166, 12.49
reg 3(1)	12.51
Sch 2 para 2	12.51
Local Authorities' Plans and Strategies (Disapplication) (England) Order 2005 SI No 157	14.3
Local Government and Public Involvement in Health Act 2007 (Commencement No 5 and Transitional, Saving and Transitory Provision) Order 2008 SI No 917—	
reg 2(1)(i)	12.122
Local Government Changes for England Regulations 1994 SI No 867	2.13, 2.15
Local Housing Authorities (Prescribed Principles for Allocation Schemes) (Wales) Regulations 1997 SI No 45—	
reg 3	11.97
Sch para 1	11.97
Sch para 2	11.97
Localism Act 2011 (Commencement No 2 and Transitional and Saving Provision) Order 2012 SI No 57	11.116
Localism Act 2011 (Commencement No 2 and Transitional Provisions) (England) Order 2012 SI No 2599—	
Art 2	4.23, 4.61, 4.141, 5.1, 7.56, 9.22, 9.157, 10.9, 10.55, 10.80, 10.84, 10.184, 10.188, 10.189, 10.196, 10.199, 10.205, 10.212
Art 3	2.110, 4.61, 4.141, 5.3, 7.6, 7.56, 9.22, 9.157, 10.9, 10.84, 10.185, 10.189, 10.199, 10.205, 10.212
Localism Act 2011 (Commencement No 2 and Transitional Provisions) Order 2013 SI No 722	12.220

Localism Act 2011 (Commencement No 3) Order 2012 SI No 411	13.89
Localism Act 2011 (Commencement No 4 and Transitional, Transitory and Saving Provisions) Order 2012 SI No 628	11.116
Localism Act 2011 (Commencement No 5 and Transitional, Savings and Transitory Provisions) Order 2012 SI No 1008	13.89
Localism Act 2011 (Commencement No 6 and Transitional, Savings and Transitory Provisions) Order 2012 SI No 1463	11.29, 11.49, 11.69
Localism Act 2011 (Consequential Amendments) Order 2012 SI No 961	3.4
National Assembly for Wales (Legislative Competence) (Housing) (Fire Safety) Order 2010 SI No 1210	1.107
National Assembly for Wales (Legislative Competence) (Housing and Local Government) Order 2010 SI No 1838	1.107, 2.11
National Assembly for Wales (Transfer of Functions) Order 1999 SI No 672	1.107, 2.11, 11.116
Regulatory Reform (Fire Safety) Order 2005 SI No 1541	10.155
Rules of the Supreme Court—	
Ord 53	1.47
Ord 53, r 4	12.120
Social Services and Well-being (Wales) Act 2014 (Commencement No 3, Savings and Transitional Provisions) Order 2016 SI No 412	13.40
Sch 1 para 2	13.8
Transfer of Housing Corporation Functions (Modifications and Transitional Provisions) Order 2008 SI No 2839	11.116
Universal Credit Regulations 2013 SI No 376—	
Sch 4	11.92

Table of international conventions

Aarhus Convention (United Nations Economic Commission for Europe (UNECE) Convention on Access to Information, Public Participation in Decision-Making and Access to Justice in Environmental Matters)	12.234
European Convention on the Protection of Human Rights and Fundamental Freedoms 1950	3.99, 3.154, 3.156, 3.158, 3.159, 10.181, 11.40, 11.120, 12.7, 12.23, 12.24, 12.26, 12.95, 12.100, 12.103, 12.104, 13.17, 13.18, 13.21, 13.32, 13.34, 13.48, 13.93
Art 2	3.135
Art 3	3.135, 3.156, 3.159, 13.20, 13.21, 13.29, 13.32
Art 6	9.174, 11.111, 12.28, 12.56–12.60, 12.95, 12.96–12.99, 12.167
Art 6(1)	9.174, 12.28, 12.97, 12.98
Art 8	1.110, 3.113, 3.119, 3.144, 3.155, 3.156, 3.157, 5.8, 9.136, 10.18, 10.42, 10.176, 12.28, 12.95, 12.100–12.102, 12.103, 12.104, 12.161, 13.19, 13.20, 13.51
Art 8(1)	10.131, 12.101
Art 14	3.113, 3.119, 5.8, 10.176, 11.40, 12.95, 12.103–12.105

Hague Convention on the Civil Aspects of International Child Abduction 1980	13.97, 13.98
Refugee Convention (United Nations Convention relating to the Status of Refugees 1951)	3.127, 3.139, 3.142, 13.29
Art 1	3.122
Art 32	3.6

Table of European legislation

Treaties and Conventions

Accession Treaty of 16 April 2003 (Cyprus, Czech Republic, Estonia, Hungary, Latvia, Lithuania, Malta, Poland, Slovakia and Slovenia)	3.60
Accession Treaty of 25 April 2005 (Bulgaria and Romania)	3.66
Annex VI	3.66
Annex VII	3.66
Accession Treaty of 9 December 2011 (Republic of Croatia)	3.24
Annex V	3.72
EC Treaty	13.6, 13.30, 13.42
Art 12	3.51
Art 18	3.79
Treaty on the Functioning of the European Union	3.23, 3.146, 3.160
Art 18	3.25, 3.38, 3.48
Art 20	3.91, 3.146
Art 21	3.23
Art 45	3.32, 3.86
Art 49	3.37

Regulations

Council Regulation (EC) No 1030/2002 of 13 June 2002 laying down a uniform format for residence permits for third-country nationals	3.126
Regulation (EEC) No 1612/68 of the Council of 15 October 1968 on freedom of movement for workers within the Community—	
Art 12	3.81, 3.82, 3.85, 3.86, 3.87, 3.88, 3.89
Regulation (EEC) No 1408/71 of the Council of 14 June 1971 on the application of social security schemes to employed persons and their families moving within the Community	3.42
Regulation (EC) No 883/2004 of the European Parliament and of the Council of 29 April 2004 on the coordination of social security systems	3.42

Regulation (EC) No 987/2009 of the European Parliament and of the Council of 16 September 2009 laying down the procedure for implementing Regulation (EC) No 883/2004 on the coordination of social security systems—
Art 11 3.105
Regulation (EU) No 492/2011 of the European Parliament and of the Council of 5 April 2011 on freedom of movement for workers within the Union 11—
Art 7(2) 3.86
Art 10 3.81, 3.85, 3.86, 3.87

Directives

Council Directive 90/364/EEC of 28 June 1990 on the right of residence 3.79
Council Directive 2003/9/EC of 27 January 2003 laying down minimum standards for the reception of asylum seekers 13.28
Council Directive 2004/83/EC of 29 April 2004 on minimum standards for the qualification and status of third country nationals or stateless persons as refugees or as persons who otherwise need international protection and the content of the protection provided 3.124
Directive 2004/38/EC of the European Parliament and of the Council of 29 April 2004 on the right of citizens of the Union and their family members to move and reside freely within the territory of the Member States 3.23, 3.24, 3.27, 3.29, 3.38, 3.41, 3.47, 3.53, 3.54, 3.59, 3.79, 3.87
Art 2(2) 3.53
Art 2(2)(c) 3.52
Art 3(1) 3.53
Art 3(2) 3.57
Art 5(1) 3.27
Art 5(2) 3.27
Art 7(1) 3.50
Art 7(1)(c) 3.43
Art 7(3) 3.38
Art 8 3.51
Art 8(5)(d) 3.53
Art 10 3.51
Art 12(1) 3.58
Art 12(2) 3.58
Art 12(3) 3.58
Art 13(1) 3.58

Art 13(2)	3.58
Art 14(1)	3.28, 3.40
Art 16	3.49, 3.50, 3.87
Art 16(1)	3.44
Art 17	3.45, 3.46
Art 17(3)	3.46
Art 19	3.51
Art 20	3.51

Abbreviations

AC(IWA) Regs 2013	Accession of Croatia (Immigration and Worker Authorisation) Regulations 2013 SI No 1460
AH(W) Regs 2003	Allocation of Housing (Wales) Regulations 2003 SI No 239
AIA 1996	Asylum and Immigration Act 1996
AIAA 1993	Asylum and Immigration Appeals Act 1993
A(IWA)Regs 2006	Accession (Immigration and Worker Authorisation) Regulations 2006 SI No 3317
A(IWR) Regs 2004	Accession (Immigration and Worker Registration) Regulations 2004 SI No 1219
A(WAWR)(A) Regs 2007	Accession (Worker Authorisation and Worker Registration) (Amendment) Regulations 2007 SI No 3012
A(WAWR)(A) Regs 2009	Accession (Worker Authorisation and Worker Registration) (Amendment) Regulations 2009 SI No 2426
ALG	Association of London Government
ARC	application registration card
AS Regs 2000	Asylum Support Regulations 2000 SI No 704
ASBCPA 2014	Anti-social Behaviour, Crime and Policing Act 2014
ASP	Asylum Support Partnership
BIA	Border and Immigration Agency
BNA 1981	British Nationality Act 1981
CA 1989	Children Act 1989
CA 2014	Care Act 2014
CACA 1985	Child Abduction and Custody Act 1985
CESC	European Social Charter
CJA 1982	Criminal Justice Act 1982
CJA 1991	Criminal Justice Act 1991
CJEU	Court of Justice of the European Union
CLG Select Committee	Communities and Local Government Select Committee
CoSLA	Convention of Scottish Local Authorities

COT	Certificate of Travel
CPR	Civil Procedure Rules
CRD	Casework Resolution Directorate
CUCK	Citizen of the United Kingdom and Colonies
DCLG	Department for Communities and Local Government
DETR	Department of the Environment, Transport and the Regions
DHSS	Department of Health and Social Security
DL	discretionary leave
DoE	Department of the Environment
DTLR	Department of Transport, Local Government and Regions
DWP	Department for Work and Pensions
EA 1996	Education Act 1996
EC	European Community
ECHR	European Convention on Human Rights
ECJ	European Court of Justice
ECtHR	European Court of Human Rights
ECSMA	European Convention on Social and Medical Assistance
EEA	European Economic Area
EEA Regs 2006	Immigration (European Economic Area) Regulations 2006 SI No 1003
EEU	Evidence and Enquiries Unit
EFTA	European Free Trade Association
Eligibility Regs 2006	Allocation of Housing and Homelessness (Eligibility) (England) Regulations 2006 SI No 1294
Eligibility (Amendment) Regs 2012	Allocation of Housing and Homelessness (Eligibility) (England) (Amendment) Regulations 2012 SI No 2588
Eligibility (Amendment) Regs 2016	Allocation of Housing and Homelessness (Eligibility) (England) (Amendment) Regulations 2016 SI No 965
Eligibility (Wales) Regs 2014	Allocation of Housing and Homelessness (Eligibility) (Wales) Regulations 2014 SI No 2603
ELR	exceptional leave to remain
English Review Procedure Regs 1999	Allocation of Housing and Homelessness (Review Procedures) Regulations 1999 SI No 71
EqA 2010	Equality Act 2010
EU	European Union
HA	Housing Act
HCA	Homes and Communities Agency

H(HP)A 1977	Housing (Homeless Persons) Act 1977
HMO	house in multiple occupation
HOS	Housing Ombudsman Service
HP	humanitarian protection
HPA 1986	Housing and Planning Act 1986
H&RA 2008	Housing and Regeneration Act 2008
HRA 1998	Human Rights Act 1998
HRA 2017	Homelessness Reduction Act 2017
H(W) Regs 2006	Homelessness (Wales) Regulations 2006 SI No 2646
H(W)A 2014	Housing (Wales) Act 2014
IA 1971	Immigration Act 1971
IA 1988	Immigration Act 1998
IAA 1999	Immigration and Asylum Act 1999
IA(PAFAS) Regs 2005	Immigration and Asylum (Provision of Accommodation to Failed Asylum Seekers) Regulations 2005 SI No 930
ILR	indefinite leave to remain
IND	Immigration and Nationality Directorate
ISD	Immigration Status Document
LA 2011	Localism Act 2011
LASPO 2012	Legal Aid, Sentencing and Punishment of Offenders Act 2012
LGA	Local Government Association
LGA 1972	Local Government Act 1972
LGA 1974	Local Government Act 1974
LGA 1985	Local Government Act 1985
LGA 2000	Local Government Act 2000
LG(MP)A 1982	Local Government (Miscellaneous Provisions) Act 1982
NAA 1948	National Assistance Act 1948
NAB	National Assistance Board
NAM	New Asylum Model
NASS	National Asylum Support Service
NHS	National Health Service
NHSCCA 1990	National Health Service and Community Care Act 1990
NIAA 2002	Nationality, Immigration and Asylum Act 2002
NIHE	Northern Ireland Housing Executive
ODPM	Office of the Deputy Prime Minister
PD	Practice Direction
PEA 1977	Protection from Eviction Act 1977
PRP	private registered provider of social housing
PSO(W)A 2005	Public Services Ombudsman (Wales) Act 2005

RA 1977	Rent Act 1977
R(A)A 1976	Rent (Agriculture) Act 1976
RSL	registered social landlord
SBC	Supplementary Benefits Commission
SEN	special educational needs
SSEN	statement of special educational needs
SSCLG	Secretary of State for Communities and Local Government
SSHD	Secretary of State for the Home Department
SSWB(W)A 2014	Social Services and Well-being (Wales) Act 2014
SSWP	Secretary of State for Work and Pensions
TFEU	Treaty on the Functioning of the European Union
TSA	Tenant Services Authority
UKBA	UK Border Agency
UKRP	UK Residence Permit
UKVI	UK Visas and Immigration
UN	United Nations
Welsh Review Procedure Regs 2015	Homelessness (Review Procedure) (Wales) Regulations 2015 SI No 1266
WLGA	Welsh Local Government Association
WRS	Worker Registration Scheme

CHAPTER 1

The policy of the provisions

1.1 **Introduction**

1.7 **National Assistance Act 1948**

1.21 **Housing (Homeless Persons) Act 1977; Housing Act 1985 Part 3**

1.27 Homelessness

1.32 Priority need

1.35 Intentional homelessness

1.43 Discharge

1.47 ***Re Puhlhofer***

1.55 **Housing and Planning Act 1986**

1.59 **Asylum and Immigration Appeals Act 1993**

1.62 ***Ex p Awua***

1.66 **Housing Act 1996 Parts 6 and 7**

1.66 Policy

1.76 Principal homelessness changes

1.77 Allocations

1.79 Other changes

1.80 **Between Acts**

1.80 Restoration of priority to homeless people

1.82 Asylum-seekers

continued

1.83 The green paper
1.89 Priority need categories

1.92 Homelessness Act 2002
1.92 Strategies
1.94 Duties
1.96 Non-priority need applicants
1.97 Other changes
1.100 Allocations

1.107 Changes following the Homelessness Act 2002

1.113 Localism Act 2011

1.119 Housing (Wales) Act 2014

1.123 Homelessness Reduction Act 2017

Introduction

1.1 This chapter outlines the history of the law on homelessness and allocations, from before the Housing (Homeless Persons) Act (H(HP)A) 1977 through Housing Act (HA) 1996 Parts 6 and 7 – the present, principal Acts in England – and Homelessness Act 2002 to changes in England under the Localism Act (LA) 2011 followed by major changes to assist the homeless in Wales under Housing (Wales) Act (H(W)A) 2014 Part 2 and the adoption of some of these in England by the Homeless Reduction Act (HRA) 2017.

1.2 Although HA 1996 Parts 6 and 7 are free-standing legislation – in the sense that they are neither consolidation nor amendment – and it is unnecessary always to approach them by reference to their evolution, both Parts are nonetheless best understood historically not least because of the adoption by Part 7 of the well-litigated, critical definitions introduced by H(HP)A 1977 which had and subsequently been consolidated into Housing Act (HA) 1985 Part 3.

1.3 Thus, the then Minister for Local Government, Housing and Urban Regeneration (Mr Curry) said of the changes to homelessness law to be made by the HA 1996:

> We shall not go back to pre-1977 days. We shall keep the 1977 Act concepts of entitlement, homelessness, priority need, intentionality and local connection. Essentially, what we are changing is the way in which the duty is to be discharged.[1]

1.4 That discharge was closely interwoven with the allocation of local authority housing – Part 6 was the first big change in allocations law since 1935, when the concept of 'reasonable preference' for certain categories of housing need was introduced: in practice, however, allocations policy had been dominated by the homeless since H(HP)A 1977.

1.5 Since HA 1996, the Homelessness Act 2002 again changed the shape of the law, introducing a new 'strategic' duty to formulate a response to homelessness and reshaping HA 1996 Part 6 to seek to include 'choice-based letting' within allocations law. Further changes have been made by regulations. Subsequently, LA 2011 reversed some of the effects of the Homelessness Act 2002 both by placing more emphasis on the use of private sector accommodation, and by introducing much greater freedom for authorities in England to determine their own criteria as to whom they will house in their own accommodation (although, as will be seen in chapter 11, the case-

1 *Hansard*, Standing Committee G, 12 March 1996, col 587.

law has rather limited this apparent freedom, see paras 11.42–11.43). Wales then led the way for further changes in H(W)A 2014, including extension of the period during which a person is threatened with homelessness from 28 to 56 days; assessment of those who need help to retain or obtain accommodation; and help to prevent them becoming homeless and a power for authorities in conjunction with Welsh Minister to abandon intentional homelessness (the most controversial of all of the homelessness provisions). The first two reforms have recently been adopted in England through what appropriately started life as a private member's bill,[2] the HRA 2017.

1.6 In this chapter, homelessness and allocations policy as embodied in law will be approached as follows:

a) National Assistance Act (NAA) 1948 Part 3;
b) H(HP)A 1977; HA 1985 Part 3;
c) *Re Puhlhofer*;[3]
d) Housing and Planning Act (HPA) 1986;
e) Asylum and Immigration Appeals Act (AIAA) 1993;
f) *ex p Awua*;[4]
g) HA 1996 Parts 6 and 7;
h) between Acts;
i) Homelessness Act 2002;
j) changes following the Homelessness Act 2002;
k) LA 2011;
l) H(W)A 2014; and
m) HRA 2017.

National Assistance Act 1948

1.7 The provisions of NAA 1948 s21(1) placed local authorities under a duty to provide:

> ... residential accommodation for persons who by reason of age, infirmity or any other circumstances are in need of care and attention which is not otherwise available to them, [and] temporary accommodation for persons who are in urgent need thereof, being need arising in circumstances which could not reasonably have been foreseen or in such other circumstances as the authority may in any particular case determine.

2 H(HP)A 1977 was itself a private member's bill.
3 *R v Hillingdon LBC ex p Puhlhofer* [1986] AC 484, (1986) 18 HLR 158, HL.
4 *R v Brent LBC ex p Awua* [1996] AC 55, (1995) 27 HLR 453, HL.

1.8 Homelessness law – starting with H(HP)A 1977 – replaces only the second limb of that duty, ie the duty to provide temporary accommodation in urgent need.[5]

1.9 The NAA 1948 duty extended to people ordinarily resident in a local authority's area.[6] The National Assistance Board (NAB) (later the Supplementary Benefits Commission (SBC)) had power to require an authority to provide accommodation where satisfied that such a person was in urgent need of it. The local authority was under a further duty to protect the property of a person to whom it provided assistance under these provisions.[7]

1.10 Local authority duties under NAA 1948 were exercised under the general guidance of the minister, who was, for these purposes, the Minister of Health.[8]

1.11 This legal structure fell far short of imposing a full and permanent duty on local authorities to protect all homeless people. Rather, it provided for emergencies, especially unforeseeable emergencies.[9] The duration of accommodation, save where the NAB/SBC was involved, was a matter for the authority. It probably meant no more than for so long as the authority considered appropriate or necessary;[10] urgent need for temporary accommodation was not to be equated with a vital but continuing need for permanent accommodation.[11]

1.12 The discretionary and temporary nature of this provision was the principal problem. Another problem was that of deciding 'ordinary residence' in an area. Reminiscent of the Poor Laws which the NAA 1948 repealed and replaced, authorities 'shuttled' homeless people between areas, claiming that they were ordinarily resident in another authority's area.

1.13 Even more problematic was the division of responsibilities between different authorities within a single geographical area: homelessness provision was to be found in NAA 1948 and was regarded as a social services problem; the duty to provide housing in any area lay, however, with the authority having responsibility under the Housing

5 H(HP)A 1977 s20 and Schedule, repealing this part of NAA 1948 s21.

6 NAA 1948 s24.

7 NAA 1948 s24.

8 NAA 1948 s33, subsequently Local Authority Social Services Act 1970 s7.

9 *Southwark LBC v Williams* [1971] Ch 734, CA; see also Ministry of Health Circular 87/48 illustrating 'urgent and unforeseen need' as homelessness arising as a result of 'fire, flood or eviction'.

10 *Bristol Corporation v Stockford* (1973), reported in Carnwath, *A guide to the Housing (Homeless Persons) Act 1977*, Knight's Annotated Acts, 1978.

11 *Roberts v Dorset CC* (1976) 75 LGR 462.

Acts.[12] This problem was exacerbated by the re-organisation effected by the Local Government Act (LGA) 1972 with effect from 1 April 1974. From that date, social services outside London, and in non-metropolitan areas, became the responsibility of county councils, while housing was the responsibility of the district council.[13] Even in London and the metropolitan areas, where social services and housing remained the responsibility of the same authority, different departments would usually handle the different responsibilities. In either event, this brought with it a different kind of shuttling, not in this case between different geographical areas, but between different authorities or different departments carrying out different functions in the same locality.

1.14 This was an unsatisfactory division. Popular perception was changing – homelessness was no longer readily regarded as a symptom of personal or social inadequacy; it had come to be recognised as part of the continuing severe housing problem (whether this is described as a crude shortage of housing or as a shortage of adequate housing where it is needed).[14]

1.15 The fact that children were commonly taken into care for no reason other than their parents' want of accommodation was itself a significant factor in the changing attitudes which produced the climate for H(HP)A 1977.

1.16 There are two other points to make concerning the pre-H(HP)A 1977 position, both of them occurring in 1974. The first is largely technical. LGA 1972 contained an amendment to the NAA 1948, additional to the redistribution of responsibilities in non-metropolitan areas. The amendment reduced to a mere power what had previously been a duty.[15] The secretary of state, however, was empowered to re-impose the duty by directive, and, following an outcry by voluntary

12 Formerly HA 1957 Part 5, now HA 1985 Part 2.

13 Formerly HA 1957 s1, as amended by LGA 1972 s193 and Sch 22, now HA 1985 s1.

14 Significant contributions to this rise in awareness included those of J Sandford and K Loach, *Cathy come home*, 'The Wednesday Play', 1966 television film; J Greve et al, *Homelessness in London*, Scottish Academic Press, 1971; Bryan Glastonbury, *Homeless near a thousand homes*, Allen & Unwin, 1971; F Berry, *Housing – the great British failure*, Charles Knight, 1974. Of less popular, but greater official, influence was the Cullingworth Report, *Council housing – purposes, procedures and priorities*, 9th report of Housing Management Sub-committee of the Central Housing Advisory Committee, 1969.

15 LGA 1972 s195 and Sch 23.

and welfare workers, lawyers and others concerned with the homeless,[16] did so in February 1974.

1.17 Second, and of more significance, was the circular issued in February 1974, which came to be known as the 'Joint Circular',[17] directed both to social services departments and authorities, and to housing departments and authorities.

1.18 The Joint Circular had two main aims: first, it urged the transfer of such stock as was held by social services authorities and social services departments for the purpose of discharging their responsibilities towards the homeless, to housing authorities or departments; second, it identified what it described as 'priority groups' who were intended to enjoy a claim on local authority stock.

1.19 The definition of 'priority groups' in the Joint Circular closely resembled the definition of 'priority need' that was adopted in H(HP)A 1977 s2, subsequently in HA 1985 s59 and now to be found in HA 1996 s189 and H(W)A 2014 s70:

> The Priority Groups comprise families with dependent children living with them or in care; and adult families or people living alone who either become homeless in an emergency such as fire or flooding or are vulnerable because of old age, disability, pregnancy or other special reasons. For these priority groups, the issue is not whether, but by what means, local authorities should provide accommodation themselves or help those concerned to obtain accommodation in the private sector . . .
>
> Where a family has children there is no acceptable alternative to accommodation in which the family can be together as a family. The social cost, personal hardship, the long-term damage to children, as well as the expense involved in receiving a child into care rules this out as an acceptable course, other than in the exceptional case when professional social work advice is that there are compelling reasons apart from homelessness for separating children from their family. The provision of shelter from which the husband is excluded is also not acceptable unless there are sound social reasons, as, for example, where a wife is seeking temporary refuge following matrimonial dispute and it is undesirable that she should be under pressure to return home.[18]

1.20 Notwithstanding this advice, many authorities failed to transfer responsibility from social services to housing, or to give the priority

16 Partington, *Housing (Homeless Persons) Act 1977*, Sweet & Maxwell, 1978, introductory notes.

17 Department of Environment (DoE) Circular 18/74; Department of Health and Social Security (DHSS) Circular 4/74.

18 DoE Circular 18/74 paras 10–12.

groups preference over their own, local priorities.[19] Accordingly, when a Liberal MP, Stephen Ross, was successful in the ballot for private members' bills, the government of the day supported him in introducing a Homeless Persons Bill and the opposition announced that it, too, would broadly support the measure. The bill was introduced and became law as the H(HP)A 1977.

Housing (Homeless Persons) Act 1977; Housing Act 1985 Part 3

1.21 These two Acts are taken together, as the HA 1985 was an exercise of consolidation of housing law – as such, save so far as there were recommendations of the Law Commission (Cmnd 9515) to effect explicit changes (of which there were none relevant to the policy of the legislation), no substantive change in homelessness law was intended or achieved.

1.22 One clear aim of H(HP)A 1977 was to place responsibility for the homeless on district councils and London borough councils.[20] Provision was made to transfer staff and stock from social services to housing: the Secretary of State for the Environment enjoyed power to compel the transfer of property and staff from one authority to another, not merely between London borough councils and district councils, but as between all 'relevant authorities', defined to include social service authorities.[21]

1.23 Another aim of H(HP)A 1977 was to provide a uniform and national definition of, or criteria for, the circumstances in which one authority could shift on to another responsibility for a homeless person, so as to end shuttling. These 'local connection' provisions included a positive link between employment and housing.[22]

1.24 The local connection provisions operated not so much to permit an authority to shift the burden of housing a homeless person on to another authority, as to prevent it from doing so once the applicant was shown to have a local connection with the area of the authority to which he or she had applied. Thus, the authority for the area in which an applicant had only an employment connection had to

19 *Hansard* HC Debs, 15 December 1975, Vol 902 cols 473–475.

20 H(HP)A 1977 s19.

21 H(HP)A 1977 s14; Housing (Consequential Provisions) Act 1985 s5 and Sch 4 para 8.

22 H(HP)A 1977 s18; HA 1985 s61.

house the applicant, even though the applicant might have had no other connections with that area, for example, family or residence.

1.25 The most important provision of H(HP)A 1977, however, was the establishment of a national criterion which required local authorities to accommodate, or to secure accommodation for, those who:

a) were homeless;
b) were in priority need of accommodation; and
c) did not become homeless intentionally.

1.26 Leaving aside the resolution of responsibility embodied in the local connection provisions, the three key questions, therefore, became:

a) what was homelessness?
b) who was in priority need? and
c) when was homelessness intentional?

Homelessness

1.27 Defining homelessness is not easy, either as a matter of law or as a matter of policy.[23] The most literal approach is to deal with those without a roof over their heads. This is not only difficult to estimate, but is likely to exclude those with children as, commonly, some form of accommodation, however inadequate, is found for them.

1.28 The most radical approach, advocated by Shelter, the National Campaign for the Homeless, was that a person was homeless if the person lived 'in conditions so bad that a civilised family life is impossible': this was homelessness 'in the true sense of the word'.[24]

1.29 Another approach is to consider those families who have no home where they can live together. This excludes both single people and childless couples, but it was at the core of the definition which was adopted.

1.30 Under H(HP)A 1977, parliament started with legal rights of occupation: a person was homeless if there was no accommodation which he or she could occupy by virtue of an interest or estate, or contract, together with anyone else who usually resided with him or her either as a member of the family, or in circumstances in which it was reasonable for that person to do so.[25]

23 This and the next paragraph are based largely on Partington, *Housing (Homeless Persons) Act 1977*, Sweet & Maxwell, 1978, introductory notes, subheading 'Definitions of homelessness and extent of homelessness'.

24 *The grief report*, Shelter, 1972.

25 H(HP)A 1977 s1; HA 1985 s58.

1.31 A person was also not to be regarded as homeless if he or she was in occupation in circumstances in which a court order was required for eviction – for example, tenants whose tenancies had been determined. A person was homeless, however, if the person had been locked out of accommodation, had to leave accommodation because of domestic violence or, in the case of mobile homes and houseboats, if there was nowhere to park/moor accommodation and to live in it.[26]

Priority need

1.32 The definition of homelessness did not create any substantive housing rights on its own. It had to be read together with the definition of priority need.

1.33 Only homeless people with a priority need for accommodation received housing assistance under H(HP)A 1977 and HA 1985:

a) those with children who were residing, or who might reasonably be expected to reside, with either the applicant or with anyone with whom the applicant might be expected to reside;
b) those who were residing, or who might reasonably be expected to reside, with someone who had become homeless as a result of an emergency;
c) those who were residing, or who might reasonably be expected to reside, with someone who was vulnerable on account of age, handicap or other special reason; and
d) a person who was residing, or who might reasonably be expected to reside, with someone who was a pregnant woman.[27]

1.34 The important point to note was this: in determining whether or not there was a priority need, not only the applicant but anyone who might reasonably be expected to reside with the applicant, regardless of whether they had hitherto lived together, had to be taken into account.

Intentional homelessness

1.35 Homeless people in priority need thus acquired a prima facie right to accommodation. To have become homeless, however, did not necessarily mean that someone had been evicted: the person might have quit of his or her own accord.

26 H(HP)A 1977 s1; HA 1985 s58.
27 H(HP)A 1977 s2; HA 1985 s59; cf para 1.19.

1.36 This provoked a hostile local authority reaction to H(HP)A 1977 as a bill and, in turn, led to the inclusion of the 'intentional homelessness' provisions.

1.37 Infamously, the bill was described as a charter for 'scroungers and scrimshankers'.[28]

1.38 Mr G Cunningham acquired a notoriety that in earlier editions of this book was described as 'unenviable' when he suggested that women would become pregnant to acquire a priority need and then terminate their pregnancies once housing had been secured.[29] 'Families who have hesitated in the past to make themselves homeless [as opposed to finding themselves homeless] need have no such reluctance now . . .' 'It will mean chaos.' 'Fifty per cent of alleged claims of homelessness are "try-ons".'[30]

1.39 Mr Cunningham's observation was nonetheless given a degree of judicial sanction by the House of Lords decision in *R v Brent LBC ex p Awua*,[31] in which Lord Hoffmann, delivering the only substantive speech, suggested that local authorities could decide to provide only temporary accommodation to a pregnant woman and 'wait and see' whether or not the child is placed for adoption.

1.40 Parliament did not wholly give in to these fears. Under H(HP)A 1977, and then HA 1985, not everyone who voluntarily quit accommodation was considered to be homeless intentionally, from which it followed that some could quit and yet be entitled to assistance from a local authority. It is when this class is considered – those who could quit of their own accord but not be deemed homeless intentionally – that the remit of H(HP)A 1977 and HA 1985 is finally defined.

1.41 For an authority to find that someone had become homeless intentionally – and, thus, had forfeited his or her right to assistance – required four preconditions:

a) the applicant had to have ceased to occupy accommodation – so that those who had never had accommodation or last had it so long ago that it could not properly be taken into account, could not be homeless intentionally; *and*
b) the applicant had to have ceased to occupy accommodation in consequence of a deliberate act or omission – an act or omission in good faith, in ignorance of a material fact (for example,

28 Per Mr W R Rees-Davies, *Hansard* HC Debs, 18 February 1977, Vol 926 col 905.

29 *Hansard* HC Debs, 8 July 1977, Vol 934 col 1689.

30 Quotes to be found in Widdowson, *Intentional homelessness*, Shelter, 1981, p6.

31 [1996] AC 55, (1995) 27 HLR 453, HL.

ignorance of security of tenure or financial assistance towards housing costs), was not to be considered deliberate; *and*

c) the accommodation had to have been such that it was reasonable to continue to occupy it, although those who left bad physical conditions were faced with the qualification that, in determining whether or not it was reasonable to remain in occupation, a housing authority could take into account housing conditions in its area generally; *and*

d) the accommodation which had been quit had to have been 'available for the occupation' of the applicant.[32] Accommodation was only 'available for occupation' if it was available both for the homeless person and for anyone who might reasonably be expected to reside with him or her.[33] In determining who might reasonably be expected to live together, no account was to be taken of want of accommodation.[34]

1.42 It followed that people who had never been able to live together but who were reasonably to be expected to do so – for example, the young couple who had to live apart for want of accommodation – and who acquired a priority need (for example, through pregnancy), could not be found to be intentionally homeless should one or other or both of them leave the separate accommodations in which they had hitherto been living. Only those who had quit accommodation which was available both for themselves and for those with whom they might reasonably be expected to live could be deemed homeless intentionally.

Discharge

1.43 Homeless people, then, for whom it was the policy of H(HP)A 1977 to ensure that any authority with which there was a local connection provided substantive assistance, were those: who had no accommodation as defined; who were in priority need of accommodation, which most commonly meant that they had children; and who did not quit accommodation which was available for themselves and for the whole of their family unit.

1.44 The right which such applicants acquired was not, however, the legal right to council housing itself. Rather, the authority's duty was

32 H(HP)A 1977 s17; HA 1985 s60.

33 H(HP)A 1977 s16; HA 1985 s75.

34 *Re Islam* [1983] 1 AC 688, (1981) 1 HLR 107, HL.

to ensure that accommodation was made available for the applicant (and for those who might reasonably be expected to reside with him or her). The authority might discharge this duty in any of the following ways:

a) by making available accommodation held by it under what is now HA 1985 Part 2 (ie, the principal part of that Act under which council housing is held)[35] or under any other enactment (for example, housing acquired in the exercise of other functions, such as education, highways, etc); or
b) by securing that the applicant obtained accommodation from some other person; or
c) by giving such advice and assistance as would secure that accommodation was obtained from some other person.[36]

1.45 Of course, the principal burden was bound to be placed on the local authority's own stock. Since 1935,[37] local authorities had been under an obligation to 'secure that in the selection of their tenants a reasonable preference is given to persons who are occupying insanitary or overcrowded houses, have large families or are living under unsatisfactory housing conditions';[38] subject to this somewhat loose obligation, they were free to determine their own priorities. To this there was now added a new group: those to whom authorities owed a duty under the homeless legislation.[39]

1.46 In principle, this did no more than require authorities to treat the homeless on the same footing as others, which in law was largely a matter of local choice. In practice, however, provision for the homeless was bound to make a significant impact – especially as no added money was made available to authorities under H(HP)A 1977.[40] Exacerbating the problem, public spending powers were severely restricted from 1980 onwards.[41] In addition, the introduction of security of tenure and the right to buy under the HA 1980 Part 1[42] meant

35 Formerly HA 1957 Part 5.

36 H(HP)A 1977 s6(1); HA 1985 s69(1).

37 HA 1935 s51.

38 As consolidated in HA 1936 s85(2).

39 H(HP)A 1977 s6(2), amending HA 1957 s113(2), subsequently HA 1985 s22.

40 A point made by Lord Brightman in *R v Hillingdon LBC ex p Puhlhofer* [1986] AC 484, (1986) 18 HLR 158, HL.

41 Local Government, Planning and Land Act 1980; subsequently, see Local Government and Housing Act 1989. See now, the somewhat more liberal regime of Local Government Act 2003 Part 1.

42 See now HA 1985 Parts 4 and 5.

that the stock of new housing available to local authorities was in decline. Inevitably, therefore, an increasing proportion of allocations went to homeless people.

Re Puhlhofer

1.47 With so much at stake for individuals, and authorities unable – and sometime unwilling – to fulfil the hope that H(HP)A 1977 appeared to hold out, it was inevitable that the courts would be needed to broker the interests of these two main parties. Because of the structure of the rights and duties created by the legislation – and following a period during which it had been considered that challenges to authorities' decisions might be mounted by ordinary civil claim (in the county court or the High Court)[43] – it was held that this was a role which could only be fulfilled by way of judicial review in the High Court.[44]

1.48 What this led to was a very substantial number of cases in what has subsequently become the Administrative Court,[45] which hears judicial review applications at first instance.[46] Any analysis runs the risk of being subjective, but there was a popular perception that the High Court (and, on appeal, the Court of Appeal) so far from maintaining a consistent bias against the homeless, were not uncommonly helpful in their interpretation of the legislation – a perception which derives much support from many of the earlier decisions referred to in the body of this book.

1.49 One body of this judge-made law developed the obviously sensible notion that if a person was occupying accommodation so poor that it could be quit without a finding of intentionality, the person ought to be treated as if already homeless. This in effect wrote into the definition of homelessness itself – with its reliance on rights of occupation[47]

43 But see, now, chapter 12, for appeal to the county court on a point of law under HA 1996 s204.

44 Under RSC Order 53, now CPR 54; *Cocks v Thanet DC* [1983] AC 286, (1983) 6 HLR 15, HL.

45 Formerly, the Crown Office List of the High Court.

46 By 1991, almost 20 per cent of all cases in the Crown Office list were homelessness cases, second only to immigration: Bridges, Meszaros and Sunkin, *Judicial review in perspective*, Public Law Project, 1995.

47 See para 1.30.

– a minimum standard below which any accommodation should be entirely disregarded, even if there was a right to occupy it.[48]

1.50 Another, related, body of judge-made law introduced the concept of 'settled accommodation'.[49] Only departure from settled accommodation could constitute intentionality, whether because of its condition, terms of occupation or temporary quality. Conversely, only acquisition of settled accommodation would, in normal circumstances, break a period of intentional homelessness and entitle an applicant to re-apply.

1.51 Sympathy – while on occasion expressed – was rarely to be seen in action, however, at the highest level, the House of Lords. Of the nine cases under the 1977/1985 legislation which reached the House of Lords,[50] the homeless were successful in only two of them.[51]

1.52 One of those nine cases was *Re Puhlhofer*,[52] in which the equiparation of homelessness and want of intentionality[53] was firmly rejected. No words such as 'appropriate' or 'reasonable' were to be imported into the term 'accommodation' in H(HP)A 1977 s1/HA 1985 s58 (definition of homelessness). The absence of any such qualification was described as something 'plainly and wisely' determined by parliament.

1.53 The House of Lords also took the opportunity forcefully to express its concern about the 'prolific' use of judicial review in this area: the courts should exercise great restraint when giving leave to proceed by way of judicial review; the courts should be used to monitor the actions of local authorities under the legislation only in exceptional

48 See *R v South Herefordshire DC ex p Miles* (1983) 17 HLR 82, QBD; *City of Gloucester v Miles* (1985) 17 HLR 292, CA; *R v Dinefwr BC ex p Marshall* (1984) 17 HLR 310, QBD; see also the judgment of Ackner LJ in *Re Puhlhofer* at the Court of Appeal (1985) 17 HLR 558.

49 The phrase was coined by Ackner LJ in *Din v Wandsworth LBC* at the Court of Appeal: [1983] 1 AC 657, (1983) 1 HLR 73, HL; see also *Dyson v Kerrier DC* [1980] 1 WLR 1205, CA. See chapter 6.

50 *Re Islam* [1983] 1 AC 688, (1981) 1 HLR 107, HL; *Din v Wandsworth LBC* [1983] 1 AC 657, (1983) 1 HLR 73; *Re Betts* [1983] 2 AC 613, (1983) 10 HLR 97; *Cocks v Thanet DC* [1983] AC 286, (1983) 6 HLR 15, HL; *Eastleigh BC v Walsh* [1985] 1 WLR 525, (1985) 17 HLR 392; *R v Hillingdon LBC ex p Puhlhofer* [1986] AC 484, (1986) 18 HLR 158, HL; *R v Oldham BC ex p G, R v Bexley LBC ex p Bentum, R v Tower Hamlets LBC ex p Begum* [1993] AC 509, (1983) 25 HLR 319; *R v Northavon DC ex p Smith* [1994] 2 AC 402, (1984) 26 HLR 659; *R v Brent LBC ex p Awua* [1996] AC 55, (1995) 27 HLR 453, HL.

51 *Re Islam* and *Eastleigh BC v Walsh*, above. Of these, *Walsh* was part of a wider issue – the distinction between tenancy and licence – which was contemporaneously being reviewed (and recast) by the House of Lords: see *Street v Mountford* [1985] AC 809, (1985) 17 HLR 402.

52 *R v Hillingdon LBC ex p Puhlhofer* [1986] AC 484, (1986) 18 HLR 158, HL.

53 See para 1.49.

cases. The speech of Lord Brightman, in particular, expressed the hope that there would be a lessening in the number of challenges under the legislation.[54]

> My Lords, I am troubled at the prolific use of judicial review for the purpose of challenging the performance by local authorities of their functions under the Act of 1977. Parliament intended the local authority to be the judge of fact. The Act abounds with the formula when, or if the housing authority are satisfied as to this, or that, or have reason to believe this, or that. Although the action or inaction of a local authority is clearly susceptible to judicial review where they have misconstrued the Act, or abused their powers or otherwise acted perversely, I think that great restraint should be exercised in giving leave to proceed by judicial review. The plight of the homeless is a desperate one, and the plight of the applicants in the present case commands the deepest sympathy. But it is not, in my opinion, appropriate that the remedy of judicial review, which is a discretionary remedy, should be made use of to monitor the actions of local authorities under the Act save in the exceptional case. The ground upon which the courts will review the exercise of an administrative discretion is abuse of power – eg bad faith, a mistake in construing the limits of the power, a procedural irregularity, or unreasonableness in the *Wednesbury* sense – unreasonableness verging on an absurdity: see the speech of Lord Scarman in *R v Secretary of State for the Environment, ex p Nottinghamshire CC*.[55] Where the existence or non-existence of a fact is left to the judgment and discretion of a public body and that fact involves a broad spectrum ranging from the obvious to the debatable to the just conceivable, it is the duty of the court to leave the decision of that fact to the public body to whom Parliament has entrusted the decision-making power save in a case where it is obvious that the public body, consciously or unconsciously, are acting perversely.
>
> . . . I express the hope that there will be a lessening in the number of challenges which are mounted against local authorities who are endeavouring, in extremely difficult circumstances, to perform their duties under the Homeless Persons Act with due regard for all their other housing problems.

1.54 Save for a relatively brief period, however, there was no appearance of any such reduction, or indeed of a lower rate of success on the part of the homeless.

54 [1986] AC 484 at 518.

55 [1986] AC 240, 247–248 – see paras 12.13, 12.22.

Housing and Planning Act 1986

1.55 In 1986, in direct response to *Puhlhofer*,[56] parliament reacted to the judgment that it had been 'wise'[57] not to qualify the accommodation the absence of which rendered a person homeless by amending the principal definition of homelessness to do precisely that, in substance to harmonise the criteria of homelessness and intentionality: the homeless were now those who, even if enjoying one of the qualifying rights of occupation, occupied accommodation so bad that it would not be reasonable to remain in occupation of it (having regard to the general housing circumstances of their area).[58]

1.56 This in substance preferred the High Court approach[59] to that of the House of Lords. In practical or applied terms, it meant that a person would now be homeless if the person enjoyed no settled accommodation.[60]

1.57 The HPA 1986 also amended HA 1985 to ensure that accommodation provided under Part 3 met broadly the same minimum criterion, likewise rejecting critical observations by Lord Brightman in *Re Puhlhofer* in relation to what had not otherwise proved to be an active area of controversy.[61] In substance and in practice, therefore, it could now also be said that accommodation to be provided had to be settled.

1.58 It may be at this point that homelessness law reached its greatest coherence or cohesiveness – the lower courts had taken the parliamentary framework and, reinforced by HPA 1986, fleshed it out to identify a level of accommodation to which all those in priority need were entitled, below which they could quit without being intentionally homeless or else they continued to be homeless; and, they were entitled to the benefit of rehousing assistance under the Act, including priority in the allocation of local authority stock, to a minimum of the same level.

56 Above.

57 See para 1.52.

58 HPA 1986 s14(2), amending HA 1985 s58. In Scotland, the equivalent amendment treated as already homeless those who were overcrowded under Scots law and in such circumstances that their health was endangered: Housing (Scotland) Act 1986 s21(2), amending H(HP)A 1977 s1(2).

59 See para 1.49.

60 See para 1.50.

61 In two cases, without drawing the same link that had been drawn between homelessness and non-intentionality, it had been held that accommodation to be provided had to be appropriate or suitable or habitable (having regard to the applicant and those to reside with him or her): *Parr v Wyre BC* (1982) 2 HLR 71, CA (disapproved in *Re Puhlhofer*); and *R v Ryedale DC ex p Smith* (1983) 16 HLR 66.

Asylum and Immigration Appeals Act 1993

1.59 For a period, homelessness and allocations law enjoyed a period of statutory stability.

1.60 Complaints of unfairness towards others awaiting public sector accommodation, or of an unduly liberal approach to intentionality, were met with revisions to the Code of Guidance issued by the Secretary of State for the Environment,[62] but neither achieved – nor sought to achieve – any substantive differences in effect.

1.61 During the 1990s, however, there was growing antagonism towards asylum-seekers, many of whom remained in the UK for years before a final decision on a claim was reached. As persons lawfully in the country pending that decision, they had at all times fallen within the protection of the legislation.[63] Under AIAA 1993, however, they were now placed on a different footing from other homeless people. Until the final determination of a claim for asylum, when authorities were bound to reach a new decision,[64] there would be no duty towards any asylum-seeker who had the benefit of some accommodation, however temporary. Likewise, accommodation to be provided did not have to be more than temporary.[65] In effect, therefore, asylum-seekers now enjoyed lesser rights, for the duration of their period as such; they did not have a right to settled accommodation.

Ex p Awua

1.62 Leaving aside the policy of AIAA 1993, as a matter of legal structure, it recognised what the courts, and the HPA 1986, had achieved in terms of quality of accommodation,[66] which is to say that it was that very achievement of which asylum-seekers were to be deprived.

1.63 This did not stop the House of Lords taking another crack at minimum standards. In *R v Brent LBC ex p Awua*,[67] it was held that 'accommodation' in both HA 1985 s58(1) (definition of homelessness) and s60(1) (definition of intentionality) meant no more than a place which could fairly be described as accommodation and which

62 Under HA 1985 s71; see now HA 1996 s182.

63 *R v Hillingdon LBC ex p Streeting (No 2)* [1980] 1 WLR 1425, CA; *R v Westminster City Council ex p Castelli, Same ex p Tristram-Garcia* (1996) 28 HLR 616, CA.

64 AIAA 1993 s4(4).

65 AIAA 1993 s4(4).

66 See paras 1.49–1.50.

67 [1996] AC 55, (1995) 27 HLR 453, HL.

it would be reasonable, having regard to general housing conditions in the local housing authority's district, for the person in question to continue to occupy. Notwithstanding the HPA 1986 amendments, there was no additional requirement that it should be permanent or settled.[68] The same was true of the accommodation which a local housing authority had to make available to an unintentionally homeless person under section 65(2); the accommodation had to be 'suitable', but there was no requirement of permanence.

1.64 Temporary accommodation was accordingly not, per se, unsuitable. If the tenure was so precarious that the person was likely to have to leave within 28 days without any alternative accommodation being available, then he or she remained threatened with homelessness[69] and the authority would not have discharged its duty. Otherwise, the period for which the accommodation was provided was a matter for the authority to decide.

1.65 The decision swept away the concept of settled accommodation, save for the purpose of defining that class of accommodation which an intentionally homeless applicant would need to secure for himself or herself before being entitled to re-apply.[70] It could no longer be used to identify accommodation which a person could quit without being found intentionally homeless or as the class of accommodation to which a qualifying applicant was entitled. The committee was not referred to – and did not refer to – AIAA 1993.[71]

Housing Act 1996 Parts 6 and 7

Policy

1.66 The decision in *Awua*:

> . . . caught most people in the housing world somewhat by surprise. It said that a housing authority's duty could be discharged in as little as 28 days. The legal landscape . . . has, therefore, changed.

This was how the Minister for Local Government, Housing and Urban Regeneration described the decision, noting that HA 1996 was neither introduced because of the *Awua* case nor was a response to it.[72]

68 Cf paras 1.57–1.58.

69 HA 1985 s58(4); see now HA 1996 s175(4).

70 See para 1.50.

71 See para 1.61.

72 *Hansard*, Standing Committee G, 19 March 1996, col 691.

1.67 Indeed, the minister suggested that it went further than the government intended, by removing the safety net of immediate help that it was its own new policy to provide,[73] in order to reduce the (increasing) proportion of (decreasing) local authority accommodation that was then being allocated to the homeless.

1.68 HA 1996 was foreshadowed by a Consultation Paper – *Access to Local Authority and Housing Association Tenancies* – in January 1994, which described:

> ... two main methods of acquiring a local authority or housing association tenancy – by making a direct application to the landlord concerned (and usually going on the relevant waiting list until a suitable property becomes available), or by being accepted as statutorily 'homeless' by a local authority ...[74]

1.69 Government research[75] published contemporaneously:

> ... shows that people rehoused from the waiting list are in many important respects (such as income, employment status and previous tenure) similar to households through the homelessness route ... But statutorily homeless households receive automatic priority over others ... As a result, in some areas – particularly in parts of London – it is almost impossible for any applicant ever to be rehoused from the waiting list ... Of those who did manage to get rehoused, people using the waiting list route had to wait nearly twice as long ... as people housed under the homelessness legislation ...[76]
>
> By giving the local authority a greater responsibility towards those who can demonstrate 'homelessness' than towards anyone else in housing need, the current legislation creates a perverse incentive for people to have themselves accepted by a local authority as homeless ... In the great majority of cases, someone accepted as homeless is in fact occupying accommodation of some sort at the time he or she approached the authority. Indeed, the largest single category of households accepted as statutorily homeless are people living as licensees of parents, relatives or friends who are no longer willing or able to accommodate them ... There is a growing belief that the

73 *Hansard*, Standing Committee G, 21 March 1996, col 776. The minister was aware of the implications of *Pepper v Hart* [1993] AC 625, HL, even if none too accurately, when he remarked, at col 769: 'The Hon Gentleman should also know that what Ministers say during the passage of a Bill is taken into consideration in legal proceedings'.

74 January 1994 Consultation Paper, para 2.5.

75 *Routes into local authority housing*, DoE Housing Research Summary No 16, 1994.

76 January 1994 Consultation Paper, para 2.6.

homelessness provisions are frequently used as a quick route into a separate home . . .[77]

Against this background, the government is proposing measures to ensure fairer access to all parts of the rented housing sector. These include measures to prevent homelessness, to remove the distorting effect that the present provisions have on the allocation of housing, and to ensure that subsidised housing is equally available to all who genuinely need it, particularly couples seeking to establish a good home in which to start and raise a family.[78]

1.70 The proposals were threefold:

a) to limit the extent of an authority's duties to the homeless;
b) to limit local authority housing allocation to the homeless; and
c) to encourage more advisory activity to help people find other accommodation.[79]

1.71 The idea was to provide an immediate safety net, while longer-term allocation to homeless people would be considered alongside others seeking council housing.[80] This would be achieved by new constraints on allocation, subject to 'broad principles' to be laid down by central government.[81]

1.72 The white paper on which the HA 1996 was based, *Our future homes*,[82] pursued the theme that homelessness was:

. . . usually a short term crisis . . . We are committed to maintaining an immediate safety net, but this should be separate from a fair system of allocating long-term accommodation in a house or flat owned by a local authority or housing association . . .[83]

Local authorities will continue to have an immediate duty to secure accommodation for families and vulnerable individuals who have nowhere to go. Where such people are found to have no alternative available accommodation, the local housing authority will have to secure suitable accommodation for not less than twelve months.[84]

77 January 1994 Consultation Paper, para 2.8.
78 January 1994 Consultation Paper, para 3.1.
79 January 1994 Consultation Paper, para 3.2.
80 January 1994 Consultation Paper, para 3.4.
81 January 1994 Consultation Paper, paras 20.2 and 22.1.
82 Cm 2901, HMSO, June 1995.
83 *Our future homes* (see footnote 82, above), p36, claiming that over 40 per cent of local authority new tenancies – over 80 per cent in some London authorities – and over 25 per cent of allocations of housing association tenancies were going to those accepted under the homelessness legislation.
84 Later changed to two years: see HA 1996 s193(2). See also *Hansard*, Standing Committee G, 21 March 1996, col 776 – reflecting a concern that, even if renewable, one year would not provide sufficient security.

> The authority may continue to secure accommodation for longer than that, although after two years it must check that the household's housing circumstances have not changed . . . These arrangements are intended to tide people over the immediate crisis of homelessness, and to give them time to find longer-term accommodation . . .[85]

1.73 The white paper was followed in January 1996 by a linked consultation paper, *Allocation of housing accommodation by local authorities*. This introduced the ideas that were to become Part 6 of HA 1996, governing the waiting list. It identified changes proposed to HA 1985 s22,[86] designed to 'create a single route into social housing',[87] in accordance with the policy[88] of putting '*all* those with long-term housing needs on the same footing, while providing a safety net for emergency and pressing needs' (emphasis in original). It will be 'the only route into social housing allocated by local authorities; it will be dynamic, and will focus on basic underlying need rather than immediate emergency'.[89]

1.74 The consultation paper proposed to retain the long-established categories of those occupying insanitary or overcrowded housing, or living in unsatisfactory housing conditions,[90] to which it would add:

a) those living in conditions of temporary or insecure tenure (including those at risk of losing accommodation, for example, tied accommodation);
b) families with dependent children or who are expecting a child ('recognising the importance of a stable home environment to children's development');
c) households containing a person with an identified need for settled accommodation (for example, those who give or need to receive care or other personal circumstances); and
d) those households with limited opportunities to secure settled accommodation (for example, low income), bearing in mind longer-term prospects.[91]

85 White paper, *Our future homes*, p37.

86 See paras 1.45 and 1.46.

87 *Hansard* (HC), Standing Committee G, 16th Sitting, 12 March 1996, Minister for Local Government, Housing and Urban Regeneration (Mr Curry), col 614.

88 White paper, *Our future homes*, chapter 6.

89 *Hansard* (HC), Standing Committee G, 15th Sitting, 12 March 1996, Minister for Local Government, Housing and Urban Regeneration (Mr Curry), col 588.

90 See para 1.45.

91 January 1996 Consultation Paper (see para 1.73), paras 26, 27, 28–31 and 33.

1.75 The principal policy change – to minimise the priority call of homeless people on local authority stock – may be addressed under its two heads: principal homelessness changes and allocation changes. In addition, there was a number of other discrete changes.

Principal homelessness changes

1.76 The principal homelessness changes[92] were:

a) persons subject to immigration control under the Asylum and Immigration Act (AIA) 1996, unless of a class prescribed by the secretary of state, were no longer eligible under HA 1996 Part 7;[93] nor were others within any class prescribed by the secretary of state; nor were such persons to be taken into consideration when determining whether someone else was homeless, threatened with homelessness or had a priority need for accommodation;[94]
b) where the authority was satisfied that there was other suitable accommodation available in its area, the duty was limited to giving 'such advice and assistance as the authority consider is reasonably required to enable' the applicant to secure such accommodation;[95]
c) in cases where such suitable accommodation was not available, the duty to secure that accommodation was made available to the applicant was limited to two years (although it could be continued in defined circumstances following a review, and – in default – a new application could otherwise be made);[96]
d) unless and until the authority could make an offer from its waiting list, the authority was prohibited from providing its own accommodation in discharge of functions under HA 1996 Part 7 for more than two years out of any three (whether continuously or in aggregate), unless it was hostel accommodation or accommodation privately leased by the authority from a private landlord.[97]

92 The exclusion of those subject to immigration control, introduced in 1993 (paras 1.59–1.61).
93 HA 1996 s185.
94 HA 1996 s185(4).
95 HA 1996 s197.
96 HA 1996 ss193 and 194.
97 HA 1996 s207; this included housing associations or, as they were to be known by HA 1996 Part 1, registered social landlords.

Allocations

1.77 Meanwhile, HA 1996 Part 6 provided that:

a) local authorities were bound to comply with Part 6 when making any allocation decision, including the selection of their own tenants and nominations to a registered social landlord;[98]
b) allocation could also[99] only be to persons qualified on their housing register, which did not include a person subject to immigration control under the AIA 1996, unless of a class prescribed by the secretary of state, nor did it include others within any class prescribed by the secretary of state; qualification was otherwise within the discretion of the authority;[100]
c) authorities had to adopt an allocation scheme for determining priority between applicants, including by whom decisions could be taken.

1.78 Subject to this, the scheme had to be framed to secure a reasonable preference not for the homeless to whom duties were owed per se, but for:

a) those occupying insanitary or overcrowded housing, or otherwise living in insanitary conditions;
b) those living in temporary accommodation or on insecure terms;
c) families with dependent children;
d) households consisting of or including someone who was expecting a child;
e) households consisting of or including someone with a particular need for settled accommodation on medical or welfare grounds, with added preference under this heading to those who could not reasonably be expected to find their own settled accommodation in the near future; and
f) households whose social or economic circumstances were such that they had difficulty in securing settled accommodation.[101]

Other changes

1.79 HA 1996 Part 6 included a number of ancillary provisions, including notification of entry on and removal from the register, review of entries and review of decisions. Part 7 also effected a number of

98 HA 1996 s159.
99 See para 1.76.
100 HA 1996 s161.
101 HA 1996 s167(2).

changes to homelessness law, of which the most significant were the introduction of a right to internal review and subsequent appeal to the county court.[102]

Between Acts

Restoration of priority to homeless people

1.80 HA 1996 Parts 6 and 7 had been in force for only a relatively short period of time when the general election of 1997 brought in a new government.

1.81 One of its first acts was to restore priority to homeless people under HA 1996 Part 6. Using a power[103] to specify further descriptions of people to whom a preference should be given, the Allocation of Housing (Reasonable and Additional Preference) Regulations 1997[104] re-afforded[105] a reasonable preference to the unintentionally homeless towards whom a duty was owed under HA 1996 Part 7 or its predecessor provisions in the HA 1985.

Asylum-seekers

1.82 The Immigration and Asylum Act 1999 set up an entirely separate national service – the National Asylum Support Service (NASS) – to deal with destitute asylum-seekers.[106] As a result, all asylum-seekers whose claims were made on or after 3 April 2000 were taken out of HA 1996 Part 7.

102 HA 1996 ss202 and 204.

103 HA 1996 s167(3).

104 SI No 1902.

105 Cf para 1.45.

106 Those who made their first asylum claim on or after 5 March 2007 were dealt with under the New Asylum Model (NAM) – see chapter 3; earlier applicants are known as 'legacy' cases and should have their asylum and support claims dealt with by the Casework Resolution Directorate (CRD).NAM was replaced by the UK Border Agency (UKBA) Local Authority Team and this, in turn, was replaced by the Home Office's UK Visa and Immigration Centre: see chapter 3, footnote 350.

The green paper

1.83 These changes were followed, in April 2000, by 'the first comprehensive review of housing policy for 23 years' – the green paper, *Quality and choice: a decent home for all.*[107]

1.84 This set out aims for reform in relation to both homelessness and allocations. The changes to the allocations provisions were given more prominence and made subject to an overall aim of encouraging 'social landlords to see themselves more as providers of a lettings service which is responsive to the needs and wishes of individuals rather than purely as housing "allocators"'.[108]

1.85 The aims were to ensure that lettings and transfer services:

a) meet the long-term housing requirements of those who need social housing most, in a way which is sustainable both for individuals and the community;
b) adopt a simple and customer-centred approach, empowering first-time applicants and existing tenants to make decisions in choosing housing which meets their requirements;
c) make better use of the national housing stock, by widening the scope for lettings and transfers across local authority boundaries, and between local authorities and registered social landlords; and
d) give local authorities more flexibility to build sustainable communities within the national context of extreme variations in local housing markets.[109]

1.86 The green paper's proposals for the reform of homelessness policy were intended to:

a) ensure that unintentionally homeless people in priority need were provided with temporary accommodation until they obtained settled accommodation (in either the public or private sector);
b) broaden the definition of priority need to ensure that the most vulnerable citizens were protected by the homelessness safety net;
c) enable local authorities to use their own housing stock to provide temporary accommodation, without the restriction that it could only be provided for two years in any three;
d) give those housed in temporary accommodation a reasonable period in which they could exercise the same degree of customer

107 Department of the Environment, Transport and the Regions (DETR), 2000.
108 *Quality and choice: a decent home for all*, para 9.3.
109 *Quality and choice: a decent home for all*, para 9.4.

choice of settled accommodation as available to other people with urgent housing needs waiting on the housing register;

e) allow local authorities greater flexibility to assist non-priority homeless households, particularly in areas of low demand; and

f) encourage a more strategic approach to the prevention of homelessness and the rehousing of homeless households.[110]

1.87 Following consultation, the government published a response, *Quality and choice: a decent home for all – The way forward,*[111] explaining how it was 'taking the agenda forward'.[112] 'The principle of choice in lettings was broadly welcomed.'[113] Indeed, the move towards choice-based lettings was already being facilitated within the existing legal framework of HA 1996 Part 6, through a series of government-funded pilot schemes.[114] In relation to the homelessness proposals, 'there was almost unanimous support, from those who responded'.[115] Legislation was promised.

1.88 This legislation originally formed part of the Homes Bill 2001, which also included provisions to improve the process of buying and selling homes through a requirement for a 'home-buyers pack'. The bill fell at committee stage in the House of Lords, as a result of the general election in May 2001. Following re-election, the government decided not to proceed immediately with the provisions relating to home-buying, but re-introduced those relating to homelessness and allocation, in the Homelessness Bill.

Priority need categories

1.89 Not all the elements of the green paper proposals required primary legislation, however. In particular, it had proposed extending the categories of priority need[116] to those leaving an institutional or care background, those fleeing domestic violence, and 16- and 17-year-olds. This could be achieved by statutory instrument, under HA 1996 s189(2).

110 *Quality and choice: a decent home for all*, para 9.42.
111 DETR, December 2000.
112 *The way forward*, p4.
113 *The way forward*, para 6.2.
114 *The way forward*, para 6.5.
115 *The way forward*, para 7.3.
116 *Quality and choice: a decent home for all*, paras 9.55 and 9.56.

1.90 An amendment was first made by the National Assembly for Wales on 1 March 2001.[117] In England, there was consultation on a draft statutory instrument during 2001, and it was not until 2002 that the changes were made, to coincide with the coming into force of most of the homelessness provisions in the Homelessness Act 2002.[118]

1.91 The Welsh and English provisions are not worded identically, illustrating an increasing divergence in housing policy following devolution.

Homelessness Act 2002

Strategies

1.92 The green paper had emphasised the need for authorities to develop a more strategic approach to the prevention and redress of homelessness.

1.93 This was embodied in Homelessness Act 2002 ss1–4, by a duty requiring each local housing authority to undertake a review of homelessness and to formulate an effective strategy to deal with it, in consultation with both social services (whether of the same authority or another) and other organisations.

Duties

1.94 One of the main changes of HA 1996 had been to limit the initial duty to house homeless people to a period of two years.[119] This limit was repealed by the Homelessness Act 2002, along with the limitation on use of an authority's stock to house the homeless.[120] Also repealed was the provision of HA 1996 s197 which allowed the main duties to be avoided[121] if other suitable accommodation was available.[122]

1.95 Nonetheless, the duty was not intended to last for an infinite time, and the circumstances which bring an authority's duty to an

117 Homeless Persons (Priority Need) (Wales) Order 2001 SI No 607.

118 See the Homelessness (Priority Need for Accommodation) (England) Order 2002 SI No 2051.

119 See para 1.76.

120 Homelessness Act 2002 s6.

121 See para 1.76.

122 Homelessness Act 2002 s9.

end under HA 1996 s193 were accordingly widened to allow more reliance on assured tenancies, and – in certain circumstances – even assured shorthold tenancies.[123]

Non-priority need applicants

1.96 Homelessness Act 2002 s5 also gave local authorities power to house the unintentionally homeless under HA 1996 Part 7, even where not in priority need.

Other changes

1.97 Further changes were made to the definitions of homelessness and intentionality, to ensure that any kind of violence – not only domestic violence – would mean that it is not reasonable to continue to occupy accommodation.[124] This helps, for example, those fleeing racial harassment or intimidation.

1.98 In addition, there was an extension in the jurisdiction of the county court to allow an applicant who appeals against an authority's decision also to appeal to that court against a refusal by the authority to provide the applicant with interim accommodation pending final outcome of the appeal process.[125]

1.99 The Homelessness Act 2002 made two other amendments to the review process: applicants are allowed both to accept an offer of accommodation and to challenge its suitability by way of review;[126] and, the county court may itself extend the 21-day time limit for appealing.[127]

Allocations

1.100 The amendments to HA 1996 Part 6 almost all reflected the government's aim of bringing greater choice to the allocation process by local authorities.

1.101 One change was to bring transfer applications (whether within the stock of a single landlord or between the stocks of more than one

123 Homelessness Act 2002 s7.
124 Homelessness Act 2002 s10.
125 Homelessness Act 2002 s11.
126 Homelessness Act 2002 s8(2).
127 Homelessness Act 2002 Sch 1 para 17.

landlord) into the ambit of HA 1996 Part 6.[128] This ensured both that existing tenants are dealt with on the same basis as new applicants and that their qualification for rehousing is not limited.[129]

1.102 The HA 1996 requirement to keep a housing register was abolished.[130]

> Removing the requirement to have a register is an important step in facilitating the development by local authorities of choice-based letting schemes that put the applicant at the centre of the decision-making process. We want to encourage authorities to move away from the rigid formulas of an often artificial points-based system, which typically becomes associated with allocation schemes based on the housing register.[131]

1.103 The government retained the ineligibility of persons from abroad for an allocation.[132] In addition, the Homelessness Act 2002 (as had the green paper) continued to reflect a widespread concern about anti-social behaviour, and the Act therefore contained provisions allowing those guilty of 'unacceptable behaviour serious enough to make him or her unsuitable to be a tenant' to be excluded from social housing.[133]

1.104 The requirement that allocation schemes reflect housing need in some way was not abandoned and the Homelessness Act 2002 retained the concept of the 'reasonable preference' to be given to certain groups, albeit subject to some changes.[134] Authorities' schemes were explicitly allowed to take into account financial resources, behaviour and local connection when determining preference and, even where those guilty of seriously unacceptable behaviour were not excluded from the allocation scheme altogether, they could be accorded no preference.

1.105 Changes were made to the ancillary provisions on notification and internal review to allow an applicant to seek an internal review in relation to any decision about the facts of the applicant's case,

128 Homelessness Act 2002 s13.

129 See *Quality and choice: a decent home for all*, DETR, 2000, para 9.8.

130 See para 1.77.

131 Standing Committee A, 12 July 2001, col 81, per Dr Alan Whitehead, Parliamentary Under-Secretary for Transport, Local Government and the Regions.

132 See para 1.77.

133 See para 1.78.

134 Including giving preference to all homeless people, whether in priority need or not, and whether or not they are intentionally homeless.

including a decision that the applicant is to be excluded or given no preference because of unacceptable behaviour.[135]

1.106 The Homelessness Act 2002 provisions still did not comprise a tightly-prescriptive framework and there remained considerable room for local variation.

> We believe the right way forward is for local authorities and registered social landlords to decide in the light of local circumstances, and drawing on the experiences of the pilot studies, the ways in which they should amend or develop their existing arrangements.[136]

Changes following the Homelessness Act 2002

1.107 Leaving aside devolution, an issue that goes far beyond this book but that has – with the increased transfer of powers to Wales[137] – substantially lengthened it as the housing policies of Westminster and Cardiff have gradually diverged, the focus of government policy following the Homelessness Act 2002 and prior to the change of administration in 2010 was primarily on its implementation.

1.108 One particular focus was on the reduction in the use of bed and breakfast accommodation. In 2003, secondary legislation made it unlawful in England for local authorities to place families in bed and breakfast accommodation for more than six weeks.[138]

1.109 Other key changes focused on issues of immigration and asylum. While it has already been noted that asylum-seekers were taken outside the existing statutory provisions in April 2000 by the establishment

135 Homelessness Act 2002 s14.

136 *The way forward,* para 6.4.

137 In Wales, ministerial functions in many areas of activity (including housing) were transferred to the National Assembly for Wales by Government of Wales Act 1998 s22, Sch 2 para 9; National Assembly for Wales (Transfer of Functions) Order 1999 SI No 672. The Government of Wales Act 2006 then transferred those functions from the Assembly to the Welsh Ministers (ss58, 161, Sch 11 para 30). The National Assembly for Wales was not granted legislative competence over housing matters but, by Government of Wales Act 2006 s95, could be given such competence by Order in Council. To date, two relevant Orders have been made: the National Assembly for Wales (Legislative Competence) (Housing) (Fire Safety) Order 2010 SI No 1210 and the National Assembly for Wales (Legislative Competence) (Housing and Local Government) Order 2010 SI No 1838.

138 Homelessness (Suitability of Accommodation) (England) Order 2003 SI No 3326. Similar (although not identical) limitations were introduced in Wales in 2006.

of NASS,[139] the question arose whether accommodation provided by NASS gave rise to a local connection under HA 1996 Part 7 if and when asylum-seekers achieved refugee status and were thus able to apply under Part 7. The House of Lords initially answered this question in the negative.[140] The government, concerned that refugees would overwhelmingly apply to areas of greatest housing stress in London and the south-east, reversed this decision by amendments to HA 1996 s199 contained in Asylum and Immigration (Treatment of Claimants, etc) Act 2004 s11.

1.110 Another immigration-related statutory change followed from the exclusion of ineligible persons when considering whether an applicant for HA 1996 Part 7 assistance was homeless, threatened with homelessness or in priority need.[141] This was held to be incompatible with the family life provisions of Article 8 of the European Convention on Human Rights (ECHR).[142] As a result, the Housing and Regeneration Act (H&RA) 2008 amended HA 1996 s185(4) so as to take such persons into account, except in those cases where, although eligible, the applicant[143] is subject to immigration control,[144] albeit that such an application would be known as a 'restricted case' to whom the authority owes a – somewhat lesser – duty by way of making a 'private accommodation offer',[145] and which is excluded from the reasonable preference afforded to the homeless under HA 1996 Part 6.[146]

1.111 The H&RA 2008 also made changes to the local connection provisions, so as to include employment in the armed forces and residence during such service as grounds for a local connection, where they had formerly been excluded.[147]

139 See para 1.82.

140 *Al-ameri v Kensington and Chelsea RLBC; Osmani v Harrow LBC* [2004] UKHL 4, [2004] HLR 20.

141 See para 1.76.

142 *R (Morris) v Westminster City Council (No 3)* [2005] EWCA Civ 1184, [2006] 1 WLR 505, [2006] HLR 8. In *Bah v UK* App No 56328/07, [2012] HLR 2, however, the European Court of Human Rights held that it was not in contravention.

143 Not being an European Economic Area (EEA) or Swiss national, who are fully eligible: see paras 3.113 and 3.116.

144 Ie, asylum-seekers, those with indefinite leave to remain: see para 3.114.

145 H&RA 2008 s314 and Sch 15 Part 1. The details of what this duty entails may be seen at paras 5.8–5.11.

146 HA 1996 s167(2ZA), inserted by H&RA 2008 s314 and Sch 15 Part 1.

147 See para 7.18.

1.112 No case-law[148] has, however, had the seminal effect of a *Puhlhofer*[149] or *Awua*,[150] with the possible exception of the HA 1996 Part 6 decision in *R (Ahmad) v Newham LBC*,[151] in which there are shades of Lord Brightman's speech in *Puhlhofer*[152] to be found in the speech of Lord Neuberger:[153]

> [A]s a general proposition, it is undesirable for the courts to get involved in questions of how priorities are accorded in housing allocation policies. Of course, there will be cases where the court has a duty to interfere, for instance if a policy does not comply with statutory requirements, or if it is plainly irrational. It seems unlikely, however, that the legislature can have intended that Judges should embark on the exercise of telling authorities how to decide on priorities as between applicants in need of rehousing, save in relatively rare and extreme circumstances. Housing allocation policy is a difficult exercise which requires not only social and political sensitivity and judgment, but also local expertise and knowledge.
>
> In relation to the provision of accommodation under the National Assistance Act 1948, my noble and learned friend, Baroness Hale of Richmond, then Hale LJ, said in *R (Wahid) v Tower Hamlets LBC*,[154] para 33, '[n]eed is a relative concept, which trained and experienced social workers are much better equipped to assess than are lawyers and courts, provided that they act rationally'. Precisely the same is true of relative housing needs under Part 6 of the 1996 Act, and trained and experienced local authority housing officers.

Localism Act 2011

1.113 The 'coalition government' which followed the general election in 2010 made a number of changes to housing, including new limits on housing benefit (and welfare benefits generally), the introduction of a new form of secure tenancy known as a 'flexible tenancy' by LA 2011,[155] and changes to both the homelessness and allocation

148 Other important decisions include *Birmingham City Council v Ali, Moran v Manchester City Council* [2009] UKHL 36, [2009] 1 WLR 1506 (see paras 4.13 and 4.70), and *Holmes-Moorhouse v Richmond upon Thames LBC* [2009] UKHL 7, [2009] HLR 34 (see para 5.29).

149 See paras 1.47–1.54.

150 See paras 1.62–1.65.

151 [2009] UKHL 14, [2009] HLR 31.

152 See para 1.53.

153 At [46]–[47].

154 [2002] EWCA Civ 287, [2003] HLR 13.

155 LA 2011 s154.

provisions of HA 1996 Part 6 (as amended by the Homelessness Act 2002).

1.114 The consultation paper which preceded the Act – *Local decisions: a fairer future for social housing*[156] – was reminiscent of the policy which preceded the HA 1996.[157]

1.115 Thus, on homelessness:

> 6.7 Under the current legislation, although local authorities have considerable flexibility in how to meet the immediate housing needs of people owed the main homelessness duty, they are very restricted in the way they can bring the duty to an end. Suitable accommodation in the private rented sector can be offered as a settled home that ends the duty, but applicants can refuse such offers without good reason, and the duty continues to be owed . . .
>
> 6.8 People owed the main homelessness duty can therefore effectively insist on being provided with temporary accommodation until offered social housing (and under housing allocation legislation, they must be given reasonable preference for social housing). We believe this encourages some households to apply as homeless in order to secure reasonable preference and an effective guarantee of being offered social housing . . .
>
> . . .
>
> 6.12 We intend to give authorities the discretion to decide in any particular case whether a person owed the homelessness duty needs social housing or whether their needs could be met with suitable accommodation in the private rented sector . . .

1.116 Likewise, on allocations:

> 4.6 The requirement to maintain open waiting lists, coupled with the introduction of choice-based lettings, may also have encouraged a commonly held – but mistaken – perception that anyone will be able to get into social housing if they wait long enough. Open waiting lists may be acceptable – should even perhaps be encouraged – where there is low demand for social housing. Where there is not enough housing, even for those who really need it, continuing to operate an open waiting list raises false expectations and is likely to fuel the belief that the allocation system is unfair.
>
> . . .
>
> 4.9 We take the view that it should be for local authorities to put in place arrangements which suit the particular needs of their local area. Some local authorities might restrict social housing to those in

156 Consultation paper, Department for Communities and Local Government (DCLG), November 2010, para 6.8. See www.gov.uk/government/consultations/a-fairer-future-for-social-housing.

157 See paras 1.68–1.69, 1.72–1.74.

housing need (e.g. homeless households and overcrowded families). Other local authorities might impose residency criteria or exclude applicants with a poor tenancy record or those with sufficient financial resources to rent or buy privately. Others may decide to continue with open waiting lists. If, having taken into account the views of their local community, local authorities decide that there are benefits in maintaining open waiting lists (for example, to stimulate demand for social housing), we believe they should be able to do so.

1.117 In relation to homelessness, the principal change was designed to allow authorities more use of the private sector, so that even the offer of an assured shorthold tenancy – without the consent of the applicant – could be used to discharge the full duty, subject to a right to a further offer within two years (even if not by then in priority need).[158] In substance, even if not in form, this reinstated the original HA 1996 s197 power,[159] which had been repealed by Homelessness Act 2002.[160]

1.118 In relation to allocations, the principal change – applicable only in England – was to allow authorities, subject to any overriding regulations, to define classes of 'qualifying' applicant,[161] ie to abandon 'open' waiting lists in favour of an authority's own criteria, no longer confined to the exclusion of the anti-social.[162] In addition, transfer applicants were removed from the allocation provisions, likewise effectively reinstating the HA 1996 as amended,[163] otherwise than where (in effect) the tenant has applied for a transfer and qualifies for a reasonable preference.[164] Thus, 'localism' took the place of the 'centralism' to which it is the antithesis, so as to restore authorities' historical discretion over to whom they allocate housing from what was something closer to a national code of preferences. This apparent freedom was, however, significantly undermined by the Court of Appeal in *Jakimaviciute*[165] (see para 11.42), in which the guidance was considered to support the conclusion of law that the qualification criteria adopted by an authority are subject to the reasonable preference duty, so that an authority cannot adopt qualification criteria

158 HA 1996 s195A.

159 See para 1.76.

160 See para 1.94.

161 HA 1996 s160ZA.

162 See para 1.103.

163 HA 1996 s159(5).

164 HA 1996 s159(4A), (4B). Cf para 1.101.

165 *R (Jakimaviciute) v Hammersmith and Fulham LBC* [2014] EWCA Civ 1438, [2015] HLR 5.

which exclude a person entitled to a reasonable preference, a conclusion that plainly conflicted with the policy intention.

Housing (Wales) Act 2014

1.119 In 2009, the Welsh Assembly Government published a Ten Year Homelessness Plan for Wales. It expressed concern that there were inconsistencies around decision-making, interpretation and implementation of the legislation, with too little attention being paid to the needs of the vulnerable. There was an undertaking to 'review . . . key areas of homelessness legislation and the duties placed on Local Authorities, especially around the areas of priority need, intentionality, local connection and the discharge of duty Into the private rented sector . . .'.[166]

1.120 As part of this process, Dr Peter Mackie[167] was commissioned to carry out a 'review of homelessness legislation in Wales in order to explore whether and how the existing legislative framework might be changed to minimise homelessness'.[168] The review concluded that the priority need categories were 'used to ration limited housing resources . . .'.[169] and that applicants found it painful and upsetting to have to 'prove' that they were vulnerable.[170] While homelessness prevention techniques were generally thought to be successful, both in terms of assisting a wide range of households and in exploring a broader range of solutions, there was concern that such prevention techniques sat uncomfortably with statutory duties.[171] Moreover, there was only limited support provided for those who became homeless after leaving care or other institutional accommodation.[172]

1.121 That report was followed, in May 2012, by the Welsh Government's white paper Homes for Wales. Chapter 8 noted that, as a result of economic decline and welfare reform, homelessness was rising in Wales. The priority of the Welsh Government was to prevent homelessness and, in the long term, eliminate it completely. The white

166 Ten Year Homelessness Plan for Wales, p26.

167 Dr Peter Mackie, Ian Thomas, Kate Hodgson Impact analysis of existing homelessness legislation in Wales, January 2012.

168 Impact analysis of existing homelessness legislation in Wales, p3.

169 Impact analysis of existing homelessness legislation in Wales, para 7.2.2.

170 Impact analysis of existing homelessness legislation in Wales, para 7.2.14.

171 Impact analysis of existing homelessness legislation in Wales, p44, second bullet point.

172 Impact analysis of existing homelessness legislation in Wales, para 7.3.6.

paper promised a 'radical shift from existing legislation' with greater focus on duties designed to prevent homelessness.[173] The period of time in which a person was considered to be 'threatened with homelessness' would be increased from 28 to 56 days, but the intention of the new legislative model would be that people should approach authorities for assistance as early as possible once they experienced a housing problem.[174] A new duty would be introduced which would require authorities to take 'all reasonable steps to achieve a suitable housing solution for all [eligible] households which are homeless or threatened with homelessness'.[175] Although the existing law on intentional homelessness would be re-enacted, authorities would be given a power to disapply the intentionality test; in time, the Welsh Government planned to prevent any consideration of intentionality where the household included children.[176] The Welsh Government also intended to 'gradually phase out' the priority need test.[177]

1.122 Save for the last of these, the proposals were introduced in the H(W)A 2014 Part 2. The majority of that Part re-enacted provisions already found in HA 1996 Part 7 and subordinate legislation, but new provisions included:

a) extending the time within which a person may be threatened with homelessness to 56 days;[178]
b) included a requirement to ensure that information and advice about was provided, in particular, to people leaving prison, youth detention, hospital after treatment for a mental disorder and young people leaving care;[179]
c) a new requirement to assess the needs of those who need help in retaining or obtaining accommodation[180] and to help to prevent an applicant from becoming homeless;[181]

173 Homes for Wales, para 8.40.
174 Homes for Wales, para 8.43.
175 Homes for Wales, para 8.44.
176 Homes for Wales, para 8.53.
177 Homes for Wales, para 8.55–8.56, as is already the case in Scotland, see Homelessness (Abolition of Priority Need Test) (Scotland) Order 2012 SI No 330.
178 H(W)A 2014 s55(4); para 1.121.
179 See para 14.22 and H(W)A 2014 s60.
180 H(W)A 2014 s62.
181 H(W)A 2014 s66.

d) power for the authorities, in conjunction with the Welsh Ministers, to resolve not to apply the intentionality test to specified categories of applicant.[182]

Homelessness Reduction Act 2017

1.123 In December 2015, the Communities and Local Government (CLG) Select Committee launched an inquiry into homelessness in England. The Committee was concerned both that homelessness, particularly rough sleeping, was increasing and that government data was not robust enough to provide an accurate picture. The final report praised the 'prevention' elements of H(W)A 2014, particularly the duty to help to prevent an applicant from becoming homeless and the extension of time within which a person is threatened with homelessness to 56 days.[183] During the inquiry, a member of the Committee (Bob Blackman MP) drew second place in the Private Members' Bill ballot and announced that he would introduce a Homelessness Reduction Bill. The government subsequently announced that it would support the bill. The general election in June 2017 affects the timetable, but it is still expected to be brought into force during the 2017/18 financial year.

1.124 The key provisions of HRA 2017 are as follows.

a) Section 1 extends the period of time within which a person is threatened with homelessness from 28 to 56 days. It also provides that a person is threatened with homelessness if he or she has been served with a valid notice under HA 1988 s21 expiring within 56 days in respect of their only home.[184]
b) Section 3 creates a new HA 1996 s189A. Where an applicant is homeless (or threatened with homelessness) and eligible for assistance, the authority must assess his or her housing needs and consider what support it can provide to ensure that the applicant has or retains suitable accommodation. The authority and applicant must try to agree a written list of the actions that each will take: if they cannot agree, the authority must produce a record of the reasons for the disagreement and specify what steps the authority will take and those that it expects of the applicant.

182 H(W)A 2014 s78; para 6.3.
183 CLG Select Committee, Homelessness, HC40, August 2016.
184 Ie notice of seeking possession in respect of an assured shorthold tenancy.

c) Section 4 amends HA 1996 s195 so that, where an applicant is threatened with homelessness and eligible for assistance, the authority will have to take reasonable steps to help him or her secure that accommodation does not cease to be available for his or her occupation, having regard to the assessment under HA 1996 s189A.

d) Section 5 introduces new HA 1996 s189B, requiring the authority to take reasonable steps for 56 days to help the applicant try to secure suitable accommodation for a minimum period of six months, regardless of whether he or she is in priority need or intentionally homeless.

1.125 The government initially indicated that it would make £35.4m available in 2017/18 and £12.1m in 2018/19 in to assist with the likely costs authorities will incur in respect of the new Act but that no funding would be provided beyond that.[185] This was subsequently increased to £61 million over the same period.[186] None of these figures takes into account any increase in legal costs[187] flowing from additional judicial review claims or HA 1996 s204 appeals. There is much concern as to whether this will be sufficient.[188]

185 House of Commons Written Statement 17 January 2017 (HCWS418). There is also the possibility of the government making 'available a small amount of further funding for local authorities in high-pressure areas to manage the transition to the new duties'.

186 House of Commons Written Statement, 15 March 2017 (HCWS538).

187 Whether to authorities or to the legal aid fund.

188 In submissions to the CLG Select Committee, Bedford BC suggested that the new duties would add c£1m pa to its homelessness costs; Kensington and Chelsea RLBC put its figure at closer to £3.5m and Redbridge BC considered that its costs (including additional staffing) could eventually reach £4.3m. The Association of Housing Advice Services put the costs in London alone at £161m.

CHAPTER 2

The provisions in outline

2.1 Introduction

2.11 Definitions

2.11 Administration

Central government • Local government

2.16 Immigration status

Information

2.21 Homelessness

Available accommodation • Reasonable to continue to occupy • Unusable accommodation • Threatened with homelessness

2.30 Priority need

2..34 Intentional homelessness

Collusive arrangements

2.39 Local connection

Residence of choice • Employment • Former asylum-seekers

2.44 Preliminary duties

Enquiries/assessment • Notification of decision • Accommodation pending decision

2.60 Principal duties

Limited duties • Full duties

2.118 Protection of property

Duty • Power • Charges and terms • Power of entry • Choice of storage • Termination • Review

continued

2.128 Homelessness strategies
Authorities • Homelessness review • Strategy
2.138 Advice, information and voluntary organisations
2.145 Code of Guidance
2.146 Code of Practice
2.147 Review and appeal
Review • Appeal
2.160 Criminal offences
2.163 Co-operation between authorities
Co-operation • Referral
2.168 Allocation
Meaning of allocation • Excluded allocations • Eligibility • Re-application • Applications • Priorities and procedures • Change and consultation • Code of Guidance • Co-operation • Information • Criminal offences

Introduction

2.1 In this chapter, the provisions of the Housing Act (HA) 1996 Parts 6 and 7, as amended by the Homelessness Act 2002 and the Localism Act (LA) 2011, will be considered, in reverse order. The amendments which will be made by the Homelessness Reduction Act (HRA) 2017 are described, though not yet in force. The Housing (Wales) Act (H(W)A) 2014 largely follows the structure of Part 7 and incorporates much of what is to be found in HRA 2017. The provisions are considered on their face; they are considered in detail in subsequent chapters.[1]

2.2 HA 1996 Part 6 extends to England and Wales, but with differences between them. HA 1996 Part 7 now only applies in England and, in Wales, the position is governed by H(W)A 2014 Part 2.[2] The provisions of the Housing (Homeless Persons) Act (H(HP)A) 1977 were consolidated in the Housing (Scotland) Act 1987 and, subject to amendment,[3] so remain; they are not considered here, but provision is made to ensure that homelessness applications in England allow for connections with Scottish authorities and for referrals by Scottish authorities.[4] In Northern Ireland, duties towards the homeless and those threatened with homelessness are imposed on the Northern Ireland Housing Executive (NIHE) by the Housing (Northern Ireland) Order 1988;[5] these duties are likewise not considered here.

1 This chapter does not cross-refer to the details in other chapters or within this, as the purpose of the chapter is to provide a simple narrative of the principal provisions, in every respect (in which there is any need or even room for any elaboration or explanation) to be considered and elaborated elsewhere in the book.

2 For applications made on or after 27 April 2015; otherwise, HA 1996 Part 7 remains applicable: Housing (Wales) Act 2014 (Commencement No 3 and Transitory, Transitional and Saving Provisions) Order 2015 SI No 1272.

3 Housing (Scotland) Act 1987 was amended by the Housing (Scotland) Act 2001. A major review of homelessness in Scotland (Scottish Executive *Homelessness Task Force Final Report* (2002)) led to further legislation in the Homelessness etc (Scotland) Act 2003. There has been increasing divergence between the law in Scotland and that in the rest of the UK. The 2003 Act provided for the eventual abolition of categories of priority need, so that a duty will be owed to all homeless persons. That reform came into force on 31 December 2012 (see the Homelessness (Abolition of Priority Need Test) (Scotland) Order 2012 SI No 330). The 2003 Act also provides for continuing duties towards the intentionally homeless.

4 HA 1996 ss201, 217.

5 SI No 1990 (NI 23). This too has been subject to review by the NIHE in 2001, and the order was amended to bring it more in line with HA 1996 Part 7 by the Housing (Northern Ireland) Order 2003 SI No 412 (NI 2). See also NIHE *Homelessness Strategy for Northern Ireland 2012–2017.*

2.3 In outline, HA 1996 Part 7 and H(W)A 2014 Part 2 place an obligation on local housing authorities to secure that suitable accommodation is made available for a person:

a) who is homeless;
b) who is in priority need of accommodation;
c) who did not become homeless intentionally,[6]

but subject to the local connection provisions.[7] The obligation is the peak housing duty under HA 1996 Part 7 or H(W)A 2014 Part 2. Where, however, discharge is to be by way of the allocation of a secure or introductory tenancy of an authority's own accommodation or nomination to such a tenancy of another authority or to an assured tenancy of a registered social landlord, it is subject to the provisions of HA 1996 Part 6.

2.4 Certain persons are ineligible for assistance on immigration grounds.[8] Special provision is made for those who, while eligible for assistance, are only homeless or in priority need by reference to others with whom they reside or might reasonably be expected to reside who are themselves ineligible.

2.5 There are also obligations in respect of those:

a) who are not yet homeless;
b) who do not have a priority need;
c) who have a priority need but become homeless intentionally; and
d) who are considered to be subject to the local connection provisions, pending determination of ultimate responsibility.

2.6 In addition, authorities have duties:

a) to make enquiries;
b) to notify the applicant of their decisions and the reasons for them; and
c) to protect the property of the homeless.

Further, in Wales, and in England once HRA 2017 comes into force:

6 Although, in Wales, authorities have a power to disapply the intentionality test: H(W)A 2014 s78.

7 HA 1996 ss193(2) and 198(1); H(W)A 2014 ss80, 81.

8 HA 1996 s185; H(W)A 2014 s61. The detail is set out in regulations. For England, see the Allocation of Housing and Homelessness (Eligibility) (England) Regulations 2006 SI No 1294 and, in Wales, see Allocation of Housing and Homelessness (Eligibility) (Wales) Regulations 2014 SI No 2603.

d) there are assessment duties designed to identify steps which applicants can take to ensure that they have and retain accommodation; and
e) there is an initial help duty, for a limited period, designed to help applicants secure accommodation for themselves,

There are ancillary provisions governing deception. There is provision for the funding of voluntary agencies. There is also provision for the internal review of decisions, and appeal to the county court on a point of law.

2.7 The approach adopted here is, first, to define the key concepts contained in HA 1996 Part 7 and H(W)A 2014 Part 2, before matching them to the duties which Part 7 and Part 2 impose, considering separately and under their own headings the ancillary provisions, review and appeal, and allocation under HA 1996 Part 6.

2.8 The definitions which must be considered are:

- 'authorities';
- 'immigration status';
- 'homelessness';
- 'priority need';
- 'intentional homelessness'; and
- 'local connection'.

2.9 The principal duties which must be considered are:

- preliminary duties;
- principal duties; and
- local connection provisions.

2.10 Further matters which must be considered are:

- protection of property;
- homelessness strategies;
- advice, information and voluntary organisations;
- Code of Guidance;
- Code of Practice;
- review and appeal;
- criminal offences;
- co-operation between authorities; and
- allocation.

Definitions

Administration

Central government

2.11 HA 1996 falls within the responsibilities of the Department of Communities and Local Government (DCLG),[9] and its secretary of state; in Wales, legislative competence over housing is now enjoyed by the National Assembly while ministerial functions are exercised by the Welsh Ministers.[10]

Local government

2.12 HA 1996 Part 7 (s217) and H(W)A 2014 Part 2 (s99) refers to three classes of authority:

a) local housing authorities;
b) relevant authorities; and
c) social services authorities.

Local housing authority

2.13 'Local housing authority' means a district council except in London where it means the London borough council or the Common Council of the City of London,[11] and in Wales where it means the county or county borough council (HA 1985 s1, as amended).[12] Where relevant, it includes a Scottish local authority for the purposes of the Housing (Scotland) Act 1987.[13] Unitary authorities under the Local Government Act 1992 or Local Government and Public Involvement in Health Act 2007, if not already local housing authorities, will invariably be housing authorities.[14]

9 Formerly the Office of the Deputy Prime Minister (ODPM) from 2002–2006, formerly the Department of Transport, Local Government and the Regions (DTLR) from 2001–2002, formerly the Department of the Environment, Transport and the Regions (DETR) from 1997–2001, formerly the Department of the Environment (DoE).

10 See Government of Wales Act 1998 s22, Sch 2 para 9; National Assembly for Wales (Transfer of Functions) Order 1999 SI No 672; Government of Wales Act 2006 ss58, 161, Sch 11 para 30; Government of Wales Act 2006 s95; National Assembly for Wales (Legislative Competence) (Housing and Local Government) Order 2010 SI No 1838.

11 HA 1996 s230 and HA 1985 s1.

12 H(W)A 2014 s99. See also Local Government (Wales) Act 1994 s17.

13 HA 1996 ss201, 217.

14 Local Government Changes for England Regulations 1994 SI No 867.

Relevant authority

2.14 'Relevant authority' means, in England and Wales, a local housing authority and a social services authority.[15]

Social services authority

2.15 'Social services authority' means a non-metropolitan county council, a metropolitan district council, a London borough council or the Common Council of the City of London, and in Wales a county or county borough council.[16] Unitary authorities will also be social services authorities, if not already social services authorities.[17] Where relevant, it includes a Scottish local authority for the purposes of the Social Work (Scotland) Act 1968.[18]

Immigration status

2.16 Persons from abroad are ineligible for assistance if they are persons who are subject to immigration control under the Asylum and Immigration Act (AIA) 1996, who have not been re-qualified by regulations.[19] No person who is excluded from entitlement to housing benefit by Immigration and Asylum Act (IAA) 1999 s115 may be re-included by such regulations.[20]

2.17 In addition, the secretary of state may, by regulation, add categories of people who are to be treated as persons from abroad for these purposes.[21] Asylum-seekers, whose position was formerly governed separately by HA 1996 s186, are now governed by the regulations, as are other immigrants. Ineligible asylum-seekers may, however, be able to access accommodation from the UK Visa and Immigration (formerly through the National Asylum Support Service (NASS)); and children in need – including those of ineligible persons from

15 HA 1996 s217; H(W)A 2014 s80. Where appropriate, it may include a Scottish housing or social services authority: HA 1996 s217.

16 HA 1996 s217; Local Authority Social Services Act 1970 s1; and, in Wales, Social Services and Well-being (Wales) Act 2014.

17 Local Government Changes for England Regulations 1994 SI No 867.

18 HA 1996 ss201, 217.

19 HA 1996 s185(1) and (2); H(W)A 2014 s61.

20 HA 1996 s185(2A); H(W)A 2014 Sch 2 para 1(3). Allocation of Housing and Homelessness (Eligibility) (England) Regulations ('Eligibility Regs') 2006 SI No 1294 and Allocation of Housing and Homelessness (Eligibility) (Wales) Regulations ('Welsh Eligibility Regs') 2014 SI No 2603.

21 HA 1996 s185(3); H(W)A 2014 Sch 2 para 1(2). See Eligibility Regs 2006 and Welsh Eligibility Regs 2014, above.

abroad – may be able to obtain assistance under local authority social service powers.

2.18 When deciding whether an eligible applicant is homeless or in priority need, provision is made governing whether persons who are themselves ineligible and subject to immigration control, and who either do not have leave to enter or remain in the UK or have leave subject to a condition of no recourse to public funds may be taken into account.[22] Such persons are not taken into account if (but only if) the applicant is him- or herself subject to immigration control (not including European Economic Area (EEA) and Swiss nationals for this purpose);[23] where reliance by an applicant is placed on such an ineligible member of his or her household, the case is known as a 'restricted case' and there are discrete provisions governing how a duty is to be discharged.[24]

Information

2.19 In order to reach a decision on the issue of eligibility, a local housing authority may seek such information as it requires from the secretary of state, who is bound to provide it (and, whether or not the original request for information was in writing, to provide it in writing if the authority, in writing, asks for it so to be provided).[25]

2.20 The secretary of state is under an additional duty to notify the authority in writing if it subsequently appears to him or her that any application, decision or other change of circumstance has affected the status of a person about whom he or she had previously provided information.[26]

Homelessness

2.21 A person is homeless for the purposes of HA 1996 Part 7 or H(W)A 2014 Part 2 if the person has no accommodation in the UK or elsewhere in the world, which is available for his or her occupation,[27] and which he or she is:

a) entitled to occupy by virtue of an interest in it (for example, as tenant or owner or under an equitable interest); or

22 HA 1996 s185(7); H(W)A 2014 s63.
23 HA 1996 s185(5); H(W)A 2014 s63.
24 HA 1996 s193(7AA); H(W)A 2014 s76.
25 HA 1996 s187(1) and (2); H(W)A 2014 Sch 2 para 3.
26 HA 1996 s187(3); H(W)A 2014 Sch 2 para 3.
27 HA 1996 s175(1); H(W)A 2014 s55.

b) entitled to occupy by virtue of a court order (for example, in the course of domestic proceedings); or
c) entitled to occupy by virtue of an express or implied licence (for example, friendly or family arrangement, contractual licence); or
d) actually occupying as a residence, 'by virtue of any enactment or rule of law giving him the right to remain in occupation or restricting the right of any other person to recover possession of it' (for example, between termination of tenancy and order for possession).[28]

Available accommodation

2.22 Accommodation is only available for an applicant's occupation if it is available for the applicant, together with any other person who normally resides with the applicant as a member of his or her family, and any other person who might reasonably be expected to reside with the applicant.[29]

Reasonable to continue to occupy

2.23 Accommodation is disregarded if it is not accommodation which it would be reasonable to continue to occupy,[30] for example, if it is in such bad condition that no one could be expected to stay in it. When deciding whether or not it would be reasonable for a person to remain in occupation, an authority to which application has been made may take into account the general housing circumstances prevailing in its area,[31] ie, to what extent others are having to live in bad conditions.

Violence/abuse

2.24 It is also not reasonable to continue to occupy accommodation if it is probable that to do so will lead to violence (domestic or otherwise) – or, in Wales, abuse – against the applicant, or against someone who normally resides with the applicant as a member of his or her family, or against anyone else who might reasonably be expected to reside with the applicant.[32]

2.25 'Violence' means violence from another person, or threats of violence from another person which are likely to be carried out.[33] 'Abuse'

28 HA 1996 s175(1); H(W)A 2014 s55.
29 HA 1996 s176; H(W)A 2014 s56.
30 HA 1996 s175(3); H(W)A 2014 s57.
31 HA 1996 s177(2); H(W)A 2014 s57.
32 HA 1996 s177(1); H(W)A 2014 s58.
33 HA 1996 s177(1A).

means physical violence, threatening or intimidating behaviour and any other form of abuse which, directly or indirectly, may give rise to the risk of harm.[34]

Domestic violence/abuse

2.26 Violence and abuse are domestic if from a person who is 'associated' with the victim.[35]

Associated people

2.27 People are associated if:

a) they are or have been married to each other;
b) they are or have been civil partners of each other;
c) they are cohabitants or former cohabitants (meaning a man and a woman who are living together without being married to one another, or two people of the same sex who are living together without being civil partners) or, in Wales, they live or have lived together in an enduring family relationship (whether they are of different sexes or the same sex);
d) they live or have lived in the same household;
e) they are relatives, meaning:
   i) parent, step-parent, child, stepchild, grandparent or grandchild of a person or of that person's spouse, civil partner, former spouse or former civil partner; or
   ii) sibling, aunt or uncle, niece or nephew of a person or that person's spouse, civil partner, former spouse or former civil partner, whether of full- or half-blood, or by marriage or civil partnership;
f) they have agreed to marry (whether or not that agreement has been terminated);
g) they have entered into a civil partnership agreement between them (whether or not that agreement has been terminated);
h) in relation to a child, each of the persons is a parent of the child, or has or has had parental responsibility (within the meaning of the Children Act (CA) 1989) for the child;
i) in relation to a child who has been adopted (or subsequently freed from adoption), if one person is a natural parent or natural parent of a natural parent, and the other is the child, or is a person who has become a parent by adoption, or who has applied for an

34 H(W)A 2014 s58(1).
35 HA 1996 s177(1A); see H(W)A 2014 s58(1).

adoption order, or with whom the child was at any time placed for adoption;[36] or

j) in Wales, the people have or have had an intimate personal relationship with each other which is or was of significant duration.[37]

Unusable accommodation

2.28 In addition, a person is homeless if the person has accommodation which he or she occupies or is entitled to occupy, and which is available for his or her occupation and reasonable to continue to occupy, but:

a) the person cannot secure entry to it; or
b) the accommodation consists of a movable structure, vehicle or vessel, designed or adapted for living in, and there is no place where the person is entitled or permitted both to place it and to reside in it (for example, houseboat or caravan).[38]

Threatened with homelessness

2.29 A person is threatened with homelessness if it is likely that the person will become homeless within 28 days (England) or 56 days (Wales).[39] Once HRA 2017 comes into force, the period of 56 days already applicable in Wales will also apply in England.[40] In addition, an assured shorthold tenant served with a valid notice under HA 1988 s21, in respect of the only accommodation which that person has which is available for his or her occupation, and which will expire within 56 days, will also be threatened with homelessness.[41]

Priority need

2.30 A person has a priority need for accommodation if the authority is satisfied that:

a) the person has dependent children who are residing with, or who might reasonably be expected to reside with, the person, for

36 HA 1996 s178, as amended by Civil Partnership Act 2004 Sch 8; H(W)A 2014 s58.
37 H(W)A 2014 s58(2)(h).
38 HA 1996 s175(2); H(W)A 2014 s55.
39 HA 1996 s175(4); in Wales, 56 days, see H(W)A 2014 s55.
40 HRA 2017 s1; HA 1996 s175(4) as amended.
41 HRA 2017 s1; HA 1996 s175(5) as added.

example, because the family is separated solely because of the need for accommodation; or

b) the person is homeless or threatened with homelessness as a result of any emergency such as flood, fire or any other disaster; or

c) the person, or any person who resides or who might reasonably be expected to reside with the person, is vulnerable – in England, this is vulnerability because of old age, mental illness, handicap or physical disability or other special reason; while in Wales it is because of some special reason of which those causes are illustrative; or

d) she is pregnant, or is a person who resides or might reasonably be expected to reside with a pregnant woman.[42]

2.31 In England, the secretary of state may specify further classes of person as having a priority need for accommodation, or amend or repeal any of the present classes.[43]

2.32 The following additional classes have been so specified:[44]

a) all 16- and 17-year-olds, provided they are not a relevant child, or a child to whom the local authority owes a duty to provide accommodation under the CA 1989 s20;[45]

b) any person who is aged 18 to 20, other than a relevant student,[46] who at any time after reaching the age of 16 but while still under 18 was, but is no longer, looked after, accommodated or fostered;[47]

c) those who are vulnerable because they have previously been looked after, accommodated or fostered;

d) those who are vulnerable as a result of service in Her Majesty's regular armed forces;

e) those who are vulnerable as a result of having served a custodial sentence, having been committed for contempt of court or having been remanded in custody;

42 HA 1996 s189(1); H(W)A 2014 s70(1)(a)–(d). Vulnerability has its own statutory definition in Wales: H(W)A 2014 s71.

43 HA 1996 s189(2).

44 Homelessness (Priority Need for Accommodation) (England) Order 2002 SI No 2051.

45 As defined by CA 1989 s23A. Relevant children remain the responsibility of social service authorities.

46 As defined by CA 1989 s24B(3).

47 The phrase 'looked after, accommodated or fostered' has the meaning given by CA 1989 s24(2).

f) those who are vulnerable because they have had to cease to occupy accommodation because of violence or threats of violence which are likely to be carried out.

2.33 In Wales, while there is power for the Welsh Ministers to add categories,[48] there are also additional categories of person who have a priority need which is defined in the legislation itself:[49]

a) a person who is homeless as a result of being subject to domestic abuse, or with whom someone other than the abuser resides, or someone who is reasonably to be expected to reside with him or her;
b) a person aged 16 or 17 when application is made or who resides or might reasonably to be expected to reside with him or her;
c) a person who has attained the age of 18 when application is made, but not the age of 21, who is at particular risk of sexual or financial exploitation, or someone other than the exploiter or potential exploiter who resides, or someone who is reasonably to be expected to reside with him or her;
d) a person who has attained the age of 18 when application is made, but not the age of 21, who was looked after, accommodated or fostered at any time while under the age of 18, or who resides or might reasonably to be expected to reside with him or her;
e) a person who has served in the regular armed forces of the Crown who has been homeless since leaving those forces, or who resides or might reasonably to be expected to reside with him or her;
f) a person who has a local connection with the area of the local housing authority and who is vulnerable as a result of having served a custodial sentence within the meaning of section 76 of the Powers of Criminal Courts (Sentencing) Act 2000, having been remanded in or committed to custody by an order of a court, or having been remanded to youth detention accommodation under section 91(4) of the Legal Aid, Sentencing and Punishment of Offenders Act (LASPO) 2012.

Intentional homelessness

2.34 A person becomes intentionally homeless if the person deliberately does or fails to do anything in consequence of which he or she ceases

48 H(W)A 2014 s72.
49 H(W)A 2014 s70(1)(e)–(j).

to occupy accommodation which is available for occupation, and which it would have been reasonable to continue to occupy.[50]

2.35 A person becomes threatened with homelessness intentionally if the person deliberately does or fails to do anything, the likely result of which is that he or she will be forced to leave accommodation which is available for occupation, and which it would have been reasonable to continue to occupy.[51]

2.36 These definitions incorporate a number of elements:

a) there must be a deliberate act or failure to act;
b) the act or omission must have a consequence;
c) the consequence must be that accommodation ceases or will cease to be occupied;
d) that accommodation must be or have been, 'accommodation available for [the] occupation' of the homeless person; and
e) it must have been reasonable to continue in occupation of that accommodation.

2.37 An act or omission in good faith, on the part of a person who was unaware of any relevant fact (for example, the availability of financial assistance towards rent, the right to remain in occupation after notice of seeking possession, notice to quit or expiry of tenancy), is not to be treated as deliberate for these purposes.[52] In Wales local housing authorities must decide whether to apply the intentionality test at all in their areas and can only be applied once the authority have notified the Welsh Government that the test will apply and have published a notice to this effect.[53] Moreover, the test may only be applied to categories of applicant specified by the Welsh Ministers, although currently all the priority need categories are so specified,[54]

Collusive arrangements

2.38 In addition, a person becomes homeless intentionally or threatened with homelessness intentionally if the person enters into an arrangement under which he or she is required to cease to occupy accommodation, which it would have been reasonable for him or her to continue to occupy, the purpose of which arrangement is to enable

50 HA 1996 s191(1); H(W)A 2014 s77(2).
51 HA 1996 s196(1).
52 HA 1996 ss191(2) and 196(2); H(W)A 2014 s77(3).
53 H(W)A 2014 s78.
54 Homelessness (Intentionality) (Specified Categories) (Wales) Regulations 2015 SI No 1265.

the person to qualify for assistance under HA 1996 Part 7 or H(W)A 2014 Part 2, and there is no other, or independent, good reason for the actual or threatened homelessness.[55]

Local connection

2.39 A person has a local connection with an area if:

a) the person is or was as a matter of choice normally resident in it; or
b) the person is employed in the area; or
c) the person has family associations with the area; or
d) there are other special circumstances which result in a local connection with the area.[56]

2.40 Once HRA 2017 is brought into force, there will in England be additional provisions applicable to those towards whom a social services authority in England has a duty under CA 1989 s23C, as a former relevant child.[57] So long as an authority in England has such a duty, then, if the authority is a local housing authority as well as a social services authority the former relevant child is deemed to have a local connection with its area, and, if the authority is not a local housing authority, with every district in its area. Further, where accommodation for a child in care has been provided under CA 1989 s22A, so that the child is normally resident in the district of a local housing authority for a continuous period of at all least two years, some or all of which falls before he or she turns 16, he or she is likewise deemed to have a local connection with that district,[58] although ceases to do so once he or she turns 21 (unless a local connection can be established on any of the other grounds for it).[59]

Residence of choice

2.41 Residence is not 'of choice' for these purposes if the person:[60]

a) became resident in it because the person or any person who might reasonably be expected to reside with him or her was detained

55 HA 1996 ss191(3) and 196(3); H(W)A 2014 s77(4).
56 HA 1996 s199(1); H(W)A 2014 s81.
57 HRA 2017 s8; HA 1996 s199(8), as added.
58 HRA 2017 s8; HA 1996 s199(9), as added.
59 HRA 2017 s8; HA 1996 s199(10), as added.
60 Residence arising from service in the armed forces was formerly also excluded, which remains the case for applications made before 1 December 2008.

under the authority of any Act of Parliament (for example, prison or mental hospital); or

b) became resident in it in such other circumstances as the secretary of state or the Welsh Ministers may specify.[61]

Employment

2.42 A person is not employed in an area if[62] the person falls within such other circumstances as the secretary of state or Welsh Ministers may specify.[63]

Former asylum-seekers

2.43 A person has a local connection with an area if the person was at any time provided with accommodation in that area under IAA 1999 s95, unless either the person was subsequently provided with accommodation in another local housing authority area under section 95, or else the accommodation was provided in an accommodation centre under Nationality, Immigration and Asylum Act (NIAA) 2002 s22.[64]

Preliminary duties

2.44 As the law currently stands, the preliminary duties described below arise where a person applies to a housing authority for accommodation, or for assistance in obtaining it,[65] and the authority has reason to believe that he or she may be homeless or threatened with homelessness.[66]

2.45 There is no requirement for any particular form of application, or even that the application should be in writing.

2.46 The three main preliminary duties are:

a) in England to make enquiries or, in Wales, to carry out an assessment of the applicant's case;
b) to notify the applicant of the decision; and

61 HA 1996 s199(3), (5); H(W)A 2014 s81(3), (4).

62 Employment in the armed forces was formerly also excluded, which remains the case for applications made before 1 December 2008.

63 HA 1996 s199(5); H(W)A 2014 s81(4)(a). This power has not been exercised to date.

64 HA 1996 s199(6) and (7), added by Asylum and Immigration (Treatment of Claimants, etc) Act 2004 s11. Note that NIAA 2002 s22 has not yet been brought into effect.

65 In Wales, help in retaining or obtaining accommodation: H(W)A 2014 s62.

66 HA 1996 s184(1).

c) in the case of an eligible homeless person in priority need,[67] to accommodate pending the outcome of enquiries and the notification.

Enquiries/assessment

2.47 Where an English authority has reason to believe that there may be actual or threatened homelessness, then it must make enquiries:

a) such as are necessary to satisfy it whether the applicant is eligible for assistance; and
b) if so, whether any, and what, duties are owed to the person under HA 1996 Part 7.[68]

2.48 The authority may also make further enquiries as to whether there is a local connection with the district of another authority.[69] Local connection enquiries about another area precede any enquiries made by an authority into the applicant's connection with its own area.

2.49 In Wales, if it appears to the authority that an applicant may be homeless or threatened with homelessness, it must carry out an assessment of his or her case.[70] The assessment must consider whether the applicant is eligible.[71] If the applicant is eligible, the assessment must then address:

a) how the applicant has become homeless or threatened with homelessness;
b) his or her housing needs and those of anyone with whom he or she lives or might reasonably be expected to live;
c) the support required to meet those needs; and
d) whether or not the authority has any duty under H(W)A 2014 Part 2 to the applicant.[72]

2.50 The assessment must seek to identify what the applicant wishes to achieve with the authority's help and the authority must consider whether the exercise of any of its powers under Part 2 can contribute to that outcome.[73] The assessment must be kept under review.[74]

67 In some circumstances, after the commencement of LA 2011, this may include people who are not in priority need.
68 HA 1996 s184(1).
69 HA 1996 s184(2).
70 H(W)A 2014 s62(1), (4), (5).
71 H(A)A 2014 s62(3).
72 H(W)A 2014 s62(5).
73 H(W)A 2014 s62(6).
74 H(W)A 2014 s62(8), (9).

Notification of decision

2.51 If an English authority is not satisfied as to eligibility, it need not proceed to make any further enquiries. If it does make further enquiries, then the authority must, on completion, notify the applicant of its decision and 'so far as any issue is decided against [the applicant's] interests' inform the applicant of the reasons for it.[75]

2.52 If the decision is to notify another authority under the local connection provisions, the applicant must also be notified of this decision and its reasons.[76]

2.53 Notification must inform the applicant of the right to request a review (within 21 days).[77] Notification must be in writing. If the applicant does not receive the notification, the applicant will be treated as having done so if the notice is made available at the authority's office for a reasonable period, for collection by or on behalf of the applicant,[78] ie, the burden is on the applicant who does not receive the decision to go to the authority's office and ask for it.

2.54 In Wales the authority must notify the applicant of the outcome of the assessment (and of any review) and, insofar as any issue is decided against his or her interests, give reasons for the decision.[79] It must also inform the applicant or his or her right to request a review.[80] Additional notification duties[81] apply where a duty under H(W)A 2014 s75 is owed only because of a restricted person or where the authority has already notified or intends to notify another authority under the local connection provisions.

Accommodation pending decision

2.55 The duty to secure that accommodation is made available pending a decision arises if the authority has reason to believe that the applicant may be homeless, and eligible for assistance, and in priority need.[82]

75 HA 1996 s184(3).
76 HA 1996 s184.
77 HA 1996 s184(5).
78 HA 1996 s184(6).
79 H(W)A 2014 s63(1).
80 H(W)A 2014 s63(4).
81 H(W)A 2014 s63(2), (3). The notification must inform the applicant of his or her right to a review and is to be given in writing; if not received by the applicant, it is to be treated as having been received if it is made available at the authority's office for a reasonable period for collection: H(W)A 2014 s63(4).
82 HA 1996 s188(1); H(W)A 2014 s68.

2.56 From commencement of LA 2011 s149 in England, an English authority's duty to house pending a decision also arises – even if there is no apparent priority need – if the authority has reason to believe that the application is a second application, following a previous application in the preceding two years which resulted in an assured shorthold tenancy which has come to an end, provided that the applicant is still eligible, and did not become homeless intentionally.[83]

2.57 The obligation is imposed on the authority to which the application has been made, whether or not the applicant may have a local connection with another authority.[84]

2.58 The accommodation must be made available for the applicant and for any other family member who normally resides with, or anyone else who might reasonably be expected to reside with, the applicant.[85]

2.59 The duty ceases on notification of a decision, even if the applicant requests a review, although the authority still has power to house pending the review.[86]

Principal duties

2.60 The extent of an authority's duty depends on its decision. Duties may be considered as:

a) limited duties; and
b) full duties.

Limited duties

Initial assessment and plan – England

2.61 Once HRA 2017 comes into force in England, there will be a new duty of assessment applicable to all applicants whom an English authority is satisfied are homeless or threatened with homelessness and eligible for assistance:[87] it therefore arises at a later stage than the corresponding Welsh duty. The duty is to 'make an assessment of the applicant's case',[88] which must include an assessment of the circumstances which resulted in the applicant's homelessness or being

83 HA 1996 s188(1A). This right only arises on one re-application: HA 1996 s195A(6).
84 HA 1996 s188(2); H(W)A 2014 s68(4).
85 HA 1996 ss176 and 188(1); H(W)A 2014 s56.
86 HA 1996 s188(2) and (3); H(W)A 2014 s69.
87 HRA 2017 s3(1); HA 1996 s189A.
88 HRA 2017 s3(1); HA 1996 s189A(1).

threatened with homelessness, his or her housing needs, and his or her needs for support[89] in order to be able to have and retain suitable accommodation.[90] The authority have to notify the applicant in writing of the assessment it makes.[91]

2.62 The authority must try to agree with the applicant what steps he or she is to be required to take in order to secure that he or she[92] has and is able to retain suitable accommodation, and what steps the authority are to take under HA 1996 Part 7 for those purposes.[93] If the authority and the applicant reach an agreement, the authority have to record it in writing.[94] If they cannot do so, the authority have to record in writing why they could not agree, what steps it considers it would be reasonable to require the applicant to take, and what steps the authority is to take under Part 7, for those purposes.[95] Either class of record can include any advice the authority consider appropriate, including as to steps which the authority think it would be 'a good idea for the applicant to take', albeit that he or she is not to be required to take.[96] The authority has to give the applicant a copy of the written record.[97]

2.63 Until the authority decides that it owes the applicant no duty under any of the remaining provisions of Part 7, the authority has to keep the assessment under review, together with the appropriateness of any agreement reached or steps recorded.[98] If the assessment of the mandatory considerations (circumstances resulting in homelessness or being threatened with homelessness, housing needs and needs for support) changes, the authority must notify the applicant, in writing, of how its assessment has changed (whether by providing a revised written assessment or otherwise); the same is true if the authority's assessment otherwise changes in a way that it considers it appropriate to notify the applicant.[99] If the authority considers that any

89 Together with anyone with whom he or she resides or might reasonably be expected to reside.
90 HRA 2017 s3(1); HA 1996 s189A(2).
91 HRA 2017 s3(1); HA 1996 s189A(3).
92 Together with anyone with whom he or she resides or might reasonably be expected to reside.
93 HRA 2017 s3(1); HA 1996 s189A(4).
94 HRA 2017 s3(1); HA 1996 s189A(5).
95 HRA 2017 s3(1); HA 1996 s189A(6).
96 HRA 2017 s3(1); HA 1996 s189A(7).
97 HRA 2017 s3(1); HA 1996 s189A(8).
98 HRA 2017 s3(1); HA 1996 s189A(9).
99 HRA 2017 s3(1); HA 1996 s189A(10).

agreement reached or any step recorded under is no longer appropriate, it must so notify the applicant in writing to this effect and that any subsequent failure to take a step that was agreed or recorded is to be disregarded.[100]

Duties to those threatened with homelessness

2.64 Once HRA 2017 comes into force, a new duty will be imposed on authorities in England in all cases where the authority is satisfied that an applicant is threatened with homelessness and eligible for assistance,[101] in place of the existing provisions of HA 1996 s195 which are only applicable to those who are threatened with homelessness and in priority need; there is no equivalent in Wales, as the duty to assess covers those who are threatened with homelessness as much as those who are already homeless.

2.65 Under the new duty, the authority will be obliged to take reasonable steps to help the applicant to secure that accommodation does not cease to be available for his or her occupation.[102] In deciding what steps to take, the authority has to have regard to its assessment of the applicant's case.[103]

2.66 The authority will be able to give notice to bring this duty to an end when it is satisfied that any one of the following circumstances is applicable.[104]

a) The applicant both has suitable accommodation which is available for his or her occupation and there is a reasonable prospect of him or having suitable accommodation available for at least six months from the date of the notice.
b) The authority has complied with the duty to take reasonable steps and the period of 56 days beginning with the day that the authority is first satisfied that the applicant is threatened with homeless and eligible has ended (whether or not he or she is still threatened with homelessness).
c) The applicant has become homeless.
d) The applicant has refused an offer of suitable accommodation and, on the date of refusal, there was a reasonable prospect that suitable accommodation would be available for occupation by the

100 HRA 2017 s3(1); HA 1996 s189A(11).
101 HRA 2017 s4; HA 1996 s195(1).
102 HRA 2017 s4; HA 1996 s195(2).
103 HRA 2017 s4; HA 1996 s195(3).
104 HRA 2017 s4; HA 1996 s195(5), (8).

applicant for at least six months or such longer period as may be prescribed.

e) The applicant has become homeless intentionally from any accommodation that has been made available to him or her as a result of the authority's exercise of its functions under this duty.

f) The applicant is no longer eligible for assistance.

g) The applicant has withdrawn the application for accommodation or assistance in obtaining it.

2.67 The notice must specify which of the circumstances applies and inform the applicant that he or she has a right to request a review of the decision to bring the duty to an end and of the time within which such a request must be made.[105] The duty can also be brought to an end under HA 1996 s193B (deliberate and unreasonable refusal to co-operate)[106] although this will not end a right to accommodation for an applicant who is homeless, eligible, in priority need and not homeless intentionally.[107]

2.68 HA 1996 s193B applies where the authority gives notice that it considers that the applicant has deliberately and unreasonably refused to take any step that he or she agreed to take or that was recorded by the authority under the assessment and plan provisions.[108] When deciding whether a refusal is unreasonable, the authority must have regard to the particular circumstances and needs of the applicant (whether identified in its assessment of his or her case or not).[109] The notice must explain why the authority is giving it, its effect and inform the applicant that he or she has a right to request a review of the decision to give the notice and of the time within which such a request must be made.[110] No notice may be given without a prior 'relevant warning' notice[111] and a reasonable period[112] must have elapsed since it was given.[113] The notice must be in writing, and, if not received by the

105 HRA 2017 s4; HA 1996 s195(7).

106 HRA 2017 s4; HA 1996 s195(10).

107 HRA 2017 s7(1); HA 1996 s193C(3), (4).

108 HRA 2017 s7(1); HA 1996 s193B(1), (2).

109 HRA 2017 s7(1); HA 1996 s193B(6).

110 HRA 2017 s7(1); HA 1996 s193B(3).

111 This is a notice given by the authority after the refusal to take the agreed or recorded step, which warns the applicant that, if he or she continues deliberately and unreasonably to refuse to take the step after receiving the notice, the authority intends to give the notice which will bring the duty to an end, and which explains the consequences of that notice: HRA 2017 s7(1); HA 1996 s193B(5).

112 This is not defined.

113 HRA 2017 s7(1); HA 1996 s193B(4).

applicant, is to be treated as having been given if made available at the authority's office for a reasonable period for collection by or on his or her behalf of the applicant.[114] The secretary of state may make provision by regulations as to the procedure to be followed in connection with notices under this section.[115]

Initial help duty

2.69 In Wales, there is an initial duty to be found in H(W)A 2014 s73. The duty does not arise if there is a local connection referral to another authority in England or Wales.[116] If an authority is satisfied that an applicant is homeless and eligible for assistance, whether or not he or she has a priority need or may be homeless intentionally, it must help to secure that accommodation is available for the applicant.[117] The duty requires the authority to take reasonable steps to help, having regard to (among other things) the need to make the best use of its resources.[118] It does not require the authority to offer accommodation, whether under HA 1996 Part 6 or otherwise.[119]

2.70 The duty only lasts for 56 days[120] although the authority can decide on a shorter period if reasonable steps to secure accommodation for the applicant have been taken.[121] Moreover, the duty will come to an end before the end of that period if one of the following occurs:

a) the authority is satisfied that the applicant has suitable accommodation available for occupation, which accommodation is likely to be available for occupation by the applicant for a period of at least six months;[122]
b) the applicant refuses an offer of accommodation from any person, having been notified in writing of the possible consequences of refusal or acceptance of the offer, provided that the authority is satisfied that the accommodation was suitable for the applicant and was likely to be available for at least the next six months;[123]
c) the applicant ceases to be eligible;[124]

114 HRA 2017 s7(1); HA 1996 s193B(8).
115 HRA 2017 s7(1); HA 1996 s193B(7).
116 H(W)A 2014 s80(1).
117 H(W)A 2014 s73.
118 H(W)A 2014 s65(a).
119 H(W)A 2014 s65(b)–(c).
120 H(W)A 2014 s74(2).
121 H(W)A 2014 s74(3).
122 H(W)A 2014 s74(4).
123 H(W)A 2014 s74(5).
124 H(W)A 2014 s79(2).

d) a mistake of fact led the authority to notify the applicant that it owed him or her a duty to help to secure accommodation for the applicant;[125]
e) the applicant has withdrawn the application;[126]
f) the applicant is unreasonably failing to co-operate with the authority.[127]

2.71 Once HRA 2017 comes into force, there will be a similar time-limited duty applicable in England, where the authority is satisfied that an applicant is homeless and eligible for assistance;[128] the duty will not arise where the authority refers the application to another local housing authority in England under the local connection provisions. The duty is to take reasonable steps to help the applicant to secure that suitable accommodation becomes available for his or her occupation for at least six months or such longer period[129] as may be prescribed.[130] In deciding what steps to take, the authority must have regard to its assessment of the applicant's case.[131]

2.72 Where the authority is satisfied that the applicant has a priority need and is not satisfied that the applicant became homeless intentionally, the duty comes to an end 56 days following the day the authority was first satisfied that the applicant was homeless and eligible.[132] The authority may also give notice bringing the duty to an end when it is satisfied that any one of certain circumstances is applicable.[133] The circumstances are as follows.[134]

a) The applicant both has suitable accommodation which is available for his or her occupation and there is a reasonable prospect of him or her having suitable accommodation available for at least six months from the date of the notice.
b) The authority has complied with the duty to take reasonable steps and the period of 56 days beginning with the day that the authority is first satisfied that the applicant was homeless and eligible has ended (whether or not he or she has secured accommodation).

125 H(W)A 2014 s79(3).
126 H(W)A 2014 s79(4).
127 H(W)A 2014 s79(5).
128 HRA 2017 s5(2); HA 1996 s189B(1).
129 Not exceeding 12 months.
130 HRA 2017 s5(2); HA 1996 s189B(2).
131 HRA 2017 s5(2); HA 1996 s189B(3).
132 HRA 2017 s5(2); HA 1996 s189B(4).
133 HRA 2017 s5(2); HA 1996 s189B(5).
134 HRA 2017 s5(2); HA 1996 s189B(7).

c) The applicant has refused an offer of suitable accommodation and, on the date of refusal, there was a reasonable prospect that suitable accommodation would be available for occupation by the applicant for at least six months or such longer period as may be prescribed.
d) The applicant has become homeless intentionally from any accommodation that has been made available to him or her as a result of the authority's exercise of its functions under this duty.
e) The applicant is no longer eligible for assistance.
f) The applicant has withdrawn the application for accommodation or assistance in obtaining it.

2.73 The notice must specify which of the circumstances applies and inform the applicant that he or she has a right to request a review of the decision to bring the duty to an end and of the time within which such a request must be made.[135] The duty can also be brought to an end under HA 1996 s193A (refusal of final offer) or s193B (unreasonable refusal to co-operate), although – by s193C – the latter will not end a right to accommodation for an applicant who is homeless, eligible, in priority need and not homeless intentionally.[136] If a final accommodation offer[137] or a final HA 1996 Part 6 offer[138] is refused, then the principal duty under s193 does not arise.[139] The authority cannot approve a final accommodation offer or make a final Part 6 offer unless it is satisfied that it is suitable for the applicant;[140] nor can it approve or make such an offer if the applicant is under contractual or other obligations in respect of his or her existing accommodation, which he or she is not able to bring to an end before he or she would have to take up the offer.[141]

135 HRA 2017 s5; HA 1996 s189B(6).
136 HRA 2017 s7(1); HA 1996 s193C(3), (4).
137 An offer of an assured shorthold tenancy made by a private landlord – including a private registered provider of social housing (England) or a registered social landlord (Wales) – in relation to any accommodation which is, or may become, available for the applicant's occupation, made, with the approval of the authority, in pursuance of arrangements made by the authority in discharge of the initial help duty, which is a fixed-term tenancy for a period of at least six months: HRA 2017 s7(1); HA 1996 s193A(4).
138 An offer of accommodation under HA 1996 Part 6 made in writing in discharge of the authority's initial help duty, which states that it is a final offer for that purpose: HRA 2017 s7(1); HA 1996 s193A(5).
139 HRA 2017 s7(1); HA 1996 s193A(3).
140 HRA 2017 s7(1); HA 1996 s193A(6).
141 HRA 2017 s7(1); HA 1996 s193A(7).

Threatened with homelessness

England

2.74 If an English authority is satisfied that an applicant is threatened with homelessness and eligible for assistance, the duties in HA 1996 s195 apply. The duties apply even though an issue of local connection may apply. If the authority is not satisfied that the applicant has a priority need, or is satisfied that he or she has a priority need but is also satisfied that he or she became threatened with homelessness intentionally, it must provide him or her, or secure that he or she is provided with, advice and assistance in any attempts he or she may make to secure that accommodation does not cease to be available for his or her occupation.[142] Before doing so, the applicant's housing needs must be assessed;[143] the advice and assistance must include information about the likely availability in the authority's district of types of accommodation appropriate to the applicant's housing needs, including, in particular, the location and sources of such types of accommodation.[144]

2.75 If the authority owes this duty because it is satisfied that the applicant has a priority need but became threatened with homelessness intentionally, of which decision the applicant seeks a review, the authority may secure that accommodation does not cease to be available for his or her occupation and, if he or she becomes homeless, secure that accommodation is available pending the decision on review.[145] If the authority is not satisfied that the applicant has a priority need, nor satisfied that he or she became threatened with homelessness intentionally, the authority has power to take reasonable steps to secure that accommodation does not cease to be available for the applicant's occupation.[146] Since LA 2011 s149(2), came into force in England, this duty may also arise even if there is no longer any priority need if the applicant becomes threatened with homelessness again within two years of acceptance of the previous offer.

2.76 If the authority is satisfied that the applicant has a priority need, and not satisfied that he or she became threatened with homelessness intentionally, it must take reasonable steps to secure that accommodation does not cease to be available for his or her

142 HA 1996 s195(5).
143 HA 1996 s195(6).
144 HA 1996 s195(7).
145 HA 1996 s195(8).
146 HA 1996 s195(9).

occupation.[147] The obligation is without prejudice to the authority's right to recover possession of any accommodation so that it cannot be used as a defence to proceedings brought for possession of an authority's own housing.[148]

2.77 Once HRA 2017 comes into force, in England, a new duty will be imposed on authorities in all cases where the authority is satisfied that an applicant is threatened with homelessness and eligible for assistance,[149] in place of the foregoing provisions. The authority will be obliged to take reasonable steps to help the applicant to secure that accommodation does not cease to be available for his or her occupation.[150] In deciding what steps to take, the authority has to have regard to its assessment of the applicant's case.[151] As before, obligation is without prejudice to the authority's right to recover possession of any accommodation.[152]

2.78 The authority will be able to give notice bringing this duty to an end when it is satisfied that any one of the following circumstances is applicable.[153]

a) The applicant both has suitable accommodation which is available for his or her occupation and there is a reasonable prospect of him or having suitable accommodation available for at least six months[154] from the date of the notice.
b) The authority has complied with the duty to take reasonable steps and the period of 56 days beginning with the day that the authority is first satisfied that the applicant is threatened with homelessness and eligible has ended (whether or not he or she is still threatened with homelessness).[155]
c) The applicant has become homeless.[156]

147 HA 1996 s195(2).
148 HA 1996 s195(3).
149 HRA 2017 s4; HA 1996 s195(1).
150 HRA 2017 s4; HA 1996 s195(2).
151 HRA 2017 s4; HA 1996 s195(3).
152 HRA 2017 s4; HA 1996 s195(4).
153 HRA 2017 s4; HA 1996 s195(5), (8).
154 Or such longer period not exceeding 12 months as may be prescribed.
155 The authority cannot give notice to the applicant in this circumstances if a valid notice has been given to the applicant under HA 1988 s21 which will expire within 56 days or has expired and is in respect of the only accommodation that is available for his or her occupation: HRA 2017 s4; HA 1996 s195(6).
156 So that the initial help duty will apply.

d) The applicant has refused an offer of suitable accommodation and, on the date of refusal, there was a reasonable prospect that suitable accommodation would be available for occupation by the applicant for at least six months or such longer period[157] as may be prescribed.
e) The applicant has become homeless intentionally from any accommodation that has been made available to him or her as a result of the authority's exercise of its functions under this duty.
f) The applicant is no longer eligible for assistance.
g) The applicant has withdrawn the application for accommodation or assistance in obtaining it.

2.79 The notice must specify which of the circumstances applies and inform the applicant that he or she has a right to request a review of the decision to bring the duty to an end and of the time within which such a request must be made.[158] The notice must be in writing, and, if not received by the applicant, is to be treated as having been given if made available at the authority's office for a reasonable period for collection by or on his or her behalf of the applicant.[159]

2.80 The duty will be able to be brought to an end under HA 1996 s193B (deliberate and unreasonable refusal to co-operate),[160] although this will not end a right to accommodation for an applicant who is homeless, eligible, in priority need and not homeless intentionally.[161]

Wales

2.81 In Wales, if an authority is satisfied that an applicant is eligible and threatened with homelessness, the duty to help comes into play, to help to secure that accommodation does not cease to be available to the applicant.[162] This duty cannot be used to prevent the authority itself obtaining vacant possession of any accommodation; accordingly, it cannot be raised as a defence by a tenant in possession proceedings by the authority.[163] The duty requires the authority to take reasonable steps to help, having regard to (amongst other things) the need to make the best use of its resources.[164] It does not require the

157 Not exceeding 12 months.
158 HRA 2017 s4; HA 1996 s195(7).
159 HRA 2017 s4; HA 1996 s195(9).
160 HRA 2017 s4; HA 1996 s195(10).
161 HRA 2017 s7(1); HA 1996 s193C(3), (4).
162 H(W)A 2014 s66(1).
163 H(W)A 2014 s66(2).
164 H(W)A 2014 s65(a).

authority to offer accommodation, whether under HA 1996 Part 6 or otherwise.[165]

2.82 An authority can help to secure that suitable accommodation does not cease to be available either by providing some form of assistance itself or arranging for someone else to provide it.[166] Examples in the H(W)A 2014 of what may be provided or arranged are: mediation; grants or loans; guarantees; support in management of debt, mortgage or rent arrears; security measures for applicants at risk of abuse; advocacy or other representation; accommodation; information and advice; and other services, goods or facilities.[167]

2.83 The authority can give notice[168] bringing this duty to and end if the authority is satisfied that:[169]

a) the applicant has become homeless;[170]
b) the applicant is no longer threatened with homelessness and suitable accommodation is likely to remain available for his or her occupation for at least another six months;[171]
c) the applicant refuses an offer of accommodation – which the authority is satisfied was suitable and was likely to be available for at least the next six months – from any person, having been notified in writing of the possible consequences of refusal or acceptance of the offer;[172]
d) the applicant ceases to be eligible;[173]
e) a mistake of fact led to authority to notify the applicant that it owed him or her a duty to help to secure accommodation for the applicant;[174]
f) the applicant has withdrawn the application;[175] or
g) the applicant is unreasonably failing to co-operate with the authority.[176]

165 H(W)A 2014 ss65(b)–(c).
166 H(W)A 2014 s64(1).
167 H(W)A 2014 s64(2)
168 H(W)A 2014 s84.
169 H(W)A 2014 s67.
170 H(W)A 2014 s67(2).
171 H(W)A 2014 s67(3).
172 H(W)A 2014 s67(4).
173 H(W)A 2014 s79(2).
174 H(W)A 2014 s79(3).
175 H(W)A 2014 s79(4).
176 H(W)A 2014 s79(5).

Other duties without priority need

2.84 If an authority in England is satisfied that an applicant is homeless – whether intentionally[177] or unintentionally[178] – or threatened with homelessness (intentionally or not),[179] and eligible for assistance, but it is also satisfied that the applicant is not in priority need, it owes an advice and appropriate assistance duty to the applicant: the duty requires the authority to assess the applicant's housing needs and provide him or her (or secure that he or she is provided) with advice and assistance,[180] which must include information about the likely availability in the authority's area of types of accommodation appropriate to the applicant's housing needs, including the location and sources of such types of accommodation.[181] In Wales, the assessment and initial help duties include power to provide advice and assistance.[182]

2.85 From commencement of LA 2011 s149, however, an English authority also owes a full duty to secure accommodation, even if there is no priority need, if the application is a renewed application, following a previous application which resulted in an assured shorthold tenancy in the preceding two years, -provided that the applicant is still eligible, and did not become homeless intentionally.[183]

2.86 In addition, if the authority is satisfied that the applicant is unintentionally homeless although not in priority need, then although there is no duty to secure that accommodation is made available for occupation by the applicant, there is power to do so.[184] Likewise, an applicant not in priority need who is unintentionally threatened with homelessness may benefit from reasonable steps taken by the authority to secure that accommodation does not cease to be available for his or her occupation.[185] These powers are not needed in Wales, and will be repealed once HRA 2017 is brought into force in England,[186] as they are subsumed into assessment and plans and the initial help duty.

177 HA 1996 s190(3).
178 HA 1996 s192.
179 HA 1996 s195(5)(a).
180 HA 1996 s190(2)(b), (4).
181 HA 1996 s190(5), added by Homelessness Act 2002 Sch 1 para 10.
182 H(W)A 2014 s64(2)(h).
183 HA 1996 s195A(1). This right only arises on one re-application: HA 1996 s195A(6).
184 HA 1996 s190(3), as added by Homelessness Act 2002 s5.
185 HA 1996 s195(6).
186 HRA 2017 s5(6).

Other duties to the intentionally homeless

2.87 In England, if the authority is satisfied that an applicant is homeless, and in priority need of accommodation, but it is also satisfied that the applicant became homeless intentionally, it has the same duty as to those not in priority need, to assess the applicant's housing needs and provide him or her (or secure that he or she is provided) with advice and assistance.[187] Once HRA 2017 comes into force, this will only apply once the duty under initial help duty under HA 1996 s189B(2) has come to an end; when discharging it, an authority will have to have regard to its assessment under HA 1996 s189A.[188]

2.88 In addition, however, the authority must secure that suitable[189] accommodation is made available for the applicant's occupation[190] for such period as it considers will give him or her a reasonable opportunity of himself or herself securing accommodation for his or her own occupation.[191] If the authority provides its own accommodation, it will not be secure unless and until the authority notifies the applicant otherwise,[192] which it may not do except in accordance with the allocation provisions considered below. If the authority secures accommodation through a landlord whose tenants are not secure, then this accommodation will not be within any statutory protection at all for a year from when the authority first gave notification of its decision, or – if there is a review (or an appeal) – from its final determination, unless the tenant is notified by the landlord that it is to be regarded either as an assured shorthold or a fully assured tenancy.[193]

2.89 In Wales, the position is somewhat different. [194] First, the authority may have decided not to apply the intentionality provisions at all. If those provisions are still being applied, then the principal duty to accommodate under H(W)A 2014 s75, will arise either if the authority is not satisfied that the applicant is homeless intentionally or if the applicant is:

a) a pregnant woman or a person with whom she resides or might reasonably be expected to reside,

187 HA 1996 s190(2)(b), (4), (5).

188 HRA 2017 s3(2); HA 1996 s190(4) as substituted.

189 See HA 1996 ss205 and 206; H(W)A 2014 s59.

190 HA 1996 s176.

191 HA 1996 s190(2)(a).

192 HA 1985 Sch 1 para 4, substituted by HA 1996 Sch 17 para 3.

193 HA 1996 s209(2).

194 H(W)A 2014 s56.

b) a person with whom a dependent child resides or might reasonably be expected to reside,
c) a person who had not attained the age of 21 when the application was made or a person with whom such a person resides or might reasonably be expected to reside, or
d) a person who had attained the age of 21, but not the age of 25, when the application was made and who was looked after, accommodated or fostered at any time while under the age of 18, or a person with whom such a person resides or might reasonably be expected to reside.[195]

2.90 In these circumstances, the full duty will arise if the applicant has no suitable accommodation available for occupation, or suitable accommodation which it is not likely will be available for occupation for at least six months starting on the day on which the applicant is notified[196] that the full duty will not apply, the applicant is eligible for help and has a priority need for accommodation, and the authority has not previously secured an offer of accommodation to the applicant under these provisions following a previous application for help, at any time within the period of five years before the day on which the applicant was notified that a duty was owed to him or her under them. If the full duty does not arise for any of these reasons, or because the applicant is not within the H(W)A 2014 s75(3) class, then the initial duty to help is all that applies and it is limited to 56 days.[197]

Local connection provisions

2.91 The local connection provisions allow one housing authority to shift the burden of making accommodation available on to another housing authority. The provisions apply when the authority is satisfied that the applicant is homeless (not merely threatened with homelessness), in priority need, and not homeless intentionally, and either:

a) in England, the applicant was placed in accommodation in its area by another authority, in pursuance of HA 1996 Part 7 functions,

195 H(W)A 2014 s75(3).
196 Under H(W)A 2014 s84.
197 H(W)A 2014 s74(2).

within such period as may be prescribed[198] for this purpose;[199] or

b) in England and Wales, the authority considers that all of the following conditions apply:
   i) neither the applicant nor anyone who might reasonably be expected to reside with him or her has a local connection with its area; and
   ii) the applicant or a person who might reasonably be expected to reside with the applicant does have a local connection with the area of another housing authority; and
   iii) neither the applicant nor any person who might reasonably be expected to reside with the applicant will run the risk of domestic violence[200] in the area of the other authority.[201]

2.92 From commencement of LA 2011 s149 in England, the provisions also apply[202] if the application is made to an English authority within the period of two years beginning with the date on which the applicant accepted an offer from the other authority under HA 1996 s193(7AC) (private rented sector offer), and neither the applicant nor any person who might reasonably be expected to reside with the applicant will run the risk of domestic violence in the district of the other authority.[203]

2.93 In addition, a local connection referral may not be made where the applicant or any person who might reasonably be expected to reside with the applicant has suffered non-domestic violence in the area of the other authority and it is probable that the return to that area of the victim will lead to further violence of a similar kind against him or her.[204]

198 By the secretary of state under HA 1996 s215. The relevant period is five years from the date of the placement together with the time between the date the application was initially made and the time the placement first became available: Allocation of Housing and Homelessness (Miscellaneous Provisions) (England) Regulations 2006 SI No 2527.

199 HA 1996 s198(4).

200 In Wales, domestic abuse.

201 HA 1996 s198(1) and (2); H(W)A 2014 s80(1)–(3).

202 Assuming homelessness, priority need and no intentionality.

203 HA 1996 s198(2ZA) as amended.

204 HA 1996 s198(2A); H(W)A 2014 s84.

Violence and domestic violence

2.94 Violence and domestic violence are defined in the same terms as when determining whether or not it is reasonable to remain in occupation.[205]

Passing and retaining responsibility

2.95 The housing duty passes to the other authority if the conditions for referral are met.[206] The other authority's obligation is to house under HA 1996 s193.[207] The housing duty under HA 1996 s193 remains with the authority to which the application was made if the conditions are not met.[208]

Interim accommodation and notification

2.96 Pending determination of final responsibility, the authority to which the application is made must provide temporary accommodation.[209]

2.97 Once the issue has been decided, it is for the authority to notify the applicant of the decision and of the reasons for it, as well as of the applicant's right to request a review (and the time within which it must be requested).[210] Notification is effected in the same way as under HA 1996 s184(6) and H(W)A 2014 s84.[211] The temporary housing duty ceases when the notification is given, even if a review is requested, although the authority may continue to provide it pending review.[212]

Arbitration

2.98 HA 1996 Part 7 and H(W)A 2014 provide elaborate machinery for the determination of disputes between authorities, by agreement or, if necessary, by reference to an independent arbitrator.[213]

205 HA 1996 s198(3); H(W)A 2014 s58.

206 HA 1996 s200(4); H(W)A 2014 s82

207 The same provisions apply under HA 1996 s200(5) as to continuation of accommodation pending review as apply if the case is referred to the other authority: H(W)A 2014 s82.

208 HA 1996 s200(3); H(W)A 2014 s82.

209 HA 1996 s200(1); H(W)A 2014 s82.

210 HA 1996 s200(2); H(W)A 2014 s82.

211 HA 1996 s200(6); H(W)A 2014 s82. The notification must be in writing and, if not received by the applicant, it is to be treated as having been received if it is made available at the authority's office for a reasonable period for collection by or on his or her behalf: HA 1996 s200(6) (England); and ss82(2), (7) and 84(3), (4) (Wales).

212 HA 1996 s200(5); H(W)A 2014 s69(11).

213 HA 1996 s198(5); H(W)A 2014 s80(5).

2.99 An arbitration decision can itself be the subject of internal review, and thence appeal to the county court.[214]

Full duties

2.100 If the authority is satisfied that the applicant is homeless, eligible for assistance, in priority need, and not intentionally homeless, then its duty is (subject to the possibility of referral to another authority) to secure that accommodation is made available for his or her occupation (and, therefore, for any other family member who normally resides with, or anyone else who might reasonably be expected to reside with, the applicant).[215]

2.101 From commencement of LA 2011 s149 in England, an English authority also owes a full duty, even if there is no priority need, if the application is a renewed application, following a previous application which resulted in an assured shorthold tenancy in the preceding two years, provided that the applicant is still eligible, and did not become homeless intentionally.[216]

2.102 In addition, an English authority must give the applicant a copy of the statement included in its allocation policy on offering choice to people allocated housing accommodation under HA 1996 Part 6.[217]

Securing accommodation

2.103 The duty to secure that accommodation is made available for the applicant's occupation can be discharged by:

a) making available suitable accommodation held by the authority under HA 1985 Part 2, or under any other powers; or
b) securing that the applicant obtains suitable accommodation from some other person; or
c) giving the applicant such advice and assistance as will secure that the applicant obtains suitable accommodation from some other person.[218]

2.104 In deciding whether accommodation is suitable, the authority must have regard to the provisions of the HAs 1985 and 2004 which govern hazardous housing, overcrowding and houses in multiple occupation

214 HA 1996 ss198(5), 202(1)(d) and (e); H(W)A 2014 ss85, 88.

215 HA 1996 s193(2); H(W)A 2014 s75.

216 HA 1996 s195A(1). This right only arises on one re-application: HA 1996 s195A(6).

217 HA 1996 s193(3A).

218 HA 1996 s206(1); H(W)A 2014 s76.

(HMOs);[219] the secretary of state has power to specify circumstances in which accommodation is, or is not, to be regarded as suitable, and as to the matters which the authority must take into account or disregard when deciding suitability.[220]

Charges

2.105 Authorities have a general power to make reasonable charges for the provision of their own accommodation under HA 1985 Part 2.[221] HA 1996 Part 7 and H(W)A 2014 Part 2 entitle them to make charges to a homeless person for accommodation which they provide, or for or towards accommodation which they arrange for some other person to provide, under HA 1996 Part 7 or H(W)A 2014 Part 2.[222]

Out-of-area accommodation

2.106 So far as reasonably practicable, authorities are bound to secure accommodation within their own area.[223]

2.107 If the authority places an applicant in another area, it must give notice to the local housing authority with responsibility for that area, stating:

a) the name of the applicant;
b) the number and description of other members of the applicant's family normally residing with him or her, or of anyone else who might reasonably to be expected to reside with him or her;
c) the address;
d) the date on which the accommodation was made available to the applicant; and
e) what HA 1996 Part 7 function the authority was discharging when securing the accommodation for him or her.[224]

2.108 The notice must be given in writing within two weeks from when the accommodation was made available.[225]

219 HA 1996 s210(1); H(W)A 2014 s59.

220 HA 1996 s210(2). A number of statutory instruments have been made under this power – see: Homelessness (Suitability of Accommodation) Order 1996 SI No 3204; Homelessness (Suitability of Accommodation) (England) Order 2003 SI No 3326; and Homelessness (Suitability of Accommodation) (England) Order 2012 SI No 2601. In Wales, the same power is given to the Welsh Ministers: H(W)A 2014 s59(3).

221 HA 1985 s24.

222 HA 1996 s206(2); H(W)A 2014 s90.

223 HA 1996 s208(1); H(W)A 2014 s91.

224 HA 1996 s208(2) and (3); H(W)A 2014 s91(3).

225 HA 1996 s208(4); H(W)A 2014 s91(4).

Security

2.109 Where an authority provides its own accommodation in discharge of the full duty, it is not secure.[226]

Discharge of duty (England pre-LA 2011; Wales pre-H(W)A 2014)

2.110 In relation to applications in England made before commencement of LA 2011 s148(3) in respect of which the duty to secure accommodation had arisen but had not ceased by that date,[227] and continuing in Wales for applications made prior to 27 April 2015,[228] the duty to secure accommodation is owed to an applicant until it is brought to an end by any of the circumstances set out in HA 1996 s193 or H(W)A 2014 s76.[229]

2.111 Those circumstances are as follows:

a) if the applicant refuses an offer under HA 1996 Part 7, which the authority is satisfied is suitable for him or her, and the authority has informed the applicant of the possible consequences of refusal, of his or her right to a review of the suitability of the accommodation and that it will regard itself as having discharged the duty;[230]
b) if the applicant ceases to be eligible for assistance;[231]
c) if the applicant becomes homeless intentionally from HA 1996 Part 7 accommodation;[232]
d) if the applicant accepts an allocation under HA 1996 Part 6;[233]
e) if the applicant accepts an offer of an assured tenancy (other than an assured shorthold tenancy) from a private landlord, ie, one whose tenants are not secure;[234]
f) if the applicant voluntarily ceases to occupy HA 1996 Part 7 accommodation as an only or principal home;[235]

226 HA 1985 Sch 1 para 4, as amended by H(W)A 2014 Sch 3 para 1.
227 Localism Act 2011 (Commencement No 2 and Transitional Provisions) (England) Order 2012 SI No 2599 article 3.
228 For applications made on or after that date, H(W)A 2014 applies: see Housing (Wales) Act 2014 (Commencement No 3 and Transitory, Transitional and Saving Provisions) Order 2015 SI No 1272 article 7.
229 HA 1996 s193(3).
230 HA 1996 s193(5).
231 HA 1996 s193(6)(a).
232 HA 1996 s193(6)(b).
233 HA 1996 s193(6)(c)
234 HA 1996 s193(6)(cc).
235 HA 1996 s193(6)(d).

g) if the applicant, having been informed of the possible consequences of refusal, and of his or her right to request a review of the suitability of accommodation refused, refuses a written final offer of HA 1996 Part 6 allocation, and the authority is satisfied that the accommodation was suitable for him or her, and that it was reasonable for him or her to accept it;[236]
h) if the applicant accepts a qualifying offer of an assured shorthold tenancy from a private landlord.[237] For this purpose, an applicant may reasonably be considered to accept an offer even though the applicant is under a contractual or other obligation in respect of his or her existing accommodation, if (but only if) the applicant can bring that other obligation to an end before he or she has to take up the offer.[238] For this purpose, an offer is qualifying if:
   i) it is made with the approval of the authority, in pursuance of arrangements made by the authority with the landlord with a view to bringing the duty towards the applicant to an end;
   ii) the offer is of a fixed-term tenancy; and
   iii) it is accompanied by a statement in writing, which states the term of the tenancy being offered and explains in ordinary language that there is no obligation on the applicant to accept it but that if it is accepted the authority will cease to be under a duty to the applicant.[239]

2.112 Acceptance of a qualifying offer is only effective if the applicant signs a statement acknowledging that he or she has understood the authority's statement.[240] An authority may not make a qualifying offer unless satisfied that the accommodation is suitable for the applicant and that it is reasonable for the applicant to accept the offer.[241] The applicant is free to reject a qualifying offer without affecting the duty owed to him or her under this section by the authority.[242]

Discharge of duty (England post-LA 2011; Wales post-H(W)A 2014)

2.113 From commencement of LA 2011 s148 in England and H(W)A 2014 in Wales, the circumstances in which the duty to secure accommodation is brought to an end as follows:

236 HA 1996 s193(7), (7A), (7F).
237 HA 1996 s193(7B).
238 HA 1996 s193(8).
239 HA 1996 s193(7D).
240 HA 1996 s193(7E).
241 HA 1996 s193(7F).
242 HA 1996 s193(7C).

a) if the applicant refuses an offer under HA 1996 Part 7 or H(W)A 2014 Part 2, which is not an offer under Part 6 (below, item g)) or a private rented sector offer (below, item h)), which the authority is satisfied is suitable for the applicant, and the authority has informed the applicant of the possible consequences of refusal or acceptance, of his or her right to a review of the suitability of the accommodation and that it will regard itself as having discharged the duty;[243]
b) if the applicant ceases to be eligible for assistance;
c) if the applicant becomes homeless intentionally from HA 1996 Part 7 or H(W)A 2014 Part 2 accommodation;[244]
d) if the applicant accepts an allocation under HA 1996 Part 6;[245]
e) if the applicant accepts an offer of an assured tenancy (other than an assured shorthold tenancy) from a private landlord, ie, one whose tenants are not secure;[246]
f) if the applicant voluntarily ceases to occupy HA 1996 Part 7 or H(W)A 2014 Part 2 accommodation as an only or principal home;[247]
g) if the applicant, having been informed:
   1) of the possible consequences of refusal or acceptance; and
   2) of his or her right to request a review of the suitability of accommodation refused,

   refuses a written final offer of HA 1996 Part 6 allocation, and the authority is satisfied that:
   i) the accommodation was suitable for the applicant, and
   ii) (in England only) the applicant was not under any contractual or other obligations in respect of his or her existing accommodation which he or she could not bring to an end before having to take up the HA 1996 Part 6 offer;[248]
h) if the applicant accepts or refuses a private rented sector offer, having been informed in writing
   1) of the possible consequence of refusal or acceptance of the offer;
   2) that the applicant has the right to request a review of the suitability of the accommodation;[249] and

243 HA 1996 s193(5) as amended; H(W)A 2014 s76(3).
244 HA 1996 s193(6)(b); H(W)A 2014 s76(6).
245 HA 1996 s193(6)(c); H(W)A 2014 s76(2)(a).
246 HA 1996 s193(6)(cc); H(W)A 2014 s76(2)(b).
247 HA 1996 s193(6)(d); H(W)A 2014 s76(7).
248 HA 1996 s193(7), (7A), (7F), as amended; H(W)A 2014 s76(3)(c).
249 H(W)A 2014 ss76(3), 84.

3) (in a case which is not a restricted case and in England only) of the effect under HA 1996 s195A of a further application to a local housing authority within two years of acceptance of the offer;

a private rented sector offer means:

i) an offer of an assured shorthold tenancy made by a private landlord to the applicant in relation to any accommodation which is, or may become, available for the applicant's occupation;
ii) made, with the approval of the authority, in pursuance of arrangements made by the authority with the landlord with a view to bringing the authority's duty under this section to an end;
iii) which is a fixed-term tenancy for a period of at least 12[250] months;[251]

the authority may not approve such an offer unless it is satisfied that:

– the accommodation was suitable for the applicant; and
– (in England only) the applicant was not under any contractual or other obligations in respect of his or her existing accommodation which he or she could not bring to an end before having to take up the offer.[252]

Restricted cases

2.114 Where the duty arises by reference to a household member who is a restricted person, the authority must, so far reasonably practicable, bring the full housing duty to an end by arranging for a private rented sector offer to be made.[253]

Homelessness Reduction Act 2017

2.115 Once HRA 2017 comes into force in England, the full duty will not arise if a final accommodation or HA 1996 Part 6 offer was refused in the course of the authority's discharge of the initial help duty.[254] In the case both of the initial help duty and the new duty that is to apply to those threatened with homelessness, an authority may serve notice bringing either duty to an end on account of the applicant's

250 In Wales, six months: see H(W)A 2014 s76(4)(c).

251 The secretary of state has power to increase the minimum term, other than in a restricted case: HA 1996 s193(10)–(12) as added.

252 HA 1996 s193(7AA)–(7AC), (7F), (8) as amended.

253 HA 1996 s193(7AD); H(W)A 2014 s76(5).

254 HRA 2017 s7(1); HA 1996 s193A(1), (2).

deliberate and unreasonable refusal to co-operate.[255] In such a case, HA 1996 s193 does not apply,[256] but a largely similar duty will arise under section 193C in relation to those applicants who are homeless, eligible for assistance, who have a priority need for accommodation and who did not become homeless intentionally.[257]

2.116 The duty is to secure that accommodation is available for occupation by the applicant.[258] The duty will cease if the applicant:

a) ceases to be eligible for assistance;
b) becomes homeless intentionally from accommodation made available for his or her occupation;
c) accepts an offer of an assured tenancy from a private landlord; or
d) otherwise voluntarily ceases to occupy, as his or her only or principal home, the accommodation made available for his or her occupation.[259]

2.117 The duty will also cease if the applicant, having been informed of the possible consequences of refusal or acceptance and of his or her right to request a review of the suitability of the accommodation, refuses or accepts a final accommodation offer,[260] or a final HA 1996 Part 6[261] offer[262] The authority cannot approve a final accommodation offer or make a final Part 6 offer unless it is satisfied that it is suitable for the applicant;[263] nor can it approve or make such an offer if the applicant is under contractual or other obligations in respect of his or her existing accommodation, which he or she is not able to bring to an end before he or she would have to take up the offer.[264]

255 HRA 2017 s7(1); HA 1996 s193B(1), (2).
256 HRA 2017 s7(1); HA 1996 s193C(4).
257 HRA 2017 s7(1); HA 1996 s193C(3).
258 HRA 2017 s7(1); HA 1996 s193C(4).
259 HRA 2017 s7(1); HA 1996 s193C(5).
260 An offer of an assured shorthold tenancy made by a private landlord – including a private registered provider of social housing (England) or a registered social landlord (Wales) – in relation to any accommodation which is, or may become, available for the applicant's occupation, made, with the approval of the authority, in pursuance of arrangements made by the authority in discharge of the HA 1996 s193C duty, which is a fixed-term tenancy for a period of at least six months: HRA 2017 s7(1); HA 1996 s193C(7).
261 An offer of accommodation under HA 1996 Part 6 made in writing in discharge of the authority's the HA 1996 s193C duty, which states that it is a final offer for that purpose: HRA 2017 s7(1); HA 1996 s193C(8).
262 HRA 2017 s7(1); HA 1996 s193C(6).
263 HRA 2017 s7(1); HA 1996 s193C(9).
264 HRA 2017 s7(1); HA 1996 s193C(10).

Protection of property

Duty

2.118 An authority may also be under a duty to take reasonable steps to prevent the loss of an applicant's property, or prevent or mitigate damage to it,[265] if it is or has been under a duty under HA 1996 s188, s190, s193, s195 or s200; or H(W)A 2014 s66, s68, s75 or s82. Once HRA 2017 is brought into force, the duty will also be owed where an English authority has become subject to the initial duty to help under HA 1996 s189B.[266]

2.119 For these purposes, an applicant's personal property includes the personal property of any person reasonably expected to reside with him or her.[267]

2.120 The duty arises if the authority has reason to believe:

a) that there is a danger of loss of or damage to property because of the applicant's inability to protect or deal with it; and
b) that no other suitable arrangements have been or are being made.[268]

Power

2.121 If the authority has not been under one of the identified duties, but has reason to believe that a relevant danger to property exists, for which there are no arrangements, it has power to protect property.[269]

Charges and terms

2.122 The authority can, however, decline to take action under these provisions other than on such conditions as it considers appropriate, including as to reasonable charges and the disposal of property.[270]

Power of entry

2.123 In connection with these provisions, the authority has power, at all reasonable times, to enter any premises which are or were the usual or last usual place of residence of the applicant, and to deal with the

265 HA 1996 s211(2); H(W)A 2014 s93(2).
266 HRA 2017 s5(12); HA 1996 s211(2) as amended.
267 HA 1996 s211(5); H(W)A 2014 s93(6).
268 HA 1996 s211(1); H(W)A 2014 s93(1).
269 HA 1996 s211(3); H(W)A 2914 s93(5).
270 HA 1996 s211(4); H(W)A 2014 s93(4).

applicant's property in any way that is reasonably necessary, including by way of storage.[271]

Choice of storage

2.124 If the applicant asks the authority to move the property to a nominated location and the authority considers the request to be reasonable, the authority may discharge its responsibilities under these provisions by complying and, therefore, treating its responsibilities as being ended.[272]

Termination

2.125 Otherwise, the responsibilities end when the authority considers that there is no longer any danger of loss or damage by reason of the applicant's inability to protect or deal with the applicant's personal property, although, if the authority has provided storage, it may continue to do so.[273]

2.126 When the authority's responsibilities end, it must notify the applicant that they have done so and of the reasons why.[274] Notification may be given by delivery, or by leaving it or sending it to the applicant's last known address.[275]

Review

2.127 These provisions are not subject to internal review or appeal to the county court.

Homelessness strategies

2.128 The Homelessness Act 2002 imposed a new duty on local housing authorities to carry out a homelessness review in their areas and formulate and publish a homelessness strategy based on its results.[276]

271 HA 1996 s212(1); H(W)A 2014 s94(1).
272 HA 1996 s212(2); H(W)A 2014 s94(4).
273 HA 1996 s212(3); H(W)A 2014 s94(6), (7).
274 HA 1996 s212(4); H(W)A 2014 s94(8).
275 HA 1996 s212(5); H(W)A 2014 s94(9).
276 Homelessness Act 2002 s1(1).

2.129 The first strategy had to be published within 12 months of Homelessness Act 2002 s1 coming into force[277] and, thereafter, a new one has to be published at least every five years.[278] Since 1 December 2014, the position in Wales has been governed by H(W)A 2014 s50. A Welsh authority must carry out a homelessness review for its area, and formulate and adopt a homelessness strategy based on the results of that review.[279] The strategy must be adopted in 2018, with a new strategy every fourth year thereafter.[280]

Authorities

2.130 Where it is a different authority, the social services authority for the area of the authority must afford such assistance in the review and in the formulation of the strategy as the housing authority may reasonably require.[281] The strategy must be taken into account by both the local housing authority and the social services authority in the exercise of their functions.[282] In Wales, the strategy must be taken into account by the authority when exercising any of its functions.[283]

Homelessness review

2.131 For these purposes, a homelessness review means a review of:

a) the level, and likely future levels, of homelessness in the authority's area;
b) the activities which are carried out in the area to:
   i) prevent homelessness in the authority's area;
   ii) secure that accommodation is or will be available for people in the area who are or may become homeless; and

277 31 July 2003 (see the Homelessness Act 2002 (Commencement No 1) (England) Order 2002 SI No 1799 article 2) and 30 September 2003 (see the Homelessness Act 2002 (Commencement) (Wales) Order 2002 SI No 1736 article 2).

278 Homelessness Act 2002 s1(3) and (4).

279 H(W)A 2014 s50(1). The strategy can form part of the Well-being Plan under the Well-being of Future Generations (Wales) Act 2015, Welsh Code para.5.4.

280 H(W)A 2014 s50(2). The Welsh Code of Guidance notes that the strategy should reflect the Welsh Government's *Ten Year Homeless Plan* (July 2009), para 5.7.

281 Homelessness Act 2002 s1(2). In Wales there is no requirement that the exercise be carried out with the assistance of the local social services authority as all Welsh authorities are unitary, ie have both housing and social service functions.

282 Homelessness Act 2002 s1(5) and (6).

283 H(W)A 2014 s50(4).

iii) provide support for people in the area who are or may become homeless or who have been homeless and need support to prevent it happening again; and

c) the resources available to the authority, the social services authority, other public authorities, voluntary organisations and other persons for such activities.[284]

2.132 On completion of the review, the authority must arrange for the results to be available for inspection at its principal office, at all reasonable hours, without charge, and provide (on payment of a reasonable charge, if required) a copy of the results.[285]

Strategy

2.133 A homelessness strategy means one formulated for:

a) preventing homelessness in the authority's area;
b) securing that sufficient accommodation is and will be available for people in the area who are or may become homeless; and
c) securing that there is satisfactory provision of support for people in the area who are or who may become homeless or who have become homeless and need support to prevent them becoming homeless again.[286]

2.134 The strategy may include specific objectives to be pursued, and specific action planned to be taken in the course of the exercise of the authority's housing functions, and also of the functions of the social services authority for the district.[287] In Wales, the strategy must include details of both general and specific actions planned by the authority, including actions expected to be taken by other public authorities and voluntary organisations, in relation to those who may be in particular need of support if they are or may become homeless, in particular:

a) people leaving prison or youth detention accommodation;
b) young people leaving care;
c) people leaving the regular armed forces of the Crown;
d) people leaving hospital after medical treatment for mental disorder as an inpatient; and

284 Homelessness Act 2002 s2(1) and (2); H(W)A 2014 s51.

285 Homelessness Act 2002 s2(3); H(W)A 2014 s51(2) – in Wales, the results must also be published on the authority's website, if it has one.

286 Homelessness Act 2002 s3(1); H(W)A 2014 s52.

287 Homelessness Act 2002 s3(2); H(W)A 2014 s52(2).

e) people receiving mental health services in the community.[288]

2.135 The strategy may also include specific action which the authority expects to be taken by any other public authority, voluntary organisation or other person, which or who can contribute to the objectives of the strategy, albeit only with the approval of the body or person in question.[289] The authority must consider how far the objectives of the strategy can be met by joint action between itself, the social services authority or any other body or persons.[290]

2.136 The strategy must be kept under review and may be modified.[291] Any modification must be published and, before adopting or modifying the strategy, the authority must consult such public or local authorities, voluntary organisations or other persons as it considers appropriate.[292]

2.137 A copy of the strategy must be available at the authority's principal office for inspection at all reasonable hours, free of charge, and be provided to members of the public on request, on payment (if required) of a reasonable charge.[293]

Advice, information and voluntary organisations

2.138 HA 1996 Part 7 makes provision for English authorities to give grants, loans, premises or goods in kind to voluntary organisations concerned with the homeless.[294]

2.139 In addition, authorities in England and Wales have an obligation to ensure that advice and assistance about homelessness and its prevention are available to any person in their area, free of charge.[295]

2.140 In Wales, the advice and information must include details about how the homelessness service operates in the authority's area, other help which might be available and how to access it.[296] Whether or not someone is threatened with homelessness, assistance must be provided to access help to prevent him or her becoming homeless.[297]

288 H(W)A 2014 s52(6).
289 Homelessness Act 2002 s3(3) and (4); H(W)A 2014 s52(3) and (4).
290 Homelessness Act 2002 s3(5); H(W)A 2014 s52(5).
291 Homelessness Act 2002 s3(6); H(W)A 2014 s52(7).
292 Homelessness Act 2002 s3(7) and (8); H(W)A 2014 s52(8).
293 Homelessness Act 2002 s3(8); H(W)A 2014 s52(9).
294 HA 1996 ss180 and 181.
295 HA 1996 s179(1); H(W)A 2014 s60(1).
296 H(W)A 2014 s60(2).
297 H(W)A 2014 s60(3).

The authority must work with other public authorities, voluntary organisations and others to ensure that the service is designed to meet the needs of groups at particular risk of homelessness, including in particular:

- people leaving prison or youth detention accommodation;
- young people leaving care;
- people leaving the regular armed forces of the Crown;
- people leaving hospital after medical treatment for mental disorder as an inpatient; and
- people receiving mental health services in the community.[298]

2.141 Two or more authorities may provide the service jointly.[299]

2.142 In England, from the commencement of HRA 2017, the general duty under HA 1996 s179 will be replaced by a more specific duty for local housing authorities to provide or secure the provision of a service, to be available free of charge to any person in its district, providing information and advice on:

- preventing homelessness;
- securing accommodation when homeless;
- the rights of persons who are homeless or threatened with homelessness, and the duties of the authority, under HA 1996 Part 7;
- any help that is available from the authority or anyone else, whether under Part 7 or otherwise, for persons in the district who are homeless or may become homeless (whether or not they are threatened with homelessness); and
- how to access that help.[300]

2.143 The service must be designed to meet the needs of persons in the authority's district including, in particular, the needs of:

- people released from prison or youth detention accommodation;
- care leavers;
- former members of the regular armed forces;
- victims of domestic abuse;
- people leaving hospital;
- people suffering from a mental illness or impairment; and
- any other group which the authority identifies as being at particular risk of homelessness in its district.[301]

298 H(W)A 2014 s60(4).
299 H(W)A 2014 s60(5).
300 HRA 2017 s2; new HA 1996 s179(1).
301 HRA 2017 s2; new HA 1996 s179(2).

2.144 The authority may provide grants or loans to someone providing the service on its behalf.[302]

Code of Guidance

2.145 In the exercise of their functions under HA 1996 Part 7 or H(W)A 2014 Part 2, authorities are bound to have regard to such guidance as may from time to time be given by the secretary of state or the Welsh Ministers.[303] Under these provisions, there have been issued Codes of Guidance for England[304] and for Wales.[305]

Code of Practice

2.146 From the commencement of HRA 2017, in England the secretary of state will have power to issue Codes of Practice relating to homelessness or homelessness prevention to local housing authorities,[306] in particular concerning the exercise by a local housing authority of functions under Part 7, staff training relating to the exercise of those functions and monitoring by the authority of the exercise of those functions.[307] A code may apply to all local housing authorities or to a local housing authority specified or described in the code, and may contain different provision for different kinds of local housing authority.[308] A local housing authority must have regard to a Code of Practice in exercising its functions.[309]

Review and appeal

Review

2.147 Applicants have a statutory right to request an internal review of what, if any, duty is owed under HA 1996 ss190–193 and 195–196; or H(W)A 2014 s66, s68, s73 or s75.[310] This expressly encompasses

302 HRA 2017 s2; new HA 1996 s179(3). Assistance may also be given by way of the use of premises, furniture or other goods and even the services of staff: HA 1996 s179(4).
303 HA 1996 s182; H(W)A 2014 s98.
304 See appendix C.
305 Reproduced in full in the ebook version of *Homelessness and Allocations*.
306 HRA 2017 s11; HA 1996 s214A(1).
307 HRA 2017 s11; HA 1996 s214A(2).
308 HRA 2017 s11; HA 1996 s214A(3).
309 HRA 2017 s11; HA 1996 s214A(12).
310 HA 1996 s202; H(W)A 2014 s85.

whether or not the applicant is eligible for assistance, in priority need, intentionally homeless, whether a duty has ceased, and whether an applicant is threatened with homelessness or threatened with homelessness intentionally; it includes the full range of questions involved in local connection referrals, issues of suitability and a range of subsidiary issues.

2.148 Once HRA 2017 comes into force, the decisions which may be the subject of review in England are expanded to include decisions under the new initial duty to help, and the new duties to those threatened with homelessness, along with the corresponding provisions governing cessation of those new duties by reference to final offers and deliberate and unreasonable refusal to co-operate.[311]

2.149 An applicant may seek a review of whether accommodation offered in discharge of a duty is suitable and, where applicable, whether it is reasonable to accept it, whether or not the applicant has accepted the offer of accommodation.[312] The right of review does not, however, entitle the applicant to a review of an earlier review.[313]

Accommodation pending review

2.150 Pending the outcome of the review, the authority may – but is not under a duty to – provide accommodation for the applicant.[314]

Request for review

2.151 A request for a review must be made within 21 days of notification of decision, or such longer period as the authority may in writing allow.[315]

Review procedure

2.152 The secretary of state and the Welsh Ministers have power to regulate review procedure, including power to require that the review be conducted by a person of 'appropriate seniority . . . not involved in the original decision', and to prescribe the 'circumstances in which the applicant is entitled to an oral hearing, and whether and by whom [the applicant] may be represented at such a hearing'.[316]

311 HRA 2017 s9(1), (2); HA 1996 s202(1), as amended.

312 HA 1996 s202(1A), added by Homelessness Act 2002 s8; H(W)A 2014 s85(3).

313 HA 1996 s202(2); H(W)A 2014 s85(4).

314 HA 1996 s188(3); H(W)A 2014 s69(11)

315 HA 1996 s202(3); H(W)A 2014 s85(2).

316 HA 1996 s203; H(W)A 2014 s86.

Notification

2.153 The authority has to notify the applicant of the outcome of the review and, if it is adverse to the applicant's interests or confirms a local connection referral, of the reasons for it.[317] The authority must also notify the applicant of the right of appeal to the county court on a point of law.[318] If either of these requirements is not fulfilled, the notification is treated as not having been given.[319] Otherwise, notification is given in the same way as under HA 1996 s184.[320] The review may also need to be carried out, and notification given, within a period to be prescribed by the regulations.[321]

Appeal

2.154 An appeal lies to the county court if the applicant either:

a) is dissatisfied with the outcome of the review; or
b) has not been notified of the outcome within any time that may be prescribed.[322]

2.155 Appeal lies only on a point of law, whether it arises from the original decision or from the decision on review.[323]

Time for appeal

2.156 The appeal must be brought within 21 days of notification, or of when the applicant ought to have been notified of the outcome.[324] The court may give permission to appeal out of time where there is good reason for the applicant being unable to bring the appeal within the 21-day limit.[325]

317 HA 1996 s203(4); H(W)A 2014 s86(4).
318 HA 1996 s203(5); H(W)A 2014 s86(5).
319 HA 1996 s203(6); H(W)A 2014 s86(6).
320 HA 1996 s203(8); H(W)A 2014 s86. Notification must be in writing and if not received by the applicant, it is to be treated as having been received if it is made available at the authority's office for a reasonable period for collection by or on his or her behalf: HA 1996 s203(8) (England) and H(W)A 2014 s86(7) (Wales).
321 HA 1996 s203(7); H(W)A 2014 s86(2)(c).
322 HA 1996 s204(1); H(W)A 2014 s88.
323 HA 1996 s204(1); H(W)A 2014 s88.
324 HA 1996 s204(2); H(W)A 2014 s88.
325 HA 1996 s204(2A); H(W)A 2014 s88(3).

Powers of court

2.157 The court may make such order as it thinks fit, confirming, quashing or varying the decision.[326]

Accommodation pending appeal

2.158 Pending an appeal (and any further appeal), the authority may, but is not obliged to, provide accommodation.[327] If the authority refuses to do so, the applicant may appeal that decision to the county court[328] and the court may order that accommodation is made available pending the outcome of the appeal (or such earlier time as it may specify), and may confirm or quash the decision of the authority not to provide accommodation.[329]

2.159 In considering whether to confirm or quash the decision, the court must apply the principles applied by the High Court on an application for judicial review.[330] If the court quashes the decision, it may order the authority to exercise the power to accommodate pending appeal in the applicant's case for such period as it specifies.[331] Such an order may, however, only be made if the court is satisfied that failure to exercise the accommodation power in accordance with its order would substantially prejudice the applicant's ability to pursue his or her substantive appeal.[332]

Criminal offences

2.160 It is a criminal offence knowingly or recklessly to make a statement which is false in a material particular, or knowingly to withhold information which an authority has reasonably required in connection with the exercise of its functions under HA 1996 Part 7 or H(W)A 2014 Part 2, with intent to induce an authority to believe that the person making the statement, or any other person, is entitled to accommodation or assistance (or accommodation or assistance of a particular kind).[333]

326 HA 1996 s204(3); H(W)A 2014 s88(4).
327 HA 1996 s204(4); H(W)A 2014 s88(5).
328 HA 1996 s204A; H(W)A 2014 s89.
329 HA 1996 s204A(4)(a), (b); H(W)A 2014 s89(4).
330 HA 1996 s204A(4); H(W)A 2014 s89(5).
331 HA 1996 s204A(5); H(W)A 2014 s89(6).
332 HA 1996 s204A(6)(a); H(W)A 2014 s89(7).
333 HA 1996 s214(1); H(W)A 2014 s97(1).

2.161 The offence is punishable on summary conviction in England by a fine of up to level five and in Wales by a fine of up to level 4 on the standard scale,[334] ie, the standard scale for the time being under Criminal Justice Act (CJA) 1982 s37.[335]

2.162 An applicant has a duty to notify an authority as soon as possible of any material change of facts material to his or her case, which occurs before the applicant receives the notification of the authority's decision on his or her application.[336] The authority is under a corresponding obligation to explain to an applicant, in ordinary language, the nature of this duty and the effect of the defence to a charge of non-compliance.[337] The defence is that no such explanation was given or that, although such an explanation was given, there is some other reasonable excuse for non-compliance.[338] In the absence of such a defence, it is a criminal offence to fail to comply with the duty to notify the authority of material changes, punishable on summary conviction at levels five and four on the standard scale.[339]

Co-operation between authorities

Co-operation

2.163 In the discharge of its functions under HA 1996 Part 7, a local housing authority in England may request assistance from another local housing authority (in England, Wales or Scotland), a private registered provider of social housing, a registered social landlord or a housing action trust, or a development corporation, registered housing association or Scottish Homes.[340] The other authority (or body) must co-operate with the housing authority by rendering such assistance as is reasonable in the circumstances.[341] The provisions also apply when a Scottish local authority seeks assistance from an English authority under Housing (Scotland) Act 1987 s38.[342]

334 HA 1996 s214(4); H(W)A 2014 s97.
335 Level 5 is presently unlimited (see CJA 1982 s37 and LASPO 2012 s85); level 4 is currently £2,500 (CJA 1982 s37).
336 HA 1996 s214(2); H(W)A 2014 s97(2).
337 HA 1996 s214(2); H(W)A 2014 s97(3), (4).
338 HA 1996 s214(3); H(W)A 2014 s97(3), (5).
339 HA 1996 s214(4); H(W)A 2014 s97(6); see above.
340 HA 1996 s213(1)(a) and (2), as amended by Housing and Regeneration Act 2008 (Consequential Provisions) Order 2010 SI No 866 Sch 2.
341 HA 1996 s213(1).
342 HA 1996 s213(3).

2.164 In Wales, where all authorities are unitary and therefore have both housing and social services functions, the corresponding provisions require each authority to make arrangements to promote co-operation between those of its officers who exercise its social services functions and those who exercise its functions as the local housing authority, with a view to achieving the following objectives in its area:

a) the prevention of homelessness,
b) that suitable accommodation is or will be available for people who are or may become homeless,
c) that satisfactory support is available for people who are or may become homeless, and
d) the effective discharge of its functions under H(W)A 2014 Part 2.[343]

2.165 In addition, the authority may request the co-operation of the following persons (whether in Wales or England): a local housing authority; a social services authority; a registered social landlord; a private registered provider of social housing; or a housing action trust.[344] The body is bound to comply with the request unless it considers that doing so would be incompatible with its own duties, or would otherwise have an adverse effect on the exercise of its functions.[345] If the authority seeks information from the body, it must likewise comply unless it considers that doing so would be incompatible with its own duties or would otherwise have an adverse effect on the exercise of the person's functions.[346] In either case, a body which decides not to comply with the request must give the local housing authority who made the request written reasons for its decision.[347]

Referral

2.166 In addition, where an English local housing authority has reason to believe that an applicant with whom children reside, or usually reside, may be ineligible for assistance, may be homeless or may have become so intentionally, or may be threatened with homelessness intentionally, they must make arrangements for ensuring that

343 H(W)A 2014 s95(1).

344 H(W)A 2014 s95(5). The Welsh Ministers may add or omit persons from this list, other than a Minister of the Crown: s95(6), (7).

345 H(W)A 2014 s95(2).

346 H(W)A 2014 s95(3).

347 H(W)A 2014 s95(4).

the applicant is invited to consent to the referral of his or her case to the social services authority (or department in the case of a unitary authority) and, if consent is given, must make the social services authority/department aware of the essential facts of the case and the subsequent decision in relation to it.[348] Following such a referral, the social services authority/department may request that the housing authority provide it with advice and assistance in the exercise of its functions under the CA 1989 Part 3 and the housing authority must provide it with such advice and assistance as is reasonable in all the circumstances.[349]

2.167 The corresponding provisions in Wales apply where the authority has reason to believe that an applicant with whom a person under the age of 18 normally resides, or might reasonably be expected to reside, may be ineligible for help, may be homeless but that a duty under H(W)A 2014 s68, s73 or s75 is not likely to apply, or may be threatened with homelessness and that a duty under s66 is not likely to apply.[350] The authority must make arrangements for ensuring that the applicant is invited to consent to the referral to the social services department of the essential facts of his or her case, and, if he or she has given that consent, that the social services department is made aware of those facts and of the subsequent decision in respect of his or her case.[351] The authority must also make arrangements to ensure that where it makes a decision that an applicant is ineligible for help, became homeless intentionally or became threatened with homelessness intentionally, its housing department provides the social services department with such advice and assistance as the social services department reasonably requests.[352]

Allocation

2.168 When allocating housing, local housing authorities are obliged to comply with the provisions of HA 1996 Part 6.[353]

348 HA 1996 s213A(1), (2).
349 HA 1996 s213A(5), (6).
350 H(W)A 2014 s96(1).
351 H(W)A 2014 s96(2).
352 H(W)A 2014 s96(4).
353 HA 1996 s159(1).

Meaning of allocation

2.169 For these purposes, 'allocation' means:

a) selecting a secure[354] or introductory tenant[355] for the authority's own accommodation. This includes notifying an existing tenant or licensee that his or her tenancy is to be secure,[356] for example, under HA 1985 Sch 1 para 2 (employment-related accommodation), para 5 (temporary accommodation for people taking up employment) or para 10 (student accommodation), as amended;
b) nominating a person to be a secure or introductory tenant of another (nomination includes formal and informal arrangements;[357]
c) nominating (in the same sense as above) a person to be an assured tenant[358] of a registered provider of social housing or a registered social landlord.[359]

Excluded allocations

2.170 Allocations to existing secure or introductory tenants are excluded, unless the allocation involves a transfer of housing accommodation for that tenant, and the transfer is made on the tenant's application.[360]

2.171 From the commencement of LA 2011 s145, this exclusion applies only in Wales. In England, the corresponding exclusion is an allocation to a person who is already a secure or introductory tenant, or an assured tenant of housing accommodation held by a private registered provider of social housing or a registered social landlord, unless the allocation involves a transfer of housing accommodation for that person, the application for the transfer is made by that person, and the authority is satisfied that the person is to be given a reasonable preference,[361] ie under HA 1996 s166A.

2.172 There is a number of other cases which are not treated as an allocation:

a) succession and devolution on death, or assignment to a potential successor;

354 HA 1985 Part 4.
355 HA 1996 Part 5 Chapter 1.
356 HA 1996 s159(3).
357 HA 1996 s159(4).
358 HA 1988 Part 1.
359 HA 1996 Part 1; s159(2), as amended by Housing and Regeneration Act 2008 (Consequential Provisions) Order 2010 SI No 866 Sch 2.
360 HA 1996 s159(5).
361 HA 1996 s159(4A), (4B), as amended.

b) assignment by way of exchange;
c) vesting under a number of family or domestic law provisions; and
d) other cases as may be prescribed by regulations.[362]

Eligibility

2.173 Any person may be allocated housing, provided that he or she is not ineligible under HA 1996 s160ZA (England) or s160A (Wales).[363] An allocation may not be made to two or more persons jointly if one of them is ineligible.[364]

Persons from abroad

2.174 Persons subject to immigration control under the AIA 1996 are ineligible unless re-included by regulations.[365] The secretary of state may not include in regulations any person who is excluded from entitlement to housing benefit by IAA 1999 s115.[366] The secretary of state may prescribe other persons from abroad who are ineligible, either in relation to local housing authorities generally or any particular local housing authority.[367]

2.175 In Wales, these provisions do not affect the eligibility of someone who is already a secure or introductory tenant or an assured tenant of housing accommodation allocated to him or her by a local housing authority.[368] In England, the disqualification does not affect the eligibility of someone who is already a secure or introductory tenant or an assured tenant of housing accommodation held by a private registered provider of social housing or a registered social landlord, if the allocation involves a transfer of housing accommodation for that person, the application for the transfer is made by that person, and the authority is satisfied that the person is to be given a reasonable preference,[369] ie under HA 1996 s166A.

362 HA 1996 s160.
363 HA 1996 ss160ZA(1), 160A(1), (2).
364 HA 1996 ss160ZA(1)(b), 160A(1)(c).
365 HA 1996 ss160ZA(2), 160A(3).
366 HA 1996 ss160ZA(3), 160A(4).
367 HA 1996 ss160ZA(4), 160A(5).
368 HA 1996 s160A(6).
369 HA 1996 ss159(4B), 160ZA(5).

Unacceptable behaviour

2.176 A local authority in Wales may decide that an applicant is to be treated as ineligible if it is satisfied that:

a) the applicant or a member of the applicant's household has been guilty of unacceptable behaviour serious enough to make the applicant unsuitable to be a tenant of the authority; and
b) by reason of the circumstances at the time that the applicant's application is considered, he or she is unsuitable to be a tenant of the authority by reason of that behaviour.[370]

2.177 'Unacceptable behaviour' is that which would (if the applicant was a secure tenant of the authority) entitle the authority to a possession order under HA 1985 s84 on any of grounds 1–7 of Schedule 2 to that Act or under the absolute ground for possession, or behaviour by a member of the applicant's household, which would (if he or she were a person residing with a secure tenant of the authority) entitle the authority to such a possession order.[371]

Re-application

2.178 An applicant who is treated as ineligible because of unacceptable behaviour may (if the applicant considers that he or she should no longer be so treated) make a fresh application.[372]

Notification

2.179 If the authority decides that the applicant is ineligible for an allocation, it must notify the applicant of that decision and the ground(s) for it.[373] Notification must be given in writing and, if not received by the applicant, shall be treated as having been given if it is made available at the authority's office for a reasonable period for collection by the applicant or on the applicant's behalf.[374] There is a right to a review of such a decision.[375]

370 HA 1996 s160A(7).
371 HA 1996 s160A(8).
372 HA 1996 s160A(11).
373 HA 1996 s160A(9).
374 HA 1996 s160A(10).
375 HA 1996 s167(4A).

Localism Act 2011

2.180 From the commencement of LA 2011 s145, these anti-social behaviour provisions are only applicable in Wales.[376] In England, the authority may determine for itself whom it will treat as a person qualifying for an allocation,[377] subject to the prohibition on persons ineligible for immigration reasons,[378] and to the power of the secretary of state by regulations to prescribe classes of person who are or who are not to be treated as qualifying, and/or to prescribe criteria that may not be used by authorities in determining who is not to qualify.[379] In the case of joint tenants, at least one of them must be a qualifying person.[380] There are analogous duties relating to notification in writing with reasons,[381] and to review,[382] and the right of re-application on the part of someone who considers that he or she should be treated as a qualifying person.[383]

Applications

2.181 Authorities must ensure that there is free advice and information available in their areas about the right to make an application for an allocation of housing.[384]

2.182 Authorities must also ensure that any necessary assistance in making an application is available free of charge to those who are likely to have difficulty in doing so without assistance.[385]

2.183 Authorities must also ensure that applicants are aware of their right to request information about the likely availability of accommodation.[386]

2.184 Every application for an allocation of housing made in accordance with the procedural requirements of the authority's allocation

376 LA 2011 s146(1).
377 HA 1996 s160ZA(6), (7).
378 HA 1996 s160ZA(7).
379 HA 1996 s160ZA(8).
380 HA 1996 s160ZA(6).
381 HA 1996 s160ZA(9), (10). If the notification is not received by the applicant, it is to be treated as having been received if it is made available at the authority's office for a reasonable period for collection by or on his or her behalf: HA 1996 s160ZA(10).
382 HA 1996 s166A(9).
383 HA 1996 s160ZA(11).
384 HA 1996 s166(1)(a).
385 HA 1996 s166(1)(b).
386 HA 1996 s166(1A) (England); s166(2) (Wales).

scheme must be considered by the authority.[387] The fact that a person is an applicant for an allocation must not be divulged by the authority to any member of the public without the applicant's consent.[388]

Priorities and procedures

2.185 An authority must maintain an allocation 'scheme' governing both priorities and procedures (including all aspects of the allocation procedure, including by whom decisions may be made).[389] An authority may not allocate accommodation otherwise than in accordance with its scheme.[390]

Procedure

2.186 The scheme must be framed so as to give an applicant the right to request general information that will enable the applicant to assess:

a) how his or her application is likely to be treated under the scheme (including whether the applicant is likely to be regarded as in one of the reasonable preference categories); and
b) whether accommodation appropriate to the applicant's needs is likely to be made available to the applicant and, if so, how long it is likely to be before such accommodation becomes available for allocation to him or her.[391]

Regulations

2.187 The secretary of state or the Welsh Ministers may require that the procedures are framed in accordance with such principles as he or she may prescribe.[392]

Choice policy

2.188 The scheme must include a statement of the authority's policy on offering people who are to be allocated housing:

a) a choice of housing accommodation; or
b) the opportunity to express preference about the housing accommodation to be allocated to them.[393]

387 HA 1996 s166(3).
388 HA 1996 s166(4).
389 HA 1996 s166A(1) (England); s167(1) (Wales).
390 HA 1996 s166A(14) (England); s167(8) (Wales).
391 HA 1996 s166A(9) (England); s167(4A)(a) (Wales).
392 HA 1996 s166A(10) (England); s167(5) (Wales).
393 HA 1996 s166A(2) (England); s167(1A) (Wales).

Priority

2.189 The scheme must be framed so as to ensure that a reasonable preference is given to the following:

a) people who are homeless;[394]
b) people who are owed a duty by an local housing authority under HA 1996 s190(2), s193(2) or s195(2) (or under HA 1985 s65(2) or s68(2)) or who are occupying accommodation secured by any such authority under HA 1996 s192(3) or, in Wales, those owed a duty under H(W)A 2014 s66, s73 or s75;[395]
c) people occupying insanitary or overcrowded housing or otherwise living in unsatisfactory housing conditions;
d) people who need to move on medical or welfare grounds (including grounds relating to disability); and
e) people who need to move to a particular locality in the authority's area, where failure to meet that need would cause hardship to themselves or to others.[396]

2.190 The scheme may also be framed so as to give additional preference to those within these categories who have an urgent housing need.[397]

2.191 The scheme may also include provision for determining priorities between those in the reasonable preference categories, taking into account:

a) the financial resources available to a person to meet his or her housing costs;
b) any behaviour of a person (or a member of the person's household) which affects his or her suitability to be a tenant;
c) any local connection which exists between a person and the authority's area.[398]

394 This does not apply if the only reason someone is homeless is because of a restricted person: HA 1996 s167(2ZA).

395 As last footnote.

396 HA 1996 s166A(3) (England); s167(2), as amended by H(W)A 2014 Sch 3 para 3 (Wales).

397 HA 1996 s166A(3) (England); s167(2) (Wales).

398 HA 1996 s166A(5) (England); s167(2A) (Wales).

Unacceptable behaviour

2.192 In Wales,[399] the scheme does not have to provide for any preference to be given to an applicant where the authority is satisfied that:

a) the applicant, or a member of his or her household, has been guilty of unacceptable behaviour serious enough to make him or her unsuitable to be a tenant of the authority; and
b) in the circumstances at the time that the applicant's case is considered, he or she deserves by reason of that behaviour not to be treated as a member of one of the groups to whom a reasonable preference is to be given.[400]

Regulations

2.193 The secretary of state and Welsh Ministers have power to add to, amend or repeal any part of the list of those to whom a reasonable preference is to be accorded.[401] They also have power to specify factors which are not to be taken into account when allocating housing.[402]

Other allocations

2.194 Subject to the reasonable preference categories, the scheme may contain provisions about the allocation of particular accommodation to a person who makes a specific application for it and to people of a particular description, whether or not they are within the reasonable preference categories.[403]

Notification

2.195 The scheme must be framed so that an applicant is notified:

a) in Wales only, in writing of any decision that he or she is a person being given no preference because of a decision as to behaviour under HA 1996 s167(2C); and
b) in England and Wales, of the right to request the authority to inform him or her about the facts of his or her case which are likely

399 This provision was considered unnecessary after changes made by LA 2011 meant that English authorities could decide for themselves who qualifies for an allocation (HA 1996 s160ZA(7)), although subsequent case-law instead means that English authorities have simply been deprived of this right.

400 HA 1996 s167(2B)–(2D).

401 HA 1996 s167(3).

402 HA 1996 s166A(8) (England); s167(4) (Wales).

403 HA 1996 s166A(6) (England); s167(2E) (Wales).

to be, or have been, taken into account in considering whether to allocate housing accommodation to the applicant.[404]

Review

2.196 The scheme must include the right for an applicant to request a review of a decision as to any decision about the facts of his or her case, whether he or she is a person who is ineligible under section 160ZA(9) (England) or section 160A (Wales), or whether (in Wales) he or she is to be given no preference under HA 1996 s167(2C).[405]

Change and consultation

2.197 Priorities and procedures are otherwise in the discretion of the authority.[406] Before adopting or making any major policy change to a scheme, the authority must send a copy of it in draft to every private registered provider and every registered social landlord with which they have nomination arrangements, and afford them a reasonable opportunity to comment.[407] When preparing or modifying its allocation scheme, an English authority must have regard to its strategy under the Homelessness Act 2002, to its current tenancy strategy under LA 2011 s150, and, if a London borough, to the London housing strategy.[408]

Code of Guidance

2.198 The secretary of state may issue guidance to which authorities must have regard.[409]

Co-operation

2.199 When an authority asks it to offer accommodation to people with priority under the authority's allocation scheme, a private registered provider of social housing or a registered social landlord is bound to co-operate to such extent as is reasonable in the circumstances.[410]

404 HA 1996 s166A(9)(b) (England); s167(4A)(b), (c) (Wales).
405 HA 1996 s166A(9)(c) (England); s167(4A)(d) (Wales).
406 HA 1996 s166A(11) (England); s167(6) (Wales.
407 HA 1996 s166A(13) (England); s167(7) (Wales).
408 HA 1996 s166A(12).
409 HA 1996 s169.
410 HA 1996 s170 as amended by Housing and Regeneration Act 2008 (Consequential Provisions) Order 2010 SI No 866 Sch 2.

Information

2.200 An authority must publish a summary of its scheme and provide a copy of it, free of charge, to any member of the public who asks for it.[411] The full scheme must be made available for inspection at the authority's principal office and a copy must be made available to any member of the public who asks for it, on payment of a reasonable fee.[412]

2.201 When the authority makes a major policy alteration to its scheme, it has to take such steps as it considers reasonable to bring the effect of the alteration to the attention of those likely to be affected by it.[413]

Criminal offences

2.202 It is a criminal offence knowingly or recklessly to make a statement – in connection with the exercise by an authority of its functions under HA 1996 Part 6 – which is false in a material particular, or knowingly to withhold information which an authority has reasonably required in connection with the exercise of its functions under HA 1996 Part 6.[414]

2.203 The offence is punishable on summary conviction by a fine of up to level 5 on the standard scale,[415] ie the standard scale for the time being under the CJA 1982 s37.[416]

411 HA 1996 s168(1).
412 HA 1996 s168(2).
413 HA 1996 s168(3).
414 HA 1996 s171(1).
415 HA 1996 s171(2).
416 Level 5 is a fine of up to an unlimited amount: see CJA 1982 s37 and LASPO 2012 s85.

CHAPTER 3

Immigration

3.1 Introduction

3.16 Immigration control

3.17 Persons subject to immigration control

3.18 Persons not subject to immigration control

British citizenship • Commonwealth citizens with the right of abode in the UK • EEA nationals with the right to reside in the UK

3.100 Habitual residence

3.106 Provision of information

3.110 Eligibility – homelessness: Housing Act 1996 Part 7 and Housing (Wales) Act 2014 Part 2

3.110 Introduction

Other members of the household

3.120 Homelessness assistance

England • Wales

3.151 Interim accommodation

Ineligibility • Exceptions to ineligibility

3.161 Eligibility – allocations: Housing Act 1996 Part 6

3.161 Introduction

3.169 England

Persons subject to immigration control • Persons not subject to immigration control

3.172 Wales

Persons subject to immigration control • Persons not subject to immigration control

Introduction

3.1 In the fourth to seventh editions of this book, this chapter was called 'eligibility'. While that title would be correct were this book concerned only with homelessness, it is not correct when it comes to allocations, which define eligibility in terms of both immigration status and conduct, ie, applicants may also be disqualified from an allocation on grounds related to 'unacceptable behaviour';[1] that subject is dealt with below.[2]

3.2 Immigration status is a key topic in relation to both homelessness and allocations. In both cases, it is determinative of eligibility, excluding certain applicants in England from the protection of Housing Act (HA) 1996 Part 7 and in Wales from the Housing (Wales) Act (H(W)A) 2014 Part 2, and, in both England and Wales, from the prospect of an allocation under the HA 1996 Part 6.

3.3 That does not mean that no assistance will ever be available from a local authority to someone thus disqualified; there remains the possibility of assistance in England under the Care Act 2014, and in Wales under the equivalent provision which is now the Social Services and Well-being (Wales) Act (SSWB(W)A) 2014, where an applicant is in need of care and attention (otherwise than as a result of destitution) – this is dealt with below.[3] In addition, some immigrants who are asylum-seekers disqualified from local authority assistance may be able to obtain housing help through the Home Office.[4] Moreover, local authorities in England[5] and Wales[6] may have to give assistance to children in need, even though they or their parents are disqualified from housing assistance under HA 1996 Parts 6 and 7 or H(W)A 2014 Part 2.[7] There are also other powers – 'general power of competence' in England, under the Localism Act (LA) 2011, and 'well-being powers' in Wales under the Local Government Act (LGA) 2000 Part 1 – which may be exercisable in some circumstances.[8]

3.4 Even if an applicant is not ineligible for assistance under HA 1996 Part 7 there are, however, additional provisions which apply in England only, which may exclude the applicant from temporary

1 HA 1996 s160A(7)–(11).
2 See paras 11.28–11.45.
3 See paras 13.7–13.26.
4 See paras 3.106, 13.27–13.39.
5 Under CA 1989.
6 Under SSWB(W)A 2014.
7 See paras 13.40–13.86.
8 See paras 13.87–13.93.

accommodation under some of the interim duties in Part 7; the same classes will also be excluded from assistance under the provisions mentioned in the last paragraph, ie, under the Care Act 2014 or the SSWB(W)A 2014, through the Home Office, under the Children Act (CA) 1989 or under LGA 2000[9] or under LA 2011. These classes are described in this chapter.[10]

3.5 Even if an applicant is not ineligible for assistance under HA 1996 Part 7 or H(W)A 2014 Part 2, if qualification for assistance relies on family or household members who would themselves be ineligible, it may affect the duty placed on the authority: this is also dealt with below.[11] Likewise, it will affect priority in the allocation of housing under HA 1996 Part 6.[12]

3.6 Historically, the Housing (Homeless Persons) Act (H(HP)A) 1977 did not contain a test of eligibility. On the face of the Act, anyone could make an application. The Court of Appeal, however, expressed the view that duties were owed only to a person who was lawfully in the country.[13] The consolidating HA 1985 Part 3, which replaced H(HP)A 1977, likewise did not limit who could apply, but the Court of Appeal interpreted the provisions so that an authority owed no duty to an applicant for housing who was an illegal entrant.[14] It was also held that where – as a result of enquiries – the authority suspected

9 LA 2011 ss1 and 2 and Sch 1, which came into force on 28 March 2012, and 6 April 2012 by operation of the Localism Act 2011 (Consequential Amendments) Order 2012 SI No 961, have repealed the well-being power in LGA 2000 s2 in England, and replaced it with a general power of competence. Nationality, Immigration and Asylum Act (NIAA) 2002 Sch 3 has not yet been amended to include the general power of competence. The position in Wales is unaffected by these changes.

10 See para 3.153.

11 See paras 3.113–3.119.

12 See paras 3.164–3.166.

13 *R v Hillingdon LBC ex p Streeting (No 2)* [1980] 1 WLR 1425, CA. Following *R v Westminster City Council ex p Castelli* (1996) 28 HLR 616, this would seem to include a European Economic Area (EEA) national who is not exercising a right to reside in the UK and has no leave to enter or remain because the Court of Appeal held that such a person was not unlawfully in the country. In *R (ST (Eritrea)) v Secretary of State for the Home Department* [2012] UKSC 12, [2012] 2 AC 135, however, the Supreme Court held that a person who had been granted temporary admission to the UK for the purposes of determining her claim for asylum, but had not yet been granted leave to enter or remain, was not lawfully in the UK within the meaning of Article 32 of the Geneva Convention relating to the Status of Refugees and was thus not entitled to the protection of that Article.

14 *Tower Hamlets LBC v Secretary of State for the Environment* [1993] QB 632, (1993) 25 HLR 524, CA.

that an applicant was an illegal entrant, it had a duty to inform the immigration authorities of its suspicion.[15]

3.7 The Asylum and Immigration Appeals Act (AIAA) 1993 was the first legislative provision explicitly to limit the rights of immigrants to housing assistance. The effect of its sections 4 and 5 was that authorities owed no duty to an asylum-seeker and the asylum-seeker's dependants if he or she had accommodation that was available for the asylum-seeker's occupation, however temporary, and which it would be reasonable for him or her to occupy. Asylum and Immigration Act (AIA) 1996 s9 additionally provided that an authority should not, so far as practicable, grant a tenancy or licence of housing accommodation to a person subject to immigration control, unless he or she is of a prescribed class.

3.8 These limitations were reproduced in HA 1996 Part 7, ss185 and 186, and in the H(W)A 2014 Sch 2 para 1, defining 'eligibility for assistance'. Subject to qualification and exception, excluded persons from abroad under HA 1996 s185,[16] and asylum-seekers under HA 1996 s186[17] were not eligible for assistance. A person ineligible for assistance could not receive 'the benefit of any function under . . . Part [7] relating to accommodation or assistance in obtaining accommodation',[18] although he or she could receive advice and assistance from any advisory service provided by the authority under its HA 1996 s179 duty.[19]

3.9 Eligibility requirements were also introduced in HA 1996 Part 6 for allocations,[20] which, so far as concerns immigration, matched those for homelessness.

3.10 Qualification as an applicant who is eligible for assistance is set out in secondary legislation in both England[21] and Wales.[22] In summary,

15 See *Tower Hamlets LBC v Secretary of State for the Environment*, above.

16 In Wales, the equivalent provision is H(W)A 2014 Sch 2 para 1.

17 This has effect in Wales until repealed, see H(W)A 2014 Sch 2 para 2.

18 HA 1996 s183(2).

19 HA 1996 s183(3); see chapter 14.

20 See now HA 1996 s160A(1)–(6), as amended by the Homelessness Act 2002.

21 Allocation of Housing and Homelessness (Eligibility) (England) Regulations ('Eligibility Regs') 2006 SI No 1294, as amended by the Allocation of Housing and Homelessness (Eligibility) (England) (Amendment) Regulations ('Eligibility (Amendment) Regs') 2012 SI No 2588 with effect from 8 November 2012, though the amendments do not affect an application for an allocation of housing or for homelessness assistance which was made before that date.

22 For allocation and homelessness applications see the Allocation of Housing and Homelessness (Eligibility) (Wales) Regulations ('Eligibility (Wales) Regs') 2014 SI No 2603 which came into force on 31 October 2014 and apply to all applications for an allocation or homelessness assistance made on or after that date.

applicants who are subject to immigration control are eligible if they come within one of the prescribed classes, and applicants who are not subject to immigration control are generally eligible, though job-seekers and those with an initial right to reside are excluded, and certain applicants are also required to be habitually resident in the UK.

3.11 The requirements imposed on applicants who are not subject to immigration control are known as the 'right to reside test'. In *Mirga and Samin*,[23] the Supreme Court upheld the lawfulness of the test and held that it would severely undermine the whole thrust and purpose of European Union (EU) free movement law if proportionality could be invoked to entitle a person to have the right of residence and social assistance in another member state, save perhaps in extreme circumstances. It would place a substantial burden on a host member state if it had to carry out a proportionality exercise in every case where the right of residence, or a right against discrimination, was invoked.[24]

3.12 This is consistent with the earlier decision of the Supreme Court in *Patmalniece*,[25] where it was held that the right to reside test is indirectly discriminatory but that the discrimination is justified because its purpose is to protect the resources of the UK against 'benefit tourism' by persons who are not economically or socially integrated. Accordingly, it was held that the application of the test does not give rise to unlawful discrimination on the grounds of nationality.[26]

3.13 This approach is also consistent with the jurisprudence of the Court of Justice of the European Union (CJEU). In *Commission v UK*[27] the court agreed with the UK's submission that the legality of the claimant's residence in its territory is a substantive condition which economically inactive persons must meet in order to be eligible for the social benefits at issue, and therefore that the 'right to reside' test did not amount to unlawful discrimination.[28] In *Dano*,[29] the court held that member states are allowed to enact legislation which excludes economically inactive nationals of other member

23 *Mirga v Secretary of State for Work and Pensions; Samin v Westminster City Council* [2016] UKSC 1, [2016] HLR 7.

24 *Mirga* at [69].

25 *Patmalniece v Secretary of State for Work and Pensions* [2011] UKSC 11, [2011] 1 WLR 783.

26 *Patmalniece* at [46], [48], [53] and [61].

27 *European Commission v United Kingdom of Great Britain and Northern Ireland*, Case C-308/14.

28 *Commission v UK* at [72] and [86].

29 *Dano v Jobcenter Leipzig*, Case C-333/13, [2015] 1 WLR 2519, CJEU.

states from entitlement to state benefits if they do not comply with the conditions for residence set down in EU law.[30]

3.14 In *Alimanovic*,[31] the court held that a member state can enact legislation which excluded entitlement to certain special non-contributory cash benefits, even though those benefits are granted to nationals of the member state concerned who are in the same situation.[32] In *Brey*,[33] however, the court held that national legislation could not automatically bar the grant of a benefit to a national of another member state who is not economically active on the grounds that, despite having been issued with a certificate of residence, he or she does not meet the necessary requirements for obtaining the legal right to reside in the host member state for a period of longer than three months, because obtaining that right of residence is conditional upon that national having sufficient resources not to apply for the benefit: this was not permitted because the automatic bar did not provide for the host member state to carry out an overall assessment of the specific burden which granting that benefit would place on the social assistance system as a whole by reference to the personal circumstances of the person concerned.[34]

3.15 In this chapter, eligibility is considered for both homelessness and allocations. Before addressing each of these, in turn, below, it is first necessary to consider the detailed rules governing the relevant classes of the various immigration statuses which may be enjoyed by – or which may limit the rights of – applicants under either HA 1996 Part 6 or Part 7, or H(W)A Part 2.

Immigration control

3.16 People in the UK are divided into two classes: persons who are subject to immigration control; and persons who are not subject to immigration control. The latter group includes all persons who have a right to reside in the UK.

30 *Dano* at [60] and [61].

31 *Jobcenter Berlin Neukolin v Alimanovic*, Case C-67/14, [2016] 2 WLR 208, CJEU.

32 *Alimanovic* at [46], [63] and [64].

33 *Pensionsversicherungsanstalt v Brey*, Case C-140/12, [2014] 1 WLR 1080, CJEU.

34 *Brey* at [77], [80] and [81].

Persons subject to immigration control

3.17 The term 'persons subject to immigration control' as used in both HA 1996 Parts 6[35] and 7[36] and H(W)A 2014 Sch 2 para 1, is based on immigration legislation[37] and means a person who, under the Immigration Act (IA) 1971, requires leave to enter or remain in the UK (whether or not such leave has been given). Generally speaking, this means anyone who requires a visa to come to the UK. It mainly applies to non-EEA (European Economic Area) nationals, but EEA nationals who are not exercising a right to reside in the UK are also subject to immigration control[38] (although they are legally present).[39]

Persons not subject to immigration control

3.18 Persons not subject to immigration control form two groups. The first group consists of those who are exempt from the requirement to have leave to enter or remain in the UK.[40] This group is relatively unimportant for eligibility purposes, and comprises three main classes:

a) diplomats and certain staff of embassies and high commissions and their families who form part of their household;[41]
b) members of UK armed forces, members of a Commonwealth or similar force undergoing training in the UK with the UK armed forces, and members of a visiting force coming to the UK at the invitation of the government;[42] and
c) members of the crew of a ship or aircraft, hired or under orders to depart as part of that ship's crew or to depart on the same or another aircraft within seven days of arrival in the UK.[43]

35 HA 1996 s160A(3).

36 HA 1996 s185(2).

37 AIA 1996 s13.

38 *Abdi v Barnet LBC and First Secretary of State; Ismail v Barnet LBC and First Secretary of State* [2006] EWCA Civ 383, [2006] HLR 23. See para 3.20. See footnote 50, below, for members of the EEA.

39 *Abdirahman v Secretary of State for Work and Pensions* [2007] EWCA Civ 657, [2008] 1 WLR 254, [2007] 4 All ER 882. A person who has temporary admission to the UK is also lawfully present: see *Szoma v Secretary of State for Work and Pensions* [2005] UKHL 64, [2006] 1 AC 564.

40 IA 1971 s8.

41 IA 1971 ss3 and 3A.

42 IA 1971 s8(4) and (6).

43 IA 1971 s8(1).

3.19 The second group is those who do not require leave to enter or remain in the UK, they include:

a) British citizens;
b) Commonwealth citizens with the right of abode in the UK;
c) EEA nationals who have a right to reside in the UK.

3.20 The IA 1971 expressly excludes a) and b) from the requirement to have leave to enter or remain in the UK;[44] c) was a later addition to the group to reflect the evolving nature of the EU.[45]

British citizenship

3.21 British citizenship was created by the British Nationality Act (BNA) 1981.[46] It came into force on 1 January 1983. Prior to that date, the most beneficial form of national status was to be a Citizen of the United Kingdom and Colonies (CUKC) with the right of abode in the UK.[47] A person can become a British citizen in a variety of ways, which include the following:

a) a person who, on 31 December 1982, was a CUKC with the right of abode in the UK because of his or her birth, adoption, naturalisation or registration in the UK, or because he or she has a parent or grandparent who was born, adopted, naturalised or registered in the UK;[48]
b) a person who, on 31 December 1982, had been ordinarily resident in the UK for five years;[49]
c) a person born in the UK after 1 January 1983 is a British citizen if at the time of the birth, the person's father or mother was a British citizen or settled in the UK.[50] In this context, 'settled' means that he or she has indefinite leave to remain or permanent residence in the UK;
d) a person born in the UK after 1 January 1983 is entitled to be registered as a British citizen if, while the person is a minor, his or

44 IA 1971 s1(1).
45 IA 1988 s7(1).
46 This has been the subject of numerous amendments including by the Borders, Citizenship and Immigration Act 2009.
47 IA 1971 s2 as it was then in force.
48 BNA 1981 s11(1).
49 IA 1971 s2(1)(c) as it was in force on 31 December 1982.
50 BNA 1981 s1(1).

her father or mother becomes a British citizen or becomes settled in the UK;[51]

e) otherwise, a person born in the UK after 1 January 1983 can apply for registration as a British citizen after the person is ten years old, providing that he or she has not been absent from the UK for more than 90 days a year;[52]

f) generally speaking, a person born outside the UK after 1 January 1983 will be a British citizen if at the time of the birth his or her father or mother was a British citizen;[53]

g) a person may also apply for naturalisation[54] as a British citizen so long as the person fulfils certain requirements set out in BNA 1981.[55]

Commonwealth citizens with the right of abode in the UK

3.22 Since the coming into force of the BNA 1981,[56] the following now have the right of abode in the UK:

a) Persons who automatically became British citizens[57] on the coming into force of the BNA 1981.[58] These will include all the former citizens of the UK and Colonies who had a right of abode because they were 'patrials', ie, citizens of the UK and Colonies born, adopted, registered or naturalised in the UK, those with the necessary ancestral connections with the UK, and those who were ordinarily resident here for five years free of immigration restrictions.[59]

b) Commonwealth citizens[60] who immediately before commencement had the right of abode by virtue of having a parent who was born in the UK under the now revoked IA 1971 s2(1)(d).

51 BNA 1981 s1(3).
52 BNA 1981 s1(4).
53 BNA 1981 s2.
54 BNA 1981 s6.
55 BNA 1981 Sch 1.
56 On 1 January 1983.
57 See para 3.21(a) and (b).
58 BNA 1981 s11.
59 IA 1971 s2(1)(c) before amendment.
60 Commonwealth citizens are all those who are citizens of the countries set out in BNA 1981 Sch 3.

c) Female Commonwealth citizens who immediately before commencement had a right of abode under the now revoked IA 1971 s2(2) by virtue of their marriage to a patrial.[61]

EEA nationals with the right to reside in the UK

3.23 The right to reside in the UK for EEA nationals now derives from the Treaty on the Functioning of the European Union (TFEU).[62] It is not an unconditional right.[63] The requirements to be met are principally[64] set out in Directive 2004/38/EC[65] ('the Directive') which has been enacted into domestic law by the Immigration (European Economic Area) Regulations ('EEA Regs') 2016.[66] The EEA Regs 2016 are not simply a repetition of the Directive: where the Directive gives a right to reside and the EEA Regs 2016 do not, an applicant is entitled to rely on the Directive.[67] Conversely, if the Directive does not give a right to reside but the EEA Regs 2016 do so, then an applicant can rely on those more favourable provisions.

3.24 There are two ways in which a person can have a right to reside in the UK. These are either

a) as an EEA[68] national who satisfies the relevant conditions,[69] who is known as a 'qualified person'[70] in the EEA Regs 2016; or

61 IA 1971 s2 before amendment. Patriality was conferred on certain citizens of the UK and Colonies and certain other Commonwealth citizens.

62 This came into force on 1 December 2009.

63 TFEU Article 21; *Minister voor Vreemdelingenzaken en Integratie v RNG Eind*, Case C-291/05 at [28]; *Trojani v Centre public d'aide sociale de Bruxelles* (CPAS), Case C-456/02, [2004] ECR I-7573 at paras [31] and [32]; *Zhu and Chen v Secretary of State for the Home Department*, Case C-200/02, [2004] ECR I-9925 at para [26]; *Ali v Secretary of State for the Home Department* [2006] EWCA Civ 484, [2006] 3 CMLR 10 at para [20].

64 Some rights of residence exist outside the scope of the Directive, see paras 3.79–3.99.

65 Of the European Parliament and of the Council of 29 April 2004, which came into force on 30 April 2004.

66 SI No 1052, which came into force on 1 February 2017.

67 IA 1988 s7(1).

68 The EEA consists of the EU plus Norway, Iceland and Liechtenstein. The EU consists of the EU15: Austria, Belgium, Denmark, Finland, France, Germany, Greece, Ireland, Italy, Luxembourg, the Netherlands, Portugal, Spain, Sweden and the UK, plus the countries which acceded on 1 May 2004, which are Cyprus, the Czech Republic, Estonia, Hungary, Latvia, Lithuania, Malta, Poland, Slovakia, Slovenia, plus the countries which acceded on 1 January 2007 (the A2), which are Bulgaria and Romania and Croatia which acceded on 1 July 2013 pursuant to the Accession Treaty signed on 9 December 2011.

69 These are either set out in the Directive or the EEA Regs 2016.

70 EEA Regs 2016 reg 6(1).

b) as a family member of an EEA national who either has a right to reside or has had a right to reside.

3.25 The right to reside exists independently of any residence documentation: the latter is merely evidence of the right,[71] although a person who is in possession of such documentation may be able to rely on Article 18 of the TFEU in order to be granted social assistance:[72] in *Sanneh*,[73] however, the Court of Appeal held that this only applied to EU citizens in possession of a residence permit.[74] This seems consistent with the judgment of the CJEU in *Ahmed*,[75] which concerned an Algerian national with a right under domestic law to be present in Belgium, which was held not to be enough to enable her to claim social assistance under EU law.[76]

3.26 There are three types of the EEA national right to reside:

a) initial right to reside;
b) extended right to reside;
c) permanent right to reside.

Initial right to reside

3.27 An EEA national must be admitted to the UK if he or she produces on arrival a valid national identity card or passport issued by an EEA state.[77] A person who is not an EEA national must produce on arrival a valid passport and an EEA family permit, a residence card or a permanent residence card.[78] An EEA family permit acts as a sort of entry clearance or visa for non-EEA nationals and its issue cannot be made subject to conditions that are more restrictive than those set out in the Directive.[79]

71 *Mario Lopes da Veiga v Staatssecretaris van Justitie*, Case 9/88; *Echternach and Moritz v Minister van Onderwijs en Wetenschappen*, Cases 389/87 and 390/87, at para [25]; *Secretary of State for Work and Pensions v Maria Dias*, Case C-325/09 at para [48].

72 *Trojani v Centre public d'aide sociale de Bruxelles* (CPAS), Case C-456/02, [2004] ECR I-7573 at para [43].

73 *Sanneh v Secretary of State for Work and Pensions* [2015] EWCA Civ 49, [2015] HLR 27.

74 *Sanneh* at [110].

75 *Office national d'allocations familiales pour travailleurs salaries (ONAFTS) v Ahmed*, Case C-45/12.

76 *Ahmed* at [40] and [41].

77 Directive 2004/38/EC Article 5(1); EEA Regs 2016 reg 11(1).

78 EEA Regs 2016 reg 11(2); see also Directive 2004/38/EC Article 5(2).

79 *Metock v Minister for Justice, Equality and Law Reform*, Case C-127/08.

3.28 The initial right to reside lasts for no longer than three months and is on condition that the EEA national or his or her family member does not become an unreasonable burden on the social assistance system of the UK.[80] The phrase 'unreasonable burden' may be thought to imply that a temporary or short-term reliance on social assistance does not deprive a person of an initial right to reside.

3.29 The term 'social assistance' is not defined in the Directive, or elsewhere in EU legislation, but has been considered by the CJEU, which has held that the grant of such assistance must essentially depend on need and not be linked to employment or contributions.[81] This is therefore likely to be considered to include social housing.[82] In England, a person who has an initial right to reside is ineligible under HA 1996 Parts 6[83] and 7.[84] In Wales, such a person is also ineligible under HA 1996 Part 6[85] and H(W)A 2014 Part 2.[86]

Extended right to reside

3.30 There are five ways in which an EEA national may have an extended right to reside in the UK.[87] These are as:

a) a jobseeker;
b) a worker;
c) a self-employed person;
d) a self-sufficient person; or
e) a student.

A jobseeker

3.31 A jobseeker is a person who:

a) entered the UK in order to seek employment; or
b) is present in the UK seeking employment, after having previously had a right to reside;

and in either case

c) provides evidence of seeking employment and having a genuine chance of being engaged.

80 Directive 2004/38/EC Article 14(1); EEA Regs 2016 reg 13.
81 *Frilli v Belgium* Case 1/72, [1972] ECR 457, [1973] CMLR 386.
82 By analogy, for the purposes of immigration law, the term 'public funds' is defined (Immigration Rules (HC 395) para 6) as including housing under HA 1996 Part 6 or Part 7 and HA 1985 Part 2.
83 Eligibility Regs 2006 reg 4(1)(b)(ii).
84 Eligibility Regs 2006 reg 6(1)(b)(ii).
85 Eligibility (Wales) Regs 2014 reg 4(1)(b)(ii).
86 Eligibility (Wales) Regs 2014 reg 6(1)(b)(ii).
87 EEA Regs 2016 reg 6(1)(a)–(e).

A person can retain the status of jobseeker for as long as he or she provides compelling evidence of continuing to seek employment and having a genuine chance of being engaged.[88] The CJEU has held that, after six months, a jobseeker must provide evidence that he or she is continuing to seek employment and has genuine chances of being engaged.[89] In English law, jobseekers are expressly excluded from eligibility under HA 1996 Parts 6[90] and 7.[91] In Wales, jobseekers are ineligible under HA 1996 Part 6[92] and H(W)A 2014 Part 2.[93]

A worker

3.32 There are three essential criteria which determine whether a person is a worker for the purposes of Article 45 of the TFEU. First, the person must perform services of some economic value.[94] The activity must be real and genuine, to the exclusion of activity on such a small scale as to be marginal and ancillary.[95] Second, the performance of such services must be for and under the direction of another person. Any activity performed outside a relationship of subordination must be classified as an activity pursued in a self-employed capacity.[96]

3.33 Third, the person concerned must receive remuneration.[97] Neither the origin of the funds from which the remuneration is paid nor the limited amount of that remuneration can have any consequences with regard to whether or not the person is a worker.[98] The fact that the income from employment is lower than the minimum required for subsistence does not prevent the person in such employment from being regarded as a worker,[99] even if the person in question seeks to supplement that remuneration by other means of subsistence such

88 EEA Regs 2016 reg 6(1).

89 *R v Immigration Appeal Tribunal ex p Antonissen,* Case C-292/98, [1991] ECR I 745.

90 Eligibility Regs 2006 reg 4(1)(b)(i).

91 Eligibility Regs 2006 reg 6(1)(b)(i).

92 Eligibility (Wales) Regs 2014 reg 4(1)(b)(i).

93 Eligibility (Wales) Regs 2014 reg 6(1)(b)(i).

94 *Lawrie-Blum v Land Baden Wurttemberg,* Case 66/85, [1986] ECR 2121; in *Bristol City Council v FV* [2011] UKUT 494 (AAC) (21 December 2011), the Upper Tribunal held that sellers of the *Big Issue* can be considered self-employed.

95 *Vatsouras and Koupatantze v Arbeitgemeinschaft (ARGE) Nurnberg 900,* Cases C-22/08 and C-23/08; *Lawrie Blum,* above.

96 *Jany v Staatssecretaris van Justitie,* Case C-268/99 at [34].

97 *Vatsouras,* above, at para [25]; and *Lawrie-Blum,* above.

98 *Vatsouras,* above, at para [27].

99 *Levin v Staatssecretaris van Justitie,* Case 53/81.

as financial assistance drawn from the public funds[100] of the host member state.[101]

3.34 The fact that the employment is of short duration does not, of itself, prevent the employee from being a worker.[102]

3.35 A person who is no longer working does not cease to be a worker if:[103]

a) the person is temporarily[104] unable to work as the result of an illness or accident;
b) the person is in duly recorded involuntary unemployed[105] after having been employed in the UK for at least one year, provided that the person has registered as a jobseeker with the relevant employment office,[106] and satisfies conditions A and B (below);

100 For the purposes of UK immigration law, the term 'public funds' is defined in the Immigration Rules (HC 395) para 6 as including housing under HA 1996 Part 6 or Part 7 and HA 1985 Part 2. The Rules have not been updated to reflect the H(W)A 2014.

101 *Kempf v Staatssecretaris van Justitie*, Case 139/85, [1986] ECR 1741.

102 *Vatsouras*, above, at para [29]; *Ninni Orasche v Bundesminster für Wissenschaft, Verkehr und Kunst*, Case C-413/01; *Barry v Southwark LBC* [2008] EWCA Civ 1140, [2009] HLR 30.

103 EEA Regs 2016 reg 6(2).

104 In *Secretary of State for the Home Department v FB* [2010] UKUT 447 (IAC), it was held that temporary means not permanent, see paras [23]–[26], followed by the Court of Appeal in *Aurelio de Brito and Lizette de Noronha v Secretary of State for the Home Department* [2012] EWCA Civ 709, [2012] 3 CMLR 24 at [30]–[35], where it was held that the test is objective and that a temporary condition could become permanent and a permanent condition could become temporary depending upon the facts of the case, such as a successful medical intervention. In *Konodyba v Royal Borough of Kensington and Chelsea* [2012] EWCA Civ 982, [2013] PTSR 13 at [22] and [23], the Court of Appeal held that whether a homeless applicant is temporarily unable to work or unlikely to be able to work in the foreseeable future is a question of fact. All these decisions were followed in *Samin v Westminster City Council* [2012] EWCA Civ 1468, [2013] 2 CMLR 6, [2013] HLR 7 where the Court of Appeal held that the question is one of fact in every case and that it will generally be helpful to ask whether there is or is not a realistic prospect of a return to work. This case has now been the subject of an appeal to the Supreme Court, [2016] UKSC 1, [2016] HLR 7, but this aspect of the case was unaffected by its judgment: see para 3.11 above.

105 In decisions of the Social Security Commissioner CH/3314/2005 and CIS/3315/2005, it was held that this phrase is concerned with why the worker is not working at the date of the decision, and not on why the worker ceased to be employed, though this may also be relevant: see para [11].

106 *Elmi v Secretary of State for Work and Pensions* [2011] EWCA Civ 1403, [2013] PTSR 780 concerned an EU citizen who had become involuntarily unemployed and then claimed income support at Jobcentre Plus. She ticked the box on the relevant form stating that she was looking for work. The Court of Appeal held that she had registered with the employment office

but he or she cannot retain such status for longer than six months without providing compelling evidence[107] of continuing to seek employment and having a genuine chance of being engaged;

c) the person is in duly recorded involuntary unemployment after having been employed in the UK for less than one year, provided he or she has registered as a jobseeker with the relevant employment office, and satisfies conditions A and B, but he or she can only retain worker status for a maximum of six months under this provision.[108]

d) the person is involuntarily unemployed and has embarked on vocational training; or

e) the person has voluntarily ceased working and embarked on vocational training that is related to his or her previous employment.

Condition A is that the person entered the UK in order to seek employment, or is present in the UK seeking employment, immediately after enjoying a right to reside other than as a jobseeker.[109] Condition B is that the person provides evidence of seeking employment and of having a genuine chance of being engaged.[110]

3.36 If a woman is incapable of working due to pregnancy, this does not constitute an illness or accident unless there is an actual associated illness.[111] The Court of Appeal adopted a similar approach to a

as a jobseeker, even though she was in receipt of income support and not jobseeker's allowance, and had therefore retained her worker status.

107 In *KS v Secretary of State for Work and Pensions* [2016] UKUT 269 (AAC), it was held that this means no more than the requirement for evidence to establish on a balance of probabilities that the claimant is continuing to seek employment and has genuine chances of being engaged. To interpret the phrase as meaning that a higher standard of proof is required would be contrary to EU law. See also *Secretary of State for Work and Pensions v MB (JSA)* [2016] UKUT 372 (AAC), where it was held that the fact that a claimant has been looking for work for six months is only one factor in determining whether he or she has a genuine chance of being engaged; 'compelling' evidence does not mean more than chances that are founded on something objective and offer real prospects of employment within a reasonable period. Given that evaluating a 'chance' necessitates a degree of looking forward, events likely to occur in the near future may be relevant to a claimant's genuine chance of being engaged. The government's guidance, the Decision Makers' Guide Volume 2: International subjects: staff guide para 073099 suggests an approach that is much higher than a mere balance of probabilities and may therefore not be correct.

108 EEA Regs 2016 reg 6(3).

109 EEA Regs 2016 reg 6(5).

110 EEA Regs 2016 reg 6(6).

111 [2009] UKUT 71 (AAC), decided in the context of a benefits appeal and *Webb v EMO Air Cargo (UK) Ltd* Case C-32/93 [1994] ECR I-3567.

woman who ceased working as a nursery school teacher because the demands of the job were too great for her because of her pregnancy, although it had not been found that she could not work because of the pregnancy.[112] It was held that the term 'worker' cannot be construed to include a person who has no contract of employment and is not therefore on maternity leave, although the issue of whether this amounted to unlawful sex discrimination was left open because it did not arise on the evidence.[113] This case was the subject of a reference to the CJEU as *St Prix*,[114] where it was held that a woman who had temporarily given up work because of the late stages of her pregnancy and aftermath of childbirth could not be regarded as a person temporarily unable to work as the result of an illness, but that she nevertheless retained the status of worker provided that she returned to work or found another job within a reasonable time after the birth of her child; in order to determine whether the period was reasonable, the national court should take account of all the specific circumstances of the case and the applicable national rules on the duration of maternity leave.[115] In a decision of the Upper Tribunal[116] it was held that it will be an unusual case in which the reasonable period is other than a 52-week period.[117] This is consistent with the concession made by the secretary of state in the Court of Appeal in *Dias*, that a woman on maternity leave retains her status as a worker, which the court assumed was correct.[118]

A self-employed person

3.37 A self-employed person means a person who establishes himself or herself in another EU state in order to pursue activity as a self-

112 *JS v Secretary of State for Work and Pensions* [2011] EWCA Civ 806. The case is now the subject of a reference to the ECJ, see [2012] UKSC 49.

113 *JS* at paras [19] and [27].

114 *St Prix v Secretary of State for Work and Pensions*, Case C-507/12, [2014] PTSR 1448.

115 *St Prix* at [29], [47] and [48].

116 *Secretary of State for Work and Pensions v SFF* [2015] UKUT 0502 (AAC) and *Weldemichael and Obulor v Secretary of State for the Home Department* [2015] UKUT 540 (IAC) at [59], where it was held, as a general proposition, that a woman will retain worker status where maternity did not commence more than 11 weeks before the expected date of birth, she did not have more than 52 weeks off and she returned to work after that period. This was a determination of the Upper Tribunal in relation to an immigration case.

117 *Secretary of State for Work and Pensions v SFF* at [35].

118 *Secretary of State for Work and Pensions v Dias* [2009] EWCA Civ 807, [2010] 1 CMLR 4 at para [18].

employed person in accordance with Article 49 of the TFEU.[119] Essentially, this means a person who is working outside a relationship of subordination.[120]

3.38 The EEA Regs 2016 provide that a person who is no longer in self-employment shall not cease to be treated as a self-employed person if he or she is temporarily unable to pursue his or her activity as the result of an illness or accident.[121] This is much narrower than the provisions of the Directive,[122] which allow a self-employed person to retain that status in the same way as a worker who is no longer working. In *Tilianu*, the Court of Appeal applied this differential treatment and held that unless a self-employed person is temporarily unable to pursue his or her activity because of illness or accident, a person who is not working is not self-employed.[123] This means that the self-employed have fewer rights than workers, because there are fewer circumstances in which they can retain that status when they are not working.[124] This is arguably discriminatory under Article 18 of the TFEU, unless there is some justification for the differential treatment.

3.39 The decision of the Court of Appeal in *Tilianu* was distinguished in a benefits appeal,[125] where the Upper Tribunal held that a self-employed person does not necessarily cease to be self-employed just because he or she does not have any contract work at that particular time. If the person is actively seeking self-employed work, then he or she can still be held to be self-employed and therefore continue to have a right to reside. The basis of the distinction was that the Court of Appeal had not considered whether self-employed status had been retained.

A self-sufficient person

3.40 A self-sufficient person is a person who has sufficient resources not to become a burden on the social assistance system of the UK during his or her period of residence, and has comprehensive sickness insurance cover in the UK.[126] The requirement not to become a burden on the social assistance system of the UK is not qualified, as in

119 EEA Regs 2016 reg 4(1)(b).

120 See *Jany*, above.

121 EEA Regs 2016 reg 6(4).

122 Directive 2004/38/EC Article 7(3).

123 *R (Tilianu) v Secretary of State for Work and Pensions* [2010] EWCA Civ 1397, [2011] PTSR 781.

124 See para 3.35.

125 *Secretary of State for Work and Pensions v AL* [2010] UKUT 451 (AAC).

126 EEA Regs 2016 reg 4(1)(c).

the case of a person who has an initial right to reside, which only requires that the person is not to be an 'unreasonable' burden.[127] A self-sufficient person is most unlikely to be eligible in England under HA 1996 Parts 6 and 7, and in Wales under HA 1996 Part 6 and H(W)A 2014 Part 2, because the need for social housing will mean that the person has become a burden on the social assistance system of the UK and therefore cannot have a right to reside on the basis of self-sufficiency.[128]

3.41 The Commission of the European Communities has published[129] guidance on the interpretation of the Directive. This states that any insurance cover, private or public, contracted in the host member state or elsewhere, is acceptable in principle, as long as it provides comprehensive coverage and does not create a burden on the public finances of the host member state.[130] This could suggest that private health insurance may not be necessary, and raised the possibility that NHS cover was sufficient.[131] In *Ahmad*,[132] however, the Court of Appeal held that access to NHS treatment was not sufficient to count as comprehensive sickness insurance. The court followed its previous decision in *W (China)*,[133] in which it was held that use of free state medical services did create a burden on the host state and that contributions towards it were not a proxy for insurance designed to remove the burden of providing health care.

3.42 In a benefits appeal,[134] a Polish national who was receiving an invalidity pension from Sweden was held to have comprehensive sickness cover by virtue of Regulation (EEC) No 1408/71[135] because

127 Directive 2004/38/EC Article 14(1); EEA Regs 2016 reg 13; see paras 3.27–3.29.

128 By analogy, for the purposes of immigration law, 'public funds' is defined (Immigration Rules (HC 395) para 6) as including housing under HA 1996 Part 6 or Part 7 and HA 1985 Part 2; the rules have not yet been amended to reflect the introduction of H(W)A 2014 Part 2.

129 On 2 July 2009.

130 At para 2.3.2.

131 In *Secretary of State for Work and Pensions v SW* [2011] UKUT 508 (AAC), 15 December 2011 at [20], the Upper Tribunal stated that a person could be self-sufficient by virtue of being entitled to treatment under the NHS by satisfying the residence and presence conditions under domestic law. In *Secretary of State for Work and Pensions v Czop*, C-147/11 at [38], the UK government conceded that the claimant was self-sufficient even though she did not have private health insurance.

132 *Ahmad v Secretary of State for the Home Department* [2014] EWCA Civ 988, [2015] 1 WLR 593.

133 *W (China) v Secretary of State for the Home Department* [2006] EWCA Civ 1494, [2007] 1 WLR 1514.

134 *SG v Tameside MBC* [2010] UKUT 243.

135 This has now been replaced by Regulation (EC) No 883/04.

these provisions allowed the UK to claim back the cost of her NHS care from Sweden. She did not, however, have sufficient resources, taking into account her housing needs and the fact that her stay in the UK was intended to be permanent.

A student

3.43 A student is a person who:

a) is enrolled, for the principal purpose of following a course of study (including vocational training), at a private or public establishment which is financed from public funds or otherwise recognised by the secretary of state as an establishment which has been accredited for the purpose of providing such courses or training within the law or administrative practice of the part of the UK in which the establishment is located;
b) has comprehensive sickness insurance cover in the UK; and
c) assures the secretary of state by means of a declaration or by such equivalent means as he or she may choose that he or she has sufficient resources not to become a burden on the social assistance system of the UK during his or her period of residence.[136]

This means that a person can have a right to reside as a student even if he or she subsequently becomes a burden on the social assistance system of the UK, ie if his or her circumstances change. If a student can have a right of residence despite having a need for social housing, then the student is likely to be eligible in England under both HA 1996 Parts 6[137] and 7,[138] and in Wales under HA 1996 Part 6 and H(W)A 2014 Part 2, so long as he or she is habitually resident in the UK.

Permanent right to reside

3.44 An EEA national who has resided in the UK for a continuous period of five years has a permanent right to reside.[139] The CJEU has held that periods of imprisonment cannot be taken into account for the purpose of acquiring the right of permanent residence, so that they interrupt continuity of residence for this purpose.[140] Family members who are

136 Directive 2004/38/EC Article 7(1)(c); EEA Regs 2016 reg 4(1)(d).

137 In England, Eligibility Regs 2006 reg 4(1); in Wales, Eligibility (Wales) Regs 2014 reg 4(1).

138 In England, Eligibility Regs 2006 reg 6(1); in Wales, Eligibility (Wales) Regs 2014 reg 6(1).

139 Directive 2004/38/EC Article 16(1); EEA Regs 2016 reg 15(1).

140 *Onuekwere v Secretary of State for the Home Department, Secretary of State for the Home Department v MG*, Cases C-378/12 and C-400/12.

not EEA nationals but who have resided with the EEA national for a continuous period of five years also obtain the right.[141]

3.45 Workers or self-employed persons who have stopped working (and their family members) also have a permanent right of residence.[142] The worker or self-employed person must have resided in the UK continuously for more than three years, must have worked for at least the last one of those years, and then stopped working at an age when he or she is entitled to a state pension or, in the case of an employed person, has ceased work in order to take early retirement.[143]

3.46 The definition also applies to a person who has stopped working as a result of a permanent incapacity to work who either resided in the UK continuously for more than two years prior to the termination, or whose incapacity is the result of an accident at work or an occupational disease that entitles him or her to a pension payable in full or in part by an institution in the UK.[144] The Court of Appeal has held that a non-EU national[145] is entitled to a permanent right to reside under Directive Article 17(3) on marrying an EU worker who has stopped working due to a permanent incapacity and who had lived in the UK for two years prior to that time, and that it was not necessary for her to have been a family member before, or as at the date of, her husband's acquisition of permanent residence.[146]

3.47 In *Lassal*,[147] the ECJ noted that the permanent right to reside did not appear in previous EU legislation; it held that continuous periods of five years' residence completed before the Directive came into force on 30 April 2006, in accordance with earlier legislation, had to be taken into account for the purposes of the acquisition of the right. It also held that absences from the host member state of less than two consecutive years, which occurred before 30 April 2006 but after a continuous period of five years' legal residence completed before that date, did not affect acquisition of the right of permanent residence.

3.48 In *Dias*,[148] the ECJ held that time spent in the UK before 30 April

141 Directive 2004/38/EC Article 16(1); EEA Regs 2016 reg 15(1)(b).

142 Directive 2004/38/EC Article 17; EEA Regs 2016 reg 15(1)(c) and (d).

143 Directive 2004/38/EC Article 17; EEA Regs 2016 reg 5(2).

144 Directive 2004/38/EC Article 17; EEA Regs 2016 reg 5(3).

145 Sometimes known as a third country national.

146 *RM (Zimbabwe) v Secretary of State for the Home Department* [2013] EWCA Civ 775, [2014] 1 WLR 2259.

147 *Secretary of State for Work and Pensions v Lassal and Child Poverty Action Group (intervener)*, Case C-162/09, [2011] 1 CMLR 31.

148 *Secretary of State for Work and Pensions v Maria Dias*, Case C-325/09, [2011] 3 CMLR 40.

2006, when Ms Dias had no right to reside but was in possession of a residence permit granted by the national authorities, did not constitute legal residence and therefore could not count towards the five years required for permanent residence. It was, however, also held that such time would not, so long as it amounted to less than two consecutive years, affect any right of permanent residence which had already been acquired. This does not seem to rule out the argument that the holder of a valid residence permit is entitled to social assistance; otherwise, there would be discrimination contrary to Article 18 of the TFEU.[149] This, however, seems only to apply to EU citizens, by virtue of what was said in *Sanneh*[150] (after consideration of what was said in *Ahmed*[151] by the CJEU).

3.49 In *Clauder*,[152] the European Free Trade Association (EFTA)[153] Court held that, although Article 16 of the Directive does not confer an autonomous right of residence on the family members of an EEA national with a permanent right to reside, it does grant them a derivative right to live with the holder of permanent residence. The admission and residence of the family members in such cases is not subject to a condition of sufficient resources, because the holder of a permanent right of residence is not subject to any such requirement and his or her enjoyment of that right would be impaired and deprived of its full effectiveness if he or she were prevented from founding a family on the basis of insufficient resources. Family members will only obtain permanent residence when they have fulfilled five years' residence.

3.50 In *Ziolkowski*,[154] the ECJ held that Article 16 of the Directive must be interpreted as meaning that an EU citizen who has been resident for more than five years in a host member state on the sole basis of the national law of that state, and without a right of residence pursuant to Article 7(1) of the Directive, cannot be regarded as having

149 *Trojani v Centre public d'aide sociale de Bruxelles (CPAS)*, Case C-456/02, [2004] ECR1-7573, ECJ at paras [43]–[46], which was followed in *R (Bidar) v London Borough of Ealing and Secretary of State for Education and Skills*, Case C-209/03, at para [37].

150 *Sanneh v Secretary of State for Work and Pensions* [2015] EWCA Civ, [2015] HLR 27 at [110].

151 *ONAFTS v Ahmed*, C-45/12 at [40] and [41].

152 Case E-4/11, 26 July 2011.

153 This was not a decision of the CJEU because it concerned a retired German citizen living in Liechtenstein which is not a member of the EU and therefore not subject to the jurisdiction of the CJEU. Liechtenstein, along with Iceland and Norway, are part of the EEA and therefore their references go to the EFTA Court instead.

154 *Ziolkowski and Szeja v Land Berlin*, Cases C-424/10 and C-425/10.

acquired permanent residence. In the same case, it also held that periods of residence completed by a national of a non-member state in the territory of a member state before its accession to the EU must, in the absence of specific provisions in the Act of Accession, count towards the period required to obtain permanent residence, provided they were completed in accordance with Article 7(1) of the Directive.

Residence documentation

3.51 An EEA national who has a right to reside in the UK is entitled to a registration certificate or derivative[155] residence card.[156] A non-EEA national who has a right to reside in the UK is entitled to a residence card or derivative residence card.[157] A person with a permanent right of residence is entitled to a permanent residence document.[158]

Family members

3.52 The EEA Regs 2016[159] define a 'family member' as:

a) a spouse[160] or civil partner;
b) direct descendants including those of a spouse or civil partner who are:
   i) under 21; or
   ii) their dependants;[161]

155 A derivative residence card is granted to a person whose right to reside in the UK is dependent upon another person's right to reside; see paras 3.79–3.99.

156 Directive 2004/38/EC Article 8; EEA Regs 2016 regs 17 and 20 ; the right to reside exists independently of any residence documentation which is merely evidence of the right, see *da Veiga v Staatssecretaris van Justitie*, Case 9/88; *Echternach and Moritz v Minister van Onderwijs en Wetenschappen*, Cases 389/87 and 390/87, at para [25]; *Secretary of State for Work and Pensions v Dias*, Case C-325/09 at para [48]; a person who is in possession of such documentation may, however, rely on EC Treaty Article 12 in order to be granted social assistance, see *Trojani v Centre public d'aide sociale de Bruxelles* (CPAS), Case C-456/02, [2004] ECR I-7573, at para [43].

157 Directive 2004/38/EC Article 10; EEA Regs 2016 regs 18 and 20.

158 Directive 2004/38/EC Articles 19 and 20; EEA Regs 2016 reg 19.

159 EEA Regs 2016 reg 7(1).

160 EEA Regs 2016 reg 7(1)(a). In *Diatta v Land Berlin* [1985] EUECJ R 267/83, the CJEU held that a marital relationship continues until terminated by the competent authority and is not affected by the fact that the spouses live separately, even where they intend to divorce at a later date. Note EEA Regs 2016 reg 2(1) states that a spouse does not include: a) a party to a marriage of convenience; or b) the spouse of a person who already has a spouse, civil partner or durable partner in the UK.

161 In *Reyes v Migrationsverket*, Case C-423/12, the CJEU held that a member state cannot require a direct descendent who is 21 years old or over to have tried to obtain employment or subsistence support from his or her home state before he or she can be treated as a dependant under the Directive Article 2(2)(c).

c) dependent[162] direct[163] relatives in the person's ascending line (ie, parents or grandparents) or those of the person's spouse or civil partner, or
d) extended family members[164] who have been issued with an EEA family permit, a registration certificate or a residence card and who satisfy the conditions in EEA Regs 2016 reg 8.

3.53 In *Jia*,[165] the CJEU defined 'dependency' to mean that the family member needs the material support of the EEA national or his or her spouse in order to meet his or her essential needs in the country of origin. Proof to establish such material support may be adduced by any appropriate means and is not confined to financial dependency.[166] This decision has been distinguished by the Court of Appeal,[167] which has held that Article 2(2) of the Directive did not specify when the dependency had to have arisen, nor did it require that the relative had to be dependent in the country of origin. Further, it was held that Article 2(2), taken together with Article 8(5)(d), suggested that dependency in the state of origin need not be proved for family members and it was sufficient if the dependency arose in the host member state. Such an interpretation, it was held, reflected the policy of the Directive to strengthen and simplify the realisation of realistic free movement rights of EU citizens compatibly with their family rights; accordingly, proof of dependency by the claimant on her son in the UK sufficed.

3.54 In *Metock*,[168] the CJEU held that it was contrary to the Directive for a member state to enact legislation which requires a non-EEA national, who is the spouse of an EU citizen residing in that member state but not possessing its nationality, to have previously been lawfully resident in another member state before arriving in the host member state, in order to benefit from the free movement rights set out in the Directive. Further, Article 3(1) must be interpreted as

162 EEA Regs 2016 reg 7(1)(c).

163 *PG and VG* [2007] UKAIT 19, where it was held that 'direct' is not confined to the first generation but can include grandchildren, although it does not include nieces, nephews, uncles and aunts. This approach was assumed to be correct in *Bigia and others v Entry Clearance Officer* [2009] EWCA Civ 79 at [4].

164 See para 3.56.

165 *Jia v Migrationsverket*, Case C-1/05, [2007] QB 545.

166 *Jia* at para [43].

167 *Pedro v Secretary of State for Work and Pensions* [2009] EWCA Civ 1358, [2010] PTSR 1504.

168 *Metock and others v Minister for Justice, Equality and Law Reform*, Case C-127/08.

meaning that a non-EEA national who is the spouse of an EU citizen residing in a member state whose nationality he or she does not possess and who accompanies or joins that EU citizen, benefits from the provisions of that Directive, irrespective of when and where the marriage took place and of how the national of a non-member country entered the host member state.

3.55 The EEA Regs 2006 were amended[169] to reflect this judgment, which change has been carried across to the EEA Regs 2016, so that the family member who is accompanying the EEA national to the UK, or joining the EEA national here, no longer has to be lawfully resident in an EEA state or meet the requirements of the Immigration Rules.

3.56 An extended family member[170] is treated as the family member of the relevant EEA national for so long as he or she holds a valid EEA family permit, a registration certificate or a residence card[171] and is one of the following:[172]

a) a relative of an EEA national, residing in a country other than the UK who is dependent on the EEA national or is a member of the EEA national's household and who either is accompanying the EEA national to the UK or wants to join him or her in the UK, or who has joined the EEA national in the UK and continues to be dependent upon him or her, or to be a member of the EEA national's household;[173]
b) a relative of an EEA national or his or her spouse or civil partner, who strictly requires his or her personal care on serious health grounds;[174]
c) a relative of an EEA national who would meet the requirements for indefinite leave to enter or remain in the UK as a dependent relative of the EEA national;[175]

169 Immigration (European Economic Area) (Amendment) Regulations 2011 SI No 1247.
170 See para 3.52(d).
171 EEA Regs 2016 reg 7(3).
172 EEA Regs 2016 reg 8.
173 EEA Regs 2016 reg 8(2).
174 EEA Regs 2016 reg 8(3).
175 EEA Regs 2016 reg 8(4).

d) a partner of an EEA national who can prove that he or she is in a durable[176] relationship with the EEA national.[177]

3.57 A number of questions about extended family members have been referred[178] to the CJEU. The CJEU has held that member states have a wide discretion in setting criteria for extended family members: Article 3(2) of the Directive does not provide a direct right to reside for such persons, and states can impose requirements in their own domestic legislation.[179] This is consistent with domestic cases which have held that extended family members have no right to reside unless they have residence documentation.[180] Subsequent to the decision of the CJEU in *Rahman*,[181] the Court of Appeal has approved the approach in that case and held that Article 3(2) requires an extended family member to show dependence that existed in the country from which the family member comes; accordingly, and is in contrast to the position of non-extended family members,[182] there is a requirement that the necessary relationship of dependency or membership of the household must have existed in another country as well as in the host state.[183]

3.58 A family member has a right to reside in the UK for so long as he or she remains the family member of an EEA national who has a right to reside in the UK.[184] The Directive provides that EEA nationals who are family members of an EEA national retain the right to reside on the death or departure of the EEA national from the host member state[185] or where there has been a divorce, annulment of marriage or termination of the registered partnership between the

176 Home Office policy suggests that a period of two years' cohabitation is required. EEA Regs 2016 reg 2(1) defines a durable partner as not including a party to a durable partnership of convenience, or the durable partner (D) of a person (P) where a spouse, civil partner or durable partner of D or P is already present in the UK and where that marriage, civil partnership or durable relationship is subsisting.

177 EEA Regs 2016 reg 8(5).

178 *MR (Bangladesh) and others* [2010] UKUT 449 (IAC).

179 *Secretary of State for the Home Department v Rahman and others*, Case C 83/11 at [26].

180 *SS v Secretary of State for Work and Pensions (ESA)* [2011] UKUT 8 (AAC).

181 *Secretary of State for the Home Department v Rahman and others*, Case C 83/11.

182 See para 3.52.

183 *Oboh and others v Secretary of State for the Home Department* [2013] EWCA Civ 1525, [2014] 1 WLR 1680.

184 EEA Regs 2016 reg 14(2).

185 Directive 2004/38/EC Article 12(1).

family member and the EEA national.[186] Under the Directive, family members who are not EEA nationals may also retain their right to reside.[187]

3.59 The EEA Regs 2016 provide that family members who are not EEA nationals may retain a right to reside in the following circumstances,[188] which are more restrictive than the Directive:

a) if the qualified person has died and the family member has resided in the UK for at least a year before the death and, if he or she were an EEA national, would be a worker, a self-employed person or a self-sufficient person or the family member of such a person;[189]
b) if the family member is the direct descendant of a qualified person who has died or left the UK, or is a direct descendant of that person's spouse or civil partner, and he or she was attending an educational course in the UK immediately before the qualified person died or left the UK, and continues to attend such a course;[190]
c) if the family member is the parent with actual custody of a child who satisfies b) above;[191]
d) if the family member ceased to be such because he or she is divorced from the qualified person[192] or their civil partnership has been terminated, he or she is not an EEA national but if he or she were, he or she would be a worker,[193] a self-employed person or

186 Directive 2004/38/EC Article 13(1).

187 Directive 2004/38/EC Articles 12(2), (3) and 13(2).

188 EEA Regs 2016 reg 10.

189 EEA Regs 2016 reg 10(2).

190 EEA Regs 2016 reg 10(3).

191 EEA Regs 2016 reg 10(4).

192 In *Singh and others v Minister for Justice and Equality and Immigrant Council of Ireland*, Case C-218/14, [2016] QB 208, the ECJ held that a third country national, divorced from an EU citizen, whose marriage had lasted for at least three years before the commencement of divorce proceedings, including at least one year in the host member state, cannot retain a right of residence in that member state, where the commencement of the divorce proceedings is preceded by the departure from that member state of the spouse who is the EU citizen. This decision was followed and applied by the CJEU in the later case of *Secretary of State for the Home Department v NA (Pakistan)*, Case C-115/15, [2017] QB 109.

193 In *Ahmed v Secretary of State for the Home Department* [2017] EWCA Civ 99, per Arden LJ at [14] to [19], the Court of Appeal held that the non-EU national former spouse must have been working at the date of the decree absolute in the divorce proceedings and that the non-EU national former spouse will not retain a right of residence if he or she only started working after that date. Both *Singh* and *NA (Pakistan)* were followed and applied; the court did not consider that there was sufficient lack of clarity on the issue to justify a reference to the CJEU.

self-sufficient person or the family member of such a person, and either:

i) the marriage or civil partnership lasted for at least three years, and the couple resided for at least one year during its duration; or
ii) the former spouse or civil partner has custody of a child of the qualified person; or
iii) the former spouse or civil partner has the right of access to a child under the age of 18, and a court has ordered that such access must take place in the UK; or
iv) the continued right of residence in the UK of the person is warranted by particularly difficult circumstances,[194] eg, he or she or another family member has been a victim of domestic violence while the marriage or civil partnership was subsisting.[195]

A8 nationals

3.60 The Accession Treaty, signed in Athens on 16 April 2003, provided that ten countries[196] would accede to the EU on 1 May 2004. The treaty provides that existing member states can, as a derogation from the usual position under EU law, regulate access to their labour markets by nationals of the accession states, other than nationals of Cyprus and Malta. The states to which this derogation applies are known as the 'A8' countries.

3.61 The derogation could be applied for a transitional period of five years from 1 May 2004, with a provision for a further two years in the case of disturbances to the labour market of the member state. In England and Wales, the derogation was extended until 30 April 2011,[197] but ended from midnight on that date.[198] The secondary

194 In *Secretary of State for the Home Department v NA (Pakistan)*, Case C-115/15, [2017] QB 109, CJEU, the former non-EU national spouse of an EU national claimed a derivative right of residence because of domestic violence, even though her former spouse had left the UK before the divorce proceedings began. The CJEU held that she did not retain any right of residence and that a non-EU national spouse of an EU national had a derivative right of residence in a member state only if the EU national spouse was resident in that member state at the start of the divorce proceedings.

195 EEA Regs 2016 reg 10(5).

196 Cyprus, the Czech Republic, Estonia, Hungary, Latvia, Lithuania, Malta, Poland, Slovakia and Slovenia.

197 Accession (Immigration and Worker Registration) (Amendment) Regulations 2009 SI No 892, which came into force on 29 April 2009.

198 By operation of the Accession (Immigration and Worker Registration) (Revocation, Savings and Consequential Provisions) Regulations 2011 SI No 544 which came into force on 1 May 2011.

legislation which abolished the derogation introduced a new regulation (reg 7A) into the EEA Regs 2006 the effect of which was that an A8 national could retain worker status if he or she became unable to work, became unemployed or ceased to work, as the case may be, on or after 1 May 2011, or on 30 April 2011 he or she had ceased working for an authorised employer in the circumstances mentioned in EEA Regs 2006 reg 6(2), during the first month of his or her employment and was still within that first month.

3.62 The treaty was given domestic effect by the European Union (Accessions) Act 2003[199] which gives the secretary of state the power to enact regulations to permit the derogation. This resulted in the Accession (Immigration and Worker Registration) Regulations ('A(IWR) Regs') 2004[200] the legality of has been unsuccessfully challenged.[201]

3.63 In certain respects, A8 nationals were worse off than nationals of the original EEA states. A8 nationals who were subject to the Worker Registration Scheme (WRS) had no right to reside in the UK as work seekers unless they were self-sufficient.[202] A8 nationals who were subject to the WRS only had a right to reside in the UK as a worker if their employment was in accordance with the requirements of the scheme.[203] A8 nationals who were subject to the WRS and who ceased to work in accordance with the requirements of the scheme ceased to have a right to reside in the UK as a worker.[204] If they ceased to work within one month of the commencement of their employment with an authorised employer, they retained the right to reside as a worker until the end of that month. A8 nationals who were subject to the WRS were not entitled to the issue of registration certificates and could not entitle non-EEA nationals to the issue of residence cards.[205]

The Worker Registration Scheme

3.64 Most A8 nationals were only able to work as employed persons in the UK if they complied with the requirements of the WRS. The following exemptions applied:

199 It received royal assent on 13 November 2003.

200 SI No 1219.

201 *Zalewska v Department for Social Development (Northern Ireland)* [2008] UKHL 67, [2008] 1 WLR 2602, HL (NI); *Putans v Tower Hamlets LBC* [2006] EWHC 1634 (Ch), [2007] HLR 10.

202 A(IWR) Regs 2004 reg 4(2) and (3). See paras 3.39–3.41.

203 A(IWR) Regs 2004 reg 5(2).

204 A(IWR) Regs 2004 reg 5(3) and (4).

205 A(IWR) Regs 2004 reg 5(5).

a) Self-employed people were exempt from the WRS.[206]
b) A8 nationals were not subject to the WRS if on 30 April 2004 they had leave to enter or remain in the UK which was not subject to any condition restricting employment.[207]
c) The WRS did not apply to A8 nationals who had worked legally in the UK without interruption for a period of 12 months up to and including 30 April 2004.[208] This could include up to 30 days during which the A8 national was not working legally in the UK.
d) A8 nationals who worked legally in the UK without interruption for a period of 12 months which ended after 30 April 2004 ceased to be subject to the WRS.[209] This could also include up to 30 days during which the A8 national was not working legally in the UK.
e) A8 nationals were not subject to the WRS during any period in which they were members of a diplomatic mission or the family member of such a person.[210]
f) A8 nationals were exempt from the WRS if their employer was not based in the UK but they had been sent here to work on that employer's behalf.[211]
g) A8 nationals were exempt from the WRS if they were also UK nationals, Swiss nationals or nationals of another EEA state except Bulgaria and Romania.[212]
h) A8 nationals were also exempt from the WRS if they were the spouse, civil partner or child under 18 of a person who had leave to enter or remain in the UK that allowed that person to work.[213]
i) A family member of a Swiss national or EEA national who had a right to reside in the UK was also exempt from the WRS. This did not include family members of nationals of the A8 or Bulgaria and

206 A(IWR) Regs 2004 regs 1(2)(k) and 2(1). See paras 3.36–3.38.
207 A(IWR) Regs 2004 reg 2(2).
208 A(IWR) Regs 2004 reg 2(3) and (8).
209 A(IWR) Regs 2004 reg 2(4) and (8).
210 A(IWR) Regs 2004 reg 2(5A), inserted by Accession (Worker Authorisation and Worker Registration) (Amendment) Regulations ('A(WAWR)(A) Regs') 2007 SI No 3012 reg 3(a), from 19 November 2007.
211 A(IWR) Regs 2004 reg 2(6)(a) and (9)(b).
212 A(IWR) Regs 2004 reg 2(5), as amended by Accession (Immigration and Worker Authorisation) Regulations ('A(IWA) Regs') 2006 SI No 3317 reg 1(3), Sch 2 para 1(1), (2)(a), from 1 January 2007.
213 A(IWR) Regs 2004 reg 2(5A), inserted by Accession (Worker Authorisation and Worker Registration) (Amendment) Regulations ('A(WAWR)(A) Regs') 2009 SI No 2426 regs 1 and 3(a), from 2 October 2009.

Romania who were subject to the relevant scheme and who only had an initial right to reside under reg 13 of the EEA Regs 2006.[214]

3.65 A8 nationals who were not exempt had to comply with the WRS. Their employment gave them a right to reside in the UK as a worker in any of the following circumstances:

a) they were working legally for an employer on 30 April 2004 and had not ceased working for that employer;[215]
b) they applied for a registration certificate[216] authorising their work within one month of starting work for an employer and had not received a valid certificate, notice of refusal or ceased working for that employer;[217]
c) they had received a valid registration certificate authorising work for that employer and the certificate is still valid;[218] or
d) they were within the first month of their employment.[219]

A2 nationals

3.66 The Treaty of Accession for Bulgaria and Romania was signed in Luxembourg on 25 April 2005. It provided for the accession of Bulgaria and Romania ('the A2') to the EU on 1 January 2007. During a transitional period of five years from 1 January 2007 to 31 December 2011, the existing member states could regulate access to their labour markets by A2 workers and restrict their rights of residence.[220] There are also provisions for member states to continue to maintain restrictions for a further two years in the case of disturbances to their labour markets.

3.67 The treaty was given domestic effect by the European Union (Accessions) Act 2006. This gave the secretary of state the power to enact regulations to permit the derogation from the provisions of EU law relating to workers. The detail of the derogation is contained in the Accession (Immigration and Worker Authorisation) Regulations

214 A(IWR) Regs 2004 reg 2(6)(b), substituted by A(WAWR)(A) Regs 2009 regs 1 and 3(b), from 2 October 2009.
215 A(IWR) Regs 2004 reg 7(2)(a).
216 In *Szpak v Secretary of State for Work and Pensions* [2013] EWCA Civ 46, the Court of Appeal held that a registration certificate did not operate retrospectively; where the claimant had not applied for the certificate within the first month of employment, his work was therefore not registered until the certificate had been issued.
217 A(IWR) Regs 2004 reg 7(2)(b).
218 A(IWR) Regs 2004 reg 7(2)(c).
219 A(IWR) Regs 2004 reg 7(3).
220 Annexes VI and VII of the Treaty of Accession.

('A(IWA) Regs') 2006.[221] On 23 November 2011, the government decided to extend the derogation for a further two years from 31 December 2011.

3.68 A2 nationals were worse off than nationals of other EEA states. A2 nationals who were subject to worker authorisation had no right to reside in the UK as jobseekers,[222] and only had a right to reside as a worker when working in accordance with an accession worker authorisation document.[223] A2 nationals subject to worker authorisation did not retain a right to reside as a worker if they ceased to work.[224] A2 nationals who were subject to worker authorisation were not entitled to the issue of registration certificates and could not entitle non-EEA nationals to the issue of residence cards.[225] This did not apply to a highly skilled person who was seeking employment in the UK who was entitled to a registration certificate which stated that he or she had unconditional access to the UK labour market. A 'highly skilled person' is defined as someone who meets the requirements of the Highly Skilled Migrant Programme or holds a certain type of qualification.[226]

Worker authorisation

3.69 The way in which the derogation worked was that certain A2 nationals were classified as 'subject to worker authorisation' and thereby restricted to authorised categories of employment.[227] The following exemptions applied:

a) Self-employed people were exempt.[228]
b) A2 nationals were not subject to worker authorisation if on 31 December 2006 they had leave to enter or remain in the UK which was not subject to any condition restricting employment.[229]
c) Worker authorisation did not apply to A2 nationals who worked legally in the UK without interruption throughout 2006.[230] This

221 SI No 3317, which came into force on 1 January 2007.
222 A(IWA) Regs 2006 reg 6(2). See para 3.31.
223 A(IWA) Regs 2006 reg 6(1).
224 A(IWA) Regs 2006 reg 6(3).
225 A(IWA) Regs 2006 reg 7(1).
226 A(IWA) Regs 2006 regs 4 and 7(2).
227 A(IWA) Regs 2006 reg 1(2)(f); these are the categories of employment listed in the first column of the table in Sch 1.
228 A(IWA) Regs 2006 reg 1(2)(t); see paras 3.37–3.39.
229 A(IWA) Regs 2006 reg 2(2), as amended by Accession (Immigration and Worker Authorisation) (Amendment) Regulations 2007 SI No 475 reg 2(1) and (2)(a), from 16 March 2007.
230 A(IWA) Regs 2006 reg 2(3).

included up to 30 days during which the A2 national was not working legally in the UK.

d) A2 nationals who worked legally in the UK without interruption for a period of 12 months which ended after 31 December 2006 ceased to be subject to worker authorisation.[231] This could also include up to 30 days during which the A2 national was not working legally in the UK.
e) A2 nationals were not subject to worker authorisation during any period in which they were members of a diplomatic mission or the family member of such a person.[232]
f) A2 nationals were also exempt if their employer was not based in the UK but they had been sent here to work on that employer's behalf.[233]
g) A2 nationals were not subject to worker authorisation if they were also nationals of the UK or an EEA state other than an A2 state. They were also exempt if they had a right of permanent residence.[234] This also applied if they were the spouse or civil partner of a national of the UK or of a person settled in the UK.[235]
h) A2 nationals were not subject to worker authorisation if they were the spouse, civil partner or child under 18 of a person who had leave to enter or remain in the UK which allowed that person to work.[236]
i) A2 nationals were not subject to worker authorisation if they were family members of an EEA national who had a right to reside in the UK. This did not include family members of A2 nationals who were subject to worker authorisation. Neither did it include family members of a person who was exempt from worker authorisation because he or she was the family member of a self-employed person, a self-sufficient person or a student. A2 nationals were nevertheless exempt if they were family members of a person who was self-employed, self-sufficient or a student.[237]

231 A(IWA) Regs 2006 reg 2(4) and (12)(c).
232 A(IWA) Regs 2006 reg 2(6A), inserted by A(WAWR)(A) Regs 2007 reg 2(1) and (2)(a), from 19 November 2007.
233 A(IWA) Regs 2006 reg 2(11) and (13)(a).
234 A(IWA) Regs 2006 reg 2(5) and (7).
235 A(IWA) Regs 2006 reg 2(6).
236 A(IWA) Regs 2006 reg 2(5A), inserted by A(WAWR)(A) Regs 2009 regs 1 and 2(2)(a), from 2 October 2009.
237 A(IWA) Regs 2006 reg 2(8), substituted by the A(WAWR)(A) Regs 2007 reg 2(1) and (2)(b), from 19 November 2007, and amended by A(WAWR)(A) Regs 2009 regs 1 and 2(2)(b), from 2 October 2009.

j) A2 nationals were not subject to worker authorisation if they were the spouse, civil partner or descendant of an A2 national who was working in accordance with the scheme, provided that the descendant was under 21 or dependent on the A2 worker.[238]
k) A2 nationals were not subject to worker authorisation if they were highly skilled persons and held a registration certificate which stated that they had unconditional access to the UK labour market.[239]
l) A2 nationals were not subject to worker authorisation if they were students, held a registration certificate that permitted employment for no more than 20 hours a week unless the work was vocational training or vacation work, and complied with that condition. This exemption was retained for four months after the end of the course of study.[240]

3.70 A2 nationals who were subject to worker authorisation had to hold an accession worker authorisation document and work in accordance with the conditions set out in that document. Such a document had to be:[241]

a) a passport or other travel document containing a visa which gave the holder the right to carry out a particular type of employment;
b) a seasonal agricultural card; or
c) an accession worker card.

3.71 An application for an A2 accession worker card could be made in two circumstances. First, if the applicant could prove that the employment concerned was within an authorised category of employment.[242] Second, an application could be made by an authorised family member, in which case there was no restriction on the type of employment.[243] An authorised family member was a family member of an A2 national who was working in accordance with the scheme, unless the worker was only authorised to work by virtue of holding an accession worker card as an authorised family member, or the

238 A(IWA) Regs 2006 reg 2(8A), inserted by A(WAWR)(A) Regs 2009 regs 1 and 2(2)(c), from 2 October 2009.
239 A(IWA) Regs 2006 reg 2(9).
240 A(IWA) Regs 2006 reg 2(10), (10A) and (10B), substituted by the Accession (Immigration and Worker Authorisation) (Amendment) Regulations 2007 SI No 475 reg 2(1) and (2)(c), from 16 March 2007.
241 A(IWA) Regs 2006 reg 9(2).
242 A(IWA) Regs 2006 reg 10(1)(a).
243 A(IWA) Regs 2006 reg 10(1)(b).

family member was the spouse or civil partner of the worker or his or her descendant who was under 21 or dependent.[244]

Croatians

3.72 On 1 July 2013 the Republic of Croatia acceded to the EU. Annex V to the Treaty of Accession, signed at Brussels on 9 December 2011, permits member states to derogate from various provisions concerning freedom of movement under EU law which relate to access to their labour markets by Croatian nationals during the accession period from 1 July 2013 to 30 June 2018. The UK has chosen to take advantage of this right to derogate and, in exercise of the powers conferred under the European Union (Croatian Accession and Irish Protocol) Act 2013[245] the secretary of state made the Accession of Croatia (Immigration and Worker Authorisation) Regulations ('AC(IWA) Regs') 2013[246] which came into force on 1 July of that year. The effect of the AC(IWA) Regs 2013 is to create a worker authorisation scheme for Croatian nationals which is almost identical to that which was in place for A2 nationals, and which will last until 30 June 2018.

3.73 The accession also necessitated an amendment to the Eligibility Regs 2006[247] on 1 July 2013 to exempt from the habitual residence test, nationals of Croatia subject to the worker authorisation scheme and are treated as workers pursuant to that scheme.

3.74 Croatian nationals are worse off than nationals of other EEA states. Croatian nationals who are subject to worker authorisation have no right to reside in the UK as jobseekers,[248] and will only have a right to right as a worker when working in accordance with the scheme, and if they hold an accession worker authorisation document and are working in accordance with the conditions set out in that document.[249] Croatian nationals subject to worker authorisation will not retain a right to reside as a worker if they cease to work.[250] Not all Croatian nationals are, however, subject to worker authorisation.

244 A(IWA) Regs 2006 reg 3, substituted by A(WAWR)(A) Regs 2009 regs 1 and 2(3), from 2 October 2009.

245 Section 4.

246 SI No. 1460.

247 Allocation of Housing and Homelessness (Eligibility) (England) (Amendment) Regulations 2013 SI No 1467 which came into force on 1 July 2013.

248 AC(IWA) Regs reg 5.

249 AC(IWA) Regs reg 5.

250 AC(IWA) Regs reg 4.

Worker authorisation

3.75 The way in which the derogation works is that certain Croatian nationals are classified as 'subject to worker authorisation' and thereby restricted to authorised categories of employment, which means:

a) employment for which a sponsor has issued the applicant with a valid certificate of sponsorship under Tier 2 or Tier 5 of the Points Based System;[251] or
b) employment as:
    i) a representative of an overseas business;
    ii) a postgraduate doctor or dentist; or
    iii) a domestic worker in a private household.[252]

3.76 The following Croatian nationals are exempt from worker authorisation:[253]

a) A Croatian national who on or after 30 June 2013 was granted leave to enter or remain in the UK not subject to any condition restricting his or her employment.[254]
b) A Croatian national who was working legally in the UK on 30 June 2013 and had been working legally in the UK for the 12 months prior to that date.[255]
c) A Croatian national who legally works in the UK without interruption for a period of 12 months which ended after 30 June 2013 ceased to be subject to the scheme at the end of the 12 months.[256]
d) A Croatian national who is also a national of the UK, or an EEA state other than Croatia, but this does not include an A2 national subject to worker authorisation.[257]
e) A Croatian national who is also an A2 national and is working in accordance with that worker authorisation scheme.[258]
f) A Croatian national who is the spouse, civil partner, unmarried or same sex partner, or child under 18, of a person who has leave to

251 The system set out in the Immigration Rules which regulates entry to the UK for work and study.
252 AC(IWA) Regs reg 1(2).
253 AC(IWA) Regs reg 2.
254 AC(IWA) Regs reg 2(2).
255 AC(IWA) Regs reg 2(3), the period of 12 months cannot be interrupted by more than 30 days.
256 AC(IWA) Regs reg 2(4), the period of 12 months cannot be interrupted by more than 30 days.
257 AC(IWA) Regs reg 2(6).
258 AC(IWA) Regs reg 2(7).

enter or remain in the UK which leave allows him or her to work in the UK.[259]

g) A Croatian national who is the spouse, civil partner, unmarried or same sex partner of a national of the UK, or a person who is settled[260] in the UK.[261]
h) A Croatian national who is a member of a diplomatic mission.[262]
i) A Croatian national who is exempt from the requirement to have leave to enter and remain in the UK.[263]
j) A Croatian national who has a permanent right of residence under the EEA Regs 2006 reg 15.[264]
k) A Croatian national who is a family member of an EEA national who has a right to reside in the UK, but where the EEA national is a Croatian or A2 national subject to worker authorisation, then he or she must be the spouse or civil partner, unmarried or same-sex partner or a direct descendant, of the EEA national, the EEA national's spouse or civil partner and, if he or she is a direct descendant, he or she must be under 21 or a dependant of the EEA national, or the EEA national's civil partner or spouse.[265]
l) A Croatian national who is a highly skilled person[266] and holds an EEA registration certificate issued in accordance with reg 7 that includes a statement that he or she has unconditional access to the UK labour market.[267]
m) A Croatian national who is in the UK as a student and either holds an EEA registration certificate which includes a statement that he or she may work[268] or he or she has leave to enter or remain as a student and works in accordance with any conditions attached to that leave.[269]
n) A Croatian national who ceases to be a student, but only for the four months after the end of his or her course and provided he or she holds an EEA registration certificate that was issued before

259 AC(IWA) Regs reg 2(8).
260 IA 1971 s33(2A).
261 AC(IWA) Regs reg 2(9).
262 AC(IWA) Regs reg 2(10) and IA 1971 s8(3) and (3A).
263 AC(IWA) Regs reg 2(11) and IA 1971 s8(2).
264 AC(IWA) Regs reg 2(12).
265 AC(IWA) Regs reg 2(13) and 2(14).
266 AC(IWA) Regs reg 3.
267 AC(IWA) Regs reg 2(15).
268 AC(IWA) Regs reg 2(17), this means he or she may only work for not more than 20 hours each week.
269 AC(IWA) Regs reg 2(16).

the end of the course and includes a statement that he or she may work during that period.[270]

o) A Croatian national who is a posted[271] worker.[272]

p) A Croatian national who is self-employed.[273]

3.77 A Croatian national subject to worker authorisation is only authorised to work in the UK during the accession period if he or she holds an accession worker authorisation document and is working in accordance with the conditions set out in that document.[274] An accession worker authorisation document means a passport or a worker authorisation registration certificate endorsed with a condition restricting the holder's employment to a particular employer and authorised category of employment.[275] This latter document ceases to be valid if the holder stops working for more than 30 days.[276] The document must be applied for in writing to the secretary of state.[277]

3.78 A Croatian national who works in breach of the authorisation scheme is liable to a penalty and commits an offence,[278] as is the case for an employer who breaches the scheme.[279]

Other rights of residence

Self-sufficient families

3.79 Rights of residence can exist outside the scope of the Directive. In *Chen*,[280] Mrs Chen and her husband were both Chinese nationals and worked for a company established in China but, for the purposes of work, Mr Chen travelled frequently to various member states of the EU, in particular the UK.[281] Their daughter was born in Belfast and had Irish nationality.[282] The child was dependent both emotionally and financially on her mother, Mrs Chen, who was her primary

270 AC(IWA) Regs reg 2(18).

271 AC(IWA) Regs reg 2(20).

272 AC(IWA) Regs reg 2(19).

273 AC(IWA) Regs reg 1(2) and the European Union (Croatian Accession and Irish Protocol) Act 2013 s4(11).

274 AC(IWA) Regs reg 8(1).

275 AC(IWA) Regs reg 8(2).

276 AC(IWA) Regs reg 8(4).

277 AC(IWA) Regs reg 9.

278 AC(IWA) Regs reg 16.

279 AC(IWA) Regs regs 11 and 15.

280 *Zhu and Chen v Secretary of State for the Home Department*, Case C-200/02, [2004] ECR I-9925.

281 *Zhu* at [7].

282 *Zhu* at [8].

carer, and she received private medical and childcare services in the UK.[283] The CJEU held that Article 18 of the EC Treaty and Council Directive 90/364/EEC[284] confer on a minor who is himself or herself an EEA national a right to reside for an indefinite period in a host member state, where that minor is covered by appropriate sickness insurance and is in the care of a parent who is not an EEA national but who has sufficient resources for that minor not to become a burden on the public finances of the host member state; in such circumstances, the parent who is the primary carer is also entitled to reside with the child in the host member state.[285]

3.80 The Court of Appeal[286] has held that the requirements to have both comprehensive sickness insurance and sufficient resources such as to avoid becoming a burden on the social assistance system of the host member state applied to the parents and the child, and must exist before any right of residence can arise. It has also been held that the right to reside in such circumstances is directly effective and exists independently of the terms of the EEA Regs 2016 and the Immigration Rules which must, in any event, be interpreted compatibly with EU law where it is possible to do so.[287]

Primary carers[288] of children in education

3.81 The CJEU has also derived a right of residence from Article 12 of Regulation (EEC) No 1612/68[289] which has now been repealed and replaced by Article 10 of Regulation (EU) No 492/2011.[290] This provides that the child of a national of a member state who is or has been

283 *Zhu* at [12]–[14].

284 Of 28 June 1990.

285 *Zhu* at [41], [46] and [47].

286 *W (China) and another v Secretary of State for the Home Department* [2006] EWCA Civ 1494, [2007] 1 WLR 1514.

287 *ECO (Dubai) v M (Ivory Coast)* [2010] UKUT 277 (IAC).

288 EEA Regs 2016 reg 16(8) defines a 'primary carer' as a person who is a direct relative or legal guardian of another person (AP), and either the person has primary responsibility for AP's care, or shares equally the responsibility for AP's care with one other person who is not an exempt person. An exempt person is a person who has a right to reside under the EEA Regs 2016, or who has a right of abode under IA 1971 s2, or to whom IA 1971 s8 applies, or in respect of whom an order has been made under IA 1971 s8(2), or who has indefinite leave to enter or remain in the UK.

289 Of 15 October 1968.

290 Of 5 April 2011. This right was recognised as a derivative right of residence in EEA Regs 2006 reg 15A as inserted by Immigration (European Economic Area) (Amendment) Regulations 2012 SI No 1547 Sch 1 para 9 with effect from 16 July 2012. This is now EEA Regs 2016 reg 16.

employed in the territory of another member state is to be admitted to that state's general educational, apprenticeship and vocational training courses on the same conditions as nationals of that state, if the child is residing in its territory.

3.82 In *Baumbast and R v Secretary of State for the Home Department*,[291] the CJEU held that children of an EU citizen who have installed themselves in a member state during the exercise by their parent of rights of residence as a migrant worker are entitled to reside there in order to attend general educational courses. The CJEU also held that Article 12 must be interpreted as entitling the parent who is the primary carer of those children, irrespective of nationality, to reside with them in order to facilitate the exercise of their right. It did not matter that the parents had divorced or that the parent who was an EU citizen had ceased to be a migrant worker in the host member state.[292]

3.83 *Baumbast* was reconsidered by the CJEU in *Ibrahim*[293] and *Teixeira*,[294] two homelessness appeals referred by the Court of Appeal[295] to the CJEU, which were heard together. Ms Ibrahim was a Somali national, married to but separated from Mr Yusuf, a Danish citizen. They had four children, who were Danish. The two eldest were at school in the UK. Initially, Mr Yusuf worked but he then ceased to enjoy a right to reside as a worker and left to live in Eastern Europe. Although he returned to live in the UK, he never regained a right to reside. Ms Ibrahim did not work, was entirely reliant on means-tested benefits and had no medical insurance. She applied with her children for homelessness assistance under HA 1996 Part 7, but was refused on the basis that she had no right to reside under EU law.

3.84 Ms Teixeira was a Portuguese national. She came to the UK in 1989 with her husband, from whom she subsequently divorced. Her daughter was born in 1991. Ms Teixeira worked from 1989 to 1991, after which time she had intermittent periods of employment. She last worked in early 2005. The daughter entered education in the UK at a time when Ms Teixeira was not a worker; in November 2006, she enrolled in a child-care course and, in March 2007, she went to live with her mother. In April 2007, Ms Teixeira applied under HA 1996 Part 7, but was refused on the basis that she had no right to reside.

291 Case C-413/99, [2002] ECR I-7091, [2002] 3 CMLR 23.

292 *Baumbast*, at [63] and [75].

293 Case C-310/08, [2010] HLR 31.

294 Case C-480/08, [2010] HLR 32.

295 *Harrow LBC and Secretary of State for the Home Department v Ibrahim* [2008] EWCA Civ 386, [2009] HLR 2; and *Teixeira v Lambeth LBC and Secretary of State for the Home Department* [2008] EWCA Civ 1088, [2009] HLR 9.

3.85 On both references, the ECJ held that where a child of an EU citizen is in education in a member state in which that citizen is or has been employed as a migrant worker, the parent who is the child's primary carer enjoys a right of residence in the host state, derived from Article 12.[296] The child also has a right to reside in those circumstances. The right of residence of the parent is not subject to a requirement that the parent should have sufficient resources and comprehensive sickness insurance cover, nor is it subject to a requirement that the parent should have been employed as a migrant worker in the host state when the child first started education. It is sufficient for the child to have been installed in the host state during the exercise by a parent of rights of residence as a migrant worker in that state. The right of residence of the parent ends when the child reaches the age of 18, unless the child continues to need the presence and care of that parent in order to be able to pursue and complete his or her education in the host member state.

3.86 The right to reside as the primary carer of a child in education who is the child of a migrant worker can apply to an A8 national, even where he or she has not completed 12 months of such work pursuant to the WRS.[297] A former self-employed worker who is the primary carer of a dependent child who is in education in the host state, does not have a right to reside.[298] It has been held that education for children, at least in England, is said to start for these purposes at around the age of five when compulsory education begins.[299] The term 'child' in Article 12 of Regulation (EEC) No 1612/68[300] should be read as including 'stepchild' as well.[301] This is consistent with the decision of the CJEU in *Depesme*,[302] that 'child' includes not only a

296 Now Article 10 of Regulation (EU) No 492/2011.

297 *Secretary of State for Work and Pensions v JS (IS)* [2010] UKUT 347 (AAC) which was approved in *Secretary of State for Work and Pensions v MP (IS)* [2011] UKUT 109 (AAC) at para [32]. See para 3.63 as to the WRS in respect of A8 nationals and their families.

298 *Czop*, Case C-147/11; and *Punakova*, Case C-148/11, at [33] and [40].

299 *Secretary of State for Work and Pensions v IM* [2011] UKUT 231 (AAC). This is reflected in the EEA Regs 2016 reg 16(7)(a) which states that education excludes nursery education but does not exclude education received before the compulsory school age where that education is equivalent to the education received at or after compulsory school age.

300 Now repealed and replaced by Article 10 of Regulation (EU) No 492/2011.

301 *Alarape and another (Article 12, EC Reg 1612/68) Nigeria* [2011] UKUT 413 (IAC) which was the subject of a reference to the ECJ, see *Alarape and Tijani v Secretary of State for the Home Department and AIRE Centre*, C-529/11.

302 *Depesme, Kerrou, Kauffmann and Lefort v Ministre de l'Enseignement superieur et de la Recherche*, Cases C-401/15 to C-403/15.

'child' in a child–parent relationship with a worker, but also a child of the spouse or registered partner of that worker, where that worker supports the child in question.[303]

3.87 The Court of Appeal has held that Article 12 of Regulation (EEC) No 1612/68[304] does not provide a qualifying right for permanent residence under Article 16 of the Directive,[305] which is in conflict with the decision of the ECJ in *Lassal,*[306] where it was held that continuous periods of five years' residence completed before the Directive came into force on 30 April 2006, in accordance with earlier legislation, had to be taken into account for the purposes of the acquisition of the right of permanent residence. In *Alarape,*[307] however, the CJEU held that the primary carer's right to reside under what was then Article 12 continued even after the child reached the age of 18, if that child remains in need of the presence and care of that parent in order to be able to continue and to complete his or her education, which it is for the referring court to assess, taking into account all the circumstances of the case. It was also held that periods of residence completed solely on the basis of Article 12, could not be counted for the purpose of acquiring permanent residence.

3.88 In *Ahmed,*[308] the CJEU held that a third country national mother could not rely on Article 12, where she was not married to the EU worker, they were merely cohabiting and the child was not the EU worker's biological child, because the daughter could not be regarded as the child of the spouse of a migrant worker or former migrant worker.

303 *Depesme* at [64] and [65], which concerned the meaning of child of a frontier worker under TFEU Article 45 and Regulation (EU) No 492/2011 Article 7(2). A frontier worker is a worker or self-employed person who, after three years of continuous employment and residence in the host member state, works in an employed or self-employed capacity in another member state, while retaining his or her place of residence in the host member state, to which he or she returns, as a rule, each day or at least once a week.

304 Now repealed and replaced by Article 10 of Regulation (EU) No 492/2011.

305 *Okafor and others v Secretary of State for the Home Department* [2011] EWCA Civ 499, [2011] 1 WLR 3071. This was reflected in the EEA Regs 2006 reg 15(1A) inserted by Immigration (European Economic Area) (Amendment) Regulations 2012 SI No 1547 Sch 1 para 8(a), with effect from 16 July 2012. This is now contained in the EEA Regs 2016 reg 15(2).

306 *Secretary of State for Work and Pensions v Lassal and Child Poverty Action Group (intervener)*, Case C-162/09, [2011] 1 CMLR 31, CJEU.

307 *Alarape and Tijani v Secretary of State for the Home Department and AIRE Centre,* Case C-529/11.

308 *ONAFTS v Ahmed,* Case C-45/12.

3.89 In *NA*,[309] the CJEU held that the right under Article 12 of Regulation No 1612/68 is a right both to commence or continue education in the host member state and, as a consequence, a right of residence. Whether the parent, the former migrant worker, did or did not reside in the host member state on the date when that child began to attend school is of no relevance.[310]

British citizens and their families[311]

3.90 In *McCarthy*,[312] the applicant had both British and Irish nationality but was born and had always lived in England. She married a Jamaican national and argued that he had a right to reside in the UK as her spouse. The CJEU held that an EU citizen cannot have a right to reside in circumstances where he or she has never exercised a right of free movement, and where he or she has always resided in a member state of which he or she is a national, even though he or she is also a national of another member state, provided that the circumstances do not include the application of measures by a member state which would deprive him or her of the genuine enjoyment of the substance of the rights conferred by virtue of his or her status as an EU citizen or would impede the exercise of her or his right of free movement and residence within the territory of the member states.

3.91 In *Zambrano*,[313] the CJEU held that Article 20 of the TFEU is to be interpreted as precluding a member state from refusing a third country national upon whom his or her minor children, who are EU citizens, are dependent, a right of residence in the member state of residence and nationality of those children, insofar as such decisions

309 *Secretary of State for the Home Department v NA (Pakistan)*, Case C-115/15, [2017] QB 109, CJEU.

310 *Secretary of State for the Home Department v NA* at [63].

311 The Immigration (European Economic Area) (Amendment) (No 2) Regulations 2012 SI No 2560 amended the EEA Regs 2006 by inserting a new reg 15A(4A) which recognised a derivative right to reside for a person who is the primary carer of a British citizen, where the relevant British citizen is residing in the UK, and the relevant British citizen would be unable to reside in the UK or in another EEA state if the person were refused a right of residence. The Eligibility (Amendment) Regs 2012 have amended the Eligibility Regs 2006 with effect from 8 November 2012 so that such a person is ineligible for an allocation of housing and for homelessness assistance. In *Pryce v Southwark LBC* [2013] EWCA Civ 1572, [2013] HLR 10, the Court of Appeal held, based on a concession made by the local authority and the government, that such a person has a right to reside and, at least in respect of applications made before 8 November 2012, is eligible for homelessness assistance.

312 *McCarthy v Secretary of State for the Home Department*, Case C-434/09.

313 *Zambrano v Office national de l'emploi (ONEm)*, Case C-34/09, [2012] QB 265.

deprive those children of the genuine enjoyment of the substance of the rights attaching to the status of an EU citizen. In that case, Mr Zambrano and his wife were Colombian citizens but their children were Belgian citizens who had been born in and never moved from Belgium. *McCarthy* was distinguished on the basis that Mrs McCarthy was not obliged to leave the territory of the EU. The *Zambrano* decision has been considered by the Upper Tribunal in both benefits appeals[314] and immigration appeals.[315]

3.92 In *Dereci*,[316] the *Zambrano* principle was applied in a number of cases where there was no risk that the EU citizens concerned would be deprived of their means of subsistence.[317] It was held that EU law, and in particular its provisions on citizenship of the EU, must be interpreted as meaning that it does not prevent a member state refusing to allow a third country national to reside on its territory, where that third country national wishes to reside with a member of his or her family who is a citizen of the EU residing in the member state of which he or she has nationality, who has never exercised his or her right to freedom of movement, provided that such refusal does not lead, for the EU citizen concerned, to the denial of the genuine enjoyment of the substance of the rights conferred by virtue of his or her status as a citizen of the EU, which is a matter for the referring court to verify.

3.93 These cases led to the Immigration (European Economic Area) (Amendment) (No 2) Regulations 2012 which amended the EEA Regs 2006 so as to recognise, in domestic law, a derivative right to reside for a person who is the primary carer of a British citizen who is residing in the UK, which citizen would be unable to reside in the UK or in another EEA state if the carer was refused a right of residence. The Eligibility Regs 2006 were, however, amended[318] so as specifically to exclude such persons from eligibility under HA 1996 Parts 6 and 7. The changes came into force on 8 November 2012 but only applied to applications under Parts 6 and 7 made on or after that date. In Wales, the equivalent changes were not made until the coming into force of the Eligibility (Wales) Regs 2014 on 31 October 2014.

314 For example, *Secretary of State for Work and Pensions v RR (IS)* [2011] UKUT 451 (AAC), though the tribunal has now set aside this determination so it is no longer good law.

315 For example, *Sanade and others v Secretary of State for the Home Department* [2012] UKUT 48 (IAC).

316 *Dereci and others v Bundesministerium fur Inneres*, Case C-256/11.

317 *Dereci*, at para [32].

318 By operation of Eligibility (Amendment) Regs 2012 with effect from 8 November 2012.

3.94 The *Zambrano* principle has been applied by the CJEU in *Iida*,[319] *O and S*[320] and *Ymeraga*,[321] In *CS*,[322] however, the CJEU held that a decision to expel a third country national who was the sole carer of minors who were citizens of the EU could be consistent with EU law where it was founded on the existence of a genuine, present and sufficiently serious threat to the requirements of public policy or of public security, provided account was taken of fundamental rights, in particular the right to respect for private and family life.

3.95 In *Pryce*,[323],based on concessions made by the local authority and the secretary of state, the Court of Appeal held that an applicant with a *Zambrano* right to reside was not subject to immigration control and was therefore eligible for homelessness assistance. The amended eligibility regulations did not apply because of the date of the application, and therefore the court did not consider their lawfulness.

3.96 In *Harrison*,[324] the Court of Appeal held that the *Zambrano* principle does not extend to cover anything short of a situation where the EU citizen is forced to leave the territory of the EU;[325] the fact that the right to family life is adversely affected, or that the presence of the non EU national is desirable for economic reasons, will not of themselves constitute factors capable of triggering the *Zambrano* principle.

3.97 In *Ahmed*,[326] the Upper Tribunal held that *Zambrano* only arises where a refusal decision would lead to an EU citizen child having to leave the EU, and only applies in exceptional circumstances.[327] *Zambrano* does, however, potentially apply even where the children are not citizens of the host member state but are nevertheless, EU citizens.[328]

3.98 In *Hines*,[329] the Court of Appeal held that where a *Zambrano* carer has applied for homelessness assistance, the reviewer must consider

319 *Iida v Stadt Ulm*, Case C-40/11, [2013] Fam 203, CJEU.

320 *O and S v Maahanmuuttovirasto*, Cases C-356/11 and C-357/11, [2013] CMLR 33, CJEU.

321 *Ymeraga and others v Ministre du Travail, de l'emploi et de l'immigration*, Case C-87/12.

322 *Secretary of State for the Home Department v Rendon Marin*, Case C-165/14; *Secretary of State for the Home Department v CS*, Case C-304/14, [2017] QB 558, CJEU.

323 *Pryce v Southwark LBC* [2013] EWCA Civ 1572, [2013] HLR 10.

324 *Harrison (Jamaica) and AB (Morocco) v Secretary of State for the Home Department* [2012] EWCA Civ 1736, [2013] 2 CMLR 23.

325 *Harrison* at [63].

326 *Ahmed v Secretary of State for the Home Department* [2013] UKUT 89 (IAC).

327 *Ahmed* at [67].

328 *Ahmed* at [68].

329 *Hines v Lambeth LBC* [2014] EWCA Civ 660, [2014] HLR 32.

the welfare of the British citizen child and the extent to which the quality or standard of his life will be impaired if the non-EU citizen is required to leave. This is for the purpose of answering the question whether the child would, as a matter of practicality, be unable to remain in the UK. This requires a consideration, amongst other things, of the impact which the removal of the primary carer would have on the child, and the child's available alternative care.[330]

3.99 In *Sanneh*,[331] the Court of Appeal considered the position of *Zambrano* carers. The court held that the *Zambrano* status is a positive right which arises as soon as the necessary conditions are satisfied, there is no need to wait until the carer is destitute or threatened with actual removal from the EU. *Zambrano* carers are not, however, entitled to the same level of social assistance as EU citizens lawfully residing in the EU. The court held that the levels of social assistance made available to *Zambrano* carers in the UK did not breach EU law. Nor did those restrictions on eligibility breach the European Convention on Human Rights (ECHR) or the Equality Act 2010. The *Zambrano* obligation is limited to providing sufficient support to meet the carer's basic needs. In the UK, section 17 of the Children Act (CA) 1989 meets the obligation to provide such basic support.

Habitual residence

3.100 The test of habitual residence applies to all persons from abroad who are not subject to immigration control and are returning to the UK. This can therefore include British citizens.

3.101 Two basic requirements need to be fulfilled to establish habitual residence. The first is that an appreciable period of time must elapse before a person can be considered habitually resident. The second is that the person concerned must have a settled intention to reside in the UK.[332]

3.102 The question whether a person is habitually resident is a question of fact to be decided by reference to all the circumstances of any particular case.[333] The requirement for an appreciable period

330 *Hines* at [6] and [23].

331 *Sanneh and others v Secretary of State for Work and Pensions and others* [2015] EWCA Civ 49, [2015] HLR 27.

332 *R (Paul-Coker) v Southwark LBC* [2006] EWHC 497 (Admin), [2006] HLR 32 at paras [19]–[28].

333 *Re J* [1990] 2 AC 562, HL per Lord Brandon at 578F–G.

of time is not for a fixed period and may be short.[334] A month can be an appreciable period of time.[335] Where the person concerned is not coming to the UK for the first time, but resuming a previous habitual residence, which frequently occurs with British citizens, no appreciable period of time is required.[336] In the context of a benefits appeal, it has been held that, in the general run of cases, the period required to establish habitual residence will lie between one and three months.[337]

3.103 The second requirement for habitual residence is settled intention. For this, there must be a degree of settled purpose; what is necessary is that the purpose of living where one does has a sufficient degree of continuity to be properly described as settled.[338]

3.104 The English Code of Guidance states that if an applicant who was previously habitually resident in the UK is returning after a period spent abroad, and it can be established that the applicant is returning to resume his or her former period of habitual residence, the applicant will be immediately habitually resident.[339] The English Code recommends that applicants who have been resident continuously for a two-year period[340] prior to their housing application will be habitually resident but enquiries will need to be conducted where an applicant has less than two years' continuous residence.[341]

3.105 A useful definition of habitual residence is also to be found in EU law, which focuses on where the centre of interest of the person concerned is to be found, based on an overall assessment of all available information relating to relevant facts, which may include, as appropriate:

a) the duration and continuity of presence; and
b) the person's situation, including the nature and the specific characteristics of any activity pursued; his or her family status and ties; the exercise of any non-remunerated activity; in the case of students the source of their income; their housing situation and

334 *Nessa v Chief Adjudication Officer* [1998] 2 All ER 728 per Lord Slynn at 682–683.

335 *Re S* [1998] AC 750 at 763A; *Re F* [1994] FLR 548 at 555.

336 *Lewis v Lewis* [1956] 1 WLR 200; *Swaddling v Adjudication Officer*, Case C-90/97, [1999] All ER (EC) 217.

337 CIS/4474/2003.

338 *Shah v Barnet LBC* [1983] 2 AC 309, HL, at 344D.

339 Code of Guidance annex 10 para 7; Welsh Code of Guidance annex 6 para 7.

340 A period of about six months appears to be applied more regularly in practice.

341 Code of Guidance para 9.16; Welsh Code of Guidance annex 6 para 1.

in particular how permanent it is; and the member state in which the person is deemed to reside for taxation purposes.[342]

Provision of information

3.106 If there are doubts about an applicant's immigration status, an authority can contact the Home Office to obtain relevant information. When a request is made, in England HA 1996 s187, and in Wales H(W)A 2014 Sch 2 para 3, place a duty on the secretary of state to provide the authority with such information as it may require to enable it to determine whether a person is eligible for assistance in England under HA 1996 Part 7, and in Wales under H(W)A 2014 Part 2, respectively.

3.107 Annex 8 of the English Code of Guidance[343] explains how to contact the Home Office.[344] The more recent[345] Welsh Code explains that contact should now be made with the Home Office's UK Visa and Immigration Centre.[346] Enquiries are dealt with by the Evidence and Enquiries Unit (EEU). The EEU's Local Authorities' Team will only assist once the authority has registered. This requires:

a) the name of the enquiring housing authority on headed paper;
b) the job title/status of the officer registering on behalf of the local housing authority;
c) the names of officers, and their job titles, who will be making the enquiries.

3.108 Once registered, enquiries can be made by letter or fax, or by email,[347] but replies will be returned by post. If the authority makes a written request, the secretary of state must confirm the information in writing.[348] The secretary of state is under a duty to update an authority in respect of any change in information that has been provided. Such a correction must be in writing, detail the change, the date on which

342 Regulation (EC) No 987/2009 Article 11, but note that this is in the context of eligibility for social security and therefore not directly applicable to housing assistance.

343 See appendix C below.

344 The UKBA was set up in February 2008. It no longer exists as an agency of the Home Office.

345 Published in March 2016.

346 See annex 5 of the Welsh Code.

347 In non-asylum cases, the email address is EvidenceandEnquiry@homeoffice.gsi.gov.uk. See the English Code of Guidance annex 8 para 2; Welsh Code of Guidance annex 5 para 2.

348 In England, HA 1996 s187(2); and in Wales, H(W)A 2014 Sch 2 para 3(2).

the previous information became inaccurate and the reason why the information changed.[349]

3.109 If the response indicates that the applicant has an outstanding asylum claim, the English Code states that enquiries should be made to the Local Authority Communications Section of the UK Border Agency (UKBA): this is no longer the case following internal reorganisation within the Home Office, and the Welsh Code states that contact should be with the UK Visa and Immigration Centre.[350]

Eligibility – homelessness: Housing Act 1996 Part 7 and Housing (Wales) Act 2014 Part 2

Introduction

3.110 In England under HA 1996 Part 7 and in Wales under H(W)A 2014 Part 2, eligibility must be determined whenever an authority has reason to believe that an applicant may be homeless or threatened with homelessness.[351] The date for establishing whether an applicant is eligible is the date of the decision and not the date of application.[352] Where there is a review, it is the date of the review decision that is key.[353]

3.111 While an authority is entitled to reach its own decision as to an applicant's immigration status, any such decision is only for housing purposes and will be subject to any contrary decision by the immigration authorities.[354] An authority is entitled to take an immigration

349 In England, HA 1996 s187(3); and in Wales, H(W)A 2014 Sch 2 para 3(3).

350 Enquiries used to be made to National Asylum Support Service (NASS) LA Comms, but NASS no longer exists. It became the UKBA Local Authority Team, but this no longer exists. Accordingly, the advice in the English Code at annex 8 para 6 cannot be relied upon. Much more helpful is the Welsh Code which states that in asylum cases, enquiries should be made to the Home Office's UK Visa and Immigration (UKVI) Centre, which can be found by following the links on www.gov.uk.

351 In England, HA 1996 s184(1)(a); and in Wales, H(W)A 2014 s62(4).

352 *R v Southwark LBC ex p Bediako* (1997) 30 HLR 22, QBD.

353 *Mohamed v Hammersmith and Fulham LBC* [2001] UKHL 57, [2002] 1 AC 547, [2002] HLR 7.

354 *R v Westminster City Council ex p Castelli and Tristan-Garcia* (1996) 28 HLR 617, CA; *Tower Hamlets LBC v Secretary of State for the Environment* [1993] QB 632, (1993) 25 HLR 524, CA.

decision of the Home Office at face value and is not required to carry out its own further investigations to determine eligibility.[355]

3.112 Where a full housing duty has been accepted in England under HA 1996 s193(2),[356] or in Wales under H(W)A 2014 s66, s68, s73 or s75, an authority may revisit the issue of eligibility and will cease to be subject to the duty if an applicant ceases to be eligible.[357]

Other members of the household

3.113 In England, HA 1996 s185(4), and in Wales, H(W)A 2014 Sch 2 para 1(5), require authorities also to consider the eligibility of household members. The section formerly required[358] authorities to disregard ineligible household members[359] when determining whether an eligible applicant was homeless or had a priority need. The provision was, however, declared incompatible with Article 14 (prohibition of discrimination) when read with Article 8 (right to respect for one's private and family life) of the ECHR, to the extent that it required a dependent child or pregnant spouse of a British citizen, habitually resident in the UK but subject to immigration control, to be disregarded when determining whether the British citizen had a priority need for accommodation.[360]

3.114 The section was accordingly amended[361] so that it now[362] applies only to eligible applicants who are themselves subject to immigration control (except for EEA and Swiss nationals) – for example, those granted refugee status, indefinite leave to remain or humanitarian

355 *R (Burns) v Southwark LBC* [2004] EWHC 1901 (Admin), [2004] NPC 127.

356 See paras 10.11–10.219.

357 In England, HA 1996 s193(6)(a); in Wales, H(W)A 2014 s79(2).

358 In respect of all applications for accommodation or assistance in obtaining accommodation, within the meaning of HA 1996 s183, made before 2 March 2009.

359 For example, in *Ehiabor v Kensington and Chelsea RLBC* [2008] EWCA Civ 1074, the applicant could not rely on the dependent child to establish a priority need because the child, although born in the UK, was not a British citizen and therefore required leave to remain under IA 1971 s1(2) and was subject to immigration control.

360 *R (Morris) v Westminster City Council (No 3)* [2005] EWCA Civ 1184, [2006] 1 WLR 505, [2006] HLR 8.

361 By operation of the Housing and Regeneration Act 2008 s314 and Sch 15 Part 1.

362 In respect of all applications for accommodation or assistance in obtaining accommodation, within the meaning of HA 1996 s183, made on or after 2 March 2009.

protection.[363] In Wales, the same approach has been followed.[364] When considering an application from such an applicant, authorities must continue to disregard any dependants or other household members who are ineligible for assistance for any reason, for the purpose of deciding whether the applicant is homeless or has a priority need[365] but, otherwise (ie, when the applicant is not himself or herself a person subject to immigration control[366]), they are to be taken into account.

3.115 The Court of Appeal granted permission for a challenge to the lawfulness of the restricted cases regime but the issue was not pursued in the substantive appeal because the appeal did not in fact involve a restricted case.[367]

3.116 It follows that applicants who are not subject to immigration control, plus EEA and Swiss nationals, will now be able to rely on ineligible household members to qualify as homeless or in priority need, and to confer an entitlement to be secured suitable accommodation in England under HA 1996 s193(2) and in Wales a duty under H(W)A 2014 s66, s68, s73 or s75. Typically, ineligible household members who could confer priority need in this way are likely to be dependent children and pregnant women who have been granted leave with a condition of no recourse to public funds.[368]

3.117 This does not, however, give such applicants the same rights as others. An application pursuant to which the authority would not be satisfied that the applicant had a priority need but for a 'restricted person' is called a 'restricted case'.[369] A restricted person is a person who is ineligible and subject to immigration control[370] who either does not have leave to enter or remain in the UK[371] or who has leave

363 See paras 3.22–3.44.

364 H(W)A 2014 Sch 2 para 1(6).

365 See the letter from the Department for Communities and Local Government (DCLG) to Chief Housing Officers dated 16 February 2009 and the accompanying guidance note.

366 See paras 3.18–3.20.

367 *Lekpo-Bozua v Hackney LBC* [2010] EWCA Civ 909, [2010] HLR 46.

368 For the purposes of UK immigration law, the term 'public funds' is defined in Immigration Rules (HC 395) para 6 as including housing under HA 1996 Part 6 or Part 7 and HA 1985 Part 2. The Rules have not yet been updated to reflect the position under the H(W)A 2014 Part 2, but there seems little doubt that the phrase will be interpreted the same way.

369 In England, HA 1996 s193(3B); in Wales, H(W)A 2014 s76(5).

370 See para 3.17.

371 See para 3.17.

subject to a condition of no recourse to public funds.[372] In a restricted case, in both England and Wales, a local housing authority must, so far as reasonably practicable, bring its duty to an end by securing a private rented sector offer.[373]

3.118 The discharge provisions governing restricted cases are considered in chapter 10 below,[374] both before and after the commencement of the LA 2011, where they may be contrasted with other applications.

3.119 It should be noted that the European Court of Human Rights[375] (ECtHR) did not follow *Morris*,[376] but held that the immigration status of the child which resulted in his mother's differential treatment was reasonably and objectively justified by the need to allocate, as fairly as possible, the scarce stock of social housing available in the UK and the legitimacy, in so allocating, of having regard to the immigration status of those who are in need of housing. Accordingly, there was no violation of Article 14, when taken in conjunction with Article 8 of the ECHR. The court expressly stated, however, that it was not ruling on the discriminatory effect of the amendments.[377]

Homelessness assistance

3.120 The division into persons subject and not subject to immigration control, set out above, applies in both England and Wales. Eligibility for both homelessness assistance and for an allocation is the same in England and Wales for persons not subject to immigration control.[378] The situation is slightly different in England and Wales for persons who are subject to immigration control.[379] This section examines the position in respect of homelessness assistance in England and Wales, starting with England.

372 In England, HA 1996 s184(7); in Wales, H(W)A 2014 s63(5).

373 In England, HA 1996 s193(7AD); in Wales, H(W)A 2014 s76(5).

374 See paras 10.205–10.211.

375 *Bah v UK*, App No 56328/07, 27 September 2011.

376 See para 3.113.

377 See para 3.114.

378 Eligibility Regs 2006 regs 4 and 6 are the same as the Eligibility (Wales) Regs 2014 regs 4 and 6.

379 Eligibility Regs 2006 regs 3 and 5 are not quite the same as the Eligibility (Wales) Regs 2014 regs 3 and 5.

England

Persons subject to immigration control

3.121 For a person subject to immigration control to be eligible for assistance, the person must fall within one of the prescribed classes.

Class A

3.122 Class A[380] is a person who is recorded by the secretary of state as a refugee within the definition set out in Article 1 of the Refugee Convention[381] and who has leave to enter or remain in the UK.

3.123 A refugee is any person:

a) who, owing to a well-founded fear of being persecuted for reasons of race, religion, nationality, membership of a particular social group or political opinion, is outside the country of his or her nationality and is unable or, owing to such fear, unwilling to avail himself or herself of the protection of that country; or
b) who, not having a nationality and being outside the country of his or her former habitual residence as a result of such events, is unable or, owing to such fear, unwilling to return to it.

3.124 A decision as to whether to recognise a person as a refugee must be taken in accordance with Council Directive 2004/83/EC[382] which lays down minimum standards for the qualification and status of third-country nationals or stateless persons as refugees or as persons who otherwise need international protection and for the protection granted. Such a decision is made by the Home Office.

3.125 Recognition as a refugee almost inevitably leads to a grant of leave to remain. Prior to 30 August 2005, refugees were granted indefinite leave to remain (ILR). From that date, the grant is normally five years' leave to remain. During the limited five-year period, refugee status can be reviewed and removed, for example, if there has been a change in circumstances in the refugee's country of origin, or he or she has returned there. Normally there is no review at the end of the five-year period, but a review can be triggered if there is evidence of criminality or if an application for settlement is made after the initial period of leave has expired. At the end of the five-year period, the refugee qualifies for indefinite leave to remain in the UK.

380 Eligibility Regs 2006 reg 5(1)(a).

381 The Convention relating to the Status of Refugees was adopted by a Conference of Plenipotentiaries of the United Nations (UN) on 28 July 1951 and entered into force on 21 April 1954.

382 Of 29 April 2004, which entered into force on 20 October 2004.

3.126 From early 2002, application registration cards (ARCs) have been issued to asylum-seekers and their dependants during the asylum screening process. The ARC is a credit card sized form of identity. If an application for asylum is successful, the applicant will be given a letter by the Home Office which explains the applicant's position as a refugee and some of his or her rights in the UK. A refugee's national passport is not stamped, because the refugee cannot use it without forfeiting his or her refugee status. Instead, the refugee will be issued with an Immigration Status Document (ISD). These were phased in during late 2003 and early 2004 and are an A4 sheet of paper, folded into four, confirming the immigration status of the holder. An ISD is also designed to hold a UK Residence Permit (UKRP). Since late 2003, the ink stamps that used to be endorsed in passports and travel documents have been progressively replaced by UKRPs which are issued to those granted more than six months' leave to enter or remain in the UK. The UKRP takes the form of a credit card sized sticker or vignette. It was introduced in accordance with Regulation (EC) No 1030/2002 which requires EU countries which have opted in to this regulation to issue uniform format vignettes to all non-EEA nationals granted more than six months' leave to enter or remain. They are a security measure.

3.127 Refugees may apply for a refugee travel document, which looks like a passport. This is issued by the Home Office under the United Nations Convention relating to the Status of Refugees and the applicant's leave will be endorsed in the document on a UKRP vignette.

Class B

3.128 Class B[383] is a person who has exceptional leave to enter or remain in the UK granted outside the provisions of the Immigration Rules, whose leave to enter or remain is not subject to a condition requiring the person to maintain and accommodate himself or herself and any person who is dependent on him or her without recourse to public funds, which includes housing and assistance under HA 1985 Part 2 or HA 1996 Parts 6 and 7.[384]

3.129 Exceptional leave to enter or remain was abolished from 1 April 2003 so that only a dwindling group now has this status. Exceptional leave to remain (ELR) describes the leave granted to applicants who were not found to be refugees but whom the Home Office, for

383 Eligibility Regs 2006 reg 5(1)(b).

384 Immigration Rules (HC 395) para 6.

humanitarian or compassionate reasons, determined it would not be right to require to return to their country of origin.

3.130 Persons with ELR should have a letter from the Home Office, sometimes known as a 'grant letter', explaining that they have been granted ELR. They should also have their status stamped in their national passport. If they do not have a national passport, they will have been issued with an ISD containing a UKRP vignette. If such persons wish to travel but do not have a national passport, they may apply to the UKBA for a travel document known as a Certificate of Travel (COT).

Class C

3.131 Class C[385] applies to a person who is habitually resident in the UK, the Channel Islands, the Isle of Man or the Republic of Ireland and whose leave to enter or remain in the UK is not subject to any limitation or condition, other than a person:

a) who has been given leave to enter or remain in the UK upon an undertaking given by his or her sponsor;
b) who has been resident in the UK, the Channel Islands, the Isle of Man or the Republic of Ireland for less than five years beginning on the date of entry or the date on which his or her sponsor gave the undertaking in respect of him or her, whichever date is the later; and
c) whose sponsor or, where there is more than one sponsor, at least one of whose sponsors, is still alive.

3.132 In summary, this class applies to any person with indefinite leave to remain in the UK unless that leave was granted on an undertaking by a sponsor less than five years ago and the sponsor is still alive.

3.133 Such a person should have a grant letter[386] from the Home Office, explaining that they have been granted indefinite leave to remain. The person should have a stamp or UKRP in his or her national passport which shows that he or she has ILR. The person may also have an ISD or a COT with a UKRP vignette which shows his or her status.

385 Eligibility Regs 2006 reg 5(1)(c).

386 See para 3.130.

Class D

3.134 Class D applies to a person who has humanitarian protection granted under the Immigration Rules.[387]

3.135 From 1 April 2003, the Home Office abolished ELR and replaced it with humanitarian protection (HP) and discretionary leave (DL). HP is granted to a person who, if removed, would face a serious risk to life or person arising from capital punishment, unlawful killing or torture or inhuman or degrading treatment or punishment in the country of return.[388] Although they do not qualify for refugee status, such persons would be at risk of treatment in violation of Articles 2 or 3 of the ECHR (right to life; and prohibition of torture, and inhuman or degrading treatment or punishment, respectively). The requirements in relation to HP can now be found in the Immigration Rules.[389]

3.136 From 30 August 2005, if a person is granted HP, he or she is also granted leave to remain for five years, after which an application can be made for settlement, at which point there is an automatic review of whether there is a continuing protection need.

3.137 Persons with HP should have a grant letter[390] from the Home Office, explaining that they have been granted HL. Their ISD or national passport will contain a UKRP vignette granting leave for a period of five years. If they do not have a national passport, they may apply for a travel document or COT which, if issued, will contain the UKRP vignette.

Class E

3.138 Class E[391] has been repealed in England, but continues[392] in force in Wales.[393] It applied to a person who was an asylum-seeker whose claim for asylum was recorded by the secretary of state as having been made before 3 April 2000 in the circumstances mentioned in one of the following:

387 Eligibility Regs 2006 reg 5(1)(d), substituted by Allocation of Housing and Homelessness (Miscellaneous Provisions) (England) Regulations 2006 SI No 2527 reg 2(1) and (3), from 9 October 2006.

388 Immigration Rules para 339C.

389 Immigration Rules para 339C.

390 See para 3.130.

391 Eligibility Regs 2006 reg 5(1)(e).

392 See para 3.149.

393 Allocation of Housing and Homelessness (Eligibility) (England) (Amendment) Regulations ('Eligibility (Amendment) Regs') 2016 SI No 965 reg 2(4)(a).

a) on arrival (other than on his or her re-entry) in the UK from a country outside the UK, the Channel Islands, the Isle of Man or the Republic of Ireland;
b) within three months from the day on which the secretary of state made a relevant declaration, and the applicant was in Great Britain on the day on which the declaration was made; or
c) on or before 4 February 1996 by an applicant who was on 4 February 1996 entitled to benefit under reg 7A of the Housing Benefit (General) Regulations 1987.[394]

3.139 For the purpose of Class E, 'asylum-seeker' means a person who is at least 18 years old, who is in the UK, and who has made a claim for asylum. A 'claim for asylum' means a claim that it would be contrary to the UK's obligations under the Refugee Convention for the applicant to be removed from, or required to leave, the UK. A person ceases to be an asylum-seeker when his or her claim for asylum is recorded by the secretary of state as having been decided, other than on appeal, or abandoned.

3.140 A 'relevant declaration' means a declaration to the effect that the country of which the applicant is a national is subject to such a fundamental change of circumstances that the secretary of state would not normally order the return of a person to that country. The only claims for asylum currently affected are those made by nationals of Sierra Leone from 16 May to 16 August 1997, and those made by nationals of the Democratic Republic of Congo between 1 July and 1 October 1997.

3.141 The significance of 3 April 2000 is that a person who claimed asylum on arrival in the UK on or after that date was no longer supported by local authorities but by the National Asylum Support Service (NASS).[395]

3.142 Applicants who come within Class E are not automatically eligible for assistance. Section 186 of HA 1996 states that such a person or his or her dependant is not eligible if the person has any accommodation in the UK, however temporary, available for his or her occupation, although it must be reasonable for the applicant to continue to occupy it.[396] For the purposes of this section, a person becomes an asylum-seeker at the time when his or her claim is recorded by the secretary of state as having been made; and ceases to be an asylum-seeker when his or her claim is recorded as having been finally

394 SI No 1971.
395 See para 3.3 above.
396 *Lismane v Hammersmith and Fulham LBC* (1998) 31 HLR 427, CA.

determined or abandoned. A 'dependant' means a spouse or child under 18, and becomes such when the secretary of state records him or her as being a dependant of the asylum-seeker; and ceases to be a dependant when the claimant ceases to be an asylum-seeker or, if earlier, when he or she is recorded by the secretary of state as ceasing to be a dependant. The section defines a claim for asylum as one made pursuant to the Refugee Convention.

Class F

3.143 Class F[397] applies to a person who is habitually resident in the UK, the Channel Islands, the Isle of Man or the Republic of Ireland and who has limited leave to enter the UK as a relevant Afghan citizen under para 276BA1 of the Immigration Rules.[398]

Class G

3.144 Class G[399] applies to a person who has limited leave to enter or remain in the UK on family or private life grounds under Article 8 of the ECHR, which leave has been granted under para 276BE(1), para 276DG or Appendix FM of the Immigration Rules and is not subject to a condition requiring the person to maintain and accommodate himself or herself and his or her dependants without recourse to public funds.[400]

Persons not subject to immigration control

3.145 Generally speaking, a person who is not subject to immigration control will only be eligible if he or she is habitually resident in the UK, but certain rights of residence are excluded and certain applicants are exempt from the habitual resident test.

3.146 A person who is not subject to immigration control is ineligible if:[401]

397 Added by the Allocation of Housing and Homelessness (Eligibility) (England) (Amendment) Regulations 2014 SI No 435 reg 2(5)(c) with effect from 31 March 2014.

398 Eligibility Regs 2006 reg 5(1)(f).

399 Added by Eligibility (Amendment) Regs 2016 reg 2(4)(c) with effect from 30 October 2016.

400 Eligibility Regs 2006 reg 5(1)(g).

401 Eligibility Regs 2006 reg 6(1), as amended by Eligibility (Amendment) Regs 2012, which inserted a new reg 6(1)(b)(iii) and (iv) and a new reg 6(1)(c), with effect from 8 November 2012, though the amendments do not have effect in relation to an application for an allocation of housing under HA 1996 Part 6 or for housing assistance under Part 7 which was made before that date. See para 3.10 above.

a) the person is not habitually resident in the UK, the Channel Islands, the Isle of Man or the Republic of Ireland;[402]
b) the person's only right to reside in the UK:
   i) is derived from his or her status as a jobseeker or as the family member of a jobseeker;[403] or
   ii) is an initial right to reside for a period not exceeding three months;[404] or
   iii) is a derivative right to reside to which he or she is entitled under EEA Regs 2006 reg 15A(1), but only in a case where the right exists under that regulation because the applicant satisfies the criteria in reg 15A(4A);[405] or
   iv) is derived from Article 20 of the TFEU in a case where the right to reside arises because a British citizen would otherwise be deprived of the genuine enjoyment of the substance of the rights attaching to the status of EU citizen;[406] or
c) the person's only right to reside in the Channel Islands, the Isle of Man or the Republic of Ireland:
   i) is a right equivalent to one of those mentioned in b) above which is derived from the TFEU;[407] or
   ii) is derived from Article 20 of the TFEU, in a case where the right to reside a) in the Republic of Ireland arises because an Irish citizen, or b) in the Channel Islands or the Isle of Man arises because a British citizen also entitled to reside there would otherwise be deprived of the genuine enjoyment of the substance of his or her rights as an EU citizen.[408]

3.147 A person who is not subject to immigration control is exempt from the habitual residence test if he or she is:[409]

a) a worker;[410]
b) a self-employed person;[411]

402 Eligibility Regs 2006 reg 6(1)(a).
403 Eligibility Regs 2006 reg 6(1)(b)(i).
404 Eligibility Regs 2006 reg 6(1)(b)(ii).
405 Eligibility Regs 2006 reg 6(1)(b)(iii).
406 Eligibility Regs 2006 reg 6(1)(b)(iv).
407 Eligibility Regs 2006 reg 6(1)(c)(i).
408 Eligibility Regs 2006 reg 6(1)(c)(ii).
409 Eligibility Regs 2006 reg 6(2).
410 Eligibility Regs 2006 reg 6(2)(a).
411 Eligibility Regs 2006 reg 6(2)(b).

c) a person who is a Croatian national who has a right to reside under the Croatian Accession Regulations;[412]
d) a person who is the family member of a person specified in a) to c) above;[413]
e) a person with a right to reside permanently in the UK by virtue of reg 15(1)(c), (d) or (e) of the EEA Regs 2006;[414]
f) (now repealed)[415] a person who left the territory of Montserrat after 1 November 1995 because of the effect on that territory of a volcanic eruption;
g) a person who is in the UK as a result of his/her deportation, expulsion or other removal by compulsion of law from another country to the UK.[416]

Wales

3.148 In Wales, as in England,[417] the issue of eligibility for assistance needs to be considered separately in relation to both those who are, and those who are not, subject to immigration control.[418]

Persons subject to immigration control

3.149 A person who is subject to immigration control is eligible if he or she falls within one of the prescribed classes A to F, as described above.[419]

Persons not subject to immigration control

3.150 The position is the same as in England, as set out above.[420]

412 Accession of Croatia (Immigration and Worker Authorisation) Regulations 2013 SI No 1460 reg 5; Eligibility Regs 2006 reg 6(2)(c); see paras 3.12–3.18.
413 Eligibility Regs 2006 reg 6(2)(d).
414 Eligibility Regs 2006 reg 6(2)(e).
415 Revoked by the Allocation of Housing and Homelessness (Eligibility) (England) (Amendment) Regulations 2014 SI No 435 reg 2(6)(c), with effect from 31 March 2014.
416 Eligibility Regs 2006 reg 6(2)(g).
417 See paras 3.121–3.147.
418 Eligibility (Wales) Regs 2014, which came into force on 31 October 2014.
419 Eligibility (Wales) Regs 2014 reg 5.
420 Eligibility (Wales) Regs 2014 reg 6.

Interim accommodation

Ineligibility

3.151 Notwithstanding prima facie eligibility for homelessness assistance as set out above, the provisions of Nationality, Immigration and Asylum Act (NIAA) 2002 Sch 3 nonetheless disqualify certain classes of immigrant in England from two types of interim accommodation. These exclusions do not apply to British citizens or to those who are under 18.[421] They also do not apply in Wales, because the two statutory provisions no longer have effect there, having been replaced by the H(W)A 2014.[422] The two types of interim accommodation excluded are:

a) HA 1996 s188(3) accommodation pending review;[423]
b) HA 1996 s204(4) accommodation pending appeal to the county court.[424]

3.152 It may be noted that these classes are also disqualified from assistance under other statutory powers which are considered below in chapter 13, which include:

a) Care Act 2014 Part 1;[425]
b) SSWB(W)A 2014 Part 4 and ss105–116;[426]
c) CA 1989 ss17, 23C, 23CA,[427] 24A and 24B;[428]
d) IAA 1999;[429]

421 NIAA 2002 Sch 3 para 2(1)(a) and (b).

422 NIAA 2002 Sch 3 para 1(1)(j) has not been amended to take account of the fact that the HA 1996 ss188(3) and 204(4) no longer apply in Wales, because of the coming into force of the H(W)A 2014. Accordingly, certain homelessness applicants in Wales are still ineligible under HA 1996 ss188(3) and 204(4) even though those provisions have no effect in Wales. The five classes of ineligible applicant (in para 3.153) are the same as in England and are set out in NIAA 2002 Sch 3 paras 4–7A.

423 NIAA 2002 Sch 3 para 1(1)(j). See paras 10.29–10.42.

424 NIAA 2002 Sch 3 para 1(1)(j). See paras 12.196–12.200.

425 NIAA 2002 Sch 3 para 1(1)(n): the Act applies only in England. See paras 13.7–13.26.

426 NIAA 2002 Sch 3 para 1(1)(o): the Act applies only in Wales.

427 Inserted by Children and Young Persons Act 2008 s22(6). See paras 13.41–13.80.

428 NIAA 2002 Sch 3 para 1(1)(g). See paras 13.41–13.80.

429 NIAA 2002 Sch 3 para 1(1)(l). See paras 13.27–13.39.

e) LA 2011 s1;[430] and
f) LGA 2000 s2.[431]

3.153 NIAA 2003 Sch 3 excludes the following five classes of persons from eligibility.

a) The first class applies to a person who has been recognised as a refugee by a European Economic Area (EEA) state other than the UK; this class also applies to a person who is the dependant of a person who is in the UK and who has such status.[432]
b) The second class applies to a person who has the nationality of an EEA state other than the UK, or who is the dependant of such a person.[433]
c) The third class applies to a person who was, but is no longer, an asylum-seeker and who is not co-operating with removal directions; it also applies to the dependant of such a person.[434]
d) The fourth class applies to a person who is in the UK in breach of NIAA 2002 s11 and who is not an asylum-seeker.[435] In summary, this means anyone who is in the UK in breach of immigration laws, ie, who does not have a right to reside under EU law, does not have leave to enter or remain, does not have a right of abode, etc.
e) The fifth class applies to a person who, although his or her asylum claim has been rejected, continues to be treated as an asylum-seeker and accommodated by the UKBA because he or she has dependent children,[436] but the Home Secretary has certified that he or she has, without reasonable excuse, not taken reasonable steps to leave the UK voluntarily or place himself or herself in a position in which he or she is able to leave the UK voluntarily. He or she must have received the certificate and have been given 14 days to act. It also applies to his or her dependants.[437]

430 NIAA 2002 Sch 3 para 1(1)(ka): the Act applies only in England.
431 NIAA 2002 Sch 3 para 1(1)(k): this part of the Act applies only in Wales. See paras 13.87–13.93.
432 NIAA 2002 Sch 3 para 4.
433 NIAA 2002 Sch 3 para 5.
434 NIAA 2002 Sch 3 para 6.
435 NIAA 2002 Sch 3 para 7.
436 See paras 13.27–13.39.
437 NIAA 2002 Sch 3 para 7A, inserted by Asylum and Immigration (Treatment of Claimants, etc) Act 2004 s9 with effect from 1 December 2004, see Asylum and Immigration (Treatment of Claimants, etc) Act 2004 (Commencement No 2) Order 2004 SI No 2999.

Exceptions to ineligibility

3.154 A person who falls within one of these classes will not, however, be ineligible if the exercise of a power or the performance of a duty is necessary for the purpose of avoiding a breach of:

a) a person's rights under the ECHR;[438] or
b) a person's rights under the Community Treaties.[439]

3.155 The ECtHR has been sympathetic to arguments based on ECHR Article 8 (right to respect for one's private and family life).[440] It has held that the right to family life includes the right of a parent and child mutually to enjoy each other's company,[441] and has found a violation of that Article where the deportation of an applicant from the Netherlands would interrupt his intermittent contact with his daughter there.[442]

3.156 Conversely, the Court of Appeal has held that neither Article 8 nor Article 3[443] (prohibition of torture and inhuman or degrading treatment or punishment) imposes a duty on the UK to provide support to foreign nationals who are in a position freely to return to their country of origin.[444] This principle was also applied in a case where the claimant had an undetermined human rights claim.[445] It has been held that the making of a purported fresh claim either for asylum or under Article 3, by a claimant whose original claim had been rejected, did not always make it necessary for support to be provided in order to avoid a breach of the ECHR. In considering the issue, the authority had to have regard to all the relevant circumstances, including where appropriate the matters which were alleged to constitute a fresh claim. It was necessary to proceed on a case-by-case basis considering the facts of each individual case with care.[446]

3.157 In *Clue*,[447] the Court of Appeal held that, when applying NIAA 2002 Sch 3, the authority should not consider the merits of an outstanding application for leave to remain unless satisfied that it was

438 See, generally, paras 12.95–12.105.
439 NIAA 2002 Sch 3 para 3.
440 See paras 12.100–12.102.
441 *Olsson v Sweden* (1988) 11 EHRR 259.
442 *Ciliz v Netherlands* [2000] 2 FLR 469.
443 See paras 12.95–12.105.
444 *R (K) v Lambeth LBC* [2003] EWCA Civ 1150, [2004] 1 WLR 272, [2004] HLR 15.
445 *R (Blackburn Smith) v Lambeth LBC* [2007] EWHC 767 (Admin), (2007) 10 CCLR 352.
446 *R (AW) v Croydon LBC* [2005] EWHC 2950 (QB), (2005) 9 CCLR 252.
447 *R (Clue) v Birmingham City Council* [2010] EWCA Civ 460, [2011] 1 WLR 99.

obviously hopeless or abusive. Otherwise, the authority should not refuse assistance if to do so would have the effect of requiring the person to leave the UK and thereby forfeiting the claim. In that case, the authority's decision to refuse assistance was unlawful because its assessment had not taken account of the application for leave to remain, nor stated that it was abusive or hopeless, and the court was of the view that the application did have merits under ECHR Article 8.

3.158 Nevertheless, an authority does have the power to fund the costs of returning an applicant and his or her family to their country of origin.[448] It would, however, be unlawful to offer to fund the cost of return travel if this is not a viable option.[449] An authority must closely scrutinise any argument that a return to the country of origin would give rise to a breach of ECHR rights.[450] It is important to take into account the potential effect of removal on each relevant family member and the impact on other family members. An authority should also take into account any relevant Home Office policy that concerns the issue of whether or not the claimant and his or her family will be able to remain in the UK.[451]

3.159 *R (De Alemeida)* is an example of where the claimant's circumstances were so dire that not providing accommodation would have breached his rights under Article 3 of the ECHR:[452] the case concerned a Portuguese man who was terminally ill with HIV. In *Paposhvili,*[453] ECtHR qualified a previous decision, *N,*[454] in order to hold that Article 3 should be understood to include the removal of a seriously ill person in which substantial grounds have been shown for believing that he or she, although not at the end of his or her life, would face a real risk, on account of the absence of appropriate treatment in the receiving country or the lack of access to such treatment, of

448 *R (Grant) v Lambeth LBC* [2005] 1 WLR 1781, [2005] HLR 27, decided under LGA 2000 Part 1 (well-being) – which continues to apply in Wales – but it would seem likely that the same would apply to exercise of the general power of competence now applicable in England, under LA 2011 Part 1 Chapter 1.

449 *R (J) v Enfield LBC* [2002] EWHC 432 (Admin); likewise under LGA 2000, but see footnote 356 on the LA 2011.

450 *R (PB) v Haringey LBC and others* [2006] EWHC 2255 (Admin), [2007] HLR 13, (2007) 10 CCLR 99; this was likewise under LGA 2000, but see penultimate footnote on the LA 2011.

451 *Clue*, above.

452 *R (De Almeida) v Royal Borough of Kensington and Chelsea* [2012] EWHC 1082 (Admin).

453 *Paposhvili v Belgium*, App No 41738/10, in particular at [181].

454 *N v UK*, App No 26565/05, (2008) 47 EHRR 39, ECtHR.

being exposed to a serious, rapid and irreversible decline in his or her state of health resulting in intense suffering; the benchmark is not, however, the health care system in the returning State and the focus should be on the individual's suffering instead. It is not decisive that the person is to be returned to a country which is a party to the ECHR (see also *MSS*[455] and *Tarakhel*[456] to the same effect as *Paposhvili*).

3.160 The exception governing EU Treaty rights[457] has also been interpreted narrowly. It appears not to apply for the benefit of work seekers[458] but probably does assist workers.[459]

Eligibility – allocations: Housing Act 1996 Part 6

Introduction

3.161 HA 1996 Part 6 is confined to allocations by authorities of secure or introductory tenancies, nominations by local authorities to registered social landlords for letting on assured tenancies, and transfers requested by tenants.[460] It does not cover, and the rules of eligibility do not apply to, the grant of or nomination to a tenancy or licence by a local authority which is not secure, or the nomination of a person to a tenancy or licence which is exempt from assured status.

3.162 Successions to and assignments of tenancies are also unaffected by eligibility because they do not involve the grant of rights of occupation by an authority.[461] Similarly unaffected are transfers of secure or introductory tenancies under the provisions of matrimonial and related domestic legislation,[462] and becoming a secure tenant following an introductory tenancy.[463]

3.163 HA 1996 Part 6 does not affect the eligibility of a person who is already a secure or introductory tenant, or an assured tenant of housing accommodation allocated to him or her by a local housing

455 *MSS v Belgium and Greece*, App No 30696/09, (2011) 53 EHRR 2, ECtHR.

456 *Tarakhel v Switzerland*, App No 29217/12, (2015) 60 EHRR 28, ECtHR.

457 See para 3.154.

458 *R (Mohamed) v Harrow LBC* [2005] EWHC 3194 (Admin), [2006] HLR 18. As to work-seekers, see para 3.31.

459 *R (Conde) v Lambeth LBC* [2005] EWHC 62 (Admin), [2005] HLR 29.

460 HA 1996 s159(2) and (5).

461 HA 1996 s160(2)(a)–(d).

462 HA 1996 s160(2)(e).

463 HA 1996 s160(3).

authority.[464] Under the legislation preceding the HA 1996, when immigration was not explicitly addressed in either homelessness or allocations law,[465] it was held that a tenancy granted to a person unlawfully in the UK was not void for that reason;[466] The same applies under Part 6: notwithstanding the prohibition in HA 1996 s167(8), it has been held that the grant of a tenancy, even though contrary to Part 6, is itself valid.[467]

3.164 The immigration status of members of the household of an applicant for an allocation under Part 6 is relevant, in particular when determining the size of the property to be allocated. It has long been said that parliament cannot have intended to require housing authorities to house those who enter the country unlawfully.[468] Similarly, in *Akinbolu,*[469] it was held that it was proper to refuse to provide public sector housing to applicants who are illegal immigrants or overstayers.

3.165 In *Ariemuguvbe,*[470] the appellant lived in a three-bedroom property with her husband, her five adult children (who had come to the UK from Nigeria but who had overstayed their visitor's visas) and three grandchildren. She contended that she was entitled to additional points under the authority's allocation scheme to take account of the five adult children.[471] The authority was held to be entitled to conclude that it was not appropriate to allocate a larger property to the appellant, because the five children were all independent adults, some having families of their own, who should have been able to make their own housing arrangements and also because they were subject to immigration control[472] in circumstances where providing

464 HA 1996 s159(5) as amended by Homelessness Act 2002 s13.

465 See paras 3.6–3.8.

466 *Akinbolu v Hackney LBC* (1996) 29 HLR 259, CA.

467 See *Birmingham City Council v Qasim* [2009] EWCA Civ 1080, [2010] HLR 19.

468 *Tower Hamlets LBC v Secretary of State for the Environment* [1993] QB 632, per Sir Thomas Bingham at p632, (1993) 25 HLR 524, CA; see also *R v Hillingdon LBC ex p Streeting (No 2)* [1980] 1 WLR 1425, CA.

469 *Akinbolu v Hackney LBC* (1996) 29 HLR 259, CA, at 269.

470 *R (Ariemuguvbe) v Islington LBC* [2009] EWCA Civ 1308. The Court of Appeal overruled the decision in *R (Kimvono) v Tower Hamlets LBC* (2001) 33 HLR 78, QBD, in which neither *Tower Hamlets* nor *Akinbolu* had been cited and in which it had been held that the immigration status of the applicant's dependent child was irrelevant to the authority's duties under HA 1996 Part 6.

471 *Ariemuguvbe* at [2] and [3].

472 See para 3.14.

accommodation for them would amount to them having recourse to public funds in breach of their conditions of entry to the UK.[473]

3.166 In a restricted case,[474] however, an applicant owed a full housing duty will not be entitled to a reasonable preference for an allocation of housing. In non-restricted cases, an applicant does enjoy such a preference.[475] Consequently, if an authority is considering making an offer of Part 6 accommodation to an applicant in a restricted case, it will need to take particular care to ensure that such an allocation is in accordance with the priorities of its published allocation scheme.[476]

3.167 Authorities must consider eligibility at the point at which an applicant is considered for an allocation.[477] Authorities are, however, advised to consider applicants' eligibility both at the time of the initial application and again when considering making an allocation to them, especially where a substantial amount of time has elapsed since the original application.[478]

3.168 Eligibility for an allocation of housing differs between England[479] and Wales.[480]

England

3.169 Eligibility for an allocation of housing depends on whether the applicant is a person subject to immigration control[481] or not subject to immigration control.[482]

Persons subject to immigration control

3.170 For a person subject to immigration control to be eligible, he or she must fall within one of the prescribed classes A–D, F or G described

473 *Ariemuguvbe* at [19].

474 See paras 3.113–3.119.

475 HA 1996 s167(2ZA), and see paras 11.62–11.63.

476 See para 17 of the guidance note that accompanied the DCLG letter dated 16 February 2009.

477 HA 1996 s160A.

478 DCLG, Allocation of accommodation: guidance for local housing authorities in England, 2012, para 3.2; available at www.communities.gov.uk/publications/housing/allocationaccommodationguide.

479 Eligibility Regs 2006 regs 3 and 4.

480 Eligibility (Wales) Regs 2014 regs 3 and 4.

481 Eligibility Regs 2006 reg 3.

482 Eligibility Regs 2006 reg 4.

above at paras 3.122–3.147 above.[483] For the purposes of an allocation, however, Class F is known as Class E,[484] and Class G as Class F.[485]

Persons not subject to immigration control

3.171 Eligibility for an allocation of housing on the part of persons who are not subject to immigration control,[486] is the same as eligibility under Part 7 of the HA 1996.[487]

Wales

3.172 As in England, eligibility for an allocation depends on whether the applicant is a person subject to immigration control[488] or not subject to immigration control.[489]

Persons subject to immigration control

3.173 A person who is subject to immigration control is eligible if the person falls within one of the prescribed classes A–D, or F, as described above (paras 3.122–3.143).[490] For the purposes of an allocation, however, Class F, as described above, is known as Class E.[491]

Persons not subject to immigration control

3.174 In Wales,[492] a person not subject to immigration control is eligible for an allocation[493] on the same basis as for homelessness assistance.[494] which is the same basis as in England.[495]

483 Eligibility Regs 2006 reg 3(a)–(f).

484 Eligibility Regs 2006 reg 3(e) as amended by the Eligibility (Amendment) Regs 2016 reg 2(3)(b)(i), with effect from 30 October 2016.

485 Eligibility Regs 2006 reg 3(f) inserted by the Eligibility (Amendment) Regs 2016 reg 2(3)(c) with effect from 30 October 2016.

486 Eligibility Regs 2006 reg 4, as amended by Eligibility (Amendment) Regs 2012, which inserted a new reg 4(1)(b)(iii) and (iv) and a new reg 4(1)(c), with effect from 8 November 2012, though the amendments do not have effect in relation to an application for an allocation of housing which was made before that date.

487 See paras 3.145–3.147.

488 Eligibility (Wales) Regs 2014 reg 3.

489 Eligibility (Wales) Regs 2014 reg 4.

490 Eligibility (Wales) Regs 2014 reg 3.

491 Eligibility (Wales) Regs 2014 reg 3(e).

492 Eligibility (Wales) Regs 2014 which came into force on 31 October 2014.

493 Eligibility (Wales) Regs 2014 reg 4.

494 This is because Eligibility (Wales) Regs 2014 reg 4 is the same as reg 6.

495 This is because Eligibility (Wales) Regs 2014 reg 4 is the same as the Eligibility Regs 2006 regs 4 and 6.

CHAPTER 4

Homelessness

4.1 Introduction

4.4 Accommodation

4.4 Location

4.6 Nature

Settled accommodation • Non-qualifying accommodation

4.16 Accommodation available for occupation

4.16 Preconditions

4.20 Accommodation for whom?

4.21 Immigration

Family • Others

4.39 Rights of occupation

4.41 Occupation under interest or order

4.44 Occupation under express or implied licence

Tied accommodation

4.48 Occupation by enactment or restriction

Actual occupation v right to occupy • Protection from Eviction Act 1977 • Rent Act protection • Secure/assured protection • Tied accommodation • Former long leaseholders • Other tenants and licensees • Spouses, civil partners and cohabitants • Non-qualifying persons • Timing

4.62 Restriction on entry or use

4.62 Entry prevented

4.66 Moveable structures

continued

4.69 Reasonable to continue to occupy

4.82 Violence and abuse

Threats • Residing with applicant • Domestic violence/abuse • Other violence

4.93 General housing circumstances of area

Other reasons • Location • Permanence • Physical conditions • Overcrowding • Legal conditions • Financial conditions • Employment • Type of accommodation • Other considerations

4.141 Threatened with homelessness

Introduction

4.1 This chapter considers the statutory definitions of 'homelessness' and of being 'threatened with homelessness'.

4.2 'Homelessness' is defined by Housing Act (HA) 1996 s175 and Housing (Wales) Act (H(W)A) 2014 s55 as:

a) accommodation, which is
b) available for the applicant's occupation, to which
c) there are rights of occupation (subsection (1)),
d) entry to or use of which is not restricted (subsection (2)), and which
e) it is reasonable for the applicant to continue to occupy (subsection (3)).[1]

4.3 The same terms also apply to:

f) what is meant by being threatened with homelessness (subsection (4)).

Accommodation

Location

4.4 Under HA 1985, only accommodation in England, Wales or Scotland was to be taken into account. This had not been stated explicitly in the original legislation – the Housing (Homeless Persons) Act 1977 – but had been accepted, albeit obiter, in *Streeting*[2] and was expressly enacted in HA 1985.

4.5 As departure from accommodation abroad could, however, qualify as intentional homelessness,[3] this did not lead to any benefit: HA 1996 s175(1) and H(W)A 2014 s55(1) now refer to accommodation in the UK 'or elsewhere'.[4]

1 See *Nipa Begum v Tower Hamlets LBC* (1999) 32 HLR 445, CA, for a discussion of the interaction of these different subsections.

2 *R v Hillingdon LBC ex p Streeting* [1980] 1 WLR 1425, CA.

3 See *de Falco, Silvestri v Crawley BC* [1980] QB 460, CA, and other cases considered at paras 6.134–6.135.

4 See, eg *Nipa Begum v Tower Hamlets LBC* (1999) 32 HLR 445, CA, where the accommodation in question was situated in Bangladesh.

Nature

4.6 The term 'accommodation' has proved one of the most controversial under the homelessness legislation, not so much as between applicant and authority, but between, on the one hand, the lower courts and the House of Lords, and, on the other, the House of Lords and parliament.

Settled accommodation

4.7 Thus, between 1977 and 1986, there was a growing tendency on the part of the courts – High Court and Court of Appeal – to equiparate a want of accommodation with accommodation of such poor quality that it could be quit without a finding of intentionality. In this context, a distinction was drawn for both purposes (and arguably for the purpose of defining the duties owed by authorities) between 'settled' and 'unsettled' accommodation.

4.8 Both applications of this approach were firmly rejected by the House of Lords, first in *Puhlhofer*,[5] and, later, in *Awua*.[6] In turn, this led to further legislation, first in the Housing and Planning Act 1986, and, to an extent, also under HA 1996 Part 7 itself.

4.9 In the more recent of these cases,[7] the House of Lords held that the only gloss on the word 'accommodation' which can properly be imported, other than pursuant to the statute itself (ie, availability and reasonableness to continue in occupation),[8] is that it must mean 'a place which can fairly be described as accommodation'.[9]

Non-qualifying accommodation

4.10 As an example of shelter which would have failed this test, Lord Brightman in *Puhlhofer* instanced Diogenes' tub.

4.11 In *Awua*, the modern equivalent was said to be the night shelter in *R v Waveney DC ex p Bowers*,[10] in which the applicant could have had a bed if one was available but where he could not remain by day – and therefore had to walk the streets.[11]

5 *R v Hillingdon LBC ex p Puhlhofer* [1986] AC 484, (1986) 18 HLR 158, HL.
6 *R v Brent LBC ex p Awua* [1996] AC 55, (1995) 27 HLR 453, HL.
7 *Awua*, above.
8 See paras 4.17–4.38 and 4.69–4.140.
9 *R v Brent LBC ex p Awua*, above, per Lord Hoffmann at 461.
10 (1982) *Times* 25 May, QBD. Not cross-appealed on this point – see further [1983] QB 238, (1983) 4 HLR 118, CA.
11 *R v Brent LBC ex p Awua*, above, at 459.

4.12 In *Sidhu*,[12] it was held that a women's refuge was not accommodation, so that a woman who left her violent partner and found temporary shelter in such a refuge was still homeless while residing there.[13]

4.13 In *Ali* and *Moran*,[14] however, the House of Lords concluded that *Sidhu* could probably not survive the decisions in *Puhlhofer*[15] and *Awua*[16] as a theoretical proposition, although the effect of the decision was preserved by reference to HA 1996 ss175(3) and 177, ie it would not normally be reasonable to continue to occupy accommodation in a women's refuge.[17] (The House of Lords declined to comment on whether a prison cell or a hospital ward could amount to accommodation.)[18]

4.14 An applicant who occupies temporary accommodation provided to him or her pending enquiries, review or appeal under HA 1996 s188 or s204(4) is nevertheless homeless for the purpose of section 175(1), because to find otherwise would create the absurd result that a homeless person who is temporarily accommodated would not be entitled to benefit from Part 7.[19]

4.15 Reference may also be made to *Miles*,[20] in which it was held that accommodation within the definition of homelessness means 'habitable'. This decision was followed by the majority in the Court of

12 *R v Ealing LBC ex p Sidhu* (1982) 2 HLR 45, QBD.

13 *Sidhu* followed a county court decision, *Williams v Cynon Valley Council*, January 1980 *LAG Bulletin* 16, CC. In addition to *Bowers* (see para 4.11 and footnote 10, above), other cases to consider the meaning of accommodation within the definition of homelessness before *Puhlhofer* and *Awua* were: *Parr v Wyre BC* (1982) 2 HLR 71, CA; *R v South Herefordshire DC ex p Miles* (1983) 17 HLR 82; *R v Preseli DC ex p Fisher* (1984) 17 HLR 147, QBD; and *R v Dinefwr BC ex p Marshall* (1984) 17 HLR 310, QBD.

14 *Birmingham City Council v Ali; Moran v Manchester City Council (Secretary of State for Communities and Local Governmentand another intervening)* [2009] UKHL 36, [2009] 1 WLR 1506 at [56].

15 *R v Hillingdon LBC ex p Puhlhofer* [1986] AC 484, (1986) 18 HLR 158, HL.

16 *R v Brent LBC ex p Awua* [1996] AC 55, (1995) 27 HLR 453, HL.

17 See para 4.72.

18 *Stewart v Lambeth LBC* [2002] HLR 747; *R (B) v Southwark LBC* [2004] HLR 40.

19 *R (Alam) v Tower Hamlets LBC* [2009] EWHC 44 (Admin), [2009] JHL D47. Approved by the House of Lords in *Ali* at [54]. See, to like effect, H(W)A 2014 ss68(1), 69(11) and 88(5). Likewise, where an authority has concluded that a person is owed the full housing duty under HA 1996 s193(2), but has not identified any specific property in which he could live there is therefore no accommodation which was available for his occupation: *Johnston v Westminster City Council* [2015] EWCA Civ 554, [2015] HLR 35.

20 *City of Gloucester v Miles* (1985) 17 HLR 292, CA.

Appeal in *Puhlhofer*,[21] which was upheld by the House of Lords without reference to *Miles*; nor was the case mentioned in *Awua*.

Accommodation available for occupation

Preconditions

4.16 The requirement that accommodation is 'available for occupation' requires consideration of a number of elements:

a) whether accommodation allows occupation 'together with' others;
b) practical accessibility; and
c) for whom the accommodation must be available.

4.17 The requirement of availability means that the accommodation must be available[22] to occupy 'together with' other members of the applicant's household: HA 1996 s176 and H(W)A 2014 s56. This can be satisfied by a single unit of accommodation in which a family can live together but may also be satisfied by two units of accommodation if they are so located that they enable the family to live 'together' in practical terms; it does not require shared living space.[23]

4.18 To be practically accessible and accordingly available to an applicant, it must be possible for the applicant physically to access the accommodation, a question which includes whether an applicant can afford to return to accommodation overseas which is otherwise available.[24]

4.19 Accommodation will not be available if the applicant is not legally entitled to live in the country in which the accommodation is situated.

21 See (1985) 17 HLR 588.

22 This requires identification of an actual property, so that where an authority has concluded that a person is owed the full housing duty under HA 1996 s193(2), but has not identified any specific property in which he could live, there was no accommodation available for his occupation: *Johnston v Westminster City Council* [2015] EWCA Civ 554, [2015] HLR 35.

23 *Sharif v Camden LBC* [2013] UKSC 10, [2013] HLR 16.

24 See *Nipa Begum v Tower Hamlets LBC* (1999) 32 HLR 445, CA. Although the authority had failed to consider this issue in the case, the Court of Appeal refused to quash the decision since the applicant had not raised the issue, and the authority was accordingly not required to investigate the matter (see para 9.100).

Accommodation for whom?

4.20 By HA 1996 s176 and H(W)A 2014 s256, accommodation is only 'available' if it is available for the applicant together[25] with:

a) any person who usually resides with the applicant as a member of his or her family; or
b) any other person who might reasonably be expected to do so.

Immigration

4.21 HA 1996 s185(4) used[26] to require local housing authorities in England and Wales to disregard household members (including dependent children) who were ineligible[27] for housing assistance when considering whether an eligible housing applicant was homeless. This provision has now[28] been amended so that it applies only to an eligible applicant who is himself or herself a person subject to immigration control[29] – for example, those granted refugee status,[30] indefinite leave to remain[31] or humanitarian protection.[32] Accordingly, when deciding whether an applicant who is a person subject to immigration control (excluding for this purpose a European Economic Area (EEA) national[33] or Swiss national), who is eligible for assistance, is homeless, a local authority must continue to disregard any dependants or other household members who are ineligible for assistance.

4.22 The effect is that HA 1996 s185(4) no longer applies to eligible[34] applicants who are not subject to immigration control[35] for example,

25 Cf para 4.17.
26 In respect of all applications for accommodation or assistance in obtaining accommodation within the meaning of HA 1996 s183, made before 2 March 2009.
27 See chapter 3.
28 By Housing and Regeneration Act 2008 s314 and Sch 15 Part 1, in respect of all applications for accommodation or assistance in obtaining accommodation within the meaning of HA 1996 s183, made on or after 2 March 2009.
29 See para 3.16.
30 See paras 3.122–3.127.
31 See paras 3.131–3.133.
32 See paras 3.134–3.137.
33 See para 3.23.
34 See chapter 3.
35 See paras 5.8–5.11.

a British citizen,[36] a Commonwealth citizen with a right of abode in the UK[37] or an EEA national or Swiss national with a right to reside in the UK.[38] This group of eligible applicants will be able to rely on ineligible household members, known as 'restricted persons',[39] to establish homelessness. A restricted person is someone who is not eligible for assistance under Part 7, who is subject to immigration control and who either does not have leave to enter or remain in the UK or who has leave subject to a condition of no recourse to public funds.

4.23 If the authority can be satisfied that the applicant is homeless only by taking into account the restricted person, the application is known as a 'restricted case'.[40] In these circumstances, the authority must, so far as reasonably practical, bring any HA 1996 s193(2) duty to an end by arranging for an offer of an assured shorthold tenancy to be made to the applicant by a private landlord.[41] This is known as a private accommodation offer.[42]

4.24 In Wales, the substantive position is the same, as the provisions of HA 1996 ss185 and 186 are deemed to apply to the H(W)A 2014.[43] It follows that, as in England, a duty owed to a restricted person must, so far as is reasonably practicable, be brought to an end by securing an offer of accommodation from a private sector landlord.[44]

Family

4.25 'Member of the family' is not defined. Both the English and Welsh Codes of Guidance say that the expression will 'include those with close blood or marital relationships and cohabiting partners (including same sex partners)'.[45]

36 See para 3.21.
37 See para 3.22.
38 See paras 3.23–3.99.
39 HA 1996 s184(7).
40 HA 1996 s193(3B).
41 HA 1996 s193(7AD). See further paras 10.166–10.168.
42 HA 1996 s193(7AC). See para 10.166. From 9 November 2012, when the Localism Act (LA) 2011 s148 came into force in England, a new offer by an English authority is to be known as a 'private rented sector offer': Localism Act 2011 (Commencement No 2 and Transitional Provisions) (England) Order 2012 SI No 2599 article 2.
43 H(W)A 2014 Sch 2 para 2.
44 H(W)A 2014 s76.
45 Code of Guidance para 8.5; Welsh Code paras 8.6–8.8.

4.26 Both Codes also state that 'any other person' (who normally resides with the applicant as a member of the family) might cover a companion for an elderly or disabled person, or children being fostered by the applicant or a member of his or her family.[46]

4.27 The English and Welsh Codes conclude:

> Persons who normally live with the applicant but who are unable to do so because there is no accommodation in which they can live together should be included in the assessment.[47]

4.28 This approach echoes the decision of the House of Lords in *Islam*,[48] where the applicant lost his right to a shared room as a result of the arrival of his wife and four children from Bangladesh. A finding of intentionality was quashed by the House of Lords on the basis that what had been lost was not accommodation 'available for his occupation', meaning that of the applicant *and* his family.[49]

4.29 Accordingly, a family which has never enjoyed accommodation in which there were rights of occupation for all of its members will at all times have been homeless. For example, a couple without a home of their own, each still living with his and her parents, will be able to assert an effective right to assistance under Part 7 or Part 2 as soon as a priority need is acquired. An authority wishing to resist the claim cannot resort to intentional homelessness based on the pregnancy itself, as this is precluded by *Islam*.[50]

4.30 Note, however, that an unborn child will not be a person with whom the applicant would be expected to reside. So the future housing needs of the unborn child need not be considered by the authority when determining homelessness,[51] save to the extent to which it had otherwise rendered the mother's accommodation unavailable in her own right.

46 Code of Guidance para 8.5; Welsh Code paras 8.6–8.8.

47 Code of Guidance para 8.6; Welsh Code para 8.8.

48 *Re Islam* [1983] 1 AC 688, (1981) 1 HLR 107, HL.

49 The argument in the Court of Appeal that Mr Islam had made the accommodation unavailable by bringing his family over was dismissed as 'circular . . . because that lack is the very circumstance which section 16 [of the Housing (Homeless Persons) Act 1977, subsequently HA 1985 s75, now s176] and the Act are designed to relieve'.

50 In *R v Eastleigh BC ex p Beattie (No 1)* (1983) 10 HLR 134, QBD, the court rejected out of hand a suggestion that pregnancy causing accommodation to cease to be reasonable to occupy could amount to intentionality.

51 See *R v Newham LBC ex p Dada* (1995) 27 HLR 502, CA.

4.31 That does not make the pregnancy irrelevant. In *Rouf*,[52] it was held that an authority could not jump to the conclusion that accommodation would continue to be available to an applicant with an increasing family. See also *Ali*,[53] in which the court found the proposition that a single, small room was 'available' for a large family (applicant, wife and five children) 'quite extraordinary'.

4.32 In other cases, hopelessly inadequate accommodation had been held not to be accommodation which it was reasonable to continue to occupy.[54]

4.33 A member of the family who usually resides with the applicant need not also be shown to do so reasonably.[55] On the other hand, where children who were not reasonably to be expected to reside with the applicant came to live with him in accommodation (a single room) that was only sufficient for him, he was (to that point) occupying accommodation that was available for him, so that he could be held intentionally homeless for allowing them to come and live with him (which made the accommodation unavailable).[56]

Others

4.34 The question of who is reasonably to be expected to reside with an applicant is a matter for the authority, challengeable on conventional grounds of public law,[57] rather than a question of fact which a court can decide for itself: see *Ly*.[58]

4.35 In *Carr*,[59] it was held that the authority had erred in law in failing to consider whether the applicant's boyfriend – the father of her child – was a person with whom she might reasonably be expected to reside. The authority had wrongly reached its decision solely on the basis that they had not lived together at the applicant's last settled accommodation.

52 *R v Tower Hamlets LBC ex p Rouf* (1989) 21 HLR 294, QBD.

53 *R v Westminster City Council ex p Ali* (1983) 11 HLR 83, QBD.

54 See paras 4.103–4.113.

55 Compare *R v Hillingdon Homeless Persons Panel ex p Islam* (1980) *Times* 10 February QBD, not cross-appealed on the proposition, as it relates to priority need.

56 *Oxford City Council v Bull* [2011] EWCA Civ 609, [2011] HLR 35.

57 See chapter 12.

58 *R v Lambeth LBC ex p Ly* (1986) 19 HLR 51, QBD. Compare *R v Newham LBC ex p Khan and Hussain* (2001) 33 HLR 29, QBD, where a decision that a grandmother, her two daughters and their respective husbands and children did not usually reside together was quashed as *Wednesbury* unreasonable.

59 *R v Peterborough City Council ex p Carr* (1990) 22 HLR 207, CA.

4.36 In *Okuneye*,[60] however, the fact that two people were intending or expecting to reside together did not mean that – when each departed from his and her separate accommodation – they were necessarily reasonably to be expected to reside together at that time. The authority was accordingly entitled to conclude that each had become homeless intentionally for ceasing to occupy available accommodation.

4.37 In *Ryder*,[61] the authority approached the question of whether a carer could reasonably be expected to reside with a disabled applicant by reference to whether the applicant was eligible for Disability Living Allowance. As the test for such an allowance was more stringent – and, it may be said, different – from what is now HA 1996 s176 (H(W)A 2014 s56), the decision was quashed. Similarly, the authority in *Tonnicodi*[62] applied the wrong test – whether the applicant needed a live-in carer – rather than whether the carer was a person who might reasonably be expected to reside with the applicant.

4.38 In *Curtis*,[63] the applicant was occupying her former matrimonial home under a separation agreement which contained a cohabitation clause to the effect that if she cohabited or remarried the property would be sold. The applicant started to cohabit and her husband enforced the power of sale. The authority found the applicant to be homeless intentionally, a decision that was quashed because it had not considered availability in the statutory sense, ie whether, if it was reasonable for her and her cohabitant to live together, the property was available to both of them (which it was not).

Rights of occupation

4.39 It is only accommodation occupied under one of three categories of occupational right which will preclude a finding of homelessness (HA 1996 s175(1); H(W)A 2014 s55(1)):

a) occupation under interest or order;
b) occupation under express or implied licence; or
c) occupation by enactment or restriction.

4.40 It has been held that accommodation in a prison does not fall within any of these rights of occupation, as the prisoner has no enforceable

60 *R v Barking and Dagenham LBC ex p Okuneye* (1995) 28 HLR 174, QBD.
61 *R v Southwark LBC ex p Ryder* (1996) 28 HLR 56, QBD.
62 *R v Hackney LBC ex p Tonnicodi* (1997) 30 HLR 916, QBD.
63 *R v Wimborne DC ex p Curtis* (1985) 18 HLR 79, QBD.

right to occupy the cell,[64] although this question has been reserved by the House of Lords.[65]

Occupation under interest or order

4.41 The right of occupation may be by virtue of an 'interest' in the accommodation: this would seem to mean a legal or equitable interest.

4.42 Those with a legal interest will include both owner-occupiers and tenants, whether under long leases or on short, periodic tenancies, and whether under an initially agreed contractual period or under the contract as statutorily extended by HA 1985 and HA 1988 (secure tenants and assured tenants). If one of a pair of joint tenants unilaterally terminates the joint tenancy, regardless of the concurrence or knowledge of the other, the remaining joint tenant no longer has an interest in the property and therefore cannot be said to have a right of occupation as a tenant.[66]

4.43 Those with an equitable interest commonly include the spouse of an owner-occupier. Spouses and civil partners, whether of owner-occupiers or of tenants, may also be given a right to occupy under an 'order of the court', ie under family legislation.[67]

Occupation under express or implied licence

4.44 Where spouses or other partners are living together, and one only has a right of occupation, such as ownership or tenancy, the other is his or her implied licensee.[68] Lodgers will usually be licensees rather than tenants; flat-sharers may be only licensees rather than joint tenants; a child in the home of his or her parents will be a licensee

64 *R (B) v Southwark LBC* [2003] EWHC 1678 (Admin), [2004] HLR 3; see further para 4.132.

65 *Birmingham City Council v Ali; Moran v Manchester City Council (Secretary of State for Communities and Local Government and another intervening)* [2009] UKHL 36, [2009] 1 WLR 1506; see para 4.13.

66 *Fletcher v Brent LBC* [2006] EWCA Civ 960, [2007] HLR 12; see further para 4.45.

67 See, in particular, Family Law Act 1996 Part 4. The powers can also be applied to cohabitants and former cohabitants.

68 *Hemans & Hemans v Windsor and Maidenhead RLBC* [2011] EWCA Civ 374, [2011] HLR 25.

rather than a tenant or sub-tenant,[69] except in the most exceptional circumstances.[70]

4.45 Where the authority claims that an applicant has a licence to occupy accommodation, it must determine its precise nature. In *Fletcher*,[71] the applicant's wife terminated their joint tenancy by service of a notice to quit. The local authority nonetheless concluded that the applicant was not homeless; on appeal to the county court, the judge concluded that the applicant had some form of licence to occupy the property – the nature of which she decided that it was unnecessary for her to determine – and was therefore not homeless. The Court of Appeal, allowing a further appeal, remitted the case to the authority to determine whether a licence existed and, if so, on what terms.

Tied accommodation

4.46 Where the applicant's licence is as a service occupier and contingent on the contract of employment, there cannot be said to be a licence to occupy once the contract of employment has been terminated.

4.47 Even where the employer of a live-in house-keeper, having terminated the contract of employment, said that the applicant could return to occupy her room, the local authority was in error in concluding that she had a licence to occupy. The licence was dependent on a contract for employment which no longer existed.[72]

Occupation by enactment or restriction

4.48 The final category of 'right of occupation' is occupation as a residence by virtue of any enactment or rule of law giving the applicant the right to remain in occupation, or restricting the right of any other person to recover possession of it.

69 On the distinction between tenant and licensee, see the decisions in *Street v Mountford* [1985] AC 809, (1985) 17 HLR 402, HL; and *AG Securities v Vaughan; Antoniades v Villiers* [1990] AC 417, (1988) 21 HLR 79, HL. See also English Code of Guidance paras 8.9–8.13 on applicants asked to leave accommodation by family or friends.

70 For example, where the house has been subdivided into two flats (self-contained or not), for one of which the parents are charging rent and there are no other criteria which lean against tenancy (such as sharing utilities).

71 *Fletcher v Brent LBC* [2006] EWCA Civ 960, [2007] HLR 12.

72 See *R v Kensington and Chelsea RLBC ex p Minton* (1988) 20 HLR 648, QBD and *Norris v Checksfield* (1991) 23 HLR 425, CA.

Actual occupation v right to occupy

4.49 This category predicates actual occupation, as distinct from a right to occupy, so that a person who walks out of accommodation occupied on this basis will be homeless, albeit at risk of a finding of intentionality.[73] In contrast, a person who walks out of a house in which he or she has an interest will, presuming it is available for his or her occupation,[74] not be homeless until such time as he or she divests himself or herself of that interest, for example, by release or sale.

Protection from Eviction Act 1977

4.50 The definition closely follows the wording of Protection from Eviction Act (PEA) 1977 s1(1).

Rent Act protection

4.51 A tenant within the protection of the Rent Act (RA) 1977 will occupy by virtue of an interest until the determination of the tenancy; thereafter, the person is a statutory tenant. A statutory tenancy is not an interest in land.[75] It is, however, a right of occupation by virtue of an enactment or rule of law, as well as one which gives the tenant the right to remain in occupation and which restricts the right of another to recover possession.

Secure/assured protection

4.52 The same approach was not taken for secure and assured tenants under HAs 1985 and 1988. Rather, there is a restriction on the landlord's right to determine the tenancy itself save by order of the court. Accordingly, the tenancy continues and, as such, occupation is under that interest.

Tied accommodation

4.53 An agricultural worker in tied accommodation, enjoying the benefit of the Rent (Agriculture) Act (R(A)A) 1976,[76] will usually occupy by virtue of a licence before its determination, and thereafter in the same way as a Rent Act statutory tenant. Those whose rights were granted after commencement of HA 1988 Part 1 may have assured agricul-

73 But see further 'Reasonable to continue to occupy' at para 4.69.

74 See para 4.62.

75 *Keeves v Dean* [1924] 1 KB 685, CA.

76 There are conditions which apply before the protection is available.

tural occupancies[77] which – as with assured tenancies[78] – cannot be terminated by the landlord without an order of the court. Those in tied accommodation who do not enjoy the benefit of R(A)A 1976 or HA 1988 derive some temporary benefits under PEA 1977.[79]

Former long leaseholders

4.54 Long leaseholders usually continue to occupy beyond what would otherwise contractually be the termination of their interests by virtue of a statutorily extended tenancy, which is thus still an interest. They will subsequently become either statutory tenants under RA 1977 or assured tenants under HA 1988.[80]

Other tenants and licensees

4.55 PEA 1977 s3 itself prohibits the eviction – otherwise than by court proceedings – of former unprotected tenants and licensees,[81] those who had licences granted on or after 28 November 1980 which qualify as restricted contracts within RA 1977 s19, as well as certain service occupiers. All these people will occupy either by virtue of an interest or a licence until determination, and subsequently by virtue of an enactment restricting the right of another to recover possession.[82]

77 As last footnote.

78 See para 4.52.

79 See PEA 1977 s8(2) applying provisions of that Act to 'a person who, under the terms of his employment, had exclusive possession of any premises other than as a tenant . . .'.

80 Landlord and Tenant Act 1954 Part 1; Local Government and Housing Act 1989 Sch 10.

81 Other than excluded tenants and licensees: see PEA 1977 s3(2B). Note that, by judicial extension, temporary accommodation provided under a licence pursuant to what is now HA 1996 ss188(1), (3), 190(2), 200(1) and 204(4) is incapable of qualifying under PEA 1977 s3: see *R (ZH and CN) v Newham LBC and Lewisham LBC* [2014] UKSC 62, [2015] HLR 6. See also *Mohamed v Manek* (1995) 27 HLR 439 CA and *Desnousse v Newham LBC* [2006] EWCA Civ 547, [2006] HLR 38. It is, however, unclear whether this proposition applies (as it was said in *Manek* to apply) to both tenancies and licences so provided, or only to licences (a difference expressly raised and left open by the court in *Desnousse*).

82 PEA 1977 ss2 and 3, as amended by HA 1980 s69(1) and HA 1988 s30.

Spouses, civil partners and cohabitants

4.56 Even where the applicant is not the tenant, Family Law Act 1996 Part 4[83] protects spouses, civil partners and some cohabitants (including those living together as civil partners) by giving them a right to remain in occupation, or restricting the right of another to recover possession.[84]

Non-qualifying persons

4.57 Those who are left outside the definition altogether are:

a) those who have been trespassers from the outset and remain so; and
b) those who have excluded tenancies and licences which have been brought to an end;[85] or who are otherwise excluded from PEA 1977.[86]

4.58 It follows that 'squatters' properly so-called, as distinct from those to whom a licence to occupy has been granted,[87] are statutorily homeless even though no possession order may yet have been made against them, for, even though they may have the benefit of a roof over their heads, they have no accommodation within any of the classes specified.

4.59 As noted above,[88] an applicant who occupies temporary accommodation provided to him or her pending enquiries, review or appeal under HA 1996 s188 or s204(4) is nevertheless homeless for the purpose of section 175(1).

Timing

4.60 The right not to be evicted otherwise than by court proceedings in PEA 1977 s3 confers protection until execution of a possession order by the court bailiff in accordance with the relevant court rules.[89]

83 As amended by the Civil Partnership Act 2004.

84 *Abdullah v Westminster City Council* [2011] EWCA Civ 1171, [2012] HLR 5.

85 *R v Blankley* [1979] Crim LR 166 and see PEA 1977 s3(2B).

86 Cf footnote 81.

87 Ie a short-life occupation agreement, usually pending redevelopment.

88 Para 4.14.

89 *Hanniff v Robinson* [1993] QB 419, CA. The relevant county court rules are found in CPR 83.

4.61 In *Sacupima*,[90] it was held that the same applied under the Civil Procedure Rules (CPR) and, therefore, under HA 1996 s175(1)(c).[91] Accordingly, an assured tenant[92] does not become homeless for the purposes of section 175(1)(c) until the warrant for possession against him or her is executed.[93] Note, however, that from 9 November 2012 when the Localism Act (LA) 2011 s149 came into force,[94] an applicant who makes a fresh application to an English authority within two years of a previous application which had resulted in the offer and acceptance of an assured shorthold tenancy,[95] in respect of which notice has been given under HA 1988 s21,[96] is homeless from the expiry of that notice, so that the applicant need not await proceedings for eviction.[97] This does not apply where the application was made before – and the duty to secure accommodation was still in existence at – that date.[98]

Restriction on entry or use

Entry prevented

4.62 A person is also homeless if he or she 'cannot secure entry to' his or her accommodation.[99]

4.63 This provision is primarily intended to benefit the illegally evicted tenant or occupier, but covers anyone else who for some reason cannot immediately be restored to occupation of a home to which he or

90 *R v Newham LBC ex p Sacupima* (2001) 33 HLR 1, QBD. See also *R v Newham LBC ex p Khan* (2001) 33 HLR 29, QBD.

91 HA 1996 s230 defines 'enactment' as including subordinate legislation.

92 Entitled to remain in occupation under HA 1988 s5 until a court order is made. The same argument will apply to secure tenancies: see HA 1985 s82.

93 In these circumstances, however, the applicant will be threatened with homelessness: see para 4.141.

94 Localism Act 2011 (Commencement No 2 and Transitional Provisions) (England) Order 2012 SI No 2599 article 2.

95 See *Manual of Housing Law*, 10th edn, Arden & Dymond, para 1.248.

96 See *Manual of Housing Law*, para 2.203.

97 HA 1996 s195A(2). This right only arises on one re-application: HA 1996 s195A(6).

98 Localism Act 2011 (Commencement No 2 and Transitional Provisions) (England) Order 2012 SI No 2599 article 3.

99 HA 1996 s175(2)(a); H(W)A 2014 s55(2)(a).

she has a legal entitlement – for example, because of occupation by squatters.[100]

4.64 This provision has not proved to be of as much practical use as was intended, because authorities have tended to consider that unless the applicant uses available legal remedies to re-enter, he or she will be considered intentionally homeless, albeit possibly provided with temporary assistance until an order from the court is obtained.

4.65 Authorities should, however, have no rigid policy to this effect,[101] for there may be circumstances in which, even though legal redress exists, both the benefits to be gained from using it and the circumstances generally suggest that it would be inappropriate, for example, illegal eviction by a resident landlord who will shortly recover possession in any event, where tensions are such that it is impracticable for the tenant to remain in the property.

Moveable structures

4.66 A person is also homeless if his or her accommodation consists of a moveable structure, vehicle or vessel designed or adapted for human habitation, and there is no place where the applicant is entitled or permitted both to place it and to reside in it – for example, a mobile home, caravan or house-boat.[102]

4.67 In *Roberts*,[103] travelling showmen were considered to be neither homeless nor threatened with homelessness while moving between fairgrounds during the fairground season, residing at each ground in caravans on a temporary basis. 'Reside' does not require permanence: it means 'live' or 'occupy'.

4.68 In *Smith v Wokingham DC*,[104] a county court considered that a caravan parked on land belonging to a county council, without express permission but in which the applicant and his family had lived for two-and-a-half years, had been the subject of an acquiescence

100 Code of Guidance para 8.16; Welsh Code para 8.16. It does not include where an applicant cannot travel to accommodation (which is otherwise available): *Nipa Begum v Tower Hamlets LBC* (1999) 32 HLR 445, CA.

101 See, eg *British Oxygen Co Ltd v Minister of Technology* [1971] AC 610, HL; *Re Betts* [1983] 2 AC 613, 10 HLR 97, HL; *Attorney-General ex rel Tilley v Wandsworth LBC* [1981] 1 WLR 854, CA; *R v Warwickshire CC ex p Williams* [1995] COD 182, QBD; *R v North Yorkshire CC ex p Hargreaves* (1997) 96 LGR 39, QBD.

102 HA 1996 s175(2)(b); H(W)A 2014 s55(2)(b).

103 *R v Chiltern DC ex p Roberts et al* (1990) 23 HLR 387, QBD.

104 April 1980 *LAG Bulletin* 92, CC. See also *Higgs v Brighton and Hove City Council* [2003] EWCA Civ 895, [2004] HLR 2.

sufficient to constitute permission for the purpose of what is now HA 1996 s175(2)(b).

Reasonable to continue to occupy

4.69 A person is homeless if his or her accommodation is such that it is not reasonable to continue to occupy it.[105] There is a relationship between reasonableness to continue to occupy and suitability of accommodation.[106] Therefore, case-law on one of these issues may be relevant to the other.[107]

4.70 The test is satisfied only if it is reasonable for the applicant to occupy the accommodation indefinitely, or at least for as long as the applicant otherwise would if the authority did not intervene to rehouse him or her: *Ali* and *Moran*.[108] Thus, an applicant may be homeless long before the situation becomes so bad that it is not reasonable for him or her to occupy the accommodation for another night.[109] What this recognises is that accommodation which it may be unreasonable for a person to occupy for a long period, may nonetheless be reasonable to occupy for a short period.[110]

4.71 The test is linked to 'suitability':[111] accommodation which is not reasonable for an applicant to continue to occupy may nevertheless be suitable for the time being; there are degrees of suitability and what is suitable for occupation in the short term may not be suitable in the longer term.[112] The point in time at which accommodation which it is not reasonable for an applicant to continue to occupy becomes unsuitable is primarily for the authority to decide, and

105 HA 1996 s175(3); H(W)A 2014 s55(3). This element of the definition was introduced into HA 1985 as s58(2A) by Housing and Planning Act 1986 s14(2), as a parliamentary response to the House of Lords decision in *R v Hillingdon LBC ex p Puhlhofer* [1986] AC 484, (1986) 18 HLR 158, HL.

106 See para 4.71; see further paras 10.145–10.163.

107 *Harouki v Kensington and Chelsea RLBC* [2007] EWCA Civ 1000, [2008] HLR 16. This is also implicit in *Birmingham City Council v Ali; Moran v Manchester City Council (Secretary of State for Communities and Local Government)* [2009] UKHL 36, [2009] 1 WLR 1506 where the House of Lords came close to eliding the two concepts.

108 *Birmingham City Council v Ali; Moran v Manchester City Council (Secretary of State for Communities and Local Government)*, above, at [37].

109 *Ali* and *Moran* at [40].

110 *Ali* and *Moran* at [42].

111 See paras 10.145–10.163.

112 *Ali* and *Moran* at [47]. See also *R (Edwards) v Birmingham City Council* [2016] EWHC 173 (Admin), [2016] HLR 11.

involves taking into account matters such as the severe constraints on budgets and personnel and the very limited number of satisfactory properties for large families.[113]

4.72 On the same basis, a woman who has left her home because of domestic or other violence[114] normally remains homeless even if she has found a temporary haven in a women's refugee[115] because it would usually not be reasonable for her to continue to occupy her place in the refuge indefinitely,[116] ie for as long as she would have to occupy it if the authority did not intervene to rehouse her.[117]

4.73 The test of reasonableness to continue to occupy does not apply only to accommodation which is actually occupied: continuation refers to the entitlement rather than the occupation. Accordingly, a person is homeless if it is – or if it would not be – reasonable to occupy the accommodation, whether or not in prior occupation of it, or in occupation of it at the time of the application or decision. Any other approach would mean that if the circumstances were so bad that the applicant had left, he or she might (in theory at least) be found not to be homeless,[118] where he or she would be found homeless if the circumstances were such that, although unreasonable to continue to occupy the accommodation, they were not so bad that the applicant had actually left it. Such a result could not have been intended: *Maloba*.[119]

4.74 Whether it would have been reasonable for an applicant to continue to occupy accommodation for the purposes of HA 1996 s191(1) is to be determined at a time before the deliberate acts or omissions which led to the loss of that accommodation. In answering this question, an authority must ignore those acts or omissions: *Denton*.[120]

4.75 The term 'reasonable to continue to occupy' is governed by HA 1996 s177 or H(W)A 2014 s57, as to both:

a) violence (HA 1996 s177(1) and (1A)) or abuse (H(W)A 2014 s57(1)); and

113 *Ali* and *Moran* at [50].
114 See paras 4.82–4.92.
115 *Ali* and *Moran* at [65].
116 *Ali* and *Moran* at [52].
117 *Ali* and *Moran* at [46].
118 In *Nipa Begum v Tower Hamlets LBC* (1999) 32 HLR 445, CA, at [41], while taking a contrary view of the statutory provisions, it was said that no reasonable authority could reach such a decision.
119 *Waltham Forest LBC v Maloba* [2007] EWCA Civ 1281, [2008] HLR 26, rejecting the majority obiter conclusion in *Nipa Begum*, in favour of the minority view.
120 *Denton v Southwark LBC* [2007] EWCA Civ 623, [2008] HLR 11.

b) the general housing circumstances of the area (HA 1996 s177(2); H(W)A 2014 s57(3)).

4.76 The secretary of state and the Welsh Ministers have power to specify other circumstances in which it is or is not to be regarded as reasonable to continue to occupy accommodation, and matters (other than the general housing circumstances of the area) which are to be taken into account when determining whether or not it is reasonable to continue in occupation (HA 1996 s177(3); H(W)A 2014 s57(4)).[121]

4.77 These considerations are not exhaustive of matters to be taken into account in determining whether or not it is reasonable to continue in occupation: *Duro-Rama*.[122] The question is not limited to consideration of the size, structural quality and amenities of accommodation.[123] It follows that, in addition to violence and the general housing circumstances of the area and any other considerations that may be specified, there is a wide range of other matters which may affect the issue.

4.78 Subject to the provisions of HA 1996 s177(2) and H(W)A 2014 s57(3), which allows regard to be had to the general housing circumstances of the area, the question whether it is reasonable to continue to occupy has been described as subjective, and not susceptible to a generalised or objective standard: *McManus*.[124] This does not mean wholly subjective in the view of the applicant, but has been construed as meaning that the issue has to be determined on all the facts of the case – not, on the one hand, determined simply by reference to local conditions or the local authority's policy, nor, on the other, looked at from the perspective of the applicant alone, so that the role of other persons or factors is ignored.[125]

121 See para 4.122 as to the regulations which have been issued.

122 *R v Hammersmith and Fulham LBC ex p Duro-Rama* (1983) 9 HLR 71, QBD.

123 *Waltham Forest LBC v Maloba* [2007] EWCA Civ 1281, [2008] HLR 26.

124 *R v Brent LBC ex p McManus* (1993) 25 HLR 643, QBD.

125 *Denton v Southwark LBC* [2007] EWCA Civ 623, [2008] HLR 11, at [13], [30] and [31]. This approach is consistent with *Ahmed v Leicester City Council* [2007] EWCA Civ 843, [2008] HLR 6, which concerned HA 1996 s193(7F) (paras 10.174–10.175), in which it was held that an applicant's genuine belief that it was not reasonable to accept an offer of accommodation was not conclusive of whether it was reasonable to do so; if the authority has evidence which entitles it to consider that the belief was not objectively reasonable, even if that evidence was not available to the applicant at the time of the refusal, the authority may nonetheless decide that it was reasonable for the applicant to accept the offer. It would seem that a similar approach may therefore be available in relation to HA 1996 s177.

4.79 The question is not, however, whether it is reasonable to leave accommodation, but whether or not it is reasonable to continue to occupy it.[126] The distinction is significant: it will commonly be reasonable (in the sense of not being unreasonable) to leave somewhere; what has to be sustained is the proposition that it is positively not reasonable to stay.

4.80 There is no presumption that an applicant's current accommodation is unsuitable, such as to impose a burden on the authority to rebut it: *McCarthy*.[127]

4.81 Whether or not it is reasonable to continue to occupy accommodation relates not only to the applicant but also to any other person who might reasonably be expected to reside with the applicant: *Bishop*.[128] This must be as true of a person residing with the applicant as a member of the family.

Violence and abuse

4.82 It is not reasonable to continue to occupy accommodation if, even though there may be a legal entitlement to do so, it is 'probable' that occupation of it will lead to domestic or other abuse (in Wales)[129] or violence or threats of violence which are likely to be carried out (in England):

a) against the applicant; or
b) against any person who usually resides with the applicant, or against any person who might reasonably be expected to reside with the applicant.[130]

4.83 In *Danesh*[131] a narrow definition of 'violence' was adopted, to mean actual physical violence, not including threats of violence or acts or gestures which lead a person to fear physical violence. In *Yemshaw*,[132] however, the Supreme Court adopted a much broader view which,

126 See *R v Kensington and Chelsea RLBC ex p Bayani* (1990) 22 HLR 406, CA; see also *R v Gravesham BC ex p Winchester* (1986) 18 HLR 208, QBD.

127 *R v Sedgemoor DC ex p McCarthy* (1996) 28 HLR 608, QBD.

128 *R v Westminster City Council ex p Bishop* (1993) 25 HLR 459, CA.

129 'Abuse' means physical violence, threatening or intimidating behaviour and any other form of abuse which, directly or indirectly, may give rise to the risk of harm: H(W)A 2014 s58(1). Given the decision in *Yemshaw* (below), the terms violence and abuse appear to be synonymous.

130 HA 1996 s177(1), (1A); H(W)A 2014 s57(1).

131 *Danesh v Kensington and Chelsea RLBC* [2006] EWCA Civ 1404, [2007] HLR 17.

132 *Yemshaw v Hounslow LBC* [2011] UKSC 3, [2011] HLR 16; see also H(W)A 2014 s58.

it held, was consistent with the purpose of the legislative scheme; accordingly, it included physical violence, threats, intimidating behaviour and any other form of abuse which, directly or indirectly, may give rise to a risk of harm.[133] It followed that the authority had erred in applying the narrow definition in *Danesh* and the case was remitted for reconsideration by them. This wider definition was subsequently incorporated into statutory guidance[134] and, in *Waltham Forest LBC v Hussein*,[135] it was held that, although *Danesh* had not been expressly overruled by *Yemshaw*, it was clear that much of the reasoning was disapproved; the wider approach in *Yemshaw* should be followed.

4.84 It is not necessary to show an actual history of violence. The test may be satisfied by the lower standard, ie, threats by someone likely to carry them out. Many authorities fail to observe this important distinction, and require a high standard of proof of actual violence in the past, as evidence of both probability and likelihood. As this section draws a careful distinction, so also must authorities.

4.85 The position is not the same as failure to use legal redress in connection with 'entry prevented'.[136] Authorities are not to concern themselves with what steps to prevent the violence applicants should (in the authority's view) take or could have taken: *Bond*.[137]

4.86 Therefore, when determining whether it is reasonable to continue to occupy under HA 1996 s177, an authority may consider only whether it was probable that continued occupation of the property would lead to violence or the threat of violence.[138] Whether a victim of violence had failed to take measures to prevent the violence (such as contacting the police or taking out an injunction) is irrelevant: if, however, the victim does take preventative measures which it is considered will probably prove effective in preventing actual or threatened violence, the level of risk may factually be reduced below probability. Those are the questions which an authority must ask itself; it may

133 The wider view had also been adopted in the English Code of Guidance para 8.21 which *Danesh* had criticised.

134 *Supplementary guidance on domestic abuse and homelessness*: CLG, November 2014.

135 [2015] EWCA Civ 14, [2015] HLR 16.

136 See para 4.62.

137 *Bond v Leicester City Council* [2001] EWCA Civ 1544, [2002] HLR 6. See also English Code of Guidance para 8.22; Welsh Code para 8.23. Compare the earlier decisions of *R v Eastleigh BC ex p Evans* (1984) 17 HLR 515, QBD; *R v Purbeck DC ex p Cadney* (1985) 17 HLR 534; and *R v Wandsworth LBC ex p Nimako-Boateng* (1984) 11 HLR 95, QBD.

138 *Bond v Leicester City Council* [2001] EWCA Civ 1544, [2002] HLR 6.

not assume that such measures will be taken or, if taken, that they will be effective.[139]

Threats

4.87 The only test that an authority may apply to establish whether threats are likely to be carried out is likewise what is probable: see *Bond*.[140] See also English Code of Guidance para 8.22:[141]

> . . . an assessment of the likelihood of a threat of violence being carried out should not be based solely on whether there has been actual violence in the past.

Residing with applicant

4.88 The violence need not be against the applicant but could be against any person who usually resides with the applicant or against any person who might reasonably be expected to do so. See above 'Accommodation available for occupation' at paras 4.16–4.38, and note that the person to whom the violence is shown need not be residing with the applicant as a member of the applicant's family, so that, for example, a carer could qualify.

Domestic violence/abuse

4.89 Domestic violence or abuse is not confined to that between spouses or cohabitants. It may come from any person with whom the applicant or other person who is the subject of it is associated.[142] The English Code of Guidance[143] suggests that 'domestic violence' should be understood to include threatening behaviour, violence or abuse

139 *Bond v Leicester City Council* [2001] EWCA Civ 1544, [2002] HLR 6. The earlier decision in *R v Wandsworth LBC ex p Nimako-Boateng*, above, in which it had been held that an authority could conclude that it would be reasonable for a woman to continue to occupy accommodation – notwithstanding domestic violence – by reference to the remedies otherwise available to her for her protection, was decided under HA 1985 s58, now HA 1996 s175(3), at a time when the question of reasonableness was at large, rather than statutorily defined as it now is in section 177. Accordingly, *Nimako-Boateng* was distinguished in *Bond*, as was the decision to like effect in *R v Purbeck DC ex p Cadney* (1985) 17 HLR 534.

140 *Bond v Leicester City Council* [2001] EWCA Civ 1544, [2002] HLR 6.

141 See Welsh Code para 8.22 to the same effect.

142 HA 1996 s177(1A), as amended by Civil Partnership Act 2004; H(W)A 2014 s58(2).

143 Code of Guidance para 8.21; see also Welsh Code para 8.21 and Violence against Women, Domestic Abuse and Sexual Violence (Wales) Act 2015 s24.

(psychological, physical, sexual, financial or emotional) between associated persons.

4.90 People are associated if:

a) they are or have been married to each other;
b) they are or have been civil partners of each other;
c) they are cohabitants or former cohabitants (meaning a man and a woman who are living together without being married to one another, or two people of the same sex who are living together without being civil partners) or, in Wales, they live or have lived together in an enduring family relationship (whether they are of different sexes or the same sex);
d) they live or have lived in the same household;
e) they are relatives, meaning:
   i) parent, step-parent, child, stepchild, grandparent or grandchild of a person or of that person's spouse, civil partner, former spouse or former civil partner; or
   ii) sibling, aunt or uncle, niece or nephew of a person or that person's spouse, civil partner, former spouse or former civil partner, whether of full- or half-blood, or by marriage or civil partnership;
f) they have agreed to marry (whether or not that agreement has been terminated);
g) they have entered into a civil partnership agreement between them (whether or not that agreement has been terminated);
h) in relation to a child, each of the persons is a parent of the child, or has or has had parental responsibility (within the meaning of the Children Act (CA) 1989) for the child;
j) in relation to a child who has been adopted (or subsequently freed from adoption), if one person is a natural parent or natural parent of a natural parent, and the other is the child, or is a person who has become a parent by adoption, or who has applied for an adoption order, or with whom the child was at any time placed for adoption;[144] and
k) in Wales, people who have or have had an intimate personal relationship with each other which is or was of significant duration.[145]

4.91 HA 1996 s178(2) and (2A) and H(W)A 2014 s58(3) and (4) contain detailed provisions governing association arising out of adoptions.

144 HA 1996 s178, as amended by Civil Partnership Act 2004 Sch 8; H(W)A 2014 s58.

145 H(W)A 2014 s58(2)(h).

Other violence

4.92 The Homelessness Act 2002 extended the application of HA 1996 s177 to 'other violence', ie, from someone not associated with the victim – covering, for example, those suffering from violent racial harassment or witnesses in trials who have been intimidated by violence or threats of violence.[146] This is a significant extension. Formerly, violence from non-associated persons was only relevant to the question of reasonableness 'at large'.[147] An authority considering reasonableness at large could therefore take into account whether an applicant could obtain protection from violence through the courts or by seeking a transfer.[148] Incorporation into HA 1996 s177, means that the proper approach to the availability of alternative remedies will be the same as set out in *Bond*.[149]

General housing circumstances of area

4.93 The comparison between accommodation occupied and the general circumstances prevailing in relation to housing accommodation in the district of the authority to which an application has been made[150] is one of the central concepts of homelessness law, albeit that most of it was developed in relation to intentionality.

4.94 Indeed, it initially bore not at all on the definition of homelessness, although it was in practice being applied by the courts at the point in the evolution of the law[151] at which an there was an equiparation between being homeless and occupation of accommodation so poor that it could be left without a finding of intentionality.

4.95 *Awua*[152] notwithstanding, it is difficult to conceive that parliament intended anything other than the importation of an identical criterion when it adopted the exact same phraseology for use in the definition (HA 1985 s58) of homelessness as had long existed in relation to intentionality (HA 1985 s60), ie whether or not it was reasonable to

146 In Wales, the extension is found in H(W)A 2014 s58(1) in respect of 'abuse'.
147 *R v Hillingdon LBC ex p H* (1988) 20 HLR 554, QBD.
148 See, eg *R v Newham LBC ex p McIlroy* (1991) 23 HLR 570, QBD.
149 See para 4.85.
150 HA 1996 s177(2); H(W)A 2014 s57(3).
151 See para 4.7 in relation to accommodation.
152 *R v Brent LBC ex p Awua* [1996] AC 55, (1995) 27 HLR 453, HL.

continue to occupy, subject to the general housing conditions of the area.[153]

4.96 The comparison is between current accommodation, wherever situated, and conditions in the area of the authority to which application is made.[154]

4.97 HA 1996 s177(2) requires the authority to carry out a balancing act between the housing conditions in the authority's area and the accommodation quit, although whether or not it is reasonable to continue to occupy accommodation involves other questions, such as the pattern of life followed by the applicant: *Monaf*.[155] Such comparisons should only be made, however, where relevant to a case.[156]

4.98 The decision in *Tickner v Mole Valley DC*,[157] in which the applicants were evicted from a caravan site because they refused to pay increased rents which they thought excessive in view of the conditions on the site, turned on what is now HA 1996 s177(2), albeit in the context of intentionality:

> That is what influenced this authority here. They had long waiting lists for housing. On those lists there were young couples waiting to be married: or young married couples sometimes staying with their in-laws: or people in poor accommodation. All those people were on the housing waiting lists – people who had been waiting for housing for years. The council thought it would be extremely unfair to all those on the waiting lists if these caravan dwellers – by coming in in this way – jumped the queue, when they were well able to pay the rent for the caravans and stay on. Those were perfectly legitimate considerations for the local authority to consider.[158]

153 Housing and Planning Act 1986 s14(2); see also para 4.75. See also *R v Wandsworth LBC ex p Wingrove*, and *R v Wandsworth LBC ex p Mansoor* [1996] 3 All ER 913, (1997) 29 HLR 801, CA. See also *Nipa Begum v Tower Hamlets LBC* (1999) 32 HLR 445, CA, at p319/H ('[T]he plain intention of Parliament was to enable a local authority to determine the question of homelessness . . . without having to go on to the corresponding question in the test of intentional homelessness . . .') and at p326/A–B.

154 *R v Tower Hamlets LBC ex p Monaf* (1988) 20 HLR 529, CA.

155 See para 4.69. See also *R v Newham LBC ex p Ajayi* (1994) 28 HLR 25, QBD, referring to matters 'of social history and national status', such as where children were born and how long a person has lived somewhere.

156 *R v Newham LBC ex p Tower Hamlets LBC* (1990) 23 HLR 62, CA.

157 August 1980 *LAG Bulletin* 187, CA.

158 The same judge – Lord Denning MR – in *de Falco, Silvestri v Crawley BC* [1980] QB 460, CA, described the provision as a 'ray of hope', allowing the authority to say: 'You ought to have stayed where you were before. You ought not to have landed yourself on us when it would have been reasonable for you to stay where you were.'

4.99 In order to rely on this provision, the authority need not consider in great detail all the information on housing conditions in its area, but may have regard to 'the generally prevailing standard of accommodation in their area, with which people have to be satisfied'.[159]

Other reasons

4.100 There is an infinite number of reasons why people may not wish to remain in accommodation; accordingly, there is no simple test of reasonableness.[160]

Location

4.101 The question is not confined to matters relating to the accommodation in itself, but can extend to its location: *Homes*.[161]

Permanence

4.102 The fact that the accommodation is not permanent is not relevant to whether or not it is reasonable to continue the occupation: *Nipa Begum*.[162]

Physical conditions

4.103 Physical conditions may produce circumstances in which it is not reasonable to continue to occupy accommodation.

4.104 It is clear that, before an applicant can claim with confidence that it would not be reasonable to continue to occupy accommodation on the ground of its physical condition, the accommodation will have to be very poor indeed, although in some cases (for example, a wheelchair user) the physical characteristics of the accommodation may make it per se unsuitable for the particular applicant.[163]

4.105 In *Miles*,[164] a hut approximately 20 feet by ten feet, with two rooms, infested by rats, and with no mains services (although services were available in a nearby caravan occupied by relatives), was held to constitute accommodation of which an authority could consider it reasonable for the applicant to continue in occupation, at a time when

159 Per Lord Denning MR in *Tickner*, para 4.98.

160 See English Code of Guidance para 8.18; Welsh Code para 8.20.

161 *R v Wycombe DC ex p Homes* (1988) 22 HLR 150, QBD.

162 *Nipa Begum v Tower Hamlets LBC* (1999) 32 HLR 445, CA.

163 English Code of Guidance para 8.34; Welsh Code para 8.27.

164 *R v South Herefordshire DC ex p Miles* (1983) 17 HLR 82, QBD.

there were two adults and two children living in it, albeit that it was on the 'borderline' of what was reasonable and would cross the border-line into what no authority could consider reasonable on the birth of a third child.

4.106 In *Fisher*,[165] the applicant and her children had been living in temporary accommodation. For a period they lived in a caravan. Immediately before her application, they lived on a boat, without bath, shower, WC, electricity, hot water system or kitchen with a sink. There was one cabin, which was kitchen, living room and bedroom combined, and the applicant occupied it with her children and two friends. This was held not to amount to accommodation of which it was reasonable to continue in occupation.

4.107 In *Winchester*,[166] the applicant and his family had left accommodation in Alderney. Among the reasons for leaving was that the accommodation was in an appalling state of disrepair, suffering from damp and a dangerous outside staircase and balcony. The family was found to be intentionally homeless. The decision of the local authority that it would have been reasonable to remain was not considered to be unreasonable or perverse.

4.108 In *Dee*,[167] a decision that it would have been reasonable for a young woman and her new baby to occupy a pre-fabricated beach bungalow which suffered severe damp problems was quashed because the authority had given too much weight to the fact that the property was not considered to be unfit for human habitation and too little to the medical advice which had been given to the applicant.[168]

4.109 In *Ben-El-Mabrouk*,[169] the want of adequate means of escape from fire did not necessarily mean that it was not reasonable for a couple with a small baby to stay in occupation of a fifth-floor flat in a house in multiple occupation (HMO), although a delay in rehousing the family under the provisions of the Land Compensation Act 1973[170]

165 *R v Preseli DC ex p Fisher* (1984) 17 HLR 147, QBD.

166 *R v Gravesham BC ex p Winchester* (1986) 18 HLR 208, QBD.

167 *R v Medina BC ex p Dee* (1992) 24 HLR 562, QBD.

168 See also the discussion of *Shala v Birmingham City Council* [2007] EWCA Civ 624, [2008] HLR 8 at para 5.41, the principle of which must apply in the same way to issues of suitability having regard to medical conditions.

169 *R v Kensington and Chelsea RLBC ex p Youssef Ben-El-Mabrouk* (1995) 27 HLR 564, CA.

170 Land Compensation Act 1973 s39 requires an authority to re-house residential occupiers displaced from their accommodation as a result of specified enforcement action taken by the authority under (now) HA 2004 Part 1, previously under HA 1985 Part 10.

might itself (in the absence of an explanation from the authority) have been challengeable.

4.110 In *Puhlhofer*,[171] at the Court of Appeal, Ackner LJ's view as to whether or not the applicants had any accommodation (within the meaning of the legislation) at all[172] was based in part on the question whether or not it would have been reasonable to continue to occupy it. He considered that accommodation for the applicant, his wife and two children in one room in a guesthouse, with no cooking or laundry facilities, was still such that it could have been reasonable to continue to occupy it in the light of the authority's evidence that there were at least 44 families on the council's waiting list for two-bedroomed accommodation considered to be of higher priority.

Overcrowding

4.111 Overcrowding is a relevant consideration: *Beattie (No 1)*.[173] An authority cannot refuse to consider an application simply because the accommodation is not statutorily overcrowded: *Alouat*.[174] The authority is, however, entitled to take into account the fact that the property is not statutorily overcrowded: *Beattie (No 2)*.[175] Even if it is, this does not prevent it being reasonable for an applicant to continue to occupy the accommodation.[176]

4.112 In *Ali*,[177] even if accommodation had been 'available', it was said:

> . . . that anyone should regard it as reasonable that a family of that size should live in one room 10ft x 12ft in size, or thereabouts, is something which I find astonishing. However, the matter has to be seen in the light of s17(4) [now HA 1996 s177(2)] which requires that reasonableness must take account of the general circumstances prevailing in relation to housing in the area. No evidence has been placed before

171 (1985) 17 HLR 588, CA.

172 See para 4.8.

173 *R v Eastleigh BC ex p Beattie (No 1)* (1983) 10 HLR 134, QBD.

174 *R v Westminster City Council ex p Alouat* (1989) 21 HLR 477, QBD. See also Code of Guidance para 8.28. The Welsh Code para 8.27 says that: 'Although statutory overcrowding, by itself, is not sufficient to determine whether it is unreasonable for the applicant to continue to live in accommodation, it can be a key factor which suggests unreasonableness.'

175 *R v Eastleigh BC ex p Beattie (No 2)* (1984) 17 HLR 168, QBD. See also, on overcrowding, *Krishnan v Hillingdon LBC* January 1981 *LAG Bulletin* 137, QBD; *R v Tower Hamlets LBC ex p Ojo* (1991) 23 HLR 488, QBD; and *R v Tower Hamlets LBC ex p Bibi* (1991) 23 HLR 500, QBD.

176 *Harouki v Kensington and Chelsea RLBC* [2007] EWCA Civ 1000, [2008] HLR 16.

177 *R v Westminster City Council ex p Ali* (1983) 11 HLR 83, QBD.

> me that accommodation in the area of the Westminster City Council is so desperately short that it is reasonable to accept overcrowding of this degree. In the absence of such evidence I am driven to the conclusion that this question could not properly have been determined against the applicant.

4.113 In *Osei*,[178] it was held that, even if the applicant's flat in Madrid had been overcrowded when he surrendered his tenancy, it was open to the authority to conclude that it was reasonable for him and his family to continue to occupy it until he had secured alternative accommodation for his family in London.

Legal conditions

4.114 The fact that accommodation had been obtained by deception meant that it would not have been reasonable to remain in occupation of it: *Gliddon*.[179]

4.115 In *Knight*,[180] and in *Li*,[181] once service occupancies had been ended and there could be no defence to an action for possession, the authorities were not able to consider that occupiers should reasonably have remained in occupation pending proceedings.

4.116 These decisions can be difficult to reconcile with the definition of rights of occupation (including the right to remain in occupation under an enactment),[182] although it is not hard to see the common sense in discouraging authorities from requiring possession orders where there would be no defence. Indeed, the Code of Guidance has long made clear that authorities should not require tenants to fight possession proceedings where the landlord has a strong prospect of success.[183] In *Ugbo*,[184] the authority's failure to consider such

178 *Osei v Southwark LBC* [2007] EWCA Civ 787, [2008] HLR 15.

179 *R v Exeter City Council ex p Gliddon* (1984) 14 HLR 103, QBD; *Chishimba v Kensington and Chelsea RLBC* [2013] EWCA Civ 786, [2013] HLR 34.

180 *R v Portsmouth City Council ex p Knight* (1983) 10 HLR 115, QBD.

181 *R v Surrey Heath BC ex p Li* (1984) 16 HLR 79, QBD.

182 See paras 4.48–4.61.

183 See paras 8.30-8.32 in the English Code paras 8.14 and 8.31 of the Welsh Code. The concept appears to have first been stated in para A1.3 of the 2nd edn of the Code, although has been strengthened and developed in subsequent editions.

184 *R v Newham LBC ex p Ugbo* (1993) 26 HLR 263, QBD, a case on para 10.12 of the 3rd edn of the Code: 'Local authorities should not require tenants to fight a possession action where the landlord has a certain prospect of success, such as an action for recovery of property let on an assured shorthold tenant, on the ground that the fixed term of the tenancy has ended. Authorities need only be satisfied that proper notice had been served with the intention to proceed.'

guidance (and the implications of the fact that that applicant was only an assured shorthold tenant rather than fully assured) invalidated its decision on this issue.

4.117 The current Code[185] suggests that where the applicant is an assured shorthold tenant who has received proper notice (under HA 1988 s21)[186] that the tenancy is to be terminated and the landlord intends to seek possession, and there is no defence to the possession proceedings, it is unlikely to be reasonable for the applicant to occupy the accommodation beyond the date given in the section 21 notice, unless he or she is taking steps to persuade the landlord to withdraw the notice.

4.118 *Ugbo* must be compared with *Jarvis*,[187] where the authority had considered the Code but was held still to be entitled to reach the conclusion that it was reasonable to continue to occupy pending a court order following termination of an assured shorthold tenancy.[188]

4.119 In *Minnett*,[189] the authority should have disregarded departure one day before the date specified in a consent order for possession.

4.120 Given the decision in *Khan and Hussain*[190] that a tenant who is subject to a possession order only becomes homeless when that order is executed, authorities should also consider cases where the applicant leaves between the possession order and physical eviction by the court bailiffs, even though – on that analysis – the applicant will not yet be homeless.[191]

185 English Code of Guidance para 8.32; Welsh Code para 8.31. See also the letter from the secretary of state to English Local Authority CEOs (June 2016, DCLG) reminding authorities that they 'should not adopt a general policy of accepting – or refusing to accept – applicants as homeless or threatened with homelessness when they are threatened with eviction but a court has not yet made an order for possession or issued a warrant of execution'.

186 See *Manual of Housing Law*, para 2.203.

187 *R v Croydon LBC ex p Jarvis* (1993) 26 HLR 194, QBD; see also *R v Bradford City Council ex p Parveen* (1996) 28 HLR 681, QBD.

188 The 2nd edn of the Code at para 1.3 read: 'Where it is clear from the facts that tenants have no defence . . . to an application for possession, authorities should not insist that an order is obtained, and a date for eviction set, before agreeing to help the tenant.'

189 *R v Mole Valley DC ex p Minnett* (1983) 12 HLR 49, QBD.

190 *R v Newham LBC ex p Khan and Hussain* (2001) 33 HLR 29, QBD.

191 *R v Newham LBC ex p Sacupima* (2001) 33 HLR 1, QBD.

Financial conditions

4.121 Financial considerations raise the question of 'affordability': see *Hawthorne*,[192] in which the authority had to consider whether the applicant's failure to pay rent had been caused by the inadequacy of her financial resources.

4.122 The secretary of state has required authorities in England to take affordability into account when determining whether or not it is reasonable to continue to occupy accommodation: Homelessness (Suitability of Accommodation) Order 1996.[193]

4.123 In reaching this decision, the authority must consider the financial resources available to a person, including, but not limited to: the costs of the accommodation; payments being made under a court order to a spouse or former spouse; any payments made to support children; whether under a court order or under the Child Support Act 1991; and the applicant's other reasonable living expenses.[194]

4.124 The order also contains a detailed list of deductible accommodation costs,[195] although authorities are not limited to considering only these.[196]

4.125 In determining the amount that an applicant requires for residual living costs, the English Code of Guidance[197] suggests that authorities may wish to have regard to the amount of benefit to which the applicant would be entitled. Both the English and Welsh Codes[198]

192 *R v Wandsworth LBC ex p Hawthorne* (1994) 27 HLR 59, CA.

193 SI No 3204 (see appendix B). In Wales, see H(W)A 2014 s59(2), to the same effect. When deciding issues of affordability, all forms of income should be considered: *Samuels v Birmingham City Council* [2015] EWCA Civ 1051, [2015] HLR 47 (rejecting an argument that all welfare benefits other than housing benefit should be left out of account).

194 1996 Order, article 2(a).

195 1996 Order, article 2(b).

196 Unlike under the 1996 Order in England, in Wales H(W)A 2014 s59(2) provides no further details. The Welsh Code requires consideration of the 'financial resources available to the applicant; the costs in respect of the accommodation; maintenance payments (in respect of ex-family members); and the applicant's other reasonable living expenses': see para 8.29; see also para 19.26.

197 English Code of Guidance para 17.40.

198 English Code of Guidance, para 8.29; Welsh Code para 8.29.

makes it clear that affordability is always an issue which must be considered.[199]

4.126 This is consistent with case-law. In *Duro-Rama*,[200] the availability of benefits was held to be a relevant consideration which the authority had ignored by confining itself to the matters set out in HA 1985 s60(4) (now HA 1996 s177(2)).

4.127 In *Griffiths*,[201] it was said that it cannot be assumed that income support is sufficient to meet housing costs.

4.128 Inadequacy of financial resources goes not merely to ability to pay the rent, but also to funding the necessities of life, including food: *Bibi*,[202] following *Tinn*.[203]

4.129 It is, however, for the authority not the court to assess whether or not accommodation is affordable: *Grossett*.[204]

Employment

4.130 In *Duro-Rama*,[205] it was also said that the issue of employment was a relevant considerations which the authority had ignored. This reflects the comment of Lord Lowry in *Islam*,[206] that:

> There will, of course, and in the interests of mobility of labour ought to be, cases where the housing authority will . . . accept that it would not have been reasonable in the circumstances for the applicant to continue to occupy the accommodation which he has left.

199 Welsh Code para 19.28 is more prescriptive: accommodation is not to be considered affordable if the applicant 'would be left with a residual income which would be significantly less than the level of income support or income-based Jobseekers allowance or Universal Credit that is applicable in respect of the applicant, or would be applicable if he or she was entitled to claim such benefit . . . Local authorities will need to consider whether the applicant can afford the housing costs without being deprived of basic essentials such as food, clothing, heating, transport and other essentials'.

200 *R v Hammersmith and Fulham LBC ex p Duro-Rama* (1983) 9 HLR 71, QBD.

201 *R v Shrewsbury BC ex p Griffiths* (1993) 25 HLR 613, QBD. See further *R v Hillingdon LBC ex p Tinn* (1988) 20 HLR 206, QBD; and *R v Camden LBC ex p Aranda* (1996) 28 HLR 672, QBD. Cf *R v Westminster City Council ex p Moklis Ali* (1996) 29 HLR 580, QBD.

202 *R v Islington LBC ex p Bibi* (1996) 29 HLR 498, QBD.

203 *R v Hillingdon LBC ex p Tinn* (1988) 20 HLR 206, QBD.

204 *R v Brent LBC ex p Grossett* (1994) 28 HLR 9, CA. See too *R v Brent LBC ex p Baruwa* (1997) 29 HLR 915, CA and *Bernard v Enfield LBC* [2001] EWCA Civ 1831, CA.

205 *R v Hammersmith and Fulham LBC ex p Duro-Rama* (1983) 9 HLR 71, QBD.

206 *Re Islam* [1983] 1 AC 688, (1981) 1 HLR 107, HL.

4.131 To the same effect, in *Ashton*,[207] it was held that no reasonable authority would have allowed the provisions of what is now HA 1996 s177(2) to have governed a decision on intentionality where a middle-aged woman who had been unemployed for six years, and who had chronic active hepatitis, left settled accommodation to take up work in another area.

Type of accommodation

4.132 It has been held that accommodation in a prison cell is not accommodation which it is reasonable for the applicant to continue to occupy (where the applicant has the opportunity to obtain early release under a tagging scheme): *B*.[208]

4.133 Both the English and Welsh Codes[209] suggest that some types of accommodation – for example, women's refuges; direct access hostels; and night shelters intended to provide very short-term temporary accommodation in a crisis – should not be regarded as reasonable for someone to continue to occupy in the medium and longer term. It may be that in some circumstances such accommodation should not be considered reasonable to occupy at all.[210]

Other considerations

4.134 In *Bassett*,[211] the court held that a woman who had followed her husband to Canada, notwithstanding the uncertainties of their prospects there, could not reasonably have remained in occupation of their secure council accommodation, when going to join him was her only chance of saving their marriage.

4.135 It would be wrong, however, to view this as anything more than an illustration of the proposition that it is the particular circumstances of applicant and household which are relevant.[212]

207 *R v Winchester City Council ex p Ashton* (1991) 24 HLR 520, CA.

208 *R (B) v Southwark LBC* [2003] EWHC 1678 (Admin), [2004] HLR 3. But cf, now, *Birmingham City Council v Ali; Moran v Manchester City Council (Secretary of State for Communities and Local Government and another intervening)* [2009] UKHL 36, [2009] 1 WLR 1506, para 4.13, where the House of Lords expressly reserved the issue of whether prison could comprise accommodation at all.

209 Para 8.34; Welsh Code para 8.27.

210 See now *Birmingham City Council v Ali; Moran v Manchester City Council (Secretary of State for Communities and Local Government and another intervening)*, para 4.13.

211 *R v Basingstoke and Deane BC ex p Bassett* (1983) 10 HLR 125, QBD.

212 Cf, above, *R v Brent LBC ex p McManus* (1993) 25 HLR 643, QBD; and *R v Shrewsbury BC ex p Griffiths* (1993) 25 HLR 613, QBD.

4.136 In *Hearn*,[213] the applicant's sense of isolation was held to be a factor relevant to deciding whether it was reasonable for her to continue to occupy premises.

4.137 In *Healiss*,[214] the authority failed to consider the applicant's reasons for concluding that it was not reasonable for her to continue in occupation of the accommodation of which she was a secure tenant, including repeated break-ins to empty flats in her block, two burglaries of her own flat, harassment involving strangers knocking at the door, stones thrown at windows, and shouting up to her windows at all hours of the day and night; in addition, gangs of youths congregated on the stairway smoking what was assumed to be drugs, the first-floor landing was used as a latrine and smelled as such, and the applicant was too frightened to allow her child to play in the block and gardens.

4.138 In *Nimako-Boateng*,[215] however, the court upheld the decision of the authority that a woman could reasonably have remained in occupation of the matrimonial home in Ghana, even though her relationship with her husband had broken down. (The court noted that it had been given no information about Ghanaian family law, and assumed that the woman's rights would have been the same as under English law. There was no complaint of domestic violence.)[216] *Nimako-Boateng* was followed in *Evans*.[217]

4.139 In *Moncada*,[218] the applicant was divorced from his wife and had custody of his two sons. The court refused to interfere with a finding that, given the shortage of accommodation in London, it was reasonable for him to continue to live in the four-bedroomed matrimonial home, notwithstanding that his ex-wife and daughter also continued to live in it.

213 *R v Swansea City Council ex p Hearn* (1990) 23 HLR 372, QBD.

214 *R v Sefton MBC ex p Healiss* (1994) 27 HLR 34, QBD.

215 *R v Wandsworth LBC ex p Nimako-Boateng* (1983) 11 HLR 95, QBD.

216 On the issue of domestic violence, as distinct from matrimonial breakdown, see now, however, *Bond*, para 4.85.

217 *R v Eastleigh BC ex p Evans* (1984) 17 HLR 515, QBD.

218 *R v Kensington and Chelsea RLBC ex p Moncada* (1996) 29 HLR 289, QBD.

4.140 All violence and threats of violence, whatever their source, will now fall to be considered under HA 1996 s177[219] rather than – as previously – under section 175(2).[220]

Threatened with homelessness

4.141 A person is threatened with homelessness for the purposes of HA 1996 Part 7 if it is likely that he or she will become homeless within 28 days.[221] In Wales, the period is 56 days.[222] Note, however, that since 9 November 2012, when LA 2011 s149 came fully into force in England,[223] an applicant who makes a fresh application to an English authority within two years of a previous application which had resulted in the offer and acceptance of an assured shorthold tenancy,[224] in respect of which notice has been given under HA 1988 s21,[225] is threatened with homelessness from when the notice is given.[226] This does not apply where the application was made before – and the duty to secure accommodation was still in existence at – that date.[227]

4.142 The period of 28 days, now only applicable in England, was originally referable to the 'normal' period granted by a court before a possession order would take effect. Since 3 October 1980, however, courts have been obliged to make orders to take effect within 14 days, save where exceptional hardship would be caused: see HA 1980 s89, although this is applicable only where the court has no other

219 See paras 4.82–4.92.

220 See, for example, *R v Hillingdon LBC ex p H* (1988) 20 HLR 559, QBD; *R v Northampton BC ex p Clarkson* (1992) 24 HLR 529, QBD; *R v Croydon LBC ex p Toth* (1987) 20 HLR 576, CA; and *R v Newham LBC ex p McIlroy and McIlroy* (1991) 23 HLR 570, QBD.

221 HA 1996 s175(4).

222 H(W)A 2014 s55(4).

223 Localism Act 2011 (Commencement No 2 and Transitional Provisions) (England) Order 2012 SI No 2599 Article 2.

224 See *Manual of Housing Law*, para 1.246.

225 See *Manual of Housing Law*, para 2.203.

226 HA 1996 s195A(4). This right only arises on one re-application: HA 1996 s195A(6). See also the letter in June 2016, from the secretary of state to all local authority chief executives reminding them that authorities 'should not adopt a general policy of accepting – or refusing to accept – applicants as homeless or threatened with homelessness when they are threatened with eviction but a court has not yet made an order for possession or issued a warrant of execution'.

227 Localism Act 2011 (Commencement No 2 and Transitional Provisions) (England) Order 2012 SI No 2599 article 3.

discretion to suspend, for example, under the RA 1977, HA 1985 or HA 1988.

4.143 Even once the date for possession has passed, the applicant will not be homeless until the warrant for possession is executed.[228] During this period, the applicant will, however, be threatened with homelessness.

4.144 There is no reason to draw any distinction of principle between the definitions of 'homelessness' and 'threatened with homelessness', other than the 28-day[229] criterion: *Dyson*.[230] This seems to be based on a concession by counsel, but must surely be correct.

4.145 Once faced with an applicant who is threatened with homelessness, the authority must start making appropriate enquiries under HA 1996 s184.[231] The duty cannot be postponed until the applicant is actually homeless: *Khan and Hussain*.[232] If enquiries are made before the 28 days, they will be non-statutory: *Hunt*.[233]

4.146 Once the Homelessness Reduction Act (HRA) 2017 comes into force, the period of 56 days currently applicable in Wales (para 4.141) will also serve to determine when a person becomes threatened with homelessness in England.[234] In addition, an assured shorthold tenant[235] served with a valid notice under HA 1988 s21,[236] in respect of the only accommodation which that person has[237] which is available for his or her occupation,[238] and which will expire within 56 days, is also threatened with homelessness.[239]

228 See *R v Newham LBC ex p Sacupima* (2001) 33 HLR 1, QBD.
229 In Wales, 56 days: H(W)A 2014 s55(4).
230 *Dyson v Kerrier DC* [1980] 1 WLR 1206, CA, at p1212.
231 In Wales, H(W)A 2014 s60. See chapter 9.
232 *R v Newham LBC ex p Khan and Hussain* (2001) 33 HLR 29, QBD.
233 *R v Rugby BC ex p Hunt* (1992) 26 HLR 1, QBD.
234 HRA 2017 s1: HA 1996 s175(4), as amended.
235 See *Manual of Housing Law*, para 1.246.
236 See *Manual of Housing Law*, para 2.203.
237 For a tenancy to be assured – including assured shorthold – it must be occupied as an only or principal home; accordingly, a tenant could have a principal home with a second home elsewhere, eg used for weekends or holidays; such a tenant will therefore not benefit from this extension. See, generally, *Manual of Housing Law*, chapter 1.
238 This will be interpreted in the usual way: paras 4.14–4.24.
239 HRA 2017 s1: HA 1996 s175(5), as added.

CHAPTER 5

Priority need

5.1 Introduction

5.8 Immigration

5.12 Pregnancy

5.13 Dependent children

5.15 Alternative tests

5.19 Dependence on applicant

5.22 Separated parents

Dependence on applicant • Residing with applicant • Reasonably expected to reside

5.30 Children in social services care

5.32 Vulnerability

England • Wales

5.38 Old age

5.39 Mental illness or handicap or physical disability

5.50 Other special reason

5.55 Multiple causes

5.56 Emergency

5.62 Other categories

5.65 16- and 17-year-olds

England • Wales

continued

5.71 18- to 20-year-old care leavers
England • Wales

5.73 Vulnerable care leavers
England • Wales

5.75 Former members of the armed forces
England • Wales

5.77 Vulnerable former prisoners
England • Wales

5.79 Persons fleeing violence
England • Wales

5.81 Young person at risk of exploitation
Wales only

Introduction

5.1 There are – normally[1] – no substantive housing rights or duties under either Housing Act (HA) 1996 Part 7 or Housing (Wales) Act (H(W)A) 2014 Part 2[2] unless the applicant has a 'priority need for accommodation'.

5.2 In England, a homeless person or a person threatened with homelessness has a priority need for accommodation if the person is within one of the following categories:[3]

a) she is a pregnant woman, or a person with whom a pregnant woman resides or might reasonably be expected to reside;
b) he or she is a person with whom dependent children reside or might reasonably be expected to reside;
c) he or she is vulnerable as a result of old age, mental illness or handicap or physical disability or other special reason, or is someone with whom such a person resides or might reasonably be expected to reside;
d) he or she is homeless or threatened with homelessness as a result of an emergency such as flood, fire or other disaster.

5.3 These categories closely follow those formerly described in Department of the Environment (DoE) Circular 18/74 as the 'priority groups' who were to have the first claim on resources available:

> The Priority Groups comprise families with dependent children living with them, or in care; and adult families or people living alone who either become homeless in an emergency such as fire or flooding or are vulnerable because of old age, disability, pregnancy or other special reasons.[4]

1 Since 9 November 2012, however, when the Localism Act (LA) 2011 s149 came into force in England (see Localism Act 2011 (Commencement No 2 and Transitional Provisions) (England) Order 2012 SI No 2599 article 2), an applicant who makes a fresh application to an English authority within two years of a previous application which resulted in an assured shorthold tenancy, will – if still eligible (see chapter 3) and not homeless intentionally (see chapter 6) – be entitled to assistance if homeless (defined as arising when the notice expires: see para 4.61) or threatened with homelessness (defined as arising when the notice is given: see para 4.141)) regardless of whether or not the applicant is still in priority need: HA 1996 s195A(1), (3). This right only arises on one re-application: HA 1996 s195A(6). It only arises where the new duty to secure accommodation has arisen and had not ceased before the relevant date (Localism Act 2011 (Commencement No 2 and Transitional Provisions) (England) Order 2012 SI No 2599 article 3).

2 But see paras 10.66–10.89.

3 HA 1996 s189(1).

4 DoE Circular 18/74 para 10; see para 1.19.

5.4 In England, the secretary of state[5] may add to these categories, which power has been exercised in the Homelessness (Priority Need for Accommodation) (England) Order 2002[6] and is discussed below.[7]

5.5 In Wales, the position is similar but not identical. The English priority need categories in HA 1996 s189 and the 2002 Order are largely mirrored in H(W)A 2014 s70. Differences are discussed in the relevant subheadings below. As in England, there is a power to add to these categories, although this has not yet been exercised.[8]

5.6 Whether in England or Wales, a local authority cannot fetter its discretion by pre-determining that people within specified groups – for example, the single or childless homeless – should never be considered 'vulnerable' within category c) in para 5.1 above.[9] Authorities are bound to provide advice and assistance even to those who are not in priority need.[10]

5.7 Authorities must, when reaching decisions, take into account all material factors up to the date of the decision and, if there is a review, up to the date of the review: *Mohamed v Hammersmith and Fulham LBC*.[11] Accordingly, a priority need can be acquired after application but before decision, or after decision but before review, eg pregnancy; thus, where children were accommodated with an applicant pending the authority's enquiries, who would not otherwise have been able to live with him or her, the applicant was still in priority need.[12]

5 HA 1996 s189(2). See also para 2.11.

6 SI No 2051.

7 See further para 5.63.

8 H(W)A 2014 s72. Unlike in England, there is an additional power for the Welsh Ministers to remove any condition that a local housing authority must have reason to believe or be satisfied that an applicant is in priority need for accommodation before any power or duty to secure accommodation arises, which would allow a court to decide that issue for itself, instead of being confined to principles of public law intervention: see paras 12.16–12.49. It is, accordingly, a power of great potential significance. No plans to exercise this power have yet been announced.

9 See also para 12.105.

10 HA 1996 s192; H(W)A 2014 s60: see paras 10.85–10.89.

11 [2001] UKHL 57, [2002] HLR 7. See para 9.177.

12 *Oxford City Council v Bull* [2011] EWCA Civ 609, [2011] HLR 35.

Immigration

5.8 HA 1996 s185(4) of used[13] to require local housing authorities in England and Wales to disregard household members (including dependent children) who were ineligible[14] for housing assistance, when considering whether any eligible housing applicant was in priority need. This provision was amended[15] so that a) it only applies on its face in England (but see para 5.11) and b) it applies only to an eligible applicant who is himself or herself a person subject to immigration control,[16] other than a European Economic Area (EEA) national[17] or Swiss national,[18] for example, those granted refugee status,[19] indefinite leave to remain[20] or humanitarian protection. Thus, the ineligible dependants or other household members of those who are not subject to immigration control, or who – though subject to immigration control – are EEA or Swiss nationals, are to be taken into account when deciding whether the applicant is in priority need, while those who are still subject to the requirement are to be disregarded when deciding that question if they are themselves ineligible for assistance.

5.9 These ineligible household members on whom – since the amendment – reliance can be made when deciding whether or not the applicant is in priority need are known as 'restricted persons':[21]

13 In respect of all applications for accommodation or assistance in obtaining accommodation within the meaning of HA 1996 s183, made before 2 March 2009.

14 See paras 3.113–3.117. For example, in *Ehiabor v Kensington and Chelsea RLBC* [2008] EWCA Civ 1074, the applicant could not rely on the dependent child to establish a priority need because the child, although born in the UK, was not a British citizen and therefore required leave to remain under the Immigration Act 1971 s1(2) and was subject to immigration control. The restriction was declared incompatible with Article 14 when read with Article 8 of the European Convention on Human Rights (ECHR) in *R (Morris) v Westminster City Council (No 3)* [2005] EWCA Civ 1184, [2006] HLR 8. Cf the different approach taken by the European Court of Human Rights (ECtHR) in *Bah v UK*, App No 56328/07, [2012] HLR 2.

15 By Housing and Regeneration Act 2008 s314 and Sch 15 Part 1, in respect of all applications for accommodation or assistance in obtaining accommodation within the meaning of HA 1996 s183, made on or after 2 March 2009.

16 See para 3.16.

17 See para 3.23.

18 See para 3.18.

19 See paras 3.122–3.127.

20 See para 3.132.

21 HA 1996 s184(7).

they are persons who are not themselves eligible for assistance under HA 1996 Part 7, who are subject to immigration control, and who either do not have leave to enter or remain in the UK or who have leave subject to a condition of no recourse to public funds.[22]

5.10 If the authority can only be satisfied that the applicant is in priority need by taking into account the restricted person, the application is known as a 'restricted case'.[23] In those circumstances, the authority must, so far as reasonably practical, bring any HA 1996 s193(2) duty to an end by arranging for an offer of an assured shorthold tenancy to be made to the applicant by a private landlord.[24] This is known as a 'private rented sector offer'.[25]

5.11 In Wales, the substantive position is the same, as the provisions of HA 1996 ss185 and 186 are deemed to apply to the H(W)A 2014.[26] It follows that, as in England, a duty owed to a restricted person must, so far as is reasonably practicable, be brought to an end by securing an offer of accommodation from a private sector landlord.[27]

Pregnancy[28]

5.12 Any stage of pregnancy qualifies as priority need. One of the objects of the Housing (Homeless Persons) Act 1977 was to eliminate the practice of some authorities, who refused to consider a woman's pregnancy as a factor until a given stage of pregnancy. Once the pregnancy is established, the priority need exists.[29]

22 See *Lekpo-Bozua v Hackney LBC* [2010] EWCA Civ 909, [2010] HLR 46.
23 HA 1996 s193(3B). See also para 3.113–3.119.
s24 HA 1996 s193(7AD). See further para 10.197.
25 HA 1996 s193, as amended.
26 H(W)A 2014 Sch 2 para 2.
27 H(W)A 2014 s76.
28 HA 1996 s189(1)(a); H(W)A 2014 s70(1)(a).
29 See also para 5.4. Both the English and the Welsh Codes consider that the 'normal letter of confirmation of pregnancy from the medical services issued to pregnant women or a midwife's letter' should be adequate evidence of pregnancy (English Code para 10.5; Welsh Code para 16.5). They note that, if the woman suffers a miscarriage, the authority may need to consider whether she remains in priority need because she is vulnerable for another special reason (English Code para 10.5; Welsh Code para 16.5).

Dependent children[30]

5.13 Dependent children do not qualify as being in priority need in their own right; nor will they qualify as vulnerable either because of their youth or because of any disability: *ex p G*.[31] Dependent children are expected to be provided for (with assistance where appropriate, ie, under HA 1996 Part 7) by those on whom they are dependent. The notion of a dependent child connotes a relationship akin to that of parent–child,[32] so that an applicant with a 17-year-old wife could not claim to be in priority need under this category on the basis of her dependency on him.[33] The same is likely to be held in relation to siblings, eg an 18-year-old applicant with a 17-year-old sibling; however, a greater age difference between siblings, giving rise to a truly dependent relationship more akin to that of parent–child, could still give rise to a priority need.[34]

5.14 Children must be 'residing' with an applicant, not merely 'staying' – that is, some degree of permanence or regularity must exist.[35]

Alternative tests

5.15 The tests are alternative. In *Islam*,[36] not cross-appealed by the authority on this point,[37] the authority unsuccessfully contended that, if reliance were placed by an applicant on dependent children living with the applicant, it was also necessary to show that such children might reasonably be expected to reside with the applicant. It was held that this is not correct; if there are dependent children actually residing with the applicant at the date of the authority's decision (not the date of application),[38] it is not relevant to consider whether or not they are reasonably expected to do so.

30 HA 1996 s189(1)(b); H(W)A 2014 s70(1)(b).

31 *R v Oldham BC ex p G; R v Bexley LBC ex p B; R v Tower Hamlets LBC ex p Begum* [1993] AC 509, (1993) 25 HLR 319, HL; and see para 9.17.

32 See Code of Guidance para 10.8; Welsh Code para 16.6.

33 *Hackney LBC v Ekinci* [2001] EWCA Civ 776, [2002] HLR 2.

34 *R (Lusamba) v Islington LBC* [2008] EWHC 1149 (Admin), [2008] JHL D89.

35 See also *R v Lewisham LBC ex p Creppy* (1991) 24 HLR 121, CA and *R v Lambeth LBC ex p Bodunrin* (1992) 24 HLR 647, QBD. But nb that this may have started in accommodation provided by the authority pending enquiries.

36 *R v Hillingdon Homeless Persons Panel ex p Islam* (1980) *Times* 10 February, QBD.

37 *Re Islam* [1983] 1 AC 688, (1981) 1 HLR 107, HL.

38 See para 9.136.

5.16 Thus, in *Sidhu*,[39] the applicant and her children were living in a women's refuge.[40] The applicant had obtained an interim custody order from the county court but the authority contended that it was entitled not to consider her to be in priority need until a full custody order was granted. The court rejected this argument: the full order was irrelevant (nor could the authority defer its decision in order to have time to assure itself that no change would take place in the future[41] – in that case, the prospective change was the remote prospect of the applicant losing custody at full hearing). The same may now be said of residence orders.[42]

5.17 An order of a court will, however, be relevant where an applicant's children are not currently residing with the applicant, but reliance is placed on a claim that they are reasonably to be expected to do so – for example, where the applicant has won custody but cannot in practice take care of the children for want of accommodation.

Dependence on applicant

5.18 There must be dependence on the applicant, so that an applicant is not in priority need where children who reside with the applicant are dependent on someone else.[43]

5.19 'Dependent' is not defined in HA 1996 Part 7 or in H(W)A 2014 Part 2. In *Amarfio*,[44] the Court of Appeal considered the Code of Guidance under HA 1985 Part 3 (reproduced so far as relevant in the current Codes),[45] which referred to children under the age of 16 as dependent, together with those under the age of 19 either receiving full-time education or training or otherwise unable to support themselves. It was held that once a child has gone into full-time employment, the child could not be dependant: a young person on a youth training scheme was considered to be in gainful employment by way of training and therefore to be regarded as being in full-time employment.

39 *R v Ealing LBC ex p Sidhu* (1982) 2 HLR 45, QBD.

40 See paras 4.10–4.16.

41 A proposition approved in *Robinson v Hammersmith and Fulham LBC* [2006] EWCA Civ 1122, [2006] 1 WLR 3295, [2006] HLR 7. See para 9.133.

42 Under Children Act 1989 s8.

43 See *R v Westminster City Council ex p Bishop* (1997) 29 HLR 546, QBD. See also *R v Camden LBC ex p Hersi* (2001) 33 HLR 52, QBD.

44 *R v Kensington and Chelsea RLBC ex p Amarfio* (1995) 27 HLR 543, CA.

45 Code of Guidance para 10.7; Welsh Code para 16.6.

5.20 The court did recognise, however, that there may be circumstances where a 16- or 17-year-old, although not financially dependent on his or her parents, is sufficiently dependent on them in other respects to fall within the subsection.[46]

5.21 In *Miah v Newham LBC*,[47] the authority had treated the Code of Guidance as limited to children up to their 18th birthday. The Court of Appeal held that the Code addresses children under 19 years old (who are in full-time education or training or otherwise unable to support themselves): the Code had therefore been misinterpreted by the authority.

Separated parents

5.22 Where parents are separated, a child may divide his or her time between parents or others.[48] Three separate issues arise:

a) whether the child is dependent on the applicant;
b) whether the child resides with the applicant; and
c) if the child is not currently residing with the applicant, whether the child may reasonably be expected to do so.

Dependence on applicant

5.23 In *Vagliviello*,[49] the authority was held to have erred by applying a 'wholly and exclusively dependent' test. For the purposes of HA 1985 s59, now HA 1996 s189, it is possible for a child to reside with and be dependent on more than one person, only one of whom may be applying for assistance.[50]

5.24 In *Bishop*,[51] where parents had agreed that the children should split their time between each of them, the authority was nonetheless

46 This accords with the conclusion in *Shortt v Secretary of State for Communities and Local Government and Tewkesbury BC* [2015] EWCA Civ 1192, [2016] 1 P&CR 15 in which the differing views expressed in the non-homelessness decision in *Fawcett Properties Ltd v Buckingham CC* [1961] AC 636, HL were considered in relation to a planning condition imposed by a local authority, the effect of which was to limit occupation of a property to persons employed in agricultural activities and their dependants: it was held that dependency was not confined to financial dependency; 'dependant' was an ordinary word, capable of referring to relationships involving non-financial dependency.

47 [2001] EWCA Civ 487.

48 See Code of Guidance paras 10.9–10.10; Welsh Code para 16.8.

49 *R v Lambeth LBC ex p Vagliviello* (1990) 22 HLR 392, CA.

50 But see *Holmes-Moorhouse v Richmond upon Thames LBC* [2009] UKHL 7, [2009] HLR 34, para 5.26.

51 *R v Westminster City Council ex p Bishop* (1997) 29 HLR 546, QBD.

entitled to conclude that the children were not dependent on one of them, the father. In reaching this decision, it took into account that the children were adequately housed with the mother, that she received income support and child benefit for them, and that the applicant, who was unemployed, did not have the financial means of supporting them.

Residing with applicant

5.25 In *Smith-Morse*,[52] the authority erred because it applied a 'main' residence test; it also failed to consider the future as well as present arrangements for the child. On the other hand, in *McCarthy*,[53] the parents were divorced and, although there was a joint custody order, care and control had been given to the mother. Although it had been agreed that the children should spend three days per week with their father, this sort of 'staying access' did not equate to residence. It was considered that it would only be in very exceptional circumstances that a child might reside with both parents living apart: this type of arrangement has become much more common since the Children Act (CA) 1989 came into force.[54]

5.26 The question is to be determined at the date of the decision.[55] Where the decision is made while the applicant is still only threatened with homelessness,[56] at which point the applicant may still be residing with children, for example, before leaving the family home, the applicant will only be in priority need if the children will be residing with the applicant once he or she is actually homeless, which may well not be the case if the authority provides no accommodation.[57]

52 *R v Kingswood BC ex p Smith-Morse* (1994) *Times* 8 December, QBD.

53 *R v Port Talbot BC ex p McCarthy* (1990) 23 HLR 208, CA.

54 See also *Holmes-Moorhouse v Richmond upon Thames LBC* [2009] UKHL 7, [2009] HLR 34. It was recognised that shared residence orders (now 'child arrangement orders') are much more common now. The policy reasons for a local authority not providing a family that previously lived under one roof with a second home are, however, considered to be overwhelming. See para 5.26.

55 See para 5.4.

56 See paras 4.141–4.146.

57 *Holmes-Moorhouse v Richmond upon Thames LBC*, above, at [20].

Reasonably expected to reside

5.27 *McCarthy*[58] also held that, while not bound to do so, the authority could conclude that children are usually reasonably to be expected to reside with the parent with care and control.

5.28 A child arrangement order[59] does not, however, mean that the children are reasonably to be expected to reside with both parents. In *Doyle,*[60] four children were to spend half the week with each parent under such an order. The father applied to the authority as homeless. The authority took the joint residence order into account but was still entitled to decide that the children could not reasonably be expected to reside with the applicant. In reaching this decision, the authority was entitled to take into account the shortage of housing stock in its area and the under-occupation for part of each week that would result.

5.29 In *Holmes-Moorhouse v Richmond upon Thames LBC,*[61] the separated parents of four children agreed to a shared residence order pursuant to which the three youngest children would spend alternate weeks and half of each school holiday with the father. The father then applied to the local authority relying on the shared residence order to demonstrate priority need. The House of Lords held that whether children are reasonably expected to reside with an applicant is a matter for the local authority to decide and cannot be dictated by a residence order, although such an order is part of the material to which an authority should have regard when making its decision.[62] The question that the local authority should ask is whether it is reasonably to be expected, *in the context of a scheme for housing the homeless,* that children who already have a home with their mother should be able also to reside with their father, ie, asking that question in the context of a scheme for the allocation of a scarce resource.[63] Only in exceptional circumstances[64] will it be reasonable to expect a child who

58 See para 5.25.

59 Under CA 1989 s8, known as a 'residence order' or 'shared/joint residence order' prior to 22 April 2014.

60 *R v Oxford City Council ex p Doyle* (1997) 30 HLR 506, QBD.

61 [2009] UKHL 7, [2009] HLR 34.

62 [2009] UKHL 7, [2009] HLR 34 at [17].

63 [2009] UKHL 7, [2009] HLR 34 at [9] and [14]–[16].

64 [2009] UKHL 7, [2009] HLR 34 at [21]: 'It seems to me that the likely needs of the children will have to be exceptional before a housing authority will decide that it is reasonable to expect an applicant to be provided with accommodation for them which will stand empty for at least half the time. I do not say that there may not be such a case; for example, if there is a child suffering from a

has a home with one parent to be provided under HA 1996 Part 7[65] with another so that the child can reside with both parents. The reference to exceptional circumstances is not a gloss on the statutory scheme, but an observation as to the probable result in the majority of cases involving separated parents.[66]

Children in social services care

5.30 The alternative limbs – 'are residing, or might reasonably be expected to reside' – avoid the difficulties which might otherwise arise where children are in temporary accommodation.

5.31 Where children are being looked after by the local social services authority, they may still be dependent on their parents and liaison with social services will be essential. 'Joint consideration with social services will ensure that the best interests of the applicant and the children are served.'[67]

Vulnerability[68]

England

5.32 The question in England is whether a person is a person vulnerable as a result of old age, mental illness or handicap or physical disability or other special reason. Much of the litigation in this area has focused on the meaning of 'vulnerable'. The 2015 Supreme Court decision in *Hotak v Southwark LBC and other appeals*[69] represented a significant change in approach, but it is best understood in the light the law as it stood previously.

5.33 It was formerly held that vulnerability meant that someone was 'less able to fend for himself than an ordinary homeless person so that injury or detriment to him will result where a less vulnerable

disability which makes it imperative for care to be shared between separated parents. But such cases, in which that child (but not necessarily any sibling) might reasonably be expected to reside with both parents, will be unusual.'

65 Or H(W)A 2014 Part 2.

66 *El Goure v Kensington and Chelsea RLBC* [2012] EWCA Civ 670, [2012] HLR 36, in which it was stressed that the question of reasonableness is primarily one for the authority.

67 Code of Guidance para 10.11; Welsh Code para 16.10.

68 H(W)A 2014 s70(1)(c).

69 *Hotak v Southwark LBC; Kanu v Southwark LBC; Johnson v Solihull MBC* [2015] UKSC 30, [2015] HLR 23.

man will be able to cope without harmful effects': *Pereira*.[70] Detriment might include a significantly increased risk of suicide or of developing a serious ailment, but it did not have to be measured in percentage terms.[71] The authority was not obliged to identify precisely the attributes of the ordinary homeless person against whom the applicant was being compared;[72] it made no difference whether the authority expressed its conclusions in terms of the applicant being at no greater risk of injury or detriment than the ordinary homeless person, or in terms of the applicant being no less able to fend for himself or herself than the ordinary homeless person: they were considered to be no more than two ways of saying the same thing.[73] The

70 *R v Camden LBC ex p Pereira* (1998) 31 HLR 317, CA at 330, applying *Bowers* (above), overruling *R v Reigate and Banstead BC ex p Di Domenico* (1987) 20 HLR 153, QBD and *Ortiz v Westminster City Council* (1993) 27 HLR 364, CA. These cases had added the gloss – amounting to a two-part test – that in addition to being less able to fend when homeless, there had to be a lessened ability to find and keep accommodation. In *R v Kensington and Chelsea RLBC, Hammersmith and Fulham LBC, Westminster City Council, and Islington LBC ex p Kihara and others* (1996) 29 HLR 147, CA, however, Simon Brown LJ doubted his own proposition to this effect in *Ortiz* (although not the outcome on the facts), which he had not intended to comprise a new statement of principle, and *Pereira* disposed of it. The issue at this stage of the law's development was whether the applicant was less able to fend with the consequences of homelessness than a less vulnerable person, without a risk of injury or detriment. The cases of *R v Bath City Council ex p Sangermano* (1984) 17 HLR 94, QBD (approved in *R v Wandsworth LBC ex p Banbury* (1986) 19 HLR 76) and *R v Lambeth LBC ex p Carroll* (1987) 20 HLR 142, QBD, which had referred to vulnerability as being 'loosely in housing terms or the context of housing', while not overruled, were not to be taken to suggest anything other than assessment of ability to cope without the risk of injury or detriment: *Pereira* at 330. See also *Osmani v Camden LBC* [2004] EWCA Civ 1706, [2005] HLR 22.

71 *Griffin v Westminster City Council* [2004] EWCA Civ 108, [2004] HLR 32. In this context, the previous edition of the English Code of Guidance (2002, para 8.13) incorrectly referred to whether the applicant 'would be likely to' suffer injury or detriment. See now the amended current edition of the Code para 10.13. In *Ajilore v Hackney LBC* [2014] EWCA Civ 1273, [2014] HLR 46, the applicant's depression and suicidal ideation were held not to make him vulnerable as statistics showed that significant numbers of homeless people had similar conditions; an appeal was unsuccessful: even though the reviewing officer had misunderstood the statistics; it still did not undermine the thrust of the decision. The decision is overtaken by *Hotak* and other appeals.

72 *Tetteh v Kingston upon Thames RLBC* [2004] EWCA Civ 1775, [2005] HLR 21. Cf *Hall v Wandsworth LBC; Carter v Wandsworth LBC* [2004] EWCA Civ 1740, [2005] HLR 23, where the authority posed the wrong question.

73 *Bellouti v Wandsworth LBC* [2005] EWCA Civ 602, [2005] HLR 46.

Periera test was considered and approved in *Osmani*,[74] although it was stressed that it was a judicial guide, not a statutory formulation: it was considered to involve a necessarily imprecise exercise in comparison between the applicant and the 'ordinary homeless person'.

> Given that each authority is charged with local application of a national scheme of priorities but against its own burden of homeless persons and finite resources, such decisions are often likely to be highly judgmental. In the context of balancing the priorities of such persons a local housing authority is likely to be better placed in most instances for making such a judgment.[75]

5.34 The authority were, however, required to be careful to assess and apply the test on the assumption that an applicant had become or would become street homeless, not on the applicant's ability to fend for himself or herself while still housed.[76]

5.35 In 2015, in *Hotak and other appeals*, the Supreme Court set a new approach, more clearly focused on the individual applicant: when assessing whether an applicant is vulnerable, an authority must pay close attention to his or her particular circumstances rather than to a statistical analysis of the homeless population; expressions such as 'street homeless' and 'fend for oneself' are not found in HA 1996 and should be avoided; whether a person is considered to be 'vulnerable' requires comparison with persons who would not be vulnerable – the correct comparator, therefore, is the ordinary person who is homeless, not the ordinary homeless person. An applicant who would otherwise be vulnerable might not be so, however, if – when homeless – he or she would be provided with support and care by a third party; whether a particular applicant will in fact receive support and, if so, what support, is a case-specific question, to which the answer must be based on evidence; even if very substantial support is provided that does not necessarily mean that an applicant is not vulnerable. Moreover, Equality Act 2010 s149 is complementary to the authority's duties under HA 1996 Part 7, and requires the authority to focus on: i) whether the applicant is under a disability (or has another relevant protected characteristic); ii) the extent of such disability; iii) the likely effect of the disability, when taken together with

74 *Osmani v Camden LBC* [2004] EWCA Civ 1706, [2005] HLR 22. The judgment of Auld LJ in *Osmani* was described by Jonathon Parker LJ in *Bellouti v Wandsworth LBC* [2005] EWCA Civ 602, [2005] HLR 46 at [57] as saying 'all that (at least for present purposes) need be said or can be said on the matter' of deciding whether an applicant is vulnerable.

75 Per Auld LJ at [38].

76 *Osmani*, above, per Auld LJ at [38].

any other features, on the applicant if and when homeless; and iv) whether the applicant is, as a result, vulnerable.

5.36 Before *Hotak*, there had been some discussion about the relationship between vulnerability and the stated reasons:[77] it had been held that it was preferably to be approached as a composite question, rather than in two separate stages,[78] ie, not asking separately whether there is vulnerability at all and, discretely, whether it was attributable to any of those factors.[79] On this aspect, *Hotak* largely disagreed as a matter of theory, although may be thought to have ended up making not much difference:[80]

> [T]he cases reveal a disagreement as to whether section 189(1)(c) gives rise to a two-stage test – (i) whether the applicant is 'vulnerable', and (ii) whether it is as a result of 'old age, mental illness or handicap or physical disability or other special reason' – or whether there is a single, composite test. This is a somewhat arid argument, and I am unconvinced that it is sensible to force housing authorities and reviewing officers into a straitjacket on this sort of issue. In any event, the correct answer may depend on the facts of the particular case. However, given the reference to 'other special reason', and given the fact that in many cases there will be a mixture of reasons as to why an applicant is said to be vulnerable, I suspect that the one-stage test will probably be more practical in most cases.

Wales

5.37 The position is slightly different in Wales. The sole question is whether a person is vulnerable as a result of some special reason.[81] The H(W)A 2014 then illustrates special reason in terms of 'old age, physical or mental illness or physical or mental disability'. The H(W)A 2014 preceded *Hotak*; it defines someone as 'vulnerable' if,

77 Old age, mental illness or handicap or physical disability or other special reason.

78 *R v Kensington and Chelsea RLBC, Hammersmith and Fulham LBC, Westminster City Council, and Islington LBC ex p Kihara and others* (1996) 29 HLR 147, CA.

79 As the court had suggested in *R v Waveney DC ex p Bowers* [1983] QB 238, (1982) 4 HLR 118, CA. *Bowers* was not overruled by *Kihara*, but it was thought that the two-stage test was capable of causing confusion, where the composite approach would not. The composite approach was approved in *Osmani v Camden LBC* [2004] EWCA Civ 1706, [2005] HLR 22 and said to have been correctly applied in *Bellouti v Wandsworth LBC* [2005] EWCA Civ 602, [2005] HLR 46. See also *Crossley v Westminster City Council* [2006] EWCA Civ 140, [2006] HLR 26.

80 At [46].

81 H(W)A 2014 s70(1)(c).

having regard to all the circumstances, he or she is less able to fend for himself or herself if he or she were to become street homeless[82] than would an ordinary homeless person who became street homeless, and this would lead to the person suffering more harm than would be suffered by the ordinary homeless person.[83] Although this was plainly a codification of the *Pereira* test effectively rejected by *Hotak*, the Welsh Code of Guidance[84] nonetheless recommends that authorities adopt *Hotak*.

Old age[85]

5.38 Both the English and Welsh Codes suggest that authorities should consider whether old age is a factor which makes it hard for applicants to fend for themselves, and that all applications from people aged 60 or over should be considered carefully.[86]

Mental illness or handicap or physical disability[87]

5.39 In considering vulnerability due to mental or physical illness or disability, both the English and Welsh Codes[88] suggest that authorities should have regard to medical advice and – where appropriate – seek social services advice. It is for the local authority to decide whether to obtain its own advice in respect of medical reports relied on by a homeless applicant; there is no absolute requirement to refer an applicant's medical reports for evaluation by a medical adviser in every case; it depends on the facts.[89] Local authorities are not, however, expected to make their own critical evaluation of an applicant's

82 'Street homelessness' means that the applicant has no accommodation available for his or her occupation in the UK or elsewhere, which he or she is entitled to occupy by virtue of an interest in it or by virtue of an order of a court, has an express or implied licence to occupy, or occupies as a residence by virtue of any enactment or rule of law giving the person the right to remain in occupation or restricting the right of another person to recover possession (see paras 4.39–4.61): H(W)A 2014 s71(2).

83 H(W)A 2014 s71.

84 Para 16.71 and following.

85 HA 1996 s189(1)(c); H(W)A 2014 s70(1)(c).

86 Code of Guidance para 10.15; Welsh Code para 16.20.

87 HA 1996 s189(1)(c); H(W)A 2014 s70(1)(c).

88 Code of Guidance, paras 10.16–10.17; Welsh Code, para 16.21.

89 *Simms v Islington LBC* [2008] EWCA Civ 1083, [2009] HLR 20.

medical evidence and should have access to specialist advice where necessary.[90]

5.40 Where the authority does decide to refer the applicant's medical reports to an adviser for specialist advice, it must take care not to appear to be using the opinion of the medical adviser to provide or support the authority's reasons for not finding a priority on medical grounds.

5.41 In *Shala v Birmingham City Council,*[91] the applicant relied on a medical report from a psychiatrist. The local authority referred that report to its own medical adviser who, although a qualified medical practitioner, was not a qualified psychiatrist. Nor did the medical adviser examine the applicant in person. When evaluating the applicant's vulnerability on the grounds of mental illness, the authority nonetheless chose the opinion of the medical adviser over that of the applicant's psychiatrist. The Court of Appeal held that – although the local authority had done nothing wrong in obtaining medical advice – it had fallen into the trap of thinking that it was comparing like with like when looking at the medical opinions. The function of the medical adviser was to assist the authority in understanding the medical issues and to evaluate the applicant's expert evidence. In the absence of an examination of the patient, the medical adviser's evidence could not itself ordinarily constitute expert evidence. The review officer had failed to take the lack of examination by the medical adviser into account when considering the medical evidence.

5.42 The local authority should also consider the nature and extent of the illness or disability, the relationship between the illness or disability and the individual's housing difficulties, and the relationship between the illness or disability and other factors such as drug/alcohol misuse, offending behaviour, challenging behaviours, age and personality disorder.[92] In *Osmani,*[93] Auld LJ said that authorities should have regard to the particular debilitating effects of depressive

90 *Shala v Birmingham City Council* [2007] EWCA Civ 624, [2008] HLR 8.

91 [2007] EWCA Civ 624, [2008] HLR 8.

92 Code of Guidance para 10.16; Welsh Code para 14.16.

93 *Osmani v Camden LBC,* above, at [38] referring to the observations of Brooke LJ in *R v Newham LBC ex p Lumley* (2001) 33 HLR 111, QBD at [63]. Cf *R (Yeter) v Enfield LBC* [2002] EWHC 2185 (Admin), [2003] JHL D19, where a decision that an applicant suffering from depression was not vulnerable – on the basis that an ordinary homeless person can be expected to suffer from depression so that the applicant was no more vulnerable than an ordinary homeless person – was upheld; this would not now survive the approach in *Hotak* and other cases (para 5.35).

disorders and the fragility of those suffering from them if suddenly deprived of the prop of their own home.

5.43 Particular reference is made in both the English and Welsh Codes[94] to those with mental health problems who have been discharged from psychiatric hospitals and local authority hostels. The need for effective liaison between housing, social services and health authorities is stressed. Authorities should also be sensitive to direct approaches from homeless discharged patients.

5.44 Cases of vulnerability due solely to the problems of drink will not usually be attributable to one of the specified causes,[95] although an extreme case may amount to a mental or physical handicap or disability. While in some cases vulnerability may be a medical question only, it may also be a question of housing and social welfare.[96] In all cases, the question must be determined by the local authority; it cannot merely 'rubber stamp' a decision of its medical experts.[97]

5.45 In *Banbury*,[98] whether epilepsy amounted to vulnerability was said to be a question of fact and degree, which would be established if attacks occurred with intense regularity. In *Leek*,[99] a decision on the vulnerability of an epileptic – comprising refusal to reconsider an earlier decision – was quashed on the ground that the position of any particular sufferer may need to be re-assessed from time to time.

5.46 A delusional condition which rendered the applicant unable to manage his own financial affairs made him vulnerable in *Dukic*.[100]

5.47 In *Sangermano*,[101] the court distinguished between mental illness that is psychotic and mental handicap. The latter is not concerned with illness, but with subnormality or severe subnormality, although not all subnormality will necessarily amount to vulnerability.

94 Code of Guidance para 10.17; Welsh Code para 16.26.

95 *R v Waveney DC ex p Bowers* [1983] QB 238, (1982) 4 HLR 118, CA.

96 *R v Lambeth LBC ex p Carroll* (1987) 20 HLR 142, QBD.

97 *R v Wandsworth LBC ex p Banbury* (1986) 19 HLR 76, QBD and *Osmani v Camden LBC* [2004] EWCA Civ 1706, [2005] HLR 22. Note, however, the comments of Auld LJ at [38] in *Osmani* stressing the need to look for and pay close regard to medical evidence submitted in support of applicants' claims of vulnerability on account of mental illness or handicap. Compare *Hall v Wandsworth LBC; Carter v Wandsworth LBC* [2004] EWCA Civ 1740, [2005] HLR 23, where the medical officer was entitled to advise that no further enquiries or specialist advice was required and *R v Newham LBC ex p Lumley* (2001) 33 HLR 11, QBD, where the medical officer failed to carry out adequate enquiries (see para 9.105).

98 *R v Wandsworth LBC ex p Banbury*, above.

99 *R v Sheffield City Council ex p Leek* (1993) 26 HLR 669, CA.

100 *R v Greenwich LBC ex p Dukic* (1996) 29 HLR 87, QBD.

101 *R v Bath City Council ex p Sangermano* (1984) 17 HLR 94.

5.48 In the same case, it was held that where medical evidence of subnormality is put before an authority, the authority ought either to accept it or make its own further enquiries.[102]

5.49 The English Code refers to those who are chronically sick, including those with HIV and AIDS.[103] It suggests that while some chronically sick people may have progressed to the point of physical or mental disability, they may also be vulnerable:

> ... because the manifestations or effects of their illness, or common attitudes to it, make it very difficult for them to find stable or suitable accommodation. This may be particularly true of people with AIDS, or even people who are infected with HIV without having any overt signs or symptoms if the nature of their infection is known.

Other special reason[104]

5.50 In *Kihara*,[105] the court rejected an *ejusdem generis*[106] approach to 'other special reason', and the argument that, therefore, it was limited to the mental or physical characteristics of an applicant. The category is free-standing, unrestricted by any notion of physical or mental weakness other than that which is inherent in the word 'vulnerable'. It can comprise a combination of circumstances.[107]

5.51 The word 'special' imports the requirement that the housing difficulties faced by an applicant are of an unusual degree of gravity, enough to differentiate the applicant from others. This does not include impecuniosity by itself, because an absence of means alone does not mark out one case from the generality of cases to a sufficient degree to render it 'special', but, eg, would include someone peculiarly in need of housing because of the risk of physical harm run from continuing homelessness.[108]

102 Furthermore, when determining priority need, the applicant's earlier rent arrears had been a wholly irrelevant consideration.

103 Code of Guidance para 10.32; see Welsh Code para 16.27, also on the chronically sick, but not given HIV/AIDS as a particular example.

104 HA 1996 s189(1)(c); H(W)A 2014 s70(1)(c); see English Code of Guidance paras 10.32–10.35 for suggestions as to groups who might fall within this category; Welsh Code paras 16.28–16.33.

105 *R v Kensington and Chelsea RLBC, Hammersmith and Fulham LBC, Westminster City Council, and Islington LBC ex p Kihara and others* (1996) 29 HLR 147, CA.

106 Ie, of the same order.

107 *R v Waveney DC ex p Bowers* [1983] QB 238, (1982) 4 HLR 118, CA.

108 *R v Kensington and Chelsea RLBC, Hammersmith and Fulham LBC, Westminster City Council, and Islington LBC ex p Kihara and others*, above.

5.52 The expression 'other special reason' requires examination of all the personal circumstances of an applicant, including physical or mental characteristics or disabilities, but is not limited to those. Accordingly, impecuniosity may still be relevant as will be opportunities to raise money (for example, whether or not a person[109] is prohibited from employment), or whether or not an applicant has family and friends and familiarity with the language, or – put another way – is subject to 'utter poverty and resourcelessness'.[110]

5.53 In *Sangermano*,[111] the court considered that language difficulties on their own would not amount to a 'special reason' within what is now HA 1996 s189(1)(c). Drug addiction alone does not amount to a 'special reason', but a likelihood of relapse into such addiction may do so.[112]

5.54 The English Code also draws attention to the position of young homeless people up to the age of 25, noting that they may be vulnerable and have a priority need for a variety of reasons.[113]

Multiple causes

5.55 In *Crossley*,[114] the applicant, as well as being a drug addict at risk of relapse and accordingly – it was contended – vulnerable for a 'special reason', had also been in care between the ages of three and 17. It was while in care that he had become a drug addict. The authority had failed to consider whether his vulnerability had arisen from the period in care. The court stated:[115]

> This appeal has not needed to address the question of how the decision-maker should deal with a case involving two of the prescribed causes of vulnerability – here, if the claimant is right, having been in care and some other special reason. We would nevertheless observe that where two such causes have produced a single set of effects, it would not seem consistent with Parliament's intention that the effects should be artificially distributed between the causes in arriving at a decision on the critical question of vulnerability.[116]

109 By reason of immigration status.

110 *Kihara*, above, at 159.

111 *R v Bath City Council ex p Sangermano*, above.

112 *Crossley v Westminster City Council* [2006] EWCA Civ 140, [2006] HLR 26.

113 Code of Guidance para 10.33.

114 *Crossley v Westminster City Council*, above.

115 At [31].

116 This is consistent with *Hotak* and other cases, at [46], see para 5.36.

Emergency[117]

5.56 This covers homelessness caused by an emergency such as flood, fire or other disaster. HA 1996 Part 7 and H(W)A 2014 Part 2 are in the same form: each requires that the event which causes the homelessness and the priority need must be both an emergency and a disaster.[118]

5.57 Fire and flood are not the only qualifying disasters. In *Noble v South Herefordshire DC*,[119] the words 'or any other disaster' (in Housing (Homeless Persons) Act 1977 s2(1)(b)) were held to mean another disaster similar to flood or fire. The omission of the word 'any' in HA 1996 s189(1)(d) would not seem to affect this.

5.58 *Noble* was concerned with a demolition order under what is now HA 1985 Part 9. This was not considered to comprise a disaster similar to flood or fire, although the facts were unhelpful to the argument insofar as the occupiers had moved in after the demolition order had been made and it is therefore distinguishable in the case of a dangerous structure notice under Building Act 1984 s77, or analogous urgency powers, imposed without any real forewarning.[120] Where a demolition order under HA 1985 is imposed, however, its procedural provisions suggest that it would not qualify as an emergency, and an occupier will in any event usually be entitled to rehousing under Land Compensation Act 1973 s39.[121]

5.59 The words 'other disaster' must be construed ejusdem generis (meaning of the same order as fire or floor).[122] Accordingly, a person

117 HA 1996 s189(1)(d); H(W)A 2014 s70(1)(d).

118 The need for the emergency to have caused the homelessness was illustrated in *Higgs v Brighton and Hove City Council* [2003] EWCA Civ 895, [2004] HLR 2: although the loss of the applicant's caravan was an emergency (see para 5.56) it had not caused his homelessness; he was already homeless – prior to the loss – because the caravan was illegally sited (see para 4.69).

119 *Noble v South Herefordshire DC* (1983) 17 HLR 80, CA.

120 But compare the provisions of Greater London Council (General Powers) Act 1984 s39, para 5.61. If these were considered both to need, and to justify, deeming emergencies, it may be implied by the courts that other provisions of a like quality do not have the same effect.

121 See also *R v Kensington and Chelsea RLBC ex p Ben-El-Mabrouk* (1995) 27 HLR 564, CA (para 4.109), in which accommodation subject to action for want of means of escape from fire could reasonably continue to be occupied, pending rehousing under the Land Compensation Act 1973. The perceived need for Greater London Council (General Powers) Act 1984 s39 (para 5.61) tends to support this result (where that Act does not apply).

122 *R v Bristol City Council ex p Bradic* (1995) 27 HLR 584, CA (following *Noble v South Herefordshire DC*, above).

who has been unlawfully evicted from his or her home is not in priority need within the subsection: it is not an emergency similar to flood or fire – *Bradic*. The subsection is not confined to emergencies amounting to force majeure, however, but embraces all emergencies consisting of physical damage: *Bradic*.

5.60 Where the applicant occupies a moving structure, such as a caravan, as his or her home, the disappearance of that structure is an emergency within the subsection because it involves the sudden and unexpected loss of the applicant's home in circumstances outside his or her control: *Higgs*.[123]

5.61 The following people are statutorily deemed to have become homeless or threatened with homelessness as a result of emergency such as flood, fire or other disaster:[124]

a) a person who resides in a building in outer London in respect of which an order has been made by a magistrates' court under the Greater London Council (General Powers) Act 1984 s37 that the occupants are to be removed because of its dangerous state;
b) a person who resides in a building in inner or outer London whose occupants are in danger by reason of its proximity to a dangerous structure or building, within Greater London Council (General Powers) Act 1984 s38(1), in respect of which an order has been made by the magistrates' court under section 38(2).

Other categories

5.62 The secretary of state and, in Wales, the Welsh Ministers[125] can add further categories of priority need, or alter or remove existing categories,[126] although only after consultation with such associations representing authorities and such other persons as the secretary of state consider or Welsh Ministers consider appropriate.[127]

5.63 In England, the categories have been supplemented so as to reflect concerns about homelessness among young people, those leaving care, those leaving institutional settings, such as prison and the armed forces, and those fleeing violence. These additional categories

123 *Higgs v Brighton and Hove City Council* [2003] EWCA Civ 895, [2004] HLR 2.

124 Greater London Council (General Powers) Act 1984 s39, as amended by HA 1996 Sch 17.

125 HA 1996 s189(2); H(W)A 2014 s72.

126 HA 1996 s189(2); H(W)A 2014 s72.

127 HA 1996 s189(3); H(W)A 2014 s72(3).

have largely been mirrored in Wales, where they are incorporated in H(W)A 2014 s70.

5.64 In England, the Homelessness (Priority Need for Accommodation) (England) Order 2002[128] came into force on 31 July 2002. It has six additional categories of priority need.[129] See also English Code of Guidance paras 10.19–10.29 and 10.36–10.41. These six categories are also relevant in Wales as they are largely adopted into H(W)A 2014 s70, although there are differences, noted in the text and footnotes. These six categories are:

a) 16- and 17-year-olds;
b) 18- to 20-year-old care leavers;
c) vulnerable care leavers;
d) former members of the armed forces;
e) vulnerable former prisoners;
f) persons fleeing violence.

Wales also has one additional category:

g) young person at risk of exploitation.

16- and 17-year-olds

England

5.65 All 16- and 17-year-olds are in priority need provided they are not classified as a relevant child[130] or its Welsh equivalent[131] (who will therefore remain the responsibility of the social services authority) or are owed a duty by a local authority under CA 1989 s20[132] or its Welsh equivalent.[133]

5.66 Whether a 16- or 17-year-old is a child in need for the purposes of CA 1989, and accordingly owed a duty under section 20, is a mixed question of law and fact for the local authority to decide: *M*.[134] When

128 SI No 2051.

129 SI No 2051 article 3.

130 As defined by CA 1989 s23A, ie a child who has left care having been an eligible child. Eligible children are those in care who have been looked after for a prescribed period of time, ie 13 weeks (see Care Leavers (England) Regulations 2010 SI No 2571 reg 3).

131 A Category 2 young person, see Social Services and Well-being (Wales) Act (SSWB(W)A) 2014 s104(2).

132 *R (S) v Sutton LBC* [2007] EWCA Civ 790. See further para 13.49.

133 SSWB(W)A 2014 s76.

134 *R (M) v Hammersmith and Fulham LBC* [2008] UKHL 14, [2008] 1 WLR 535, (2008) 4 All ER 271, HL, per Baroness Hale at [29].

considering whether to house a 16- or 17-year-old applicant under HA 1996 s188 pending enquiries,[135] a housing officer is not required to assess whether the applicant is a child in need, but – if required – should provide interim accommodation while a decision is reached by social services,[136] to whom the child should be referred.[137] It is unlawful for a social services department to sidestep their responsibilities under section 20 by assuming that a child in need can be suitably accommodated as a homeless person.[138]

5.67 If an authority's normal enquiry time would mean that an applicant will have turned 18 by the time of the decision, the authority cannot take the view that the applicant will not be in priority need and refuse all assistance, or simply provide accommodation until the birthday, even though, if enquiries in fact take the applicant to 18, the applicant will not be in priority need at the time of the decision.[139] Nor may the authority postpone its decision to that date.[140] Nor can an authority take the benefit of an invalid decision which forces the applicant into a review, by which time the applicant has turned 18: the principle in *Mohamed v Hammersmith and Fulham LBC*,[141] that the reviewer takes into account all facts to the date of the review,[142] cannot apply in this way, for:

135 See chapter 10.

136 The assessment should be reached within ten days: Provision of accommodation for 16- and 17-year-old people who may be homeless and/or require accommodation, Department for Communities and Local Government (DCLG) / Department for Children, Schools and Families, April 2010.

137 See also *R (M) v Hammersmith and Fulham LBC*, above, at [33], [36] and [42].

138 *R (S) v Sutton LBC* [2007] EWCA Civ 790. See also *R (M) v Hammersmith and Fulham LBC*, above, HL, per Baroness Hale at [33] and [42]. Although there was no evidence of a deliberate policy, to seek 'to avoid its responsibilities under the 1989 Act by shifting them on to the housing department . . . would be unlawful'. The observation was made in connection with *any* duty under the CA 1989, not section 20 alone. Social services authorities may, however, enter into an arrangement with another authority for assistance in discharge of the section 20 duty: *R (G) v Southwark LBC* [2009] UKHL 26, [2009] 1 WLR 1299.

139 *Robinson v Hammersmith and Fulham LBC* [2006] EWCA Civ 1122, [2006] 1 WLR 3295, [2007] HLR 7.

140 *Robinson v Hammersmith and Fulham LBC*, above, even for a short period.

141 [2001] UKHL 57, [2002] HLR 7.

142 See para 5.5; para 9.176.

> If the original decision was unlawful . . . the review decision maker should have so held and made a decision that would have restored to the appellant the rights she would have had if the decision had been lawful.[143]

5.68 The English Code of Guidance[144] suggests that for some young homeless applicants the most appropriate solution may be reconciliation with their families so that they can return home. It recognises that in some cases, however, relationships may have broken down irretrievably, and in others that it may not be safe for a young person to return to the family home. Accordingly, any mediation or reconciliation will need careful brokering, and social services should be involved.[145] Temporary accommodation may need to be provided while the process takes place.[146]

5.69 If mediation would take an applicant beyond his or her 18th birthday, however, the authority is bound to reach its decision without awaiting the outcome, as – if unsuccessful – the effect would otherwise be to deprive the applicant of his or her right to a full duty.[147] Mediation and enquiries are separate processes:

> The two processes may of course proceed in parallel; and if mediation is successful while the section 184 inquiry process is still on foot, then of course there will be no need for the latter process to continue any further. On the other hand, a local housing authority has . . . no power to defer making inquiries pursuant to section 184 on the ground that there is a pending mediation.[148]

143 *Robinson v Hammersmith and Fulham LBC*, above, per Waller LJ at [32].

144 Code para 12.8; Welsh Code para 14.39 simply suggests that this should be considered for 16- and 17-year-olds.

145 See also the comments of Baroness Hale who approved the 'wisdom of this guidance' in *R (M) v Hammersmith and Fulham LBC* [2008] UKHL 14, [2008] 1 WLR 535, [2008] 4 All ER 271, HL at [27].

146 Provision of accommodation for 16- and 17-year-old people who may be homeless and/or require accommodation, DCLG / Department for Children, Schools and Families, April 2010.

147 *Robinson v Hammersmith and Fulham LBC*, above.

148 *Robinson*, above, at [42], per Jonathan Parker LJ. See also per Jacob LJ at [45], who additionally relied on the HA 1996 s179 duty (para 14.18) to provide advice and information: 'A near-18-year-old who came to the authority could obviously not be properly be advised to mediate if the effect of mediation would be to delay the actual s184 decision past the 18th birthday.'

Wales

5.70 Any child who is aged 16 or 17 when he or she applies to a local housing authority for accommodation or help in obtaining or retaining accommodation is in priority need.[149]

18- to 20-year-old care leavers

England

5.71 Any person who is aged 18 to 20 (other than a relevant student)[150] who at any time after reaching the age of 16, but while under 18, was, but is no longer, looked after, accommodated or fostered[151] is in priority need.

Wales

5.72 Any person who is aged 18 to 20 who was looked after, accommodated or fostered at any time while under the age of 18 is in priority need. [152]

149 H(W)A 2014 s70(1)(f). The Welsh Code similarly stresses that it is in the best interests of most 16- and 17-year-olds to live in the family home unless this is unsafe or it is unsuitable for them because of risk of violence or abuse; in recognition of this, authorities are encouraged to consider the possibility of reconciliation through mediation, para 16.44.

150 'Relevant student' is defined by the CA 1989 as a care leaver under 24 to whom CA 1989 s24B(3) applies, who is in full-time further or higher education and whose term time accommodation is not available to him or her during a vacation. Relevant students remain the responsibility of social services authorities.

151 As defined by CA 1989 s22, ie, looked after by a local authority (ie, has been subject to a care order or voluntarily accommodated); accommodated by or on behalf of a voluntary organisation; accommodated in a private children's home; accommodated for a consecutive period of at least three months by a health authority, special health authority, primary care trust or local education authority or in any care home or independent hospital or in any accommodation provided by the National Health Service Trust; or, privately fostered. See para 13.69.

152 H(W)A 2014 s70(1)(h). 'Looked after' within the meaning of SSWB(W)A 2014 s74 or CA 1989 s22, accommodated by or on behalf of a voluntary organisation; accommodated in a private children's home; accommodated for a continuous period of at least three months by a local health board, special health authority, primary care trust or local education authority, or in any care home or independent hospital or in any accommodation provided by the National Health Service Trust; or, privately fostered: Welsh Code para16.49. See also Provision of Accommodation for 16 and 17 year old young people who may be homeless (Welsh Assembly Government, September 2010) and Welsh Code paras 16.41–16.43.

Vulnerable care leavers

England

5.73 Where a person has previously been looked after, accommodated or fostered,[153] the person will be in priority need no matter what his or her age, if this has resulted in the person being vulnerable.[154]

Wales

5.74 There is no equivalent in Wales. The Welsh Code does, however, stress that care leavers who are over 20 are 'likely to be vulnerable as a result of being in care' and so in priority need in their own right.[155]

Former members of the armed forces

England

5.75 Those who have been members of Her Majesty's regular armed forces[156] are in priority need, but only if they are vulnerable[157] as a result of that service.

Wales

5.76 A person who has served in the regular armed forces of the Crown who has been homeless since leaving those forces is in priority need (ie, there is no need for the applicant also to be vulnerable).[158]

153 See footnote 150, above.

154 As to whether someone is vulnerable, see paras 5.29–5.32. See also *Crossley v Westminster City Council* [2006] EWCA Civ 140, [2006] HLR 26.

155 Welsh Code para 16.52

156 See HA 1996 s199(4), para 7.16.

157 As to whether someone is vulnerable, see paras 5.32–5.55.

158 H(W)A 2014 s70(1)(i).

Vulnerable former prisoners

England

5.77 A person who is vulnerable[159] as a result of having served a custodial sentence,[160] having been committed for contempt of court or having been remanded in custody[161] is also in priority need.

Wales

5.78 The position is the same, save that the prisoner must also have a local connection with the area of the local authority.[162]

Persons fleeing violence

England

5.79 If an applicant has had to cease to occupy accommodation because of violence[163] or threats of violence which are likely to be carried out, the applicant will be in priority need if he or she is vulnerable[164] as a result.

Wales

5.80 If an applicant is homeless as a result of being subject to domestic abuse,[165] he or she will be in priority need, ie, there is no need that he or she also be vulnerable.[166]

159 It should not be assumed that a person released from prison will always be vulnerable: *Johnson v Solihull MBC* [2013] EWCA Civ 752, [2013] HLR 39 (not considered on appeal: [2015] UKSC 30, [2015] HLR 23).

160 Within the meaning of Powers of Criminal Courts (Sentencing) Act 2000 s76.

161 Within the meaning of Criminal Justice Act 2003 s242(2).

162 H(W)A 2014 s70(1)(j); as to local connection, see chapter 7.

163 See the definition of violence in HA 1996 s177(1), paras 4.83–4.88.

164 As to whether someone is vulnerable, see paras 5.32–5.55.

165 'Abuse' is probably synonymous with 'violence' (see H(W)A 2014 s58, *Yemshaw v Hounslow LBC* [2011] UKSC 3, [2011] HLR 16 and *Waltham Forest LBC v Hussein* [2015] EWCA Civ 14, [2015] HLR 16.

166 H(W)A 2014 s70(1)(e).

Young person at risk of exploitation

Wales only

5.81 A person aged between 18 and 21 who requires help in obtaining or retaining accommodation and who is at particular risk of sexual or financial exploitation is in priority need.[167]

167 H(W)A 2014 s70(1)(g); Welsh Code para 16.48. If a person turns 21 while still being assessed, this category of vulnerability remains applicable: Welsh Code para 16.46.

CHAPTER 6

Intentional homelessness

6.1 Introduction

6.4 Principal definition

6.7 Elements of principal definition

6.10 Whose conduct?

Burden • Non-acquiescent applicants • Findings of acquiescence • Rent arrears • Non-cohabitants

6.26 Deliberate act or omission

6.26 General principles

6.27 Good faith

Ignorance of facts • Carelessness v deliberate conduct • Act causing loss of accommodation • Bad faith

6.55 Illustrations

Rent/mortgage arrears • Nuisance and annoyance • Pregnancy • Failure to use other remedies • Loss of tied accommodation • Sale of jointly owned home • Overlap with 'reasonable to continue to occupy'

6.83 In consequence

6.85 Cause and effect

6.101 Breaking the chain of causation

Settled accommodation • Breaking the chain by other means

6.134 Cessation of occupation

6.134 Accommodation abroad

6.136 Short-term accommodation

continued

6.138 Notional occupation

6.142 Available for occupation

6.143 Reasonable to continue to occupy

6.149 Extended definition – collusive arrangements

Introduction

6.1 This chapter concerns the provision which at one time attracted most attention and controversy in homelessness law, intentional homelessness, although with so many issues related to it fairly well settled in law, much recent attention has passed to the definition of vulnerability in relation to priority need,[1] and otherwise to the suitability of accommodation.[2] The issue nonetheless remains of considerable importance as, where a person is homeless intentionally, the authority's duty is to provide temporary accommodation only for as long as it thinks is reasonable for the applicant to get his or her own accommodation.[3]

6.2 The principal definition of intentionality is the same under both the Housing Act (HA) 1996 and the Housing (Wales) Act (H(W)A) 2014 as it was under HA 1985. It was, however, extended by HA 1996 to include arrangements under which an applicant is required to cease to occupy accommodation which it would have been reasonable for the applicant to continue to occupy, being an arrangement entered into so as to entitle the applicant to assistance under HA 1996 Part 7, where there is no other good reason for the applicant to be homeless.[4] The same extension is to be found in the H(W)A 2014.[5]

6.3 In Wales there is, however, this critical distinction: local housing authorities must decide whether to apply the intentionality test at all in their areas;[6] and it can only be applied once the authority have notified the Welsh Government that the test will apply and have published a notice to this effect.[7] Moreover, the test may only be applied to categories of applicant specified by the Welsh Ministers, although currently all the priority need categories are specified.[8] An authority

1 See paras 5.32–5.55.

2 See paras 4.71 and 10.145–10.177.

3 See chapter 10.

4 HA 1996 s191(3). A further extension – to include persons to whom advice and assistance had been given under HA 1996 s197 (where the authority was satisfied that other suitable accommodation was available for the applicant's occupation in its area) but who failed to secure accommodation in circumstances where it was reasonable to be expected to do so (section 191(4)) – was repealed by the Homelessness Act 2002.

5 H(W)A 2014 s77(4).

6 H(W)A 2014 s78.

7 H(W)A 2014 s78(3).

8 Homelessness (Intentionality) (Specified Categories) (Wales) Regulations 2015 SI No 1265.

may choose to adopt none, some, or all of the specified categories.[9] The Welsh Government does not appear to publish a centralised list of decisions made by authorities, and it is accordingly necessary to check the website of each authority.

Principal definition

6.4 A person is homeless intentionally if he or she has deliberately done or failed to do something, in consequence of which he or she ceases to occupy accommodation which is available for his or her occupation, and which it would have been reasonable for him or her to continue to occupy.[10]

6.5 A person is threatened with homelessness intentionally if the person has deliberately done or failed to do something, the likely result of which is that the person will be forced to leave accommodation ,which is available for his or her occupation, and which it would have been reasonable for him or her to continue to occupy.[11] There is no reason for drawing any distinction of principle between the operation of the two definitions.[12]

6.6 Before an applicant can be considered homeless intentionally, the authority must satisfy itself that *all* the elements of this definition apply: for example, if the applicant left accommodation that was not available for the applicant's occupation, there can be no finding of intentionality.[13]

Elements of principal definition

6.7 The elements of the definition are:

a) the applicant must deliberately have done something or failed to do something;
b) the loss of accommodation must be in consequence of the act or omission;

9 Welsh Code paras 17.6–17.11.

10 HA 1996 s191(1); H(W)A 2014 s77(2).

11 HA 1996 s196(1); there is no direct equivalent in Wales, but see H(W)A 2014 s55 which defines 'threatened with homelessness'.

12 *Dyson v Kerrier DC* [1980] 1 WLR 1205, CA, at 1212. This seems to be based on a concession by counsel, but must surely be correct.

13 *Re Islam* [1983] 1 AC 688, (1981) 1 HLR 107, HL; see also, eg, *R v Eastleigh BC ex p Beattie (No 1)* (1983) 10 HLR 134, QBD.

c) there must be a cessation of occupation, as distinct from a failure to take up accommodation;
d) the accommodation must have been available for the occupation of the homeless person; and
e) it must have been reasonable for the homeless person to continue to occupy the accommodation.

6.8 Each of these elements, some of which are subject to further statutory definition or qualification, must be considered carefully and in the light of the case-law.

6.9 Before turning to these questions, there is one preliminary issue which requires discussion: that is, when an application is by or on behalf of more than one person, the question of *whose conduct* is to be taken into account.

Whose conduct?

6.10 A number of cases have considered how an authority should treat an application where one of the applicants, or a member of the applicant's household, has either already been adjudged homeless intentionally, or is susceptible to a finding of intentionality. The point tends to arouse strong views for, as will be seen below,[14] the duty to a homeless person is also owed to anyone who might reasonably be expected to reside with him or her, which may well include the putatively intentionally homeless member of the household.[15]

6.11 The question was first considered in *Lewis*,[16] where a man quit his employment and lost his tied accommodation. He applied to the authority, which held that he had become homeless intentionally.[17] Thereupon, the woman with whom he lived applied in her own name. The court rejected the authority's argument that it need only consider one application for the family unit as a whole: each applicant was entitled to individual consideration.[18]

6.12 The court did, however, uphold the authority's argument that, in considering whether or not the women had become homeless intentionally, it could take into account conduct to which she had been a party or in which she had acquiesced:

14 See para 10.12.

15 See also the English Code of Guidance para 11.9; Welsh Code para 17.3.

16 *R v North Devon DC ex p Lewis* [1981] 1 WLR 328, QBD.

17 See further paras 6.67–6.75.

18 See paras 9.36–9.37.

> In my view, the fact that the Act requires consideration of the family unit as a whole indicates that it would be perfectly proper in the ordinary case for the housing authority to look at the family as a whole and assume, in the absence of material which indicates to the contrary, where the conduct of one member of the family was such that he should be regarded as having become homeless intentionally, that was conduct to which the other members of the family were a party . . .
>
> If, however, at the end of the day because of material put before the housing authority by the wife, the housing authority are not satisfied that she was a party to the decision, they would have to regard her as not having become homeless intentionally. In argument the housing authority drew my attention to the difficulties which could arise in cases where the husband spent the rent on drink. If the wife acquiesced to his doing this then it seems to me it would be proper to regard her, as well as him, as having become homeless intentionally. If, on the other hand, she had done what she could to prevent the husband spending his money on drink instead of rent then she had not failed to do anything (the likely result of which would be that she would be forced to leave the accommodation) and it would not be right to regard her as having become homeless intentionally.

Burden

6.13 This creates something of a shift in the normal burden that lies on an authority to make enquiries, because it imposes on an applicant seeking to avail himself or herself of the principle of non-acquiescence something of a positive obligation to show why acquiescence should not be presumed.[19] See also *Caine*,[20] in which the Court of Appeal held that the authority was entitled to look at the family as a whole, to infer that the applicant was aware that her partner had been withholding rent, and – even though there was no direct evidence that they had done so – to infer that the couple would have discussed the matter. The authority could not be criticised for proceeding on the basis that what it was considering was a normal family/couple in which such information would be shared.

19 See chapter 9.

20 *R v Nottingham City Council ex p Caine* (1995) 28 HLR 374, CA. See too *R v Hillingdon LBC ex p Thomas* (1987) 19 HLR 196, QBD.

Non-acquiescent applicants

6.14 *Lewis* was applied to the benefit of the applicant in *Sidhu*,[21] where the authority additionally[22] sought to rely on an earlier finding of intentionality relating to rent arrears which had occurred while the applicant was still living with her husband, even though the couple had since separated.

6.15 *Lewis* was also applied to the applicant's benefit in *Beattie (No 2)*,[23] a case of non-payment of mortgage arrears,[24] even though the applicants were still living together as a couple, and in *Phillips*,[25] a case of rent arrears caused by the husband's drinking, likewise even though the applicants were still living together as a couple.

6.16 In *Trevena*,[26] a wife – the sole tenant of a flat – surrendered the tenancy in order to move in with another man in another town, leaving her husband in (unlawful) occupation. Possession proceedings had to be taken for his eviction. Subsequently, the couple were reconciled and he was able to rely on his lack of acquiescence in (indeed, opposition to) the surrender.

6.17 An attempt to raise a finding of intentionality against a wife for her husband's conduct, dating from before she even met him, was (unsurprisingly) rejected by the court in *Puhlhofer*.[27]

Findings of acquiescence

6.18 In *Thomas*,[28] however, Woolf J (who had decided *Lewis*), while restating the principle, upheld 'acquiescence' on the part of a male joint tenant whose cohabitant had caused the loss of their council tenancy by nuisance and annoyance, even though he had been in prison both at the time of the conduct and at the time of the proceedings for possession.

6.19 The factors which influenced the court were:

a) that the man had been offered, but had declined, an opportunity to attend the hearing; and

21 *R v Ealing LBC ex p Sidhu* (1982) 2 HLR 45, QBD.
22 See paras 4.12 and 5.16.
23 *R v Eastleigh BC ex p Beattie (No 2)* (1984) 17 HLR 168, QBD.
24 See further, paras 6.56–6.59.
25 *R v West Dorset DC ex p Phillips* (1984) 17 HLR 336, QBD.
26 *R v Penwith DC ex p Trevena* (1984) 17 HLR 526, QBD.
27 *R v Hillingdon LBC ex p Puhlhofer* (1985) 17 HLR 278, QBD, not appealed on this point; cf [1986] AC 484, CA and HL, (1985) 17 HLR 588, CA, (1986) 18 HLR 158, HL.
28 *R v Swansea City Council ex p Thomas* (1983) 9 HLR 64, QBD.

b) that there was no evidence of attempts by him to persuade the woman to desist in the conduct, which had persisted up until the hearing.

6.20 In *Khatun*,[29] it was unsuccessfully argued on behalf of a Bangladeshi wife that she had not acquiesced in her husband's conduct in leaving accommodation which it would have been reasonable to continue to occupy, on the basis that – as a matter of culture and practice – she had no choice but to abide by her husband's decision. Dismissing her appeal, the court held that, as she had been content to leave decisions to her spouse and to co-operate in implementing those decisions, she could properly be regarded as having acquiesced.

Rent arrears

6.21 It may be the case, particularly in arrears cases, that the spouse has found out too late to be able to do anything about rent arrears. So, for example, arrears may be so substantial when the spouse discovers them that simple awareness of the debt before homelessness cannot be said to amount to acquiescence: see *Spruce*.[30]

6.22 On the other hand, in *O'Connor*[31] the authority was entitled to conclude that there had been acquiescence, and in *Salmons*[32] the authority had addressed the critical question of whether it was entitled to conclude that the applicant must have known about, or at least turned a blind eye to, the arrears, and was accordingly entitled to reach the view that the applicant had either not been honest about his knowledge of the arrears, or that he had at the least been reckless about the true situation.

Non-cohabitants

6.23 The acquiescence point is not confined to cohabitants. In *Smith v Bristol City Council*,[33] a woman was held responsible for acts of nuisance caused by her son and lodgers, which resulted in her eviction. Similarly, the basis for the order for possession which resulted[34] in a finding of intentionality in *Devenport*[35] was conduct by the children

29 *R v Tower Hamlets LBC ex p Khatun* (1993) 27 HLR 344, CA.
30 *R v East Northamptonshire DC ex p Spruce* (1988) 20 HLR 508, QBD.
31 *R v Barnet LBC ex p O'Connor* (1990) 22 HLR 486, QBD.
32 *R v Ealing LBC ex p Salmons* (1990) 23 HLR 272, QBD.
33 See discussion at December 1981 *LAG Bulletin* 287.
34 But see para 6.26.
35 *Devenport v Salford City Council* (1983) 8 HLR 54, CA.

of the family; conduct by children was included in the reasons for the finding of intentionality in *Ward*.[36]

6.24 In *Bannon*,[37] acquiescence was upheld in relation to nuisance by the family as a whole, which the applicant had either been a party to or else had done nothing to prevent. In *John*,[38] nuisance and annoyance by a lodger caused the eviction of the tenant even though it occurred only when she was out of the flat, and the lodger was both younger and considerably stronger than she, so that she was unable to control his behaviour. Her 'acquiescence' was the failure to evict him.[39]

6.25 An attempt to use the principle of non-acquiescence on behalf of child applicants failed on the basis that the children were not in priority need in their own right: *ex p G*.[40]

Deliberate act or omission

General principles

6.26 The issue is not whether a person deliberately became homeless but whether he or she deliberately did (or failed to do) something as a result of which he or she became homeless. The word 'deliberate' only governs the act or omission: *Devenport*.[41] The link between the

36 *R v Southampton City Council ex p Ward* (1984) 14 HLR 114, QBD.

37 *R v East Hertfordshire DC ex p Bannon* (1986) 18 HLR 515, QBD.

38 *R v Swansea City Council ex p John* (1982) 9 HLR 56, QBD.

39 In *Darlington BC v Sterling* (1997) 29 HLR 309, CA, it was taken for granted that eviction on the grounds of nuisance and annoyance by – in that case – the tenant's son was capable of giving rise to a finding of intentionality (which should not, however, have prevented an order for possession being made against the tenant).

40 *R v Oldham MBC ex p G; R v Bexley LBC ex p B* (1993) 25 HLR 319, HL, see para 5.10. See also *R v Camden LBC ex p Hersi* (2001) 33 HLR 52, CA. On the applicability of the Children Act 1989 in such cases, see paras 13.49–13.87. Children Act 2004 s11 (duty on authorities to have regard to the need to safeguard and promote the welfare of children when discharging any functions) adds nothing to the assessment of whether someone is intentionally homeless: *Huzrat v Hounslow LBC* [2013] EWCA Civ 1865, [2014] HLR 17. The correct forum for deploying arguments about section 11 is at the application and/or review stage: *Mohamoud v Kensington and Chelsea RLBC; Saleem v Wandsworth LBC* [2015] EWCA Civ 780, [2015] HLR 38.

41 *Devenport v Salford City Council*, above. Cf the obiter comments of the Master of the Rolls in *R v Slough BC ex p Ealing LBC* [1981] QB 801, CA.

act and the homelessness must be judged objectively: *Robinson v Torbay BC*.[42]

Good faith

6.27 That said, 'an act or omission in good faith on the part of a person who was unaware of any relevant fact shall not be treated as deliberate' for the purposes of establishing intentional homelessness.[43] This statutory qualification introduces a subjective element into the analysis of intentionality.[44] Subsections HA 1996 191(1) and (2) pose 'serial questions': whether an act is in good faith *and* in ignorance of relevant facts must be considered separately: *O'Connor*.[45] In that case, the authority had merged the two subsections and obscured the critical, good faith question.

6.28 If it is established that the applicant was unaware of a relevant fact, the question is not whether the ignorance was reasonable, but whether it was in good faith.[46] Good faith includes circumstances where the applicant's ignorance of a relevant fact was due to his or her own unreasonable conduct,[47] even where the applicant could be said to have been foolish or imprudent.[48] The good faith requirement will not, however, be satisfied where an applicant has shut his or her eyes to the obvious, or has acted with wilful ignorance or on little more than a wing and a prayer.[49] Want of 'good faith' carries the connotation of some kind of impropriety, or an element of misuse or abuse of the legislation.[50] Dishonesty will not constitute good faith.[51]

Ignorance of facts

6.29 An applicant's failure properly to appreciate his or her prospects (or lack of prospects) of future housing can be treated as 'awareness of a relevant fact' for the purposes of HA 1996 s191(2),[52] provided that

42 *Robinson v Torbay BC* [1982] 1 All ER 726, QBD.

43 HA 1996 ss191(2) and 196(2); H(W)A 2014 s77(3).

44 *R v Exeter City Council ex p Tranckle* (1993) 26 HLR 244, CA. See the examples in the English Code of Guidance para 11.27; Welsh Code para 17.26.

45 *O'Connor v Kensington and Chelsea RLBC* [2004] EWCA Civ 394, [2004] HLR 37.

46 *F v Birmingham City Council* [2006] EWCA Civ 1427, [2007] HLR 18 at [17].

47 *F*, above, at [17].

48 *Ugiagbe v Southwark LBC* [2009] EWCA Civ 31, [2009] HLR 35 at [26].

49 *F*, above, at [17].

50 *Ugiagbe*, above, at [27].

51 *Ugiagbe*, above, at [27].

52 *F v Birmingham City Council*, above, at [17].

it is sufficiently specific and based on a degree of genuine investigation, not mere aspiration.[53] If the prospect of future housing rests on next to nothing but hope, it cannot be said that a decision falls into legal error by not invoking section 191(2) in the applicant's favour;[54] in such a case, the subsection is a non-starter and no specific reference to it is needed.[55]

6.30 In *Ugiagbe*,[56] the applicant was unaware of a relevant fact because she did not know that she could not be required to leave without a court order.[57] It is, however, ignorance of a relevant fact which must not have been deliberate, not ignorance of the legal consequences.[58]

6.31 Where an applicant temporarily went to live with her mother while at college but was warned by her father that she would not be allowed to return, it was held that the authority had misdirected itself in disregarding her genuine belief that he did not mean it, ie, that she would be able to go back. The father's state of mind was a relevant fact and so his daughter's action – taken in genuine ignorance of her father's true intent – could not be classified as deliberate: *Wincentzen v Monklands DC*.[59]

6.32 It was unawareness of a relevant fact here a person was misled as to business prospects, which caused him to move abroad: *Lusi*.[60]

6.33 In *Sukhija*,[61] a distinction was drawn between a mistake of fact (which could be within the good faith defence) and a mere unfulfilled hope (which was held not to be). The decision that the applicant – who had come to England in the mistaken belief that she would be able to find employment and a home – was intentionally homeless was accordingly upheld. See also *Khatun*,[62] in which the applicant was described as having no more than an expectation of being able to live

53 *R v Westminster City Council ex p Obeid* (1996) 29 HLR 389, QBD at 398; *Aw-Aden v Birmingham City Council* [2005] EWCA Civ 1834 at [10] and [11].

54 *Aw-Aden*, above, at [11].

55 *Aw-Aden*, above, at [12].

56 *Ugiagbe v Southwark LBC* [2009] EWCA Civ 31, [2009] HLR 35 at [8].

57 For the facts, see further para 6.40.

58 *R v Eastleigh BC ex p Beattie (No 2)* (1984) 17 HLR 168, QBD; *R v Croydon LBC ex p Toth* (1988) 20 HLR 576, CA; cf *R v Mole Valley DC ex p Burton* (1988) 20 HLR 479, QBD, where the applicant's belief in assurances by her husband that they would be rehoused under a union agreement was held to be a belief of fact, not of law.

59 *Wincentzen v Monklands DC* (1988) SLT (Court of Session) 259, September 1988 *LAG Bulletin* 13.

60 *R v Hammersmith and Fulham RLBC ex p Lusi* (1991) 23 HLR 460, QBD.

61 *R v Ealing LBC ex p Sukhija* (1994) 26 HLR 726, QBD.

62 *R v Tower Hamlets LBC ex p Khatun* (1994) 27 HLR 465, CA.

temporarily with her parents-in-law on her return to the UK, which was not a fact to which the good faith defence could be applied.

6.34 In *Ashton*,[63] a middle-aged woman moved from her home in Tunbridge Wells to take up a temporary job in Winchester, where the authority provided her with a one-year tenancy subject to the exception in HA 1985 Sch 1 para 5.[64] After a year, the authority obtained possession of the premises. A finding that the applicant was intentionally homeless was quashed on the basis, inter alia, that, in leaving Tunbridge Wells, the applicant had acted in good faith because she was unaware that she would be unable to find either housing or employment after the initial year. Accordingly, her action in surrendering the tenancy at Tunbridge Wells should not have been treated as deliberate.

6.35 In *Conway*,[65] a woman erroneously but genuinely believed that she had a further period of a year in which to decide whether or not to extend her existing shorthold tenancy. This was ignorance of a material fact, ie, the time remaining in which to make her decision.

6.36 In *Obeid*,[66] the applicant had taken private-sector accommodation in the belief that her rent would be covered by housing benefit, in ignorance of (and without making enquiries about) the provisions of the (then) Housing Benefit (General) Regulations 1987 which could limit her benefit to a proportion of her rent. This was held to be capable of constituting ignorance of a relevant fact.

6.37 Carnwath J, considering, inter alia, the decisions in *Lusi*[67] and *Sukhija*,[68] said that:

> The effect of those judgments, as I understand them, is that an applicant's appreciation of the prospects of future housing or future employment can be treated as 'awareness of a relevant fact' for the purposes of this subsection, provided it is sufficiently specific (that

63 *R v Winchester City Council ex p Ashton* (1991) 24 HLR 48, QBD. The decision of Kennedy J was upheld by the Court of Appeal (see (1991) 24 HLR 520) on the additional basis that, although the authority had stated that they had had regard to the general circumstances prevailing in relation to housing in their area (H(HP)A 1977 s60, now HA 1996 s177), they had failed to balance that against the 'quite exceptional circumstances' of the applicant (ie that she had left her previous accommodation in Tunbridge Wells in order to take up employment in Winchester and resume employment after six years of involuntary unemployment).

64 Temporary accommodation for people taking up employment.

65 *R v Christchurch BC ex p Conway* (1987) 19 HLR 238, QBD.

66 *R v Westminster City Council ex p Obeid* (1996) 29 HLR 389, QBD.

67 *R v Hammersmith and Fulham LBC ex p Lusi*, above; see para 6.32.

68 *R v Ealing LBC ex p Sukhija*, above, at 398; see para 6.33.

is related to specific employment or specific housing opportunities) and provided it is based on some genuine investigation and not mere 'aspiration'.

This statement was approved in *Aw-Aden*,[69] where the applicant's unfulfilled hope of finding employment in this country was insufficiently specific; rather, it was a mere aspiration.

6.38 Leaving settled accommodation to move into unsettled accommodation may form part of the circumstances amounting to intentional homelessness, under the HA 1996 extended definition of intentionality – see further below.[70] Ignorance about the unsettled nature of intended accommodation would, however, amount to ignorance of a relevant fact and as such should mean that the move would not be caught, because 'the purpose of the arrangement' implies an element of intention ('to enable [the applicant] to become entitled to assistance').

Carelessness v deliberate conduct

6.39 In deciding whether the ignorance is in good faith, an authority must distinguish between honest blundering or carelessness on the one hand, which can still amount to good faith conduct; and dishonesty, where there can be no question of good faith: *Lusi*;[71] *Ali and Bibi*.[72] The question is whether the action is taken in good faith, not whether it was reasonable.

6.40 In *Ugiagbe*,[73] the applicant was asked by her landlord to leave; she went to her local authority's 'One-Stop Shop' and was told to go to the Homeless Persons' Unit to get temporary accommodation; as she did not want to be treated as homeless, she returned to the property. Eventually, her landlord again asked her to leave, which she did, and she applied for homelessness assistance. Her conduct could be described as foolish or imprudent, yet it was the opposite of bad faith because her subjective motivation in not going to the Homeless Persons' Unit was because she had been led to believe that she would be treated as homeless, which was the last thing she wanted.[74]

69 *Aw-Aden v Birmingham City Council* [2005] EWCA Civ 1834.

70 See paras 6.149–6.154.

71 *R v Hammersmith and Fulham LBC ex p Lusi* (1991) 23 HLR 460, QBD.

72 *R v Westminster City Council ex p Ali and Bibi* (1992) 25 HLR 109, QBD.

73 *Ugiagbe v Southwark LBC* [2009] EWCA Civ 31, [2009] HLR 35 at [3].

74 *Ugiagbe*, above, at [25], [26] and [28].

6.41 In *F*,[75] the applicant surrendered a secure tenancy of a two-bedroom flat, ignoring advice from her social worker that she risked being found intentionally homeless, and took a tenancy of a three-bedroom house, from which she was evicted for arrears which accrued because she did not receive housing benefit. She was found, at best, to have proceeded on a wing and a prayer; her conduct was described as wilful ignorance or shutting her eyes to the obvious and she therefore could not satisfy the good faith test; HA 1996 s191(2) did not arise for consideration.[76]

6.42 In *Rouf*,[77] a finding of intentionality against an applicant who returned to a flat that had been repossessed after an absence of three years, but who had nonetheless believed that it would still be available to him, was quashed. The authority had failed to consider whether the belief was genuine, wrongly approaching the question as one of the reasonableness of his conduct.

6.43 In *Onwudiwe*,[78] however, an unemployed applicant's conduct in taking on large mortgage commitments in order to fund a business for which there had been no market-testing took the case beyond the stage of honest incompetence and provided material on which it could be said that he was deliberately putting his house at risk.

6.44 In *Beattie (No 2)*,[79] persistent failure to pay mortgage arrears was upheld as deliberate, notwithstanding that the applicant had been advised by his solicitors that it would not be.

6.45 On the other hand, in *White*,[80] the applicant believed that the then Department of Health and Social Security (DHSS) was, or ought to be, paying the whole of the interest element on the mortgage instalments by direct deduction from his benefit. In fact, his supplementary benefit entitlement was so low that it did not cover the full amount of the interest, so that arrears continued to mount. The court held that – for most of the period in question – the applicant was under a genuine misapprehension as to a relevant fact (whether or not the DHSS was paying the whole of the interest payments), and that he had acted in good faith in failing to make the payments himself. There was, accordingly, no deliberate omission and, in consequence, no intentional homelessness.

75 *F v Birmingham City Council* [2006] EWCA Civ 1427, [2007] HLR 18 at [9].
76 *F*, above, at [19].
77 *R v Tower Hamlets LBC ex p Rouf* (1991) 23 HLR 460, QBD.
78 *R v Wandsworth LBC ex p Onwudiwe* (1994) 26 HLR 302, CA.
79 *R v Eastleigh BC ex p Beattie (No 2)* (1984) 17 HLR 168, QBD.
80 *White v Exeter City Council*, December 1981 *LAG Bulletin* 287, QBD.

6.46 In *O'Connor v Kensington and Chelsea RLBC*,[81] the applicant husband and wife believed that a friend, who was staying at their flat while they were visiting Ireland for a funeral and while the husband recovered from depression, was paying the rent. He was not in fact doing so; a suspended possession order was obtained in their absence and subsequently enforced after their return. The Court of Appeal held that it is not necessary for the ignorance of the relevant fact to be reasonable before an omission qualifies to be treated as non-deliberate. A person's ignorance may well be due to unreasonable behaviour, yet what the person does in consequence may still be in good faith. The dividing line is not at the point where an applicant's ignorance of a relevant fact is due to the applicant's own unreasonable conduct, but at the point where by shutting his or her eyes to the obvious the applicant cannot be said to have acted in good faith.

Act causing loss of accommodation

6.47 The act of good faith referred to in HA 1996 s191(2) is the act or omission causing homelessness, which is the act that has to be considered under section 191(1).[82]

6.48 In *Stewart*,[83] the authority found that the deliberate act which caused the homelessness was the commission of a criminal act by the applicant, following which he was imprisoned and a warrant executed (without notice) on the basis of an earlier possession order for arrears. The authority accepted that, after his imprisonment, the applicant had made an arrangement with his sister to maintain the tenancy, but no rent was in fact paid under it. He sought to argue that the deliberate act or omission was the failure to pay the rent, which was an act in good faith because he had been unaware of a relevant fact, ie, his sister's failure to keep to the arrangement. The Court of Appeal held that, given a proper finding that the deliberate act which caused the homelessness was the offence, the subsequent acts in good faith were irrelevant and the authority was not obliged to investigate them.

6.49 Where the cause of homelessness was an applicant's inability to meet mortgage repayments as a result of a severe downturn in business, the homelessness was intentional because the mortgage itself

81 *O'Connor v Kensington and Chelsea RLBC* [2004] EWCA Civ 394, [2004] HLR 37.

82 Which is why it is important correctly to identify the date when the (putatively intentional) homelessness began – cf *O'Connor v Kensington and Chelsea RLBC*, above. See also *Ugiagbe v Southwark LBC*, above at [6].

83 *Stewart v Lambeth LBC* [2002] EWCA Civ 753, [2002] HLR 40.

had been obtained as a result of the applicant's fraudulent misrepresentation of her income: *Rughooputh*.[84]

6.50 In *Chishimba v Kensington and Chelsea RLBC*,[85] however, the appellant had used a counterfeit passport to secure assistance under HA 1996 Part 7, which fraud was only discovered at a later date. The Court of Appeal held that the immediate cause of her homelessness was the discovery that she had obtained her tenancy by deception; proceeding back in time from that immediate cause, the effective cause of her homelessness was that she had been ineligible for assistance, so that she was not intentionally homeless as it could not have been reasonable for her to continue to occupy accommodation to which she never had any lawful right. In *Tranckle*,[86] the applicant entered into an imprudent financial arrangement in good faith, because she was unaware of the (un)reality of the prospects of success for the public house which she was purchasing, which had been concealed from her by the brewery; it followed that her decision to purchase the public house was made in good faith.

6.51 In *Watchman*,[87] the applicant was a secure tenant who exercised the right to buy with the aid of a mortgage on which the repayments were significantly higher than the rent she had previously been paying in respect of which there was a history of arrears. Her husband subsequently lost his job but, although he found another at a lower salary, mortgage arrears built up and the mortgagee repossessed the property. The review found that the applicant had become intentionally homeless by taking on the mortgage when it was inevitable that she would get into severe financial difficulties within a short time; her husband's employment problems had not caused the repossession but merely accelerated the inevitable eviction.[88] Upholding that decision, it was held that – when deciding whether an applicant is intentionally homeless where there are several potential causes of the homelessness – the authority has to make a careful judgment on the particular facts, to decide whether the homelessness is a likely consequence of a deliberate act on the part of the applicant, bearing in mind that it is the applicant's responsibility for the homelessness

84 *R v Barnet LBC ex p Rughooputh* (1993) 25 HLR 607, CA.

85 [2013] EWCA Civ 786, [2013] HLR 34.

86 *R v Exeter City Council ex p Tranckle* (1993) 26 HLR 244, CA.

87 *Watchman v Ipswich BC* [2007] EWCA Civ 348, [2007] HLR 33 at [6].

88 *Watchman*, above, at [9].

that is in question.[89] While the authority has to consider the time when the applicant in fact became homeless,[90] it is entitled to take account of events prior to that date.[91]

6.52 Ironically, it may even be the case that a person who takes the trouble to find out relevant facts, and reaches a decision on them, is more vulnerable to a finding of intentionality than a person who has omitted to make any such enquiries at all.[92]

Bad faith

6.53 Where bad faith is suspected, it has been suggested that it may not invariably be necessary to put the matter to the applicant (*Hobbs v Sutton LBC*)[93] – but see *Moozary-Oraky*,[94] in which good faith relative to awareness of housing benefit was considered to be a question of jurisdictional fact, without which no reasonable authority could reach a conclusion on intentionality, into which the authority was accordingly required to make explicit enquiry of the applicant (as to whether or not she had seen a letter informing her that her benefit had been stopped).

6.54 In *Joyce*,[95] the authority did not even ask the applicant why mortgage arrears had arisen. This failure was accordingly fatal to its decision as it had omitted to take something relevant into account, ie, the applicant's explanation or answer.

Illustrations

6.55 There is much guidance and a large number of cases on intentionality, which can conveniently be approached under a series of headings – but it is essential to remember that the cases are all illustrative of the operation of the provisions rather than precedents on their facts, and that guidance is not binding.[96]

89 *Watchman*, above, at [22]; see also *Carthew v Exeter City Council* [2012] EWCA Civ 1913, [2013] HLR 19, in which the authority failed to consider why Ms Carthew had transferred her interest in a property to her former partner.

90 *Din v Wandsworth LBC* [1983] 1 AC 657, HL.

91 *Watchman* at [23].

92 *R v Westminster City Council ex p Obeid* (1996) 29 HLR 389, QBD.

93 (1993) 26 HLR 132, CA.

94 *R v Westminster City Council ex p Moozary-Oraky* (1993) 26 HLR 214, QBD.

95 *R v Wyre BC ex p Joyce* (1983) 11 HLR 73, QBD.

96 As to departing from guidance, see *De Falco v Crawley* BC [1980] QB 460, CA, at 478; see also the recent summary of authorities in relation to departing from statutory guidance in *R (X) v Tower Hamlets LBC* [2013] EWHC 480 (Admin), at [27]–[35]: see generally para 12.41.

Rent/mortgage arrears

6.56 The English Code gives as an example of homelessness which should not be treated as deliberate:

> . . . where an applicant has lost his/her home or was obliged to sell it because of rent or mortgage arrears resulting from significant financial difficulties, and the applicant was genuinely unable to keep up the rent or mortgage payments even after claiming benefits, and no further financial help was available.[97]

6.57 This is to be contrasted with cases where an applicant:

> . . . chooses to sell his/her home in circumstances where he or she is under no risk of losing it, or has lost it because of wilful and persistent refusal to pay rent or mortgage repayments.[98]

6.58 The previous Code issued under HA 1985 Part 3 was in similar terms. In *Hawthorne*,[99] it was considered not to misstate the law. In *Bryant*,[100] it was said that the Code drew a distinction 'between those who can, or could reasonably be expected to, pay mortgage payments or rent but do not do so, and those who in reality cannot pay because of real financial difficulties'. It was a question of fact for the authority to decide into which category an applicant fell, open only to challenge on usual public law principles.[101]

6.59 Supplemental guidance[102] on intentional homelessness is specifically directed to applicants who are homeless following difficulties in meeting mortgage commitments, in the light of national economic circumstances. An authority should not refuse to accommodate people whose homelessness has been brought about without fault on their part[103] – for example, if the home was not affordable because the applicant could not meet the cost of his or her mortgage commitments.[104] By way of further example, in *Noel v Hillingdon*

97 English Code of Guidance para 11.18; see Welsh Code para 17.18 to like effect.

98 English Code of Guidance para 11.20(ii); Welsh Code para 17.23.

99 *R v Wandsworth LBC ex p Hawthorne* (1994) 27 HLR 59, CA. See also *Ekwuru v Westminster City Council* [2003] EWCA Civ 1293, [2004] HLR 14, where arrears arose because of a housing benefit cap.

100 *R v Warrington BC ex p Bryant* (2001) JHL D5, QBD.

101 As to which, see chapter 12. See also *William v Wandsworth LBC; Bellamy v Hounslow LBC* [2006] EWCA Civ 535, on failure to make mortgage payments after taking out a further loan.

102 *Homelessness code of guidance for local authorities: supplementary guidance on intentional homelessness* ('Supplementary Guidance') was published by the Department for Communities and Local Government (DCLG) in August 2009.

103 Supplementary Guidance para 7.

104 Supplementary Guidance para 11.

LBC,[105] the applicant had taken a tenancy which he could not afford; his partner and child then moved in and he failed to apply for an increase in his housing benefit; both the decision to take an unaffordable tenancy and the failure to apply for an increase in housing benefit were held to amount to intentional homelessness. In *Viackiene v Tower Hamlets* LBC,[106] the failure to seek a joint tenant who could have assisted with paying the rent – as suggested by the landlord – was held to amount to intentional homelessness.

Nuisance and annoyance

6.60 Nuisance and annoyance can clearly be considered 'deliberate' for this purpose.[107] In *ex p P*,[108] a finding of intentionality was upheld in relation to alleged criminal and anti-social behaviour[109] (confirmed by the authority's own enquiries) which had led to threats from the IRA that the applicants would be killed if they did not leave their accommodation.

6.61 In *Bell*,[110] a possession order was obtained against the applicant on the grounds of nuisance and annoyance. She was accepted by Wirral MBC as having a priority need because of the state of her mental health. Applying a test to be found in the Code of Guidance under HA 1985 Part 3 – which referred to capacity to manage affairs[111] – the authority nonetheless found that she had become homeless intentionally. Her application for judicial review was dismissed. It was said to be one thing to be less able to fend for oneself (for the purpose of establishing vulnerability)[112] and another to be incapable

105 [2013] EWCA Civ 1602, [2014] HLR 10.

106 [2013] EWCA Civ 1764, [2014] HLR 13.

107 *Devenport v Salford City Council* (1983) 8 HLR 54, CA; *R v Swansea City Council ex p John* (1982) 9 HLR 56, QBD; and *R v East Hertfordshire DC ex p Bannon* (1986) 18 HLR 515, QBD. See also English Code of Guidance para 11.20(v); Welsh Code para 17.23.

108 *R v Hammersmith and Fulham LBC ex p P* (1989) 22 HLR 21, QBD.

109 In *Bristol City Council v Mousah* (1997) 30 HLR 32, CA, allowing premises to be used in connection with the sale of drugs, even though the tenant was himself absent and was not charged, appears to have been presumed to be capable of giving rise to a finding of intentionality (which should not have prevented the making of an order for possession on the basis of 'reasonableness'; compare also the details of *Darlington BC v Sterling* (1997) 29 HLR 309, CA, summarised above at footnote 39).

110 *R v Wirral MBC ex p Bell* (1994) 27 HLR 234, QBD.

111 Now repeated in the current English Code of Guidance para 11.17(ii). There is no equivalent in the Welsh Code.

112 See paras 5.32–5.55.

of managing one's own affairs (for the purpose of intentionality); the two findings were accordingly not inconsistent.

6.62 In *Denton,*[113] the applicant's mother asked him to leave the family home because of his behaviour. The authority found that he had become homeless intentionally, a decision upheld by the Court of Appeal: when people live together, they must show appropriate respect for each other's needs and follow reasonable requests; there had been nothing inappropriate about the rules the mother had laid down.[114] It was relevant that the applicant's last accommodation had been a family home rather than rented accommodation because a child has no enforceable right to remain in his or her family home and therefore has to obey the house rules.[115] Accordingly, when deciding the issue of intentionality, the reasonableness of those rules should be considered.

Pregnancy

6.63 A person does not become homeless intentionally by becoming pregnant,[116] for example, because accommodation is lost (on account of size or for other reasons, such as terms of accommodation), or because it is the family home and the family reject the pregnant woman.

Failure to use other remedies

6.64 Two common examples of omission alleged to amount to intentional homelessness are:

a) failure by an evicted private tenant to take civil proceedings to secure re-entry; and
b) failure by a cohabitant or spouse to use domestic remedies.

Each of these examples merits closer consideration.

6.65 Under HA 1996 s175(2), 'a person is also homeless if he has accommodation but . . . he cannot secure entry to it'.[117] This defines as homeless a person who has been locked out of his or her home, and is generally taken to refer to the illegally evicted occupier.[118] While it

113 *Denton v Southwark LBC* [2007] EWCA Civ 623, [2008] HLR 11 at [1].
114 *Denton,* above, at [21].
115 *Denton,* above, at [14].
116 *R v Eastleigh BC ex p Beattie (No 1)* (1983) 10 HLR 134, QBD.
117 In Wales, H(W)A 2014 s55(2); see paras 4.62–4.65.
118 English Code of Guidance para 8.16; Welsh Code para 8.16.

is open to an authority to treat an occupier who does not use his or her civil remedies as intentionally homeless, it would be unlawful to adopt a blanket policy that all such occupiers must do so.[119]

6.66 Detailed provision is now made for cases of domestic and non-domestic violence,[120] and – since the decision in *Bond*[121] – it is clear that in such cases authorities cannot require an applicant to use civil remedies. A person who knows what can be done to prevent violence but deliberately fails to do it has not caused the probability of the domestic violence which makes the continued occupation of that accommodation unreasonable.[122] The probability of violence is to be assessed objectively, by the person carrying out the assessment.[123]

Loss of tied accommodation

6.67 Another common example is loss of tied accommodation.[124] It was not merely accepted in the High Court in *Lewis*[125] that the man's departure from his job, and consequent loss of accommodation, qualified as intentional, but an earlier (and otherwise unreported) challenge to that decision had been, albeit reluctantly, dismissed. Loss of tied accommodation also amounted to intentionality in *Goddard*[126] and *Jennings*,[127] but the cases were determined on the meaning of 'in consequence' and are, as such, considered below.

6.68 Detailed consideration was given to this problem in *Williams*.[128] The manager of a public house was dismissed for stock and profit irregularities, which he denied. In the course of an appeals procedure, which he pursued with the assistance of his union representative,

119 See para 4.65, see also paras 12.44–12.45.

120 See paras 4.82–4.92.

121 *Bond v Leicester City Council* [2001] EWCA Civ 1544, (2002) HLR 6. See also *Supplementary guidance on domestic abuse and homelessness*, DCLG, November 2014.

122 *Bond*, above, at [33].

123 *Danesh v Kensington and Chelsea RLBC* [2006] EWCA Civ 1404, [2007] HLR 17.

124 See Code of Guidance para 11.20(vii); Welsh Code para 17.23. Note, however, English Code of Guidance at para 11.15, which states that the secretary of state considers that service personnel required to vacate service quarters as a result of taking up an option to give notice to leave the service should not be considered to have become homeless intentionally. There is no direct equivalent in the Welsh Code.

125 See para 6.11.

126 *Goddard v Torridge DC* January 1982 *LAG Bulletin* 9, QBD.

127 *Jennings v Northavon DC* January 1982 *LAG Bulletin* 9, QBD.

128 *R v Thurrock DC ex p Williams* (1981) 1 HLR 128, QBD.

his employers offered him the choice of resigning or dismissal. He resigned and, while threatened with homelessness, applied to the local authority for accommodation.

6.69 The authority made enquiries of the former employers and concluded:

> My understanding of the circumstances of your resignation lead me to the conclusion that, had you not resigned, the end result would be the same, ie, that events leading up to your appeal against dismissal would be regarded as something 'the likely result of which is that you will be forced to leave accommodation which is available for your occupation and which it would have been reasonable for you to continue to occupy'.

The court interpreted this as:

> . . . saying it was intentional because he resigned. It also seems to go on to say that in any event 'even if you had not resigned you would have been dismissed because of your own faults.' In either event, it would have been an intentional homelessness.

6.70 During the course of the judgment, the court likened the position of the applicant to that of a person who had been constructively dismissed for the purposes of employment law:

> Had he gone to an industrial tribunal and complained that he had been unfairly dismissed, it would not have been open to the employers to say by way of answer . . . you resigned, because he would have been able to reply that he resigned only because he had been told that if he did not do so, he would be dismissed.

6.71 This is clearly one basis for distinguishing a resignation from dismissal. But what the authority was seeking to do was to say: either the applicant resigned (intentional homelessness) or he was dismissed (intentional homelessness), and it ignored the 'grey area' of dispute, which had led to the compromise.

6.72 The court analysed the case in stages. It asked:

a) why the applicant was homeless (because there had been a possession order against him);
b) why a possession order was made (because his contract of employment came to an end);
c) why did it end (because he resigned);
d) why did he resign (because if he did not do so, he would be dismissed);
e) why would he have been dismissed, was it his fault (this was in dispute).

The authority was therefore bound to reach a view as to fault, however hard it was for it to do so.

6.73 The court approved the authority's initial approach to 'job loss cases'. An act the consequences of which can be construed as a deliberate departure can qualify within the provisions; but someone who loses his or her job for incompetence, which will usually comprise a course of conduct spread over a period of time, cannot be said to be carrying out a deliberate act. This would seem to be because the person would lack the necessary intention, or state of mind, in the absence of clear proof that a course of incompetent conduct had been adopted in order to provoke dismissal.

6.74 *Reeve*[129] was also a case on loss of tied accommodation, although it was as much on the meaning of 'in consequence' as 'deliberate'. A woman worked as a receptionist for a car hire firm and lived above the office. She was living with a man. She told her employers that he was not disqualified from driving; in fact he was. When the employers found out, they dismissed her. The authority found that she lost her accommodation because of the misconduct leading to loss of employment, which misconduct was the statement made to the employers.

6.75 This allegation was, at the time of dismissal and indeed at the time of the local authority's decision and of the hearing at the High Court, disputed. Nonetheless, the authority had investigated, and it had concluded that the dismissal was 'for that deliberate act of misconduct'. This was the crucial point of distinction from *Williams* (above):

> Some acts which a person does will lead indirectly to their becoming homeless . . . Other acts will be sufficiently proximate to render the person within the category of those who become homeless intentionally . . . It is my view that this case probably comes close to the borderline. For it to fall on the right side so far as the local authority are concerned it seems to me that the termination of the employment . . . must be lawful. It must be some conduct on the part of the applicant which justifies the employer treating the contract as at an end . . .

Sale of jointly owned home

6.76 In *Bellamy*,[130] the applicant was the joint owner of a property with her mother. She applied as homeless when the property was sold, having waived all rights to any of the proceeds of sale in favour of her

129 *R v Thanet DC ex p Reeve* (1981) 6 HLR 31, QBD.

130 *William v Wandsworth LBC; Bellamy v Hounslow LBC* [2006] EWCA Civ 535, [2006] HLR 42.

mother. The authority found her intentionally homeless. On review, the authority rejected the applicant's assertion that she had intended her mother to be the sole owner of the property and concluded that the she had been aware that she had the right to object to the sale and had also been aware that – as a beneficial owner – she had a right to an interest in the property. They found that her failure to object to the sale constituted a deliberate act which caused her to become homeless.

6.77 The decision was quashed at first instance but restored by the Court of Appeal, which held that the authority had been entitled, on the basis of the evidence before it, to conclude that the appellant was a joint legal owner of the property with rights over it, including the right to object to the sale under Trusts of Land and Appointment of Trustees Act 1996 ss14 and 15. The question for the judge had not been what the appellant and the mother intended when jointly purchasing the property but whether the authority had been obviously wrong in its understanding of that intention.

Overlap with 'reasonable to continue to occupy'

6.78 The question whether there has been a deliberate act or omission frequently overlaps with the question whether it was reasonable for the applicant to continue to occupy the accommodation.[131] Whether accommodation is accommodation which it would have been reasonable for an applicant to continue to occupy must of course be determined at a time before – and without regard to – the deliberate acts or omissions which led to the loss of that accommodation.[132]

6.79 In *Tinn*,[133] Kennedy J expressed the view that, as a matter of common sense, it cannot be reasonable for someone to continue to occupy accommodation the financial obligations in relation to which the person can no longer discharge without so straining his or her resources as to deprive himself or herself of the ordinary necessities of life.

6.80 Likewise, in *Hawthorne*,[134] the authority's omission to consider whether the applicant's failure to pay rent was caused by the inadequacy of her financial resources allowed her to succeed in her

131 See paras 4.69–4.140, and, in particular, now the Homelessness (Suitability of Accommodation) Order 1996 SI No 3204: see para 4.122 and paras 6.143–6.144.

132 *Denton v Southwark LBC* [2007] EWCA Civ 623, [2008] HLR 11 at [2] and [25].

133 *R v Hillingdon LBC ex p Tinn* (1988) 20 HLR 305, QBD.

134 *R v Wandsworth LBC ex p Hawthorne* (1994) 27 HLR 59, CA.

application to quash a finding of intentionality: it was a question the authority was bound to address.

6.81 See also *Griffiths*,[135] in which the authority was held to have failed to have regard to the family's particular circumstances, and *Bibi*,[136] where the authority had failed to make a finding whether the applicant could reasonably have continued to occupy accommodation, in the light of her stated financial inability to feed her family.

6.82 On the other hand, in *Khan*,[137] the authority was entitled to reach the view that the applicants had not been forced to sell their previous home by reason of financial pressure and, in *Baruwa*,[138] it was said that deciding what were the necessities of life for any particular family permitted a substantial 'margin of appreciation' for authorities. The authority was accordingly entitled to be satisfied that the applicant had sufficient income, given that – though no longer in work – she was spending £954 on a university course for herself and over £50 per week on nursery education for her child. In *Samuels*,[139] the argument that only housing benefit should be taken into account when deciding whether a property was affordable for the applicant was rejected; all household income should be taken into account.

In consequence

6.83 The homelessness must be 'in consequence of' the deliberate act or omission. This is a question of 'cause and effect',[140] and the principal issue which has arisen is the attribution of present homelessness to past act or omission. That is to say, there is commonly an act which has or could have been the subject of a finding of intentionality and the argument then becomes whether or not it (that act or omission) is the cause of this homelessness. See also *Bashir Hassan*,[141] where

135 *R v Shrewsbury and Atcham BC ex p Griffiths* (1993) 25 HLR 613, QBD.

136 *R v Islington LBC ex p Bibi* (1996) 29 HLR 498, QBD.

137 *R v Westminster City Council ex p Khan* (1991) 23 HLR 230, QBD. See also *R v Leeds City Council ex p Adamiec* (1991) 24 HLR 138, QBD; and *R v Westminster City Council ex p Moklis Ali* (1996) 29 HLR 580, QBD.

138 *R v Brent LBC ex p Baruwa* (1997) 29 HLR 915, CA.

139 *Samuels v Birmingham City Council* [2015] EWCA Civ 1051, [2015] HLR 47.

140 *Dyson v Kerrier DC* [1980] 1 WLR 1205, CA; *Din v Wandsworth LBC* [1983] 1 AC 657, (1981) 1 HLR 73, HL.

141 *R v Islington LBC ex p Bashir Hassan* (1995) 27 HLR 485, although compare *R v Newham LBC ex p Campbell* (1993) 26 HLR 183, QBD.

the authority wrongly sought to rely on events which post-dated the onset of homelessness.

6.84 Where there are potentially multiple causes of an applicant's homelessness, the authority must make a careful judgment on the particular facts, looking to see whether homelessness is shown to have been a likely consequence of the applicant's deliberate act, bearing in mind that it is the applicant's own responsibility for his or her homelessness at which the statute is looking.[142] The precise question to be asked and answered relates to the time when the applicant in fact became homeless[143] but the authority is entitled to have regard to events prior to that date.[144]

Cause and effect

6.85 A causal link may continue to subsist following the act of intentionality even though the applicant ceases to be homeless in the interim – for example, because he or she finds some temporary accommodation from which he or she is subsequently evicted: *Awua*.[145]

6.86 The authority must look back to the original cause of the homelessness and determine whether it was intentional.[146] This derives from the wording of the provisions and the distinction between tenses within what is now HA 1996 s191(1) – 'is' homeless, but 'became' homeless intentionally; see also HA 1996 s189(2) – 'has' a priority need', and s191 'is homeless . . . and has a priority need, and did not become homeless intentionally'. Thus, in *Bull*,[147] the applicant allowed his children to come to live with him in a single room (rather than continuing to live with their mother in a property with sufficient rooms for them), from which they were then evicted: the authority having provided accommodation pending enquiries for them all, he was in priority need (at the date of decision), regardless of whether

142 *Watchman v Ipswich BC* [2007] EWCA Civ 348, [2007] HLR 33 at [22]. It is for the authority to determine the act which is said to be the cause of the homelessness; *Enfield LBC v Najim* [2015] EWCA Civ 319, [2015] HLR 19.

143 *Din v Wandsworth LBC* [1983] 1 AC 657. Although a later event constituting an involuntary cause of homelessness can supersede the earlier conduct where, in view of the later event, it cannot reasonably be said that, but for the deliberate conduct, the applicant would not have become homeless: *Haile v Walham Forest LBC* [2015] UKSC 34, [2015] HLR 24. See further para 6.133.

144 *Watchman*, above, at [23].

145 *R v Brent LBC ex p Awua* [1996] AC 55, (1995) 27 HLR 453, HL. See also *Bratton v Croydon LBC* [2002] EWCA Civ 1494, [2002] All ER (D) 404.

146 *Din v Wandsworth LBC*, above.

147 *Oxford City Council v Bull* [2011] EWCA Civ 609, [2011] HLR 35.

the children were reasonably to be expected to reside with him,[148] but because the accommodation had been available for him when he allowed them to join him,[149] he was homeless intentionally for allowing them to reside with him when they were not reasonably to be expected to do so – it was allowing them to come to live with him which had caused his homelessness.

6.87 In *Reeve*,[150] Woolf J said:

> It seems to me that the answer to the question of whether or not the council were entitled to take the view which they did of the applicant's conduct depends on the proper interpretation of s17(1) [now HA 1996 s191(1)]. It appears to me that the use of the words 'in consequence' in that subsection does raise problems of causation. Really, what is involved in deciding whether or not the applicant is right is a decision as to remoteness . . .

6.88 In *ex p P*,[151] Schiemann J observed that causation was a notorious minefield in jurisprudence and philosophy. The authority was entitled to conclude that the misbehaviour of the applicants – resulting in threats from the IRA causing them to have to leave their home – was something 'in consequence of which' the applicants had ceased to occupy accommodation.

6.89 In *Hinds*,[152] the applicant undertook to leave the matrimonial home to avoid an ouster order; this led to termination of the secure tenancy. The authority's conclusion that his violence towards his wife had caused the loss of accommodation was upheld.

6.90 In *Aranda*,[153] the judge applied a 'but for' test. The applicant and her husband received a grant of £20,000 from the authority to give up a secure tenancy. That money was used to partially fund the purchase of a family home in Colombia. Shortly after the family arrived in Colombia, the marriage failed. The house was transferred to a relative and the applicant and her children returned to the UK, where she applied as homeless. The authority concluded that she was intentionally homeless. The matters relied on by the authority, including the grant, were matters 'but for' which she might never have gone to Colombia at all, rather than matters but for which the applicant would have continued in occupation of the property in Colombia.

148 See para 5.2.
149 See para 4.33.
150 *R v Thanet DC ex p Reeve* (1981) 6 HLR 31, QBD.
151 *R v Hammersmith and Fulham LBC ex p P* (1989) 22 HLR 21, QBD.
152 *R v Islington LBC ex p Hinds* (1995) 28 HLR 302, CA.
153 *R v Camden LBC ex p Aranda* (1996) 28 HLR 672, QBD.

Accordingly, they could not be considered deliberate acts which had caused the applicant's loss of (the Colombian) accommodation.

6.91 In *Robinson v Torbay BC*,[154] it was said that the loss of the home must be the 'reasonable result' of the deliberate act. This approach was adopted in *Reid*.[155]

6.92 Thus, in *R v Hounslow LBC ex p R*,[156] the applicant had terminated his tenancy when he was sentenced to seven years' imprisonment for indecent assault, as he could no longer pay his rent. In considering whether he was intentionally homeless, the test correctly applied was whether ceasing to occupy the accommodation would reasonably have been regarded at the time as a likely consequence of the deliberate conduct.[157]

6.93 *Ex p R* was approved in *Stewart v Lambeth LBC*,[158] where the applicant lost his home after being convicted of drug dealing. In *Goodger v Ealing LBC*,[159] the Court of Appeal described the decision of a review panel that an applicant had become homeless intentionally by breaching a prohibition in his tenancy agreement against drug dealing from the property – which had led to a term of six years' imprisonment – as being the only decision possible in the circumstances, so much so that what might otherwise have been the procedural unfairness[160] of failing to disclose his housing file until a few days before the review hearing was irrelevant.

6.94 The decision in *City of Gloucester v Miles*[161] may also be considered to turn on cause and effect. The applicant had left her home for a period of time, but had not clearly or certainly quit it. During her absence, her estranged husband returned and caused damage which rendered the property entirely uninhabitable. As she was not a party to the vandalism, she had done nothing that could be classed as intentional, even though she might subsequently have lost the property either through failing to resume residence or because arrears had accrued and there was a threat of proceedings.

154 [1982] 1 All ER 726, QBD.

155 *R v Westminster City Council ex p Reid* (1994) 26 HLR 691, QBD.

156 (1997) 29 HLR 939, QBD.

157 Which, on the facts, it was.

158 *Stewart v Lambeth LBC* [2002] EWCA Civ 753, [2002] HLR 40.

159 [2002] EWCA Civ 751, [2003] HLR 6.

160 See para 12.57.

161 (1985) 17 HLR 292, CA, referred to in the Court of Appeal in *Puhlhofer* (1985) 17 HLR 558, CA, but not criticised either in that case at the House of Lords ([1986] AC 484, 18 HLR 158) or in *R v Brent LBC ex p Awua* [1996] AC 55, (1995) 27 HLR 453, HL.

6.95 The authority must clearly act reasonably in regarding present homelessness as being caused by a departure from earlier accommodation. In *Krishnan*,[162] Birmingham City Council was putting pressure on owner-occupiers to reduce overcrowding in their premises. A family of relatives sharing the home were offered accommodation by another relative in Uxbridge until such time as they could afford to buy their own house. At the same time, there was a possibility of promotion if the family could move to London. Subsequently, the Uxbridge relative decided to sell his house and move to Canada, at which point the family became homeless.

6.96 The authority considered that the family could reasonably have gone on occupying the Birmingham property – on which point its decision was not upheld – and took the view that the Uxbridge arrangement was only temporary.[163] On this, too, its decision was set aside by the court:

> I also hold that the Council's officers made insufficient enquiry as to the state of knowledge and expectations of the Plaintiff with regard to the availability of his accommodation at Uxbridge at the time when he moved here. Mrs Bates states in her note . . . that the Plaintiff did not deny that his accommodation at [Uxbridge] was temporary. That, however, was not the point. The word 'temporary' can aptly cover a considerable period. Thus, accommodation held on a tenancy for a year or more can rightly be described as temporary.
>
> As I have already indicated, the Plaintiff's expectation at the time when he moved . . . was that the accommodation there would be available for him for at least a year. It follows as it seems to me that if the Council's officers had been aware of that fact they might well have taken the view that the Plaintiff became homeless not because he moved to [Uxbridge] from . . . Birmingham, but because the Plaintiff's cousin changed his mind about the length of time for which he was willing to accommodate the Plaintiff and his family . . .

6.97 Similarly, in *Rose*,[164] although decided on the meaning of 'deliberate', the point may as easily be made that an earlier departure had not caused the homelessness: what had caused the homelessness was the loss of the intervening, temporary accommodation, which the applicant had not appreciated was – or was likely to be – temporary.

6.98 In *Gliddon*,[165] the applicants quit private-sector accommodation. Initially, they had been granted a tenancy. The landlord alleged that

162 *Krishnan v Hillingdon LBC* January 1981 *LAG Bulletin* 137, QBD.

163 Ie, unsettled; cf para 6.102.

164 *R v Wandsworth LBC ex p Rose* (1983) 11 HLR 105, QBD.

165 *R v Exeter City Council ex p Gliddon* (1984) 14 HLR 103, QBD.

they had obtained it by deception and compelled them to enter into a licence agreement in substitution. It was the loss of accommodation under licence which was the immediate cause of the homelessness.

6.99 At first, the authority advised the applicants to await court proceedings for determination of their status; the court held that this was a valid approach.[166] On the applicants' failure to follow this advice, however, the authority reached a new decision, based on the deception pursuant to which the accommodation had been obtained, and concluded that it had therefore been lost by the applicants' own fault.

6.100 In the light of this finding of fact by the authority, however, the authority could no longer conclude that the applicants could reasonably have remained in occupation. Accordingly, the accommodation obtained by deception ought to have been ignored and the authority was obliged to look back instead to the loss of the applicants' previous accommodation.

Breaking the chain of causation

6.101 The question, then, becomes one of how the chain of causation between an act causing homelessness and current homelessness may be broken.

6.102 Where the applicant has enjoyed a period of 'settled accommodation'[167] or 'other than temporary accommodation',[168] this will break the chain.[169] There is no reverse corollary: acquisition and loss of settled accommodation is not the only means of breaking the chain; the fact that what has been lost is unsettled does not mean that the applicant is still homeless intentionally.[170]

Settled accommodation

6.103 The concept of settled accommodation was developed by the judiciary – under the Housing (Homeless Persons) Act 1977 and under HA 1985 Part 3 – and was used in a number of different contexts:

a) HA 1985 s58(1) – definition of homelessness;

166 See paras 6.144–6.148.

167 *Din v Wandsworth LBC* [1983] 1 AC 657, (1981) 1 HLR 73, HL, per Lord Wilberforce, adopting Ackner LJ in the Court of Appeal.

168 *Din*, above, per Lord Lowry.

169 *R v Brent LBC ex p Awua*, above. See also *Mohammed v Westminster City Council* [2005] EWCA Civ 796, [2005] HLR 47.

170 See paras 6.120–6.133.

b) HA 1985 s60(1) – intentionality: whether what was quit could give rise to a finding of intentionality/whether there had been a break in a period of intentionality;
c) HA 1985 s65(2) – discharge of duty in relation to unintentionally homeless.

Following the decision in *Awua*,[171] however, the distinction between settled and unsettled accommodation is now only relevant to the question of whether the chain of causation has been broken.[172]

6.104 In *Din*, in which the concept of settled accommodation first emerged, it was said to be a question of 'fact and degree'.

6.105 Different circumstances may lead to accommodation being found to be unsettled. One circumstance relates to the physical conditions in the property; another, to the security of tenure which an applicant had, which is often linked to how long the applicant has occupied the accommodation.

Physical conditions

6.106 If these are so poor as to be unfit for human habitation[173] or otherwise in such a condition that no reasonable person could consider it to be capable of amounting to accommodation,[174] then it should not be treated as settled.[175] In *Mohammed*,[176] one of the reasons that accommodation occupied by the applicant was not settled was because it was severely overcrowded.

171 *R v Brent LBC ex p Awua*, above. See para 6.85.

172 See para 6.102. As *Awua* preserved this use of the concept of settled accommodation, albeit only for the purpose of determining whether the chain of causation has been broken, it is appropriate to consider pre-*Awua* cases alongside subsequent decisions.

173 As it was put in *R v South Herefordshire DC ex p Miles* (1983) 17 HLR 82, QBD; *City of Gloucester v Miles* (1985) 17 HLR 292, CA, to the same effect, asked whether the property was 'uninhabitable'. It is doubtful, however, that this test would be met because a property does not meet the *statutory* definition of unfitness (Landlord and Tenant Act 1985 s8) as distinct from a common sense view of it, or if the causes of the unfitness are such as to qualify as hazards which the local authority could require to be remedied under HA 2004 Part 1.

174 (1983) 17 HLR 82, QBD.

175 See the early cases of *R v South Herefordshire DC ex p Miles* (1983) 17 HLR 82, QBD; *City of Gloucester v Miles* (1985) 17 HLR 292, CA; *R v Dinefwr BC ex p Marshall* (1984) 17 HLR 310, which – notwithstanding their disapproval in *R v Hillingdon LBC ex p Puhlhofer* [1986] AC 484, HL, on the question of whether the accommodation was so physically poor that the applicant was already homeless – remain illustrative of when the physical condition of a property is so bad that it cannot be considered settled.

176 *Mohammed v Westminster City Council*, above. See para 6.118.

Security/temporal conditions

6.107 Most of the cases have turned on security.

6.108 *Ruffle*[177] concerned a family who had earlier applied to the authority and been found intentionally homeless. That decision was not contested. The applicants subsequently moved into the flat of a council tenant under an arrangement which was intended to be permanent but which broke down after a few months through no fault of their own. The family returned to the authority, which decided that they were still intentionally homeless because the intervening period had not 'been one in settled occupation which would give rise to a new cause of homelessness'.

6.109 The applicants argued that the authority had asked the wrong question: it should have asked not whether the intervening accommodation was settled, but whether it was obviously temporary. There was a spectrum of accommodation of which 'settled' and 'obviously temporary' were only the extremes. The applicants contended that they needed only to have secured something more than the least secure type of accommodation in order to have ended homelessness and broken the chain, not the most secure.

6.110 The judge disagreed:[178]

> I think that one or the other term encompasses all states of accommodation. Thus, it is correct to contrast, as the various cases do, settled or permanent accommodation on the one hand with less than secure accommodation, variously described as precarious or temporary or transient on the other . . . [For] the authority to ask themselves . . . has the intervening period been one of settled accommodation occupation, involves asking the same question as whether the accommodation was only temporary. These questions are merely the opposite sides of the same coin.[179]

6.111 In *Evans*,[180] a couple left a secure tenancy for larger premises in the private sector, purportedly on a bed and breakfast basis. There was, however, a strong argument that they had full Rent Act protection. Following threats of – and actual – violence from their landlord, the

177 *R v Merton LBC ex p Ruffle* (1989) 21 HLR 361, QBD.

178 *Ruffle*, above, at 366.

179 Simon Brown J (given the later decision in *Awua*, somewhat presciently) contemplated an alternative analysis, which he considered contains possible tensions, of three possible types of accommodation: one so tenuous that it is discounted altogether; one which is sufficient to preclude homelessness; and a further type, 'settled' accommodation, which is required to break the chain of intentionality.

180 *R v Swansea City Council ex p Evans* (1990) 22 HLR 467, CA.

couple left the new accommodation. The authority's decision that they were intentionally homeless was quashed because the authority had failed to consider whether the new accommodation, with security, had been settled.

6.112 Authorities are not bound to accept the applicant's view as to whether accommodation was settled. In *Cadney*,[181] a woman sought to rely on a period of three months during which she had moved out of the matrimonial home and into the home of another man. Their relationship was not successful and she left. She sought to rely on this as a period of intervening accommodation, because she had intended to stay with him permanently. The court considered this too subjective an approach. The authority had been entitled to take the view that it was a transient or precarious arrangement, ie that an objective test could be applied.[182]

6.113 In *Ashton*,[183] the authority's decision that occupation of premises under a tenancy falling within the exception in HA 1985 Sch 1 para 5[184] was not occupation of settled accommodation was upheld, entitling the authority to look back to the previous accommodation.

6.114 Length of time will be important in establishing whether accommodation is settled: see *Easom*,[185] in which it was open to the authority to conclude that accommodation was not settled – over several years – because the applicants had at all times been illegal immigrants to Australia who might have been deported at any moment.

6.115 In *Ajayi*,[186] Dyson J reiterated that whether accommodation was settled is a question of fact and degree. The applicant had lived with family friends (in the first instance for a period of 20 months, and in the second for some nine months) since leaving her family home in Nigeria. The authority concluded that in neither case had the accommodation been settled. The term 'settled accommodation' was an ordinary English expression, not a term of art. Although when the applicant moved in with her friends the duration of the accommodation had been uncertain, the authority was entitled – having regard to the circumstances – to conclude that it had been precarious.

181 *R v Purbeck DC ex p Cadney* (1985) 17 HLR 534, QBD.

182 See also *R v Merton LBC ex p Ruffle*, above.

183 *R v Winchester City Council ex p Ashton* (1991) 24 HLR 48, QBD, (1991) 24 HLR 520, CA.

184 Temporary accommodation for persons taking up employment.

185 *R v Croydon LBC ex p Easom* (1992) 25 HLR 262, QBD.

186 *R v Hackney LBC ex p Ajayi* (1997) 30 HLR 473, QBD.

6.116 The fact and degree test was restated in *Knight*,[187] where the question was whether occupation of a property under a six-month assured shorthold tenancy could amount to settled accommodation for the purpose of breaking the chain of causation. Although the Court of Appeal accepted that such occupation was capable of constituting settled accommodation, it did not as a matter of law always do so.[188] The question remained one of fact and degree to be determined by the authority. In the circumstances of the particular case, it was open to the authority to find that the accommodation was not settled, because the applicant had known from the outset that the tenancy was only for six months and would not be renewed.

6.117 In *Huda*[189] the applicant had been provided with temporary accommodation by the authority under a licence agreement with a third party. He was subsequently found to be intentionally homeless but, due to an administrative oversight, no steps were taken to evict him. After four years he re-applied for assistance, contending that his lengthy occupation of the temporary accommodation amounted to settled accommodation. The authority decided that it was not settled accommodation as it had been due to administrative error and was of a precarious nature with no security of tenure; the Court of Appeal repeated that settled accommodation was a matter of fact and degree and concluded held that the decision was one the authority were entitled to reach.

Combination of factors

6.118 The applicant in *Mohammed*[190] also took an assured shorthold tenancy. She was evicted after 12 months because of a shortfall in housing benefit leading to arrears of rent. The authority on review considered that the accommodation was not settled for three reasons:

a) the applicant had obtained the accommodation with a view to making a second application to the authority as homeless;[191]
b) she could not afford the rent for the accommodation; and
c) the accommodation was overcrowded.

The Court of Appeal held that the reviewing officer was entitled to have regard to all these matters in reaching his decision.

187 *Knight v Vale Royal BC* [2003] EWCA Civ 1258, [2004] HLR 9.
188 It was suggested at [25] that, where accommodation is let on an assured shorthold tenancy, it is normally a significant pointer to it being settled.
189 *Huda v Redbridge LBC* [2016] EWCA Civ 709, [2016] HLR 30.
190 *Mohammed v Westminster City Council* [2005] EWCA Civ 796, [2005] HLR 47.
191 See now para 6.149.

6.119 An argument that a period of imprisonment could amount to settled accommodation was rejected in *Stewart*.[192]

Breaking the chain by other means

6.120 Whether acquisition of settled accommodation is the only means of breaking the causal link was expressly reserved in *Awua*.[193]

6.121 That question was considered by the Court of Appeal in *Fahia*.[194] The applicant had been found intentionally homeless by the authority and housed temporarily in a guest house. She remained in the guest house for over a year, her rent paid by housing benefit. A subsequent review of her housing benefit led to payments being cut and she was, in consequence, evicted from the guest house.

6.122 The authority decided that it had no new duty towards the applicant because the accommodation at the guest house did not constitute intervening settled accommodation such as to break the causal link with the applicant's original intentional homelessness.

6.123 The Court of Appeal rejected this approach and decided that events other than securing settled accommodation could break the chain; it remitted the case to the authority to decide whether the change in housing benefit had constituted such an event.

6.124 The court expressly approved the earlier decision in *Bassett*[195] as an example of a break in the chain of causation otherwise than by settled accommodation. In that case, temporary accommodation had been lost not because of its temporary quality, but because the applicant had been staying with her sister-in-law and had to leave when she separated from her husband.

6.125 Although *Fahia* went to the House of Lords, the authority abandoned its appeal on this aspect.[196]

6.126 In subsequent cases, following *Fahia* at the Court of Appeal (and its approval of *Bassett*), it has been held that the subsequent event must be unconnected to the temporary nature of the accommodation.

6.127 Thus, in *Harvey*,[197] the applicant was evicted from his home for noise nuisance and moved in with a friend. After four months, the friend was taken into hospital and the applicant had to move out.

192 *Stewart v Lambeth LBC* [2002] EWCA Civ 753, [2002] HLR 40.

193 *Stewart v Lambeth LBC*, above.

194 *R v Harrow LBC ex p Fahia* (1997) 29 HLR 974, CA (not overruled by the House of Lords on this point, see [1998] 1 WLR 1396, (1998) 30 HLR 1124).

195 *R v Basingstoke and Deane BC ex p Bassett* (1983) 10 HLR 125, QBD.

196 *R v Harrow LBC ex p Fahia*, above, at p1130.

197 *R v Brighton BC ex p Harvey* (1997) 30 HLR 670, QBD.

The loss of the friend's accommodation did not break the chain of causation because it could not be said to be unconnected with the temporary or unsettled nature of the accommodation the applicant had been occupying.[198]

6.128 Likewise, in *Ajayi*,[199] the applicant left accommodation in Nigeria and moved to London where she stayed with various friends and acquaintances. She moved in with one friend in January 1996, at the same time as she discovered she was pregnant and, on the birth of the baby, was asked to leave. The chain of causation had not been broken. The real and effective cause of her homelessness was not the pregnancy but leaving her accommodation in Nigeria.

6.129 A term of imprisonment cannot amount to a supervening event which breaks the chain of causation.[200]

6.130 A slightly different question was posed in *Din*[201] – whether an act which at its inception was one causing intentional homelessness can cease to qualify as such merely through the passage of time, ie, whether it can become 'spent'?

6.131 In that case, a family were living in accommodation under extremely trying circumstances, and would ultimately have had to leave, but they were advised by the authority to remain in occupation until a court order was made.[202] It was common ground, at least on appeal, that if an application had been made immediately after the departure, the authority could have found the family to be homeless intentionally, because at that date it would have been reasonable to remain in occupation (see further below), whereas, on application at a later date, it was conceded by the authority that the family would by then have become homeless in any event, and not intentionally so.[203]

6.132 During the interim period, the family had stayed with relatives and it was not argued that there had, on that account, been a break in the homelessness. Rather, it was argued that the original cause of

198 For instance, because the hospitalisation was no different from being asked to leave, which could have happened at any time due to the temporary nature of the accommodation: *Harvey*, above, at 678.

199 *R v Hackney LBC ex p Ajayi* (1997) 30 HLR 473, QBD.

200 *Stewart v Lambeth LBC*, above. See also para 6.119 – prison is not settled accommodation. In *Birmingham City Council v Ali; Moran v Manchester City Council (Secretary of State for Communities and Local Government and another intervening)* [2009] UKHL 36, [2009] 1 WLR 1506, the House of Lords expressly reserved the issue of whether prison could comprise accommodation at all.

201 *Din v Wandsworth LBC* [1983] 1 AC 657, (1981) 1 HLR 73, HL.

202 Paras 6.143–6.148.

203 There was no defence to the landlord's proposed proceedings for possession and the order would have already taken effect.

homelessness had ceased to be effective because the family would have become homeless unintentionally by the time of application. This argument was upheld in the county court, but dismissed on appeal. The question was whether the present period of homelessness had, at its inception, been intentional. The fact that the applicants would have become homeless unintentionally by the date of application was held to be irrelevant.[204]

6.133 *Din* was re-considered in *Haile*.[205] The Supreme Court, while stating that *Din* remained good law, held that, when considering whether an applicant is intentionally homeless, the authority must look at the conduct which caused the present homelessness unless a later event (which is not itself an act of voluntary homelessness) supersedes the earlier conduct, so that it cannot reasonably be said that 'but for' that earlier conduct, the applicant would not have become homeless, in which case the causal connection between current homelessness and earlier conduct will have been interrupted. In the absence of any such event, the question is whether the proximate cause of the homelessness is an event which is unconnected to the earlier conduct. The question may be approached in two stages: first, was the homelessness intentional at its inception; second, has it been superseded by a later (unconnected) event which means that the authority must ignore the origins of the homelessness because the applicant would have been homeless in any event. The connection between the initial event and the immediate cause is therefore a critical element in the analysis. It has to be said that it is not easy to square this decision in *Haile* with *Din*:[206] in particular, it is extremely difficult – if even possible – to distinguish the reasoning adopted in *Haile* from the homeless person's submissions which were rejected in *Din*.[207]

204 See also *R v Brent LBC ex p Yusuf* (1995) 29 HLR 48, QBD.

205 *Haile v Waltham Forest LBC* [2015] UKSC 34, [2015] AC 1471, [2015] HLR 24.

206 Lord Carnwath in the minority commented that the majority had engaged in a re-analysis of *Din* that had not been contended for by the appellant. Moreover, it is extremely difficult – if even possible – to distinguish the reasoning adopted in *Haile* from the homeless person's argument which was rejected in *Din*.

207 See, in particular, pp658/F–661/B, and, at 660/A and 661/A, the reliance in *Din* on precisely the 'but for' approach that is at the heart of the majority decision in *Haile*.

Cessation of occupation

Accommodation abroad

6.134 The accommodation which has been lost can be accommodation abroad and the act causing its loss can be an act abroad.

6.135 In *de Falco*,[208] the reason given by the authority for finding intentional homelessness was that the family in question had come to the UK without arranging permanent accommodation. That reason was patently bad on its face. It was upheld by the Court of Appeal, however, by expanding it – against the factual background – to refer to a departure from accommodation in Italy. That this approach had been devised by the Court of Appeal was made clear in *Paris*,[209] where the authority used the same wording as in *de Falco* but was held to have erred because it had failed actually to consider the accommodation which had been quit and the circumstances of departure from it.

Short-term accommodation

6.136 Where the authority is providing temporary housing pending a permanent allocation, its loss may lead to a finding of intentionality: *Hunt*.[210]

6.137 In *Conway*,[211] the applicant failed to renew a protected shorthold tenancy. It was held that this could amount to a deliberate omission (although on the facts, it had not been).[212]

Notional occupation

6.138 In *Islam*,[213] at the Court of Appeal, it was argued that the accommodation lost had not been available for the occupation of the applicant and his family (who had recently arrived from Bangladesh).[214] One of the grounds advanced for upholding the decision in the court

208 *De Falco, Silvestri v Crawley BC* [1980] QB 460, CA.

209 *R v Reigate and Banstead BC ex p Paris* (1984) 17 HLR 103, QBD.

210 *R v East Hertfordshire DC ex p Hunt* (1985) 18 HLR 51, QBD. The basis for the decision was politely criticised (described as 'heroic') in *Awua*, but the outcome remains correct. In any event, in such circumstances the authority will now be considered to have discharged its duty to the applicant: see HA 1996 s193(6)(b) – para 10.152.

211 *R v Christchurch BC ex p Conway* (1987) 19 HLR 238, QBD.

212 See para 6.35.

213 *Re Islam* [1983] 1 AC 688, (1981) 1 HLR 107, HL.

214 See para 4.28.

below was that the applicant – while living in a shared single room in Uxbridge – had at all material times nonetheless been in 'notional occupation' of the family home in Bangladesh, through his wife and children. Another suggestion was that the accommodation available for, and occupied by, the family was made up of the family home in Bangladesh and the room in Uxbridge.

6.139 The House of Lords rejected both of these approaches:

> The Master of the Rolls was . . . using the word occupation in an artificial sense, which . . . is quite inconsistent with its ordinary meaning and with the probably narrower sense in which it is used in the Act. When it speaks of occupying accommodation, the Act has in contemplation people who are residing in that accommodation . . .

6.140 It has been held, however, that an applicant may be occupying accommodation even though not physically residing in it. Thus, in *Khan*,[215] the applicants represented to immigration authorities that they would be living in a house which the first applicant subsequently sold. The applicants never occupied the house, although the first applicant's family had done so. This was held to be sufficient occupation for the purposes of intentionality so that, on sale of the house, the applicants could be considered to have ceased to occupy it.

6.141 In *Lee-Lawrence*,[216] the applicant had to leave his home because it became uninhabitable following an arson attack. He accepted the offer of a tenancy elsewhere, on which he claimed housing benefit, but, when he subsequently applied as homeless, he asserted that he had never in fact occupied the new property. The Court of Appeal held that the fact that a person had a legal right to possession or held the keys was not, of itself, sufficient to establish occupation; nonetheless, those factors combined with the claim for housing benefit and other representations by the applicant that he had been resident in the premises, were sufficient to support a finding of occupancy.

Available for occupation

6.142 This has been considered in chapter 4.[217]

215 *R v Westminster City Council ex p Khan* (1991) 23 HLR 230, QBD.
216 *Lee-Lawrence v Penwith DC* [2006] EWCA Civ 507.
217 See paras 4.16–4.38.

Reasonable to continue to occupy

6.143 It must have been reasonable to continue to occupy the accommodation which has been lost. This has also been considered in chapter 4,[218] to which reference should be made, but there are circumstances which are particular to findings of intentionality which merit mention. This is particularly so where advice has been given to the applicant by the authority prior to departure from the accommodation.[219]

6.144 In *Hughes*,[220] it appeared that an alleged winter letting might not fall within the provisions of Rent Act 1977 Sch 15 case 13, so that there would be no mandatory ground for possession available to the landlord. The occupier was accordingly advised to await the outcome of proceedings but did not do so:

> The important point which this application raises . . . is the question as to what extent an authority exercising its powers under [the] Act is entitled to say to a person . . . 'You should remain in accommodation which you at present occupy and not leave that accommodation until there is a court order made against you requiring you to vacate . . .'
>
> [W]here there is a situation which is doubtful or difficult, it is reasonable for the authority to give advice to a person who is a prospective candidate for assistance under the . . . Act . . . that they should not vacate the accommodation which they are at present occupying without the order of the court because otherwise they may be regarded as persons intentionally homeless.

6.145 In *Adamiec*,[221] the failure of an applicant to heed advice not to sell his home resulted in a finding of intentionality which was upheld as, although he might ultimately have been forced to sell because of his financial circumstances, that was a stage he had not yet reached.

6.146 Whether it is reasonable for an applicant to continue to occupy the accommodation is to be judged at the time that the conduct in consequence of which the accommodation was lost took place, not at some later date when the applicant actually left the accommodation: *ex p P*.[222]

218 See paras 4.69–4.140.

219 See also *F v Birmingham City Council* [2006] EWCA Civ 1427, [2007] HLR 18, para 6.41, and *Ugiagbe v Southwark LBC* [2009] EWCA Civ 31, [2009] HLR 35, para 6.40.

220 *R v Penwith DC ex p Hughes* August 1980 *LAG Bulletin* 187, QBD.

221 *R v Leeds City Council ex p Adamiec* (1991) 24 HLR 138, QBD. See too *R v Westminster City Council ex p Moklis Ali* (1996) 29 HLR 580, QBD.

222 *R v Hammersmith and Fulham LBC ex p P* (1989) 22 HLR 21, QBD. See also *Denton v Southwark LBC* [2007] EWCA Civ 623, [2008] HLR 11.

6.147 Whether it is reasonable to continue to occupy may be affected by whether alternative accommodation will be available if the applicants remain in their present accommodation in the short term.[223] See also *McIlory*,[224] in which Catholic applicants left accommodation in Northern Ireland after being subjected to several years of harassment by Protestant factions, culminating in a shooting incident. A finding of intentionality was upheld on the ground that they had failed to wait and see whether they would be rehoused by the Northern Ireland Housing Executive. This may be contrasted with *McManus*,[225] where the applicant lived in a house in Belfast just off a road which was the dividing line between the two main religious groups and the scene of much sectarian violence. The applicant left her home and went to London where she applied for homelessness assistance; the authority found her to have become homeless intentionally. Her challenge was successful: the authority should have examined the effect of the situation in Belfast on the applicant and her daughter and focused on the particular area of Belfast where they lived, which the evidence suggested was particularly prone to the worst sectarian violence in the city.[226]

6.148 In *Wilson*,[227] the court, albeit with some hesitation, held that it had not been reasonable for a woman to remain in accommodation in Australia because a) she had no legal permission to remain; and b) she was pregnant and would shortly have reached the stage of pregnancy when she would not have been able to fly back to the UK.

Extended definition – collusive arrangements

6.149 HA 1996 s191(3) and H(W)A 2014 s77(4) contain the extended definitions of intentionality, under which a person is to be treated as intentionally homeless if he or she enters into an arrangement pursuant to which he or she has to cease to occupy accommodation, which it would have been reasonable for the person to continue to occupy,[228] and the purpose of the arrangement is to enable the person to become entitled to assistance under HA 1996 Part 7 or H(W)A

223 *R v Hammersmith and Fulham LBC ex p P* (1989) 22 HLR 21, QBD.
224 *R v Newham LBC ex p McIlroy* (1991) 23 HLR 570, QBD.
225 *R v Brent LBC ex p McManus* (1993) 25 HLR 643, QBD at 645 and 646.
226 *McManus*, above, at 648.
227 *R v Hillingdon LBC ex p Wilson* (1983) 12 HLR 61, QBD.
228 See paras 4.69–4.140 and 6.143–6.148.

2014 Part 2, and there is no other good reason why the applicant is homeless.

6.150 This provision is aimed at arrangements designed to give the impression of being obliged to leave accommodation[229] which would have been reasonable to continue to occupy, so as to create an apparent right to assistance under HA 1996 Part 7 or H(W)A 2014 Part 2.

6.151 If it would not have been accommodation which it was reasonable to continue to occupy in any event, the arrangement may be disregarded, although this would not prevent the authority looking back to the loss of any previous accommodation which may properly be considered to be the cause of the present homelessness.

6.152 The English Code[230] suggests that collusion is not confined to those staying with friends or relatives, but can also arise between landlords and tenants:

> Housing authorities, while relying on experience, nonetheless need to be satisfied that collusion exists, and must not merely rely on hearsay or unfounded suspicions.[231]

6.153 Even if the subsection is prima facie applicable, there must also be no other 'good reason' for the homelessness. Examples of 'other good reasons' include overcrowding or an obvious breakdown in relationships between the applicant and the 'host' household or landlord.[232]

6.154 It seems that authorities do not frequently find collusive arrangements. A rare example is to be found in *Lomotey v Enfield LBC*,[233] where the claimant surrendered her joint interest in a property to her brother, who then evicted her.

229 Note that it does not also have to have been 'available for . . . occupation'.

230 English Code of Guidance para 11.28; Welsh Code para 17.30 is in similar terms.

231 This is true for all decision-making (see chapter 9) but may be a particular problem in reaching decisions on collusion.

232 Code of Guidance para 11.28; Welsh Code para 17.30.

233 [2004] EWCA Civ 627, [2004] HLR 45.

CHAPTER 7

Local connection

7.1 Introduction

7.9 What is a local connection?

7.16 Relevant time for determining local connection

7.17 Residence

7.223 Employment

7.26 Family associations

7.30 Other special circumstances

7.33 Former asylum-seekers

7.37 When are the local connection provisions applicable?

7.53 England: additional application of provisions

7.59 Procedure on prospective reference

7.68 Initial help duty

7.73 Resolution of disputes

7.75 Local Authority Agreement

7.82 Arbitration

7.89 Post-resolution procedure

Introduction

7.1 The local connection provisions of Housing Act (HA) 1996 Part 7 and Housing (Wales) Act (H(W)A) 2014 Part 2 allow one authority to pass on to another the burden of securing that permanent accommodation is made available to an applicant. The provisions operate only in specified circumstances. It was one of the principal aims of the Housing (Homeless Persons) Act (H(HP)A) 1977 to end 'shuttling' homeless people between different local authorities, each alleging there was 'greater' connection with the other.[1] The provisions have been described[2] as 'curiously reminiscent of one of the features of the old Poor Law 1601, whereby paupers could be sent back to the parishes where they had a settlement'.

7.2 The local connection provisions represent a mixture of substance and procedure, and of binding law and voluntary agreement. In this chapter, reference will be made not only to HA 1996 Part 7 and H(W)A 2014 Part 2, and the Codes of Guidance (see appendix C), but also to the document known as the Local Authority Agreement[3] and the statutory instrument governing arbitration of disputes between authorities.[4]

7.3 It may be helpful to restate, in outline, how and when these provisions operate, before proceeding to consider them in detail. The local connection provisions exempt an authority to which application has been made (the 'notifying' authority) from the duty to secure that accommodation is made available under HA 1996 s193[5] or H(W)A 2014 ss68 and 73.[6] This duty passes to the 'notified' authority.[7]

7.4 The circumstances in which this may occur are that:

a) there must be no local connection with the area of the notifying authority;
b) there must be a local connection with the area of the notified authority; and

1 See chapter 1.
2 *R v Slough BC ex p Ealing LBC* [1981] QB 801, CA, per Lord Denning MR.
3 See Code of Guidance annex 18 in appendix C, below.
4 Homelessness (Decisions on Referrals) Order 1998 SI No 1578.
5 HA 1996 s200(1).
6 H(W)A 2014 s82(1).
7 HA 1996 s200(4); H(W)A 2014 s82(4). See also *Johnson v City of Westminster City Council* [2015] EWCA Civ 554, [2015] HLR 35.

c) there must be no risk of violence[8] in the area of the notified authority.[9]

7.5 All three conditions must usually be fulfilled before the local connection provisions can be relied on. There are two other conditions for referral which apply in more detailed circumstances. First, where the applicant has previously applied to another authority – within a specified period – which authority has (in pursuance of its duties under Part 7 or Part 2) accommodated the applicant in the area of the authority to which the applicant has now made a new application, the authority to which the new application is made may make a referral back to the first authority regardless of whether any of the other conditions is established.[10]

7.6 Second, the conditions for referral will be met in England if the applicant had accepted a private sector offer of accommodation[11] from another authority, in the area of the authority to which application is now made, within the two years before the application in question and neither the applicant nor anyone who might reasonably be expected to reside with the applicant runs the risk of domestic violence in the district of that other authority.[12]

7.7 In the event of a dispute between the two (or more) authorities, the first stage in both England and Wales will be to try to resolve it by reference to the Local Authority Agreement.[13] In default of agreement, the matter must be referred to arbitration.[14] Pending the resolution of the dispute, principal responsibility for the homeless person or family rests with the authority to which application was initially made, ie, the notifying authority.[15]

8 In Wales, 'domestic abuse' rather than 'violence', but given the definition of 'abuse' in H(W)A 2014 s58 and the decisions in *Yemshaw v Hounslow LBC* [2011] UKSC 3, [2011] HLR 16 and *Waltham Forest LBC v Hussein* [2015] EWCA Civ 14, [2015] HLR 16, the two terms appear to be synonymous.

9 HA 1996 s198(2) and (2A); H(W)A 2014 s80(3).

10 HA 1996 s198(4), (4A). There is no equivalent of this duty in Wales.

11 See paras 10.199–10.204.

12 HA 1996 s198(2ZA), added by Localism Act (LA) 2011 s149(6). This does, however, only apply where the private sector offer had been made before – and the duty to secure accommodation was still in existence at – 9 November 2012: Localism Act 2011 (Commencement No 2 and Transitional Provisions) (England) Order 2012 SI No 2599 article 3. This could now only apply to an application made before 9 November 2014 and still undetermined.

13 HA 1996 s198(5); H(W)A 2014 s80(5).

14 HA 1996 s198(5); H(W)A 2014 s80(5).

15 HA 1996 s200(1); H(W)A 2014 s82(1). See, eg *R (Tanushi) v (1) Westminster City Council (2) Hillingdon LBC*, CO/156/2016, High Court (QBD), 22 January

7.8 Against the background of this outline, the matters which must be considered are:

a) What is a local connection?
b) When are the local connection provisions applicable?
c) Procedure on prospective reference.
d) Resolution of disputes.
e) Post-resolution procedure.

What is a local connection?

7.9 The term 'local connection' is defined in HA 1996 s199 and H(W)A 2014 s81.[16] A person may have a local connection with the district of a local housing authority[17] based on one of four grounds:

a) because the person is, or in the past was, normally resident in it, and the person's residence is or was of his or her own choice;
b) because the person is employed in it;
c) because of family associations; and
d) because of any special circumstances.[18]

7.10 In addition, special provisions apply to applicants who have previously been housed by UK Visas and Immigration (UKVI).[19] There are also additional provisions applicable in England.[20]

2016, in which Westminster sought to refer the application to Hillingdon, who had not accepted it; Ms Tanushi was granted interim relief requiring Westminster to continue to provide her with accommodation.

16 It may be noted that the provisions do not apply in relation to the Isles of Scilly, where there is a requirement of residence of two years and six months during the previous three years: Homelessness (Isles of Scilly) Order 1997 SI No 797.

17 For these purposes, this includes a local authority within the meaning of the Housing (Scotland) Act 1988: HA 1996 ss201, 217.

18 HA 1996 s199(1); H(W)A 2014 s81(1).It is possible for a person to have no local connection with any authority (eg if he or she has just arrived in the country), in which case these provisions will not be applicable and the applicant will be the responsibility of the authority to whom s/he applied, see English Code para 18.22; Welsh Code para 18.19.

19 As it has been since 2013. Between 2008 and 2013, the UK Borders Agency (UKBA) dealt with such matters. Asylum support was previously administered by the National Asylum Support Service (NASS) which was part of the Home Office. See paras 7.33–7.36; see further paras 13.36–13.487.

20 Paras 7.83–7.88. There are no equivalent provisions in Wales.

7.11 It is important not to pay so much attention to the four grounds that insufficient regard is had to the governing phrase 'local connection' itself: see *Re Betts*.[21]

7.12 In that case, the applicant was living with his family in the area of Blaby DC between 1978 and 1980. In August 1980, he got a job in Southampton, and moved into a houseboat in the area, where he was joined by his family. In October 1980, he was given a house by Eastleigh BC. Soon after, however, he lost his job through no fault of his own, fell into arrears with his rent, and was evicted. In February 1981, shortly before the order for possession expired, he applied under H(HP)A 1977. Eastleigh BC referred the application to Blaby DC. The reason given for the decision was that the family had lived in Eastleigh BC's district for less than six months, and, accordingly, was not normally resident in its area. The applicant challenged this decision.

7.13 The Court of Appeal allowed the challenge.[22] The only reason given for the finding that the family was not normally resident in the area was that the family had lived in the area for less than six months, and this decision had been reached by rigid application of the Local Authority Agreement.[23] Normal residence was where a person intended to settle, not necessarily permanently or indefinitely, and a person may have more than one normal residence at different times. It requires consideration of many features of residence, not merely the application of a six-month, or any other arbitrary, period.

7.14 Allowing the authority's appeal, the House of Lords held that the fundamental question was whether or not the applicant had a local connection with the area. This meant more than 'normal residence'. Normal residence, and the other specified grounds of local connection, are subsidiary components of the formula to be applied. The formula is governed by the proposition that residence of any sort will be irrelevant unless and until it is such as to establish a local connection.[24]

7.15 The House of Lords did not dissent from the Court of Appeal's analysis of 'residence' (based on the decision in *R v Barnet LBC ex p Shah*,[25] under the Education Act 1962). Nor did it dissent from the

21 *Re Betts* [1983] 2 AC 613, (1983) 10 HLR 97, HL.

22 *Betts v Eastleigh BC* [1983] 1 WLR 774, (1983) 8 HLR 28, CA.

23 See paras 7.75–7.88. See also Welsh Code para 18.8.

24 This approach was taken in *R v Islington LBC ex p Adigun* (1986) 20 HLR 600, QBD and *R v Westminster City Council ex p Benniche* (1996) 29 HLR 230, CA.

25 [1983] 2 AC 309, HL.

proposition that a rigid application of the Local Authority Agreement would constitute a fetter on the authority's discretion.[26] The Agreement could, however, certainly be taken into account, and applied as a guideline, provided an authority does not shut out the particular facts of the individual case, ie, provided its *application* is given individual consideration.[27] In the present case, the House of Lords found that the authority had not misdirected itself in this respect.

Relevant time for determining local connection

7.16 When seeking to establish whether an applicant has a local connection with a particular area, the authority must look at the facts at the time of the decision. If there is a review of the decision,[28] it is the facts at the date of the review which must be considered.[29] An applicant may not have a local connection with an authority at the time of his or her application, but may acquire one subsequently, either prior to a decision or between decision and review – for example, by obtaining permanent employment or through normal residence in the area.[30]

Residence

7.17 Residence has to be 'of choice'.[31] There is no residence of choice if the applicant, or a person who might reasonably be expected to reside with the applicant, is detained under the authority of any Act of Parliament.[32] Thus, prisoners (whether or not convicted) and those detained under the Mental Health Act 1983 will not acquire a local connection with the area in which the prison or hospital is situated. The secretary of state has power to specify further circumstances in which residence is not to be considered 'of choice',[33] although this

26 See para 12.44.

27 See also *Ozbek v Ispwich BC* [2006] EWCA Civ 534, [2006] HLR 41, at [39] where Chadwick LJ stated that the need for a common basis of decision-making meant that there was an 'imperative for all authorities to apply the guidelines generally to all applications which come before them'.

28 See chapter 9.

29 *Mohamed v Hammersmith and Fulham LBC* [2001] UKHL 57, [2002] HLR 7, HL.

30 See further paras 9.184–9.186.

31 HA 1996 s199(1)(a); H(W)A 2014 s81(2)(a). See *Wandsworth LBC v NJ* [2013] EWCA Civ 1373, [2014] HLR 6 as to whether accommodation in a refuge is 'of choice'.

32 HA 1996 s199(3); H(W)A 2014 s81(3) and Welsh Code para 18.14.

33 HA 1996 s199(5).

power has not been exercised. In Wales, the Welsh Ministers have the same power, which has likewise not been exercised.[34]

7.18 Prior to 1 December 2008, residence resulting from service in the armed forces did not constitute residence 'of choice' for serving members of the armed forces.[35] This still applies to applications made before 1 December 2008;[36] for applications made on or after that date, residence resulting from service in the armed forces is now to be treated as 'of choice' for the purposes of HA 1996 s199 or H(W)A 2014 s82.[37]

7.19 In *Mohamed*,[38] the House of Lords considered whether occupation of interim accommodation provided[39] by a local authority during enquiries and pending review could amount to normal residence. Lord Slynn, concluding that it did, said:

> . . . the prima facie meaning of normal residence is a place where at the relevant time the person in fact resides. That therefore is the question to be asked . . . So long as that place where he eats and sleeps is voluntarily accepted by him, the reason why he is there rather than somewhere else does not prevent that place from being his normal

34 H(W)A 2014 s81(4)(b).

35 The armed forces were defined as the Royal Navy, the regular armed forces as defined by Army Act 1955 s225, and the regular air forces as defined by Air Force Act 1955 s223: HA 1996 s199(4). From 31 October 2009, the armed forces are defined as Royal Navy, the Royal Marines, the regular army or the Royal Air Force: Armed Forces Act 2006 s374. The repealed provision was addressed in *R v Vale of White Horse DC ex p Smith and Hay* (1984) 17 HLR 160, QBD, two cases heard together which considered the usual practice of the armed forces to allow a period of time after the termination of service before recovering possession of married quarters; it was held that the exclusion of residence as a result of service in the armed forces referred to the time residence commenced; a fresh residence after leaving the armed forces could be established, even in the same premises, but would not usually be established merely by holding over after the right to occupy married quarters had come to an end.

36 While now long ago, someone may have remained in housing provided under HA 1996 Part 7, without cessation of the duty under section 193, whether by a final offer of accommodation or otherwise.

37 HA 1996 s199(2) repealed with effect from 1 December 2008. See also Circular 04/2009 *Housing allocations – members of the armed forces* from the Department for Communities and Local Government (DCLG). No such restriction was included in H(W)A 2014; see Welsh Code para 18.11.

38 *Mohamed v Hammersmith and Fulham LBC*, above. Cf *Al-ameri v Kensington and Chelsea RLBC; Osmani v Harrow LBC* [2004] UKHL 4, [2004] HLR 20 where accommodation provided by NASS to asylum-seekers was not residence of choice. The effect of this latter decision has now been statutorily overturned: see para 7.33.

39 Usually under HA 1996 s188(1) but also potentially under s200(1) or s188(3) or s200(5) pending the review.

> residence. He may not like it, he may prefer some other place, but that place is for the relevant time the place where he normally resides . . . Where he is given interim accommodation by a local housing authority even more clearly is that the place where for the time being he is normally resident. The fact that it is provided subject to statutory duty does not . . . prevent it from being such.

7.20 The Local Authority Agreement suggests a working (or extended) definition of 'normal residence' as six months in an area during the previous 12 months, or not less than three years during the previous five-year period.[40] In *Re Betts*, this was described as 'eminently sensible and proper to have been included in the agreement'.

7.21 In *Smith and Hay*,[41] a period of a few months, some ten years before application, during which one of the spouses had been employed – and therefore resident – in an area, was considered too short necessarily to have established a local connection.

7.22 Compare, however, *Hughes*,[42] where the applicant had moved into the area to set up a permanent home with the man by whom she became pregnant. The relationship broke down owing to domestic violence after only two months and the applicant applied as homeless. A decision made some months later – during which the applicant had resided in a local women's aid refuge – that the applicant did not have a local connection with the area was quashed as one to which no reasonable authority could have come.

Employment

7.23 The Local Authority Agreement suggests that an authority should seek confirmation from the employer both of the employment and that it is not of a casual nature.[43] This implies that 'employment' is to be given a restrictive meaning, ie, one in the employ of another, but neither HA 1996 Part 7 nor H(W)A 2014 suggests that self-employed people should be excluded or that employment need be full-time.

7.24 Given that employment is a subsidiary consideration, and merely one of the grounds for establishing a local connection,[44] it is clearly open to an authority to exclude casual work, but not, it is submitted, self-employment. In *Smith and Hay* (above), the same few months'

40 Local Authority Agreement para 4.1(i).

41 *R v Vale of White Horse DC ex p Smith and Hay* (1984) 17 HLR 160, QBD.

42 *R v Southwark LBC ex p Hughes* (1998) 30 HLR 1082, QBD.

43 Local Authority Agreement para 4.1(i).

44 See also paras 7.9–7.15.

employment, some ten years before the application, was described as limited and of short duration and the authority did not err in finding that it did not give rise to a local connection, but – especially in this day and age when employment relationships are markedly more diverse than traditional – to suggest, say, that someone who has been a self-employed trader (eg a local builder) for a period of time long enough to be considered a connection is not employed in an area would not only be a gloss on the legislation but would fly in its face.

7.25 A person used not to be regarded as employed in an area either if he or she was serving in the regular armed forces,[45] or in such other circumstance as the secretary of state or Welsh Ministers[46] may by order specify.[47] (This power has not been exercised.) For applications made on or after 1 December 2008, a person serving as a member of the regular armed forces is regarded as employed so as to give rise to a local connection.[48]

Family associations

7.26 There is no statutory definition of the phrase 'family associations'. The English Code of Guidance[49] suggests that, in addition to parents, adult children or siblings, it may include associations with family members such as step-parents, grandparents, grandchildren, aunts or uncles 'provided there are sufficiently close links in the form of frequent contact, commitment or dependency'. This goes further than the Local Authority Agreement which suggests that it arises where an applicant or a member of the applicant's household has parents, adult children, brothers or sisters currently residing in the area in question.[50]

45 HA 1996 s199(2). This subsection was repealed with effect from 1 December 2008: Housing and Regeneration Act 2008 s315(a), s321(1) and Sch 16, and Housing and Regeneration Act 2008 (Commencement No 2 and Transitional, Saving and Transitory Provisions) Order 2008 SI No 3068.

46 See H(W)A 2014 s81(4)(a).

47 HA 1996 s199(5).

48 Housing and Regeneration Act 2008 s315(a), s321(1) and Sch 16 and Housing and Regeneration Act 2008 (Commencement No 2 and Transitional, Saving and Transitory Provisions) Order 2008 SI No 3068. See also para 7.18. See Welsh Code para.18.11.

49 Code para 18.10. The Welsh Code does not comment on this matter.

50 Local Authority Agreement para 4.1(ii). It continues that 'only in exceptional circumstances would the residence of relatives other than those listed above be taken to establish a local connection'.

7.27 In *Avdic*,[51] a claim based on a first cousin once removed was insufficient. The decision is not, however, to be interpreted as limiting family associations to those mentioned in the Agreement: see *Ozbek*,[52] where it was said that the character of the family association was a least as relevant – if not more relevant – than the degree of consanguinity.[53] In that case, the applicants sought to establish their local connection with the borough to which they had applied through brothers who had lived in the area for only 18 months, and cousins and other extended family members who had lived there for over five years. The relevant question for the authority in these circumstance was 'whether, in the particular circumstances of the individual case, the bond between the applicant and one or more members of the extended family was of such a nature that it would be appropriate to regard those members of the extended family as "near relatives" in the sense in which that concept is recognised in [the Local Authority Agreement]'.[54] The authority had correctly asked itself this question in reaching its conclusion that there was no local connection.

7.28 The Local Authority Agreement continues by saying that the relatives must have been resident for a period of at least five years and that the applicant must indicate a wish to be near them.[55] It also says that an applicant who objects to being referred to an area on account of family associations should not be so referred.[56]

7.29 Once family association has been raised by the applicant, the authority should address the issue. A decision letter which failed to do so after the issue had been raised was held to be defective in *Khan*[57] (because it appeared from the letter that only residence had been addressed).

51 *R v Hammersmith and Fulham LBC ex p Avdic* (1996) 28 HLR 897, QBD; (1998) 30 HLR 1, CA.

52 *Ozbek v Ispwich BC* [2006] EWCA Civ 534, [2006] HLR 41. This is now reflected in the Code of Guidance, see previous para. See also the first instance decision of *Munting v Fulham LBC* [1998] JHL D91, where the authority had wrongly concluded that a step-father could not be a close relative.

53 At [64].

54 At [49].

55 Local Authority Agreement para 4.1(ii).

56 Local Authority Agreement para 4.1(ii), but compare, *R v McCall and others ex p Eastbourne BC*, unreported, but referred to at (1981) 8 HLR 48, QBD, in which it was observed that though the applicant's wishes are relevant, where other factors are equally balanced, they cannot override the words of the statute.

57 *R v Slough BC ex p Khan* (1995) 27 HLR 492, QBD.

Other special circumstances

7.30 'Other special circumstances' is a phrase likewise left undefined in HA 1996 Part 7 or H(W)A 2014 Part 2. The English Code[58] suggests as an example the need to be near special medical or support services which are only available in a particular district. The Welsh Code suggests that young adults leaving the care system should be considered to have a local connection either to their original area of residence or to the area where they were placed.[59] The Local Authority Agreement mentions[60] those who have been in prison or in hospital or those who wish to return to an area where they were brought up or had lived for a considerable length of time in the past. It stresses that an authority must exercise its discretion when considering whether special circumstances apply.

7.31 In *Smith and Hay*,[61] one of the families attempted to place some reliance on membership of an evangelical church, around which their lives revolved. Following *Betts* (see para 7.11) – which held that the fundamental test is whether or not there is a local connection – the authority had not erred in concluding as a matter of fact that this association did not amount to a special circumstance giving rise to a local connection in their case. Nor does a mere desire not to return to an area with which the applicant has a local connection amount to a special circumstance giving rise to a local connection with a different area: *Adigun*.[62]

7.32 It has been suggested that family associations too weak to qualify under HA 1996 s199(1)(c) cannot amount to a special circumstance under this subsection: see *Khan* and *Avdic*.[63] This also seems too rigid. If a connection of importance exists, which could be based on what might also be described as a weak family association, it should not automatically rule out qualification as a special circumstance. Indeed, it would seem that if the exclusion of a range of family members from qualification as family association is correct, this category ought to be capable of catching it. That is not to say that a mere distant relation would automatically qualify as a connection under this

58 Code of Guidance para 18.10; the Welsh Code does not comment on this.

59 Welsh Code para 18.9.

60 Local Authority Agreement para 4.1(iii).

61 *R v Vale of White Horse DC ex p Smith and Hay* (1984) 17 HLR 160, QBD. See also *R v Westminster City Council ex p Benniche* (1996) 29 HLR 230, CA.

62 *R v Islington LBC ex p Adigun* (1986) 20 HLR 600, QBD.

63 *R v Slough BC ex p Khan* (1995) 27 HLR 492, QBD; *R v Hammersmith and Fulham LBC ex p Avdic* (1996) 28 HLR 897, QBD; (1998) 30 HLR 1, CA.

head but, if the connection is of particular significance, nor should it automatically be disqualified.

Former asylum-seekers

7.33 In *Al-ameri*,[64] the House of Lords held that a former asylum-seeker who subsequently applied as homeless did not have a local connection with the area in which he had been provided with accommodation by the National Asylum Support Service (NASS),[65] because residence in that accommodation was not 'of choice'.[66] HA 1996 Part 7 was amended by Asylum and Immigration (Treatment of Claimants, etc) Act 2004 s11 to reverse this.[67] The H(W)A 2014 adopted the same approach.[68]

7.34 By HA 1996 s199(6), (7) and H(W)A 2014 s81(5), (6), a person has a local connection with an authority's district if s/he was at any time provided with accommodation in that district under Immigration and Asylum Act 1999 s95[69] unless:

a) the applicant was subsequently provided with accommodation under section 95 in another authority's district; or
b) the accommodation was provided in an accommodation centre under Nationality, Immigration and Asylum Act 2002 s22.[70]

7.35 The amendments apply only to accommodation provided by UKVI in England or Wales.[71] Accordingly, a former asylum-seeker who has been housed by UKVI in Scotland will not have a local connection in the district where the accommodation was provided.

64 *Al-ameri v Kensington and Chelsea RLBC; Osmani v Harrow LBC* [2004] UKHL 4, [2004] HLR 20.

65 Now UKVI, as it has been since 2013. Between 2008 and 2013, the UKBA dealt with such matters. Asylum support was previously administered by the NASS which was part of the Home Office.

66 See paras 7.17–7.22.

67 Given the statutory amendment, the absence of support from family and friends in the area in which an asylum-seeker has been housed by UKBA does not provide sufficient reason for an authority to decide against making a referral which it is otherwise entitled to make: *Ozbek v Ispwich BC* [2006] EWCA Civ 534, [2006] HLR 41.

68 H(W)A 2014 s81(5), (6), in the same terms as HA 1996 s199(6), (7); Welsh Code paras18.16–18.18.

69 See further paras 13.27–13.39, on the provision of accommodation by UKVI under this section.

70 This provision has not yet been brought into force.

71 See paras 13.27–13.39.

7.36 In those circumstances – where a former asylum-seeker who has been housed by UKVI in Scotland[72] applies to an authority in England[73], and has no local connection with the authority to which he or she has applied nor any with an authority in Scotland – the principal housing duty under section 193[74] is disapplied.[75] Instead, the local authority has a discretion to secure accommodation for a reasonable period and may provide advice and assistance.[76]

When are the local connection provisions applicable?

7.37 The local connection provisions exempt an authority from duties under HA 1996 s193 and H(W)A 2014 s73, ie, the responsibility for securing that housing is made available. They do not affect the provision of temporary accommodation for a person who is homeless and in priority need, but whom the authority to which application has been made has determined is homeless intentionally.[77]

7.38 It has been held that the local connection provisions are not applicable when the authority's duty arises because of threatened homelessness under HA 1996 s195(2). In *Williams v Exeter City Council*,[78] a woman was occupying army property let to her husband, a serviceman, in the Exeter area. As such, she had no connection with Exeter on the basis of residence of choice,[79] nor on any other ground. The Ministry of Defence secured an order for possession against her and, before it was executed, she applied to the authority.

72 Other than in an accommodation centre under Nationality, Immigration and Asylum Act 2002 s22. This provision has not yet been brought into force.

73 The position appears to be different in Wales. The Asylum and Immigration (Treatment of Claimants, etc) Act 2004 s11 has not been amended in the light of the H(W)A 2014, so that the disapplication provisions do not apply to Wales, with the effect that a former asylum-seeker who was housed in Scotland is potentially entitled to the full range of services and support if he or she applies to a Welsh local housing authority.

74 See paras 10.109–10.119.

75 Asylum and Immigration (Treatment of Claimants, etc) Act 2004 s11(2), (3)(a).

76 Asylum and Immigration (Treatment of Claimants, etc) Act 2004 s11(3)(b). This discretion is framed in the same terms as the duty towards the intentionally homeless; see para 10.54.

77 HA 1996 s198(1); *Delahaye v Oswestry BC* (1980) *Times* 28 July, QBD; H(W)A 2014 s80(1); Welsh Code para 18.3.

78 *Williams v Exeter City Council* September 1981 *LAG Bulletin* 211.

79 Under the provisions at that time: see now para 7.18.

7.39 The authority agreed that she was threatened with homelessness but referred her case to East Devon DC. As the applicant did not wish to leave the area, she challenged this decision: it was held that the local connection provisions applied only once the duty arose under HA 1985 s65(2) (now HA 1996 s193), not under s195(2), ie once she was actually homeless. It is unclear from the short report, however, whether the authority could have used the local connection provisions once actual homelessness occurred, or whether what was being held was that the structure of the provisions implies that if a decision is made while the applicant is still only threatened with homelessness, the local connection provisions will remain irrelevant once it does so: the former construction seems more likely.

7.40 An authority will be entitled to rely on the local connection provisions when it is:

a) satisfied that the applicant is homeless and in priority need;
b) not satisfied that the applicant became homeless intentionally; and
c) of the opinion that the conditions for referral apply.[80]

7.41 The conditions are that:

a) neither the applicant nor any person who might reasonably be expected to reside with the applicant has a local connection with their area; and
b) the applicant or a person who might reasonably be expected to reside with the applicant does have a local connection with the area of another housing authority; and
c) neither the applicant nor any person who might reasonably be expected to reside with the applicant will run the risk of domestic violence[81] in that other authority's area.[82]

7.42 Nor are the conditions met if the applicant or any person who might reasonably be expected to reside with the applicant has suffered non-domestic violence (in Wales, non-domestic abuse) in the authority's area, and it is probable that the return to the area will lead to further violence (or abuse) of a similar kind against the victim.[83]

80 HA 1996 s198(1); H(W)A 2014 s80(1).

81 In Wales, 'domestic abuse': H(W)A 2014 s80(3)(c). The difference in wording does not appear to make any substantive difference, see footnote 8, above.

82 HA 1996 s198(2); H(W)A 2014 s80(3). On the meaning of 'domestic violence' see Supplementary Guidance on Domestic Abuse and Homelessness, DCLG, November 2014, endorsing the broad approach taken in *Yemshaw v Hounslow* LBC [2011] UKSC 3, [2011] HLR 16.

83 HA 1996 s198(2A); H(W)A 2014 s80(4); see also footnotes 8, 81, above.

7.43 For the purposes of HA 1996 s198, 'violence' is not confined to actual physical violence but can include physical violence, threats, intimidating behaviour and any other form of abuse which, directly or indirectly, may give rise to a risk of harm.[84] For the purposes of H(W)A 2014 s80, 'abuse' is similarly defined to include physical violence, threatening or intimidating behaviour and any other form of abuse which, directly or indirectly, may give rise to the risk of harm.[85]

7.44 It is clear that all criteria must be satisfied. There must be:

a) no local connection with the one area; *and*
b) a local connection with the other area; *and*
c) no risk of domestic violence/abuse; *and*
d) no risk of non-domestic violence/abuse.

7.45 Thus, the procedure is unavailable if there is a local connection with the area to which application has been made, but the authority is of the opinion that the applicant has a greater or closer local connection elsewhere.[86] This was one of the mischiefs which H(HP)A 1977 was intended to end.[87]

7.46 The decision to make enquiries into local connection, and, therefore, whether or not to refer, is discretionary and, as such, may be vulnerable to challenge if exercised unreasonably.[88] Given the discretionary nature of the exercise, however, authorities are under no obligation to investigate local connection, even where the applicant indicates that he or she wishes to live in another area.[89]

7.47 In *Tower Hamlets*,[90] a decision by Newham LBC to refer an applicant to Tower Hamlets LBC was quashed. The referral concerned a Bangladeshi man who had originally applied to Tower Hamlets LBC

84 *Yemshaw v Hounslow LBC* [2011] UKSC 3, [2011] HLR 16 and *Waltham Forest LBC v Hussein* [2015] EWCA Civ 14, [2015] HLR 16, overruling *Danesh v Kensington and Chelsea RLBC* [2006] EWCA Civ 1404, [2007] HLR 17. See para 4.83.

85 H(W)A 2014 s56; Welsh Code paras 18.20–18.21.

86 See *Re Betts* [1983] 2 AC 613, (1983) 10 HLR 97, HL; the House of Lords did not overrule the Court of Appeal on this point. See also Welsh Code para 18.10.

87 See chapter 1.

88 HA 1996 s184(2). *R v Newham LBC ex p Tower Hamlets LBC* (1990) 23 HLR 62, CA; *Ozbek v Ispwich BC* [2006] EWCA Civ 534, [2006] HLR 41. See also *R v East Devon DC ex p Robb* (1997) 30 HLR 922, QBD, where the authority failed to consider whether it had a discretion to refer the applicant.

89 *Hackney LBC v Sareen* [2003] EWCA Civ 351, [2003] HLR 54.

90 *R v Newham LBC ex p Tower Hamlets LBC*, above, CA. See also Local Authority Agreement para 3.4, advising on this decision.

for housing but was found to be intentionally homeless. He subsequently applied to Newham LBC who found him not to be intentionally homeless. In reaching its decision, Newham LBC made a comparison between the housing conditions in Bangladesh and housing conditions in its own area. The Court of Appeal decided that a referring authority must satisfy itself that the applicant was homeless, in priority need and not intentionally homeless, but that if a finding of non-intentionality was flawed, to the extent that in appropriate judicial review proceedings it would have been quashed, the decision could not form a proper foundation for referral. Newham LBC's decision in the case was flawed because it had failed to take account of the general circumstances prevailing in relation to housing in Tower Hamlets LBC.

7.48 The circumstances in which a person runs the risk of domestic violence or non-domestic violence are the same as those considered in relation to whether or not it would have been reasonable – on this ground – to continue to occupy accommodation, pursuant to HA 1996 s177.[91] The authority is under a positive duty to enquire whether the applicant is subject to such a risk.[92]

7.49 One point which may be made here relates to the interaction with intentional homelessness. It is not uncommon for women not merely to leave home on account of domestic violence, but to want to leave the area. Some authorities who find that a person in these circumstances is not homeless intentionally will nonetheless seek to refer her back. It is true that there is no necessary conflict between finding that a woman is homeless (perhaps on account of the domestic violence) and finding that she will not run the risk of domestic violence in the area from which she has fled; an authority could take the view that while domestic violence drove her out, the risk is no longer present: nonetheless, it is a relatively fine distinction, for which there needs to be a material basis, and to refer her back without reaching the conclusion that this distinction may properly be drawn (which necessarily imports the requirement that there is a foundation for it) will be a bad decision in law.

7.50 In *Browne*,[93] which for these purposes and on this issue may be treated as if a local connection case,[94] the authority had not found intentional homelessness, but appeared to have addressed itself

91 HA 1996 s198(3); H(W)A 2014 s57; see paras 4.82–4.92.

92 *Patterson v Greenwich LBC* (1993) 26 HLR 159, CA.

93 *R v Bristol City Council ex p Browne* [1979] 1 WLR 1437, DC.

94 See para 10.128.

expressly to the point made in the last paragraph. In *Adigun*,[95] it was stressed that the task of determining whether or not there was a risk of domestic violence is one for the local authority: so long as there was material on which it could base its decision, the court would not intervene.

7.51 Although it is lawful for an authority to have a policy about how it proposes to exercise its discretion, it cannot decide in advance that every applicant who qualifies for referral should be referred: *Carter*.[96]

7.52 If a person has no local connection with any housing authority in England, Wales or Scotland, he or she will be entitled to housing from the authority to which the application has been made.[97]

England: additional application of provisions

7.53 By HA 1996 s198(4), the conditions for referral are deemed to be fulfilled – regardless, therefore, of local connection with the authority to which the application was made (on any of the foregoing grounds), and regardless of risk of domestic or other violence – if:

a) the applicant was placed by another authority[98] in accommodation in the area of the authority to which the application has been made;
b) in discharge of its functions under HA 1996 Part 7 or H(W)A 2014 Part 2;
c) within such period as may be prescribed.

7.54 The relevant period is five years from the date of the placement, plus the time between the date the application was initially made to the time of the first placement in the area of the authority to which the application has now been made.[99]

95 *R v Islington LBC ex p Adigun* (1986) 20 HLR 600, QBD. See also *R v Newham LBC ex p Smith* (1996) 29 HLR 213, QBD.

96 *R v Harrow LBC ex p Carter* (1992) 26 HLR 32, QBD.

97 *R v Hillingdon LBC ex p Streeting (No 2)* [1980] 1 WLR 1425, CA. Although note the limitations in relation to former asylum-seekers at para 7.33

98 Including a Welsh authority, see HA 1996 s198(4A), added by H(W)A 2014 Sch 3 para 11.

99 Allocation of Housing and Homelessness (Miscellaneous Provisions) (England) Regulations 2006 SI No 2527.

7.55 In relation to eligible asylum-seekers[100] in England, the provisions are amended to permit a referral in any case where another authority has agreed to accept the referral and there is no risk of violence.[101]

7.56 From 9 November 2012, when the Localism Act (LA) 2011 s149(6) came into force in England,[102] the conditions for referral are also met (in England) if the applicant had accepted a private sector offer of accommodation[103] from another authority, in the area of the authority to which the application has now been made, within the previous two years and neither the applicant nor anyone who might reasonably be expected to reside with the applicant runs the risk of domestic violence in the district of that other authority.[104] As this only applies where the private sector offer had been made before – and the duty to secure accommodation was still in existence at – that date,[105] it can now only apply to an application made before 9 November 2014 and still undetermined.

7.57 Once the Homelessness Reduction Act (HRA) 2017 is brought into force, there are also additional provisions governing those towards whom a social services authority[106] in England has a duty under Children Act (CA) 1989 s23C,[107] as a former relevant child.[108] So long as an authority in England has such a duty, then, if the authority is a local housing authority as well as a social services authority[109] the former relevant child is deemed to have a local connection with its area, and if the authority is not a local housing authority,[110] with every district in its area.

7.58 Further, where accommodation for a child in care has been provided under CA 1989 s22A,[111] so that the child is normally resident

100 See paras 3.138–3.142.

101 Homelessness (Asylum-seekers) (Interim Period) (England) Order 1999 SI No 3126.

102 Localism Act 2011 (Commencement No 2 and Transitional Provisions) (England) Order 2012 SI No 2599 article 2.

103 See paras 10.199–10.204.

104 HA 1996 s198(2ZA), added by LA 2011 s149(6).

105 Localism Act 2011 (Commencement No 2 and Transitional Provisions) (England) Order 2012 SI No 2599 article 3.

106 See para 13.59.

107 See paras 13.74–13.86.

108 HRA 2017 s8; HA 1996 s199(8), as added.

109 Which will mean all London Boroughs and the Common Council of the City of London, all unitary authorities and all district councils in metropolitan areas.

110 Ie county council in non-metropolitan areas.

111 See para 13.74.

in the district of a local housing authority for a continuous period of at all least two years, some or all of which falls before he or she turns 16, he or she is likewise deemed to have a local connection with that district,[112] although ceases to do so once he or she turns 21 unless a local connection can be established on any of the other grounds for it.[113]

Procedure on prospective reference

7.59 The obligation to house passes to the notified authority[114] when the conditions for referral[115] are – or are deemed to be[116] – fulfilled.[117] The duty to make all preliminary enquiries into:

a) homelessness;
b) priority need; and
c) intentional homelessness

lies on the authority to which application is made.[118] This is so even if it becomes apparent that the local connection provisions may apply,[119] and even if the homeless person has already applied to the other authority and been rejected by it as homeless intentionally.[120]

7.60 Furthermore, even if the notified authority has already made a previous, different decision, it will be bound by the decision arising on the new application to the notifying authority. This leads to what has been described as a 'merry-go-round',[121] in which a person may apply to authority A, be found homeless intentionally, move across to the area of authority B, make a new application, be found homeless

112 HRA 2017 s8; HA 1996 s199(9), as added.

113 HRA 2017 s8; HA 1996 s199(10), as added.

114 Which may include a Scottish local authority: under Housing (Scotland) Act 1987: HA 1996 ss201, 217.

115 See para 7.46.

116 Under HA 1996 s198(4): see paras 7.53–7.57.

117 HA 1996 s200(2); H(W)A 2014 s82(4). They apply to referrals by a local authority in Scotland under the provisions of Housing (Scotland) Act 1987 ss33, 34: HA 1996 s201.

118 HA 1996 s194; H(W)A 2014 s82(1); Welsh Code para.18.3.

119 *Delahaye v Oswestry BC* (1980) *Times* 29 July, QBD.

120 *R v Slough BC ex p Ealing LBC* [1981] QB 801, CA, but see *R v Newham LBC ex p Tower Hamlets LBC* (1990) 23 HLR 62, CA.

121 *R v Slough BC ex p Ealing LBC*, above.

unintentionally and then be referred back for permanent housing to authority A.[122]

7.61 A referral under HA 1996 s198 (or H(W)A 2014 s80) gives rise to a new section 193 (or H(W)A 2014 s73) duty, so that if an applicant applies to authority A, is not found homeless intentionally but rejects its offer of accommodation, and then applies to authority B which refers the applicant back to authority A, authority A cannot rely on its earlier offer.[123]

7.62 An authority that finds an applicant homeless intentionally but wrongly refers the applicant to another authority is not bound by its error; the erroneous reference may simply be ignored: just because the local connection provisions are inapplicable if there is intentionality, it does not follow that the erroneous referral in some way nullifies the intentionality decision.[124]

7.63 Until the completion of enquiries, the applicant will have been housed under HA 1996 s188 or H(W)A 2014 s68.[125] This duty arises irrespective of local connection.[126]

7.64 If the authority concludes that the applicant is homeless, in priority need and has not become homeless intentionally, but decides to enquire into local connection[127] and to make a referral by notifying another authority of the application under HA 1996 s198(1), it must notify the applicant of this and of its reasons.[128] Pending resolution of the issue, it is the duty of the notifying authority to continue to secure that accommodation is available for the applicant and the applicant's family until he or she is notified of the outcome of the referral.[129]

122 *R v Slough BC ex p Ealing LBC*, above.

123 *R v Tower Hamlets LBC ex p Ali; R v Tower Hamlets LBC ex p Bibi* (1992) 25 HLR 158, CA (overruling *R v Hammersmith and Fulham LBC ex p O'Brian* (1985) 17 HLR 471, QBD on this point).

124 This is consistent with the approach and decision in *Crawley BC v B* (2000) 32 HLR 636, CA: see paras 9.127–9.129.

125 See paras 10.8–10.24.

126 HA 1996 s188(2); H(W)A 2014 s68(2).

127 In its discretion, cf HA 1996 s184(2); H(W)A 2014 s80(2).

128 HA 1996 s184(4); H(W)A 2014 s84. In the usual way, notices must be in writing and, if not received by the applicant, are treated as given if made available at the authority's office for a reasonable period for collection by him or her or on his or her behalf: HA 1996 s194(6).

129 HA 1996 s200(1); H(WA) 2014 s82(1). The duty is not, however, under either HA 1996 s188 (pending enquiries) or s193 (principal duty), each of which ceases, but under s200(1) itself. Once HRA 2017 comes into force, its s5(10) adds a s200(1A) that no notification of a referral, which is what activating s200(1), may be given unless any initial help duty on the part of the authority under s189B(2) has come to an end. This is difficult to understand as, by

So long as it remains under a duty towards the applicant, whether to accommodate pending enquiries or pending resolution of a local connection referral, the notifying authority also has duties in relation to the protection of the applicant's property.[130]

7.65 The law applicable to the provision of temporary accommodation under other provisions of HA 1996 Part 7 is considered in chapter 10, and will be applicable to temporary accommodation to those potentially (pending enquiries) or actually to be referred to another authority (pending resolution of any dispute): see the observations on quality (paras 10.19–10.22) and termination made in relation to accommodation pending decision (paras 10.17–10.32), those on availability (para 10.8), payment (para 10.12) and security (para 10.15), exclusion from Protection from Eviction Act 1977 (para 10.16) and defences on eviction (para 10.17). How accommodation may be provided,[131] suitability[132] and the constraints on out-of-area placements,[133] which are all considered in chapter 10 in relation to the principal housing duty under HA 1996 s193 and H(W)A 2014 s75, also apply to discharge under this section.

7.66 Where the authority to which the applicant is referred accepts the referral, the discussion in chapter 10 relating to unintentionally homeless applicants will apply.[134]

7.67 If a local connection referral results in the transfer of the applicant to another authority, which had made an earlier offer under HA 1996 s193, then – assuming that the earlier offer was sustainable as a discharge of duties[135] – the applicant will be entitled to a further offer; moreover, if the authority to which the applicant is referred had earlier found that he or she was homeless intentionally, so that no earlier section 193 offer was made, it will nonetheless usually be bound by the finding of unintentionality made by the second authority and

s189B(2), the duty for which it provides does not arise if the authority refers the application to another authority; see also HA 1996 s198(A1), when added by HRA 2017 s5(8), talks of a referral when the authority 'would be' under a s189B(2) duty; and s199A(1), when added by HRA 2017 s5(9), says that when an authority notifies another authority that it intends to refer or has referred – the same wording as in s200(1) – it is not subject to a s189B duty.

130 HA 1996 s211(2); H(W)A 2014 s93; see chapter 8.

131 See paras 10.121–10.133.

132 See paras 10.145–10.177.

133 See para 10.136.

134 See para 10.108.

135 See chapter 10.

will accordingly now be required to ensure that suitable accommodation is made available.[136]

Initial help duty

7.68 Once HRA 2017 comes into force in England, a new initial help duty is introduced for the homeless who are eligible for assistance (regardless of priority need or intentionality): paras 10.66–10.74. The HRA 2017 provisions are similar to those already in force in Wales in H(W)A 2014.[137] If the authority to which applicant is made would be subject to the initial help duty, but considers that the conditions for referral are met, it will not be subject to the initial help duty,[138] but may instead notify the other authority of its opinion, in which case it ceases to be under any HA 1996 s188 temporary duty pending enquiries for applicants whom the authority has reason to believe may be in priority need,[139] is instead subject to the same duty under HA 1996 s199A(2) to secure that accommodation is available until the applicant is notified of the decision as to whether the conditions for referral are met,[140] regardless of whether there is a request for a review, although the authority has a discretion to continue it pending the decision on review.[141]

7.69 Once it has been decided whether the conditions for referral are met, the notifying authority must give the applicant notice of the decision and its reasons and must inform him or her of his or her right to request a review of the decision[142] and of the time within which such a request must be made.[143]

7.70 If it is decided that the conditions for referral are not met, the notifying authority is subject to the initial help duty[144] and, if the authority has reason to believe that the applicant has a priority need, it must secure that accommodation is available for occupation by the

136 See paras 9.157–9.160.

137 H(W)A 2014 s73, and see paras 10.74–10.76.

138 HRA 2017 s5; HA 1996 ss189B(2), 199A(1). In Wales, H(W)A 2014 s73.

139 HRA 2017 s5(8); HA 1996 s198(A1). In Wales, H(W)A 2014 s73(2).

140 HRA 2017 s5(9); HA 1996 s199A(2). In Wales, H(W)A 2014 s82(1).

141 HRA 2017 s5(9); HA 1996 s199A(6). In Wales, H(W)A 2014 s82(6).

142 See paras 9.149–9.161.

143 HRA 2017 s5(9); HA 1996 s199A(3). In Wales, H(W)A 2014 ss82(2) and 84.

144 HRA 2017 s5(9); HA 1996 s199A(4). The references in HA 1996 s189B(4) and (7) – in the context of the duty being brought to an end – to dates when the authority is first satisfied as to the s189B criteria (paras 10.66–10.67) are to be read as references to the day on which notice is given under s199A(3): ibid. In Wales, see H(W)A 2014 s82(3).

applicant until the later of when the HA 1996 s189B duty itself comes to an end (paras 10.68–10.74) or when the authority decides what other duty (if any) it owes the applicant under HA 1996 Part 7 following the duty under s189B,[145] regardless of whether there is a request for a review, although the authority has a discretion to continue it pending the decision on review.[146]

7.71 If it is decided that the conditions for referral are met, then the applicant is treated as having made an application to the notified authority on the date on which he or she was given notice of the decision (para 7.69), from which date the notifying authority owes no duties under HA 1996 Part 7 and the notified authority is bound by the decisions of the notifying authority as to eligibility, homelessness and intentionality unless satisfied that the applicant's circumstances have changed or that further information has come to light since the notifying authority made its decision, which change in circumstances or further information justifies a different decision.[147] In substance, this embodies the case-law on re-applications.[148] In addition, the notifying authority must give the notified authority copies of any notifications that it gave the applicant as to its assessment of his or her case (paras 10.42, 10.45).[149]

7.72 Notices under these provisions, if not received by the applicant, are to be treated as having been given if made available at the authority's office for a reasonable period for collection by or on behalf of the applicant:[150] see also para 9.146.

Resolution of disputes

7.73 The question whether the conditions for referral of an application[151] are satisfied is to be determined by agreement between the notifying authority and the notified authority or, in default of agreement, in accordance with such arrangements as the secretary of state or Welsh Ministers

145 HRA 2017 s5(9); HA 1996 s199A(4). For the position in Wales, see para 10.76 for the circumstances in which the initial help duty may be brought to an end.

146 HRA 2017 s5(9); HA 1996 s199A(6).

147 HRA 2017 s5(9); HA 1996 s199A(5). In Wales, the authority to which the applicant has been referred becomes subject to the initial help duty: H(W)A 2014 s82(4).

148 Paras 9.23–9.35. See also paras 7.60, 7.61, 7.67.

149 HRA 2017 s5(9); HA 1996 s199A(5). There is no equivalent in Wales.

150 HRA 2017 s5(9); HA 1996 s199A(7). In Wales, see H(W)A 2014 s84.

151 See para 7.46.

may order by statutory instrument.[152] 'Arrangements' are those agreed by the authorities, or by associations of authorities, or in default of agreement such as appears to the secretary of state and/or Welsh Ministers to be suitable, after consultation with the local authority associations and such other persons as he or she thinks appropriate.[153]

7.74 The current arrangements are to be found in the Homelessness (Decisions on Referrals) Order 1998[154] and the agreement reached by the Association of London Government (ALG), the Convention of Scottish Local Authorities (CoSLA), the Local Government Association (LGA) and the Welsh Local Government Association (WLGA) in 2006 – the Local Authority Agreement.

Local Authority Agreement

7.75 The substantive provisions of the Local Authority Agreement in relation to the four grounds for local connections have been noted above. The Local Authority Agreement reminds authorities that, if there is any local connection with the area of the authority to which application is made, the local connection provisions will not be relevant, even though the household may have a greater local connection elsewhere. The degree of local connection is irrelevant except where an applicant has no local connection with the notifying authority but does have a local connection with more than one other local authority.[155]

7.76 The authority to which application has been made is urged to investigate all circumstances with the same thoroughness that it would use if it did not have it in mind to refer the application to another authority. These enquiries may be of another authority, one

152 HA 1996 s198(5), (5A) (added by H(W)A 2014 Sch 3 para 11); H(W)A 2014 s80(5). This applies only to disputes about whether the applicant has a local connection. If an authority wishes to challenge a referral, eg because it believes the applicant should have been found intentionally homeless, it must do so by judicial review. In the absence of such a challenge, the authority cannot simply reject the referral: *R (Bantamagbari) v Westminster City Council* [2003] EWHC 1350 (Admin), [2003] JHL D70.

153 HA 1996 s198(6); H(W)A 2014 s80(6).

154 SI No 1578. There is no order that directly deals with referrals to Scotland. See, however, the Homelessness (Decisions on Referrals) (Scotland) Order 1998 SI No 1603, made under Housing (Scotland) Act 1987 s33 and Local Authority Agreement para 10.8, which provides for the appointment of a referee to be by CoSLA where the notified authority is in Scotland (in the case of referrals from England or Wales) and by the LGA where the referral is from Scotland to England or Wales.

155 Local Authority Agreement para 4.11.

to which it may be making a referral, and such enquiries should be made as soon as possible.[156]

7.77 Where an applicant has a local connection with a number of authorities, the Local Authority Agreement says that the notifying authority should weigh up all relevant factors.[157] The English Code of Guidance[158] suggests that the wishes of the applicant should be taken into account in deciding which authority to notify.

7.78 In *McCall*,[159] it was held that, although an arbitrator[160] will not – without the consent of the authorities – usually be entitled to apply the criteria set out in the Local Authority Agreement, it is proper for him or her to have regard to the wishes of the applicant if issues are evenly balanced. Indeed, where all other considerations give no indication one way or another, the court described it as 'perfectly reasonable and perfectly sensible, and within the spirit of the statutory provisions', to have regard to the wishes of the family.

7.79 Under the terms of the Local Authority Agreement, each authority should nominate one person to receive notifications of referral from other authorities.[161] Unless it has clear evidence to the contrary, the notified authority should accept all statements of the facts of the case as stated by the notifying authority.[162]

7.80 If the notified authority provides new information which causes the notifying authority to want to reconsider questions of homelessness, priority need or intentionality, the position will be the same as in other reconsideration cases.[163] The Local Authority Agreement stresses that the disputes procedures should be used only where there is a disagreement over the existence of a local connection, not for resolving disagreement on any other matter, and that – once enquiries have been completed – a challenge to the notifying authority's decision that the applicant is eligible, homeless, in priority need and not intentionally homeless can only be made by judicial review.[164]

156 Local Authority Agreement para 5.1.

157 Local Authority Agreement para 4.11.

158 Code of Guidance para 18.14.

159 *R v McCall and others ex p Eastbourne BC*, unreported, but referred to at (1981) 8 HLR 48, QBD, in which it was observed that though the applicant's wishes are relevant, where other factors are equally balanced, they cannot override the words of the statute.

160 See paras 7.73–7.79.

161 Local Authority Agreement para 6.2.

162 Local Authority Agreement para 6.3.

163 See paras 9.123–9.129.

164 Local Authority Agreement para 5.5. See also chapter 12.

7.81 If the Local Authority Agreement resolves the issue, then the notified authority should, if it has accepted responsibility, provide accommodation for the applicant and the applicant's family immediately. Once the notified authority has accepted responsibility, it is liable to repay the notifying authority for expenses incurred in the provision of temporary accommodation, although if the notifying authority has delayed unduly[165] the notified authority need only reimburse it for expenses incurred since notification of the referral was received.[166]

Arbitration

7.82 Where a notified authority disputes the referral, it should set out its reasons in full within ten days.[167] If there is still no agreement, the authorities must seek, within 21 days of receipt of the referral, to agree on an arbitrator who will make the decision.[168] The LGA maintains an independent panel of persons – generally known as referees – for this purpose.[169] In default of agreement as to the referee, the authorities must jointly request the chairman of the LGA or his or her nominee (the proper officer) to appoint a person from the panel.[170] If an arbitrator has not been appointed within six weeks of the date of notification, the notifying authority must request the proper officer to appoint a referee from the panel.[171]

7.83 The referee must invite written representations from both the notifying and the notified authority.[172] The referee may also invite further written representations from the authorities, written representations from any other person[173] and oral representations from any person.[174]

165 Usually a period of more than 30 days from the date of initial application: Local Authority Agreement para 7.3.

166 Local Authority Agreement.

167 Local Authority Agreement para 10.2.

168 Homelessness (Decisions on Referrals) Order ('Homelessness Order') 1998 SI No 1578 Schedule paras 1 and 2.

169 Homelessness Order 1998 Schedule para 3.

170 Homelessness Order 1998 Schedule para 4(1).

171 Homelessness Order 1998 Schedule para 4(2).

172 Homelessness Order 1998 Schedule para 5(2).

173 Most obviously the applicant, who the Local Authority Agreement suggests (para 13.4), should be supplied with copies of the authorities' submissions. Representations may be made by someone, whether or not legally qualified, acting on behalf of the person invited to submit them: Homelessness Order 1998 Schedule para 5(4).

174 Homelessness Order 1998 Schedule para 5(3).

7.84 The Local Authority Agreement suggests[175] that, where an oral hearing is necessary or more convenient (for example, where the applicant is illiterate, where English is not the applicant's first language or where further information is necessary to resolve the dispute), the notifying authority should be invited to present its case first, followed by the notified authority and any other persons whom the referee wishes to hear. It is for the referee to arrange the venue, although it is suggested that the offices of the notifying authority will often be the most convenient location.[176] Where a person has made oral representations, the referee may direct that reasonable travelling expenses are paid by either or both authorities.[177]

7.85 It is not part of the referee's duties to enquire into matters preceding a local connection reference: homelessness, eligibility, priority need or intentional homelessness.[178]

7.86 The referee must notify both authorities of his or her decision and the reasons for it.[179] The Local Authority Agreement[180] suggests a target of one month for the decision, from receipt of the authorities' written submissions. There is no obligation on the referee to notify the applicant of his or her decision – that is the notifying authority's duty.[181]

7.87 The previous regulations[182] specifically provided that the decision of the referee was final and binding on the authorities. No such provision is included in the current regulations, although the Local Authority Agreement does state[183] that it is binding on the participating authorities, subject to the applicant's right to review.[184] Once a referee has made the determination, the referee should not reopen the case, even though facts may be presented to him or her, unless it is to rectify an error arising from a mistake or omission.[185] The proviso that the decision is final and binding on the authority does

175 Local Authority Agreement para 14.1.
176 Local Authority Agreement para 14.2.
177 Homelessness Order 1998 Schedule para 7(2).
178 *R v Slough BC ex p Ealing LBC* [1981] QB 801, CA.
179 Homelessness Order 1998 Schedule para 6.
180 Local Authority Agreement para 13.5.
181 HA 1996 s200(2); H(W)A 2014 s82(2).
182 Housing (Homeless Persons) (Appropriate Arrangements) Order 1978 SI No 69.
183 Local Authority Agreement para 15.1.
184 See para 9.149.
185 Local Authority Agreement para 19.1.

not, however, prevent challenge on the grounds that the decision is ultra vires.[186]

7.88 The notifying and notified authorities each pay their own costs of the determination.[187] Unlike the 1978 order,[188] there is no explicit discretion for the referee to make a costs order against either party. The Local Authority Agreement suggests,[189] however, that the referee's fees and expenses, and any third party costs, would usually be recovered from the unsuccessful party to the dispute, although the referee may choose to apportion expenses between the authorities if the referee considers it warranted.

Post-resolution procedure

7.89 If the resolution of the dispute results in the burden of housing lying on the notified authority, it is still the duty of the notifying authority to provide notification of the result and the reasons for it to the applicant.[190] The notification must also inform the applicant of the applicant's right to a review of whether the conditions[191] are met.[192] Notices under these provisions, if not received by the applicant, are to be treated as having been given if made available at the authority's office for a reasonable period for collection by or on behalf of the applicant:[193] see also para 9.146.

7.90 It is not entirely clear whether a review can encompass the 'decision' of the arbitrator. If it does, it would open the way to an applicant to appeal that decision to the county court on a point of law.[194]

7.91 If the burden of providing housing does not shift to the notified authority, it will remain with the notifying authority[195] and the principal housing duty under HA 1996 s193[196] will apply.[197]

186 See chapter 12.
187 Homelessness Order 1998 Schedule para 7(1).
188 Housing (Homeless Persons) (Appropriate Arrangements) Order 1978 SI No 69.
189 Local Authority Agreement para 18.3.
190 HA 1996 s200(2); H(W)A 2014 s82(2). See paras 9.142–9.148.
191 See para 7.46.
192 HA 1996 s202(1)(d); H(W)A 2014 s85(1)(c).
193 HA 1996 s200(6).
194 HA 1996 s204; H(W)A 2014 s88. See chapter 12.
195 HA 1996 s200(3); H(W)A 2014 s82(3).
196 In Wales, H(W)A 2014 s73.
197 See chapter 10.

7.92 The mere fact that an authority has unsuccessfully sought to shift the burden on to another authority is not a basis on which to alter the original decision that the applicant has not become homeless intentionally. If the duty does pass to the notified authority, it will (in the case of an English authority) be a HA 1996 s193 duty and (in Wales) be a duty under either H(W)A 2014 s68 or s73.[198]

198 Where an English authority refers to another English authority, see HA 1996 s200(4), added by H(W)A 2014 Sch 3 para 12; where an English authority refers to a Welsh authority, see H(W)A 2014 s83; where a Welsh authority refers to an English authority, see HA 1996 s201A, added by H(W)A 2014 Sch 3 para 13; and, where a Welsh authority refers to another Welsh authority, see H(W)A 2014 s82(4).

CHAPTER 8

Protection of property

8.1 Introduction

8.3 To whom is a duty owed?

8.5 When is the duty owed?

8.10 What is the duty?

8.19 The power to protect property

8.20 Notification of cessation of responsibility

Introduction

8.1 Both Housing Act (HA) 1996 Part 7 and Housing (Wales) Act (H(W)A) 2014 Part 2 make provision for local housing authorities to take steps to protect the property of homeless people. These provisions – which appeared in both the Housing (Homeless Persons) Act 1977 and the HA 1985 – are of considerable practical importance. Failure to take steps to protect the belongings of those who are homeless or threatened with homelessness can only have the effect of prolonging or worsening their economic position.

8.2 HA 1996 Part 7 and H(W)A 2014 Part 2 each contain:

a) a duty to protect property in some circumstances; and
b) a power to do so in others.

The discharge of this duty and the power[1] are not co-extensive with the discharge of housing duties and it is necessary, therefore, to consider these property provisions in their own right. Authorities do not necessarily have to discharge duties themselves, but can contract them out – this is discussed at the start of chapter 9.

To whom is a duty owed?

8.3 In England, the duty is owed[2] to an applicant towards whom the authority has become subject to a duty under one of the following provisions of the HA 1996:

a) section 188 – accommodation pending enquiries;
b) section 193 – full duty;
c) section 190 – temporary accommodation for the intentionally homeless in priority need;
d) section 195 – accommodation for those threatened with homelessness, in priority need and not so threatened intentionally; and
e) section 200 – accommodation for those who are or have been the subject of a local connection issue.

In addition, the duty is owed under to someone who is reasonably to be expected to reside with the applicant, ie, for whom housing must also be provided.[3] Once the Homelessness Reduction Act (HRA)

1 Both of which may be contracted out; see para 9.5.
2 HA 1996 s211(2).
3 HA 1996 s211(5).

2017 is brought into force, the property duty will also be owed where the authority has become subject to the initial duty to help under HA 1996 s189B (paras 10.66–10.74).[4]

8.4 In Wales, the duty is owed[5] to an applicant towards whom the authority has become subject to a duty under one of the following provisions of the H(W)A 2014:

a) section 66 – duty to prevent an applicant who is in priority need from becoming homeless;
b) section 68 – accommodation pending enquiries;
c) section 75 – full duty; and
d) section 82 – accommodation for those who are or have been the subject of a local connection issue.

In addition, the duty is also owed to someone who might reasonably be expected to reside with the applicant.[6]

When is the duty owed?

8.5 The duty is owed when the authority has reason to believe that:

a) by reason of the applicant's inability to protect or deal with it, there is a danger of loss of, or damage to, any personal property of the applicant, or other person to whom the duty is owed; and
b) no other suitable arrangements have been or are being made.[7]

'Danger' of loss or damage means a likelihood of harm, not merely a possibility.[8]

8.6 The duty continues until the authority is of the opinion that there is no longer any reason to believe that there is a danger of loss of, or damage to, that property by reason of the applicant's inability to protect or deal with it, or that of someone else to whom the duty is owed.[9]

8.7 The duty is owed not only when the authority is subject to one of the prescribed duties, but also when it has been so subject.[10] For example, a person may be evicted from accommodation, and subsequently held to be homeless intentionally. The former landlord may

4 HRA 2017 s5(12); HA 1996 s211(2), as amended.
5 H(W)A 2014 s93(2).
6 H(W)A 2014 s93(6).
7 HA 1996 s211(1); H(W)A 2014 s93(1).
8 *Deadman v Southwark LBC* (2001) 33 HLR 75, CA.
9 HA 1996 s212(3); H(W)A 2014 s94(6)).
10 HA 1996 s211(2); H(W)A 2014 s93(3).

have been willing to hold on to the person's property for a period of time. That period may be no longer than the period for which accommodation has been provided under HA 1996 s190(2)(a). If, after the expiry of section 190(2)(a) accommodation, the property duty has not expired, application may yet be made for assistance under section 211 and, if the relevant conditions are fulfilled, the authority will be obliged to provide that assistance.

8.8 Even when the property duty has expired, because the authority has formed the view that there is no further danger of loss of or damage to the property, or that the applicant is no longer unable to protect or deal with it, the authority has power to continue to protect that property.[11] Property may be kept in store, and the conditions on which it was taken into store will continue to have effect, with any necessary modifications.[12]

8.9 Both the English and Welsh Codes of Guidance illustrate inability to protect property with the example of a person who is ill or who cannot afford to have his or her property placed in store.[13] The English Code also suggests that a person could be deemed capable of taking back responsibility if the person is no longer ill, or has obtained accommodation, or is able to afford the cost of storage.[14]

What is the duty?

8.10 The duty is to take reasonable steps to prevent loss or prevent or mitigate damage to the property.[15] In order to discharge the duty, the authority has power of entry on to private property.[16] At all reasonable times, it may enter any premises which are 'the usual place of residence of the applicant or which were his last usual place of residence', and deal with the applicant's property in any way that is reasonably necessary, including by storing or arranging to store the property.[17]

11 HA 1996 s212(3); H(W)A 2014 s94(7).
12 HA 1996 s212(3); H(W)A 2014 s94(7).
13 Code of Guidance para 20.6; Welsh Code para 11.16.
14 Code of Guidance para 20.11; there is no equivalent example in the Welsh Code.
15 HA 1996 s211(2); H(W)A 2014 s93(1).
16 HA 1996 s212(1); H(W)A 2014 s94(1). Such provisions were also to be found in the National Assistance Act 1948 s48.
17 HA 1996 s212(1); H(W)A 2014 s94(1).Under H(W)A 2014 s94(2), where the authority proposes to exercise a power of entry, the officer it authorises to do so must, on request, produce valid documentation setting out the authorisation. A person who without reasonable excuse obstructs the exercise of the power of

8.11 The duty is owed in respect of 'personal property'. In *Roberts*,[18] there are dicta that suggest that this would not extend to equipment used by an applicant in his or her business, at any rate where the business is conducted other than at the accommodation.

8.12 The authority generally has responsibility for arranging storage. It may, however, refuse to exercise the duty, except on appropriate conditions.[19] This means such conditions as it considers appropriate in a particular case, and can include conditions empowering it:

a) to charge for discharge of the duty; and
b) to dispose of the property in respect of which it discharged the duty, in such circumstances as may be specified.[20]

8.13 Both the English and the Welsh Codes suggest[21] that the authority might dispose of the property if it loses touch with the person concerned and is unable to trace him or her after a specified period. Whether or not a charge is made or a duty to store exists, the authority must, as bailee of the property, take reasonable care of it, and deliver it up when reasonably requested to do so. Failure to do this will render the authority liable to damages, even if the failure to deliver up is accidental, albeit a negligent accident.[22] The standard of care is high, and the burden of disproving negligence when damage has resulted from an accident lies on the authority, as bailee.[23]

8.14 The position set out in the above paragraphs may, however, need to be considered in the light of Local Government (Miscellaneous Provisions) Act (LG(MP)A) 1982 s41. That section applies wherever property comes into the possession of a local authority, after being found on premises owned or managed by it, or property has been deposited with the local authority and is not collected from it in accordance with the terms on which it was deposited.

8.15 LG(MP)A 1982 s41 entitles the authority to give the owner or depositor of the property notice in writing that it requires him or her to collect the property by a date specified in the notice, and that if he or she does not do so the property will vest in the authority as from

entry commits an offence and, on summary conviction, is liable for a fine not exceeding level 4 on the standard scale (currently £2,500) (H(W)A 2014 s94(3)). There is no equivalent to either of these provisions in England.

18 *R v Chiltern DC ex p Roberts et al* (1990) 23 HLR 387, QBD.

19 HA 1996 s211(4); H(W)A 2014 s93(4).

20 HA 1996 s211(4); H(W)A 2014 s93(4).

21 Code of Guidance para 20.10; Welsh Code para 11.19.

22 *Mitchell v Ealing LBC* [1979] QB 1.

23 *Port Swettenham Authority v TW Wu & Co* [1979] AC 580, PC.

that date. If the person notified then fails to comply with the notice, the property does vest in the authority on that date.

8.16 The date to be specified is to be not less than one month from the date of the notice. When an authority finds property, as distinct from when property is deposited with it, and it appears to it that it is impossible to serve a notice, the property vests in it one month from the date when it so finds the property. In any other case, including deposit, when the authority is satisfied after reasonable enquiry that it is impossible to serve notice, the property vests in it six months after the property was deposited with it or six months from the date when the period from which the property was deposited with it expired, whichever is the later.

8.17 Perishable property, and property the continued storage of which would involve the authority in unreasonable expense or inconvenience, may, in any event, be sold or otherwise disposed of by the authority as it thinks fit. In such a case, the proceeds of sale vest in the authority on the same date as the property itself would have done were it not perishable or too inconvenient or expensive to store. If property is claimed by its owner prior to the date when it vests in the authority, the owner can collect it on payment to the authority of its costs in storing the property, and in making enquiries or carrying out any of the other steps referred to in this section.

8.18 There was no express reference in the LG(MP)A 1982 to the provisions of the Housing (Homeless Persons) Act 1977, nor (by way of amendment) to the HA 1985 nor HA 1996 Part 7 nor H(W)A 2014 Part 2. The courts may therefore consider that references to the LG(MP)A 1982 to 'property deposited' with the authority do not include property taken into safe-keeping under HA 1996 s211 or H(W)A 2014 s93. If so, the HA 1996 Part 7 (or H(W)A 2014 Part 2) provisions only will apply. Otherwise, the LG(MP)A 1982 makes it somewhat easier for authorities to limit the impact of their HA 1996 s211 or H(W)A 2014 s93 duties.

The power to protect property

8.19 The authority has power to take the identical steps to prevent loss of property, or to prevent or mitigate damage to it, as it is obliged to take under the duty described above, in any case where there is no duty to do so.[24] This power might benefit those not in priority

24 HA 1996 s211(3); H(W)A 2014 s93(5).

need of accommodation, and also those who, though in priority need of accommodation, are only threatened with homelessness, and in respect of whom no decision on intentionality has yet been taken. Where the authority exercises this power, it has the same ancillary powers as in relation to the duty – ie, entry into premises, imposing conditions, etc.

Notification of cessation of responsibility

8.20 When the authority considers that it no longer has a duty or a power to protect property, it is obliged to notify the person towards whom it was subject to the duty, or in relation to whose property it has exercised the power:

a) that it has ceased to be subject to the duty, or to enjoy the power; and
b) why it is of the opinion that the duty or power has come to an end.[25]

The notification must be by personal delivery to the person to be notified or by leaving it or sending it by post to his or her last known address.[26]

25 HA 1996 s212(4); H(W)A 2014 s94(8).
26 HA 1996 s212(5); H(W)A 2014 s94(9).

CHAPTER 9

Homelessness decisions

9.1 Introduction
9.3 Changes in law
9.4 Decision-making
9.6 Relationship between decision and review

9.9 Applications
9.9 Who can apply?
Generally • Qualifications
9.45 How to apply
9.46 Provision of accommodation on application

9.48 Enquiries
9.49 The duty to make enquiries
9.58 Who must make the enquiries?
9.62 Conduct of enquiries
9.66 Ambit of enquiries
Whose circumstances? • Burden of proof • Adequacy of enquiries • Reliance on particular circumstances • Medical evidence • Blanket policies • Loss of employment
9.112 Fairness
9.122 Doubt
9.123 Further enquiries and reconsideration
9.130 Time-scales

9.132 Decisions
9.132 Postponement

continued

9.135 Gatekeeping
9.136 Material to be taken into account
9.140 Own decision
9.142 Notification
Reasons • Local connection • Review • Relationship of notification duty and substantive duty • Written notification • Restricted cases • Oral explanation

9.149 Review
9.151 Eligibility
9.152 Duties
9.154 Local connection
9.157 Suitability and availability of offers
9.160 Further review

9.162 Review procedure
9.165 Identity of the reviewer
Local connection reviews
9.174 Impact of the Human Rights Act 1998
9.175 Procedure on review
9.191 Time
9.194 Notification of review decision
9.197 Housing pending review
9.198 Reasons

Introduction

9.1 The previous chapters have addressed the elements of entitlement as homeless. This and the following chapters are concerned with the procedure by which an applicant applies as homeless; the procedures to be followed by an authority on receipt of the application; the formal requirements concerning the decision-making process (including the right to request an internal review of an adverse decision); and the method by which the duty (if any) is discharged.

9.2 The next chapter is concerned with the discharge of duty – this chapter is therefore concerned with the steps from application to decision and (if any) to review. This process involves a number of steps:

a) application;
b) enquiry into the application;
c) initial decision;
d) request for a review;
e) further enquiries on review;
f) 'minded to find' letter where necessary;
g) review decision.

Changes in law

9.3 A number of points may be made at the outset. First, it is to be remembered that the body of homelessness law is organic and develops over time, whether court-led, by the introduction of new legislation and/or through the relationship between housing and other areas of public law.[1] The procedural aspects discussed in this chapter are therefore liable to change as issues are subjected to further scrutiny by the courts or are amended by Parliament to reflect cross-discipline policies.[2]

Decision-making

9.4 The second point of general significance is the question of who may discharge the various duties under Housing Act (HA) 1996 Part 7

1 Including the impact of immigration law and European law on the issue of eligibility (chapter 3) and of human rights law on the extent of housing duties. See generally chapter 12.

2 Consider the impact of the anti-social behaviour agenda on all aspects of housing law, including intentional homelessness (chapter 6) and allocations (chapter 11).

or Housing (Wales) Act (H(W)A) 2014. It is common for decision-making in relation to homelessness to be delegated to an individual officer; the reviewing function – which in England[3] must in any event be conducted by a person senior to the person carrying out the initial decision – is sometimes reserved to a panel rather than an individual, whether a panel of members, officers or both.

9.5 Under the Local Authorities (Contracting Out of Allocation of Housing and Homelessness Functions) Order 1996,[4] an authority may 'contract out' all or part[5] of its homelessness functions (including, for example, enquiries or reviews), save for functions relating to[6] the provision of advisory services,[7] assistance for voluntary organisations,[8] and the duty to co-operate with relevant housing authorities and bodies.[9] A contract may be for a period of up to ten years, but 'may be revoked at any time' by the authority.[10] The 1996 Order continues to apply in Wales, even after the commencement of the H(W)A 2014.[11]

Relationship between decision and review

9.6 A third point should be made in relation to enquiries. Authorities are under obligations to conduct all relevant enquiries when an application is received – it would nonetheless be wrong to proceed on the basis that a failure to do so (or that there is a defect in the enquiries process) is sufficient immediately to vitiate the decision-making process.

9.7 The availability of a review of a decision affords an applicant an opportunity to remedy any perceived failure to conduct enquiries; it goes further than this, because it can be said positively to require

3 But not in Wales, where regulations only require that the reviewing officer be someone who was not involved in the original decision, see Homelessness (Review Procedure) (Wales) Regulations 2015 SI No 1266 reg 3; see also Welsh Code para 20.9.

4 SI No 3205. See further para 12.47. See, by way of example, *Tachie v Welwyn Hatfield BC* [2013] EWHC 3972 (QB).

5 Deregulation and Contracting Out Act 1994 ss70(4) and 69(5).

6 SI No 3205 article 3 and Sch 2.

7 See para 14.18.

8 See para 14.24.

9 See para 9.59.

10 Local Authorities (Contracting Out of Allocation of Housing and Homelessness Functions) Order 1996 article 3 and Sch 2.

11 See Housing (Wales) Act 2014 (Consequential Amendments) Regulations 2015 SI No 752, amending the 1996 Order.

the applicant to draw to the authority's attention all matters that the applicant wishes to be considered or in relation to which he or she believes there to be a need for enquiries.[12] In this sense, the review process serves to remedy any failures in the initial enquiry process, without necessarily vitiating it.

9.8 Otherwise, although the substance of the duties on enquiries is discussed below in relation to the application itself,[13] the same principles as apply to enquiries are as relevant on review.

Applications

Who can apply?

Generally

9.9 Applications as homeless may in principle be made by any person who is lawfully in the country. 'Lawfully' in this context means 'not unlawfully', ie, someone who is not an offender under Immigration Act 1971 s14 – see *Castelli and Tristran-Garcia, Tower Hamlets* and *Streeting.*[14]

9.10 Accordingly, 'applicant' under HA 1996 Part 7 means any person who applies to a local housing authority for accommodation, or for assistance in obtaining accommodation, whom the authority has reason to believe is or may be homeless, or threatened with homelessness.[15]

9.11 In Wales, 'applicant' means any person who applies to a local housing authority for accommodation or help in *retaining or obtaining* accommodation, and whom it appears to the authority may be homeless or threatened with homelessness.[16] If the person has previously been assessed for assistance under H(W)A 2014 Part 2, then there must have been a material change in circumstances since the

12 See *Bellouti v Wandsworth LBC* [2005] EWCA Civ 602, [2005] HLR 46.

13 Under HA 1996 s184(1).

14 *R v Westminster City Council ex p Castelli and Tristran-Garcia* (1996) 28 HLR 617, CA; *R v Secretary of State for the Environment ex p Tower Hamlets LBC* [1993] QB 632, 25 HLR 524, CA; *R v Hillingdon LBC ex p Streeting (No 2)* [1980] 1 WLR 1425, CA. A person is lawfully here even where the person has only been given temporary permission to enter, eg, as an asylum-seeker: *Szoma v Secretary of State for Work and Pensions* [2005] UKHL 64, [2006] 1 All ER 1.

15 HA 1996 s183(1) and (2); See *R (Edwards and others) v Birmingham City Council* [2016] EWHC 173 (Admin), [2016] HLR 11.

16 H(W)A 2014 s62(1).

previous assessment or new information which materially affects the assessment must have come to light, before he or she will be considered an applicant again.[17]

9.12 Subject to these qualifications, it follows that anyone – regardless as to whether he or she has a local connection with the authority (or any other authority in the UK)[18] – is entitled to make an application, and refusal to permit him or her to do so is a breach of duty. There is, however, a number of qualifications which merit consideration.

Qualifications

Immigrants

9.13 As noted,[19] a person unlawfully in the UK will not be permitted to make an application. An authority is entitled to reach its own decision as to whether or not an applicant for assistance is disqualified as such an illegal immigrant, albeit:

a) only for its own purposes; and
b) subject to a contrary decision by the Home Secretary.[20]

9.14 If, after the housing authority has decided the issue against an applicant, the immigration authorities later determine the issue of legality in the applicant's favour, or else decide not to take immigration action against the applicant, he or she will cease to be an illegal immigrant for the purposes of HA 1996 Part 7 (or H(W)A 2014 Part 2), and will be entitled to apply. The question of more detailed immigration status will then govern the question of eligibility.[21]

9.15 If a person has already been granted accommodation by the authority, questions of status do not serve to deprive the person of his or her rights under the accommodation agreement: see *Akinbolu v Hackney LBC*.[22]

9.16 In *Tower Hamlets*,[23] it was held – by concession – that, in addition to making enquiries of the immigration authorities and providing them with information, the authority was also under a positive duty to report suspected illegal immigrants to the immigration authorities.

17 H(W)A 2014 s62(2).
18 *R v Hillingdon LBC ex p Streeting (No 2)*, above.
19 See para 9.9.
20 See *Castelli and Tristran-Garcia* and *ex p Tower Hamlets LBC*, above.
21 See chapter 3.
22 (1996) 29 HLR 259, CA.
23 *R v Secretary of State for the Environment ex p Tower Hamlets LBC*, above.

Dependent children

9.17 A dependent child cannot apply in his or her own right: see *Garlick* and *Bentum*.[24] Children are expected to be provided for by those on whom they are dependent (with – where appropriate and qualifying – assistance under HA 1996 Part 7 or H(W)A 2014 Part 2).

9.18 The emphasis here is on 'dependent' children. The statutory scheme itself envisages the possibility of minors – 16- or 17-year-olds – applying as homeless.[25] It may be that subsequent enquiries disclose a family home to which the minor can return, but the absence of such at the date of the application is sufficient to require an application to be received and considered.

Capacity

9.19 A person must be capable of accepting or rejecting an offer of accommodation or assistance in order to qualify as an applicant: see *Begum*.[26] Persons so disabled that they have neither the capacity themselves to apply nor to authorise an agent on their behalf do not qualify. There must be the capacity to understand and respond to the offer, and to undertake its responsibilities; whether or not a person so qualifies is a matter for the authority.

Transfers

9.20 In *Pattinson*,[27] it was suggested that an application for housing by an existing tenant of the authority is usually to be presumed to be an application for transfer, rather than for assistance under HA 1996 Part 7. That approach was, however, rejected in *ex p B*,[28] in which it was noted than an application for a transfer could overlap with what may on its facts require to be treated as an application as a homeless person. Although the point was not taken in it, the latter approach

24 *R v Oldham MBC ex p Garlick; R v Bexley LBC ex p Bentum; R v Tower Hamlets LBC ex p Begum* [1993] AC 509, (1993) 25 HLR 319, HL.

25 See Homelessness (Priority Need for Accommodation) (England) Order 2002 SI No 2051 articles 3 and 4 and H(W)A 2014 s70(1)(f); see paras 5.65–5.70.

26 *R v Tower Hamlets LBC ex p Begum* [1993] AC 509, (1993) 25 HLR 319, HL. This remains good law notwithstanding Article 14 ECHR (which has been applied to disability, even though not specifically mentioned in it: see *AM (Somalia) v Entry Clearance Officer* [2009] EWCA Civ 634, [2009] UKHRR 1073): see *R (MT, by his father as litigation friend) v Oxford City Council* [2015] EWHC 795 (Admin).

27 *R v Lambeth LBC ex p Pattinson* (1985) 28 HLR 214, QBD.

28 *R v Islington LBC ex p B* (1997) 30 HLR 706, QBD.

may be considered to have been put beyond doubt by the decision (and its factual basis) in *Ali*.[29]

9.21 The question in each case is whether the conditions are satisfied. Even if an existing tenant is accepted as homeless, however, an authority may nonetheless continue to consider his or her transfer application and may resolve the homelessness by that means.[30]

Renewed applications

9.22 From 9 November 2012 when the Localism Act (LA) 2011 s149 came fully into force in England,[31] an applicant who makes a fresh application[32] within two years of a previous application to an English authority, which resulted in an assured shorthold tenancy in respect of which tenancy notice has been given under HA 1988 s21, is:

a) homeless from the expiry of that notice;[33]
b) threatened with homelessness from service of that notice;[34]
c) entitled to further assistance by way of accommodation provided that the applicant is still eligible[35] and did not become homeless intentionally,[36] even if no longer in priority need;[37] and
d) entitled to accommodation pending enquiries if there is reason to believe that the applicant may qualify under this provision.[38]

29 *Birmingham City Council v Ali; Moran v Manchester City Council (Secretary of State for Communities and Local Government and another intervening)* [2009] UKHL 36, [2009] HLR 41 at [56].

30 *Ali* and *Moran*, at para 4.71; and see also *R (Bilverstone) v Oxford City Council* [2003] EWHC 2434 (Admin), [2004] JHL D12.

31 Localism Act 2011 (Commencement No 2 and Transitional Provisions) (England) Order 2012 SI No 2599 Article 2.

32 Provided that the authority's duty to secure accommodation had not ceased before that date: Localism Act 2011 (Commencement No 2 and Transitional Provisions) (England) Order 2012 SI No 2599 Article 3.

33 HA 1996 s195A(2), cf the normal position (which usually means when actual eviction occurs) at para 4.61 above.

34 HA 1996 s195A(4), cf the current normal position (likely to be homeless within 28 days or 56 in Wales) at para 4.141 above (although this will also be 56 days in England once the provisions of the HRA 2017 s1 come into force: para 4.146. Once that Act is in force, however, s195A(4) will be repealed and new duties will apply (paras 10.58–10.61): HRA 2017 s4(4).

35 HA 1996 s195A(1), (3). Subsection (3) concerns those threatened with homelessness and, once HRA 2017 is in force, however, s195A(3) will be repealed and new duties will apply (paras 10.58–10.61): HRA 2017 s4(4).

36 HA 1996 s195A(1), (3). See also last footnote.

37 HA 1996 s195A(1), (3). See also penultimate footnote.

38 HA 1996 s188(1A). This right only arises on one re-application: HA 1996 s195A(6).

Repeat applications

9.23 This is an area which has attracted much litigation. Where an applicant who was refused assistance in the past, or in respect of whom a duty has been discharged because the applicant abandoned accommodation offered by the authority following a previous application, applies again to the authority for assistance, there is a conflict between:

a) the absolute right of a person to make an application as homeless and the fact that the HA 1996 'does not place any express limitation on who can make an application or as to how many applications can be made';[39] and
b) the need to prevent repetitive applications on the same grounds which serve only to waste the authority's resources, which applications entitle the applicant to temporary accommodation[40] pending the authority's enquiries,[41] and which may have arisen as a result of the applicant's own actions – for example, because the applicant refused accommodation previously offered to him or her by the authority.[42]

9.24 In many cases, an authority will have to accept a repeat application. A number of separate questions arise:

a) Who may make a repeat application?
b) What needs to have occurred before an applicant can re-apply?
c) Where one member of a household has, or may be treated as having, become homeless intentionally, but another member seeks 'separate treatment',[43] does he or she have to make a separate application, or does a duty to consider this issue arise whoever makes the application?
d) What is the position when there are applications to different authorities?

Who may make a repeat application?

9.25 A person who has become homeless intentionally[44] from accommodation provided under HA 1996 s193 or who loses its benefits for

39 *R v North Devon DC ex p Lewis* [1981] 1 WLR 328, QBD, under HA 1985 Part 3.
40 See para 10.8 onwards.
41 *Delahaye v Oswestry BC* (1980) *Times* 29 July, QBD.
42 *R v Westminster City Council ex p Chambers* (1982) 6 HLR 24, QBD.
43 See para 6.9 onwards.
44 See chapter 6.

some other reason has a statutory right to re-apply.[45] Other applicants, including those in respect of whom the authority has previously refused assistance and those who have previously refused assistance offered by the authority under HA 1996 Part 7, are not governed by statutory provisions and must therefore be considered in the light of the case-law.

What needs to have occurred before an applicant can re-apply?

9.26 Until the decision of the House of Lords in *Fahia*,[46] it had been held that what was needed before an applicant could make a repeat application was a material change of circumstances.[47] In *Fahia*, the applicant, who had one year previously been found intentionally homeless, made a new application for assistance, after being evicted from the bed and breakfast accommodation in which she had initially been placed by the authority and in which she had remained. There had been no intervening settled accommodation.[48] The application was refused by the authority.

9.27 In the House of Lords it was decided that, if an authority has reason to believe that an applicant is homeless, the authority is bound to accept the application and make necessary enquiries. Lord Browne-Wilkinson said:

> [W]hen an applicant has been given temporary accommodation . . . and is then found to be intentionally homeless, he cannot then make a further application based on exactly the same facts as his earlier application . . . But those are very special cases when it is possible to say that there is no application before the local authority and therefore the mandatory duty under [HA 1996 s184] has not arisen. But in the present case there is no doubt that when Mrs Fahia made her further application for accommodation she was threatened with homelessness. Moreover in my judgment her application could not be treated as identical with the earlier 1994 application. She was relying on her eviction from the guesthouse which, for one year, she had been occupying as the direct licensee of the guesthouse proprietor, paying

45 HA 1996 s193(9). The position is different in Wales: a person has a right to apply for assistance (and the authority must carry out an assessment) (H(W)A 2014 s62(1)). The duty to assess does not arise, however, if a person has previously been assessed and there has been no material change in his or her circumstances and no new material information (H(W)A 2014 s62(2)).

46 *R v Harrow LBC ex p Fahia* [1998] 1 WLR 1396, (1998) 30 HLR 1124, HL.

47 See *R v Westminster City Council ex p Chambers* (1982) 6 HLR 24, QBD; *R v Ealing LBC ex p McBain* [1985] 1 WLR 1351, (1985) 18 HLR 59, CA; *R v Southwark LBC ex p Campisi* (1998) 31 HLR 560, CA.

48 See paras 6.101–6.119.

the rent for that accommodation . . . It is impossible to say that there has been no relevant change in circumstances at all.[49]

9.28 This introduced a test of whether the application is 'identical', but it begged the question of how that was to be approached – change of *circumstances* or change of facts. In the post-*Fahia* case of *J*,[50] the applicant was living with a friend who had asked her to leave. J was found not to be threatened with homelessness. More than a year later, when possession proceedings were issued against the friend, she re-applied. The authority refused to conduct any enquiries, contending that there had been no material change in circumstances. The decision was quashed. *Fahia* was authority for the proposition that an authority is not under a duty to make enquiries in relation to an application based on exactly the same *facts* as an earlier application but it did not entitle an authority to refuse to make enquiries where there had been a material change of *circumstances*. There had clearly been a material change in circumstances: possession proceedings against the friend were imminent.

9.29 In *Rikha Begum*,[51] the applicant, who had been living with her parents when she initially applied as homeless, refused an offer of accommodation made under HA 1996 s193 and the authority decided that it had discharged its duty towards her. She returned to live with her family. Nearly two years later, she re-applied. She claimed there had been a change in circumstances since her first application, because she had given birth to a second child[52] and other family members had come to live at her parents' home so that it was now overcrowded. The authority decided there had been no material change of circumstances and refused to accept an application. It was held that this was the wrong test: the authority ought to have asked whether the application was based on exactly the same *facts* as the previous application, not whether there had been a material change in *circumstances*.

9.30 The decisions raise as many questions as they resolve, for example, what constitutes a change of fact and when must the change have occurred. Most importantly, they could have re-opened

49 At WLR 1402/D–E, HLR 1130. *Delahaye v Oswestry BC* (1980) *Times* 29 July, QBD, which appeared to have decided to the contrary was distinguished on the basis of the requirement for there to be a change in the facts.

50 *R (J) v Waltham Forest LBC* [2002] EWHC 487 (Admin), [2002] JHL D38.

51 *Rikha Begum v Tower Hamlets LBC* [2005] EWCA Civ 340, [2005] HLR 34.

52 The child had been born between the previous application and the refusal of an offer, and the decision by the authority that it had discharged its duty.

the flood-gates to repeat applications, which could not be summarily dismissed, regardless of how insignificant the factual change was.

9.31 To address those concerns, the Court of Appeal in *Rikha Begum* offered guidance to assist authorities in identifying when an application may be refused on the ground that it is not on exactly the same facts:

a) while it is for the applicant to identify in any subsequent application the facts which he or she contends render the application different from prior applications, it is for the authority to assess whether the circumstances of the two applications are exactly the same;
b) if a subsequent application for assistance purports to reveal new facts but those facts are, to the authority's knowledge (and without the need for further enquiry), not new, or else they are fanciful or trivial, the authority may reject the application as 'incompetent'; and
c) if a subsequent application reveals new facts which, in the light of the information then available to the authority, are neither fanciful nor trivial, the authority must accept the application; it is not open to the authority to investigate the accuracy of the alleged new facts before deciding whether to treat the application as valid, even if it suspects (but does not know) that the new facts are inaccurate.

9.32 While there plainly is a difference, at least in theory and occasionally in practice, between a change of circumstances and new facts, the reality is that the distinction will rarely be possible for an authority to rely on with any confidence as a basis for refusing to entertain a new application, unless it falls within the second limb of this guidance. In *Gardiner v Haringey LBC*,[53] the applicant was a British national living in Colombia, where she had a house. Her daughter suffered from autism and needed care and support – including educational support – that was not available in Colombia. She came to the UK and applied to the authority as homeless. That authority refused the application because it was considered reasonable for the applicant to continue to occupy the house in Colombia, and she was accordingly not homeless. Almost a year later, the applicant made another application to the authority and provided new information about her daughter's special needs and an updated medical report in support of the application. The new information included a statement that since the daughter had been in the UK she had demonstrated 'considerable

53 *Gardiner v Haringey LBC* [2009] EWHC 2699 (Admin).

and dramatic improvements'. The authority sought to rely on *Rikha Begum* in refusing to accept the application on the ground that there had been no change in the facts since the previous application. The claimant successfully applied for judicial review: the new information amounted to new facts which rendered it different from the earlier application.

9.33 To determine whether a subsequent application is based on exactly the same facts as an earlier application, the comparison is not between the facts as they existed at the time of the original application and those existing at the time of the second application. Rather, it is between the circumstances as they were at the time of the authority's original decision (or review if there was one) on the earlier application, and the circumstances revealed by the subsequent application.[54]

9.34 There is a mild discrepancy within *Rikha Begum*: although reference is made to 'the date of the authority's *decision*'[55] as the appropriate date for comparison, there is also reference to 'the circumstances as they were known to be when the earlier application was *disposed of*' as the appropriate date for comparison;[56] and, when disposing of the appeal,[57] there is reference to the facts at the date of *discharge* of the original decision.

9.35 This discrepancy might seem to suggest that – where the original application was determined by way of discharge by the authority of its duty by means of an offer that was not accepted – the time for comparison is the date of discharge rather than of the authority's decision. That theory draws some support from *Griffin*,[58] in which a new application was properly held to have been based on the same facts: the change – relationship breakdown – had been known to the authority and taken into account at the time when the earlier offer of accommodation had been made, but had occurred subsequently to the decision on the original application.

54 *Rikha Begum* at [43]. See, by way of example, *R (Hoyte) v Southwark LBC* [2016] EWHC 1665 (Admin), [2016] HLR 35 in which the applicant had attempted suicide between the first and second applications. See also *R (Abdulrahman) v Hillingdon LBC* [2016] EWHC 2647 (Admin), [2017] HLR 1 in which the new facts were that the applicant's husband had left her and three of her nine children no longer lived with her.

55 *Rikha Begum* at [43].

56 *Rikha Begum* at [44].

57 *Rikha Begum* at [54].

58 *R (Griffin) v Southwark LBC* [2004] EWHC 2463 (Admin), [2005] HLR 12.

Applications by other family members

9.36 There is no bar to a family member of an unsuccessful applicant making a fresh application in his or her own name. Commonly this occurs where an applicant is found intentionally homeless and a member of the applicant's family claims not to have acquiesced in the act which gave rise to the intentionality.[59]

9.37 An application by another member of the family cannot, however, be used to circumvent a decision that the authority has discharged its duty towards the family: it is considered irrelevant that the member of the family making the new application did not acquiesce in or agree to the refusal of accommodation which led to the decision that the duty had been discharged.[60]

Applications to other authorities

9.38 In *R v Slough BC ex p Ealing LBC*,[61] two applicants had been found homeless intentionally in Slough. One applicant moved and applied to Ealing, the other to Hillingdon; both authorities concluded that the applicants were not homeless intentionally. In each case, however, the local connection provisions entitled them to refer the applicants back to Slough.[62] It was held that Slough BC was bound by the unintentionally decisions of Ealing and Hillingdon.

9.39 There is therefore nothing in principle to stop an applicant moving around until he or she finds an authority which concludes that the applicant is not homeless intentionally, and – unless the second authority's decision can be vitiated as a matter of public law[63] – there is no way in which the authority fixed with final responsibility for the applicant can defeat the decision, even though it conflicts with its own finding.

9.40 *Ex p Ealing LBC* was applied in *ex p Camden LBC*,[64] which was on like facts. In its discretion, however, the court refused judicial review to quash the original authority's refusal to accept the referral, because the referring authority had failed to make adequate enquiries either of the applicant or of the other authority to resolve certain factual discrepancies between the applicant's statements to the two

59 *R v North Devon DC ex p Lewis* [1981] 1 WLR 328, QBD. See also paras 6.14–6.17.

60 *R v Camden LBC ex p Hersi* (2001) 33 HLR 52, CA.

61 *R v Slough BC ex p Ealing LBC* [1981] QB 801, CA.

62 The case is a reminder that different authorities can reach different conclusions on the same question.

63 See paras 12.21–12.105.

64 *R v Tower Hamlets LBC ex p Camden LBC* (1988) 21 HLR 197, QBD.

authorities. Authorities should therefore examine with care applications by people who have been declared homeless intentionally elsewhere. They should afford the first authority to which application was made (and which will bear the burden if a second application is successful) an opportunity to comment on any discrepancies between the applications.

9.41 The Court of Appeal went somewhat further in *ex p Tower Hamlets LBC*:[65] where an application is made to a second authority, that authority's enquiries should extend to examination of the reasons for the first authority's refusal to assist, and should take into account the general housing circumstances prevailing in the first authority's district, just as it may take into account the housing circumstances in its own.[66]

9.42 In *Ali and Bibi*,[67] it was held that, when the duty to house an applicant on a first application was discharged by reference to another authority under what is now HA 1996 s198, there was no discharge of duty (by the first authority) under what is now section 193. Accordingly, assuming there had been no take-up of an accommodation offer from the other authority, the acquisition of a local connection with the area of the first authority entitled an applicant to re-apply. This was consistent with the early decision in *Wyness v Poole BC*,[68] in which the family declined to accept a reference to another authority, but 'made do' until one of its members had acquired employment and – thence – a local connection.

9.43 In practice, both *Ali and Bibi* and *Wyness* are overtaken by – and absorbed into – the post-*Fahia* position:[69] *Wyness* was decided on the basis of 'change of circumstance' but it was also a change of facts and *Ali and Bibi*, while on a somewhat different point (whether there had been any previous discharge such as to prevent a new application) becomes somewhat redundant.

9.44 In any event, it was explicitly decided that the principle derived from *ex p Ealing LBC*[70] applies both where the application to the second authority is made after the first authority had accepted a duty

65 *R v Newham LBC ex p Tower Hamlets LBC* (1990) 23 HLR 62, QBD.

66 See para 4.97.

67 *R v Tower Hamlets LBC ex p Ali*; *R v Tower Hamlets LBC ex p Bibi* (1992) 25 HLR 158, CA, overruling: *R v Hammersmith and Fulham LBC ex p O'Brian* (1985) 17 HLR 471, QBD.

68 *Wyness v Poole DC* July 1979 *LAG Bulletin* 166, CC.

69 Paras 9.26–9.35.

70 See para 9.40.

and made an offer[71] as much as where the first authority referred the applicant to another authority.

How to apply

9.45 Authorities have a duty to hear and adjudicate on applications[72] made by people who are potentially homeless and they must therefore make provision to receive applications. In heavily populated areas, reasonable provision would be expected to comprise some form of 24-hour cover.[73] There is, however, no requirement that applications be in writing or in any particular form and an authority is therefore not at liberty to refuse an application on that basis.[74] Once the authority have enough information to comprise reason to believe[75] that the applicant may be homeless or threatened with homelessness, its duties arise,[76] although circumstances – including action taken by

71 *R (Kensington and Chelsea RLBC) v Ealing LBC* [2017] EWHC 24 (Admin), [2017] HLR 13.

72 The English Code of Guidance (para 6.6) suggests that applications can be made 'to any department of the local authority', but it is submitted that this in wrong. It is inconsistent with paras 6.8–6.10, all of which envisage (leaving aside out-of-hours provision) a dedicated and expert service with sole responsibility for accepting and processing applications; taken literally, it would also mean that applications could be made at library or a school, the leisure department or even the waste collection department. Such departments are manifestly unsuitable for dealing with such an application, could not arrange interim accommodation where necessary and may not even recognise that an application is being made at all, for which failure an authority should surely not be held to be legally in default. It is submitted that the correct position is that an application is not made until there is an approach to a suitable or appropriate department or service which a homeless person could reasonably think might be able to help: this does not necessarily mean a *housing* department or service, but would include, eg, a general help line or an out-of-hours emergency service for all the functions of the authority.

73 *R v Camden LBC ex p Gillan* (1988) 21 HLR 114, QBD.

74 *R v Chiltern DC ex p Roberts* (1990) 23 HLR 387, QBD. See also *R (Aweys) v Birmingham City Council* [2007] EWHC 52 (Admin), [2007] HLR 27 (point not taken in Court of Appeal or House of Lords – see *Birmingham City Council v Aweys and others* [2008] EWCA Civ 48, [2008] HLR 32 and *Birmingham City Council v Ali and others; Moran v Manchester City Council* [2009] UKHL 36, [2009] HLR 41).

75 Whether this standard is met is a matter for the authority, subject to challenge on conventional *Wednesbury* grounds: see *R (Edwards and others) v Birmingham City Council* [2016] EWHC 173 (Admin), [2016] HLR 11.

76 Thus, in *Bury MBC v Gibbons* [2010] EWCA Civ 327, [2010] HLR 33, an approach to the authority asking for assistance when the applicant had been given notice meant that he was threatened with homelessness and the authority should at that stage have treated the approach as an application

the authority – may mean that the applicant is no longer homeless or threatened with homelessness by the time a decision is taken on the application.[77]

Provision of accommodation on application

9.46 Once an application has been received and accepted, the preliminary consideration for any local authority is whether it must provide accommodation pending the decision on the application, because the applicant appears to it to be eligible for assistance and in priority need.[78] The threshold test for the provision of accommodation pending decision is very low:[79] it only requires authority to have 'reason to believe' that an applicant may be homeless, eligible for assistance and have a priority need for the duty to secure accommodation to be activated,[80] although – again[81] – note that the authority itself may take action that obviates the homelessness before a decision is taken.[82]

9.47 A local housing authority may be able to leave an applicant in current accommodation (where it remains available) in satisfaction of the duty under HA 1996 s188(1).[83] It is a question of fact, to be

under HA 1996 Part 7. See also *R (Edwards and others) v Birmingham City Council* [2016] EWHC 173 (Admin), [2016] HLR 11: an authority is entitled to question an applicant to clarify whether, in fact, there is reason to believe that any accommodation presently occupied is such that it may not be reasonable to continue to occupy it; it is not the case that every complaint about the condition is sufficient to meet the 'reason to believe' threshold.

77 See paras 9.132–9.135.

78 HA 1996 s188(1); H(W)A 2014 s68. Priority need is not a precondition in the case of a first renewed application (ie within two years of acceptance of a private sector offer on a previous application, see HA 1996 s195A(6)): see para 9.22.

79 *R (M) v Hammersmith and Fulham LBC* [2006] EWCA Civ 917. The case was appealed to the House of Lords (*R (M) v Hammersmith and Fulham LBC* [2008] UKHL 14, [2008] 1 WLR 535, [2008] 4 All ER 271, HL; see also para 5.66) but the point on the threshold for HA 1996 s188(1) was not in issue. A similar point on the threshold was made in the High Court in *R (Aweys) v Birmingham City Council* [2007] EWHC 52 (Admin), [2007] HLR 27, not pursued on appeal, see above; see also para 9.47.

80 HA 1996 s188(1), H(W)A 2014 s68.

81 See para 9.45.

82 See para 9.135.

83 *Birmingham City Council v Ali and others; Moran v Manchester City Council.* See also *R (Edwards and others) v Birmingham CC* [2016] EWHC 173 (Admin), [2016] HLR 11 in which the authority were entitled to rely on an applicant's 'self-certification' as to the suitability of property he or she was occupying on a 'homeless at home' application; this was not objectionable so long as the applicant was aware of his or her right to interim accommodation and knew he or she could return to request it at a later date.

determined by the authority, as to for how long accommodation will remain suitable.[84]

Enquiries

9.48 Once an application has been received, in England, the next stage in the application process is for the authority to make enquiries into the application to determine what (if any) duty is owed: the duty arises when the authority considers that an applicant is or may be homeless or threatened with homelessness. In Wales, this first stage duty has been replaced by a duty to make an assessment of the applicant's housing needs,[85] a duty which – once HRA 2017 is in force – will also apply in England but only at a later stage when the authority is satisfied that the applicant is homeless or threatened with homelessness and eligible for assistance. These assessment duties are more substantive than the current enquiry duty, and are therefore considered in chapter 10: para 10.43 onwards.

The duty to make enquiries

9.49 The duty to make enquiries arises in England if the authority:

a) receives an application for accommodation or for assistance in obtaining accommodation; and
b) has 'reason to believe' that the applicant may be homeless or threatened with homelessness.[86]

84 *Birmingham City Council v Ali and others; Moran v Manchester City Council*; see also HA 1996 ss188(1) and 206.

85 H(W)A 2014 s62.

86 HA 1996 s184(1). See also *R (Edwards and others) v Birmingham City Council* [2016] EWHC 173 (Admin), [2016] HLR 11: the authority is entitled to question an applicant to clarify whether, in fact, there is reason to believe that any accommodation presently occupied is such that it may be reasonable to continue to occupy it; it is not the case that every complaint about the condition is sufficient to meet the 'reason to believe' threshold. Note the different dates when the application is a first renewed application (see s195A(6)), ie following an earlier application which resulted in a private sector letting; if an assured shorthold, homelessness arises once notice under HA 1988 s21 has expired, and the applicant is threatened with homelessness once it has been served – see para 9.22. Note also the possibility that an assured shorthold applicant in England may be threatened with homelessness as a result of service of a valid s21 notice which will expire within 56 days, once HRA 2017 s1 is brought into force: para 4.146.

(As noted, if the authority is also satisfied that there is reason to believe that the applicant may be eligible for assistance and in priority need, there is a duty to house pending a decision.[87])

9.50 These conditions arise relatively easily: the authority need only 'have reason to believe' that the applicant 'may' be homeless or threatened with homelessness.[88] Once the Homelessness Reduction Act (HRA) 2017 is brought into force, the second of the conditions (para 9.49) may be fulfilled if another public authority notifies[89] the housing authority[90] of its opinion that someone in relation to whom it exercises functions is or may be homeless or threatened with homelessness and provides his or her contact information: paras 13.92–13.93.[91] Indeed, if another public authority, or anyone whom the housing authority considers a credible source of information, provides such information, that condition would appear to be fulfilled regardless of whether they are under any duty to do so. In neither case, however, is the first condition on its face fulfilled unless the notification – statutory or voluntary – also asserts, in whatever terms, that the individual is applying to the housing authority for accommodation or assistance in obtaining it. In the case of a post-HRA 2017 statutory notification (only), however, it is strongly arguable that this is the intention of HA 1996 s213B and that section 184 should be construed commensurately with it; it is difficult to see what other purpose s213B could have sought to achieve.

9.51 Failure to undertake the necessary enquiries does not, however, give rise to an action in damages: *Palmer*.[92]

9.52 Where there is no reason to believe that an applicant is yet threatened with homelessness, the duty to make enquiries has not been triggered and the authority cannot make a decision whether or not an applicant is threatened with homelessness intentionally: *Hunt*.[93]

9.53 In *Jarvis*,[94] notice that possession would be required of premises let on an assured shorthold tenancy was not of itself sufficient to trigger a duty under HA 1996 s184.

87 See paras 10.8–10.28. Again, priority need is not a requirement in the case of a first renewed application (see HA 1996 s195A(6) and last footnote): see para 9.49.

88 HA 1996 s184(1).

89 With the consent of the individual in question.

90 Being the authority which the individual has chosen to be notified.

91 HRA 2017 s10; HA 1996 s213B.

92 *R v Northavon DC ex p Palmer* (1995) 27 HLR 576, CA.

93 *R v Rugby BC ex p Hunt* (1992) 26 HLR 1, QBD.

94 *R v Croydon LBC ex p Jarvis* (1993) 26 HLR 194, QBD.

9.54 The enquiries must be sufficient to satisfy the authority whether the applicant is eligible for assistance and if so what (if any) duty is owed to the applicant under HA 1996 Part 7 or H(W)A 2014 Part 2.

9.55 If the authority considers that there may be a local connection, it is still under a duty to make the preliminary[95] enquiries,[96] which are exclusively in the province of the authority to which application has been made: *ex p Ealing LBC*.[97] The authority may also make enquiries whether or not the applicant has a local connection with the area of another housing authority.[98] As referrals are discretionary, authorities are under no duty to investigate local connection, even where the applicant indicates that he or she wishes to live in another area,[99] although it is submitted that if such an applicant gives the authority sufficient cause to think that a local connection referral is available, the authority should have reasons for refusing to do so.[100]

9.56 If local connection enquiries are to be made, the first must be whether the applicant has a local connection with the area of another authority rather than whether there is one with the authority to which the application has been made. If there is no such local connection, it will not be relevant to consider whether or not there is one with the authority to which application has been made. People without a connection elsewhere remain the responsibility of that authority: *Streeting*.[101]

9.57 The authority can start local connection enquiries without awaiting the conclusion of its other enquiries, but the issue has to be determined by the date of the decision,[102] and it may become necessary to reconsider a decision to refer on local connection grounds if the other enquiries are prolonged,[103] as the connection itself may be based on factors arising during the enquiries.[104]

95 See para 9.54.
96 *Delahaye v Oswestry BC* (1980) *Times* 29 July, QBD.
97 *R v Slough BC ex p Ealing LBC* [1981] QB 801, CA; see para 9.41.
98 HA 1996 s184(2); H(W)A 2014 s80.
99 *Hackney LBC v Sareen* [2003] EWCA Civ 351, [2003] HLR 54.
100 In practice, of course, most authorities are keen to refer; that said, there can be reciprocal arrangements between authorities which militate against a referral and it remains to be decided whether this would be sufficient to justify a decision not to do so.
101 *R v Hillingdon LBC ex p Streeting (No 2)* [1980] 1 WLR 1425, DC and CA. See further para 9.9.
102 *Mohamed v Hammersmith and Fulham LBC* [2001] UKHL 57, [2002] HLR 7.
103 *R v Newham LBC ex p Smith* (1996) 29 HLR 213, QBD.
104 See *Mohamed*, above.

Who must make the enquiries?

9.58 The burden of making enquiries rests with the authority to whom the application was made. In the absence of a contracting out agreement,[105] the duty to enquire may not be delegated to another organisation although the authority may ask another housing authority or relevant body,[106] or a social services authority,[107] to assist in discharging the enquiry duty. That body is obliged to co-operate in the discharge of the function to which the request relates, to the extent that is reasonable in the circumstances.[108]

9.59 In *Gerrard*,[109] the authority had transferred all of its housing stock to a registered housing association,[110] and had reached an agreement pursuant to which the association was to carry out the enquiries under what is now HA 1996 s184, on the basis of which enquiries the authority would make its decisions. Quashing the authority's decision that the applicant was not homeless, it was held that, although entitled under what is now HA 1996 s213 to enlist assistance from third parties (including a registered housing association) in making enquiries, the authority must nonetheless take an active and dominant role in the investigative process.

9.60 On the other hand, in *Woolgar*,[111] it was held that it is only the decision-making function which is exclusive to the authority (absent a contracting out arrangement), so that the investigative function involved in making enquiries could properly be delegated to an outside body (at least, one recognised by statute, such as a registered housing association, now private registered provider or, in Wales, registered social landlord).[112]

9.61 The cases are not irreconcilable: as a matter of law, authorities are not bound to carry out all their functions through employees but may

105 See para 9.5.

106 Registered provider (in Wales, registered social landlord) or housing action trust, or in Scotland a local authority, development corporation, registered housing association or Scottish Homes: HA 1996 s213(2); H(W)A 2014 s95(5).

107 In the case of 16- and 17-year-olds, the English Code of Guidance (para 6.19) recommends joint assessments with social services; (see the Welsh Code para 11.10). See also *R (M) v Hammersmith and Fulham LBC* [2008] UKHL 14, [2008] 1 WLR 535, [2008] 4 All ER 271.

108 HA 1996 s213; H(W)A 2014 s95.

109 *R v West Dorset DC, West Dorset HA ex p Gerrard* (1994) 27 HLR 150, QBD. Both this and *Woolgar*, below, preceded the contracting out power: see para 9.5.

110 As private registered proprietors of social housing were then known.

111 *R v Hertsmere BC ex p Woolgar* (1995) 27 HLR 703, QBD.

112 HA 1996 s213(2)(a).

retain outside contractors; if it can be said, however, that the contractor has determined what enquiries need to be made, and takes them to such a point that the decision is 'all but' made before the authority exercises its decision-making function, then the authority will improperly have delegated rather than properly used an outside service in order to lay the ground for its decision.

Conduct of enquiries

9.62 It is for the authority, not the courts, to determine how the necessary enquiries are made, including who should conduct interviews and what questions should be asked.[113] Enquiries should nonetheless be carried out in a sympathetic way:[114] *Phillips*.[115]

9.63 Whether an interview is necessary is likewise primarily for the authority to decide.[116] In *Tetteh*,[117] the applicant had set out his position in correspondence and there was nothing which required the authority to interview him; failure to do so could therefore not be seen to be a breach of the principles of natural justice.[118] A number of authorities – and/or contractors – now carry out interviews by telephone: while this may be proper where all that is needed is to establish or check facts, it is submitted that this will nonetheless not be sufficient where the matter under consideration calls for a face-to-face

113 Subject to *Wednesbury* review: see *R(IA) v Westminster City Council* [2013] EWHC 1273 (QB) where a short interview with the applicant was considered insufficient, leading to 'irrational and, indeed, perverse' conclusions.

114 See English Code para 6.15. Previous versions of the Code referred to carrying out enquiries in a caring and sympathetic manner; the current version does not explicitly do so, but does refer to enquiries being carried out quickly and applicants having an opportunity to explain their circumstances fully: see Code para 6.15. In *Supplementary Guidance on domestic abuse and homelessness*, Department for Communities and Local Government (DCLG), November 2014, authorities are cautioned to ensure that – in cases of domestic violence or abuse – enquiries do not provoke further such behaviour.

115 *R v West Dorset DC ex p Phillips* (1984) 17 HLR 336, QBD. See also comments in the decision in *R v Camden LBC ex p Gillan* (1988) 21 HLR 114, QBD. The change to the Code in England (see footnote 114, above) does not appear to derogate from these cases; the same conclusion would probably have been reached by the courts in any event, as a matter of construction of HA 1996 and its purposes.

116 If an interview is needed, the interviewer must speak fluent English, see Immigration Act 2016 s77(1) and the Code of Practice (English Language Requirements for Public Sector Workers) Regulations 2016 SI No 1157.

117 *Tetteh v Kingston upon Thames RLBC* [2004] EWCA Civ 1775, [2005] HLR 21.

118 See paras 12.56–12.60.

interview,[119] for example, vulnerability.[120] Thus, many people find it difficult to express themselves on the telephone, whether because of language difficulties or mental competence or through unease at being asked to talk about potentially sensitive issues without forewarning, as is often the case on receipt of a telephone call. Likewise, the interviewer is deprived of the ability to assess 'body language', a concept that may be difficult to describe but that is well-recognised and that is essential to the overall evaluative exercise in which the interviewer is engaged. It may be observed that the interviewee, too, is also deprived of the element of 'reading' the interviewer that is likewise central to comprehension (and to assessing reactions).[121] Furthermore, the interviewee may, without the knowledge of the interviewer, be distracted by other people or events;[122] indeed, the interviewee may be temporarily impaired, for example, through drink or drugs.[123] Nor is it impossible for someone else to be answering questions, eg in a hostel or house in multiple occupation (HMO), whether maliciously or through mistake: such conversations are ripe for misunderstanding.

9.64 Inconsistencies will frequently be found when someone's native language is not English: *Li*.[124] Previous editions of the Code recommended that authorities secure access to competent interpreters for the community languages of their area, but that recommendation is not found in either the current English Code or the Welsh Code.[125]

119 In *R v Camden LBC ex p Gillan* (1988) 21 HLR 114, QBD, the Divisional Court referred to the expectation of a 'face to face' opportunity to explain an applicant's situation, in contrast to a telephone-based system, and criticised the authority's 'cavalier treatment' of applicants who were required to explain their circumstances by telephone. See also the position on review, para 9.187.

120 An authority must approach vulnerability with 'great care' – see *Crossley v Westminster City Council* [2006] EWCA Civ 140, [2006] HLR 26, at [30].

121 An interviewee may – is likely to – wish to appear co-operative, and/or may be suggestible, at least to a point; in a telephone interview, an interviewee cannot gauge how his or her answers are impacting on the interviewer.

122 Particularly if the interview is with someone in a hostel, taking the call on a telephone in the common parts.

123 It is not impossible, including in cases such as those referred to in the previous footnotes, for there to be a mistake in identity, whether by misunderstanding or even deliberate conduct by a third party.

124 *R v Surrey Heath BC ex p Li* (1984) 16 HLR 79, QBD.

125 The English Code does, however, suggest that information on homelessness procedures should be made available in the main languages spoken in the area, and that for languages less frequently spoken that there should be access to interpreters: Code para 6.10. The Welsh Code also recommends that consideration be given to producing Information in minority languages, see Welsh Code para 7.17.

9.65 Where there is doubt about the competence of an interpreter, the test is whether it has been shown that the interpreter is not – to the knowledge of the authority – competent to conduct the interview: *Jalika Begum*.[126] In *Khatun*,[127] interviews with an applicant (without the applicant's own independent adviser or counsellor) were not inherently flawed on the basis that they had been conducted by an employee of the council who would be inclined to protect the employer's limited resources.[128]

Ambit of enquiries

9.66 The burden of making enquiries is squarely on the authority.[129] Enquiries must cover all the relevant factors, for example, priority need,[130] or risk of domestic violence in another area.[131] Enquiries need not, however, amount to 'CID-type' enquiries.[132] The approach is summarised in *Winchester*:[133]

> The burden lies upon the local authority to make appropriate enquiries . . . in a caring and sympathetic way . . . These enquiries should be pursued rigorously and fairly albeit the authority are not under a duty to conduct detailed CID-type enquiries . . . The applicant must be given an opportunity to explain matters which the local authority is minded to regard as weighing substantially against him . . .

9.67 It follows that there may be some limited circumstances where a local housing authority need not make enquiries into some matters. For example, in *Green v Croydon LBC*[134] the applicant had been evicted

126 *R v Tower Hamlets LBC ex p Begum* (1990) 24 HLR 188, QBD.

127 *R v Tower Hamlets LBC ex p Khatun* (1994) 27 HLR 465, CA.

128 Cf the 'fairness' discussions in *Runa Begum v Tower Hamlets LBC* [2003] UKHL 5, [2003] 2 AC 430, [2003] HLR 32; *Feld v Barnet LBC* [2005] EWCA Civ 1307, [2005] HLR 9 (see also see paras 9.168–9.169); *De-Winter Heald and others v Brent LBC* [2009] EWCA Civ 930, [2010] HLR 8. See para 12.62.

129 *R v Woodspring DC ex p Walters* (1984) 16 HLR 73, QBD; *R v Reigate and Banstead DC ex p Paris* (1984) 17 HLR 103, QBD; *R v Barnet LBC ex p Babalola* (1995) 28 HLR 196, QBD; *R v Wandsworth LBC ex p Dodia* (1997) 30 HLR 562, QBD. See also English Code of Guidance para 6.15.

130 *R v Ryedale DC ex p Smith* (1983) 16 HLR 66, QBD.

131 *Patterson v Greenwich LBC* (1993) 26 HLR 159, CA.

132 *Lally v Kensington and Chelsea RLBC* (1980) *Times* 27 March, QBD. They must, however, address obviously relevant factors, see *Wandsworth LBC v NJ* [2013] EWCA Civ 1373, [2014] HLR 6, in which the authority failed to make any enquiries into the possibility that a violent man would be able to locate his ex-partner (the applicant), despite clear evidence that he was attempting to do so.

133 *R v Gravesham BC ex p Winchester* (1986) 18 HLR 208, QBD, at 214–215.

134 [2007] EWCA Civ 1367, [2008] HLR 28.

from a privately rented property for rent arrears; when she applied as homeless, the authority decided that she was intentionally homeless. She contended that the possession order was wrongly made as the possession proceedings had proceeded on the basis of a monthly rent of £700, whereas the true rent was only £650 per month. It was held that the authority did not have to make enquiries of the landlord, applicant or District Judge but were entitled to rely on the possession order which was only consistent with a rent of £700 per month. This is, however, an unusual case. In most cases where accommodation has been lost as a result of rent (or mortgage) arrears, the authority will need to make enquires of the applicant's financial affairs, If only to be satisfied as to whether the accommodation that was lost was affordable.[135] Nor, when considering whether an applicant has been occupying what was asserted by her to be settled accommodation, does an authority necessarily have to enquire into its legal character.[136] In *Gilby v Westminster City Council*,[137] the applicant occupied accommodation either as an unlawful subtenant or as a bare licensee. The question was whether the occupation constituted settled accommodation, for which purpose the relevant question was whether the applicant had the basis for a reasonable expectation of continued occupation: the difference between bare license and unlawful sub-tenancy was irrelevant to that question; the authority had been entitled to determine that the accommodation was not settled either way.

9.68 Enquiries may extend to other departments within the authority, for example, the housing department (referable to an earlier tenancy): *Adair*.[138] Where an application is made by an occupier of property owned by the authority, the duty to make enquiries does not, however, fetter any decision to recover possession. In *Grumbridge*,[139] a trespasser sought judicial review of the authority's decision to evict him before determining his application for housing: it was held that there was no requirement or statutory obligation on the authority to determine whether a person is either homeless or in priority need or, indeed, as to any of the other matters under (then) HA 1985 Part 3 (now HA 1996 Part 7), before deciding whether to obtain possession of property.

135 As to which, see the Homelessness (Suitability of Accommodation) Order 1996 SI No 3204 and H(W)A 2014 s59(2). See further English Code para 8.29 and Welsh Code paras 8.29–8.30 and 17.18–17.19.

136 *Gilby v Westminster City Council* [2008] EWCA Civ 604, [2008] HLR 7.

137 [2007] EWCA Civ 604, [2008] HLR 7.

138 *R v Camden LBC ex p Adair* (1996) 29 HLR 236, QBD.

139 *R v Barnet LBC ex p Grumbridge* (1992) 24 HLR 433, QBD.

9.69 Where the facts relating to an application are fairly placed before the applicant for the applicant to agree, dispute or supplement, and the applicant agrees them, it is not unfair for the decision-maker or the reviewing officer to proceed on the basis that the agreed facts are accurate,[140] bearing particularly in mind that the burden is normally on the applicant to put forward the matters and evidence which he or she wishes to be taken into account: see *Cramp*.[141] Note, however, that if reliance is placed on a disability, Equality Act (EqA) 2010 s149 – the public sector equality duty[142] – may[143] oblige the authority to carry out further inquiries if some feature of the evidence presents a real possibility that an applicant is within it.[144]

140 *Rowley v Rugby BC* [2007] EWCA Civ 483, [2007] HLR 40. See para 9.199. See also *R (Lynch) v Lambeth LBC* [2007] HLR 15 at [32]: 'All the medical evidence was accepted, and the housing authority did not consider, either before the s184 or the review, that any further inquiries were necessary. No suggestion was made by the claimant or her advisers that further information should be sought, nor was any more offered. No response was made to the minded to find letter of the reviewing officer. In line with the decision of the *Cramp* case, . . . the Housing Authority were not unreasonable in failing to make further inquiries. It is difficult to envisage what other inquiries needed to be made, given the wealth of information with the original application.'

141 *Cramp v Hastings BC, Phillips v Camden LBC* [2005] EWCA Civ 1005, [2005] HLR 48, see para 9.92. See also *Mohamoud v Kensington and Chelsea RLBC; Saleem v Wandsworth LBC* [2015] EWCA Civ 780, [2015] HLR 38: where an applicant seeks to rely on Children Act 2004 s11 (duty on authorities to safeguard and promote the welfare of children when discharging any functions), he or she must notify the authority of any relevant matters relating to the child on which he or she wishes to rely.

142 In the exercise of functions, to have due regard to the need to eliminate unlawful discrimination, harassment and victimisation and to advance equality of opportunity and foster good relations between persons with protected characteristics (age, disability, gender reassignment, pregnancy or maternity, race, sex, sexual orientation, religion or belief) and other persons.

143 In *Wilson v Birmingham City Council* [2016] EWCA Civ 1137, [2017] HLR 4, it was held that a review officer was entitled to expect the appellant to bring forward any information which might be relevant to show that her children had a disability; the absence of any response from the appellant to invitations to submit information meant that the officer had been entitled to conclude that any problems experienced by the children were not such as to engage the EqA 2010.

144 *Pieretti v Enfield LBC* [2010] EWCA Civ 1104, [2011] HLR 3, rejecting arguments a) that the predecessor provisions of Disability Discrimination Act 1995 s49A had no application to homelessness applications, but only to the formulation of policy; b) that HA 1996 Part 7 was a complete code that comprehensively addressed the rights and needs of disabled people so that section 49A added nothing; c) that a determination under Part 7 was not a 'function' within the meaning of section 49A; and d) that neither the original decision-maker nor the review officer had been asked to consider section 49A.

9.70 In *Hackney LBC v Haque*,[145] it was held, in the context of a suitability review, that what EqA 2010 s149 required was for the authority: i) to recognise that the appellant had a disability; ii) to focus on specific aspects of his impairments to the extent that they were relevant to the suitability of the accommodation; iii) to focus on the disadvantages he might suffer when compared to a person without those impairments; iv) to focus on his accommodation needs arising from those impairments and the extent to which the accommodation met those needs; v) to recognise that the appellant's particular needs might require him to be treated more favourably than a person without a disability; and vi) to review the suitability of the accommodation, paying due regard to those matters.[146]

Whose circumstances?

9.71 The section refers to 'a person making . . . an application', and enquiries under HA 1996 s184[147] are whether 'he is' eligible for assistance, or whether 'he has a local connection' with another authority. The wording might therefore be said to suggest that it is only the applicant who is to be considered.[148]

9.72 On the other hand, enquiries into the local connection of the applicant alone would not suffice, for the local connections of a person reasonably to be expected to reside with the applicant are relevant,[149] and priority need may likewise arise by reference to non-applicants.[150] The circumstances of a person reasonably to be expected to reside with the applicant may also affect the issue of intentionality – for example, if those circumstances meant that the accommodation which has been quit was not available or reasonable to continue to be occupied.[151] The suitability of accommodation offered will also require regard to be had to those reasonably to be expected to reside with the applicant.[152]

9.73 It would introduce a surprising – and inconsistent – degree of legality or formality into HA 1996 Part 7 and H(W)A 2014 Part 2 if

145 [2017] EWCA Civ 4, [2017] HLR 14.

146 There is no need to refer in terms to EqA 2010 s149, what matters is whether the substance has been complied with: *Haque*, above, *Poshteh v Kensington and Chelsea RLBC* [2015] EWCA Civ 711, [2015] HLR 36.

147 See para 9.48.

148 In Wales, the H(W)A 2014 speaks of an assessment of 'a person's case': s62.

149 See para 7.34.

150 See para 5.2.

151 See paras 6.77 and 6.140.

152 See para 10.170.

anything turned on who actually approaches the authority or signs an application form.

9.74 It seems clear, therefore, that any person whose circumstances will, under HA 1996 Part 7 (or H(W)A 2014 Part 2), necessarily be taken into consideration in determining either eligibility for assistance or the level of that assistance, should be considered within the ambit of an application and its enquiries.[153]

Burden of proof

9.75 It is not for the applicant to 'prove' his or her homelessness. In *Walters*,[154] the applicant's solicitor gave the authority information which, if confirmed, would have led to a finding that the applicant was homeless; the authority said that she had not established that she was homeless. This wrongly treated the burden as being on the applicant to prove homelessness.

Relevant matters

9.76 It is a trite proposition that enquiries must cover all relevant matters; this means more than merely 'touching on' relevant matters: an authority must engage with the issues that are germane to the application.[155]

9.77 A relevant matter may evolve from the factual background provided by the applicant or of the authority's own motion. In *Paris*,[156] it was held that enquiries into matters relevant to a finding of intentionality have to be made whether or not the applicant provides information which suggests that there may be something to follow up – for example, whether or not the last accommodation occupied was

153 In turn, this could lead to a finding that there had not been intentional homelessness – where one member is or could be held to have become homeless intentionally but another is or could not be. At that point, assuming that there is at least a minimal degree of knowledge that the 'second' person is asking the authority for housing assistance, there is in substance an 'application', and that person is entitled to his or her separate consideration: see para 9.72.

154 *R v Woodspring DC ex p Walters* (1984) 16 HLR 73, QBD.

155 See *Islington LBC v Mohammed* [2013] EWCA Civ 739, [2013] HLR 41 (not engaged with whether applicant would be vulnerable because fainting attacks more likely if street homeless). See also *Farah v Hillingdon LBC* [2014] EWCA Civ 359, [2014] HLR 24 (intentional homelessness because of arrears which could have been avoided by unnecessary expenditure, including taxis: authority had not engaged with whether the applicant's argument that some of the fares were necessary expenditure because of her mobility difficulties). See further paras 12.11 and 12.41–12.42.

156 *R v Reigate and Banstead BC ex p Paris* (1984) 17 HLR 103, QBD.

available and whether it was reasonable to continue in occupation of it.

9.78 Thus, in *Silchenstedt*,[157] the applicant was asked to leave accommodation consisting of two bedrooms on the ground of rent arrears, but was offered alternative accommodation by the same landlord, which he refused on the ground that it was not suitable. The authority found the applicant intentionally homeless and that the *alternative* accommodation was available for him and reasonable for him to occupy.[158] The applicant successfully challenged the decision on the basis that the authority had not conducted sufficient enquiries into the size and nature of the accommodation which the applicant had refused.

9.79 By way of contrast, in *de Falco*,[159] the applicants gave their reason for leaving Italy as unemployment and did not put forward any material from which it might have been inferred that the accommodation that they had left was not accommodation which had been reasonable to continue to occupy.[160] The authority was held not to have erred in drawing the inference that what they had left had been suitable,[161] even though it had made no express enquiry to this effect. *De Falco* was, however, an interlocutory application and was treated as such in *Paris*.[162] On this aspect, it is somewhat out of harmony with subsequent decisions.

9.80 In *Fisher*,[163] it was held that intentionality enquiries may have to go back over several years, to the last accommodation occupied by the applicant (if any) which was available and reasonable. See also *Iqbal*,[164] where insufficient enquiries were made into the applicant's claim that he was a political refugee.

157 *R v Kensington and Chelsea RLBC ex p Silchenstedt* (1996) 29 HLR 728, QBD.

158 For reasons that are not apparent on the face of the report, the argument (described as 'legalistic, although it may be a perfectly proper, approach') that the applicant could not be homeless intentionally as a result of a failure to take up accommodation 'has not been pressed in this application before me': *Silchenstedt*, at 731.

159 *De Falco, Silvestri v Crawley BC* [1980] QB 460, CA.

160 Although Bridge LJ considered the reason for leaving Italy to be 'not their lack of suitable accommodation, but their lack of employment' (at 482F; a phrase then picked up by the headnote writer), the correct test was reasonable to continue to occupy, as is recognised later in the same paragraph.

161 Ie reasonable for them to continue to occupy, see last footnote.

162 *R v Reigate and Banstead BC ex p Paris* (1984) 17 HLR 103, QBD.

163 *R v Preseli DC ex p Fisher* (1984) 17 HLR 147, QBD.

164 *R v Westminster City Council ex p Iqbal* (1988) 22 HLR 215, QBD.

Adequacy of enquiries

9.81 The requirement to enquire into all relevant matters does not, however, mean that a failure to enquire into every matter raised will necessarily make the enquiry process flawed. What is relevant will be different in every case. The duty to make enquiries means enquiries appropriate to the facts known to the authority, or of which it ought reasonably to have been aware;[165] the applicant should normally put forward the matters and evidence which he or she wishes to be taken into account.[166]

9.82 Enquiries can only be attacked as inadequate if they are enquiries that no reasonable authority could have failed to make; the court should not intervene merely because further enquiries would have been sensible or desirable, only if they were such that no reasonable authority could be satisfied had been sufficient – see *Costello*,[167] *Bayani*[168] and *Kassam*.[169]

Examples – unsuccessful challenge

9.83 In *Adamiec*,[170] where the applicant alleged that he had been constrained to sell his home because of financial circumstances, the court refused to quash the decision that he was intentionally homeless either on the basis that a reasonable authority would have further tested the financial material before it or that a reasonable authority would have made further enquiries.

9.84 Likewise in *Baruwa*,[171] where the applicant claimed that she could not afford her rent because of other necessary outgoings, the Court of Appeal held that it was not necessary for the authority to investigate every detail and every inconsistency in the income and expenditure figures provided by the applicant before reaching its decision.[172]

9.85 In *Bariise*,[173] the applicant complained that insufficient enquiries had been made into her allegations that those she had shared a house

165 *R v Sedgemoor DC ex p McCarthy* (1996) 28 HLR 608, QBD.

166 *Cramp v Hastings BC; Phillips v Camden LBC* [2005] EWCA Civ 1005, [2005] HLR 48; see para 9.92.

167 *R v Nottingham City Council ex p Costello* (1989) 21 HLR 301, QBD.

168 *R v Kensington and Chelsea RLBC ex p Bayani* (1990) 22 HLR 406, CA.

169 *R v Kensington and Chelsea RLBC ex p Kassam* (1993) 26 HLR 455, QBD. See also *R v Nottingham City Council ex p Edwards* (1998) 31 HLR 33, QBD.

170 *R v Leeds City Council ex p Adamiec* (1991) 24 HLR 138, QBD.

171 *R v Brent LBC ex p Baruwa* (1997) 29 HLR 915, CA.

172 Contrast *R v Tower Hamlets LBC ex p Ullah* (1992) 24 HLR 680, QBD, where further enquiries were held to have been necessary on very similar facts to *Baruwa*.

173 *R v Brent LBC ex p Bariise* (1998) 31 HLR 50, CA.

with had stolen her food and had scolded her children, making them cry. All the allegations were, however, known to the authority; there were no further enquiries which it could usefully have made.

9.86 In *McDonagh*,[174] a failure to enquire into the applicant's British nationality could not be criticised, as the applicant had informed the authority that his family was a large Irish travelling family just arrived from Dublin, and only claimed to be British after the decision that he was intentionally homeless had been made.

9.87 In *Augustin*,[175] it could not be said – on the material before it – that the authority could not have been satisfied that the applicant was homeless intentionally. In the circumstances, it could not be said that it had not made necessary enquiries.

Examples – successful challenge

9.88 In *Beattie (No 2)*,[176] affidavit evidence in earlier proceedings was considered to be material which the authority ought to have taken into account, even though it had not expressly been referred to during the course of a further application.

9.89 In *Krishnan v Hillingdon LBC*,[177] the authority had made inadequate enquiries when it failed to chase up its letter to another authority, or to follow up the applicant's own description of pressure on him to leave his earlier accommodation because of overcrowding.

9.90 In *Phillips*,[178] the applicant burst out at her husband during their interview that she had always told him his drinking would get them into trouble. This was said not to be capable of being construed as acquiescence,[179] even by the most hard-hearted of officers; it was astonishing that the officer had not made further enquiries. If he had, for example, of social services, it would inevitably have led to the conclusion that the applicant could not be blamed. In *Ajayi*,[180] the authority had failed to enquire into 'important matters of social history and national status', such as for how long the applicant had been away from the UK and where her children were born, which failure led the authority to consider that the applicant was an immigrant, whereas she had actually been born in the UK.

174 *R (McDonagh) v Hounslow LBC* [2004] EWHC 511 (Admin), [2004] JHL D61.
175 *R v Westminster City Council ex p Augustin* (1993) 25 HLR 281, CA.
176 *R v Eastleigh BC ex p Beattie (No 2)* (1984) 17 HLR 168, QBD.
177 *Krishnan v Hillingdon LBC* June 1981 *LAG Bulletin* 137, QBD.
178 *R v West Dorset DC ex p Phillips* (1984) 17 HLR 336, QBD.
179 See para 6.14.
180 *R v Newham LBC ex p Ajayi* (1994) 28 HLR 25, QBD.

9.91 In *Tickner v Mole Valley DC*,[181] Lord Denning MR criticised the enquiries made as to whether or not the applicants were actually homeless. The applicants, while living in mobile homes, had given permanent addresses to the site manager, on which the authority based its conclusion that they were not homeless:

> They made that finding because each couple gave their permanent address elsewhere. One gave a mother-in-law's address. Another gave a divorced husband's address. I think that was not sufficient. Enquiries should have been made at the addresses given as permanent addresses. If the mother-in-law was asked – or if the divorced husband was asked – the answer would have been: 'We are not going to have that person back.' So Mole Council should have found these couples were homeless.

9.92 As presaged above,[182] the right to review is likely to cure any deficiency or failure to conduct adequate enquiries. In *Cramp*,[183] Brooke LJ said:[184]

> Given the full-scale nature of the review, a court whose powers are limited to considering points of law should now be even more hesitant than the High Court was encouraged to be at the time of *ex p Bayani*[185] if the appellant's ground of appeal relates to a matter which the reviewing officer was never invited to consider, and which was not an obvious matter he should have considered.

9.93 Although *Cramp* has undoubtedly raised the bar which an applicant must cross in order to establish illegality on the grounds of the adequacy of enquiries, that is not to say that the issue can no longer be raised. Challenges are frequently pursued on the basis of failure to make enquiries and the obligation to do so remains extant and, if a failure to make an enquiry remains uncorrected on review, the right to challenge remains available. Moreover, in *Pieretti v Enfield LBC*[186] it was said that the dictum of Brooke LJ requires qualification in circumstances where the applicant is a disabled[187] person; even

181 *Tickner v Mole Valley DC* August 1980 *LAG Bulletin* 187, CA.

182 See para 9.7.

183 *Cramp v Hastings BC, Phillips v Camden LBC*, above.

184 *Cramp* at [14].

185 *R v Kensington and Chelsea RLBC ex p Bayani* (1990) 22 HLR 406, CA.

186 [2010] EWCA Civ 1104, [2011] HLR 3.

187 *Pieretti* concerned Disability Discrimination Act 1995 s49A; this has been replaced with the broader 'public sector equality duty' in EqA 2010 s149 and, as such, the full range of 'protected characteristics' should be considered, ie age, disability, gender reassignment; pregnancy or maternity, race, sex, sexual orientation, religion or belief.

where a decision maker (whether under HA 1996 s184 or s202) is not expressly invited to consider a putative[188] disability, he or she must still have due regard to the need to take steps to take account of it.

9.94 The pre-*Cramp* case-law still provides useful guidance as to the matters which will influence the court's decision. It should, however, be read with the limitations of *Cramp* in mind.

Reliance on particular circumstances

9.95 If reliance is sought to be placed on some eventuality which is not to be taken for granted – eg some idiosyncratic or uncommon circumstance which would alter the decision – of which not even a suspicion has come to the authority's attention, it is much harder to complain of its failure to ask a relevant question.[189] Note, however, the possibility that EqA 2010 s149 – the public sector equality duty – may oblige the authority to carry out further inquiries if some feature of the evidence presents a real possibility that an applicant is within its provisions.[190]

9.96 Advisers should therefore be careful to put all relevant matters before an authority. An authority will not be criticised for failing to make enquiries of someone they have no reason to believe will provide relevant information, for example, a doctor or a school where health or education did not appear to be in issue, especially if an experienced adviser has not raised the point.

9.97 In *Holland*,[191] a couple applied as homeless. They had been living at a series of temporary addresses since leaving a caravan site, which the authority was satisfied had been quit in circumstances which amounted to intentional homelessness. At the Court of Appeal, the couple sought to rely on a suggestion that the man had enjoyed an intervening period of what would have been permanent accommodation in a boarding-house (because he and his wife had at that time separated), but which he had lost for reasons beyond his control, so that he could not be treated as being intentionally homeless. This argument was rejected: the authority had been given no reason to suspect that the accommodation might have been permanent or

188 The decision-maker is, however, entitled to ask for evidence of an alleged disability and, if none is provided, may conclude that there is no disability: *Birmingham City Council v Wilson* [2016] EWCA Civ 1137, [2017] HLR 4.

189 See *Cramp*. See also *Bellouti v Wandsworth LBC* [2005] EWCA Civ 602, [2005] HLR 46.

190 *Pieretti v Enfield LBC* [2010] EWCA Civ 1104, [2011] HLR 3.

191 *R v Harrow LBC ex p Holland* (1982) 4 HLR 108, CA.

acceptable to the man, whose separation from his wife had never been mentioned.

9.98 In *Henderson*,[192] the applicants contended that they were unaware of material facts when they agreed to an order for possession being made against them. The authority could not, however, be faulted for failing to make appropriate enquiries when, on the facts available to it (including what it had been told by the applicants), it had no reason to be aware of this.

9.99 See also *Mahsood*,[193] in which it was held that the authority had no reason to be aware of the applicant's ignorance of housing benefit entitlement during a period of absence. See further *Cunha*,[194] where there had been little or no reference to the illness of the applicant's child as a reason for her return from Brazil; in contrast, see *Ajayi*,[195] where the authority had failed to enquire into 'important matters of social history and national status', such as for how long the applicant had been away from the UK and where her children were born, which failure led to an error in the way in which the application was considered

9.100 In *Nipa Begum*,[196] although relevant to consider whether an applicant could afford to travel to accommodation in deciding whether it was available to her,[197] the challenge failed because the applicant had not raised the issue, nor was it evident from any of the information before the authority that it was an issue. It was accordingly entitled to conclude without further enquiries that she could return to it.

Medical evidence

9.101 In cases where vulnerability is claimed for medical reasons, it will be both proper and a necessary part of an authority's enquiries to consider a medical opinion. The authority must, however, still decide the question of vulnerability for itself: *Carroll*.[198]

9.102 A medical report obtained in pursuance of enquiries is not necessarily required to be disclosed to an applicant. In *R (Lynch) v*

192 *R v Wandsworth LBC ex p Henderson* (1986) 18 HLR 522, QBD.
193 *R v Wycombe DC ex p Mahsood* (1988) 20 HLR 683, QBD.
194 *R v Kensington and Chelsea RLBC ex p Cunha* (1988) 21 HLR 16, QBD.
195 *R v Newham LBC ex p Ajayi* (1994) 28 HLR 25, QBD.
196 *Nipa Begum v Tower Hamlets LBC* (1999) 32 HLR 445, CA.
197 See para 4.18.
198 *R v Lambeth LBC ex p Carroll* (1987) 20 HLR 142, QBD; *Osmani v Camden LBC* [2004] EWCA Civ 1706, [2004] HLR 22.

Lambeth LBC,[199] the authority made reference to extracts of its medical officer's report within the 'minded to find' letter sent in compliance with the Allocation of Housing and Homelessness (Review Procedures) Regulations 1999.[200] The applicant had the opportunity to make representations in response to the letter on any matter with which she disagreed, including the references to the medical officer's report. She did not do so. The failure by the authority to provide the applicant with a copy of the medical report was therefore 'not conclusive of any error of public law'.[201]

9.103 In *Sangermano*,[202] the authority ought either to have accepted medical evidence which was submitted by the applicant's advisers, or to have made its own further enquiries. Once medical evidence has been provided to an authority and properly considered, however, it is open to the authority to reject it.[203]

9.104 Medical evidence may also be rejected if it does not relate to a relevant time. In *Hijazi*,[204] a psychiatrist's opinion was rejected because it did not relate to the applicant's condition at the material time of his eviction.

9.105 In *Lumley*,[205] the authority was provided with a questionnaire completed by the applicant's GP which confirmed that the applicant suffered from severe depression for which he was on medication. The information was passed to the authority's medical officer, who was not qualified in psychiatric medicine, and who neither saw the applicant nor made any further enquiries. He concluded, without giving any reasons, that the applicant was not vulnerable on medical grounds. The enquiries made by the medical officer were held to be inadequate.

9.106 In *Kacar*,[206] however, the applicant claimed that it was not reasonable for him to continue to live away from London because of his wife's depression and phobia of being alone. His wife was not receiving any medical treatment, nor had she consulted her GP, nor had she spoken to her social worker. There were no further enquiries which a reasonable authority could have been expected to make; it had sufficient information to assess the seriousness of the wife's depression.

199 [2006] EWHC 2737 (Admin), [2007] HLR 15.

200 SI No 71. See paras 9.178–9.180.

201 *R (Lynch) v Lambeth LBC* [2006] EWHC 2737 (Admin), [2007] HLR 15, at [33].

202 *R v Bath City Council ex p Sangermano* (1984) 17 HLR 94, QBD.

203 *Noh v Hammersmith and Fulham LBC* [2001] JHL D54, CA.

204 *Hijazi v Kensington and Chelsea RLBC* [2003] EWCA Civ 692, [2003] HLR 73.

205 *R v Newham LBC ex p Lumley* (2001) 33 HLR 11, QBD.

206 *Kacar v Enfield LBC* (2001) 33 HLR 5, CA.

9.107 In *Shala v Birmingham City Council*,[207] the applicants – a husband and wife – applied as homeless and asserted that the wife had mental health issues which meant that she had a priority need. Information was provided from a GP setting out the diagnosis and treatment of post-traumatic stress disorder and depression. The authority concluded that the wife was not in priority need. The couple asked for a review and obtained medical evidence from a psychiatrist stating that the wife was 'very depressed'. The local authority referred this to a medical adviser who provided an opinion that 'there was no particular assertion of severity' and no suggestion of admission to a psychiatric hospital or of other significant treatment being necessary. The medical adviser did not carry out any examination of the wife. Further information was subsequently provided as to the wife's vulnerability from the psychiatrist and the GP. None of that information was referred to the medical adviser. The authority upheld the original decision that there was no priority need.

9.108 On appeal, quashing the authority's decision, it was said that:

a) where an authority's medical expert lacks parity of qualification with the appellant's expert, as here the authority's medical adviser did not have the qualifications of the psychiatrist, the authority 'must not fall into the trap of thinking that it is comparing like with like';[208] and
b) if one medical expert advises on the implications of another expert's report without examining the patient, 'his advice cannot itself ordinarily constitute expert evidence of the applicant's condition' and, if he or she does advise without examination 'the decision-maker needs to take the absence of an examination into account'.[209]

Blanket policies

9.109 A decision reached without proper enquiries will be invalid. A decision reached pursuant to a policy to treat all those evicted for arrears as homeless intentionally will be plainly void as a failure to exercise properly the duty to reach an individual decision: *Williams v Cynon Valley Council*.[210] Nor may an authority automatically or invariably treat as homeless intentionally all those who have been evicted from

207 *Shala v Birmingham City Council* [2007] EWCA Civ 624, [2008] HLR 8. See also para 5.37.
208 *Shala* at [22].
209 *Shala* at [22]–[23].
210 January 1980 *LAG Bulletin* 16, CC.

premises on grounds which reflect tenant default, for example, nuisance and annoyance; the authority must take the reasons for the eviction into account and look at the circumstances giving rise to the order.[211]

9.110 An authority must also bear in mind that some possession orders are within the discretion of the county court judge, who may have taken into account matters for which the applicant has no responsibility. In *Stubbs v Slough BC*,[212] a county court ordered the authority to reconsider its finding of intentionality because an element in the decision to order possession on the ground of nuisance had been the proximity of landlord and tenant, and their relationship, over which the tenant had no control.

Loss of employment

9.111 If the cause of an application is loss of employment, the authority must enquire why the job was lost: *Williams*.[213] Consider also *Cosmo*,[214] where there was a successful challenge on the ground that the authority had failed to make enquiries into whether the loss of accommodation was due to the failure of the applicant's business. In *Cunha*,[215] however, the claimant sought to require the authority to consider the difficulties in sustaining employment in Brazil before deciding that she had become intentionally homeless when she had left employment there to come to the UK; it was held that there was no requirement for the authority to enquire into local employment conditions in Brazil. Likewise in *Bayani*,[216] the failure of the local authority to make full enquiries into the applicant's employment situation in the Philippines was not fatal to its finding of intentionality.

Fairness

9.112 It is a trite proposition that fairness calls for all basic issues (that may be decided adversely to the applicant) to be put to an applicant. When conducting enquiries fairly, authorities are not bound to treat the

211 *Devenport v Salford City Council* (1983) 8 HLR 54, CA; *R v Cardiff City Council ex p John* (1982) 9 HLR 56, QBD.

212 January 1980 *LAG Bulletin* 16, CC.

213 *R v Thurrock DC ex p Williams* (1981) 1 HLR 128, QBD; see para 6.67.

214 *R v Camden LBC ex p Cosmo* (1997) 30 HLR 817, QBD.

215 *R v Kensington and Chelsea RLBC ex p Cunha* (1988) 21 HLR 16, QBD.

216 *R v Kensington and Chelsea RLBC ex p Bayani* (1990) 22 HLR 406, CA.

issue as if in a court of law: *Ward*.[217] They act reasonably if they act on responsible material from responsible people who might reasonably be expected to provide a reliable account. An authority can rely on hearsay, in the sense that it is not obliged to confine itself to direct evidence – for example, where an authority relied on evidence from a social worker's supervisor, rather than the social worker herself.[218]

9.113 In *Goddard v Torridge DC*,[219] the authority discussed with the applicant's former employers the circumstances in which he had quit his job and, accordingly, had lost his tied accommodation, and went into these matters fully with the applicant on three separate occasions, which was sufficient for these purposes.

9.114 In the Divisional Court hearing in *Islam*,[220] an allegation of want of natural justice failed because – by the time of the decision – the authority had given the applicant the benefit of no fewer than six interviews. The judgment nonetheless takes for granted that a want of natural justice would be fatal to an authority's decision.

9.115 The authority is, however, not obliged to put every detail to an applicant, although the applicant must have an opportunity to deal with at least the generality of material which will adversely affect him or her, which will usually mean matters of factual detail.[221] Where facts are agreed by an applicant, however, which facts form the basis of the decision, the decision-maker is entitled to take the applicant's acceptance of the facts at face value.[222]

9.116 A failure to ask why the applicant fell into mortgage arrears,[223] or a failure to enquire into the applicant's state of mind when she quit her previous accommodation, ie, what she had believed about the accommodation that she was coming to (which turned out to be less than settled),[224] have both been held to have been errors on the part of an authority.

217 *R v Southampton City Council ex p Ward* (1984) 14 HLR 114, QBD.

218 *Ward*, above. See also *R v Nottingham City Council ex p Costello* (1989) 21 HLR 301, QBD.

219 January 1982 *LAG Bulletin* 9, QBD.

220 *R v Hillingdon Homeless Persons Panel ex p Islam* (1980) *Times* 10 February, QBD (not forming part of the subsequent appeals – see [1983] 1 AC 688, CA and HL, (1981) 1 HLR 107, HL).

221 On the requirements of fairness, see paras 12.56–12.60.

222 *Rowley v Rugby BC* [2007] EWCA Civ 483, [2007] HLR 40.

223 *R v Wyre BC ex p Joyce* (1983) 11 HLR 73, QBD.

224 *R v Wandsworth LBC ex p Rose* (1983) 11 HLR 105, QBD.

9.117 Where matters are put, they must be put to the applicant himself or herself[225] and, if during interview, a record of the interview should be kept: *Brown*.[226]

9.118 All matters that are ultimately decided against the applicant should be put to the applicant,[227] whether the matter is related to an admission by the applicant of which he or she is aware[228] (regardless of whether it was provided on a 'confidential' basis)[229] or where the authority obtains information from a third party on which it intends to rely, such as a bank,[230] or information from the applicant's GP which is inconsistent with that which the applicant has himself or herself provided.[231]

9.119 The duty is not, however, absolute. A finding of intentionality was upheld in *Reynolds*,[232] even though important but ultimately not decisive issues had not been put directly to the applicant, who had refused both a home visit and an interview and requested that all communication be made through her solicitors. Nor, in *Jaafer*,[233] was the authority required to put to the applicant its conclusion that her husband and child were illegal immigrants, as it had given her every opportunity to offer her version of events in an interview.

9.120 Where the facts are uncontested, there is no general obligation to inform each and every applicant in advance of any negative decision; this would place an unrealistically heavy burden on authorities: *Tetteh*.[234]

9.121 Nor is there an obligation to give the applicant the last word in every case. Whether or not it is unfair not to do so depends on the facts of the particular case. Thus in *Bellouti*,[235] medical evidence from

225 *R v Tower Hamlets LBC ex p Saber* (1992) 24 HLR 611, QBD.

226 *R v Dacorum BC ex p Brown* (1989) 21 HLR 405, QBD.

227 *R v Tower Hamlets LBC ex p Rouf* (1989) 21 HLR 294, QBD.

228 *Robinson v Brent LBC* (1998) 31 HLR 1015, CA. See also *R v Wandsworth LBC ex p Dodia* (1997) 30 HLR 562, QBD and *R v Camden LBC ex p Mohammed* (1998) 30 HLR 315, QBD on inconsistent statements given by applicants.

229 *R v Poole BC ex p Cooper* (1995) 27 HLR 605, QBD.

230 *R v Shrewsbury and Atcham BC ex p Griffiths* (1993) 25 HLR 613, QBD. See also *R v Brent LBC ex p McManus* (1993) 25 HLR 643, QBD and *R v Hackney LBC ex p Decordova* (1994) 27 HLR 108, QBD.

231 *R (Begum) v Tower Hamlets LBC* [2002] EWHC 633 (Admin), [2003] HLR 8.

232 *R v Sevenoaks DC ex p Reynolds* (1989) 22 HLR 250, CA.

233 *R v Westminster City Council ex p Jaafer* (1997) 30 HLR 698, QBD.

234 *Tetteh v Kingston upon Thames RLBC* [2004] EWCA Civ 1775, [2005] HLR 21.

235 *Bellouti v Wandsworth LBC* [2005] EWCA Civ 602, [2005] HLR 46. See also *Hall v Wandsworth LBC; Carter v Wandsworth LBC* [2004] EWCA Civ 1740, [2005] HLR 23.

the applicant's GP was submitted to the authority's medical adviser, who advised that it did not make the applicant vulnerable. Taking into account the evidence and the views of the medical adviser, a decision that the applicant was not vulnerable was upheld on review. The Court of Appeal held that the views of the medical adviser did not have to be put to the applicant, because they were not factual material obtained from a third party; all the authority had done was to refer material on which the applicant relied to its own medical adviser for comment. There was accordingly no unfairness in the comments not being shown to the applicant.

Doubt

9.122 If enquiries suggest that the applicant may have become homeless intentionally, but any doubt or uncertainty remains, the issue must be resolved in favour of the applicant.[236]

Further enquiries and reconsideration

9.123 Once a decision has been made, there is no statutory power to make further enquiries unless application is made for a review[237] or on a new application.[238] The local authority is entitled to take as its starting point the matters which the applicant has specifically raised on review.[239] If a decision taken has been adverse to an applicant, the authority can nonetheless re-open its enquiries of its own motion if it receives new information.[240] This will cure any defects in its earlier procedure, for example, failure to consider relevant matters.

9.124 If the authority has power to reopen enquiries of its own motion, then it is hard to see how any reasonable authority could refuse to exercise it, ie, at the request of a disappointed applicant, provided that the new information has some degree of credibility and could (if accepted) affect the decision. If an authority refuses to do so, however, the correct course is not to seek judicial review but to appeal the original decision.[241]

236 *R v North Devon DC ex p Lewis* [1981] 1 WLR 328, QBD; see also *R v Thurrock BC ex p Williams* (1982) 1 HLR 71, QBD and *R v Gravesham BC ex p Winchester* (1986) 18 HLR 208, QBD.

237 *Mohamed v Hammersmith and Fulham LBC* [2001] UKHL 57, [2002] HLR 7, HL.

238 *R v Lambeth LBC ex p Miah* (1994) 27 HLR 21, QBD.

239 *Williams v Birmingham City Council* [2007] EWCA Civ 691, [2008] HLR 4.

240 Consider *R v Hambleton DC ex p Geoghan* [1985] JPL 394, QBD.

241 *Demetri v Westminster City Council* (2000) 32 HLR 470, CA; and see para 9.161.

9.125 In *Walsh*,[242] further enquiries led the authority to the conclusion that an earlier account of being locked out of accommodation was entirely false: while there was no general right to make a new decision on the same facts, the authority could do so if there was a material change, including new facts or the ascertained falsity of former facts.

9.126 In *Dagou*,[243] however, it was suggested that only fraud and deception could entitle the authority to re-open enquiries once its decision had been reached, although new information might still be relevant to the accommodation which was to be provided.

9.127 In *Crawley BC v B*,[244] the authority decided initially that an applicant was not in priority need and had so notified her (without reaching a decision on intentionality). Subsequently, during an appeal, it changed the priority need decision. It was still entitled to go on to consider whether the applicant had become intentionally homeless. This was, however, not so much a case of revising a decision as completing it. Some dicta in the case do, however, suggest that an authority may revisit a decision whenever, on public law grounds, it would be reasonable to do so.[245]

9.128 *Crawley* was distinguished in *Sadiq*.[246] Once a duty had been accepted under HA 1996 s193,[247] the section provides a complete code of when an authority ceases to be subject to its requirements, so that, for example, loss of priority need after acceptance of a section 193 duty does not entitle the authority to make a new decision that no further duty is owed.

9.129 Nonetheless, in *Porteous*,[248] the authority was permitted to change its decision even after a duty had been accepted under section 193. Rejecting the proposition in *Dagou*[249] that decisions could only be re-opened in cases of fraud or deception, it was held that they could also be revisited where the original decision was based on a fundamental

242 *R v Dacorum BC ex p Walsh* (1991) 24 HLR 401, QBD. Under HA 1985, there was no statutory review process.

243 *R v Southwark LBC ex p Dagou* (1995) 28 HLR 72, QBD.

244 (2000) 32 HLR 636, CA.

245 See per Buxton LJ at 645.

246 *R v Brent LBC ex p Sadiq* (2000) 33 HLR 47, QBD.

247 See paras 10.109–10.219.

248 *Porteous v West Dorset DC* [2004] EWCA Civ 244, [2004] HLR 30.

249 *R v Southwark LBC ex p Dagou* (1995) 28 HLR 72, QBD; see para 9.126.

mistake of fact.[250] Likewise, in *Slaiman*,[251] the return of an applicant to her husband following domestic violence was held to go to the existence or non-existence of the original allegation of domestic violence, rather than comprising a change of circumstances arising after acceptance of a full duty.

Time-scales

9.130 Although there is no statutory requirement that enquiries be carried out within any specific time, the English Code[252] says that authorities should deal with enquiries as quickly as possible. It suggests that authorities should aim to achieve the following:

a) interview and initial assessment of the eligibility of applicants on the day of application;
b) wherever possible, complete enquiries and notify applicant within 33 working days of accepting the duty to make enquiries.

9.131 The target does not entitle an authority to take the view that because enquiries take an average period of time, or are due to be completed with a target period, it owes no duty to a person whose priority need will be lost before that period expires, as where a young person with an automatic priority need because he or she is 16 or 17 years old[253] will turn 18 during that period.[254]

250 Both applicant and authority had operated under a fundamental mistake of fact relating to a tenancy which neither had realised the applicant still held. See also *R (Sambotin) v Brent LBC* [2017] EWHC 1190 (Admin), in which it was held that a decision could only be revisited in the event of fraud or deception (*Dagou*) or if there were a fundamental mistake of fact (*Porteous*). In *Sambotin*, neither was present. The claimant had provided correct information about his immigration status, including an earlier decision letter from a different authority who had concluded that he was not eligible for assistance. If there was any error, it would have been a failure on Brent's part properly to apply the eligibility criteria to those facts, something which Brent did not contend entitled it to reach a new decision; moreover, Brent was under a duty to give reasons for reaching a second decision, with which duty it had failed to comply (see also para 12.64, n160).

251 *R (Slaiman) v Richmond upon Thames LBC* [2006] EWHC 329 (Admin), [2006] HLR 20.

252 Code of Guidance para 6.16; see the Welsh Code para 10.54 to similar effect.

253 See paras 5.65–5.70.

254 *Robinson v Hammersmith and Fulham LBC* [2006] EWCA Civ 1122, [2006] 1 WLR 3295, [2007] HLR 7 at [35].

Decisions

Postponement

9.132 Although the obligation to reach a decision is not spelled out in the section, it is implicit: *Sidhu*.[255] An authority may not defer the obligation in the hope or expectation of a change in circumstances such as might reduce its duties, for example, by loss of priority need.[256]

9.133 Nor can an authority seek to use mediation (to reconcile a 17-year-old with his or her family) to prolong the decision-making process, so that the child turns 18 and loses his or her automatic priority need. Where mediation cannot take place without depriving the child of a right he or she would otherwise have had, the authority must perform its full duty, although it may be able to use mediation in order to fulfil that duty.[257] Mediation and enquiries are entirely independent processes.[258]

9.134 If the issue is eligibility for accommodation,[259] there would in any event be no point in deferring because the authority's housing duty under HA 1996 Part 7 ceases if the applicant's eligibility ends.[260]

Gatekeeping

9.135 An authority's decision on completion of its enquiries is taken on the basis of the information known to it at the time it is reached. It follows that changed circumstances – including those generated

255 *R v Ealing LBC ex p Sidhu* (1982) 2 HLR 45, QBD, approved in *Robinson v Hammersmith and Fulham LBC*, above, at [36].

256 *R v Ealing LBC ex p Sidhu* (1982) 2 HLR 45, QBD. A suggestion in the *Encyclopaedia of Housing Law and Practice*, Sweet & Maxwell, that in an appropriate case, a de minimis deferral, perhaps a few days, may be permissible where there is a substantive basis (as distinct from speculation or a remote chance) for the authority to anticipate a material change was not disapproved, but 'in the case of a 17 year old child, it would not seem to me to be lawful for a local authority to postpone the taking of a decision even for a short period on the basis that by postponing that decision the child will have reached the age of 18 before the decision is taken': per Waller LJ in *Robinson v Hammersmith and Fulham LBC* at [38]. The effect would seem to be that the proposition will not apply if it will cause loss of the priority need (as where priority need will, absent other grounds, be lost on reaching 18, see paras 5.63–5.70).

257 *Robinson v Hammersmith and Fulham LBC*, above, per Waller LJ at [41].

258 *Robinson v Hammersmith and Fulham LBC*, above, per Jonathan Parker LJ at [42] and [45].

259 See chapter 3.

260 HA 1996 s193(6)(a).

by the authority itself – may lead to a different finding than might have been taken had the decision immediately followed the application. This, in turn, opens the way for authorities to engage in forms of 'gatekeeping', ie action which obviates homelessness by ensuring that the applicant finds accommodation otherwise than through HA 1996 Part 7 or H(W)A 2014 Part 2. There is a number of reasons why authorities engage in this: to help to ensure that targets are achieved for the purposes of audit or performance criteria and/or in the interests of returns to central government; for local presentational purposes; and to avoid the need to comply with ancillary provisions, including written decision with reasons, right to review and a reasonable preference in relation to allocations. In *Hanton-Rhouila*,[261] a challenge based on failure to advise the applicant of the implications of accepting private accommodation[262] without completing the HA 1996 Part 7 process failed on the facts, and the review officer had been entitled to conclude that the applicant was no longer homeless.

Material to be taken into account

9.136 An authority must always take into account all that is relevant up to the date of its decision. An applicant cannot complain of a decision which failed to take into account a matter which only came to the knowledge of the authority after it had made its final decision: *Islam*.[263] If it comes to light after the initial decision, but before the review, it must be taken into account on the review.[264] If it comes to light after the review, the technically proper course would appear to be to put the further information before the authority for it to re-open its enquiries and to consider judicial review of a refusal to do so,[265] although in practice, if the information and request are included in a pre-action protocol letter before appeal, it would be very difficult indeed for an authority to resist the appeal if the information was decisive; it may even be that the power to raise an Article 8 issue on

261 *Hanton-Rhouila v Westminster City Council* [2010] EWCA Civ 1334, [2011] HLR 12.

262 An assured shorthold tenancy arranged by the authority's Private Sector Housing Initiatives team under its Finders Payment Scheme (a discretionary scheme for helping people find suitable accommodation in the private sector).

263 *R v Hillingdon Homeless Persons Panel ex p Islam* (1981) *Times* 24 February, QBD (not forming part of the subsequent appeals [1983] 1 AC 688, [1981] 1 HLR 107, HL).

264 See para 9.177.

265 See para 9.101.

appeal[266] could be used as a legal basis for the court to have regard to the information if none other is available.

9.137 In *Crossley*,[267] the decision was so at odds with the evidence put before the authority that it was considered that the authority must have failed to take it into account. As the court put it:[268]

> . . . there were also stark facts, or appraisals of fact, pointing towards vulnerability for a statutorily recognised reason; and these the decision-maker had an obligation to acknowledge, take into account and evaluate along with everything else.

9.138 An authority must consider those matters which sensibly arise on the facts of a case. In *F*,[269] the applicant took a tenancy of a property that she could not afford and contended that she had made appropriate enquiries with the housing benefit department before doing so. The authority found that she had not acted in good faith when accepting the tenancy.[270] Although it had not explicitly been invited to consider whether the applicant had acted in good faith, the court held that it was a matter that was sensibly capable of arising on the facts and therefore required consideration by the authority – which the authority had undertaken.

9.139 In *Elrify*,[271] the applicant applied as homeless by reason of overcrowding. Both in its original decision and on review, the authority had applied only one part of the statutory test for overcrowding under HA 1985 Part 10. The review decision was accordingly flawed because the authority had had failed properly to apply the statutory test and had therefore miscalculated the level of statutory overcrowding in the applicant's flat.

Own decision

9.140 The authority must reach its own decision. Even though other authorities from which an authority requests assistance must cooperate,[272] one authority cannot simply 'rubber-stamp' the decision of another: *Miles*.[273] There may, for example, be information about

266 See para 6.103 onwards.

267 *Crossley v Westminster City Council* [2006] EWCA Civ 140, [2006] HLR 26.

268 At [28].

269 *F v Birmingham City Council* [2006] EWCA Civ 1427, [2007] HLR 18.

270 Within the meaning of HA 1996 s191(2); see paras 6.27–6.28.

271 *Elrify v Westminster City Council* [2007] EWCA Civ 332, [2007] HLR 36.

272 HA 1996 s213.

273 *R v South Herefordshire DC ex p Miles* (1983) 17 HLR 82, QBD. See also *Eren v Haringey LBC* [2007] EWCA Civ 409.

what has occurred between the two applications, such as a separation which means that intervening accommodation was 'settled' for the purposes of the separated parts of a family.[274]

9.141 This principle applies even to decisions of a court[275] – thus, while an authority must take into consideration decisions by family courts relating to with whom children are to live, the authority is not bound by them but must reach its own decision in the context of its own duties in the (different) legislative context in which they arise: *Holmes-Moorhouse*.[276]

Notification

Reasons

9.142 Once the authority has reached its decision, it must notify the applicant.[277] While there will generally be no reason to distinguish between when the decision is made and notification of reasons, these do not necessarily occur on the same date: ascertaining the date of the decision is essentially a question of fact.[278] If the authority decides an issue – relating either to eligibility or to level of duty – adversely to an applicant, it must also notify the applicant of its reasons.[279]

Local connection

9.143 A decision to refer an application to another authority under the local connection provisions, and the reasons for doing so, must likewise be notified.[280]

Review

9.144 Notifications must inform applicants of the right to request a review of a decision and of the time within which the request must be made.[281]

274 See para 6.100.

275 Otherwise than so far as they are decisions of a court directly relating to the decision, ie, appeal against it or on judicial review.

276 *Holmes-Moorhouse v Richmond upon Thames LBC* [2009] UKHL 7, [2009] HLR 34.

277 HA 1996 s184(3); H(W)A 2014 s63.

278 *Robinson v Hammersmith and Fulham LBC* [2006] EWCA Civ 1122, [2006] 1 WLR 3295, [2007] HLR 7, at [25], referring (at [24]) to *R v Beverley BC ex p McPhee* (1978) *Times* 27 October, QBD.

279 *Robinson v Hammersmith and Fulham LBC*, above. And see para 9.182.

280 HA 1996 s184(4); H(W)A 2014 s82(2). Once HRA 2017 comes into force, the duty applies when the referral is under section 198(A1) (referral of cases where section 189B applies): HRA 2017 s5(3), amending HA 1996 s184(4).

281 HA 1996 s184(5); H(W)A 2014 s84; see further below.

Relationship of notification duty and substantive duty

9.145 Duties to notify and to give reasons for decisions arise independently of the substantive duties to which they refer: *R v Beverley BC ex p McPhee*.[282] It is not open to an authority to claim that it has no duty under, for example, HA 1996 s193[283] or s200,[284] on the basis that it has not yet given notice. To hold otherwise would in substance be to permit an authority to rely on its own wrong, ie its failure to provide notice 'on completion' of enquiries.

Written notification

9.146 Notification, and reasons, must be given in writing; if not received by the applicant, notification will be treated as having been given only if made available at the authority's office for a reasonable time for collection by the applicant or on the applicant's behalf.[285] This appears to be so even if a copy of the notice is sent by registered post to one of the authority's own hostels or other property.[286]

Restricted cases[287]

9.147 If the authority decides that a duty is owed under HA 1996 s193(2) or s195(2)[288] or H(W)A 2014 s75,[289] but only because of a restricted person, the notification is subject to additional requirements.[290] It must inform the applicant that the decision was reached on this basis, include the name of the restricted person, explain why the person is a restricted person, and explain the effect of section 193(7AD)[291] or, as the case may be, section 195(4A),[292] or, in Wales, H(W)A 2014 s76(5).

282 (1978) *Times* 27 October, QBD.

283 See para 10.111.

284 See para 7.71.

285 HA 1996 s184(6); H(W)A 2014 s84.

286 The express requirement for writing was added to HA 1985 pursuant to Law Commission Recommendations (Cmnd 9515), No 5.

287 See paras 3.113–3.119.

288 This will no longer apply in England once HRA 2017 s4(3) comes into force.

289 See paras 10.111–10.119.

290 HA 1996 s184(3A); H(W)A 2014 s63(2). Once HRA 2017 comes into force, this duty also arises if the authority decides that a duty would be owed after its duty under s189B(2) comes to an end: HRA 2017 s5(3), amending s184(3A),

291 See paras 10.205–10.211.

292 See paras 10.205–10.211. This will also no longer apply in England once HRA 2017 s4(3) comes into force.

Oral explanation

9.148 In cases where the applicant may have difficulty understanding the implications of the decision, authorities 'should consider arranging for a member of staff to provide and explain the notification in person'.[293]

Review

9.149 Neither the Housing (Homeless Persons) Act 1977 nor HA 1985 Part 3 made any provision for an applicant to seek an internal review of the authority's decision. The third edition of the Code of Guidance issued under HA 1985 Part 3 had, however, recommended[294] that authorities 'should have in place arrangements to review decisions on homelessness cases where an applicant wishes to appeal against the decision'. That recommendation is now a statutory requirement.[295] An applicant is statutorily entitled to request a review, provided that the decision complained of falls within those specified in HA 1996 s202 or H(W)A 2014 s85.

9.150 The request for a review should be interpreted generously. In *Nzamy*,[296] the authority informed the applicant that if he did not accept an offer of alternative accommodation, it would treat its duty as discharged:[297] a request for a review of the suitability of the offer, in the course of which the applicant made clear that the family was willing to remain in their current temporary accommodation pending a permanent offer, should also have been treated as a request for a review of the discharge decision. The right to request a review arises in relation to the following decisions.

Eligibility[298]

9.151 A decision on eligibility may be reviewed.[299] This includes whether or not the applicant is a person subject to immigration control.[300]

293 English Code of Guidance para 6.23; see Welsh Code para 15.95 to similar effect.
294 Code of Guidance para 9.6.
295 HA 1996 s202(4); H(W)A 2014 s85.
296 *Nzamy v Brent LBC* [2011] EWCA (Civ) 283, [2011] HLR 20.
297 See paras 10.185–10.188.
298 See generally chapter 3.
299 HA 1996 s202(1)(a); H(W)A 2014 s85(1).
300 See paras 3.10–3.109.

Duties[301]

9.152 An applicant may also seek review of any decision on what, if any, duty is owed under HA 1996 ss190–193 and 195–196 or H(W)A 2014 ss66, 68, 73 or 75.[302] This expressly encompasses whether or not the applicant is in priority need,[303] whether intentionally homeless,[304] whether a duty has ceased under HA 1996 s193(6) or (7)[305] and whether an applicant is threatened with homelessness or threatened with homelessness intentionally.[306] Whether an authority has complied with the requirement to notify the applicant of the consequences of refusal and the right to request a review under HA 1996 s193(7) and (7A)[307] is also subject to review under this provision.[308]

9.153 Once HRA 2017 comes into force, HA 1996 s196 (duties to those threatened with homelessness intentionally) will be repealed,[309] but the decisions which may be the subject of review are otherwise expanded to include decisions[310] under the new initial duty to help (paras 10.66–10.74) and the new duties to those threatened with

301 See generally chapter 10.

302 HA 1996 s202(1)(b); in Wales, see H(W)A 2014 s85(1)(b) and (c).

303 HA 1996 ss190(3) and 192; and also by inference whether the applicant is homeless. See also H(W)A 2014 ss70, 71. Once HRA 2017 is in force, s192 will be repealed (HRA 2017 s5(6)) and replaced by new provisions: see paras 10.52–10.61.

304 HA 1996 ss190(1) and 191; and H(W)A 2014 s77.

305 HA 1996 s193 encompasses a decision that a duty, once owed, is no longer owed: *Warsame v Hounslow LBC* (1999) 32 HLR 335, CA, affirmed notwithstanding intervening legislative changes under Homelessness Act 2002 in *Ravichandran v Lewisham LBC* [2010] EWCA Civ 755, [2010] HLR 42 (discussed below). In Wales, see H(W)A 2014 s85(1)(c).

306 HA 1996 ss195 and 196. Section 195 will be replaced, and s196 repealed, once HRA 2017 is in force and replaced with new provisions see paras 10.52–10.61: HRA 2017 s4(2), (5).

307 See para 10.190.

308 *Tower Hamlets LBC v Rahanara Begum* [2005] EWCA Civ 116, [2006] HLR 9. The applicant had failed to seek an internal review and the matter could not be raised as a defence to eviction proceedings being brought against her. Cf *R (Zaher) v Westminster City Council* [2003] EWHC 101 (Admin), where the failure of the authority to inform the applicant of his right to review entitled the applicant to challenge the decision on suitability by judicial review. In Wales, the equivalent to s193(7) and (7A) is now H(W)A 2014 s76(3)(c) and it is likely that the cases cited in this footnote will apply with equal force.

309 HRA 2017 s5(5); see also s9(2).

310 This includes decisions as to steps to be taken, as to the giving of notice to bring either duty to an end and as to the suitability of final offers. The latter may be the subject of a review whether or not the offer has been accepted: HRA 2017 s9(1), (2); HA 1996 s202(1B) as added.

homelessness (paras 10.52–10.61) along with the corresponding provisions of ss193A–193C governing cessation of those new duties by reference to final offers (para 10.59) or deliberate and unreasonable refusal to co-operate (para 10.78).[311]

Local connection[312]

9.154 Review may be sought of a number of local connection decisions.[313] The decision to notify another authority under HA 1996 s198(1) can be reviewed; the decision that the conditions for referral are met under section 198(5) can itself also be reviewed.

9.155 A decision that the conditions of referral are met may be reached either as a result of an agreement between the authorities, or as the result of an arbitration between them.[314] It may at first glance seem somewhat surprising to find provision for review of a decision that the conditions for referral are met, when it is statutorily provided that this is to be a matter for agreement or approved arbitration arrangements.[315] It needs, however, to be remembered that the applicant is himself or herself party to neither agreement nor arbitration: this is accordingly the applicant's opportunity to dispute the outcome.

9.156 Decisions on how the duty is to be discharged may themselves also be reviewed. This includes discharge both where the local connection referral conditions are met[316] and where they are not.[317]

Suitability and availability of offers

9.157 An applicant may seek a review of whether accommodation offered in discharge of duty under HA 1996 s190, s193[318] or s200 is 'suitable'[319]

311 HRA 2017 s9(1), (2); HA 1996 s202(1) as amended.

312 See generally chapter 7.

313 HA 1996 s202(1)(c), (d), (e); H(W)A 2014 s85(1)(c). It may not be sought against a decision not to make a local connection referral: *Hackney LBC v Sareen* [2003] EWCA Civ 351, [2003] HLR 54.

314 See paras 7.73–7.88.

315 See paras 7.73–7.88.

316 HA 1996 s200(4).

317 HA 1996 s200(3).

318 Including expressly HA 1996 s193(7) (see para 10.179) to clear up any residual doubt following the decision in *Warsame v Hounslow LBC* (1999) 32 HLR 335, CA, which had the effect of confining application of HA 1996 s202(1)(f) to the question of the suitability of an offer under section 193(6). In Wales, see H(W)A 2014 s85(1)(c).

319 HA 1996 s202(1)(f); H(W)A 2014 s59.

and, where applicable,[320] whether it is reasonable to accept it. An applicant may also seek a review of a decision of an authority as to the suitability of accommodation offered by way of a private accommodation offer,[321] ie, in a restricted case;[322] from the commencement of LA 2011 s148,[323] there is likewise a right to seek a review of a decision as to the suitability of a private rented sector offer,[324] in a restricted case or otherwise.[325]

9.158 It had formerly been held that, where an applicant accepted an offer of accommodation, the applicant could not also seek a review as to its suitability: *Alghile*.[326] The result of this was that an applicant to whom an unsatisfactory offer of accommodation had been made had to face 'an unwholesome opportunity to gamble',[327] either to refuse – which gave rise to the risk that, if unsuccessful on the review, the applicant would end up with nowhere to live – or to accept, which meant putting up with accommodation that the applicant considered unsatisfactory.[328] There is, however, now a right to seek an internal review of the suitability of accommodation offered under HA 1996 s193(5) or (7), whether or not the applicant has accepted the offer of accommodation.[329]

9.159 The date at which suitability of accommodation should be considered on a review will differ depending whether the accommodation was accepted or refused. If an offer of accommodation was accepted,

320 HA 1996, s193(7F). See, in particular, *Ravichandran v Lewisham LBC* [2010] EWCA Civ 755, [2010] HLR 42, where the authority had considered suitability at a previous review, but at no time had considered whether it was reasonable for the applicant to accept it, for which reason its decision could not stand.

321 HA 1996 s202(1)(g), inserted by Housing and Regeneration Act 2008 Sch 15 para 7; H(W)A 2014 s76(2) requires all private rented sector offers to be suitable, ie the position in Wales is the same as the post-LA 2011 position in England.

322 See above, paras 3.113–3.119 and 9.147; see paras 10.68–10.69.

323 Localism Act 2011 (Commencement No 2 and Transitional Provisions) (England) Order 2012 SI No 2599 article 2.

324 Provided that the authority's duty to secure accommodation has not ceased before that date: Localism Act 2011 (Commencement No 2 and Transitional Provisions) (England) Order 2012 SI No 2599 article 3.

325 See paras 10.205–10.211.

326 *Alghile v Westminster City Council* (2001) 33 HLR 57, CA, overruling *R v Kensington and Chelsea RLBC ex p Byfield* (1997) 31 HLR 913, QBD.

327 *Alghile v Westminster City Council* [2001] EWCA Civ 363, (2001) 33 HLR 57 per Tuckey LJ at [28].

328 This contrasts with the outcome in *R v Wycombe DC ex p Hazeltine* (1993) 25 HLR 313, CA; see para 10.216.

329 HA 1996 s202(1A), added by Homelessness Act 2002 s8; H(W)A 2014 s85(3).

then the authority should consider the facts at the date of review because the accommodation is still available.[330] Conversely, however, where an offer of accommodation has been refused, then the council has taken the decision that it has fulfilled its duty and the property will no longer be available; in those circumstances, the issue has to be tested by reference to the circumstances as they existed at the date of that decision.[331]

Further review

9.160 There is no right to request a review of a decision reached on an earlier review;[332] it is highly likely that the courts would so have limited the entitlement in any event.

9.161 Although HA 1996 s202(2) does not prevent an authority from further reconsidering a decision if asked and willing to do so, a refusal to exercise the discretion to reconsider has been held not to be judicially reviewable.[333] The correct forum for challenge remains by way of appeal to the county court of the original review decision.[334]

Review procedure

9.162 A request for a review should be made within 21 days of notification of a decision under HA 1996 s184.[335] The applicant must be told about the right to request a review in the decision notification;[336] if the notification does not do so, time cannot be considered to have started to run.

330 *Omar v Westminster City Council* [2008] EWCA Civ 421, [2008] HLR 36.

331 *Omar*, above, per Waller LJ at [25].

332 HA 1996 s202(2); H(W)A 2014 s85(4).

333 *R v Westminster City Council ex p Ellioua* (1998) 31 HLR 440, CA. See also *R (C) v Lewisham LBC* [2003] EWCA Civ 927, [2004] HLR 4.

334 See *Demetri v Westminster City Council* (2000) 32 HLR 470, CA as to the effects of reconsideration on time limits to appeal to the county court, discussed at paras 12.168–12.170.

335 HA 1996 s202(3); H(W)A 2014 s85(5). The wording need not be followed slavishly – thus, saying that the appeal 'must be made within 21 days of the date of this letter' rather than of when the applicant was notified of the decision did not vitiate the letter in *Dharmaraj v Hounslow LBC* [2011] EWCA Civ 312, [2011] HLR 18.

336 HA 1996 s202(3); H(W)A 2015 s85(5). Notification to an applicant's solicitor suffices: *Dharmaraj v Hounslow LBC*, above. See also *Dragic v Wandsworth LBC* [2011] JHL D59.

9.163 If the notification does inform the applicant of the right to review, then on the face of it, the applicant who fails to exercise it in time will lose it. The authority has power to extend time.[337] This discretion must be exercised in furtherance of its statutory purpose, which is to establish procedures and time limits necessary to enable the authority to manage its housing stock in an orderly way, and – where appropriate – to grant an indulgence to an applicant where the merits of the applicant's claim for review are deserving enough to override the failure to request a review in time. Accordingly, the authority is entitled but not bound to take into account the prospect of the review's success.[338]

9.164 The secretary of state has power to make regulations as to the procedure to be followed in connection with a review:[339] see the Allocation of Housing and Homelessness (Review Procedures) Regulations ('English Review Procedure Regs') 1999.[340] In Wales, the Welsh Ministers have the same power: see Homelessness (Review Procedure) (Wales) Regulations ('Welsh Review Procedure Regs') 2015.[341]

Identity of the reviewer

9.165 Both sets of regulations may require that the decision on review be made by a person of appropriate seniority who was not involved in the original decision.[342] The Welsh regulations do not do so, and only require that the review officer be someone who was not involved in the original decision.[343]

9.166 The English regulations,[344] however, do require that, when the original decision was made by an officer of the authority[345] and the

337 HA 1996 s202(3); H(W)A 2014 s85(5).

338 *R (C) v Lewisham LBC* [2003] EWCA Civ 927, [2004] HLR 4. See also *R (Slaiman) v Richmond upon Thames LBC* [2006] EWHC 329 (Admin), [2006] HLR 20.

339 HA 1996 s203(1); in Wales, the Welsh Ministers have the same power, see H(W)A 2014 s86 and Homelessness (Review Procedure) (Wales) Regulations 2015 SI No 1266.

340 SI No 71.

341 See H(W)A 2014 s86 and SI No 1266.

342 HA 1996 s203(2)(a); H(W)A 2014 s86(2)(a).

343 Welsh Review Procedure Regs 2015 reg 3; see also Welsh Code para 20.9.

344 English Review Procedure Regs 1999 reg 2.

345 The decision must be made by the authority by its executive (single member, committee, sub-committee or officer) to whom the function is delegated: see Local Government Act 2000 ss13–15 and Local Authorities (Functions and Responsibilities) (England) Regulations 2000 SI No 2853.

review is also to be carried out by an officer of the authority, the latter must be someone who was not involved in the original decision and who is senior to the original decision-maker:

> Seniority for these purposes means seniority in rank within the authority's organisational structure.[346]

9.167 The officer who is undertaking the review may, however, enlist the assistance of a more junior officer, even where that junior officer made the original decision.[347] A view expressed by a more senior officer about the type of allocation for which an applicant qualified under the authority's HA 1996 Part 6 allocation scheme was not a decision for the purposes of the English Review Procedure Regs 1999 reg 2, nor could it be subject to a section 202 review, nor therefore did it disqualify a more junior officer from conducting the review: *Feld*.[348]

9.168 If elected members are involved in the review process,[349] neither the English nor the Welsh regulations set any particular requirements.

9.169 There may be more than one review on a single application, for example, following a successful county court appeal or where – following a finding that an original offer of accommodation was unsuitable – the applicant seeks to challenge a further offer. The fact that a review officer has conducted an earlier review does not prevent him or her conducting a second review; there is no apparent bias and any actual unfairness can be cured on appeal to the county court: *Feld*.[350]

9.170 There is nothing in HA 1996 Part 7 or H(W)A 2014 Part 2 that requires a decision as to whether or not to secure interim accommodation under HA 1996 s188(3) or H(W)A 2014 s85[351] pending a review[352] to be made by an officer who is senior to the officer who made the original decision on the application; nor is there anything necessarily objectionable in the same officer who made the decision under review also making the decision on Interim accommodation.[353]

346 English Code of Guidance para 19.8; the Welsh regulations only require that the review officer be someone who was not involved in the original decision (reg 3; see also Welsh Code para 20.9).

347 English Review Procedure Regs 1999 reg 2; and see *Butler v Fareham BC* May 2001 *Legal Action* 24, CA.

348 *Feld v Barnet LBC; Pour v Westminster City Council* [2004] EWCA Civ 1307, [2005] HLR 9.

349 These will have to be members of the executive.

350 *Feld v Barnet LBC; Pour v Westminster City Council*, above.

351 See Welsh Code para 20.29.

352 See para 10.29.

353 *R (Abdi) v Lambeth LBC* [2007] EWHC 1565 (Admin), [2008] HLR 5.

9.171 The review function may be contracted out.[354]

Local connection reviews

9.172 While most reviews will be carried out by the authority to which the original homelessness application was made, there is an exception in the case of a review sought under HA 1996 s202(1)(d) or H(W)A 2014 s85(1)(c), against a decision under HA 1996 s198(5) or H(W)A 2014 s80(3) that the conditions for a local connection referral are met.[355] In these cases, the review must be carried out either:

a) jointly by the notifying and notified authorities where the decision was reached by agreement;[356] or
b) by a further referee, where the matter had been determined by a referee under the Homelessness (Decisions on Referrals) Order 1998.[357]

9.173 In the latter case, the further referee must be appointed within five working days.[358] If a referee is not appointed by agreement, then a person must be appointed in accordance with the both the English and Welsh Review Procedure Regs.

Impact of the Human Rights Act 1998

9.174 The review procedure is not the determination of a civil right for the purposes of Article 6[359] of the European Convention on Human Rights (ECHR).[360] Even if it was, it was considered in *Runa Begum*[361] that an internal review coupled with the right to an appeal to the county

354 See para 9.5; and English Code of Guidance para 19.8. See Housing (Wales) Act 2014 (Consequential Amendments) Regulations 2015 SI No 752, amending the Local Authorities (Contracting Out of Allocation of Housing and Homelessness Functions) Order 1996 SI No 3205 so as to continue to apply it to H(W)A 2014 Part 2.

355 See para 7.58.

356 English Review Procedure Regs 1999 reg 1; Welsh Review Procedure Regs 2015 reg 4.

357 SI No 1578.

358 English Review Procedure Regs 1999 reg 7(1) and (2); Welsh Review Procedure Regs 2015 reg 4.

359 'In the determination of his civil rights and obligations . . . everyone is entitled to a fair and public hearing within a reasonable time by an independent and impartial tribunal established by law . . .'

360 See paras 12.96–12.100.

361 *Runa Begum v Tower Hamlets LBC* [2003] UKHL 5, [2003] 2 AC 430, [2003] HLR 32.

court under HA 1996 s204 comprised compliance with Article 6, an approach followed in *Ali v Birmingham City Council*.[362] In *Ali v UK*,[363] the latter case at the European Court of Human Rights, *Runa Begum* was qualified to the extent that it was held that Article 6(1) is engaged once an authority has decided that a duty is owed under s193 because there is a sufficiently certain right to amount to a 'civil right'; in agreement with *Runa Begum* and *Ali* at the Supreme Court, however, it was also held that there was no violation of Article 6 as the rights to a reasoned decision, review and appeal were adequate safeguards. In *Poshteh v Kensington and Chelsea RLBC*,[364] the Supreme Court refused to depart from its decision in *Ali v Birmingham City Council*, notwithstanding *Ali v UK*: the decision in *Ali v UK* did not engage in any detail with the decision in *Ali v Birmingham City Council*; the scope and limit of the concept of a 'civil right' was suitable for consideration by the Grand Chamber of the European Court of Human Rights; without such a decision, it was not appropriate to depart from the fully reasoned decision in *Ali v Birmingham City Council*.

Procedure on review

9.175 Once the applicant has requested a review, the authority must notify the applicant that he or she – or someone acting on the applicant's behalf – may make representations in writing.[365]

9.176 The purpose of this requirement is to invite the applicant to state his or her grounds for requesting a review (if the applicant has not already done so) and to elicit any new information that the applicant may have in relation to it.[366] Where the applicant's legal representatives requested information from the authority prior to making representations, and the authority failed to provide the information or await the representations prior to making a review decision, the decision was unlawful.[367] If the applicant has not already been informed

362 [2010] UKSC 8.

363 App No 40378/10, [2015] HLR 46.

364 [2017] UKSC 36.

365 English Review Procedure Regs 1999 reg 6(2)(a). Where the case concerns a local connection referral that has been referred to a referee (see para 9.171), it is the referee who must make the notification: reg 6(3)(a). Welsh Review Procedure Regs 2015 reg 2, gives a right to make representations in writing, orally, or both.

366 English Code of Guidance para 19.10; Welsh Code para 20.11.

367 *Aw-Aden v Birmingham City Council* [2005] EWCA Civ 1834 at [21], although as the authority subsequently reconsidered the decision it was in fact upheld by the Court of Appeal.

of the procedure to be followed,[368] then the notification must also set out what it is.[369]

9.177 The original regulations[370] required the reviewer to consider any representations made by the applicant and to carry out the review on the basis of the facts known to him or her at its date. The latter requirement is not explicit in the current English Review Procedure Regs 1999.[371] This change notwithstanding, the reviewing officer 'is not simply considering whether the initial decision was right on the material before it at the date it was made. He may have regard to information relevant to the period before the decision but only obtained thereafter and to matters occurring after the initial decision': *Mohamed*.[372]

9.178 If there is a deficiency or irregularity in the original decision, or in the way it was made, but the reviewer is nonetheless minded to make a decision which is against the interests of the applicant, the reviewer must notify the applicant that the reviewer is so minded and of the reasons why, and that the applicant or someone on the applicant's behalf may make representations to the reviewer, orally or in writing or both, which representations the reviewer must consider.[373] If the applicant is represented, notification to his or her solicitor suffices for the purposes of this requirement.[374] This procedure is capable of remedying any defect in the original decision letter and is suitable

368 English Review Procedure Regs 1999 reg 6(2)(b) and (3)(b); Welsh Review Procedure Regs 2015 reg 2(2)(b).

369 A requirement in the 1996 edition of the Code of Guidance that authorities should have an approved document setting out their procedure available to the public is not included in the present Code.

370 Allocation of Housing and Homelessness (Review Procedures and Amendment) Regulations 1996 SI No 3122 reg 8(1).

371 The former is included: English Review Procedure Regs 1999 reg 8(1). Where the review is being conducted by a referee (see para 9.171, above) the referee must send any representations to both authorities involved and seek their comments: reg 7(5). The position is the same in Wales, reg 4.

372 *Mohamed v Hammersmith and Fulham LBC* [2001] UKHL 57, [2002] HLR 7 at [26]. As to reviews of suitability, see paras 9.156–9.158.

373 English Review Procedure Regs 1999 reg 8(1)(b) and (2). The Court of Appeal has assumed – without argument – that the wording of reg 8(2)(b) gives the applicant the right to choose how representations are made – orally, in writing, or orally and in writing: see *Lambeth LBC v Johnston* [2008] EWCA Civ 690, [2009] HLR 10 at [53]; and *Hall v Wandsworth LBC; Carter v Wandsworth LBC* [2004] EWCA Civ 1740, [2005] HLR 23 at [25]–[26]. In Wales, see Welsh Review Procedure Regs 2015 reg 5(2).

374 *Maswaku v Westminster City Council* [2012] EWCA Civ 669; *El Goure v Kensington and Chelsea RLBC* [2012] EWCA Civ 670.

as a means for challenging the original decision of a local authority, rather than judicial review.[375]

9.179 The duty is two-fold:

a) first, to consider whether there was a deficiency or irregularity in the original decision or in the manner in which it was made; and
b) second, if there was – and if the review officer is nonetheless minded to make a decision adverse to the applicant on one or more issues – to serve a 'minded to find' notice on the applicant explaining the reasons for the reviewer's provisional views.[376]

The review officer is only under a duty to 'consider' the representations, not necessarily to give any notification or indication of that consideration.[377] Where consideration of deficiency and/or irregularity has taken place, but no reasons have been given for an adverse conclusion in relation to it,[378] the review procedure could still be susceptible on public law grounds.[379] Accordingly, in practice a local authority is now effectively obliged to state in every review decision letter why there is no deficiency or irregularity in the original decision, and consequently why no 'minded to find' letter was sent.

9.180 Neither 'deficiency' nor 'irregularity' is defined in either the English or Welsh Review Procedure Regulations.[380] 'Deficiency' is not confined to an error of law in the original decision; there is a deficiency if there is 'something lacking' in it which is of sufficient importance to the fairness of the procedure to justify the additional procedural safeguard: *Hall* and *Carter*.[381] Accordingly, a reviewing officer should apply English Review Procedure Regs reg 8(2) whenever the officer considers that an important aspect of the case was

375 *R (Lynch) v Lambeth LBC* [2007] HLR 15.

376 *Lambeth LBC v Johnston*, above.

377 *Johnston*, above, per Rimer LJ at [51].

378 A poorly worded letter which, however, had addressed all the important aspects of the case which meant that a reasonable reader would have had no doubt about the basis of the decision sufficed in one (*Nagi*) of the three cases heard together in *Makisi v Birmingham City Council; Yosief v Birmingham City Counci; Nagi v Birmingham City Council* [2011] EWCA Civ 355, [2011] HLR 27.

379 *Johnston*, per Rimer LJ at [54].

380 See English Code of Guidance para 19.13 which suggests matters which might be included (eg failure to take into account relevant considerations; failure to base decision on the facts; bad faith or dishonesty; error of law; decisions which are contrary to the purpose of the HA 1996; irrational or unreasonable decisions; procedurally unfair decisions); see also Welsh Code para 20.13, which contains the same list of examples as in the English Code.

381 *Hall v Wandsworth LBC; Carter v Wandsworth LBC*, above. See now English Code of Guidance para 19.14, Welsh Code para 21.9 reflecting this decision.

either not addressed or was not addressed adequately by the original decision-maker. A lack of clarity as to whether the correct test of vulnerability[382] had been applied was one such deficiency. In *Mitu*,[383] the original decision held both that the applicant was not in priority need and that he had become homeless intentionally; the review concluded that he was not homeless intentionally but upheld the finding on priority need; there was nonetheless a deficiency in the original decision and reg 8(2) therefore applied. This may be contrasted with *Mohamoud v Birmingham City Council*,[384] in which the applicant had rejected a flat and the authority decided that its duty towards her had been discharged; on review, she claimed for the first time that she had misunderstood what she had originally been told by the authority and that she had thought that she would receive up to three offers of accommodation, a confusion that could have arisen as English was not her first language. The review officer rejected these contentions and upheld the original decision but it was held that this should have triggered a 'minded to' letter under reg 8(2).

9.181 If circumstances have changed between the original decision and decision on review,[385] reviewers will need to undertake further enquiries before reaching a decision and may need to serve a 'minded to find' letter.[386]

9.182 Applicants should be aware that it is not only new circumstances which count in the applicant's favour which are to be taken into account, but also any developments which adversely affect the applicant's entitlement.[387] A change of circumstances may yet lead to the loss of a qualifying element in the previous decision, for example,

382 See paras 5.29–5.32.

383 *Mitu v Camden LBC* [2011] EWCA Civ 1249, [2012] HLR 10.

384 [2014] EWCA Civ 227, [2014] HLR 22

385 As in *Mohamed v Hammersmith and Fulham LBC* [2001] UKHL 57, [2002] HLR 7, HL.

386 *Banks v Kingston Upon Thames RLBC* [2008] EWCA Civ 1443, [2009] HLR 29. In the original decision, the applicant was found to be not homeless. Between the original decision and the review decision, the applicant was served with notice to quit by his landlord. The reviewer found that the applicant was homeless, and went on to consider the question of priority need without giving the applicant the opportunity to make representations on that issue, before deciding it against the applicant. The applicant successfully appealed to the Court of Appeal that the change in question under consideration invoked his right to receive a 'minded to find' letter in accordance with English Review Procedure Regs 1999 reg 8(2).

387 See further para 9.189.

priority need.[388] In such a case, the requirement to allow further representations, including an oral hearing,[389] will apply.

9.183 An adverse change will not, however, cause the loss of an element in the first decision if that decision was itself unlawful. In *Robinson*,[390] the authority unlawfully decided that the applicant was not in priority need, notwithstanding that she was only 17 years old at the time.[391] By the time of the review, she was 18 and no longer in priority need. The authority unsuccessfully sought to uphold its original decision on that basis: the proper decision on the review was that an unlawful decision had been made such as to have denied the applicant her rights; she should therefore have been given the rights to which she was entitled had a lawful decision been made, and the reviewer should accordingly have found her to be in priority need.[392] The court applied the *dictum* of Chadwick LJ in *Crawley BC v B*[393] that:

> . . . an applicant ought not to be deprived, by events which had occurred between the date of the original decision and the date of the appeal, of some benefit or advantage to which he would have been entitled if the original decision had been taken in accordance with the law.

9.184 Points made earlier about enquiries before the first decision are equally relevant here.[394] For example, if the reviewer fails to make sufficient enquiries into a matter or fails to make those enquiries that a reasonable authority would make, the decision is susceptible to challenge. The point of the review is to cure any defects in the original decision and therefore a failure to conduct sufficient enquiries can be resolved at this stage by the person conducting the review.

9.185 It is incumbent on the applicant to put forward the matters and evidence which the applicant wishes to be taken into account: see *Cramp*.[395] This is particularly important where a 'minded to find' letter has been sent because a failure to challenge anything in it is likely to bar any argument on appeal that the authority had failed to carry out further enquiries in respect of the matters raised in the letter.[396]

388 For example, a dependent child leaving home, death of a vulnerable co-resident.

389 See para 9.187.

390 *Robinson v Hammersmith and Fulham LBC* [2006] EWCA Civ 1122, [2006] 1 WLR 3295, [2007] HLR 7.

391 See para 5.67.

392 *Robinson v Hammersmith and Fulham LBC*, above, at [32].

393 (2000) 32 HLR 636, CA, at 651.

394 See paras 9.48–9.131.

395 See para 9.92.

396 *R (Lynch) v Lambeth LBC* 16 October 2006, [2007] HLR 15.

In *Pieretti v Enfield LBC*,[397] however, it was said that the approach in *Cramp* requires qualification where the applicant is a disabled[398] person; where a decision maker (whether under HA 1996 s184 or s202) is not expressly invited to consider a putative[399] disability, he or she must still have due regard to the need to take steps to take account of it.

9.186 In *Bellouti*, 'it was for Mr Bellouti to put forward the material on which he relied in support of his assertion of priority need'.[400] Bearing in mind that a decision can only be based on the information available to the authority, there may therefore be difficulty complaining to the county court (on appeal) of a failure to make enquiries if a matter has not been raised before the review, at least sufficiently to put the reviewer on notice, or to call for him or her to make such further enquiries as are necessary.

9.187 The review must be carried out fairly. Applicants should be given the opportunity to refute matters on which the authority wishes to rely: *Robinson*.[401] The right to make representations 'orally or in writing or both orally and in writing' is not satisfied by a telephone interview: the right includes a right exercisable at a face-to-face meeting, although amounts to no more than a 'simple and relatively brief opportunity' for the applicant (with or without someone acting on his or her behalf) to make oral representations to the review officer; it does not authorise the calling of third party witnesses or cross-examination.[402]

397 [2010] EWCA Civ 1104, [2011] HLR 3.

398 *Pieretti* concerned Disability Discrimination Act 1995 s49A; this has been replaced with the broader 'public sector equality duty' in EqA 2010 s149 and, as such, the full range of 'protected characteristics' should be considered, ie age, disability, gender reassignment; pregnancy or maternity, race, sex, sexual orientation, religion or belief.

399 The decision-maker is, however, entitled to ask for evidence of an alleged disability and, if none is provided, may conclude that there is no disability: *Birmingham City Council v Wilson* [2016] EWCA Civ 1137, [2017] HLR 4.

400 *Bellouti v Wandsworth LBC* [2005] EWCA Civ 602, [2005] HLR 46, at [59].

401 *Robinson v Brent LBC* (1999) 31 HLR 1015, CA. See further, para 9.118, on the fairness of conducting enquiries by authorities.

402 *Makisi v Birmingham City Council; Yosief v Birmingham City Council; Nagi v Birmingham City Council* [2011] EWCA Civ 355, [2011] HLR 27. The court does not appear to have been assisted by *Bury MBC v Gibbons* [2010] EWCA Civ 327, [2010] HLR 33, in which it had been said that, while there were some cases (such as that) in which the requirements of English Review Procedure Regs 1999 reg 8(2) could not be satisfied without a face-to-face meeting with the applicant, in other cases it would be sufficient for representations to be made over the telephone. There is no reference in the judgment to *Lomotey v Enfield LBC* [2004] EWCA Civ 627, [2004] HLR 45 in which it had been said

9.188 What comprises fairness in carrying out a review has to be determined having regard to the basis of the decision under review. In *Goodger*,[403] the authority's decision-making file was not disclosed to the applicant's advisers until a few days before the review. There was no procedural unfairness, however, as the applicant had known the case against him and the decision of intentional homelessness had been the only one possible in the circumstances.

9.189 Where an applicant deliberately withholds information so as to hinder the authority's enquiries, the authority may be entitled to decide matters against the applicant.[404]

9.190 As at the initial enquiry stage,[405] authorities may obtain expert medical opinion. If this raises new issues or contentious points on which the applicant has not been able to comment, the applicant should normally be given a chance to do so in the interests of fairness. If, however, the advice is merely directed to assisting the authority to assess the weight to be given to evidence on matters which are already fully in play, there is no automatic obligation to disclose it to the applicant before the authority reaches its decision.[406]

Time

9.191 The English and Welsh Review Procedure Regs[407] generally require authorities to notify applicants of their decision within eight weeks of the request for the review being made.[408]

9.192 The exceptions are:

a) where an applicant is seeking to review an agreement between two authorities that the conditions for a local connection referral

that a refusal to hold a face-to-face hearing had not been unfair, but in that case it was not argued that reg 8(2) gave a right to an oral hearing (to the contrary, it was conceded that it did not apply).

403 *Goodger v Ealing LBC* [2002] EWCA Civ 751, [2003] HLR 6.

404 *R (Abdi) v Lambeth LBC* [2007] EWHC 1565 (Admin), [2008] HLR 5, although a case about accommodation pending review. This issue commonly arises in the context of assessments under the Children Act (CA) 1989, ie where a parent appears to the authority to be withholding information for the purposes of trying to secure accommodation with a child under CA 1989 s17(6): see eg *R (MN and KN) v Hackney LBC* [2013] EWHC 1205 (Admin), para 13.46.

405 See para 9.66.

406 *Hall v Wandsworth LBC; Carter v Wandsworth LBC* [2004] EWCA Civ 1740, [2005] HLR 23. See also *Shala v Birmingham City Council* [2007] EWCA Civ 624, [2008] HLR 8, in particular [19]–[23].

407 See para 9.114.

408 English Review Procedure Regs 1999 reg 9(1)(a); in Wales, reg 6(1)(a).

are met, in which case the decision must be notified within ten weeks;[409] and

b) where the review is being conducted by a referee,[410] the period is 12 weeks.[411]

9.193 The parties may, however, agree a longer period. Both the English and Welsh Codes suggest that this may be appropriate where further enquiries are required about information which the applicant has provided or where an applicant has been invited to make oral representations which require additional time to arrange.[412]

Notification of review decision

9.194 The authority must notify the applicant of the outcome of the decision.[413]

9.195 Where the decision is against the interests of the applicant,[414] reasons for the decision must be included.[415]

9.196 The notification of the decision on the review must also inform the applicant of his or her right of appeal to the county court on a point of law.[416] There is no obligation to give reasons for deciding the review in the applicant's favour nor, therefore, any appeal from such a decision (or its reasoning).[417]

Housing pending review

9.197 This is considered in chapter 10.[418]

409 English Review Procedure Regs 1999 reg 9(1)(b); in Wales, reg 6(1)(b).

410 See para 9.132.

411 English Review Procedure Regs 1999 reg 9(1)(c). In such a case, the referee must notify the two authorities within 11 weeks (reg 9(3)), in order to give them time to notify the applicant. In Wales, see reg 6(1)(c) and (3).

412 English Code of Guidance para 19.16; in Wales, see also reg 6(2).

413 HA 1996 s203(4); H(W)A 2014 s86(3).

414 Identifying decisions to refer to another authority separately out of an abundance of caution, as the applicant may be presumed so to have considered it when he or she elected to seek a review under HA 1996 s203.

415 See para 9.198.

416 See chapter 12.

417 *Akhtar v Birmingham City Council* [2011] EWCA Civ 383, [2011] HLR 28, in which the applicant rejected a second offer on an erroneous assumption as to why an earlier review had been successful; nor had it been unfair to explain the basis of the first review decision. See also *Solihull MBC v Khan* [2014] EWCA Civ 41, [2014] HLR 33.

418 See paras 10.29–10.42.

Reasons

9.198 Both the original decision and a decision reached on a review the outcome of which is adverse to the applicant[419] must contain sufficient reasons.[420] In cases where there has been an internal review,[421] it is likely to be the reasons in the review decision which will be the focus of any challenge, although these may well rely on, reflect or be elaborated by, the first decision, which may therefore remain relevant. What is imported by the requirement to give reasons is considered below, in chapter 12.[422] There is nothing in the 1999 regulations which prevents a reviewing officer from making a decision which is less favourable to the applicant than the original decision.[423]

419 See last footnote.
420 HA 1996 ss184(3) and 203(4); H(W)A 2014 s86(4).
421 See para 9.194.
422 See paras 12.64–12.91.
423 *Temur v Hackney LBC* [2014] EWCA Civ 877, [2014] HLR 39.

CHAPTER 10

Discharge of homelessness duties

10.1 Introduction
10.4 Contracting out of functions
10.5 Co-operation
10.8 Accommodation pending decision
10.16 Security
10.19 Quality
10.23 Area
10.24 Termination of accommodation
10.29 Accommodation pending review
10.43 Assessment and plan
10.43 England
10.49 Wales
10.52 Duties to those threatened with homelessness
10.52 England
10.62 Wales
10.66 Initial help duty
10.66 England
When the duty comes to an end
10.75 Wales
When the duty comes to an end
10.79 Other duties without priority need

continued

10.80 Homelessness Act 2002
10.84 Localism Act 2011
10.85 Advice and assistance
Wales

10.90 Other duties to the intentionally homeless
10.95 Time
10.107 Policies

10.108 Duties where local connection referral

10.109 Other duties towards the unintentionally homeless in priority need
10.111 Housing Act 1996 s193/Housing (Wales) Act 2014 s75
Postponement of the duty • Means of discharge • Out-of-area placements • Suitability of accommodation • Cessation of the duty
10.220 Homelessness Reduction Act 2017 – England
HA 1996 s193A • HA 1996 s193C

Introduction

10.1 The Housing Act (HA) 1996 Part 7 and the Housing (Wales) Act (H(W)A) 2014 Part 2 impose duties on local authorities:

a) to make enquiries or carry out an assessment;
b) to make and notify decisions;
c) to protect property; and
d) to secure that accommodation is made available.

10.2 Duties relating to property have already been considered (see chapter 8); so also have the duties to entertain applications, make enquiries and reach decisions (see chapter 9). Other statutory duties, eg under children and social care legislation, are considered in chapter 13.

10.3 This chapter is accordingly concerned with the remaining duties under HA 1996 Part 7 and H(W)A 2014 Part 2. These will be considered under the following headings:

a) accommodation pending decision;
b) accommodation pending review;
c) assessment and plan;
d) duties to those threatened with homelessness;
e) initial help duty;
f) duties to those not in priority need;
g) duties to the intentionally homeless;
h) duties on local connection referral; and
i) duties to the unintentionally homeless.

Contracting out of functions

10.4 The power of an authority to contract out functions under HA 1996 Part 7 and H(W)A 2014 Part 2 has been discussed at the start of chapter 9.

Co-operation

10.5 In discharging their duties, an English authority is entitled to call for co-operation from another local housing authority (in England, Wales or Scotland), a private registered provider of social housing, a registered social landlord or a housing action trust, or a development corporation, registered housing association or Scottish Homes.[1] The

1 HA 1996 s213(1)(a) and (2), as amended by Housing and Regeneration Act 2008 (Consequential Provisions) Order 2010 SI No 866 Sch 2.

other authority (or body) must co-operate with the housing authority by rendering such assistance as is reasonable in the circumstances.[2]

10.6 In Wales, where all authorities are unitary and therefore have both housing and social services functions, the corresponding provisions require each authority to make arrangements to promote co-operation between those of its officers who exercise its social services functions and those who exercise its functions as the local housing authority, with a view to achieving the following objectives in its area:

a) the prevention of homelessness;
b) that suitable accommodation is or will be available for people who are or may become homeless;
c) that satisfactory support is available for people who are or may become homeless; and
d) the effective discharge of its functions under H(W)A 2014 Part 2.[3]

10.7 In addition, the authority may request the co-operation of the following persons (whether in Wales or England): a local housing authority, a social services authority, a registered social landlord, a private registered provider of social housing or a housing action trust.[4] The body is bound to comply with the request unless it considers that doing so would be incompatible with its own duties, or would otherwise have an adverse effect on the exercise of its functions.[5] If the authority seeks information from the body, it must likewise comply unless it considers that doing so would be incompatible with its own duties or would otherwise have an adverse effect on the exercise of the person's functions.[6] In either case, a body which decides not to comply with the request must give the local housing authority who made the request written reasons for its decision.[7]

2 HA 1996 s213(1).
3 H(W)A 2014 s95(1).
4 H(W)A 2014 s95(5). The Welsh Ministers may add or omit persons from this list, other than a Minister of the Crown: s95(6), (7).
5 H(W)A 2014 s95(2).
6 H(W)A 2014 s95(3).
7 H(W)A 2014 s95(4).

Accommodation pending decision

10.8 If an authority has reason to believe that an applicant may be eligible for assistance, homeless and in priority need, it has to secure that accommodation is made available for his or her occupation pending any decision that it may make as a result of its enquiries.[8] This duty exists irrespective of questions of local connection.[9] The test is exhaustive: the authority cannot qualify it by adding any further criteria, for example, that an applicant must be at risk of harm in his or her current accommodation if not provided with other accommodation pending the decision.[10]

10.9 From 9 November 2012, when the Localism Act (LA) 2011 s149(2) came into force in England,[11] the duty also arises if the authority has reason to believe that the new duty in HA 1996 s195A may apply to the applicant:[12] consequent on the extended powers of an authority to discharge the full duty in HA 1996 s193[13] by using private sector accommodation,[14] the full duty recurs even if there is no priority need,[15] if the applicant becomes homeless[16] again within two years of acceptance of the offer, provided that he or she is found still to be eligible for assistance, and not to have become homeless intentionally,

8 HA 1996 s188(1); H(W)A 2014 s68. This duty is met by an offer of suitable accommodation. If the application does not take up the offer then – absent a material change in circumstances which affects the suitability of the accommodation – he or she cannot require the authority to make a further offer: *R (Brooks) v Islington LBC* [2015] EWHC 2657 (Admin), [2016] HLR 2.

9 HA 1996 s188(2); H(W)A 2014 s68(4).

10 *R (Kelly and Mehari) v Birmingham City Council* [2009] EWHC 3240 (Admin), [2009] JHL D24.

11 Localism Act 2011 (Commencement No 2 and Transitional Provisions) (England) Order 2012 SI No 2599 Article 2.

12 HA 1996 s188(1A) added by LA 2011 s149(2). This is only applicable where the duty to secure accommodation had arisen but had not ceased before 9 November 2012: Localism Act 2011 (Commencement No 2 and Transitional Provisions) (England) Order 2012 SI No 2599 Article 3.

13 Paras 10.111–10.219.

14 LA 2011 s148, amending HA 1996 s193.

15 Ie, it has been lost since the original application, eg if a child leaves home.

16 Defined to mean when valid notice under HA 1988 s21, expires (see *Manual of Housing Law*, 10th edn, Arden & Dymond, para 2.203: there is no need for the applicant to await proceedings for possession or an order: HA 1996 s195A(2), added by LA 2011 s149(4).

on that new application.[17] When assessing whether this duty has arisen, the authority must disregard any restricted person.[18]

10.10 Once the Homelessness Reduction Act (HRA) 2017 comes into force, in England, the duty will end on different dates, depending on whether or not the authority concludes that the applicant is or is not in priority need.[19] If the authority concludes that the applicant is not in priority need, and the authority decides that it does not owe him or her a duty under HA 1996 s189B(2) (initial help duty – paras 10.66–10.74), the duty ends when the authority notifies the applicant of that decision; otherwise, it ends when the authority notify the applicant of its decision that it owes the applicant no duty under either section 190 (duties to the intentionally homeless – paras 10.90–10.107) or section 193 (principal duty – paras 10.111–10.219).[20] In any other case, the duty comes to an end on the later of either when the section 189B(2) comes to an end or it notifies the applicant that it does not owe him or her a duty under that section, or when the authority notifies the applicant of its decision as to what other duty (if any) it owes to the applicant under Part 7 following the duty under section 189B(2) coming to an end.[21] The latter alternatives will also apply to the duty under HA 1996 s188(1A) (para 10.6).[22]

10.11 The threshold – 'reason to believe'[23] – is designedly low; the authority should provide the accommodation when it is needed and then make further enquiries.[24] Even this threshold was not reached in *Burns*,[25] however, where the authority had no reason to believe that the applicant was eligible. The applicant, who had married a European Union (EU) national, had been refused a residence permit by the Home Office, which refusal it was not unreasonable for

17 This duty applies only to the first re-application: HA 1996 s195A(6).

18 HA 1996 s195(1), (5), added by LA 2011 s149. As to restricted person, see paras 10.168–10.173.

19 HRA 2017 s5(4). Once the HRA 2017 comes into force, this will no longer apply: HRA 2017 s4(2).

20 HRA 2017 s5(4); HA 1996 s188(1ZA).

21 HRA 2017 s5(4); HA 1996 s188(1ZB).

22 HRA 2017 s5(4); HA 1996 s188(1A), as amended.

23 Whether this threshold is met is primarily a matter for the authority, with any review on conventional *Wednesbury* grounds: *R (Edwards) v Birmingham City Council* [2016] EWHC 173 (Admin), [2016] HLR 11.

24 *R (M) v Hammersmith and Fulham LBC* [2008] UKHL 14, [2008] 1 WLR 535 at [36].

25 *R (Burns) v Southwark LBC* [2004] EWHC 1901 (Admin), [2004] JHL D105; see also, by way of example *R (Omar) v Wandsworth LBC* [2015] EWHC 4110 (Admin).

the authority to take at face value so that it was reasonable for the authority to have refused interim accommodation without making any further enquiries. In *R (Edwards) v Birmingham City Council*,[26] it was held that although the threshold is a low one: the authority is entitled to question a person who claims to be homeless at home to clarify whether in fact there is reason to believe that the accommodation occupied by that person is such that it may not be reasonable for him or her to continue to occupy it.

10.12 The requirement to make accommodation available for the applicant's occupation is, by definition, a requirement to make it available for the applicant and for any person who might reasonably be expected to reside with him or her.[27] The meaning of this has been considered in chapter 4, above.[28]

10.13 An authority may discharge its duties pending enquiries by providing its own accommodation; by arranging for it to be provided by someone else; or by giving advice such as will secure that it is provided by someone else.[29] These provisions are considered below, in relation to the principal housing duty.[30]

10.14 The requirement calls for some action on the part of the authority. In *Sidhu*,[31] a women's refuge, not even in the same area, provided accommodation, but as the authority had not been involved in procuring it, it could not rely on it as a discharge of its duty. The fact that the accommodation was in another area was not itself fundamental to the result, but it may not be without relevance. Many such refuges are funded by local authorities. In such circumstances, there are two reasons why accommodation provided voluntarily and other than at the arrangement of the authority may be less susceptible to challenge:

a) as a matter of practice, the refuge is not entirely independent of the authority; and
b) the provision of funds for the refuge may be held to denote a sufficient degree of participation or assistance by the authority,[32]

26 [2016] EWHC 173 (Admin), [2016] HLR 11.
27 HA 1996 s176; H(W)A 2014 s68.
28 Paras 4.17–4.38 and see, in particular, *Sharif v Camden LBC* [2013] UKSC 10, [2013] HLR 16 in which it was held that two flats yards apart in the same building can comprise accommodation in which a household can live together.
29 HA 1996 s206(1); H(W)A 2014 ss95, 96; see further para 10.121.
30 Paras 10.111–10.219.
31 *R v Ealing LBC ex p Sidhu* (1982) 2 HLR 45, QBD.
32 It may depend on the circumstances, including the powers under which assistance was provided and the terms of assistance.

although probably only if the accommodation is provided at the express request of the authority, or it is agreed – or at the lowest 'understood' – that the organisation will accommodate those referred to it by the authority; anything more vague would probably not qualify.

10.15 The authority may require a person housed under this provision to pay such reasonable charges[33] as it may determine, or to pay an amount towards the payment made by the authority to a third party for accommodation – for example, a contribution towards the cost of private sector accommodation.[34] If the authority provides its own accommodation, it can in any event make a reasonable charge under HA 1985 s24. The provision of assistance under HA 1996 Part 7 or H(W)A 2014 Part 2 is not, however, contingent on ability to pay,[35] although there is no reason why – even if the applicant is unable to make a payment – an authority should not reserve the right to payment, eg against a future change of fortunes on the part of an applicant.

Security

10.16 In *Miah*,[36] *Buscombe*[37] and *Hayden*,[38] some doubt was cast on whether accommodation provided under the Housing (Homeless Persons) Act (H(HP)A) 1977 amounted to a tenancy or licence within the security provisions of what is now HA 1985 Part 4. In *Walsh*,[39] however, the authority's argument that any temporary accommodation so provided would necessarily be by way of licence was rejected by the House of Lords and the letting was held to amount to a tenancy.[40]

33 Which can be 'nil': *R (Yekini) v Southwark LBC* [2014] EWHC 2096 (Admin).

34 HA 1996 s206(2); H(W)A 2014 s90. It must be arguable that, if accommodation is provided or secured by the authority but is subsequently found not to be suitable on grounds of costs (para 10.153), it cannot have been a 'reasonable charge' so that the applicant could seek to resist a claim for arrears.

35 *R v Secretary of State for Social Security ex p B and Joint Council for the Welfare of Immigrants* (1996) 29 HLR 129, CA.

36 *Family Housing Association v Miah* (1982) 5 HLR 94, CA.

37 *Restormel DC v Buscombe* (1982) 14 HLR 91, CA.

38 *Kensington and Chelsea RLBC v Hayden* (1984) 17 HLR 114, CA.

39 *Eastleigh DC v Walsh* [1985] 1 WLR 525, (1985) 17 HLR 392, HL.

40 See also *Street v Mountford* [1985] AC 809, (1985) 17 HLR 402, HL.

10.17 The importance of this issue is diminished[41] by the exclusion of security of tenure under the HAs 1985[42] and 1988[43] for homeless applicants, although it may still bear on determination of the right of occupation at common law, disrepair claims and whether or not court proceedings are required to evict an occupier.[44] The exclusion from assured protection under the HA 1988 lasts for a period of 12 months beginning on the date on which the applicant is notified of the decision on his or her application,[45] unless the landlord notifies him or her to the contrary, either that it is to be a fully assured tenancy or an assured shorthold tenancy.[46] For these purposes, a private sector landlord is any landlord who is not within the HA 1985 s80(1);[47] the term therefore includes registered providers of social housing and registered social landlords.[48] It follows that someone initially accommodated pending enquiries but left in it for long enough afterwards could become assured through the passage of time; secure protection under the HA 1985 is not, however, likewise limited by time, only by whether or not it is provided under HA 1996 Part 7 or H(W)A 2014 Part 2.

10.18 Accommodation provided under HA 1996 Part 7 or H(W)A 2014 Part 2 is not protected by Protection from Eviction Act (PEA) 1977 s3, and the applicant may be evicted without a court order; any challenge based on Article 8 of the European Convention on Human Rights (ECHR) can, however, be raised on appeal to the county court against the decision which means that a full duty is not to be accepted.[49]

41 If not eliminated: see next paragraph.

42 HA 1985 Sch 1 para 4 as amended by H(W)A 2014 Sch 3 para 1; such a tenancy will become secure if the authority notifies the tenant that the tenancy is to be regarded as a secure tenancy. In *Tompkins v Wandsworth LBC* [2015] EWCA Civ 846, [2015] HLR 44, use of an incorrect form of tenancy agreement was held not to amount to 'notification' for these purposes.

43 HA 1996 s209; H(W)A 2014 s92.

44 A homeless person who has been granted a daily licence to occupy a room with a lock in a local authority hostel is entitled to exclude trespassers: *Thomas v Director of Public Prosecutions* [2009] EWHC 3906 (Admin).

45 Or in the case of a review or appeal to the county court, of the date on which he or she is notified of the outcome of the review or of when the appeal is finally determined.

46 HA 1996 s209(2); H(W)A 2014 s92(2).

47 Ie, local authorities, new town corporations, housing action trusts, urban development corporations, or housing co-operatives within the meaning of HA 1985 s27B.

48 HA 1996 s217; H(W)A 2014 s99.

49 *R (ZH and CN) v Newham LBC and Lewisham LBC* [2014] UKSC 62, [2015] HLR 6.

Moreover, if court proceedings are used, it seems likely that they can still be resisted both on the basis that the authority's decision to seek possession is ultra vires in domestic public law,[50] or on the basis of Article 8[51] or that it would amount to unlawful discrimination under the Equality Act 2010.[52]

Quality

10.19 Under H(HP)A 1977 and HA 1985, as unamended, there was no statutory standard as to the quality of accommodation provided.[53] Under HA 1985, as amended by Housing and Planning Act 1986,[54] statutory requirements for suitability were introduced, but were not applicable to temporary accommodation pending enquiries. The suitability requirements[55] of HA 1996 and H(W)A 2014 are, however, applicable to every requirement to secure that accommodation is available, including the temporary duties. An authority does not have to give reasons why it considers that a property offered under these provisions is suitable.[56] Suitability is considered below in relation to the principal housing duty.[57]

10.20 In *Ali* and *Moran*,[58] however, it was observed that 'what is regarded as suitable for discharging the interim duty may be rather different from what is regarded as suitable for discharging the more open-ended duty in section 193(2)'. This accords with two earlier decisions on the quality of temporary accommodation under the H(HP)A 1977, even though there was then no statutory suitability requirement,[59] although both related to temporary accommodation for the intentionally homeless.[60]

50 *Barber v Croydon LBC* [2010] EWCA Civ 51, [2010] HLR 26.
51 *Powell v Hounslow LBC; Frisby v Birmingham CC; Hall v Leeds CC* [2011] UKSC 8, [2011] HLR 23.
52 *Akerman-Livingstone v Aster Communities Ltd* [2015] UKSC 15, [2015] HLR 20.
53 *R v Hillingdon LBC ex p Puhlhofer* [1986] AC 484, (1986) 18 HLR 158, HL.
54 Section 14(3).
55 See HA 1996 ss206(1) and 210(1) and H(W)A 2014 s59, and paras 10.145 onwards.
56 *Akhtar v Birmingham City Council* [2011] EWCA Civ 383, [2011] HLR 28; *Solihull MBC v Khan* [2014] EWCA Civ 41, [2014] HLR 33.
57 See paras 10.145–10.179.
58 *Birmingham City Council v Ali; Moran v Manchester City Council (Secretary of State for Communities and Local Government and another intervening)* [2009] UKHL 36, [2009] 1 WLR 1506 at [18].
59 See para 10.19.
60 See para 10.91.

10.21 In *Gliddon*,[61] the authority was alleged to have been in breach of its temporary duty because the accommodation provided was in substantial disrepair, requiring works to prevent it becoming statutorily unfit for human habitation. It was held that the authority was entitled to have regard to the time for which accommodation was likely to be occupied when determining whether the accommodation was appropriate: while some quality of accommodation would fall below the line of acceptable discharge of even a temporary duty, accommodation needing works to pre-empt statutory unfitness did not necessarily do so; accommodation so unfit that it is not even repairable, however, might well have been inadequate even for a temporary purpose.

10.22 In *Ward*,[62] accommodation on a caravan site described by a social worker as being in appalling condition was nonetheless an adequate discharge of the temporary duty, having regard to the family's wish to live on a site, rather than in a permanent structure.

Area

10.23 There are constraints on out-of-area placements, considered below in relation to the full duty,[63] which apply to discharge under this section.

Termination of accommodation

10.24 On occasion, in particular when enquiries have taken some time (for example, into accommodation abroad), a local authority will wish to terminate a right of occupation, either because it wants to move the applicant elsewhere or because of some default on the part of the applicant (for example, non-payment of charges, nuisance and annoyance, damage to property) or it will have to deal with the position which arises if another landlord providing accommodation on its behalf has taken or wants to take such action. It is clear that the authority may move the occupier, for example, for reasons of cost, provided the new accommodation is also suitable, and it is otherwise acting reasonably.

10.25 Where the accommodation is lost because of the applicant's default, it is not open to an authority to conclude that the applicant

61 *R v Exeter City Council ex p Gliddon* (1984) 14 HLR 103, QBD.

62 *R v Southampton City Council ex p Ward* (1984) 14 HLR 114, QBD.

63 See paras 10.136–10.149.

has thereby become homeless intentionally, as this would not have been the accommodation the loss of which gives rise to the homelessness application requiring a decision: see *Din*.[64]

10.26 Intervening accommodation under this section does not create a new period of homelessness. This survives the decision in *Awua*,[65] where what had been lost, although interim in quality, was accommodation provided to the applicant (by another authority) in discharge of the full housing duty (ie post-decision), withdrawn when that other authority offered – and the applicant refused – a more permanent offer.[66] Until a decision is reached, however, what is in issue is the loss of the accommodation that gave rise to the (as yet undetermined) application.

10.27 Where the applicant refuses the accommodation offered (under HA 1996 s188), the authority may nonetheless be able to conclude that it has discharged its duty under this section, and decline to provide further accommodation pursuant to it, by parity of reasoning with the decision under what is now HA 1996 s193 in *Chambers*,[67] albeit that it will still be bound to consider and discharge the appropriate section 193 duty following its decision under HA 1996 s184, based on the accommodation lost which led to the homelessness which gave rise to the application.[68]

10.28 In reaching its decision on whether or not that loss amounted to intentionality, the loss of the intervening accommodation will therefore not be relevant,[69] save if and so far as the conduct involved can

64 *Din v Wandsworth LBC* [1983] 1 AC 657, (1983) 1 HLR 73, HL. Consider, too, that HA 1996 s193(6)(b) makes explicit provision for an authority to determine that its duty towards a homeless applicant – following a decision that the applicant is homeless, in priority need and not intentionally homeless – has been discharged in the event of becoming intentionally homeless from *that* accommodation; it would be anomalous to reach the same conclusion in relation to temporary accommodation *pending* a decision.

65 *R v Brent LBC ex p Awua* [1996] AC 55, (1995) 27 HLR 453, HL.

66 See also *R v East Hertfordshire DC ex p Hunt* (1985) 18 HLR 51, QBD, the reasoning in which was criticised in *Awua* as 'heroic', but the result of which was not doubted. See now HA 1996 s193(6), (7).

67 *R v Westminster City Council ex p Chambers* (1982) 6 HLR 15, QBD; see para 10.156.

68 In *R v Kensington and Chelsea RLBC ex p Kujtim* (2000) 32 HLR 579, (1999) 2 CCLR 460, CA, the duty to provide accommodation under National Assistance Act 1948 s21 (see now chapter 13 for the provisions replacing that section) was held not to be absolute. Where the applicant manifests a persistent and unequivocal refusal to observe the authority's reasonable requirements in relation to occupation of the accommodation, the authority is entitled to treat its duty as discharged and to refuse to provide further accommodation.

69 *R v Islington LBC ex p Hassan* (1995) 27 HLR 485, QBD.

properly be considered to have some evidential value in reaching a view on the earlier loss of accommodation, for example, analogous conduct.[70]

Accommodation pending review

10.29 Once the HA 1996 s184 decision has been notified to the applicant, the authority ceases to be under any duty to provide interim accommodation under HA 1996 s188,[71] even if a review is sought.[72] The duty is, however, replaced with a power to provide accommodation pending the review.[73] Once HRA 2017 comes into force, in England, however, the duty under HA 1996 s189B(2) (initial help duty – paras 10.66–10.79) will not end where the applicant requests a review of the authority's decision as to the suitability of accommodation offered by way of a final accommodation offer[74] or a final Part 6 offer,[75] until the decision on the review has been notified.[76] In the case of any other review, however, the duty ends as described above (para 10.7) but a power to secure accommodation pending a decision on the review will remain.[77]

10.30 The observations on quality[78] and termination made in relation to accommodation pending decision (paras 10.8–10.24) also apply to accommodation pending review, as do those on availability (para 10.12), payment (para 10.15), security (paras 10.16–10.18), exclusion from PEA 1977 (para 10.18) and defences on eviction (para 10.18). How accommodation may be provided,[79] suitability[80] and the constraints on out-of-area placements[81] (which are all considered below in relation to the principal duty) also apply to discharge under this section.

70 See *R v Newham LBC ex p Campbell* (1993) 26 HLR 183, QBD.
71 See para 10.29.
72 HA 1996 s188(3); H(W)A 2014 s69. See also *R (Faizi) v Brent LBC* [2015] EWHC 2449 (Admin).
73 HA 1996 s188(3); H(W)A 2014 s69(11).
74 See para 10.71.
75 See para 10.71.
76 HRA 2017 s5(4); HA 1996 s188(2A), as added.
77 HRA 2017 s5(4); HA 1996 s188(3), as substituted.
78 See also paras 10.19–10.22.
79 See para 10.121.
80 See paras 10.145–10.178.
81 See para 10.136.

10.31 Until amendment by Homelessness Act 2002, HA 1996 s188(3) only permitted an authority to 'continue to' house. This led to the argument that it could not be used where the applicant's temporary accommodation under HA 1996 s188(1) had come to an end before a request to exercise the section 188(3) power was made. The repeal of the words 'continue to' was intended to close this gap. In particular, where an applicant has been found to be intentionally homeless, and accommodation has been provided under HA 1996 s190(2)(a),[82] which comes to an end before the review is completed, the amended section 188(3) will permit authorities to provide accommodation pending outcome of the review.

10.32 Similar provisions apply where the applicant has been housed under HA 1996 s200 pending the outcome of a local connection referral: where the applicant seeks a review, the duty to house ceases and is replaced by a power.[83]

10.33 The authority is not obliged of its own motion to consider whether to exercise its power under HA 1996 s188(3) but may await a request from the applicant before deciding whether to do so.[84] As a refusal to house pending a review is not a decision that is itself susceptible to the statutory review process, any challenge has to be by way of judicial review.[85]

10.34 As an applicant has an unfettered right to a review,[86] HA 1996 s188(3) does not envisage that the discretion to house pending review will be exercised as a matter of course. An authority may therefore decide to exercise the discretion only in exceptional circumstances: *Mohammed*.[87]

10.35 In exercising its discretion, the authority must balance the objective of maintaining fairness between other homeless persons – in circumstances where it has decided that no duty is owed to the applicant

82 See para 10.191.

83 HA 1996 s200(5); H(W)A 2014 s82(5), (6).

84 *R (Ahmed) v Waltham Forest LBC* [2001] EWHC (Admin) 540, [2001] JHL D89.

85 *R v Camden LBC ex p Mohammed* (1998) 30 HLR 315, QBD. This sets a high bar: consider *R (Abdusemed) v Lambeth LBC*, High Court (Administrative Court), February 19, 2016; *HousingView*, 29 February 2016, where interim relief on judicial review was refused to a woman whom the authority had declined to house pending review even though she was walking the streets during the day and spending the night at a local mosque. See para 12.147.

86 Paras 9.149–9.158.

87 *R v Camden LBC ex p Mohammed*. See also *R v Hammersmith and Fulham LBC ex p Fleck* (1997) 30 HLR 679, QBD and *R v Newham LBC ex p Bautista* April 2001 *Legal Action* 22. See, however, English Code of Guidance para 15.19 on applying such a policy flexibly.

– and proper consideration of the possibility that the applicant may be right.[88]

10.36 In carrying out this balancing exercise, certain matters will always require consideration, although other matters may also be relevant:

a) the merits of the case and the extent to which it can properly be said that the decision was one which was either contrary to the apparent merits or was one which involved a very fine balance of judgment;
b) whether consideration is required of new material, information or argument which could have a real effect on the decision under review;
c) the personal circumstances of the applicant and the consequences to him or her of a decision not to exercise the discretion.[89]

10.37 In *Lumley*,[90] Brooke LJ explained the merits of the case as meaning 'the merits of the applicant's case that the council's original decision was flawed'. In that case, the decision was quashed because the initial decision that the applicant was not in priority need was seriously flawed and the authority had failed to take the flaws into account when considering the exercise of its discretion to house pending review.

10.38 In each case, the principles must be applied to the relevant facts and a properly reasoned decision provided.[91] In *Mohammed*,[92] the judge found that the council had considered the matters set out properly, but he nonetheless quashed its decision not to house the applicant pending review, because it had failed to give her an opportunity to explain inconsistencies in her statements and had therefore failed to take into account a relevant and material consideration in exercising its discretion.

10.39 In *Nacion*,[93] the Court of Appeal applied *Mohammed* to a decision under the discretion to house pending an appeal.[94] Housing pending

88 *R v Camden LBC ex p Mohammed* (1998) 30 HLR 315, QBD.

89 *R v Camden LBC ex p Mohammed* (1998) 30 HLR 315, QBD.

90 *R v Newham LBC ex p Lumley* (2001) 33 HLR 11, QBD.

91 See *R (Paul-Coker) v Southwark LBC* [2006] EWHC 497 (Admin), [2006] HLR 32.

92 *R v Camden LBC ex p Mohammed* (1997) 30 HLR 315, QBD.

93 *R v Brighton and Hove Council ex p Nacion* (1999) 31 HLR 1095, CA.

94 HA 1996 s204(4). But see now section 204A, allowing an appeal from such a refusal to be made to the county court itself – paras 12.196–12.202.

appeal is considered in chapter 12, below, as part of the machinery for enforcement of duties.[95]

10.40 There is, however, a difference between housing pending review and housing pending appeal, as recognised by Brooke LJ in *Lumley*:[96] in *Nacion* there had already been a review, so that 'most of the errors, if any, made on the first consideration of the case should have been put right by the senior officer who conducted the review,' while pending review, there will only have been the one decision and consideration. Accordingly, the bar is a little lower when considering housing pending review than when considering housing pending appeal.

10.41 In deciding when to terminate accommodation provided under HA 1996 s188(3) following an unsuccessful review, an authority must give the person reasonable notice so that he or she can have an opportunity to make alternative arrangements.[97]

10.42 It was previously held that there is no requirement for a local housing authority to take into consideration possible duties owed to the children of an applicant under Children Act (CA) 1989, or the potential break-up of the family, when deciding whether to continue to provide accommodation under HA 1996 s188(3),[98] although the correctness of this must now be in doubt given the impact of ECHR Article 8 and CA 2004 s11.[99]

Assessment and plan

England

10.43 Once HRA 2017 comes into force, there will be a new duty[100] of 'assessment' applicable to all applicants whom an English authority

95 Para 12.202.

96 (2001) 33 HLR 11, QBD.

97 *R v Newham LBC ex p Ojuri (No 5)* (1998) 31 HLR 631, QBD.

98 *R (Hassan) v Croydon LBC* [2009] JHL D56, Administrative Court.

99 Local authorities must have regard 'to the need to safeguard and promote the welfare of children' when discharging their functions: CA 2004 s11 (England) s28 (Wales). This includes functions under HA 1996 Part 7: *Huzrat v Hounslow LBC* [2013] EWCA Civ 1865, [2014] HLR 17. See also *Nzolameso v Westminster City Council* [2015] UKSC 22, [2015] HLR 22: when considering whether accommodation is suitable for a family, the authority must identify the principal needs of the children both individually and collectively when making the decision.

100 Based on provisions already in force in Wales, see H(W)A 2014 s62: paras 10.49–10.51.

is satisfied are homeless or threatened with homelessness[101] and eligible[102] for assistance.[103] The duty is to 'make an assessment of the applicant's case',[104] which must include an assessment of the circumstances which resulted in the applicant's homelessness or being threatened with homelessness, his or her housing needs,[105] and his or her needs for support[106] in order to be able to have and retain suitable accommodation.[107] The authority have to notify the applicant in writing of the assessment it makes.[108]

10.44 The next stage is for the authority to try to agree with the applicant what steps he or she is to be required to take in order to secure that he or she[109] has and is able to retain suitable accommodation, and what steps the authority are to take under HA 1996 Part 7 for those purposes.[110]

10.45 If the authority and the applicant reach an agreement, the authority have to record it in writing.[111] If they cannot do so, the authority have to record in writing why they could not agree, what steps it considers it would be reasonable to require the applicant to take, and what steps the authority is to take under HA 1996 Part 7, for those purposes.[112] Either class of record can include any advice the authority

101 Chapter 4.
102 Chapter 3.
103 HRA 2017 s3(1); HA 1996 s189A.
104 HRA 2017 s3(1); HA 1996 s189A(1).
105 In particular, what accommodation would be suitable for him or her and anyone with whom he or she resides or might reasonably be expected to reside.
106 Together with anyone with whom he or she resides or might reasonably be expected to reside.
107 HRA 2017 s3(1); HA 1996 s189A(2).
108 HRA 2017 s3(1); HA 1996 s189A(3).
109 Together with anyone with whom he or she resides or might reasonably be expected to reside.
110 HRA 2017 s3(1); HA 1996 s189A(4). This could include the applicant and the authority working together to ensure that the applicant is receiving all welfare benefits to which he or she might be entitled, whether as of right or pursuant to any discretionary scheme. For example, if the applicant is entitled to housing benefit or universal credit and requires further financial assistance in order to meet his housing costs then the authority has power to make a discretionary housing payment: Discretionary Financial Assistance Regulations 2001 SI No 1167 and Discretionary Housing Payments (Grants) Order 2001 SI No 2340. Such payments can be made in any amount and for any period of time and are a legitimate tool for preventing homelessness: *R (Halvai) v Hammersmith and Fulham LBC* [2017] EWHC 802 (Admin).
111 HRA 2017 s3(1); HA 1996 s189A(5).
112 HRA 2017 s3(1); HA 1996 s189A(6).

consider appropriate, including as to steps which the authority think it would be 'a good idea for the applicant to take' albeit that he or she is not to be required to take.[113] The authority has to give the applicant a copy of the written record.[114]

10.46 Until the authority decides that it owes the applicant no duty under any of the remaining provisions of Part 7, the authority has to keep the assessment under review, together with the appropriateness of any agreement reached or steps recorded.[115] If the assessment of the mandatory considerations (circumstances resulting in homelessness or being threatened with homelessness, housing needs and needs for support)[116] changes, the authority must notify the applicant, in writing, of how its assessment has changed (whether by providing a revised written assessment or otherwise); the same is true if the authority's assessment otherwise changes in a way that it considers it appropriate to notify the applicant.[117]

10.47 If the authority considers that any agreement reached or any step recorded under is no longer appropriate, it must so notify the applicant in writing to this effect and that any subsequent failure to take a step that was agreed or recorded is to be disregarded; the provisions governing attempt to reach agreement, or to record a failure to do so, described above (paras 10.44–10.45) reapply.[118]

10.48 Notification and written records under these provisions, if not received by the applicant, are to be treated as having been given if made available at the authority's office for a reasonable period for collection by or on behalf of the applicant:[119] see also para 9.146.

Wales

10.49 In Wales, H(W)A 2014 contains similar – but not identical – duties which are already in force.[120] If it appears to the authority that an applicant may be homeless or threatened with homelessness it must

113 HRA 2017 s3(1); HA 1996 s189A(7).
114 HRA 2017 s3(1); HA 1996 s189A(8).
115 HRA 2017 s3(1); HA 1996 s189A(9).
116 See para 10.43.
117 HRA 2017 s3(1); HA 1996 s189A(10).
118 HRA 2017 s3(1); HA 1996 s189A(11).
119 HRA 2017 s3(1); HA 1996 s189A(12).
120 Since 27 April 2015, H(W)A 2014 applies: see Housing (Wales) Act 2014 (Commencement No 3 and Transitory, Transitional and Saving Provisions) Order 2015 SI No 1272.

carry out an assessment of the person's case.[121] The assessment must consider whether the applicant is eligible.[122] If the applicant is eligible, the assessment must then address:

- how the applicant has become homeless or threatened with homelessness;
- his or her housing needs and those of anyone with whom he or she lives or might reasonably be expected to live;
- the support required to meet those needs; and
- whether or not the authority has any duty under H(W)A 2014 Part 2 to the applicant.[123]

The assessment must seek to identify what the applicant wishes to achieve with the authority's help and the authority must consider whether the exercise of any of its powers under Part 2 can contribute to that outcome.[124] The assessment must be kept under review.[125]

10.50 The authority must notify the applicant of the outcome of the assessment (and of any review) and, insofar as any issue is decided against his or her interests, give reasons for the decision.[126] It must also inform the applicant or his or her right to request a review.[127] Additional notification duties[128] apply where a duty under H(W)A 2014 s75[129] is owed only because of a restricted person[130] or where the authority has already notified or intends to notify another authority under the local connection provisions.[131]

10.51 Notice must be in writing,[132] and if not received by the applicant, is to be treated as having been given if made available at the authority's office for a reasonable period for collection by or on behalf of the applicant.[133]

121 H(W)A 2014 s62(1), (4), (5).
122 H(W)A 2014 s62(3).
123 H(W)A 2014 s62(5).
124 H(W)A 2014 s62(6).
125 H(W)A 2014 s62(8), (9).
126 H(W)A 2014 s63(1).
127 H(W)A 2014 s63(4).
128 H(W)A 2014 s63(2), (3).
129 Ie the full duty.
130 As to which, see para 3.117.
131 As to which, see paras 7.37–7.58.
132 H(W)A 2014 s63(4)(a).
133 H(W)A 2014 s63(4)(b).

Duties to those threatened with homelessness

England

10.52 If the authority is satisfied that an applicant is threatened with homelessness and eligible for assistance,[134] the duties in HA 1996 s195 apply. The duties apply even although an issue of local connection may apply.[135] The duties will be replaced by new provisions once HRA 2017 comes into force (paras 10.58–10.61).[136]

10.53 If the authority is not satisfied that the applicant has a priority need,[137] or is satisfied that he or she has a priority need but is also satisfied that he or she became threatened with homelessness intentionally, it must provide him or her, or secure that he or she is provided with, advice and assistance in any attempts he or she may make to secure that accommodation does not cease to be available for his or her occupation.[138] Before doing so, the applicant's housing needs must be assessed,[139] and the advice and assistance must include information about the likely availability in the authority's district of types of accommodation appropriate to the applicant's housing needs, including, in particular, the location and sources of such types of accommodation.[140]

10.54 If the authority owes this duty because it is satisfied that the applicant has a priority need but became threatened with homelessness intentionally, of which decision the applicant seeks a review, the authority may secure that accommodation does not cease to be available for his or her occupation and, if he or she becomes homeless, secure that accommodation is available pending the decision on review.[141]

10.55 If the authority is not satisfied that the applicant has a priority need, nor satisfied that he or she became threatened with homelessness intentionally, the authority has power to take reasonable steps to secure that accommodation does not cease to be available for the

134 Chapter 3.

135 *Williams v Exeter City Council*, September 1981 *LAG Bulletin* 211, CC.

136 HRA 2017 s4(2).

137 Even though the applicant is at this point only threatened with homelessness, priority need is to be determined as at the date when homelessness will occur: *Holmes-Moorhouse v Richmond upon Thames LBC* [2009] UKHL 7, [2009] HLR 34 – see para 5.23.

138 HA 1996 s195(5).

139 HA 1996 s195(6).

140 HA 1996 s195(7).

141 HA 1996 s195(8).

applicant's occupation.[142] Since LA 2011 s149(2), came into force in England,[143] this duty may also arise even if there is no longer any priority need if the applicant becomes threatened with homelessness again within two years of acceptance of the previous offer: see para 10.49, above.

10.56 If the authority is satisfied that the applicant has a priority need, and not satisfied that he or she became threatened with homelessness intentionally, it must take reasonable steps to secure that accommodation does not cease to be available for his or her occupation,[144] or, if the authority secures accommodation other than that being occupied when the application is made, then HA 1996 s193(3)–(9) apply as if the applicant was already homeless and the authority had a duty under section 193(2).[145] The obligation is without prejudice to the authority's right to recover possession of any accommodation so that it cannot be used as a defence to proceedings brought for possession of an authority's own housing.[146] Authorities cannot refuse as a matter of policy to take any action in relation to applicants who are threatened with homelessness until physical eviction: each case must be considered on its merits and where it is obvious that homelessness will ensue steps taken to prepare for it.[147] A discharge of duty which means that an applicant is already threatened with homelessness anew will not constitute an adequate discharge.[148]

10.57 The position is adapted for restricted cases[149] of threatened homelessness: if other accommodation is secured, HA 1996 s193(3)–(9) apply as if the applicant was only owed a duty under section 193(2) because he or she was a restricted case,[150] ie, the authority must, so

142 HA 1996 s195(9).

143 9 November 2012: Localism Act 2011 (Commencement No 2 and Transitional Provisions) (England) Order 2012 SI No 2599 Article 2.

144 HA 1996 s195(2).

145 HA 1996 s195(4).

146 HA 1996 s195(3). The provision does not make an authority's refusal to withdraw 'stop notices', under planning legislation perverse, even though it would render the applicants, a group of travelling showmen, homeless: *R v Chiltern DC ex p Dyason* (1990) 23 HLR 387, QBD.

147 *R v Newham LBC ex p Khan* (2001) 33 HLR 29, QBD.

148 *R v Brent LBC ex p Awua* [1996] AC 55, (1995) 27 HLR 453, HL.

149 HA 1996 s195(4A) and (4B) – ie, where the authority is only satisfied that the applicant is threatened with homelessness and eligible because of a restricted person: see para 3.117.

150 See para 3.117.

far as is reasonably practicable, bring its duty to an end by making a private accommodation offer.[151]

10.58 Once HRA 2017 comes into force, in England, a new duty will be imposed on authorities in all cases where the authority is satisfied that an applicant is threatened with homelessness[152] and eligible[153] for assistance,[154] in place of the foregoing provisions of HA 1996 s195. The authority will be obliged to take reasonable steps to help the applicant to secure that accommodation does not cease to be available for his or her occupation.[155] In deciding what steps to take, the authority has to have regard to its assessment (paras 10.43–10.47) of the applicant's case.[156] As before, the obligation is without prejudice to the authority's right to recover possession of any accommodation.[157]

10.59 The authority will be able to give notice bringing this duty to an end when it is satisfied that any one of the following circumstances is applicable:[158]

a) the applicant both has suitable accommodation which is available for his or her occupation[159] and there is a reasonable prospect of him or her having suitable accommodation[160] available for at least six months[161] from the date of the notice;
b) the authority has complied with the duty to take reasonable steps and the period of 56 days beginning with the day that the authority is first satisfied that the applicant is threatened with homeless and eligible has ended (whether or not he or she is still threatened with homelessness);[162]
c) the applicant has become homeless;[163]

151 HA 1996 s193(7AD); para 10.169.
152 See paras 4.141–4.146.
153 Chapter 3.
154 HRA 2017 s4; HA 1996 s195(1).
155 HRA 2017 s4; HA 1996 s195(2).
156 HRA 2017 s4; HA 1996 s195(3).
157 HRA 2017 s4; HA 1996 s195(4).
158 HRA 2017 s4; HA 1996 s195(5), (8).
159 See paras 4.16–4.38.
160 It need not be the same accommodation.
161 Or such longer period not exceeding 12 months as may be prescribed.
162 The authority cannot give notice to the applicant in this circumstances if a valid notice has been given to the applicant under HA 1988 s21 (see *Manual of Housing Law*, para 2.203) which will expire within 56 days or has expired and is in respect of the only accommodation that is available for his or her occupation (see para 4.146): HRA 2017 s4; HA 1996 s195(6).
163 So that the initial help duty will apply: see paras 10.66–10.74.

d) the applicant has refused an offer of suitable accommodation and, on the date of refusal, there was a reasonable prospect that suitable accommodation would be available for occupation by the applicant for at least six months or such longer period[164] as may be prescribed;
e) the applicant has become homeless intentionally[165] from any accommodation that has been made available to him or her as a result of the authority's exercise of its functions under this duty;
f) the applicant is no longer eligible for assistance; or
g) the applicant has withdrawn the application for accommodation or assistance in obtaining it.

10.60 The notice must specify which of the circumstances applies, and inform the applicant that he or she has a right to request a review of the decision to bring the duty to an end and of the time within which such a request must be made.[166] The notice must be in writing, and, if not received by the applicant, is to be treated as having been given if made available at the authority's office for a reasonable period for collection by or on his or her behalf of the applicant:[167] see also para 9.146.

10.61 The duty will also be able to be brought to an end under HA 1996 s193B (deliberate and unreasonable refusal to co-operate: paras 10.72–10.74),[168] although this will not end a right to accommodation for an applicant who is homeless, eligible, in priority need and not homeless intentionally (para 10.74).[169]

Wales

10.62 In Wales, if an authority is satisfied that an applicant is eligible and threatened with homelessness, it must 'help to secure' that accommodation does not cease to be available to the applicant.[170] This duty cannot be used to prevent the authority itself obtaining vacant possession of any accommodation; accordingly, it cannot be raised as a defence by a tenant in possession proceedings by the authority.[171]

164 Not exceeding 12 months.
165 Chapter 6.
166 HRA 2017 s4; HA 1996 s195(7).
167 HRA 2017 s4; HA 1996 s195(9).
168 HRA 2017 s4; HA 1996 s195(10).
169 HRA 2017 s7(1); HA 1996 s193C(3), (4).
170 H(W)A 2014 s66(1).
171 H(W)A 2014 s66(2).

10.63 The duty to help to secure that accommodation does not cease to be available requires the authority to take reasonable steps to help, having regard to (amongst other things) the need to make the best use of its resources.[172] It does not require the authority to offer accommodation, whether under H(W)A 2014 Part 6 or otherwise.[173]

10.64 An authority can help to secure that suitable accommodation does not cease to be available either by providing some form of assistance itself or arranging for someone else to provide it.[174] Examples in the Act of what may be provided or arranged are:

- mediation;
- grants or loans;
- guarantees;
- support in management of debt, mortgage or rent arrears;
- security measures for applicants at risk of abuse;
- advocacy or other representation;
- accommodation;
- information and advice; and
- other services, goods or facilities.[175]

10.65 The authority can give notice[176] bringing this duty to and end if the authority is satisfied that:[177]

a) the applicant has become homeless;[178]
b) the applicant is no longer threatened with homelessness and suitable accommodation is likely to remain available for his or her occupation for at least another six months;[179]
c) the applicant refuses an offer of accommodation – which the authority is satisfied was suitable and was likely to be available for at least the next six months – from any person, having been notified in writing of the possible consequences of refusal or acceptance of the offer;[180]
d) the applicant ceases to be eligible;[181]

172 H(W)A 2014 s65(a).
173 H(W)A 2014 ss65(b)–(c)
174 H(W)A 2014 s64(1).
175 H(W)A 2014 s64(2).
176 H(W)A 2014 s84.
177 H(W)A 2014 s67.
178 H(W)A 2014 s67(2).
179 H(W)A 2014 s67(3).
180 H(W)A 2014 s67(4).
181 H(W)A 2014 s79(2).

e) a mistake of fact led to authority to notify the applicant that it owed him or her a duty to help to secure accommodation for the applicant;[182]
f) the applicant has withdrawn the application;[183] or
g) the applicant is unreasonably failing to co-operate with the authority.[184]

Initial help duty

England

10.66 Once the HRA 2017 comes into force, there will be a new – and time-limited (para 10.67) – duty[185] applicable where the authority is satisfied that an applicant is homeless[186] and eligible[187] for assistance;[188] the duty will not, however, arise where the authority refers the application to another local housing authority in England under the local connection provisions (see paras 7.59–7.72).[189] The duty is to take reasonable steps to help the applicant to secure that suitable accommodation becomes available for his or her occupation[190] for at least six months or such longer period[191] as may be prescribed.[192] In deciding what steps to take, the authority must have regard to its assessment of the applicant's case (paras 10.43–10.48).[193]

10.67 It may be stressed that, while the authority could fulfil the duty by providing accommodation,[194] it is only a duty to take reasonable steps to help to secure accommodation. It seems highly likely that the courts will take the view that what is reasonable for the authority to do is a matter for the authority, rather than the court: compare

182 H(W)A 2014 s79(3).
183 H(W)A 2014 s79(4).
184 H(W)A 2014 s79(5).
185 Also based on provisions already in force in Wales: see paras 10.49–10.51.
186 Chapter 4.
187 Chapter 3.
188 HRA 2017 s5(2); HA 1996 s189B(1).
189 HRA 2017 s5(2); HA 1996 s189B(2).
190 See paras 4.16–4.38.
191 Not exceeding 12 months.
192 HRA 2017 s5(2); HA 1996 s189B(2).
193 HRA 2017 s5(2); HA 1996 s189B(3).
194 Although this is not explicitly stated, it is not merely implied but supported by other provisions of the HRA 2017, amending HA 1996: see, in particular, HRA 2017 s6, amending HA 1996 s205, and s7(1) adding s193A.

the duty in HA 1996 s213,[195] to render 'such assistance . . . as is reasonable in the circumstances' in which the authority's decision to refuse to assist was upheld on the basis that it was for it to decide whether or not to do so would unduly prejudice the discharge of its functions.[196]

When the duty comes to an end

Generally

10.68 Where the authority is satisfied that the applicant has a priority need[197] and is not satisfied that the applicant became homeless intentionally,[198] the duty comes to an end 56 days following the day the authority was first satisfied that the applicant was homeless and eligible.[199] The authority may also give notice bringing the duty to an end when it is satisfied that any one of certain circumstances is applicable.[200] The circumstances are as follows:[201]

a) the applicant both has suitable accommodation which is available for his or her occupation and there is a reasonable prospect of him or her having suitable accommodation[202] available for at least six months[203] from the date of the notice;
b) the authority has complied with the duty to take reasonable steps and the period of 56 days beginning with the day that the authority is first satisfied that the applicant was homeless and eligible has ended (whether or not he or she has secured accommodation);
c) the applicant has refused an offer of suitable accommodation and, on the date of refusal, there was a reasonable prospect that suitable accommodation would be available for occupation by the applicant for at least 6 months or such longer period[204] as may be prescribed;
d) the applicant has become homeless intentionally from any accommodation that has been made available to him or her as a result of the authority's exercise of its functions under this duty;
e) the applicant is no longer eligible for assistance; or

195 See paras 13.66–13.73.
196 *R v Northavon DC ex p Smith* [1994] 2 AC 402, (1994) 26 HLR 659, HL.
197 Chapter 5.
198 Chapter 6.
199 HRA 2017 s5(2); HA 1996 s189B(4).
200 HRA 2017 s5(2); HA 1996 s189B(5).
201 HRA 2017 s5(2); HA 1996 s189B(7).
202 It need not be the same accommodation.
203 Or such longer period not exceeding 12 months as may be prescribed.
204 Not exceeding 12 months.

f) the applicant has withdrawn the application for accommodation or assistance in obtaining it.

10.69 The notice must specify which of the circumstances applies and inform the applicant that he or she has a right to request a review of the decision to bring the duty to an end and of the time within which such a request must be made.[205] The notice must be in writing, and, if not received by the applicant, is to be treated as having been given if made available at the authority's office for a reasonable period for collection by or on his or her behalf of the applicant:[206] see also para 9.146.

Additional circumstances

10.70 The duty can also be brought to an end under HA 1996 s193A (refusal of final offer: para 10.71) or s193B (deliberate and unreasonable refusal to co-operate: see paras 10.72–10.74),[207] although – by section 193C – the latter will not end a right to accommodation for an applicant who is homeless, eligible, in priority need and not homeless intentionally: para 10.74.[208]

Refusal of final offer

10.71 The first of these additional circumstances in which the initial help duty can be brought to an end is if the applicant, having been informed of the consequences of refusal and of his or her right to request a review of the suitability of the accommodation,[209] refuses either a final accommodation offer,[210] or a final Part 6[211] offer.[212] If it is brought to an end on this basis, the principal housing duty in

205 HRA 2017 s5; HA 1996 s189B(6).

206 HRA 2017 s5; HA 1996 s189B(8).

207 HRA 2017 s5; HA 1996 s189B(9)

208 HRA 2017 s7(1); HA 1996 s193C(3), (4).

209 Paras 9.157–9.159.

210 This is an offer of an assured shorthold tenancy made by a private landlord – including a private registered provider of social housing (England) or a registered social landlord (Wales) – in relation to any accommodation which is, or may become, available for the applicant's occupation, made, with the approval of the authority, in pursuance of arrangements made by the authority in discharge of the initial help duty, which is a fixed term tenancy for a period of at least six months: HRA 2017 s7(1); HA 1996 s193A(4).

211 This is an offer of accommodation under Part 6 made in writing in discharge of the authority's initial help duty, which states that it is a final offer for that purpose: HRA 2017 s7(1); HA 1996 s193A(5).

212 HRA 2017 s7(1); HA 1996 s193A(1), (2).

HA 1996 s193 (paras 10.111–10.219) does not apply.[213] The authority cannot approve a final accommodation offer or make a final Part 6 offer unless it is satisfied that it is suitable for the applicant;[214] nor can it approve or make such an offer if the applicant is under contractual or other obligations in respect of his or her existing accommodation, which he or she is not able to bring to an end before he or she would have to take up the offer.[215] The provisions are modelled on, and similar to, those which may determine that a section 193 duty has ceased.[216]

Deliberate and unreasonable refusal to co-operate

10.72 The second of the additional circumstances in which the initial help duty can be brought to an end – which can also bring to an end the new duty to those threatened with homelessness (paras 10.57–10.60) – arises where the authority gives notice to an applicant that it considers that the applicant has deliberately and unreasonably refused to take any step that he or she agreed to take or that was recorded by the authority under the assessment and plan provisions considered above (paras 10.43–10.51).[217] Note that the refusal must be both deliberate and unreasonable. When deciding whether a refusal is unreasonable, the authority must have regard to the particular circumstances and needs of the applicant (whether identified in its assessment of his or her case or not).[218]

10.73 The notice must explain why the authority is giving it, its effect and inform the applicant that he or she has a right to request a review[219] of the decision to give the notice and of the time within which such a request must be made.[220] Moreover, no notice may be given without a prior 'relevant warning' notice[221] and a reasonable period[222] has

213 HRA 2017 s7(1); HA 1996 s193A(3).
214 HRA 2017 s7(1); HA 1996 s193A(6).
215 HRA 2017 s7(1); HA 1996 s193A(7).
216 See paras 10.111–10.211.
217 HRA 2017 s7(1); HA 1996 s193B(1), (2).
218 HRA 2017 s7(1); HA 1996 s193B(6).
219 See paras 9.149–9.161.
220 HRA 2017 s7(1); HA 1996 s193B(3).
221 This is a notice given by the authority after the refusal to take the agreed or recorded step, which warns the applicant that, if he or she continues deliberately and unreasonably to refuse to take the step after receiving the notice, the authority intends to give the notice which will bring the duty to an end, and which explains the consequences of that notice: HRA 2017 s7(1); HA 1996 s193B(5).
222 This is not defined.

elapsed since it was given.[223] The notice must be in writing, and, if not received by the applicant, is to be treated as having been given if made available at the authority's office for a reasonable period for collection by or on his or her behalf of the applicant:[224] see also para 9.146. The secretary of state may make provision by regulations as to the procedure to be followed in connection with notices under this section.[225]

10.74 If either duty[226] is brought to an end on this basis,[227] then while the principal housing duty in HA 1996 s193 (paras 10.111–10.219) will not apply,[228] the homeless who are eligible and in priority need but not homeless intentionally will be entitled to accommodation under section 193C (para 10.24).[229] This is considered below, alongside other duties to the unintentionally homeless in priority need.[230]

Wales

10.75 If an authority is satisfied that an applicant is homeless and eligible for assistance, whether or not he or she has a priority need or may be homeless intentionally, it must help to secure that accommodation is available for the applicant.[231] The duty does not apply if the authority refers the application to another local housing authority[232] in England or Wales.[233]

10.76 The duty requires the authority to take reasonable steps to help, having regard to (among other things) the need to make the best use of its resources.[234] It does not require the authority to offer accommodation, whether under Part 6 or otherwise.[235]

223 HRA 2017 s7(1); HA 1996 s193B(4).
224 HRA 2017 s7(1); HA 1996 s193B(8)
225 HRA 2017 s7(1); HA 1996 s193B(7).
226 HA 1996 ss189B(2), 195(2), as added or substituted by HRA 2017 ss4, 5.
227 Which will be the effect of a notice which fulfils all its requirements: HRA 2017 s7(1); HA 1996 s193C(1), (2).
228 HRA 2017 s7(1); HA 1996 s193C(3).
229 HRA 2017 s7(1); HA 1996 s193C(4).
230 See para 10.109.
231 H(W)A 2014 s73(1).
232 H(W)A 2014 s73(2).
233 H(W)A 2014 s18(1).
234 H(W)A 2014 s65(a).
235 H(W)A 2014 s65(b)–(c).

When the duty comes to an end

10.77 This duty lasts for 56 days[236] although the authority can decide on a shorter period if reasonable steps to secure accommodation for the applicant have been taken.[237] Moreover, the duty will come to an end before the end of that period if one of the following occurs:

a) the authority is satisfied that the applicant has suitable accommodation available for occupation, which accommodation is likely to be available for occupation by the applicant for a period of at least six months;[238]
b) the applicant refuses an offer of accommodation from any person, having been notified in writing of the possible consequences of refusal or acceptance of the offer, provided that the authority is satisfied that the accommodation was suitable for the applicant and was likely to be available for at least the next six months;[239]
c) the applicant ceases to be eligible;[240]
d) a mistake of fact led the authority to notify the applicant that it owed him or her a duty to help to secure accommodation for the applicant;[241]
e) the applicant has withdrawn the application;[242]
f) the applicant is unreasonably failing to co-operate with the authority.[243]

Unreasonable failure to co-operate

10.78 While HRA 2017 contains detailed provisions governing the refusal of an applicant in England to co-operate (paras 10.72–10.74), H(W)A 2014 has no equivalent. The Welsh Code of Guidance suggests that authorities should satisfy themselves that the applicant is not failing to co-operate because he or she is vulnerable, has an unmet support need or has difficulty communicating and recommends a 'minded to' letter be sent before discharging any duty.[244]

236 H(W)A 2014 s74(2).
237 H(W)A 2014 s74(3).
238 H(W)A 2014 s74(4).
239 H(W)A 2014 s74(5).
240 H(W)A 2014 s79(2).
241 H(W)A 2014 s79(3).
242 H(W)A 2014 s79(4).
243 H(W)A 2014 s79(5).
244 Paras 15.86–15.89.

Other duties without priority need

10.79 HA 1996 Part 7 and H(W)A 2014 Part 2 distinguish between those without priority need who are, and those who are not, intentionally homeless.[245] It is a distinction which did not appear in HA 1985 Part 3, as those without a priority need could not obtain substantive housing assistance under it, whether or not homeless intentionally.

Homelessness Act 2002

10.80 The distinction was designed for use in connection with the allocation provisions of HA 1996 Part 6 (see chapter 11). HA 1996 s167(3) gave the secretary of state power to make regulations specifying people to whom preference is to be given in allocating housing accommodation.[246]

10.81 The Homelessness Act 2002 built on the distinction by introducing a power to secure that accommodation is made available for those who are not in priority need and not intentionally homeless.[247] The power will be repealed once HRA 2017 is brought into force in England[248] as it is replaced by assessment and plans (paras 10.43–10.48) and the initial help duty (paras 10.66–10.74).

10.82 The observations on quality[249] and termination made in relation to accommodation pending decision (paras 10.17–10.32) also apply to accommodation provided under this power, as do those on availability (para 10.12) and payment (para 10.18); such accommodation, while excluded from security under the HA 1985, is not however excluded from assured protection under HA 1988;[250] there is also no basis for thinking that the observations on exclusion from PEA 1977 (para 10.16) will apply here, although the defences available on

245 So also does HRA 2017.

246 HA 1996 s167(3) (from commencement of LA 2011 s147, in England, s166A(7), on 9 November 2012: Localism Act 2011 (Commencement No 2 and Transitional Provisions) (England) Order 2012 SI No 2599 Article 2).

247 HA 1996 s192(3), as amended. As this power to house falls within HA 1996 Part 7, authorities can accordingly provide housing on a non-secure basis to this group. Previously, any allocation would have fallen within Part 6 and, as such, would have been or become secure (see chapter 11). Hence, authorities can now afford assistance to the homeless not in priority need, without needing to go as far as to provide them with full security. As to Wales, such persons are entitled to support under H(W)A 2014 s73: see para 10.74.

248 HRA 2017 s5(6).

249 See also paras 10.19–10.22.

250 See HA 1996 s209(1).

eviction (para 10.17) will. How accommodation may be provided,[251] suitability[252] and the constraints on out-of-area placements[253] (which are all considered below in relation to the principal duty) also apply to discharge under this section. There is no right to seek an internal review of a refusal to exercise this power: a challenge would therefore have to be by way of judicial review.[254]

10.83 Where an applicant who is not in priority need is threatened with homelessness unintentionally, the authority may correspondingly take reasonable steps to secure that accommodation does not cease to be available to him or her, although is not obliged to do so.[255] Once HRA 2017 comes into force in England, this power is also replaced by assessment and plans (paras 10.43–10.48) and the initial help duty (paras 10.66–10.74).[256]

Localism Act 2011

10.84 As noted above,[257] since LA 2011 s149(2) came into force in England,[258] there is one substantive housing duty now applicable (in England) to those who are no longer in priority need, which is consequent on the extended powers of an authority to discharge the full duty in HA 1996 s193[259] by using private sector accommodation.[260] The duty arises if the applicant becomes homeless[261] again within two years of acceptance of the previous offer, provided that the applicant is found still to be eligible for assistance, and not to have become

251 See para 1.21.

252 Paras 10.145–10.178.

253 See para 10.112.

254 See para 10.136.

255 HA 1996 s195(2). In Wales, an applicant who is eligible and threatened with homelessness is owed the H(W)A 2014 s66 duty, above: para 10.61.

256 HRA 2017 s4 substituting a new HA 1996 s195.

257 See para 10.9.

258 9 November 2012: Localism Act 2011 (Commencement No 2 and Transitional Provisions) (England) Order 2012 SI No 2599 article 2. This does not apply where the application was made and the duty to secure accommodation arose before, and the duty had not ceased by, that date: Localism Act 2011 (Commencement No 2 and Transitional Provisions) (England) Order 2012 SI No 2599 article 3.

259 Paras 10.152–10.181.

260 LA 2011 s48, amending HA 1996 s93.

261 Defined to mean when valid notice under HA 1988 s21 expires (see *Manual of Housing Law*, para 2.203), ie, there is no need for the applicant to await proceedings for possession or an order: HA 1996 s195A(2), added by LA 2011 s149(4).

homeless intentionally, on that second application, nor was found to be ineligible or homeless intentionally on any preceding application,[262] nor has the authority had regard to a restricted person[263] when concluding that the applicant is homeless again.[264] There is likewise a duty[265] to those who are threatened with homelessness,[266] even if not in priority need, within two years of acceptance of the previous offer, subject to the same qualifications.[267]

Advice and assistance

10.85 Having distinguished between those in priority need who are, and those who are not, intentionally homeless, the relevant sections currently lead in England[268] to the same HA 1996 Part 7 duty[269] in each case, which is to provide or secure that the applicant is provided with 'advice and assistance' in any attempts the applicant may make to secure that accommodation becomes available for his or her occupation.[270] Once HRA 2017 comes into force, however, this duty will not

262 HA 1996 s195A(6), ie, it will not be possible to circumvent the intention by making two successive applications within the two-year period.

263 See para 3.17.

264 HA 1996 s195A(1), (5), added by LA 2011 s149.

265 To take reasonable steps to secure that accommodation does not cease to be available: see para 10.75.

266 Defined to mean service of a valid notice under HA 1988 s21 (see *Manual of Housing Law*, para 2.203), even though such a notice is of a minimum period of two months, and being threatened with homelessness normally means homelessness within 28 days or 56 days in Wales (para 4.141), 56 days in England, too, once HRA 2017 s1 comes into force (para 4.146): HA 1996 s159A(4).

267 HA 1996 s195A(3), (5), (6) added by LA 2011 s149. Subsection (3) concerns those threatened with homelessness and, once HRA 2017 is in force, it will be repealed and new duties will apply (paras 10.52–10.61): HRA 2017 s4(4).

268 The position is different in Wales: see para 10.88.

269 Ie, as distinct from power.

270 HA 1996 s192(2) (unintentionally homeless) and s190(3) (intentionally homeless), as amended by the Homelessness Act 2002. See, on this, *Crawley BC v B* (2000) 32 HLR 636, CA, in which the authority – having made a decision that the applicant was not in priority need and therefore not gone on to consider intentionality – was still able to investigate and reach a conclusion on intentionality once the priority need had been successfully challenged; whether this could stand today in light of the power may be open to argument. Assistance could include paying a rent deposit: see Code of Guidance para 14.29; Welsh Code para 16.3. Once HRA 2017 is in force, however, HA 1996 s192 will be repealed (HRA 2017 s5(6)) and replaced by new provisions: see paras 10.50–10.61.

apply to those who are not in priority need,[271] but they benefit instead from the assessment and plan duty (paras 10.43–10.48) and the initial help duty (paras 10.66–10.74).

10.86 Before advice and assistance are provided, the applicant's housing needs must be assessed, and the advice and assistance should identify factors that make it difficult for the applicant to secure accommodation for himself or herself (eg, poverty, health and disabilities).[272] This assessment does not require a fresh or discrete investigation; it can be carried out by having regard to the information already obtained during the determination of the application.[273]

10.87 Even as strengthened by the Homelessness Act 2002, the right to advice and assistance is not of much substance or one therefore that is likely to be worth enforcing. In relation to the equivalent duty towards the intentionally homeless,[274] it has been held that, while an authority may provide financial assistance, there is no obligation so to do; a refusal to provide such assistance could only be challenged on conventional public law grounds: *Conville*.[275]

10.88 Nor does the right to advice and assistance give rise to a duty of care on the part of the authority to ensure that any accommodation towards which the applicant is directed is safe. Thus, in *Ephraim v Newham LBC*,[276] the plaintiff had been directed by the authority – by way of advice and assistance – to a guesthouse, a house in multiple occupation (HMO). She took up occupation in a bedsitting room in it. The HMO lacked proper fire precautions. Subsequently, there was a fire in the property and she suffered severe injuries. She sued, unsuccessfully alleging that Newham LBC was under a duty of care to satisfy itself that the premises to which it had referred her were reasonably safe, particularly in relation to fire. It was held that the imposition of such a duty would put the authority in the dilemma of having either to inspect a particular property, or else not advise people to seek available accommodation; it was more desirable that

271 HRA 2017 s5(5) as amended.

272 HA 1996 s192(4) and (5) (unintentionally homeless) and s190(4) and (5) (intentionally homeless), added by the Homelessness Act 2002. See generally Code of Guidance para 14.4; Welsh Code para 16.5. See also *R (Savage) v Hillingdon LBC* [2010] EWHC 88 (Admin), [2010] JHL D44. See last note as to HA 1996 s192 and HRA 2017.

273 *R (Savage) v Hillingdon LBC* [2010] EWHC 88 (Admin), [2010] JHL D44.

274 See para 10.54.

275 *Conville v Richmond upon Thames LBC* [2005] EWHC 1430 (Admin), [2006] HLR 1, not appealed on this point, see [2006] EWCA Civ 718, [2006] HLR 45; see chapter 12.

276 *Ephraim v Newham LBC* (1992) 25 HLR 208, CA.

the authority should give advice which enables homeless people to obtain accommodation, even though some of the properties where they obtain accommodation might prove not to be properly equipped, than it was to restrict the range of advice and make it more difficult for homeless people to find housing.

Wales

10.89 In Wales, an applicant who is not in priority need is entitled to the benefit of duties in H(W)A 2014 s66 (help to prevent him or her from becoming homeless)[277] and s73 (help to secure accommodation).[278] In each case, the duty includes power to provide advice and assistance.[279]

Other duties to the intentionally homeless

10.90 The same duty to provide advice and assistance arises when an applicant is homeless, in priority need, but has become homeless intentionally;[280] indeed, once HRA 2017 is brought into force, it will *only* apply to those in priority need, and then only once the duty under HA 1996 s189B(2) (initial help duty: paras 10.66–10.74) has come to an end; when discharging it, an authority must have regard to its assessment under HA 1996 s189A (paras 10.43–10.47).[281]

10.91 If in priority need, however, this class of applicant currently benefits – and will continue to benefit – from the additional duty imposed on the authority to secure that suitable[282] accommodation is made available for the applicant's occupation[283] – which means for the occupation of the applicant and of any person who might reasonably be expected to reside with him or her – 'for such period as they consider will give him a reasonable opportunity of himself securing accommodation for his occupation'.[284]

277 See para 10.62.
278 See para 10.75.
279 H(W)A 2014 s64(2)(h).
280 HA 1996 s190(2)(b), (4) and (5). The same is true in Wales, see last para.
281 HRA 2017 s3(2); HA 1996 s190(4), as substituted.
282 See HA 1996 ss205 and 206; H(W)A 2014 s59.
283 HA 1996 s176; H(W)A 2014 s56.
284 HA 1996 s190(2)(a). In Wales, the position is different: where the authority decides that a person is eligible for assistance, homeless and in priority need, it has a duty to secure that accommodation is made available for his or her occupation (unless it refers the applicant to another authority under the local

10.92 In Wales, the position is somewhat different.[285] First, the authority may have decided not to apply the intentionality provisions at all.[286] If those provisions are still being applied, then the principal duty to accommodate under H(W)A 2014 s75,[287] will arise either if the authority is not satisfied that the applicant is homeless intentionally or if the applicant is:

a) a pregnant woman or a person with whom she resides or might reasonably be expected to reside;
b) a person with whom a dependent child resides or might reasonably be expected to reside;
c) a person who had not attained the age of 21 when the application was made or a person with whom such a person resides or might reasonably be expected to reside; or
d) a person who had attained the age of 21, but not the age of 25, when the application was made and who was looked after, accommodated or fostered at any time while under the age of 18, or a person with whom such a person resides or might reasonably be expected to reside.[288]

10.93 In these circumstances, the full duty will arise if the applicant has no suitable accommodation available for occupation, or suitable accommodation which it is not likely will be available for occupation for at least six months starting on the day on which the applicant is notified[289] that the full duty will not apply, the applicant is eligible for help and has a priority need for accommodation, and the authority has not previously secured an offer of accommodation to the applicant under these provisions following a previous application for help, at any time within the period of five years before the day on which the

connection provisions of the legislation): H(W)A 2014 s75(1), (2). When discharging this duty, however, the authority has power to consider whether or not the applicant became homeless intentionally: H(W)A 2014 s78. If the authority decides to exercise that power, its duty to the applicant is to secure that accommodation is available for his or her occupation for 56 days: H(W)A 2014 s74(2). If the Welsh Authority has decided that the relevant intentionality category is to be disregarded, then the full duty in H(W)A 2014 s75 will be owed. See further para 6.3.

285 H(W)A 2014 s56.

286 Para 6.3.

287 Paras 10.111–10.219.

288 H(W)A 2014 s75(3).

289 Under H(W)A 2014 s84.

applicant was notified[290] that a duty was owed to him or her under them.[291] If the full duty does not arise for any of these reasons, or because the applicant is not within the H(W)A 2014 s75(3) class,[292] then the initial duty to help[293] is limited to 56 days.[294]

10.94 The observations on quality[295] and termination made in relation to accommodation pending decision (paras 10.17–10.32) also apply to accommodation provided under this power, as do those on availability (para 10.2), payment (para 10.15), security (para 10.18), exclusion from PEA 1977 (para 10.18) and defences on eviction (para 10.17). How accommodation may be provided,[296] suitability[297] and the constraints on out-of-area placements[298] (which are all considered below in relation to the principal duty) also apply to discharge under this section.

Time

10.95 This duty has given rise to a number of problems. The first question is from when does time run when determining what comprises a reasonable opportunity. Whether or not an applicant seeks internal review does not affect this issue: time runs from the date of the decision regardless of whether an internal review is sought: *Conville*.[299]

10.96 In *Dyson*,[300] the applicant was told on 21 May that she would be provided with one month's accommodation from 25 May (the date when her homelessness would actually occur). This decision appears to have been taken by an official but appears to have required ratification by a committee. The time was subsequently extended to 6 July, but it was not until 3 July that committee ratification was communicated to the applicant. Time was nonetheless held to run from

290 The applicant is to be treated as notified on the day the notice is sent or first made available for collection: H(W)A 2014 s75(4).

291 H(W)A 2014 s75(3).

292 See para 10.92.

293 See paras 10.75–10.78.

294 H(W)A 2014 s74(2).

295 See also paras 10.19–10.22.

296 See para 10.121.

297 See para 10.145–10.178.

298 See para 10.136.

299 *R (Conville) v Richmond upon Thames LBC* [2005] EWHC 1430 (Admin), [2006] HLR 1, not appealed on this point see [2006] EWCA Civ 718, [2006] HLR 45.

300 *Dyson v Kerrier DC* [1980] 1 WLR 120, CA.

the notification by the official, of which the letter of 3 July was mere confirmation.

10.97 In *de Falco*,[301] only four days had been allowed between notification of decision and the expiry of what is now HA 1996 s188 accommodation. The Master of the Rolls thought that this period was probably adequate, having regard to several weeks in accommodation provided by the authority prior to its decision. He was, however, also influenced by the time during which the applicants had been accommodated between the issue of proceedings and the hearing before the Court of Appeal. As *de Falco* was the hearing of an interlocutory appeal for an interlocutory injunction to house until trial, he treated that matter as conclusive as a matter of the court's discretion.

10.98 The same point influenced Bridge LJ, although he was otherwise of the view that time prior to communication of the local authority's decision was irrelevant so that only time since that decision was communicated could count. As the purpose of the provisions is to give the applicant time to find somewhere else to live once it has been decided that the authority need not provide full assistance, this view seems preferable.[302]

10.99 The courts may be less generous towards an applicant who lives with another person who has previously been found homeless intentionally, and who has already enjoyed a period of HA 1996 s190(2)(a) accommodation, although such a person may indeed reapply and it seems to be an irresistible inference from *Lewis*[303] and the other cases on this point[304] that such a person will then be entitled to a new period of section 190(2)(a) accommodation; it is strongly arguable that he or she can and should benefit from the reasoning of Bridge LJ in *de Falco*.

10.100 Some reconciliation of merits and principle may be found in the extent of acquiescence or participation in the act which results in the finding of intentionality and therefore the extent to which an adverse finding should have been anticipated.

301 *de Falco, Silvestri v Crawley BC* [1980] QB 460, CA.

302 Sir David Cairns thought that the decision was unreviewable, although this proposition does not find any support elsewhere and is wholly out of line with a more modern approach in public law.

303 *R v North Devon DC ex p Lewis* [1981] 1 WLR 328, QBD.

304 See paras 6.9–6.24. See also *R (Savage) v Hillingdon LBC* [2010] EWHC 88 (Admin), [2010] JHL D44, where it was held that it was for the authority to determine what period of time afforded a reasonable opportunity of securing accommodation.

10.101 In *Smith v Bristol City Council*,[305] a county court judge held that, even where a substantial period of warning had been given to the applicant, the authority was still obliged to give more time:

> I cannot accept that 'no time' can in any circumstances be a reasonable period . . . [A] reasonable time must be given to the applicant after she actually becomes homeless . . .

10.102 When an authority decides for how long it should secure that accommodation is available so as to give an applicant a reasonable opportunity of securing accommodation for himself or herself, pursuant to its duty under HA 1996 s190(2)(a), it may not have regard to considerations peculiar to itself, ie the extent of its resources and other demands.[306] While it is for the authority to decide what is a reasonable opportunity, subject to the usual principles of intervention,[307] what is reasonable for these purposes is to be assessed by reference to the particular needs and circumstances of the applicant, including the availability of other accommodation; if the applicant is not making reasonable efforts to pursue other possibilities, however, that will be a strong indication that he or she should not be given more time; and, even if the applicant makes reasonable efforts, a moment will normally be reached when time will expire if those possibilities have not come to fruition; the opportunity is no more than that – it can not be converted into a duty to provide long-term accommodation.[308]

10.103 The Code no longer suggests any particular time frame:[309]

> A few weeks may provide the applicant with a reasonable opportunity to secure accommodation for him or herself. However, some applicants might require longer, and others, particularly where the housing authority provides pro-active and effective advice and assistance, might require less time.[310]

10.104 It continues that 'authorities will need to take account of local circumstances, including how readily other accommodation is available in the district, and will need to have regard to the particular circumstances of the applicant', including the resources available to him or

305 December 1981 *LAG Bulletin* 287, CC.

306 *R (Conville) v Richmond upon Thames LBC* [2006] EWCA Civ 718, [2006] HLR 45.

307 See chapter 12.

308 *R (Conville) v Richmond upon Thames LBC* [2006] EWCA Civ 718, [2006] HLR 45.

309 Previous editions referred to 28 days being adequate in most cases.

310 English Code of Guidance para 14.28; Welsh Code paras 9.27 and 17.45–17.46.

her to provide rent in advance or a rent deposit where this may be required by private landlords.[311]

10.105 This much is clear: an applicant's circumstances must be individually considered, and if it can be shown that the time allowed has been reached without regard to them or was such a short period that no authority could have considered that it gave the applicant a reasonable opportunity to find somewhere for himself or herself, the courts will order sufficient time.[312]

10.106 It would seem from *Monaf*[313] that – at least where the housing authority is also a social services authority – the authority ought to have regard to its duties under the CA 1989 s20(1)[314] when determining this period.[315] Prior to this stage, the housing authority should in any event have sought the applicant's consent to refer the case to the social services authority,[316] so that the latter authority can consider exercise of its powers under the CA 1989.[317]

Policies

10.107 A further problem is posed by 'policies'. In particular, the frequency with which all kinds of applicants receive identical offers of 28 days' accommodation suggests that many authorities operate a policy under this provision.[318] If an inflexible policy can be proven, it can be set aside.[319] If, however, the 28-day rule is merely a guideline, genuinely reconsidered in each case, it will be valid.

311 English Code of Guidance para 14.28; Welsh Code paras 9.27 and 17.45–17.46.

312 *Lally v Kensington and Chelsea RLBC* (1980) *Times* 27 March, ChD.

313 *R v Tower Hamlets LBC ex p Monaf* (1988) 20 HLR 529, CA.

314 See paras 13.58–13.72.

315 Moreover, local authorities must now have regard 'to the need to safeguard and promote the welfare of children' when discharging their functions: CA 2004 s11 (England); s28 (Wales). This includes functions under HA 1996 Part 7: *Huzrat v Hounslow LBC* [2013] EWCA Civ 1865, [2014] HLR 17. See also *Nzolameso v Westminster City Council* [2015] UKSC 22, [2015] HLR 22: when considering whether accommodation is suitable for a family, the authority must identify the principal needs of the children both individually and collectively when making the decision.

316 See further HA 1996 s213A; and para 13.73.

317 See further paras 13.49–13.87.

318 In *Birmingham City Council v Ali; Moran v Manchester City Council (Secretary of State for Communities and Local Government and another intervening)* [2009] UKHL 36, [2009] 1 WLR 1506 at [17], Baroness Hale commented: 'We are told that up to six weeks is usually thought enough for this although there is no statutory limit.'

319 See paras 12.44–12.45.

Duties where local connection referral

10.108 The allocation of housing responsibilities when the homeless person falls within the local connection provisions has been considered in chapter 7.[320]

Other duties towards the unintentionally homeless in priority need

10.109 Duties towards those whom the authority is satisfied are eligible, homeless, in priority need and not intentionally homeless, are currently governed by HA 1996 s193 and H(W)A 2014 s75. Once HRA 2017 comes into force, in England, the duty does not arise until the authority's duty under HA 1996 s189B(2) (initial help duty: paras 10.66–10.74) has come to an end.[321] Likewise, in Wales, the H(W)A 2014 s75 duty does not arise until the section 73 duty has come to an end.[322] Moreover, the duty will not arise at all either if it has been disapplied by HA 1996 s193A(3) (refusal of final offer: para 10.71) or the authority has given notice to the applicant under s193B(2) (deliberate and unreasonable refusal to co-operate: para 10.72),[323] although in the latter case it is replaced by duties under s193C (paras 10.221–10.225).

10.110 In Wales, the H(W)A 2014 s75 duty can only arise where the section 73 duty has come to an end and the applicant is eligible, in priority need, not intentionally homeless[324] and does not have suitable accommodation available for his or her occupation or, if he or she does have suitable accommodation, it is not likely that It will be available for at least six months: accordingly, if the section 73 duty has come to an end because the applicant accepted other accommodation or refused an offer or unreasonably refused to co-operate with the authority, the section 75 duty will not be owed.[325]

320 Paras 7.59–7.72.

321 HRA 2017 s5(7); HA 1996 s193(1), as substituted.

322 H(W)A 2014 s75(1).

323 HRA 2017 s7(2), adding HA 1996 s193(1A).

324 Assuming the authority is applying the intentionality provisions: H(W)A 2014 ss77, 78. See also H(W)A 2014 s75(3).

325 H(W)A 2014 s75(1).

Housing Act 1996 s193/Housing (Wales) Act 2014 s75

10.111 Under HA 1996 s193, the duty towards the unintentionally homeless is to secure that accommodation is available for occupation by the applicant until the duty ceases in accordance with the sections;[326] it is the principal – or 'highest' – duty under the Acts, sometimes referred to as permanent or indefinite although it will be seen that neither description is wholly accurate.

10.112 The observations on availability (para 10.12), payment (para 10.15) and security (para 10.18) made in relation to accommodation pending decision (paras 10.8–10.28) in principle also apply to accommodation provided under this power, save that there is no exclusion from assured security under HA 1996 s209 for accommodation provided under these provisions although as it is likely to be provided on a shorthold basis[327] it is not required. It is thought, however, that the exclusion from PEA 1977 (para 10.18) does not apply once the principal duty is owed.[328] Observations on defences on eviction (para 10.18) will apply should an authority seek to evict an applicant while he or she is still being housed under HA 1996 Part 7 or H(W)A 2014 Part 2.

10.113 A number of issues fall to be considered:

a) postponement of the duty;
b) means of discharge;
c) out-of-area placements;
d) suitability of accommodation;
e) cessation of duty.

326 HA 1996 s193(2) and (3); s193(3) was amended by the Homelessness Act 2002 to remove the restriction on the duty to a period of two years. In Wales, see H(W)A 2014 ss75 and 76; as in England, there is no 'two-year' restriction.

327 See *Manual of Housing Law*, para 1.246.

328 *R (ZH and CN) v Lewisham LBC* [2014] UKSC 62, [2015] AC 1259, [2015] HLR 6; It would seem to follow from Lord Hodge at [16] and [45]. Lady Hale referred at [165] to the 'generally accepted view that the protection of section 3 of the 1977 Act will apply once the local authority have accepted that they owe the family the "full housing duty"', presumably picking up the local authorities' submission that the 'licences were expressly limited to the period to be taken to provide a decision' (at 1287F) and the secretary of state's submission that the premises were 'temporary accommodation while the council made inquiries' (at 1288D).

Postponement of the duty

10.114 Discharge of the duty may not be postponed for any extraneous reason: see *Khalique*,[329] where the authority sought to postpone making an offer of accommodation pending a reduction in arrears of rent owed by the applicant.[330] This does not mean that the applicant's arrears may not be taken into account when deciding whether or not to make a Part 6 allocation,[331] which is governed by its own provisions.[332]

10.115 There are, however, apparently conflicting decisions as to whether the duty under HA 1996 s193 to secure suitable accommodation may be postponed, although these have tended to conflate the provision of suitable accommodation on a temporary basis with an allocation or other final offer of suitable accommodation.

10.116 In *Anderson*,[333] the authority had failed to make any suitable offers to the applicant in 16 months after accepting that she was homeless because of overcrowding in her current accommodation. A number of offers of accommodation had been made, but it was accepted by the authority that these had been reasonably refused. One offer remained outstanding and subject to review. Moses J said:[334]

> The statutory scheme under the Housing Act shows that there is no time limit within which a housing authority is obliged under the statute to comply with a duty to secure available accommodation for those who fall within section 193 . . . The provisions within the Housing Act, which require housing authorities to put in place an allocations policy and to comply with that policy, are contained in Part 6 of the Housing Act. They demonstrate that there will be those to whom a duty is owed under section 193 of the Act who will not be housed immediately or within any particular time-limit. There may be those in respect of whom, the housing authority will be under an obligation, in accordance with their allocations policy, to give a greater priority.

10.117 In *Sembi*,[335] the applicant, a woman of 52 who was confined to a wheelchair, was accepted as homeless and offered accommodation in a nursing home occupied mainly by the elderly and terminally ill.

329 *R v Tower Hamlets LBC ex p Khalique* (1994) 26 HLR 517, QBD.

330 See also *R v Newham LBC ex p Miah* (1995) 28 HLR 279, QBD.

331 Both *Khalique* and *Miah* preceded HA 1996: accordingly, discharge and offer of permanent accommodation were commonly synonymous. The proposition in the text applies the principle in *Khalique* to the provisions *post*-1996.

332 See paras 11.23–11.53.

333 *R v Southwark LBC ex p Anderson* (1998) 32 HLR 96, QBD.

334 *R v Southwark LBC ex p Anderson* (1998) 32 HLR 96 at 98, QBD.

335 *R v Merton LBC ex p Sembi* (1999) 32 HLR 439, QBD.

The authority accepted that the nursing home was not suitable in the long term, but considered it suitable as temporary accommodation. The judge held that there had been no failure by the authority to discharge its duty under HA 1996 s193. Jowitt J cited the passage from *Anderson* with approval.

10.118 However, in *Begum*,[336] Collins J held that duties under the HA 1996 – whether under section 193 or otherwise[337] – could not be deferred. Accordingly, the authority could not defer providing accommodation which was suitable for the applicant and his family, including for the applicant's mother who used a wheelchair. He accepted that where there were great difficulties in finding suitable accommodation, a court would not enforce the duty unreasonably, for example within a few days, but only if the authority was doing all that it could to comply with it.[338]

10.119 This conflict has in practice now been resolved by the House of Lords in *Ali* and *Moran*,[339] where a clearer distinction was drawn between the duty to secure that suitable accommodation is available for a homeless family under HA 1996 s193(2) and allocation under Part 6. Thus, suitability for the purpose of section 193(2) does not imply permanence or security of tenure; there are degrees of suitability and what is suitable in the short term may not be suitable for a longer period; when the time comes that the applicant cannot continue to occupy his or her current accommodation for another night, the authority must act immediately.[340] Accordingly, Birmingham CC could decide that applicants were homeless even though they could remain in their current accommodation for a while.[341] When

336 *R v Newham LBC ex p Begum* (1999) 32 HLR 808, QBD. See also *R (Khan) v Newham LBC* [2001] EWHC (Admin) 589, [2001] JHL D90, where Newham LBC conceded that it was in breach of the duty (through the provision of inadequate bed and breakfast-type accommodation), and a mandatory order requiring the authority to provide suitable accommodation within two months was made. Cf *Begum v Tower Hamlets LBC* [2002] EWHC 633 (Admin), [2002] JHL D58, where, again, the authority acknowledged that the accommodation was unsuitable but the court refused to make a mandatory order in the absence of any evidence of the time within which suitable accommodation could be provided.

337 Ie, also under HA 1996 ss188, 190 and 200.

338 The authority had not, however, done all that it could, because it had adopted a policy not to consider its own stock to discharge its duty under HA 1996 s193.

339 *Birmingham City Council v Ali; Moran v Manchester City Council (Secretary of State for Communities and Local Government and another intervening)* [2009] UKHL 36, [2009] 1 WLR 1506.

340 At [47].

341 At [48].

considering the question whether a local housing authority has left an applicant in accommodation which it would not be reasonable for him or her to continue to occupy for too long a period, the question is primarily one for the authority; a court should normally be slow to accept that the authority has left an applicant in unsatisfactory accommodation for too long; in resolving this issue it is necessary to take account of the severe constraints on budgets and personnel, and the limited housing stock.[342]

10.120 The decision allows an authority to conclude that an applicant is already homeless, without necessarily providing fresh accommodation at once, on the basis that current accommodation is suitable in the short term: hence, no question of postponement of duty arises.

Means of discharge

10.121 By HA 1996 s206 or H(W)A 2014 s76, a local authority may discharge its duty under section 193 in one of three ways:[343]

a) by securing that suitable accommodation provided by it is available for the applicant;
b) by securing that the applicant obtains suitable accommodation from some other person; or
c) by giving the applicant such advice and assistance as will secure that suitable accommodation is available from some other person.

10.122 As a matter of language, and construction, HA 1996 s206 is exhaustive of the means of providing accommodation, and so it cannot be used – even in conjunction with Local Government Act 1972 s111 – to guarantee the provision of accommodation by another.[344]

10.123 Once HRA 2017 is in force in England, bringing with it the new initial help duty (paras 10.66–10.74) and new duties to those in priority need (paras 10.220–10.225), HA 1996 s206 only applies where the authority decides to discharge those duties by securing that accommodation is available for an applicant's accommodation.[345]

342 At [50].

343 HA 1996 s206(1); H(W)A 2014 ss64, 76.

344 *Crédit Suisse v Waltham Forest LBC* (1996) 29 HLR 115, CA. It may, however, be that the general power of competence in LA 2011 s1, could be used, although this depends on construction of the limits on that power in LA 2011 s2. See paras 13.90–13.94.

345 HRA 2017 s6, adding HA 1996 s205(3).

Resources

10.124 The issue of resources is not irrelevant to how an authority decides to discharge its duty. Thus, if an applicant has a particular and perhaps unusual need, the authority can – in deciding whether to meet it by purchasing a property on the open market – take into account the cost of doing so.[346] In *Calgin*,[347] the cost of providing accommodation was likewise held to be a factor that the authority could take into account in deciding how to discharge its duty.

10.125 In *Sheridan v Basildon BC*,[348] the applicants were travellers living at unauthorised sites in Basildon's area; they applied under HA 1996 Part 7; the authority accepted that they were owed the full housing duty under HA 1996 s193(2). Having decided that there were no suitable traveller sites in their area, Basildon offered them tenancies of conventional properties, which were refused, relying, inter alia, on a regional planning strategy which had recommended that the authority provide further pitches, so that Basildon ought to be required to purchase land to be used as a traveller site, an argument that failed: whilst it might be said that, as a matter of planning policy, Basildon should have provided suitable sites, it was unrealistic to expect a HA 1996 s202 review to consider such matters; planning policy was outside the expertise of housing officers and Parliament could not have intended such matters to fall within the scope of a section 202 review; nor was there any basis for requiring Basildon to purchase land; the section 193 duty was to be discharged within the existing resources of the authority.

Advice and assistance

10.126 Advice and assistance such that the applicant secures accommodation from another under HA 1996 s206(1)(c) or H(W)A 2014 s64 seems wide enough to cover advice and assistance leading to house purchase by an applicant who is financially able to undertake it.[349] It may

346 *R v Lambeth LBC ex p Ekpo-Wedderman* (1999) 31 HLR 498, QBD. See also *R v Lambeth LBC ex p A1* (1997) 30 HLR 933, CA, where the homeless applicant's challenge to a decision of the authority not to exercise its powers under HA 1985 ss9 and 17 to add to its stock failed.

347 *R (Calgin) v Enfield LBC* [2005] EWHC 1716 (Admin), [2006] HLR 4.

348 [2012] EWCA Civ 335, [2012] HLR 29. See also *Slattery v Basildon BC* [2014] EWCA Civ 30, [2014] HLR 16, following *Sheridan*.

349 See English Code of Guidance para 16.33, including through shared equity or similar schemes for low cost home ownership: see Code of Guidance para 16.34. There is no equivalent in the Welsh Code.

also cover the provision of mediation designed to ensure that a 16- or 17-year-old applicant returns to live in his or her family home.[350]

Discharge through another

10.127 Some other person, in the context of HA 1996 s206(1), may be a person or body – or an authority – abroad.

10.128 In *Browne*,[351] a woman with no local connection with Bristol, and no local connection with the area of any other housing authority in England, Wales or Scotland, was offered assistance to return to her home town of Tralee, Eire, where the authorities were prepared to ensure that she was housed. In order to sustain its decision, Bristol CC did not need to know the exact details of the accommodation to be made available to her.[352] The arrangement was, however, only appropriate once it was established by Bristol CC that, in its opinion, the woman ran no risk of domestic violence in Tralee. It would seem from the report that had there been a risk of domestic violence, the arrangement would not have been acceptable, for otherwise Bristol CC would have managed to circumvent the spirit of the local connection provisions,[353] even though, not being a referral to another authority in the UK, its letter did not apply. On the same basis, other statutory considerations governing suitability, considered below, would now have to be applied in principle.

10.129 In *Wyness v Poole BC*,[354] a county court rejected an attempt to house an applicant in the area of another authority, when the local connection provisions were inapplicable because of an employment connection, because living in the area of that other authority would have meant that the employment would have to be given up. The court held that no reasonable authority could so discharge the duty.[355]

10.130 In *Parr v Wyre BC*,[356] an authority sought to discharge its duty by securing an offer of accommodation in Birmingham, an area with which the applicants had no connection at all. There were no details

350 See *Robinson v Hammersmith and Fulham LBC* [2006] EWCA Civ 1122, [2007] HLR 7 at [39].

351 *R v Bristol City Council ex p Browne* [1979] 1 WLR 1437, DC.

352 The decision preceded the introduction of the requirement of suitability. Today, an authority would be bound to take steps to satisfy itself about suitability, even if only by appropriate enquiries – this accords with the approach taken in *Browne* to domestic violence: see text.

353 See para 7.50.

354 July 1979 *LAG Bulletin* 166, CC.

355 See also paras 10.136–10.144, on out-of-area placements.

356 (1982) 2 HLR 71, CA.

available of the accommodation to be provided and the applicants had a limited time in which to accept. While it was common ground that discharge could be in another area (but consider now the provisions that govern out-of-area placements[357]), the Court of Appeal, distinguishing *Browne*, did not uphold the offer: the offer had to be of 'appropriate accommodation', in terms both of size of family and of area. In *Puhlhofer*,[358] however, the House of Lords rejected introduction of the qualification 'appropriate'.[359]

10.131 Nonetheless, the result may well have been the same, so far as it related to relocation to another, altogether distant, area. Thus, a decision by Enfield LBC, in whose area the applicant had lived for the previous eight years since arriving as an asylum-seeker[360] and where her children were in school, to secure accommodation for an applicant in bed and breakfast accommodation in Birmingham, with which city the applicant had no connection, was held to be irrational and an infringement of the applicant's rights under ECHR Article 8(1): *Yumsak*.[361]

10.132 In *Cafun*,[362] the authority purported to discharge its duty by referring the applicant to another (neighbouring) authority with which it had a reciprocal agreement. It failed to consider either whether accommodation in the neighbouring area would be suitable for the particular applicant, or the limits on out-of-area placements.[363] The decision was quashed.

10.133 The provision of successful mediation which enables a 16- or 17-year-old applicant to return to live in the family home may be considered to secure 'accommodation from some other person'.[364]

10.134 The authority may discharge the duty by securing an assured shorthold tenancy from a private sector landlord.[365]

357 See paras 10.136–10.144.

358 *R v Hillingdon LBC ex p Puhlhofer* [1986] AC 484, (1986) 18 HLR 158, HL.

359 See paras 4.7–4.9.

360 Acceptance of her refugee status, bringing an end to her assistance from the social services department of the council, prompted her homelessness application.

361 *R (Yumsak) v Enfield LBC* [2002] EWHC 280 (Admin), [2002] JHL D38; see also *R (Calgin) v Enfield LBC* [2005] EWHC 1716 (Admin), [2006] HLR 4, para 10.114. See also now, para 10.154: distance from the authority's area is a mandatory consideration under the Homelessness (Suitability of Accommodation) (England) Order 2012 SI No 2601.

362 *R (Cafun) v Bromley LBC* 17 October 2000, CO/1481/2000, QBD (unreported).

363 See paras 10.136–10.144.

364 See *Robinson v Hammersmith and Fulham LBC* [2006] EWCA Civ 1122 at [39].

365 HA 1996 s193(7AC); H(W)A 2014 s76(2)(b).

Discharge by authority

10.135 Although an authority may now use its own stock without limit of time to house an applicant under HA 1996 Part 7 or H(W)A 2014 Part 2,[366] applicants do not become secure tenants, unless and until so notified.[367]

Out-of-area placements

10.136 'So far as reasonably practicable', the authority must secure accommodation in its own area.[368]

10.137 In *Sacupima*,[369] Latham LJ stated[370] that 'the clear and sensible purpose' of HA 1996 s208 is 'to ensure that so far as possible that authorities do not simply decant homeless persons into areas for which other authorities are responsible'.[371] A failure to consider section 208 was a significant factor in rendering the decision in *Cafun*[372] unlawful.

10.138 In *Calgin*,[373] the authority, a London borough, had a policy of providing accommodation to some homeless households outside its district because of an acute shortage of affordable housing locally. The applicant was offered accommodation in Birmingham and challenged its suitability. On review, the authority decided that the accommodation was suitable and that its policy was not incompatible with HA 1996 s208 because it was not reasonably practical to provide accommodation locally. The decision was upheld: it was for the authority to decide whether or not it was reasonably practical to obtain accommodation within its district, an assessment with which

366 Cf HA 1996 s207, which was repealed by the Homelessness Act 2002.

367 HA 1985 Sch 1 para 4, as amended by H(W)A 2014 Sch 3 para 1. Notification that the tenancy is to be secure is an allocation under Part 6 (see para 11.13).

368 HA 1996 s208(1). Note that this requirement is disapplied in England in relation to eligible asylum-seekers, if there is written agreement with another authority that it may place asylum-seekers in its area: HA 1996 s208(1A) added by Homelessness (Asylum-seekers) (Interim Period) (England) Order 1999 SI No 3126.

369 *R v Newham LBC ex p Sacupima* (2001) 33 HLR 2, CA.

370 *R v Newham LBC ex p Sacupima* (2001) 33 HLR 2, CA, at [31].

371 A failure by one authority to notify another under s.208 made a significant contribution to the problems that arose in conducting a needs assessment under CA 1989 s17: see *R (AM) v Havering LBC and Tower Hamlets LBC* [2015] EWHC 1004 (Admin).

372 See para 10.132.

373 *R (Calgin) v Enfield LBC* [2005] EWHC 1716 (Admin), [2006] HLR 4.

the court would only interfere on *Wednesbury* grounds.[374] The decision to use out-of-district accommodation for a small proportion of those seeking accommodation was not *Wednesbury* unreasonable.

10.139 If it is not reasonably practicable to accommodate in its own district, an authority must try to place the household as close as possible to where it had previously been living.[375]

10.140 Authorities should adopt policies relating to the procurement of temporary accommodation, which should be approved by elected members and made available to the public; the policy should explain how accommodation will be allocated and what factors will be taken into account in allocating out-of-borough units.[376]

10.141 Under HA 1996 s208(2), if the authority accommodates someone in another area, it must – within 14 days of the accommodation being made available to the applicant[377] – give notice to the local housing authority for the area in which that accommodation is situated.

10.142 The notice must state:

a) the name of the applicant;
b) the number and description of the persons residing with the applicant;
c) the address of the accommodation;
d) the date on which it became available; and
e) the function under which it was made available.[378]

10.143 The notification function is designed to allow the notified authority to refer the applicant back under the local connection provisions,[379] should a later application be made to it for assistance: as such, it is considered in chapter 7.[380]

10.144 Once HRA 2017 is in force in England, bringing with it the new initial help duty (paras 10.66–10.74) and new duties to those in priority need (paras 10.220–10.225), HA 1996 s208 only applies where the authority decide to discharge those duties by securing that accommodation is available for an applicant's accommodation.[381]

374 See chapter 12.
375 *Nzolameso v Westminster City Council* [2015] UKSC 22, [2015] HLR 22.
376 *Nzolameso v Westminster City Council* [2015] UKSC 22, [2015] HLR 22.
377 HA 1996 s208(4); in Wales, see H(W)A 2014 s91(2)–(3).
378 HA 1996 s208(3). For example, under HA 1996 s193, s200 or s190. In Wales, see H(W)A 2014 s91(3).
379 See HA 1996 s198(4); H(W)A 2014 s75.
380 See para 7.59.
381 HRA 2017 s6, adding HA 1996 s205(3).

Suitability of accommodation

10.145 Suitability is statutorily governed by HA 1996 s210 and H(W)A 2014 s59,[382] which identify considerations which must be taken into account – the law governing housing conditions, overcrowding and HMOs.[383] The obligation is to 'have regard to' these provisions of the HAs 1985 and 2004. The obligation was introduced by Housing and Planning Act 1986 s14, in direct response to the decision of the House of Lords in Puhlhofer,[384] in which both the Court of Appeal and the House of Lords had rejected the first instance decision that, inter alia, accommodation which was statutorily overcrowded was incapable of comprising accommodation for the purposes of what is now HA 1996 s175.

10.146 Even now, and save so far as overtaken by the specific grounds of unsuitability in the secondary legislation,[385] the statutory wording is not strong enough to prevent an authority using overcrowded[386] or hazardous property[387] or an HMO which falls below standard, although it will vitiate a decision in relation to which the authority had ignored these considerations; it may be thought that the wording is sufficient, however, to require the authority to justify its decision to use such substandard accommodation.[388]

382 See also para 10.150 where asylum-seekers are concerned.

383 Additionally, in Wales, regard must be had to H(W)A 2014 Part 1 (landlord licencing).

384 *Re Puhlhofer* [1986] AC 484, (1986) 18 HLR 158.

385 In England, there are three such orders: Homelessness (Suitability of Accommodation) (England) Order 2012 SI No 2601; Homelessness (Suitability of Accommodation) (England) Order 2003 SI No 3326; Homelessness (Suitability of Accommodation) Order 1996 SI No 3204. There is also a specific order for accommodation provided for asylum-seekers: Homelessness (Asylum-seekers) (Interim Period) (England) Order 1999 SI No 3126. In Wales, there is only one order: Homelessness (Suitability of Accommodation) (Wales) Order 2015 SI No 1268.

386 See *Harouki v Kensington and Chelsea RLBC* [2007] EWCA Civ 1000, [2008] HLR 16 in which it was said that the wording of HA 1996 s210 recognises that accommodation is not necessarily unsuitable because it is statutorily overcrowded.

387 The English Code of Guidance para 17.15 recommends that, when determining the suitability of accommodation, authorities should, as a minimum, ensure that all accommodation is free of category 1 hazards under HA 2004 Part 1. See now the Homelessness (Suitability of Accommodation) (England) Order 2012 SI No 2601 Article 3 – private sector accommodation which the authority is of the view is not in a reasonable physical condition is not suitable.

388 Consider *Padfield v Minister of Agriculture, Fisheries and Food* [1968] AC 997, HL.

10.147 In *Campbell*,[389] a cockroach-infested property was not suitable for the applicant, a decision which, on its facts, could still stand post-*Awua*. On the other hand, in *Jibril*,[390] an offer of a five-bedroom house with only one toilet – situated in the bathroom – to a family of 12 was held to be within the 'margin of appreciation' of that which an authority could consider suitable.

10.148 In *Khan*,[391] the authority conceded that a bed and breakfast property with communal kitchen and bathroom facilities – in which the applicant, his wife and their four children occupied two bedrooms on different floors – was unsuitable. Ordering the authority to find alternative accommodation, the judge stressed that bed and breakfast accommodation should only be used in the short term and that authorities should look for alternative ways to discharge their HA 1996 s193 duty. This has now been embodied in statutory constraints on use of bed and breakfast: see paras 10.156–10.162.

10.149 The duty to provide suitable accommodation is a continuing one; authorities must consider any changes in circumstances which occur while they are discharging their duty: *Zaher*.[392]

Asylum-seekers

10.150 In relation to eligible asylum-seekers in England,[393] HA 1996 s210 is modified[394] so that in considering whether accommodation is suitable for the applicant or any person who might reasonably be expected to reside with him or her, the authority must have regard to the fact that the accommodation is to be temporary, pending the applicant's claim for asylum; the authority may not have regard to any preference the applicant, or any person who might reasonably be expected to reside with him or her, may have as to the locality of the accommodation; the authority must, however, have regard to the desirability, in general, of securing accommodation in areas in

389 *R v Lambeth LBC ex p Campbell* (1994) 26 HLR 618, QBD.

390 *R v Camden LBC ex p Jibril* (1997) 29 HLR 785, QBD.

391 *R (Khan) v Newham LBC* [2001] EWHC (Admin) 589, [2001] JHL D90.

392 *R (Zaher) v Westminster City Council* [2003] EWHC 101 (Admin), [2003] JHL D41.

393 See paras 3.138–3.142.

394 HA 1996 s210(1A), inserted by the Homelessness (Asylum Seekers) (Interim Period) (England) Order 1999 SI No 3126 Article 6.

which there is a ready supply of accommodation: see Homelessness (Asylum-seekers) (Interim Period) (England) Order 1999.[395]

Added considerations

10.151 The secretary of state has power to specify circumstances in which accommodation is (or is not) to be regarded as suitable and to specify other matters to be taken into account or disregarded.[396]

England

10.152 In England, this power has been used to require authorities to take affordability into account when determining suitability: see Homelessness (Suitability of Accommodation) (England) Order 1996.[397]

10.153 This requires the authority to consider:

a) the financial resources available to the person;
b) the costs of the accommodation;
c) payments being made under a court order to a spouse, or former spouse;
d) any payments made to support children, whether under a court order or under the Child Support Act 1991; and
e) the applicant's other reasonable living expenses.[398]

395 SI No 3126. HA 1996 s206(1A), added by Homelessness (Asylum-seekers) (Interim Period) (England) Order 1999 SI No 3126. This is intended to encourage authorities in areas of high demand for social housing to seek accommodation outside the district: see 2002 edition of the Code of Guidance annex 12 para 7.

396 HA 1996 s210(2). In Wales, the same power is given to the Welsh Ministers: H(W)A 2014 s59(3).

397 SI No 3204 (appendix B). The English Code does not directly address the impact of the 'benefit cap' (Welfare Reform Act 2012 s96), although government policy is for Discretionary Housing Payments to be used to cover any shortfall between the contractual rent and the housing benefit/housing element of universal credit: see Department for Work and Pensions (DWP) Circular HB/CTB G6/12 – Annex A, June 2012.

398 See further paras 4.122–4.125. See also English Code of Guidance paras 17.39–17.40. The authority can take into account all forms of income (including social security benefits of all kinds, not just housing benefit/housing element of universal credit): *Samuels v Birmingham City Council* [2015] EWCA Civ 1051, [2015] HLR 47.

10.154 The power has also been used in England[399] to require the authority to consider the location of accommodation,[400] including:

a) where it is outside the authority's own area, its distance from that area;[401]
b) the significance of any disruption to employment, caring responsibilities or education;[402]
c) proximity and accessibility to medical facilities and other support which is currently used by or provided to the applicant or a member of his or her household and which is essentially to that person's well-being;[403] and,

399 Homelessness (Suitability of Accommodation) (England) Order 2012 SI No 2601 article 2, in force from 9 November 2012: it was brought into force contemporaneously with the new provisions governing private sector discharge: paras 10.202–10.204.

400 From the point of view of all members of the household – Supplementary Suitability Guidance 2012 para 47. Authorities are urged to seek accommodation as close as possible to previous accommodation as 'accommodation for an applicant in a different location can cause difficulties for some applicants. . . . Where possible the authority should seek to retain established links with schools, doctors, social workers and other key services and support': para 49.

401 Where otherwise suitable and affordable accommodation is available nearer to the authority's own district 'the accommodation which it has secured is not likely to be suitable unless the authority has a justifiable reason or the applicant has specified a preference' – Supplementary Suitability Guidance 2012 para 48.

402 '[A]ccount should be taken of the type and importance of the care household members provide and the likely impact the withdrawal would cause. Authorities may want to consider the cost implications of providing care where an existing care arrangement becomes unsustainable due to a change of location': Supplementary Suitability Guidance 2012 para 51. 'Authorities should also take into account the need to minimise disruption to the education of young people, particularly at critical points in time such as leading up to taking GCSE (or their equivalent) examinations': para 52.

403 'Housing authorities should consider the potential impact on the health and well being of an applicant or any person reasonably expected to reside with them, were such support removed or medical facilities were no longer accessible. They should also consider whether similar facilities are accessible and available near the accommodation being offered and whether there would be any specific difficulties in the applicant or person residing with them using those essential facilities, compared to the support they are currently receiving. Examples of other support might include support from particular individuals, groups or organisations located in the area where the applicant currently resides: for example essential support from relatives or support groups which would be difficult to replicate in another location': Supplementary Suitability Guidance 2012 para 53.

d) proximity and accessibility to local services, amenities and transport.[404]

10.155 Additionally, the authority may not consider private rented sector accommodation[405] as suitable if any of the following applies.[406]

a) the authority considers that the accommodation is not a reasonable physical condition;[407]
b) the authority considers that any electrical equipment supplied with the accommodation does not meet Electrical Equipment (Safety) Regulations 1994 regs 5 and 7;[408]
c) the authority considers that the landlord has not taken reasonable fire safety precautions with the accommodation and furnishings;[409]

404 'Housing authorities should avoid placing applicants in isolated accommodation away from public transport, shops and other facilities where possible': Supplementary Suitability Guidance 2012 para 54.

405 Once HRA 2017 comes into force, article 3 is amended to spell out that the requirements apply not only to private sector offers under HA 1996 s193(7F) (paras 10.202–10.204) but also to the suitability of final offers under HA 1996 ss193A (para 10.220) and 193C (para 10.201) and of accommodation for applicants in priority need by way of arrangements with private landlords under the initial help duty in s189B (paras 10.66–10.74) and the replacement provisions governing threatened with homelessness in s195 (paras 10.52–10.61): HRA 2017 s12. The amendments are without prejudice to any power by order to amend or revoke article 3: HRA 2017 s12(5).

406 Homelessness (Suitability of Accommodation) (England) Order 2012 SI No 2601 article 3, likewise in force from 9 November 2012 (see last footnote).

407 'Authorities should ensure that the property has been visited by either a local authority officer or someone acting on their behalf to determine its suitability before an applicant moves in': Supplementary Suitability Guidance 2012 para 62. 'In determining whether the property is in reasonable physical condition attention should be paid to signs of damp, mould, indications that the property would be cold, for example cracked windows, and any other physical signs that would indicate the property is not in good physical condition': para 63.

408 SI No 3260. Supplementary Suitability Guidance 2012 para 64 suggests visual inspection of the property, checking for signs of loose wiring, cracked or broken electrical sockets, light switches that do not work as well as evidence of portable appliance testing as indicative that the regulations have been applied.

409 Eg, consideration of Regulatory Reform (Fire Safety) Order 2005 SI No 1541, which applies to the common or shared parts of multi-occupied residential buildings, and Furniture and Furnishings (Fire) (Safety) Regulations 1988 SI No 1324, as amended: see Supplementary Suitability Guidance 2012 para 65. 'Local authorities and fire and rescue authorities should work together to ensure the safety of domestic premises including the provision of fire safety advice to households (such as the benefits of a working smoke alarm)' and that the regulations have been adhered to: para 66.

d) the authority considers that the landlord has not taken reasonable precautions to prevent carbon monoxide poisoning in the accommodation;[410]
e) the authority considers that the landlord is not a fit and proper person to act as landlord, after considering if he or she has committed any one of a number of specified categories of offence,[411] or has practiced unlawful discrimination in or in connection with carrying on any business,[412] contravened any provision of housing law,[413] or acted otherwise than in accordance with any approved[414] and applicable code of practice for the management of an HMO;
f) the accommodation is an unlicensed HMO which ought to be licensed;[415]
g) the accommodation is or forms part of residential property which does not have a valid energy performance certificate[416] or a current gas safety record;[417]
h) the landlord has not provided the authority with a written tenancy agreement which he or she proposes to use for the purposes of the private rented sector offer and which the authority considers adequate.[418]

410 The Supplementary Suitability Guidance 2012 para 67, suggests that the installation of a carbon monoxide alarm – taken together with a valid gas safety record – would constitute reasonable precaution to prevent the possibility of carbon monoxide poisoning, where such a risk exists.

411 Offences involving fraud or other dishonest, violence or illegal drugs, or offences attracting notification requirements in Sexual Offences Act 2003 Sch 3. When placing households outside of their own district, authorities should check with the authority for the receiving district to see whether it has taken enforcement activity against the landlord: Supplementary Suitability Guidance 2012 para 71.

412 On the grounds of sex, race, age, disability, marriage or civil partnership, pregnancy or maternity, religion or belief, sexual orientation, gender identity of reassignment.

413 Including landlord and tenant law.

414 Under HA 2004 s133.

415 Under HA 2004 s54 or s55.

416 As required by the Energy Performance of Buildings (Certificates and Inspections) (England and Wales) Regulations 2007 SI No 991, as amended. Authorities should have sight of a current certificate to ensure that the requirement has been met: Supplementary Suitability Guidance 2012 para 68.

417 In accordance with Gas Safety (Installation and Use) Regulations 1998 SI No 2451 reg 36. Authorities should request sight of a valid Gas Safety certificate: Supplementary Suitability Guidance 2012 para 69.

418 'It is expected that the local authority should review the tenancy agreement to ensure that it sets out, ideally in a clear and comprehensible way, the tenant's obligations, for example a clear statement of the rent and other charges, and the responsibilities of the landlord, but does not contain unfair

10.156 Bed and breakfast accommodation is not in itself necessarily unsuitable,[419] but the Homelessness (Suitability of Accommodation) (England) Order 2003[420] limits the use of it: where it is provided to families (including pregnant women), it is not to be regarded as suitable, save where there is no other accommodation available and then only for a period not exceeding six weeks (or periods not exceeding six weeks in total).[421]

10.157 Bed and breakfast accommodation is defined[422] as accommodation (whether or not breakfast is provided) which is not separate and self-contained and in which more than one household share one or more of the following:

a) a toilet;
b) personal washing facilities; or
c) cooking facilities.

Accommodation owned or managed by an authority, a registered provider of social housing or a voluntary organisation[423] is exempt from the prohibition.

Wales

10.158 There is no need for an affordability statutory instrument in Wales because H(W)A 2014 s59(2) requires authorities to have regard to whether or not accommodation is affordable.[424]

10.159 The Homelessness (Suitability of Accommodation) (Wales) Order 2015[425] requires Welsh authorities to take into account the following additional matters when considering suitability of accommodation for a person in priority need:

or unreasonable terms, such as call-out charges for repairs or professional cleaning at the end of the tenancy': Supplementary Suitability Guidance 2012 para 72. 'Whilst a local authority will not be able to check that a tenant's deposit has been placed in a tenancy deposit protection scheme prior to them taking the tenancy' it is recommended 'that local authorities remind prospective landlords and tenants of their responsibilities in this area': para 73.

419 See English Code of Guidance para 7.6 suggesting its use in emergencies, but also stating that authorities should avoid using it wherever possible. See also English Code of Guidance paras 17.24–17.38.

420 SI No 3326 (appendix B).

421 See further para 10.48.

422 Suitability Order 2003 article 2.

423 See para 14.34 as to the definition of voluntary organisation.

424 See also see Welsh Code para 19.26 on factors to be taken into account when assessing affordability under H(W)A 2014 s59(2).

425 SI No 1268 (Welsh Suitability Order).

a) the specific health needs of the person;
b) the proximity and accessibility of the support of the family or other support services;
c) any disability of the person;
d) the proximity and accessibility of medical facilities, and other support services which–
   i) are currently used by or provided to the person; and
   ii) are essential to the well-being of the person;
e) where the accommodation is situated outside the area of the authority, the distance of the accommodation from the area of the authority;
f) the significance of any disruption which would be caused to the employment, caring responsibilities or education of the person by the location of the accommodation; and
g) the proximity of alleged perpetrators and victims of domestic abuse.

10.160 Additionally, the authority may not consider private rented sector accommodation as suitable if any of the following applies.[426]

a) the authority is of the view that the accommodation is not in a reasonable physical condition;
b) the authority is of the view that the accommodation does not comply with all statutory requirements (such as, where applicable, requirements relating to fire, gas, electrical, carbon monoxide and other safety; planning; and licences for HMOs);
c) the authority is of the view that the landlord is not a fit and proper person within the meaning of H(W)A 2014 s20, to act in the capacity of landlord.

10.161 As in England,[427] bed and breakfast accommodation is not in itself necessarily unsuitable,[428] but, since 27 April 2015, there have been restrictions on its use and that of other shared accommodation, both as regards quality and duration.[429] Bed and breakfast or shared accommodation will be unsuitable for a person who is, or who may be, in priority need unless:

426 Welsh Suitability Order, Part 3.
427 See para 10.156.
428 See Welsh Code paras 5.40 and 19.56–19.62.
429 Homelessness (Suitability of Accommodation) (Wales) Order 2015 SI No 1268. See also the previous restrictions in the Homelessness (Suitability of Accommodation) (Wales) Order 2006 SI No 650.

a) offered in response to an emergency (eg fire, flood) and no other accommodation is reasonably available;
b) the applicant has been offered other suitable accommodation but has chosen bed and breakfast; or
c) it is used for less than a fixed period (two weeks, or six weeks if the accommodation meets a 'higher standard', as defined in the Schedule to the Order, taking into account, inter alia, room size, heating facilities, storage facilities, toilet and washing facilities).

10.162 Bed and breakfast accommodation is defined in substantially the same way as under the 2003 English Suitability Order; shared accommodation is likewise defined as accommodation which is not separate and self-contained premises; or in which a toilet, personal washing facilities or cooking facilities are not available to the applicant or are shared by more than one household.[430]

Other considerations

10.163 In *Awua*,[431] it was said that suitability is primarily a matter of space and arrangement, but that other matters, such as whether the applicant can afford the rent, may also be material:[432] The statutory considerations (primary and subordinate)[433] are accordingly not exhaustive. In *Maloba*,[434] on the related issue of whether accommodation was reasonable to continue to occupy, it was held that the question was not limited to consideration of the size, structural quality and amenities of accommodation. Thus, in *Kaur*,[435] (decided before the Homelessness (Suitability of Accommodation) (England) Order 1996 required consideration of affordability) (see para 10.154), it had been held that accommodation secured for the applicant in the private sector was not suitable because the contractual rent exceeded the amount which would be met in housing benefit and the shortfall could not be afforded from the applicant's own resources.

430 Welsh Suitability Order 2015 reg 2. The only differences from the English order are that the accommodation must be 'commercially provided' and must not be registered under the Care Standards Act 2000.

431 *R v Brent LBC ex p Awua* [1996] AC 55, (1995) 27 HLR 453, HL.

432 This decision preceded the statutory instrument (see para 10.125) requiring authorities to take affordability into account.

433 Paras 10.145–10.157.

434 *Waltham Forest LBC v Maloba* [2007] EWCA Civ 1281, [2008] HLR 26 at [59]–[61].

435 *R v Tower Hamlets LBC ex p Kaur* (1994) 26 HLR 597, QBD.

Personal circumstances

10.164 In deciding the question of suitability, the authority must consider the individual needs of the applicant and his or her family, including needs as to work, education and health.[436]

10.165 In *Omar*,[437] a political refugee was offered accommodation in a basement flat in an estate. The condition of the premises and the layout of the estate strongly reminded the applicant of the prisons in which she had been held and abused, to such an extent that she maintained that she would rather commit suicide than live there. The court held that the accommodation must be suitable for the person to whom the duty was owed, in determining which the authority should have regard to the relevant circumstances of the applicant as well as to the matters set out in HA 1996 s210.

10.166 *Omar* was considered in *Dolan*,[438] where the authority's decision to offer accommodation was flawed because it had separated out medical and social considerations and had not taken an overall view of the applicant's needs: 'the ultimate decision as to suitability must be the result of a composite assessment'.

10.167 *Omar* was also considered in *Karaman*,[439] where the applicant's terror of her husband's domestic violence was such that the authority's decision to house her within two miles of where her husband was believed to be living was held to be *Wednesbury* unreasonable.

10.168 In *Slater*,[440] Ward LJ said of a young single mother who was fleeing domestic violence 'that the particular needs of the applicant, for example, to be protected from domestic violence and to be located near to support networks, are relevant when considering suitability'.

10.169 In *Haque*,[441] it was held where a person has a disability (or other protected characteristic under the Equality Act 2010), then the 'public sector equality duty' in Equality Act 2010 s149 requires the authority:

i) to recognise that the appellant has a disability;
ii) to focus on specific aspects of his or her impairments to the extent that they are relevant to the suitability of the accommodation;

436 *R v Newham LBC ex p Sacupima* (2001) 33 HLR 1, QBD and (2001) 33 HLR 2, CA. See also *R v Newham LBC ex p Ojuri (No 3)* (1998) 31 HLR 452, QBD.

437 *R v Brent LBC ex p Omar* (1991) 23 HLR 446, QBD.

438 *R v Lewisham LBC ex p Dolan* (1992) 25 HLR 68, QBD.

439 *R v Haringey LBC ex p Karaman* (1996) 29 HLR 366, QBD. Cf *R v Lambeth LBC ex p Woodburne* (1997) 29 HLR 836, QBD.

440 *Slater v Lewisham LBC* [2006] EWCA Civ 394, [2006] HLR 37 at [30].

441 *Hackney LBC v Haque* [2017] EWCA Civ 4, [2017] HLR 14.

iii) to focus on the disadvantages he or she might suffer when compared to a person without those impairments;
iv) to focus on his or her accommodation needs arising from those impairments and the extent to which the accommodation meets those needs;
v) to recognise that the appellant's particular needs might require him or her to be treated more favourably than a person without a disability; and
vi) to review the suitability of the accommodation, paying due regard to those matters.[442]

Family

10.170 An authority has a wide discretion to determine who is within an applicant's household.[443] In *Ariemuguvbe*,[444] the claimant was living in a three-bedroom property with her husband, five adult children who had come to the UK from Nigeria in 1998 who had overstayed their visitor's visas, and three grandchildren. The claimant argued that the points allocated to her under the authority's allocation scheme should be increased to take account of the five adult children.[445] It was held that the authority was entitled to conclude that it was not appropriate to allocate a larger property to the claimant, because her five children were all independent adults, some having their own families, who should have been able to make their own housing arrangements; also, they were subject to immigration control[446] in circumstances where providing accommodation for them would amount to them having recourse to public funds in breach of their conditions of entry to the UK.[447]

Racial harassment

10.171 Issues of racial harassment and violence are also relevant. In *Abdul Subhan*,[448] Tower Hamlets LBC offered a Bangladeshi applicant accommodation in a block of flats in which there was active racial

442 There is no need to refer in terms to Equality Act 2010 s149, what matters is whether the substance has been complied with: *Haque*; *Poshteh v Kensington and Chelsea RLBC* [2015] EWCA Civ 711, [2015] HLR 36.

443 *R (Ariemuguvbe) v Islington LBC* [2009] EWCA Civ 1308.

444 *R (Ariemuguvbe) v Islington LBC* [2009] EWCA Civ 1308.

445 *R (Ariemuguvbe) v Islington LBC* [2009] EWCA Civ 1308 at [2] and [3].

446 See para 3.16.

447 *R (Ariemuguvbe) v Islington LBC* [2009] EWCA Civ 1308 at [19].

448 *R v Tower Hamlets LBC ex p Abdul Subhan* (1992) 24 HLR 541, QBD; see also *R v Southwark LBC ex p Solomon* (1994) 26 HLR 693, QBD.

harassment. The authority had itself set up a Racial Incidents Panel, had been provided with details of incidents of racial harassment by the local law centre, and had received reports from a research project set up by the Home Office Crime Prevention Unit. The decision to make the offer was quashed because the authority had failed to take into account the material on harassment which was before it.

Separation

10.172 Accommodation which split a family between two hostels was held not to be suitable in *Surdonja*.[449] In *Flash*,[450] a one-bedroom flat provided to the applicant and her grandson was suitable: the grandson could sleep in the living room.

Location

10.173 Independently of the requirement, applicable in England, to consider locality under the Homelessness (Suitability of Accommodation) (England) Order 2012,[451] location will in any event impact on suitability,[452] and an authority must consider how location will affect employment, education and healthcare for the applicant and his or her family.[453] In *Abdullah*,[454] the review officer had taken into account the appellant's submissions and the medical evidence provided and was entitled to conclude that the medical evidence meant no more than that it would be advantageous for the appellant to live near to her family and friends, rather than meaning that was being necessary

449 *R v Ealing LBC ex p Surdonja* (1998) 31 HLR 686, QBD; cf *Camden LBC v Sharif* [2013] UKSC 10, [2013] HLR 16, where the accommodation was split between two flats, yards apart in the same building. The decision that the flats were suitable was not challenged. The challenge was confined to whether it was accommodation which was available: see paras 4.16–4.38.

450 *R (Flash) v Southwark LBC* [2004] EWHC 717 (Admin), [2004] JHL D60.

451 SI No 2601 article 2.

452 See also the discussion at paras 10.136–10.149, on discharging the duty by securing accommodation outside the authority's area.

453 *R v Newham LBC ex p Sacupima* (2001) 33 HLR 1, QBD and (2001) 33 HLR 2, CA; *R v Newham LBC ex p Ojuri (No 3)* (1998) 31 HLR 452, QBD; *R (Yumsak) v Enfield LBC* [2002] EWHC 280 (Admin), [2002] JHL D38. The English Code of Guidance is somewhat less generous, referring to 'relevant needs, requirements and circumstances' and otherwise focusing on health considerations and matters such as violence (domestic or otherwise) and racial harassment (paras 17.4–17.6), but the Welsh Code adds 'Authorities should also consider factors such as access to schools and other services and facilities (eg, GPs and informal support networks) with a view to maintaining stability for the household, particularly in respect of children's schooling, wherever possible' (para 19.11).

454 *Abdullah v Westminster City Council* [2007] EWCA Civ 1566, [2007] JHL D89.

for her to do so; it was also open to the reviewer to assume that social services would provide assistance where necessary, regardless of where the appellant lived.[455]

Adaptations

10.174 The suitability of accommodation offered by an authority pursuant to HA 1996 s193(2) is not to be judged exclusively by reference to the condition of the accommodation at the time of the offer, so regard may be had to proposed adaptations or alterations provided that the proposals can fairly be regarded as certain, binding and enforceable; adaptations that are proposed after the date of the offer are, however, irrelevant to the question of suitability.[456]

Security

10.175 In *Wingrove* and *Mansoor*,[457] Evans LJ thought that the tenure, or time element, of suitability had to be proportionate to the circumstances of the case, including the needs of the applicant – for example, the need for the applicant's children to remain in an area to attend the same school for a number of years. Suitability for the purpose of HA 1996 s193(2) does not imply permanence or security of tenure;[458] thus, even pre-LA 2011,[459] an assured shorthold tenancy could be suitable: see *Wingrove* and *Mansoor*[460] and *Griffiths*.[461]

Gypsies

10.176 Where the applicant is a gypsy, authorities must give special consideration to securing accommodation that will facilitate his or her traditional way of life: *Codona*.[462] Nonetheless, in *Codona*, the authority

455 The decision in *Shala v Birmingham City Council* [2007] EWCA Civ 624, [2008] HLR 8 was not considered: see para 5.36. While this may not have led to a different result, the same principles must surely apply to how the authority approaches the medical evidence.

456 *Boreh v Ealing LBC* [2008] EWCA Civ 1176, [2009] HLR 22 at [31].

457 *R v Wandsworth LBC ex p Wingrove* and *R v Wandsworth LBC ex p Mansoor* [1997] QB 953, CA.

458 *Birmingham City Council v Ali; Moran v Manchester City Council (Secretary of State for Communities and Local Government and another intervening)* [2009] UKHL 36, [2009] 1 WLR 1506 at [47].

459 See paras 10.202–10.204.

460 *R v Wandsworth LBC ex p Wingrove* and *R v Wandsworth LBC ex p Mansoor* [1997] QB 953, CA, per Sir Thomas Bingham MR at 923G.

461 *Griffiths v St Helens MBC* [2006] EWCA Civ 160, [2006] 1 WLR 2233, [2006] HLR 29.

462 *Codona v Mid-Bedfordshire DC* [2005] EWCA Civ 925, [2005] HLR 1. See also *R (Price) v Carmarthenshire CC* [2003] EWHC 42 (Admin), [2003] JHL D43.

was unable to find any suitable accommodation other than bed and breakfast accommodation in the short term, and a decision that it was suitable was not unlawful and did not violate the applicant's rights under ECHR Articles 8 and 14.[463]

10.177 A person who has adopted a lifestyle similar to that of a gypsy, but is not a gypsy, is not entitled to the special protection afforded to gypsies under human rights jurisprudence.[464]

Enquiries into suitability

10.178 Although there is no explicit statutory duty to enquire into questions of suitability, it is implicit: authorities cannot otherwise reach a decision that accommodation is suitable for the particular applicant.[465] The principles developed in relation to HA 1996 s184 enquiries[466] therefore also apply to enquiries as to suitability: *Thomas*.[467]

Viewing property

10.179 There is no requirement[468] that authorities provide applicants with an opportunity to view and comment on the suitability of any accommodation before moving into it or before a decision is made on its suitability: *Khatun*.[469] It is not oppressive, perverse or disproportionate to the fair and efficient administration of HA 1996 Part 7 for an authority to require an applicant who has not viewed a property to decide whether or not to accept it on pain of immediate cancellation of his or her current accommodation if he or she does not do so, as applicants can challenge suitability by internal review after moving in.[470]

Challenges to suitability

10.180 Challenge to the suitability of an offer is by review under HA 1996 s202 (H(W)A 2014 s85)[471] and appeal under s204 (H(W)A 2014 s88).[472]

463 See also paras 12.100–12.105.

464 *Steward v Kingston Upon Thames LBC* [2007] EWCA Civ 565, [2007] HLR 42.

465 Likewise, if a complaint is made, the authority must decide whether an inspection is required: *Firoozmand v Lambeth LBC* [2015] EWCA Civ 952, [2015] HLR 45.

466 See para 9.62.

467 *R v Islington LBC ex p Thomas* (1997) 30 HLR 111, QBD. See also *R v South Holland DC ex p Baxter* (1998) 30 HLR 1069, QBD.

468 The current edition of the English Code (para 14.22) refers to a 'period of consideration'; see also Welsh Code para 3.65.

469 *Khatun v Newham LBC* [2004] EWCA Civ 55, [2004] HLR 29.

470 See para 9.149.

471 See paras 9.149–9.161.

472 See para 12.159.

Save in exceptional circumstances, a decision on suitability of offer may not be challenged in a defence to eviction from temporary accommodation.[473]

Cessation of the duty

10.181 The duty under HA 1996 s193 or H(W)A 2014 s75 will terminate in the following circumstances.[474]

Eligibility

10.182 The duty will cease if the applicant ceases to be eligible for assistance,[475] for example, if his or her immigration status changes.[476]

Loss of accommodation

10.183 If the applicant becomes homeless intentionally from the accommodation made available, or otherwise voluntarily ceases to occupy it as his or her only or principal home,[477] the duty will cease.[478]

Offers

10.184 A number of instances terminate the duty through offers of accommodation outside of HA 1996 Part 7 or H(W)A 2014 Part 2. Although the LA 2011, which made a number of changes to the provisions governing subsequent applications, came into force on 9 November 2012,[479] the length of time during which applicants may remain in Part 7/Part 2 accommodation before the duty towards them is discharged means that it continues to be necessary to consider the position both before and since the LA 2011, as well as before and since the H(W)A 2014.

Refusal of suitable offers

10.185 **England pre-LA 2011 and Wales pre-H(W)A 2014.** By HA 1996 s193(5), in relation to applications made before commencement of the LA 2011 s148(3)[480] in respect of which the duty to secure accommodation had

473 *Tower Hamlets LBC v Rahnara Begum* [2005] EWCA Civ 116, [2006] HLR 9.

474 But see also para 10.18, on the possibility of a public law defence (whether on domestic grounds or under the ECHR).

475 See chapter 3.

476 HA 1996 s193(6)(a); H(W)A 2014 s79(2).

477 See *Crawley BC v Sawyer* (1998) 20 HLR 98, CA.

478 HA 1996 s193(6)(b) and (d); H(W)A 2014 s76(6).

479 9 November 2012: Localism Act 2011 (Commencement No 2 and Transitional Provisions) (England) Order 2012 SI No 2599 article 2.

480 See last footnote.

arisen but had not ceased by that date,[481] and continuing in Wales for applications made prior to 27 April 2015,[482] the duty ceases if the applicant is made an offer of suitable accommodation which he or she refuses, having been warned that the authority will regard itself as having discharged its duty if he or she does so[483] and having been informed of the right to an internal review.[484] This provision operates to bring to an end the full housing duty regardless of whether the accommodation offered to the applicant is temporary or permanent.[485]

10.186 Where an authority has placed an applicant in accommodation pursuant to its duty under HA 1996 s193(2), pending a final offer, but that accommodation becomes unsuitable because of the applicant's change of circumstances so that the applicant has to move, the authority's duty will cease under subsection (5) if the applicant refuses a new offer of suitable alternative section 193(2) accommodation.[486] In *Muse*, the authority had not acted unfairly because it had followed the procedural safeguards set out in the subsection and had not led the applicant to believe that she was entitled to any additional procedural protection.[487]

10.187 The authority must notify the applicant that it considers the duty to have been discharged.[488] As such notification comprises a decision

481 Localism Act 2011 (Commencement No 2 and Transitional Provisions) (England) Order 2012 SI No 2599 article 3.

482 For applications made on or after that date, H(W)A 2014 applies: see Housing (Wales) Act 2014 (Commencement No 3 and Transitory, Transitional and Saving Provisions) Order 2015 SI No 1272 article 7.

483 In *Maswaku v Westminster City Council* [2012] EWCA Civ 669, [2012] HLR 37 an offer letter which informed the applicant that, should she refuse it, she would have to find her own accommodation, was a sufficient warning for this purpose.

484 HA 1996 s193(5). This condition even applies to an offer of an assured shorthold tenancy unless it is held out as an offer of a 'qualifying' offer under section 193(7B): see *Griffiths v St Helens BC* [2006] EWCA Civ 160, [2006] 1 WLR 2233, [2006] HLR 29; but this premises that the offer is only a stage in the rehousing exercise. Section 193(5) embodies the effect of *R v Westminster City Council ex p Chambers* (1982) 6 HLR 24, QBD. In Wales, H(W)A 2014 s76(2) also permits the offer of an assured shorthold tenancy in discharge of the duty.

485 *Griffiths v St Helens MBC* [2006] EWCA Civ 160, [2006] 1 WLR 2233, [2006] HLR 29.

486 *Muse v Brent LBC* [2008] EWCA Civ 1447.

487 *Muse v Brent LBC* [2008] EWCA Civ 1447.

488 HA 1996 s193(5). Given the applicant's right to challenge the suitability of the offer, the reasons should encompass why the authority considers the accommodation to be suitable for the applicant. Surprisingly there is no express requirement that the notification has to be in writing. In Wales, see H(W)A 2014 s84.

as to what duty is owed to the applicant, ie that there is no duty because it has ceased,[489] it must comply with HA 1996 s184, which means that it must give reasons, inform the applicant of his or her right to a review and be in writing.[490]

10.188 **England post-LA 2011 and Wales post-H(W)A 2014.** Since LA 2011 s148(3) came into force in England,[491] the duty does not cease by reason of HA 1996 s193(5), in the case either of an offer of accommodation under Part 6[492] or of private sector accommodation,[493] but is governed instead by discrete provisions which will determine when those duties come to an end: these are considered below.[494] Thus, in effect, HA 1996 s193(5) is now limited to a refusal of a suitable offer of interim accommodation. In Wales, the position is the same: the refusal of an offer of suitable interim accommodation brings the duty to an end.[495]

Part 6 offer

10.189 **England pre-LA 2011 and Wales pre-H(W)A 2014.** In relation to applications made before commencement of LA 2011 s148(3),[496] in respect of which the duty to secure accommodation had arisen but had not ceased by that date,[497] and continuing in Wales for applications made prior to 27 April 2015,[498] the duty will cease if the applicant accepts an offer of accommodation under Part 6.[499]

489 HA 1996 s184(1); H(W)A 2014 s84.

490 See para 9.144.

491 9 November 2012: Localism Act 2011 (Commencement No 2 and Transitional Provisions) (England) Order 2012 SI No 2599 article 2.

492 Paras 10.196–10.198.

493 Paras 10.202–10.204.

494 Paras 10.196–10.198 and 10.202–10.204.

495 H(W)A 2014 s76(3)(a).

496 9 November 2012: Localism Act 2011 (Commencement No 2 and Transitional Provisions) (England) Order 2012 SI No 2599 article 2.

497 Localism Act 2011 (Commencement No 2 and Transitional Provisions) (England) Order 2012 SI No 2599 article 3.

498 For applications made on or after that date, the H(W)A 2014 applies: see Housing (Wales) Act 2014 (Commencement No 3 and Transitory, Transitional and Saving Provisions) Order 2015 SI No 1272 article 7.

499 HA 1996 s193(6)(c); see chapter 11. Such an offer could have been made by way of nomination to become the assured tenant of a private registered provider of social housing (England) or a registered social landlord (Wales): HA 1996 s159(1)(c).

10.190 The duty will also cease if the applicant, having been informed of the possible consequences of refusal[500] and of his or her right to request a review of the suitability of the accommodation, refuses a final offer of accommodation under Part 6.[501] A final offer of accommodation cannot be made unless the authority is satisfied that the accommodation is suitable for the applicant and that it is reasonable for him or her to accept it:[502] The questions of suitability and whether it is reasonable for the applicant to accept the offer have to be considered separately.[503] In judging whether it is unreasonable to refuse an offer:

> . . . the decision-maker must have regard to all the personal characteristics of the applicant, her needs, her hopes and her fears and then taking account of those individual aspects, the subjective factors, ask whether it is reasonable, an objective test, for the applicant to accept. The test is whether a right-thinking local housing authority would conclude that it was reasonable that *this applicant* should have accepted the offer of *this* accommodation.[504]

10.191 An offer is a final offer for this purpose if it is in writing and states that it is a final offer for the purposes of HA 1996 s193(7).

10.192 The exact wording of section 193(7) does not need to be followed, provided that the notification contains every matter of substance which the subsection requires; the authority should, however, convey to the applicant that it is satisfied both that the accommodation is suitable for him or her and that it is reasonable for him or her to accept it.[505] In *Begum*,[506] the notification was inadequate because it merely stated that the accommodation offered was a reasonable and suitable offer of permanent accommodation. The requirements may, however, be fulfilled by information in more than one document, provided that they can properly be read together.[507]

500 HA 1996 s193(7).

501 HA 1996 s193(7); in Wales, see H(W)A 2014 s76(3).

502 HA 1996 s193(7F)(a).

503 *Slater v Lewisham LBC* [2006] EWCA Civ 934, [2006] HLR 37, where the authority had failed to apply its mind to the element of reasonableness.

504 Ward LJ in *Slater v Lewisham LBC* (emphasis in original).

505 *Tower Hamlets LBC v Rahanara Begum* [2005] EWCA Civ 116, [2006] HLR 9 at [27], though that case concerned HA 1996 s193(7)(b) prior to its amendment by the Homelessness Act 2002.

506 *Tower Hamlets LBC v Rahanara Begum* [2005] EWCA Civ 116, [2006] HLR 9.

507 *Vilvarasa v Harrow LBC* [2010] EWCA Civ 1278, [2010] HLR 11 – the information was spread across two letters, one in July (which did not specify the property in question) and one in August (which did so); the two documents could be read together.

10.193 An applicant's genuine belief that it was not reasonable to accept an offer of accommodation is not conclusive of whether it was reasonable to do so; if the authority has evidence which entitles it to consider that the belief was not objectively reasonable, even if that evidence was not available to the applicant at the time of the refusal, the authority may nonetheless decide that it was reasonable for the applicant to accept the offer: *Ahmed*.[508]

10.194 It had been held that an offer under Part 6 which does not satisfy the requirements of subsection (7) may nonetheless serve to discharge the authority's duty if it satisfied the requirements of section 193(5) (paras 10.156–10.158): *Omar*.[509] In *Ravichandran*,[510] however, it was said that *Omar* should be confined to its own facts. It is submitted that this is correct: it is difficult to see how compliance with the less stringent requirements of section 193(5) could properly be considered compliance with the detailed requirements of section 193(7).[511]

10.195 The courts will not easily interfere with an authority's allocation scheme,[512] nor, therefore, with its policy in relation to Part 6 offers to homeless persons: thus, once a homeless person housed in temporary accommodation achieved the requisite number of points to qualify to bid on an appropriate property, he was given only two months in which to make a voluntary bid before a successful 'auto-bid' was generated on his behalf,[513] which could be treated as a final offer, refusal of which meant that the authority's duty could lawfully be treated as discharged.[514] It would seem, however, to have been central to the court's decision that, before the two months began, a housing officer would visit, which would allow any particular personal considerations or difficulties to be taken into account before the bid was placed on his behalf.

508 *Ahmed v Leicester City Council* [2007] EWCA Civ 843, [2008] HLR 6.

509 *Omar v Birmingham City Council* [2007] EWCA Civ 610, [2007] HLR 43 at [29] and [36]; see also *Tower Hamlets LBC v Rahanara Begum* [2005] EWCA Civ 116, [2006] HLR 9 at [27].

510 *Ravichandran v Lewisham LBC* [2010] EWCA Civ 755, [2010] HLR 42.

511 The issue does not arise in relation to the post-LA 2011/H(W)A 2014 applications considered under the next heading, in respect of whom HA 1996 s193(5) is expressed only to apply to an offer which is neither a Part 6 offer nor an offer of private sector accommodation.

512 See *R (Ahmad) v Newham LBC* [2009] UKHL 14, [2009] HLR 31; paras 11.79–11.87.

513 Ie a bid by an officer of the authority on his behalf.

514 *R (Tout a Tout) v Haringey LBC; R (Heff) v Haringey LBC* [2012] EWHC 873 (Admin), [2012] JHL D77.

10.196 **England post-LA 2011 and Wales post-H(W)A 2014.** The law considered in relation to pre-LA 2011/H(W)A 2014 applicants is largely the same for applications in relation to which the duty had not arisen before commencement of LA 2011 s148(3)[515] and those in Wales made prior to 27 April 2015.

10.197 The duty will cease if the applicant accepts an offer of accommodation under Part 6.[516] The duty will also cease if the applicant, having been informed of the possible consequences of refusal and acceptance[517] and of his or her right to request a review of the suitability of the accommodation, refuses a final offer of accommodation under Part 6.[518] An offer is a final offer for this purpose if it is in writing and states that it is a final offer for the purposes of HA 1996 s193(7).[519] Accordingly, the earlier cases considered at paras 10.189–10.195 will remain relevant.

10.198 Apart from the requirement in England to inform the applicant about the possible consequences of acceptance as well as of refusal (para 10.190), the other difference is that the issue considered at para 10.194 – whether an offer under Part 6 which does not satisfy the requirements of subsection (7) may nonetheless serve to discharge the authority's duty if it satisfied the requirements of section 193(5) – is not relevant to these post-LA 2011/H(W)A 2014 applications, as HA 1996 s193(5) is now expressed only to apply to an offer which is neither a Part 6 offer nor an offer of private sector accommodation.[520]

Private sector accommodation offers

10.199 **England pre-LA 2011 and Wales pre-H(W)A 2014.** The following provisions applied until LA 2011 s148 came into force in England,[521] and continue to apply to applications made before that date, in relation to which the duty to secure accommodation had arisen but had not

515 9 November 2012: Localism Act 2011 (Commencement No 2 and Transitional Provisions) (England) Order 2012 SI No 2599 article 2.

516 HA 1996 s193(6)(c); H(W)A 2014 s76(2). See chapter 11.

517 HA 1996 s193(7) as amended from 9 November 2012, by LA 2011 s148(4) . In Wales, see H(W)A 2014 s76(3).

518 HA 1996 s193(7); in Wales, see H(W)A 2014 s76(3). Such an offer may include a nomination to become the assured tenant of a private registered provider of social housing (England) or a registered social landlord (Wales): HA 1996 s159(1)(c).

519 HA 1996 s193(7A). There is no such requirement in Wales.

520 See also Supplementary Suitability Guidance 2012 para 19.

521 9 November 2012: Localism Act 2011 (Commencement No 2 and Transitional Provisions) (England) Order 2012 SI No 2599 article 2.

ceased by it;[522] in Wales they apply to applications made prior to 27 April 2015.[523]

10.200 The duty will cease if the applicant accepts an offer of an assured (but not an assured shorthold) tenancy from a private landlord.[524] The duty will also cease if the applicant accepts a 'qualifying offer' of an assured shorthold.[525] An offer qualifies if:

a) it is made with the approval of the authority,[526] pursuant to arrangements made between it and the private landlord in order to bring the HA 1996 s193 duty to an end;
b) the tenancy is a fixed-term tenancy;[527] and
c) it is accompanied by a statement in writing, which states the term of the tenancy being offered and explains in ordinary language that there is no obligation to accept the offer, but that if it is accepted the duty under HA 1996 s193 will cease.[528]

10.201 An applicant is free to reject a qualifying offer without meaning that the duty under HA 1996 s193 is discharged,[529] and acceptance is only effective if the applicant signs a statement acknowledging that he or she has read and understood the statement made with the offer.[530] An offer of accommodation let on an assured shorthold tenancy which does not comply with the requirements of HA 1996 s193(7D) (para 10.200) cannot be a qualifying offer but, if refused, can nevertheless operate to bring the authority's duty under section 193(2) to an end under section 193(5), provided that the requirements of the latter subsection have been fulfilled, as qualified in the case of an assured shorthold.[531] If an applicant accepts an offer of an assured shorthold

522 Localism Act 2011 (Commencement No 2 and Transitional Provisions) (England) Order 2012 SI No 2599 article 3.

523 For applications made on or after that date, the H(W)A 2014 applies: see Housing (Wales) Act 2014 (Commencement No 3 and Transitory, Transitional and Saving Provisions) Order 2015 SI No 1272 article 7.

524 HA 1996 s193(6)(cc); as defined by HA 1996 s217(1). A private landlord is any landlord other than one within HA 1985 s80 and therefore includes a private registered provider of social housing (England) or a registered social landlord (Wales): HA 1996 s217 and H(W)A 2014 s99.

525 HA 1996 s193(7B).

526 The offer may not be approved unless the authority is satisfied that the accommodation is suitable for the applicant and that it is reasonable for him or her to accept the offer: HA 1996 s193(7F)(b).

527 As defined by HA 1988 s45(1), ie, any tenancy other than a periodic tenancy.

528 HA 1996 s193(7D).

529 HA 1996 s193(7C).

530 HA 1996 s193(7E).

531 *Griffiths v St Helens MBC* [2006] EWCA Civ 160, [2006] 1 WLR 2233.

tenancy that is not a qualifying offer, which accommodation subsequently ceases to be available, the authority will continue to owe him or her a duty under section 193(2) (provided that the applicant's circumstances have not otherwise materially changed).[532]

10.202 **England post-LA 2011 and Wales post-H(W)A 2014.** An offer of private rented sector accommodation by an authority leads to cessation of the duty even if the tenancy is an assured shorthold.[533] A private rented sector accommodation offer is of an assured shorthold tenancy, from a private landlord[534] to the applicant in respect of any accommodation which is, or may become, available for the applicant's occupation, which is made with the approval of the authority in pursuance of arrangements made between it and the landlord, with a view to bringing its duty to an end; the tenancy must be for a fixed term of at least 12 months[535] or – otherwise than in a restricted case – such longer period as the secretary of state may by regulations prescribe.[536]

10.203 In England, the offer must comply with specified qualifying conditions: the applicant must be informed in writing of the consequences of refusal or acceptance, that he or she has the right to a review of the suitability of the accommodation and – otherwise than in a restricted case – that he or she will be entitled to further assistance from the authority if a new application is made within two years of acceptance,[537] even if he or she is no longer in priority need, provided that he or she is not ineligible when that application is made nor had become homeless intentionally.[538] In Wales, he need only be informed in writing of the consequences of refusal and acceptance and of his or her right to seek a review.[539]

532 *Griffiths v St Helens MBC* [2006] EWCA Civ 160, [2006] 1 WLR 2233.

533 HA 1996 s193(7AA), as amended; H(W)A 2014 s76(2)–(4).

534 Ie any landlord other than one within HA 1985 s80 and thus including a private registered provider of social housing (England) or a registered social landlord (Wales): HA 1996 s217.

535 In Wales, six months: see H(W)A 2014 s76(4)(c).

536 HA 1996 s193(7AC), as amended. There is no equivalent in Wales.

537 Homelessness in this case arises when a valid notice under HA 1988 s21, expires (HA 1996 s195A(2)); see *Manual of Housing Law*, para 2.203.

538 HA 1996 s193(7AA)–(7AD) , as amended, s195A(1), (5), (6). Similar provision is made for those threatened with homelessness, which is defined as arising arises once a valid notice under HA 1988 s21 is served (see *Manual of Housing Law*, para 2.203): HA 1996 s195A(3)–(5). Subsection (3) concerns those threatened with homelessness and, once HRA 2017 is in force, it will be repealed and new duties will apply (paras 10.52–10.61): HRA 2017 s4(4).

539 H(W)A 2014 ss76(3), 84.

10.204 While there is still a requirement that the authority considers the accommodation suitable[540] for the applicant, there is no longer a requirement that the authority additionally considers it reasonable[541] for the applicant to accept the offer. The latter is replaced by a prohibition on the offer if the applicant is under contractual or other obligations in respect of his or her existing accommodation which he or she cannot bring to an end before being required to take up the offer.[542]

Restricted cases

10.205 **England pre-LA 2011 and Wales pre-H(W)A 2014.** The following provisions governing restricted cases applied until the LA 2011 s148 came into force in England,[543] and continue to apply to applications made before that date, in relation to which the duty to secure accommodation had arisen but had not ceased by it,[544] and in Wales they apply to applications made prior to 27 April 2015.[545] A restricted case[546] is one where the authority is only satisfied that the applicant is homeless, threatened with homelessness or in priority need because of a restricted person.[547]

10.206 If the authority only owes a full housing duty[548] to the applicant because of the restricted person, then, so far as reasonably practicable, it must bring the duty to an end by making a private accommodation offer.[549] Where it is not reasonably practicable to do so, the authority may discharge its duty under the other provisions of HA 1996 s193 but should continue to try to bring the duty to an end with a private accommodation offer.[550] A private accommodation

540 HA 1996 s193(7F) as amended by the LA 2011; H(W)A 2014 s76(2).

541 HA 1996 193(7F) as it read prior to amendment by LA 2011.

542 HA 1996 s193(7F), (8), as amended: see 'Reasonable refusals', below.

543 9 November 2012: Localism Act 2011 (Commencement No 2 and Transitional Provisions) (England) Order 2012 SI No 2599 article 2.

544 Localism Act 2011 (Commencement No 2 and Transitional Provisions) (England) Order 2012 SI No 2599 article 3.

545 For applications made on or after that date, the H(W)A 2014 applies: see Housing (Wales) Act 2014 (Commencement No 3 and Transitory, Transitional and Saving Provisions) Order 2015 SI No 1272 article 7. As to applications under H(W)A 2014, see paras 10.179–10.182.

546 HA 1996 s193(3B). See para 3.117.

547 HA 1996 s184(7). See para 3.117.

548 Under HA 1996 s193(2).

549 HA 1996 s193(7AD).

550 Department of Communities and Local Government (DCLG) Guidance Note, 16 February 2009, para 14.

offer is of an assured shorthold tenancy made by a private landlord[551] to the applicant in relation to any accommodation which is, or may become, available for the applicant's occupation, which is made with the approval of the authority in pursuance of arrangements made between it and the landlord with a view to bringing the authority's duty to an end; the tenancy must be for a fixed term of at least 12 months.[552]

10.207 When making a private accommodation offer, the authority must inform the applicant of the possible consequences of refusal and of the right to request a review of the suitability of the accommodation.[553] The duty ceases if the applicant either accepts or refuses the private accommodation offer.[554]

10.208 **England post-LA 2011 and in Wales post-H(W)A 2014.** In a restricted case,[555] the authority must, so far as is reasonably practicable, bring the full housing duty to an end by arranging for a private accommodation offer to be made.[556] This means an offer of an assured shorthold tenancy made by a private landlord to the applicant, made with the approval of the authority in pursuance of arrangements made by between it and the landlord with a view to bringing the authority's duty to an end; the tenancy must be a fixed tenancy for a period of at least 12 months.[557]

10.209 In a restricted case, the full housing duty ends if the applicant, having been informed of the possible consequences of refusal of the offer and the right to request a review of the suitability of the accommodation,[558] either accepts or refuses a private accommodation offer.[559]

10.210 If the authority decides that a duty is owed to the applicant under section 193(2) or section 195(2), but only because of a restricted person, it must inform the applicant that this was the basis for the

551 Ie any landlord other than one within HA 1985 s80 and thus including a private registered provider of social housing (England) or a registered social landlord (Wales): HA 1996 s217 and H(W)A 2014 s99.
552 HA 1996 s193(7AC).
553 HA 1996 s193(7AB).
554 HA 1996 s193(7AA).
555 See para 3.117.
556 HA 1996 s193(7AD).
557 HA 1996 s193(7AC).
558 HA 1996 s193(7AB).
559 HA 1996 s193(7AA).

decision,[560] identify the restricted person by name, and explain both why the person is a restricted person and that it is necessary to bring the duty to an end with a private accommodation offer.[561]

10.211 In Wales, as in England, a duty owed to a restricted person must, so far as is reasonably practicable, be brought to an end by securing an offer of accommodation from a private sector landlord.[562]

Reasonable refusals

10.212 Until LA 2011 s148 came into force in England,[563] an authority was not to make a final offer of accommodation under Part 6,[564] approve a private accommodation offer[565] or approve an offer of an assured shorthold tenancy,[566] unless satisfied that the accommodation was suitable for the applicant and that it was reasonable for him or her to accept the offer:[567] this is of continuing application to an application made before that date in respect of which the accommodation duty had arisen but had not ceased by that date.[568] It is also of continuing application for applications made to Welsh authorities prior to 27 April 2015.[569]

10.213 From LA 2011, the requirement that it is reasonable to accept the offer is replaced by a prohibition on making the offer if the applicant is under contractual or other obligations in respect of his or her existing accommodation which he or she cannot bring to an end before

560 HA 1996 s184(3A). Once HRA 2017 comes into force in England, this duty also arises if the authority decides that a duty would be owed after its duty under s189B(2) comes to an end: HRA 2017 s5(3), amending HA 1996 s184(3A).

561 HA 1996 s184(3).

562 H(W)A 2014 s76.

563 9 November 2012: Localism Act 2011 (Commencement No 2 and Transitional Provisions) (England) Order 2012 SI No 2599 article 2.

564 HA 1996 s193(7F)(a).

565 HA 1996 s193(7F)(ab), inserted by the Housing and Regeneration Act 2008 s314 and Sch 15 Part 1 paras 1, 5(1) and (6), from 2 March 2009 except in relation to applications for an allocation of social housing or housing assistance or for accommodation made before that date, see the Housing and Regeneration Act 2008 (Commencement No 1 and Saving Provisions) Order 2009 SI No 415 article 2.

566 HA 1996 s193(7F)(b).

567 HA 1996 s193(7F).

568 Localism Act 2011 (Commencement No 2 and Transitional Provisions) (England) Order 2012 SI No 2599 article 3.

569 For applications made on or after that date, H(W)A 2014 applies: see Housing (Wales) Act 2014 (Commencement No 3 and Transitory, Transitional and Saving Provisions) Order 2015 SI No 1272 article 7.

being required to take up the offer.[570] This does not, however, mean that:

> . . . those subjective suitability issues which have become associated with 'reasonable to accept', such as those discussed in *Ravichandran and another v Lewisham LBC*[571] or *Slater v Lewisham LBC*[572] are not to be taken into account. The intention is that these factors . . . (for example, fear of racial harassment; risk of violence from ex-partner's associates) continue to be part of those factors/elements an authority consider in determining suitability of accommodation.[573]

10.214 In Wales, there is no analogous restriction on the offer.

Keeping offers open

10.215 In *Khatun*,[574] the Court of Appeal reviewed earlier cases in which it had been held that an offer (under HA 1985 Part 3) should remain open for consideration by the applicant for a reasonable time.[575] It was held that they did not support a proposition that the applicant's subjective views on suitability are a mandatory factor in the authority's decision-making process. Given the right to seek a review of suitability after moving in, authorities may insist that an applicant makes a decision whether or not to accept an offer at the time that it is made, without holding it open to afford him or her an opportunity to view it. The letter making the offer comprises the decision under HA 1996 s193(5) that the offer is suitable for the applicant, which pre-empts any opportunity for the applicant to make representations about it, whether based on viewing it or otherwise. The decision assumes that, at the time of making the offer, all the relevant information about suitability is known by the authority, or else that the review process will cure any defects.

10.216 The position is different where the authority knows that admittedly relevant material, for example, medical evidence, is to be

570 HA 1996 s193(7F), (8), as amended.

571 [2010] EWCA Civ 755, [2010] HLR 42.

572 [2006] EWCA Civ 394, [2006] HLR 37.

573 Supplementary Suitability Guidance 2012 para 22.

574 *Khatun v Newham LBC* [2004] EWCA Civ 55, [2004] HLR 29.

575 *R v Wandsworth LBC ex p Lindsay* (1986) 18 HLR 502, QBD. The same had been held in *Parr v Wyre BC* (1982) 2 HLR 71, CA, which was disapproved in *R v Hillingdon LBC ex p Puhlhofer* [1986] AC 484, (1986) 18 HLR 158, HL, so far as it was based on the introduction of the word 'appropriate'. See also *R v Ealing LBC ex p Denny* (1995) 27 HLR 424, QBD.

produced. In *Hazeltine*,[576] the applicant challenged suitability on medical grounds; the authority agreed to keep the offer open, but only for a limited period, before the end of which it would not have received or evaluated the medical reports that it had requested from her. The authority's proposal was that, if she accepted the offer, she should abandon her challenge to it, but that, if she did not do so, the authority would determine the issue of suitability retrospectively, ie, if considered unsuitable she would get another offer, but if suitable she would not and the authority would take the position that it had discharged its duty to her. The court held that this procedure was not fair.

10.217 Where an authority notifies an applicant that it has ceased to be subject to the duty under HA 1996 s193(2), because the applicant has refused an offer of suitable accommodation under section 193(5), the authority is not obliged to keep the accommodation available during the period when the applicant has the right to request a review or until the authority has reached its review decision.[577]

Review

10.218 There is a right to seek an internal review of the suitability of accommodation offered under HA 1996 s193(5) or (7),[578] which may be exercised whether or not the applicant has accepted the offer of accommodation.[579] See generally chapter 12.

Re-application

10.219 A person towards whom the authority has been under a duty under HA 1996 s193 which has ceased, may re-apply.[580] This prevents an authority from simply relying on the previous discharge.[581] Rather, the authority must reconsider the case, so that a new duty will arise unless the authority can properly conclude that the applicant no

576 *R v Wycombe DC ex p Hazeltine* (1993) 25 HLR 313, CA. See *Khatun v Newham LBC*, above, at [37] where *Hazeltine* was held to be consistent with the decision in that case.

577 *Osseily v Westminster City Council* [2007] EWCA Civ 1108, [2008] HLR 18 at [11].

578 HA 1996 s202(1A); H(W)A 2014 s85.

579 HA 1996 s202(1A); reversing the effect of *Alghile v Westminster City Council* (2001) 33 HLR 57, CA, so as to afford the applicant the option of moving into the property while still contesting its suitability. In Wales, see H(W)A 2014 s85.

580 HA 1996 s193(9); H(W)A 2014 s62(2).

581 Cf paras 9.23–9.35. The case-law discussed there would suggest that, notwithstanding HA 1996 s193(9), an authority may refuse to accept a new application from an applicant who has refused a suitable offer of accommodation if the application is based on exactly the same facts.

longer fulfils the preconditions, for example, is not eligible or became intentionally homeless.[582] This is, however, subject to the discussion in *Fahia*[583] and *Rikha Begum*[584] of when a further application may be made and when it may be said to be identical with a previous application, such that there is no application before the authority at all.[585]

Homelessness Reduction Act 2017 – England

HA 1996 s193A

10.220 As noted,[586] once HRA 2017 is brought into force, the initial help duty can be brought to an end if the applicant, having been informed of the consequences of refusal and of his or her right to request a review of the suitability of the accommodation,[587] refuses either a final accommodation offer,[588] or a final Part 6[589] offer.[590] If it is brought to an end on this basis, the principal housing duty in section 193 does not apply.[591] The authority cannot approve a final accommodation offer or make a final Part 6 offer unless it is satisfied that it is suitable for the applicant;[592] nor can it approve or make such an offer if the applicant is under contractual or other obligations in respect of his or

582 See also para 10.171, for the right to re-apply with two years even if not in priority need.

583 *R v Harrow LBC ex p Fahia* [1998] 1 WLR 1396, (1998) 30 HLR 1124, HL.

584 *Rikha Begum v Tower Hamlets LBC* [2005] EWCA Civ 340, [2005] HLR 34: HA 1996 s193(9) is expressly considered at [53]. See also *R (Kensington and Chelsea RLBC) v Ealing LBC* [2017] EWHC 24 (Admin), [2017] HLR 13 at [18].

585 See the full discussion of repeat applications at paras 9.23–9.35 and, in particular, the conclusion in para 9.32 that the distinction is rarely one on which an authority can rely, ie a new application will normally need to be accepted. The corollary is that ss193(9) and 85 add little.

586 See para 10.10.

587 See paras 9.149–9.161.

588 This is an offer of an assured shorthold tenancy made by a private landlord – including a private registered provider of social housing (England) or a registered social landlord (Wales) – in relation to any accommodation which is, or may become, available for the applicant's occupation, made, with the approval of the authority, in pursuance of arrangements made by the authority in discharge of the initial help duty, which is a fixed term tenancy for a period of at least 6 months: HRA 2017 s7(1); HA 1996 s193A(4).

589 This is an offer of accommodation under Part 6 made in writing in discharge of the authority's initial help duty, which states that it is a final offer for that purpose: HRA 2017 s7(1); HA 1996 s193A(5).

590 HRA 2017 s7(1); HA 1996 s193A(1), (2).

591 HRA 2017 s7(1); HA 1996 s193A(3).

592 HRA 2017 s7(1); HA 1996 s193A(6).

her existing accommodation, which he or she is not able to bring to an end before he or she would have to take up the offer.[593]

HA 1996 s193C

10.221 Once HRA 2017 is brought into force, then HA 1996 s193 will also not apply when either the duty towards those threatened with homelessness (para 10.58) or the initial help duty (paras 10.66–10.74) is brought to an end by reason of the applicant's deliberate and unreasonable refusal to co-operate (paras 10.72–10.74).[594] In either case, however, an applicant who is homeless, eligible, in priority need and not homeless intentionally will be entitled to accommodation under HA 1996 s193C instead.[595]

10.222 The authority's duty under HA 1996 s193C is to secure that accommodation is available for occupation by the applicant.[596] Much of the law considered in relation to section 193 will apply: the general provisions referred to at para 10.112 (observations on availability: para 10.12; payment: para 10.12; and security: para 10.18), subject to the same qualification applicable to assured security as in para 10.112, and it remains to be seen whether the exclusion from PEA 1977 (para 10.18) applies to this duty:[597] it is submitted that the close relationship between sections 193 and 193C suggests that it should also not do so.

10.223 Observations on defences on eviction (para 10.118) will likewise apply should an authority seek to evict an applicant while he or she is still being housed under this provision. In addition, the following headings in relation to section 193 should also apply save so far as qualified for the commencement of HRA 2017 or by specific statutory qualification: postponement of the duty (paras 10.114–10.120); means of discharge (paras 10.121–10.123); out-of-area placements (paras

593 HRA 2017 s7(1); HA 1996 s193A(7).

594 HRA 2017 ss4, 5; HA 1996 ss195(10), 189B(9).

595 HRA 2017 s7(1); HA 1996 s193C(3), (4).

596 HRA 2017 s7(1); HA 1996 s193C(3), (4).

597 *R (ZH and CN) v Lewisham LBC* [2014] UKSC 62, [2015] AC 1259, [2015] HLR 6; it would seem to follow from Lord Hodge at [16] and [45]. Lady Hale referred at [165] to the 'generally accepted view that the protection of section 3 of the 1977 Act will apply once the local authority have accepted that they owe the family the "full housing duty"', presumably picking up the local authorities' submission that the 'licences were expressly limited to the period to be taken to provide a decision' (at 1287F) and the secretary of state's submission that the premises were 'temporary accommodation while the council made inquiries' (at 1288D).

10.145–10.177); suitability of accommodation (paras 10.145–10.177); keeping offers open (paras 10.215–10.217).

10.224 The duty will cease if the applicant:

a) ceases to be eligible for assistance;
b) becomes homeless intentionally from accommodation made available for his or her occupation;
c) accepts an offer of an assured tenancy from a private landlord; or
d) otherwise voluntarily ceases to occupy, as his or her only or principal home,[598] the accommodation made available for his or her occupation.[599]

10.225 The duty will also cease if the applicant, having been informed of the possible consequences of refusal or acceptance and of his or her right to request a review[600] of the suitability of the accommodation, refuses or accepts a final accommodation offer,[601] or a final Part 6[602] offer[603] The authority cannot approve a final accommodation offer or make a final Part 6 offer unless it is satisfied that it is suitable for the applicant;[604] nor can it approve or make such an offer if the applicant is under contractual or other obligations in respect of his or her existing accommodation, which he or she is not able to bring to an end before he or she would have to take up the offer.[605]

598 See *Manual of Housing Law*, paras 1.62–1.73.

599 HRA 2017 s7(1); HA 1996 s193C(5).

600 See paras 9.149–9.161.

601 This is an offer of an assured shorthold tenancy made by a private landlord – including a private registered provider of social housing (England) or a registered social landlord (Wales) – in relation to any accommodation which is, or may become, available for the applicant's occupation, made, with the approval of the authority, in pursuance of arrangements made by the authority in discharge of the HA 1996 s193C duty, which is a fixed term tenancy for a period of at least six months: HRA 2017 s7(1); HA 1996 s193C(7).

602 This is an offer of accommodation under Part 6 made in writing in discharge of the authority's HA 1996 s193C duty, which states that it is a final offer for that purpose: HRA 2017 s7(1); HA 1996 s193C(8).

603 HRA 2017 s7(1); HA 1996 s193C(6).

604 HRA 2017 s7(1); HA 1996 s193C(9).

605 HRA 2017 s7(1); HA 1996 s193C(10).

CHAPTER 11

Allocations

11.1 Introduction

11.10 Meaning of 'allocation'
11.11 Selecting a person to be a secure or introductory tenant
11.14 Nominations
11.19 Exemptions

11.23 Eligibility and qualification
11.27 Transfer applicants
11.28 Serious unacceptable behaviour in Wales
11.39 Disqualification in England
11.46 Notification
11.47 Re-applications
11.52 Existing applicants

11.54 Applications for housing
11.54 Housing register
11.55 Consideration of applications
11.56 Advice and information
11.58 Disclosure of information

11.59 The allocation scheme
11.60 Choice-based housing
11.61 Unlawful allocations
11.62 Categories of reasonable preference

continued

11.68 Considerations
11.69 Anti-social behaviour
11.73 Consultation
11.74 Reasonable preference
R (Ahmad) v Newham LBC
11.88 Children
11.89 Carers, adopters and fosterers
11.90 Armed forces
11.91 Households in or seeking work
11.92 Under-occupation
11.93 Choice-based and local lettings

11.95 Procedure
11.98 Enquiries
11.103 Information
Scheme
11.106 Applications

11.110 Internal review and challenge

11.115 Allocations by private registered providers of social housing (England) and registered social landlords (Wales)
11.122 England
11.127 Wales

Introduction

11.1 Local authorities hold the bulk of their housing stock under the Housing Act (HA) 1985 Part 2.

11.2 Until 1996, the statutory constraints on the allocation of that stock were to be found in HA 1985 s22, which required that in the selection of tenants certain groups were to be given a reasonable preference, including homeless people, a formulation so loose that there was negligible case-law under it.

11.3 Under HA 1985 Part 3, duties towards the homeless could be discharged by allocating housing held by the authority under HA 1985 Part 2 or any other power.[1] The Housing Act (HA) 1996 was designed to reduce the proportion of permanent housing which went directly to homeless people, whether from an authority's own stock or by way of nomination to the stock of registered providers of social housing; accordingly, it repealed and replaced HA 1985 s22.[2] Homelessness was not per se a ground of preference, although the homeless could qualify along with others, on the grounds of, for example, unsatisfactory housing conditions, temporary or insecure housing, a particular need for settled accommodation, or social or economic circumstances which made it difficult for them to secure settled accommodation.[3]

11.4 HA 1996 also introduced a statutory requirement to maintain a housing register, which the authority could keep in such form as it thought fit and which it could, if it wished, maintain in common with other landlords, eg other social housing landlords.[4]

11.5 In 1997, a degree of direct priority for homeless people was restored in the allocation of permanent stock by regulations.[5] The Homelessness Act 2002 extensively amended HA 1996 Part 6,[6] primarily:

1 HA 1985 s69(1)(a).

2 See paras 1.66–1.75.

3 HA 1996 s167 as enacted.

4 See generally, HA 1996 ss162–166 as enacted; as to common registers, see HA 1996 s162(3).

5 Allocation of Housing (Reasonable and Additional Preference) Regulations 1997 SI No 1902.

6 The amendments came into force in Wales on 27 January 2003 (Homelessness Act 2002 (Commencement) (Wales) Order 2002 SI No 1736) and 31 January 2003 in England (Homelessness Act 2002 (Commencement No 3) (England) Order 2002 SI No 3114).

a) to remove the detailed requirements governing the housing register;
b) to remove the power of local authorities to impose blanket restrictions on groups of people;[7]
c) to introduce arrangements to exclude or give a lower priority to those guilty of 'serious unacceptable behaviour'; and
d) to advance the policy of more applicant choice in the allocation of housing.

11.6 In England, the provisions were changed again by the Localism Act (LA) 2011, primarily by re-introducing a right for local authorities to determine for themselves who qualifies for an allocation, subject to any regulations which require them to include or exclude specified classes of person.

11.7 This chapter addresses allocations under the following headings:
a) meaning of 'allocation';
b) qualifying persons;
c) applications for housing;
d) the allocation scheme;
e) procedure;
f) internal reviews and challenges; and
g) allocation of housing by registered providers of social housing/registered social landlords.

11.8 Criminal offences which may be committed in relation to housing applications under HA 1996 Part 6 – as under Part 7 – are considered in chapter 15. The secretary of state and Welsh Ministers have power – which has been exercised – to issue guidance to local authorities on the exercise of their functions under Part 6.[8]

7 A practice facilitated by the wording of the former HA 1996 s161(4), which provided that authorities could decide what classes of persons were or were not 'qualifying persons' for the purposes of an allocation of housing.

8 *Allocation of accommodation: guidance for local housing authorities in England*, Department for Communities and Local Government (DCLG), 2012, replacing all previous guidance (see para.1.2 of the guidance), although note that earlier codes will be relevant to applications which precede it (ie before commencement of the changes effected by the LA 2011, which came into force on 18 June 2012 – see para 11.52), as to which see previous editions of this book. In Wales, see the *Code of guidance for local authorities: allocation of accommodation and homelessness*, Welsh Government, March 2016 ('Welsh Code'). See also the Housing Association Circular RSL 004/15 (replacing circular RSL 003/12, which itself replaced RLS 023/09) which requires all housing associations registered in Wales to take account of the Welsh Code.

11.9 The interaction of allocation schemes with other statutory duties, in particular Care Act 2014 and Children Act 1989 ss17 and 20, is considered in chapter 13.

Meaning of 'allocation'

11.10 The provisions of HA 1996 Part 6 apply only to the allocation of housing accommodation, as defined by HA 1996 s159(2).[9]

Selecting a person to be a secure or introductory tenant

11.11 Any selection of a person to be a secure[10] or introductory tenant,[11] whether or not of property held under HA 1985 Part 2, is an allocation.[12] It has been held that selection is not synonymous with the grant of a tenancy:[13] the provisions accordingly govern how people are selected to become tenants, but the grant itself is a separate process under HA 1985 Part 2; it follows that a grant that is not in accordance with the HA 1996 Part 6 allocations policy of the authority is not invalid[14] for that reason.[15]

11.12 For this purpose, 'tenancy' includes 'licence'.[16]

11.13 'Selection' includes notifying a tenant or licensee who is not currently secure that he or she is to become so.[17] The transition from introductory to secure tenant, effected by the passage of time,[18] is not, however, a selection.

9 An authority will not normally owe a duty of care to anyone seeking an allocation under HA 1996 Part 6; the remedy for a person dissatisfied with a decision is to seek internal review or use the ombudsman service: *R (Darby, as administratix of the estate of Lee Rabbetts) v Richmond upon Thames LBC* [2015] EWHC 909 (QB). As to internal review, see paras 11.110–11.114, and see para 11.118 on the ombudsman. Ultimately, judicial review may be available.

10 HA 1985 Part 4.

11 Introductory tenancies were brought in by HA 1996 Part 5 Chapter 1.

12 HA 1996 s159(2)(a).

13 Ie, the disposal of stock by way of the grant of a tenancy, under HA 1985 s32.

14 Cf para 11.61.

15 *Birmingham City Council v Qasim* [2009] EWCA Civ 1080, [2010] HLR 19.

16 HA 1996 s159(3); see HA 1985 s79(3).

17 HA 1996 s159(3). For example, under HA 1985 Sch 1 paras 4 (homeless persons), 5 (temporary accommodation for persons taking up employment) and 10 (student lettings), as amended by HA 1996 Schs 16 and 17.

18 HA 1996 s125.

Nominations

11.14 Nomination of a person to be the secure or introductory tenant (or licensee) of another, for example, of a housing action trust, is an allocation.[19]

11.15 Likewise, the nomination of a person to be an assured tenant of a private registered provider of social housing or registered social landlord is an allocation: accordingly, this does not include a nomination to a tenancy that will not be assured under HA 1988 Sch 1, but does include nomination to an assured shorthold.[20]

11.16 Nominations include those made in pursuance of an arrangement (whether or not legally enforceable) to require that accommodation is made available to a person or a number of persons nominated by the authority.[21]

11.17 These provisions reflect long-standing arrangements with housing associations and trusts to which funding has been provided,[22] linked to a right on the part of an authority to nominate a proportion (or even all) of the tenants to a particular property, group of properties (for example, block of flats), or to an association's stock as a whole.

11.18 The wording of HA 1996 s159(4) is oxymoronic: if the entitlement is to 'require' that accommodation is made available to a person or number of persons, it is 'legally enforceable'. It may be that what was in mind is that a particular nomination is not legally enforceable, because such arrangements commonly work by way of proportions of voids, but the wording does not lend itself to this, because it is the arrangement that must 'require' – even if putatively not 'legally enforceable'. To give the wording some meaning (within the apparent intention of the provision), it would seem that a voluntary nomination arrangement not made by deed and for which there is no consideration will still qualify.

19 HA 1996 s159(2)(b).

20 HA 1996 s159(2)(c).

21 HA 1996 s159(4).

22 Whether under Local Government Act 1988 Part 3 or HA 1996 s22. (Since 1 April 2010, the latter provision has only been applicable in Wales as a result of amendments by Housing and Regeneration Act 2008.)

Exemptions

11.19 In England, HA 1996 s159(4A) and (4B)[23] provide that the allocation provisions do not apply to anyone who is already a secure or introductory tenant, or an assured tenant of a private registered provider of a social housing or registered social landlord, unless the person has applied to the authority for a transfer and the authority decide that the applicant is entitled to a reasonable preference[24] in the allocation.[25] The position is different in Wales:[26] HA 1996 s159(5) exempts from these allocation provisions an allocation to anyone who is already a secure or introductory tenant (whether or not of the same landlord), unless the allocation involves a transfer of housing accommodation for that person which has been made on his or her application.[27] Those moved at the behest of the landlord – for example, for redevelopment – are exempt from both sets of provisions.

11.20 Also exempt from HA 1996 Part 6 are the categories specified in HA 1996 s160:

a) succession to secure tenancy on death, or devolution of a fixed term in such circumstances that the tenancy remains secure;[28]
b) assignment by way of exchange of secure tenancy or to a person who could have succeeded to it;[29]
c) transfers by way of surrender and re-grant where one of the tenancies is a flexible tenancy[30] or an assured shorthold tenancy;[31]

23 As amended by the Homelessness Act 2002 s13 and the LA 2011 s145.

24 See paras 11.74–11.78.

25 HA 1996 s159(4A), (4B), as amended by LA 2011 s145(2). So far as concerns assured tenants, the wording is difficult: HA 1996 s159(4B) refers to someone within section 159(4A)(a) or (b), the former referring to local authority tenants, the latter to private registered providers and registered social landlords; it is, however, an unusual use of the word 'transfer' and if section 159(4B) had only referred to section 159(4A), it may have been assumed that it applied only to local authority tenants.

26 HA 1996 s159(5), as amended by the Homelessness Act 2002 s13.

27 Before amendment, transfers were also exempt. The re-inclusion within the provisions of transfer applications accords with the practice of many local authorities to deal with transfer applications on the same basis as those of new applicants (see, eg *R v Islington LBC ex p Reilly and Mannix* (1998) 31 HLR 651, QBD).

28 HA 1985 ss87–90.

29 HA 1985 s92.

30 See HA 1985 s107A.

31 LA 2011 s158.

d) transfers of secure or introductory tenancies under the provisions of matrimonial and related domestic legislation;[32]
e) becoming a secure tenant following an introductory tenancy;[33]
f) succession to an introductory tenancy;[34]
g) assignment of an introductory tenancy to a person who could have succeeded to it.[35]

11.21 The secretary of state (in Wales, the Welsh Ministers) may prescribe other categories of allocation which are to fall outside HA 1996 Part 6, subject to restrictions or conditions, including by reference to a specific category or proportion of housing.[36]

11.22 This power has been exercised to exempt allocation of housing to:[37]

a) those entitled to rehousing under Land Compensation Act 1973 s39;[38]
b) those whose homes are repurchased under HA 1985 s554 or s555;[39] and
c) in England, those to whom accommodation is let on a family intervention tenancy.[40]

Eligibility and qualification

11.23 The principal class of person to whom a property cannot be allocated is someone who is ineligible because of immigration status.[41] This has been considered in chapter 3. It is suggested that eligibility be considered both when an initial application is made and when

32 Matrimonial Causes Act 1973 s24; Matrimonial and Family Proceedings Act 1984 s17; Children Act 1989 Sch 1 para 1 and Part 2 of Schedule 5 or paragraph 9(2) or 9(3) of Schedule 7 to the Civil Partnerships Act 2004.
33 HA 1996 s125.
34 HA 1996 s133.
35 HA 1996 s134.
36 HA 1996 s160(4) and (5).
37 Allocation of Housing (England) Regulations 2002 SI No 3264 reg 3 and Allocation of Housing (Wales) Regulations 2003 SI No 239 reg 3.
38 Following compulsory purchase or a number of specified actions leading to loss of the home, eg a demolition order under HA 1985 or a prohibition order under HA 2004.
39 Repurchase of a designated defective dwelling.
40 As to Family Intervention Tenancies, see Housing and Regeneration Act 2008 s297.
41 HA 1996 s160ZA(1) in England; HA 1996 s160A(1) in Wales.

considering making an allocation, especially where a substantial period of time has elapsed since the application.[42]

11.24 If a person is ineligible, then the authority is not permitted to allocate a tenancy to the person, even jointly with someone else who is qualified.[43]

11.25 This does not prevent an allocation to someone who is eligible simply because a member of his or her household is not, although the ineligibility of members of the family may in some circumstances need to be taken into account when determining an applicant's housing needs under an allocation scheme.[44] Although, in principle, an allocation can be made to a household which includes an ineligible person, that is unlikely to occur In practice as, under Part 2 of the Housing (Wales) Act (H(W)A) 2014 or Part 7 of the HA 1996, such cases (known as 'restricted cases') are, so far as is reasonably practicable, to be dealt with by way of an offer of private sector accommodation (see paras 5.8–5.11).

11.26 Unless a person is ineligible, he or she may *prima facie* – subject to the following paragraphs – be allocated housing accommodation by an authority.[45]

Transfer applicants

11.27 Where an applicant[46] is an existing secure or introductory tenant, or an assured tenant of housing accommodation allocated[47] to him or her by a local housing authority, the applicant is not disqualified on the basis of his or her immigration status.[48]

Serious unacceptable behaviour in Wales

11.28 Additionally, local authorities in Wales may disqualify those who – or whose household members[49] – have been guilty of unacceptable behaviour serious enough to make them unsuitable to be tenants of

42 *Allocation of accommodation: guidance for local housing authorities in England*, para 3.2. There is no similar advice in the Welsh Code.

43 HA 1996 s160ZA(1)(b); HA 1996 s160A(1)(c) in Wales.

44 See paras 3.164–3.168.

45 HA 1996 s160A(2).

46 In England only, an applicant whom the authority considers is entitled to a reasonable preference, HA 1996 s160ZA(5), referring to s159(4B). See para 11.19.

47 See para 11.19.

48 HA 1996 s160ZA(5) (England) and s160A(6) (Wales).

49 'Household' is not defined, but is presumably wider than 'family'.

the authority and who – in the circumstances at the time their application is considered – are unsuitable to be tenants of the authority because of the unacceptable behaviour.[50]

11.29 An English authority which wanted to adopt such a restriction would *prima facie* appear free to do so as part of their allocation scheme, although, in practice, such restrictions would need to be carefully framed, given the development through case-law of a prohibition on excluding persons entitled to a reasonable preference (see paras 11.39–11.45).[51]

11.30 'Unacceptable behaviour' is defined as behaviour which would, if the person was either a secure tenant or a member of a secure tenant's household, entitle a landlord to a possession order under any of grounds 1–7 of HA 1985 Sch 2[52] or the 'absolute' ground for possession in HA 1985 s84A.[53] Accordingly, a former assured or protected tenant evicted on analogous grounds could be treated as disqualified. There need not have been an eviction on the particular ground, only behaviour which would entitle the landlord to a possession order.[54] HA 1985 Sch 2 grounds 1–7 are the discretionary (fault) grounds for possession and, as such, the court has to be satisfied that it is reasonable to make a possession order before an order can be made.[55]

11.31 The grounds are:

Ground 1[56] – Rent arrears or breach of tenancy.

Ground 2[57] – Behaviour which caused or is likely to cause a nuisance or annoyance to those persons residing, visiting or otherwise engaging in a lawful activity in the locality of the dwelling, or to any person employed (whether or not by the landlord) in

50 HA 1996 s160A(7). It has been held that this does not entitle an authority to take into account criminal convictions which are 'spent' under the Rehabilitation of Offenders Act 1974: see R *(YA) v Hammersmith and Fulham LBC* [2016] EWHC 1850 (Admin), [2016] HLR 39. Even if – contrary to the apparent effect of the Rehabilitation of Offenders Act 1974 – an argument could be mounted to the contrary, it is very difficult indeed to see how it could be reasonable to in public law terms to take it into account.

51 Prior to 18 June 2012, the restriction also applied in England, but was removed by the LA 2011, see Localism Act 2011 (Commencement No 6 and Transitional, Savings and Transitory Provisions) Order 2012 SI No 1463. As to the power to impose restrictions as part of the allocation scheme, see HA 1996 s160ZA(6), (7), as amended by LA 2011 s146. See also para 11.41.

52 HA 1996 s160A(8)(a).

53 HA 1996 s160A(8)(aa).

54 See Welsh Code para 2.33.

55 HA 1985 s84(2).

56 HA 1988 Sch 2 grounds 8, 10, 11 and 12; Rent Act (RA) 1977 Sch 15 case 1.

57 HA 1988 Sch 2 ground 14; RA 1977 Sch 15 case 2.

connection with the exercise of the landlord's housing management functions, and which behaviour is directly or indirectly related to or affects those functions; or, conviction for using the dwelling for immoral or illegal purposes or committing an indictable offence in or in the locality of the dwelling house.[58]

Ground 2A[59] – Domestic violence causing a partner or other family member to leave the property.[60]

Ground 3[61] – Deterioration of the dwelling-house due to waste, neglect or default.

Ground 4[62] – Deterioration of furniture provided by the landlord due to ill-treatment;

Ground 5[63] – Tenancy induced by a false statement.[64]

Ground 6[65] – Premium received or paid in connection with a mutual exchange.

58 A number of cases have relied on this ground and the Court of Appeal has either upheld possession orders or substituted possession where it has originally been refused: see *Kensington and Chelsea RLBC v Simmonds* (1996) 29 HLR 507; *Bristol City Council v Mousah* (1997) 30 HLR 32; *Darlington LBC v Sterling* (1997) 29 HLR 309; *West Kent HA v Davies* (1998) 31 HLR 415; *Camden LBC v Gilsenan* (1998) 31 HLR 81; *Portsmouth City Council v Bryant* (2000) 32 HLR 906; *Newcastle City Council v Morrison* (2000) 32 HLR 891; *Lambeth LBC v Howard* (2001) 33 HLR 58; *New Charter HA v Ashcroft* [2004] EWCA Civ 310, [2004] HLR 36; *London and Quadrant Housing Trust v Root* [2005] EWCA Civ 43, [2005] HLR 28; *Manchester City Council v Higgins* [2006] HLR 14; *Sandwell MBC v Hensley* [2008] HLR 22. These cases reflect a hardening of attitudes towards those guilty of anti-social behaviour and, in turn, make it easier for authorities to conclude that an applicant is disqualified on this ground, although authorities will need to be careful to consider each case and, in particular, the issue of reasonableness on its own merits not on the basis of policy. For the equivalent provision under HA 1988 Sch 2 ground 14, see eg, *Knowsley Housing Trust v Prescott* [2009] EWHC 924 (QB), [2009] L&TR 24. See also *Brent LBC v Corcoran* [2010] EWCA Civ 774, [2010] HLR 43 concerning breach of licence conditions for caravan pitches by reason of anti-social behaviour.

59 HA 1988 Sch 2 ground 14A; there is no equivalent under the RA 1977.

60 See *Camden LBC v Mallett* (2001) 33 HLR 20, CA.

61 HA 1988 Sch 2 ground 13; RA 1977 Sch 15 case 3.

62 HA 1988 Sch 2 ground 15; RA 1977 Sch 15 case 4.

63 HA 1988 Sch 2 ground 17; there is no equivalent under the RA 1977.

64 Including those made as part of a homelessness application. Cf *Rushcliffe BC v Watson* (1991) 24 HLR 124, CA; *Shrewsbury and Atcham BC v Evans* (1997) 30 HLR 123, CA; and *Lewisham LBC v Akinsola* (1999) 32 HLR 414, CA; *Waltham Forest LBC v Roberts* [2004] EWCA Civ 940, [2005] HLR 2.

65 There is no equivalent under the HA 1988 or RA 1977, although in each case, if the tenancy agreement prohibit assignment (whether absolutely or only with the consent of the landlord), an assignment in breach of such a term may give rise to a basis for possession under HA 1988 Sch 2 ground 12 or RA 1977 Sch 15 case 1.

Ground 7[66] – Eviction from a dwelling within the curtilage of a building held for non-housing purposes due to conduct such that given the nature of the building it would not be right for occupation to continue.

Absolute ground[67] – Anti-social Behaviour, Crime and Policing Act (ASBCPA) 2014 s94, introduced a new 'absolute ground for possession' where a secure tenant (or a person residing in or visiting the property) has engaged in certain specified anti-social behaviour (eg breached an injunction under ASBCPA 2014 s1, convicted of a breach of a criminal behaviour order under ASBCPA 2014 s30).

11.32 The overriding test is whether the authority is satisfied that the applicant or member of the applicant's household has been guilty of behaviour 'serious enough to make [the applicant] unsuitable to be' its tenant, and that – in the circumstances at the time of his or her application – the applicant is thus unsuitable (still or, eg if there has been a period of good behaviour, again). The latter qualification means that the fact that an order for possession has been made on a relevant ground will not be sufficient on its own,[68] nor will a fixed rule or practice to treat all those evicted on one of the relevant grounds as qualifying under the first limb of the test (ie past unsuitability) be lawful.[69] The separation in HA 1996 s160A(7) between past conduct and suitability at time of application is likely to be strictly applied.

11.33 Criminal convictions for drug-related offences can be sufficient.[70] Convictions for sexual offences, including offences against children, were sufficient to render an applicant for a transfer ineligible, even though he had been assessed as having a critical need for ground floor accommodation and, due to his disabilities, was unable to climb stairs; if he had been allocated the ground floor flat that he had identified, then he would have easy access to a playground, which posed an obvious risk to children in the area.[71]

11.34 HA 1985 Sch 2 grounds 1–7 are discretionary grounds for possession, and as such the court has to be satisfied that it is reasonable to grant possession before an order can be made.[72] Authorities will therefore need to address this issue of reasonableness for

66 There is no equivalent under either the HA 1988 or RA 1977.
67 HA 1988 Sch 2 ground 7A.
68 See Welsh Code para 2.35.
69 See para 12.44.
70 *R (Dixon) v Wandsworth LBC* [2007] EWHC 3075 (Admin), [2008] JHL D21.
71 *R (M) v Hackney LBC* [2009] EWHC 2255 (Admin), [2010] JHL D1.
72 HA 1985 s84(2).

themselves,[73] ie they will need to reach a public law decision (that in itself is not so unreasonable as to be irrational or perverse)[74] on whether or not a county court would have found it reasonable to make the order.

11.35 Conduct leading to an outright, a suspended or a postponed order can suffice, because postponement and suspension are under HA 1985 s85, which does not come into play unless an order under section 84 is available. There is a difficult relationship here. In *Portsmouth City Council v Bryant*,[75] it was said that: 'In deciding whether it is reasonable to make an order under section 84(2) the judge can properly take into account his power under section 85(2) to suspend that order.' The burden of the decision was that a court could decide to make an order because it had power to suspend or postpone knowing that it intended to do so, where if there were no such power it might not make an order at all.

11.36 It follows that there is a material difference between an outright order made under HA 1996 s84 and one made in contemplation of the exercise of the section 85 power to suspend or postpone. On the face of it, any such order could suffice; on the other hand, if the conduct was such that a court would have been likely to suspend or postpone, it is tantamount to recognising that a court would have been operating from the premise that the conduct had not yet reached the point at which the occupier was – in terms of the overriding issue for the authority – unsuitable to be a tenant. In turn, it is submitted that this should impact on the overriding issue (whether or not the conduct was sufficient to make the applicant unsuitable to be a tenant). Accordingly, it must be the best practice for the authority to ask itself whether it was likely that an outright, suspended or postponed order would have been made: if one of the latter two, while it still has the right to treat the applicant as unsuitable, it should nonetheless be able to justify why. The Welsh Code of Guidance suggests that the authority needs 'to satisfy itself that if a possession order were granted it would have been an outright order'.[76] It may be contended that this is an overstatement of the law; the essential issue is selection of tenants, to which conduct is, on the face of it, not irrelevant;[77] on the other hand, there is much practical merit in this reconciliation.

73 See Welsh Code para 2.34.

74 Cf paras 12.52–12.55.

75 (2000) 32 HLR 906, CA, per Simon Brown LJ at 916.

76 At para 2.35.

77 See also para 12.39.

11.37 Relevant too would seem to be the distinction drawn in some of the anti-social behaviour cases between conduct by the tenant himself or herself and conduct by a member of the tenant's household which the tenant had failed to control, such that an outright order might be made in the first case but a suspended order in the second, depending on the degree of acquiescence.[78] Thus, a transfer applicant against whom a suspended order has been made (which has not subsequently led to eviction) would prima facie still be suitable, even if the decision is that of the authority. Likewise, a person against whom a suspended order was made on the ground of, for example, nuisance and annoyance, but put into effect because of arrears,[79] would be in a different class from an applicant whose order was put into effect because of continued nuisance or annoyance.

11.38 Consider also the position of a former tenant who has abandoned a property owing several hundred pounds of arrears. On application for housing from the local authority, the authority may consider that the arrears are such that an order would have been made, so that the applicant can be considered to have committed unacceptable behaviour. The authority should, it is submitted, also consider whether it was an outright or a suspended order that would have been made if the tenant had decided not to abandon but had instead waited and defended a possession action based on the arrears.[80]

Disqualification in England

11.39 The previous class of ineligibility based on anti-social behaviour has been replaced in England by a power entitling the local authority to decide for itself who does – or does not – qualify for an allocation,[81] and accommodation can only be allocated to someone who qualifies according to those local criteria (or to joint tenants, one of whom so qualifies).[82] The power is, however, subject to the overriding immigration criteria considered in chapter 3, ie there can be no allocation

78 See, eg *Gallagher v Castle Vale HAT* [2001] EWCA Civ 944, (2001) 33 HLR 72; see also *Kensington and Chelsea RLBC v Simmonds* (1996) 29 HLR 507, CA, per Simon Brown LJ at 512; *Newcastle City Council v Morrison* (2000) 32 HLR 891, CA; *Manchester City Council v Higgins* [2005] EWCA Civ 1423, [2006] HLR 14; and *Knowsley Housing Trust v McMullen (by her litigation friend)* [2006] EWCA Civ 539, [2006] HLR 43. Cf *London and Quadrant Housing Trust v Root* [2005] EWCA Civ 43, [2005] HLR 28.

79 See *Sheffield City Council v Hopkins* [2001] EWCA Civ 1023, [2002] HLR 12.

80 See, eg *Lambeth LBC v Henry* (2000) 32 HLR 874, CA.

81 HA 1996 s160ZA(7), added by LA 2011 s146.

82 HA 1996 s160ZA(6), added by LA 2011 s146.

in contravention of them.[83] It has been held that this power cannot be used to disqualify a person entitled to a reasonable preference.[84] Moreover, an authority cannot rely on 'spent' criminal convictions to exclude an otherwise qualified applicant.[85]

11.40 An authority must be careful not to offend anti-discrimination legislation in relation to those with protected characteristics[86] under equalities legislation. Authorities are under a duty to seek to eliminate discrimination.[87] Discrimination may be direct, ie treating a person less favourably because of a protected characteristic[88] – although treating the disabled more favourably is not discrimination;[89] or, it may be indirect, as defined:[90] this occurs if the authority applies to an applicant a provision, criterion or practice which is discriminatory in relation to a relevant protected characteristic,[91] meaning a provision, criterion or practice which, while applied to others, puts, or would put, persons with that characteristic at a particular disadvantage

83 HA 1996 s160ZA(7), added by LA 2011 s146; see paras 11.23–11.26.

84 Under HA 1996 s166A(3), see *R (Jakimaviciute) v Hammersmith and Fulham LBC* [2014] EWCA Civ 1438, [2015] HLR 5; *R (Alemi) v Westminster City Council* [2014] EWHC 3858 (Admin); *R (HA) v Ealing LBC* [2015] EWHC 2375 (Admin).

85 *R (YA) v Hammersmith and Fulham LBC* [2016] EWHC 1850 (Admin), [2016] HLR 39. Given the statutory and policy background, this was a surprising conclusion, leaving Wales in a position to exclude the anti-social with a reasonable preference where English authorities cannot do so: the judgment rejected an approach based on examination of the previous statutory position in England and analysis of what the subsequent legislation had intended to change; it may be that this conclusion would not withstand Supreme Court consideration. The court also rejected Guidance advising against such policies, which, however, implied that the Secretary of State thought that legally they were possible, see para 11.42.

86 Equality Act (EqA) 2010 s4: age, disability, gender reassignment, marriage and civil partnership, pregnancy and maternity, race, religion and belief, sex and sexual orientation. Some of these (age, marriage and civil partnership) are not protected in relation to the disposal and management of premises, but it may be doubted whether disposal here goes as far as formulating an allocation scheme: see EqA 2010 s38: '(3) A reference to disposing of premises includes, in the case of premises subject to a tenancy, a reference to– (a) assigning the premises, (b) sub-letting them, or (c) parting with possession of them. (4) A reference to disposing of premises also includes a reference to granting a right to occupy them.'

87 EqA 2010 s149.

88 EqA 2010 s13.

89 EqA 2010 s13(3).

90 EqA 2010 s19.

91 EqA 2010 s19(1). Indirect discrimination does not apply to the protected characteristic of pregnancy and maternity: EqA 2010 s19(3).

when compared to persons without it, which provision, criterion or practice cannot be shown to be a proportionate means of achieving a legitimate aim.[92] Nor can authorities otherwise discriminate under Article 14 of the European Convention on Human Rights (ECHR).[93]

11.41 The power to decide who qualifies to apply is also subject to the power of the secretary of state by regulations to prescribe classes of persons who are, or are not, to be treated as qualifying persons and to prescribe criteria that may not be used in deciding what classes of persons are not qualifying persons.[94] Authorities may not disqualify – on the basis that they have no local connection with their areas – the following applicants:

a) someone who is serving in the regular forces,[95] or who has served in the regular forces within five years of the date of application;

92 EqA 2010 s19(2). In *R (XC) v Southwark LBC* [2017] EWHC 736 (Admin) an allocation scheme which gave priority to people who were working or volunteered in the local community was held to be indirectly discriminatory against disabled persons (who would be less likely to be able to work or to volunteer), but that the discrimination was justified: it was legitimate for the authority to seek to ensure that their tenants included a reasonable proportion of working people and to encourage volunteering. The scheme accorded with para 4.27 of the Allocation of Accommodation: guidance for local housing authorities in England (which encourages authorities to 'consider how they can use their allocation policies to support those households who want to work as well as those who . . . are contributing . . . through voluntary work'). There was no alternative measure which could have been applied to achieve these legitimate aims. See also *R (C) v Islington LBC* [2017] EWHC 1288 (Admin), in which it was held that provisions of an allocation scheme which prioritised existing social housing tenants who wanted to move were potentially discriminatory against homeless people, victims of domestic violence and women, but that any discrimination was justified as it served the legitimate purpose of encouraging existing tenants to move to smaller homes and free up larger units. The claim was, however, allowed in part on a different point, see n244.

93 Article 14 provides that the rights protected by the ECHR must be enjoyed by all persons without discrimination on 'any ground such as sex, race, colour, language, religion, political or other opinion, national or social origin, association with a national minority, property, birth or other status'. Although disability discrimination is not expressly mentioned in Article 14, it has been held that it is also prohibited under Article 14: *AM (Somalia) v Entry Clearance Officer* [2009] EWCA Civ 634, [2009] UKHRR 1073. See, eg *R (HA) v Ealing LBC* [2015] EWHC 2375 (Admin), where a requirement that an applicant had lived in the borough for five years was held to violate Article 14 in respect of female victims of domestic violence (itself held to be a 'status' for Article 14 purposes).

94 HA 1996 s160ZA(8), added by LA 2011 s146.

95 The Royal Navy, the Royal Marines, the regular army or the Royal Air Force: see Armed Forces Act 2006 s374 (applied by Allocation of Housing (Qualification Criteria for Armed Forces) (England) Regulations 2012 SI No 1869 reg 2).

b) someone who has recently ceased, or will cease, to be entitled to reside in accommodation provided by the Ministry of Defence following the death of that person's spouse or civil partner, which spouse or civil partner had served in the regular forces and whose death was attributable (wholly or partly) to that service;

c) someone who is serving or has served in the reserve forces[96] and who is suffering from a serious injury, illness or disability which is attributable (wholly or partly) to that service; or[97]

d) a person with the 'right to move'.[98]

11.42 Guidance suggests that authorities should avoid setting qualifying criteria which disqualify groups of people whose members are likely to qualify for a reasonable preference[99] (eg on medical or welfare grounds[100]), although the guidance does appear to consider that authorities *could* adopt criteria which would disqualify individuals who do so (eg if they are disqualified on the basis of anti-social behaviour).[101] In *Jakimaviciute*,[102] however, the Court of Appeal – relying on these passages in the guidance – held that they supported the conclusion

96 The Royal Fleet Reserve, the Royal Naval Reserve, the Royal Marines Reserve, the Army Reserve, the Territorial Army, the Royal Air Force Reserve or the Royal Auxiliary Air Force: see Armed Forces Act 2006 s374 (applied by Allocation of Housing (Qualification Criteria for Armed Forces) (England) Regulations 2012 SI No 1869 reg 2).

97 Allocation of Housing (Qualification Criteria for Armed Forces) (England) Regulations 2012 SI No 1869 reg 3. It is intended that such persons will be given additional preference (see para 11.64) – see *Allocation of accommodation: guidance for local housing authorities in England*, para 4.14.

98 Allocation of Housing (Qualification Criteria for Right to Move) (England) Regulations 2015 SI No 967. This is a three-stage test. First, the person must be a secure or introductory tenant or an assured tenant of a social landlord (reg 4(a)). Second, he or she must be entitled to a reasonable preference because he or she needs to move to a particular locality in the authority's district, where failure to meet that need would cause hardship (reg 4(b)). Third, he or she must have a 'need to move', either because he works in the authority's district or he has been offered work in their district and has a genuine intention of taking up the offer (regs 4(c) and 5). See also Right to Move: Statutory guidance on social housing allocations for local housing authorities in England, DCLG, March 2015.

99 See paras 11.74–11.78. Following *R (Jakimaviciute) v Hammersmith and Fulham LBC* [2014] EWCA Civ 1438, [2015] HLR 5, such a policy would likely be unlawful in any event: see paras 11.29 and 11.39–11.45.

100 *Allocation of accommodation: guidance for local housing authorities in England*, para 3.21.

101 *Allocation of accommodation: guidance for local housing authorities in England*, para 3.21.

102 *R (Jakimaviciute) v Hammersmith and Fulham LBC* [2014] EWCA Civ 1438, [2015] HLR 5, at [40].

that the qualification criteria adopted by an authority were subject to the reasonable preference duty, so that an authority cannot adopt qualification criteria which exclude a person entitled to a reasonable preference. Guidance also indicates that, in deciding what classes of people do not qualify for an allocation, authorities should consider the implications of excluding a whole class and should ensure that there are suitable exceptions; the guidance specifically envisages that where an authority uses a residence criteria to exclude people from an allocation, it may wish to consider the position of people moving into the area to take up work or to escape violence, or homeless applicants or children in care placed out of borough.[103] The need for exceptions was underscored by subsequent guidance which stressed that, while authorities are encouraged to consider prioritising those with a local connection to their area, they should ensure that people who have not lived in the area for some time but who have family or work commitments in it are not excluded.[104]

11.43 Guidance also suggests that authorities should avoid allocating to people who already own their own homes, save in exceptional circumstances, eg, elderly owner occupiers who cannot stay in their own home and need to move into sheltered accommodation.[105] It also notes that there may be reasons for applying different qualification criteria in relation to existing tenants from those which apply to new applicants, eg, to ensure that residency requirements do not restrict existing social tenants moving to take up work or downsizing to a smaller home; and, authorities could apply different qualification criteria in relation to different stock, eg, properties which are hard to let.[106]

11.44 The guidance reminds authorities that there may always be exceptional circumstances when it will be necessary not to apply criteria in the case of an individual applicant, eg, an intimidated witness who needs to move quickly to another area; authorities are encouraged

103 *Allocation of accommodation: guidance for local housing authorities in England*, para 3.22. Following *Jakimaviciute*, a residence test cannot not be used so as to exclude people entitled to a reasonable preference: *R (HA) v Ealing LBC* [2015] EWHC 2375 (Admin).

104 Providing Social Housing for Local People: Statutory Guidance, paras 12, 13, 15 and 26–27.

105 *Allocation of accommodation: guidance for local housing authorities in England*, para 3.23.

106 *Allocation of accommodation: guidance for local housing authorities in England*, para 3.24.

to include provision for dealing with exceptional cases within their qualification rules.[107]

11.45 As with eligibility,[108] authorities are advised to consider whether an applicant qualifies for an allocation at the time of the initial application and when considering making an allocation, 'particularly where a long time has elapsed since the original application'.[109]

Notification

11.46 An authority which decides that an applicant is ineligible must notify[110] him or her of the decision and of the grounds for it in writing.[111] This duty is identical to that which applies to a decision on a homelessness application and the reasons for it: see chapters 9[112] and 12.[113]

Re-applications

11.47 In Wales, an applicant who is treated as ineligible due to serious unacceptable behaviour may make a fresh application if he or she considers that he or she should no longer be treated as ineligible[114] – for example, because rent arrears have been cleared, or because someone who had been guilty of anti-social behaviour is no longer part of his or her household.[115]

11.48 Likewise, in England, an applicant who is not being treated as a qualifying person by an English authority may (if he or she considers that he or she should now be treated as a qualifying person) make a fresh application to the authority for an allocation.[116]

107 *Allocation of accommodation: guidance for local housing authorities in England*, para 3.25.

108 See para 11.23.

109 *Allocation of accommodation: guidance for local housing authorities in England*, para 3.26.

110 If the notification is not received by the applicant, it is to be treated as having been received if it is made available at the authority's office for a reasonable period for collection: HA 1996 s160ZA(10) (England) and s160(10) (Wales).

111 HA 1996 s160ZA(9) and (10) (England); s160A(9) and (10) (Wales).

112 See paras 9.132–9.148.

113 See paras 12.65–12.91.

114 HA 1996 s160A(11).

115 Cf the distinction drawn at para 11.37 – see *Gallagher v Castle Vale HAT* [2001] EWCA Civ 944, (2001) 33 HLR 72; *Kensington and Chelsea RLBC v Simmonds* (1996) 29 HLR 507, CA.

116 HA 1996 s160ZA(11), added by LA 2011 s146.

11.49 Superficially, the entitlement to re-apply might seem to suggest an analogy with the law on re-applications for assistance under HA 1996 Part 7.[117] This would, however, be wrong because, while the test – whether the application is made on exactly the same facts – in relation to a homelessness re-application is in principle a question for the authority to determine,[118] the obligation to reconsider qualification for an allocation arises when the applicant considers that he or she should no longer be treated as ineligible or (in England)[119] that he or she should be treated as a qualifying person.

11.50 That said, it is unlikely that an authority has to reconsider application after application, week in week out, each to be followed by a review,[120] without some basis for suggesting a relevant change. There are two broad approaches: either a) the courts will oblige authorities to engage in consideration (and review), but they will be entitled to do no more than ask whether there has been a change 'in the [applicant's] circumstances'[121] and what that change is, so that if the applicant fails to put forward anything which could justify reconsideration, the authority may reach the same decision on that basis alone;[122] or b) the courts will impose a somewhat more rigorous test along the lines of whether 'a reasonable applicant' could himself or herself consider that there had been any material change such as to lead him or her to consider that he or she should no longer be treated as ineligible or should not be treated as qualifying, in which case reconsideration and, if needs be, review must follow. The latter seems less likely.

11.51 In practice, the issue is only likely to get to court where there has been something that could lead the applicant to re-apply, both because a challenge will have to be by way of judicial review for which permission will be required and in order to procure public funding to make a claim. Nonetheless, authorities need to determine a proper response to such applications. The safest course is for authorities to ask the applicant to identify the putative change and ensure that that

117 See paras 9.24–9.39.

118 See *Rikha Begum v Tower Hamlets LBC* [2005] EWCA Civ 340, [2005] HLR 34; see paras 9.29–9.30.

119 18 June 2012: Localism Act 2011 (Commencement No 6 and Transitional, Savings and Transitory Provisions) Order 2012 SI No 1463.

120 See para 11.110.

121 Cf the wording of HA 1996 s160(7)(b).

122 Consider by way of analogy the homelessness cases where the applicant has failed to put forward a matter for the authority to enquire into, or something to put the authority on notice of an enquiry which needs to be made – see paras 9.95–9.100.

they consider along with any other material changes of which they are aware, including, for example, to their own policies and/or in the overall demographics of an area.[123] The Welsh Code of Guidance suggests that unless there has been a considerable lapse of time, it will be for the applicant to show that his or her circumstances or behaviour have changed,[124] ie, the first approach in para 11.50.

Existing applicants

11.52 The eligibility provisions of HA 1996 s160A came into force on 27 January 2003 in Wales and 31 January 2003 in England. All applicants who were on a local authority housing register immediately before that date, or who had made an application which had not yet been determined, were to be treated as persons who had applied for an allocation of housing, which had the effect of applying the provisions of section 160A to them.

11.53 From 18 June 2012, local authorities in England may only allocate accommodation in accordance with the provisions of HA 1996 s160ZA and their own allocation scheme. Any entitlement to an allocation of housing will largely depend on the allocation scheme of the local housing authority to which the applicant has applied.[125] An authority must take steps to bring to the attention of those likely to be affected by it any alteration to its allocation scheme which reflects a major change of policy.[126] Some applicants may therefore find that, following a change in allocation scheme by the local housing authority, they are no longer be entitled to an allocation of housing either because they are ineligible or because they do not satisfy the authority's qualification criteria. If an authority decides that an applicant is ineligible or is not a qualifying person, the local housing authority must serve the applicant with a written notice of that decision together with the reasons for it.[127] An applicant has a right to a statutory review of that decision.[128] The applicant may reapply to the local housing authority if the applicant considers that he or she should (now) be treated as a qualifying person.[129]

123 See, in particular, HA 1996 s166(3).
124 Welsh Code para 2.40.
125 See paras 11.39–11.51.
126 HA 1996 s168(3).
127 HA 1996 s160ZA(9).
128 HA 1996 s166A(9)(c).
129 HA 1996 s160ZA(11).

Applications for housing

Housing register

11.54 Prior to amendment by the Homelessness Act 2002, HA 1996 Part 6 required all local authorities to establish and maintain a housing register. That requirement has now been repealed.

Consideration of applications

11.55 All applications must, if made in accordance with the procedures laid down in an authority's allocation scheme,[130] be considered by that authority.[131] It is a matter for the authority how it records that application and the information contained in it.

Advice and information

11.56 All authorities must make available, free of charge, advice and information about the right to make an application for an allocation of housing.[132] They must also provide the necessary assistance in making an application to those who are likely otherwise to have difficulty in doing so.[133]

11.57 All applicants must be informed of the right to request information about their applications,[134] and about any decisions made in relation to them,[135] and to seek an internal review.[136]

Disclosure of information

11.58 The fact that a person is an applicant for housing must not be disclosed – without the consent of the applicant – to any other member of the public.[137]

130 See para 11.59.
131 HA 1996 s166(3). Provided proper consideration has been given, a court will not interfere with the authority's findings or how it decides to treat the application: see, eg *R (Heaney) v Lambeth LBC* [2006] EWHC 3332 (Admin), [2007] JHL D25.
132 HA 1996 s166(1)(a).
133 HA 1996 s166(1)(b).
134 Under HA 1996 s166A(9)(a) (England) or s167(4A)(a) (Wales): see paras 11.106 and 11.107.
135 Under HA 1996 s166A(9)(b) (England) or s167(4A)(b) (Wales): see para 11.109.
136 Under HA 1996 s167(4A)(c); see para 11.110.
137 HA 1996 s166(4).

The allocation scheme

11.59 Each local housing authority must establish an allocation scheme for determining priorities between qualifying persons[138] and for the procedure to be followed in allocating housing accommodation.[139] Authorities in England must – when preparing or modifying their schemes – have regard to their homelessness strategy,[140] as well as to their 'current tenant strategy';[141] London boroughs will also have to have regard to the London housing strategy,[142] prepared by the Mayor.[143]

Choice-based housing

11.60 The scheme must include a statement of the authority's policy on offering applicants a 'choice of housing accommodation' or 'the opportunity to express preferences' about the accommodation to be allocated to them.[144]

Unlawful allocations

11.61 Allocation from the waiting list must be in accordance with the scheme.[145] An allocation which is not in accordance with the scheme will be ultra vires.[146] Notwithstanding what might be thought the obvious purpose of this provision to constrain lettings that are not in

138 See paras 11.23–11.45.

139 HA 1996 s167(1) (from commencement of LA 2011 s147, in England, s166A(1)).

140 Under Homelessness Act 2002 s1: see paras 14.3–14.17.

141 This is the strategy under LA 2011 s150, pursuant to which authorities decide, among other matters, whether and when to grant flexible tenancies, ie outside of full security.

142 Under LA 2011 s151.

143 HA 1996 s166A(12).

144 HA 1996 s166A(2) (England); s167(1A) (Wales).

145 HA 1996 s166A(14) (England). See *Sarhadid v Camden LBC* [2004] EWCA Civ 1485, [2005] HLR 11; *R (Bibi) v Camden LBC* [2004] EWHC 2527 (Admin), [2005] HLR 18, where failures by the local authority to apply the scheme led to the quashing of its decisions. Cf *R (Osei) v Newham LBC* [2010] EWHC 368 (Admin), [2010] JHL D37.

146 See *R v Macclesfield BC ex p Duddy* [2001] JHL D16, QBD (allocation to a former employee outside the provisions of the scheme).

accordance with the scheme, it has been held that a non-compliant tenancy is nonetheless valid.[147]

Categories of reasonable preference

11.62 When establishing priorities, a reasonable preference must be given to:[148]

a) those who are homeless (within the meaning of HA 1996 Part 7 or, in Wales, H(W)A 2014 Part 2);[149]
b) those who are owed a duty by any local housing authority under HA 1996 s190(2),[150] s193(2)[151] or s195(2)[152] (or under HA 1985 s65(2) or s68(2))[153] or who are occupying accommodation secured under HA 1996 s192(3),[154] or, in Wales, those who are owed any duty under H(W)A 2014 s66, s73 or s75;[155]
c) those in insanitary or overcrowded housing or otherwise in unsatisfactory housing conditions;
d) those who need to move on medical or welfare grounds (including grounds relating to a disability);[156] and

147 *Birmingham City Council v Qasim* [2009] EWCA Civ 1080, [2010] HLR 19.

148 HA 1996 s166A(3) (England); s167(2) (Wales)).

149 See chapter 4. The class is not qualified in any way (cf HA 1996 ss167(2)(b) and 166A(3)(b)), and therefore encompasses those who are homeless but not in priority need. There is no requirement that an applicant should have applied as homeless before an authority must consider whether or not he or she qualifies under this ground (again, cf HA 1996 s167(2)(b)/s166A(3)(b)): *R (Alam) v Tower Hamlets LBC* [2009] EWHC 44 (Admin), [2009] JHL D47.

150 See para 10.54. This is the duty to those who are in priority need but intentionally homeless. Prior to this amendment, intentionally homeless people did not receive any statutory preference and many authorities either excluded them altogether or gave them little or no priority. Any exclusion or reduction of preference for this group must now be in accordance with HA 1996 s160ZA(7) or s166A(5) (England) or s160A(7) (see para 11.28) or s167(2A) or (2B) (Wales) (see paras 11.69–11.72).

151 The duty to those who are eligible, in priority need and not intentionally homeless: see para 10.85.

152 The duty to those threatened with homelessness unintentionally: see para 10.89.

153 The equivalent duties under the HA 1985 to the unintentionally homeless.

154 Those unintentionally homeless who are not in priority need but who are offered housing under the discretionary power: see para 10.47.

155 H(W)A 2014 s66 – duty to help to secure accommodation for those threatened with homelessness; s73 – initial duty owed to those who are eligible and homeless; s75 – full duty equivalent to HA 1996 s193(2).

156 The express reference to disability was added by HA 2004 s223 because of concerns that local authorities were interpreting the need for a move on

e) those who need to move to a particular locality in the district of the authority, where failure to meet that need would cause hardship (to themselves or others).[157]

11.63 Reasonable preference must not be given to an applicant who only falls within any of the reasonable preference categories because of a restricted person.[158] A restricted person is someone who is ineligible,[159] subject to immigration control,[160] and who either does not have leave to enter or remain in the UK, or whose leave is subject to a condition to maintain and accommodate him or herself, and any dependants, without recourse to public funds.[161] An authority should take care that their published allocation scheme reflects the position of restricted cases.[162]

11.64 The secretary of state and the Welsh Ministers have power to specify further categories of reasonable preference or to amend or repeal any part of HA 1996 s166A(3) (England) or s167(2) (Wales).[163] This power has not been exercised in relation to the amended section 167(2) in Wales. In England, it has been used as to provide that additional preference should be given to former members of the armed forces, serving members who need to move because of a serious injury, medical condition or disability sustained as a result of service, bereaved spouses and civil partners of members of the armed forces leaving services accommodation following the death, and serving or former members of the reserve forces who need to move because of

'medical' grounds too narrowly. *Allocation of accommodation: guidance for local housing authorities in England*, para 4.10, envisages that this head could include care leavers, a person moving on from a drug or alcohol recovery programme, young adults with learning disabilities and those who provide care or support, eg foster carers, those approved to adopt, or those being assessed to foster or adopt, special guardians, and family and friend carers who – without fostering or adopting – have taken care of a child because the parents are unable to do so. The extension to disability is not found in H(W)A 2014, but see also Welsh Code paras 3.31–3.33.

157 'This would include, for example, a person who needs to move to a different locality in order to give or receive care, to access specialised medical treatment, or to take up a particular employment or training opportunity': *Allocation of accommodation: guidance for local housing authorities in England*, para 4.11; Welsh Code para 4.23.

158 HA 1996 s166A(4) (England); s167(2ZA) (Wales).

159 See paras 3.113–3.119.

160 See para 3.16.

161 HA 1996 s184(7); and see para 3.116.

162 DCLG Guidance Note, 16 February 2009, para 17.

163 HA 1996 s166A(7) (England); s167(3) (Wales).

a serious injury, medical condition or disability sustained as a result of service, who have urgent housing needs.[164]

11.65 Additional preference may be given to sub-groups within those groups, being persons with urgent housing needs.[165] This means giving those applicants 'additional weight' or 'an extra head start, but does not require an allocation to be made to applicants entitled to it ahead of all others'.[166] The English guidance reminds authorities to 'consider, in the light of local circumstances, the need to give effect to this provision', offering, by way of illustration, those who need to move suddenly because of a life-threatening illness or sudden disability, families in such severe overcrowding that it poses a serious health hazard, and those who require urgent rehousing as a result of violence or threats of violence, whether intimidated witnesses or as a result of serious anti-social behaviour or domestic violence.[167]

11.66 There is no requirement for a local authority to frame an allocation scheme to provide for cumulative preference, ie affording greater priority to applicant who falls into more than one reasonable preference category.[168]

164 Housing Act 1996 (Additional Preference for Armed Forces) (England) Regulations 2012 SI No 2989. See also *Allocation of accommodation: guidance for local housing authorities in England*, para 4.14.

165 HA 1996 s166A(3) (England); s167(2) (Wales). See also *R (Heaney) v Lambeth LBC* [2006] EWHC 3332 (Admin), [2007] JHL D25, where the applicant asserted that she had an urgent housing need arising out of the distress caused by continuing to live in a property in which one of her daughters had died and, as such, that she qualified within the authority's category for transfer on an urgent basis, a claim which the authority rejected. Recognising that the authority had set a high threshold for inclusion in the relevant category, and that it had considered all the evidence, the court held that the authority was entitled to reach the conclusion that the applicant did not meet the criteria.

166 *R (L and D) v Lambeth LBC* [2001] EWHC (Admin) 900, (2002) JHL D1 (upheld on appeal, *Lambeth LBC v A; Lambeth LBC v Lindsay* [2002] EWCA Civ 1084, [2002] HLR 57). There is nothing objectionable in an authority adopting a 'points threshold', below which an applicant cannot bid under the authority's choice procedures (as to which, see para 11.60): *R (Woolfe) v Islington LBC* [2016] EWHC 1907 (Admin), [2016] HLR 42.

167 *Allocation of accommodation: guidance for local housing authorities in England*, para 4.13.

168 *R (Ahmad) v Newham LBC* [2009] UKHL 14, [2009] HLR 31. See also *Allocation of accommodation: guidance for local housing authorities in England*, para 4.5. See further paras 11.79–11.87.

11.67 The English guidance encourages authorities to take advantage of the flexibility available to them to meet local needs and local priorities.[169]

Considerations

11.68 For the purpose of defining how preference is to be awarded to those within these categories, an authority's allocation scheme may take into account:[170]

a) the financial resources open to an applicant to meet his or her housing costs;
b) any behaviour of an applicant (or a member of the applicant's household) which affects his or her suitability to be a tenant;[171]
c) any local connection[172] which exists between an applicant and the authority's area.[173]

Anti-social behaviour

11.69 The discrete anti-social behaviour provisions which formerly applied both in England and in Wales apply, since full commencement of LA 2011 s147,[174] only in Wales,[175] as in England the issue can – to some extent – now be dealt with under the new discretion to decide who is a person qualifying for an allocation (save that an authority cannot exclude a person who is entitled to a reasonable preference).[176]

11.70 Under the provision as it continues to operate in Wales, the allocation scheme need not afford any preference at all for an applicant who – in the circumstances at the time his or her case is considered – does not deserve to be treated as a member of a group who are to be given preference, because the applicant, or a member of the applicant's household, has been guilty of such serious unacceptable

169 *Allocation of accommodation: guidance for local housing authorities in England*, para 4.19.

170 HA 1996 s166A(5) (England), s167(2A) (Wales).

171 See further paras 11.69–11.72.

172 As defined by HA 1996 s199; see paras 7.9–7.15.

173 Accordingly, a scheme is not unlawful because it includes reference to whether an applicant has a local connection when determining priority as between two applicants otherwise in the same band of priority: *R (Boolen) v Barking and Dagenham LBC* [2009] EWHC 2196 (Admin), [2009] JHL D113.

174 18 June 2012: Localism Act 2011 (Commencement No 6 and Transitional, Savings and Transitory Provisions) Order 2012 SI No 1463.

175 LA 2011 s147(5)(b).

176 See paras 11.29 and 11.39–11.45.

behaviour that he or she is unsuitable to be a tenant of the authority.[177] Such behaviour is defined in the same way as for ineligibility.[178]

11.71 Welsh authorities thus have a choice whether to exclude applicants altogether because of serious unacceptable behaviour,[179] or to permit them to join the allocation scheme but downgrade their preference.

11.72 An applicant must be notified in writing of a decision that he or she is a person to whom HA 1996 s167(2C) applies,[180] and of the grounds for it.[181] There is provision for review of such a decision.[182]

Consultation

11.73 By HA 1996 s166A(13) (England) and s167(7) (Wales), the authority must afford all registered providers of social housing and registered social landlords with whom it has nomination arrangements the opportunity to comment on an allocation scheme before it is adopted or before it is altered in any way that reflects 'a major change of policy'. The expression 'major change of policy' is not statutorily defined.[183] In an appropriate case, it may be that a person awaiting an allocation will have a legitimate expectation that they will enjoy the same priority under the new scheme as the old.[184]

Reasonable preference

11.74 The requirement to give a 'reasonable preference' to certain groups was also to be found in HA 1985 s22. In relation to that section, it was said that to give a reasonable preference meant that the criteria must be an 'important factor in making a decision about the allocation of housing',[185] and that 'positive favour should be shown to applications

177 HA 1996 s167(2B) and (2C).
178 See paras 11.28–11.38.
179 See para 11.28.
180 HA 1996 s167(4A)(b).
181 HA 1996 s167(4A)(c).
182 See paras 11.110–11.114.
183 *Allocation of accommodation: guidance for local housing authorities in England*, para 5.2 suggests any amendment affecting the relative priority of a large number of applicants or a significant alteration to procedures. See also Welsh Code para 4.26.
184 See, eg *R (Alansi) v Newham LBC* [2013] EWHC 3722 (Admin), [2014] HLR 25.
185 Per Tucker J in *R v Lambeth LBC ex p Ashley* (1996) 29 HLR 385, QBD at 387.

which satisfy any of the relevant criteria'.[186] More recently, HA 1996 s167(2)[187] was said to provide those within it with a 'reasonable head start', although still not guaranteed an allocation.[188] The test is whether they are given a reasonable preference relative to persons who are not so entitled; whether a preference is reasonable is a decision for the authority; a scheme may still give reasonable preference to applicants who do not fall within HA 1996 s166A(3) (England) or s167(2) (Wales) provided that such non-statutory preferences do not dominate the scheme at the expense of the statutory preference categories.[189]

11.75 Reasonable preference does, however, imply a power to choose between different applicants on 'reasonable grounds ... it is not unreasonable to prefer good tenants to bad tenants'.[190] There is therefore no reason why an authority's own principles of allocation should not include reference to arrears of rent[191] (but not, it is suggested, other categories of debt, such as arrears of local taxation).[192] It has been held that there was no impropriety in requiring a victim of domestic violence, whom the authority agreed ought to be rehoused, to clear her arrears from a previous tenancy before being made an offer – the

186 Per Judge LJ in *R v Wolverhampton MBC ex p Watters* (1997) 29 HLR 931, CA at 938.

187 Which in England, is now found in HA 1996 s166A(3).

188 See per Collins J in *R (A) v Lambeth LBC; R (Lindsay) v Lambeth LBC* [2002] EWCA Civ 1084, [2002] HLR 57 at [15].

189 *R (Lin) v Barnet LBC* [2007] EWCA Civ 132, [2007] HLR 30.

190 Per Carnwath J in *R v Newham LBC ex p Miah* (1995) 28 HLR 279, at 288. In *R (Cranfield-Adams) v Richmond Upon Thames LBC* [2012] EWHC 3334 (Admin), [2012] All ER(D) 114 (Jun), JHL D10, the authority could lawfully remove priority and defer any further allocation for a period of two years from the refusal of a previous, suitable offer; the refusal was a matter the authority was entitled to take into account. It may be that, post-LA 2011, this needs reconsideration, at least insofar as it applies to persons entitled to a reasonable preference. In *R (Alemi) v Westminster City Council* [2014] EWHC 3858 (Admin), the allocation policy provided that people who were owed the full duty under HA 1996 s193(2) were not able to bid for an allocation from a social landlord for the first 12 months, ie during the first year of waiting, only tenancies with private landlords were available. That was held to be unlawful because, rather than give a reasonable preference, it created a group of persons who had no preference at all for the first 12 months.

191 *R v Newham LBC ex p Miah*, above; *R v Lambeth LBC ex p Njomo* (1996) 28 HLR 737, QBD; *R v Islington LBC ex p Aldabbagh* (1994) 27 HLR 271, QBD. See now HA 1996 s167(2A)(b), (2B) and (2C) specifically allowing behaviour to be taken into account; see paras 11.69–11.72. They may also go to discretionary disqualification under section 160A(7) in Wales only.

192 *R v Forest Heath DC ex p West and Lucas* (1991) 24 HLR 85, CA: all local taxpayers are to be treated the same way, regardless of their need for housing.

authority was entitled to have regard to the fact that the claimant was one of a number of persons in need of emergency re-housing; as other such persons did not have such debts, it was not irrational to conclude that she should be given a lower priority than them.[193] On the other hand, an authority – whose allocation scheme provided for overpayments of housing benefit to be taken into account when determining priority – could not take them into account when the applicant's overpayment was statute-barred under the Limitation Act 1980: it was unlawful and irrational to reduce the applicant's preference on account of debts which were not recoverable.[194]

11.76 The secretary of state and Welsh Ministers may specify factors which the local authority may not take into account when allocating housing accommodation.[195] This power has not been exercised.

11.77 Insofar as authorities can and do adopt their own policies, they cannot adopt policies so rigid as to fetter their consideration of the individual circumstances of particular applicants for housing.[196]

11.78 The requirement to give a reasonable preference to the specified groups does not prevent an authority allocating a quota of all vacancies to one particular group (for example, homeless persons).[197]

R (Ahmad) v Newham LBC

11.79 A line of cases on reasonable preference within local authority allocation schemes was reversed by the House of Lords in *Ahmad*.[198]

193 *R (Osei) v Newham LBC Lettings Agency* [2010] EWHC 368 (Admin), [2010] JHL D37. Arrears also prevented an allocation (on the basis of overcrowding) in *R (Babakandi) v Westminster City Council* [2011] EWHC 1756 (Admin), [2011] JHL D105, though the Director of Housing had a discretion not to apply the policy of not allocating to those in arrears in 'exceptional circumstances', the fact that those circumstances were not spelled out did not make the scheme unlawful.

194 *R (Joseph) v Newham LBC* [2009] EWHC 2983 (Admin), [2010] JHL D37.

195 HA 1996 s166A(8) (England); s167(4) (Wales).

196 See *R v Canterbury City Council ex p Gillespie* (1987) 19 HLR 7, QBD; *R v Bristol City Council ex p Johns* (1992) 25 HLR 249, QBD; *R v Newham LBC ex p Campbell* (1993) 26 HLR 183, QBD; *R v Newham LBC ex p Watkins* (1993) 26 HLR 434, QBD; *R v Newham LBC ex p Dawson* (1994) 26 HLR 747, QBD; *R v Islington LBC ex p Aldabbagh* (1994) 27 HLR 271, QBD; *R v Lambeth LBC ex p Njomo* (1996) 28 HLR 737, QBD; *R v Southwark LBC ex p Melak* (1996) 29 HLR 223, QBD; *R v Gateshead MBC ex p Lauder* (1997) 29 HLR 360, QBD; and *R v Lambeth LBC ex p Ashley* (1996) 29 HLR 385, QBD. See also para 12.44.

197 *R v Islington LBC ex p Reilley and Mannix* (1998) 31 HLR 651, QBD; *R v Westminster LBC ex p Al-Khorshan* (2000) 33 HLR 6, QBD; *R (Babakandi) v Westminster City Council* [2011] EWHC 1756 (Admin), [2011] JHL D105.

198 [2009] UKHL 14, [2009] HLR 31.

Those cases had held that a reasonable authority is bound to include within its scheme a mechanism for identifying, and giving added preference, to those with 'cumulative need', ie, who qualified within more than one category of reasonable preference.[199]

11.80 In *Ahmad*, Newham LBC's allocations policy was challenged on two principal grounds: first, that it failed to determine priority between people in the reasonable preference groups in accordance with the gravity of their individual needs, ie, cumulative needs; and second, that the policy of allocating up to five per cent of properties advertised under the authority's choice-based lettings scheme to existing tenants (without a reasonable preference) who wished to transfer to another similar property failed to give reasonable preference to those within HA 1996 s167(2).[200]

11.81 In both the High Court and the Court of Appeal, the scheme was held to be unlawful, principally because the mechanism for determining priority between those with a reasonable preference was by length of time since registration, not by relative need.[201] The scheme was also found to be unlawful because of the allocation of five per cent of properties to tenants seeking a transfer.

11.82 The House of Lords held that an authority cannot be required to afford preference by reference to cumulative need,[202] as HA 1996 s167(2) provides only that a local authority may afford additional preference to those within the priority groups who have an urgent need,[203] and section 167(2A) provides only that it may determine priorities between those within priority groups by reference to other considerations.[204]

11.83 In relation to the challenge to its choice-based scheme, the authority was entitled to allocate properties to people who did not fall within a category of reasonable preference; HA 1996 s167(2)[205] only requires that the categories set out in that subsection are given a 'reasonable preference' – it does not require that they should be given absolute

199 *R v Islington LBC ex p Reilly and Mannix* (1998) 31 HLR 651, QBD; *R v Westminster City Council ex p Al-Khorsan* (1999) 33 HLR 77; *R (A) v Lambeth LBC* [2002] EWCA Civ 1084, [2002] HLR 57. See also *R (Cali and others) v Waltham Forest LBC* [2006] EWHC 2950 (Admin), [2007] HLR 1. See, generally, the 7th edition of this book, at paras 11.70–11.83.

200 In England, see now HA 1996 s166A(3).

201 Per Richards LJ [2008] EWCA Civ 140 at [69].

202 See Baroness Hale at [14] and Lord Neuberger at [39]–[43].

203 See para 11.65. In England, see now HA 1996 s166A(5).

204 See para 11.69.

205 In England, see now HA 1996 s166A(3).

priority over everyone else.[206] Moreover, allocating a proportion of the available housing stock to transfer applicants who were already tenants of the local authority neither increased nor decreased the available housing stock – the property left by the transferring tenant becomes available to others.[207]

11.84 The importance of the case is not merely the dismissal of the judicially created requirement of provision for cumulative need, but its statement about judicial intervention generally:

> ... as a general proposition, it is undesirable for the courts to get involved in questions of how priorities are accorded in housing allocation policies. Of course, there will be cases where the court has a duty to interfere, for instance if a policy does not comply with statutory requirements, or if it is plainly irrational. However, it seems unlikely that the legislature can have intended that Judges should embark on the exercise of telling authorities how to decide on priorities as between applicants in need of rehousing, save in relatively rare and extreme circumstances. Housing allocation policy is a difficult exercise which requires not only social and political sensitivity and judgment, but also local expertise and knowledge.[208]
>
> In relation to the provision of accommodation under the National Assistance Act 1948, my noble and learned friend, Baroness Hale of Richmond, then Hale LJ, said in *R (Wahid) v Tower Hamlets London Borough Council* [2002] EWCA Civ 287, [2003] HLR 13, para 33, '[n]eed is a relative concept, which trained and experienced social workers are much better equipped to assess than are lawyers and courts, provided that they act rationally'. Precisely the same is true of relative housing needs under Part 6 of the 1996 Act, and trained and experienced local authority housing officers.
>
> If section 167[209] carries with it the sort of requirements which can be said to be implied by the decisions of the Court of Appeal and the Deputy Judge in this case, then Judges would become involved in considering details of housing allocation schemes in a way which would be both unrealistic and undesirable. Because of the multifarious factors involved, the large number of applicants, and the relatively small number of available properties at any one time, any scheme would be

206 See Baroness Hale at [18]–[19].

207 At [17]–[21].

208 This judicial restraint was applied in the planning case of *R (McDonagh) v Hackney LBC* [2012] EWHC 373, [2012] JHL D60, upholding a policy whereby Gypsies and Travellers who wanted a pitch on a caravan site had to provide documentary evidence of an address in the authority's area at which correspondence could be sent to them and to re-register every year; there was nothing irrational about the policy as it ensured that applicants had connections to the local area and that the waiting list was up-to-date.

209 In England, see now HA 1996 s166A.

open to attack, and it would be a difficult and very time-consuming exercise for a Judge to decide whether the scheme before him was acceptable. If it was not, then the consequences would also often be unsatisfactory: either the authority would be in a state of some uncertainty as to how to reformulate the scheme, or the Judge would have to carry out the even more difficult and time-consuming (and indeed inappropriate) exercise of deciding how the scheme should be reformulated to render it acceptable. As Baroness Hale said, that point is well made by looking at the Deputy Judge's order in this case, which requires the Scheme to be reconsidered 'in accordance with the law set out in this judgment'.[210]

11.85 In contrast, however, in *Birmingham City Council v Ali*,[211] the same committee of the House of Lords as in *Ahmad* – cognisant that in that case it has 'made it clear that the courts should be very slow indeed to interfere with a local housing authority's allocation policy, unless it breached the requirements of Part 6'[212] – nonetheless held that Birmingham City Council's allocations policy was unlawful by reason of irrationality.

11.86 Under that policy, where it was accepted that a family was homeless because of overcrowding in, or the condition of, its current accommodation, so that a 'full' duty was owed,[213] the authority would discharge its duty under HA 1996 s193(2) by leaving the family in the existing accommodation until suitable permanent accommodation could be found; they were, however, awarded a lower priority than where the authority placed a homeless family in temporary accommodation. There was little argument on this part of the case.[214] While the conclusion of the Court of Appeal that those who were homeless in their current accommodation could not lawfully be left in it under HA 1996 Part 7[215] was not supported by the House of Lords,[216] it was nonetheless irrational on a 'relatively narrow aspect': the authority had not justified the difference in treatment – its 'bald statement' that 'those in greatest need are dealt with first' was insufficient; on the face of it, those in (their current) unsuitable accommodation were in greater need than those in other temporary accommodation which

210 Lord Neuberger, with whom the other members of the Committee agreed, at [46]–[48].

211 [2009] UKHL 36, [2009] HLR 41.

212 At [62].

213 See paras 10.85–10.89.

214 See Baroness Hale at [57].

215 See paras 10.96 and 10.136.

216 At [61].

had not been subject to an unsuitability finding; if there was evidence to that effect, it had not been put forward.[217]

11.87 In the post-*Ahmad* decision of *Kabashi*,[218] the scheme took waiting time into account but re-set the date whenever a change of circumstances led to a re-assessment of an applicant's rehousing needs (with no residual discretion to disapply that provision). The applicant's need for a three-bedroom property changed to a need for two bedrooms, with the result that her waiting time was re-set to a later date. This was not unlawful: the authority had explained that, in its experience, those adversely affected by applicants moving from the waiting list for three-bed properties to two-bed properties perceived such interloping as unfair queue jumping; it was not for the court to second-guess that policy.

Children

11.88 Where an authority – as it will invariably do – takes children into account for the purposes of determining priority and nature of accommodation under its HA 1996 Part 6 scheme, a child arrangement order under Children Act 1989 s8 will be relevant in deciding whether or not a child is to be taken into account, but it is not determinative of the authority's allocation decision.[219]

Carers, adopters and fosterers

11.89 Carers who need to stay overnight should, where possible, merit a spare room;[220] likewise, applications from prospective fosterers or adopters 'who would require an extra bedroom to accommodate a foster or adoptive child', should lead authorities 'to weigh up the risk that the application to foster or adopt may be unsuccessful (leading to the property being under-occupied), against the wider benefits which would be realised if the placement was successful'.[221] Authorities are encouraged to work with children's services to meet the needs of prospective

217 At [62]–[63].

218 *R (Kabashi) v Redbridge LBC* [2009] EWHC 2984 (Admin), [2011] JHL D1.

219 *R (Bibi) v Camden LBC* [2004] EWHC 2527 (Admin), [2005] HLR 18. See also *Holmes-Moorhouse v Richmond Upon Thames LBC* [2009] UKHL 7, [2009] HLR 34.

220 *Allocation of accommodation: guidance for local housing authorities in England*, para 4.29.

221 *Allocation of accommodation: guidance for local housing authorities in England*, para 4.30.

and approved foster carers and adopters, so that children's services can fulfil their duties under Children Act 1989 s22G, to ensure sufficient accommodation in the area to meet the needs of 'looked after children',[222] eg by setting aside a quota of properties for people who need to move to larger accommodation in order to foster or adopt.[223]

Armed forces

11.90 Authorities are 'strongly encouraged' to take into account the needs of current and former members of the armed forces when determining their allocation policies, 'and to give sympathetic consideration to the housing needs of family members of serving or former service personnel who may have been disadvantaged by the requirements of military service and, in particular, the need to move from base to base'[224] – eg by affording preference to those who have recently left or who are close to leaving the service, or to determine priorities between those with a reasonable preference, or, if using financial resources to determine priorities, disregarding any lump sum received as compensation for injury or disability sustained on active service, or by setting aside a proportion of properties for them under a local lettings policy.[225]

Households in or seeking work

11.91 Authorities are also 'urged' to consider using policies to support households in or seeking work, 'as well as those who – while unable to engage in paid employment – are contributing to their community in other ways, for example, through voluntary work'[226] – eg, by giving preference to those in low paid work, or employment-related training, or greater priority to those with a reasonable preference who

222 See para 13.75.

223 *Allocation of accommodation: guidance for local housing authorities in England*, para 4.31.

224 *Allocation of accommodation: guidance for local housing authorities in England*, para 4.24. See also paras 11.41, 11.64.

225 *Allocation of accommodation: guidance for local housing authorities in England*, para 4.25. As to local lettings, see paras 11.93–11.109.

226 *Allocation of accommodation: guidance for local housing authorities in England*, para 4.27. In *R (XC) v Southwark LBC* [2017] EWHC 736 (Admin) an allocation scheme which gave priority to people who were working or volunteered in the local community was held to be indirectly discriminatory against disabled persons (who would be less likely to be able to work or to volunteer), but that the discrimination was justified. The court considered it significant that the scheme adopted this paragraph of the guidance. See further footnote 92.

are working or actively seeking work, or using local lettings policies to allocate to households 'in particular types of employment where, for example, skills are in short supply',[227] or by using 'flexible tenancies'[228] either to support households in low paid work or to incentivise people 'to take up employment opportunities'.[229]

Under-occupation

11.92 When determining their criteria for property sizes, authorities should take account of the provisions in the Welfare Reform Act 2012 which reduce housing benefit to under-occupiers.[230]

Choice-based and local lettings

11.93 Subject to the 'reasonable preference' categories, the allocation scheme may contain provisions about the allocation of particular housing accommodation either to a person who makes a specific application for it[231] or to persons of a particular description, whether or not within the reasonable preference groups.[232]

11.94 Allocation to persons 'of a particular description' comprises the statutory basis for local lettings policies outside the general priorities of HA 1996 s166A(3) or s167(2).[233]

Procedure

11.95 Allocations are a matter for an authority's executive.[234]

11.96 The secretary of state (in Wales, the Welsh Ministers) may prescribe the principles of procedure to be followed when framing allocation schemes.[235]

227 *Allocation of accommodation: guidance for local housing authorities in England*, para 4.27. As to local lettings, see paras 11.93–11.109.
228 See para 1.113; para 14.10.
229 *Allocation of accommodation: guidance for local housing authorities in England*, para 4.28.
230 *Allocation of accommodation: guidance for local housing authorities in England*, para 4.22; see Housing Benefit Regulations 2006 SI No 213 reg B13; and Universal Credit Regulations 2013 SI No 376 Sch 4.
231 Eg through advertisement and 'bidding'.
232 HA 1996 s166A(6) (England); s167(2E) (Wales).
233 *Allocation of accommodation: guidance for local housing authorities in England*, para 4.21. See further, Welsh Code, para 3.71–3.74 on local lettings policies.
234 See para 9.165.
235 HA 1996 s166A(10) (England); s167(5) (Wales).

11.97 In Wales, local housing authority officers must be included among the persons by whom allocation decisions can be taken, except where an express decision has been made not to delegate the decision, ie, to retain it as an executive decision.[236] In both England and Wales, elected members may not be involved in allocation decisions where the accommodation to be allocated, or the applicant's sole or main residence, is in the member's ward.[237]

Enquiries

11.98 Unlike under HA 1996 Part 7 or H(W)A 2014 Part 2,[238] there is no express provision requiring an authority to make enquiries before determining an application. Nevertheless, a body charged with a statutory function must make or cause to be made such enquiries as will allow it to be satisfied that it can properly discharge its role.[239]

11.99 In *Crowder*,[240] a decision that the applicant's daughter was no longer living with her – and that she should accordingly only be considered for single person accommodation – was quashed because of the authority's failure to make adequate enquiries.

11.100 In *Maali*,[241] the authority's decision was quashed because of flaws in the medical assessment. The claimant, an asthmatic, occupied a third-floor maisonette under a secure tenancy granted by the authority. She occupied the property with her three children, the eldest of whom also suffered from asthma. She applied to the authority to be

236 Local Housing Authorities (Prescribed Principles for Allocation Schemes) (Wales) Regulations 1997 SI No 45 reg 3 and Sch para 2.

237 1997 SI No 45 reg 3 and Sch para 1; and Allocation of Housing (Procedure) Regulations 1997 SI No 483 reg 3. *Allocation of accommodation: guidance for local housing authorities in England*, para 5.8, reminds authorities of this, but at para 5.9 also notes that : 'The regulations do not prevent an elected Member from representing their [sic] constituents in front of the decision making body, or from participating in the decision making body's deliberations prior to its decision. The regulations also do not prevent elected Members' involvement in policy decisions that affect the generality of housing accommodation in their division or electoral ward rather than individual allocations; for example, a decision that certain types of property should be prioritised for older people.' See also Welsh Code paras 4.35–4.37.

238 See paras 9.49–9.60.

239 See *R v Islington LBC ex p Thomas* (1997) 30 HLR 111, QBD, per Roger Henderson QC at 120 (in relation to whether accommodation provided under HA 1985 s65(2) was suitable). See also *Secretary of State for Education and Science v Tameside BC* [1977] AC 1014, per Lord Diplock at 1065.

240 *R v Oxford City Council ex p Crowder* (1998) 31 HLR 485, QBD.

241 *R (Maali) v Lambeth LBC* [2003] EWHC 2231 (Admin), [2003] JHL D83.

transferred to another property, contending that she and her eldest daughter were having difficulty climbing the stairs and that therefore she fell within the emergency medical category (group B) of the authority's allocation scheme. In August 2003, the authority's housing medical adviser concluded that the claimant's and her child's medical conditions were not severe enough to justify the need for an emergency transfer because: i) the fact that the claimant and her child had to climb stairs was positive because exercise helped alleviate the symptoms of asthma; and ii) when the claimant's asthma worsened, she went to stay with friends in order to obtain help with childcare and would continue to do so even if transferred to another property. The authority accordingly assessed her as being within a mainstream category (group D) of its allocation scheme. The court concluded that the assessment was *Wednesbury* unreasonable: the medical adviser had wrongly attributed the claimant's stays with friends to a need for assistance with childcare rather than to the difficulties that she was experiencing in reaching the third floor. Nor was there any basis for the adviser's conclusion that, because exercise was beneficial to asthmatics, the climbing of stairs was positive.

11.101 In *Bauer-Czarnomski*,[242] the applicant lived in a four-bedroom house with his parents, both of whom suffered from mental health problems and required 24-hour assistance which he provided. In 2004, he applied to the authority for his own accommodation and was placed in the lowest band. In 2006, he submitted a report from his doctor which explained that, because he was required to be permanently available to assist his parents, his sleep was frequently disturbed and he was not able to rest, with the result that his own health was being harmed. The authority obtained a report from a different doctor which accepted that the living arrangements had adverse implications for the applicant's health, but went on to advise that there was no need to place him in a higher band as the physical condition of the house did not affect his well-being. In particular, it noted that he had his own bedroom and was able to maintain a degree of independence and separation from other family members. In reliance on that report, the authority refused to put the applicant into a higher band, a decision which was quashed because the authority's medical report had gone beyond an assessment of the applicant's medical need; it had not been for a doctor to advise on the priority to be afforded to him and in taking account of it, the authority therefore had regard to an immaterial and irrelevant consideration; in any event, having

242 *R (Bauer-Czarnomski) v Ealing LBC* [2010] EWHC 130 (Admin), [2010] JHL D38.

regard to the medical evidence, the decision to leave the applicant in band D was perverse.

11.102 In *Adow*,[243] the authority's allocation scheme provided that every application which claimed a medical need would be 'assessed on its merits by the medical assessment officer in the quality and review team'. The applicant was the respondent's tenant in a one-bedroom flat in which she lived with her partner and her four children; she adduced evidence from a paediatrician and her family GP to show that the cramped conditions in which she was living were having an adverse impact on her health and that of her family. The authority – contrary to its policy – did not refer the case to a medical assessment officer, but instead engaged an external doctor to evaluate the medical evidence and make a decision as to her housing needs: the authority accepted that this was unlawful.

Information

Scheme

11.103 Since the HA 1980, authorities have been obliged to publish details of their allocation provisions: see HA 1985 s106. The details must be sufficient both to enable applicants to ascertain how the practices of a local authority will affect them and so that the legality of the practice may be determined.[244] Lack of publication does not, however, make a policy ultra vires.[245]

11.104 There is a similar and overlapping duty under HA 1996 Part 6, that an authority must publish a summary of its scheme and provide

243 *R (Adow) v Newham LBC* [2010] EWHC 951 (Admin), [2010] JHL D101.

244 *R (Faarah) v Southwark LBC* [2008] EWCA Civ 807, [2009] HLR 12 (how registration dates were determined). Cf *R (Yazar) v Southwark LBC* [2008] EWHC 515 (Admin), [2008] JHL D55: it was sufficient for a social services procedure for making housing nominations to be provided in a short and comprehensible form; nor did the social services department have to give reasons for refusing to make a nomination to housing unless asked to do so; and *R (Boolen) v Barking and Dagenham LBC* [2009] EWHC 2196 (Admin), [2009] JHL D113 where the local authority was entitled to adopt its local connection policy so long as it was rational and like cases were treated alike: the policy did not have to be set out in the allocations scheme itself because it was not a central feature of the scheme. See, however, *R (C) v Islington LBC* [2017] EWHC 1288 (Admin), where the scheme wrongly suggested that the applicant could not bid for a property, but there was in fact a separate policy which would have allowed her to do so: the claim for judicial review was allowed on this basis, although not on the basis of the principal challenge (see above, n92). See also para 11.68.

245 *R v Newham LBC ex p Miah* (1995) 28 HLR 279, QBD.

a copy of the summary free of charge to any member of the public who asks for one.[246] The authority must keep the full scheme available for inspection at its principal office, although a reasonable fee may be charged to any member of the public who asks for a copy.[247]

11.105 Where an authority makes an alteration to the scheme reflecting a major change in policy,[248] it must, within a reasonable period, take such steps as it considers reasonable to bring the effect of the alteration to the attention of those likely to be affected by it.[249]

Applications

11.106 The scheme must include a right for an applicant to request such general information as enables him or her to assess how his or her application is likely to be treated under the scheme. This must, in particular, include whether the applicant is likely to be a member of a group to which a preference will be given.[250]

11.107 A person is also entitled to be given general information that will enable him or her to assess whether accommodation appropriate to his or her needs is likely to be made available and, if so, how long it is likely to be before housing accommodation actually becomes available.[251]

11.108 The Welsh Code of Guidance suggests[252] that it is important for authorities to provide 'regular, accurate and generalised information on how housing is allocated and how waiting lists are managed, working actively to dispel any myths and misconceptions which may arise'. English guidance encourages authorities to consider how accurate and anonymised information on waiting list applicants and lettings outcomes could be published.[253]

11.109 The scheme must also afford an applicant the opportunity to request information about any decision about the facts of his or her case.[254]

246 HA 1996 s168(1). This is not confined to a member of the public in the authority's area.

247 HA 1996 s168(2).

248 Cf para 11.73.

249 HA 1996 s168(3).

250 HA 1996 s166A(9)(a)(i) (England); s167(4A)(a)(i) (Wales).

251 HA 1996 s166A(9)(a)(ii) (England); s167(4A)(a)(ii) (Wales).

252 Welsh Code para 3.58.

253 *Providing Social Housing for Local People: Statutory Guidance.*

254 HA 1996 s166A(9)(b) (England); s167A(4A)(c) (Wales).

Internal review and challenge

11.110 An applicant in England has the right to request an internal review of any decision taken under HA 1996 s166A(9)(b) (decision about the facts of his or her case) or under s160ZA(9) (eligibility) and to be notified of the outcome and the grounds for it.[255] Likewise, an applicant in Wales has the same rights in respect of a decision under HA 1996 s167(4A)(b) (unacceptable conduct) or under s160A(9) (eligibility, whether on the grounds of immigration status or conduct).[256]

11.111 Prior to its repeal, HA 1996 s165 permitted regulations to be made governing the conduct of internal reviews under Part 6.[257] There is no such provision in connection with section 166A(9) or section 167(4A). Authorities will nonetheless want to ensure that any review is fair to the applicant.[258] A decision on an application under Part 6 is not, however, a determination of a civil right or obligation for the purposes of Article 6 of the ECHR (right to a fair trial).[259]

11.112 There is no appeal to the county court against the review decision;[260] any challenge has to be by way of judicial review.[261]

11.113 There is, however, nothing to prevent authorities establishing a voluntary review or appeal process that goes beyond the statutory right to review.[262]

11.114 If the authority does add such a voluntary review process, it is likely to be considered necessary for anyone who is dissatisfied with the priority which he or she has been given to use this before seeking judicial review.[263]

255 HA 1996 s166A(9)(c) (England).

256 HA 1996 s167(4A)(d) (Wales).

257 Allocation of Housing and Homelessness (Review Procedures) Regulations 1999 SI No 71.

258 Cf para 12.56.

259 See paras 12.96–12.100.

260 Cf paras 12.159–12.219.

261 See chapter 12.

262 See, eg *R v Southwark LBC ex p Mason* (1999) 32 HLR 88, QBD (panel reviewing the suitability of offers).

263 See chapter 12. The person could, of course, also complain to the local government ombudsman – see paras 12.220–12.226.

Allocations by private registered providers of social housing (England) and registered social landlords (Wales)

11.115 Private registered providers (PRPs) of social housing (England) and registered social landlords (RSLs) (Wales) are obliged to co-operate with local housing authorities in offering accommodation to people with priority under the authority's allocation scheme, to such extent as is reasonable in the circumstances.[264] In practice, many local authorities now maintain no housing stock of their own, but have transferred it either to private registered providers specially formed for the purpose, or to other providers, by way of large-scale voluntary stock transfers, in connection with which they will necessarily have reserved rights to ensure that they can discharge their homelessness duties, ie, by way of nomination. Even where the authority has retained some or all of its housing stock, it is likely also to have nomination arrangements with private registered providers in its area.[265] Such registered providers are amongst the partners with which local authorities will normally develop their homelessness strategies.[266]

11.116 Private registered providers of social housing in England are regulated under Part 2 of the Housing and Regeneration Act (H&RA) 2008;[267] those in Wales[268] are still regulated under HA 1996 Part 1.[269] Registered providers of social housing in England were formerly regulated by the Housing Corporation – which had been the regulator of

264 HA 1996 s170. See also *Allocation of accommodation: guidance for local housing authorities in England*, para 6.1. See also the Housing Association Circular RSL 004/15 (replacing circular RSL 003/12, which itself replaced RLS 023/09) which requires all housing associations registered in Wales to take account of the Welsh Code.

265 *Allocation of accommodation: guidance for local housing authorities in England*, para 6.3: 'Nomination agreements should set out the proportion of lettings that will be made available; any criteria which the Private Registered Provider has adopted for accepting or rejecting nominees; and how any disputes will be resolved. Housing authorities will want to put in place arrangements to monitor effective delivery of the nomination agreement so they can demonstrate they are meeting their obligations under Part 6.' In Wales, see paras 1.7 and 4.18 of the Welsh Code, reminding associations to have regard to the *Regulatory Framework for Housing Associations Registered in Wales*.

266 See paras 14.9–14.17.

267 As amended by LA 2011 Part 7 Chapter 5 and Schs 16 and 17.

268 Still called 'registered social landlords' under HA 1996 Part 1; the term 'registered provider' is, however, used for both England and Wales.

269 Albeit amended in parts by H&RA 2008.

housing associations and trusts since the HA 1974[270] – until it was abolished and replaced[271] by what was statutorily called the Office for Tenants and Social Landlords,[272] known as the Tenant Services Authority (TSA).[273] From 1 April 2012, however, the TSA was itself abolished and its functions transferred to the Regulation Committee of the Homes and Communities Agency (HCA).[274] In Wales, regulation was the responsibility of the National Assembly for Wales ('the Assembly') from 1 July 1999.[275] The regulatory function was transferred to the Welsh Ministers on 1 April 2012.[276] The Welsh Ministers remain responsible for regulation in Wales.

11.117 It is not possible to describe either system of regulation here in any detail,[277] although a small number of matters affecting allocation

270 The original role of the Housing Corporation under HA 1964 was only that of funding a small category of 'housing society' (cost rent and co-ownership).

271 H&RA 2008 s64. The Housing Corporation closed on 30 November 2008 and was replaced by the TSA from 1 December 2008, on which date the regulatory functions of the Housing Corporation transferred to the TSA: Transfer of Housing Corporation Functions (Modifications and Transitional Provisions) Order 2008 SI No 2839. Thereafter, the Housing Corporation was formally dissolved on 1 April 2009: see Housing Corporation (Dissolution) Order 2009 SI No 484.

272 H&RA 2008 s81.

273 It is worth noting that, unlike the former Housing Corporation, the TSA did not have power to provide financial assistance to registered providers; that role is now undertaken by the Homes and Communities Agency (HCA).

274 From 15 January 2012, the HCA was required to set up a Regulation Committee pursuant to H&RA 2008 s94B, brought into force by Localism Act 2011 (Commencement No 2 and Transitional and Saving Provision) Order 2012 SI No 57. The Regulation Committee took over the functions previously undertaken by the TSA on 1 April 2012 – the same date on which the TSA was abolished: see Localism Act 2011 (Commencement No 4 and Transitional, Transitory and Saving Provisions) Order 2012 SI No 628. At time of writing, it is proposed that the regulatory functions of the HCA will be transferred to a new non-departmental public body (see Proposal on using a Legislative Reform Order to establish the social housing regulator as an independent body, DCLG, November 2016) and the HCA will be re-branded as 'Homes England' (see Fixing our broken housing market, DCLG, February 2017).

275 National Assembly for Wales (Transfer of Functions) Order 1999 SI No 672.

276 Housing and Regeneration Act 2008 (Commencement No 7 and Transitional and Saving Provisions) Order 2010 SI No 862 Article 2. The Welsh Ministers remain the 'relevant authority' for the purposes of HA 1996 Part 1. The regulatory framework is that published in 2011.

277 See, generally, Arden and Partington's *Housing Law*, Sweet & Maxwell, paras 1-203 onwards; and *Manual of Housing Law*, 10th edn, Arden & Dymond, chapter 8. In general terms, the HCA may set managements standards requiring local authorities and PRPs to comply with rules about, inter alia, allocating accommodation (H&RA 2008 s193, as amended by LA 2011); the

are considered below.[278] It suffices to say that registered providers are subject to regulatory regimes under one or other Act – HA 1996 or H&RA 2008. This means that, while not subject to direct statutory rules on allocation in the same way that local authorities are, their actions, including in relation to allocations, are nonetheless susceptible to review by their regulators and, in turn, susceptible to complaints to those regulators by those adversely affected by their actions and/or inaction.[279] Regulators have a range of sanctions available, including powers of inspection of performance by and/or enquiry into private registered providers, extending ultimately to the de-registration or winding up of providers whose performance is inadequate.[280]

11.118 Complaints can also be made to an independent scheme approved by the secretary of state.[281] HA 1996 Sch 2 sets out the general provisions governing the membership, approval and registration of such a scheme. In England, the Housing Ombudsman Service (HOS) is the approved scheme of which every social landlord must be a member.[282] Failure to comply with the requirement to be a member of the scheme may result in an application to the High Court by the secretary of state for an order directing the provider to comply.[283]

11.119 Where a complaint is made to the HOS,[284] the ombudsman has the power to investigate and determine that complaint by reference to what is, in the opinion of the ombudsman, 'fair in all the

standards are presently contained in Tenancy Involvement and Empowerment Standard (April 2012).

278 See paras 11.121–11.130.

279 In some cases, contracts governing the transfer of stock from authorities to registered providers may themselves contain complaint provisions and – although not commonly – even provisions enabling direct enforcement, although this is unlikely to assist a would-be tenant complaining of failure to allocate and/or disappointed with the nature of an allocation so much as an existing tenant. In such circumstances, an existing tenant seeking a transfer may be able to avail himself or herself of such provisions.

280 See H&RA 2008 Part 1 Chapters 4, 6 and 7; HA 1996 Part 1 and Sch 1.The enforcement powers are different as between local authorities and PRPs, for example, the HCA can require a PRP (but not a local authority) to transfer its stock to another PRP (H&RA 2008 s253).

281 HA 1996 Sch 2 para 3. In Wales, the function was transferred to the Public Services Ombudsman in 2006.

282 HA 1996 Sch 2 para 1(1). If the relevant provisions of the LA 2011 are ever brought into force, local authorities will also fall within the jurisdiction of the housing ombudsman, see para 12.222.

283 HA 1996 Sch 2 para 1(2).

284 As to which, see para 12.228 as to the procedure for making a complaint through a 'designated person' rather than directly.

circumstances of the case'.[285] If the complaint is upheld, the ombudsman has the power to order the private relevant registered provider of social housing to pay compensation to the complainant or even to order that the member or the complainant is not to exercise or require the performance of contractual or other obligations or rights existing between them.[286] If the private registered provider fails to comply with the ombudsman's determination, the ombudsman has the power to order the private registered provider to publish that failure in such manner as he or she sees fit.[287] If the private registered provider fails to comply with the order to publish, the ombudsman has the power to take such steps as he or she thinks appropriate to publish what the private registered provider ought to have published and to recover the costs of doing so from the provider.[288]

11.120 It has been held that private registered providers may qualify as public authorities within the Human Rights Act 1998, in respect of some aspects of their management of their social housing stock (including service of notice to quit or of seeking possession) and, in addition to the requirement to conform to the ECHR rights, that in such circumstances they are also susceptible to the principles of domestic public law in respect of such activities, even if they would not otherwise be capable of challenge on that basis.[289]

11.121 At first instance, those aspects explicitly included the allocation of social housing; while this was not overruled per se, it was not the basis on which the decision that such providers may be public authorities for the purposes of the Human Rights Act 1998 was upheld: rather, it was held that service of notice to quit or to seek possession is a public function for the purposes of that Act, which means that registered providers are public authorities in respect of such service; while allocation was not directly in issue, however, it seems also to qualify; and, in *R (McIntyre) v Gentoo Group Ltd*,[290] it was held to include allocation. Whether or not other acts of management qualify may well depend on a detailed investigation into and assessment of

285 HA 1996 Sch 2 para 7.

286 HA 1996 Sch 2 para 7(2). There is no power to enforce against the complainant.

287 HA 1996 Sch 2 para 7(3).

288 HA 1996 Sch 2 para 7(5).

289 *R (Weaver) v London & Quadrant Housing Trust* [2008] EWHC 1377 (Admin), [2008] JHL D94 and on appeal [2009] EWCA Civ 587, [2010] 1 WLR 363, [2009] HLR 40. See para 12.8. The proposition as to susceptibility was conceded on appeal.

290 [2010] EWHC 5 (Admin), [2010] JHL D22 and D40, in particular at [25].

the functions of allocating and managing housing of the particular registered provider.[291]

England

11.122 The Regulation Committee of the HCA enjoys a range of powers in relation to the provision of social housing, including that of setting standards, which may include requiring registered providers to comply with rules about, inter alia, allocation criteria,[292] in relation to which it may issue codes of practice amplifying the standard.[293] The statutory objectives of the Regulation Committee include economic and consumer objectives, the latter of which include ensuring that actual or potential tenants of social housing have an appropriate degree of choice and protection.[294]

11.123 The secretary of state may direct the HCA to issue a standard, or make directions about its content or to require regard to be had to specified objectives when setting a standard.[295] The Regulation Committee must comply with any such direction.[296] Standards issued by the HCA may require registered providers of social housing to comply with specified rules about a wide range of matters including criteria for allocating accommodation.[297]

11.124 Failure to meet a standard is a ground for action by the Regulation Committee,[298] including enforcement powers ranging from notices, fines and compensation, to orders to require the appointment of a manager over the whole of a registered provider's functions or specified functions, or the transfer of functions to another, and to the removal or suspension of officers or employees or their disqualification.[299]

11.125 Specific provision is made for the Regulation Committee to exercise any of the powers of regulation where there is a failure (or an

291 *Weaver* at [68]–[72]. See also *Aston Cantlow and Wilmcote with Billisley Parochial Church Council v Wallbank* [2003] UKHL 37, [2004] 1 AC 546.
292 H&RA 2008 s193(2)(a).
293 H&RA 2008 s195.
294 H&RA 2008 s92K.
295 H&RA 2008 s197.
296 H&RA 2008 s197(7).
297 H&RA 2008 s193(2)(a).
298 H&RA 2008 s198.
299 H&RA 2008 Part 1 Chapter 7. The enforcement powers are different as between Local Authorities and PRPs: eg the HCA can require a PRP to transfer stock to another PRP but cannot require a local authority to transfer its stock (H&RA 2008 s253).

anticipated failure) to meet any of the consumer standards where the Regulation Committee has reason to believe that there has been or may be a serious detriment caused to a tenant or potential tenant.[300]

11.126 In March 2015, the Regulation Committee issued *The regulatory framework for social housing in England from April 2015*[301] which took effect from 1 April 2015. The framework covers key areas of regulation including the regulation of consumer standards. The framework specifies outcomes and expectations of standards relating to economic and consumer standards that reflect the statutory objectives of the HCA.[302]

Wales

11.127 The statutory framework governing registered providers[303] in Wales under HA 1996 Part 1 has been the responsibility of the Welsh Ministers since 1 April 2010.[304] The Welsh Ministers have responsibility for maintaining a register of providers, financial regulation, setting of performance standards and the power to issue guidance. The Welsh Ministers also now have some enforcement powers, although not as extensive as the powers granted to the HCA. From October 2011, the Welsh Ministers have had the power to set standards to be met by registered social landlords in Wales.[305] Welsh Ministers have the power to issue guidance that relates to a matter addressed by a standard and which amplifies the standard.[306]

11.128 In December 2011, the Welsh Ministers issued *The regulatory framework for housing associations registered in Wales*[307] ('Welsh Framework'). The purpose of the Welsh Framework is to 'ensure that housing associations provide good quality homes and services to tenants and others who use their services'.[308] The framework does not set out any expectations that relate specifically to allocations, but its principles include close working relationships between the Welsh

300 H&RA 2008 ss198A, 198B.

301 The Social Housing Regulator, March 2015. It replaced the 2012 guidance.

302 H&RA 2008 s92K. See para 11.121.

303 Ie RSLs. For the position in respect of Welsh local housing authorities, see H(W)A 2014 Part 4.

304 Prior to that, it was the responsibility of the Welsh Assembly. See para 11.116.

305 HA 1996 s33A.

306 HA 1996 s33B.

307 Pursuant to HA 1996 s36.

308 Welsh Framework para 1.9.

Ministers, housing associations, their tenants and service users and their key partners.[309]

11.129 Enforcement powers include service of an enforcement notice in specified cases,[310] prosecution in relation to matters relied on in enforcement notices,[311] imposition of penalties,[312] and a power to require a landlord to pay compensation to an affected person for failure to meet a standard or comply with an undertaking given by a landlord to the Welsh Ministers.[313] The Welsh Ministers also have powers of inspection[314] and inquiry[315] into the affairs of landlords. There is also power for Welsh Ministers to remove[316] and appoint[317] officers in certain circumstances, to petition for the winding up of a registered social landlord[318] and to take control of assets following dissolution or winding up of a landlord.[319]

11.130 Housing Association Circular RSL 004/15 requires all housing associations registered in Wales to take account of the Welsh Code (ie the Code under Part 6) governing allocations[320] when 'addressing key delivery outcomes' for the Welsh Framework.

309 Welsh Framework para 2.1.
310 HA 1996 s50C.
311 HA 1996 s50G.
312 HA 1996 s50H.
313 HA 1996 s50O.
314 HA 1996 Sch 1 Part 3A.
315 HA 1996 Sch 1 Part 4.
316 HA 1996 Sch 1 Part 2 para 4.
317 HA 1996 Sch 1 Part 2 paras 6–8.
318 HA 1996 Sch 1 Part 2 para 14.
319 HA 1996 Sch 1 Part 2 paras 15–15A.
320 See para 11.8.

CHAPTER 12

Enforcement

12.1 Introduction

12.5 Substantive law

12.5 Introduction

12.12 The nature of a challenge

12.16 Ultra vires

12.20 The general principles of administrative law

Wednesbury • CCSU

12.23 Human Rights Act 1998 and proportionality

12.31 Grounds for challenge – practical classification

Illegality • Irrationality • Procedural impropriety

12.95 Human Rights Act 1998

Article 6 • Article 8 • Article 14

12.106 Procedural law

12.106 Introduction

12.107 Which court?

12.116 Judicial review

Procedure • Remedies and relief • Confidentiality

12.159 Appeal to county court

Procedure • Remedies and relief

12.220 Ombudsman

12.234 Annex: Specimen documents

Introduction

12.1 Housing Act (HA) 1996 Parts 6 and 7 and Housing (Wales) Act (H(W)A) 2014 Part 2 all contain provision for the *internal* review of decisions, which are considered elsewhere in this book.[1] This chapter is concerned with the *external* enforcement of an applicant's rights, ie, what an applicant, who remains dissatisfied with the decision of the authority after internal review, can do to challenge or change it by way of recourse to the courts or the ombudsman.

12.2 The only route available to a dissatisfied applicant for an allocation of housing under HA 1996 Part 6 is by way of a claim for judicial review in the High Court, which means that permission must be obtained from the court to bring the claim; HA 1996 Part 7 and H(W)A 2014 Part 2, however, provide for a statutory appeal to the county court[2] on a 'point of law' but as of right, and this is the procedure that will normally be used in homelessness cases, although there are circumstances in which judicial review either remains available or may be the only recourse.[3]

12.3 The divergence is practical rather than substantive because an appeal on a point of confers on the county court a like jurisdiction to that available on a claim for judicial review, engaging the same legal basis for challenge.

12.4 This chapter is divided into two parts: The first part contains the substantive law, applicable either on judicial review or on statutory appeal. The second part deals with the procedure governing how to bring a claim in either court and when to do so. In an annex, a number of specimen documents have been produced, both to illustrate the principles under consideration here, and to assist when applying them.

Substantive law

Introduction

12.5 The general principles which underlie a challenge on a point of law are those of administrative – or public – law, which have been largely,

1 Discussed in chapter 11 (HA 1996 Part 6) and chapter 10 (HA 1996 Part 7 and H(W)A 2014 Part 2).

2 HA 1996 s204; H(W)A 2014 s88.

3 Para 12.112.

but far from exclusively,[4] developed in the course of proceedings for judicial review, and comprise a significant area of law in its own right.[5] The overwhelming bulk of homelessness and allocations case-law is of this order, ie an illustration of the operation of the principles of administrative law, in relation to the statutes governing homelessness and allocations: the issue is whether the decision reached can be said to be *ultra vires*, ie outwith the powers of the body making the decision, rather than whether or not it is the decision which the court would have reached on an application. This is so regardless of whether the challenge is brought by way of judicial review or as a statutory appeal.[6]

12.6 The underlying principles of administrative law – developed across a range of areas of law and the activities of government, central and local – are accordingly relevant when determining appeals as they are on judicial review; conversely, the jurisprudence that the courts develop in the contexts of homelessness appeals has itself added to the general body of administrative law, as well as contributing to the growth of housing law.

12.7 Domestic administrative law includes the obligations imposed on public bodies by the Human Rights Act (HRA) 1998 and the rights from the European Convention on Human Rights ('the Convention'/ ECHR) that the HRA 1998 imports. This has three consequences: first, it adds to the categories of illegality – if an administrative law decision is unlawful under the provisions of HRA 1998, it is ultra vires; second, it reinforces and develops existing administrative law; third, public authorities within its purview include registered providers of social housing in respect of some aspects of their management of social housing stock (including service of notice to quit or of seeking possession), which means that, in addition to the requirement

4 The important Court of Appeal decision in *Crédit Suisse v Allerdale MBC* [1997] QB 306, [1996] 4 All ER 129, CA, was an appeal from a decision of the Commercial Court; *Boddington v British Transport Police* [1999] 2 AC 143, HL, was a criminal prosecution.

5 See the two leading text-books in the area: Wade and Forsyth, *Administrative law*, 11th edn, OUP, 2014; and de Smith, Woolf and Jowell, *Judicial review of administrative action*, 7th edn, Sweet & Maxwell, 2016.

6 *Nipa Begum v Tower Hamlets LBC* [2000] 1 WLR 306, (2000) 32 HLR 445, CA, approved by the House of Lords in *Runa Begum v Tower Hamlets LBC* [2003] UKHL 5, [2003] 2 AC 430, [2003] HLR 32, see particularly Lord Bingham at [7]. *Runa Begum* was followed in *Ali v Birmingham City Council* [2010] UKSC 8, [2010] HLR 22. This did not, however, allow a firm of solicitors with a Legal Aid Agency contract for public law work (but not housing) to conduct HA 1996 s204 appeals: *Bhatia Best Ltd v Lord Chancellor* [2014] EWHC 746 (QB), [2014] 1 WLR 3487.

to conform to the Convention rights, they are (in these respects) also susceptible to the principles of domestic public law, even if they would not otherwise be.[7] At least so far as it has yet developed in housing law,[8] and even though it may be its less well-known point of reference, it is the second impact of HRA 1998 with which we are most concerned here – its own influence on the development of domestic administrative law.[9]

12.8 This developing – and expanding – body of 'administrative law' is that with which this part of this chapter is concerned. It is addressed as follows.

a) the nature of a challenge;
b) the general principles of administrative law;
c) substantive grounds for challenge;
d) procedural grounds for challenge.

12.9 This caveat needs to be entered at the start. Public law is not about absolutes: many aspects of it engage degrees of right and wrong, which will depend on the facts of the individual challenge, rather than 'rules': as it has been said, 'in law, context is everything'.[10]

12.10 Thus, a general duty to make enquiries will differ depending on the context: a duty to make enquiries under the homelessness provisions will import different practical obligations than will a duty to make enquiries into another, entirely different area – for example, a

7 *R (Weaver) v London & Quadrant Housing Trust* [2008] EWHC 1377, [2008] JHL D94 and on appeal [2009] EWCA Civ 587, [2010] 1 WLR 363, [2009] HLR 40. The proposition as to susceptibility was conceded. The decision of the High Court that the public functions of registered providers extend to the management and allocation of social housing, while not overruled per se, was not the basis on which the decision that they are public authorities for the purposes of the HRA 1998 was upheld: nonetheless, allocation would seem also to qualify as a public function (see in particular *Weaver* at [76]) and it is not difficult to argue that other acts of management will also do so. In *R (Macleod) v Peabody Trust Governors* [2016] EWHC 737 (Admin), [2016] HLR 27, it was held that the association was not amenable to judicial review in connection with the refusal to allow an assignment of a tenancy which, however, did not fall to be treated as social housing because i) it had been acquired by the association without the use of any public funds; ii) although the rent was not a full market rent, it was nonetheless higher than would have been the case in social housing; and iii) it was not made accommodation which was provided in order to meet the needs of people who were not adequately served by the commercial market, see *Macleod* at [20] and Housing and Regeneration Act 2008 s69.

8 See paras 12.95–12.105.

9 See paras 12.24–12.30.

10 *R (Daly) v Secretary of State for the Home Department* [2001] UKHL 26, [2001] 2 AC 532.

police enquiry into the commission of a crime (hence, the proposition that local authority enquiries do not have to amount to 'CID-type enquiries').[11] Likewise, and plainly, what is factually relevant to one area of activity will not necessarily be relevant to another.

12.11 Because administrative law derives from a variety of sources and is applied to (and therefore continues to be developed in relation to) a wide range of activities, many of which are very far from the specific issues raised by HA 1996 Parts 6 and 7 and H(W)A 2014 Part 2, cases which have been developed in other areas do need to be treated with some caution: there may be more room for manoeuvre (either way) over how they function under Parts 6, 7 or 2 than may at first appear. Decisions on the specific statutory provisions are one thing; decisions on principles of decision-making quite another.

The nature of a challenge

12.12 At the heart of administrative law is the proposition that Parliament intends public bodies always to act properly, in the sense of reasonably and lawfully. The role of the courts is, however, supervisory rather than appellate: the court[12] must review the decision-making processes of the body in question, rather than determine for itself what decision the authority should make.[13] Provided that the authority does not err in how it reaches the decision,[14] the substance of the

11 *Lally v Kensington and Chelsea RLBC* (1980) *Times* 26 March, QBD.

12 Whether Administrative Court on judicial review or county court on appeal. The Court of Appeal has expressed its disapproval of county court judges who have overstepped their role (*Kruja v Enfield LBC* [2004] EWCA Civ 1769, [2005] HLR 13 – see para 12.151) and emphasised that decision-making on matters such as the vulnerability of applicants is for the local authority: *Osmani v Camden LBC* [2004] EWCA Civ 1706, [2005] HLR 22.

13 See, eg *R v Northumberland Compensation Appeal Tribunal ex p Shaw* [1952] 1 KB 338, CA, per Denning LJ at 346–7: 'The Court of King's Bench has an inherent jurisdiction to control all inferior tribunals, not in an appellate capacity but in a supervisory capacity. This control extends not only to seeing that the inferior tribunals keep within their jurisdiction, but also to seeing that they observe the law . . . The King's Bench does not substitute its own views for those of the tribunal, as a Court of Appeal would do. It leaves it to the tribunal to hear the case again, and in a proper case may command it to do so.' See also *R v Secretary of State for Trade and Industry ex p Lonrho plc* [1989] 1 WLR 525, HL per Lord Keith of Kinkel at 535: 'The question is not whether the Secretary of State came to . . . a conclusion which meets with the approval of the . . . Court but whether the discretion was properly exercised.' This is the same approach as the appellate court adopts when considering an appeal against a discretionary decision of a judge: eg, *Woodspring DC v Taylor* (1982) 4 HLR 95.

14 In any of the acknowledged senses – see paras 12.16–12.105.

decision is for the authority, not for the court, and it is the authority's view or decision which must prevail.[15] There is rarely only one decision which an authority may reach: one individual's view of what is reasonable will often quite properly differ from that of another, and parliament has entrusted decision-making under HA 1996 Parts 6 and 7 and H(W)A 2014 Part 2 to authorities, not to the courts.

12.13 In *Puhlhofer*,[16] Lord Brightman said, at 518:

> I am troubled at the prolific use of judicial review for the purpose of challenging the performance by local authorities of their functions under the Act of 1977. Parliament intended the local authority to be the judge of fact. The Act abounds with the formula when, or if, the housing authority are satisfied as to this, or that, or have reason to believe this, or that. Although the action or inaction of a local authority is clearly susceptible to judicial review where they have misconstrued the Act, or abused their powers or otherwise acted perversely, I think that great restraint should be exercised in giving leave to proceed by judicial review. The plight of the homeless is a desperate one, and the plight of the applicants in the present case commands the deepest sympathy. But it is not, in my opinion, appropriate that the remedy of judicial review, which is a discretionary remedy, should be made use of to monitor the actions of local authorities under the Act save in the exceptional case. The ground upon which the courts will review the exercise of an administrative discretion is abuse of power, for example, bad faith, a mistake in construing the limits of the power, a procedural irregularity, or unreasonableness in the *Wednesbury*[17] sense – unreasonableness verging on an absurdity: see the speech of Lord Scarman in *R v Secretary of State for the Environment ex p Nottinghamshire CC*.[18] Where the existence or non-existence of a fact is left to

15 See, eg *R v Secretary of State for the Home Department ex p Khawaja* [1984] AC 74, HL per Lord Scarman at 100, referring to the *Wednesbury* principle: 'The principle excluded the court from substituting its own view of the facts for that of the authority'; *R v Secretary of State for the Home Department ex p Brind* [1991] AC 696, HL per Lord Lowry at 767: 'The judges are not, generally speaking, equipped by training or experience or furnished with the necessary knowledge and advice, to decide the answer to an administrative problem where the scales are evenly balanced, but they have a much better chance of reaching the right answer where the question is put in a *Wednesbury* form'; see also *Wednesbury* itself, below, footnote 17 and para 12.20, where Lord Greene MR, at 234, refers to the court as 'a judicial authority which is concerned, and concerned only, to see whether the local authority have contravened the law by acting in excess of the powers which Parliament has confided in them'.

16 *R v Hillingdon LBC ex p Puhlhofer* [1986] AC 484, (1986) 18 HLR 158, HL.

17 *Associated Provincial Picture Houses Ltd v Wednesbury Corporation* [1948] 1 KB 223, CA.

18 *Nottinghamshire CC v Secretary of State for the Environment* [1986] 1 AC 240, HL.

the judgment and discretion of a public body and that fact involves a broad spectrum ranging from the obvious to the debatable to the just conceivable, it is the duty of the court to leave the decision of that fact to the public body to whom Parliament has entrusted the decision-making power save in a case where it is obvious that the public body, consciously or unconsciously, are acting perversely.

. . . I express the hope that there will be a lessening in the number of challenges which are mounted against local authorities who are endeavouring, in extremely difficult circumstances, to perform their duties under the Homeless Persons Act with due regard for all their other housing problems.[19]

12.14 There are echoes of this in the HA 1996 Part 6 decision of the House of Lords in *R (Ahmad) v Newham LBC*.[20]

46. . . . [A]s a general proposition, it is undesirable for the courts to get involved in questions of how priorities are accorded in housing allocation policies. Of course, there will be cases where the court has a duty to interfere, for instance if a policy does not comply with statutory requirements, or if it is plainly irrational. However, it seems unlikely that the legislature can have intended that Judges should embark on the exercise of telling authorities how to decide on priorities as between applicants in need of rehousing, save in relatively rare and extreme circumstances. Housing allocation policy is a difficult exercise which requires not only social and political sensitivity and judgment, but also local expertise and knowledge.

47. In relation to the provision of accommodation under the National Assistance Act 1948, my noble and learned friend, Baroness Hale of Richmond, then Hale LJ, said in *R (Wahid) v Tower Hamlets LBC*[21] '[n]eed is a relative concept, which trained and experienced social workers are much better equipped to assess than are lawyers and courts, provided that they act rationally'. Precisely the same is true of relative housing needs under Part 6 of the 1996 Act, and trained and experienced local authority housing officers.

48. If section 167 carries with it the sort of requirements which can be said to be implied by the decisions of the Court of Appeal and the Deputy Judge in this case, then Judges would become involved in considering details of housing allocation schemes in a way which would be both unrealistic and undesirable . . .

. . .

19 The same principles apply on a statutory appeal – the county court must at all times bear in mind the public law exercise in which it is engaged: *Crawley BC v B* (2000) 32 HLR 636, CA.

20 [2009] UKHL 14, [2009] NPC 36.

21 [2002] EWCA Civ 287, [2003] HLR 2 at [33].

55. This is not to say that there could never be circumstances in which a scheme, which complies with the statutory requirements, could be susceptible to judicial review on grounds of irrationality. Such a suggestion would be unmaintainable not least because it would represent an abdication of judicial responsibility. However, what is important is to emphasise that once a housing allocation scheme complies with the requirements of section 167 and any other statutory requirements, the courts should be very slow to interfere on the ground of alleged irrationality.

12.15 The discretion conferred by parliament, embodied in this more limited,[22] supervisory approach, does not lead to the conclusion that an authority's decision under HA 1996 Part 6 or Part 7 or H(W)A 2014 Part 2 is above reproach.[23] It is the purpose of public law to ensure that public authorities, entrusted with an apparently blanket power to reach 'subjective' decisions, nonetheless do so in accordance with the law. A discretionary decision may still be ultra vires and without effect in law: it may be unreasonable in the *Wednesbury* sense – ie, a decision which no reasonable authority, properly directing itself, could have reached; it may be a decision that is contrary to the law; it may be a decision which has been reached without affording the applicant his or her due procedural safeguards; or it may be a decision which is not based on all the relevant information.

Ultra vires

12.16 Local authorities may only act within their powers. If they do not do so, they are acting unlawfully, and their actions and decisions will be so treated[24] – this is the ultra vires doctrine and a decision so made will be unlawful because:

a) on the face of the statute there was no authority to engage in the action at all; or
b) the statute has been misconstrued; or
c) the authority has misapplied the statute, for example, by failing to use the powers to implement the purpose of the statute; or

22 Than when an appeal approach allows a court to substitute its own view of the facts.

23 See per Lord Wilberforce in *Secretary of State for Education and Science v Tameside MBC* [1977] AC 1014, HL, at 1047: 'The section is framed in a "subjective" form . . . This form of section is quite well-known and *at first sight* might seem to exclude judicial review . . .' (emphasis added).

24 Subject to issues of forum: cf *Wandsworth LBC v Winder* [1985] AC 461, HL; *Avon CC v Buscott* [1988] QB 656, CA; and *Hackney LBC v Lambourne* (1992) 25 HLR 172, CA; *Manchester City Council v Cochrane* [1999] 1 WLR 809, CA.

d) a decision has been reached under the statute by reference to something which is irrelevant, or in ignorance of something which is relevant, to the way the power under the statute is intended to be operated, or which is so unreasonable – or irrational or perverse – that no reasonable authority could have reached it.

12.17 If it can be shown that a public body such as a local authority has approached its decision unlawfully then, regardless of the reason, the decision will be void and the courts will not give effect to it.

12.18 The propositions in the last two paragraphs assume:

a) that there are no differences between the legal consequences of decisions which there was no power at all to take (ie, those which are said to be outside the four corners of a statute) and those which there was power to take but which have been taken in some way improperly;[25] and
b) that once it is decided that a decision was ultra vires, it must be treated as if it had at all times been void for all purposes.

12.19 There have been several cases which have considered these two (overlapping) issues, and they are issues which will doubtless continue to be discussed.[26] For the purposes of this book, however, those propositions normally probably suffice in practice.[27]

25 See, in particular, *Crédit Suisse plc v Allerdale MBC* [1997] QB 306, CA, per Neill LJ at 343: 'I know of no authority for the proposition that the *ultra vires* decisions of local authority can be classified into categories of invalidity . . .' But cf *Charles Terence Estates Ltd v Cornwall CC* [2012] EWCA Civ 1439, [2013] 1 WLR 466, [2013] HLR 12, at [27]–[37], [44]–[53].

26 *Anisminic Ltd v Foreign Compensation Commission* [1969] 2 AC 147, HL, would nonetheless seem to be definitive: a decision wrongly reached, for whatever reason, was considered to be void and a nullity, because decision-makers have no jurisdiction to make unlawful decisions (see, in particular, per Lord Reid, at 171, using similar terms to describe unlawfulness as the classic definition by Lord Greene MR in *Wednesbury*, see para 12.20). In *Boddington v British Transport Police* [1999] 2 AC 143, HL, however, the majority of the Committee was not willing simply to assume invalidity for all purposes and at all times, because people would in the meantime have regulated their lives on the basis of a decision's validity.

27 It today appears to be accepted in homelessness law that a decision improperly taken may be retaken: see *Crawley LBC v B*, above (see further para 12.207); *Porteous v West Dorset DC* [2004] EWCA Civ 244, HLR 30 at [7]–[9] (fundamental mistake of fact); and *Islington LBC v Uckac* [2006] EWCA Civ 340, [2006] HLR 35 (on mistake of fact, but by counsel's concession). Although the discussion in *Porteous* is in terms of revisiting and changing or rescinding an earlier decision, the basis of the argument in both cases was that the earlier decision was void and it is hard to see any other basis: unless void, the authority is what is known as functus officio, ie, it has no further function – it has had an application and it has reached its decision.

The general principles of administrative law

Wednesbury

12.20 The classic statement of the court's role and function when addressing public law issues is that of Lord Greene MR in *Wednesbury*:[28]

> What, then, is the power of the courts? They can only interfere with an act of executive authority if it be shown that the authority has - contravened the law. It is for those who assert that the local authority has contravened the law to establish that proposition . . . It is not to be assumed prima facie that responsible bodies like the local authority in this case will exceed their powers; but the court, whenever it is alleged that the local authority have contravened the law, must not substitute itself for that authority . . . When an executive discretion is entrusted by Parliament to a body such as the local authority in this case, what appears to be an exercise of that discretion can only be challenged in the courts in a strictly limited class of case . . . When discretion of this kind is granted the law recognises certain principles upon which that discretion must be exercised, but within the four corners of those principles the discretion . . . is an absolute one and cannot be questioned in any court of law. What then are those principles? They are well understood. They are principles which the court looks to in considering any question of discretion of this kind. The exercise of such a discretion must be a real exercise of the discretion. If, in the statute conferring the discretion, there is to be found expressly or by implication matters which the authority exercising the discretion ought to have regard to, then in exercising the discretion it must have regard to those matters. Conversely, if the nature of the subject-matter and the general interpretation of the Act make it clear that certain matters would not be germane to the matter in question, the authority must disregard those irrelevant collateral matters. [at 228]
>
> There have been in the cases expressions used relating to the sort of things that authorities must not do . . . I am not sure myself whether the permissible grounds of attack cannot be defined under a single head . . . Bad faith, dishonesty – those of course, stand by themselves – unreasonableness, attention given to extraneous circumstances, disregard of public policy and things like that have all been referred to, according to the facts of individual cases, as being matters which are relevant to the question. If they cannot all be confined under one head, they at any rate . . . overlap to a very great extent. For instance, we have heard in this case a great deal about the meaning of the word 'unreasonable'.
>
> It is true the discretion must be exercised reasonably. Now what does that mean? . . . It has frequently been used and is frequently

28 *Associated Provincial Picture Houses Ltd v Wednesbury Corporation* [1948] 1 KB 223, CA.

used as a general description of the things that must not be done . . . A person entrusted with a discretion must . . . direct himself properly in law. He must call his own attention to the matters which he is bound to consider. He must exclude from his consideration matters which are irrelevant to what he has to consider. If he does not obey those rules, he may truly be said, and often is said, to be acting 'unreasonably'. Similarly, there may be something so absurd that no sensible person could ever dream that it lay within the powers of the authority. Warrington LJ in *Short v Poole Corporation*[29] gave the example of the red-haired teacher, dismissed because she had red hair. That is unreasonable in one sense. In another sense it is taking into consideration extraneous matters. It is so unreasonable that it might almost be described as being done in bad faith; and, in fact, all these things run into one another . . . [at 229]

It is true to say that, if a decision on a competent matter is so unreasonable that no reasonable authority could ever have come to it, then the courts can interfere . . . But to prove a case of that kind would require something overwhelming . . . [The] proposition that the decision of the local authority can be upset if it is proved to be unreasonable, really meant that it must be proved to be unreasonable in the sense that the court considers it to be a decision that no reasonable body could have come to. It is not what the court considers unreasonable, a different thing altogether . . . The effect of the legislation is not to set up the court as an arbiter of the correctness of one view over another. It is the local authority that are set in that position and, provided they act, as they have acted, within the four corners of their jurisdiction, this court . . . cannot interfere . . . [at 230–231]

The court is entitled to investigate the action of the local authority with a view to seeing whether they have taken into account matters which they ought not to take into account, or, conversely, have refused to take into account or neglected to take into account matters which they ought to take into account. Once that question is answered in favour of the local authority, it may still be possible to say that, although the local authority have kept within the four corners of the matters which they ought to consider, they have nevertheless come to a conclusion so unreasonable that no reasonable authority could ever have come to it. In such a case, again, I think the court can interfere. The power of the court to interfere in each case is not as an appellate authority to override a decision of the local authority, but as a judicial authority which is concerned, and concerned only, to see whether the local authority have contravened the law by acting in excess of the powers which Parliament has confided in them. [at 233–234]

12.21 This statement, in particular the last passage, remains the cornerstone of domestic administrative law.

29 [1926] Ch 66, CA.

CCSU

12.22 The central principles of public law derived from Lord Greene's comments in *Wednesbury* were subsequently re-classified by Lord Diplock under the headings of 'illegality', 'irrationality' and 'procedural impropriety' in *CCSU*:[30]

> By 'illegality' as a ground of judicial review I mean that the decision-maker must understand correctly the law that regulates his decision-making power and must give effect to it. Whether he has or not is par excellence a justiciable question to be decided, in the event of dispute, by those persons, the judges, by whom the judicial power of the state is exercisable.
>
> By 'irrationality' I mean what can by now be succinctly referred to as '*Wednesbury* unreasonableness' . . . It applies to a decision which is so outrageous in its defiance of logic or of accepted moral standards that no sensible person who had applied his mind to the question to be decided could have arrived at it. Whether a decision falls within this category is a question that judges by their training and experience should be well-equipped to answer, or else there would be something badly wrong with our judicial system . . . 'Irrationality' by now can stand upon its own feet as an accepted ground on which a decision may be attacked by judicial review.
>
> I have described the third head as 'procedural impropriety' rather than failure to observe basic rules of natural justice or failure to act with procedural fairness towards the person who will be affected by the decision. This is because susceptibility to judicial review under this head covers also failure by an administrative tribunal to observe procedural rules that are expressly laid down in the legislative instrument by which its jurisdiction is conferred, even where such failure does not involve any denial of natural justice . . .

Human Rights Act 1998 and proportionality

12.23 As noted above,[31] HRA 1998 is relevant in a number of ways, including, first, that it imports specific articles of the ECHR; and, second, because of its influence on the development of the principles of

30 *Council of Civil Service Unions v Minister for the Civil Service* [1985] 1 AC 374, HL ('*CCSU*'). The statement was described by Lord Scarman as 'a valuable and already "classical"' statement of the law, albeit 'certainly not exhaustive': *R v Secretary of State for the Environment ex p Nottinghamshire CC* [1986] AC 240, HL at 249.

31 See para 12.7.

domestic administrative law. It is the second of these aspects which is relevant under this heading. The first is considered below.[32]

12.24 In *CCSU*,[33] Lord Diplock had raised – but did not answer – the question whether or not the principle of 'proportionality'[34] might be imported into domestic law from Europe.[35]

12.25 From the early 1990s, doubt began to be cast on whether the *Wednesbury* test – affording a decision-maker a wide ambit of discretion – was suitable to deal with cases that involved what were recognisable as fundamental rights, and it began to be suggested that the *Wednesbury* test required adaptation so as to subject such cases to what has been called 'anxious scrutiny',[36] requiring a closer degree of factual scrutiny than the conventional *Wednesbury* approach.[37]

12.26 Comparing the differences, it has been observed that there are three potential approaches to the standard of review that may be applied when there is challenge on public law grounds:[38]

a) the conventional *Wednesbury* approach;
b) an approach based on fundamental rights which requires the court to 'insist that that fact be respected by the decision-maker, who is accordingly required to demonstrate either that his proposed action does not in truth interfere with the right, or, if it does, that there exist considerations which may reasonably be accepted as amounting to a substantial objective justification for the interference'; and

32 See paras 12.95–12.105.

33 See para 12.22.

34 'Proportionality' is the doctrine that there has to be a reasonable relationship between the governmental (including local) action under review and its purpose in a given context.

35 At 410. What Lord Diplock had in mind was not the ECHR but European Union (EU) law, in which proportionality also plays a substantial part. Some have considered that proportionality was in any event already inherent in *Wednesbury* unreasonableness: *R v Secretary of State Home Department ex p Leech* [1994] QB 198, CA; *R v Chief Constable of Sussex ex p International Trader's Ferry* [1999] 2 AC 418, HL.

36 *R v Ministry of Defence ex p Smith* [1996] QB 517, CA; *Bugdaycay v Secretary of State for the Home Department* [1987] AC 514, HL; sometimes referred to as 'Super-*Wednesbury*' – *Vilvarajah v UK* (1991) 14 EHRR 248, ECtHR.

37 See *R v Ministry of Agriculture, Fisheries and Food ex p First City Trading Limited* [1997] 1 CMLR 250, QBD; see also *R v Secretary of State for Health ex p Eastside Cheese Co* [1999] 3 CMLR 123, CA.

38 *R (Mahmood) v Secretary of State for the Home Department* [2001] 1 WLR 840, CA.

c) an approach based on claims which directly engage rights guaranteed by the ECHR, which requires the court to decide whether there has been a violation of a convention right.[39]

12.27 This trend towards different standards of review depending on the rights in issue appears to imply a weakening of the dominance of the *Wednesbury* test for determining public law challenges. In *Daly*,[40] Lord Steyn (although suggesting that in most cases the courts would reach the same conclusion regardless of the basis on which the decision was scrutinised) said that:

> . . . the day will come when it will be more widely recognised that [*Wednesbury*] was an unfortunately retrogressive decision in English administrative law, insofar as it suggested that there are degrees of unreasonableness and that only a very extreme degree can bring an administrative decision within the legitimate scope of judicial invalidation. The depth of judicial review and the deference due to administrative discretion vary with the subject matter. It may well be, however, that the law can never be satisfied in any administrative field merely by a finding that the decision under review is not capricious or absurd.[41]

12.28 The reference to subject-matter is the key element for present purposes: see also Lord Steyn's comment in the same case that 'in law, context is everything'.[42] In *Runa Begum*,[43] it could accordingly still be

39 Those categories were not 'hermitically sealed': 'There is, rather, what may be called a sliding scale of review; the graver the impact of the decision in question upon the individual affected by it, the more substantial the justification that will be required . . . [C]ases where, objectively, the individual is most gravely affected will be those where what we have come to call his fundamental rights are or are said to be put in jeopardy' (at [19]).

40 *R (Daly) v Secretary of State for the Home Department* [2001] UKHL 26, [2001] 2 AC 532. In *R (Pro-Life Alliance) v British Broadcasting Corporation* [2003] UKHL 23, [2004] 1 AC 185, Lord Walker extensively cited with approval the passages under consideration here: see [134]–[135]. See also per Lord Bingham in *A and others v Secretary of State for the Home Department; X and another v Secretary of State for the Home Department* [2004] UKHL 56, [2005] 2 AC 68, at [40].

41 Per Lord Cooke at [32]. The Court of Appeal has observed that 'the *Wednesbury* test is moving closer to proportionality' but also said that 'it is not for this court to perform the burial rights' – *R (Association of British Civilian Internees (Far East Region)) v Secretary of State for Defence* [2003] EWCA Civ 473, [2003] 3 WLR 80.

42 *Daly*, at [28].

43 *Runa Begum v Tower Hamlets LBC* [2003] UKHL 5, [2003] 2 AC 430, [2003] HLR 32. *Runa Begum* was followed in *Ali v Birmingham City Council* [2010] UKSC 8, [2010] HLR 22. In *Ali v UK* App No 40378/10, [2015] HLR 46, however, it was held that Article 6(1) was engaged once the authority decided that a duty was

held that it was appropriate for the decision-maker to make findings of fact without any scrutiny other than the usual grounds for judicial review, because homelessness decisions are administrative in nature and do not engage substantive Convention rights:[44] there was therefore no need for any intensification of the traditional approach to review, or for anxious scrutiny[45] of, the decision.

12.29 In *R (Association of British Civilian Internees (Far East Region)) v Secretary of State for Defence*,[46] the Court of Appeal suggested that the time had come for the *Wednesbury* approach to be dispensed with, noting that its strictness had been relaxed in recent years so that it was, in any event, moving closer to proportionality, so much so that in some cases it was not possible to see daylight between the two tests. In *R (Keyu) v Secretary of State for Foreign and Commonwealth Affairs*,[47] however, Lord Neuberger said that reconsideration of the basis on which courts review decisions of the executive, specifically whether *Wednesbury* rationality should be replaced by a structured proportionality assessment, would require a panel of nine Supreme Court justices because the move from rationality to proportionality could have far-reaching consequences and implications which were profound in constitutional terms.[48]

12.30 What then is the current position? *Runa Begum* concludes that what may be called the highest standard of judicial scrutiny of the three identified[49] is not applicable to challenges under Part 7. It implies that nothing more than conventional *Wednesbury* is applicable. Nonetheless, it remains open to argument that housing is a fundamental right, within the 'middle' standard of review. Even if forced back to *Wednesbury*, that may not be the end of it: the *Wednesbury* approach is clearly under pressure or, as it has been put, the

owed under HA 1996 s193 as that was a sufficiently certain right to amount to a 'civil right'; but it was also held that there was no violation of Article 6 as the right to a reasoned decision, review and appeal were adequate safeguards.

44 See further paras 12.95–12.105.

45 See *R v Ministry of Agriculture, Fisheries and Food ex p First City Trading Limited* [1997] 1 CMLR 250, QBD; see also *R v Secretary of State for Health ex p Eastside Cheese Co* [1999] 3 CMLR 123, CA.

46 [2003] EWCA Civ 473, [2003] QB 1397, per Lord Phillips at [34]–[35].

47 [2015] UKSC 69.

48 At [132]–[133]. Lord Kerr, at [271] agreed with the need for a panel of nine but also said that the question would have to be addressed by the Supreme Court sooner rather than later.

49 See para 12.26.

law is engaged in a 'long trek away from *Wednesbury* irrationality'.[50] Perhaps the simplest approach is to view the *Wednesbury* approach as an absolute minimum, while acknowledging that, sometimes, it will not be enough.

Grounds for challenge – practical classification

12.31 Having considered the general principles on which public law decisions may be challenged, we turn to consider the practical classification of grounds for challenge, utilising *CCSU*,[51] supplemented by the specific (relevant) provisions of the HRA 1998, to which attention has not yet been paid.[52]

12.32 As effectively recognised in *Wednesbury*,[53] when applied in a practical context, grounds tend to overlap one another: thus a failure to have regard to a relevant fact may also be an error of law; a failure to give reasons for a decision may not only be unlawful for failure to comply with the duty to do so but may also found a challenge based on the fairness of the procedure.[54]

12.33 Moreover, the distinction between a point of law (challengeable on administrative law principles) and a question of fact (which is not) is not a straightforward distinction and there will be cases where matters of pure fact arise:

> The cases do not support the proposition that *any* conclusion that a legal or statutory concept applies to a particular set of facts is a question of law, although in practice they permit considerable elasticity in their application.[55]

50 Per Lord Walker in *R (ProLife Alliance) v British Broadcasting Corporation* [2003] UKHL 23, [2004] 1 AC 185, at [131].

51 See para 12.22.

52 Cf paras 12.23–12.30.

53 See para 12.20.

54 The overlapping nature of grounds is illustrated by the specimen documents annexed to this chapter.

55 *Adan v Newham LBC* [2001] EWCA Civ 1916, [2002] HLR 28, per Hale LJ at [66] (emphasis in original).

Illegality

Misdirection of law

12.34 A decision-maker must 'understand correctly the law that regulates his or her decision-making power and must give effect to it'[56], ie, the decision-maker must understand and apply the law correctly. Thus in *Islam*,[57] the authority's misunderstanding of the test to be applied when determining whether a person was homeless intentionally under the Housing (Homeless Persons) Act 1977 was a misdirection of law sufficient to vitiate the decision.[58]

Decisions must be based on the facts

12.35 While it is of the essence of *Puhlhofer*[59] that matters of fact are for the decision-maker, this does not mean that factual errors are irrelevant. In *Adan*,[60] Brooke LJ commented:[61]

> In very many cases, although it could be said that an administrative body had made a material mistake of fact the decision is vulnerable on other more conventional grounds: for procedural impropriety . . . or because a factor had been taken into account which should not have been taken into account . . . or because there was no evidence on which the decision could have been safely based . . . What is quite clear is that a court of supervisory jurisdiction does not, without more, have the power to substitute its own view of the primary facts for the view reasonably adopted by the body to whom the fact-finding power has been entrusted.

12.36 If it can be shown that a decision proceeded on the basis of an incorrect understanding of the facts, that there was no evidence to support the finding of fact made, or that there was no account taken of the facts, there may be scope for a challenge on the basis that the decision was at odds with the factual matrix,[62] in particular where there

56 *CCSU* at 410F, per Lord Diplock.

57 *R v Hillingdon LBC ex p Islam* [1983] 1 AC 688, HL. See also *Anisminic Ltd v Foreign Compensation Commission* [1969] 2 AC 147, HL and *R (Q) v Secretary of State for the Home Department* [2003] EWCA Civ 364, [2004] QB 36.

58 If the decision-maker incorrectly thinks that it does not have a power, that is also a misdirection of law: *National Aids Trust v National Health Service Commissioning Board (NHS England)* [2016] EWHC 2005 (Admin).

59 See para 12.13.

60 *Adan v Newham LBC*, above.

61 At [41].

62 *Secretary of State for Education and Science v Tameside MBC* [1977] AC 1014, HL, at 1047.

are fundamental rights at stake.[63] It has also for some time been recognised that the court is entitled to decide what the facts are if they comprise 'precedent facts' or as they are sometimes called, 'jurisdictional facts',[64] ie, if the facts establish the right to exercise a power or the obligation to perform a duty,[65] the court is entitled to reach a decision for itself as to what the facts are.[66] Where there has been a review,[67] however, the issue will be whether the reviewer could, as a matter of public law, have reached the relevant decision on the facts, rather than whether those facts exist,[68] as the scheme of the HA 1996 means that 'there is no jurisdiction . . . for the County Court to set itself up as a finder of the relevant primary facts for itself'.[69] See also the discussion of the judgment of the Supreme Court in *Ali v Birmingham City Council*[70] below.[71]

63 In *R (Wilkinson) v Broadmoor Special Hospital Authority* [2001] EWCA Civ 1545, [2002] 1 WLR 419, it was suggested that, where fundamental rights were at issue, the court 'must now inevitably reach its own view' on the facts. See also *R (Murphy) v Secretary of State for the Home Department* [2005] EWHC 140 (Admin), [2005] 1 WLR 3516.

64 Eg, *R v Secretary of State for the Environment ex p Powis* [1981] 1 WLR 584, CA per Dunn LJ at 595H.

65 *R v Secretary of State for Home Department ex p Khawaja* [1984] AC 74, HL. See also per Baroness Hale in *R (A) (FC) v Croydon LBC; R (M) (FC) v Lambeth LBC* [2009] UKSC 8, at [29]–[30].

66 See *Khawaja*, above, per Lord Wilberforce at 105; *R v Oldham BC ex p Garlick* [1993] AC 509, HL, per Lord Griffiths at 520E.

67 See para 9.149 and following.

68 *Bubb v Wandsworth LBC* [2011] EWCA Civ 1285, [2012] HLR 13, where the issue was whether the applicant had received the authority's letter warning her of the possible consequences of refusal of an offer, and of her right to request a review of the suitability of the accommodation, under HA 1996 s193(7), (7F); the reviewing officer had been entitled to conclude that she had done so. Cf *R (A) v Croydon LBC* [2009] UKSC 8, [2009] 1 WLR 2557, where the question of the age of a child for the purposes of Children Act 1989 s20 was held to be one for the court, distinguishing (at [28]) between 'a number of different value judgments' contained in the CA 1989 and 'a different kind of question [to which there] is a right or a wrong answer' (of which age was an example).

69 *Bubb* at [20]. See also *Richmond upon Thames v Kubickek* [2012] EWHC 3292 (QB) where It was held that the county court judge had been wrong to list a trial of a preliminary issue (and hear factual evidence) to resolve a dispute between the authority and the applicant as to what had been said during s184 enquiries.

70 [2010] UKSC 8.

71 See para 12 96–12.99.

12.37 In *Tameside* at the Court of Appeal,[72] Scarman LJ suggested that an error of fact – not merely precedent fact – might be sufficient of itself to vitiate an authority's decision where that error could be said to be a 'misunderstanding or ignorance of an established and relevant fact': this approach has found significant subsequent support.[73] There are now several examples of administrative decisions quashed because they were reached on a material error[74] of fact,[75] although opinions differ as to whether they are examples of failing to take into account a relevant consideration,[76] a stand-alone ground[77] or indeed are as an

72 *Secretary of State for Education and Science v Tameside MBC* (1976) 120 *SL* 539, CA.

73 Lord Slynn, in *R v Criminal Injuries Compensation Board ex p A* [1999] 2 AC 330, CA accepted the existence of such a doctrine, a view he re-affirmed in *R (Alconbury Developments Ltd) v Secretary of State for the Environment, Transport and the Regions* [2001] UKHL 23, [2003] 2 AC 295 at [53], but in neither case was this reasoning adopted by the Committee and, in the first, Lord Slynn himself 'preferred' to decide the case on the alternative ground of breach of natural justice amounting to unfairness (at 345). In *E v Secretary of State for the Home Department* [2004] EWCA Civ 49, [2004] QB 1044, Carnwath LJ considered the history in some detail. How far the House of Lords can be said to have endorsed Scarman LJ's approach may be in some doubt: see *E* at [55].

74 Or 'fundamental mistake of fact': see *Porteous v West Dorset DC* [2004] EWCA Civ 244, per Mantell LJ at [9].

75 See also *Mason v Secretary of State for the Environment and Bromsgrove DC* [1984] JPL 332; *Jagendorf & Trott v Secretary of State for the Environment and Krasucki* [1986] JPL 771; *R v Hillingdon LBC ex p Thomas* (1987) 19 HLR 196; *R v Legal Aid Committee No 10 (East Midlands) ex p McKenna* [1990] COD 358, (1989) *Times* 20 December, DC; *Simplex GE (Holdings) Ltd v Secretary of State for the Environment* [1988] 3 PLR 25, CA; *R v London Residuary Body ex p ILEA* (1987) *Times* 3 July, CA. See also *R (Meredith) v Merthyr Tydfil CBC* [2002] EWHC 634 (Admin), unreported; *R (Kathro) v Rhondda Cynon Taff CBC* [2001] EWHC (Admin) 527, [2002] Env LR 196; *R (McLellan) v Bracknell Forest BC* [2001] EWCA Civ 1510, [2002] QB 1129; *Martin Hill v Bedfordshire CC* [2007] EWHC 2435 (Admin), [2008] ELR 191; *R (March) v Secretary of State for Health* [2010] EWHC 765 (Admin); *Manydown Ltd v Basingstoke and Deane BC* [2012] EWHC 977 (Admin); *R (Watt) v Hackney LBC* [2016] EWHC 1978 (Admin).

76 *Secretary of State for Education and Science v Tameside MBC*, above, per Lord Diplock at 1066F–1067A. See also *Crake v Supplementary Benefits Commission* [1982] 1 All ER 498, QBD at 508, cited in *Aslam v South Bedfordshire DC* [2001] EWCA Civ 514, [2001] RVR 65, itself cited in *E v Secretary of State for the Home Department* [2004] EWCA Civ 49, [2004] QB 1044, at [38].

77 *R (Alconbury Developments and others) v Secretary of State for the Environment, Transport and the Regions*, above at [53], [169]; *R v Criminal Injuries Compensation Board ex p A*, above, at [344]; *Runa Begum v Tower Hamlets LBC* [2003] UKHL 5, [2003] 2 AC 430, at [7]–[11].

aspect of fairness.[78] It must nonetheless be said that mistake of fact is still some way from a generally accepted ground of judicial review.[79]

Taking into account irrelevant considerations

12.38 It is sufficient to void a decision on the basis that an irrelevant factor has been taken into account if the factor is significant, or potentially of influence, meaning that, if it had not been taken into account, the decision might have been different. The authority must take such steps as are reasonable to find out the relevant facts.[80] When housing is in issue, 'consideration of common humanity' is a relevant consideration in its own right.[81] While the resources available to an authority will be relevant to how it discharges its duty,[82] they are not

78 *E v Secretary of State for the Home Department* [2004] EWCA Civ 49, [2004] QB 1044 and see further, paras 12.56–12.60. 'What mattered was that, because of their failure, and through no fault of her own, the claimant had not had "a fair crack of the whip" (see *Fairmount Investments v Secretary of State for the Environment* [1976] 1 WLR 1255, HL per Lord Russell at 1266/A). If it is said that this is taking "fairness" beyond its traditional role as an aspect of procedural irregularity it is no further than its use in cases such as *HTV Ltd v Price Commission* [1976] ICR 170, CA approved by the House of Lords in *R v IRC ex p Preston* [1985] AC 825, at 865–866). In our view, the time has now come to accept that a mistake of fact giving rise to unfairness is a separate head of challenge in an appeal on a point of law, at least in those statutory contexts where the parties share an interest in co-operating to achieve the correct result. Asylum law is undoubtedly such an area.' Per Carnwath LJ in *E* at [65]–[66].

79 See *Wandsworth LBC v A* [2000] 1 WLR 1246, CA, at 1255/H–1256/C: 'While there may, possibly, be special considerations that apply in the more formalised area of planning inquiries . . . and while the duty of "anxious scrutiny" imposed in asylum cases by *R v Secretary of State for the Home Department ex p Bugdaycay* [[1987] AC 514, HL] renders those cases an uncertain guide for other areas of public law; none the less . . . there is still no general right to challenge the decision of a public body on an issue of fact alone. The law in this connection continues, in our respectful view, to be as stated for a unanimous House of Lords by Lord Brightman in *R v Hillingdon LBC ex p Puhlhofer . . .*'

80 Per Lord Diplock in *Secretary of State for Education and Science v Tameside MBC* [1977] AC 1014, HL, at p1065; see also *R v Lincolnshire CC and Wealden DC ex p Atkinson* [1995] 8 Admin LR 529, DC and *R v Hillingon LBC ex p McDonagh* (1998) 31 HLR 531.

81 *Ex p Atkinson, ex p McDonagh*, above; *R v Kerrier ex p Uzell* (1995) 71 P&CR 566; *R v Brighton and Hove Council ex p Marmont* (1998) 30 HLR 1046, QBD.

82 *R v Lambeth LBC ex p A and G* (1998) 30 HLR 933, CA. Consider, however, *Conville v Richmond upon Thames LBC* [2006] EWCA Civ 718, [2006] HLR 45, where it was held that financial considerations were not relevant when determining the period for which an authority must provide an applicant with accommodation under section 190(2)(a) to afford her or him 'reasonable opportunity to secure accommodation'. Nonetheless, homelessness and allocations must be considered in their context: 'But the social norm must be applied in the context of a scheme for allocating scarce resources. It is

relevant[83] to the question whether there is a duty at all.[84]

12.39 There is no general proposition which governs the question of what is a relevant consideration: the question is what the Act requires to be taken into account, not what the court thinks may be relevant.[85]

Disproportionate weight for relevant considerations

12.40 It is not just taking something irrelevant into account that may vitiate the decision, but also giving disproportionate weight to a relevant consideration. In *Ashton*,[86] excessive reliance had been placed on the prevailing housing circumstances of the area when considering intentional homelessness;[87] the decision-maker had not appreciated that 'it is something that must be weighed carefully in the balance with the other factors upon which the decision . . . is reached'.[88]

impossible to consider only what would be desirable in the interests of the family if resources were unlimited . . .'; 'There seems to me no reason in logic why the fact that Parliament has made the question of priority need turn upon whether a dependent child might reasonably be expected to reside with the applicant should require that question to be answered without regard to the purpose for which it is being asked, namely, to determine priority in the allocation of a scarce resource. To ignore that purpose would not be a rational social policy. It does not mean that a housing authority can say that it does not have the resources to comply with its obligations under the Act. Parliament has placed upon it the duty to house the homeless and has specified the priorities it should apply. But so far as the criteria for those priorities involve questions of judgment, it must surely take into account the overall purpose of the scheme': per Lord Hoffmann in *Holmes-Moorhouse v Richmond upon Thames LBC* [2009] UKHL 7, [2009] HLR 34, at [12] and [16].

83 Save so far as it may be said that consideration of the general housing circumstances of an area as an element in a decision on homelessness, and on intentionality, might be said to import 'resources' by the back-door (see para 4.93).

84 Cf *R v Birmingham City Council ex p Mohammed* [1999] 1 WLR 33, QBD, (1999) 31 HLR 392, QBD where it was said that to treat resources as relevant when deciding whether or not to approve a disabled facilities grant would be to downgrade a duty to a discretion. See, generally, *R v East Sussex CC ex p Tandy* [1998] AC 714, HL; see also *R v Bristol City Council ex p Penfold* (1997–98) 1 CCLR 315, QBD. Compare also *Conville v Richmond upon Thames LBC* [2006] EWCA Civ 718, [2006] HLR 1, and *Holmes-Moorhouse v Richmond upon Thames LBC* [2009] UKHL 7, [2009] HLR 34.

85 *Re Findlay* [1985] AC 318, HL, at 333; see also *R v Hillingdon LBC ex p McDonagh* (1999) 31 HLR 531, QBD.

86 *R v Winchester City Council ex p Ashton* (1991) 24 HLR 520, CA.

87 See para 6.34.

88 At p526.

Failure to take into account relevant considerations

12.41 Just as taking into account the irrelevant may vitiate a decision, so may a failure to take into account the relevant, such as the effect of a medical condition on the need for a transfer from accommodation.[89] The authority must take reasonable steps to acquaint itself with what is relevant.[90] Some considerations derive from statute and therefore must be taken into account: consider the requirements under HA 1996 ss169(1) and 182(1) and H(W)A 2014 s98(1) to have regard to Codes of Guidance when determining applications under HA 1996 Parts 6 and 7 and H(W)A 2014 Part 2.[91] The requirement to 'have regard' to the Code of Guidance does not mean that the authority is bound by it, or bound to apply it: it simply means that the Code is a relevant consideration to which regard must be had.[92] An authority may depart from the Code eg because it considers the Code to be incorrect[93] or in conflict with the requirements of statute[94] but the reasons for any departure should be explained.[95] If the decision-maker wrongly takes the view that a consideration is not relevant, and therefore has no regard to it, his or her decision cannot stand and he or she must be required to think again.[96]

12.42 A failure to take into account a relevant consideration will be sufficient to found a claim only if consideration of the relevant fact would have made a difference to the decision.[97]

89 *R v Islington LBC ex p Aldabbagh* (1995) 27 HLR 271, QBD.

90 Per Lord Diplock in *Secretary of State for Education and Science v Tameside MBC* [1977] AC 1014, HL, at 1065.

91 As to which, see *R v Wandsworth LBC ex p Hawthorne* [1994] 1 WLR 1442, CA.

92 An authority need not, however, spell out every paragraph of the Code to which it has had regard, see eg *Birmingham City Council v Balog* [2013] EWCA Civ 1582, [2014] HLR 14 and footnote 187, below.

93 See, eg, *R v Brent LBC ex p Awua* [1996] AC 55, (1995) 27 HLR 453, HL.

94 In which case, it is always the statute which prevails: see, eg, *R v Waveney DC ex p Bowers* [1983] QB 238; (1982) 4 HLR 118, CA; *Griffin v Westminster City Council* [2004] EWCA Civ 108, [2004] HLR 32.

95 See, eg *de Falco, Silvestri v Crawley BC* [1980] QB 460, CA; *Khatun v Newham LBC* [2004] EWCA Civ 55; [2005] QB 37. In *R v Newham LBC ex p Bones* (1992) 25 HLR 357, QBD, it was held that regard to the wrong (earlier) Code would invalidate a decision, if there was a substantive point of difference, including a change of emphasis.

96 *Tesco Stores Ltd v Secretary of State for the Environment* [1995] 1 WLR 759, at 764G–H.

97 *R v Wandsworth LBC ex p Onwudiwe*; *R v Secretary of State for Health ex p Eastside Cheese Co* [1999] EuLR 968.

Promoting the object of legislation[98]

12.43 Powers conferred for public purposes must be used in a way that parliament can be presumed to have intended.[99] In *Khalique,*[100] the authority was entitled to provide temporary accommodation (in discharge of the HA 1996 Part 7 duty) provided the entitlement to permanent accommodation was not deferred so as 'to frustrate the purpose of the legislation and the rights which it gives to individuals, nor deferred or withheld for some improper or illicit reason'.[101] Likewise, in *Robinson v Hammersmith and Fulham LBC,*[102] the authority could not defer a decision until the applicant, a child, reached an age at which she would not be in priority need so that she would no longer be entitled to assistance.[103]

Fettering discretion

12.44 An authority must reach its own decision on each individual case; it may not fetter its discretion by approaching a decision with a predetermined policy on how it will deal with cases that fall within a particular class.[104] That is not to say that – if good administration requires it – an authority cannot adopt a policy in order to guide the future exercise of its discretion. Where it does so, however, it must consider the application of that policy individually in every case where it is sought to make an exception.[105] This approach was adopted and applied by the House of Lords in *Re Betts.*[106]

12.45 A policy of requiring all applicants who were joint tenants of an authority to serve notice to quit (thereby terminating the tenancy) before they could be accepted as homeless owing to domestic violence under HA 1996 Part 7 was held to be unlawful in *Hammia.*[107] In *Savage,*[108] the applicant was refused assistance by way of a rent

98 See, generally, *Padfield v Minister of Agriculture, Fisheries and Food* [1968] AC 997, HL; see also *Meade v Haringey LBC* [1979] 1 WLR 1, CA, and *R v Braintree DC ex p Halls* (2000) 32 HLR 770, CA.

99 *R v Tower Hamlets LBC ex p Chetnik Developments Ltd* [1988] AC 858, HL.

100 *R v Tower Hamlets LBC ex p Khalique* (1994) 26 HLR 517, QBD.

101 *Khalique*, at 522.

102 [2006] EWCA Civ 1122, at [31].

103 See paras 5.67–5.69.

104 *British Oxygen Co Ltd v Minister of Technology* [1971] AC 610, HL. See also *R v Secretary of State for the Environment ex p Brent LBC* [1982] QB 593, DC.

105 *British Oxygen Co Ltd v Minister of Technology*, above, at 625E.

106 [1983] 2 AC 613, 10 HLR 97, HL; see chapter 8.

107 *R (Hammia) v Wandsworth LBC* [2005] EWHC 1127 (Admin), [2005] HLR 46.

108 *R (Savage) v Hillingdon LBC* [2010] EWHC 88 (Admin), [2010] JHL D44.

deposit in order to secure private rented accommodation because she had been found to be homeless intentionally; although the authority's policy was not unlawful, because it required officers to consider its application in every case, it had been misunderstood and misapplied in the present case.

Unlawful delegation or dictation

12.46 The authority cannot avoid its duties by adopting the decision of another body.[109] A distinction must be drawn, however, between adoption of the decision of another body and the proper use of others to assist in reaching a decision.[110] The authority may employ staff,[111] and have implied power to employ contractors or agents and to enter into contracts with them.[112] These resources can all be used when reaching a decision. What cannot be abdicated – save so far as statutorily permitted – is responsibility for the essential elements of a decision, which are to determine what is to be done or what is to happen (in contrast to – even if overlapping with – *how* something is to be done), ie, the underlying decision rather than its day-to-day management.[113]

12.47 Statute may permit functions to be designated by order as capable of being exercised by others who are not members or employees of the authority.[114] Under this provision, the Local Authorities (Contracting Out of Allocation of Housing and Homelessness Functions) Order 1996[115] permits a wide range of functions under both HA 1996 Parts 6 and 7 and H(W)A 2014 Part 2 to be contracted out, including enquiry and even decision-making on homelessness.[116]

109 *Lavender & Sons v Minister of Housing and Local Government* [1970] 1 WLR 1231, QBD.

110 In *R v West Dorset DC ex p Gerrard* (1994) 27 HLR 150, QBD, under HA 1985 Part 3, the authority could enlist the assistance of a third party but had to take the 'active and dominant' part in the investigative process. But cf the approach in *R v Hertsmere BC ex p Woolgar* (1995) 27 HLR 703, QBD, likewise under HA 1985 Part 3. The actual results are now overtaken by statutory provision: see para 12.47.

111 Local Government Act (LGA) 1972 s112.

112 *Crédit Suisse v Allerdale BC* [1997] QB 306, CA, at 346. There is now express power to contract, in Local Government (Contracts) Act 1997 s1.

113 *Crédit Suisse v Allerdale BC* [1995] 1 Lloyds LR 315, Comm Ct; [1997] QB 306, CA.

114 Deregulation and Contracting Out Act 1994 s70. See chapter 10.

115 SI No 3205; as amended by Housing (Wales) Act 2014 (Consequential Amendments) Regulations 2015 SI No 752 so as to extend to H(W)A 2014 Part 2. See generally *Tachie v Welwyn Hatfield BC* [2013] EWHC 3972 (QB).

116 See chapter 9.

The authority's decision must be reached properly

12.48 Under the Local Government Act (LGA) 1972, it is the full authority[117] which is entrusted with functions, including the function of reaching decisions, and only the authority can do so[118] – save so far as the authority is permitted to delegate it: the general power of delegation in local government (LGA 1972 s101) permits delegation to a committee, subcommittee or officer. That power does not permit delegation to a single member, because there cannot be a committee or subcommittee of one.[119] It does, however, permit delegation to an officer, to be exercised in consultation with a member, so long as the member does not play the dominant role to the extent that the officer cannot be said to have reached the decision himself or herself.[120]

12.49 Under LGA 2000, however, local authorities function in what may be described as two parts: an executive and the full authority. Decisions not conferred on the authority by statute, statutory instrument or (where the matter is left to the authority to decide) under what is known as 'local choice',[121] *must* be taken by the executive.[122] Decisions on allocations and homelessness are – by this route – matters for the executive.[123] Decisions to be taken by the executive may be dealt with in any way that the LGA 2000 permits, which includes delegation to an individual member of the executive, or to a committee or sub-committee of the executive, or to an officer (or, in some circumstances, an area committee not of the executive but of the authority itself).[124]

117 Subject to exceptions.

118 *Gardner v London Chatham and Dover Railway Co (No 1)* (1867) LR 2 Ch App 201; *Marshall v South Staffordshire Tramways Co* [1895] 2 Ch 36; *Parker v Camden LBC* [1986] 1 Ch 162, CA; *Crédit Suisse plc v Waltham Forest LBC* [1997] QB 362, CA.

119 *R v Secretary of State for the Environment ex p Hillingdon LBC* [1986] 1 WLR 807, CA. There is statutory power to delegate to a single member in circumstances which do not apply here: see Local Government and Public Involvement in Health Act 2007 s236.

120 *R v Port Talbot BC ex p Jones* [1988] 2 All ER 208, QBD. See also *R v Tower Hamlets LBC ex p Khalique* (1994) 26 HLR 517, QBD.

121 LGA 2000 s9D(3) (England); s13(3)(b) (Wales).

122 LGA 2000 s9D(2) (England); s13(2), (10) (Wales).

123 LGA 2000 ss9D and 13; Local Authorities (Functions and Responsibilities) (England) Regulations 2000 SI No 2853; and Local Authorities (Executive Arrangements) (Functions and Responsibilities) (Wales) Regulations 2007 SI No 399.

124 LGA 2000 ss9E–9EB (England); ss14–16 and 18 (Wales).

12.50 A decision of an executive is treated as that of, and is binding on, the authority;[125] it is not a delegation to the executive but a decision taken on behalf of the authority:[126] the authority cannot 'overrule' it in the way that, for example, it can 'overrule' one of its own committees or officers (and could formerly overrule all committees and -officers), although it does have power to consider an executive decision and to require the executive to reconsider it.[127] Nor, conversely, can the executive overrule a decision of the authority.[128]

12.51 A general category of 'appeals' is within the 'local choice' class.[129] It does not seem that this includes reviews under HA 1996 Parts 6 and 7 because a review can take into account facts arising subsequent to the original decision[130] which means that it is not exclusively an 'appeal' and there remain issues of judgment that fall within the 'execution' of functions that should fall on the executive.

Irrationality

Wednesbury

12.52 As noted,[131] the authority may not reach a decision which no reasonable authority could have reached – such a decision, sometimes referred to as a perverse decision, is conclusive evidence that the decision is irrational and therefore void. There is a high threshold to cross.[132]

Bad faith/improper purposes or motives

12.53 A decision will be unlawful if it can be shown that the decision-maker acted in bad faith or was motivated by some aim or purpose that is not

125 LGA 2000 s9D (England); s13(9) and (10)(a) (Wales).

126 LGA 2000 s9D (England); s13(9) (Wales).

127 LGA 2000 s9F (England); s21 (Wales). All authorities must maintain at least one 'overview and scrutiny' committee to exercise such powers, on which the executive cannot be represented; they may, however, maintain more than one, referable to different functions.

128 This is implicit in the allocation of functions to the different parts of the authority.

129 Local Authorities (Functions and Responsibilities) (England) Regulations 2000 SI No 2853 reg 3(1) and Sch 2 para 2; and Local Authorities (Executive Arrangements) (Functions and Responsibilities) (Wales) Regulations 2007 SI No 399, Sch 2 para 2.

130 *Mohamed v Hammersmith and Fulham LBC* [2001] UKHL 57, [2002] 1 AC 547. As to decisions, see chapter 9.

131 See para 12.20.

132 See *El-Dinnaoui v Westminster City Council* [2013] EWCA Civ 231, [2013] HLR 23 for an example.

considered legitimate. This is part of the (obvious) principle that the decision-maker may not use the powers entrusted to him or her for purposes which fall outwith his or her authority.[133] Acting in bad faith stands alone as a ground and will automatically vitiate a decision.[134]

12.54 Although frequently alleged by dissatisfied applicants, both grounds are difficult to establish[135] and must be fully particularised and proven by the applicant.[136]

12.55 A power conferred on a local authority may not lawfully be exercised to promote the electoral advantage of a political party.[137] If several purposes are being pursued and the dominant purpose is legitimate, however, the decision will not be unlawful.[138]

Procedural impropriety

Fairness and Article 6

12.56 A decision-maker must act fairly and in accordance with the principles of natural justice, which are supplemented and developed by Article 6 of the ECHR (right to a fair trial).[139]

12.57 What constitutes fairness has been described as 'essentially an intuitive judgment'[140] and what it demands will depend on the context of the decision, the statute which confers the decision-making power on the decision-maker, and the legal and administrative system within which the decision is taken. Fairness will also commonly require that a person adversely affected by the decision should have an opportunity to make representations on his or her own behalf either before the decision is taken or with a view to procuring its modification; that requirement necessarily carries with it a need on the part of the applicant to be informed of the gist of the case which he or she has to answer.[141]

12.58 The influence of Article 6 in this area generally has been considerable, but has not yet had a significant impact in relation to claims

133 *R v Tower Hamlets LBC ex p Chetnik Developments Ltd* [1988] AC 858, HL.

134 *Wednesbury*, see para 12.20; *Smith v East Elloe Rural DC* [1956] AC 736, HL.

135 In *Cannock Chase DC v Kelly* [1978] 1 WLR 1, CA, it was suggested that the term should be used only in respect of a dishonest misuse of power.

136 *Cannock Chase DC v Kelly* [1978] 1 WLR 1, CA.

137 *Magill v Porter* [2001] UKHL 67, [2002] 2 AC 357.

138 *Magill v Porter* [2001] UKHL 67, [2002] 2 AC 357.

139 As to which, see paras 12.96–12.99.

140 *R v Secretary of State for the Home Department ex p Doody* [1994] 1 AC 531, HL, at 560/D.

141 *R v Secretary of State for the Home Department ex p Doody* [1994] 1 AC 531, HL.

under HA 1996 Part 6 or Part 7 or H(W)A 2014 Part 2.[142] Any defects which may exist in the statutory procedure for internal review are rectified by the right of an applicant to appeal to the county court or by judicial review.[143]

12.59 That is not to say that the existence of a statutory scheme will always be deemed sufficient. The courts may, if they consider the circumstances of the case justify it, impose more stringent requirements to ensure that a matter has been decided fairly.[144] Thus, while review of a homelessness decision has to be carried out by a senior officer not involved in the original decision,[145] mere compliance with this would per se not prevent a challenge to the review[146] if the reviewer – though senior and not involved – could, for other reasons,[147] be said to be biased against the applicant.

12.60 Leaving aside Article 6, the principles of natural justice require both that no one should be a judge in his or her own cause (bias); and that an applicant has the right to be heard.[148]

Bias

12.61 For a decision to be quashed on the ground of bias, it is not necessary to show that the decision-maker was in fact biased; it is sufficient for there to be an apparent bias.[149] In *R v Gough*[150] it had been held that, in

142 See further paras 12.96–12.99.

143 See also *R (Alconbury Developments Ltd) v Secretary of State for the Environment, Transport and the Regions* [2001] UKHL 23, [2003] 2 AC 295.

144 *Wiseman v Boreman* [1971] AC 297, HL; *R v Hull Prison Visitors ex p St Germain (No 2)* [1979] 1 WLR 1401, QBD; *Lloyd v McMahon* [1987] AC 625, HL; *R v Civil Service Appeal Board ex p Cunningham* [1991] 4 All ER 310, CA; *R v Secretary of State for the Home Department ex p Doody et al* [1994] 1 AC 531, HL; *R v Higher Education Funding Council ex p Institute of Dental Surgery* [1994] 1 WLR 242, DC; *R v Kensington and Chelsea RLBC ex p Grillo* (1995) 28 HLR 94, CA; and *R v Ministry of Defence ex p Murray* [1998] COD 134, QBD.

145 See HA 1996 s202 and Allocation of Housing and Homelessness (Review Procedures) Regulations 1999 SI No 71 reg 2. The Welsh regulations only require that the review officer be someone who was not involved in the original decision (Homelessness (Review Procedure) (Wales) Regulations 2015 SI No 1266 reg 3; see also Welsh Code, para 20.9).

146 Cf *Feld v Barnet LBC* [2005] EWCA Civ 1307, [2005] HLR 9.

147 Eg, past contact/dealings suggesting something other than full disinterestedness, or even some private or personal reason.

148 *Ridge v Baldwin* [1964] AC 40, HL.

149 By Localism Act (LA) 2011 s25, there is no apparent bias in relation to a decision taken after 12 January 2012 (but capable of referring to things done beforehand) simply because the decision-maker has previously done something that directly or indirectly indicates what view he or she took, or would or might take, in relation to a matter relevant to the decision.

150 [1993] AC 646, HL.

the absence of actual bias, the court should decide for itself whether, in all of the circumstances relevant to the issue of bias, there was a real danger that the decision-maker/decision-making body had been biased. In *Re Medicaments and Related Classes of Goods (No 2)*,[151] however, it was said that the court should ask whether a fair-minded and informed observer would conclude that there was a real possibility or danger of bias. The House of Lords has approved this 'modest adjustment of the test in *Gough*',[152] subject to omission of the phrase 'real danger'; accordingly, the appropriate test for bias is now 'whether the fair-minded and informed observer, having considered the facts, would conclude that there was a real possibility that the tribunal was biased'.[153]

12.62 In *Feld*,[154] the authority had only one reviewing officer, who conducted both an initial review and a subsequent re-review following a successful complaint to the ombudsman (of which she was not the subject, and in the report on which she was not criticised). The applicant asserted that this gave rise to the appearance of bias. The Court of Appeal dismissed the claim. The fair-minded and informed observer would take into account that a decision under HA 1996 s202, is an administrative decision which parliament has entrusted to senior local authority officers, who have received training; the observer would also consider the practical constraints (financial and administrative) imposed on local housing authorities. Taking those factors into account, there would not be said to have been any bias in the decision-making process, based either on the officer's conduct of the previous review or on the successful complaint to the ombudsman.[155]

12.63 In *De-Winter Heald v Brent LBC*,[156] the Court of Appeal held that an objective and well informed observer would not think that there was a real danger of bias on the part of a contracted-out reviewer, and therefore rejected the contention that the review decisions in the

151 [2001] 1 WLR 700, CA.

152 See *Magill v Porter* [2001] UKHL 67, [2002] 2 AC 357, at [103].

153 *Magill v Porter*, at [103].

154 *Feld v Barnet LBC*, above.

155 'Adopting a balanced approach such an observer will accept that investigation by and even adverse comment from the Ombudsman is one of the slings and arrows of local government misfortune with which broad shouldered officials have to cope. [The officer] was not herself involved nor the subject of criticism. She could be expected to bear criticism of the department not only with fortitude but with indifference . . .': per Ward LJ at [49].

156 [2009] EWCA Civ 930, [2010] HLR 8.

appeals were marred by apparent bias; there was no reason why a person contracted to carry out a review on an authority's behalf should necessarily be less impartial than an authority employee; whether he may be regarded as less independent depends on the facts, in particular the terms of the contract between the authority and the reviewer; eg a long contractual term terminable only for serious breach would suggest that there was a high degree of independence on the part of the reviewer (at [52]).

Right to be heard

12.64 This has two elements: first, to inform the party affected about what is being said; and second, to afford him or her the opportunity to answer it.[157] This does not equate to a requirement for an oral hearing – so as to require any internal review to be a full hearing[158] – but does require, where a decision is reached without an hearing, that the applicant is given an opportunity to put his or her case in response to adverse findings.[159]

Reasons

12.65 While there is no universal obligation to give reasons in all circumstances, the common law is moving to the position that, in general, they should be given unless there is a proper justification for not doing so.[160] The internal review requirements in both HA 1996 Parts 6 and 7 and H(W)A 2014 Part 2, however, contain express provision for reasons to be given for decisions.[161] A failure to provide reasons would give rise to a ground of challenge and would suffice to quash

157 *Board of Education v Rice* [1911] AC 179, HL; *Kanda v Government of the Federation of Malaya* [1962] AC 362, PC.

158 Consider *Runa Begum* and *Ali v Birmingham City Council*, paras 12.96–12.99.

159 This is not a limitless right and there is no absolute right to the last word: *Bellouti v Wandsworth LBC* [2005] EWCA Civ 602, [2005] HLR 46.

160 Thus, reasons will be required where fairness requires it, or a particular decision is aberrant, where the failure to give reasons may frustrate a right of appeal (because without reasons a party will not know whether there is an appealable ground or not) and where a party has a legitimate expectation that reasons will be given: *Oakley v South Cambridgeshire DC* [2017] EWCA Civ 71 at [30]–[31]. See also *R (Sambotin) v Brent LBC* [2017] EWHC 1190 (Admin), para 9.129, n250, in which the authority sought to revisit and change its own earlier decision without a lawful basis for doing so (fraud nor deception, or fundamental mistake of fact): the court additionally held that the authority had been under a duty to give reasons for reaching a second decision, with which duty it had failed to comply.

161 HA 1996 ss167(4A) and 203(4); H(W)A 2014 s86(4).

the decision.[162] The requirement is a manifestation of the need for the applicant to be aware of the decision against him or her and to be able to challenge that decision if necessary,[163] so that it is the substance rather than the form that is of importance.

12.66 The authority must apply the facts to the legal background and reach a 'properly or adequately reasoned decision'.[164] In *Paul-Coker*, the applicant successfully claimed judicial review of the authority's decision to refuse her accommodation pending review, on the grounds that the authority had not applied the legal criteria to her circumstances and that there was a 'complete absence of any explanation or reasoning' in the authority's decision letter. This success, based on inadequacy of reasons, was 'an exceptional case'.[165]

12.67 The nature and extent of reasons must relate to the substantive issues raised by an applicant (or by an applicant's adviser): see *Re Poyser & Mills Arbitration*,[166] approved by the House of Lords in *Westminster City Council v Great Portland Estates plc*,[167] and again in *Save Britain's Heritage v Secretary of State for the Environment*.[168] 'The reasons that are set out must be reasons which will not only be intelligible, but which deal with the substantive points that have been raised', per Megaw J in *Posyer*. 'The three criteria suggested in the dictum of Megaw J are that the reasons should be proper, intelligible and adequate', per Lord Bridge in *Save Britain's Heritage*. In *Edwin H Bradley & Sons Ltd v Secretary of State for the Environment*,[169] Glidewell J added to the dictum of Megaw J that reasons can be briefly stated (also approved in *Great Portland Estates*).

12.68 In *Baruwa*[170] it was said to be:

> . . . trite law that where, as here, an authority is required to give reasons for its decision it is required to give reasons which are proper, adequate, and intelligible and enable the person affected to know why they have won or lost. That said, the law gives decision-makers

162 *R v Westminster City Council ex p Ermakov* [1996] 2 All ER 302, CA. Reasons should be 'proper, adequate and intelligible': *Westminster City Council v Great Portland Estates plc* [1985] 1 AC 661, HL.

163 *R v Islington LBC ex p Hinds* (1995) 27 HLR 65, QBD.

164 *R (Paul-Coker) v Southwark LBC* [2006] EWHC 497 (Admin), [2006] HLR 32.

165 *R (Paul-Coker) v Southwark LBC*, at [52].

166 [1964] 2 QB 467, QBD.

167 [1985] AC 661, HL.

168 [1991] 1 WLR 153. See also *Givaudan v Minister of Housing and Local Government* [1967] 1 WLR 250, QBD; *Mountview Court Properties Ltd v Devlin* (1970) 21 P&CR 689, QBD.

169 (1982) 264 EG 926, QBD.

170 *R v Brent LBC ex p Baruwa* (1997) 29 HLR 915, CA.

> a certain latitude in how they express themselves and will recognise that not all those taking decisions find it easy in the time available to express themselves with judicial exactitude.

12.69 The purpose of the obligation to give reasons is to enable the recipient to see whether they might be challengeable in law: see *Thornton v Kirklees MBC*.[171] In *Mohammed*,[172] Latham J considered the role of reasons in the light of the right to seek an internal review of the decision:

> . . . the purpose to be served by the giving of such reasons . . . is to enable the applicant to put before the local housing authority a proper case based upon a full understanding of the council's previous[173] decision to refuse accommodation.

12.70 The reasons should accordingly be sufficient to enable the applicant to form a view as to whether to challenge the decision on a point of law.[174] Merely stating the words of the Act 'parrot-fashion', with no substantive explanation for the decision, is insufficient.[175] Reasons should be in sufficient detail to show the principles on which the decision-maker has acted and that have led to his or her decision; they need not be elaborate nor need they deal with every argument presented in support of the case.[176] Not every factor which weighed with the decision-maker in the appraisal of the evidence has to be identified and explained, but the issues which were vital to the conclusion should be identified, and the manner in which they were resolved, explained.[177] The question is whether it is possible to understand the decision-maker's thought processes when he or she was making material findings.[178]

171 [1979] QB 626, CA, which appears to have been a judicial summary of counsel's submission, rather than a judicial observation in its own right. See further *R v Tynedale DC ex p Shield* (1987) 22 HLR 144, QBD.

172 *R v Camden LBC ex p Mohammed* (1998) 30 HLR 315, QBD at p323.

173 Ie, initial.

174 *Osmani v Camden LBC* [2004] EWCA Civ 1706, [2005] HLR 22. See also *R v Croydon LBC ex p Graham* (1993) 26 HLR 286, at 291–292.

175 *R v Newham LBC ex p Lumley* (2001) 33 HLR 124: this was a concession by counsel, but is again obviously correct. The decision in *Kelly v Monklands DC* (1985) 12 July, Ct of Session (OH), that a mere recital of the words of the Act was sufficient, is unlikely to be followed unless the relevant factual issues for determination by the authority are both clear and confined to something which the wording of HA 1996 serves to address.

176 *Eagil Trust Co Ltd v Pigott Brown* [1985] 3 All ER 119, CA.

177 *English v Emery Reimbold & Strick Ltd* [2002] EWCA Civ 605, [2002] 1 WLR 2409.

178 *R (Iran) and others v Secretary of State for the Home Department* [2005] EWCA Civ 982.

12.71 Authorities are entitled to give their reasons quite simply:

> . . .their decision and their reasons are not to be analysed in minute detail. They are not to be gone through as it were with a fine-tooth comb. They are not to be criticised by saying: 'They have not mentioned this or that'.[179]

In the context of a decision on review, it has been said that reasons contained in the decision letter are not to be treated as if they are statutes or judgments and that it is important to read a decision letter as a whole to get its full sense: *Osmani*.[180] Nevertheless, if a decision-maker fails to address in his or her decision letter an issue 'so startling that one would not expect it to pass without individual comment', the court may be justified in inferring that it has not received any or any sufficient consideration: *Bariise*.[181]

12.72 In *Graham*,[182] Sir Thomas Bingham MR said:

> I readily accept that these difficult decisions are decisions for the housing authority and certainly a pedantic exegesis of letters of this kind would be inappropriate. There is, nonetheless, an obligation under the Act to give reasons and that must impose on the council a duty to give reasons which are intelligible and which convey to the applicant the reasons why the application has been rejected in such a way that if they disclose an error of reasoning the applicant may take such steps as may be indicated.

12.73 This passage was cited with approval in *Hinds*,[183] in which the duty had been complied with because the reasons were intelligible and conveyed clearly to the applicant why his application had been rejected. In *Carpenter*,[184] in contrast, the decision letter was considered 'manifestly defective' because it failed to address the reasons why the applicant had left his previous accommodation and, accordingly, defeated the purpose of the section, 'to enable someone who is entitled to a decision to see what the reasons are for that decision and to challenge those reasons if they are apparently inadequate'.

12.74 A court should not approve incomprehensible or misguided reasoning, but a judge should not adopt an unfair or unrealistic approach

179 *Tickner v Mole Valley DC* [1980] 2 April, CA transcript.

180 *Osmani v Camden LBC* [2004] EWCA Civ 1706, [2004] HLR 22. See also *William v Wandsworth LBC; Bellamy v Hounslow LBC* [2006] EWCA Civ 535, [2006] HLR 42.

181 *R v Brent LBC ex p Bariise* (1998) 31 HLR 50, CA, per Millett LJ at 58.

182 *R v Croydon LBC ex p Graham* (1993) 26 HLR 286, CA at 291–292.

183 *R v Islington LBC ex p Hinds* (1996) 28 HLR 302, CA. See also *R v Camden LBC ex p Adair* (1996) 29 HLR 236, QBD; and *R v Wandsworth LBC ex p Dodia* (1997) 30 HLR 562, QBD.

184 *R v Northampton BC ex p Carpenter* (1992) 25 HLR 349, QBD.

when considering or interpreting review decisions;[185] a decision can often survive despite the existence of an error in the reasoning advanced to support it – for example, the error may be irrelevant to the outcome; it may be too trivial to affect the outcome; it may be obvious from the rest of the reasoning, read as a whole, that the decision would have been the same notwithstanding the error; there may be more than one reason for the conclusion, while the error only undermines one of the reasons; or, the decision may be the only one which could rationally have been reached: in all such cases, the error should not, save perhaps in wholly exceptional circumstances, justify the decision being quashed.[186]

12.75 Although they may be checked by people with legal experience or qualifications before they are sent out, review decisions are prepared by housing officers, who occupy a post of considerable responsibility and who have substantial experience in the housing field, but they are not lawyers; it is not therefore appropriate to subject their decisions to the same sort of analysis as may be applied to a contract drafted by solicitors, to an Act of Parliament, or to a court's judgment; rather, a benevolent approach should be adopted. Nor should the court take too technical view of the language used, or search for inconsistencies, or adopt a nit-picking approach when confronted with an appeal against a review decision.[187] This approach does, however, need to be read subject to the requirements of the public sector equality duty[188] where it is engaged,[189] not only when the issue is vulnerability[190] but by parity of reasoning in all cases where it falls for consideration, ie it must be possible to see how the authority has addressed that duty.

12.76 In *City of Gloucester v Miles*,[191] the Court of Appeal held that – to comply with the requirement to state reasons – a notification of intentional homelessness[192] ought to have stated:

185 *Holmes-Moorhouse v Richmond upon Thames LBC* [2009] UKHL 7, [2009] HLR 34, at [47].

186 *Holmes-Moorhouse* at [51].

187 *Holmes-Moorhouse* at [50]; a review officer need not refer to every relevant passage of the Code of Guidance, see. *Birmingham City Council v Balog* [2013] EWCA Civ 1582, [2014] HLR 14 and *Samuels v Birmingham City Council* [2015] EWCA Civ 1051, [2015] HLR 47.

188 See para 9.69.

189 *Hotak v Southwark LBC and other appeals* [2015] UKSC 30, [2015] 2 WLR 1341, [2015] HLR 23, at [79].

190 See also para 5.32.

191 (1985) 17 HLR 292, CA.

192 See chapter 6.

a) that the authority was satisfied that the applicant for accommodation became homeless intentionally;
b) when the applicant was considered to have become homeless;
c) why the applicant was said to have become homeless at that time, ie, what is the deliberate act or omission in consequence of which it is concluded that at that time the applicant ceased to occupy accommodation which was available for his or her occupation; and
d) that it would have been reasonable for the applicant to continue to occupy that accommodation.

12.77 In *ex p H*,[193] it was held that, while the authority was entitled to express itself quite simply and could not be criticised for not having gone into great detail, it was nonetheless incumbent on it to say what was the deliberate act or omission in consequence of which it had been concluded that the applicant had ceased to occupy accommodation available for his occupation and which it would have been reasonable for him to continue to occupy. In the context of the case, that required more than a statement that he could have continued to occupy under his council tenancy in Northern Ireland.

12.78 Likewise, in *Baruwa*,[194] the decision letter should have clarified why the applicant was regarded as having spent money on non-essential items and why the authority regarded this as having caused the applicant's homelessness. It is not necessary, however, that the decision letter set out arithmetical calculations or itemised what an applicant could or could not afford.[195]

12.79 In *Monaf*,[196] the court quashed the decision of the authority on the basis that its letters did not disclose that it had carried out the proper balancing act called for, to determine whether or not it would have been reasonable for applicants to remain in accommodation in Bangladesh or to come back to the UK.

12.80 In *Adair*,[197] the court described a decision letter, which merely recited that the authority had taken into account all the evidence and that the applicant did not fall within any of the categories of priority need, as being completely devoid of reasoning and inadequate.[198] The

193 *R v Hillingdon LBC ex p H* (1988) 20 HLR 554, QBD. See also *R v Southwark LBC ex p Davies* (1993) 26 HLR 677, QBD.

194 *R v Brent LBC ex p Baruwa* (1997) 29 HLR 915, CA. See also *Robinson v Brent LBC* (1999) 31 HLR 1015, CA.

195 *Bernard v Enfield LBC* [2001] EWCA Civ 1831, CA.

196 *R v Tower Hamlets LBC ex p Monaf* (1988) 20 HLR 529, CA.

197 *R v Camden LBC ex p Adair* (1996) 29 HLR 236, QBD.

198 See also *R v Brent LBC ex p Bariise* (1998) 31 HLR 50, CA, at 58.

decision letter should have set out why the applicant was considered not to be a vulnerable person in the light of the medical evidence which he had put forward.

12.81 In *Khan*,[199] a decision letter which addressed only one of a number of grounds on which local connection was being claimed was held to be defective. In *McCarthy*,[200] however, the decision letter was upheld, even though it had not dealt with the suitability of the applicant's current accommodation, because the applicant had not raised that issue with the authority.

12.82 In *O'Connor*,[201] the authority concluded that the applicants were intentionally homeless. Both initial and review decision letters, however, failed to identify the date at which the authority considered that the homelessness had commenced and therefore had not considered whether the omission at that time had been in good faith. Although the letter was 'thoughtful and factually sound', the decision was quashed because it failed to address the questions raised by HA 1996 s191(2).

12.83 In *Augustin*,[202] it was held that a later letter from the authority could rectify the shortcomings of an earlier notification (which, however, was not itself considered defective, albeit 'sparse' – per Auld J in the court below – or 'cryptic' and brief – per Glidewell LJ in the Court of Appeal; the notification had given the applicant the information she needed).

12.84 The courts may be slow to intervene on the basis of want of adequate reasons unless the applicant, or the applicant's adviser, offers the authority an opportunity to remedy a defective decision letter, by way of a 'prompt request for details', to which the authority has failed to respond.[203] In judicial review cases, the pre-action protocol[204] requires a letter before action[205] and the same is expected before a county court appeal is launched.[206]

12.85 The issue of additional evidence to amplify reasons arises in the context of appeals where the person undertaking the review sometimes

199 *R v Slough BC ex p Khan* (1995) 27 HLR 492, QBD.

200 *R v Sedgemoor DC ex p McCarthy* (1996) 28 HLR 608, QBD.

201 *O'Connor v Kensington and Chelsea RLBC* [2004] EWCA Civ 394, [2004] HLR 37.

202 *R v Westminster City Council ex p Augustin* (1993) 25 HLR 281, CA.

203 *R v Camden LBC ex p Mohammed* (1997) 30 HLR 315, at 323, cited with approval in *R v Newham LBC ex p Lumley* (2000) 33 HLR 124, at 136–137.

204 See para 12.116.

205 See para 12.117.

206 See para 12.170.

submits a witness statement containing further reasoning for his or her decision. Such evidence cannot be admitted as of right. Statements which are aimed at clarification and do not alter or contradict anything in the decision letter are, however, properly admitted.[207]

12.86 In *Graham*[208] and *Ermakov*,[209] the Court of Appeal held that – save in exceptional circumstances – the courts will not permit the reasons given in the notification to be supplemented.[210] In *John*,[211] however, non-disclosure of the proper reasons for the decision in the decision letter did not prevent the authority from relying on proper reasons and justifying its decision accordingly and, in *Hobbs*,[212] the Court of Appeal upheld the High Court decision to admit affidavit evidence amplifying and explaining earlier evidence as to reasons.

12.87 In *Baruwa*,[213] it was recognised that there are cases:

> . . . where . . . one could look at the affidavit[214] . . . by way of amplification of the reasons for the decision. Looking at such an affidavit is often a sensible course and saves the bother and expense of going back to the decision-maker to make a new decision which will incorporate the material which appears in the affidavit.

12.88 Nonetheless, the courts have not invariably held authorities to the reasons given. The decision in *de Falco*[215] was, so far as relevant, that:

> . . . the council is of the opinion that you became homeless intentionally because you came to this country without having ensured that you had permanent accommodation to come to.

207 *Hijazi v Kensington and Chelsea RLBC* [2003] EWCA Civ 692, [2003] HLR 73. See also *Hall v Wandsworth LBC; Carter v Wandsworth LBC* [2004] EWCA Civ 1740, [2005] HLR 23.

208 *R v Croydon LBC ex p Graham* (1993) 26 HLR 286, CA.

209 *R v Westminster City Council ex p Ermakov* (1995) 28 HLR 819, CA; see also *R v Southwark LBC ex p Dagou* (1995) 28 HLR 72, QBD.

210 These were pre-county court appeal, judicial review cases, but the same principles apply: *Samuels v Birmingham City Council* [2015] EWCA Civ 1051, [2015] HLR 47.

211 *R v Cardiff City Council ex p John* (1982) 9 HLR 56, QBD. Another judicial review, pre-appeal case.

212 *Hobbs v Sutton LBC* (1993) 26 HLR 132, CA. See also *R v Bradford City Council ex p Parveen* (1996) 28 HLR 681, QBD.

213 *R v Brent LBC ex p Baruwa* (1997) 29 HLR 915, QBD at 929. See also *Samuels v Birmingham City Council* [2015] EWCA Civ 1051, [2015] HLR 47 where the authority was entitled to lead evidence to rebut an allegation of factual error made for the first time the afternoon before the HA 1996 s204 appeal hearing.

214 Or, witness statement or evidence on an appeal to the county court.

215 *De Falco, Silvestri v Crawley BC* [1980] QB 460, CA.

12.89 This was clearly, and has since expressly been held to be, wrong.[216] The court upheld it by finding that the applicants were homeless intentionally because they had left accommodation (in Italy) before coming to this country.

12.90 In *Islam*,[217] at the Court of Appeal, the court was similarly willing to disregard the express words used by the authority, and consider whether there had been what in substance could be considered intentional homelessness. In *Chambers*,[218] the decision that applicants had become homeless intentionally was not sustainable, but relief was refused on the alternative approach that the authority had discharged its duties to the applicants by an earlier offer.

12.91 These earlier cases should be treated with some caution. *De Falco* could as easily be described as a decision (at an interlocutory hearing) on discretion. The result in *Islam* was overturned on appeal.[219] *Chambers* was explicitly a decision on relief (discretion).

Legitimate expectation

12.92 The requirement of fairness means that an authority must respect any legitimate expectation which an applicant may enjoy.[220] Conventionally, legitimate expectation refers to a legitimate *procedural* expectation, ie, as to how a matter is to be handled, such as an assurance that no decision will be taken, at all or on an aspect of a matter, until there has been a further opportunity to comment or until the authority has managed to contact someone, or that it will only be taken by an officer of a particular level of seniority or by a panel (member or officer),[221] provided that to conform to the expectation would not interfere or conflict with the authority's statutory duty.[222]

12.93 At its most narrow, it may refer only to the procedure to be adopted before an existing right or privilege is removed,[223] although as the concept is a part of the overall duty of fairness, it may equally be used to infer the loss of an opportunity to acquire a benefit or

216 See paras 6.134–6.138.

217 *R v Hillingdon LBC ex p Islam* [1983] 1 AC 688, (1981) 1 HLR 107, HL.

218 *R v Westminster City Council ex p Chambers* (1982) 6 HLR 24, QBD.

219 *R v Hillingdon LBC ex p Islam*, above, see para 6.138.

220 *R v North and East Devon Health Authority ex p Coughlan* [2001] QB 213, CA.

221 *Schmidt v Secretary of State for Home Affairs* [1969] 2 Ch 149, CA; *R v Devon CC ex p Baker* [1995] 1 All ER 73, CA.

222 *R v Attorney General of Hong Kong ex p Ng Yuen Shiu* [1983] 2 AC 629, PC, at 638/f.

223 *Council of Civil Service Unions v Minister for the Civil Service* [1985] 1 AC 374, HL, per Lord Diplock at 413.

advantage. This does not easily translate into a legitimate substantive expectation, ie, of a particular outcome of a decision-making process, as opposed to its procedure. For legitimate expectation to give rise to a substantive entitlement would require a clear and unambiguous representation, devoid of qualification, on which it was reasonable to rely.[224] There is, however, no requirement that an applicant should detrimentally have changed his or her position in reliance on the promise.[225] The question is whether it would be an abuse of power to frustrate the legitimate expectation. It is for the court to determine whether there is a sufficient overriding interest to justify a departure from what has previously been promised.[226] In one case, the substantive right to take over a tenancy was upheld.[227]

12.94 No appeal to legitimate expectation can, however, widen an authority's duties under either HA 1996 Part 6 or Part 7 or H(W)A 2014 Part 2.[228] Nonetheless, where a promise of a 'permanent' home had been made to homeless applicants, a legitimate expectation had arisen which was sufficient to justify derogation from the authority's housing allocation scheme, and which required the authority to provide reasons if the expectation was not to be fulfilled.[229]

Human Rights Act 1998

12.95 The scheme of HRA 1998 is to require all domestic legislation to be read and given effect (as far as is possible) in a manner that is compatible with the Convention rights contained in the Act[230] and to render it unlawful for a 'public authority'[231] – including local authorities and registered providers of social housing in respect of some

224 *R v IRC ex p MFK Underwriting* [1990] 1 WLR 1545, QBD at 1569/G.

225 *R v Newham LBC ex p Bibi and Al-Nashed* [2001] EWCA Civ 607, (2001) 33 HLR 84.

226 *R v North and East Devon Health Authority ex p Coughlan*, above.

227 *R v Lambeth LBC ex p Trabi* (1997) 30 HLR 975, QBD.

228 *R v Lambeth LBC ex p Ekpo-Wedderman* (1998) 31 HLR 498, QBD; *Obiorah v Lewisham LBC* [2013] EWCA Civ 325, [2013] HLR 35. The same must be true of H(W)A 2014 Part 2.

229 *R v Newham LBC ex p Bibi and Al-Nashed* [2001] EWCA Civ 607, (2001) 33 HLR 84; cf. *Obiorah v Lewisham LBC* [2013] EWCA Civ 325 where a similar claim was not upheld on the facts. See also *R (Alansi) v Newham LBC* [2013] EWHC 3722 (Admin), [2014] HLR 25: authority entitled to resile from a clear promise as a result of changes made to its allocation scheme.

230 HRA 1998 s3(1). *R (Morris) v Westminster City Council (No 3)* [2005] EWCA Civ 1184, [2006] 1 WLR 505, [2006] HLR 8.

231 As defined in HRA 1998 s6(3).

aspects of their management of their social housing stock, including service of notice to quit or of seeking possession[232] – to act in a way which is incompatible with one or more of the Convention rights.[233] A person who claims that a public authority has acted in such a way may bring proceedings against the authority or rely on the Convention right in any legal proceedings.[234] The Convention rights which are relevant to a claim brought against HA 1996 Part 6 or Part 7 or H(W)A 2014 Part 2 decisions are:

- *Article 6* – Everyone, in the determination of his or her civil rights and obligations, is entitled to a fair and public hearing within a reasonable time by an independent and impartial tribunal established by law.
- *Article 8 – Rights to respect for private and family life and home,* interference with which is permitted to the extent that it is in accordance with law and necessary in a democratic society in the interests of national security, public safety, economic well-being of the country, the prevention of disorder or crime, the protection of health or morals or the rights and freedoms of others.
- *Article 14 – Prohibition on discrimination* on grounds of sex, race, colour, language, religion, political or other opinion, national or social origin, association with a national minority, property, birth or other status.

Article 6

12.96 Internal reviews do not need to be compliant with Article 6, as homelessness rights are not civil rights within it.[235] Even if they were, it was held in *Runa Begum*[236] that an internal review coupled with the right to an appeal to the county court under HA 1996 s204 comprised compliance with Article 6. This approach was followed in *Ali v Birmingham City Council*.[237]

232 *R (Weaver) v London & Quadrant Housing Trust* [2008] EWHC 1377 (Admin), [2008] JHL D94 and on appeal [2009] EWCA Civ 587, [2009] HLR 40; see para 12.7: see also footnote 7 to that paragraph on other acts of management and allocation.

233 HRA 1998 s6(1).

234 HRA 1998 s7(1).

235 *Ali v Birmingham City Council* [2010] UKSC 8, [2010] HLR 22.

236 *Runa Begum v Tower Hamlets LBC* [2003] UKHL 5, [2003] 2 AC 430, [2003] HLR 32.

237 [2010] UKSC 8.

12.97 In *Ali v UK*,[238] the same case at the European Court of Human Rights, it was held that Article 6(1) was engaged once the authority decided that a duty was owed under HA 1996 s193 because there was a sufficiently certain right to amount to a 'civil right'; in agreement with *Runa Begum* and *Ali* at the Supreme Court, however, it was also held that there was no violation of Article 6 as the rights to a reasoned decision, review and appeal were adequate safeguards. In *Poshteh v Kensington and Chelsea RLBC*,[239] the Supreme Court refused to depart from its decision in *Ali v Birmingham City Council*, notwithstanding *Ali v UK*, for the reasons referred to at para 9.174.

12.98 For the purpose of illustrating the principle, the position may be contrasted with *Tsfayo*,[240] a challenge at the European Court of Human Rights to a decision of a housing benefit review board to refuse to find good reason for backdating a claim, in which it was held that judicial review had not provided the claimant with access to a court of full jurisdiction for the purpose of Article 6(1), because the question in issue for the board – which lacked independence[241] – was a simple one of fact, not involving professional knowledge or specialist experience; judicial review was considered an inappropriate jurisdiction for the resolution of factual issues. This was distinguished in *Ali v Birmingham City Council*, where the issue whether the homeless person had received a letter warning her – in accordance with HA 1996 s193(5) – that if she did not accept the accommodation offered, the authority would consider that its duty had been discharged,[242] was held not to be a matter of simple fact required by *Tsfayo* to be considered by a court of full jurisdiction: see also the discussion of *Bubb v Wandsworth LBC*,[243] above.[244]

12.99 Article 6 was also relied on in a challenge to the legality of contracting out review decisions.[245] The Court of Appeal rejected the argument that a third party would be any less impartial than an employee of the authority; in any event, the authority accepted the contracted

238 App No 40378/10, [2015] HLR 46.

239 [2017] UKSC 36.

240 *Tsfayo v UK* App no 60860/00, [2007] HLR 19, ECtHR.

241 And perhaps impartiality: it was relevant to the decision that – had the claim been allowed – the authority (of some of whose members the board was comprised) would have received only 50 per cent rather than 95 per cent subsidy: at [19].

242 See para 10.184.

243 [2011] EWCA Civ 1285, [2011] HLR 13.

244 See para 12.36 and footnote 68, above.

245 *De-Winter Heald and others v Brent LBC* [2009] EWCA Civ 930 at [4].

out review as its own decision and the availability of an appeal to the county court under HA 1996 s204 ensured compliance with Article 6, following *Runa Begum*.[246]

Article 8

12.100 Article 8 does not comprise a right to housing to be provided by the state.[247] Given this, it does not currently seem likely that a claim for breach of the right to respect for the home under Article 8 will succeed[248] where an authority has properly applied the provisions of HA 1996 Part 7 or H(W)A 2014 Part 2 and reached the conclusion that there is no substantive duty to house an applicant, because the provisions of HA 1996 Part 7 and H(W)A 2014 Part 2 are themselves compliant with the ECHR (and, indeed, go further than any duties under Article 8).

12.101 Thus, in *Hackney LBC v Ekinci*,[249] the Court of Appeal rejected the applicant's argument that he was in priority need through his 17-year-old wife.[250] Pill LJ said, at [16]:

> There is no breach of article 8(1) in Parliament enacting a scheme of priorities whereby applications for accommodation by homeless persons are to be determined by local housing authorities whose - resources will inevitably be limited . . .

12.102 Claims may also be made under Article 8 in relation to the right to respect for family life. Generally, social welfare measures provided by the state do not fall within the ambit of Article 8, as they are not specifically designed to promote or protect family life.[251] Although

246 *Runa Begum v Tower Hamlets LBC*, above.

247 *X v Federal Republic of Germany* (1965) 8 Yearbook of the ECHR 158; *Chapman v UK* (2001) 33 EHRR 18, (2001) 10 BHRC 48; *O'Rourke v UK* App No 39022/97, ECtHR. See also *Lambeth LBC v Kay; Leeds City Council v Price* [2006] UKHL 10, [2006] 2 AC 465, [2006] HLR 22. Cf *Mazari v Italy* (2000) 30 EHRR CD 218, suggesting that a right may arise in some limited, extreme circumstances, where there is a positive obligation towards the applicant under Article 8.

248 See *R (Morris) v Newham LBC* [2002] EWHC 1262 (Admin), [2002] JHL D77, where a claim that the failure to comply with the authority's duty under HA 1996 s193 was a breach of ECHR Article 8 and gave rise to a right to damages was rejected.

249 [2001] EWCA Civ 776, (2002) HLR 2.

250 See, further, chapter 5.

251 See *R (Carson) v Secretary of State for Work and Pensions* [2003] EWCA Civ 797, [2003] 3 All ER 577 at [28], upheld [2005] UKHL 37, [2006] 1 AC 173. See also *R (Couronne and others) v (1) Crawley BC (2) Secretary of State for Work and Pensions (3) First Secretary of State; R (Bontemps and others) v Secretary of State*

this principle was applied to HA 1996 Part 7 generally in *Morris* and *Badu*,[252] the Court of Appeal considered that the particular section under consideration, section 185(4),[253] nonetheless fell within the ambit of Article 8 'because it sets out to give effect to a legislative policy of preserving family life for the homeless'.[254]

Article 14

12.103 Article 14 will be breached if it applies directly to another Convention right or if it can be said to fall within the ambit of another Convention right, even if no specific right under that article is said to have been breached.[255] Courts should approach Article 14 in a structured way, considering: whether the facts fall within the ambit of one or more Convention rights;[256] whether there is a difference in treatment of the claimant and persons put forward for comparison; whether chosen comparators are in an analogous situation to the complainant; and whether the difference in treatment has an objective and reasonable justification.[257]

for Work and Pensions [2006] EWHC 1514 (Admin), [2006] JHL D106, in which the application of the 'habitual residence' test in deciding whether a homeless applicant is eligible (see chapter 3) was held to have nothing to do with promoting respect for private and/or family life; accordingly, the claimants' case was not within the ambit of Article 8.

252 *R (Morris) v Westminster City Council; R (Badu) v Lambeth LBC and First Secretary of State* [2005] EWCA Civ 1184, [2006] 1 WLR 505, [2006] HLR 8.

253 Section 185(4) provides that a person from abroad who is ineligible is to be disregarded in determining whether another person is homeless or in priority need.

254 *R (Morris) v Westminster City Council; R (Badu) v Lambeth LBC and First Secretary of State* [2005] EWCA Civ 1184, [2006] 1 WLR 505, [2006] HLR 8 at 25.

255 *M v Secretary of State for Work and Pensions* [2006] UKHL 11, [2006] 2 AC 91, at [11]–[14].

256 The right does not, however, have to be engaged – thus, even if there is no claim under Article 8, there may be a claim under Article 14 because the subject-matter is family, private life or home: *M v Secretary of State for Work and Pensions* [2006] UKHL 11, [2006] 2 AC 91, at [11]–[14].

257 *Wandsworth LBC v Michalak* [2002] EWCA Civ 271, [2003] 1 WLR 617 (see also *Ghaidan v Godin-Mendoza* [2004] UKHL 30, [2004] HLR 46). In *R (Carson) v Secretary of State for Work and Pensions* [2005] UKHL 37, [2006] 1 AC 173, Lord Nicholls said that the criteria derived from *Michalak* may not be appropriate in every case and that it may be appropriate simply to consider whether the alleged discrimination can withstand scrutiny.

12.104 In *Morris (No 2)*,[258] it was held that – in addition – the courts should ask whether any difference in treatment between the complainant and his or her comparator is based on one or more of the grounds set out in Article 14.[259] Having found that HA 1996 s185(4)[260] fell within the ambit of Article 8, the court went on to consider whether the section was in breach of Articles 8 and 14. As the distinction in section 185(4) in effect discriminated on the ground of nationality, and could not be justified,[261] the section was declared incompatible with ECHR under HRA 1998 s4.[262]

12.105 In *R (RJM) v Secretary of State for Work and Pensions*,[263] the House of Lords accepted that being a homeless person was a 'personal characteristic', and accordingly that being a homeless person fell within the category of 'other status' within the meaning of Article 14. In view of the reach of Article 14,[264] the decision might yet, therefore, have wider implications in future homelessness cases than has yet been realised.

Procedural law

Introduction

12.106 There are two courts to which a dissatisfied applicant will be able to turn: a) the Administrative Court, by of proceedings for judicial review; and b) the county court, by way of a statutory appeal against a decision made under HA 1996 Part 7 or H(W)A 2014 Part 2. In this section, we consider the procedure to be followed in relation to each.

258 *R (Morris) v Westminster City Council (No 3)* [2004] EWHC 2191 (Admin), [2005] HLR 7. The decision was upheld on appeal: [2005] EWCA Civ 1184, [2006] 1 WLR 505, [2006] HLR 8.

259 See also *R (S) v Chief Constable of South Yorkshire Police* [2004] UKHL 39, [2004] 1 WLR 2196.

260 See para 3.113.

261 The government sought to justify the section on the basis that it was a necessary element of immigration control in order to prevent benefit tourism. This was rejected on the basis that the parent applicants in the cases (both of whom had children who were ineligible and were thus held not in priority need because of the application of section 185(4)) were both lawfully and habitually resident here. In *Bah v UK* App No 56328/07, [2012] HLR 2, however, ECtHR held that there was no contravention.

262 Some changes were made as a result of the declaration – see para 3.114.

263 [2008] UKHL 63, [2009] 1 AC 311.

264 See paras 12.103–12.105.

Which court?

12.107 Decisions made by local authorities under HA 1996 Parts 6 and 7 and H(W)A 2014 Part 2 are administrative law decisions and therefore, without more, would *prima facie* only be justiciable by way of judicial review in the Administrative Court. Judicial review is, however, a remedy of 'last resort'[265] and the provision of a statutory appeal (or any form of alternative remedy) generally precludes recourse to it unless the case can in some way be distinguished from the category for which the appeal – or alternative – procedure is provided.[266] Thus, the existence of a scheme of internal review under Parts 6 and 7 and Part 2 requires the applicant – save in exceptional cases – to pursue that review before going to court. More significantly for current purposes, the existence of a statutory appeal against a decision under HA 1996 Part 7 and H(W)A 2014 Part 2 will generally preclude a dissatisfied applicant from seeking to challenge that decision by proceedings for judicial review.

12.108 Examples of decisions outside HA 1996 Parts 6 and 7 and H(W)A 2014 Part 2, where judicial review has proceeded notwithstanding the existence of an alternative – or internal – procedure, include cases where it is not the individual decision that is in issue but the underlying legality of a decision – for example, a policy – to which the individual case is a mere application,[267] and where the decision was made without jurisdiction or contained an error of law.[268]

12.109 In *R v East Yorkshire Borough of Beverley Housing Benefits Review Board ex p Hare*,[269] the court allowed judicial review proceedings to continue – and granted relief – even though the applicant had an alternative remedy by way of appeal (under the then provisions) to a housing benefit review board, because the point raised was in part a point of statutory interpretation of general importance on which it was therefore appropriate for the court to rule.

12.110 Even these circumstances are, however, unlikely to lead to the grant of permission to seek judicial review under HA 1996 Part 7 or

265 Ie, any proper alternative remedy should be exhausted before the Administrative Court will permit a case to be heard: *R v Hammersmith and Fulham LBC ex p Burkett* [2002] UKHL 23, [2002] 1 WLR 1593; *R (Bancoult) v Secretary of State for the Foreign and Commonwealth Office* [2001] QB 1067, CA.

266 *R v Secretary of State for the Home Department ex p Swati* [1986] 1 WLR 477, CA.

267 *R v Paddington Valuation Officer ex p Peachey Property Corporation Ltd* [1966] 1 QB 380, CA.

268 *R v Hillingdon LBC ex p Royco Homes Ltd* [1974] 1 QB 720, DC.

269 (1995) 27 HLR 637, QBD.

H(W)A 2014 Part 2 to a homeless person aggrieved by a decision on his or her application which could otherwise be appealed to the county court,[270] because the appeal procedure itself – being on a 'point of law'[271] – embraces the same grounds as those on which judicial review would be available.[272]

12.111 The intention could not have been clearer, to transfer the bulk of the work from the High Court to the county court.[273] Accordingly, permission to bring a challenge by way of judicial review was refused where the reason the applicant could not appeal to the county court simply was because the applicant was out of time[274] to do so: while the court did not rule out *ever* granting permission where an applicant was out of time, the applicant would have to show 'really exceptional circumstances'.[275]

12.112 It would nonetheless be wrong to think that the High Court – through the Administrative Court – has nothing to do with homelessness. A number of HA 1996 Part 7 cases have come before it and the use of judicial review has been approved where:

a) an authority refused to house pending an internal review;[276]
b) an authority refused to consider a request for accommodation pending review;[277]
c) the decision letter from the authority was so unsatisfactory, and the authority refused to rectify the deficiency in the letter, so that any internal review would be unfair to the applicant;[278]

270 The issue does not arise if the issue raised *cannot* be brought by way of appeal to the county court, as there is no 'alternative remedy'.

271 HA 1996 s204(1); H(W)A 2014 s88(1).

272 See paras 12.31–12.105.

273 'Prior to 1997, many of these unhappy cases fell to be considered by nominated judges dealing with the Crown Office list. Such was the pressure that a particular deputy High Court judge sat almost continuously dealing with homelessness cases and other such cases frequently had to be referred to other deputy High Court judges. Therefore, Parliament incorporated into the Housing Act 1996 another route whereby complaints could be dealt with': per Tucker J in *R v Brent LBC ex p O'Connor* (1998) 31 HLR 923, QBD, at 924.

274 See para 12.166.

275 *R v Brent LBC ex p O'Connor*, above, at 925.

276 *R v Camden LBC ex p Mohammed* (1998) 30 HLR 315, QBD (see further para 12.147). Prior to the county court acquiring power to make an interim order to house (see para 12.197), this would also have been true of a refusal to house pending appeal to the county court.

277 *R (Casey) v Restormel BC* [2007] EWHC 2554 (Admin), [2008] JHL D27.

278 *R v Camden LBC ex p Mohammed*, above.

d) the challenge was to the legality of a policy of the authority: see *Byfield*,[279] a challenge to a policy that applicants could not seek an internal review of the suitability of an offer of accommodation unless the offer was rejected; this was an unlawful fetter on their right to an internal review and was accordingly properly brought by way of judicial review;[280]
e) the case raised an important matter of law: *Sadiq*;[281]
f) an authority had not made a decision in response to a request for accommodation: *Lusamba*;[282]
g) the decision was to refuse to make a local connection referral to another authority, which decision is not reviewable under HA 1996 s202:[283] *Sareen*;[284]
h) the authority refused to extend time to apply for an internal review under HA 1996 s202(3):[285] *Lewisham*,[286] *Slaiman*;[287]

279 (1997) 31 HLR 913, QBD. It is conceivable that such a challenge might be brought by an interested pressure group; see, eg, *R v Inland Revenue Commissioners ex p National Federation of Self-employed and Small Businesses Ltd* [1982] AC 617, HL; *R v Secretary of State for Social Services ex p Child Poverty Action Group* [1990] 2 QB 540, CA; *R v Her Majesty's Inspectorate of Pollution ex p Greenpeace Ltd* [1994] 4 All ER 329, QBD; *R v Secretary of State for Foreign and Commonwealth Affairs ex p World Development Movement Ltd* [1995] 1 WLR 386, QBD.

280 The substance of this decision was overruled in *Alghile v Westminster City Council* [2001] EWCA Civ 363, 33 HLR 57; in turn, *Alghile* was overturned by the statutory amendment that permits an applicant to seek a review of accommodation while accepting it: HA 1996 s202(1A). These do not, however, affect the underlying point being made here, that a challenge to an unlawful policy may yet be brought by judicial review.

281 *R v Brent LBC ex p Sadiq* (2000) 33 HLR 47, QBD. Moses J, while acknowledging that the applicant should have sought a review and county court appeal, referred to the residual jurisdiction of the High Court and said that the case raised an important point, which might well have had to be considered by the Court of Appeal in any event.

282 *R (Lusamba) v Islington LBC* [2008] EWHC 1149 (Admin), [2008] JHL D89. If, however, a decision is subsequently made by the authority, then there is no point in pursuing the substantive hearing.

283 In Wales, H(W)A 2014 s85. See also see also *R (Savage) v Hillingdon LBC* [2010] EWHC 88 (Admin) where it was said that it was doubtful that the manner in which an authority chose to discharge their duties under HA 1996 s190(2) and (4) (duties to persons who are eligible, homeless, in priority need but became homeless intentionally) could be dealt with by way of review under HA 1996 s202.

284 *Hackney LBC v Sareen* [2003] EWCA Civ 351, [2003] HLR 54. See further para 9.153.

285 In Wales, H(W)A 2014 s85(5); see further chapter 10.

286 *R (C) v Lewisham LBC* [2003] EWCA Civ 927, [2004] HLR 4.

287 *R (Slaiman) v Richmond upon Thames LBC* [2006] EWHC 329 (Admin), [2006] HLR 20.

i) an appeal under HA 1996 s204 would not provide an effective remedy: in *Aguiar*,[288] the applicant received his costs on a compromised judicial review application, in part because the remedy being sought[289] would not have been available in appeal proceedings under HA 1996 s204;

j) the person seeking judicial review was a third party, not the applicant: in *Hammia*,[290] the authority applied a policy that victims of domestic violence, if a joint tenant of the authority, must first serve a notice to quit their existing home as a condition of acceptance as homeless; the applicant's husband, who lost his security of tenure because of the notice, successfully challenged this policy by proceedings for judicial review;

k) following a local connection referral, the authority to which the applicant had been referred wished to challenge a substantive finding, for example, that the applicant is unintentionally homeless: *Bantamagbari*;[291]

l) there were exceptional circumstances: *Van der Stolk*.[292]

12.113 In addition, there remain a number of circumstances, not yet considered by the courts, in which it is likely that judicial review will continue to be available, for example:

a) in circumstances where, otherwise than so far as governed by the local connection provisions of HA 1996 ss200–201,[293] two authorities are at odds, eg under the co-operation provisions of HA 1996 s213;[294]

288 *R (Aguiar) v Newham LBC* [2002] EWHC 1325 (Admin), [2002] JHL D92.

289 An order that the authority carries out a HA 1996 s202 review.

290 *R (Hammia) v Wandsworth LBC* [2005] EWHC 1127 (Admin), [2005] HLR 46.

291 *R (Bantamagbari) v Westminster City Council* [2003] EWHC 1350 (Admin), [2003] JHL D70.

292 *R (Van der Stolk) v Camden LBC* [2002] EWHC 1261 (Admin), [2002] JHL D77, where the authority had failed properly to consider medical evidence provided after the time limit to appeal had passed and the applicant's mental health was deteriorating. See also *R (W) v Sheffield City Council* [2005] EWHC 720 (Admin), where two local authorities were disputing responsibility for the applicant under the local connection provisions, and neither would house in the interim. '[T]he claimant having been caught between two stools and faced with an exceptional situation, I consider that it is appropriate, notwithstanding the existence of alternative remedies, to entertain judicial review proceedings': per Gibb J at [34].

293 In Wales, H(W)A 2014 ss80–83. See para 7.37 onwards. Cf *Sheffield*, last footnote, where the dispute was not covered by the statutory arbitration provisions.

294 See chapter 13.

b) where what is in issue is discharge of the property duties, which are not subject to internal review or, therefore, to appeal (see HA 1996 ss211 and 212[295]);

c) where an applicant seeks an internal review on the facts alone, ie, without reference to a point of law, but the authority does not conduct the internal review (or notify the applicant of the outcome) within the prescribed time: there may need to be an application for judicial review to compel the authority to conduct the internal review or to notify the applicant of the outcome.[296]

12.114 Accordingly, judicial review is far from an obsolete process in cases under HA 1996 Parts 6 and 7 and H(W)A 2014 Part 2. Permission to pursue a judicial review for a 'pre-emptive' declaration in advance of any homelessness or threatened homelessness, that the applicant should not be considered intentionally homeless, while not within the review or appeal provisions (for want of any decision), would, however, seem likely to be refused.[297]

12.115 In the following paragraphs, the procedural steps to be followed when challenging a decision either in the Administrative Court – by way of judicial review against a decision under HA 1996 Part 6 or in those circumstances where decisions under HA 1996 Part 7 or H(W)A 2014 Part 2 may still be challenged by way of proceedings for judicial review – or the county court, by way of statutory appeal, are considered; see also the annex to this chapter for specimen documents.

Judicial review

Procedure

12.116 The procedure for claiming judicial review is to be found in Civil Procedure Rules (CPR) Part 54.[298] Cases are now commonly – but not invariably – heard by a single High Court judge. All parties should comply with the pre-action protocol for judicial review. Compliance or non-compliance will be taken into account when giving directions for the case management of proceedings or when making an order for costs.[299] The protocol will not, however, be appropriate where

295 In Wales, H(W)A 2014 ss93, 94. See chapter 8.

296 See further para 12.162.

297 See *R v Hillingdon LBC ex p Tinn* (1988) 20 HLR 305, QBD. Like every 'absolute' proposition, there may yet be exceptions, for example, where the court apprehends – with a degree of reason – *such* unlawful conduct by an authority that it feels impelled to intervene, even if the conditions for a prohibiting order are not fulfilled.

298 See also the accompanying PD and Senior Courts Act 1981 s31.

299 See Judicial Review Pre-action Protocol para 7 and CPR Costs PDs.

there is an urgent need for an interim order, for example, to secure interim accommodation under HA 1996 s188(3), although informal (or 'short') notice should nonetheless be given.[300]

Letter before claim

12.117 The pre-action protocol requires the claimant to send a letter to the defendant before making the claim, to identify the issues in dispute and to establish whether litigation can be avoided.[301] The letter should contain the date and details of the decision, act or omission being challenged and a clear summary of the facts on which the claim is based. It should also contain the details of any relevant information that the claimant is seeking to obtain and an explanation of why this is considered relevant.[302] The letter should set out a date for reply, which in most circumstances will be 14 days.[303] A claim should not usually be made until the proposed reply date has passed.[304]

Letter of response

12.118 The authority should respond within 14 days.[305] If this is not possible, an interim reply should be sent and a reasonable extension proposed.[306] The reply must indicate clearly whether or not the claim is being conceded.[307] Failure to comply with the requirement to respond may lead to a costs order. In *R v Kensington and Chelsea RLBC ex p Ghebregiogis*,[308] a comprehensive letter before action had been sent to the authority by the applicant's solicitors explaining the applicant's position and dealing with the authority's adverse contentions, following which the applicant commenced judicial review proceedings. Just before the application for permission came on for hearing, the authority changed its mind. The applicant successfully sought his costs: the authority should properly have considered the case when it received the letter.

300 Judicial Review Pre-action Protocol para 6. See further para 12.148 onwards on challenges to refusals to house pending internal review.

301 Judicial Review Pre-action Protocol para 14. A suggested standard format is provided at annex A to the Protocol.

302 Judicial Review Pre-action Protocol para 16.

303 See standard letter, annex A, para 13.

304 Judicial Review Pre-action Protocol para 18.

305 Judicial Review Pre-action Protocol para 20. A standard format letter is provided at annex B to the Protocol.

306 Judicial Review Pre-action Protocol para 21.

307 Judicial Review Pre-action Protocol para 22.

308 (1994) 27 HLR 602, QBD.

Permission

12.119 Permission must be sought to bring an application for judicial review.[309] Where a claim has become academic, even if as a result of a change of circumstances between issue and hearing,[310] it is only in exceptional circumstances, and where there is good reason to do so in the public interest, that permission to claim judicial review will be granted; such exceptional circumstances include where a large number of similar cases either exist or are anticipated or where there is a discrete point of statutory construction which does not involve detailed consideration of the facts.[311] In *Adow*,[312] the applicant had obtained alternative accommodation before the hearing. The authority failed to file an acknowledgement of service and only produced a witness statement the day before the hearing. It contended that no remedy should be granted because it was in the process of revising the relevant policy. A declaration was nonetheless granted: the conduct of the authority in failing to file an acknowledgement of service and producing a witness statement shortly before the substantive hearing was unacceptable; the court had the distinct impression that the authority was anxious to hide its position as far as possible. It was right that the court should mark its disapproval of such conduct.

Time

12.120 Application for permission must be made 'promptly and in any event within three months from the date when grounds for the application

309 The requirement for permission represents the most significant difference between the procedure to be followed on a claim for judicial review and an appeal under HA 1996 s204 or H(W)A 2014 s88, which is as of right.

310 See *R v Secretary of State for the Home Department, ex p Salem* [1999] 1 AC 450; *R (Rushbridger) v Attorney-General* [2004] 1 AC 357, HL.

311 *R (McKenzie) v Waltham Forest LBC* [2009] EWHC 1097 (Admin), [2009] JHL D94. See *R (Raw) v Lambeth LBC* [2010] EWHC 507 (Admin), [2010] JHL D40, D104 where the authority conceded the applicant's entitlement to assistance under its rent deposit scheme after the issue of his claim, which it invited him to withdraw, which he refused to do. The Administrative Court dismissed the claim as it was not in the public interest to hear academic claims and the court's resources were better spent on cases directly affecting the rights and obligations of the parties; nor was there evidence of other cases in which the authority had applied its policy or that the issue raised would need to be resolved by the courts in the near future. If a claim is fact-sensitive, it will not be permitted to proceed: *R (Zoolife International Ltd) v Secretary of State for the Environment* [2007] EWHC 2995 (Admin), [2008] ACD 44.

312 *R (Adow) v Newham LBC* [2010] EWHC 951 (Admin), [2010] JHL D101; for the facts, see para 11.102.

first arose'.[313] The three-month period runs from the time when application for permission can first be made.[314] The former explicit power (to be found in RSC Order 53 r4) to extend time for 'good reason' has not been retained, although the general jurisdiction of the court to extend time under CPR 3.1 is available. Any application to extend time must be set out in the claim form with grounds.[315] The parties may not agree to extend time,[316] nor will the court be enthusiastic about granting permission when an application has grown stale.[317] Delay in obtaining legal aid may constitute an acceptable reason for granting permission belatedly.[318] Where the challenge is to the lawfulness of a policy and the relief sought is to restrain its further implementation, the need to ensure that a prima facie unlawful policy is discontinued is likely to comprise a good reason for extending time.[319]

12.121 When permission to pursue judicial review out of time is granted, it is not a final decision on the time question: it may still be raised at the full hearing of the application for judicial review itself.[320]

Form of application

12.122 An application must be made on form N461, in accordance with CPR Part 54. The claim form must include or be accompanied by a detailed statement of the grounds and a statement of the facts relied on.[321]

313 CPR 54.5.

314 PD 54A, para 4.1. When what is under challenge is a policy, time only begins to run when it affects the individual applicant: *R v Tower Hamlets LBC ex p Mohib Ali* (1993) 25 HLR 218, DC; *R v Newham LBC ex p Ajayi* (1994) 28 HLR 25, QBD.

315 PD 54A, para 54.6.

316 CPR 54.5(2).

317 See *R v Rochester City Council ex p Trotman* (1983) *Times* 13 May.

318 *R v Stratford on Avon DC ex p Jackson* [1985] 1 WLR 1319, CA; see also *R v Dacorum BC ex p Brown* (1989) 21 HLR 405, QBD.

319 *R (Lin) v Barnet LBC* [2006] EWHC 1041 (Admin), [2006] HLR 44.

320 *R v Dairy Produce Quota Tribunal ex p Caswell* [1990] 2 AC 738, HL; caution should, however, be exercised when re-opening the issue of delay at the substantive hearing: *R (Lichfield Securities Ltd) v Lichfield DC* [2001] EWCA Civ 304, [2001] 3 PLR 33.

321 A form of N461, including the statement of grounds and statement of facts is annexed to this chapter.

Supporting documents

12.123 In addition, any written evidence in support of the claim, a copy of the decision that the applicant[322] seeks to have quashed, any documents which will be relied on, copies of relevant statutory material and a list of essential documents for advance reading must also be supplied. Two copies of the relevant documents in a paginated and indexed bundle must be filed.[323] Where it is not possible to file all of the documents, the applicant must say which are to follow and explain why they are not currently available.

12.124 In the usual case, the applicant's full case will have to be made out in the initial application, without anticipating additional oral evidence or later elaboration. This makes the initial papers very important indeed. This means that the case must be made out from the outset.

Duty of care

12.125 There is a high duty of care on the part of all applicants to make full and frank disclosure in an application for permission, even if it is unhelpful to the case.[324] Non-disclosure is not necessarily fatal if it causes no advantage to the applicant and no prejudice to the respondent but, even if it does not lead to the refusal of permission, it could still affect relief at the end of the day.[325] The obligation is to make full and candid disclosure of the material facts known to the applicant and to make proper enquiries before making the application; there is a breach of the disclosure duty if he or she has not disclosed any additional material facts which he or she would have known if he or she had made proper enquiries before making the application.[326] Proper disclosure for this purpose means specifically identifying all relevant documents for the judge, taking him or her to the particular passages in the documents which are material and taking appropriate steps to ensure that the judge correctly appreciates the significance of what he or she is being asked to read; that burden of full and frank

322 Under the CPR, a person claiming judicial review is now (as in other cases) a claimant (see CPR 2.3(1): 'a claimant is a person who makes a claim' and CPR 54.1 referring to a 'claim for judicial review'); the term 'applicant' is, however, used in this book to denote applicant under either HA 1996 Part 6 or Part 7 or H(W)A 2014 Part 2.

323 PD 54A, paras 5.6–5.9.

324 See also para 12.149, on an application for interim relief, where there is an analogous duty of disclosure.

325 See *R v Wirral MBC ex p Bell* (1994) 27 HLR 234, QBD.

326 *R (Lawer) v Restormel BC* [2007] EWHC 2299 (Admin), [2008] HLR 20.

disclosure is more onerous where a telephone application is being made to a judge who has none of the papers before him or her, nor is it removed by giving informal notice to the other party.[327]

Service

12.126 The claim form (and accompanying documents) must be served on the defendant(s) within seven days of the date of issue,[328] together with an acknowledgment of service form, which must be filed by the respondent authority not more than 21 days after service of the claim form.[329]

Pre-permission response

12.127 In the acknowledgement of service, the defendant must set out a summary of the grounds for contesting the claim, any directions which will be sought and other applications which will be made at the permission stage. A respondent who does not return the acknowledgment of service form within 14 days of service will lose the right to take part in the permission hearing (although not the right to take part in the substantive application) without the court's express permission to do so.[330] A respondent authority may not apply to set aside permission where it has been served with the claim form,[331] but may do so where there has been a failure to serve by the applicant.[332]

Paper applications

12.128 Applications for permission to proceed will, unless the court directs otherwise, be decided by a judge without hearing oral submissions.

Interim applications

12.129 Any applications for interim relief should be made in accordance with CPR Parts 23 and 25 and may be considered with the application for permission.[333] Even where an interim application – for example, to

327 See para 12.116.

328 CPR 54.7. Where the relief sought in the claim form includes a declaration of incompatibility under HRA 1998 s4, the Crown must be given 21 days' notice and/or joined as an interested party or second defendant to the claim: CPR 19.4A(1), and see *R (Morris) v Westminster City Council* [2003] EWHC 2266 (Admin), [2004] HLR 18.

329 CPR 54.8.

330 CPR 54.9.

331 CPR 54.13.

332 *R (Webb) v Bristol City Council* [2001] EWHC (Admin) 696, [2001] JHL D90.

333 There is a duty of full disclosure – see para 12.148.

house pending the substantive hearing – is made at the same time as permission is sought, there does not have to be an oral hearing if the court does not consider it appropriate.[334] Failure to comply with any order of the court – or an undertaking given in lieu of an order – may amount to contempt of court.[335]

Attendance of respondent

12.130 The respondent authority does not need to attend any permission hearing, unless the court directs otherwise. Where it does so, the court will not generally make an order for costs against the applicant.[336]

Post-permission response

12.131 If permission is granted, the respondent must, within 35 days of service of the order granting permission, file and serve detailed grounds for contesting the claim and any written evidence on which reliance is to be placed.[337]

Further stages

12.132 At least 21 days prior to the hearing, the applicant must file a full skeleton argument. The respondent must file a skeleton at least 14 days in advance.[338] Where permission is, on the papers, refused or granted only subject to conditions or on certain grounds, the applicant may, within seven days, request that the decision be reconsidered at an oral hearing.[339] An appeal against a refusal of permission – generally or on specific grounds, or against conditions – lies to the Court of Appeal, but only with its permission.[340]

334 CPR 23.8.

335 See *R (Bempoa) v Southwark LBC* [2002] EWHC 153 (Admin), [2002] JHL D44, where, in proceedings under the National Assistance Act 1948 s21, the authority through its social services department undertook not to evict the applicant, pending an assessment of his needs. Notwithstanding this, the authority's housing department evicted him from his accommodation and refused to reinstate him. The undertaking bound all departments in the authority, which was held to be in contempt.

336 PD 54A, paras 8.5–8.6.

337 CPR 54.14.

338 PD 54A, para 15.

339 CPR 54.12. No such application may be made, however, if the refusal of permission records that the application is totally without merit: CPR 54.12(7). As to the meaning of 'totally without merit' in this context see *R (Wasif) v Secretary of State for the Home Department* [2016] EWCA Civ 82, [2016] 1 WLR 2793. Such a litigant can still seek permission to appeal from the Court of Appeal: *Wasif.*

340 CPR 52.8.

Disclosure

12.133 Application for disclosure of documents may be made (by either party) at the same time that permission is sought, or after it has been granted.[341] Unless the court makes an order for disclosure, it is not required.[342] On discovery, only material which is privileged – because it has been produced in the course of, or in anticipation of, the proceedings – may be withheld.

12.134 The applicant will accordingly be able to inspect the authority's minutes, emails and other memoranda dealing with his or her application. An examination of the authority's standing orders should be undertaken in every case, as these may reveal a want of authorised delegation or sub-delegation.[343] It may be said that few authorities can withstand such close legal scrutiny without revealing *some* flaws in their procedure, although these flaws may do no more than cause minor embarrassment without invalidating the whole process.

Further appeal

12.135 If permission is refused, the refusal may be appealed to the Court of Appeal; this must be pursued within seven days.[344] If successful, the Court of Appeal, rather than giving permission to appeal, may give permission to apply for judicial review[345] and will usually order that the case should proceed in the High Court.[346] Appeals from a full judicial review application require permission from either the High Court, or – if refused – from the Court of Appeal.[347]

Hearing

12.136 In the usual course, evidence will be that which was served (in writing) with the application for permission,[348] supplemented by any evidence in reply and any further evidence in response; not uncommonly there will be two or three exchanges of evidence. Oral evidence

341 CPR 54.16.
342 PD 54A.12(1).
343 See chapter 9.
344 CPR 52.8(3).
345 CPR 52.8(5).
346 CPR 52.8(6).
347 CPR 52.3(1). Permission may only be granted where there is a real prospect of success or some other compelling reason: CPR 52.6.
348 See para 12.123.

is possible, but only at the discretion of the court.[349] Permission to cross-examine witnesses is rarely granted.[350]

Burden of proof

12.137 As noted,[351] the burden of proof lies on a person seeking to show that a decision is void; the allegations must be both substantiated and particularised: *Wednesbury*[352] and *Cannock Chase DC v Kelly*.[353] Thus, it is never enough to say simply that the applicant is a homeless person and in priority need, because this would not be enough to raise the inference of a duty. The duty arises only when the authority is satisfied, or has reason to believe, or considers that the fact or state of affairs is as it is claimed to be. It must be alleged that it has refused or failed to reach a decision, or that such decision as has been reached must be treated by the courts as void, for want of compliance with such of the foregoing principles as are identified; the factual basis for this allegation must be set out.

Costs

12.138 The general provisions concerning costs (ie, those contained in CPR 44) are applicable to judicial review proceedings.[354] Accordingly, the usual order is for costs to follow the event so that the successful party will be able to recover costs.[355] The court, however, has a broad discretion to take into account all factors, including the conduct of the parties; thus, where either party's conduct has prolonged litigation or has had the effect of increasing the costs burden on the other, the

349 The court has an inherent power to give directions requiring oral evidence and cross-examination in a claim for judicial review: *R (G) v Ealing LBC (No 2)* [2002] EWHC 250 (Admin), [2002] MHLR 140. See further CPR 54.16 (referring to CPR 8.6(1)).

350 *Bubb v Wandsworth LBC* [2011] EWCA Civ 1285, [2012] HLR 13 at [24]–[25].

351 See para 12.123.

352 *Associated Provincial Picture Houses Ltd v Wednesbury Corporation* [1948] 1 KB 223, CA.

353 [1978] 1 WLR 1, CA.

354 This includes the wasted costs jurisdiction under Senior Courts Act 1981 s51 and CPR 48.7, where a legal representative has acted improperly, unreasonably or negligently, causing another party to incur unnecessary costs and it is just to make such an order: see generally *Ridehalgh v Horsefield* [1994] Ch 205, CA: see *R (Grimshaw) v Southwark LBC* [2013] EWHC 4504 (Admin) (proceedings challenging decision to terminate provision of temporary accommodation followed by accepted offer of accommodation about which claimant's solicitors failed to inform the court).

355 CPR 44.2(2)(a). See, eg *Mendes and another v Southwark LBC* [2009] EWCA Civ 594, [2010] HLR 3, at [23] and [24].

court may deprive the successful party of all or a proportion of the costs.[356] The courts will depart from the general rule on an issue-by-issue basis: where a party unsuccessfully raises an issue that takes up a significant part of the hearing, the party may be denied costs in relation to that issue, even if successful in the claim overall.[357]

12.139 Publicly funded litigants should not be treated differently from those who are not; nonetheless, the consequences for solicitors who do such work is a factor which must be taken into account: it is one thing for solicitors who do a substantial amount of publicly funded work, and who have to fund the substantial overheads that sustaining a legal practice involves, to take the risk of being paid at lower rates if a publicly funded case turns out to be unsuccessful, but quite another for them to be unable to recover remuneration at inter partes rates in the event that it is successful.[358]

12.140 Where a claim for judicial review is settled (most commonly, in the present context, where an authority agrees to withdraw its decision and reconsider it) but the costs remain in dispute, the principles – additional to the point that it will ordinarily be irrelevant that the claimant is in receipt of public funding for his or her claim – derive from *R (Boxall) v Waltham Forest LBC*:[359]

a) the court has power to make a costs order even where parties have settled the substantive claim;
b) it will ordinarily be irrelevant that the claimant is in receipt of public funding for his or her claim;
c) the overriding objective is to do justice between the parties without incurring unnecessary court time and costs;
d) how far the court will be prepared to look into the substantive issues will depend on the circumstances of the particular case,

356 CPR 44.2(1)–(5).

357 *AEI Rediffusion Music v Phonographic Performance Ltd* [1999] 1 WLR 1507, CA; *R (Bateman) v Legal Services Commission* [2001] EWHC 797 (Admin), [2002] ACD 29.

358 *R (E) v Governing Body of JFS and the Admissions Appeal Panel of JFS and others; R (E) v Governing Body of JFS and the Admissions Appeal Panel of JFS (United Synagogue) and others* [2009] UKSC 1 at [25]. The dicta of Scott Baker J in *R (Boxall) v Waltham Forest LBC* (2001) 4 CCLR 258, QBD that the fact that the claimants were legally aided was immaterial when deciding what, if any, costs order to make between the parties in a case where they were successful, was approved. See also *Bunning v King's Lynn and West Norfolk Council* [2016] EWCA Civ 1037, accepting the general principle, but, on the facts, making no order as to costs (claimant had prima facie been in breach of an injunction but her subsequent compliance rendered the committal proceedings academic).

359 (2001) 4 CCLR 258, QBD.

including the amount of costs at stake and the conduct of the parties;

e) in the absence of a good reason to make any other order, the fall-back position is to make no order as to costs; and

f) the court should take care not to discourage parties from settling judicial review proceedings.

A number of other cases approved and applied *Boxall*, drawing out the proposition that where the claimant has secured the substantive relief sought, it would normally comprise a good reason to award him or her his or her costs;[360] a judge should not be tempted too readily to adopt the fall-back position of making no order.[361]

12.141 The *Boxall* approach was applied by the Court of Appeal in *Haripaul v Lewisham LBC*:[362] the applicant was dissatisfied with both the original section 184 decision and the subsequent section 202 review and unsuccessfully appealed to the county court under section 204, from which the Court of Appeal granted permission to appeal, in response to which the authority offered to carry out a fresh review. The appeal was dismissed by consent but the parties were unable to agree who should bear the costs of the appeal. The Court of Appeal held that the authority should pay the costs of the appeal: the case was akin to a judicial review and the *Boxall* principles applied; the applicant had obtained the substantive relief that she sought and it was for the authority to show why it should not pay the costs; no such reasons existed on the facts.

12.142 In *R (M)*,[363] the Court of Appeal went somewhat further, holding that where a claimant obtains all the relief which he or she seeks

360 *Brawley v Marczynski & Business Lines Ltd* [2002] EWCA Civ 756, [2002] 4 All ER 1060; *R (Scott) v Hackney LBC* [2009] EWCA Civ 217; *Mendes v Southwark LBC* [2009] EWCA Civ 594, [2010] HLR 3; *R (Bhata) v Secretary of State for the Home Department* [2011] EWCA Civ 895. In *R (J) v Hackney LBC* [2010] EWHC 3021 (Admin), [2010] JHL D20, under Children Act 1989, the good reason was not only the rejection of the authority's argument that its concession followed a recent decision resulting from a development in the law (rejected on the basis that the law had not radically altered the legal landscape) but also flowed from the conduct of the authority which was sufficiently poor to justify an award of costs: it had taken 12 months to file an acknowledgement of service and five months after the new case to settle the matter; it had also been unreasonable for the authority to require an oral hearing to determine costs.

361 *R (Scott) v Hackney* LBC, above, at [51].

362 [2012] EWCA Civ 266, [2012] HLR 24.

363 *R (M) v Croydon LBC* [2012] EWCA Civ 595; see further *R (Dempsey) v Sutton LBC* [2013] EWCA Civ 863.

(whether by consent or after a contested hearing),[364] he or she is ordinarily[365] entitled to all his or her costs unless there is a good reason to the contrary; where, however, the claimant obtains only some of the relief which he or she is seeking, the issue is more complex: it may be appropriate to make an order for costs based on individual issues in proceedings; in many cases, the correct order will be 'no order as to costs'; each case will turn on its own facts.[366]

12.143 The court has power to order that costs be set off.[367] This may permit an order to set off costs against damages or costs to which a legally aided person has become or becomes entitled in the action; the set-off is no different from and no more extensive than the set-off available to or against parties who are not legally aided; the broad criterion is that the claims of both claimant and defendant claim are so closely connected that it would be inequitable to allow the claimant's claim without taking into account the defendant's claim;[368] the costs of and incidental to all proceedings in the High Court are in the discretion of the court.[369] While an assisted person is protected against the making of enforceable orders for payment of costs, that protection is not available to prevent an order for costs being set off.[370] While there will rarely be claim and counterclaim in HA 1996 Parts 6 and 7 (or H(W)A 2014 Part 2) cases,[371] the implication is that it may be possible to set off costs orders made in different judicial reviews, and perhaps even costs orders made in the county court against orders made in the High Court, if the proceedings are closely connected.

364 But not where the relief is obtained as the result of the actions of a third party, see *R (Naureen) v Salford City Council* [2012] EWCA Civ 1795 – the claimant became entitled to housing benefit because the Secretary of State granted her leave to remain, rather than because of any act or concession on the part of the authority.

365 See also *R (Hunt) v North Somerset Council* [2015] UKSC 51, [2015] 1 WLR 3575 in which it was held that a person who establishes that a public authority has acted unlawfully should ordinarily recover his costs, even if no relief is obtained.

366 As to the procedure to be adopted where the parties have settled a judicial review claim but cannot agree costs, see Guidance as to how the parties should assist the court when applications for costs are made following settlement of claims for judicial review, Administrative Court Office, December 2013.

367 CPR 44.12.

368 *Lockley v National Blood Transfusion Service* [1992] 1 WLR 492, CA.

369 *R (Burkett) v Hammersmith and Fulham* LBC [2004] EWCA Civ 1342.

370 *Hill v Bailey* [2003] EWHC 2835 (Ch).

371 Whether formally so or in practice.

Remedies and relief

Interim relief

12.144 Where a challenge is made by judicial review, the normal principle on an application for an interim injunction is that an order will be granted if it can be shown that the balance of convenience is in its favour.[372] In *de Falco, Silvestri v Crawley BC*,[373] however, Lord Denning MR said that in a homeless person's action it is necessary to show that there was a strong prima facie case of breach by the authority. The justification offered for this difference was that, almost invariably, the applicant would be unable to give a worthwhile undertaking in damages should the applicant eventually lose, although the House of Lords had in *Cyanamid*[374] already included ability to give a meaningful undertaking in damages as a factor to be weighed up in determining the balance of convenience.

12.145 The *de Falco* approach would also seem to conflict with Lord Denning MR's own approach in *Allen v Jambo Holdings Ltd*,[375] a case in which the owners of an aircraft sought discharge of a *Mareva* injunction on the ground that the plaintiff, who was legally-aided, could not give a valuable cross-undertaking in damages.

> It is said that whenever a *Mareva* injunction is granted the plaintiff has to give the cross-undertaking in damages. Suppose the widow should lose this case altogether. She is legally-aided. Her undertaking is worth nothing. I would not assent to that argument . . . A legally-aided plaintiff is by our statutes not to be in any worse position by reason of being legally-aided than any other plaintiff would be. I do not see why a poor plaintiff should be denied a *Mareva* injunction just because he is poor, whereas a rich plaintiff would get it . . .

12.146 In *R v Kensington and Chelsea RLBC ex p Hammell*,[376] it was contended by the authority that, following *Puhlhofer*,[377] it would be necessary to show something akin to 'exceptional circumstances' before an interim injunction could be granted. The court rejected this argument: interim relief is discretionary, although the discretion is one that must be exercised in accordance with principles of law; in a clear case of breach, there is therefore likely to be no issue of whether or

372 *American Cyanamid v Ethicon* [1975] AC 396, HL; *Fellowes v Fisher* [1976] QB 122, CA.

373 *De Falco, Silvestri v Crawley BC* [1980] QB 460, CA.

374 *American Cyanamid v Ethicon*, above.

375 [1980] 1 WLR 1252, CA.

376 [1989] QB 518, (1988) 20 HLR 666, CA.

377 *R v Hillingdon LBC ex p Puhlhofer* [1986] AC 484, (1986) 18 HLR 158.

not such relief should be granted. In *R v Cardiff City Council ex p Barry*,[378] it was held that, as a strong prima facie case had to be made out for a court to grant leave to move for judicial review of an authority's decision, interim relief would be the usual concomitant of the grant of leave.

12.147 In relation to a challenge to a refusal to house pending review,[379] however, this approach was rejected in *R v Camden LBC ex p Mohammed*[380] (approved in *R v Brighton and Hove Council ex p Nacion*[381]) because a review is as of right, available to everyone who is the subject of an adverse decision, and so no prima facie case has to be made out, as in the case of an application for judicial review.[382]

12.148 The principles on which the discretion to house pending review is to be exercised by the authority have been considered in chapter 10;[383] their application to housing pending appeal[384] is considered below.[385] Whether the development of those principles will have an impact in other cases in which permission is sought to claim judicial review – on other grounds – is unclear, but there is no apparent reason why they should do so, or why *Hammell*[386] should not continue to apply.

12.149 Orders granted without notice should be for a defined and short period, though sometimes it may be appropriate to decline to make an immediate order and direct instead an oral hearing within one or two days. This would give the defendant the opportunity to mount an effective opposition to the application.[387] There is a duty of full and frank disclosure of all relevant facts and law on an application for interim relief:[388] thus, in *Konodyba*,[389] an interim order for interim accommodation was set aside for breach of the duty of disclosure because the applicant had failed to disclose that she was the tenant of a property in Bishop's Stortford in which she could live pending determination of her application under HA 1996 Part 7.

378 (1989) 22 HLR 261, CA.
379 Under the power in HA 1996 s188(3); or H(W)A 2014 s69(10), (11).
380 (1998) 30 HLR 315, QBD.
381 (1999) 31 HLR 1095, CA.
382 (1998) 30 HLR 315, at 320.
383 See paras 10.29–10.42.
384 Under HA 1996 s204A or H(W)A 2014 s88(1), (5).
385 See paras 12.196–12.202.
386 See para 12.146.
387 *R (Casey) v Restormel BC* [2007] EWHC 2554 (Admin), [2008] JHL D27.
388 *R (Lawer) v Restormel BC* [2007] EWHC 2299 (Admin), [2008] HLR 20.
389 *R (Konodyba) v Kensington and Chelsea RLBC* [2011] EWHC 2653 (Admin), [2011] JHL D10. Upheld on appeal [2012] EWCA Civ 982.

Substantive hearing

12.150 The Administrative Court may:

a) quash a decision (a quashing order);
b) compel an authority to make a decision or a particular decision, or re-take a decision that has been quashed (a mandatory order);[390]
c) prohibit an authority from taking some action (a prohibiting order); or
d) make a declaration,[391] for example, to declare a decision ultra vires or void.

12.151 Although the Administrative Court, no more than the county court, cannot substitute its own decision for that of the authority, the findings of fact or law it makes may on occasion be such that there is only one decision that the authority can lawfully make, ie, with which it is left. In such cases, either directly or indirectly, the court will (in substance) order the authority to come to that decision.[392] Such circumstances would comprise circumstances in which the county court could use its powers to vary a decision instead of remitting the matter to the authority to reconsider.[393] It may also be that the Administrative Court would order the authority to come to a particular decision where it is necessary in order to restore a right of which the claimant has been unlawfully deprived.[394]

12.152 In an appropriate case, the Administrative Court may award damages as compensation for wrongful action or wrongful refusal to act.[395] This is not available where damages are the sole remedy claimed; the court must be satisfied that, if the claim had been made in a private law action, the claimant would have been awarded damages.

390 Where the court does so, the authority is bound by its conclusions and cannot go behind the findings of the High Court; if it disagrees with that decision, its recourse is to appeal: *Kuteh v Secretary of State for Education* [2014] EWCA Civ 1586.

391 CPR 54.3(1).

392 See *Barty-King v Ministry of Defence* [1979] 2 All ER 80, ChD. See also, eg *R v Ealing LBC ex p Parkinson* (1997) 29 HLR 179, QBD per Laws J at 185–186; *R (Cunningham) v Exeter Crown Court* [2003] EWHC 184 (Admin), [2003] 2 Cr App R (S) 64, per Clarke LJ at [22]; *R (S) v Secretary of State for the Home Department* [2007] EWCA Civ 546, [2007] Imm AR, 781, per Carnwath LJ at [46].

393 See paras 12.203–12.214.

394 Consider *Crawley LBC v B* (2000) 32 HLR 636, CA, at 651–652, see para 12.207; and *Robinson v Hammersmith and Fulham LBC* [2006] EWCA Civ 1122, [2006] 1 WLR 3295, [2007] HLR 7, at [31], see para 12.209.

395 CPR 54.3(2).

Refusal of relief

12.153 It is accepted in judicial review cases that a court may refuse relief, notwithstanding a finding of procedural error on the part of the authority, if the error would plainly have made no difference to the authority's decision.[396] This will not be so, however, if reconsideration *could* lead to a different decision, ie, it is not enough for the authority to assert that it could reach the same decision on reconsideration; the error must be such that it *would* have made no difference.[397]

Confidentiality

12.154 Both the High Court and the county court[398] have inherent jurisdiction to make an order granting anonymity to an applicant, and to support it with an order under the Contempt of Court Act 1981 s11 preventing publication of an applicant's name, address and photograph.[399] Such an order should be made, however, only where it can be shown that a failure to do so would render the attainment of justice doubtful or, in effect, impracticable.[400]

12.155 If no order is sought and obtained before proceeding, then:

a) no subsequent order could relate back, with the result that
b) it might become inappropriate to make an order in relation to the substantive proceedings themselves simply by reason of any publicity properly derived from preliminary proceedings.

12.156 The proper course, therefore, is to apply to the court without notice under Contempt of Court Act 1981 s11 at the same time as proceedings are to be issued, if appropriate asking for a hearing to be in camera. If there is power to make an order because the pre-conditions are satisfied, the court can grant it for a short time, for notice to be given

396 *R (Bibi) v Newham LBC* [2001] EWCA Civ 607, [2002] 1 WLR 237, at [40]: 'The court has two functions – assessing the legality of actions by administrators and, if it finds unlawfulness on the administrators' part, deciding what relief it should give.' See also *R v Secretary of State for the Environment ex p Walters; R v Brent LBC ex p O'Malley* (1997) 30 HLR 328, CA; *R v Islington LBC ex p B* (1997) 30 HLR 706, QBD. See also Senior Courts Act 1981 s31(2A), providing that the court must refuse relief if it is 'highly likely that the outcome for the applicant would not have been substantially different' notwithstanding the conduct complained of.

397 See, by analogy in the context of statutory appeals under HA 1996 s204.

398 *Norman v Mathews* (1916) 85 LJKB 857, *affirmed* (1916) 23 TLR 369, CA.

399 *R v Westminster City Council ex p Castelli; R v Same ex p Tristran-Garcia* (1995) 27 HLR 125.

400 *In the matter of D* (1997–98) 1 CCLR 190, at 196K.

to the press.[401] In some cases, it may be necessary for papers not to be lodged until the application can be dealt with immediately, so as to prevent disclosure by way of inspection of office documents.[402]

12.157 Additionally, the court has power under CPR 39.2(4) to order that the identity of any party or witness should not be disclosed if it considers non-disclosure necessary in order to protect the interests of that party or witness.

Minors

12.158 A court may also require reports not to identify parties for the purpose of protecting the interests of children indirectly involved in a case.[403]

Appeal to county court

Procedure

Point of law

12.159 An appeal to the county court lies on a point of law.[404] 'Point of law' includes 'not only matters of legal interpretation but also the full range of issues[405] which would otherwise be the subject of an application to the High Court for judicial review, such as procedural error and questions of vires, to which I add, also of irrationality and (in)adequacy of reasons'.[406]

12.160 The jurisdiction does not permit judges to reach their own decisions of fact; to do so is in excess of the statutory jurisdiction.[407] Where an authority considered that an applicant was not vulnerable[408] because of mental illness, it was not for the judge to conclude

401 *In the matter of D* (1997–98) 1 CCLR 190.

402 *In the matter of D* (1997–98) 1 CCLR 190.

403 See *Crawley BC v B* (2000) 32 HLR 636, CA, at 638. See CPR 39.2(3)(d).

404 HA 1996 s204(1); H(W)A 2014 s88(1).

405 Cf the first part of this chapter: 'Substantive law', paras 12.5–12.105.

406 *Nipa Begum v Tower Hamlets LBC* [2000] 1 WLR 306, (1999) 32 HLR 445, CA per Auld LJ at 452. *Nipa Begum* was approved by the House of Lords in *Runa Begum v Tower Hamlets LBC* [2003] UKHL 5, [2003] 2 AC 430, [2003] HLR 32, see particularly Lord Bingham at [7].

407 *Kruja v Enfield LBC* [2004] EWCA Civ 1769, [2005] HLR 13. See also *Aw-Aden v Birmingham City Council* [2005] EWCA Civ 1834, in which it was held that the judge had made inappropriate findings of fact. See also *Bubb v Wandsworth LBC* [2011] EWCA Civ 1285, [2012] HLR 13 and *Richmond Upon Thames LBC v Kubickek* [2012] EWHC 3292 (QB), again reiterating that the county court should not set Itself up as a finder of fact.

408 And accordingly not in priority need – see chapter 5.

that he was mentally ill (and accordingly vulnerable): 'Some decision-makers might have arrived at a different conclusion. It is elementary that matters of that kind were not for the judge . . .'[409]

12.161 There are, however, exceptions to this. First, the discussion of when error of fact may comprise a public law failure sufficient to vitiate a decision is as applicable in the county court as otherwise: this may involve the court considering the facts from the perspective of whether there has been such an error.[410] Second, an applicant who will face eviction from temporary accommodation if his or her HA 1996 s204 appeal is unsuccessful is entitled to raise his or her Article 8 rights[411] during that appeal,[412] provided occupation can be said to be as a home, [413] which, on the basis of how Article 8 is understood and applied domestically,[414] means that, if what is asserted is that the authority has come to the wrong decision in concluding, eg that the applicant is not in priority need or is intentionally homeless, because it has erred in relation to the facts,[415] the court may be required independently to determine the facts for itself.[416]

409 *Kruja v Enfield LBC* [2004] EWCA Civ 1769, [2005] HLR 13 at [23]. See also *Wandsworth LBC v Watson* [2010] EWCA Civ 1558, [2011] HLR 9, where the authority's appeal was allowed because the recorder had effectively substituted her own decision as to risk of violence in relation to an offer of accommodation for that of the authority.

410 Para.12.37.

411 Para.12.95.

412 *R (ZH and CN) v Newham LBC and Lewisham LBC* [2014] UKSC 62, [2015] AC 1259, [2015] HLR 6 at [64].

413 This is an autonomous test which requires 'the existence of sufficient and continued links with a specific place': see, eg, *Hounslow LBC v Powell* [2011] UKSC 8, [2011] 2 AC 186, [2011] HLR 23, per Lord Hope at [33] but is not a high bar and will commonly be fulfilled by homeless people (who, after all, of definition have nowhere else to call home) who have been in the accommodation for a relatively short time, perhaps as little as a month.

414 *Manchester City Council v Pinnock* [2010] UKSC 45, [2011] 2 AC 104, [2011] HLR 7; *Hounslow LBC v Powell* (above).

415 Because it is strongly arguable that it would not be disproportionate to evict someone on a materially erroneous assessment of his or her circumstances.

416 'A fair procedure requires the occupant to have a right to raise the issue of the proportionality of the interference and to have that issue determined by an independent tribunal': *Manchester* at [45] cited in *R (ZH and CN) v Newham LBC and Lewisham LBC* at [63]. 'It is only in very exceptional cases that the applicant will succeed in raising an arguable case of a lack of proportionality where an applicant has no right under domestic law to remain in possession of a property' which 'is so particularly where an authority seeks to recover possession of interim accommodation provided under s.188 of the 1996 Act'; and, it is for the occupier to raise the question: nonetheless, 'In an appropriate case the court, if satisfied that eviction was disproportionate, could prohibit

From what decision?

12.162 The point of law under challenge will usually be one made in relation to the internal review rather than the original decision, as any error on the original decision will either have been remedied on or replaced by the review (with or without the same or an alternative error of law).

12.163 One exception to this is[417] if a time has been prescribed for notification of a decision on an internal review[418] and no such notification has been given (or, if notification has been given, if it does not comply with the minimum statutory requirements, ie, to give reasons and advise of the right to appeal and the time for appeal – see HA 1996 s203(4) and (5) and H(W)A 2014 s86(4) and (5) – so that it is treated as not having been given: see HA 1996 s203(6) and H(W)A 2014 s88(2)). In such a case, the appeal will be against the original decision.

12.164 Another exception is if the review simply ignores an original error which continues to have an effect, whether because it has been adopted or because – even if expressed differently – it influences how the court should construe the decision on review. In either event, however, the appeal must be on a point of law, whether it is in relation to the internal review or – for want of review decision within time – in relation to the original decision.[419]

Review and reconsideration

12.165 There is no right to a review of a decision on an earlier review.[420] Not uncommonly, however, even where there has been a review, a local authority will be willing to reconsider its decision, for example, following receipt of a letter before action.[421] A complaint about the decision on such a reconsideration may still lie to the county court[422] if, but only if, the complaint can be described as still comprising an appeal from the original review decision[423] (which in turn will raise the issue of whether it is still in time).[424] In the alternative, it is

the eviction for as long as that was the case, for example if the local authority did not provide alternative accommodation': *R (ZH and CN) v Newham LBC and Lewisham LBC* at [65]–[66].

417 HA 1996 s204(1)(b); H(W)A 2014 s88(1)(b).

418 HA 1996 s203(7); H(W)A 2014 s85.

419 HA 1996 s204(1); H(W)A 2014 s88(1).

420 HA 1996 s202(2); H(W)A 2014 s85(4).

421 See para 12.170.

422 *R v Westminster City Council ex p Ellioua* (1998) 31 HLR 440, CA.

423 *Demetri v Westminster City Council* [2000] 1 WLR 772, CA, at 780/A–B.

424 See para 12.166.

possible that the decision to reconsider can in context be construed as a withdrawal of the original review decision.[425]

Time for appeal

12.166 The appeal must be brought within 21 days of the applicant being notified of the decision on the internal review, or when the applicant should have been so notified.[426] Where the court office is closed on the final day for lodging the appeal, the time is extended until the next day that the office is open.[427] Delivery of the notice of appeal is sufficient to constitute filing; there is no requirement that a court officer receive or authenticate the notice.[428]

Extension of time

12.167 The 21-day limit has been acknowledged as short, indeed 'draconian, as some might think'.[429] Prior to amendment by the Homelessness Act 2002 there was no power for the court to extend time.[430] By HA 1996 s204(2A) and H(W)A 2014 s88(3), the county court now has power to extend time – before or after the 21-day period has expired – for 'good reason'. Delay in obtaining public funding to bring an appeal may well constitute an acceptable reason for extension of time[431] as may incompetent legal advice, although there has to be evi-

425 See para 12.169.

426 HA 1996 s204(2); H(W)A 2014 s88(2).

427 *Calverton Parish Council v Nottingham City Council* [2015] EWHC 503 (Admin); *Aadan v Brent LBC* (2000) 32 HLR 848, CA; *Pritam Kaur v S Russell & Sons Ltd* [1973] QB 336. See also *Croke v Secretary of State for Communities and Local Government* [2016] EWHC 248 (Admin) in which the claimant's agent arrived at the court office at 4.25pm on the last day for lodging an appeal. A security guard refused him entry to the court building. The documents were filed a few days later. The High Court held that the principle in *Calverton, Aadan* and *Kaur* did not apply. The court office had been open and available to accept the papers. Litigants had to appreciate that there would be security procedures to be completed before being allowed access to the court and had to allow sufficient time to deal with those matters.

428 *Van Aken v Camden LBC* [2002] EWCA Civ 1724, [2003] 1 WLR 684, [2003] HLR 33.

429 *R v Brent LBC ex p O'Connor* (1998) 31 HLR 923, QBD, per Tucker J at 925.

430 *Honig v Lewisham LBC* (1958) 122 JPJ 302; and *Gwynedd CC v Grunshaw* (1999) 32 HLR 610, CA. See also *O'Connor*, above.

431 *R v Stratford on Avon DC ex p Jackson* [1985] 1 WLR 1319, CA; see also *R v Dacorum BC ex p Brown* (1989) 21 HLR 405, QBD. Cf *Peake v Hackney LBC* [2013] EWHC 2528 (QB) (that time for appeal expired on Christmas Day did not necessarily comprise good reason: nor did the imposition of a time limit give rise to any arguable issue under Article 6).

dence of the latter – it does not automatically follow from the failure to issue in time.[432] Where the applicant was profoundly deaf and had been seeking legal assistance that she could understand and follow, there was a good reason for her appeal not to have been brought within the 21-day time limit.[433]

12.168 The merits of the appeal are irrelevant to deciding whether there is good reason to extend time; the merits come in at the next stage, when – having decided that there is a good reason – the court has to decide whether it should exercise its discretion to extend time.[434]

Agreement to further review

12.169 Where an authority agrees to reconsider the review decision, it is possible that the agreement will in substance comprise an agreement on the part of the authority to revoke or withdraw its original decision. Alternatively, it may comprise an agreement to waive, extend or suspend the time limit for appeal from it, or to take no time point.[435] Such an agreement does, however, need to be clearly spelled out:[436] where an applicant seeking reconsideration is not represented, the authority should take it on itself to make clear the basis on which it is agreeing to reconsider and, in particular, should point out if time to appeal is not being extended.[437]

Letter before action

12.170 The provisions of CPR Part 52 do not require the applicant (or the applicant's legal advisers) to write a letter before action setting out the applicant's case on appeal. Prior to the introduction of the statutory appeal,[438] however – when challenges against adverse decisions were made by way of judicial review – a letter before claim should

432 *Poorsalehy v Wandsworth LBC* [2013] EWHC 3687 (QB).

433 *Barrett v Southwark LBC* [2008] EWHC 1568 (QB), [2008] JHL D107.

434 *Short v Birmingham City Council* [2004] EWHC 2112 (QB), [2005] HLR 6. If a judge is minded to strike out an appeal as being outside the 21-day time limit, the applicant is entitled to proper notice so as to enable him or her to meet the point: *Dawkins v Central Bedfordshire Council* [2013] EWHC 4757 (QB).

435 *Demetri v Westminster City Council* [2000] 1 WLR 772, CA, at 780/C–D and 781/E–G. An agreement to conduct a further review could constitute a good reason for the applicant being unable to bring the appeal in time, and would be likely to do so if public funding was not available until after its outcome.

436 *Demetri*.

437 *Demetri*, at 781/H–782/A.

438 And prior to the introduction of the requirement for a pre-action protocol letter in judicial review cases.

have been written.[439] Given the introduction of a requirement for a pre-action letter in judicial review proceedings,[440] and the fact that the question of costs is a matter for the discretion of the court,[441] the same principles should be applied (in the absence of special circumstances rendering such a letter impossible, or impracticable or pointless).

Supporting documents

12.171 The appeal will need to be brought in accordance with CPR Part 52 and the associated Practice Directions (PDs).[442] Three copies of the appellant's notice (plus a further copy for each respondent) must be filed, together with grounds of appeal[443] and a copy of the decision under appeal. Any amendment to the appellants notice or grounds of appeal requires the permission of the court.[444] When issuing an appeal, the appellant must file and serve proposed case management directions, with which – within 14 days – the authority must either agree or to which it must propose alternatives.[445] Within the same period, the authority must also disclose any relevant documents which have not previously been disclosed; within 14 days of their receipt, the grounds of appeal may be amended as of right to deal with any new material.[446]

12.172 Notwithstanding the discretion to amend the notice of appeal (other than as of right to deal with new material),[447] the Court of Appeal has emphasised the importance of the grounds in setting the agenda for the appeal hearing and in enabling the respondent (and the court) to understand that agenda from the outset. Brooke LJ concluded that:

> It is thoroughly bad practice to state the barest possible grounds in the original notice of appeal . . ., and then to delay formulating and serving very substantial amended grounds of appeal for five months so that they surfaced for the first time less than a week before the appeal hearing.[448]

439 *R v Horsham DC ex p Wenman* [1995] 1 WLR 680, QBD; *R v Secretary of State for the Home Department ex p Begum* [1995] COD 177.
440 See para 12.117.
441 See Senior Courts Act 1981 s51 and CPR 44.2.
442 See in particular, PD 52D, para 28.1.
443 PD 52B, para 4.1; see form N161.
444 CPR 52.17.
445 CPR Part 52, PD 52D, para 28.1(5)(a), (b).
446 CPR Part 52, PD 52D, para 28.1(5)(c), (d).
447 See para 12.171.
448 *Cramp v Hastings BC; Phillips v Camden LBC*, above, at [72].

Response

12.173 While a respondent's notice may be filed where a respondent seeks to uphold a decision for reasons different from, or additional to, those previously given,[449] this is unlikely to be appropriate in a homelessness appeal. If the review (or, on occasion, the original) decision is wrong, then the authority should consent to it being quashed, and proceed to make a fresh decision on the correct basis. The only obvious circumstance when the authority could ask the court to substitute one (wrong) decision with a fresh decision is if the fresh decision is the only decision open to the authority as a matter of law.[450]

12.174 While an authority may well need to concede one or more elements of a challenge before the appeal comes to a hearing, the authority may not withdraw its decision so as to pre-empt the appeal if continuing the appeal could lead to an enduring benefit to the applicant. Thus, in *Deugi*,[451] the applicant not only sought to quash the original decision but also sought a variation of it; its withdrawal would have deprived the applicant of the opportunity to seek the variation.

District judges

12.175 Once it was appreciated that the CPR permitted district judges to hear Part 52 appeals,[452] a new PD was introduced to prevent them doing so.[453]

12.176 As with judicial review,[454] it is only exceptionally that the court will hear oral evidence,[455] eg where relevant evidence has come to light since the review was concluded.[456]

Costs

12.177 The general rule that costs should follow the event applies even where the matter is remitted to the authority for a fresh decision. It is not appropriate for the county court judge to refuse costs on the basis that it is considered inevitable that the authority will reach the same adverse decision (and that it will be upheld on review and appeal); it is inappropriate for the judge to reach any conclusion on

449 CPR 52.13.

450 See paras 12.203–12.214.

451 *Tower Hamlets LBC v Deugi* [2006] EWCA Civ 159, [2006] HLR 28.

452 See the comments of Sir Richard Scott V-C in *Crawley BC v B* (2000) 32 HLR 636, CA.

453 CPR 2, PD 2B.9.

454 See para 12.136.

455 *Bubb v Wandsworth LBC* [2011] EWCA Civ 1285, [2012] HLR 13 at [24]–[25].

456 *Bubb* at [26].

that issue.[457] The principles applicable to costs where a claim for judicial review is settled[458] – that if the claimant has secured the substantive relief sought, he or she should normally be awarded his or her costs[459] – is also applicable to appeals under HA 1996 s204.[460]

12.178 The court has power to order that costs be set off.[461] The implication of this – discussed above – is that it may be possible to set off costs orders made in the county court against orders made in the High Court, if the proceedings are closely connected,[462] as well as costs in other county court proceedings.

12.179 In *Maloba*,[463] the county court ordered the authority to pay two-thirds of the appellant's costs in relation to a section 204 appeal and refused the authority's application for a stay of enforcement pending the outcome of any future appeal against its fresh review decision, in which it hoped to be successful and therefore to secure a costs award in its favour, to be set off against those awarded against it in the present case.[464] The Court of Appeal accepted that the court's discretion was wide enough in principle to enable it to grant such a stay if it considers it just to do so, but refused to overturn the judge's decision.[465] It was cautious about introducing a general practice which would have the effect of depriving solicitors who acted for successful Legal Services Commission funded clients of payment at normal commercial rates without being able to assess properly the potential wider consequences that this would have.[466]

12.180 It may be observed that it is hard to see that such an anticipatory order could ever be successful unless there was a history of unsuccessful challenges, in which the instant success was a rare or only

457 *Rikha Begum v Tower Hamlets LBC* [2005] EWCA Civ 340, [2005] HLR 34.

458 See paras 12.138–12.143.

459 *R (M) v Croydon LBC* [2012] EWCA Civ 595, [2012] 1 WLR 2607.

460 *Harripaul v Lewisham LBC* [2012] EWCA Civ 266, [2012] HLR 24. See also *Unichi v Southwark LBC* [2013] EWHC 3681 (QB) (authority refused to await conclusion of review pending receipt of psychologist's report which was provided after review issued and on receipt of which authority agreed to carry out a fresh review: the applicant had obtained the substantive relief she had sought; the authority had been alerted to the importance of the report but had decided to conclude the review before it was available; the costs were payable immediately rather than held against any further proceedings).

461 CPR 44.12.

462 See para 12.143.

463 *Waltham Forest LBC v Maloba* [2007] EWCA Civ 1281, [2008] HLR 26.

464 *Maloba* at [65].

465 *Maloba* at [71].

466 *Maloba* at [73].

occurrence. Even so, it would necessarily assume that the same solicitors would be acting, for those who had been successful should surely not properly be deprived of their success-based costs in the event that other solicitors pursued an unsuccessful case.

Wasted costs

12.181 In *Wilson*,[467] a first-instance decision that non-legal officers of an authority could be ordered personally to pay costs, in substance for causing unnecessary legal expenditure by failing to respond to litigation, was overturned and held to have been wrongly made. Lawyers, however, are susceptible to such orders ('wasted costs orders') under Senior Courts Act 1981 s51[468] and CPR 46.8.

12.182 It is appropriate to make a wasted costs order against a legal representative only if:

a) the legal representative acted improperly, unreasonably or negligently;[469]
b) the legal representative's conduct caused a party to incur unnecessary costs; and
c) it is just in all the circumstances to order the legal representative to compensate that party for the whole or part of the costs.[470]

12.183 The test is a moderately high one. Improper conduct is that which would attract a sanction from a professional body or which would fairly be stigmatised as being improper; unreasonable conduct is that which is vexatious or is designed to harass the other side rather than to advance a resolution of the case or which does not have a reasonable explanation;[471] negligent conduct is not that which would found a common law action for damages,[472] but a question as to whether the legal representative conducted himself or herself with the competence to be expected of a professional person.[473] It must be

467 *R v Lambeth LBC ex p Wilson* (1997) 30 HLR 64, CA.

468 Inserted by Courts and Legal Services Act 1990 s4.

469 *KOO Golden East Mongolia v Bank of Nova Scotia* [2008] EWHC 1120 (QB), per Silber J; *Hallam Peel & Co v Southwark LBC* [2008] EWCA Civ 1120.

470 The test derives from *Re A Barrister (wasted costs order) (No 1 of 1991)* [1992] 3 All ER 429, CA, and is now incorporated into the PD accompanying CPR Part 48 (at para 53.5).

471 '[The] courts can be trusted to differentiate between errors of judgment and true negligence': *Arthur JS Hall & Co (a firm) v Simons* [2002] 1 AC 615, HL.

472 This is not negligence in any technical sense, see *Re Sternberg, Reed, Taylor and Gill* (1999) *Times* 26 July, CA and *Dempsey v Johnstone* [2003] EWCA Civ 1134, [2003] All ER (D) 515.

473 See *Ridehalgh v Horsefield* [1994] Ch 205, CA.

something akin to abuse of process; a breach of the lawyer's duty to the court.[474]

12.184 The rising tendency to seek an order for wasted costs was curtailed by the Court of Appeal in *Ridehalgh v Horsefield*,[475] where it was said that the courts should be anxious to avoid satellite litigation. Reinforcing the point, the House of Lords has held[476] that wasted costs orders should be confined to questions which are apt for summary disposal by the courts:[477]

> Save in the clearest case, applications against the lawyers acting for an opposing party are unlikely to be apt for summary determination, since any hearing to investigate the conduct of a complex action is itself likely to be expensive and time-consuming. The desirability of compensating litigating parties who have been put to unnecessary expense by the unjustified conduct of their opponents' lawyers is, without doubt, an important public interest, but it is, as the Court of Appeal pointed out in *Ridehalgh v Horsefield* . . . only one of the public interests which have to be considered.[478]

12.185 As a general rule, only matters such as the following are apt for wasted costs: failure to appear, conduct which leads to an otherwise avoidable step in the proceedings or the prolongation of a hearing by gross repetition or extreme slowness in the presentation of evidence or argument, wasting court time and abuse of process which results in excessive cost.[479]

12.186 Costs that arise as a consequence of difficulties with public funding are unlikely to lead to an order for wasted costs. Where a solicitor sought an adjournment on the day before the hearing because of difficulties with his client's funding, his failure was an error of judgment, not an act which attracted liability for wasted costs.[480]

474 *Persaud (Luke) v Persaud (Mohan)* [2003] EWCA Civ 394, [2003] PNLR 26, CA at [27].

475 [1994] Ch 205, CA; see also *Re A Barrister (wasted costs order)* [1993] QB 293, CA. See *Arthur JS Hall & Co v Simons* [2002] 1 AC 615 and *R v Camden LBC ex p Martin* [1997] 1 WLR 359, QBD, where it was held that there was no power to make a wasted costs order in favour of a person who elects to oppose an ex parte application for permission to seek judicial review.

476 *Medcalf v Mardell* [2002] UKHL 27, [2003] 1 AC 120.

477 See *Wall v Lefever* [1998] 1 FCR 605, CA, where wasted costs orders were said to provide a 'salutary and summary remedy' in clear cases. See also *R v Luton Family Proceedings Court Justices ex p R* [1998] 1 FCR 605, CA.

478 *Medcalf v Mardell* [2002] UKHL 27, [2003] 1 AC 120, per Lord Bingham at [24].

479 *Medcalf*, approving *Harley v McDonald* [2001] 2 AC 678, PC.

480 *Re a Solicitor (wasted costs order)* [1993] 2 FLR 959, CA.

12.187 Where a court refuses to make a wasted costs order, it will only be in very rare circumstances that an appeal court will intervene.[481]

Further appeal

12.188 Under the Access to Justice Act 1999 (Destination of Appeals) Order 2016,[482] the appropriate forum for appeal from a county court section 204 or section 88 appeal is to the Court of Appeal. The basis for this requirement is that the section 204 or section 88 appeal is itself an 'appeal' (from the decision of the authority), and so an appeal against the county court judge is a second appeal, to be determined by the Court of Appeal.[483]

12.189 A consequence of the 'second appeal' status is that permission cannot be granted by the county court; it must be obtained from the Court of Appeal.[484] An application for permission to appeal must be made in accordance with CPR Part 52. Permission must be requested in an appellant's notice, which must be served within such period as directed by the lower court,[485] or – if no such direction is made – within 21 days of the decision being appealed.[486] Witness statements in support of an application for permission to appeal are only appropriate for relevant and admissible evidence (if any) going to the issue before the court and nothing else: submissions in support of the appeal are for advocates to make in skeleton arguments.[487]

12.190 Where a county court has ordered a further review and the authority seeks permission to appeal, the parties should agree that the obligation to undertake a fresh review is suspended pending outcome of the appeal. If agreement is not reached, an authority may apply to the Court of Appeal to stay the effect of the quashing order made by the county court. In the event that an authority does undertake a fresh

481 *Persaud v Persaud*, above.

482 SI No 917.

483 An appeal against a decision on costs is, however, treated as a first appeal and is therefore to the High Court: see *Handley v Lake Jackson Solicitors* [2016] EWCA Civ 465, [2016] HLR 23; and Access to Justice Act 1999 (Destination of Appeals) Order 2016 reg 5. The county court judge can therefore grant permission to appeal; indeed, it is good practice to ask for permission: *P v P* [2015] EWCA Civ 447.

484 CPR 52.7.

485 Which may be longer or shorter than the period of 21 days required under the CPR: CPR 52.12.

486 CPR 52.12.

487 *William v Wandsworth LBC; Bellamy v Hounslow LBC* [2006] EWCA Civ 535, [2006] HLR 42.

review pending the appeal, however, it is verging on an abuse for the authority not to inform the Court of Appeal that it has done so.[488]

12.191 Permission to bring a second appeal will be granted only if the court is satisfied that:

a) the appeal has a real prospect of success and raises an important point of principle or practice;[489] or
b) there is some other compelling reason for the appeal to be heard.[490]

12.192 Where an appeal raises an important point of principle which has not previously been determined, permission will normally be granted under CPR 52.7(2)(a).[491] When determining whether there is some other compelling reason to grant permission under CPR 52.7(2)(b), the court should apply the following principles:

a) the prospects of success on appeal must be very high;
b) even where the prospects of success are very high, the court may nonetheless conclude that justice does not require the appellant to have the opportunity of a second appeal; but, conversely,
c) if the prospects of success are not very high, there may nevertheless be a compelling reason for a second appeal if the court is satisfied that the first appeal was tainted by procedural irregularity such as to render it unfair.[492]

12.193 In the context of a homelessness appeal, permission was refused in *Azimi*,[493] where the decision of the county court was reached primarily on the facts. By contrast, in *Cramp*,[494] the Court of Appeal gave permission to appeal against a decision that an authority's enquiries had been inadequate because the appeal raised an important point of practice. Brooke LJ said:[495]

488 *William*, above.

489 CPR 52.7(2)(a).

490 CPR 52.7(2)(b).

491 *Uphill v BRB (Residuary) Ltd* [2005] EWCA Civ 60, [2005] 1 WLR 2070. Uphill does not comment on the 'real prospect of success' limb as that was only introduced for appeals issued after 3 October 2016: see Civil Procedure (Amendment No 3) Rules 2016 SI No 788.

492 *Upill*, above.

493 *Azimi v Newham LBC* (2000) 33 HLR 51, CA. See also *Ryde v Enfield LBC* [2005] EWCA Civ 1281 (no important point of principle or practice) and *Gentle v Wandsworth LBC* [2005] EWCA Civ 1377 (no obvious injustice).

494 *Cramp v Hastings BC; Phillips v Camden LBC* [2005] EWCA Civ 1005, [2005] HLR 48.

495 At [66].

> In view of the amount of public money that is in issue in cases like this, it would in my judgment be quite wrong for this court to feel that the judgment in *Uphill*[496] represented a fetter on its power to put things right if it has occasion to believe that things are going wrong in an important way in the practical operation of the statutory scheme in Part 7 of the 1996 Act (up to and including the appeal on a point of law to the county court).

12.194 In *Elrify*,[497] it was pointed out that the second appeal is really only the first appeal from a judicial decision because the appeal to the county court is not in respect of a judicial decision but from the authority's review decision; this does not mean that CPR 52.7 is inapplicable but does mean that the court can take a somewhat more relaxed approach to a second appeal in a homelessness case that has clear merits.[498]

12.195 On an appeal to the Court of Appeal, the primary question is normally not whether the county court judge deciding the first appeal was right, but whether the decision being appealed is right, or at least one that the decision-maker was entitled to reach.[499]

Remedies and relief

Interim relief

12.196 Authorities have power under HA 1996 s204(4) and H(W)A 2014 s88(5) to house pending any appeal (and any subsequent appeal). Interim relief will not be needed on a county court appeal if the authority agrees to use this power.

12.197 Prior to amendment by the Homelessness Act 2002, if an authority refused to exercise this power, the county court could not grant an interim injunction because the applicant had no substantive rights to which an interim injunction could properly be said to be ancillary;[500] accordingly, the only recourse was by way of judicial review. Under HA 1996 s204A or H(W)A 2014 s89, an applicant with a right to appeal to the county court against a local authority's decision on review[501] may now also appeal to the county court if the authority refuses to exercise its power to secure interim accommodation under section 204(4) or section 88 or is only willing to do so for a limited

496 See para 12.192.

497 *Elrify v Westminster City Council* [2007] EWCA Civ 332, [2007] HLR 36.

498 *Elrify*, at [24].

499 *Danesh v Kensington and Chelsea RLBC* [2006] EWCA Civ 1404, [2007] HLR 17 at [30].

500 *Ali v Westminster City Council* (1998) 31 HLR 349, CA.

501 HA 1996 s204A(1); H(W)A 2014 s89(1).

period ending before the final determination of the main appeal.[502] Once the county court has dismissed an appeal under section 204, it has no remaining function under section 204A so cannot consider an appeal against an authority's decision not to secure interim accommodation for the appellant pending a further appeal to the Court of Appeal.[503]

12.198 This right to appeal under HA 1996 s204A or H(W)A 2014 s89 may be exercised even before the applicant has appealed under section 204 or section 88, provided the latter appeal is against the authority's decision on review: this excludes the possibility of a section 204A or section 89 appeal where the applicant only has a right to appeal against the section 184 or section 86 decision because the authority has not notified the review decision in time.[504] In those circumstances, judicial review remains the only remedy.

12.199 As a matter of good practice, however, an applicant should include appeals under section 204 and section 204A in one appellant's notice[505] although, if this is not possible, the appeals may be included in separate notices.[506] An appeal under section 204A or section 89 may[507] include an application for an order under section 204A(4)(a) or section 89(4)(a) requiring the authority to secure that accommodation is available for the applicant's occupation.[508] If the court makes such an order without notice, the appellant's notice must be served on the authority together with the order. Such an order will normally require the authority to secure that accommodation is available until a hearing date when the authority can make representations as to whether the order should be continued.[509]

12.200 The primary power given to the county court[510] is to order the authority to secure accommodation for the applicant pending determination of the appeal or such earlier time that the court may specify. The court is bound either to quash the authority's section 204(4)

502 HA 1996 s204A(2); H(W)A 2014 s89(2).

503 *Johnson v Westminster City Council* [2013] EWCA Civ 773, [2013] HLR 45. The appropriate course of action is to seek judicial review.

504 HA 1996 s204(1)(b); H(W)A 2014 s88(1)(b).

505 CPR Part 52D PD para 24.2(1). The PD has not been amended to reflect the position in Wales, but it seems unlikely that a different approach would be thought to apply.

506 CPR Part 52D PD para 24.2(2).

507 And usually will.

508 PD 52D, para 28.1(4).

509 PD 52D, para 28.1(4).

510 HA 1996 s204A(4)(a); H(W)A 2014 s89(4)(a).

decision on accommodation pending appeal, or to confirm it.[511] If the county court decides to quash, it may order the authority to exercise the power for such period as may be specified in the order, up to but not beyond the determination of the main appeal.[512] The power may be exercised only if the court is satisfied that failure to exercise the section 204(4) power would substantially prejudice the applicant's ability to pursue the main appeal.

12.201 Contempt of Court Act 1981 s2(2) uses a similar, although not identical, phrase of 'substantial risk that the course of justice will be seriously prejudiced'. In this context it has been held that:

> . . . 'substantial' as a qualification of 'risk' does not have the meaning 'weighty' but rather means 'not insubstantial' or 'not minimal'.[513]

12.202 In deciding whether to confirm or quash, the court must apply judicial review principles.[514] In effect, this means applying the approach to decisions to provide interim accommodation in *R v Camden LBC ex p Mohammed*,[515] and described above,[516] so that the court can order the provision of accommodation only if the authority has failed to direct itself in accordance with it: *Francis*.[517]

Powers on appeal

12.203 Under its appeal powers, the county court can confirm a decision, or quash it; or, it can vary the decision as it thinks fit.[518]

511 HA 1996 s204A(4)(b); H(W)A 2014 s89(4)(b).

512 HA 1996 s204A(5) and (6)(b); H(W)A 2014 s89(6) and (7).

513 Per Donaldson MR in *Attorney-General v News Group Newspapers Ltd* [1987] QB 1, CA.

514 HA 1996 s204A(4); H(W)A 2014 s89(5).

515 (1998) 30 HLR 315, QBD, as approved in *R v Brighton and Hove Council ex p Nacion* (1999) 31 HLR 1095, CA in relation to challenges under HA 1996 s204 prior to the addition of s204A (see para 12.146).

516 See para 10.39. When considering an application for interim accommodation pending an appeal against an authority's review decision, an authority must take into account the grounds of appeal: *Lewis v Havering LBC* [2006] EWCA Civ 1793, [2007] HLR 20.

517 *Francis v Kensington and Chelsea RLBC* [2003] EWCA Civ 443, [2003] HLR 50.

518 HA 1996 s204(3); H(W)A 2014 s88(4). Whether the court can refuse to grant relief when the appeal has been overtaken by events and is accordingly pointless is still open. Compare the difference of views in *O'Connor v Kensington and Chelsea RLBC* [2004] EWCA Civ 394, [2004] HLR 37 between the proposition that the court can only refuse to grant relief where the appeal is an abuse of process and that the court ought to be able to make no order if the appeal is pointless.

12.204 The power to vary gives the county court a somewhat wider range of powers than a court on judicial review.[519] This does not, however, empower the court to extend its scope beyond the 'point of law' (within the meaning given to that phrase that has already been considered).[520] It follows that the power can usually only be used to quash a decision, remitting the matter back to the authority for re-determination, unless – the point of law having been determined – there is only one decision which the authority could lawfully take.[521]

12.205 It may, however, be argued that – while the appeal is confined to a point of law – once the applicant has been successful on the appeal, the power to vary allows the court to substitute its own decision for that of the authority (even where matters of judgment or evaluation of facts are inherent). It is not a complete answer to this to say that, since the appeal itself has been on a point of law, there will not be the evidential material before the court on which to do so, because:

a) that will not be true in all cases (and would therefore merely limit the occasions when the power could be used); and
b) it is, in any event, a chicken-and-egg point, for if the court has the wider powers, then material can still be put before it even if only directed or relevant to the exercise of its powers.

12.206 Although this argument is consistent with parliament having conferred wider powers on the county court than are available on judicial review,[522] it would nonetheless not seem to be available in most cases.[523] The 'decision' which the court has jurisdiction to vary, is a decision for the authority under HA 1996 s202(1) or H(W)A 2014 s85(1), as to eligibility, suitability or local connection or – most relevantly here – 'as to what duty (if any) is owed' to the applicant, under the principal sections.

12.207 Thus, in *Crawley BC v B*,[524] it was held that, once the existing decision had been quashed because of an error of law (admitted by the authority), the authority had to reconsider, which required it to make enquiries and reach a further decision. This will, of course, require

519 As noted in *Nipa Begum v Tower Hamlets LBC* (1999) 32 HLR 445, CA, [2000] 1 WLR 306, (1999) 32 HLR 445, CA at 313F: see further para 12.159.

520 See para 12.159.

521 See para 12.150.

522 Sedley LJ in *Begum* agreed with Auld LJ as to the ambit of the powers (see para 12.204): 'The jurisdiction of the county court is *at least* as wide as that of a court of judicial review': at 327/B–C, emphasis added.

523 See further para 12.210.

524 *Crawley BC v B* (2000) 32 HLR 636, CA.

the authority to establish (properly) whether or not it has reason to believe, or is of the opinion, or is satisfied as to a particular state of affairs. It is only once the relevant precondition (state of mind of the authority) exists, that the decision about duty can be taken:[525]

> The question, therefore, is whether the judge was entitled, or required, on the material before him, to do more than simply quash the decision . . . I would accept that, if that material had shown that the only decision as to its duty to provide accommodation or assistance that the Council, acting rationally, could reach was that the duty was that imposed by section 193(2) of the Act, the judge could properly have pre-empted further consideration by making an order to that effect . . .[526]

12.208 There is, however, an exception to this, where the power to vary may be used to substitute a decision in the applicant's favour, without remission back to the authority, in order to reinstate a benefit of which the applicant should not have been deprived:

> I would accept, also, that there could be circumstances in which a judge might properly take the view that an applicant ought not to be deprived, by events which had occurred between the date of the original decision and the date of the appeal, of some benefit or advantage to which he would have been entitled if the original decision had been taken in accordance with the law . . .[527]

12.209 This passage was adopted in *Robinson v Hammersmith and Fulham LBC*[528] in support of the proposition – in relation to a decision on a review – that:

> If the original decision was unlawful . . . the review decision maker should have so held and made a decision that would have restored to the appellant the rights she would have had if the decision had been lawful.

525 'The decision that the authority has to make is . . . as to the category into which its duty falls under the 1996 Act. Although subject to the discipline of sections 202 and 204, that remains a decision based on the satisfaction of the authority as to the issues (which are issues of fact and judgment) of priority need and intentionality. As is well-established, a conclusion as to a public body's satisfaction can only be challenged on public law grounds . . . The application of the jurisprudence of public law to the process of decision-making in homelessness cases does not, therefore, necessarily lead to the conclusion that a decision, once taken, cannot be revisited': *Crawley BC v B*, above, per Buxton LJ at 645.

526 *Crawley BC v B*, above, per Chadwick LJ at 651.

527 *Crawley BC v B*, above, at 651–652.

528 [2006] EWCA Civ 1122, at [31].

12.210 It would therefore seem that the power to vary does import an alternative to quashing a decision – and its remission to the authority – *either*:

a) where the variation relates to, reflects or rectifies the error of law itself, for example, where the decision can be identified in light of the authority's factual findings and/or evaluation, so that remission to the authority is unnecessary;[529] *or*
b) where it restores rights of which the applicant has been deprived.

12.211 Thus, in *Ekwuru*,[530] the authority could not, on the material before it, lawfully conclude that the applicant was intentionally homeless. The applicant had twice successfully appealed against the decision of the local authority, upheld on review, that he was intentionally homeless and on each occasion the decision had been quashed and remitted to the authority. Following the second appeal, the authority again found him intentionally homeless and for a third time upheld this decision on review. On appeal, the county court judge again quashed the decision and remitted it. The applicant appealed against the failure of the judge to vary the decision. The Court of Appeal concluded that on the material before the authority at the date of the third review decision, it could not lawfully have concluded that the applicant was intentionally homeless. Accordingly, nothing could be gained by remitting the application for further investigation because there was no real prospect that the authority would discover further material which permitted it properly to conclude that the applicant was intentionally homeless. The circumstances of the case were, however, described as 'exceptional'.[531]

12.212 In *Deugi*,[532] the authority's decision on eligibility and priority need was at issue on appeal, but the judge, having quashed the authority's decision, varied it to include a finding that the applicant was not intentionally homeless:

> The question for the judge was whether there was any real prospect that Tower Hamlets, acting rationally and with the benefit of further enquiry, might have been satisfied that Mrs Deugi was intentionally homeless.[533]

529 Ie, where the only rational conclusion that the authority can reach is that proposed by the applicant: *Slater v Lewisham LBC* [2006] EWCA Civ 394.

530 *Ekwuru v Westminster City Council* [2003] EWCA Civ 1293, [2004] HLR 14.

531 Per Schiemann LJ at [31].

532 *Tower Hamlets LBC v Deugi* [2006] EWCA Civ 159, [2006] HLR 28.

533 Per May LJ at [36]. This formulation was said (at [37]) 'to be seen as an amalgam of Chadwick LJ [in *Crawley BC v B*] and Schiemann LJ [in *Ekwuru*], [and] is intended to reflect the fact that this appeal process is in the nature of judicial review'.

12.213 Only if there had been no such prospect could the judge properly have varied the decision. On the facts of the case, however, there remained a possibility that further enquiries could yet have led to a finding of intentional homelessness, for which reason the decision could only be quashed.[534]

12.214 In *Robinson*,[535] the initial decision ought to have been that the applicant was in priority need (because she was 17),[536] but she had turned 18 by the time of the review. On a strict application of *Mohamed*,[537] the review decision would therefore have concluded that the applicant was – regardless of the correctness of the first decision – not in priority need. The Court of Appeal in *Robinson* rejected this:

> I am not persuaded that the above passages[538] have any application to a situation such as the present. It was not in issue in *Mohamed* whether an unlawful decision by the original decision maker had denied rights to the person affected by the decision to which he would otherwise have been entitled.[539]

Damages

12.215 Damages can only be awarded in the county court in respect of a claim within its jurisdiction arising in contract or tort. An award of compensation is not one of the powers conferred on the county court in relation to a section 204 or section 88 appeal.

12.216 Notwithstanding some differences of opinion over the years,[540] no action will lie for breach of statutory duty for failure properly to

534 See also *R (P) v Ealing LBC* [2013] EWCA Civ 1579, [2014] HLR 5 (county court judge wrong to vary a decision to find that an applicant was homeless as it was 'quite impossible' to say that there was no real prospect of any other conclusion) and *R (Woolfe) v Islington LBC* [2016] EWHC 1907 (Admin) (authority had wrongly applied their allocation policy so that the refusal to award the applicant points based on her residence in the borough was quashed and remitted for further investigation and consideration) for further examples of cases where quashing, rather than variation, was the appropriate remedy.

535 [2006] EWCA Civ 1122.

536 See para 5.67.

537 *Mohamed v Hammersmith and Fulham LBC* [2001] UKHL 57, [2002] 1 AC 547 – see paras 9.176–9.180.

538 From *Mohamed*.

539 At [31].

540 *Thornton v Kirklees MBC* [1979] QB 626, CA; *Cocks v Thanet DC* [1983] AC 286, 6 HLR 15, HL; *Mohram Ali v Tower Hamlets LBC* [1993] QB 407, (1992) 24 HLR 474, CA; *Tower Hamlets LBC v Abdi* (1992) 25 HLR 80, CA; *R v Lambeth LBC ex p Barnes* (1992) 25 HLR 140, QBD; *Hackney LBC v Lambourne* (1992) 25 HLR 172, CA; *R v Northavon DC ex p Palmer* (1995) 27 HLR 576, CA.

perform duties under HA 1996 Part 7,[541] absent some separate cause of action, for example, negligence,[542] or indeed contract.[543] Nor will action for misfeasance in public office[544] be easy to maintain.[545]

Confidentiality

12.217 As noted above,[546] the court has inherent jurisdiction to make an order granting anonymity to an applicant. The same principles as discussed above in relation to judicial review proceedings are applicable here.[547]

Ancillary relief

12.218 Ancillary relief in the county court is available only where final relief is available.[548] It follows that if the authority has failed to carry out the review but the only basis for complaining about the original decision is on the facts, ie, if there is still no appeal to the county court on a point of law, then – notwithstanding the provisions of HA 1996 s204(1) or H(W)A 2014 s88(1)[549] – the county court cannot make a mandatory order to require the authority to carry out the review.[550]

541 *O'Rourke v Camden LBC* [1998] AC 188, HL; *R (Morris) v Newham LBC* [2002] EWHC 1262 (Admin), [2002] JHL D77; *R (Darby) v Richmond Upon Thames LBC* [2015] EWHC 909 (QB). The same must be true of H(W)A 2014 Part 2.

542 See further *Ephraim v Newham LBC* (1993) 25 HLR 207, CA.

543 For example, in respect of the conditions in accommodation occupied under contract (tenancy or licence), under which the authority is the landlord.

544 Where an officer of a public authority either: i) maliciously exercises a power with the intent to injure a person or persons; or ii) acts knowing that he or she has no power to act where to do so will probably injure a third party: *Three Rivers DC v Bank of England (No 3)* [2003] 2 AC 1, HL. Authorities can themselves be liable for the misfeasance of an officer on the basis of vicarious liability, cf *AA v Southwark LBC* [2014] EWHC 500 (QB) where the authority were liable for the behaviour of housing officers who had engaged in a tortious conspiracy to evict Mr AA.

545 Consider *R (Khazai and others) v Birmingham City Council* [2010] EWHC 2576 (Admin), [2011] JHL D9, where it was held that an email containing unlawful instructions was the product of 'oversight and ill-considered drafting' rather than 'anything more sinister' and as being the work of one person rather than an institutional decision.

546 See para 12.154.

547 See paras 12.154–12.157.

548 County Courts Act 1984 s38.

549 See para 12.159.

550 See para 12.204.

Refusal of relief

12.219 As in the Administrative Court on a claim for judicial review, a county court judge on a homelessness appeal may refuse relief on the basis that, notwithstanding a procedural error on the part of the authority, the error would have made no difference to the authority's decision. Where a court identifies procedural flaws in an authority's decision-making process, that decision may, however, only be upheld where the court is satisfied that a properly directed authority would *inevitably* have reached the same decision. The test of inevitability is a strict test; regardless of how slight, if the possibility exists that a proper assessment of the circumstances might produce a different decision, the authority must conduct and consider such an assessment.[551]

Ombudsman

12.220 One further forum for challenge which is to be mentioned[552] is the Local Government Ombudsman,[553] who may investigate claims of maladministration against local authorities, where the claimant can show that he or she has sustained injustice in consequence of the maladministration.[554] If the provisions of Localism Act (LA) 2011 ss180–183 are brought fully into force,[555] jurisdiction over maladministration in England in actions taken in relation to the provision or management of social housing will transfer to the Housing Ombudsman.[556]

12.221 'Maladministration' is not defined. In *Eastleigh BC*,[557] Lord Donaldson stated that:[558]

551 *Ali v Newham LBC* [2002] HLR 20, CA.

552 For reasons of space, it is not practicable to describe the procedure here in any detail.

553 LGA 1974 Part 3. In England this is called the Commission for Local Administration in England or the 'ombudsman'.

554 LGA 1974 s26.

555 Localism Act 2011 (Commencement No 2 and Transitional Provisions) Order 2013 SI No 722 brought the relevant provisions into force for limited purposes only and no further commencement order has been made: jurisdiction therefore remains with the Local Government Ombudsman.

556 Jurisdiction for all other complaints relating to maladministration generally (such as matters relating to health or education) will remain with the local government ombudsman. See paras 12.228–12.230.

557 *R v Local Commissioner for the South etc ex p Eastleigh BC* [1988] 1 QB 855, CA.

558 *Eastleigh BC* at 863E/F, as a summary of the decision in *R v Local Commissioner for Administration for the North etc ex p Bradford MBC* [1979] QB 287, CA. Emphasis in original.

> . . . administration and maladministration in the context of the work of a local authority is concerned with the *manner* in which decisions by the authority are reached and the *manner* in which they are or are not implemented. Administration has nothing to do with the nature, quality or reasonableness of the decision itself.

12.222 The powers of the ombudsman in England were extended by the Local Government and Housing Act 1989[559] and by the Local Government and Public Involvement in Health Act 2007.[560] The latter extends jurisdiction in England from maladministration to include alleged or apparent maladministration in connection with the authority's administrative functions, alleged or apparent failure in a service which the authority has the function to provide, and alleged or apparent failure to provide such a service.[561]

12.223 The ombudsman can recommend that compensation be paid to a complainant. Where maladministration is found, this will usually be ordered, and compensation has commonly been recommended in homelessness cases.

12.224 Complaint to the ombudsman may be particularly appropriate where there are delays in making decisions and inadequacies in decision letters. Even where the applicant is eventually adequately housed, it may be worthwhile proceeding with the complaint in order to obtain compensation.

12.225 Complaints must generally be made within 12 months of the maladministration complained of, although there is discretion to take complaints outside that period, if the ombudsman considers it reasonable so to do.[562]

12.226 Currently, any person (or his or her representative) can make a direct complaint to the ombudsman.[563] The complaint must generally be made in writing.[564] A complaint may also be made by way of referral from a member of a local authority,[565] and a matter may even be considered if it comes to the attention of the ombudsman during

559 LGA 1972 Part 2, substituted by the Local Government and Housing Act 1989.

560 Part 9.

561 LGA 1972 s26(1), substituted by Local Government and Public Involvement in Health Act 2007 s173(2) with effect from 1 April 2008, by virtue of Local Government and Public Involvement in Health Act 2007 (Commencement No 5 and Transitional, Saving and Transitory Provision) Order 2008 SI No 917 reg 2(1)(i).

562 LGA 1974 s26B.

563 LGA 1974 s26A.

564 Although the LGO also accepts complaints through an online form or via telephone, see: www.lgo.org.uk/make-a-complaint/how-to-complain.

565 LGA 1974 s26C.

the course of an investigation and it appears to the ombudsman that a member of the public has, or may have, suffered injustice in consequence of the matter.[566] The ombudsman has a wide discretion to conduct any investigation in any manner he or she deems appropriate, and to make such inquiries as he or she thinks fit.[567]

12.227 At the conclusion of the investigation, the ombudsman will usually produce a report.[568] If the ombudsman concludes that there has been maladministration, a failure in a service or a failure to provide a service, then the report is laid before the local authority concerned,[569] which must consider the report and, within three months beginning with the date on which they received the report, notify the ombudsman of what action the authority has taken or proposes to take.[570] If the ombudsman is not satisfied by the steps taken or proposed to be taken, he or she will produce a further report including his or her own recommendations as to the action the authority should take.[571] The ombudsman has power to publish a copy of the further report, and a separate power to require the authority to publish a statement in a local newspaper about the complaint, including details of the ombudsman's recommendations.[572] Authorities have power to make payments to those who have suffered injustice as a result of maladministration, whether or not recommended to do so by the ombudsman.[573]

12.228 If LA 2011 ss180–182 come fully into force,[574] the complaints procedure in England[575] will change considerably.[576] The primary change is in the way complaints are commenced. Under the new procedure, complaints to the housing ombudsman will usually have to be made by a member of the public writing to a 'designated person' and for the designated person to refer the complaint to the ombudsman.[577]

566 LGA 1974 s26D.
567 LGA 1974 s28.
568 LGA 1974 s30(1).
569 LGA 1974 s31.
570 LGA 1974 s31(2).
571 LGA 1974 s31(2A).
572 LGA 1974 s31(2D).
573 LGA 2000 s92.
574 See para 12.220.
575 The complaints procedure in Wales will remain the same: see para 12.232. There are currently no plans to change this.
576 By inserting new paras 7A–7D into HA 1996 Sch 2, as well as making amendments to the LGA 1974.
577 LA 2011 s180, new HA 1996 Sch 2 para 7A.

Designated persons will include an MP, a member of the local housing authority for the district in which the property concerned is located, or a designated tenant panel. The 'designated tenant panel' is a new entity: it is defined as a group of tenants recognised by a social landlord for the purpose of referring complaints against it.[578]

12.229 Exceptionally, there will be no requirement that the complaint be made by such a referral:

a) where the social landlord has its own complaints procedure and more than eight weeks have elapsed since that procedure was exhausted;[579]
b) where a designated person refused in writing to refer the complaint to the ombudsman;[580]
c) where a designated person has agreed in writing to the complaint being made otherwise than by referral.[581]

12.230 Enforcement of decisions by the housing ombudsman will be strengthened. Under the new scheme, the secretary of state will have the power to make provision (by statutory instrument) for the housing ombudsman to be able to apply to a court or tribunal for an order that his or her determination is to be enforced as if it were an order of the court.[582]

12.231 The local government ombudsman has published a report following an analysis of complaints about councils dealing with applications under HA 1996 Part 7.[583] The recommendations, based on an analysis of recent complaints, include the following.

a) authorities should decide on the same day an application is received whether to offer interim accommodation;
b) appropriate arrangements should be put in place to ensure that vulnerable applicants are referred to social services;
c) there should be a proactive approach to identifying actual or potential homelessness when applicants join the housing register and/or provide new information;
d) clear records should be kept of all interviews with applicants, advice given to applicants and decisions made on applications.

578 LA 2011 s180, new HA 1996 Sch 2 para 7C(1).
579 LA 2011 s180, new HA 1996 Sch 2 para 7B(1).
580 LA 2011 s180, new HA 1996 Sch 2 para 7B(2)(a)(i).
581 LA 2011 s180, new HA 1996 Sch 2 para 7B(2)(a)(ii).
582 LA 2011 s180, new HA 1996 Sch 2 para 7D(1).
583 *Homelessness: how councils can ensure justice for homeless people*, July 2011.

12.232 The ombudsman also indicates that maladministration is likely to be found where authorities:

a) use homelessness prevention techniques to block or delay consideration of an application;
b) insist that applicants complete a specific form or be interviewed by a specialist homelessness assessment officer;
c) place a burden of proof on the applicant to demonstrate that he or she is homeless; or
d) defer taking an application merely because it does not appear that the applicant would be in priority need.

12.233 In Wales, the Public Services Ombudsman for Wales has responsibility not only for local administration but also for the health service in Wales, social housing in Wales and for the functions of the former Welsh Administration Ombudsman. He or she therefore has power to investigate maladministration and service failure by the Welsh Assembly, Welsh health service, health service providers in Wales, local authorities in Wales and Welsh registered providers of social housing.[584] He or she has power to investigate[585] complaints by or on behalf of a person who claims to have suffered injustice or hardship[586] arising from maladministration by an authority in connection with a relevant action,[587] failure in a relevant service[588] provided by an authority and failure by an authority to provide a relevant service.[589] The Public Services Ombudsman for Wales also has power, subject to consultation, to issue guidance to local authorities about good administrative practice.[590]

584 Public Services Ombudsman (Wales) Act (PSO(W)A) 2005 Sch 3.
585 PSO(W)A 2005 ss8 and 10.
586 PSO(W)A 2005 s4.
587 PSO(W)A 2005 s7(3).
588 PSO(W)A 2005 s7(4).
589 PSO(W)A 2005 s7.
590 PSO(W)A 2005 s31.

Annex: Specimen documents

12.234 The following are examples of the forms[591] and pleadings used in both judicial review proceedings, based on an allocation decision, and an appeal against a homelessness decision in the county court:

a) judicial review pre-action protocol letter before claim;
b) judicial review claim form;
c) judicial review statement of grounds and facts relied on;
d) judicial review acknowledgement of service;
e) judicial review summary grounds for contesting the claim;
f) county court appellant's notice and draft directions;
g) county court grounds of appeal.

591 The forms in this section are all © Crown Copyright.

Leo & Nevil Solicitors
2404 Nashville Road
Warden
WAR7 8QB

Warden Drane District Council
Legal Services Department
Civic Centre
Warden High Road
Warden
WAR1 9SX

20 June 2016

Your ref: LE/HSG/FIELDS/86915
Our ref: LH/H/FIELDS/01533

Dear Sir/Madam

The following is a letter before claim written in accordance with the pre action protocol for judicial review claims and follows the structure of the model letter in Annex A.

1. Proposed claim for judicial review
To: Warden Drane District Council, Housing Department, Civic Centre, Warden High Road, Warden, WAR1 9SX
Copied to: Warden Drane District Council, Legal Services Department, Civic Centre, Warden High Road, Warden, WAR1 9SX

2. The claimant
The proposed claimant is Ms Jane Fields, 16A Maxwell Square, Warden WAR16 1AB.

3. Reference details
Your ref: LE/HSG/FIELDS/86915.

4. The Claimant's Legal Advisors
Leo & Nevil Solicitors, 2404 Nashville Road, Warden WAR7 8QB. Our ref: LH/H/FIELDS/01533

5. The details of the matter being challenged
The assessment of the claimant by the defendant under its allocation scheme, and the defendant's refusal to increase her points.

6. Interested Parties
None

7. The issue(s)
There are five. First, whether the claimant has been awarded a reasonable

preference in accordance with section 166A(3) of the Housing Act 1996 ('the Act'). Secondly, whether the defendant's allocation scheme is in breach of section 166A(3) of the Act. Thirdly, whether the defendant's discretion to award additional preference complies with section 166A(3) of the Act. Fourthly, whether the defendant has properly applied its allocation scheme to the claimant and, in particular, whether it has acted lawfully by refusing to exercise its residual discretion in her favour, and whether it has properly assessed the issue of overcrowding. Fifthly, whether the defendant's allocation scheme, and the application of it to the claimant's case, has been perverse.

8. The details of the action that the defendant is expected to take
The defendant is required to reassess the claimant and award her more than 250 points under its allocation scheme, and redraft its scheme so that reasonable and additional preference is properly awarded.

9. ADR Proposals
The claimant is prepared to have a without prejudice meeting and/or negotiations to try to resolve this matter without litigation, as suggested by para.9 of the pre-action protocol for judicial review claims. If the defendant has other suggestions for alternative dispute resolution, the claimant is willing to consider them.

10. The details of information sought
An explanation by the defendant of how its allocation scheme purports to operate lawfully in relation to the award of reasonable and additional preference.

11. The details of any documents that are considered relevant and necessary
A full copy of the defendant's allocation scheme so that the claimant can satisfy herself that the copy that she has seen is the one being applied by the defendant.

12. The address for reply and service of court documents
This is set out at 7 above.

13. Proposed reply date
The claimant expects a reply within 14 days of receipt of this letter.

Yours sincerely,

Print form | Reset form

Judicial Review
Claim Form

Notes for guidance are available which explain how to complete the judicial review claim form. Please read them carefully before you complete the form.

In the High Court of Justice
Administrative Court

Help with Fees - Ref no. (if applicable) H W F - [ ] - [ ]

For Court use only	
Administrative Court Reference No.	
Date filed	

Seal

Is your claim in respect of refusal of an application for fee remission? ☐ Yes ☐ No

SECTION 1 Details of the claimant(s) and defendant(s)

Claimant(s) name and address(es)

name
Jane Fields

address
16A Maxwell Square
Warden
WAR16 1AB

Telephone no. 012557 932831
Fax no. n/a
E-mail address jane.fields@googliemail.com

Claimant's or claimant's legal representatives' address to which documents should be sent.

name
Leo & Nevil Solicitors

address
2404 Nashville Road
Warden
WAR7 8QB

Telephone no. 012557 168932
Fax no. n/a
E-mail address housing@leoandnevil.co.uk

Claimant's Counsel's details

name
Julia Clunes

address
Justice Chambers
Warden Drane
Warden, WAR 1AA

Telephone no. 012557 204204
Fax no. n/a
E-mail address julia.clunes@justicechambers.com

1st Defendant

name
Warden Drane District Council

Defendant's or (where known) Defendant's legal representatives' address to which documents should be sent.

name
Warden Drane District Council – Legal Services

address
Civic Centre
Warden High Road
Warden, WAR1 9SX

Telephone no. 012557 132000
Fax no. n/a
E-mail address legal@warden.gov.uk

2nd Defendant

name

Defendant's or (where known) Defendant's legal representatives' address to which documents should be sent.

name

address

Telephone no.
Fax no.
E-mail address

SECTION 2 Details of other interested parties

Include name and address and, if appropriate, details of DX, telephone or fax numbers and e-mail

name	name
address	**address**
Telephone no. / **Fax no.**	**Telephone no.** / **Fax no.**
E-mail address	**E-mail address**

SECTION 3 Details of the decision to be judicially reviewed

Decision:
Failure by the defendant authority to operate a lawful allocation scheme and properly to afford the claimant the appropriate preference within the terms of the scheme

Date of decision:
30 May 2016 and continuing

Name and address of the court, tribunal, person or body who made the decision to be reviewed.

name
Housing Department, Warden Drane DC

address
Civic Centre
Warden High Road
Warden, WAR1 9SX

SECTION 4 Permission to proceed with a claim for judicial review

I am seeking permission to proceed with my claim for Judicial Review.

Question	Yes	No
Is this application being made under the terms of Section 18 Practice Direction 54 (Challenging removal)?	☐ Yes	☑ No
Are you making any other applications? If Yes, complete Section 8.	☐ Yes	☑ No
Is the claimant in receipt of a Civil Legal Aid Certificate?	☑ Yes	☐ No
Are you claiming exceptional urgency, or do you need this application determined within a certain time scale? If Yes, complete Form N463 and file this with your application.	☐ Yes	☑ No
Have you complied with the pre-action protocol? If No, give reasons for non-compliance in the box below.	☑ Yes	☐ No

Question	Yes	No
Have you issued this claim in the region with which you have the closest connection? (Give any additional reasons for wanting it to be dealt with in this region in the box below). If No, give reasons in the box below.	☑ Yes	☐ No

Does the claim include any issues arising from the Human Rights Act 1998?
If Yes, state the articles which you contend have been breached in the box below. ☐ Yes ☑ No

SECTION 5 Detailed statement of grounds

☐ set out below ☑ attached

Please see attached statement of facts and grounds

SECTION 6 Aarhus Convention claim

I contend that this claim is an Aarhus Convention claim ☐ Yes ☑ No

If Yes, indicate in the following box if you do not wish the costs limits under CPR 45.43 to apply.

If you have indicated that the claim is an Aarhus claim set out the grounds below, including (if relevant) reasons why you want to vary the limit on costs recoverable from a party.

SECTION 7 Details of remedy (including any interim remedy) being sought

1) Quashing order to quash the defendant's allocation scheme.

2) Further or alternatively, a declaration that the scheme is unlawful in that it failed to afford the statutory preferences required by s.166A(3), Housing Act 1996

3) Further or other relief

4) Costs

SECTION 8 Other applications

I wish to make an application for:-

SECTION 9 Statement of facts relied on

Please see attached

Statement of Truth

I believe (The claimant believes) that the facts stated in this claim form are true.

Full name ____

Name of claimant's solicitor's firm ______________________________

Signed __________________________ Position or office held ____________________

Claimant ('s solicitor) (if signing on behalf of firm or company)

SECTION 10 Supporting documents

If you do not have a document that you intend to use to support your claim, identify it, give the date when you expect it to be available and give reasons why it is not currently available in the box below.

Please tick the papers you are filing with this claim form and any you will be filing later.

☑ Statement of grounds	☐ included	☑ attached
☑ Statement of the facts relied on	☐ included	☑ attached
☐ Application to extend the time limit for filing the claim form	☐ included	☐ attached
☐ Application for directions	☐ included	☐ attached
☐ Any written evidence in support of the claim or application to extend time		
☐ Where the claim for judicial review relates to a decision of a court or tribunal, an approved copy of the reasons for reaching that decision		
☑ Copies of any documents on which the claimant proposes to rely		
☑ A copy of the legal aid or Civil Legal Aid Certificate *(if legally represented)*		
☑ Copies of any relevant statutory material		
☑ A list of essential documents for advance reading by the court *(with page references to the passages relied upon)*		
☐ Where a claim relates to an Aarhus Convention claim, a schedule of the claimant's financial resources.	☐ included	☐ attached

If Section 18 Practice Direction 54 applies, please tick the relevant box(es) below to indicate which papers you are filing with this claim form:

☐ a copy of the removal directions and the decision to which the application relates	☐ included	☐ attached
☐ a copy of the documents served with the removal directions including any documents which contains the Immigration and Nationality Directorate's factual summary of the case	☐ included	☐ attached
☐ a detailed statement of the grounds	☐ included	☐ attached

Reasons why you have not supplied a document and date when you expect it to be available:-

Signed ______________________ Claimant ('s Solicitor)______________________

Print form Reset form

IN THE HIGH COURT OF JUSTICE **Claim No.**
QUEEN'S BENCH DIVISION
ADMINISTRATIVE COURT

BETWEEN

THE QUEEN
(on the application of
JANE FIELDS) **Claimant**

–and–

WARDEN DRANE
DISTRICT COUNCIL **Defendant**

STATEMENT OF FACTS AND GROUNDS

STATEMENT OF FACTS

Introductory

1. The claimant is a 33 year old woman with 3 children – Sally (aged 12), Margaret (aged 11) and Peter (aged 10). Peter is quadriplegic and is confined to a wheel-chair. Sally suffers from severe attention-deficit and hyper-activity disorder. The claimant is unable to work as she is the sole carer of Peter.
2. On 14 July 2015, she applied to the defendant authority for accommodation under Part 6 of the Housing Act 1996, and was duly registered on the authority's housing register.

Background

3. The claimant has resided in the authority's area since childhood. Until January 2012, she and her children lived in a privately rented house in the area.
4. In January 2012, the claimant left the accommodation that she shared with her former partner, due to domestic violence. The claimant secured her current accommodation, which is a one-bedroom flat, occupied under a private tenancy. The flat is located on the second-floor. There is no lift.
5. She applied to the authority as homeless under Part 7 of the Housing 1996. The authority found that – although she was eligible for assistance and in priority need – the claimant was not homeless as she had accommodation that was available for her occupation and that is was

reasonable for her to continue to occupy it. That decision was upheld on review and the claimant did not appeal.

6. The claimant applied to be registered on the authority's housing register. She provided medical evidence as to her children's medical needs and information on the overcrowded nature of her current accommodation, in particular that:
   (a) there are two girls, a disabled boy and the claimant living in a one-bedroom flat, the girls share the only bedroom and the claimant and her son sleep in the living room;
   (b) the bedroom is 8 foot x 8 foot – there is room for two single beds but no other furniture;
   (c) Sally's severe ADHD causes her to act impulsively and without regard to the consequences of her actions, this can have dangerous consequences in a confined space and places the other members of the household at risk; and,
   (d) the claimant has severe difficulties taking Peter out of the flat as she has to carry him down two flights of stairs and return for his wheelchair – although she is currently able to carry Peter, it is unlikely that she will be able to do so as he grows.
7. In September 2015, the authority assessed the medical needs of Peter and Sally and visited the flat to assess its size and determine whether it was overcrowded. As a result of those assessments (and expert evidence obtained by the claimant), the authority found that both children had medical needs and that the family had a need for accommodation with an additional bedroom.
8. The current position is that the claimant is registered on the authority's housing register, awaiting an allocation of two-bedroom accommodation, in accordance with Part 6 of the Housing 1996.

The authority's allocation scheme

9. The authority's allocation scheme operates, principally – but not exclusively – by means of 'choice-based lettings'. In broad terms, this means that applicants are given points to reflect their priority according to criteria set out in the scheme, and are informed of the types of property for which they are eligible. They may then bid for any properties of the appropriate type which are advertised as available to let. The bidding applicant with the highest number of points is offered the property. It is estimated by the authority that an applicant requires a minimum of 250 points before there is any realistic possibility that he will be able successfully to bid for accommodation.
10. In summary, the principal material provisions of the scheme are as follows.
11. Part 1 of the Scheme governs applications under Part 6 of the Housing Act 1996. The scheme provides that all applications are to be assessed using a points system.

12. Paragraphs 1.3 and 1.4 of the scheme make provision for various categories of applicant (those owed a duty as homeless under Pt 7, Housing Act 1996; young people leaving care; people moving to larger accommodation to foster or adopt a child; people with learning disabilities; applicants who have successfully completed rehabilitation from drug or alcohol dependency) to be afforded 300 points, thereby essentially obtaining an overriding priority for accommodation.

Points for overcrowding

13. Where an applicant claims to reside in overcrowded accommodation, the application is referred to a panel which assesses the accommodation. The panel has power to award a maximum of 12 points. Those points are awarded on the basis of a space assessment; the scheme assumes that a room which is 60 square feet can accommodate two persons of any age and no account is taken of the sex of the occupants or their relationship to one another.

14. On the basis of the space assessment, the panel calculates the number of bedrooms required and may award an applicant three points for each extra bedroom required.

Medical and Welfare points

15. The scheme allows 10 points to be awarded on medical or welfare grounds. Paragraph. 2.4 provides:

> 'The panel may award a set 10 points on medical or welfare grounds. In calculating the amount of points (if any) to award, the panel shall have regard to any medical reports supplied but ultimately shall use their absolute discretion to award a household points on this basis.'

General points

16. All applicants are entitled to 'time points' awarded at the rate of 10 points for every year spent on the waiting list for accommodation.

17. Additionally, all applicants may receive 100 income points if they are 'unable (on financial grounds) to meet their own housing needs'.

18. Local connection points, at the rate of 50, are awarded to those applicants who live in the Borough and have done so by choice for two years.

19. The authority retains an absolute discretion to award up to 75 additional points, if it considers the circumstances justify doing so. Provision is also made for the award of other points, including for existing tenants of the authority who apply for a transfer to smaller accommodation.

The claimant's points

20. The claimant has been awarded the following points:

    100 income points
    50 residence points
    10 time points
    10 medical and welfare points
    3 overcrowding points

21. The overcrowding panel calculated the claimant's entitlement to points on the basis that the household requires only one additional bedroom as the house comprises only four persons.

22. In assessing the need for medical and welfare points, the panel had regard to medical reports submitted in relation to both Peter and Sally. The panel accepted that both children had medical and welfare needs that were not being met in their current accommodation. On the basis of that conclusion they awarded the set 10 points.

23. The claimant has bid for a number of properties under the choice-based scheme, but 173 points has been insufficient for her bid to be successful.

Pre-claim correspondence

24. The claimant has been in correspondence with the authority since September 2015, seeking to negotiate the award of additional points. The claimant has sought three additional overcrowding points, on the basis that her household requires a three bedroom property. She has also sought to obtain additional medical and welfare points on the basis that two of her children have (accepted) medical and welfare needs, such that she should be entitled to a further 10 points on that basis.

25. The claimant has also asked the authority to exercise its residual discretion to award 50 further points on the grounds that her household's need for alternative accommodation is severe.

26. The authority has refused those requests. In letters dated 12 December 2015, 14 February 2016, and 16 May 2016, the authority has consistently stated that the claimant is not entitled to further points and has refused to exercise the residual discretion.

27. The only suggestions offered by the letters were that the claimant take up a council scheme to obtain a private sector tenancy or else move to another area where accommodation is in greater supply.

28. On 20 June 2016, the claimant's legal representatives sent the authority a pre-action protocol letter before action, which asserted (a) that the authority's allocation scheme was unlawful, alternatively (b) that the way in which the allocation scheme had been applied to the claimant was unlawful. The authority was invited to withdraw its scheme or to award the claimant sufficient points

STATEMENT OF GROUNDS

Allocations Law

29. The claimant and her children remain in the flat, awaiting an allocation of accommodation under Part 6. By section 166A(14) of the Housing Act 1996, the authority may only lawfully allocate such accommodation in accordance with the provisions of its allocation scheme.

30. This section provides that every local housing authority shall have an allocation scheme for determining priorities, and as to the procedure to be followed in allocating housing accommodation (s166A(1)).

31. As a person who resides in overcrowded and unsatisfactory housing conditions and as a person who needs to move on medical or welfare grounds, the claimant is entitled to a reasonable preference in the allocation of Part 6 accommodation. Section 166A(3) provides that such preference must be afforded to certain priority groups, in the following terms.

> '(2) As regards priorities, the scheme shall be framed so as to secure that reasonable preference is given to –
>
> > . . .
> >
> > (c) people occupying insanitary or overcrowded housing or otherwise living in unsatisfactory housing conditions;
> >
> > (d) people who need to move on medical or welfare grounds (including any grounds relating to a disability); and
>
> . . . '.

The scheme may also be framed so as to give additional preference to particular descriptions of people within this subsection (being descriptions of people with urgent housing needs).'

32. Although the courts should be slow to interfere with the allocation policy of a local authority (*R (Ahmad) v Newham LBC* [2009] UKHL 14, [2009] HLR 31), where an allocation scheme is clearly irrational, even on a relatively narrow aspect, it should be struck down. The purpose of an allocation scheme should be justified properly and authorities should not rely on 'bald statements': *Birmingham City Council v Ali; Moran v Manchester City Council (Secretary of State for Communities and Local Government and another intervening)* [2009] UKHL 36, [2009] HLR 41.

GROUND ONE Error of law – no reasonable preference

33. The effect of the scheme is not to confer any reasonable preference at all on the claimant; unless and until the claimant has resided in the authority's area for two years, she has and will have no preference at all in practical terms.

34. The claimant has been awarded 10 points on medical grounds and a further 3 on the grounds of overcrowding. Those additional points give her no increased priority in practice; although the claimant and her family could remain in their current accommodation, when she is evicted or has to leave because she can no longer physically manage with her disabled son on the second floor, she will be entitled to apply as homeless and receive an additional 300 points.

35. The claimant and her family have no chance whatsoever of bidding successfully for a property unless or until they become homeless. Thus the claimant is in an even worse position than if she were to be evicted from her accommodation, as she would then receive 300 points as a homeless person.

36. In the context of the scheme, the award of a maximum 12 overcrowding points and 10 medical points is *de minimis* and has no effect on priority whatsoever, unless the applicant has a preference in another category.

37. The absence of any real preference can be seen by analysis of the points awarded to the claimant. Aside from the 10 medical points and the 3 overcrowding points, she has received 100 income points, 10 time points, 50 residence point (the maximum available).

38. Residency points are available to anyone who has resided in the authority's area for 2 years, regardless of whether or not that person is entitled to any statutory preference. Likewise, the income points are available to anyone, it seems, whose income is low. Waiting points are available to everyone.

39. Thus the only points which are related to the claimant's statutory right to a reasonable preference are the 13 points received for overcrowding and medical need. The claimant's 173 points have reached the maximum available to her, save for the possibility of 10 points a year for the next four years, giving her a maximum of 223. She will not be able to increase her points total at all, unless her circumstances change and she falls within another category of need.

40. The claimant's points total is at least 75 points short of any possibility of successfully bidding for a property under Part 6. The only option that the authority has been able to suggest is that, with three children, one of whom is disabled, she could move out of the area where she has lived since childhood.

41. To describe a scheme which operates in this way as securing a reasonable preference to persons who have a medical need or a need based on overcrowding (section 166A(3)(c) and (d)), is a misuse of language.

GROUND TWO Error of law – frustrating the purpose of the 1996 Act

42. The provision of a maximum of 23 points to families with medical needs in overcrowded accommodation does not amount to securing a reasonable or any preference, and is contrary to – and frustrates – the scheme of Part 6 of the Housing 1996.

43. It is plain from the scheme itself, from the correspondence referred to above, and indeed from the manner in which the scheme is operated, that the scheme is designed to keep families in overcrowded accommodation or with medical needs from being eligible for accommodation for as long as possible before permitting them sufficient points to have any prospect at all of bidding successfully for a tenancy under Part 6.

44. This is demonstrated by the following matters:
    (a) the availability of only 10 points on medical grounds;
    (b) the availability of only 12 points on the grounds of overcrowding, regardless of how overcrowded the property is;
    (c) the availability of 300 points where an alternative statutory preference category (homelessness) exists.

45. This is unlawful and conflicts with and frustrates the purposes of the 1996 Act, in particular the statutory intention concerning the statutory preference to be afforded to those with medical need or those in overcrowded accommodation.

GROUND THREE Irrationality – discretion

46. The scheme purports to confer 'additional preference' on persons who, in the absolute discretion of the defendant, have circumstances that give them 'urgent housing needs'. The only provision under the scheme for the award of additional points (other than waiting time) is the defendant's residual discretion to award up to 75 points. This is not a rational means by which to assess need, nor is it a rational means by which a person in the position of the claimant could ever achieve an additional preference, having regard to the maximum points available under the 'additional preference discretion'.

GROUND FOUR Policy applied unlawfully

47. In the alternative, if the policy is not unlawful, the application of the policy to the claimant's circumstances has been unlawful.

Failure to exercise the residual discretion

48. It is unlawful to fail to give any proper priority to the claimant's claim, not least because to do so requires her to remain in statutorily overcrowded accommodation that is fundamentally unsuitable to the medical needs of her household.
49. In the claimant's case, there were compelling factors which ought to have led to an exercise of discretion in her favour: namely the matters set out at paragraph 6, above.

Failure properly to assess the issue of overcrowding

50. The claimant has been awarded 3 points on the grounds of overcrowding, on the basis that her household only requires one additional bedroom (ie two bedrooms in total). If that conclusion is correct, the claimant would be required to share a bedroom with her disabled son, while her two daughters – one of whom has a medical need – would also be required to share a room.
51. In concluding that two-bedroom accommodation would suffice for the claimant's household, the authority has acted irrationally and contrary to the medical evidence that was before it when making its decision on overcrowding.

GROUND FIVE Perversity

52. Further, or alternatively, the defendant's policy, and the treatment which the defendant has given to the claimant's application are both unreasonable in the *Wednesbury* sense.

Julia Clunes
Justice Chambers, Warden Drane

Print form | Reset form

N462
Judicial Review
Acknowledgment of Service

In the High Court of Justice Administrative Court	
Claim No.	
Claimant(s) (including ref.)	Jane Fields (LH/H/fields/01533)
Defendant(s)	Warden Drane DC (LE/HSG/Fields/86915)
Interested Parties	

Name and address of person to be served

name: Warden Drane DC

address: Civic Centre
Warden High Rd
Warden
WAR 1 96X

SECTION A

Tick the appropriate box

1. I intend to contest all of the claim ☑ } complete sections B, C, D and F
2. I intend to contest part of the claim ☐ }
3. I do not intend to contest the claim ☐ complete section F
4. The defendant (interested party) is a court or tribunal and **intends** to make a submission. ☐ complete sections B, C and F
5. The defendant (interested party) is a court or tribunal and **does not intend** to make a submission. ☐ complete sections B and F
6. The applicant has indicated that this is a claim to which the Aarhus Convention applies. ☐ complete sections E and F
7. The **Defendant** asks the Court to consider whether the outcome for the claimant would have been **substantially different** if the conduct complained of had not occurred [see s.31(3C) of the Senior Courts Act 1981] ☐ A summary of the grounds for that request must be set out in/accompany this Acknowledgment of Service

Note: If the application seeks to judicially review the decision of a court or tribunal, the court or tribunal need only provide the Administrative Court with as much evidence as it can about the decision to help the Administrative Court perform its judicial function.

SECTION B

Insert the name and address of any person you consider should be added as an interested party.

name

address

Telephone no. | Fax no.

E-mail address

name

address

Telephone no. | Fax no.

E-mail address

SECTION C

Summary of grounds for contesting the claim. If you are contesting only part of the claim, set out which part before you give your grounds for contesting it. If you are a court or tribunal filing a submission, please indicate that this is the case.

Please see attached summary grounds of resistance

SECTION D

Give details of any directions you will be asking the court to make, or tick the box to indicate that a separate application notice is attached.

None

If you are seeking a direction that this matter be heard at an Administrative Court venue other than that at which this claim was issued, you should complete, lodge and serve on all other parties Form N464 with this acknowledgment of service.

SECTION E

Response to the claimant's contention that the claim is an Aarhus claim

Do you deny that the claim is an Aarhus Convention claim? ☐ Yes ☑ No

If Yes, please set out your grounds for denial in the box below.

SECTION F

*delete as appropriate

*(I believe)(The defendant believes) that the facts stated in this form are true.

*I am duly authorised by the defendant to sign this statement.

(if signing on behalf of firm or company, court or tribunal)

Position or office held

(To be signed by you or by your solicitor or litigation friend)

Signed

Date

Give an address to which notices about this case can be sent to you	If you have instructed counsel, please give their name address and contact details below.
name Legal Services	**name** Clare Ronethun
address Warden Drane DC Civic Centre Warden High Rd Warden WAR1 96X	**address** Smith Chambers 96 Smith Lane London ECR1 9SS
Telephone no. 012557 123000 **Fax no.** n/a	**Telephone no.** 0207 999 8118 **Fax no.** n/a
E-mail address Legal@warden.gov.uk	**E-mail address** clairer@smithchambers.law.co.uk

Completed forms, together with a copy, should be lodged with the Administrative Court Office (court address, over the page), at which this claim was issued within 21 days of service of the claim upon you, and further copies should be served on the Claimant(s), any other Defendant(s) and any interested parties within 7 days of lodgement with the Court.

Print form Reset form

Administrative Court addresses

- Administrative Court in **London**

  Administrative Court Office, Room C315, Royal Courts of Justice, Strand, London, WC2A 2LL.

- Administrative Court in **Birmingham**

  Administrative Court Office, Birmingham Civil Justice Centre, Priory Courts, 33 Bull Street, Birmingham B4 6DS.

- Administrative Court in **Wales**

  Administrative Court Office, Cardiff Civil Justice Centre, 2 Park Street, Cardiff, CF10 1ET.

- Administrative Court in **Leeds**

  Administrative Court Office, Leeds Combined Court Centre, 1 Oxford Row, Leeds, LS1 3BG.

- Administrative Court in **Manchester**

  Administrative Court Office, Manchester Civil Justice Centre, 1 Bridge Street West, Manchester, M3 3FX.

IN THE HIGH COURT OF JUSTICE **Claim No.**
QUEEN'S BENCH DIVISION
ADMINISTRATIVE COURT

BETWEEN

THE QUEEN
(on the application of
JANE FIELDS) **Claimant**

–and–

WARDEN DRANE
DISTRICT COUNCIL **Defendant**

SUMMARY GROUNDS FOR CONTESTING THE CLAIM

Lawfulness of the allocations policy

1. The defendant's allocation policy is lawful and cannot successfully be challenged for the following reasons.

Error of law – reasonable preference

2. The scheme complies with the requirements of Part 6 of the Housing Act 1996. A reasonable preference is afforded in accordance with section 166A(3) as all of the priority groups are afforded points that would not be available to persons who did not qualify under those categories.
3. It cannot be said that the preference awarded on overcrowding or medical grounds is not a reasonable preference. When affording a reasonable preference the requirement is that persons entitled to such a preference must be given a 'head start' over other applicants (*R (A) v Lambeth LBC* [2002] EWCA Civ 1084, [2002] HLR 57). The scheme achieves this by providing additional points for need arising on medical or overcrowding grounds.
4. In designing the allocations scheme the authority has determined – as it is entitled to do – that priority on those grounds should be given less (but still reasonable) preference when compared with other categories of need such as the homeless. The extent of the reasonable preference is a matter for the authority to determine and can be challenged only on *Wednesbury* grounds.

Error of law – frustration of the purpose of the 1996 Act

5. An additional preference is given to, *inter alia*, the homeless. That is

permissible under the terms of the statute (s166A) and accords with the purpose of the interrelationship between Parts 6 and 7 of the Act. The authority cannot be criticised for deciding to award additional preference to the homeless over those in other priority groups.

6. It is absurd to suggest that the scheme is designed to keep families in overcrowded accommodation or with medical needs from being eligible for accommodation for as long as possible. Families falling within those groups are awarded additional points, thereby enhancing their possibility of successfully bidding for accommodation under the choice-based lettings scheme.

Irrationality – discretion

7. It is not irrational to have a residual discretion (*R v Islington LBC, ex p Reilly and Mannix* (1998) 31 HLR 651, QBD see also *R (Ahmad) v Newham LBC* [2009] UKHL 14, [2009] HLR 31), such a discretion is necessary to ensure that the scheme operates efficiently and can be adapted to unforeseen or individual circumstances.

Unlawful application of the policy

8. The authority's failure to exercise the residual discretion can only be challenged on *Wednesbury* grounds. It is for local authorities to determine the allocation of accommodation and they are afforded a wide margin of appreciation when doing so and when applying the scheme. It is not possible for the claimant to demonstrate that the decision not to exercise the residual discretion is so unreasonable as to be perverse.

9. Further, the issue of overcrowding has been considered in accordance with the scheme and the authority's policy for assessing overcrowding. There is no challenge to that policy and the claim under this head must fail. On the claimant's own case, the authority had regard to the medical evidence submitted and it is a matter for the authority – applying its policies – to determine the weight to be given to that medical evidence.

Challenge futile

10. In any event, the defendant is currently in the process of updating its scheme in accordance with its modernisation agenda and its commitment to continuous improvements in its services. It is envisaged that the new allocations scheme will be in place some time during 2017/18. The defendant cannot move any more quickly to replace its existing policy than this, whatever rulings the court may make on this application.

11. The claimant should await adoption of the new policy and challenge that within three months of its adoption if she believes that she has grounds for so doing.

12. For those reasons, it is submitted that the claimant is not entitled to the relief claimed, or to any relief.

Claire Ronethun
Smith Chambers, London

Click here to reset form | Click here to print form

Appellant's notice

(All appeals except small claims track appeals and appeals to the Family Division of the High Court)

For Court use only	
Appeal Court Ref. No.	
Date filed	

Notes for guidance are available which will help you complete this form. Please read them carefully before you complete each section.

SEAL

Section 1 Details of the claim or case you are appealing against

Claim or Case no.

Fee Account no. (if applicable)

Help with Fees - Ref no. (if applicable) HWF- -

Name(s) of the ☐ Claimant(s) ☑ Applicant(s) ☐ Petitioner(s)

JANE FIELDS

Name(s) of the ☐ Defendant(s) ☑ Respondent(s)

WARDEN DRANE DC

Details of the party appealing ('The Appellant')

Name

Elizabeth Leahy

Address (including postcode)

16A Maxwell Square
Warden
WAR 16 6AB

Tel No.	012557 932831
Fax	n/a
E-mail	elizabeth.leahy@googliemail.com

Details of the Respondent to the appeal

Name

Warden Drane District Council

Address (including postcode)

Housing Department
Civic Centre
Warden High Rd
Warden
WAR1 96X

Tel No.	012557 132000
Fax	n/a
E-mail	housing@warden.gov.uk

Details of additional parties (if any) are attached ☐ Yes ☑ No

Section 2 Details of the appeal

From which court is the appeal being brought?

☐ The County Court at

☐ The Family Court at

☐ High Court

- ☐ Queen's Bench Division
- ☐ Chancery Division
- ☐ Family Division

☑ Other (please specify)

A decision of Warden Drane DC under s.202 Housing Act 1996

What is the name of the Judge whose decision you want to appeal?

n/a

What is the status of the Judge whose decision you want to appeal?

☐ District Judge or Deputy	☐ Circuit Judge or Recorder	☐ Tribunal Judge
☐ Master or Deputy	☐ High Court Judge or Deputy	☐ Justice(s) of the Peace

What is the date of the decision you wish to appeal against?

28 July 2017

Is the decision you wish to appeal a previous appeal decision? ☐ Yes ☑ No

Section 3	Legal representation

Are you legally represented? ☑ Yes ☐ No

If Yes, is your legal representative (please tick as appropriate)

☑ a solicitor

☐ direct access counsel instructed to conduct litigation on your behalf

☐ direct access counsel instructed to represent you at hearings only

Name of your legal representative

Leo & Nevil Solicitors

The address (including postcode) of your legal representative

23204 Nashville Road
Warden
WAR7 8QB

Tel No.	012557 168932
Fax	n/a
E-mail	housing@leoandnevil.co.uk
DX	896432 Warden 2
Ref.	LN/h/fields/01532

Are you, the Appellant, in receipt of a Civil Legal Aid Certificate? ☑ Yes ☐ No

Is the respondent legally represented? ☑ Yes ☐ No
If 'Yes', please give details of the respondent's legal representative below

Name and address (including postcode) of the respondent's legal representative

Legal Services
Warden Drane DC
Civic Centre
Warden High Road
Warden
WAR1 96X

Tel No.	012557 132000
Fax	n/a
E-mail	legal@warden.gov.uk
DX	162 Warden 1
Ref.	LE/HSG/Fields/86914

Section 4 Permission to appeal

Do you need permission to appeal? ☐ Yes ☑ No

Has permission to appeal been granted?

☐ **Yes** (Complete Box A) ☐ **No** (Complete Box B)

Box A

Date of order granting permission

Name of Judge granting permission

Box B

I

the Appellant('s legal representative) seek permission to appeal.

If permission to appeal has been granted **in part** by the lower court, do you seek permission to appeal in respect of the grounds refused by the lower court? ☐ Yes ☐ No

Section 5 Other information required for the appeal

Please set out the order (or part of the order) you wish to appeal against

Decision of the local authority that the appellant is intentionally homeless.

Have you lodged this notice with the court in time? (There are different types of appeal - see Guidance Notes N161A) ☑ Yes ☐ No

If **'No'** you must also complete **Part B of Section 10 and Section 11**

Section 6 Grounds of appeal

Please state, in numbered paragraphs, **on a separate sheet** attached to this notice and entitled 'Grounds of Appeal' (also in the top right hand corner add your claim or case number and full name), why you are saying that the Judge who made the order you are appealing was wrong.

☑ I confirm that the grounds of appeal are attached to this notice.

Section 7 Arguments in support of grounds for appeal

☐ I confirm that the arguments (known as a 'Skeleton Argument') in support of the 'Grounds of Appeal' are set out **on a separate sheet** and attached to this notice.

OR (in the case of appeals other than to the Court of Appeal)

☑ I confirm that the arguments (known as a 'Skeleton Argument') in support of the 'Grounds of Appeal' will follow within 14 days of filing this Appellant's Notice. A skeleton argument should only be filed if appropriate, in accordance with CPR Practice Direction 52B, paragraph 8.3.

Section 8 Aarhus Convention Claim

For applications made under the Town and Country Planning Act 1990 or Planning (Listed Buildings and Conservation Areas) Act 1990

I contend that this claim is an Aarhus Convention Claim ☐ Yes ☑ No

If Yes, and you are appealing to the Court of Appeal, any application for an order to limit the recoverable costs of an appeal, pursuant to CPR 52.19, should be made in section 10.

If Yes, indicate in the following box if you do not wish the costs limits under CPR 45 to apply. If you have indicated that the claim is an Aarthus claim set out the grounds below

Section 9 What are you asking the Appeal Court to do?

I am asking the appeal court to:-
(please tick the appropriate box)

☐ set aside the order which I am appealing

☑ vary the order which I am appealing and substitute the following order. Set out in the following space the order you are asking for:-

The court is asked to allow the appeal and substitute a decision that the appellant is not intentionally homeless. Alternatively, the court is asked to quash the decision and remit the matter back to the defendant for further consideration and redetermination

☐ order a new trial

Section 10 Other applications

Complete this section **only** if you are making any additional applications.

Part A

☐ I apply for a stay of execution. (You must set out in Section 11 your reasons for seeking a stay of execution and evidence in support of your application.)

Part B

☐ I apply for an extension of time for filing my appeal notice. (You must set out in Section 11 the reasons for the delay and what steps you have taken since the decision you are appealing.)

Part C

☑ I apply for an order that:

The court make case management directions in the form attached

(You must set out in Section 11 your reasons and your evidence in support of your application.)

Section 11 Evidence in support

In support of my application(s) in Section 10, I wish to rely upon the following reasons and evidence:

By CPR PD 52D para 28, the appellant is required to serve proposed case management directions with this appeal. The appellant proposes:

1) The defendant shall, by [insert date 14/21 days hence], disclose a full copy of the housing file (and any other document relevant to this appeal if not otherwise contained in the housing file) to the appellant.

2) Any application by the appellant to amend the grounds of appeal must be made within 14 days of receipt of the documents referred to in (1), above.

3) Any witness statements of fact must be exchanged by 4pm on [insert date 21 days after the date in (1), above]

4) The appellant must liaise with the respondent and seek to agree paginated and indexed bundle for use at the appeal. Such bundle must be filed and served not less than 14 days before the hearing of this appeal.

5) Each party must file and serve a skeleton argument not less than 7 days before the hearing of this appeal. The advocates who will argue the appeal must lodge an agreed bundle of authorities not less than 3 days before the hearing of this appeal.

Statement of Truth – This must be completed in support of the evidence in Section 11

I believe (The appellant believes) that the facts stated in this section are true.

Full name

Name of appellant's legal representative firm

signed   position or office held

Appellant ('s legal representative)   (if signing on behalf of firm or company)

Section 12 Supporting documents

To support your appeal you should file with this notice all relevant documents listed below. To show which documents you are filing, please tick the appropriate boxes.

If you do not have a document that you intend to use to support your appeal complete the box over the page.

In the County Court or High Court:

- [x] three copies of the appellant's notice for the appeal court and three copies of the grounds of appeal;
- [x] one additional copy of the appellant's notice and grounds of appeal for each of the respondents;
- [ ] one copy of the sealed (stamped by the court) order being appealed;
- [ ] a copy of any order giving or refusing permission to appeal; together with a copy of the judge's reasons for allowing or refusing permission to appeal; and
- [x] a copy of the Civil Legal Aid Agency Certificate (if legally represented).

In the Court of Appeal:

- [ ] three copies of the appellant's notice and three copies of the grounds of appeal on a separate sheet attached to each appellant's notice;
- [ ] one additional copy of the appellant's notice and one copy of the grounds of appeal for each of the respondents;
- [ ] one copy of the sealed (stamped by the court) order or tribunal determination being appealed;
- [ ] a copy of any order giving or refusing permission to appeal together with a copy of the judge's reasons for allowing or refusing permission to appeal;
- [ ] one copy of any witness statement or affidavit in support of any application included in the appellant's notice;
- [ ] where the decision of the lower court was itself made on appeal, a copy of the first order, the reasons given by the judge who made it and the appellant's notice of appeal against that order;
- [ ] in a claim for judicial review or a statutory appeal a copy of the original decision which was the subject of the application to the lower court;
- [ ] one copy of the skeleton arguments in support of the appeal or application for permission to appeal;
- [ ] a copy of the approved transcript of judgment; and
- [ ] a copy of the Civil Legal Aid Certificate (if applicable)
- [ ] where a claim relates to an Aarhus Convention claim, a schedule of the claimant's financial resources

Reasons why you have not supplied a document and date when you expect it to be available:-

Title of document and reason not supplied	**Date when it will be supplied**
Skeleton argument - it is proposed to file and serve this once the full housing file has been disclosed	14 days after the disclosure of the housing file

Section 13 The notice of appeal must be signed here

Signed [ ] Appellant('s legal representative)

Click here to reset form | Click here to print form

IN THE COUNTY COURT AT WARDEN **Claim No. WXN1234**

BETWEEN

ELIZABETH LEAHY **Appellant**

–and–

WARDEN DRANE DISTRICT COUNCIL **Respondent**

GROUNDS OF APPEAL

This is an appeal under the Housing Act 1996 s204, against the decision of the authority's reviewing officer (under HA 1996 s202) to uphold the decision that the appellant had made herself homeless intentionally homeless from 1 Warden Lane, Warden, WD9 9ZX.

A person is intentionally homeless if he deliberately does or fails to do anything in consequence of which he ceases to occupy settled accommodation which is available for his occupation and which it would have been reasonable for him to continue to occupy: Housing Act 1996 s191(1). In each case, the ground of appeal raises a point of law.

GROUND ONE: The authority misdirected itself in law in finding that it would be reasonable for the appellant to continue to occupy the matrimonial home because she could exclude her husband

1.1 A person is homeless if he has no accommodation which he has a legal entitlement to occupy (s175(1)), but shall not be treated as having accommodation unless it is accommodation which it would be reasonable for him to continue to occupy: s175(3). Section 177(1) provides that it is not reasonable for a person to continue to occupy accommodation if it is probable that such occupation will lead to domestic or other violence or threats of violence against him or against a person who might reasonably be expected to reside with him.

1.2 The only question that an authority should ask when determining – whether accommodation is suitable on the grounds of violence or threats of violence is whether it is probable that continued occupation of the accommodation will lead to violence or threats of violence against the applicant; it is irrelevant whether the applicant has or could have availed him/herself of any alternative remedies to address the domestic violence: *Bond v Leicester City Council* [2001] EWCA Civ 1544, [2002] HLR 6 (see paras 6.18 onwards of the Homelessness Code of Guidance 2006).

1.3 In its review decision letter, the authority states that it would be reasonable for the Appellant to continue to occupy the matrimonial home because:

> *'There are steps which Ms Leahy may take to ask the court to oust her husband, John Jones, from their jointly owned property. It does not make sense to consider the first option in such cases to be rehousing by a local authority when a home-owner has suitable accommodation which they may use the process of law to secure and to protect them in residence there yet chooses not to do so.'*

1.4 In so finding, the authority misdirected itself in law by concluding that it was reasonable for the Appellant to continue to occupy the matrimonial home because the Appellant should have considered obtaining and/or obtained an injunction excluding her husband from the matrimonial home.

GROUND TWO: The authority gave inadequate reasons for finding that it was not probable that occupation of the marital home by the Appellant would lead to violence or threats of violence from her husband

2.1 Where on review under section 202 of the Housing Act 1996, a local authority confirms an earlier decision, it is required to give reasons for doing so: s203(4), and see *R v Croydon LBC, ex p Graham* (1993) 26 HLR 286, CA, and *R v Brent LBC ex p Bariise* (1998) 31 HLR 50, CA.

2.2 In its decision letter, the authority disputes whether the Appellant would be at risk of violence from her husband were she to return to live at the matrimonial home:

> *That she says she is in fear – and for the sake of argument I am willing to accept that she is – does not mean that it is likely or probable that violence or threats of violence will be carried out. Just because Ms Leahy fears it does not make it so . . . Whilst I do not dispute Ms Leahy version of past events, ie that violence occurred in the past, it does not mean that it is probable that domestic violence, other violence or threats of violence are likely to be carried out against her, or those who normally reside with her.*

2.3 No reasons are given for not accepting the Appellant's belief that she would be subjected to violence or for disregarding the evidence submitted on her behalf and, accordingly, the authority has failed to provide any or any adequate reasoning for its decision.

GROUND THREE: the authority failed to make sufficient enquiries

3.1 The obligation on a reviewing officer is to have regard to all matters as they appear to him at the date of the review: *Sahardid v Camden LBC* [2004] EWCA Civ 1485, [2005] HLR 11. The officer is also under an obligation to make sufficient enquiries into all matters relevant to an application, including the risk of domestic violence (*Patterson v Greenwich LBC* (1993) 26 HLR 159, CA).

3.2 On 9 September 2016, representations were made on behalf of the Appellant. Those representations detailed the Appellant's history of violence from her husband and her concerns about the likely repetition of that violence since her husband was released from prison. The Appellant – and her then advisers – provided the authority with details of persons who could support her application and her account, including details of a next-door neighbour, Becky Dodgson, who was aware of the domestic violence suffered by the Appellant.

3.3 Once the issue of the husband's release from prison had been drawn to the authority's attention, it was obliged to make reasonable inquiries into the Appellant's concern that there was a probability of threats of violence towards her. In failing to do so, the authority acted in breach of its duties under Part 7.

3.4 In circumstances where the authority was minded not to believe that the Appellant was at risk of domestic violence, it was incumbent on it to make enquiries of the neighbour in order to determine whether the Appellant's assertions could be corroborated. In failing to do so, the authority erred in law by failing to make sufficient enquiries into the Appellant's application.

GROUND FOUR: The authority failed to put adverse findings to the Appellant

4.1 In conducting its inquiries, the authority must put basic issues to the applicant that may be decided against him to enable him to comment on them (*R v Tower Hamlets LBC ex p Rouf* (1989) 21 HLR 294, QBD); the applicant must have an opportunity to deal with the generality of material which will adversely affect him: *R v Gravesham BC ex p Winchester* (1986) 18 HLR 208, QBD.

4.2 The authority found that it was not probable that the Appellant and her daughter were not at risk of violence or threats of violence if they returned to the property; in so finding they dismissed the evidence put forward by the Appellant as to her belief and the evidence put forward in support of the Appellant. That finding was a finding that was central to the authority's decision. The authority failed, however, to put that finding to the Appellant and in so doing breached the principles of natural justice and/or acted unfairly towards the Appellant by failing to put adverse findings to her and allow her an opportunity to comment on them.

GROUND FIVE: Failure to have regard to relevant considerations

5.1 In the representations put to the authority on behalf of the Appellant, the authority was informed that the Appellant's husband had been released from prison and had been seen in the vicinity of 1 Warden Lane and had been associating with the Appellant's neighbours.

5.2 The authority's decision letter is silent on this point or its effect. In failing to consider the effect which this would have on the Appellant's application, the authority failed to have regard to a relevant consideration.

GROUND SIX: Error of fact

6.1 The authority made a number of findings when reaching its decision that the Appellant did a deliberate act that rendered her intentionally homeless which are based on errors of fact.

6.2 In reaching its conclusions, the authority makes a number of key findings: '*You took no steps to oust your husband from the property*'; '*you did not report the alleged incidents to anyone*', and '*Your daughter has not expressed any symptoms of being scared of your husband*'.

6.3 These findings are factually incorrect:

(a) the Appellant did take steps to exclude her husband from the marital home, by contacting a solicitor and discussing her options regarding an exclusion order;
(b) the Appellant did report incidents of domestic violence to the police and to her doctor; copies of the crime incident numbers and a letter from her doctor were supplied to the authority;
(c) the authority received evidence that the Appellant's daughter was receiving counselling for stress consequent upon her experiences of violence from her husband.

6.4 Accordingly, the decision is based on errors of fact, which are so fundamental to the authority's conclusions that the decision that there was an intentional act cannot be said to be sustainable.

GROUND SEVEN: Reasonableness

7.1 When authorities make decisions, they must have regard to all relevant matters, ignore irrelevant matters and not come to a decision that no reasonable authority could make ('*Wednesbury* unreasonableness'): *Associated Provincial Picture House v Wednesbury Corporation* [1948] 1 KB 223, CA, *per* Lord Greene MR at 229, 234.

7.2 The decision that the accommodation at 1 Warden Lane Road was suitable as permanent accommodation was a decision which no reasonable authority, properly directing itself, could have reached, because, *inter alia*:

- the authority did not consider that accommodation which may be suitable on a temporary basis may not be suitable on a permanent basis;
- the authority did not have any or any adequate regard to the fact that the Appellant's husband had been released from prison; and,
- the authority failed to have regard to the Appellant's concerns for her own safety and that of her family.

7.3 Further or alternatively, the decision to dismiss the Appellant's belief that she would be subject to domestic violence were she to return was – on the basis of the facts and the evidence before the authority – a decision that no reasonable authority could have reached. Having regard to all the circumstances, the decision was so unreasonable as to be perverse.

Julia Clunes
Justice Chambers

CHAPTER 13

Other statutory provisions

13.1 Introduction

13.7 Care Act 2014/Social Services and Well-being (Wales) Act 2014

13.9 Duty and power to meet needs for care and support

Duty • Power

13.14 Assessment of need

13.15 Immigrants and asylum-seekers

13.22 Provision of housing accommodation

13.26 Discharge of the duty

13.27 Immigration and Asylum Act 1999

13.40 Children Act 1989/Social Services and Well-being (Wales) Act 2014

13.41 Children Act 1989

CA 1989 s17 • CA 1989 s20

13.66 Co-operation between social services and housing authorities

13.74 Children leaving care

13.81 Social Services and Well-being (Wales) Act 2014

13.87 Local Government Act 2000/Localism Act 2011

13.94 Specified public authorities

13.97 Other statutory provisions

13.97 Child Abduction and Custody Act 1985

Introduction

13.1 The National Assistance Act (NAA) 1948 was the direct precursor of homeless persons legislation.[1] That Act was also a precursor of the Children Act (CA) 1989.[2] Two factors placed a much greater housing emphasis on those Acts in recent years:[3]

a) the exclusion from housing assistance of categories of immigrants;[4] and
b) the stricter controls on housing under Housing Act (HA) 1996 Parts 6 and 7.[5]

13.2 The NAA 1948 has recently been replaced, in England by the Care Act (CA) 2014 and in Wales by the Social Services and Well-being (Wales) Act (SSWB(W)A) 2014; the CA 1989 now only applies in England, with the equivalent provisions in Wales to be found in SSWB(W)A 2014. This book is not a comprehensive study of the broader welfare provisions of any of this legislation. There is, however, an overlap: the facts of many of the cases often suggest circumstances that would, but for legislative change, formerly have been dealt with under homelessness legislation; indeed, many of those cases refer directly to that legislation.

13.3 Also overlapping with homelessness is the asylum support scheme under the Immigration and Asylum Act (IAA) 1999.

13.4 In addition, because it has been held to be an available source of power with which to assist in appropriate circumstances, reference must also be made to the power of general competence under the Localism Act (LA) 2011 in England, replacing the well-being powers of the Local Government Act (LGA) 2000, which remain available in Wales.

13.5 In this chapter, we therefore consider the relevant provisions of the following Acts:

a) CA 2014/SSWB(W)A 2014;
b) IAA 1999;
c) CA 1989/SSWB(W)A 2014;
d) LGA 2000/LA 2011;
e) other statutory provisions.

1 See paras 1.7–1.20.

2 See NAA 1948 ss21 and 29, as enacted, amended to apply only to persons aged 18 and over by CA 1989 s108(5) and Sch 13 para 11; see the observations of Laws LJ in *R (A) v Lambeth LBC* [2001] EWCA Civ 1624, [2002] HLR 13 at [1].

3 It seems likely that benefit caps and other recent measures will also enhance dependence on social welfare duties.

4 See paras 1.59–1.61 and 1.82.

5 See paras 1.66–1.79.

13.6 As with interim accommodation under Part 7 of the HA 1996, however, it is important to note that some classes of immigrant are wholly excluded from assistance even under these provisions. These classes – and the exceptions from them, including the over-arching exception for British citizens,[6] and the human rights/EC Treaty exceptions[7] – are the same as those considered in chapter 3.[8]

Care Act 2014/Social Services and Well-being (Wales) Act 2014

13.7 Adults with needs for care and support may be provided with residential care by local authorities under the CA 2014 in England or the SSWB(W)A 2014 in Wales.[9]

13.8 In England, CA 2014 Part 1 came into force on 1 April 2015.[10] In Wales, SSWB(W)A 2014 came fully into force on 6 April 2016.[11]

6 See para 3.21.

7 See paras 3.154–3.160.

8 See paras 3.154–3.160.

9 Cases decided under NAA 1948 are, however, likely to have some bearing on the application of the new legislative schemes under CA 2014 and SSWB(W)A 2014. In *R (GS) v Camden LBC* [2016] EWHC 1762 (Admin), [2016] HLR 43 it was held that the case law on the meaning of 'care and attention' in NAA 1948 s21, applies to 'care and support' in CA 2014 s9; thus a need for accommodation is not itself a need for care and support; to be eligible for accommodation under Part 1 of the 2014 Act, an applicant must have other needs which mean that he is not capable of living independently. For case-law on the NAA 1948, see the 9th edition of this work, Legal Action Group, 2012, paras 13.7–13.35.

10 Where a person was being provided with assistance under NAA 1948 Part 3, on 1 April 2015, the authority had one year in which to assess his needs under the CA 2014 by carrying out a review of his case: The Care Act 2014 (Transitional Provision) Order 2015 SI No 995 Article 2. Until such a review was completed, the NAA 1948 continued to apply to that person. If the authority failed to complete a review under the 2014 Act before 1 April 2016, the person is automatically treated as having needs which he or she is entitled to have met under the CA 2014. That automatic entitlement continues until the authority complete a review.

11 Social Services and Well-being (Wales) Act 2014 (Commencement No 3, Savings and Transitional Provisions) Order 2016 SI No 412 Sch 1 para 2 provides that SSWB(W)A 2014 does not apply where a person was receiving support or services prior to 6 April 2016 but that the authority must carry out a review of that person's case by 1 April 2017. Once the review has been carried out, the SSWB(W)A 2014 will apply. If the authority fails to complete a review by 1 April 2017, the person will automatically be treated as having needs

Under both Acts, local authorities[12] have both a duty and a power to meet needs for care and support.[13] In order to meet needs, authorities may provide, inter alia, accommodation in a care home or in premises of some other type.[14]

Duty and power to meet needs for care and support

Duty

13.9 In respect of both CA 2014 and SSWB(W)A 2014, the duty to meet needs arises where an adult is ordinarily resident[15] in the local authority's area (or present in its area and of no settled residence)[16] and that adult has needs which meet the eligibility criteria.[17] The duty is not, however, triggered where there would be a charge for meeting the needs,[18] unless one of three conditions is met:[19]

which he is entitled to have met under the SSWB(W)A 2014. That automatic entitlement continues until the authority completes a review.

12 A county council in England, a district council for an area in England for which there is no county council, a London borough council, or the Common Council of the City of London: CA 2014 s1(4); the council of a county or county borough in Wales: SSWB(W)A 2014 s197(1).

13 CA 2014 ss18 and 19; SSWB(W)A 2014 ss35 and 36. There is also a duty and a power to meet a carer's needs for support: CA 2014 s20; SSWB(W)A 2014 ss40 and 45.

14 CA 2014 s8(1)(a); SSWB(W)A 2014 s34(2)(a).

15 A person's ordinary residence is determined in accordance with CA 2014 s39 or SSWB(W)A 2014 s194. In particular, both Acts provide for a person provided with accommodation under certain statutory provisions to be treated as ordinarily resident in the area in which he or she was ordinarily resident before being provided with that accommodation. The statutory provisions include the National Health Service Act 2006 and National Health Service (Wales) Act 2006 thereby addressing *R (Kent CC) v Secretary of State for Health* [2015] EWCA Civ 81, [2015] 1 WLR 1221 (person ordinarily resident for purposes of NAA 1948 in Kent, despite not having lived there prior to having been placed in NHS accommodation). In determining where someone is resident, any period and place of detention in hospital is to be disregarded: *R (Hertfordshire CC) v Hammersmith and Fulham LBC* [2011] EWCA Civ 77; *R (Wiltshire CC) v Hertfordshire CC* [2014] EWCA Civ 712, [2014] HLR 41.

16 CA 2014 s18(1)(a); SSWB(W)A 2014 s35(2).

17 CA 2014 s18(1); SSWB(W)A 2014 s35(3)(a). In Wales, the duty may arise even if the adult's needs do not meet the eligibility criteria, provided that the authority considers it necessary to meet those needs in order to protect the adult from abuse or neglect or a risk of abuse or neglect: SSWB(W)A 2014 s35(3)(b).

18 Under CA 2014 s14 or SSWB(W)A 2014 s59.

19 CA 2014 s18(1)(c); SSWB(W)A 2014 s35(4)(a). There is also a cap on care costs in England but this has not yet been brought into force: CA 2014 ss15 and 18(1)(b).

a) The first condition is that the adult's financial resources are at or below the financial limit.
b) The second condition is that, if the adult's financial resources are above the financial limit, the adult nonetheless asks the authority to make the arrangements to meet his or her needs.[20]
c) The third condition is that the adult lacks capacity to arrange for the provision of care and support and there is no person authorised under the Mental Capacity Act 2005 to make such provision for him or her or otherwise in a position to do so on his or her behalf.[21]

13.10 The phrase 'ordinarily resident'. was considered in *Shah*,[22] under the Education Act 1962: it was held that a person's long-term future intentions or expectations are not relevant; the test is not what is a person's real home, but whether a person can show a regular, habitual mode of life in a particular place, the continuity of which has persisted despite temporary absences; a person's attitude is only relevant in two respects – the residence must be voluntarily adopted and there must be a settled purpose in living in the particular residence.[23] In *R (Cornwall CC) v Secretary of State for Health*,[24] this was said to be 'the leading modern authority on the meaning' of ordinary residence[25] although 'the meaning of the term . . . may be strongly influenced by the particular statutory context'.[26]

13.11 In England, an adult's needs meet the eligibility criteria if:

i) they arise from or are related to a physical or mental impairment or illness;
ii) as a result of those needs the adult is unable to achieve two or more specified personal outcomes;[27] and

20 The costs both of meeting the care needs and of making the arrangements to do so being met by the adult, see CA 2014 s14 and SSWB(W)A 2014 s59.

21 CA 2014 s18(2)–(4); SSWB(W)A 2014 s35(4)(b). The financial limit is set by regulations: Care and Support (Charging and Assessment of Resources) Regulations 2014 SI No 2672 (England); Care and Support (Charging) (Wales) Regulations 2015 SI No 1843) (Wales).

22 *R v Barnet LBC ex p Shah* [1983] 2 AC 309, HL.

23 *Shah* at 349C.

24 [2015] UKSC 46, [2015] HLR 32.

25 *Cornwall* at [41].

26 *Cornwall* at [43].

27 The specified outcomes are: managing and maintaining nutrition; maintaining personal hygiene; managing toilet needs; being appropriately clothed; being able to make use of the adult's home safely; maintaining a habitable home environment; developing and maintaining family or other personal relationships; accessing and engaging in work, training, education

iii) as a consequence there is (or is likely to be) a significant impact on the adult's well-being.[28]

In Wales, the need of an adult meets the eligibility criteria if:

i) it arises from the adult's physical or mental ill-health, age, disability, dependence on alcohol or drugs, or other similar circumstances;
ii) it relates to one or more of a list of specified matters;[29] and
iii) the adult is not able to meet the need.[30]

Power

13.12 In England, the power to meet needs is engaged where the adult is ordinarily resident in the authority's area[31] or is present in its area but of no settled residence, and the authority is satisfied that it is not under a duty to meet the adult's needs,[32] ie not under the duty considered at para 13.9, above.[33] The power may also be exercised to support an adult who is ordinarily resident in another authority's area[34] Finally, the power may be exercised where the adult has needs which appear to the authority to be urgent even though an assessment has not yet been carried out.[35]

or volunteering; making use of necessary facilities or services in the local community including public transport, and recreational facilities or services; and, carrying out any caring responsibilities the adult has for a child: Care and Support (Eligibility Criteria) Regulations 2015 SI No 313 reg 2(2).

28 Care and Support (Eligibility Criteria) Regulations 2015 SI No 313 reg 2(1).

29 The ability to carry out self-care or domestic routines; the ability to communicate; protection from abuse or neglect; involvement in work, education, learning or in leisure activities; maintenance or development of family or other significant personal relationships; development and maintenance of social relationships and involvement in the community; and, fulfilment of caring responsibilities for a child: Care and Support (Eligibility) (Wales) Regulations 2015 SI No 1578 reg 3(b).

30 Care and Support (Eligibility) (Wales) Regulations 2015 SI No 1578 reg 3.

31 See para 13.10.

32 Ie not under a duty pursuant to CA 2014 s18: CA 2014 s19(1).

33 The only restrictions on this power are those found in CA 2014 ss21–23 (exclusions for certain illegal immigrants, NHS services and housing services) discussed below (see paras 13.15–13.21). In Wales, see SSWB(W)A 2014 ss46–48, to the same effect.

34 This power cannot be used unless the authority which is exercising the power has notified the authority for the area where the adult is ordinarily resident that they intend to provide support (CA 2014 s14(2)(c)) and, in any event, is subject to limitations as to what charges the authority may impose on the adult (s14(2)(b)).

35 CA 2014 s19.

13.13 In Wales, the power is expressed rather more broadly. An authority may meet an adult's needs for care and support if he or she is either within its area or ordinarily resident in its area but presently outside of it.[36] The power to meet needs may be used whether or not an assessment has been completed.[37]

Assessment of need

13.14 Where it appears[38] to a local authority that an adult may have needs for care and support, the authority must assess whether he or she does have such needs and, if so, what those needs are.[39] If a person refuses an assessment, the authority need not carry one out.[40] Where the authority is satisfied, on the basis of the needs assessment, that a person has needs for care and support, it must determine whether his or her needs meet the eligibility criteria and, if satisfied that they do so, it must, inter alia, consider what could be done to meet those needs.[41]

Immigrants and asylum-seekers

13.15 A local authority may not meet the needs for care and support of an adult to whom IAA 1999, s115, applies if his or her needs for care and support have arisen solely because he or she is destitute or because of the physical effects (or anticipated physical effects) of being destitute.[42]

36 SSWB(W)A 2014 s36(1).

37 SSWB(W)A 2014 s36(3).

38 Under the pre-CA 2014 law, it was held that there was no need to request an assessment so long as the person had come to the attention of the local authority: *R v Gloucester CC ex p RADAR* (1997–98) 1 CCLR 476. It must, however, 'appear' to the authority that a person has a need: *R (NM) v Islington LBC* [2012] EWHC 414 (Admin).

39 CA 2014 s9(1); SSWB(W)A 2014 s19(1). Statutory guidance on assessments under CA 2014 has been issued, see CA 2014 s78 and *Care and support statutory guidance* (last updated 27 February 2017), chapter 6. In Wales, see SSWB(W)A 2014 s145 and the Code of Practice on the exercise of social services functions in relation to SSWB(W)A 2014 Part 3 (Assessing the needs of individuals).

40 CA 2014 s11(1); SSWB(W)A 2014 s20(1). A lack of capacity does not, in itself, amount to a refusal (CA 2014 s11(2)(a); SSWB(W)A 2014 s20(2)). A person who refuses an assessment is entitled to change his or her mind and require one at a later date, see CA 2014 s11(3) and SSWB(W)A 2014 s20(3).

41 CA 2014 s13; SSWB(W)A 2014 s32.

42 CA 2014 s21(1); SSWB(W)A 2014 s46(1). These provisions follow a similar exclusion contained in NAA s21(1A). See also Nationality, Immigration and Asylum Act (NIAA) 2002 Sch 3 para 1.

13.16 The effect of this is to exclude those who are subject to immigration control (unless re-included by regulations) from making an application for assistance under CA 2014 or SSWB(W)A 2014, where the need for care and attention arises solely from destitution. Their needs are, instead, intended to be met under the IAA 1999. Local authorities have no power to provide any accommodation for non-asylum-seeking immigrants who are merely destitute, and who do not have children. In the case of asylum-seekers whose need for care and attention does not arise because of destitution, however, but because of, eg, disability, responsibility for meeting their care needs remains with the local authority.[43]

13.17 These exclusions are subject to what is commonly known as the 'human rights'[44] exception:[45] ie they do not prevent the exercise of a power or the performance of a duty if, and to the extent that, its exercise or performance is necessary for the purpose of avoiding a breach of a person's rights under the European Convention on Human Rights ('the Convention'/ECHR).

13.18 A similar exclusion was found in the (now repealed) NAA 1948 s21(1A). Under that Act, it was held that the starting-point was to ask whether support should be provided in order to avoid a violation of a right under the ECHR, before applying any eligibility criteria or assessing the applicant's need for care and attention.[46]

13.19 In *PB*,[47] the claimant was a homeless Jamaican woman and an illegal overstayer. She had contact with her oldest child who lived with his father in the UK but the other four children, all born in the UK, were the subject of care proceedings and not living with her at the time. The authority refused to assist her under NAA 1948 s21, on the basis that she could return to Jamaica. The High Court held that this decision was unlawful because the authority had not considered

43 *Westminster City Council v National Asylum Support Service* [2002] UKHL 38, [2002] 1 WLR 2958; *O v Wandsworth LBC* (2001) 33 HLR 39, CA. See also *R (M) v Slough BC* [2008] UKHL 52, [2008] 1 WLR 1808, where *O* was applied and *R (Murua) v Croydon LBC* [2001] EWHC Admin 830, QBD; *R (Mani) v Lambeth LBC* [2003] EWCA Civ 836, (2003) 6 CCLR 376; and *R (SL) v Westminster City Council* [2013] UKSC 27, [2013] 1 WLR 1445.

44 It is not limited to human rights but also extends to rights under the EU treaties: see NIAA 2002, Sch 3 para 3(b).

45 NIAA 2002 Sch 3 para 3(a).

46 *R (N) v Lambeth LBC* [2006] EWHC 3427 (Admin).

47 *R (PB) v Haringey LBC and (1) Secretary of State for Health (2) Secretary of State for Communities and Local Government (interested parties)* [2006] EWHC 225 (Admin), [2007] HLR 13.

whether her right to respect for family life under ECHR Article 8[48] would be breached if she were forced to leave the UK while care proceedings were pending.

13.20 In *Binomugisha*,[49] the authority withdrew CA 1989[50] support from a 19-year-old failed asylum-seeker with mental health problems who had made a further application for leave to remain in the UK on the basis that it would be a breach of Article 8 to remove him to Uganda. The Home Office had not yet made a decision on that application. The claimant asserted that the authority owed him a duty under the leaving care provisions of the CA 1989[51] and under NAA 1948 s21. The court held that where there is an outstanding Article 8 claim, the question for the authority is whether that application was manifestly unfounded; while responsibility for making decisions on such applications lay with the Home Office, pending that decision the authority would have to consider whether it was necessary to provide a service in order to prevent a breach of ECHR Article 3 (prohibition of torture and inhuman or degrading treatment or punishment).

13.21 In *AW*[52] it was held that a purported fresh claim, either for asylum or under Article 3, by an asylum-seeker whose original claim had been rejected, did not always necessitate the provision of support in order to avoid a breach of the Convention; in considering the issue, it was necessary to have regard to all the relevant circumstances, including – where appropriate – the matters which were alleged to give rise to the fresh claim; it was necessary to proceed on a case-by-case basis.[53] Accordingly, the human rights exception does not bite simply because a human rights claim has been made to the UK Borders Agency (UKBA): it only applies where the provision of community care service is necessary for the purpose of avoiding a breach of a person's human rights,[54] eg where an applicant has limited life expectancy and could die at any time.[55]

48 See paras 12.100–12.102.

49 *R (Gordon Binomugisha) v Southwark LBC* [2006] EWHC 2254 (Admin), [2007] ACD 35.

50 See paras 13.41–13.80.

51 See paras 13.74–13.80.

52 *R (AW) v Croydon LBC* [2005] EWHC 2950 (QB), (2006) 9 CCLR 252.

53 *R (AW) v Croydon LBC*. The decision on appeal did not affect this part of the judgment below – see *Croydon LBC and Hackney LBC v R (AW, A and Y)* [2007] EWCA Civ 266, [2007] 1 WLR 3168.

54 NIAA 2002 Sch 3 para 3.

55 *R (De Almeida) v Kensington and Chelsea RLBC* [2012] EWHC 1082 (Admin).

Provision of housing accommodation

13.22 A local authority may not meet needs for care and support by doing anything which they, or another local authority, are required to do under HA 1996,[56] or Housing (Wales) Act (H(W)A) 2014.[57] In relation to NAA 1948 s21, it was held that once the local authority had assessed an applicant's needs as satisfying the relevant criteria, it must provide accommodation on a continuing basis so long as the need of the applicant remains as originally assessed: *R v Kensington and Chelsea RLBC ex p Kujtim*.[58] It was also held that residential accommodation could include 'ordinary' housing accommodation.[59] A duty to supply such accommodation arose where a person needed care and attention, including housing accommodation, that was not otherwise available. The need for care and attention was, however, a precondition of such a duty.[60] Although both CA 2014 and SSWB(W)A 2014 use the phrase 'care and support' instead of NAA 1948's 'care and attention', it has been held that the case-law on the NAA 1948 still applies.[61]

13.23 Under NAA 1948, the courts adopted a relatively generous approach to this phrase.[62] In the context of psychiatric care, it was held[63] that the question is whether the individual's need for care and attention by way of the provision of residential accommodation is made materially more acute by reason of his or her psychiatric disorder. A claimant may, however, have mental health needs that do not necessitate the provision of accommodation, for example where

56 CA 2014 s21(1)(a).

57 SSWB(W)A 2014 s48(a).

58 [1999] 4 All ER 161, (1999) 32 HLR 579, CA.

59 See *R v Bristol City Council ex p Penfold* (1998) 1 CCLR 315, QBD; *R v Wigan MBC ex p Tammadge* (1998) 1 CCLR 581, QBD; *R (Batantu) v Islington LBC* (2001) 33 HLR 76, QBD; and *Khana v Southwark LBC* [2001] EWCA Civ 999, CA; cf *R (Wahid) v Tower Hamlets LBC* [2001] EWHC Admin 641, QBD, where Stanley Burnton J doubted the correctness of the proposition, but felt constrained by the existing case-law.

60 *Khana*, above. It should not be used to circumvent the controls in HA 1996 Part 6.

61 See *R (SG) v Haringey LBC* [2015] EWHC 2579 (Admin), (2015) CCLR 444 (the appeal did not deal with this issue: [2017] EWCA Civ 322); *R (GS) Camden LBC* [2016] EWHC 1762 (Admin), [2016] HLR 43.

62 *R v Hammersmith LBC ex p M; R v Lambeth LBC ex p P and X; R v Westminster City Council ex p A* (1998) 30 HLR 10.

63 *R (Pajaziti and Pajaziti) v Lewisham LBC and Secretary of State for the Home Department (interested party)* [2007] EWCA Civ 1351.

the claimant is able to manage the practicalities of day-to-day life and does not need looking after.[64]

13.24 *R (M)*[65] comprises a comprehensive review of the meaning of 'care and attention' in NAA 1948: the natural and ordinary meaning of the words 'care and attention' in that context is 'looking after', which means doing something for the person being cared for which the person cannot or should not be expected to do for himself or herself, such as household tasks, protection from risks, or personal care – eg feeding, washing or toileting. In *R (SL) v Westminster City Council*,[66] the Supreme Court stressed that it was not enough that the authority were doing something that the applicant could not do for himself as that could lead to absurd conclusions (eg if the authority had to buy a refrigerator for him if he had no money); the need in question had to be linked to the provision of accommodation.

13.25 In *R (Nassery) v Brent LBC*,[67] the claimant suffered from mental health problems, had previously self-harmed and had made a number of suicide attempts. He sought accommodation under NAA 1948 s21 on the basis that he needed the assistance of a social worker to access medical help and that he had difficulty cooking as he suffered lapses in concentration. The authority carried out an assessment of his needs and concluded that he did not need such assistance and was not in need of care and attention. The claimant unsuccessfully sought judicial review of this conclusion:[68] the authority had considered all relevant evidence and had been entitled to reach its conclusion that he was not in need of care and attention; he had previously been able to access medical services via his GP and his mental health had been stable for some time; his contention that he was unable to cook was contrary to earlier statements made by him; the authority was entitled to conclude that the risk of self-harm did not amount to a need for care and attention. In the Court of Appeal, the claimant unsuccessfully sought to raise a new issue (that he had become obsessive and anxious about the most basic of decisions in life that he was essentially unable to function): new matters that had arisen since the initial assessment should be the subject of a request for a new assessment.

64 *R (Okil) v Southwark LBC* [2012] EWHC 1202 (Admin).

65 *R (M) v Slough BC* [2008] UKHL 52, [2008] 1 WLR 1808.

66 [2013] UKSC 27, [2013] HLR 30.

67 [2011] EWCA Civ 539, [2011] PTSR 1639.

68 [2010] EWHC 2326 (Admin).

Discharge of the duty

13.26 The duty to meet needs is not absolute. Where an applicant manifests a persistent and unequivocal refusal to observe the authority's reasonable requirements in relation to occupation of accommodation, the authority is entitled to treat its duty as discharged and to refuse to provide further accommodation.[69] The duty may also be discharged by the unreasonable refusal of an offer of accommodation. In *Khana v Southwark LBC*,[70] the applicant was a severely disabled elderly Kurdish woman. She lived with her husband and daughter in the latter's one-bedroom flat. Following assessment, the authority offered her and her husband a placement in a residential home on the basis that it was the only form of residential accommodation which would meet her needs for care and attention. The offer was refused by the applicant and her husband, who asserted they would only accept a two-bedroom, ground floor flat, where the family could continue to live together. Given its conclusion as to needs, the authority was held to have discharged its duty and, in any event, the refusal was unreasonable and as such discharged the authority from any further duty for so long as the refusal was maintained.

Immigration and Asylum Act 1999

13.27 IAA 1999 Part 6 came into force on 3 April 2000. It excludes persons subject to immigration control[71] from social security benefits and most other welfare provisions.[72] At the same time, however, it also set up a scheme for asylum support. The National Asylum Support Service (NASS) was established within the Immigration and Nationality Directorate (IND) of the Home Office, to administer the scheme. In July 2006 the Home Office announced that NASS no longer existed as a separate department. Asylum support is now administered in two separate ways:

a) those who made their first asylum claim on or after 5 March 2007 have their support processed by the New Asylum Model (NAM) 'case owner' who is processing his or her asylum claim; and

69 *R v Kensington and Chelsea RLBC ex p Kujtim* (2000) 32 HLR 579.

70 *Khana v Southwark LBC* [2001] EWCA Civ 999, (2001) 4 CCLR 267. See also *R (Patrick) v Newham LBC* (2001) 4 CCLR 48, QBD.

71 See para 3.16.

72 IAA 1999 s115.

b) those who claimed before that date are known as 'legacy cases' and have their asylum and support claims dealt with by the Casework Resolution Directorate (CRD).

In April 2007, the Border and Immigration Agency (BIA) replaced the IND. The BIA was replaced by the UKBA, which, in turn has been replaced by the Home Office's UK Visas and Immigration (UKVI) centre.

13.28 The EU has attempted to implement a common policy for the treatment of asylum-seekers across Europe by enacting Council Directive 2003/9/EC[73] which lays down minimum standards for their reception. The directive has been implemented into domestic law by amending the Immigration Rules[74] and enacting new regulations[75] which apply to a person whose claim for asylum is recorded on or after 5 February 2005.[76]

13.29 Under the IAA 1999 s95(1) the secretary of state may provide, or arrange for the provision of support for asylum-seekers or dependants of asylum-seekers who appear to him or her to be destitute or to be likely to become destitute within the prescribed period. That period is 14 days, or 56 days if they are already receiving asylum support.[77] The power to provide support is now a duty.[78] An asylum-seeker is a person who is not under 18 and who has made a claim for asylum which has been recorded by the secretary of state but which has not been determined.[79] A claim for asylum means a claim that it would be contrary to the UK's obligations under the Refugee Convention, or under ECHR Article 3, for the claimant to be removed from, or required to leave, the UK.[80] Dependants include a spouse, a child of the claimant or the claimant's spouse, who is under 18 and dependent on the claimant,[81] and various other prescribed persons.[82]

13.30 Assistance under these provisions is in theory excluded in the case of some classes of immigrant, being those classes (subject to exceptions, including the over-arching exception for British citizens

73 The directive came into force on 6 February 2003.

74 HC 395.

75 Asylum Seekers (Reception Conditions) Regulations 2005 SI No 7 and Asylum Support (Amendment) Regulations 2005 SI No 11.

76 Asylum Seekers (Reception Conditions) Regulations 2005 SI No 7 reg 1(2).

77 Asylum Support Regulations ('AS Regs') 2000 SI No 704 reg 7.

78 Asylum Seekers (Reception Conditions) Regulations 2005 SI No 7 reg 5.

79 IAA 1999 s94(1).

80 IAA 1999 s94(1).

81 IAA 1999 s94(1).

82 The list is set out in the AS Regs 2000 reg 2(4).

and persons under the age of 18,[83] and the human rights/EC Treaty exceptions)[84] considered in chapter 3.[85] In practice, the government does not usually apply these eligibility criteria when making asylum support decisions but applies the principles set out in these paragraphs.[86]

13.31 A person is destitute if he or she does not have adequate accommodation or any means of obtaining it, or has adequate accommodation or the means of obtaining it but cannot meet his or her other essential living needs.[87] This test involves a consideration of the claimant and the claimant's dependants.[88]

13.32 The secretary of state may not arrange or provide asylum support unless satisfied that the claim for asylum was made as soon as reasonably practicable after the person's arrival in the UK.[89] This does not apply if support is necessary to avoid a breach of the ECHR or if the household includes a dependent child who is under 18 years old.[90] The House of Lords has held that there would be a breach of ECHR Article 3 when an individual faces an imminent prospect of serious suffering caused or materially aggravated by denial of shelter, food or the most basic necessities of life: *R (Limbuela) v Secretary of State of the Home Department*.[91] The government has interpreted the judgment as meaning that support 'should be provided under [NIAA 2002] section 55(5)(a) when an applicant (or his adult dependant(s)) faces an imminent prospect of serious suffering caused or materially aggravated by denial of support'.[92] The judgment, however, also requires the decision-maker to be satisfied that the asylum-seeker has some means of meeting his or her need for food and washing facilities.

13.33 The secretary of state may provide, or arrange for the provision of, temporary support to destitute asylum-seekers and their dependants until a decision is reached on eligibility for support under IAA 1999 s95.[93] This is usually in a hotel or hostel, arranged by one of

83 See para 3.151.
84 See para 3.154.
85 See paras 3.101–3.160.
86 See paras 13.36–13.39.
87 IAA 1999 s95(3).
88 IAA 1999 s95(4).
89 NIAA 2002 s55(1).
90 NIAA 2002 s55(5).
91 [2005] UKHL 66, [2006] 1 AC 396.
92 UKVI, *Section 55 guidance*, Version 12, 1 June 2015.
93 IAA 1999 s98.

the voluntary organisations funded by the Home Office, which are known as the Asylum Support Partnership (ASP) and which provide reception assistance.

13.34 The secretary of state should arrange for the asylum-seeker to be offered support under IAA 1999 s95, as soon as it has been decided that he or she is eligible. This support can include providing accommodation that appears to be adequate for the needs of the supported person and his or her dependants, and providing for their essential living needs.[94] Before deciding what form of support to provide or continue to provide, the secretary of state must take certain matters into account and ignore others.[95] The asylum-seeker's resources must be taken into account when deciding the kind and level of support.[96]

13.35 An asylum-seeker stops being an asylum-seeker for support purposes 28 days after the secretary of state notifies him or her of a favourable asylum decision, or 21 days after notification of a refusal. If there is an appeal, the period ends 28 days after any final appeal is disposed of.[97] This does not apply if the asylum-seeker has a dependent child under 18 in the household: in those circumstances, he or she continues to be treated as an asylum-seeker for support purposes so long as the child is under 18 and within the household.[98] An asylum-seeker will not benefit from this provision if he or she is a refused asylum-seeker with a dependent child under 18 but is refusing to leave the UK and the secretary of state has certified that this is the case.[99]

13.36 A person who is ineligible for asylum support under IAA 1999 s95 or s98 may nevertheless be entitled to what used to be known as 'hard cases' support.[100] Under IAA 1999 s4(1), the secretary of state has powers to provide, or arrange for the provision of, support to any person who has arrived in the UK and been granted temporary admission[101] or who has been detained, whether or not they are also a former asylum-seeker. Under IAA 1999 s4(2), the secretary of state may provide, or arrange for the provision of, facilities for the accommodation of a person if the person was, but is no longer, an

94 IAA 1999 s96(1).

95 IAA 1999 s97(1), (2) and (4).

96 AS Regs 2000 reg 12.

97 IAA 1999 s94(3) and AS Regs 2000 reg 2(2).

98 IAA 1999 s94(5).

99 NIAA 2002 Sch 3 para 7A, substituted by the Asylum and Immigration (Treatment of Claimants, etc) Act 2004, with effect from 1 December 2004.

100 IAA 1999 s4.

101 Immigration Act 1971 Sch 2 para 21.

asylum-seeker, and the person's claim for asylum was rejected, if he or she can satisfy one of the five conditions set out in the applicable regulations.[102]

13.37 Those conditions are that:

a) the person is taking all reasonable steps to leave the UK or place himself or herself in a position in which he or she is able to leave, which may include complying with attempts to obtain a travel document to facilitate his or her departure;
b) the person is unable to leave the UK because he or she cannot travel for physical reasons or for some other medical reason;
c) the person is unable to leave the UK because in the opinion of the secretary of state there is currently no viable route of return available;
d) the person has made an application for judicial review of a decision in relation to his or her asylum claim,[103] and has been granted permission to proceed pursuant to Civil Procedure Rules (CPR) Part 54;
e) the provision of accommodation is necessary for the purpose of avoiding a breach of rights under the ECHR.[104]

13.38 The power to provide support under IAA 1999 s4 is expressed in terms of 'facilities for accommodation' so it may be provided in the form of accommodation with living expenses attached. Unlike support under IAA 1999 s95, it is not possible for an applicant to stay with a friend and only claim a subsistence allowance. The support usually comprises vouchers for living expenses with a room in a communal private rented house arranged by an accommodation provider. Sometimes the package is full board in hostel accommodation. The accommodation provider will issue weekly supermarket vouchers, which may be delivered to the applicant, or the applicant may need to collect them from an office. Unlike accommodation under IAA 1999 s95, there is no requirement for IAA 1999 s4 accommodation to be adequate – section 4 is a more limited and less advantageous duty for the applicant than the duty imposed by section 95: *R (Kiana) v Secretary of State for the Home Department.*[105]

102 Immigration and Asylum (Provision of Accommodation to Failed Asylum-Seekers) Regulations ('IA(PAFAS) Regs') 2005 SI No 930.

103 *R (NS) v First Tier Tribunal (Social Security Entitlement Chamber) and Secretary of State for the Home Department* [2009] EWHC 3819 (Admin), Staden J, on 6 November 2009.

104 IA(PAFAS) Regs 2005 reg 3(2).

105 [2010] EWHC 1002 (Admin).

13.39 In *R (VC) v Newcastle City Council*,[106] the High Court confirmed the statutory interpretation of IAA 1999 s4 as a 'residuary power', but added that the mere fact that support is or may be available under section 4 does not, of itself, exonerate a local authority from what would otherwise be a power or duty under other statutory provisions: thus, where a local authority had assessed a child as being in need within CA 1989 s17 or was already providing services under that power, it would not be able to justify the non-provision or discontinuance of assessed services on the ground that support under IAA 1999 s4 is available unless it can be shown that the secretary of state is actually able and willing (or if not willing could be compelled) to provide support, which support would meet the assessed needs of the child.

Children Act 1989/Social Services and Well-being (Wales) Act 2014

13.40 CA 1989 Part 3 confers general powers and imposes general duties on local authorities in England exercising social service functions in respect of children and families in their area.[107] From 6 April 2016, SSWB(W)A 2014 applies in Wales in its place.[108]

Children Act 1989

CA 1989 s17

13.41 Under CA 1989 s17(1), authorities are required to safeguard and promote the welfare of children within their areas[109] whom they assess as

106 [2011] EWHC 2673 (Admin), [2012] PTSR 546. The other statutory powers and duties in *VC* referred in particular to CA 1989 s17. See para 13.41.

107 A local authority exercising a social services function in respect of children and families in their area is a 'children's services authority' as defined by CA 2004 s65(1). This mirrors the definition of a 'social services authority' save for the addition of the Council of the Isles of Scilly. See para 13.8.

108 Social Services and Well-being (Wales) Act 2014 (Commencement No 3, Savings and Transitional Provisions) Order 2016 SI No 412.

109 A child will be within an authority's area if physically present: it is not necessary that the child be 'ordinarily resident' in the area; it is possible for a child to be 'within' more than one authority's area for the purposes of CA 1989 s17, eg where the child is living in one area but attends school in another – see *R (Sandra Stewart) v Wandsworth LBC and others* [2001] EWHC 709 (Admin), [2002] 1 FLR 469; *R (N) v (1) Newham LBC (2) Essex CC* [2013] EWHC 2475 (Admin). Although an authority needs only assess those children within its area, it can provide services outside of the area in order to meet those assessed

being in need and, insofar as is consistent with that duty, to promote the upbringing of such children by their families.[110] The section sets out duties of a general character intended for the benefit of children in need in the area of the social services authority.[111] Other duties – and specific duties in subsequent provisions of the Act – must be performed in individual cases by reference to the general duty under section 17(1), but section 17(1) does not itself impose an individual duty.[112]

13.42 The provision is excluded in the case of some classes of immigrant, being those classes (subject to exceptions, including the overarching exception for British citizens and persons under the age of 18,[113] and the human rights/EC Treaty exceptions)[114] considered in chapter 3.[115] In view of the exception for persons under the age of 18, the exclusion has no effect on them, but it may prevent the use of CA 1989 s17 for adult members of the family.

13.43 Although CA 1989 s17(1) is a general duty, when discharging it authorities have available the specific powers and duties set out in Schedule 2 Part 1, including assessment of the child's needs.[116] By section 17(6), such services may include assistance in kind or, in exceptional circumstances, cash, and may include the provision

needs: *R (J) v Worcestershire CC* [2014] EWCA Civ 1518 (services provided to Romany Gypsy child).

110 CA 1989 s17(1)(b).

111 In *R (AM) v Havering LBC and Tower Hamlets LBC* [2015] EWHC 1004 (Admin), [2015] PTSR 1242, an application under Part 7 was made to Tower Hamlets who provided temporary accommodation in Havering without notifying the latter under HA 1996 s208 (see paras 10.136–10.144), which accommodation was withdrawn following a decision that the applicant was intentionally homeless; Tower Hamlets started but did not complete an assessment under CA 1989 s17, but referred the applicant to Havering, who refused to conduct an assessment under section 17 on the basis that Tower Hamlets should do it; claims for judicial review against both authorities were allowed – having started the assessment, Tower Hamlets should have completed it; and, Havering had a duty since the family had moved to its area. The problems which had arisen were 'significantly aggravated' by the failure of Tower Hamlets to give notice to Havering under HA 1996 s208. Had that been done, the two authorities would have been able to co-operate by, for example, one conducting the Children Act assessment on behalf of both.

112 *R (G) v Barnet LBC; R (W) v Lambeth LBC; R (A) v Lambeth LBC* [2003] UKHL 57, [2004] AC 208, [2004] HLR 10. See also *R (Bates) v Barking and Dagenham LBC* [2012] EWHC 4218 (Admin).

113 See para 3.151.

114 See para 3.154.

115 See paras 3.151–3.160.

116 Section 17(2).

of accommodation, possibly together with family.[117] Local Authority Circular 2003/13 (Guidance on accommodating children in need and their families) provides that 'social services departments might find it helpful to refer . . . to Chapter 12 of the [Homelessness Code of Guidance]' when considering what accommodation to provide for families under section 17(6). The English Code confirms[118] that bed and breakfast accommodation is not suitable for families and should only be used as a last resort and, even then, for no more than six weeks (para 12.14). This is, however, only guidance and does not render a decision to provide accommodation under section 17 in bed and breakfast accommodation unlawful under section 17.[119] A child in need within section 17(10) is eligible for the provision of assistance, but has no absolute right to it.[120]

13.44 In *R (G) v Barnet LBC*,[121] the House of Lords held that it was unlawful for a local authority to adopt a general policy of only accommodating homeless children pursuant to their duty under CA 1989 s20[122] while refusing to exercise its power under section 17 to accommodate other members of the family. The provisions of CA 1989 s17(6), and in particular the inclusion of the power to provide accommodation,[123] should now be read in the light of Local Authority Circular, *Guidance on accommodating children in need and their families*[124] and the observations of Baroness Hale in *R (G) v Southwark LBC*,[125]

117 The Act was amended by Adoption and Children Act 2002 s116(1) to include references to accommodation following the decision of the Court of Appeal in *R (A) v Lambeth LBC* [2001] EWCA Civ 1624, [2002] HLR 13, which suggested that there was no power to provide accommodation (although this was subsequently held to have been decided per incuriam: *R (W) v Lambeth LBC* [2002] EWCA Civ 613, [2002] HLR 41, (2002) 5 CCLR 203). See para 13.89.

118 See paras 14-252 to 14-254.

119 *R (C, T, M, U) v Southwark LBC* [2014] EWHC 3983 (Admin); on appeal, this issue was not pursued: [2016] EWCA Civ 707, [2016] HLR 36.

120 *Barnet*.

121 [2003] UKHL 57, [2004] AC 208, [2004] HLR 10. See also paras 13.50 and 13.65.

122 See paras 13.58–13.72. In *R (Bates) v Barking and Dagenham LBC* [2012] EWHC 4218 (Admin), a refusal to use CA 1989 s17 instead of making an offer to accommodate the claimant's children (without her) under section 20 was upheld where the authority was trying to prompt the claimant to organise herself better and seek appropriate assistance, which was a legitimate aim and a lawful decision on the facts.

123 Adoption and Children Act 2002 s116(1).

124 Para 13.53.

125 [2009] UKHL 26, [2009] 1 WLR 1299 at [30].

suggesting that children in need of accommodation will almost always involve children needing to be accommodated with their families.

13.45 The assessment of need carried out under CA 1989 s17 should not be dealt with summarily and requires proper enquiry and consideration: *R (MM) v Lewisham LBC*.[126] In that case, the claimant, a 17-year-old girl, had been living in a women's refuge for four months when she was referred to the social services department of Lewisham LBC by a support worker at the refuge. The support worker informed the social services department that the reasons for the referral were that the claimant was fleeing domestic violence, vulnerable, lacking life-skills and that she was shortly to be placed in hostel accommodation. The social services department made no enquiries of its own and determined that the referral was 'vague'. It also decided that, as the claimant was in receipt of benefits and had accommodation provided for her, she was not a child in need under CA 1989 s17 and was not therefore entitled to assistance from social services. The claimant applied for judicial review of that decision on the basis that the authority had failed to carry out a proper assessment. The High Court agreed that the decision could not stand. The consideration given to the referral was no more than 'cursory' and 'fell far below' the standard required by law.[127]

13.46 An authority is, however, entitled to draw adverse inferences from a failure by the parents to co-operate with the assessment: *R (MN and KN) v Hackney LBC*[128] in which the parents had failed to provide information about their income and other sources of assistance from friends or relatives, entitling the authority to conclude that there was no immediate risk of homelessness and that the children were not 'in need'.

13.47 A local authority must consider the policy of the secretary of state when deciding whether to withdraw accommodation provided under CA 1989 s17(6): *R (Clue) v Birmingham City Council*[129] In that case, the claimant and her eldest son were Jamaican citizens who had come to the UK as visitors and overstayed. The claimant was refused leave to remain. No action was taken to remove her and her son back to Jamaica. She subsequently had three more children in the UK. Accommodation for the entire family was being funded by the local

126 *R (MM) v Lewisham LBC* [2009] EWHC 416 (Admin).

127 *R (MM)* at [14].

128 [2013] EWHC 1205 (Admin).

129 *R (Clue) v Birmingham City Council* [2010] EWCA Civ 460, [2011] 1 WLR 99, [2010] 2 FLR 1011, (2010) 13 CCLR 276.

authority under CA 1989 s17(6). After the birth of her youngest child, the claimant made a further application for leave to remain, by which time her eldest child had been continuously in the UK for seven years. The policy of the secretary of state for the Home Department was that it would normally be inappropriate forcibly to remove a family with a child who had been continuously in the country for seven years because such a child would, in most cases, have established ties which rendered it right and fair that the family should be allowed to remain.[130] The authority nonetheless decided to withdraw funding for the accommodation and pay the cost of returning the family to Jamaica, even though no action had been taken by immigration authorities to remove the claimant and her family from the country.

13.48 It was held[131] that the authority was required by NIAA 2002 Sch 3 para 1 to determine whether its proposed course of action would breach the ECHR rights of the claimant or any of her family members. Although the policy of the secretary of state was not binding, the authority had failed to give sufficient weight to it, in light of which it was likely that the claimant and her eldest daughter would be permitted to remain in the UK. If the claimant and her family were to return to Jamaica, that would render the application for indefinite leave to remain academic and defeat the purpose of the policy; the authority was not intended to pre-empt the decision of the secretary of state on applications for leave to remain. In *R (KA) v Essex CC*[132] it was held that the effect of *Clue* was that, save where the case was obviously hopeless or abusive, an authority could not deny support under the CA 1989 if the effect would be to negate a Convention right.

13.49 A local authority cannot automatically withdraw, or decline to offer, support under the CA 1989 s17(6) to a child whom it had assessed to be 'in need' simply on the basis that support is available under the IAA 1999 s4.[133] It could only do so in the unlikely event that it could be shown that the secretary of state was able and willing, or could be compelled, to provide IAA 1999 s4 support, which support would suffice to meet the child's assessed needs.

130 DP 56/96.

131 *Clue*.

132 [2013] EWHC 43 (Admin), [2013] 1 WLR 1163.

133 *R (VC) v Newcastle City Council* [2011] EWHC 2673 (Admin), [2012] JHL D3, QBD.

CA 1989 s20

13.50 CA 1989 s20 provides:

> (1) Every local authority shall provide accommodation for any child in need within their area who appears to them to require accommodation as a result of:
> (a) there being no person who has parental responsibility for him;
> (b) his being lost or having been abandoned; or
> (c) the person who has been caring for him being prevented (whether or not permanently, and for whatever reason) from providing him with suitable accommodation or care.
>
> . . .
>
> (3) Every local authority shall provide accommodation for any child in need within their area who has reached the age of sixteen and whose welfare the authority consider is likely to be seriously prejudiced if they do not provide him with accommodation.
> (4) A local authority may provide accommodation for any child within their area (even though a person who has parental responsibility for him is able to provide him with accommodation) if they consider that to do so would safeguard or promote the child's welfare.

13.51 CA 1989 s20 therefore contains both a power and a duty to provide accommodation for the child.[134] The duty is imposed on social services authorities to house children in the circumstances set out in section 20(1) and to house young people in the circumstances set out in section 20(3); the power arises under section 20(4). An authority may enter into arrangements with another local authority for assistance in the discharge of the duty under CA 1989 s20, but that does not permit it to pass the child 'from pillar to post' between authorities: *R (G) v Southwark LBC*.[135]

13.52 Following this decision,[136] the Department for Communities and Local Government (DCLG) issued new guidance in April 2010, the Provision of accommodation for 16 and 17 year old people who may be homeless and/or require accommodation ('DCLG Guidance').[137]

134 When deciding how to discharge the duty, and, in particular, whether or not to house parents with the child or children, the authority must consider the family rights of the child/children under Article 8 ECHR: *R (PK and another) v Harrow LBC* [2014] EWHC 584 (Admin).

135 [2009] UKHL 26, [2009] 1 WLR 1299, per Baroness Hale at [28].

136 *R (G) v Southwark LBC*, above.

137 Available at: www.gov.uk/government/publications/provision-of-accommodation-for-16-and-17-year-olds-who-may-be-homeless-and-or-require-accommodation.

In particular, the guidance sets out that if the young person makes an initial approach to housing services, the authority should commence inquiries under HA 1996 Part 7 and, if appropriate, secure interim accommodation, which should not normally be in bed and breakfast accommodation. The accommodation should be provided until the children's services authority has assessed whether a duty is owed under CA 1989 s20. Such an assessment should be carried out as soon as possible and no later than ten days after being notified by the housing authority. If no duty is owed under CA 1989 s20, then the housing authority should consider whether any duty is owed under HA 1996 Part 7.

13.53 The guidance stresses the importance of preventative work, including mediation, in seeking to resolve family problems which may have led the young person to become homeless. It recognises that such steps should be undertaken alongside the statutory assessment procedures and that it is unlawful to delay the statutory assessment in order to attempt mediation.[138] The guidance supersedes those parts of circular 2003/13 (guidance on accommodating children in need and their families) that related to homeless 16- and 17-year-olds.

13.54 Whether a person is a child is a question of jurisdictional fact which the court determines for itself, ie the court is not confined to the judicial review approach of asking whether or not the authority could have reached its decision on that point: *R (A) v Croydon LBC and (1) Secretary of State for the Home Department (2) Children's Commissioner; R (M) v Lambeth LBC and (1) Secretary of State for the Home Department (2) Children's Commissioner.*[139] Whether a child is 'in need', however, is an evaluative question to be determined by the authority, subject to judicial review on conventional public law grounds: *R (A); R (M)*.

13.55 Where the age of a person is in dispute the approach to be taken is that set out in *CJ v Cardiff City Council*:[140] in determining a person's age for the purposes of the CA 1989, the court's role is inquisitorial and it must decide, on the balance of probabilities, if the person in question was a child at the material time; there is no burden of proof for either party to overcome.[141]

138 *Robinson v Hammersmith and Fulham LBC* [2006] EWCA Civ 1122, [2006] 1 WLR 3295, [2007] HLR 7; see paras 9.131, 9.183 and 12.43.

139 [2009] UKSC 8, [2009] 1 WLR 2557, [2010] 1 All ER 469. See, in particular, the opinions of Lady Hale at [14]–[33] and Lord Hope at [51]–[54].

140 [2011] EWCA Civ 1590, [2012] HLR 20.

141 [2011] EWCA Civ 1590, [2012] HLR 20, per Lord Justice Pitchford at [21]–[24].

13.56 In *R (FZ) v Croydon LBC*,[142] the Court of Appeal issued general procedural guidance to local authorities to be applied in age assessment cases:

a) Where an authority is minded to reach a decision that is adverse to the applicant, it must give the applicant a fair and proper opportunity to deal with important points prior to reaching any final conclusion.
b) Applicants are entitled to have an adult present at any interview.
c) The correct test for the court to apply is not whether the authority had reached a reasonable decision but what determination the court makes of the claimant's age for itself.
d) The court is not required to come to the same conclusions as the local authority on all matters, eg credibility.
e) Considering the balance of probabilities at the permission stage is unhelpful.
f) The burden on the Administrative Court in deciding disputes of fact in age assessment cases is a significant use of resources. In the majority of cases, it would be appropriate to transfer age assessment disputes to the Upper Tribunal, which has sufficient judicial review jurisdiction for this purpose.[143]

13.57 Where an authority provides a child with accommodation pursuant to its duty under CA 1989 s20, it is not obliged by section 23(6)[144] to

142 [2011] EWCA Civ 59, [2011] HLR 22. See also *R (AK) v Secretary of State for the Home Department* [2011] EWHC 3188 (Admin) and *R (K) v Birmingham City Council* [2011] EWHC 1559 (Admin). The guidance given in *FZ* has not yet been incorporated into any government guidance. The UKBA guidance *Assessing age* still refers to *R (B) v Merton LBC* [2003] EWHC 1689 (Admin), [2003] 4 All ER 280. The UKBC guidance is available at: www.ukba.homeoffice.gov.uk/sitecontent/documents/policyandlaw/asylumprocessguidance/specialcases/guidance/assessing-age?view=Binary. See also *Age Assessment: Joint Working Guidance* (June 2015), which also still refers to the *Merton* case, while recognising that there have been subsequent decisions. It is available at www.gov.uk/government/uploads/system/uploads/attachment_data/file/432724/Age_Assessment_Joint_Working_Guidance__April_2015__Final_agreed_v2_EXT.pdf.

143 A local authority undertaking age assessments for the purposes of the CA 1989 is not bound by any previous age assessment carried out by the secretary of state or the First-tier Tribunal (Immigration and Asylum Chamber) on appeal: *R (Kadri) v Birmingham City Council* [2012] EWCA Civ 1432, [2013] HLR 4.

144 CA 1989 s23(6) provided that an authority may provide accommodation with a child's family, relatives or any other suitable person and, so far as is reasonably practicable and consistent with the child's welfare, the authority must make the placement with a parent, person with parental responsibility, relative, friend or other person connected with him or her; see now CA 1989 s22C.

make arrangements to enable the child to live with a parent, relative, friend or other person connected with him or her.[145]

13.58 A duty is only owed under CA 1989 s20 to a 'child in need'. Once a social services department has determined that it owes a duty to a child to provide accommodation under section 20, it cannot sidestep that duty by securing accommodation pursuant to a different statutory provision, eg, CA 1989 s17, HA 1996 Part 7[146] or Education Act (EA) 1996 Part 4.[147] If, however, a child approaches a local housing authority directly and asks for accommodation which is then provided under HA 1996 Part 7, such accommodation can be taken into consideration at the point that the authority carries out its assessment of the child's needs in order to determine if a duty under CA 1989 s20 exists; accordingly, a determination that adequate housing is already being provided under an alternative legislative provision – so that no duty is owed – is not an unlawful or irrational conclusion.[148] Likewise, where a child leaves home in order to live on his or her own, there is no duty on the authority to house the child under CA 1989 s20.[149] A duty may, however, be owed under HA 1996 Part 7.[150]

13.59 To activate the duty to provide accommodation under CA 1989 s20, notice must be given or a referral made to the social services

145 *R (G) v Barnet LBC; R (W) v Lambeth LBC; R (A) v Lambeth LBC* [2003] UKHL 57, [2004] AC 208, [2004] HLR 10. But see the obiter comments of Lord Nichols at [52] and [55]–[56] on the best interests of the child(ren) and the importance of maintaining the relationship between parent(s) and child(ren). In *R (Bates) v Barking and Dagenham LBC* [2012] EWHC 4128 (Admin), a refusal to house the claimant with her children under CA 1989 s20 was upheld: the authority was trying to prompt the claimant to organise herself better and seek appropriate assistance, which was a legitimate aim and a lawful decision on the facts.

146 *R (S) v Sutton LBC* [2007] EWCA Civ 790, (2007) 10 CCLR 615 considered and applied in *R (G) v Southwark LBC* [2009] UKHL 26, [2009] 1 WLR 1299.

147 *R (O) v East Riding of Yorkshire CC* [2011] EWCA Civ 196, [2011] 3 All ER 137. EA 1996 Part 4, makes provision for the assessment of a child with special educational needs within the meaning of EA 1996 s312 (EA 1996 s323), and maintenance of a statement of special educational needs (SSEN) (EA 1996 s342) by a local authority. Where such a SSEN is maintained by a local authority (EA 1996 s324) and the SSEN requires the arrangement of 'non-educational provision', the authority may arrange such provision, which can include the arrangement and provision of accommodation (EA 1996 s324(5)).

148 *R (B) v Nottingham City Council* [2011] EWHC 2933 (Admin), [2012] JHL D2, QDB.

149 *R (AH) v Cornwall Council* [2010] EWHC 3192 (Admin), [2011] PTSR, D23. An appeal to the Court of Appeal was dismissed.

150 *R (AH) v Cornwall Council* [2010] EWHC 3192 (Admin), [2011] PTSR, D23.

authority;[151] a social services authority cannot be criticised for not doing something that it had not been given notice it should be doing.[152] Nonetheless, where a child assessed as being in need is erroneously referred to the housing department rather than the social services department of a unitary authority, the accommodation provided by the authority should be treated as having been provided under CA 1989 s20.[153]

13.60 It is a question of fact what statutory power has been used to secure accommodation, so that it is not open to a court to deem a child to have been accommodated under CA 1989 s20 where some other power was, in fact, used to provide accommodation.[154] Where a local authority is found to have wrongly failed to provide accommodation to someone under section 20 (eg, due to an erroneous assessment of age), it can exercise discretionary powers (such as under LGA 2000 or LA 2011)[155] in order to provide him or her with some or all of the support services to which he or she would otherwise have been entitled[156] as a formerly looked after child.[157]

13.61 In considering discharge of the duty under CA 1989 s20, CA 1989 s1[158] does not apply to judicial review proceedings involving a challenge to a local authority decision on where to accommodate a child:

151 All Welsh authorities – counties and county boroughs – are social services authorities; all London borough councils and the Common Council of the City of London, and all other unitary authorities in England, whether termed district, county or otherwise, are social services authority; where there remains two-tier local government, the position depends on whether the area is a metropolitan area or not – in the former, a district council will be the social services authority; in the latter, it will be the county council. See London Government Act 1963, Local Authority Social Services Act 1970, LGA 1972 and LGA 1985.

152 *R (M) v Hammersmith and Fulham LBC* [2008] UKHL 14, [2008] 1 WLR 535.

153 *R (TG) v Lambeth LBC* [2011] EWCA Civ 526, [2011] HLR 33.

154 *R (M) v Hammersmith and Fulham LBC* [2008] UKHL 14, [2008] 1 WLR 535; *R (GE (Eritrea)) v Secretary of State for the Home Department* [2014] EWCA Civ 1490, [2015] 1 WLR 4123.

155 Paras 13.87–13.93.

156 Such as having a priority need (and therefore a greater entitlement to homelessness assistance).

157 *R (GE (Eritrea)) v Secretary of State for the Home Department*, [2014] EWCA Civ 1490, [2015] 1 WLR 4123; *R (A) v Enfield LBC* [2016] EWHC 567 (Admin); [2016] HLR 33. As to looked after – and formerly looked after – children, see paras 13.74–13.80.

158 This provides that when a court determines any question with respect to the upbringing of a child or the administration of a child's property or the application of any income arising from it, the child's welfare is the court's paramount consideration.

the role of the court is to review the decision of the local authority. As such, it is not determining a question with respect to the upbringing of the child; there is a number of ways in which the authority could meet the needs of the child and it is for the authority to choose between them.[159]

13.62 A child in need provided with accommodation pursuant to the duty or power in CA 1989 s20 is a 'looked after child' for the purposes of the general duty in CA 1989 s22. A 'looked after child' may be either a child in the care of the local authority,[160] or a child provided with accommodation by the authority in the exercise of a social services function within the meaning of the Local Authority Social Services Act 1970, other than a function exercised pursuant to CA 1989 ss17, 23B and 23C.[161] The duty under CA 1989 s22 towards a 'looked after' child is to safeguard and promote the child's welfare and to make such use of services available for children cared for by his or her own parents as appears reasonable to the authority for a particular child.[162] The duty was extended by section 52 of the Children Act 2004 inserting section 22(3A) to include a particular duty to promote the child's educational achievement.

13.63 An authority may discharge of the duty under CA 1989 s22 by the provision of accommodation for children in care by the authority,[163] or by the maintenance of looked after children (other than by provision of accommodation);[164] the provisions also deal with the class of persons with whom a local authority is permitted to make arrangements for a looked after child to be accommodated and the matters to which an authority should have regards when placing a looked after child in accommodation,[165] the circumstances in which an authority must carry out a review before placing a looked after child in accommodation,[166] and terms under which a child may be placed in a children's home.[167]

13.64 Whether a child has been a 'looked after child' for the purposes of CA 1989 Part 3 is germane to the nature and extent of the duty

159 *R (O) v Hammersmith and Fulham LBC* [2011] EWCA Civ 925, [2012] 1 WLR 1057.

160 CA 1989 s22(1)(a).

161 CA 1989 s22(1)(b).

162 CA 1989 s22(3).

163 CA 1989 s22A.

164 CA 1989 s22B.

165 CA 1989 s22C.

166 CA 1989 s22D.

167 CA 1989 s22E.

owed to any child by a local authority once the child attains the age of 16 or 17 and becomes a 'relevant child' entitled to advice and assistance under different statutory provisions relating to duties owed by authorities to children leaving care[168] which may include the provision of accommodation.[169]

13.65 Once the Homelessness Reduction Act (HRA) 2017 is brought into force, where accommodation for a child in care has been provided under CA 1989 s22A,[170] so that the child is normally resident in the district of a local housing authority for a continuous period of at all least two years, some or all of which falls before he or she turns 16, he or she is deemed to have a local connection with that district, although ceases to do so once he or she turns 21, unless a local connection can be established on any of the other grounds for it:[171] paras 7.9–7.36.

Co-operation between social services and housing authorities

13.66 Just as housing authorities can seek the co-operation of social services authorities under HA 1996 s213,[172] social services authorities can ask housing authorities to assist them, in which event the housing authority must comply with the request if it is compatible with its own statutory or other duties and obligations and does not unduly prejudice the discharge of any of its own functions.[173] Such joint working is encouraged by the DCLG in its guidance for local authorities: Joint working between Housing and Children's Services: preventing homelessness and tackling its effects on children and young people.[174] The duty to co-operate does not apply where one

168 See paras 13.82–13.87.

169 CA 1989 s24A.

170 See para 13.63.

171 HRA 2017 s8; HA 1996 s199(10), as added.

172 See para 9.58.

173 CA 1989 s27. See also CA 2004 s10 which places a duty on 'children's services authorities' (see footnote 107) to make arrangements to promote co-operation between the authority, relevant partners (including district authorities) and other persons or bodies engaged in activities in relation to children, to improve the well-being of children and young people in the authority's area.

174 DCLG, May 2008. Available at: www.communities.gov.uk/documents/housing/pdf/jointworkinghomelessness.

department of a local authority seeks help from another department of the same authority.[175]

13.67 In *Smith*,[176] the housing authority refused a request from the social services authority for assistance in housing a family with children whom the housing authority had previously found to be intentionally homeless. In the Court of Appeal, it was held that the housing authority could not simply refuse to help by reference to the finding of intentionality. The House of Lords allowed an appeal: although housing and social services authorities were expected to co-operate, if the housing authority could not assist – because no solution was forthcoming which did not unduly prejudice the discharge of its functions – then in the final analysis the children remained the responsibility of the social services authority.

13.68 A further referral and co-operation duty is imposed on English local housing authorities by amendment of HA 1996 Part 7 by the Homelessness Act 2002,[177] which arises[178] where the local housing authority has reason to believe that a homeless applicant with children may be:

a) ineligible for assistance;[179]
b) homeless intentionally;[180] or
c) threatened with homelessness intentionally.[181]

13.69 Given the low standard of satisfaction needed ('have reason to believe'),[182] the housing authority may reach this conclusion prior to a final decision on the homelessness application, and the procedures for referral put into place by CA 1989 s27 should commence before the applicant is notified of the decision under HA 1996 s184.[183] In anticipation of this duty, the housing authority must have in place

175 *R v Tower Hamlets LBC ex p Byas* (1992) 25 HLR 105, CA; *R (C1) v Hackney LBC* [2014] EWHC 3670 (Admin); [2015] PTSR 1011; and, *R (M and A) v Islington LBC* [2016] EWHC 332 (Admin), [2016] HLR 19.

176 *R v Northavon DC ex p Smith* [1994] 2 AC 402, (1994) 26 HLR 659, HL.

177 This followed the decision of the Court of Appeal in *R (A) v Lambeth LBC* [2001] EWCA Civ 1624, [2002] HLR 13, subsequently upheld in the House of Lords at [2003] UKHL 57, [2004] AC 208, [2004] HLR 10.

178 HA 1996 s213A(1).

179 See chapter 3.

180 See chapter 6.

181 See para 6.4. The reference to threatened with homelessness will, however, be repealed once HRA 2017 is in force in England, as it will be replaced with new provisions (paras 10.58–10.61): HRA 2017 s4(7).

182 The same standard as triggers the homelessness enquiry duty: see para 9.50.

183 See para 9.142.

arrangements to invite the applicant to give his or her consent to a referral either to the social services authority for the area (where a separate authority) or to the social services department (in the case of a unitary authority).[184] Where consent is obtained, the social services authority or department, as may be, must be made aware of the case and notified of any subsequent decision by the authority.[185] These provisions do not affect any other power to disclose information to social services, with or without the consent of the applicant, for example, where the housing authority receives information which might indicate that a child in the family is at risk of significant harm.[186]

13.70 Once a social services authority is made aware that an applicant is ineligible for assistance and homeless intentionally or threatened with homelessness intentionally, it may request the local housing authority to provide it with advice and assistance in the exercise of its functions under CA 1989 Part 3;[187] the housing authority must provide 'such advice and assistance as is reasonable in the circumstances'.[188] A unitary authority must likewise make arrangement for ensuring that its housing department provides its social services department with such advice and assistance as is reasonably requested.[189] These duties are additional to those in CA 1989 s27.[190] They do not, however, reverse the position in *Smith*,[191] that where the housing authority/department is unable to provide any assistance, the ultimate responsibility for ensuring that the needs of the children are met remains with the social services authority/department.

13.71 Once the provisions of the HRA 2017 are in force, an English social services authority is likely to be one of the public authorities specified as being under a duty[192] to notify a local housing authority if

184 HA 1996 s213(2)(a) and (3)(a).
185 HA 1996 s213A(2)(b) and (3)(b).
186 HA 1996 s213A(4). See also English Code of Guidance para 13.7.
187 HA 1996 s213A(5). The reference to threatened with homelessness will, however, be repealed once HRA 2017 is in force in England, as it will be replaced with new provisions (paras 10.58–10.61): HRA 2017 s4(7).
188 HA 1996 s213A(5).
189 HA 1996 s213A(6). This overturns the decision in *R v Tower Hamlets LBC ex p Byas* (1992) 25 HLR 105, CA, where it was held that the previous duty requiring authority to co-operate (HA 1996 s213) did not apply where one department of a local authority sought help from another department of the same authority.
190 See para 13.66.
191 See para 13.67. See also English Code of Guidance para 13.9.
192 Subject to conditions: see paras 13.92–13.93.

it considers that someone in relation to whom it exercises functions is or may be homeless or threatened with homelessness.[193]

13.72 The corresponding provisions in Wales apply where the authority has reason to believe that an applicant with whom a person under the age of 18 normally resides, or might reasonably be expected to reside, may be ineligible for help, may be homeless but that a duty under H(W)A 2014, s68,[194] s73[195] or s75[196] is not likely to apply, or may be threatened with homelessness and that a duty under section 66[197] is not likely to apply.[198]

13.73 The authority must make arrangements for ensuring that the applicant is invited to consent to the referral to the social services department of the essential facts of his or her case, and, if he or she has given that consent, that the social services department is made aware of those facts and of the subsequent decision in respect of his or her case.[199] The authority must also make arrangements to ensure that where it makes a decision that an applicant is ineligible for help, became homeless intentionally or became threatened with homelessness intentionally, its housing department provides the social services department with such advice and assistance as the social services department reasonably requests.[200]

Children leaving care

13.74 In certain circumstances, local social services authorities are under a duty to provide services[201] to children who are about to leave the care of the local authority and to children who were previously in its care. The statutory scheme governing these duties was introduced by the Children (Leaving Care) Act 2000. There are three categories towards whom a local authority might owe a duty:

193 HRA 2017 s10; HA 1996 s213B.
194 Paras 10.8–10.15.
195 Paras 10.75–10.77.
196 Paras 10.111–10.219.
197 Para 10.62.
198 H(W)A 2014 s96(1).
199 H(W)A 2014 s96(2).
200 H(W)A 2014 s96(4).
201 When Children and Social Work Act 2017 Part 1 is brought into force, authorities will also be under a duty to publish information about what support is available to eligible, relevant and former relevant children, including information about what accommodation is available from the authority (Children and Social Work Act 2017 s2).

a) eligible child;
b) relevant child;
c) former relevant child.

13.75 An 'eligible child' is a child aged 16 or 17 who has been 'looked after'[202] by a local authority[203] for a prescribed period,[204] which is 13 weeks.[205] The duty owed to an eligible child is not the provision of accommodation per se, but to arrange for the child to have a personal advisor[206] and to carry out an assessment of the child's needs to determine what advice, assistance and support it would be appropriate for the authority to provide both while it is still looking after the eligible child and after it ceases to do so.[207] Such assistance and support might include the provision of accommodation. The authority must complete a pathway plan following the assessment which the authority must keep under regular review.[208]

13.76 A 'relevant child' is a child aged 16 or 17 who would otherwise be an eligible child because he or she was looked after by a local authority for a prescribed period, but whom the authority has ceased to look after and who is not being looked after by any other authority.[209] The duty owed to a relevant child is the same as that owed to an eligible child, but includes a requirement for the authority to 'stay in touch'[210] with the relevant child; the duty requires the authority to provide the relevant child with suitable accommodation unless the authority is satisfied that the relevant child's welfare is such

202 See para 13.62.

203 It must be by the authority and not (for example), pursuant to an informal agreement by a family member during care proceedings (*Re B (a child) (looked-after child)* [2013] EWCA Civ 964, [2014] FLR 277; *R (O) v Doncaster MBC* [2014] EWHC 2309 (Admin); *R (T) v Hertfordshire CC* [2016] EWCA Civ 1108, [2017] HLR 10. The position would be different if the child had been placed by the authority pursuant to its power to place children with a relative under CA 1989 s22C.

204 CA 1989 Sch 2 Part 2 para 19B.

205 Care Planning, Placement and Case Review (England) Regulations 2010 SI No 959 from 1 April 2011. For a child who was an eligible child prior to 1 April 2011, see the Children (Leaving Care) (England) Regulations 2001 SI No 2874. The prescribed period is the same under both sets of regulations. The period need not be continuous, see CA 1989 Sch 2 para 19B(2)(b).

206 CA 1989 Sch 2 Part 2 para 19C.

207 CA 1989 Sch 2 Part 2 para 19B.

208 CA 1989 Sch 2 Part 2 para 19B.

209 CA 1989 s23A.

210 CA 1989 s23B(1).

that it is not needed.[211] Under CA 1989 s23B(10), regulations may be made which govern the meaning of 'suitable accommodation'. Schedule 2 to the Care Leavers (England) Regulations 2010[212] provides that matters to be taken into consideration when determining the suitability of accommodation include the facilities and services provided, the state of repair of the accommodation, safety, location, support, tenancy status and the financial commitments involved for the relevant child and their affordability.[213] The authority should also take into consideration the child's views about the accommodation, his or her understanding of rights and responsibilities in relation to the accommodation, and his or her understanding of funding arrangements.[214]

13.77 A 'former relevant child' is a person aged 18 years or over who was previously a relevant child[215] or who was an eligible child[216] immediately before he ceased to be looked after by the local authority.[217] The duty owed to a former relevant child is for the local authority to take reasonable steps to stay in touch or if it loses touch to re-establish contact, and to appoint a personal advisor, carry out an assessment and create a care plan which it must keep under review.[218] While there is no duty to provide accommodation, there is power for the authority to provide other assistance,[219] which is wide enough to include a contribution towards accommodation expenses in connection with education expenses.[220] When considering whether to exercise that power, the authority cannot take into account the possibility of support that might be provided under IAA 1999 s95.[221] Nor can the authority withdraw support in circumstances where to do would be tantamount to pre-empting a decision on an asylum application.[222]

211 CA 1989 s23B.

212 SI No 2571.

213 Care Leavers (England) Regulations 2010 SI No 2571 Sch 2 para 1.

214 Care Leavers (England) Regulations 2010 SI No 2571 Sch 2 para 2.

215 See para 13.64.

216 See para 13.75.

217 CA 1989 s23C.

218 CA 1989 s23C.

219 Under CA 1989 s23C(4).

220 *R (Sabiri) v Croydon LBC* [2012] EWHC 1236 (Admin).

221 *R (O) v Barking and Dagenham LBC* [2010] EWCA Civ 1101, [2011] 1 WLR 1283, [2011] 1 FLR 734, [2011] HLR 4, (2010) 13 CCLR 591.

222 *R (Birara) v Hounslow LBC* [2010] EWHC 2113 (Admin), [2010] 3 FCR 21, (2010) 13 CCLR 685.

13.78 In *R (TG) v Lambeth LBC*,[223] the a social worker employed by the authority's Youth Offending Team[224] correctly identified the applicant as a child in need for the purposes of CA 1989 Part 3,[225] but failed to make the necessary referral to the social services department. Accommodation was instead provided by the housing department. The authority accordingly denied that the claimant was a former relevant child as it had not provided the accommodation pursuant to CA 1989 s20 and refused to provide services to the claimant as if he or she was a relevant child or former relevant child. The Court of Appeal held that the social worker was to be regarded as the 'eyes and ears' of the social services department and that, as she had assisted the applicant to find accommodation, it should be 'treated or deemed'[226] to have been provided under CA 1989 s20; the claimant was therefore, and was to be treated as, a former relevant child for the purposes of CA 1989 with all the rights and benefits that flowed from that. See also *R (R) v Croydon LBC*,[227] where the court held that, in circumstances where the local authority undoubtedly knew that the claimant was a child and entitled to accommodation under CA 1989 s20, accommodation provided by the UKBA should be deemed to have been provided by the local authority.[228]

13.79 The courts will, however, only intervene where litigation is necessary; thus, judicial review was not available where the authority, while denying that claimants were 'former relevant children' for the purposes of CA 1989 s23C, had nevertheless agreed voluntarily to offer them all the services equivalent to those to which they would have been entitled if they had been.[229]

223 [2011] EWCA Civ 526, [2011] HLR 33.

224 Local authorities – as defined in Crime and Disorder Act 1998 s42(1) – must establish youth offending teams, who are responsible for, inter alia, the supervision and rehabilitation of young offenders: ss38(4) and 39(7). A youth offending team must include at least one person who is a social worker in the local authority's social services department: s39(5)(a).

225 See para 13.54.

226 At [43]. In *R (GE (Eritrea)) v Secretary of State for the Home Department* [2014] EWCA Civ 1490, [2015] 1 WLR 4123, it was said that *TG* was not a case of (impermissible – see para 13.54) deeming, but, rather, a case where the 'provision of accommodation by the local authority could be attributed to its social services function' (at [33]).

227 [2013] EWHC 4243 (Admin), [2012] JHL D58.

228 Although this decision was doubted in *R (GE (Eritrea)) v Secretary of State for the Home Department* [2014] EWCA Civ 1490, [2015] 1 WLR 4123, which reiterated that 'deeming' is impermissible, cf para 13.54.

229 *R (C) v Nottingham City Council* [2010] EWCA Civ 790, [2011] 1 FCR 127.

13.80 Note that, once the HRA 2017 is brought into force, so long as an authority in England has a duty under CA 1989 s23C towards a former relevant child, then, if the authority is a local housing authority as well as a social services authority[230] the former relevant child is deemed to have a local connection with its area, and if the authority is not a local housing authority,[231] with every district in its area:.[232] paras 7.57–7.58.

Social Services and Well-being (Wales) Act 2014

13.81 From 6 April 2016, the position in respect of children in Wales has been governed by the SSWB(W)A 2014. Welsh local authorities[233] have a duty and a power to meet the care and support needs of a child.[234] In order to meet needs, authorities may provide, inter alia, 'accommodation in a care home, children's home or premises of some other type'.[235]

13.82 Where it appears to a local authority that a child may need care and support in addition to, or instead of, the care and support provided by his or her family, the authority must assess whether he or she does have such needs and, if so, what those needs are.[236] As part of that assessment, the authority must seek to identify outcomes that the child wishes to achieve, that persons with parental responsibility wish to achieve for the child, and that persons specified in regulations[237] wish to achieve for the child.[238] Where the authority is satisfied, on the basis of the needs assessment, that a person has needs for care and support, it must determine whether his or her needs meet the eligibility criteria and, if satisfied that they do so, it must, inter alia, consider what could be done to meet those needs.[239]

230 Which will mean all London boroughs and the Common Council of the City of London, all unitary authorities and all district councils in metropolitan areas, cf footnote 12.

231 Ie county council in non-metropolitan areas.

232 HRA 2017 s8; HA 1996 s199(8), as added.

233 The council of a county or county borough in Wales: SSWB(W)A 2014 s197(1).

234 SSWB(W)A 2014 ss37 and 38. There is also a duty and a power to meet the needs for care and support of a child carer: SSWB(W)A 2014 ss42 and 45.

235 SSWB(W)A 2014 s34(2)(a).

236 SSWB(W)A 2014 s21(1).

237 No such regulations have yet been made.

238 SSWB(W)A 2014 s21(4)(b).

239 SSWB(W)A 2014 s32.

13.83 Subject to exceptions,[240] the duty to meet a child's needs arises where:

i) the child is in the authority's area;[241] and
ii) either the child's needs meet the eligibility criteria or the local authority considers it necessary to meet the child's needs in order to protect the child from abuse or neglect (or a risk of abuse or neglect), or other harm (or a risk of such harm).[242]

13.84 The child's needs meet the eligibility criteria if:

i) the need arises from the child's physical or mental ill-health, age, disability, dependence on alcohol or drugs, or other similar circumstances, or if the need is one that if unmet is likely to have an adverse effect on the child's development;[243]
ii) the need relates to one or more of a list of specified matters;[244]
iii) the need is one that neither the child, the child's parents nor other persons in a parental role is able to meet;[245] and
iv) the child is unlikely to meet one or more of his personal outcomes unless, inter alia, care and support is provided.[246]

13.85 The power to meet a child's needs for care and support is expressed in very broad terms. An authority may meet any child's needs for care and support if he or she is either within its area or ordinarily resident

240 The duty does not apply if the authority is satisfied that the child's needs are being met by the child's family or a carer, or if the child is being looked after by a local authority or a Health and Social Care Trust: SSWB(W)A 2014 s37(5), (6).

241 SSWB(W)A 2014 s37(2).

242 SSWB(W)A 2014 s37(3).

243 Care and Support (Eligibility) (Wales) Regulations 2015 SI No 1578 reg 4(1)(a). References to a child's development include the physical, intellectual, emotional, social and behavioural development of that child: reg 4(2)(i).

244 The ability to carry out self-care or domestic routines; the ability to communicate; protection from abuse or neglect; involvement in work, education, learning or in leisure activities; maintenance or development of family or other significant personal relationships; development and maintenance of social relationships and involvement in the community; and, achieving developmental goals: Care and Support (Eligibility) (Wales) Regulations 2015 SI No 1578 reg 4(1)(b).

245 Care and Support (Eligibility) (Wales) Regulations 2015 SI No 1578 reg 4(1)(c).

246 Care and Support (Eligibility) (Wales) Regulations 2015 SI No 1578 reg 4(1)(d). The personal outcomes are those identified under SSWB(W)A 2014 s21(4)(b): reg 1(3).

in its area but presently outside of it.[247] The power to meet needs may be used whether or not an assessment has been completed.[248]

13.86 Further duties to provide accommodation for children are contained in SSWB(W)A 2014 s76. These are, so far as material, in the same terms as CA 1989 s20.[249]

Local Government Act 2000/Localism Act 2011

13.87 The LGA 2000 provided a new power of 'well-being' applicable in both England and Wales. Section 2 provided, so far as relevant:

> (1) Every local authority are to have power to do anything which they consider is likely to achieve any one or more of the following objects –
>
> ...
>
> (b) the promotion or improvement of the social well being of their area.

13.88 The power continues to apply in Wales. It can be exercised for the benefit of the whole or any part of the local authority's area,[250] or of all or any persons resident or present in it.[251] Well-being powers cannot, however, be used where there is a prohibition, restriction or limitation on the authority's power to act 'contained in' any enactment, whenever passed or made.[252] The courts have inclined against finding implied restrictions and have tended to interpret the limitation as referring only to cases where these is an express provision.[253] Use of the provision is, however, excluded in the case of some classes of immigrant, being those classes (subject to exceptions, including the

247 SSWB(W)A 2014 s38(1).

248 SSWB(W)A 2014 s38(3).

249 Likewise, similar duties exist for those leaving care, see SSWB(W)A 2014 Part 6; and the Care Leavers (Wales) Regulations 2015 SI No 1820.

250 LGA 2000 s2(2)(a).

251 LGA 2000 s2(2)(b).

252 LGA 2000 s3(1).

253 *R (J) v Enfield LBC* [2002] EWHC Admin 432, [2002] HLR 38; *R (Theophilus) v Lewisham LBC* [2002] EWHC 1371 (Admin), [2002] 3 All ER 851; *R (W) v Lambeth LBC* [2002] EWCA Civ 613, [2002] HLR 41, (2002) 5 CCLR 203, per Brooke LJ at [75]; *R (Khan) v Oxfordshire CC* [2004] EWCA Civ 309, [2004] HLR 41; *R (Grant) v Lambeth LBC* [2004] EWCA Civ 1711, [2005] HLR 27; *R (Richards) West Somerset Council* [2008] EWHC 3215 (Admin). The power under LGA 2000 s2 does not, however, enable an authority to promote its own economic well-being: *Brent LBC v Risk Management Partners Ltd* [2009] EWCA Civ 490 (the point did not arise on the subsequent Supreme Court appeal: [2011] UKSC 7, [2011] 2 AC 34).

overarching exception for British citizens and persons under the age of 18,[254] and the human rights/EC Treaty exceptions)[255] considered in chapter 3.[256]

13.89 From 18 February 2012, LA 2011 s1 introduced a further new power, to replace well-being in England (but not Wales), being a 'power of general competence'.[257] The repeal of well-being powers in England, and the amendment of the LGA 2000 to confine its operation to Wales, however, did not take effect until 4 April 2012.[258]

13.90 The power of general competence is a power to do anything that individuals – with full capacity – generally may do, even though they are in nature, extent or otherwise unlike anything the authority may do without the power, or unlike anything that other public bodies may do. The power may be exercised anywhere in the UK or elsewhere, and is not limited by the existence of any other power of the authority which overlaps the general power, just as any such other power is not limited by the existence of the general power.[259]

13.91 By LA 2011 s2, however, if exercise of the power 'overlaps with' a pre-commencement power which is subject to restrictions, those restrictions apply to exercise of the power 'so far as it is overlapped' by the pre-commencement power; nor can the authority do anything which they are unable to do by reason of a pre-commencement limitation; nor can the general power be used to do anything which they are unable to do by virtue of a post-commencement limitation which is expressed to apply to it or to all of the authority's powers (or to all of the authority's powers subject to exceptions which do not include the general power).[260]

13.92 While LGA 2000 s2 was primarily intended for strategic use,[261] cases under it affirmed its availability for use as a 'safety-net',

254 See para 3.101.

255 See paras 3.154–3.160.

256 See paras 3.154–3.160.

257 Localism Act 2011 (Commencement No 3) Order 2012 SI No 411.

258 Localism Act 2011 (Commencement No 5 and Transitional, Savings and Transitory Provisions) Order 2012 SI No 1008.

259 LA 2011 s1.

260 On the difference in treatment between a pre- and post-commencement limitation, see *R (GS) Camden LBC* [2016] EWHC 1762 (Admin), [2016] HLR 43 at [61]: only an express limitation can comprise a post-commencement limitation.

261 See the requirement in LGA 2000 s2(3) to have regard to the authority's community strategy (made under LGA 2000 s4) in determining whether and how to use the power.

including the provision of accommodation.[262] These cases will be applicable under LA 2011, which has likewise been held to encompass the provision of accommodation.[263]

13.93 The power in LGA 2000 s2 was likewise held to be wide enough to permit an authority to fund travel arrangements for a person unlawfully in the UK, where exercising that power was necessary to avoid breaching the person's rights under the ECHR.[264] There is no reason to believe that LA 2011 s1 will be interpreted differently. The power will not, however, become a duty even if use of the power is the only way to avoid a breach of human rights: *Morris*,[265] applying the decision of the House of Lords in *Hooper*,[266] and overruling the decision in *J*.[267]

Specified public authorities

13.94 Once HRA 2017 is brought into force, in England the secretary of state will have power to specify by regulations a public authority, or public authorities of a particular description, who will be under notification duties under HA 1996 s213B;[268] public authority means anyone – other than a local housing authority – with functions of a public nature.[269]

13.95 The duty arises if the authority considers that a person in England in relation to whom the authority exercises any functions is or may be homeless or threatened with homelessness, and asks the person to agree to it notifying a local housing authority in England of its opinion and of how he or she may be contacted by the local housing authority.[270] Moreover, the duty does not arise unless the person identified a local housing authority in England to which he or she would like the notification to be made.[271] If these conditions are

262 See, eg *R (J) v Enfield LBC* [2002] EWHC 432 (Admin), [2002] HLR 38.
263 *R (GS) Camden LBC* [2016] EWHC 1762 (Admin), [2016] HLR 43.
264 *R (Grant) v Lambeth LBC*, above; see also *R (Theophilus) v Lewisham LBC*, above, authorising a student loan to someone not otherwise entitled to assistance.
265 *R (Morris) v Westminster City Council (No 3)* [2005] EWCA Civ 1184, [2006] 1 WLR 505, [2006] HLR 8.
266 *R (Hooper) v Secretary of State for Work and Pensions* [2005] UKHL 29, [2005] 1 WLR 1681.
267 *R (J) v Enfield LBC* [2002] EWHC 432 (Admin), [2002] HLR 38.
268 HRA 2017 s10; HA 1996 s213B(4), (5).
269 This is likely to rely on the same phrase in the definition of public authority under Human Rights Act 1998 s6(3); see para 12.95.
270 HRA 2017 s10; HA 1996 s213B(2).
271 HRA 2017 s10; HA 1996 s213B(3).

fulfilled, the public authority must notify that local housing authority of its opinion and the of the contact information.[272]

13.96 Note, however, that unless the notification also asserts, in whatever terms, that the individual is applying to the housing authority for accommodation or assistance in obtaining it, the duty to make enquiries under HA 1996 s184[273] does not on the face of it appear to arise, although it is strongly arguable that this is the intention of HA 1996 s213B and that section 184 should be construed commensurately with it; it is difficult to see what other purpose section 213B could have sought to achieve.

Other statutory provisions

Child Abduction and Custody Act 1985

13.97 Child Abduction and Custody Act (CACA) 1985 s5 provides:

> Where an application has been made to a court in the United Kingdom under the Convention, the court may, at any time before the application is determined, give such interim directions as it thinks fit for the purpose of securing the welfare of the child concerned or of preventing changes in the circumstances relevant to the determination of the application.

13.98 The convention referred to in section 5 is the Hague Convention.[274] The word 'directions' refers to orders of the court directing the provision of accommodation.[275] In *Re A (children) (abduction: interim powers)*,[276] the Court of Appeal held that the provisions of CACA 1985 s5 should be construed widely and that the court has the power to direct a local authority to provide accommodation for an alleged abductor and an allegedly abducted child, pending determination of an application for the return of the child. Moreover, it held that an order for the provision of accommodation is an order made for the purpose of securing the welfare of the child; accordingly, interim directions can include an order that a child, or a child's family, are provided with accommodation.[277]

272 HRA 2017 s10; HA 1996 s213B(3).

273 See para 9.50.

274 CACA 1985 s1.

275 *Re A (children) (abduction: interim powers), sub nom EA v GA* [2010] EWCA Civ 586, [2011] 2 WLR 1269.

276 [2010] EWCA Civ 586, [2011] Fam 179, [2011] 2 WLR 1269.

277 [2010] EWCA Civ 586, [2011] Fam 179, [2011] 2 WLR 1269.

CHAPTER 14

Strategy, practice, aid and advice

14.1 Introduction

14.3 Homelessness strategies

14.6 Reviews

Guidance • Publication

14.9 Strategies

Functions • Partnership • Guidance • Review of strategy • Publication

14.20 Code of Practice – England

14.23 Provision of advisory services

14.31 Advice and assistance, England – Homelessness Reduction Act 2017

14.34 Aid to voluntary organisations

Introduction

14.1 In this chapter, we consider what might be called the 'general' functions related to homelessness, imposed on local housing authorities for the benefit of their areas. There are three such functions:

a) to maintain a homelessness strategy;
b) to provide advisory services; and
c) to provide assistance to the voluntary sector.

14.2 In addition, once the Homelessness Reduction Act (HRA) 2017 has been brought into force, in England the secretary of state will have power to issue codes of practice relating to homelessness or the prevention of homelessness about the exercise by a local housing authority of functions under Part 7 of the Housing Act (HA) 1996, staff training and monitoring, which power is also considered in this chapter.

Homelessness strategies

14.3 By Homelessness Act 2002 s1, all local housing authorities are required to carry out a homelessness review and formulate and publish a strategy based on that review:[1] by Homelessness Act 2002 s1(3) and (4), the first such strategy had to be drawn up within a year of the section coming into force,[2] and thereafter at least every five years.[3]

14.4 This exercise is to be carried out with the assistance of the local social services authority.[4] Both the housing and social services

1 Homelessness Act 2002 s1(1). Para 20 of *Fair and flexible: statutory guidance on social housing allocations for local authorities in England* (Department for Communities and Local Government (DCLG), December 2009) spells out the importance the government places on prevention of homelessness and the encouragement given to local authorities to use their allocations policies to assist with homeless strategies. In Wales, see the Welsh Code of Guidance chapter 5.

2 That was by 31 July 2003 in England, and 30 September 2003 in Wales.

3 An English authority which has been categorised as an 'excellent authority' under an order made under Local Government Act 2003 s99(4) (previously Comprehensive Performance Assessment, but, since 1 April 2009, Comprehensive Area Assessment) is exempt from the requirement to publish further strategies: Local Authorities' Plans and Strategies (Disapplication) (England) Order 2005 SI No 157.

4 Homelessness Act 2002 s1(2). Within the meaning of the Local Authority Social Services Act 1970 (see para 2.15).

authorities have to take the strategy into account in exercising their functions.[5]

14.5 Initially, these provisions applied to both England and Wales: since 1 December 2014, the position in Wales has been governed by the Housing (Wales) Act (H(W)A) 2014 s50. A Welsh authority must carry out a homelessness review for its area, and formulate and adopt a homelessness strategy based on the results of that review.[6] There is no requirement that the exercise be carried out with the assistance of the local social services authority as all Welsh authorities are unitary, ie have both housing and social service functions. The strategy must be taken into account by the authority when exercising any of its functions.[7] The strategy must be adopted in 2018, with a new strategy every fourth year thereafter.[8]

Reviews

14.6 'Homelessness review' is defined in Homelessness Act 2002 s2 and H(W)A 2014 s51 as a review of:

a) the current and likely future levels of homelessness in an authority's district;[9]
b) the activities carried out in the authority's area for:[10]
    i) preventing homelessness;
    ii) securing that accommodation is or will be available in the area for people who are or may become homeless; and
    iii) providing support[11] for such people or for those who have been homeless and need support to prevent it recurring;[12] and

5 Homelessness Act 2002 s1(5) and (6).

6 H(W)A 2014 s50(1). The strategy can form part of the Well-Being Plan under the Well-being of Future Generations (Wales) Act 2015; Welsh Code para.5.4.

7 H(W)A 2014 s50(4).

8 H(W)A 2014 s50(2). The Welsh Code of Guidance notes that the strategy should reflect the Welsh Government's Ten Year Homeless Plan (July 2009), para.5.7.

9 See English Code of Guidance paras 1.13–1.18; Welsh Code paras 5.17–5.37.

10 See English Code of Guidance paras 1.19–1.25.

11 Support means 'advice, information or assistance': Homelessness Act 2002 s4.

12 In Wales, the requirement is for 'satisfactory support': H(W)A 2014 s51(1)(b)(iii).

c) the resources available to the authority, the social services authority,[13] other public authorities, voluntary organisations[14] and other persons for such activities.[15]

Guidance

14.7 Guidance on carrying out a review is available in *Homelessness strategies: a good practice handbook*[16] and, in Wales, in the *Code of Guidance for Local Authorities on the Allocation of Accommodation and Homelessness*.[17] The review should include an assessment of the needs of all homeless people, including those who have become homeless intentionally and those who are not in priority need. The review of needs and an audit of services should identify both where needs are not being met, and where there is unnecessary duplication in the supply of services. The review of resources should cover staff, property and funding and include existing provision as well as plans for the future.

Publication

14.8 On completion of the review, an authority must arrange for the results to be available for inspection by members of the public, at reasonable hours, without charge, and provide a copy on payment of a reasonable charge.[18]

Strategies

14.9 'Homelessness strategy' is defined in Homelessness Act 2002 s3(1) and H(W)A 2014 s52(1) as one formulated in order to:

13 This is omitted from H(W)A 2014 s51(1)(c), although a Welsh authority is required to have regard to any resources available to it in the exercise of other statutory functions, so that, as each authority is itself a social services authority, it will be required to have regard to social service as well as housing resources.

14 By Homelessness Act 2002 s4, this has the same definition as HA 1996 s180(3).

15 See English Code of Guidance paras 1.25–1.29; Welsh Code para 5.38.

16 Department of Transport, Local Government and Regions (DTLR), February 2002. See, in particular, chapter 4. See also *Local authorities' homelessness strategies: evaluation and good practice,* Office of the Deputy Prime Minister (ODPM), 2004.

17 March 2016, see chapter 5.

18 Homelessness Act 2002 s2(3); H(W)A 2014 s51(2). The results must also be published on the authority's website, if it has one.

a) prevent homelessness in an authority's area;[19]
b) secure that accommodation is and will be available in that area for people who are or may become homeless; and
c) provide support[20] for such people or those who have been homeless and need support to prevent it recurring.

14.10 In England, there is no requirement that specific objectives or plans, such as housing a proportion of homeless applicants outside an authority's district, should be included in the strategy: it is a matter of discretion for the authority whether or not to include such matters.[21] Since 7 June 2012[22], however, an authority in England must – when formulating or modifying a homelessness strategy – have regard to its current allocation scheme under HA 1996 s166A,[23] and its current tenancy strategy under Localism Act (LA) 2011 s150,[24] and (in the case of a London borough council) the current London Housing Strategy.[25]

14.11 In Wales, the strategy must include details of both general and specific actions planned by the authority, including actions expected to be taken by other public authorities and voluntary organisations, in relation to those who may be in particular need of support if they are or may become homeless, in particular:

a) people leaving prison or youth detention accommodation;
b) young people leaving care;
c) people leaving the regular armed forces of the Crown;

19 On prevention, see further Code of Guidance chapter 2; Welsh Code paras 5.45–5.48.

20 In England, 'support' means 'advice, information or assistance': Homelessness Act 2002 s4. It is undefined in Wales.

21 *R (Calgin) v Enfield LBC* [2005] EWHC 1716 (Admin), [2006] HLR 4. In *Nzolameso v Westminster City Council* [2015] UKSC 22, [2015] HLR 22, however, the Supreme Court held that an authority should have a policy for procuring sufficient units of temporary accommodation to meet the anticipated demand for the coming year; that policy should reflect the authority's duties under the HA 1996 and the Children Act (CA) 2004 ; it should be approved by the democratically accountable members of the authority; the authority should also have a policy for allocating those units; where there is an anticipated shortfall of accommodation in its district, the policy should explain the factors which will be taken into account in offering accommodation further away; and, both policies should be publicly available. It would clearly be possible to include this policy in the Homelessness Strategy.

22 Ie the commencement of LA 2011 s153.

23 See para 11.59.

24 Ie flexible tenancies.

25 Homelessness Act 2002 s3(7A).

d) people leaving hospital after medical treatment for mental disorder as an inpatient; and
e) people receiving mental health services in the community.[26]

Functions

14.12 The strategy may encompass specific objectives or action falling within both housing and social service functions.[27]

Partnership

14.13 The strategy may also include provision for action to be taken by other public authorities, voluntary organisations[28] or persons who might be capable of contributing to the achievement of any of the strategic objectives,[29] but only if given approval to include such provision by that contributing authority, organisation or person,[30] ie, an authority cannot rely on what others might do, otherwise than with their consent.

14.14 In order to encourage partnership working, an authority is under a duty positively to consider the extent to which any of the objectives of the strategy can be achieved through action involving two or more of the local authority, social services authority, another public authority, any voluntary organisation or any person.[31]

Guidance

14.15 In England, in addition to the needs assessment and audit of services emerging from the homelessness review, the strategy should include action on planning and implementing the strategy, including:[32]

a) the involvement of partner agencies – public, voluntary and private – in formulating and implementing the strategy;

26 H(W)A 2014 s52(6); see also Welsh Code para 5.65

27 Homelessness Act 2002 s3(2); H(W)A 2014 s52(2). See the English Code of Guidance annex 4 for a list of specific objectives and action that might be included. See also the guidance on developing action plans in *Local authorities' homelessness strategies: evaluation and good practice* (ODPM, 2004). See Welsh Code chapter 5.

28 By Homelessness Act 2002 s4, this has the same definition as HA 1996 s180(3). In Wales, see H(W)A 2014 ss52(3) and 99.

29 See the English Code of Guidance annexes 3 and 6; for other authorities, organisations and persons who may be able to contribute and specific action that might be expected to be taken by others.

30 Homelessness Act 2002 s3(3) and (4); H(W)A 2014 s52(3) and (4).

31 Homelessness Act 2002 s3(5); H(W)A 2014 s52(5).

32 *Homelessness strategies: a good practice handbook*, DTLR, 2002, para 2.1.5.

b) consultation with other agencies in contact with homeless people, even if not involved in service provision;
c) consultation with service-users and other homeless people;
d) defining key aims and objectives of the strategy;
e) agreeing priorities for action;
f) a timetabled and costed programme;
g) identification of which agencies will do what and when;
h) mechanisms for joint and partnership work;
i) mechanisms of monitoring and evaluation of the strategy and individual elements of the programme, including targets and performance indicators; and
j) mechanisms for regular review and amendment of the strategy in the light of the monitoring and evaluation.

On strategies to prevent homelessness, further guidance is also available in *Homelessness prevention: a guide to good practice.*[33]

14.16 As the allocation of accommodation under HA 1996 Part 6 is one of the ways in which the main homelessness duty can be discharged, allocation policies and procedures should be consistent with the local authority's homelessness strategy.[34] In addition, since 7 June 2012, see also the obligation for an authority to have regard to its allocation scheme, and its current tenancy strategy, and – in the case of a London borough council – the current London housing strategy.[35]

14.17 In Wales, the strategy should 'prioritise the need for prevention' and adequate consideration and resources should be devoted to preventative services, eg information, advice, short term support and mediation.[36] Related areas such as money advice and debt counselling should also be included.[37] Discretionary Housing Payments are particularly important and ought to be prioritised where they can be used most effectively to prevent homelessness.[38] The private rented sector plays a 'critical role' and strategic planning 'must reflect' that, both as regards prevention and sustaining tenancies and helping the homeless to move into accommodation.[39]

33 DCLG, June 2006.
34 *Allocation of accommodation: guidance for local housing authorities in England*, DCLG, 2012, para 4.2.
35 See para 14.10.
36 Welsh Code para 5.44.
37 Welsh Code para 5.45.
38 Welsh Code para 5.47.
39 Welsh Code para 5.53.

Review of strategy

14.18 The strategy must be kept under review by the authority,[40] and may be modified.[41] Any modifications must be published.[42] Any public or local authorities, voluntary organisations or other persons as the authority considers appropriate must be consulted prior to both adopting or modifying the strategy.[43]

Publication

14.19 The published strategy, and any modifications, must be available for inspection, at reasonable hours, without charge, by members of the public and available for purchase on payment of a reasonable charge.[44]

Code of Practice – England

14.20 From the commencement of HRA 2017, in England the secretary of state will have power to issue codes of practice relating to homelessness or homelessness prevention to local housing authorities,[45] in particular concerning the exercise by a local housing authority of functions under HA 1996 Part 7, staff training relating to the exercise of those functions and monitoring by the authority of the exercise of those functions.[46] A code may apply to all local housing authorities or to a local housing authority specified or described in the code, and may contain different provision for different kinds of local housing authority.[47]

14.21 The secretary of state must lay a draft of the code before parliament, which is subject to negative resolution by either House of Parliament not to approve it; if none is made within 40 days[48] of

40 See *Preventing homelessness: a strategy health check*, non-statutory guidance published in September 2006 by the DCLG.

41 Homelessness Act 2002 s3(6); H(W)A 2014 s52(7).

42 Homelessness Act 2002 s3(7); H(W)A 2014 s52(9), (10), (11).

43 Homelessness Act 2002 s3(8); H(W)A 2014 s52(8).

44 Homelessness Act 2002 s3(9); H(W)A 2014 s52(9).

45 HRA 2017 s11; HA 1996 s214A(1).

46 HRA 2017 s11; HA 1996 s214A(2).

47 HRA 2017 s11; HA 1996 s214A(3).

48 No account is taken of any period during which parliament is dissolved or prorogued, or both Houses are adjourned for more than four days.

the date the code is laid,[49] then the code may issue.[50] A code may be revised from time to time revise and reissued or revoked: the procedural requirements do not apply to the reissue of a code;[51] accordingly, they do apply to revision or revocation. The secretary of state must publish the current version of each code of practice in whatever manner he or she thinks fit.[52]

14.22 A local housing authority must have regard to a code of practice in exercising its functions.[53] As to the effect of this, see para 12.41.

Provision of advisory services

14.23 Until commencement of the HRA 2017,[54] HA 1996 s179[55] and H(W)A 2014 s60 require authorities to ensure that provision of advice and information about homelessness and the prevention of homelessness is available free of charge in their areas.

14.24 In England, 'Advice' and 'information' are not defined, but the Code of Guidance[56] suggests that 'it will need to be wide ranging and comprehensive in its coverage and may require a full multi-disciplinary assessment . . . Advice services should provide information on the range of housing options that are available in the district'. Such services may also include an advocacy service, which may include providing legal representation for people facing the loss of their home.[57] Where advice is provided by the authority, it is trite – but should be borne in mind – that accurate advice in the interests of the applicant must be given.[58]

49 If laid before the two Houses on different dates, the later such date.

50 HRA 2017 s11; HA 1996 s214A(4)–(8).

51 HRA 2017 s11; HA 1996 s214A(9)–(10).

52 HRA 2017 s11; HA 1996 s214A(11).

53 HRA 2017 s11; HA 1996 s214A(12).

54 Paras 14.31–14.33.

55 See also HA 1996 s166, as amended by the Homelessness Act 2002 and the LA 2011; see para 11.55.

56 Code of Guidance paras 2.10 and 2.11.

57 Code of Guidance para 2.12.

58 *Robinson v Hammersmith and Fulham LBC* [2006] EWCA Civ 1122, [2006] 1 WLR 3295, [2007] HLR 7, per Jacob LJ at [45], considering – with reference to HA 1996 s179 – advice to mediate offered to a 17-year-old: 'A near 18 [year] old who came to the authority could obviously not be properly advised to mediate if the effect of mediation would be to delay the actual s.184 decision past the 18th birthday' (thus causing the loss of automatic priority need – see para 5.67).

14.25 The advice given to applicants must provide information about the applicant's rights in HA 1996 s166A(9).[59] They are:

a) the right to request information to enable the applicant to assess how his or her application for housing is likely to be treated;
b) the right to request information to enable the applicant to assess whether housing accommodation appropriate to the applicant's needs is likely to be made available to him or her and, if so, how long it is likely to be before such accommodation becomes available for allocation to the applicant;
c) the right to request that the authority inform the applicant of the facts of his or her case taken into account by the authority;
d) the right to request a review of the authority's decision about the facts of the applicant's case that the authority have taken into account, and to be informed of the decision on review and the grounds for the decision on review;
e) the right to request a review of the authority's decision that the applicant is ineligible for housing or not a qualifying person, and to be informed of the decision on review and the grounds for the decision on review.[60]

14.26 In Wales, the advice and information must include details about how the homelessness service operates in the authority's area, other help which might be available and how to access it.[61] Whether or not someone is threatened with homelessness, assistance must be provided to access help which is available to prevent him or her becoming homeless.[62] The authority must work with other public authorities, voluntary organisations and other to ensure that the service is designed to meet the needs of groups at particular risk of homelessness, including in particular:[63]

a) people leaving prison or youth detention accommodation;
b) young people leaving care;
c) people leaving the regular armed forces of the Crown;
d) people leaving hospital after medical treatment for mental disorder as an inpatient; and
e) people receiving mental health services in the community.

59 Introduced by amendment under LA 2011 s147(4), with effect from 15 January 2012.
60 See HA 1996 s160ZA(9).
61 H(W)A 2014 s60(2).
62 H(W)A 2014 s60(3).
63 H(W)A 2014 s60(4).

14.27 In neither England nor Wales does the authority have to provide this service itself but may secure that it is provided on its behalf by or in partnership with some other organisation.[64]

14.28 To facilitate this, it may provide grants or loans to a person providing the service on its behalf.[65] Assistance may also be given by way of the use of premises, furniture or other goods and even the services of staff.[66]

14.29 To ensure that they are providing an effective service to a high standard, housing authorities may wish to refer to the quality assurance systems applied by the National Association of Citizens Advice Bureaux and the Shelter Network of housing advice centres, the national Disabled Housing Services Ltd (HoDis) accreditation scheme and the Community Legal Service Quality Mark. Housing authorities are also advised to monitor the provision of advisory services to ensure that they continue to meet the needs of all sections of the community and help deliver the aims of their homelessness strategy.[67]

14.30 The duty to provide advice and information to persons in the area is applicable even to those who are ineligible for assistance.[68]

Advice and assistance, England – Homelessness Reduction Act 2017

14.31 In England, from the commencement of the HRA 2017, the duty under HA 1996 s179 is replaced by a more specific duty to imposed on local housing authorities to provide, or secure the provision of, a service, to be available free of charge to any person in its district, providing information and advice on:

- preventing homelessness;
- securing accommodation when homeless;
- the rights of persons who are homeless or threatened with homelessness;
- the duties of the authority, under Part 7;

64 See further, English Code of Guidance paras 2.17–2.19. In Wales, two or more authorities may provide a combined service: H(W)A 2014 s60(5); see further: Welsh Code paras 9.9–9.12.

65 HA 1996 s179(2). There is no equivalent in Wales.

66 HA 1996 s179(3). There is no equivalent statutory provision in Wales.

67 English Code of Guidance para 2.20.

68 HA 1996 s183(3); see chapter 3. H(W)A 2014 s60.

- any help that is available from the authority or anyone else, whether under Part 7 or otherwise, for persons in the district who are homeless or may become homeless (whether or not they are threatened with homelessness); and
- how to access that help.[69]

14.32 The service has to be designed to meet the needs of persons in the authority's district including, in particular, the needs of:

- people released from prison or youth detention accommodation;[70]
- care leavers;[71]
- former members of the regular armed forces;[72]
- victims of domestic abuse;[73]
- people leaving hospital;[74]
- people suffering from a mental illness or impairment; and
- any other group which the authority identifies as being at particular risk of homelessness in its district.[75]

14.33 As under the pre-HRA 2017 provision,[76] the authority may provide grants or loans to a person providing the service on its behalf.[77] Assistance may also be given by way of the use of premises, furniture or other goods and even the services of staff.[78]

69 HRA 2017 s2; new HA 1996 s179(1).

70 Youth detention accommodation means a secure children's home, a secure training centre, a secure college, a young offender institution, accommodation provided by or on behalf of a local authority for the purpose of restricting the liberty of children, accommodation provided for that purpose under CA 1989 s82(5), or accommodation, or accommodation of a description, for the time being specified by order under Powers of Criminal Courts (Sentencing) Act 2000 s107(1)(e): HRA 2017 s2; new HA 1996 s179(5).

71 People who are former relevant children within CA 1989 s23C(1) – see para 13.74.

72 The regular forces as defined by Armed Forces Act 2006 s374 – see para 7.18.

73 For this purpose, domestic abuse means physical violence, threatening, intimidating, coercive or controlling behaviour, emotional, financial, sexual or any other form of abuse, where the victim is associated with the abuser. Financial abuse includes having money or other property stolen, being defrauded, being put under pressure in relation to money or other property, and having money or other property misused.

74 Hospital has the same meaning as in the National Health Service Act 2006 s275(1).

75 HRA 2017 s2; new HA 1996 s179(2).

76 Para 14.28.

77 HRA 2017 s2; new HA 1996 s179(3).

78 HRA 2017 s2; new HA 1996 s179(4).

Aid to voluntary organisations[79]

14.34 Voluntary organisations have long played an important role in assisting homeless people. Bodies such as housing associations have provided significant assistance to local authorities in the discharge of their obligations towards the homeless, especially those in 'special categories'. A voluntary organisation is, for the purposes of HA 1996 Part 7, a body whose activities are carried on otherwise than for profit, but not including a public or local authority.[80] This definition is wide enough to include housing associations and other non-profit-making social landlords.[81]

14.35 The powers permit the secretary of state, or local housing authorities, to give money by way of grant or loan to such a voluntary organisation.[82]

14.36 A local housing authority may also assist by letting a voluntary organisation use premises belonging to it, on such terms and conditions as may be agreed, and by making available furniture or other goods – by way of gift, loan or otherwise – or the services of staff employed by it.[83]

14.37 Assistance under HA 1996 s179 or s180 may be given on such terms and conditions as the secretary of state or authority may determine.[84]

14.38 No assistance of any kind is to be given, however, unless the voluntary organisation first gives an undertaking:

a) to use the money, furniture or other goods or premises made available to it for a purpose to be specified in the undertaking; and
b) that – if required to do so by the body providing the assistance – it will, within 21 days of notice served upon it, certify such information as may reasonably be required by the notice as to the manner in which assistance given to it is being used.[85]

79 There is no equivalent to these provisions in Wales, although the Welsh Code does discuss the circumstances in which an authority might provide assistance to a voluntary body, at paras 9.13–9.16.

80 HA 1996 s180(3).

81 *Goodman v Dolphin Square Trust Ltd* (1979) 38 P&CR 257, CA.

82 HA 1996 s180(1).

83 HA 1996 s180(2).

84 HA 1996 s181(2).

85 HA 1996 s181(3).

14.39 In every case in which assistance is provided, the conditions must include a requirement that the voluntary organisation: keeps proper books of account and has them audited in a specified manner; keeps records indicating how the assistance has been used; and submits accounts and records for inspection by the body providing the assistance.[86]

14.40 If it appears to the body providing the assistance that the voluntary organisation is not using the assistance for the purposes specified in the undertaking, it is obliged to take all reasonable steps to recover an amount of money equal to the amount of the assistance from the organisation. No such amount is recoverable, however, unless there has first been served on the voluntary organisation a notice specifying the amount alleged to be recoverable and the basis on which it has been calculated.[87]

86 HA 1996 s181(4).
87 HA 1996 s181(5) and (6).

CHAPTER 15

Criminal offences

15.1 Introduction

15.3 Making a false statement

15.5 Homelessness

15.6 Allocations

15.7 Withholding information

15.9 Homelessness

15.10 Allocations

15.11 Failure to notify changes

Introduction

15.1 To prevent abuse of Housing Act (HA) 1996 Parts 6 and 7 and Housing (Wales) Act (H(W)A) 2014 Part 2, some attempts to obtain accommodation are classified as criminal offences. There are three such offences:[1]

a) making a false statement;
b) withholding information; and
c) failing to notify changes.

15.2 Offences under these provisions are prosecuted in the magistrates' court, and are punishable by a fine.[2]

Making a false statement

15.3 In all cases, the offence is sufficiently widely drafted to catch, for example, an adviser who makes representations on behalf of an applicant. Since the homelessness offences requires proof of intent to induce the authority to believe something which is not true, the prosecutor must, accordingly, include proof of such intent as part of the prosecution, so this would be a rare event. Advisers should, however, bear the possibility in mind when deciding in what terms to relay information to an authority.[3]

15.4 The elements of the offence differ depending on whether made in connection with an allocation (HA 1996 Part 6) or homelessness application (HA 1996 Part 7, H(W)A 2014 Part 2).

Homelessness

15.5 The offence is committed by anyone – not only an applicant – who knowingly or recklessly makes a statement which is false in a material particular with intent to induce an authority, in connection with the exercise of its functions under HA 1996 Part 7 or H(W)A Part 2, to

1 HA 1996 ss171, 214; H(W)A 2014 s97.

2 For HA 1996 Parts 6 and 7, the fine may not exceed level 5 on the standard scale, but level 5 is presently unlimited (see Criminal Justice Act 1982 s37 and Legal Aid, Sentencing and Punishment of Offenders Act 2012 s85). For H(W)A 2014 Part 2, the fine may not exceed level 4 on the standard scale, currently £2,500: Criminal Justice Act 1982 s37.

3 As a criminal offence, the standard of proof is beyond reasonable doubt but the element of intent may be proved by natural inference from acts.

believe that the person making the statement or any other person is entitled to accommodation or assistance[4] in accordance with the provisions of HA 1996 Part 7 or H(W)A 2014 Part 2.[5]

Allocations

15.6 The offence is committed by anyone – not only an applicant – who knowingly or recklessly makes a statement which is false in any material particular in connection with the exercise by an authority of its functions under HA 1996 Part 6 (ie there is no requirement that there be an intent to induce an authority to believe anything).[6]

Withholding information

15.7 The offence is committed by anyone – again, not just an applicant – who knowingly withholds information which the authority has reasonably required the person to give in connection with the exercise of its functions under HA 1996 Parts 6 and 7 or H(W)A 2014 Part 2.[7] This is a widely drafted provision, allowing an authority to require information from, for example, a relative or a former landlord.

15.8 As with the 'false statement' offence (above), the offence is different as between 'allocations' and 'homelessness' cases.

Homelessness

15.9 Under HA 1996 s214(1) and H(W)A 2014 s97(1), an intent must be shown to induce the authority, in connection with the exercise of its HA 1996 Part 7 or H(W)A 2014 Part 2 functions, to believe that the person withholding the information, or any other person, is entitled to accommodation or assistance.[8] Accordingly, it is directed at the person withholding information that would be harmful to an

4 Defined for the purposes of HA 1996 s214 as 'the benefit of any duty under HA 1996 Part 7, which relates to accommodation or to assistance in obtaining accommodation' (s183). There is no equivalent definitional provision in HA 1996 Part 6 or H(W)A 2014 Part 2.

5 HA 1996 s214(1); H(W)A 2014 s97(1).

6 HA 1996 s171(1).

7 HA 1996 ss171(1) and 214(1); H(W)A 2014 s97(1).

8 Defined for the purposes of HA 1996 s214 as 'the benefit of any duty under HA 1996 Part 7, which relates to accommodation or to assistance in obtaining accommodation' (s183). There is no equivalent definition in HA 1996 Part 6 or H(W)A 2014 Part 2.

applicant, rather than at someone who refuses to provide helpful information.

Allocations

15.10 There is no equivalent 'intent' provision in HA 1996 s171(1), ie the offence is committed where a person knowingly withholds information which the authority have reasonably required him to give in connection with the exercise of its functions under HA 1996 Part 6.

Failure to notify changes

15.11 The offence arises only in relation to HA 1996 Part 7 and H(W)A 2014. It may be committed only by an applicant.

15.12 An applicant is under a positive duty to inform the authority as soon as possible of any change of facts material to his or her application, which occurs before receipt of notification under HA 1996 s184 or H(W)A 2014 s63 of the authority's decision on his or her application.[9] This is so even though the circumstances to be taken into account on an internal review include any that have changed between that decision and the decision on the review.[10] It follows on the face of it that a failure to notify the authority of a change adverse to the applicant's interests after the decision would seem to be exempt from this obligation, even though the authority is entitled to take it into account,[11] but as the point has never been explicitly tested, it may yet be that this is (from the perspective of the homeless person) an over-optimistic or over-legalistic interpretation of the effect of case-law on statute.

15.13 The extent of the obligation is less straightforward than the two offences previously considered. Of particular difficulty is the issue of what constitutes a 'material change of facts'. In accordance with

9 HA 1996 s214(2). The statutory language would not seem to be capable of being extended to the decision on the review, especially bearing in mind that as a criminal offence is involved, it is to be interpreted narrowly.

10 See para 9.177.

11 Although there is no reference to HA 1996 s214 in *Mohamed v Hammersmith and Fulham LBC* [2001] UKHL 57, [2002] HLR 7, it formed a substantive part of the argument and it would therefore seem that Lord Slynn's conclusion at [25] confirms this analysis: 'I find nothing in the statutory language which requires the review to be confined to the date of the initial application or determination.'

the usual principles of criminal law, the courts should interpret the provisions narrowly, ie in favour of the accused.

15.14 A related duty is imposed on authorities: to explain to an applicant, in ordinary language, the nature of the applicant's duty to notify them of material changes and that failure to do so is a criminal offence.[12] The English Code of Guidance[13] suggests that this obligation is 'explained in ordinary language, and conveyed sensitively to avoid intimidating applicants'.

15.15 It is a defence for the applicant to show that he or she was not given such an explanation. It is also a defence to show that the applicant had a reasonable excuse for non-compliance.[14]

12 HA 1996 s214(2); H(W)A 2014 s97(3), (4).

13 Code of Guidance para 6.11. There is no equivalent In the Welsh Code.

14 HA 1996 s214(3); H(W)A 2014 s97(4)–(5).

APPENDICES

A Statutes 699

Homelessness Reduction Act 2017 700

Housing Act 1996 Parts 6 and 7 718

B Statutory instruments 771

Allocation of Housing (Qualification Criteria for Right to Move) (England) Regulations 2015 772

Allocation of Housing (Qualification Criteria for Armed Forces) (England) Regulations 2012 773

Homelessness (Suitability of Accommodation) (England) Order 2012 774

Allocation of Housing and Homelessness (Miscellaneous Provisions) (England) Regulations 2006 776

Allocation of Housing and Homelessness (Eligibility) (England) Regulations 2006 777

Homelessness (Suitability of Accommodation) (England) Order 2003 782

Homelessness (Priority Need for Accommodation) (England) Order 2002 784

Allocation of Housing and Homelessness (Review Procedures) Regulations 1999 786

Homelessness (Suitability of Accommodation) Order 1996 790

C Guidance 793

Right to move: statutory guidance on social housing allocations for local housing authorities in England (March 2015) 794

Supplementary guidance on domestic abuse and homelessness (November 2014) 800

continued

Providing social housing for local people: statutory guidance on social housing allocations for local authorities in England (December 2013) 812

Supplementary Guidance on the homelessness changes in the Localism Act 2011 and on the Homelessness (Suitability of Accommodation) (England) Order 2012 (November 2012) 816

Allocation of accommodation: guidance for local housing authorities in England (June 2012) 827

Provision of Accommodation for 16 and 17 year old young people who may be homeless and/or require accommodation (April 2010) 861

Homelessness Code of Guidance for Local Authorities: Supplementary Guidance on Intentional Homelessness (August 2009) 878

Homelessness Code of Guidance for Local Authorities (July 2006) 881

APPENDIX A

Statutes[1]

Homelessness Reduction Act 2017 700
Housing Act 1996 Parts 6 and 7 718

In addition to these statutes, Housing (Wales) Act 2014 Part 2 is reproduced in the ebook version of *Homelessness and Allocations*

HOMELESSNESS REDUCTION ACT 2017

Threatened homelessness

1 Meaning of 'threatened with homelessness'

(1) Section 175 of the Housing Act 1996 (homelessness and threatened homelessness) is amended as follows.

(2) In subsection (4), for '28' substitute '56'.

(3) After subsection (4) insert–

'(5) A person is also threatened with homelessness if–

(a) a valid notice has been given to the person under section 21 of the Housing Act 1988 (orders for possession on expiry or termination of assured shorthold tenancy) in respect of the only accommodation the person has that is available for the person's occupation, and

(b) that notice will expire within 56 days.'

Advisory services

2 Duty to provide advisory services

For section 179 of the Housing Act 1996 (duty of local housing authority to provide advisory services) substitute–

'179 Duty of local housing authority in England to provide advisory services

(1) Each local housing authority in England must provide or secure the provision of a service, available free of charge to any person in the authority's district, providing information and advice on–

(a) preventing homelessness,

(b) securing accommodation when homeless,

(c) the rights of persons who are homeless or threatened with homelessness, and the duties of the authority, under this Part,

(d) any help that is available from the authority or anyone else, whether under this Part or otherwise, for persons in the authority's district who are homeless or may become homeless (whether or not they are threatened with homelessness), and

(e) how to access that help.

(2) The service must be designed to meet the needs of persons in the authority's district including, in particular, the needs of–

(a) persons released from prison or youth detention accommodation,

(b) care leavers,

(c) former members of the regular armed forces,

(d) victims of domestic abuse,

(e) persons leaving hospital,

(f) persons suffering from a mental illness or impairment, and

(g) any other group that the authority identify as being at particular risk of homelessness in the authority's district.

(3) The authority may give to any person by whom the service is provided on behalf of the authority assistance by way of grant or loan.

(4) The authority may also assist any such person–

(a) by permitting the person to use premises belonging to the authority,
(b) by making available furniture or other goods, whether by way of gift, loan or otherwise, and
(c) by making available the services of staff employed by the authority.

(5) In this section–

'care leavers' means persons who are former relevant children (within the meaning given by section 23C(1) of the Children Act 1989);

'domestic abuse' means–
(a) physical violence,
(b) threatening, intimidating, coercive or controlling behaviour, or
(c) emotional, financial, sexual or any other form of abuse,

where the victim is associated with the abuser;

'financial abuse' includes–
(a) having money or other property stolen,
(b) being defrauded,
(c) being put under pressure in relation to money or other property, and
(d) having money or other property misused;

'hospital' has the same meaning as in the National Health Service Act 2006 (see section 275(1) of that Act);

'regular armed forces' means the regular forces as defined by section 374 of the Armed Forces Act 2006;

'youth detention accommodation' means–
(a) a secure children's home,
(b) a secure training centre,
(c) a secure college,
(d) a young offender institution,
(e) accommodation provided by or on behalf of a local authority for the purpose of restricting the liberty of children;
(f) accommodation provided for that purpose under section 82(5) of the Children Act 1989, or
(g) accommodation, or accommodation of a description, for the time being specified by order under section 107(1)(e) of the Powers of Criminal Courts (Sentencing) Act 2000 (youth detention accommodation for the purposes of detention and training orders).'

Assessments and plans

3 Duty to assess all eligible applicants' cases and agree a plan

(1) After section 189 of the Housing Act 1996, but before the heading after that section (duties to persons found to be homeless or threatened with homelessness), insert–

'Duty to assess every eligible applicant's case and agree a plan

189A Assessments and personalised plan

(1) If the local housing authority are satisfied that an applicant is–
(a) homeless or threatened with homelessness, and
(b) eligible for assistance,
the authority must make an assessment of the applicant's case.

(2) The authority's assessment of the applicant's case must include an assessment of–
(a) the circumstances that caused the applicant to become homeless or threatened with homelessness,
(b) the housing needs of the applicant including, in particular, what accommodation would be suitable for the applicant and any persons with whom the applicant resides or might reasonably be expected to reside ('other relevant persons'), and
(c) what support would be necessary for the applicant and any other relevant persons to be able to have and retain suitable accommodation.

(3) The authority must notify the applicant, in writing, of the assessment that the authority make.

(4) After the assessment has been made, the authority must try to agree with the applicant–
(a) any steps the applicant is to be required to take for the purposes of securing that the applicant and any other relevant persons have and are able to retain suitable accommodation, and
(b) the steps the authority are to take under this Part for those purposes.

(5) If the authority and the applicant reach an agreement, the authority must record it in writing.

(6) If the authority and the applicant cannot reach an agreement, the authority must record in writing–
(a) why they could not agree,
(b) any steps the authority consider it would be reasonable to require the applicant to take for the purposes mentioned in subsection (4)(a), and
(c) the steps the authority are to take under this Part for those purposes.

(7) The authority may include in a written record produced under subsection (5) or (6) any advice for the applicant that the authority consider appropriate (including any steps the authority consider it would be a good idea for the applicant to take but which the applicant should not be required to take).

(8) The authority must give to the applicant a copy of any written record produced under subsection (5) or (6).

(9) Until such time as the authority consider that they owe the applicant no duty under any of the following sections of this Part, the authority must keep under review–
(a) their assessment of the applicant's case, and

(b) the appropriateness of any agreement reached under subsection (4) or steps recorded under subsection (6)(b) or (c).

(10) If–

(a) the authority's assessment of any of the matters mentioned in subsection (2) changes, or

(b) the authority's assessment of the applicant's case otherwise changes such that the authority consider it appropriate to do so,

the authority must notify the applicant, in writing, of how their assessment of the applicant's case has changed (whether by providing the applicant with a revised written assessment or otherwise).

(11) If the authority consider that any agreement reached under subsection (4) or any step recorded under subsection (6)(b) or (c) is no longer appropriate–

(a) the authority must notify the applicant, in writing, that they consider the agreement or step is no longer appropriate,

(b) any failure, after the notification is given, to take a step that was agreed to in the agreement or recorded under subsection (6)(b) or (c) is to be disregarded for the purposes of this Part, and

(c) subsections (4) to (8) apply as they applied after the assessment was made.

(12) A notification under this section or a copy of any written record produced under subsection (5) or (6), if not received by the applicant, is to be treated as having been given to the applicant if it is made available at the authority's office for a reasonable period for collection by or on behalf of the applicant.'

(2) In section 190 of that Act (duties to persons becoming homeless intentionally), for subsection (4) substitute–

'(4) In deciding what advice and assistance is to be provided under this section, the authority must have regard to their assessment of the applicant's case under section 189A.'

Duties to those who are homeless or threatened with homelessness

4 Duty in cases of threatened homelessness

(1) The Housing Act 1996 is amended as follows.

(2) For section 195 (duties in case of threatened homelessness) substitute–

'195 Duties in cases of threatened homelessness

(1) This section applies where the local housing authority are satisfied that an applicant is–

(a) threatened with homelessness, and

(b) eligible for assistance.

(2) The authority must take reasonable steps to help the applicant to secure that accommodation does not cease to be available for the applicant's occupation.

(3) In deciding what steps they are to take, the authority must have regard to their assessment of the applicant's case under section 189A.

(4) Subsection (2) does not affect any right of the authority, whether by

virtue of contract, enactment or rule of law, to secure vacant possession of any accommodation.

(5) If any of the circumstances mentioned in subsection (8) apply, the authority may give notice to the applicant bringing the duty under subsection (2) to an end.

(6) But the authority may not give notice to the applicant under subsection (5) on the basis that the circumstances in subsection (8)(b) apply if a valid notice has been given to the applicant under section 21 of the Housing Act 1988 (orders for possession on expiry or termination of assured shorthold tenancy) that–
   (a) will expire within 56 days or has expired, and
   (b) is in respect of the only accommodation that is available for the applicant's occupation.

(7) The notice must–
   (a) specify which of the circumstances apply, and
   (b) inform the applicant that the applicant has a right to request a review of the authority's decision to bring the duty under subsection (2) to an end and of the time within which such a request must be made.

(8) The circumstances are that the authority are satisfied that–
   (a) the applicant has–
      (i) suitable accommodation available for occupation, and
      (ii) a reasonable prospect of having suitable accommodation available for occupation for at least 6 months, or such longer period not exceeding 12 months as may be prescribed, from the date of the notice,
   (b) the authority have complied with the duty under subsection (2) and the period of 56 days beginning with the day that the authority are first satisfied as mentioned in subsection (1) has ended (whether or not the applicant is still threatened with homelessness),
   (c) the applicant has become homeless,
   (d) the applicant has refused an offer of suitable accommodation and, on the date of refusal, there was a reasonable prospect that suitable accommodation would be available for occupation by the applicant for at least 6 months or such longer period not exceeding 12 months as may be prescribed,
   (e) the applicant has become homeless intentionally from any accommodation that has been made available to the applicant as a result of the authority's exercise of their functions under subsection (2),
   (f) the applicant is no longer eligible for assistance, or
   (g) the applicant has withdrawn the application mentioned in section 183(1).

(9) A notice under this section must be given in writing and, if not received by the applicant, is to be treated as having been given to the applicant if it is made available at the authority's office for a reasonable period for collection by or on behalf of the applicant.

(10) The duty under subsection (2) can also be brought to an end under sections 193B and 193C (notices in cases of applicant's deliberate and unreasonable refusal to co-operate).'

(3) In section 184 (inquiry into cases of homelessness or threatened homelessness), in subsection (3A)–
(a) omit 'or 195(2)';
(b) omit 'or (as the case may be) section 195(4A)'.
(4) In section 195A (re-application after private rented sector offer)–
(a) omit subsections (3) and (4);
(b) in subsection (5), omit 'or (3)';
(c) in subsection (6), omit 'or (3)' (in both places).
(5) Omit section 196 (becoming threatened with homelessness intentionally).
(6) In section 204 (right of appeal to the county court on point of law), in subsection (4), omit 'or had the power under section 195(8) to do so,'.
(7) In section 213A (co-operation in certain cases involving children)–
(a) in subsection (1)–
(i) at the end of paragraph (a) insert 'or';
(ii) omit paragraph (c) and the 'or' preceding it;
(b) in subsection (5)(a), for the words from 'assistance' to the second 'intentionally' substitute 'assistance or became homeless intentionally'.
(8) In section 218 (index of defined expressions: Part 7), in the Table, omit the entry for 'intentionally threatened with homelessness'.

5 Duties owed to those who are homeless

(1) The Housing Act 1996 is amended as follows.
(2) Before section 190, but after the heading before that section (duties to persons found to be homeless or threatened with homelessness), insert–

'189B Initial duty owed to all eligible persons who are homeless

(1) This section applies where the local housing authority are satisfied that an applicant is–
(a) homeless, and
(b) eligible for assistance.
(2) Unless the authority refer the application to another local housing authority in England (see section 198(A1)), the authority must take reasonable steps to help the applicant to secure that suitable accommodation becomes available for the applicant's occupation for at least–
(a) 6 months, or
(b) such longer period not exceeding 12 months as may be prescribed.
(3) In deciding what steps they are to take, the authority must have regard to their assessment of the applicant's case under section 189A.
(4) Where the authority–
(a) are satisfied that the applicant has a priority need, and
(b) are not satisfied that the applicant became homeless intentionally,

the duty under subsection (2) comes to an end at the end of the period of 56 days beginning with the day the authority are first satisfied as mentioned in subsection (1).
(5) If any of the circumstances mentioned in subsection (7) apply, the authority may give notice to the applicant bringing the duty under subsection (2) to an end.

(6) The notice must–
(a) specify which of the circumstances apply, and
(b) inform the applicant that the applicant has a right to request a review of the authority's decision to bring the duty under subsection (2) to an end and of the time within which such a request must be made.

(7) The circumstances are that the authority are satisfied that–
(a) the applicant has–
(i) suitable accommodation available for occupation, and
(ii) a reasonable prospect of having suitable accommodation available for occupation for at least 6 months, or such longer period not exceeding 12 months as may be prescribed, from the date of the notice,
(b) the authority have complied with the duty under subsection (2) and the period of 56 days beginning with the day that the authority are first satisfied as mentioned in subsection (1) has ended (whether or not the applicant has secured accommodation),
(c) the applicant has refused an offer of suitable accommodation and, on the date of refusal, there was a reasonable prospect that suitable accommodation would be available for occupation by the applicant for at least 6 months or such longer period not exceeding 12 months as may be prescribed,
(d) the applicant has become homeless intentionally from any accommodation that has been made available to the applicant as a result of the authority's exercise of their functions under subsection (2),
(e) the applicant is no longer eligible for assistance, or
(f) the applicant has withdrawn the application mentioned in section 183(1).

(8) A notice under this section must be given in writing and, if not received by the applicant, is to be treated as having been given to the applicant if it is made available at the authority's office for a reasonable period for collection by or on behalf of the applicant.

(9) The duty under subsection (2) can also be brought to an end under–
(a) section 193A (consequences of refusal of final accommodation offer or final Part 6 offer at the initial relief stage), or
(b) sections 193B and 193C (notices in cases of applicant's deliberate and unreasonable refusal to co-operate).'

(3) In section 184 (inquiry into cases of homelessness)–
(a) in subsection (3A), after 'duty is' insert ', or after the authority's duty to the applicant under section 189B(2) comes to an end would be,';
(b) in subsection (4), for 'under section 198 (referral of cases)' substitute 'in England under section 198(A1) (referral of cases where section 189B applies)'.

(4) In section 188 (interim duty to accommodate in case of apparent priority need)–
(a) for subsection (1) substitute–

'(1) If the local housing authority have reason to believe that an applicant may be homeless, eligible for assistance and have a priority need, they must secure that accommodation is available for the applicant's occupation.

(1ZA) In a case in which the local housing authority conclude their inquiries under section 184 and decide that the applicant does not have a priority need–

(a) where the authority decide that they do not owe the applicant a duty under section 189B(2), the duty under subsection (1) comes to an end when the authority notify the applicant of that decision, or

(b) otherwise, the duty under subsection (1) comes to an end upon the authority notifying the applicant of their decision that, upon the duty under section 189B(2) coming to an end, they do not owe the applicant any duty under section 190 or 193.

(1ZB) In any other case, the duty under subsection (1) comes to an end upon the later of–

(a) the duty owed to the applicant under section 189B(2) coming to an end or the authority notifying the applicant that they have decided that they do not owe the applicant a duty under that section, and

(b) the authority notifying the applicant of their decision as to what other duty (if any) they owe to the applicant under the following provisions of this Part upon the duty under section 189B(2) coming to an end.';

(b) in subsection (1A), for 'pending a decision of the kind referred to in subsection (1)' substitute 'until the later of paragraph (a) or (b) of subsection (1ZB).';

(c) for subsection (3) substitute–

'(2A) For the purposes of this section, where the applicant requests a review under section 202(1)(h) of the authority's decision as to the suitability of accommodation offered to the applicant by way of a final accommodation offer or a final Part 6 offer (within the meaning of section 193A), the authority's duty to the applicant under section 189B(2) is not to be taken to have come to an end under section 193A(2) until the decision on the review has been notified to the applicant.

(3) Otherwise, the duty under this section comes to an end in accordance with subsections (1ZA) to (1A), regardless of any review requested by the applicant under section 202.

But the authority may secure that accommodation is available for the applicant's occupation pending a decision on review.'

(5) In section 190 (duties to persons becoming homeless intentionally)–

(a) for subsection (1) substitute–

'(1) This section applies where–

(a) the local housing authority are satisfied that an applicant–

(i) is homeless and eligible for assistance, but

(ii) became homeless intentionally,

(b) the authority are also satisfied that the applicant has a priority need, and

(c) the authority's duty to the applicant under section 189B(2) has come to an end.';

(b) in subsection (2), for the words before paragraph (a) substitute 'The authority must–';
(c) omit subsection (3);
(d) in subsection (5), omit 'or (3)'.

(6) Omit section 192 (duty to persons not in priority need who are not homeless intentionally).

(7) In section 193 (duty to persons with priority need who are not homeless intentionally), for subsection (1) substitute–

'(1) This section applies where–
(a) the local housing authority–
(i) are satisfied that an applicant is homeless and eligible for assistance, and
(ii) are not satisfied that the applicant became homeless intentionally,
(b) the authority are also satisfied that the applicant has a priority need, and
(c) the authority's duty to the applicant under section 189B(2) has come to an end.'

(8) In section 198 (referral of case to another local housing authority), before subsection (1) insert–

'(A1) If the local housing authority would be subject to the duty under section 189B (initial duty owed to all eligible persons who are homeless) but consider that the conditions are met for referral of the case to another local housing authority in England, they may notify that other authority of their opinion.'

(9) After section 199 insert–

'199A Duties to the applicant whose case is considered for referral or referred under section 198(A1)

(1) Where a local housing authority ('the notifying authority') notify an applicant that they intend to notify or have notified another local housing authority in England ('the notified authority') under section 198(A1) of their opinion that the conditions are met for referral of the applicant's case to the notified authority, the notifying authority–
(a) cease to be subject to any duty under section 188 (interim duty to accommodate in case of apparent priority need), and
(b) are not subject to the duty under section 189B (initial duty owed to all eligible persons who are homeless).

(2) But, if the notifying authority have reason to believe that the applicant may have a priority need, they must secure that accommodation is available for occupation by the applicant until the applicant is notified of the decision as to whether the conditions for referral of the applicant's case are met.

(3) When it has been decided whether the conditions for referral are met,

the notifying authority must give notice of the decision and the reasons for it to the applicant.

The notice must also inform the applicant of the applicant's right to request a review of the decision and of the time within which such a request must be made.

(4) If it is decided that the conditions for referral are not met–
  (a) the notifying authority are subject to the duty under section 189B,
  (b) the references in subsections (4) and (7)(b) of that section to the day that the notifying authority are first satisfied as mentioned in subsection (1) of that section are to be read as references to the day on which notice is given under subsection (3) of this section, and
  (c) if the notifying authority have reason to believe that the applicant may have a priority need, they must secure that accommodation is available for occupation by the applicant until the later of–
    (i) the duty owed to the applicant under section 189B coming to an end, and
    (ii) the authority deciding what other duty (if any) they owe to the applicant under this Part after the duty under section 189B comes to an end.

(5) If it is decided that the conditions for referral are met–
  (a) for the purposes of this Part, the applicant is to be treated as having made an application of the kind mentioned in section 183(1) to the notified authority on the date on which notice is given under subsection (3),
  (b) from that date, the notifying authority owes no duties to the applicant under this Part,
  (c) where the notifying authority have made a decision as to whether the applicant is eligible for assistance, is homeless or became homeless intentionally, the notified authority may only come to a different decision if they are satisfied that–
    (i) the applicant's circumstances have changed, or further information has come to light, since the notifying authority made their decision, and
    (ii) that change in circumstances, or further information, justifies the notified authority coming to a different decision to the notifying authority, and
  (d) the notifying authority must give to the notified authority copies of any notifications that the notifying authority have given to the applicant under section 189A(3) or (10) (notifications of the notifying authority's assessments of the applicant's case).

(6) A duty under subsection (2) or paragraph (c) of subsection (4) ceases as provided in the subsection or paragraph concerned even if the applicant requests a review of the authority's decision upon which the duty ceases.

The authority may secure that accommodation is available for the applicant's occupation pending the decision on review.

(7) A notice under this section must be given in writing and, if not received by the applicant, is to be treated as having been given to the

applicant if it is made available at the authority's office for a reasonable period for collection by or on behalf of the applicant.'

(10) In section 200 (duties to the applicant whose case is considered for referral or referred)–
(a) in the heading, after 'referred' insert 'under section 198(1)';
(b) in subsection (1), after 'another local housing authority' insert 'under section 198(1)';
(c) after that subsection insert–

'(1A) A local housing authority in England may not notify an applicant as mentioned in subsection (1) until the authority's duty to the applicant under section 189B(2) (initial duty owed to all eligible persons who are homeless) has come to an end.';

(d) in subsection (6), omit 'required to be'.

(11) In section 204 (right of appeal to county court on point of law), in subsection (4), after '190' insert ', 199A'.

(12) In section 211 (protection of property of homeless persons and persons threatened with homelessness), in subsection (2), after 'accommodate),' insert–

'section 189B (initial duty owed to all eligible persons who are homeless),'.

6 Duties to help to secure accommodation

In section 205 of the Housing Act 1996 (discharge of functions: introductory), after subsection (2) insert–

'(3) For the purposes of this section, a local housing authority's duty under section 189B(2) or 195(2) is a function of the authority to secure that accommodation is available for the occupation of a person only if the authority decide to discharge the duty by securing that accommodation is so available.'

Failure to co-operate by an applicant for assistance

7 Deliberate and unreasonable refusal to co-operate: duty upon giving of notice

(1) After section 193 of the Housing Act 1996 insert–

'193A Consequences of refusal of final accommodation offer or final Part 6 offer at the initial relief stage

(1) Subsections (2) and (3) apply where–
(a) a local housing authority owe a duty to an applicant under section 189B(2), and
(b) the applicant, having been informed of the consequences of refusal and of the applicant's right to request a review of the suitability of the accommodation, refuses–
(i) a final accommodation offer, or
(ii) a final Part 6 offer.

(2) The authority's duty to the applicant under section 189B(2) comes to an end.

(3) Section 193 (the main housing duty) does not apply.

(4) An offer is a 'final accommodation offer' if–

(a) it is an offer of an assured shorthold tenancy made by a private landlord to the applicant in relation to any accommodation which is, or may become, available for the applicant's occupation,

(b) it is made, with the approval of the authority, in pursuance of arrangements made by the authority in the discharge of their duty under section 189B(2), and

(c) the tenancy being offered is a fixed term tenancy (within the meaning of Part 1 of the Housing Act 1988) for a period of at least 6 months.

(5) A 'final Part 6 offer' is an offer of accommodation under Part 6 (allocation of housing) that–

(a) is made in writing by the authority in the discharge of their duty under section 189B(2), and

(b) states that it is a final offer for the purposes of this section.

(6) The authority may not approve a final accommodation offer, or make a final Part 6 offer, unless they are satisfied that the accommodation is suitable for the applicant and that subsection (7) does not apply.

(7) This subsection applies to an applicant if–

(a) the applicant is under contractual or other obligations in respect of the applicant's existing accommodation, and

(b) the applicant is not able to bring those obligations to an end before being required to take up the offer.

193B Notices in cases of an applicant's deliberate and unreasonable refusal to co-operate

(1) Section 193C applies where–

(a) a local housing authority owe a duty to an applicant under section 189B(2) or 195(2), and

(b) the authority give notice to the applicant under subsection (2).

(2) A local housing authority may give a notice to an applicant under this subsection if the authority consider that the applicant has deliberately and unreasonably refused to take any step–

(a) that the applicant agreed to take under subsection (4) of section 189A, or

(b) that was recorded by the authority under subsection (6)(b) of that section.

(3) A notice under subsection (2) must–

(a) explain why the authority are giving the notice and its effect, and

(b) inform the applicant that the applicant has a right to request a review of the authority's decision to give the notice and of the time within which such a request must be made.

(4) The authority may not give notice to the applicant under subsection (2) unless–

(a) the authority have given a relevant warning to the applicant, and

(b) a reasonable period has elapsed since the warning was given.

(5) A 'relevant warning' means a notice–
  (a) given by the authority to the applicant after the applicant has deliberately and unreasonably refused to take any step–
    (i) that the applicant agreed to take under subsection (4) of section 189A, or
    (ii) that was recorded by the authority under subsection (6)(b) of that section,
  (b) that warns the applicant that, if the applicant should deliberately and unreasonably refuse to take any such step after receiving the notice, the authority intend to give notice to the applicant under subsection (2), and
  (c) that explains the consequences of such a notice being given to the applicant.

(6) For the purposes of subsections (2) and (5), in deciding whether a refusal by the applicant is unreasonable, the authority must have regard to the particular circumstances and needs of the applicant (whether identified in the authority's assessment of the applicant's case under section 189A or not).

(7) The Secretary of State may make provision by regulations as to the procedure to be followed by a local housing authority in connection with notices under this section.

(8) A notice under this section must be given in writing and, if not received by the applicant, is to be treated as having been given to the applicant if it is made available at the authority's office for a reasonable period for collection by or on behalf of the applicant.

193C Notice under section 193B: consequences

(1) In the circumstances mentioned in section 193B(1), this section applies in relation to a local housing authority and an applicant.

(2) The authority's duty to the applicant under section 189B(2) or 195(2) comes to an end.

(3) Subsection (4) applies if the authority–
  (a) are satisfied that the applicant is homeless, eligible for assistance and has a priority need, and
  (b) are not satisfied that the applicant became homeless intentionally.

(4) Section 193 (the main housing duty) does not apply, but the authority must secure that accommodation is available for occupation by the applicant.

(5) The authority cease to be subject to the duty under subsection (4) if the applicant–
  (a) ceases to be eligible for assistance,
  (b) becomes homeless intentionally from accommodation made available for the applicant's occupation,
  (c) accepts an offer of an assured tenancy from a private landlord, or
  (d) otherwise voluntarily ceases to occupy, as the applicant's only or principal home, the accommodation made available for the applicant's occupation.

(6) The authority also cease to be subject to the duty under subsection (4)

if the applicant, having been informed of the possible consequences of refusal or acceptance and of the applicant's right to request a review of the suitability of the accommodation, refuses or accepts–

(a) a final accommodation offer, or

(b) a final Part 6 offer.

(7) An offer is 'a final accommodation offer' if–

(a) it is an offer of an assured shorthold tenancy made by a private landlord to the applicant in relation to any accommodation which is, or may become, available for the applicant's occupation,

(b) it is made, with the approval of the authority, in pursuance of arrangements made by the authority with a view to bringing the authority's duty under subsection (4) to an end, and

(c) the tenancy being offered is a fixed term tenancy (within the meaning of Part 1 of the Housing Act 1988) for a period of at least 6 months.

(8) A 'final Part 6 offer' is an offer of accommodation under Part 6 (allocation of housing) that is made in writing and states that it is a final offer for the purposes of this section.

(9) The authority may not approve a final accommodation offer, or make a final Part 6 offer, unless they are satisfied that the accommodation is suitable for the applicant and that subsection (10) does not apply.

(10) This subsection applies to an applicant if–

(a) the applicant is under contractual or other obligations in respect of the applicant's existing accommodation, and

(b) the applicant is not able to bring those obligations to an end before being required to take up the offer.'

(2) In section 193 (duty to persons with priority need who are not homeless intentionally), after subsection (1) insert–

'(1A) But this section does not apply if–

(a) section 193A(3) disapplies this section, or

(b) the authority have given notice to the applicant under section 193B(2).'

Local connection

8 Local connection of a care leaver

In section 199 of the Housing Act 1996 (local connection), after subsection (7), insert–

'(8) While a local authority in England have a duty towards a person under section 23C of the Children Act 1989 (continuing functions in respect of former relevant children)–

(a) if the local authority is a local housing authority, the person has a local connection with their district, and

(b) otherwise, the person has a local connection with every district of a local housing authority that falls within the area of the local authority.

(9) In subsection (8), 'local authority' has the same meaning as in the Children Act 1989 (see section 105 of that Act).

(10) Where, by virtue of being provided with accommodation under section 22A of the Children Act 1989 (provision of accommodation for children in care), a person is normally resident in the district of a local housing authority in England for a continuous period of at least two years, some or all of which falls before the person attains the age of 16, the person has a local connection with that district.

(11) A person ceases to have a local connection with a district under subsection (10) upon attaining the age of 21 (but this does not affect whether the person has a local connection with that district under any other provision of this section).'

Reviews of local housing authority decisions etc

9 Reviews

(1) Section 202 of the Housing Act 1996 (right to request review of decision) is amended as follows.

(2) In subsection (1)–

(a) in paragraph (b)–

(i) for '190 to 193' substitute '189B to 193C';

(ii) omit 'and 196';

(b) after paragraph (b) insert–

'(ba) any decision of a local housing authority–

(i) as to the steps they are to take under subsection (2) of section 189B, or

(ii) to give notice under subsection (5) of that section bringing to an end their duty to the applicant under subsection (2) of that section,

(bb) any decision of a local housing authority to give notice to the applicant under section 193B(2) (notice given to those who deliberately and unreasonably refuse to co-operate),

(bc) any decision of a local housing authority–

(i) as to the steps they are to take under subsection (2) of section 195, or

(ii) to give notice under subsection (5) of that section bringing to an end their duty to the applicant under subsection (2) of that section,';

(c) omit the 'or' at the end of paragraph (f);

(d) after paragraph (g) insert', or

(h) any decision of a local housing authority as to the suitability of accommodation offered to the applicant by way of a final accommodation offer or a final Part 6 offer (within the meaning of section 193A or 193C).'

(3) After subsection (1A) insert–

'(1B) An applicant may, under subsection (1)(h), request a review of the suitability of the accommodation offered whether or not the applicant has accepted the offer.'

Duty on public authorities in England to refer cases

10 Duty of public authority to refer cases to local housing authority

After section 213A of the Housing Act 1996, but before the heading after that section (general provisions), insert–

'213B Duty of public authority to refer cases in England to local housing authority

(1) This section applies if a specified public authority considers that a person in England in relation to whom the authority exercises functions is or may be homeless or threatened with homelessness.

(2) The specified public authority must ask the person to agree to the authority notifying a local housing authority in England of–

(a) the opinion mentioned in subsection (1), and

(b) how the person may be contacted by the local housing authority.

(3) If the person–

(a) agrees to the specified public authority making the notification, and

(b) identifies a local housing authority in England to which the person would like the notification to be made,

the specified public authority must notify that local housing authority of the matters mentioned in subsection (2)(a) and (b).

(4) In this section 'specified public authority' means a public authority specified, or of a description specified, in regulations made by the Secretary of State.

(5) In subsection (4) 'public authority' means a person (other than a local housing authority) who has functions of a public nature.'

Codes of practice

11 Codes of practice

After section 214 of the Housing Act 1996 insert–

'214A Codes of practice

(1) The Secretary of State may from time to time issue one or more codes of practice dealing with the functions of a local housing authority in England relating to homelessness or the prevention of homelessness.

(2) The provision that may be made by a code of practice under this section includes, in particular, provision about–

(a) the exercise by a local housing authority of functions under this Part;

(b) the training of an authority's staff in relation to the exercise of those functions;

(c) the monitoring by an authority of the exercise of those functions.

(3) A code of practice may–

(a) apply to all local housing authorities or to the local housing authorities specified or described in the code;

(b) contain different provision for different kinds of local housing authority.

(4) The Secretary of State may issue a code of practice under this section only in accordance with subsections (5) and (6).
(5) Before issuing the code of practice, the Secretary of State must lay a draft of the code before Parliament.
(6) If–
(a) the Secretary of State lays a draft of the code before Parliament, and
(b) no negative resolution is made within the 40-day period,
the Secretary of State may issue the code in the form of the draft.
(7) For the purposes of subsection (6)–
(a) a 'negative resolution' means a resolution of either House of Parliament not to approve the draft of the code, and
(b) 'the 40-day period' means the period of 40 days beginning with the day on which the draft of the code is laid before Parliament (or, if it is not laid before each House of Parliament on the same day, the later of the two days on which it is laid).
(8) In calculating the 40-day period, no account is to be taken of any period during which–
(a) Parliament is dissolved or prorogued, or
(b) both Houses are adjourned for more than four days.
(9) The Secretary of State may–
(a) from time to time revise and reissue a code of practice under this section;
(b) revoke a code of practice under this section.
(10) Subsections (4) to (6) do not apply to the reissue of a code of practice under this section.
(11) The Secretary of State must publish the current version of each code of practice under this section in whatever manner the Secretary of State thinks fit.
(12) A local housing authority must have regard to a code of practice under this section in exercising their functions.'

Suitability of accommodation

12 Suitability of private rented sector accommodation

(1) Article 3 of the Homelessness (Suitability of Accommodation) (England) Order 2012 (SI 2012/2601) (circumstances in which accommodation is not to be regarded as suitable for a person) ('the 2012 Order') is amended in accordance with subsections (2) to (4).
(2) The existing text becomes paragraph (1).
(3) For 'of a private rented sector offer under section 193(7F) of the Housing Act 1996' substitute 'mentioned in paragraph (2)'.
(4) After paragraph (1) insert–

'(2) The purposes are–
(a) determining, in accordance with section 193(7F) of the Housing Act 1996, whether a local housing authority may approve a private rented sector offer;
(b) determining, in accordance with section 193A(6) or 193C(9) of

that Act, whether a local housing authority may approve a final accommodation offer made by a private landlord;

(c) determining whether any accommodation–

(i) secured for a person who has a priority need by a local housing authority in discharge of their functions under section 189B(2) or 195(2) of that Act, and

(ii) made available for occupation under a tenancy with a private landlord,

is suitable for the purposes of the section concerned.'

(5) The amendments made by this section are without prejudice to any power to make an order or regulations amending or revoking article 3 of the 2012 Order.

General

13 Extent, commencement and short title

(1) This Act extends to England and Wales only.

(2) This section comes into force on the day on which this Act is passed.

(3) The rest of this Act comes into force on such day or days as the Secretary of State may by regulations made by statutory instrument appoint.

(4) Regulations under subsection (3) may make transitional, transitory or saving provision.

(5) This Act may be cited as the Homelessness Reduction Act 2017.

HOUSING ACT 1996

PART 6: ALLOCATION OF HOUSING ACCOMMODATION

Introductory

159 Allocation of housing accommodation

(1) A local housing authority shall comply with the provisions of this Part in allocating housing accommodation.

(2) For the purposes of this Part a local housing authority allocate housing accommodation when they–

(a) select a person to be a secure or introductory tenant of housing accommodation held by them,

(b) nominate a person to be a secure or introductory tenant of housing accommodation held by another person, or

(c) nominate a person to be an assured tenant of housing accommodation held by a private registered provider of social housing or a registered social landlord.

(3) The reference in subsection (2)(a) to selecting a person to be a secure tenant includes deciding to exercise any power to notify an existing tenant or licensee that his tenancy or licence is to be a secure tenancy.

(4) The references in subsection (2)(b) and (c) to nominating a person include nominating a person in pursuance of any arrangements (whether legally enforceable or not) to require that housing accommodation, or a specified amount of housing accommodation, is made available to a person or one of a number of persons nominated by the authority.

(4A) Subject to subsection (4B), the provisions of this Part do not apply to an allocation of housing accommodation by a local housing authority in England to a person who is already–

(a) a secure or introductory tenant, or

(b) an assured tenant of housing accommodation held by a private registered provider of social housing or a registered social landlord.

(4B) The provisions of this Part apply to an allocation of housing accommodation by a local housing authority in England to a person who falls within subsection (4A)(a) or (b) if–

(a) the allocation involves a transfer of housing accommodation for that person,

(b) the application for the transfer is made by that person, and

(c) the authority is satisfied that the person is to be given reasonable preference under section 166A(3).

(5) The provisions of this Part do not apply to an allocation of housing accommodation by a local housing authority in Wales to a person who is already a secure or introductory tenant unless the allocation involves a transfer of housing accommodation for that person and is made on his application.

(7) Subject to the provisions of this Part, a local housing authority may allocate housing accommodation in such manner as they consider appropriate.

160 Cases where provisions about allocation do not apply

(1) The provisions of this Part about the allocation of housing accommodation do not apply in the following cases.

(2) They do not apply where a secure tenancy–
- (a) vests under section 89 of the Housing Act 1985 (succession to periodic secure tenancy on death of tenant),
- (b) remains a secure tenancy by virtue of section 90 of that Act (devolution of term certain of secure tenancy on death of tenant),
- (c) is assigned under section 92 of that Act (assignment of secure tenancy by way of exchange),
- (d) is assigned to a person who would be qualified to succeed the secure tenant if the secure tenant died immediately before the assignment,
- (da) is granted in response to a request under section 158 of the Localism Act 2011 (transfer of tenancy), or
- (e) vests or is otherwise disposed of in pursuance of an order made under–
  - (i) section 24 of the Matrimonial Causes Act 1973 (property adjustment orders in connection with matrimonial proceedings),
  - (ii) section 17(1) of the Matrimonial and Family Proceedings Act 1984 (property adjustment orders after overseas divorce, etc),
  - (iii) paragraph 1 of Schedule 1 to the Children Act 1989 (orders for financial relief against parents), or
  - (iv) Part 2 of Schedule 5, or paragraph 9(2) or (3) of Schedule 7, to the Civil Partnership Act 2004 (property adjustment orders in connection with civil partnership proceedings or after overseas dissolution of civil partnership, etc).

(3) They do not apply where an introductory tenancy–
- (a) becomes a secure tenancy on ceasing to be an introductory tenancy,
- (b) vests under section 133(2) (succession to introductory tenancy on death of tenant),
- (c) is assigned to a person who would be qualified to succeed the introductory tenant if the introductory tenant died immediately before the assignment, or
- (d) vests or is otherwise disposed of in pursuance of an order made under–
  - (i) section 24 of the Matrimonial Causes Act 1973 (property adjustment orders in connection with matrimonial proceedings),
  - (ii) section 17(1) of the Matrimonial and Family Proceedings Act 1984 (property adjustment orders after overseas divorce, etc),
  - (iii) paragraph 1 of Schedule 1 to the Children Act 1989 (orders for financial relief against parents), or
  - (iv) Part 2 of Schedule 5, or paragraph 9(2) or (3) of Schedule 7, to the Civil Partnership Act 2004 (property adjustment orders in connection with civil partnership proceedings or after overseas dissolution of civil partnership, etc).

(4) They do not apply in such other cases as the Secretary of State may prescribe by regulations.

(5) The regulations may be framed so as to make the exclusion of the provisions of this Part about the allocation of housing accommodation subject to such restrictions or conditions as may be specified.

In particular, those provisions may be excluded–
(a) in relation to specified descriptions of persons, or
(b) in relation to housing accommodation of a specified description or a specified proportion of housing accommodation of any specified description.

Eligibility for allocation of housing accommodation

160ZA Allocation only to eligible and qualifying persons: England

(1) A local housing authority in England shall not allocate housing accommodation–
(a) to a person from abroad who is ineligible for an allocation of housing accommodation by virtue of subsection (2) or (4), or
(b) to two or more persons jointly if any of them is a person mentioned in paragraph (a).
(2) A person subject to immigration control within the meaning of the Asylum and Immigration Act 1996 is ineligible for an allocation of housing accommodation by a local housing authority in England unless he is of a class prescribed by regulations made by the Secretary of State.
(3) No person who is excluded from entitlement to universal credit or housing benefit by section 115 of the Immigration and Asylum Act 1999 (exclusion from benefits) shall be included in any class prescribed under subsection (2).
(4) The Secretary of State may by regulations prescribe other classes of persons from abroad who are ineligible to be allocated housing accommodation by local housing authorities in England.
(5) Nothing in subsection (2) or (4) affects the eligibility of a person who falls within section 159(4B).
(6) Except as provided by subsection (1), a person may be allocated housing accommodation by a local housing authority in England (whether on his application or otherwise) if that person–
(a) is a qualifying person within the meaning of subsection (7), or
(b) is one of two or more persons who apply for accommodation jointly, and one or more of the other persons is a qualifying person within the meaning of subsection (7).
(7) Subject to subsections (2) and (4) and any regulations under subsection (8), a local housing authority may decide what classes of persons are, or are not, qualifying persons.
(8) The Secretary of State may by regulations–
(a) prescribe classes of persons who are, or are not, to be treated as qualifying persons by local housing authorities in England, and
(b) prescribe criteria that may not be used by local housing authorities in England in deciding what classes of persons are not qualifying persons.
(9) If a local housing authority in England decide that an applicant for housing accommodation–
(a) is ineligible for an allocation by them by virtue of subsection (2) or (4), or
(b) is not a qualifying person,
they shall notify the applicant of their decision and the grounds for it.
(10) That notice shall be given in writing and, if not received by the applicant,

shall be treated as having been given if it is made available at the authority's office for a reasonable period for collection by him or on his behalf.

(11) A person who is not being treated as a qualifying person may (if he considers that he should be treated as a qualifying person) make a fresh application to the authority for an allocation of housing accommodation by them.

160A Allocation only to eligible persons: Wales

(1) A local housing authority in Wales shall not allocate housing accommodation–

(a) to a person from abroad who is ineligible for an allocation of housing accommodation by virtue of subsection (3) or (5);

(b) to a person who the authority have decided is to be treated as ineligible for such an allocation by virtue of subsection (7); or

(c) to two or more persons jointly if any of them is a person mentioned in paragraph (a) or (b).

(2) Except as provided by subsection (1), any person may be allocated housing accommodation by a local housing authority in Wales (whether on his application or otherwise).

(3) A person subject to immigration control within the meaning of the Asylum and Immigration Act 1996 (c 49) is (subject to subsection (6)) ineligible for an allocation of housing accommodation by a local housing authority in Wales unless he is of a class prescribed by regulations made by the Secretary of State.

(4) No person who is excluded from entitlement to universal credit or housing benefit by section 115 of the Immigration and Asylum Act 1999 (c 33) (exclusion from benefits) shall be included in any class prescribed under subsection (3).

(5) The Secretary of State may by regulations prescribe other classes of persons from abroad who are (subject to subsection (6)) ineligible for an allocation of housing accommodation, either in relation to local housing authorities in Wales generally or any particular local housing authority in Wales.

(6) Nothing in subsection (3) or (5) affects the eligibility of a person who is already–

(a) a secure or introductory tenant;

(b) an assured tenant of housing accommodation allocated to him by a local housing authority in Wales.

(7) A local housing authority in Wales may decide that an applicant is to be treated as ineligible for an allocation of housing accommodation by them if they are satisfied that–

(a) he, or a member of his household, has been guilty of unacceptable behaviour serious enough to make him unsuitable to be a tenant of the authority; and

(b) in the circumstances at the time his application is considered, he is unsuitable to be a tenant of the authority by reason of that behaviour.

(8) The only behaviour which may be regarded by the authority as unacceptable for the purposes of subsection (7)(a) is–

(a) behaviour of the person concerned which would (if he were a secure tenant of the authority) entitle the authority to a possession order under section 84 of the Housing Act 1985 (c 68) on any ground mentioned in Part 1 of Schedule 2 to that Act (other than ground 8); or

(aa) behaviour of the person concerned which would (if he were a secure tenant of the authority) entitle the authority to a possession order under section 84A of the Housing Act 1985; or

(b) behaviour of a member of his household which would (if he were a person residing with a secure tenant of the authority) entitle the authority to a possession order of the type referred to in paragraph (a) or (aa).

(9) If a local housing authority in Wales decide that an applicant for housing accommodation–

(a) is ineligible for an allocation by them by virtue of subsection (3) or (5); or

(b) is to be treated as ineligible for such an allocation by virtue of subsection (7),

they shall notify the applicant of their decision and the grounds for it.

(10) That notice shall be given in writing and, if not received by the applicant, shall be treated as having been given if it is made available at the authority's office for a reasonable period for collection by him or on his behalf.

(11) A person who is being treated by a local housing authority in Wales as ineligible by virtue of subsection (7) may (if he considers that he should no longer be treated as ineligible by the authority) make a fresh application to the authority for an allocation of housing accommodation by them.

161–165 [Repealed].

Applications for housing accommodation

166 Applications for housing accommodation

(1) A local housing authority shall secure that–

(a) advice and information is available free of charge to persons in their district about the right to make an application for an allocation of housing accommodation; and

(b) any necessary assistance in making such an application is available free of charge to persons in their district who are likely to have difficulty in doing so without assistance.

(1A) A local housing authority in England shall secure that an applicant for an allocation of housing accommodation is informed that he has the rights mentioned in section 166A(9).

(2) A local housing authority in Wales shall secure that an applicant for an allocation of housing accommodation is informed that he has the rights mentioned in section 167(4A).

(3) Every application made to a local housing authority for an allocation of housing accommodation shall (if made in accordance with the procedural requirements of the authority's allocation scheme) be considered by the authority.

(4) The fact that a person is an applicant for an allocation of housing accommodation shall not be divulged (without his consent) to any other member of the public.

(5) In this Part 'district' in relation to a local housing authority has the same meaning as in the Housing Act 1985 (c 68).

Allocation schemes

166A Allocation in accordance with allocation scheme: England

(1) Every local housing authority in England must have a scheme (their 'allocation scheme') for determining priorities, and as to the procedure to be followed, in allocating housing accommodation.

For this purpose 'procedure' includes all aspects of the allocation process, including the persons or descriptions of persons by whom decisions are taken.

(2) The scheme must include a statement of the authority's policy on offering people who are to be allocated housing accommodation–

(a) a choice of housing accommodation; or

(b) the opportunity to express preferences about the housing accommodation to be allocated to them.

(3) As regards priorities, the scheme shall, subject to subsection (4), be framed so as to secure that reasonable preference is given to–

(a) people who are homeless (within the meaning of Part 7);

(b) people who are owed a duty by any local housing authority under section 190(2), 193(2) or 195(2) (or under section 65(2) or 68(2) of the Housing Act 1985) or who are occupying accommodation secured by any such authority under section 192(3);

(c) people occupying insanitary or overcrowded housing or otherwise living in unsatisfactory housing conditions;

(d) people who need to move on medical or welfare grounds (including any grounds relating to a disability); and

(e) people who need to move to a particular locality in the district of the authority, where failure to meet that need would cause hardship (to themselves or to others).

The scheme may also be framed so as to give additional preference to particular descriptions of people within one or more of paragraphs (a) to (e) (being descriptions of people with urgent housing needs).

The scheme must be framed so as to give additional preference to a person with urgent housing needs who falls within one or more of paragraphs (a) to (e) and who–

(i) is serving in the regular forces and is suffering from a serious injury, illness or disability which is attributable (wholly or partly) to the person's service,

(ii) formerly served in the regular forces,

(iii) has recently ceased, or will cease to be entitled, to reside in accommodation provided by the Ministry of Defence following the death of that person's spouse or civil partner who has served in the regular forces and whose death was attributable (wholly or partly) to that service, or

(iv) is serving or has served in the reserve forces and is suffering from a serious injury, illness or disability which is attributable (wholly or partly) to the person's service.

For this purpose 'the regular forces' and 'the reserve forces' have the meanings given by section 374 of the Armed Forces Act 2006.

(4) People are to be disregarded for the purposes of subsection (3) if they would

not have fallen within paragraph (a) or (b) of that subsection without the local housing authority having had regard to a restricted person (within the meaning of Part 7).

(5) The scheme may contain provision for determining priorities in allocating housing accommodation to people within subsection (3); and the factors which the scheme may allow to be taken into account include–
  (a) the financial resources available to a person to meet his housing costs;
  (b) any behaviour of a person (or of a member of his household) which affects his suitability to be a tenant;
  (c) any local connection (within the meaning of section 199) which exists between a person and the authority's district.

(6) Subject to subsection (3), the scheme may contain provision about the allocation of particular housing accommodation–
  (a) to a person who makes a specific application for that accommodation;
  (b) to persons of a particular description (whether or not they are within subsection (3)).

(7) The Secretary of State may by regulations–
  (a) specify further descriptions of people to whom preference is to be given as mentioned in subsection (3), or
  (b) amend or repeal any part of subsection (3).

(8) The Secretary of State may by regulations specify factors which a local housing authority in England must not take into account in allocating housing accommodation.

(9) The scheme must be framed so as to secure that an applicant for an allocation of housing accommodation–
  (a) has the right to request such general information as will enable him to assess–
    (i) how his application is likely to be treated under the scheme (including in particular whether he is likely to be regarded as a member of a group of people who are to be given preference by virtue of subsection (3)); and
    (ii) whether housing accommodation appropriate to his needs is likely to be made available to him and, if so, how long it is likely to be before such accommodation becomes available for allocation to him;
  (b) has the right to request the authority to inform him of any decision about the facts of his case which is likely to be, or has been, taken into account in considering whether to allocate housing accommodation to him; and
  (c) has the right to request a review of a decision mentioned in paragraph (b), or in section 160ZA(9), and to be informed of the decision on the review and the grounds for it.

(10) As regards the procedure to be followed, the scheme must be framed in accordance with such principles as the Secretary of State may prescribe by regulations.

(11) Subject to the above provisions, and to any regulations made under them, the authority may decide on what principles the scheme is to be framed.

(12) A local housing authority in England must, in preparing or modifying their allocation scheme, have regard to–
  (a) their current homelessness strategy under section 1 of the Homelessness Act 2002,

(b) their current tenancy strategy under section 150 of the Localism Act 2011, and

(c) in the case of an authority that is a London borough council, the London housing strategy.

(13) Before adopting an allocation scheme, or making an alteration to their scheme reflecting a major change of policy, a local housing authority in England must–

(a) send a copy of the draft scheme, or proposed alteration, to every private registered provider of social housing and registered social landlord with which they have nomination arrangements (see section 159(4)), and

(b) afford those persons a reasonable opportunity to comment on the proposals.

(14) A local housing authority in England shall not allocate housing accommodation except in accordance with their allocation scheme.

167 Allocation in accordance with allocation scheme: Wales

(1) Every local housing authority in Wales shall have a scheme (their 'allocation scheme') for determining priorities, and as to the procedure to be followed, in allocating housing accommodation.

For this purpose 'procedure' includes all aspects of the allocation process, including the persons or descriptions of persons by whom decisions are to be taken.

(1A) The scheme shall include a statement of the authority's policy on offering people who are to be allocated housing accommodation–

(a) a choice of housing accommodation; or

(b) the opportunity to express preferences about the housing accommodation to be allocated to them.

(2) As regards priorities, the scheme shall, subject to subsection (2ZA), be framed so as to secure that reasonable preference is given to–

(a) people who are homeless (within the meaning of Part 2 of the Housing (Wales) Act 2014);

(b) people who are owed any duty by a local housing authority under section 66, 73 or 75 of the Housing (Wales) Act 2014;

(c) people occupying insanitary or overcrowded housing or otherwise living in unsatisfactory housing conditions;

(d) people who need to move on medical or welfare grounds (including grounds relating to a disability); and

(e) people who need to move to a particular locality in the district of the authority, where failure to meet that need would cause hardship (to themselves or to others).

The scheme may also be framed so as to give additional preference to particular descriptions of people within this subsection (being descriptions of people with urgent housing needs).

(2ZA) People are to be disregarded for the purposes of subsection (2) if they would not have fallen within paragraph (a) or (b) of that subsection without the local housing authority having had regard to a restricted person (within the meaning of Part 2 of the Housing (Wales) Act 2014).

(2A) The scheme may contain provision for determining priorities in allocating housing accommodation to people within subsection (2); and the factors which the scheme may allow to be taken into account include–

(a) the financial resources available to a person to meet his housing costs;
(b) any behaviour of a person (or of a member of his household) which affects his suitability to be a tenant;
(c) any local connection (within the meaning of section 81 of the Housing (Wales) Act 2014) which exists between a person and the authority's district.

(2B) Nothing in subsection (2) requires the scheme to provide for any preference to be given to people the authority have decided are people to whom subsection (2C) applies.

(2C) This subsection applies to a person if the authority are satisfied that–

(a) he, or a member of his household, has been guilty of unacceptable behaviour serious enough to make him unsuitable to be a tenant of the authority; and
(b) in the circumstances at the time his case is considered, he deserves by reason of that behaviour not to be treated as a member of a group of people who are to be given preference by virtue of subsection (2).

(2D) Subsection (8) of section 160A applies for the purposes of subsection (2C)(a) above as it applies for the purposes of subsection (7)(a) of that section.

(2E) Subject to subsection (2), the scheme may contain provision about the allocation of particular housing accommodation–

(a) to a person who makes a specific application for that accommodation;
(b) to persons of a particular description (whether or not they are within subsection (2)).

(3) The Secretary of State may by regulations–

(a) specify further descriptions of people to whom preference is to be given as mentioned in subsection (2), or
(b) amend or repeal any part of subsection (2).

(4) The Secretary of State may by regulations specify factors which a local housing authority in Wales shall not take into account in allocating housing accommodation.

(4A) The scheme shall be framed so as to secure that an applicant for an allocation of housing accommodation–

(a) has the right to request such general information as will enable him to assess–
    (i) how his application is likely to be treated under the scheme (including in particular whether he is likely to be regarded as a member of a group of people who are to be given preference by virtue of subsection (2)); and
    (ii) whether housing accommodation appropriate to his needs is likely to be made available to him and, if so, how long it is likely to be before such accommodation becomes available for allocation to him;
(b) is notified in writing of any decision that he is a person to whom subsection (2C) applies and the grounds for it;
(c) has the right to request the authority to inform him of any decision about the facts of his case which is likely to be, or has been, taken into account in considering whether to allocate housing accommodation to him; and
(d) has the right to request a review of a decision mentioned in paragraph

(b) or (c), or in section 160A(9), and to be informed of the decision on the review and the grounds for it.

(5) As regards the procedure to be followed, the scheme shall be framed in accordance with such principles as the Secretary of State may prescribe by regulations.

(6) Subject to the above provisions, and to any regulations made under them, the authority may decide on what principles the scheme is to be framed.

(7) Before adopting an allocation scheme, or making an alteration to their scheme reflecting a major change of policy, a local housing authority in Wales shall–

(a) send a copy of the draft scheme, or proposed alteration, to every private registered provider of social housing and registered social landlord with which they have nomination arrangements (see section 159(4)), and

(b) afford those persons a reasonable opportunity to comment on the proposals.

(8) A local housing authority in Wales shall not allocate housing accommodation except in accordance with their allocation scheme.

168 Information about allocation scheme

(1) A local housing authority shall publish a summary of their allocation scheme and provide a copy of the summary free of charge to any member of the public who asks for one.

(2) The authority shall make the scheme available for inspection at their principal office and shall provide a copy of the scheme, on payment of a reasonable fee, to any member of the public who asks for one.

(3) When the authority make an alteration to their scheme reflecting a major change of policy, they shall within a reasonable period of time take such steps as they consider reasonable to bring the effect of the alteration to the attention of those likely to be affected by it.

Supplementary

169 Guidance to authorities by the Secretary of State

(1) In the exercise of their functions under this Part, local housing authorities shall have regard to such guidance as may from time to time be given by the Secretary of State.

(2) The Secretary of State may give guidance generally or to specified descriptions of authorities.

170 Co-operation between certain social landlords and local housing authorities

Where a local housing authority so request, a private registered provider of social housing or registered social landlord shall co-operate to such extent as is reasonable in the circumstances in offering accommodation to people with priority under the authority's allocation scheme.

171 False statements and withholding information

(1) A person commits an offence if, in connection with the exercise by a local housing authority of their functions under this Part–

(a) he knowingly or recklessly makes a statement which is false in a material particular, or

(b) he knowingly withholds information which the authority have reasonably required him to give in connection with the exercise of those functions.

(2) A person guilty of an offence under this section is liable on summary conviction to a fine not exceeding level 5 on the standard scale.

172 Regulations

(1) Regulations under this Part shall be made by statutory instrument.

(2) No regulations shall be made under section 166A(7) or 167(3) (regulations amending provisions about priorities in allocating housing accommodation) unless a draft of the regulations has been laid before and approved by a resolution of each House of Parliament.

(3) Any other regulations under this Part shall be subject to annulment in pursuance of a resolution of either House of Parliament.

(4) Regulations under this Part may contain such incidental, supplementary and transitional provisions as appear to the Secretary of State appropriate, and may make different provision for different cases including different provision for different areas.

173 Consequential amendments: Part VI

The enactments mentioned in Schedule 16 have effect with the amendments specified there which are consequential on the provisions of this Part.

174 Index of defined expressions: Part VI

The following Table shows provisions defining or otherwise explaining expressions used in this Part (other than provisions defining or explaining an expression used in the same section)–

allocation (of housing)	section 159(2)
allocation scheme	Section 166A and 167
assured tenancy	section 230
district (of local housing authority)	section 166(5)
introductory tenancy and introductory tenant	section 230 and 124
local housing authority	section 230
registered social landlord	section 230 and 2
secure tenancy and secure tenant	section 230

PART 7: HOMELESSNESS: ENGLAND

Homelessness and threatened homelessness

175 Homelessness and threatened homelessness

(1) A person is homeless if he has no accommodation available for his occupation, in the United Kingdom or elsewhere, which he–

(a) is entitled to occupy by virtue of an interest in it or by virtue of an order of a court,

(b) has an express or implied licence to occupy, or

(c) occupies as a residence by virtue of any enactment or rule of law giving him the right to remain in occupation or restricting the right of another person to recover possession.

(2) A person is also homeless if he has accommodation but–
(a) he cannot secure entry to it, or
(b) it consists of a moveable structure, vehicle or vessel designed or adapted for human habitation and there is no place where he is entitled or permitted both to place it and to reside in it.
(3) A person shall not be treated as having accommodation unless it is accommodation which it would be reasonable for him to continue to occupy.
(4) A person is threatened with homelessness if it is likely that he will become homeless within [28] *56*[2] days.
(5) A person is also threatened with homelessness if–
(a) a valid notice has been given to the person under section 21 of the Housing Act 1988 (orders for possession on expiry or termination of assured shorthold tenancy) in respect of the only accommodation the person has that is available for the person's occupation, and
(b) that notice will expire within 56 days.[3]

176 Meaning of accommodation available for occupation

Accommodation shall be regarded as available for a person's occupation only if it is available for occupation by him together with–
(a) any other person who normally resides with him as a member of his family, or
(b) any other person who might reasonably be expected to reside with him.
References in this Part to securing that accommodation is available for a person's occupation shall be construed accordingly.

177 Whether it is reasonable to continue to occupy accommodation

(1) It is not reasonable for a person to continue to occupy accommodation if it is probable that this will lead to domestic violence or other violence against him, or against–
(a) a person who normally resides with him as a member of his family, or
(b) any other person who might reasonably be expected to reside with him.
(1A) For this purpose 'violence' means–
(a) violence from another person; or
(b) threats of violence from another person which are likely to be carried out;
and violence is 'domestic violence' if it is from a person who is associated with the victim.
(2) In determining whether it would be, or would have been, reasonable for a person to continue to occupy accommodation, regard may be had to the general circumstances prevailing in relation to housing in the district of the local housing authority to whom he has applied for accommodation or for assistance in obtaining accommodation.
(3) The Secretary of State may by order specify–
(a) other circumstances in which it is to be regarded as reasonable or not reasonable for a person to continue to occupy accommodation, and

2 Reference to '28' repealed and '56' substituted by Homelessness Reduction Act 2017 s1(1), (2). Not yet in force: see Homelessness Reduction Act 2017 s13(3).

3 Inserted by Homelessness Reduction Act 201 s1(1), (3). Not yet in force: see Homelessness Reduction Act 2017 s13(3).

(b) other matters to be taken into account or disregarded in determining whether it would be, or would have been, reasonable for a person to continue to occupy accommodation.

178 Meaning of associated person

(1) For the purposes of this Part, a person is associated with another person if–

(a) they are or have been married to each other;

(aa) they are or have been civil partners of each other;

(b) they are cohabitants or former cohabitants;

(c) they live or have lived in the same household;

(d) they are relatives;

(e) they have agreed to marry one another (whether or not that agreement has been terminated);

(ea) they have entered into a civil partnership agreement between them (whether or not that agreement has been terminated);

(f) in relation to a child, each of them is a parent of the child or has, or has had, parental responsibility for the child.

(2) If a child has been adopted or falls within subsection (2A), two persons are also associated with each other for the purposes of this Part if–

(a) one is a natural parent of the child or a parent of such a natural parent, and

(b) the other is the child or a person–

(i) who has become a parent of the child by virtue of an adoption order or who has applied for an adoption order, or

(ii) with whom the child has at any time been placed for adoption.

(2A) A child falls within this subsection if–

(a) an adoption agency, within the meaning of section 2 of the Adoption and Children Act 2002, is authorised to place him for adoption under section 19 of that Act (placing children with parental consent) or he has become the subject of an order under section 21 of that Act (placement orders), or

(b) he is freed for adoption by virtue of an order made–

(i) in England and Wales, under section 18 of the Adoption Act 1976,

(ii) in Scotland, under section 18 of the Adoption (Scotland) Act 1978, or

(iii) in Northern Ireland, under Article 17(1) or 18(1) of the Adoption (Northern Ireland) Order 1987.

(3) In this section–

'adoption order' means an adoption order within the meaning of section 72(1) of the Adoption Act 1976 or section 46(1) of the Adoption and Children Act 2002;

'child' means a person under the age of 18 years;

'civil partnership agreement' has the meaning given by section 73 of the Civil Partnership Act 2004;

'cohabitants' means–

(a) a man and a woman who, although not married to each other, are living together as husband and wife, or

(b) two people of the same sex who, although not civil partners of each other, are living together as if they were civil partners;

and 'former cohabitants' shall be construed accordingly;

'parental responsibility' has the same meaning as in the Children Act 1989; and

'relative', in relation to a person, means–

(a) the father, mother, stepfather, stepmother, son, daughter, stepson, stepdaughter, grandmother, grandfather, grandson or granddaughter of that person or of that person's spouse, civil partner, former spouse or former civil partner, or

(b) the brother, sister, uncle, aunt, niece or nephew (whether of the full blood or of the half blood or by marriage or civil partnership) of that person or of that person's spouse, civil partner, former spouse or former civil partner,

and includes, in relation to a person who is living or has lived with another person as husband and wife, a person who would fall within paragraph (a) or (b) if the parties were married to each other.

General functions in relation to homelessness or threatened homelessness

179 Duty of local housing authority to provide advisory services[4]

[(1) Every local housing authority in England shall secure that advice and information about homelessness, and the prevention of homelessness, is available free of charge to any person in their district.

(2) The authority may give to any person by whom such advice and information is provided on behalf of the authority assistance by way of grant or loan.

(3) A local housing authority may also assist any such person–

(a) by permitting him to use premises belonging to the authority,

(b) by making available furniture or other goods, whether by way of gift, loan or otherwise, and

(c) by making available the services of staff employed by the authority.]

(1) Each local housing authority in England must provide or secure the provision of a service, available free of charge to any person in the authority's district, providing information and advice on–

(a) preventing homelessness,

(b) securing accommodation when homeless,

(c) the rights of persons who are homeless or threatened with homelessness, and the duties of the authority, under this Part,

(d) any help that is available from the authority or anyone else, whether under this Part or otherwise, for persons in the authority's district who are homeless or may become homeless (whether or not they are threatened with homelessness), and

(e) how to access that help.

(2) The service must be designed to meet the needs of persons in the authority's district including, in particular, the needs of–

(a) persons released from prison or youth detention accommodation,

(b) care leavers,

(c) former members of the regular armed forces,

4 Subsections (1)-(3) in square brackets repealed and subsections (1)-(5) in italics substituted by Homelessness Reduction Act 2017 s2. Not yet in force: see Homelessness Reduction Act 2017 s13(3).

(d) victims of domestic abuse,
(e) persons leaving hospital,
(f) persons suffering from a mental illness or impairment, and
(g) any other group that the authority identify as being at particular risk of homelessness in the authority's district.

(3) The authority may give to any person by whom the service is provided on behalf of the authority assistance by way of grant or loan.

(4) The authority may also assist any such person–
(a) by permitting the person to use premises belonging to the authority,
(b) by making available furniture or other goods, whether by way of gift, loan or otherwise, and
(c) by making available the services of staff employed by the authority.

(5) In this section–
'care leavers' means persons who are former relevant children (within the meaning given by section 23C(1) of the Children Act 1989);
'domestic abuse' means–
(a) physical violence,
(b) threatening, intimidating, coercive or controlling behaviour, or
(c) emotional, financial, sexual or any other form of abuse,
where the victim is associated with the abuser;
'financial abuse' includes–
(a) having money or other property stolen,
(b) being defrauded,
(c) being put under pressure in relation to money or other property, and
(d) having money or other property misused;
'hospital' has the same meaning as in the National Health Service Act 2006 (see section 275(1) of that Act);
'regular armed forces' means the regular forces as defined by section 374 of the Armed Forces Act 2006;
'youth detention accommodation' means–
(a) a secure children's home,
(b) a secure training centre,
(c) a secure college,
(d) a young offender institution,
(e) accommodation provided by or on behalf of a local authority for the purpose of restricting the liberty of children;
(f) accommodation provided for that purpose under section 82(5) of the Children Act 1989, or
(g) accommodation, or accommodation of a description, for the time being specified by order under section 107(1)(e) of the Powers of Criminal Courts (Sentencing) Act 2000 (youth detention accommodation for the purposes of detention and training orders).

180 Assistance for voluntary organisations

(1) The Secretary of State or a local housing authority in England may give assistance by way of grant or loan to voluntary organisations concerned with homelessness or matters relating to homelessness.

(2) A local housing authority may also assist any such organisation–
(a) by permitting them to use premises belonging to the authority,

(b) by making available furniture or other goods, whether by way of gift, loan or otherwise, and
(c) by making available the services of staff employed by the authority.

(3) A 'voluntary organisation' means a body (other than a public or local authority) whose activities are not carried on for profit.

181 Terms and conditions of assistance

(1) This section has effect as to the terms and conditions on which assistance is given under section 179 or 180.

(2) Assistance shall be on such terms, and subject to such conditions, as the person giving the assistance may determine.

(3) No assistance shall be given unless the person to whom it is given undertakes–

(a) to use the money, furniture or other goods or premises for a specified purpose, and
(b) to provide such information as may reasonably be required as to the manner in which the assistance is being used.

The person giving the assistance may require such information by notice in writing, which shall be complied with within 21 days beginning with the date on which the notice is served.

(4) The conditions subject to which assistance is given shall in all cases include conditions requiring the person to whom the assistance is given–

(a) to keep proper books of account and have them audited in such manner as may be specified,
(b) to keep records indicating how he has used the money, furniture or other goods or premises, and
(c) to submit the books of account and records for inspection by the person giving the assistance.

(5) If it appears to the person giving the assistance that the person to whom it was given has failed to carry out his undertaking as to the purpose for which the assistance was to be used, he shall take all reasonable steps to recover from that person an amount equal to the amount of the assistance.

(6) He must first serve on the person to whom the assistance was given a notice specifying the amount which in his opinion is recoverable and the basis on which that amount has been calculated.

182 Guidance by the Secretary of State

(1) In the exercise of their functions relating to homelessness and the prevention of homelessness, a local housing authority or social services authority in England shall have regard to such guidance as may from time to time be given by the Secretary of State.

(2) The Secretary of State may give guidance either generally or to specified descriptions of authorities.

Application for assistance in case of homelessness or threatened homelessness

183 Application for assistance

(1) The following provisions of this Part apply where a person applies to a local housing authority in England for accommodation, or for assistance in

obtaining accommodation, and the authority have reason to believe that he is or may be homeless or threatened with homelessness.

(2) In this Part–

'applicant' means a person making such an application,

'assistance under this Part' means the benefit of any function under the following provisions of this Part relating to accommodation or assistance in obtaining accommodation, and

'eligible for assistance' means not excluded from such assistance by section 185 (persons from abroad not eligible for housing assistance) [or section 186 (asylum seekers and their dependants)].[5]

(3) Nothing in this section or the following provisions of this Part affects a person's entitlement to advice and information under section 179 (duty to provide advisory services).

184 Inquiry into cases of homelessness or threatened homelessness

(1) If the local housing authority have reason to believe that an applicant may be homeless or threatened with homelessness, they shall make such inquiries as are necessary to satisfy themselves–

(a) whether he is eligible for assistance, and

(b) if so, whether any duty, and if so what duty, is owed to him under the following provisions of this Part.

(2) They may also make inquiries whether he has a local connection with the district of another local housing authority in England, Wales or Scotland.

(3) On completing their inquiries the authority shall notify the applicant of their decision and, so far as any issue is decided against his interests, inform him of the reasons for their decision.

(3A)[6] If the authority decide that a duty is, *or after the authority's duty to the applicant under section 189B(2) comes to an end would be,*[7] owed to the applicant under section 193(2) [or 195(2)][8] but would not have done so without having had regard to a restricted person, the notice under subsection (3) must also–

(a) inform the applicant that their decision was reached on that basis,

(b) include the name of the restricted person,

(c) explain why the person is a restricted person, and

(d) explain the effect of section 193(7AD) [or (as the case may be) section 195(4A)].[9]

(4) If the authority have notified or intend to notify another local housing authority

5 Words 'or section 186 (asylum seekers and their dependants)' in square brackets repealed by Immigration and Asylum Act 1999 s169(1), (3), Sch 14, para 116, Sch 16. Not yet in force: see Immigration and Asylum Act 1999 s170(4).

6 Subs (3A) in force except in relation to applications for an allocation of social housing or housing assistance (homelessness) or for accommodation made before that date): see SI 2009/415 art 2.

7 Word in italics inserted by Homelessness Reduction Act 2017 s5(1), (3)(a). Not yet in force: see Homelessness Reduction Act 2017 s13(3).

8 Words 'or 195(2)' in square brackets repealed by Homelessness Reduction Act 2017 s 4(1), (3)(a). Not yet in force: see Homelessness Reduction Act 2017 s13(3).

9 Words 'or (as the case may be) section 195(4A)' in square brackets repealed by Homelessness Reduction Act 2017 s4(1), (3)(b). Not yet in force: see Homelessness Reduction Act 2017 s13(3).

[under section 198 (referral of cases)] *in England under section 198(A1) (referral of cases where section 189B applies),*[10] they shall at the same time notify the applicant of that decision and inform him of the reasons for it.

(5) A notice under subsection (3) or (4) shall also inform the applicant of his right to request a review of the decision and of the time within which such a request must be made (see section 202).

(6) Notice required to be given to a person under this section shall be given in writing and, if not received by him, shall be treated as having been given to him if it is made available at the authority's office for a reasonable period for collection by him or on his behalf.

(7) In this Part 'a restricted person' means a person–
- (a) who is not eligible for assistance under this Part,
- (b) who is subject to immigration control within the meaning of the Asylum and Immigration Act 1996, and
- (c) either–
  - (i) who does not have leave to enter or remain in the United Kingdom, or
  - (ii) whose leave to enter or remain in the United Kingdom is subject to a condition to maintain and accommodate himself, and any dependants, without recourse to public funds.

Eligibility for assistance

185 Persons from abroad not eligible for housing assistance

(1) A person is not eligible for assistance under this Part if he is a person from abroad who is ineligible for housing assistance.

(2) A person who is subject to immigration control within the meaning of the Asylum and Immigration Act 1996 is not eligible for housing assistance unless he is of a class prescribed by regulations made by the Secretary of State.

(2A) No person who is excluded from entitlement to universal credit or housing benefit by section 115 of the Immigration and Asylum Act 1999 (exclusion from benefits) shall be included in any class prescribed under subsection (2).

(3) The Secretary of State may make provision by regulations as to other descriptions of persons who are to be treated for the purposes of this Part as persons from abroad who are ineligible for housing assistance.

(4) A person from abroad who is not eligible for housing assistance shall be disregarded in determining for the purposes of this Part whether a person falling within subsection (5)–
- (a) is homeless or threatened with homelessness, or
- (b) has a priority need for accommodation.

(5) A person falls within this subsection if the person–
- (a) falls within a class prescribed by regulations made under subsection (2); but
- (b) is not a national of an EEA State or Switzerland.

10 Words 'under section 198 (referral of cases)' in square brackets repealed and subsequent words in italics substituted by Homelessness Reduction Act 2017 s5(1), (3)(b). Not yet in force: see Homelessness Reduction Act 2017 s13(3).

[186 Asylum-seekers and their dependants]

[(1) An asylum-seeker, or a dependant of an asylum-seeker who is not by virtue of section 185 a person from abroad who is ineligible for housing assistance, is not eligible for assistance under this Part if he has any accommodation in the United Kingdom, however temporary, available for his occupation.

(2) For the purposes of this section a person who makes a claim for asylum–

(a) becomes an asylum-seeker at the time when his claim is recorded by the Secretary of State as having been made, and

(b) ceases to be an asylum-seeker at the time when his claim is recorded by the Secretary of State as having been finally determined or abandoned.

(3) For the purposes of this section a person–

(a) becomes a dependant of an asylum-seeker at the time when he is recorded by the Secretary of State as being a dependant of the asylum-seeker, and

(b) ceases to be a dependant of an asylum-seeker at the time when the person whose dependant he is ceases to be an asylum-seeker or, if it is earlier, at the time when he is recorded by the Secretary of State as ceasing to be a dependant of the asylum-seeker.

(4) In relation to an asylum-seeker, 'dependant' means a person–

(a) who is his spouse or a child of his under the age of eighteen, and

(b) who has neither a right of abode in the United Kingdom nor indefinite leave under the Immigration Act 1971 to enter or remain in the United Kingdom.

(5) In this section a 'claim for asylum' means a claim made by a person that it would be contrary to the United Kingdom's obligations under the Convention relating to the Status of Refugees done at Geneva on 28 July 1951 and the Protocol to that Convention for him to be removed from, or required to leave, the United Kingdom.][11]

187 Provision of information by Secretary of State

(1) The Secretary of State shall, at the request of a local housing authority in England, provide the authority with such information as they may require–

(a) as to whether a person is a person to whom section 115 of the Immigration and Asylum Act 1999 (exclusion from benefits) applies, and

(b) to enable them to determine whether such a person is eligible for assistance under this Part under section 185 (persons from abroad not eligible for housing assistance).

(2) Where that information is given otherwise than in writing, the Secretary of State shall confirm it in writing if a written request is made to him by the authority.

(3) If it appears to the Secretary of State that any application, decision or other change of circumstances has affected the status of a person about whom information was previously provided by him to a local housing authority under this section, he shall inform the authority in writing of that fact, the reason for it and the date on which the previous information became inaccurate.

11 Section 186 repealed by the Immigration and Asylum Act 1999 ss117(5), 169(3), Sch 16. Not yet in force: see Immigration and Asylum Act 1999 s170(4).

Interim duty to accommodate

188 Interim duty to accommodate in case of apparent priority need

[(1) If the local housing authority have reason to believe that an applicant may be homeless, eligible for assistance and have a priority need, they shall secure that accommodation is available for his occupation pending a decision as to the duty (if any) owed to him under the following provisions of this Part.][12]

(1) If the local housing authority have reason to believe that an applicant may be homeless, eligible for assistance and have a priority need, they must secure that accommodation is available for the applicant's occupation.

(1ZA) In a case in which the local housing authority conclude their inquiries under section 184 and decide that the applicant does not have a priority need–

(a) where the authority decide that they do not owe the applicant a duty under section 189B(2), the duty under subsection (1) comes to an end when the authority notify the applicant of that decision, or

(b) otherwise, the duty under subsection (1) comes to an end upon the authority notifying the applicant of their decision that, upon the duty under section 189B(2) coming to an end, they do not owe the applicant any duty under section 190 or 193.

(1ZB) In any other case, the duty under subsection (1) comes to an end upon the later of–

(a) the duty owed to the applicant under section 189B(2) coming to an end or the authority notifying the applicant that they have decided that they do not owe the applicant a duty under that section, and

(b) the authority notifying the applicant of their decision as to what other duty (if any) they owe to the applicant under the following provisions of this Part upon the duty under section 189B(2) coming to an end.

(1A) But if the local housing authority have reason to believe that the duty under section 193(2) may apply in relation to an applicant in the circumstances referred to in section 195A(1), they shall secure that accommodation is available for the applicant's occupation [pending a decision of the kind referred to in subsection (1)] *until the later of paragraph (a) or (b) of subsection (1ZB)* regardless of whether the applicant has a priority need.[13]

(2) The duty under this section arises irrespective of any possibility of the referral of the applicant's case to another local housing authority (see sections 198 to 200).

[(3) The duty ceases when the authority's decision is notified to the applicant, even if the applicant requests a review of the decision (see section 202). The authority may secure that accommodation is available for the applicant's occupation pending a decision on a review.][14]

12 Subs (1) substituted, by subsequent subss (1), (1ZA), (1ZB) in italics by Homelessness Reduction Act 2017 s5(1), (4)(a). Not yet in force: see the Homelessness Reduction Act 2017 s13(3).

13 Subs (1A) not in force in relation to Wales. Words 'pending a decision of the kind referred to in subsection (1)' in square brackets repealed and subsequent words in italics substituted by Homelessness Reduction Act 2017 s5(1), (4)(b). Not yet in force: see Homelessness Reduction Act 2017 s13(3).

14 Subs (3) substituted, by subsequent subss (2A), (3), by Homelessness Reduction Act 2017 s5(1), (4)(c). Not yet in force: see the Homelessness Reduction Act 2017 s13(3).

(2A) For the purposes of this section, where the applicant requests a review under section 202(1)(h) of the authority's decision as to the suitability of accommodation offered to the applicant by way of a final accommodation offer or a final Part 6 offer (within the meaning of section 193A), the authority's duty to the applicant under section 189B(2) is not to be taken to have come to an end under section 193A(2) until the decision on the review has been notified to the applicant.

(3) Otherwise, the duty under this section comes to an end in accordance with subsections (1ZA) to (1A), regardless of any review requested by the applicant under section 202.

But the authority may secure that accommodation is available for the applicant's occupation pending a decision on review.

189 Priority need for accommodation

(1) The following have a priority need for accommodation–

(a) a pregnant woman or a person with whom she resides or might reasonably be expected to reside;

(b) a person with whom dependent children reside or might reasonably be expected to reside;

(c) a person who is vulnerable as a result of old age, mental illness or handicap or physical disability or other special reason, or with whom such a person resides or might reasonably be expected to reside;

(d) a person who is homeless or threatened with homelessness as a result of an emergency such as flood, fire or other disaster.

(2) The Secretary of State may by order–

(a) specify further descriptions of persons as having a priority need for accommodation, and

(b) amend or repeal any part of subsection (1).

(3) Before making such an order the Secretary of State shall consult such associations representing relevant authorities, and such other persons, as he considers appropriate.

(4) No such order shall be made unless a draft of it has been approved by resolution of each House of Parliament.

Duty to assess every eligible applicant's case and agree a plan[15]

189A Assessments and personalised plan

(1) If the local housing authority are satisfied that an applicant is–

(a) homeless or threatened with homelessness, and

(b) eligible for assistance,

the authority must make an assessment of the applicant's case.

(2) The authority's assessment of the applicant's case must include an assessment of–

(a) the circumstances that caused the applicant to become homeless or threatened with homelessness,

(b) the housing needs of the applicant including, in particular, what accommodation would be suitable for the applicant and any persons with whom the applicant resides or might reasonably be expected to reside ('other relevant persons'), and

15 Inserted by Homelessness Reduction Act 2017 s3(1). Not yet in force: see Homelessness Reduction Act 2017 s13(3).

(c) what support would be necessary for the applicant and any other relevant persons to be able to have and retain suitable accommodation.

(3) The authority must notify the applicant, in writing, of the assessment that the authority make.

(4) After the assessment has been made, the authority must try to agree with the applicant–

(a) any steps the applicant is to be required to take for the purposes of securing that the applicant and any other relevant persons have and are able to retain suitable accommodation, and

(b) the steps the authority are to take under this Part for those purposes.

(5) If the authority and the applicant reach an agreement, the authority must record it in writing.

(6) If the authority and the applicant cannot reach an agreement, the authority must record in writing–

(a) why they could not agree,

(b) any steps the authority consider it would be reasonable to require the applicant to take for the purposes mentioned in subsection (4)(a), and

(c) the steps the authority are to take under this Part for those purposes.

(7) The authority may include in a written record produced under subsection (5) or (6) any advice for the applicant that the authority consider appropriate (including any steps the authority consider it would be a good idea for the applicant to take but which the applicant should not be required to take).

(8) The authority must give to the applicant a copy of any written record produced under subsection (5) or (6).

(9) Until such time as the authority consider that they owe the applicant no duty under any of the following sections of this Part, the authority must keep under review–

(a) their assessment of the applicant's case, and

(b) the appropriateness of any agreement reached under subsection (4) or steps recorded under subsection (6)(b) or (c).

(10) If–

(a) the authority's assessment of any of the matters mentioned in subsection (2) changes, or

(b) the authority's assessment of the applicant's case otherwise changes such that the authority consider it appropriate to do so,

the authority must notify the applicant, in writing, of how their assessment of the applicant's case has changed (whether by providing the applicant with a revised written assessment or otherwise).

(11) If the authority consider that any agreement reached under subsection (4) or any step recorded under subsection (6)(b) or (c) is no longer appropriate–

(a) the authority must notify the applicant, in writing, that they consider the agreement or step is no longer appropriate,

(b) any failure, after the notification is given, to take a step that was agreed to in the agreement or recorded under subsection (6)(b) or (c) is to be disregarded for the purposes of this Part, and

(c) subsections (4) to (8) apply as they applied after the assessment was made.

(12) A notification under this section or a copy of any written record produced under subsection (5) or (6), if not received by the applicant, is to be treated as having been

given to the applicant if it is made available at the authority's office for a reasonable period for collection by or on behalf of the applicant.[16]

Duties to persons found to be homeless or threatened with homelessness

189B Initial duty owed to all eligible persons who are homeless

(1) This section applies where the local housing authority are satisfied that an applicant is–
(a) homeless, and
(b) eligible for assistance.

(2) Unless the authority refer the application to another local housing authority in England (see section 198(A1)), the authority must take reasonable steps to help the applicant to secure that suitable accommodation becomes available for the applicant's occupation for at least–
(a) 6 months, or
(b) such longer period not exceeding 12 months as may be prescribed.

(3) In deciding what steps they are to take, the authority must have regard to their assessment of the applicant's case under section 189A.

(4) Where the authority–
(a) are satisfied that the applicant has a priority need, and
(b) are not satisfied that the applicant became homeless intentionally,
the duty under subsection (2) comes to an end at the end of the period of 56 days beginning with the day the authority are first satisfied as mentioned in subsection (1).

(5) If any of the circumstances mentioned in subsection (7) apply, the authority may give notice to the applicant bringing the duty under subsection (2) to an end.

(6) The notice must–
(a) specify which of the circumstances apply, and
(b) inform the applicant that the applicant has a right to request a review of the authority's decision to bring the duty under subsection (2) to an end and of the time within which such a request must be made.

(7) The circumstances are that the authority are satisfied that–
(a) the applicant has–
(i) suitable accommodation available for occupation, and
(ii) a reasonable prospect of having suitable accommodation available for occupation for at least 6 months, or such longer period not exceeding 12 months as may be prescribed, from the date of the notice,
(b) the authority have complied with the duty under subsection (2) and the period of 56 days beginning with the day that the authority are first satisfied as mentioned in subsection (1) has ended (whether or not the applicant has secured accommodation),
(c) the applicant has refused an offer of suitable accommodation and, on the date of refusal, there was a reasonable prospect that suitable accommodation would be available for occupation by the applicant for at least 6 months or such longer period not exceeding 12 months as may be prescribed,

16 Inserted by the Homelessness Reduction Act 2017 s3(1). Not yet in force: see Homelessness Reduction Act 2017 s13(3).

(d) the applicant has become homeless intentionally from any accommodation that has been made available to the applicant as a result of the authority's exercise of their functions under subsection (2),

(e) the applicant is no longer eligible for assistance, or

(f) the applicant has withdrawn the application mentioned in section 183(1).

(8) A notice under this section must be given in writing and, if not received by the applicant, is to be treated as having been given to the applicant if it is made available at the authority's office for a reasonable period for collection by or on behalf of the applicant.

(9) The duty under subsection (2) can also be brought to an end under–

(a) section 193A (consequences of refusal of final accommodation offer or final Part 6 offer at the initial relief stage), or

(b) sections 193B and 193C (notices in cases of applicant's deliberate and unreasonable refusal to co-operate).[17]

190 Duties to persons becoming homeless intentionally

[(1) This section applies where the local housing authority are satisfied that an applicant is homeless and is eligible for assistance but are also satisfied that he became homeless intentionally.][18]

(1) This section applies where–

(a) the local housing authority are satisfied that an applicant–

(i) is homeless and eligible for assistance, but

(ii) became homeless intentionally,

(b) the authority are also satisfied that the applicant has a priority need, and

(c) the authority's duty to the applicant under section 189B(2) has come to an end.

(2) [If the authority are satisfied that the applicant has a priority need, they shall–] *The authority must–*[19]

(a) secure that accommodation is available for his occupation for such period as they consider will give him a reasonable opportunity of securing accommodation for his occupation, and

(b) provide him with (or secure that he is provided with) advice and assistance in any attempts he may make to secure that accommodation becomes available for his occupation.

[(3) If they are not satisfied that he has a priority need, they shall provide him with (or secure that he is provided with) advice and assistance in any attempts he may make to secure that accommodation becomes available for his occupation.][20]

17 Section 189B inserted by Homelessness Reduction Act 2017 s5(1), (2). Not yet in force: see Homelessness Reduction Act 2017 s13(3).

18 Subs (1) in square brackets substituted by words in italics by Homelessness Reduction Act 2017 s5(1), (5)(a). Not yet in force: to be appointed: see Homelessness Reduction Act 2017 s13(3).

19 Words from 'If the authority' to 'need, they shall–' in square brackets repealed and subsequent words in italics substituted by Homelessness Reduction Act 2017 s5(1), (5)(b). Not yet in force: see Homelessness Reduction Act 2017 s13(3).

20 Repealed by Homelessness Reduction Act 2017 s 5(1), (5)(c). Not yet in force: see Homelessness Reduction Act 2017 s13(3).

[(4) The applicant's housing needs shall be assessed before advice and assistance is provided under subsection (2)(b) or (3).][21]

(4) In deciding what advice and assistance is to be provided under this section, the authority must have regard to their assessment of the applicant's case under section 189A.

(5) The advice and assistance provided under subsection (2)(b) [or (3)] must include information about the likely availability in the authority's district of types of accommodation appropriate to the applicant's housing needs (including, in particular, the location and sources of such types of accommodation).[22]

191 Becoming homeless intentionally

(1) A person becomes homeless intentionally if he deliberately does or fails to do anything in consequence of which he ceases to occupy accommodation which is available for his occupation and which it would have been reasonable for him to continue to occupy.

(2) For the purposes of subsection (1) an act or omission in good faith on the part of a person who was unaware of any relevant fact shall not be treated as deliberate.

(3) A person shall be treated as becoming homeless intentionally if–

(a) he enters into an arrangement under which he is required to cease to occupy accommodation which it would have been reasonable for him to continue to occupy, and

(b) the purpose of the arrangement is to enable him to become entitled to assistance under this Part,

and there is no other good reason why he is homeless.

(4) [Repealed.]

[192 Duty to persons not in priority need who are not homeless intentionally

(1) This section applies where the local housing authority–

(a) are satisfied that an applicant is homeless and eligible for assistance, and

(b) are not satisfied that he became homeless intentionally,

but are not satisfied that he has a priority need.

(2) The authority shall provide the applicant with (or secure that he is provided with) advice and assistance in any attempts he may make to secure that accommodation becomes available for his occupation.

(3) The authority may secure that accommodation is available for occupation by the applicant.

(4) The applicant's housing needs shall be assessed before advice and assistance is provided under subsection (2).

(5) The advice and assistance provided under subsection (2) must include information about the likely availability in the authority's district of types of

21 Subs (4) in square brackets substituted by words in italics by Homelessness Reduction Act 2017 s3(2). Not yet in force: see Homelessness Reduction Act 2017 s13(3).

22 Words 'or (3)' in square brackets repealed by Homelessness Reduction Act 2017 s5(1), (5)(d). Not yet in force: see Homelessness Reduction Act 2017 s13(3).

accommodation appropriate to the applicant's housing needs (including, in particular, the location and sources of such types of accommodation).][23]

193 Duty to persons with priority need who are not homeless intentionally[24]

[(1) This section applies where the local housing authority are satisfied that an applicant is homeless, eligible for assistance and has a priority need, and are not satisfied that he became homeless intentionally.][25]

(1) This section applies where–

(a) the local housing authority–

(i) are satisfied that an applicant is homeless and eligible for assistance, and

(ii) are not satisfied that the applicant became homeless intentionally,

(b) the authority are also satisfied that the applicant has a priority need, and

(c) the authority's duty to the applicant under section 189B(2) has come to an end.

(1A) But this section does not apply if–

(a) section 193A(3) disapplies this section, or

(b) the authority have given notice to the applicant under section 193B(2).

(2) Unless the authority refer the application to another local housing authority (see section 198), they shall secure that accommodation is available for occupation by the applicant.

(3) The authority are subject to the duty under this section until it ceases by virtue of any of the following provisions of this section.

(3A) The authority shall, on becoming subject to the duty under this section in a case which is not a restricted case, give the applicant a copy of the statement included in their allocation scheme by virtue of section 167(1A) (policy on offering choice to people allocated housing accommodation under Part 6).

(3B) In this section 'a restricted case' means a case where the local housing authority would not be satisfied as mentioned in subsection (1) without having had regard to a restricted person.

(5) The local housing authority shall cease to be subject to the duty under this section if–

(a) the applicant, having been informed by the authority of the possible consequence of refusal or acceptance and of the right to request a review of the suitability of the accommodation, refuses an offer of accommodation which the authority are satisfied is suitable for the applicant,

(b) that offer of accommodation is not an offer of accommodation under Part 6 or a private rented sector offer, and

(c) the authority notify the applicant that they regard themselves as ceasing to be subject to the duty under this section.

(6) The local housing authority shall cease to be subject to the duty under this section if the applicant–

(a) ceases to be eligible for assistance,

23 Repealed by Homelessness Reduction Act 2017 s 5(1), (6). Not yet in force: see Homelessness Reduction Act 2017 s13(3).

24 Reproduced as relates to England only.

25 Subs (1) words in square brackets substituted by subsequent (1) and (1A) in italics by Homelessness Reduction Act 2017 s 5(1), (7). Not yet in force: see Homelessness Reduction Act 2017 s13(3).

(b) becomes homeless intentionally from the accommodation made available for his occupation,
(c) accepts an offer of accommodation under Part VI (allocation of housing), or
(cc) accepts an offer of an assured tenancy (other than an assured shorthold tenancy) from a private landlord,
(d) otherwise voluntarily ceases to occupy as his only or principal home the accommodation made available for his occupation.

(7) The local housing authority shall also cease to be subject to the duty under this section if the applicant, having been informed of the possible consequence of refusal or acceptance and of his right to request a review of the suitability of the accommodation, refuses a final offer of accommodation under Part 6.

(7A) An offer of accommodation under Part 6 is a final offer for the purposes of subsection (7) if it is made in writing and states that it is a final offer for the purposes of subsection (7).

(7AA) In a restricted case the authority shall also cease to be subject to the duty under this section if the applicant, having been informed in writing of the matters mentioned in subsection (7AB)–
(a) accepts a private rented sector offer, or
(b) refuses such an offer.

(7AB) The matters are–
(a) the possible consequence of refusal or acceptance of the offer, and
(b) that the applicant has the right to request a review of the suitability of the accommodation, and
(c) in a case which is not a restricted case, the effect under section 195A of a further application to a local housing authority within two years of acceptance of the offer.

(7AC) For the purposes of this section an offer is a private rented sector offer if–
(a) it is an offer of an assured shorthold tenancy made by a private landlord to the applicant in relation to any accommodation which is, or may become, available for the applicant's occupation,
(b) it is made, with the approval of the authority, in pursuance of arrangements made by the authority with the landlord with a view to bringing the authority's duty under this section to an end, and
(c) the tenancy being offered is a fixed term tenancy (within the meaning of Part 1 of the Housing Act 1988) for a period of at least 12 months.

(7AD) In a restricted case the authority shall, so far as reasonably practicable, bring their duty under this section to an end as mentioned in subsection (7AA).

(7B) In a case which is not a restricted case, the authority shall also cease to be subject to the duty under this section if the applicant accepts a qualifying offer of an assured shorthold tenancy which is made by a private landlord in relation to any accommodation which is, or may become, available for the applicant's occupation.

(7C) In a case which is not a restricted case, the applicant is free to reject a qualifying offer without affecting the duty owed to him under this section by the authority.

(7D) For the purposes of subsection (7B) an offer of an assured shorthold tenancy is a qualifying offer if–

(a) it is made, with the approval of the authority, in pursuance of arrangements made by the authority with the landlord with a view to bringing the authority's duty under this section to an end;
(b) the tenancy being offered is a fixed term tenancy (within the meaning of Part 1 of the Housing Act 1988 (c 50)); and
(c) it is accompanied by a statement in writing which states the term of the tenancy being offered and explains in ordinary language that–
(i) there is no obligation to accept the offer, but
(ii) if the offer is accepted the local housing authority will cease to be subject to the duty under this section in relation to the applicant.

(7E) An acceptance of a qualifying offer is only effective for the purposes of subsection (7B) if the applicant signs a statement acknowledging that he has understood the statement mentioned in subsection (7D).

(7F) The local housing authority shall not–
(a) make a final offer of accommodation under Part 6 for the purposes of subsection (7); or
(ab) approve a private rented sector offer; or
(b) approve an offer of an assured shorthold tenancy for the purposes of subsection (7B),
unless they are satisfied that the accommodation is suitable for the applicant and subsection (8) does not apply to the applicant.

(8) This subsection applies to an applicant if–
(a) the applicant is under contractual or other obligations in respect of the applicant's existing accommodation, and
(b) the applicant is not able to bring those obligations to an end before being required to take up the offer.

(9) A person who ceases to be owed the duty under this section may make a fresh application to the authority for accommodation or assistance in obtaining accommodation.

(10) The Secretary of State may provide by regulations that subsection (7AC)(c) is to have effect as if it referred to a period of the length specified in the regulations.

(11) Regulations under subsection (10)–
(a) may not specify a period of less than 12 months, and
(b) may not apply to restricted cases.

(12) [Repealed].

193A Consequences of refusal of final accommodation offer or final Part 6 offer at the initial relief stage

(1) Subsections (2) and (3) apply where–
(a) a local housing authority owe a duty to an applicant under section 189B(2), and
(b) the applicant, having been informed of the consequences of refusal and of the applicant's right to request a review of the suitability of the accommodation, refuses–
(i) a final accommodation offer, or
(ii) a final Part 6 offer.

(2) The authority's duty to the applicant under section 189B(2) comes to an end.

(3) Section 193 (the main housing duty) does not apply.

(4) An offer is a 'final accommodation offer' if–

(a) it is an offer of an assured shorthold tenancy made by a private landlord to the applicant in relation to any accommodation which is, or may become, available for the applicant's occupation,

(b) it is made, with the approval of the authority, in pursuance of arrangements made by the authority in the discharge of their duty under section 189B(2), and

(c) the tenancy being offered is a fixed term tenancy (within the meaning of Part 1 of the Housing Act 1988) for a period of at least 6 months.

(5) A 'final Part 6 offer' is an offer of accommodation under Part 6 (allocation of housing) that–

(a) is made in writing by the authority in the discharge of their duty under section 189B(2), and

(b) states that it is a final offer for the purposes of this section.

(6) The authority may not approve a final accommodation offer, or make a final Part 6 offer, unless they are satisfied that the accommodation is suitable for the applicant and that subsection (7) does not apply.

(7) This subsection applies to an applicant if–

(a) the applicant is under contractual or other obligations in respect of the applicant's existing accommodation, and

(b) the applicant is not able to bring those obligations to an end before being required to take up the offer.[26]

193B Notices in cases of an applicant's deliberate and unreasonable refusal to co-operate

(1) Section 193C applies where–

(a) a local housing authority owe a duty to an applicant under section 189B(2) or 195(2), and

(b) the authority give notice to the applicant under subsection (2).

(2) A local housing authority may give a notice to an applicant under this subsection if the authority consider that the applicant has deliberately and unreasonably refused to take any step–

(a) that the applicant agreed to take under subsection (4) of section 189A, or

(b) that was recorded by the authority under subsection (6)(b) of that section.

(3) A notice under subsection (2) must–

(a) explain why the authority are giving the notice and its effect, and

(b) inform the applicant that the applicant has a right to request a review of the authority's decision to give the notice and of the time within which such a request must be made.

(4) The authority may not give notice to the applicant under subsection (2) unless–

(a) the authority have given a relevant warning to the applicant, and

(b) a reasonable period has elapsed since the warning was given.

(5) A 'relevant warning' means a notice–

(a) given by the authority to the applicant after the applicant has deliberately and unreasonably refused to take any step–

26 Sections 193A–193C inserted by Homelessness Reduction Act 2017 s7(1). Not yet in force: see the Homelessness Reduction Act 2017 s13(3).

(i) that the applicant agreed to take under subsection (4) of section 189A, or
(ii) that was recorded by the authority under subsection (6)(b) of that section,

(b) that warns the applicant that, if the applicant should deliberately and unreasonably refuse to take any such step after receiving the notice, the authority intend to give notice to the applicant under subsection (2), and

(c) that explains the consequences of such a notice being given to the applicant.

(6) For the purposes of subsections (2) and (5), in deciding whether a refusal by the applicant is unreasonable, the authority must have regard to the particular circumstances and needs of the applicant (whether identified in the authority's assessment of the applicant's case under section 189A or not).

(7) The Secretary of State may make provision by regulations as to the procedure to be followed by a local housing authority in connection with notices under this section.

(8) A notice under this section must be given in writing and, if not received by the applicant, is to be treated as having been given to the applicant if it is made available at the authority's office for a reasonable period for collection by or on behalf of the applicant.[27]

193C Notice under section 193B: consequences

(1) In the circumstances mentioned in section 193B(1), this section applies in relation to a local housing authority and an applicant.

(2) The authority's duty to the applicant under section 189B(2) or 195(2) comes to an end.

(3) Subsection (4) applies if the authority–

(a) are satisfied that the applicant is homeless, eligible for assistance and has a priority need, and

(b) are not satisfied that the applicant became homeless intentionally.

(4) Section 193 (the main housing duty) does not apply, but the authority must secure that accommodation is available for occupation by the applicant.

(5) The authority cease to be subject to the duty under subsection (4) if the applicant–

(a) ceases to be eligible for assistance,

(b) becomes homeless intentionally from accommodation made available for the applicant's occupation,

(c) accepts an offer of an assured tenancy from a private landlord, or

(d) otherwise voluntarily ceases to occupy, as the applicant's only or principal home, the accommodation made available for the applicant's occupation.

(6) The authority also cease to be subject to the duty under subsection (4) if the applicant, having been informed of the possible consequences of refusal or acceptance and of the applicant's right to request a review of the suitability of the accommodation, refuses or accepts–

(a) a final accommodation offer, or

(b) a final Part 6 offer.

(7) An offer is 'a final accommodation offer' if–

27 Inserted by Homelessness Reduction Act 2017 s7(1). Not yet in force: see Homelessness Reduction Act 2017 s13(3).

(a) it is an offer of an assured shorthold tenancy made by a private landlord to the applicant in relation to any accommodation which is, or may become, available for the applicant's occupation,

(b) it is made, with the approval of the authority, in pursuance of arrangements made by the authority with a view to bringing the authority's duty under subsection (4) to an end, and

(c) the tenancy being offered is a fixed term tenancy (within the meaning of Part 1 of the Housing Act 1988) for a period of at least 6 months.

(8) A 'final Part 6 offer' is an offer of accommodation under Part 6 (allocation of housing) that is made in writing and states that it is a final offer for the purposes of this section.

(9) The authority may not approve a final accommodation offer, or make a final Part 6 offer, unless they are satisfied that the accommodation is suitable for the applicant and that subsection (10) does not apply.

(10) This subsection applies to an applicant if–

(a) the applicant is under contractual or other obligations in respect of the applicant's existing accommodation, and

(b) the applicant is not able to bring those obligations to an end before being required to take up the offer.[28]

194 [Repealed.]

[195 Duties in case of threatened homelessness

(1) This section applies where the local housing authority are satisfied that an applicant is threatened with homelessness and is eligible for assistance.

(2) If the authority–

(a) are satisfied that he has a priority need, and

(b) are not satisfied that he became threatened with homelessness intentionally,

they shall take reasonable steps to secure that accommodation does not cease to be available for his occupation.

(3) Subsection (2) does not affect any right of the authority, whether by virtue of a contract, enactment or rule of law, to secure vacant possession of any accommodation.

(3A) The authority shall, on becoming subject to the duty under this section in a case which is not a restricted threatened homelessness case, give the applicant a copy of the statement included in their allocation scheme by virtue of section 167(1A) (policy on offering choice to people allocated housing accommodation under Part 6).

(4) Where , in a case which is not a restricted threatened homelessness case, in pursuance of the duty under subsection (2) the authority secure that accommodation other than that occupied by the applicant when he made his application is available for occupation by him, the provisions of section 193(3) to (9) (period for which duty owed) . . . apply, with any necessary modifications, in relation to the duty under this section as they apply in relation to the duty under section 193 in a case which is not a restricted case (within the meaning of that section).

28 Inserted by Homelessness Reduction Act 2017 s7(1). Not yet in force: see Homelessness Reduction Act 2017 s13(3).

(4A) Where, in a restricted threatened homelessness case, in pursuance of the duty under subsection (2) the authority secure that accommodation other than that occupied by the applicant when he made his application is available for occupation by him, the provisions of section 193(3) to (9) (period for which duty owed) apply, with any necessary modifications, in relation to the duty under this section as they apply in relation to the duty under section 193 in a restricted case (within the meaning of that section).

(4B) In subsections (3A) to (4) and (4A) 'a restricted threatened homelessness case' means a case where the local housing authority would not be satisfied as mentioned in subsection (1) without having had regard to a restricted person.

(5) If the authority–
  (a) are not satisfied that the applicant has a priority need, or
  (b) are satisfied that he has a priority need but are also satisfied that he became threatened with homelessness intentionally,

they shall provide him with (or secure that he is provided with) advice and assistance in any attempts he may make to secure that accommodation does not cease to be available for his occupation.

(6) The applicant's housing needs shall be assessed before advice and assistance is provided under subsection (5).

(7) The advice and assistance provided under subsection (5) must include information about the likely availability in the authority's district of types of accommodation appropriate to the applicant's housing needs (including, in particular, the location and sources of such types of accommodation).

(8) If the authority decide that they owe the applicant the duty under subsection (5) by virtue of paragraph (b) of that subsection, they may, pending a decision on a review of that decision–
  (a) secure that accommodation does not cease to be available for his occupation; and
  (b) if he becomes homeless, secure that accommodation is so available.

(9) If the authority–
  (a) are not satisfied that the applicant has a priority need; and
  (b) are not satisfied that he became threatened with homelessness intentionally,

the authority may take reasonable steps to secure that accommodation does not cease to be available for the applicant's occupation.][29]

(1) This section applies where the local housing authority are satisfied that an applicant is–
  (a) threatened with homelessness, and
  (b) eligible for assistance.

(2) The authority must take reasonable steps to help the applicant to secure that accommodation does not cease to be available for the applicant's occupation.

(3) In deciding what steps they are to take, the authority must have regard to their assessment of the applicant's case under section 189A.

29 Section 195 substituted by the subsequent words in italics by Homelessness Reduction Act 2017 s4(1), (2). Not yet in force: see Homelessness Reduction Act 2017 s13(3).

(4) Subsection (2) does not affect any right of the authority, whether by virtue of contract, enactment or rule of law, to secure vacant possession of any accommodation.

(5) If any of the circumstances mentioned in subsection (8) apply, the authority may give notice to the applicant bringing the duty under subsection (2) to an end.

(6) But the authority may not give notice to the applicant under subsection (5) on the basis that the circumstances in subsection (8)(b) apply if a valid notice has been given to the applicant under section 21 of the Housing Act 1988 (orders for possession on expiry or termination of assured shorthold tenancy) that–

(a) will expire within 56 days or has expired, and

(b) is in respect of the only accommodation that is available for the applicant's occupation.

(7) The notice must–

(a) specify which of the circumstances apply, and

(b) inform the applicant that the applicant has a right to request a review of the authority's decision to bring the duty under subsection (2) to an end and of the time within which such a request must be made.

(8) The circumstances are that the authority are satisfied that–

(a) the applicant has–

(i) suitable accommodation available for occupation, and

(ii) a reasonable prospect of having suitable accommodation available for occupation for at least 6 months, or such longer period not exceeding 12 months as may be prescribed, from the date of the notice,

(b) the authority have complied with the duty under subsection (2) and the period of 56 days beginning with the day that the authority are first satisfied as mentioned in subsection (1) has ended (whether or not the applicant is still threatened with homelessness),

(c) the applicant has become homeless,

(d) the applicant has refused an offer of suitable accommodation and, on the date of refusal, there was a reasonable prospect that suitable accommodation would be available for occupation by the applicant for at least 6 months or such longer period not exceeding 12 months as may be prescribed,

(e) the applicant has become homeless intentionally from any accommodation that has been made available to the applicant as a result of the authority's exercise of their functions under subsection (2),

(f) the applicant is no longer eligible for assistance, or

(g) the applicant has withdrawn the application mentioned in section 183(1).

(9) A notice under this section must be given in writing and, if not received by the applicant, is to be treated as having been given to the applicant if it is made available at the authority's office for a reasonable period for collection by or on behalf of the applicant.

(10) The duty under subsection (2) can also be brought to an end under sections 193B and 193C (notices in cases of applicant's deliberate and unreasonable refusal to co-operate).

195A Re-application after private rented sector offer[30]

(1) If within two years beginning with the date on which an applicant accepts an offer under section 193(7AA) (private rented sector offer), the applicant re-

30 Not in force in Wales.

applies for accommodation, or for assistance in obtaining accommodation, and the local housing authority–

(a) is satisfied that the applicant is homeless and eligible for assistance, and

(b) is not satisfied that the applicant became homeless intentionally,

the duty under section 193(2) applies regardless of whether the applicant has a priority need.

(2) For the purpose of subsection (1), an applicant in respect of whom a valid notice under section 21 of the Housing Act 1988 (orders for possession on expiry or termination of assured shorthold tenancy) has been given is to be treated as homeless from the date on which that notice expires.

[(3) If within two years beginning with the date on which an applicant accepts an offer under section 193(7AA), the applicant re-applies for accommodation, or for assistance in obtaining accommodation, and the local housing authority–

(a) is satisfied that the applicant is threatened with homelessness and eligible for assistance, and

(b) is not satisfied that the applicant became threatened with homelessness intentionally,

the duty under section 195(2) applies regardless of whether the applicant has a priority need.

(4) For the purpose of subsection (3), an applicant in respect of whom a valid notice under section 21 of the Housing Act 1988 has been given is to be treated as threatened with homelessness from the date on which that notice is given.][31]

(5) Subsection (1) [or (3)] does not apply to a case where the local housing authority would not be satisfied as mentioned in that subsection without having regard to a restricted person.

(6) Subsection (1) [or (3)] does not apply to a re-application by an applicant for accommodation, or for assistance in obtaining accommodation, if the immediately preceding application made by that applicant was one to which subsection (1) [or (3)] applied.[32]

[196 Becoming threatened with homelessness intentionally

(1) A person becomes threatened with homelessness intentionally if he deliberately does or fails to do anything the likely result of which is that he will be forced to leave accommodation which is available for his occupation and which it would have been reasonable for him to continue to occupy.

(2) For the purposes of subsection (1) an act or omission in good faith on the part of a person who was unaware of any relevant fact shall not be treated as deliberate.

(3) A person shall be treated as becoming threatened with homelessness intentionally if–

(a) he enters into an arrangement under which he is required to cease to

31 Subss (3), (4) repealed by Homelessness Reduction Act 2017 s4(1), (4)(a). Not yet in force: see Homelessness Reduction Act 2017 s13(3).

32 Words 'or (3)' in square brackets in subs (5), (6) repealed by Homelessness Reduction Act 2017 s4(1), (4)(b), (c). Not yet in force: see Homelessness Reduction Act 2017 s13(3).

occupy accommodation which it would have been reasonable for him to continue to occupy, and

(b) the purpose of the arrangement is to enable him to become entitled to assistance under this Part,

and there is no other good reason why he is threatened with homelessness.

(4) [Repealed.]][33]

197 [Repealed.]

Referral to another local housing authority

198 Referral of case to another local housing authority

(A1) If the local housing authority would be subject to the duty under section 189B (initial duty owed to all eligible persons who are homeless) but consider that the conditions are met for referral of the case to another local housing authority in England, they may notify that other authority of their opinion.[34]

(1) If the local housing authority would be subject to the duty under section 193 (accommodation for those with priority need who are not homeless intentionally) but consider that the conditions are met for referral of the case to another local housing authority, they may notify that other authority of their opinion.

(2) The conditions for referral of the case to another authority are met if–

(a) neither the applicant nor any person who might reasonably be expected to reside with him has a local connection with the district of the authority to whom his application was made,

(b) the applicant or a person who might reasonably be expected to reside with him has a local connection with the district of that other authority, and

(c) neither the applicant nor any person who might reasonably be expected to reside with him will run the risk of domestic violence in that other district.

(2ZA) The conditions for referral of the case to another authority are also met if–

(a) the application is made within the period of two years beginning with the date on which the applicant accepted an offer from the other authority under section 193(7AA) (private rented sector offer), and

(b) neither the applicant nor any person who might reasonably be expected to reside with the applicant will run the risk of domestic violence in the district of the other authority.[35]

(2A) But the conditions for referral mentioned in subsection (2) or (2ZA) are not met if–

(a) the applicant or any person who might reasonably be expected to reside with him has suffered violence (other than domestic violence) in the district of the other authority; and

(b) it is probable that the return to that district of the victim will lead to further violence of a similar kind against him.

33 Section 196 repealed by Homelessness Reduction Act 2017 s4(1), (5). Not yet in force: see Homelessness Reduction Act 2017 s13(3).

34 Inserted by Homelessness Reduction Act 2017, s 5(1), (8). Not yet in force: see Homelessness Reduction Act 2017 s13(3).

35 Not in force in Wales.

(3) For the purposes of subsections (2), (2ZA) and (2A) 'violence' means–
   (a) violence from another person; or
   (b) threats of violence from another person which are likely to be carried out;

and violence is 'domestic violence' if it is from a person who is associated with the victim.

(4) The conditions for referral of the case to another authority are also met if–
   (a) the applicant was on a previous application made to that other authority placed (in pursuance of their functions under this Part) in accommodation in the district of the authority to whom his application is now made, and
   (b) the previous application was within such period as may be prescribed of the present application.

(4A) Subsection (4) is to be construed, in a case where the other authority is an authority in Wales, as if the reference to 'this Part' were a reference to Part 2 of the Housing (Wales) Act 2014.

(5) The question whether the conditions for referral of a case which does not involve a referral to a local housing authority in Wales are satisfied shall be decided by agreement between the notifying authority and the notified authority or, in default of agreement, in accordance with such arrangements as the Secretary of State may direct by order.

(5A) The question whether the conditions for referral of a case involving a referral to a local housing authority in Wales shall be decided by agreement between the notifying authority and the notified authority or, in default of agreement, in accordance with such arrangements as the Secretary of State and the Welsh Ministers may jointly direct by order.

(6) An order may direct that the arrangements shall be–
   (a) those agreed by any relevant authorities or associations of relevant authorities, or
   (b) in default of such agreement, such arrangements as appear to the Secretary of State or, in the case of an order under subsection (5A), to the Secretary of State and the Welsh Ministers to be suitable, after consultation with such associations representing relevant authorities, and such other persons, as he thinks appropriate.

(7) An order under this section shall not be made unless a draft of the order has been approved by a resolution of each House of Parliament and, in the case of a joint order, a resolution of the National Assembly for Wales.

199 Local connection

(1) A person has a local connection with the district of a local housing authority if he has a connection with it–
   (a) because he is, or in the past was, normally resident there, and that residence is or was of his own choice,
   (b) because he is employed there,
   (c) because of family associations, or
   (d) because of special circumstances.

(2) A person is not employed in a district if he is serving in the regular armed forces of the Crown.

(3) Residence in a district is not of a person's own choice if–

(a) he becomes resident there because he, or a person who might reasonably be expected to reside with him, is serving in the regular armed forces of the Crown, or

(b) he, or a person who might reasonably be expected to reside with him, becomes resident there because he is detained under the authority of an Act of Parliament.

(4) [In subsections (2) and (3) 'regular armed forces of the Crown' means the Royal Navy, the regular forces as defined by section 225 of the Army Act 1955 or the regular air force as defined by section 223 of the Air Force Act 1955][36] *the regular forces as defined by section 374 of the Armed Forces Act 2006.*

(5) The Secretary of State may by order specify *other* circumstances in which–

(a) a person is not to be treated as employed in a district, or

(b) residence in a district is not to be treated as of a person's own choice.

(6) A person has a local connection with the district of a local housing authority if he was (at any time) provided with accommodation in that district under section 95 of the Immigration and Asylum Act 1999 (support for asylum seekers).

(7) But subsection (6) does not apply–

(a) to the provision of accommodation for a person in a district of a local housing authority if he was subsequently provided with accommodation in the district of another local housing authority under section 95 of that Act, or

(b) to the provision of accommodation in an accommodation centre by virtue of section 22 of the Nationality, Immigration and Asylum Act 2002 (c 41) (use of accommodation centres for section 95 support).

(8) While a local authority in England have a duty towards a person under section 23C of the Children Act 1989 (continuing functions in respect of former relevant children)–

(a) if the local authority is a local housing authority, the person has a local connection with their district, and

(b) otherwise, the person has a local connection with every district of a local housing authority that falls within the area of the local authority.

(9) In subsection (8), 'local authority' has the same meaning as in the Children Act 1989 (see section 105 of that Act).

(10) Where, by virtue of being provided with accommodation under section 22A of the Children Act 1989 (provision of accommodation for children in care), a person is normally resident in the district of a local housing authority in England for a continuous period of at least two years, some or all of which falls before the person attains the age of 16, the person has a local connection with that district.

(11) A person ceases to have a local connection with a district under subsection (10) upon attaining the age of 21 (but this does not affect whether the person has a local connection with that district under any other provision of this section).[37]

36 Words from 'the Royal Navy,' to the end repealed and subsequent words in italics substituted by the Armed Forces Act 2006, s 378(1), Sch 16, para 139. Not yet in force: see Armed Forces Act 2006 s383(2).

37 Inserted by Homelessness Reduction Act 2017 s8. Not yet in force: see Homelessness Reduction Act 2017 s13(3).

199A Duties to the applicant whose case is considered for referral or referred under section 198(A1)

(1) Where a local housing authority ('the notifying authority') notify an applicant that they intend to notify or have notified another local housing authority in England ('the notified authority') under section 198(A1) of their opinion that the conditions are met for referral of the applicant's case to the notified authority, the notifying authority–

(a) cease to be subject to any duty under section 188 (interim duty to accommodate in case of apparent priority need), and

(b) are not subject to the duty under section 189B (initial duty owed to all eligible persons who are homeless).

(2) But, if the notifying authority have reason to believe that the applicant may have a priority need, they must secure that accommodation is available for occupation by the applicant until the applicant is notified of the decision as to whether the conditions for referral of the applicant's case are met.

(3) When it has been decided whether the conditions for referral are met, the notifying authority must give notice of the decision and the reasons for it to the applicant. The notice must also inform the applicant of the applicant's right to request a review of the decision and of the time within which such a request must be made.

(4) If it is decided that the conditions for referral are not met–

(a) the notifying authority are subject to the duty under section 189B,

(b) the references in subsections (4) and (7)(b) of that section to the day that the notifying authority are first satisfied as mentioned in subsection (1) of that section are to be read as references to the day on which notice is given under subsection (3) of this section, and

(c) if the notifying authority have reason to believe that the applicant may have a priority need, they must secure that accommodation is available for occupation by the applicant until the later of–

(i) the duty owed to the applicant under section 189B coming to an end, and

(ii) the authority deciding what other duty (if any) they owe to the applicant under this Part after the duty under section 189B comes to an end.

(5) If it is decided that the conditions for referral are met–

(a) for the purposes of this Part, the applicant is to be treated as having made an application of the kind mentioned in section 183(1) to the notified authority on the date on which notice is given under subsection (3),

(b) from that date, the notifying authority owes no duties to the applicant under this Part,

(c) where the notifying authority have made a decision as to whether the applicant is eligible for assistance, is homeless or became homeless intentionally, the notified authority may only come to a different decision if they are satisfied that–

(i) the applicant's circumstances have changed, or further information has come to light, since the notifying authority made their decision, and

(ii) that change in circumstances, or further information, justifies the notified authority coming to a different decision to the notifying authority, and

(d) the notifying authority must give to the notified authority copies of any notifications that the notifying authority have given to the applicant under section 189A(3) or (10) (notifications of the notifying authority's assessments of the applicant's case).

(6) A duty under subsection (2) or paragraph (c) of subsection (4) ceases as provided

in the subsection or paragraph concerned even if the applicant requests a review of the authority's decision upon which the duty ceases.
The authority may secure that accommodation is available for the applicant's occupation pending the decision on review.

(7) A notice under this section must be given in writing and, if not received by the applicant, is to be treated as having been given to the applicant if it is made available at the authority's office for a reasonable period for collection by or on behalf of the applicant.[38]

200 Duties to the applicant whose case is considered for referral or referred *under section 198(1)*[39]

(1) Where a local housing authority notify an applicant that they intend to notify or have notified another local housing authority *under section 198(1)*[40] of their opinion that the conditions are met for the referral of his case to that other authority–
  (a) they cease to be subject to any duty under section 188 (interim duty to accommodate in case of apparent priority need), and
  (b) they are not subject to any duty under section 193 (the main housing duty),

but they shall secure that accommodation is available for occupation by the applicant until he is notified of the decision whether the conditions for referral of his case are met.

(1A) A local housing authority in England may not notify an applicant as mentioned in subsection (1) until the authority's duty to the applicant under section 189B(2) (initial duty owed to all eligible persons who are homeless) has come to an end.[41]

(2) When it has been decided whether the conditions for referral are met, the notifying authority shall notify the applicant of the decision and inform him of the reasons for it.
The notice shall also inform the applicant of his right to request a review of the decision and of the time within which such a request must be made.

(3) If it is decided that the conditions for referral are not met, the notifying authority are subject to the duty under section 193 (the main housing duty).

(4) If it is decided that those conditions are met and the notified authority is not an authority in Wales, the notified authority are subject to the duty under section 193 (the main housing duty); for provision about cases where it is decided that those conditions are met and the notified authority is an authority in Wales, see section 83 of the Housing (Wales) Act 2014 (cases referred from a local housing authority in England).

(5) The duty under subsection (1), ceases as provided in that subsection even if the applicant requests a review of the authority's decision (see section 202).

38 Inserted by Homelessness Reduction Act 2017 s5(1), (9). Not yet in force: see Homelessness Reduction Act 2017 s13(3).

39 Words 'under section 198(1)' in italics inserted by Homelessness Reduction Act 2017 s5(1), (10)(a).

40 Words 'under section 198(1)' in italics inserted by Homelessness Reduction Act 2017 s5(1), (10)(b). Not yet in force: see Homelessness Reduction Act 2017 s13(3).

41 Inserted by Homelessness Reduction Act 2017 s5(1), (10)(c). Not yet in force: see Homelessness Reduction Act 2017 s13(3).

The authority may secure that accommodation is available for the applicant's occupation pending the decision on a review.

(6) Notice [required to be][42] given to an applicant under this section shall be given in writing and, if not received by him, shall be treated as having been given to him if it is made available at the authority's office for a reasonable period for collection by him or on his behalf.

201 Application of referral provisions to cases arising in Scotland

Sections 198 and 200 (referral of application to another local housing authority and duties to applicant whose case is considered for referral or referred) apply–

(a) to applications referred by a local authority in Scotland in pursuance of sections 33 and 34 of the Housing (Scotland) Act 1987, and

(b) to persons whose applications are so transferred,

as they apply to cases arising under this Part (the reference in section 198 to this Part being construed as a reference to Part II of that Act).

201A Cases referred from a local housing authority in Wales

(1) This section applies where an application has been referred by a local housing authority in Wales to a local housing authority in England under section 80 of the Housing (Wales) Act 2014 (referral of case to another local housing authority).

(2) If it is decided that the conditions in that section for referral of the case are met, the notified authority are subject to the duty under section 193 of this Act in respect of the person whose case is referred (the main housing duty); for provision about cases where it is decided that the conditions for referral are not met, see section 82 of the Housing (Wales) Act 2014 (duties to applicant whose case is considered for referral or referred).

(3) References in this Part to an applicant include a reference to a person to whom a duty is owed by virtue of subsection (2).

Right to request review of decision

202 Right to request review of decision

(1) An applicant has the right to request a review of–

(a) any decision of a local housing authority as to his eligibility for assistance,

(b) any decision of a local housing authority as to what duty (if any) is owed to him under sections [190 to 193][43] *189B to 193C* and 195 [and 196][44] (duties to persons found to be homeless or threatened with homelessness),

(ba) any decision of a local housing authority–

(i) as to the steps they are to take under subsection (2) of section 189B, or

42 Words 'required to be' in square brackets repealed by Homelessness Reduction Act 2017 s5(1), (10)(d). Not yet in force: see Homelessness Reduction Act 2017 s13(3).

43 Words '190 to 193' in square brackets repealed and subsequent words in italics substituted by Homelessness Reduction Act 2017 s9(1), (2)(a)(i). Not yet in force: see Homelessness Reduction Act 2017 s13(3).

44 Words 'and 196' in square brackets repealed by Homelessness Reduction Act 2017 s9(1), (2)(a)(ii). Not yet in force: see Homelessness Reduction Act 2017 s13(3).

(ii) to give notice under subsection (5) of that section bringing to an end their duty to the applicant under subsection (2) of that section,

(bb) any decision of a local housing authority to give notice to the applicant under section 193B(2) (notice given to those who deliberately and unreasonably refuse to co-operate),

(bc) any decision of a local housing authority–

(i) as to the steps they are to take under subsection (2) of section 195, or

(ii) to give notice under subsection (5) of that section bringing to an end their duty to the applicant under subsection (2) of that section,[45]

(c) any decision of a local housing authority to notify another authority under section 198(1) (referral of cases),

(d) any decision under section 198(5) whether the conditions are met for the referral of his case,

(e) any decision under section 200(3) or (4) (decision as to duty owed to applicant whose case is considered for referral or referred),

(f) any decision of a local housing authority as to the suitability of accommodation offered to him in discharge of their duty under any of the provisions mentioned in paragraph (b) or (e) or as to the suitability of accommodation offered to him as mentioned in section 193(7), [or][46]

(g) any decision of a local housing authority as to the suitability of accommodation offered to him by way of a private rented sector offer[47] (within the meaning of section 193)*, or*

(h) any decision of a local housing authority as to the suitability of accommodation offered to the applicant by way of a final accommodation offer or a final Part 6 offer (within the meaning of section 193A or 193C).[48]

(1A) An applicant who is offered accommodation as mentioned in section 193(5), (7) or (7AA) may under subsection (1)(f) or (as the case may be) (g) request a review of the suitability of the accommodation offered to him whether or not he has accepted the offer.

(1B) An applicant may, under subsection (1)(h), request a review of the suitability of the accommodation offered whether or not the applicant has accepted the offer.[49]

(2) There is no right to request a review of the decision reached on an earlier review.

(3) A request for review must be made before the end of the period of 21 days beginning with the day on which he is notified of the authority's decision or such longer period as the authority may in writing allow.

(4) On a request being duly made to them, the authority or authorities concerned shall review their decision.

45 Paras (ba)–(bc) inserted by Homelessness Reduction Act 2017 s9(1), (2)(b). Not yet in force: see Homelessness Reduction Act 2017 s13(3).

46 Word 'or' in square brackets repealed by Homelessness Reduction Act 2017 s9(1), (2)(c). Not yet in force: see Homelessness Reduction Act 2017 s13(3).

47 Not in force in Wales.

48 Para (h) and word ', or' preceding it inserted by Homelessness Reduction Act 2017 s9(1), (2)(d). Not yet in force: see Homelessness Reduction Act 2017 s13(3).

49 Inserted by Homelessness Reduction Act 2017 s9(1), (3). Not yet in force: see Homelessness Reduction Act 2017 s13(3).

203 Procedure on a review

(1) The Secretary of State may make provision by regulations as to the procedure to be followed in connection with a review under section 202.
Nothing in the following provisions affects the generality of this power.

(2) Provision may be made by regulations–
  (a) requiring the decision on review to be made by a person of appropriate seniority who was not involved in the original decision, and
  (b) as to the circumstances in which the applicant is entitled to an oral hearing, and whether and by whom he may be represented at such a hearing.

(3) The authority, or as the case may be either of the authorities, concerned shall notify the applicant of the decision on the review.

(4) If the decision is–
  (a) to confirm the original decision on any issue against the interests of the applicant, or
  (b) to confirm a previous decision–
    (i) to notify another authority under section 198 (referral of cases), or
    (ii) that the conditions are met for the referral of his case,

they shall also notify him of the reasons for the decision.

(5) In any case they shall inform the applicant of his right to appeal to the county court on a point of law, and of the period within which such an appeal must be made (see section 204).

(6) Notice of the decision shall not be treated as given unless and until subsection (5), and where applicable subsection (4), is complied with.

(7) Provision may be made by regulations as to the period within which the review must be carried out and notice given of the decision.

(8) Notice required to be given to a person under this section shall be given in writing and, if not received by him, shall be treated as having been given if it is made available at the authority's office for a reasonable period for collection by him or on his behalf.

204 Right of appeal to county court on point of law

(1) If an applicant who has requested a review under section 202–
  (a) is dissatisfied with the decision on the review, or
  (b) is not notified of the decision on the review within the time prescribed under section 203,

he may appeal to the county court on any point of law arising from the decision or, as the case may be, the original decision.

(2) An appeal must be brought within 21 days of his being notified of the decision or, as the case may be, of the date on which he should have been notified of a decision on review.

(2A) The court may give permission for an appeal to be brought after the end of the period allowed by subsection (2), but only if it is satisfied–
  (a) where permission is sought before the end of that period, that there is a good reason for the applicant to be unable to bring the appeal in time; or
  (b) where permission is sought after that time, that there was a good reason for the applicant's failure to bring the appeal in time and for any delay in applying for permission.

(3) On appeal the court may make such order confirming, quashing or varying the decision as it thinks fit.

(4) Where the authority were under a duty under section 188, 190, *199A*[50] or 200 to secure that accommodation is available for the applicant's occupation, [or had the power under section 195(8) to do so,][51] they may secure that accommodation is so available–

(a) during the period for appealing under this section against the authority's decision, and

(b) if an appeal is brought, until the appeal (and any further appeal) is finally determined.

204A Section 204(4): appeals

(1) This section applies where an applicant has the right to appeal to the county court against a local housing authority's decision on a review.

(2) If the applicant is dissatisfied with a decision by the authority–

(a) not to exercise their power under section 204(4) ('the section 204(4) power') in his case;

(b) to exercise that power for a limited period ending before the final determination by the county court of his appeal under section 204(1) ('the main appeal'); or

(c) to cease exercising that power before that time,

he may appeal to the county court against the decision.

(3) An appeal under this section may not be brought after the final determination by the county court of the main appeal.

(4) On an appeal under this section the court–

(a) may order the authority to secure that accommodation is available for the applicant's occupation until the determination of the appeal (or such earlier time as the court may specify); and

(b) shall confirm or quash the decision appealed against,

and in considering whether to confirm or quash the decision the court shall apply the principles applied by the High Court on an application for judicial review.

(5) If the court quashes the decision it may order the authority to exercise the section 204(4) power in the applicant's case for such period as may be specified in the order.

(6) An order under subsection (5)–

(a) may only be made if the court is satisfied that failure to exercise the section 204(4) power in accordance with the order would substantially prejudice the applicant's ability to pursue the main appeal;

(b) may not specify any period ending after the final determination by the county court of the main appeal.

50 Words in italics inserted by Homelessness Reduction Act 2017 s5(1), (11). Not yet in force: see Homelessness Reduction Act 2017 s13(3).

51 Words 'or had the power under section 195(8) to do so,' in square brackets repealed by Homelessness Reduction Act 2017 s4(1), (6). Not yet in force: see Homelessness Reduction Act 2017 s13(3).

Supplementary provisions

205 Discharge of functions: introductory

(1) The following sections have effect in relation to the discharge by a local housing authority of their functions under this Part to secure that accommodation is available for the occupation of a person–

section 206 (general provisions),
section 208 (out-of-area placements),
section 209 (arrangements with private landlord).

(2) In sections 206 and 208 those functions are referred to as the authority's 'housing functions under this Part'.

(3) For the purposes of this section, a local housing authority's duty under section 189B(2) or 195(2) is a function of the authority to secure that accommodation is available for the occupation of a person only if the authority decide to discharge the duty by securing that accommodation is so available.[52]

206 Discharge of functions by local housing authorities

(1) A local housing authority may discharge their housing functions under this Part only in the following ways–

(a) by securing that suitable accommodation provided by them is available,
(b) by securing that he obtains suitable accommodation from some other person, or
(c) by giving him such advice and assistance as will secure that suitable accommodation is available from some other person.

(2) A local housing authority may require a person in relation to whom they are discharging such functions–

(a) to pay such reasonable charges as they may determine in respect of accommodation which they secure for his occupation (either by making it available themselves or otherwise), or
(b) to pay such reasonable amount as they may determine in respect of sums payable by them for accommodation made available by another person.

207 [Repealed].

208 Discharge of functions: out-of-area placements

(1) So far as reasonably practicable a local housing authority shall in discharging their housing functions under this Part secure that accommodation is available for the occupation of the applicant in their district.

(2) If they secure that accommodation is available for the occupation of the applicant outside their district, they shall give notice to the local housing authority in whose district the accommodation is situated.

(3) The notice shall state–

(a) the name of the applicant,
(b) the number and description of other persons who normally reside with him as a member of his family or might reasonably be expected to reside with him,
(c) the address of the accommodation,

52 Inserted by Homelessness Reduction Act 2017 s6. Not yet in force: see Homelessness Reduction Act 2017 s13(3).

(d) the date on which the accommodation was made available to him, and
(e) which function under this Part the authority was discharging in securing that the accommodation is available for his occupation.

(4) The notice must be in writing, and must be given before the end of the period of 14 days beginning with the day on which the accommodation was made available to the applicant.

209 Discharge of interim duties: arrangements with private landlord

(1) This section applies where in pursuance of any of their housing functions under section 188, 190, 200 or 204(4) (interim duties) a local housing authority make arrangements with a private landlord to provide accommodation.

(2) A tenancy granted to the applicant in pursuance of the arrangements cannot be an assured tenancy before the end of the period of twelve months beginning with–
(a) the date on which the applicant was notified of the authority's decision under section 184(3) or 198(5); or
(b) if there is a review of that decision under section 202 or an appeal to the court under section 204, the date on which he is notified of the decision on review or the appeal is finally determined,

unless, before or during that period, the tenant is notified by the landlord (or in the case of joint landlords, at least one of them) that the tenancy is to be regarded as an assured shorthold tenancy or an assured tenancy other than an assured shorthold tenancy.

210 Suitability of accommodation

(1) In determining for the purposes of this Part whether accommodation is suitable for a person, the local housing authority shall have regard to Parts 9 and 10 of the Housing Act 1985 (slum clearance and overcrowding) and Parts 1 to 4 of the Housing Act 2004).

(2) The Secretary of State may by order specify–
(a) circumstances in which accommodation is or is not to be regarded as suitable for a person, and
(b) matters to be taken into account or disregarded in determining whether accommodation is suitable for a person.

211 Protection of property of homeless persons and persons threatened with homelessness

(1) This section applies where a local housing authority have reason to believe that–
(a) there is danger of loss of, or damage to, any personal property of an applicant by reason of his inability to protect it or deal with it, and
(b) no other suitable arrangements have been or are being made.

(2) If the authority have become subject to a duty towards the applicant under–
section 188 (interim duty to accommodate),
section 189B (initial duty owed to all eligible persons who are homeless),[53]
section 190, 193 or 195 (duties to persons found to be homeless or threatened with homelessness), or

53 Inserted by Homelessness Reduction Act 2017 s5(12). Not yet in force: see Homelessness Reduction Act 2017 s13(3).

section 200 (duties to applicant whose case is considered for referral or referred),

then, whether or not they are still subject to such a duty, they shall take reasonable steps to prevent the loss of the property or prevent or mitigate damage to it.

(3) If they have not become subject to such a duty, they may take any steps they consider reasonable for that purpose.

(4) The authority may decline to take action under this section except upon such conditions as they consider appropriate in the particular case, which may include conditions as to–

(a) the making and recovery by the authority of reasonable charges for the action taken, or

(b) the disposal by the authority, in such circumstances as may be specified, of property in relation to which they have taken action.

(5) References in this section to personal property of the applicant include personal property of any person who might reasonably be expected to reside with him.

(6) Section 212 contains provisions supplementing this section.

212 Protection of property: supplementary provisions

(1) The authority may for the purposes of section 211 (protection of property of homeless persons or persons threatened with homelessness)–

(a) enter, at all reasonable times, any premises which are the usual place of residence of the applicant or which were his last usual place of residence, and

(b) deal with any personal property of his in any way which is reasonably necessary, in particular by storing it or arranging for its storage.

(2) Where the applicant asks the authority to move his property to a particular location nominated by him, the authority–

(a) may, if it appears to them that his request is reasonable, discharge their responsibilities under section 211 by doing as he asks, and

(b) having done so, have no further duty or power to take action under that section in relation to that property.

If such a request is made, the authority shall before complying with it inform the applicant of the consequence of their doing so.

(3) If no such request is made (or, if made, is not acted upon) the authority cease to have any duty or power to take action under section 211 when, in their opinion, there is no longer any reason to believe that there is a danger of loss of or damage to a person's personal property by reason of his inability to protect it or deal with it.

But property stored by virtue of their having taken such action may be kept in store and any conditions upon which it was taken into store continue to have effect, with any necessary modifications.

(4) Where the authority–

(a) cease to be subject to a duty to take action under section 211 in respect of an applicant's property, or

(b) cease to have power to take such action, having previously taken such action,

they shall notify the applicant of that fact and of the reason for it.

(5) The notification shall be given to the applicant–
  (a) by delivering it to him, or
  (b) by leaving it, or sending it to him, at his last known address.

(6) References in this section to personal property of the applicant include personal property of any person who might reasonably be expected to reside with him.

213 Co-operation between relevant housing authorities and bodies

(1) Where a local housing authority in England–
  (a) request another relevant housing authority or body, in England, Wales or Scotland, to assist them in the discharge of their functions under this Part, or
  (b) request a social services authority, in England, Wales or Scotland, to exercise any of their functions in relation to a case which the local housing authority are dealing with under this Part,

the authority or body to whom the request is made shall co-operate in rendering such assistance in the discharge of the functions to which the request relates as is reasonable in the circumstances.

(2) In subsection (1)(a) 'relevant housing authority or body' means–
  (a) in relation to England and Wales, a local housing authority, a new town corporation, a private registered provider of social housing a registered social landlord or a housing action trust;
  (b) in relation to Scotland, a local authority, a development corporation, a registered housing association or Scottish Homes.

Expressions used in paragraph (a) have the same meaning as in the Housing Act 1985; and expressions used in paragraph (b) have the same meaning as in the Housing (Scotland) Act 1987.

(3) Subsection (1) above applies to a request by a local authority in Scotland under section 38 of the Housing (Scotland) Act 1987 as it applies to a request by a local housing authority in England and Wales (the references to this Part being construed, in relation to such a request, as references to Part II of that Act).

213A Co-operation in certain cases involving children

(1) This section applies where a local housing authority have reason to believe that an applicant with whom a person under the age of 18 normally resides, or might reasonably be expected to reside–
  (a) may be ineligible for assistance; *or*[54]
  (b) may be homeless and may have become so intentionally; [or
  (c) may be threatened with homelessness intentionally.][55]

(2) A local housing authority shall make arrangements for ensuring that, where this section applies–
  (a) the applicant is invited to consent to the referral of the essential facts of his case to the social services authority for the district of the housing authority (where that is a different authority); and

54 Word 'or' in italics inserted by Homelessness Reduction Act 2017 s4(1), (7)(a)(i). Not yet in force: see Homelessness Reduction Act 2017 s13(3).

55 Words in square brackets repealed by Homelessness Reduction Act 2017 s4(1), (7)(a)(ii). Not yet in force: see Homelessness Reduction Act 2017 s13(3).

(b) if the applicant has given that consent, the social services authority are made aware of those facts and of the subsequent decision of the housing authority in respect of his case.

(3) Where the local housing authority and the social services authority for a district are the same authority (a 'unitary authority'), that authority shall make arrangements for ensuring that, where this section applies–

(a) the applicant is invited to consent to the referral to the social services department of the essential facts of his case; and

(b) if the applicant has given that consent, the social services department is made aware of those facts and of the subsequent decision of the authority in respect of his case.

(4) Nothing in subsection (2) or (3) affects any power apart from this section to disclose information relating to the applicant's case to the social services authority or to the social services department (as the case may be) without the consent of the applicant.

(5) Where a social services authority–

(a) are aware of a decision of a local housing authority that the applicant is ineligible for [assistance, became homeless intentionally or became threatened with homelessness intentionally] *assistance or became homeless intentionally*,[56] and

(b) request the local housing authority to provide them with advice and assistance in the exercise of their social services functions under Part 3 of the Children Act 1989 or Part 6 of the Social Services and Well-being (Wales) Act 2014,

the local housing authority shall provide them with such advice and assistance as is reasonable in the circumstances.

(6) A unitary authority shall make arrangements for ensuring that, where they make a decision of a kind mentioned in subsection (5)(a), the housing department provide the social services department with such advice and assistance as the social services department may reasonably request.

(7) In this section, in relation to a unitary authority–

'the housing department' means those persons responsible for the exercise of their housing functions; and

'the social services department' means those persons responsible for the exercise of their social services functions under Part 3 of the Children Act 1989 or Part 6 of the Social Services and Well-being (Wales) Act 2014.

213B Duty of public authority to refer cases in England to local housing authority

(1) This section applies if a specified public authority considers that a person in England in relation to whom the authority exercises functions is or may be homeless or threatened with homelessness.

(2) The specified public authority must ask the person to agree to the authority notifying a local housing authority in England of–

(a) the opinion mentioned in subsection (1), and

(b) how the person may be contacted by the local housing authority.

56 Words 'assistance, became homeless intentionally or became threatened with homelessness intentionally' in square brackets repealed and subsequent words in italics substituted by Homelessness Reduction Act 2017 s4(1), (7)(b). Not yet in force: see Homelessness Reduction Act 2017 s13(3).

(3) If the person–
(a) agrees to the specified public authority making the notification, and
(b) identifies a local housing authority in England to which the person would like the notification to be made,
the specified public authority must notify that local housing authority of the matters mentioned in subsection (2)(a) and (b).
(4) In this section 'specified public authority' means a public authority specified, or of a description specified, in regulations made by the Secretary of State.
(5) In subsection (4) 'public authority' means a person (other than a local housing authority) who has functions of a public nature.[57]

General provisions

214 False statements, withholding information and failure to disclose change of circumstances

(1) It is an offence for a person, with intent to induce a local housing authority to believe in connection with the exercise of their functions under this Part that he or another person is entitled to accommodation or assistance in accordance with the provisions of this Part, or is entitled to accommodation or assistance of a particular description–
(a) knowingly or recklessly to make a statement which is false in a material particular, or
(b) knowingly to withhold information which the authority have reasonably required him to give in connection with the exercise of those functions.
(2) If before an applicant receives notification of the local housing authority's decision on his application there is any change of facts material to his case, he shall notify the authority as soon as possible.
The authority shall explain to every applicant, in ordinary language, the duty imposed on him by this subsection and the effect of subsection (3).
(3) A person who fails to comply with subsection (2) commits an offence unless he shows that he was not given the explanation required by that subsection or that he had some other reasonable excuse for non-compliance.
(4) A person guilty of an offence under this section is liable on summary conviction to a fine not exceeding level 5 on the standard scale.

214A *Codes of practice*

(1) The Secretary of State may from time to time issue one or more codes of practice dealing with the functions of a local housing authority in England relating to homelessness or the prevention of homelessness.
(2) The provision that may be made by a code of practice under this section includes, in particular, provision about–
(a) the exercise by a local housing authority of functions under this Part;
(b) the training of an authority's staff in relation to the exercise of those functions;
(c) the monitoring by an authority of the exercise of those functions.
(3) A code of practice may–

57 Inserted by Homelessness Reduction Act 2017 s10. Not yet in force: see Homelessness Reduction Act 2017 s13(3).

(a) apply to all local housing authorities or to the local housing authorities specified or described in the code;

(b) contain different provision for different kinds of local housing authority.

(4) The Secretary of State may issue a code of practice under this section only in accordance with subsections (5) and (6).

(5) Before issuing the code of practice, the Secretary of State must lay a draft of the code before Parliament.

(6) If–

(a) the Secretary of State lays a draft of the code before Parliament, and

(b) no negative resolution is made within the 40-day period,

the Secretary of State may issue the code in the form of the draft.

(7) For the purposes of subsection (6)–

(a) a 'negative resolution' means a resolution of either House of Parliament not to approve the draft of the code, and

(b) 'the 40-day period' means the period of 40 days beginning with the day on which the draft of the code is laid before Parliament (or, if it is not laid before each House of Parliament on the same day, the later of the two days on which it is laid).

(8) In calculating the 40-day period, no account is to be taken of any period during which–

(a) Parliament is dissolved or prorogued, or

(b) both Houses are adjourned for more than four days.

(9) The Secretary of State may–

(a) from time to time revise and reissue a code of practice under this section;

(b) revoke a code of practice under this section.

(10) Subsections (4) to (6) do not apply to the reissue of a code of practice under this section.

(11) The Secretary of State must publish the current version of each code of practice under this section in whatever manner the Secretary of State thinks fit.

(12) A local housing authority must have regard to a code of practice under this section in exercising their functions.[58]

215 Regulations and orders

(1) In this Part 'prescribed' means prescribed by regulations of the Secretary of State.

(2) Regulations or an order under this Part may make different provision for different purposes, including different provision for different areas.

(3) Regulations or an order under this Part shall be made by statutory instrument.

(4) Unless required to be approved in draft, regulations or an order under this Part shall be subject to annulment in pursuance of a resolution of either House of Parliament.

216 Transitional and consequential matters

(1) The provisions of this Part have effect in place of the provisions of Part III of the Housing Act 1985 (housing the homeless) and shall be construed as one with that Act.

58 Inserted by Homelessness Reduction Act 2017 s11. Not yet in force: see Homelessness Reduction Act 2017 s13(3).

(2) Subject to any transitional provision contained in an order under section 232(4) (power to include transitional provision in commencement order), the provisions of this Part do not apply in relation to an applicant whose application for accommodation or assistance in obtaining accommodation was made before the commencement of this Part.

(3) The enactments mentioned in Schedule 17 have effect with the amendments specified there which are consequential on the provisions of this Part.

217 Minor definitions: Part VII

(1) In this Part, subject to subsection (2)–

'private landlord' means a landlord who is not within section 80(1) of the Housing Act 1985 (c 68) (the landlord condition for secure tenancies);

'relevant authority' means a local housing authority or a social services authority; and

'social services authority' means–

(a) in relation to England, a local authority for the purposes of the Local Authority Social Services Act 1970, as defined in section 1 of that Act;

(b) in relation to Wales, a local authority exercising social services functions for the purposes of the Social Services and Well-being (Wales) Act 2014.

(2) In this Part, in relation to Scotland–

(a) 'local housing authority' means a local authority within the meaning of the Housing (Scotland) Act 1988, and

(b) 'social services authority' means a local authority for the purposes of the Social Work (Scotland) Act 1968.

(3) References in this Part to the district of a local housing authority–

(a) have the same meaning in relation to an authority in England or Wales as in the Housing Act 1985, and

(b) in relation to an authority in Scotland, mean the area of the local authority concerned.

218 Index of defined expressions: Part VII

The following Table shows provisions defining or otherwise explaining expressions used in this Part (other than provisions defining or explaining an expression used in the same section)–

accommodation available for occupation	section 176
applicant	section 183(2)
assistance under this Part	section 183(2)
associated (in relation to a person)	section 178
assured tenancy and assured shorthold tenancy	section 230
district (of local housing authority)	section 217(3)
eligible for assistance	section 183(2)
homeless	section 175(1)
housing functions under this Part (in sections 206 and 208)	section 205(2)
intentionally homeless	section 191

[intentionally threatened with homelessness]	[section 196][59]
local connection	section 199
local housing authority-	
–in England and Wales	section 230
–in Scotland	section 217(2)(a)
Prescribed	section 215(1)
priority need	section 189
private landlord	section 217(1)
Reasonable to continue to occupy accommodation	section 177
registered social landlord	section 230
relevant authority	section 217(1)
restricted person	section 184(7)
social services authority	section 217(1) and (2)(b)
threatened with homelessness	section 175(4)

59 Repealed by Homelessness Reduction Act 2017 s4(1), (8). Not yet in force: see Homelessness Reduction Act 2017 s13(3).

APPENDIX B

Statutory instruments[1]

Allocation of Housing (Qualification Criteria for Right to Move) (England) Regulations 2015 772
Allocation of Housing (Qualification Criteria for Armed Forces) (England) Regulations 2012 773
Homelessness (Suitability of Accommodation) (England) Order 2012 774
Allocation of Housing and Homelessness (Miscellaneous Provisions) (England) Regulations 2006 776
Allocation of Housing and Homelessness (Eligibility) (England) Regulations 2006 777
Homelessness (Suitability of Accommodation) (England) Order 2003 782
Homelessness (Priority Need for Accommodation) (England) Order 2002 784
Allocation of Housing and Homelessness (Review Procedures) Regulations 1999 786
Homelessness (Suitability of Accommodation) Order 1996 790

In addition to these statutory instruments, the following Welsh SIs are reproduced in the ebook version of *Homelessness and Allocations*:

- Homelessness (Intentionality) (Specified Categories) (Wales) Regulations 2015
- Homelessness (Review Procedure) (Wales) Regulations 2015
- Homelessness (Suitability of Accommodation) (Wales) Order 2015
- Allocation of Housing and Homelessness (Eligibility) (Wales) Regulations 2014

Allocation of Housing (Qualification Criteria for Right to Move) (England) Regulations 2015 SI No 967

1 Citation, commencement and application

(1) These Regulations may be cited as the Allocation of Housing (Qualification Criteria for Right to Move) (England) Regulations 2015.

(2) These Regulations come into force on 20th April 2015.

(3) These Regulations apply in relation to England only.

2 Interpretation

Any reference in these Regulations to a section is a reference to a section of the Housing Act 1996.

3 Criterion that may not be used in deciding what classes of persons are not qualifying persons

(1) In deciding whether a person is a qualifying person under section 160ZA(7), a local housing authority may not use the criterion set out in paragraph (2) if the allocation involves a transfer of housing accommodation for that person from the district of another local housing authority in England.

(2) The criterion is that a relevant person must have a local connection with the district of the local housing authority.

(3) In this regulation 'local connection' has the meaning given by section 199.

4 Relevant person

For the purposes of regulation 3, a relevant person is a person who–

(a) falls within section 159(4A)(a) or (b),

(b) is to be given reasonable preference under section 166A(3)(e), and

(c) has a need to move falling within regulation 5(1).

5 Need to move

(1) Subject to paragraph (2), for the purposes of regulation 4, a relevant person has a need to move because the relevant person–

(a) works in the district of the local housing authority, or

(b)

(i) has been offered work in the district of the local housing authority, and

(ii) the authority is satisfied that the relevant person has a genuine intention of taking up the offer of work.

(2) This regulation does not apply if the need to move is associated with work or the offer of work which is–

(a) short-term or marginal in nature,

(b) ancillary to work in another district, or

(c) voluntary work.

(3) In this regulation 'voluntary work' means work where no payment is received by the relevant person or the only payment due to be made to the relevant person by virtue of being so engaged is a payment in respect of any expenses reasonably incurred by the relevant person in the course of being so engaged.

Allocation of Housing (Qualification Criteria for Armed Forces) (England) Regulations 2012 SI No 1869

1 Citation and commencement

(1) These Regulations may be cited as the Allocation of Housing (Qualification Criteria for Armed Forces) (England) Regulations 2012.

(2) These Regulations come into force on 24th August 2012.

2 Interpretation

In these Regulations–

'the 1996 Act' means the Housing Act 1996;

'local connection' has the meaning given by section 199 of the 1996 Act; and

'regular forces' and 'reserve forces' have the meanings given by section 374 of the Armed Forces Act 2006.

3 Criterion that may not be used in deciding what classes of persons are not qualifying persons

(1) In deciding what classes of persons are not qualifying persons under section 160ZA(7) of the 1996 Act, a local housing authority in England may not use the criterion set out in paragraph (2).

(2) The criterion is that a relevant person must have a local connection to the district of a local housing authority.

(3) A relevant person is a person who–

(a) is serving in the regular forces or who has served in the regular forces within five years of the date of their application for an allocation of housing under Part 6 of the 1996 Act;

(b) has recently ceased, or will cease to be entitled, to reside in accommodation provided by the Ministry of Defence following the death of that person's spouse or civil partner where–

(i) the spouse or civil partner has served in the regular forces; and

(ii) their death was attributable (wholly or partly) to that service; or

(c) is serving or has served in the reserve forces and who is suffering from a serious injury, illness or disability which is attributable (wholly or partly) to that service.

Homelessness (Suitability of Accommodation) (England) Order 2012 SI No 2601

1 Citation, commencement and application

(1) This Order may be cited as the Homelessness (Suitability of Accommodation) (England) Order 2012 and comes into force on 9th November 2012.

(2) This Order applies in relation to England only.

2 Matters to be taken into account in determining whether accommodation is suitable for a person

In determining whether accommodation is suitable for a person, the local housing authority must take into account the location of the accommodation, including–

(a) where the accommodation is situated outside the district of the local housing authority, the distance of the accommodation from the district of the authority;

(b) the significance of any disruption which would be caused by the location of the accommodation to the employment, caring responsibilities or education of the person or members of the person's household;

(c) the proximity and accessibility of the accommodation to medical facilities and other support which–

(i) are currently used by or provided to the person or members of the person's household; and

(ii) are essential to the well-being of the person or members of the person's household; and

(d) the proximity and accessibility of the accommodation to local services, amenities and transport.

3 Circumstances in which accommodation is not to be regarded as suitable for a person

(1)[2] For the purposes [of a private rented sector offer under section 193(7F) of the Housing Act 1996] *mentioned in paragraph (2)*,[3] accommodation shall not be regarded as suitable where one or more of the following apply–

(a) the local housing authority are of the view that the accommodation is not in a reasonable physical condition;

(b) the local housing authority are of the view that any electrical equipment supplied with the accommodation does not meet the requirements of Schedule 1 to the Electrical Equipment (Safety) Regulations 2016;

(c) the local housing authority are of the view that the landlord has not taken reasonable fire safety precautions with the accommodation and any furnishings supplied with it;

(d) the local housing authority are of the view that the landlord has not taken reasonable precautions to prevent the possibility of carbon monoxide poisoning in the accommodation;

2 Numbered as para (1) by Homelessness Reduction Act 2017 s12(1), (2). Not yet in force: see Homelessness Reduction Act 2017 s13(3).

3 Words in square brackets revoked and subsequent words in italics substituted by Homelessness Reduction Act 2017 s12(1), (3). Not yet in force: see Homelessness Reduction Act 2017 s13(3).

(e) the local housing authority are of the view that the landlord is not a fit and proper person to act in the capacity of landlord, having considered if the person has:
   (i) committed any offence involving fraud or other dishonesty, or violence or illegal drugs, or any offence listed in Schedule 3 to the Sexual Offences Act 2003 (offences attracting notification requirements);
   (ii) practised unlawful discrimination on grounds of sex, race, age, disability, marriage or civil partnership, pregnancy or maternity, religion or belief, sexual orientation, gender identity or gender reassignment in, or in connection with, the carrying on of any business;
   (iii) contravened any provision of the law relating to housing (including landlord or tenant law); or
   (iv) acted otherwise than in accordance with any applicable code of practice for the management of a house in multiple occupation, approved under section 233 of the Housing Act 2004;

(f) the accommodation is a house in multiple occupation subject to licensing under section 55 of the Housing Act 2004 and is not licensed;

(g) the accommodation is a house in multiple occupation subject to additional licensing under section 56 of the Housing Act 2004 and is not licensed;

(h) the accommodation is or forms part of residential property which does not have a valid energy performance certificate as required by the Energy Performance of Buildings (Certificates and Inspections) (England and Wales) Regulations 2007;

(i) the accommodation is or forms part of relevant premises which do not have a current gas safety record in accordance with regulation 36 of the Gas Safety (Installation and Use) Regulations 1998; or

(j) the landlord has not provided to the local housing authority a written tenancy agreement, which the landlord proposes to use for the purposes of a private rented sector offer, and which the local housing authority considers to be adequate.

(2) The purposes are–

(a) determining, in accordance with section 193(7F) of the Housing Act 1996, whether a local housing authority may approve a private rented sector offer;

(b) determining, in accordance with section 193A(6) or 193C(9) of that Act, whether a local housing authority may approve a final accommodation offer made by a private landlord;

(c) determining whether any accommodation–
   (i) secured for a person who has a priority need by a local housing authority in discharge of their functions under section 189B(2) or 195(2) of that Act, and
   (ii) made available for occupation under a tenancy with a private landlord,

is suitable for the purposes of the section concerned.[4]

4 Inserted by Homelessness Reduction Act 2017 s12(1), (4). Not yet in force: see Homelessness Reduction Act 2017 s13(3).

Allocation of Housing and Homelessness (Miscellaneous Provisions) (England) Regulations 2006 SI No 2527

1 Citation, commencement, interpretation and application

(1) These Regulations may be cited as the Allocation of Housing and Homelessness (Miscellaneous Provisions) (England) Regulations 2006 and shall come into force on 9th October 2006.

(2) In these Regulations, 'the 1996 Act' means the Housing Act 1996.

(3) These Regulations apply to England only.

2 Amendment of the classes of person from abroad who are eligible for an allocation of accommodation and for housing assistance

(1) The Allocation of Housing and Homelessness (Eligibility) (England) Regulations 2006 are amended as follows.

(2) For regulation 3(d), substitute–

'(d) Class D–a person who has humanitarian protection granted under the Immigration Rules.'.

(3) For regulation 5(1)(d), substitute–

'(d) Class D–a person who has humanitarian protection granted under the Immigration Rules; and'.

3 Prescribed period for referral of case to another local housing authority

For the purposes of section 198(4)(b) of the 1996 Act (referral of case to another local housing authority), the prescribed period is the aggregate of–

(a) five years; and

(b) the period beginning on the date of the previous application and ending on the date on which the applicant was first placed in pursuance of that application in accommodation in the district of the authority to whom the application is now made.

4 Transitional provisions

The amendments made by these Regulations shall not have effect in relation to an applicant whose application for–

(a) an allocation of housing accommodation under Part 6 of the 1996 Act; or

(b) housing assistance under Part 7 of the 1996 Act,

was made before 9th October 2006.

Allocation of Housing and Homelessness (Eligibility) (England) Regulations 2006 SI No 1294

1 Citation, commencement and application

(1) These Regulations may be cited as the Allocation of Housing and Homelessness (Eligibility) (England) Regulations 2006 and shall come into force on 1st June 2006.

(2) These Regulations apply to England only.

2 Interpretation

(1) In these Regulations–

'the 1996 Act' means the Housing Act 1996;

'the Accession Regulations 2013' means the Accession of Croatia (Immigration and Worker Authorisation) Regulations 2013;

'the EEA Regulations' means the Immigration (European Economic Area) Regulations 2006;

'the Human Rights Convention' means the Convention for the Protection of Human Rights and Fundamental Freedoms, agreed by the Council of Europe at Rome on 4thNovember 1950 as it has effect for the time being in relation to the United Kingdom;

'the Immigration Rules' means the rules laid down as mentioned in section 3(2) of the Immigration Act 1971 (general provisions for regulation and control);

'the Refugee Convention' means the Convention relating to the Status of Refugees done at Geneva on 28th July 1951, as extended by Article 1(2) of the Protocol relating to the Status of Refugees done at New York on 31st January 1967; and

'sponsor' means a person who has given an undertaking in writing for the purposes of the Immigration Rules to be responsible for the maintenance and accommodation of another person.

(2) For the purposes of these Regulations–

(a) 'jobseeker', 'self-employed person', and 'worker' have the same meaning as for the purposes of the definition of a 'qualified person' in regulation 6(1) of the EEA Regulations; and

(b) subject to paragraph (3), references to the family member of a jobseeker, self-employed person or worker shall be construed in accordance with regulation 7 of those Regulations.

(3) For the purposes of regulations 4(2)(d) and 6(2)(d) 'family member' does not include a person who is treated as a family member by virtue of regulation 7(3) of the EEA Regulations.

(4) [Revoked].

3 Persons subject to immigration control who are eligible for an allocation of housing accommodation

The following classes of persons subject to immigration control are persons who are eligible for an allocation of housing accommodation under Part 6 of the 1996 Act–

(a) Class A–a person who is recorded by the Secretary of State as a refugee within the definition in Article 1 of the Refugee Convention and who has leave to enter or remain in the United Kingdom;

(b) Class B–a person–
  (i) who has exceptional leave to enter or remain in the United Kingdom granted outside the provisions of the Immigration Rules; and
  (ii) who is not subject to a condition requiring him to maintain and accommodate himself, and any person who is dependent on him, without recourse to public funds;
(c) Class C–a person who is habitually resident in the United Kingdom, the Channel Islands, the Isle of Man or the Republic of Ireland and whose leave to enter or remain in the United Kingdom is not subject to any limitation or condition, other than a person–
  (i) who has been given leave to enter or remain in the United Kingdom upon an undertaking given by his sponsor;
  (ii) who has been resident in the United Kingdom, the Channel Islands, the Isle of Man or the Republic of Ireland for less than five years beginning on the date of entry or the date on which his sponsor gave the undertaking in respect of him, whichever date is the later; and
  (iii) whose sponsor or, where there is more than one sponsor, at least one of whose sponsors, is still alive;
(d) Class D–a person who has humanitarian protection granted under the Immigration Rules;
(e) Class E–a person who is habitually resident in the United Kingdom, the Channel Islands, the Isle of Man or the Republic of Ireland and who has limited leave to enter the United Kingdom as a relevant Afghan citizen under paragraph 276BA1 of the Immigration Rules; and
(f) Class F–a person who has limited leave to enter or remain in the United Kingdom on family or private life grounds under Article 8 of the Human Rights Convention, such leave granted–
  (i) under paragraph 276BE(1), paragraph 276DG or Appendix FM of the Immigration Rules, and
  (ii) who is not subject to a condition requiring that person to maintain and accommodate himself, and any person dependent upon him, without recourse to public funds.

4 Other persons from abroad who are ineligible for an allocation of housing accommodation

(1) A person who is not subject to immigration control is to be treated as a person from abroad who is ineligible for an allocation of housing accommodation under Part 6 of the 1996 Act if–
  (a) subject to paragraph (2), he is not habitually resident in the United Kingdom, the Channel Islands, the Isle of Man, or the Republic of Ireland;
  (b) his only right to reside in the United Kingdom–
    (i) is derived from his status as a jobseeker or the family member of a jobseeker; or
    (ii) is an initial right to reside for a period not exceeding three months under regulation 13 of the EEA Regulations; or
    (iii) is a derivative right to reside to which he is entitled under regulation 15A(1) of the EEA Regulations, but only in a case where the right exists under that regulation because the applicant satisfies the criteria in regulation 15A(4A) of those Regulations; or

(iv) is derived from Article 20 of the Treaty on the Functioning of the European Union, in a case where the right to reside arises because a British citizen would otherwise be deprived of the genuine enjoyment of the substance of their rights as a European Union citizen; or

(c) his only right to reside in the Channel Islands, the Isle of Man or the Republic of Ireland–

(i) is a right equivalent to one of those mentioned in sub-paragraphs (b)(i),(ii) or (iii) which is derived from the Treaty on the Functioning of the European Union; or

(ii) is derived from Article 20 of the Treaty on the Functioning of the European Union, in a case where the right to reside–

(a) in the Republic of Ireland arises because an Irish citizen, or

(b) in the Channel Islands or the Isle of Man arises because a British citizen also entitled to reside there

would otherwise be deprived of the genuine enjoyment of the substance of their rights as a European Union citizen.

(2) The following are not to be treated as persons from abroad who are ineligible for an allocation of housing accommodation pursuant to paragraph (1)(a)–

(a) a worker;

(b) a self-employed person;

(c) a person who is treated as a worker for the purpose of the definition of 'qualified person' in regulation 6(1) of the EEA Regulations pursuant to –

(i) [Revoked].

(ii) regulation 5 of the Accession Regulations 2013 (right of residence of an accession State national subject to worker authorisation);

(d) a person who is the family member of a person specified in sub-paragraphs (a)-(c);

(e) a person with a right to reside permanently in the United Kingdom by virtue of regulation 15(c), (d) or (e) of the EEA Regulations; and

(f) [Revoked].

(g) a person who is in the United Kingdom as a result of his deportation, expulsion or other removal by compulsion of law from another country to the United Kingdom;

(h) [Revoked].

(i) [Revoked].

5 Persons subject to immigration control who are eligible for housing assistance

(1) The following classes of persons subject to immigration control are persons who are eligible for housing assistance under Part 7 of the 1996 Act–

(a) Class A – a person who is recorded by the Secretary of State as a refugee within the definition in Article 1 of the Refugee Convention and who has leave to enter or remain in the United Kingdom;

(b) Class B – a person–

(i) who has exceptional leave to enter or remain in the United Kingdom granted outside the provisions of the Immigration Rules; and

(ii) whose leave to enter or remain is not subject to a condition requiring him to maintain and accommodate himself, and any person who is dependent on him, without recourse to public funds;

(c) Class C – a person who is habitually resident in the United Kingdom, the Channel Islands, the Isle of Man or the Republic of Ireland and whose leave to enter or remain in the United Kingdom is not subject to any limitation or condition, other than a person–

(i) who has been given leave to enter or remain in the United Kingdom upon an undertaking given by his sponsor;

(ii) who has been resident in the United Kingdom, the Channel Islands, the Isle of Man or the Republic of Ireland for less than five years beginning on the date of entry or the date on which his sponsor gave the undertaking in respect of him, whichever date is the later; and

(iii) whose sponsor or, where there is more than one sponsor, at least one of whose sponsors, is still alive;

(d) Class D – a person who has humanitarian protection granted under the Immigration Rules;

(e) [Revoked].

(f) Class F – a person who is habitually resident in the United Kingdom, the Channel Islands, the Isle of Man or the Republic of Ireland and who has limited leave to enter the United Kingdom as a relevant Afghan citizen under paragraph 276BA1 of the Immigration Rules; and

(g) Class G – a person who has limited leave to enter or remain in the United Kingdom on family or private life grounds under Article 8 of the Human Rights Convention, such leave granted–

(i) under paragraph 276BE(1), paragraph 276DG or Appendix FM of the Immigration Rules, and

(ii) who is not subject to a condition requiring that person to maintain and accommodate himself, and any person dependent upon him, without recourse to public funds.

(2) [Revoked].

(3) [Revoked].

6 Other persons from abroad who are ineligible for housing assistance

(1) A person who is not subject to immigration control is to be treated as a person from abroad who is ineligible for housing assistance under Part 7 of the 1996 Act if–

(a) subject to paragraph (2), he is not habitually resident in the United Kingdom, the Channel Islands, the Isle of Man, or the Republic of Ireland;

(b) his only right to reside in the United Kingdom–

(i) is derived from his status as a jobseeker or the family member of a jobseeker; or

(ii) is an initial right to reside for a period not exceeding three months under regulation 13 of the EEA Regulations; or

(iii) is a derivative right to reside to which he is entitled under regulation 15A(1) of the EEA Regulations, but only in a case where the right exists under that regulation because the applicant satisfies the criteria in regulation 15A(4A) of those Regulations; or

(iv) is derived from Article 20 of the Treaty on the Functioning of the European Union in a case where the right to reside arises because a British citizen would otherwise be deprived of the genuine enjoyment of the substance of the rights attaching to the status of European Union citizen; or

(c) his only right to reside in the Channel Islands, the Isle of Man or the Republic of Ireland–
  (i) is a right equivalent to one of those mentioned in sub-paragraph (b)(i),(ii) or (iii) which is derived from the Treaty on the Functioning of the European Union; or
  (ii) is derived from Article 20 of the Treaty on the Functioning of the European Union, in a case where the right to reside–
    (a) in the Republic of Ireland arises because an Irish citizen, or
    (b) in the Channel Islands or the Isle of Man arises because a British citizen also entitled to reside there

  would otherwise be deprived of the genuine enjoyment of the substance of their rights as a European Union citizen.

(2) The following are not to be treated as persons from abroad who are ineligible for housing assistance pursuant to paragraph (1)(a)–
  (a) a worker;
  (b) a self-employed person;
  (c) a person who is treated as a worker for the purpose of the definition of 'qualified person' in regulation 6(1) of the EEA Regulations pursuant to –
    (i) [Revoked].
    (ii) regulation 5 of the Accession Regulations 2013 (right of residence of an accession State national subject to worker authorisation);
  (d) a person who is the family member of a person specified in sub-paragraphs (a)-(c);
  (e) a person with a right to reside permanently in the United Kingdom by virtue of regulation 15(c), (d) or (e) of the EEA Regulations; and
  (f) [Revoked].
  (g) a person who is in the United Kingdom as a result of his deportation, expulsion or other removal by compulsion of law from another country to the United Kingdom;
  (h) [Revoked].
  (i) [Revoked].

7 Revocation

Subject to regulation 8, the Regulations specified in column (1) of the Schedule are revoked to the extent mentioned in column (3) of the Schedule.

8 Transitional provisions

The revocations made by these Regulations shall not have effect in relation to an applicant whose application for–

(a) an allocation of housing accommodation under Part 6 of the 1996 Act; or

(b) housing assistance under Part 7 of the 1996 Act,

was made before 1st June 2006.

Homelessness (Suitability of Accommodation) (England) Order 2003 SI No 3326

1 Citation, commencement and application

(1) This Order may be cited as the Homelessness (Suitability of Accommodation) (England) Order 2003 and shall come into force on 1st April 2004.

(2) This Order applies in relation to the duties of local housing authorities in England to make accommodation available for occupation by applicants under Part 7 of the Housing Act 1996.

2 Interpretation

In this Order–

'applicant with family commitments' means an applicant–

(a) who is pregnant;

(b) with whom a pregnant woman resides or might reasonably be expected to reside; or

(c) with whom dependent children reside or might reasonably be expected to reside;

'B&B accommodation' means accommodation (whether or not breakfast is included)–

(a) which is not separate and self-contained premises; and

(b) in which any one of the following amenities is shared by more than one household–

(i) a toilet;

(ii) personal washing facilities;

(iii) cooking facilities,

but does not include accommodation which is owned or managed by a local housing authority, a non-profit registered provider of social housing or a voluntary organisation as defined in section 180(3) of the Housing Act 1996; and

any reference to a numbered section is a reference to a section of the Housing Act 1996.

3 Accommodation unsuitable where there is a family commitment

Subject to the exceptions contained in article 4, B&B accommodation is not to be regarded as suitable for an applicant with family commitments where accommodation is made available for occupation–

(a) under section 188(1), 190(2), 193(2) or 200(1); or

(b) under section 195(2), where the accommodation is other than that occupied by the applicant at the time of making his application.

4 Exceptions

(1) Article 3 does not apply–

(a) where no accommodation other than B&B accommodation is available for occupation by an applicant with family commitments; and

(b) the applicant occupies B&B accommodation for a period, or a total of periods, which does not exceed 6 weeks.

(2) In calculating the period, or total period, of an applicant's occupation of B&B accommodation for the purposes of paragraph (1)(b), there shall be disregarded–

(a) any period before 1st April 2004; and
(b) where a local housing authority is subject to the duty under section 193 by virtue of section 200(4), any period before that authority became subject to that duty.

Homelessness (Priority Need for Accommodation) (England) Order 2002 SI No 2051

1 Citation, commencement and interpretation

(1) This Order may be cited as the Homelessness (Priority Need for Accommodation) (England) Order 2002 and shall come into force on the day after the day on which it is made.

(2) This Order extends to England only.

(3) In this Order–

'looked after, accommodated or fostered' has the meaning given by section 24(2) of the Children Act 1989 or, as the case may be, section 104(3) of the Social Services and Well-being (Wales) Act 2014; and

'relevant student' means a person to whom section 24B(3) of the Children Act 1989 or, as the case may be, section 114(5) or 115(6) of the Social Services and Well-being (Wales) Act 2014 applies–

(a) who is in full-time further or higher education; and

(b) whose term-time accommodation is not available to him during a vacation.

2 Priority need for accommodation

The descriptions of person specified in the following articles have a priority need for accommodation for the purposes of Part 7 of the Housing Act 1996.

3 Children aged 16 or 17

(1) A person (other than a person to whom paragraph (2) below applies) aged sixteen or seventeen who is not a relevant child for the purposes of section 23A of the Children Act 1989 or, as the case may be, is not a category 2 young person within the meaning of section 104(2) of the Social Services and Well-being (Wales) Act 2014.

(2) This paragraph applies to a person to whom a local authority owe a duty to provide accommodation under section 20 of that Act (provision of accommodation for children in need) or, as the case may be, section 76 of the Social Services and Well-being (Wales) Act 2014 (accommodation for children without parents or who are lost or abandoned etc).

4 Young people under 21

(1) A person (other than a relevant student) who–

(a) is under twenty-one; and

(b) at any time after reaching the age of sixteen, but while still under eighteen, was, but is no longer, looked after, accommodated or fostered.

5 Vulnerability: institutional backgrounds

(1) A person (other than a relevant student) who has reached the age of twenty-one and who is vulnerable as a result of having been looked after, accommodated or fostered.

(2) A person who is vulnerable as a result of having been a member of Her Majesty's regular naval, military or air forces.

(3) A person who is vulnerable as a result of–

(a) having served a custodial sentence (within the meaning of section 76 of the Powers of Criminal Courts (Sentencing) Act 2000);
(b) having been committed for contempt of court or any other kindred offence;
(c) having been remanded in custody (within the meaning of paragraph (b), (c) or (d) of section 88(1) of that Act).

6 Vulnerability: fleeing violence or threats of violence
A person who is vulnerable as a result of ceasing to occupy accommodation by reason of violence from another person or threats of violence from another person which are likely to be carried out.

Allocation of Housing and Homelessness (Review Procedures) Regulations 1999 SI No 71[5]

PART I: GENERAL

1 Citation, commencement and interpretation

(1) These Regulations may be cited as the Allocation of Housing and Homelessness (Review Procedures) Regulations 1999 and shall come into force on 11th February 1999.

(2) In these Regulations –

'the authority' means the local housing authority which has made the decision whose review under section 164 or 202 has been requested;

'the Decisions on Referrals Order' means the Homelessness (Decisions on Referrals) Order 1998;

'the reviewer' means –

(a) where the original decision falls within section 202(1)(a), (b), (c), (e) or (f), the authority;

(b) where the original decision falls within section 202(1)(d) (a decision under section 198(5) whether the conditions are met for referral of a case) –

(i) the notifying authority and the notified authority, where the review is carried out by those authorities;

(ii) the person appointed to carry out the review in accordance with regulation 7, where the case falls within that regulation.

(3) In these Regulations, references to sections are references to sections of the Housing Act 1996.

2 Who is to make the decision on the review

Where the decision of the authority on a review of an original decision made by an officer of the authority is also to be made by an officer, that officer shall be someone who was not involved in the original decision and who is senior to the officer who made the original decision.

PART II: THE HOUSING REGISTER

3 Notification of review procedure

Following a duly made request for a review under section 164, the authority shall –

(a) notify the person concerned that he, or someone acting on his behalf, may make representations in writing to the authority in connection with the review; and

(b) if they have not already done so, notify the person concerned of the procedure to be followed in connection with the review.

4 Procedure on a review

The authority shall, subject to compliance with the provisions of regulation 5, consider any representations made under regulation 3.

5 Revoked in relation to Wales.

5 Notification of the decision on a review

The period within which the authority shall notify the person concerned of the decision on a review under section 164 is eight weeks from the day on which the request for a review is made to the authority or such longer period as the authority and the person concerned may agree in writing.

PART III: HOMELESSNESS

6 Request for a review and notification of review procedure

(1) A request for a review under section 202 shall be made –
   (a) to the authority, where the original decision falls within section 202(1)(a), (b), (c), (e) or (f);
   (b) to the notifying authority, where the original decision falls within section 202(1)(d) (a decision under section 198(5) whether the conditions are met for referral of a case).

(2) Except where a case falls within regulation 7, the authority to whom a request for a review under section 202 has been made shall –
   (a) notify the applicant that he, or someone acting on his behalf, may make representations in writing to the authority in connection with the review; and
   (b) if they have not already done so, notify the applicant of the procedure to be followed in connection with the review.

(3) Where a case falls within regulation 7, the person appointed in accordance with that regulation shall –
   (a) notify the applicant that he, or someone acting on his behalf, may make representations in writing to that person in connection with the review; and
   (b) notify the applicant of the procedure to be followed in connection with the review.

7 Initial procedure where the original decision was made under the Decisions on Referrals Order

(1) Where the original decision under section 198(5) (whether the conditions are met for the referral of the case) was made under the Decisions on Referrals Order, a review of that decision shall, subject to paragraph (2), be carried out by a person appointed by the notifying authority and the notified authority.

(2) If a person is not appointed in accordance with paragraph (1) within five working days from the day on which the request for a review is made, the review shall be carried out by a person –
   (a) from the panel constituted in accordance with paragraph 3 of the Schedule to the Decisions on Referrals Order ('the panel'), and
   (b) appointed in accordance with paragraph (3) below.

(3) The notifying authority shall within five working days from the end of the period specified in paragraph (2) request the chairman of the Local Government Association or his nominee ('the proper officer') to appoint a person from the panel and the proper officer shall do so within seven days of the request.

(4) The notifying authority and the notified authority shall within five working days of the appointment of the person appointed ('the appointed person')

provide him with the reasons for the original decision and the information and evidence on which that decision was based.

(5) The appointed person shall –
(a) send to the notifying authority and the notified authority any representations made under regulation 6; and
(b) invite those authorities to respond to those representations.

(6) The appointed person shall not be the same person as the person who made the original decision.

(7) For the purposes of this regulation a working day is a day other than Saturday, Sunday, Christmas Day, Good Friday or a bank holiday.

8 Procedure on a review

(1) The reviewer shall, subject to compliance with the provisions of regulation 9, consider –
(a) any representations made under regulation 6 and, in a case falling within regulation 7, any responses to them; and
(b) any representations made under paragraph (2) below.

(2) If the reviewer considers that there is a deficiency or irregularity in the original decision, or in the manner in which it was made, but is minded nonetheless to make a decision which is against the interests of the applicant on one or more issues, the reviewer shall notify the applicant –
(a) that the reviewer is so minded and the reasons why; and
(b) that the applicant, or someone acting on his behalf, may make representations to the reviewer orally or in writing or both orally and in writing.

9 Notification of the decision on a review

(1) The period within which notice of the decision on a review under section 202 shall be given under section 203(3) to the applicant shall be –
(a) eight weeks from the day on which the request for the review is made, where the original decision falls within section 202(1)(a), (b), (c), (e) or (f);
(b) ten weeks from the day on which the request for the review is made, where the original decision falls within section 202(1)(d) and the review is carried out by the notifying authority and the notified authority;
(c) twelve weeks from the day on which the request for the review is made in a case falling within regulation 7.

(2) The period specified in paragraph (1) may be such longer period as the applicant and the reviewer may agree in writing.

(3) In a case falling within paragraph (1)(c), the appointed person shall notify his decision on the review, and his reasons for it, in writing to the notifying authority and the notified authority within a period of eleven weeks from the day on which the request for the review is made, or within a period commencing on that day which is one week shorter than that agreed in accordance with paragraph (2).

PART IV: REVOCATION

10 Revocation and transitional provisions

(1) Subject to paragraph (2), the following provisions are hereby revoked –

(a) regulations 2 to 8 of the Allocation of Housing and Homelessness (Review Procedures and Amendment) Regulations 1996;

(b) the definition of 'the Review Regulations' in regulation 1(3) of the Allocation of Housing and Homelessness (Amendment) Regulations 1997 and regulation 6 of those Regulations.

(2) The provisions revoked by paragraph (1) shall continue in force in any case where a request for a review under section 164 or 202 is made prior to the date these Regulations come into force.

Homelessness (Suitability of Accommodation) Order 1996 SI No 3204[6]

1 Citation and commencement

This Order may be cited as the Homelessness (Suitability of Accommodation) Order 1996 and shall come into force on 20th January 1997.

2 Matters to be taken into account

In determining whether it would be, or would have been, reasonable for a person to continue to occupy accommodation and in determining whether accommodation is suitable for a person there shall be taken into account whether or not the accommodation is affordable for that person and, in particular, the following matters –

(a) the financial resources available to that person, including, but not limited to –
- (i) salary, fees and other remuneration;
- (ii) social security benefits;
- (iii) payments due under a court order for the making of periodical payments to a spouse or a former spouse, or to, or for the benefit of, a child;
- (iv) payments of child support maintenance due under the Child Support Act 1991;
- (v) contributions to the costs in respect of the accommodation which are or were made or which might reasonably be expected to be, or have been, made by other members of his household;
- (vi) pensions
- (vii) financial assistance towards the costs in respect of the accommodation, including loans, provided by a local authority, voluntary organisation or other body;
- (viii) benefits derived from a policy of insurance;
- (ix) savings and other capital sums;

(b) the costs in respect of the accommodation, including, but not limited to, –
- (i) payments of, or by way of, rent;
- (ii) payments in respect of a licence or permission to occupy the accommodation;
- (iii) mortgage costs;
- (iv) payments of, or by way of, service charges;
- (v) mooring charges payable for a houseboat;
- (vi) where the accommodation is a caravan or a mobile home, payments in respect of the site on which it stands;
- (vii) the amount of council tax payable in respect of the accommodation;
- (viii) payments by way of deposit or security in respect of the accommodation;
- (ix) payments required by an accommodation agency;

(c) payments which that person is required to make under a court order for

6 Revoked in relation to Wales.

the making of periodical payments to a spouse or a former spouse, or to, or for the benefit of, a child and payments of child support maintenance required to be made under the Child Support Act 1991;

(d) that person's other reasonable living expenses.

APPENDIX C

Guidance[1]

Right to move: statutory guidance on social housing allocations for local housing authorities in England (March 2015) 794
Supplementary guidance on domestic abuse and homelessness (November 2014) 800
Providing social housing for local people: statutory guidance on social housing allocations for local authorities in England (December 2013) 812
Supplementary Guidance on the homelessness changes in the Localism Act 2011 and on the Homelessness (Suitability of Accommodation) (England) Order 2012 (November 2012) 816
Allocation of accommodation: guidance for local housing authorities in England (June 2012) 827
Provision of Accommodation for 16 and 17 year old young people who may be homeless and/or require accommodation (April 2010) 861
Homelessness Code of Guidance for Local Authorities: Supplementary Guidance on Intentional Homelessness (August 2009) 878
Homelessness Code of Guidance for Local Authorities (July 2006) 881

In addition to this guidance, the following Welsh guidance is reproduced in the ebook version of *Homelessness and Allocations*:

- Code of Guidance to Local Authorities on the Allocation of Accommodation and Homelessness 2016 (March 2016)
- Provision of Accommodation for 16 and 17 year old young people who may be homeless (September 2010)

1 © Crown copyright. All guidance available at www.gov.uk.

Right to move: statutory guidance on social housing allocations for local housing authorities in England (March 2015)

Introduction

1. This is guidance by the Secretary of State for Communities and Local Government under section 169 of the Housing Act 1996 ('the 1996 Act'). Local housing authorities housing authorities) are required to have regard to it in exercising their functions under Part 6 of the 1996 Act.
2. It is in addition to the Guidance for Local Housing Authorities in England on the Allocation of Accommodation issued in June 2012 ('the 2012 guidance').
3. References to sections in this guidance are references to sections in the 1996 Act.
4. Housing authorities are encouraged to review their existing allocation policies and revise them, where appropriate, in the light of this guidance as soon as possible.

PURPOSE OF THE GUIDANCE

5. The Government is committed to increasing mobility for social tenants to enable tenants to meet their aspirations, and to support them into work. We want to ensure that tenants are not prevented from taking up an employment opportunity because they cannot find a suitable place to live, recognising that long term unemployment is damaging for individuals and communities. That is why in the Autumn Statement 2013 we set out our intention to introduce a Right to Move for social tenants who need to move to take up a job or live closer to employment or training.
6. We've already taken some important steps in the right direction. *HomeSwap* Direct is helping social tenants search for a new home across the country. Through the Localism Act, we have given local authorities the freedom to make better use of the social housing stock by taking transferring tenants who are not in housing need out of the allocation legislation, allowing authorities to develop appropriate policies for transferring tenants, without the risk of challenge from those in greater need on the waiting list.
7. The Government has also taken decisive steps to increase the supply of affordable housing. The current Affordable Homes Programme is on track to deliver 170,000 homes between 2011 and 2015 with £19.5 billion of public and private investment. A further £38 billion of public and private investment will help deliver another 275,000 new affordable homes between 2015 and 2020.
8. To give effect to the Right to Move we have introduced regulations to prevent local authorities applying a local connection test that could disadvantage tenants who need to move across local authority boundaries for work related reasons. This guidance is intended to assist local authorities to implement these regulations.
9. The Government has made clear that we expect social homes to go to people who genuinely need and deserve them. That is why the Localism Act has maintained the protection provided by the statutory reasonable preference

criteria which ensure that priority for social housing continues to be given to those in the greatest housing need.

10. Another important aim of this guidance, therefore, is to assist local authorities to apply the allocation legislation to ensure that tenants who need to move within or across local authority boundaries are given appropriate priority under local authorities' allocation schemes.

QUALIFICATION

11. Section 160ZA(7) provides that local authorities may decide who does or does not qualify for an allocation of social housing, subject to any regulations made under subsection 8 which provides that the Secretary of State may prescribe that certain classes of persons are or are not qualifying persons, or that certain criteria cannot be taken into account in deciding who qualifies.
12. Subject to parliamentary scrutiny, the Allocation of Housing (Qualification Criteria for Right to Move) (England) Regulations 2015 SI No 967 ('the qualification regulations 2015') will come into force on 20 April. These provide that local authorities must not disqualify certain persons on the grounds that they do not have a local connection with the authority's district. Specifically, a local connection may not be applied to existing social tenants seeking to transfer from another local authority district in England who:
    - have reasonable preference under s166(3)(e) because of a need to move to the local authority's district to avoid hardship, and
    - need to move because the tenant works in the district, or
    - need to move to take up an offer of work
13. This will ensure that existing tenants who are seeking to move between local authority areas in England in order to be closer to their work, or to take up an offer of work (hereafter referred to together as 'work related reasons'), will not be disadvantaged.
14. We have made a similar provision for certain members of the Armed Forces community, by regulating to prevent local authorities from applying a local connection requirement to disqualify them,[1] in order to give effect to the Government's commitment that those who serve in the Armed Forces are not disadvantaged in their access to social housing by the need to move from base to base. Aside from members of the Armed Forces and transferring tenants who will benefit from the Right to Move, the Government has made clear that we expect local authorities to ensure that only long standing local residents, or those with a well established local association should qualify for social housing, and has issued statutory guidance to ensure that local authorities apply a residency test to social housing of at least two years.[2]

Local connection

15. Local connection is defined by s199. A person has a local connection because of normal residence (current or previous) of their own choice, employment, family associations, or special circumstances.

1 Allocation of Housing (Qualification Criteria for Armed Forces) (England) Regulations 2012 SI 1869.

2 Providing Social Housing for Local People: Statutory guidance on social housing allocations for local authorities in England.

Need to move

16. The qualification regulations 2015 apply to transferring tenants who have reasonable preference under s166A(3)(e), that is to say the local authority is satisfied that they need to move to a particular locality in the district of the housing authority, where failure to meet that need would cause hardship (to themselves or others).
17. The local authority must ensure, therefore, not simply that the tenant needs to move for work, but that, if they were unable to do so, it would cause them hardship.
18. Local authorities must be satisfied that the tenant needs, rather than wishes, to move for work related reasons. In the Secretary of State's view the factors that local authorities should take into account in determining whether a tenant needs to move to be closer to work or to take up a job offer include:
    - the distance and/or time taken to travel between work and home
    - the availability and affordability of transport, taking into account level of earnings
    - the nature of the work and whether similar opportunities are available closer to home
    - other personal factors, such as medical conditions and child care, which would be affected if the tenant could not move
    - the length of the work contract
    - whether failure to move would result in the loss of an opportunity to improve their employment circumstances or prospects, for example, by taking up a better job, a promotion, or an apprenticeship
19. This is not an exhaustive list and local authorities may wish to consider providing for other appropriate factors to take into account in the light of local circumstances.

Work

20. The qualification regulations 2015 only apply if work is not short-term or marginal in nature, nor ancillary to work in another district. Voluntary work is also excluded.

Short-term

21. In determining whether work is short-term, the Secretary of State considers that the following are relevant considerations:
    - *whether work is regular or intermittent*

    This is likely to be particularly relevant in the case of the self-employed.
    - *the period of employment and whether or not work was intended to be short-term or long-term at the outset*

    In the Secretary of State's view a contract of employment that was intended to last for less than 12 months could be considered to be short-term.

Marginal

22. The following considerations would be relevant in determining whether work is marginal:
    - *the number of hours worked*

    In the Secretary of State's view employment of less than 16 hours a week could be considered to be marginal in nature. This is the threshold below which a person may be able to claim Income Support and the threshold for a single person's entitlement to Working Tax Credit.

- *the level of earnings*

23. Local authorities should take into account all the relevant factors when reaching a decision. The fact that a tenant only works 15 hours a week, for example, may not be determinative if they are able to demonstrate that the work is regular and the remuneration is substantial.

Ancillary

24. Work must not be ancillary to work in another local authority's district. This means that, if the person works occasionally in the local authority's district, even if the pattern of work is regular, but their main place of work is in a different local authority's district, the work is excluded from the ambit of these regulations.
25. A further relevant consideration would be whether the tenant is expected eventually to return to work in the original local authority district. If a local authority has reason to believe this is the case, they should seek verification from the tenant's employer.
26. A person who seeks to move into a local authority to be closer to work in a neighbouring authority – for example, where the transport links are better in the first local authority's area – is also excluded from these regulations. However, there is nothing to prevent local authorities looking sympathetically on tenants seeking to move into their authority's district for this reason, if they choose to do so.

Voluntary work

27. The regulations exclude voluntary work. Voluntary work means work where no payment is received or the only payment is in respect of any expenses reasonably incurred.

Apprenticeship

28. The term 'work' includes an apprenticeship. This is because an apprenticeship normally takes place under an apprenticeship agreement which is an employment contract (specifically a contract of service).

Genuine intention to take up an offer of work

29. Where the tenant has been offered a job and needs to move to take it up, they must be able to demonstrate to the local authority's satisfaction that they have a genuine intention to take up the offer.
30. Local authorities may wish to ask to see a letter of acceptance and may wish to contact the employer to verify the position. Authorities may also wish to seek clarification from the tenant by interviewing them over the telephone or in person.

Verification and evidence

31. Local authorities will want to satisfy themselves that the work or job-offer is genuine and should seek appropriate documentary evidence.
32. Appropriate evidence could include:
    - a contract of employment

- wage/salary slips covering a certain period of time, or bank statements (this is likely to be particularly relevant in the case of zero-hours contracts)
- tax and benefits information – eg proof that the applicant is in receipt of working tax credit (if eligible)
- a formal offer letter

33. Additionally, local authorities may wish to contact the employer to verify the position.
34. Authorities are strongly advised to consider whether an applicant qualifies for an allocation under the qualification regulations 2015 both at the time of the initial application and when considering making an allocation.

PRIORITISATION

35. The qualification regulations will ensure that tenants who need to move between local authority districts for work related reasons are not disadvantaged by a local connection test. However, to deliver the Right to Move, it is also important that tenants who need to move for work, within or across local authority boundaries, are given appropriate priority under local authorities' allocation schemes.

Hardship reasonable preference

36. Section 166A(3) provides that housing authorities must frame their allocation scheme to ensure that reasonable preference is given to people who need to move to a particular locality in the authority's district, where failure to meet that need would cause hardship (to themselves or others).
37. Paragraph 4.11 of the 2012 guidance sets out the Secretary of State's view that 'hardship' would include, for example, a person who needs to move to a different locality to take up a particular employment, education or training opportunity.
38. This guidance goes further and strongly encourages all local authorities to apply the hardship reasonable preference category to tenants who are seeking to transfer and who need to move within the local authority district or from another local authority district to be closer to work, or to take up an offer of work.
39. In considering whether a transferring tenant needs to move for work related reasons to avoid hardship to themselves (or others), they may wish to take account of the guidance set out in paragraphs 16 to 34 above.
40. Where a tenant is seeking to move within the same local authority district, local authorities are encouraged to take a more flexible approach. This is because the tenant is already accommodated in the district and any move to another social home will therefore be broadly stock neutral (that is to say the transfer creates another void which can be used to meet other housing needs). In particular, local authorities should consider whether or not the issue of whether work is short-term, marginal, ancillary or voluntary carries the same weight in relation to a within district move.

Setting aside a proportion of lets for cross-boundary moves

41. In framing their allocation scheme to determine their allocation priorities, local authorities will wish to strike a balance between the interests of

transferring tenants who need to move into their district for work related reasons and the demand from other applicants in identified housing need.

42. The Secretary of State considers that an appropriate way to do so would be for a local authority to set a quota for the proportion of properties that it expects to allocate each year to transferring tenants who need to move into their district for work related reasons ('the Right to Move quota'). The Secretary of State strongly encourages all local authorities to adopt such an approach and considers that an appropriate quota would be at least 1%.
43. Local authorities should publish the quota as part of their allocation scheme, together with their rationale for adopting the specific percentage. They should review and revise the proportion as appropriate, in the light of changing circumstances.
44. Local authorities may wish to set aside a higher proportion than 1%. Authorities that decide to set a quota that is lower than 1%, should be ready to explain publicly why they have chosen to do so.
45. It is important that local authorities are open and accountable, to their own tenants and the wider community as well as to tenants seeking to move into the area for work related reasons. Accordingly, local authorities are encouraged to report locally on demand for and lettings outcomes in relation to the Right to Move quota.

Area based choice based lettings schemes

46. We are aware that in some parts of the country, local authorities participate in area-based choice based lettings schemes that bring together a number of authorities and Private Registered Providers of social housing, often with a common allocation policy that applies to all the partner local authorities.
47. We consider that such schemes provide an excellent basis for cross-boundary mobility, particularly as housing and employment markets are likely to be similar across the partner authorities. Accordingly, we strongly encourage all local authorities that participate in area-based choice based lettings schemes to consider how they can provide for tenants to move between partner authorities for work related reasons, for example, by providing for a quota of lettings to be made available for this group.

Supplementary guidance on domestic abuse and homelessness (November 2014)

Introduction

1. This guidance is issued to local housing authorities ('housing authorities') in England under section 182(1) of the Housing Act 1996 ('the 1996 Act'). Housing authorities are required to have regard to it in exercising their functions under Part 7 of the 1996 Act ('Part 7').
2. This statutory guidance supplements the relevant sections of the Homelessness Code of Guidance for Local Authorities issued in July 2006, and the Supplementary Guidance on the homelessness changes in the Localism Act 2011 and on the Homelessness (Suitability of Accommodation) (England) Order 2012 issued in November 2012 which deal with domestic abuse. This guidance should be read in conjunction with existing guidance.
3. This guidance looks at domestic abuse and homelessness. In this guidance the term violence is shorthand for all types of abuse.
4. Domestic abuse is an insidious crime against a partner within an intimate or family relationship. The Government is committed to protecting those at risk of or fleeing domestic abuse. More information about the Government's Ending Violence Against Women and Girls strategy is available here: https://www.gov.uk/government/policies/ending-violence-against-women-and-girls-in-the-uk

What is domestic abuse?

5. Domestic violence and abuse is not simply physical violence. When working with victims of domestic abuse local authorities must take account of the cross-government definition of domestic violence and abuse. This defines domestic violence an d abuse as:

   any incident or pattern of incidents of controlling, coercive, threatening behaviour, violence or abuse between those aged 16 or over who are, or have been, intimate partners or family members regardless of gender or sexuality. The abuse can encompass, but is not limited to:

   - psychological
   - physical
   - sexual
   - financial
   - emotional

6. **Psychological** – including: Intimidation, insults, isolating the person from friends and family, criticising, denying the abuse, treating the person as an inferior, threatening to harm children or take them away, forced marriage.
7. **Physical** – this can include: Shaking, smacking, punching, kicking, presence of finger or bite marks, bruising, starving, tying up, stabbing, suffocation, throwing things, using objects as weapons, female genital mutilation. Physical effects are often in areas of the body that are covered and hidden (ie breasts, legs and stomach).
8. **Sexual** – such as: rape (including the threat of rape), sexual assault, forced prostitution, ignoring religious prohibitions about sex, refusal to practise

safe sex, sexual insults, passing on sexually transmitted diseases, preventing breastfeeding.

9. **Financial** – such as: Not letting the person work, undermining efforts to find work or study, refusing to give money, asking for an explanation of how every penny is spent, making the person beg for money, gambling, not paying bills, building up debt in the other person's name.
10. **Emotional** – including: Swearing, undermining confidence, making racist, sexist or other derogatory remarks, making the person feel unattractive, calling the person stupid or useless, eroding the person's independence, keeping them isolated from family or friends.
11. So-called honour-based abuse is also a form of domestic abuse. Honour-based abuse is explained by the perpetrator of the abuse on the grounds that it was committed as a consequence of the need to protect or defend the honour of the family, it can include all the types of abuse listed below and specific crimes such as forced marriage and female genital mutilation.
12. Over the years as we have understood more about the nature of domestic abuse the definition of domestic abuse has changed. Housing authorities should be alert to any future developments and should never adopt a narrow definition.

What do we mean by controlling behaviour and coercive behaviour?

13. Controlling behaviour is a range of acts designed to make a person subordinate and/or dependent by isolating them from sources of support, exploiting their resources and capacities for personal gain, depriving them of the means needed for independence, resistance and escape and regulating their everyday behaviour. There may be single or multiple perpetrators of domestic abuse.
14. Coercive behaviour is an act or a pattern of acts of assault, threats, humiliation and intimidation or other abuse that is used to harm, punish, or frighten their victim.

Who experiences domestic abuse?

15. People may experience domestic abuse regardless of ethnicity, religion, class, age, sexuality, disability or lifestyle. Domestic violence can also occur in a range of relationships including heterosexual, gay, lesbian, bisexual and transgender relationships, and also within extended families. Housing authorities should bear in mind that the provisions of the Equality Act 2010 for public authorities apply to policies, practice and procedures relating to homelessness and domestic violence. This includes commissioning and procurement. For example as statistics show that women are more likely than men to experience domestic violence the gender equality duty needs to be considered.[1]

Understanding domestic abuse

16. An important factor in ensuring that an authority develops a strong and appropriate response to domestic abuse is understanding what it is, the context in which it takes place in and what the impacts are on victims; as well as how the impacts may be different on different groups of people. For example, victims from black and minority ethnic communities may present with a range of specific needs, including fear of rejection by the community, loss of

1 www.equalityhumanrights.com/public-sector-equality-duty

access to faith and community spaces and may lack English skills to engage in processes. Lesbian, gay, bisexual, and transgender victims may present with different needs again including fear of being outed or being excluded from community spaces.

17. Specialist training for frontline staff, managers and commissioners will help housing advisers to understand how best to tackle the issues victims face and provide or commission the appropriate support. Your local specialist domestic abuse service provider for example local black and minority ethnic, youth and lesbian, gay, bisexual, and transgender service provider or national agencies such as Women's Aid and Co-ordinated Action Against Domestic Abuse can provide training on domestic abuse, and offer support to commission better local services.

Victims with no recourse to public funds

18. People who have no recourse to public funds are not eligible for homelessness assistance. The Government operates the Destitute Domestic Violence Concession to support those who have entered or stayed in the UK as a spouse, unmarried partner, same-sex or civil partner of a British Citizen, or settled citizen and this relationship has broken down due to domestic violence and abuse.
19. A victim may be eligible if:
    - They came to the UK or were granted leave to stay in the UK as the spouse or partner of a British Citizen or someone settled in the UK
    - Their relationship has broken down due to domestic violence and abuse.
20. They can then apply to the Home Office for limited leave to remain under the Destitute Domestic Violence Concession to enable them to access public funds whilst they prepare and submit an application for indefinite leave to remain.

Preventing homelessness

21. Gaining a good understanding of the causes of homelessness will help to inform the range of preventative measures that need to be put in place. Many statutory and non-statutory services can contribute to preventing homelessness. Housing authorities should adopt an open approach and recognise that there will be a broad range of organisations operating in fields other than housing including, for example, organisations working to tackle domestic abuse.
22. Households at risk of domestic abuse often have to leave their homes because of the risk of abuse. 70% of referrals to refuge services in England are from local authority areas outside the one in which the services is located.[2] There is a clear need for women and their children to be able to travel to different areas in order for them to be safe from the perpetrator. We would expect local areas to extend the same level of support to those from other areas as they do to their own residents.
23. Refuges and other forms of emergency and temporary accommodation can provide a safe and supportive environment for households fleeing violence

2 Meeting the needs of households at risk of domestic violence in England: The role of accommodation and housing-related support services, DCLG 2010.

but many households do not wish to leave their homes or choose to return to their homes after a short stay in temporary accommodation despite the risks.

24. Sanctuary Schemes are an additional accommodation option for households at risk of domestic violence which can, where suitable and appropriate, offer households the choice of remaining in their homes. Putting in place a Sanctuary Scheme should not be seen as a replacement for refuge provision. A Sanctuary Scheme must only be used where it is the victim's choice, where it is safe (i.e. subject to a thorough risk assessment) and where the perpetrator no longer lives in the property.
25. A Sanctuary Scheme is a multi-agency victim centred initiative which aims to enable households at risk of violence to remain safely in their own homes by installing a 'Sanctuary' in the home and through the provision of support to the household. A 'Sanctuary' comprises enhanced security measures designed to enable households to remain safely in their homes.
26. Based on extensive research Government published guidance to assist local practitioners in developing strategies to prevent homelessness and support for households at risk of domestic abuse: www.gov.uk/government/publications/sanctuary-schemes-for-households-at-risk-of-domestic-violence-guide-for-agencies.

Identifying domestic abuse early and responding appropriately

27. By better understanding domestic abuse housing authorities will begin to see the strategic links and discover more opportunities to work with others to help tackle and prevent domestic abuse. Housing authorities should have strong policies in place to identify domestic abuse. Alongside their role in tackling homelessness local authorities should take an active role in identifying victims and referring them for help and support. They are key partners in local domestic violence partnerships and should be represented at their local multi-agency risk assessment conference. Every area in England now has a multi-agency risk assessment conference.
28. The multi-agency risk assessment conference leads multi-agency safety planning for high-risk victims of domestic abuse. It brings together the police, independent domestic violence advisers, children's social services, health, social landlords and other relevant agencies. They share information and write a safety plan for each victim and family, which may include actions by any agency present. The housing authority should be consistently represented at the multi-agency risk assessment conference, and should make sure relevant social landlords are also represented.
29. Where a disclosure of domestic abuse is made to a housing advisor, whether or not in the context of a homelessness presentation, the housing advisor should refer to the authority's domestic violence policy and act appropriately.
30. Many housing authorities are landlords but even where they have transferred their stock they will still maintain strong links with local landlords, whether private or registered providers. Housing providers are uniquely placed to spot signs and respond to domestic abuse as they are often on the frontline in communities and in tenants' homes. Authorities should consider how they might identify potential victims of abuse. For example, housing organisations are ideally placed as they have access to people's homes for maintenance purposes and can spot domestic abuse through an analysis of repairs and also

through community development work where trained staff can spot signs of abuse.

31. Those experiencing domestic abuse often only report to Police after more informal routes have been exhausted. Victims can experience many, many incidents of abuse before calling the Police. Housing providers are in a position to identify abuse at earlier stages and should consider how they can best provide support to their residents. By understanding the indicators of domestic abuse through training and professional development, housing officers can increase their confidence to speak to people experiencing abuse, risk assess and safety plan alongside them. Organisations such as the Domestic Abuse Housing Alliance have developed practical approaches to service delivery based on national research to enable landlords to analyse and improve their existing response to domestic abuse. These help practitioners to spot the early signs of domestic abuse and enable them to take action to stop any further escalation.

32. Local authorities should also be alert to the wider role they play in ensuring victim safety. Procedures should be in place to keep all information on victims safe and secure. In many cases, particularly where extended family members or multiple perpetrators may be involved, for example in female genital mutilation, forced marriage and so called honour-based violence cases, perpetrators go to great lengths to seek information on victims. The authority must be alert to the possibility that employees could have links to perpetrators. We would recommend that all cases where any domestic abuse is indicated must be flagged to alert any officer accessing the file that information is not to be given to anyone other than the applicant. Consideration should also be given to restricting access to cases where abuse is disclosed to only named members of staff. Housing authorities should also consider how they flag case files so they can identify those victims who have been referred to a multi-agency risk assessment conference and who may once again present as homeless.

Securing services

33. Support services play an essential role in preventing and tackling homelessness. The Homelessness Code of Guidance for local authorities outlines the types of housing-related and other support services that might be required.

34. In formulating their homelessness strategies, housing authorities need to recognise that for some households, homelessness cannot be tackled, or prevented, solely through the provision of accommodation. Some households will require a range of support services, which may include housing-related support to help them sustain their accommodation, as well as personal support relating to factors such as relationship breakdown, domestic violence, mental health problems, drug and alcohol addiction, poverty, debt and unemployment.

35. There will be a number of accommodation options for victims of domestic abuse. Housing authorities should consider which are most appropriate for each person on a case by case basis taking into account their needs. This may include temporary accommodation or a managed transfer, as well as refuge.

36. For some victims with severe needs and with highly dangerous perpetrators, refuges will be the most appropriate choice. Refuges provide key short term, intensive support for those who flee from abuse. Given the intensity of the

support and the vulnerability of the victims attention should be paid to the length of time they spend in a refuge. Refuges are not simply a substitute for other forms of temporary accommodation. Working with the service provider the housing authority should consider how long a person needs to stay before the provision of other accommodation (which may be temporary in the absence of settled accommodation) with floating support may be more appropriate.

37. When commissioning services for victims of domestic abuse the Secretary of State recommends that authorities adhere to the following standards around:
- Safety, security and dignity;
- Rights and access;
- Physical and emotional help;
- Stability, resilience and autonomy;
- Children and young people;
- Prevention.

38. These standards[3] set out the minimum levels of service we would expect to see in a refuge:

Safety, Security and Dignity
- Victims can access crisis support at any time and receive a timely response.
- Victims are assessed and offered services on the basis of their individual need for safety and support
- Victims are assisted to move geographical location if necessary for their safety
- Provision for male victims is located separately from women's services, within dedicated men's services.

Rights and Access
- Service users are believed and listened to and service interventions are respectful of their rights to self-determination
- Service users with protected characteristics under the Equality Act 2010 can access dedicated specialist services addressing their particular needs
- Resources are allocated to addressing barriers to access.

Health and Wellbeing
- The physical, mental and sexual health needs of service users are addressed
- Service users can access individual counselling or group work to build their confidence and resources
- The organisation works with partners in the sexual violence sector to provide specialist therapeutic support
- The safety and wellbeing of staff teams is attended to.

3 These standards are derived from the Women's Aid National Quality Standards. Service providers may find the full standards of use: www.womensaid.org.uk/page.asp?section=0001000100350002%C2%A7ionTitle=National+Service+Standards&

Stability, resilience and autonomy

- Service users are supported to take charge of decision-making processes in their lives
- Service users are encouraged to identify goals and access education, training and employment to maximise their stability and independence
- Service users have access to resettlement and follow-up services with exit strategies tailored to individual need.

Children and young people

- The safety and wellbeing of children and young people is addressed in risk assessment and support planning
- Children are able to access support to understand their experiences and build their resilience and confidence.
- Support is provided to mothers to develop their parenting resources and maintain their relationships with their children.
- Services are responsive to the needs and views of children and young people.

Prevention

- Children and young people are better informed and educated around consent, healthy relationships, gender inequality and violence against women and girls
- The organisation contributes to training and awareness-raising activities with other professionals and within local communities
- The organisation contributes to local strategies for ending violence against women and girls.

39. Housing authorities should also consider working with other local authorities and other commissioners to commission or provide services to tackle domestic abuse. When they are developing homelessness strategies that tackle domestic abuse they should also involve the local Domestic Violence Forum and local domestic violence service provider(s).

Duties to those homeless of threatened with homelessness

40. The Housing Act 1996 sets out clearly those duties a housing authority owes vulnerable victims of domestic abuse and other violence.
41. Section 177(1) provides that it is not reasonable for a person to continue to occupy accommodation if it is probable that this will lead to domestic violence or other violence against:
    i) the applicant;
    ii) a person who normally resides as a member of the applicant's family; or
    iii) any other person who might reasonably be expected to reside with the applicant.
42. Section 177(1A) provides that violence means violence from another person or threats of violence from another person which are likely to be carried out. Domestic violence is violence from a person who is associated with the victim and also includes threats of violence which are likely to be carried out. Domestic violence is not confined to instances within the home but extends to violence outside the home.

43. Section 178 provides that, for the purposes of defining domestic violence, a person is associated with another if:
    a) they are, or have been, married to each other;
    b) they are or have been civil partners of each other;
    c) they are, or have been, cohabitants (including same sex partners);
    d) they live, or have lived, in the same household;
    e) they are relatives, i.e. father, mother, stepfather, stepmother, son, daughter, stepson, stepdaughter, grandmother, grandfather, grandson, granddaughter, brother, sister, uncle, aunt, niece or nephew (whether of full blood, half blood or by affinity) of that person or of that person's spouse or former spouse. A person is also included if he or she would fall into any of these categories in relation to cohabitees or former cohabitees if they were married to each other;
    f) they have agreed to marry each other whether or not that agreement has been terminated;
    g) they have entered into a civil partnership agreement between them whether or not that agreement has been terminated;
    h) in relation to a child, each of them is a parent of the child or has, or has had, parental responsibility for the child (within the meaning of the Children Act 1989). A child is a person under 18 years of age;
    i) if a child has been adopted or freed for adoption (Adoption Act 1976 s16(1)), two persons are also associated if one is the natural parent or grandparent of the child and the other is the child of a person who has become the parent by virtue of an adoption order (Adoption Act 1976 s72(1)) or has applied for an adoption order or someone with whom the child has been placed for adoption.
44. The Secretary of State considers that the term 'violence' should not be given a restrictive meaning, and that 'domestic violence' should be understood to include threatening behaviour, violence or abuse (psychological, physical, sexual, financial or emotional) between persons who are, or have been, intimate partners, family members or members of the same household, regardless of gender or sexuality. This matter was dealt with in *Yemshaw v London Borough of Hounslow*.[4]
45. An assessment of the likelihood of a threat of violence or abuse being carried out should not be based on whether there has been actual violence or abuse in the past. An assessment must be based on the facts of the case and devoid of any value judgements about what an applicant should or should not do, or should or should not have done, to mitigate the risk of any violence and abuse (eg seek police help or apply for an injunction against the perpetrator). Inquiries into cases where violence and abuse is alleged will need careful handling.
46. It is essential that inquiries do not provoke further violence and abuse. It is not advisable for the housing authority to approach the alleged perpetrator, since this could generate further violence and abuse, and may delay the assessment. Housing authorities may, however, wish to seek information from friends and relatives of the applicant, social services and the police, as appropriate. In some cases, corroborative evidence of actual or threatened violence may

4 [2011] UKSC 3.

not be available, for example, because there were no adult witnesses and/or the applicant was too frightened or ashamed to report incidents to family, friends or the police. In many cases involving violence, the applicant may be in considerable distress and an officer trained in dealing with the particular circumstances should conduct the interview. Applicants should be given the option of being interviewed by an officer of the same sex if they so wish. Be aware that this may be the first time a victim has disclosed their abuse and that the period during which a victim is planning or making their exit, is often the **most dangerous time** for them and their children.

47. In cases where violence is a feature and the applicant may have a local connection elsewhere, the housing authority, in considering whether to notify another housing authority about a possible referral of the case, must be aware that s198 provides that an applicant cannot be referred to another housing authority if he or she, or any person who might reasonably be expected to reside with him or her, would be at risk of violence in the district of the other housing authority.

48. In cases involving violence and abuse, housing authorities may wish to inform applicants of the option of seeking an injunction, but should make clear that there is no obligation on the applicant to do so. The authority may want to consider working with other organisations, for example local or national specialist domestic abuse service providers, such as Women's Aid or Refuge, or a local Independent Domestic Violence Adviser. Victims should be allowed sufficient time and space to absorb and understand the options available to them. Where applicants wish to pursue this option, authorities should inform them that they should seek legal advice and that legal aid for non-molestation orders remains in scope and there is no longer a fee payable for these applications. Further information about Legal Aid is available here: www.gov.uk/check-legal-aid/.

49. Housing authorities should recognise that injunctions ordering a person not to molest, or enter the home of an applicant may not be effective in deterring some habitual perpetrators from carrying out further violence or incursions, and applicants may not have confidence in their effectiveness. Consequently, applicants should not be expected to return home on the strength of an injunction. To ensure applicants who have experienced actual or threatened violence get the support they need, authorities should inform them of appropriate specialist organisations in the area, as above, as well as agencies offering counselling and support.

50. When dealing with cases involving violence, or threat of violence, from outside the home, housing authorities should consider the option of improving the security of the applicant's home to enable him or her to continue to live there safely, where that is an option that the applicant wishes to pursue. In some cases, immediate action to improve security within the victim's home may prevent homelessness. A fast response combined with support from the housing authority, police and the voluntary sector may provide a victim with the confidence to remain in their home.

51. When dealing with domestic violence within the home, where the authority is the landlord, housing authorities should consider the scope for evicting the perpetrator and allowing the victim to remain in their home. **However, where there would be a probability of violence if the applicant continued to**

occupy his or her present accommodation, the housing authority must treat the applicant as homeless and should not expect him or her to remain in, or return to, the accommodation. In all cases involving violence the safety of the applicant and his or her household should be the primary consideration at all stages of decision making as to whether or not the applicant remains in their own home.

Having left accommodation because of violence

52. A person has a priority need if he or she is vulnerable as a result of having to leave accommodation because of violence from another person, or threats of violence from another person that are likely to be carried out. It will usually be apparent from the assessment of the reason for homelessness whether the applicant has had to leave accommodation because of violence or threats of violence. **In cases involving violence, the safety of the applicant and ensuring confidentiality must be of paramount concern.** It is not only domestic violence and abuse that is relevant, but all forms of violence, including racially motivated violence or threats of violence likely to be carried out. Inquiries of the perpetrators of violence should not be made. In assessing whether it is likely that threats of violence are likely to be carried out, a housing authority should only take into account the probability of violence, and not actions which the applicant could take (such as injunctions against the perpetrators).

53. In considering whether applicants are vulnerable as a result of leaving accommodation because of violence or threats of violence likely to be carried out, a housing authority may wish to take into account the following factors:
   i) the nature of the violence or threats of violence (there may have been a single but significant incident or a number of incidents over an extended period of time which have had a cumulative effect);
   ii) the impact and likely effects of the violence or threats of violence on the applicant's current and future well being;
   iii) whether the applicant has any existing support networks, particularly by way of family or friends
   iv) the continuing threat from the perpetrator.

Suitability of accommodation

54. Account will need to be taken of any social considerations relating to the applicant and his or her household that might affect the suitability of accommodation. Any risk of violence or racial harassment in a particular locality must also be taken into account. Where domestic violence is involved and the applicant is not able to stay in the current home, housing authorities may need to consider the need for alternative accommodation whose location can be kept a secret and which has security measures and appropriately trained staff to protect the occupants. For applicants who have suffered domestic violence who are accommodated in an emergency in hostels or bed and breakfast accommodation, the accommodation should be gender-specific as well as have security measures.

Location

55. Whilst authorities should, as far as is practicable, aim to secure accommodation within their own district, they should also recognise that there can be

clear benefits for some applicants to be accommodated outside of the district. This could occur, for example, where the applicant, and/or a member of his or her household, would be at risk of domestic or other violence in the district and need to be accommodated elsewhere to reduce the risk of further contact with the perpetrator(s) or where ex-offenders or drug/alcohol users would benefit from being accommodated outside the district to help break links with previous contacts which could exert a negative influence. Any risk of violence or racial harassment in a particular locality must also be taken into account. Where domestic violence is involved and the applicant is not able to stay in the current home, housing authorities may need to consider the need for alternative accommodation whose location can be kept a secret and which has security measures and staffing to protect the occupants.

Risk of violence

56. A housing authority cannot refer an applicant to another housing authority if that person or any person who might reasonably be expected to reside with him or her would be at risk of violence. The housing authority is under a positive duty to enquire whether the applicant would be at such a risk and, if he or she would, it should not be assumed that the applicant will take steps to deal with the threat.
57. Section 198(3) defines violence as violence from another person or threats of violence from another person which are likely to be carried out. This is the same definition as appears in s.177 in relation to whether it is reasonable to continue to occupy accommodation and the circumstances to be considered as to whether a person runs a risk of violence are the same.
58. Housing authorities should be alert to the deliberate distinction which is made in s.198(3) between actual violence and threatened violence. A high standard of proof of actual violence in the past should not be imposed. The threshold is that there must be:
    (a) no risk of domestic violence (actual or threatened) in the other district; and
    (b) no risk of non-domestic violence (actual or threatened) in the other district. Nor should 'domestic violence' be interpreted restrictively.

Support from other organisations and useful links

If you are a victim of domestic violence and abuse, other organisations can offer you help and support.

The National Domestic Violence Freephone Helpline

(Partnership with Refuge & Women's Aid) 0808 2000 247
www.nationaldomesticviolencehelpline.org.uk

Women's Aid: www.womensaid.org.uk
Women's Aid has an A-Z of local services that can help you locate your local provider
www.womensaid.org.uk/azrefuges.
asp?section=00010001000800060002&itemTitle=A-Z+of+services

Broken Rainbow (Lesbian Gay Bisexual And Transgender domestic violence charity)
0303 999 5428
www.brokenrainbow.org.uk

The National Stalking Helpline (Support and help for stalking victims)
0808 802 0300
www.stalkinghelpline.org

Male Advice Line (Support for male victims of domestic violence)
0808 801 0327
www.mensadviceline.org.uk

Respect (Perpetrators helpline to help stop their violence and change their abusive behaviours)
0808 802 4040
www.respect.uk.net/

Useful links

Find out about domestic violence and abuse, coercive control, disclosure scheme, protection notices, domestic homicide reviews and advisers.
www.gov.uk/domestic-violence-and-abuse

Application for Destitution Domestic Violence concession
www.gov.uk/government/publications/application-for-benefits-for-visa-holder-domestic-violence

Government's Ending Violence Against Women and Girls strategy is available here: www.gov.uk/government/policies/ending-violence-against-women-and-girls-in-the-uk

The government have funded Co-ordinated Action Against Domestic Abuse to support multi agency risk assessment conferences. More information is available at www.caada.org.uk/marac/Information_about_MARACs.html, and specific guidance for housing representatives is available at www.caada.org.uk/marac/Toolkit-Housing-Feb-2012.pdf. If your authority is not represented at your multi agency risk assessment conferences, please contact your local multi agency risk assessment conferences co-ordinator (their contact details are available at www.caada.org.uk/marac/findamarac.html

The Domestic Abuse and Housing Alliance seeks to improve the housing sector's response to domestic abuse through the introduction and adoption of an established set of national domestic abuse service standards. See www.peabody.org.uk/resident-services/safer-communities/domestic-abuse/daha

Providing social housing for local people: statutory guidance on social housing allocations for local authorities in England (December 2013)

Introduction

1. This is guidance by the Secretary of State for Communities and Local Government under section 169 of the Housing Act 1996 (the 1996 Act). Local housing authorities (housing authorities) are required to have regard to it in exercising their functions under Part 6 of the 1996 Act.
2. It is in addition to the Guidance for Local Housing Authorities in England on the Allocation of Accommodation issued in June 2012 (the 2012 guidance).
3. References to sections in this guidance are references to sections in the 1996 Act.
4. Housing authorities are encouraged to review their existing allocation policies and revise them, where appropriate, in the light of this guidance as soon as possible.

Purpose of the guidance

5. Social housing – stable and affordable – is of enormous importance for the millions who live in it now and for those who look to it to provide the support they need in future. The way it is allocated is key to creating communities where people choose to live and are able to prosper.
6. The Government has made clear that we expect social homes to go to people who genuinely need and deserve them. That is why the Localism Act has maintained the protection provided by the statutory reasonable preference criteria which ensure that priority for social housing continues to be given to those in the greatest housing need.
7. The Localism Act has also given back to local authorities the freedom to better manage their social housing waiting list, as well as providing authorities with greater flexibility to enable them to tackle homelessness by providing homeless households with suitable private sector accommodation. Local authorities can now decide who qualifies for social housing in their area, and can develop solutions which make best use of the social housing stock. This guidance is intended to assist housing authorities to make full use of the flexibilities within the allocation legislation to better meet the needs of their local residents and their local communities.
8. The Government has also taken decisive steps to increase the supply of affordable housing, with £19.5 billion of public and private investment in the current Spending Review, and up to £23.3 billion more money invested from 2015 to 2018 alongside receipts from Right to Buy sales.
9. This investment in new affordable housing will help to meet housing need. We now want to see local authorities take an approach to social housing allocations which gives greater priority to those in need who have invested in and demonstrated a commitment to their local community.
10. The Prime Minister has made clear the Government's determination to tackle the widespread perception that the way social housing is allocated is unfair, and to address concerns that the system favours households who have little

connection to the local area over local people and members of the Armed Forces. Another important aim of this guidance, therefore, is to encourage authorities to be open and transparent about who is applying for and being allocated social housing in their area.

Qualification for social housing

11. Section 160ZA(6) provides that housing authorities may only allocate accommodation to people who are defined as 'qualifying persons' and section 160ZA(7) gives them the power to decide the classes of people who are, or are not, qualifying persons.
12. The Government is of the view that, in deciding who qualifies or does not qualify for social housing, local authorities should ensure that they prioritise applicants who can demonstrate a close association with their local area. Social housing is a scarce resource, and the Government believes that it is appropriate, proportionate and in the public interest to restrict access in this way, to ensure that, as far as possible, sufficient affordable housing is available for those amongst the local population who are on low incomes or otherwise disadvantaged and who would find it particularly difficult to find a home on the open market.
13. Some housing authorities have decided to include a residency requirement as part of their qualification criteria, requiring the applicant (or member of the applicant's household) to have lived within the authority's district for a specified period of time in order to qualify for an allocation of social housing. The Secretary of State believes that including a residency requirement is appropriate and strongly encourages all housing authorities to adopt such an approach. The Secretary of State believes that a reasonable period of residency would be at least two years.
14. We are aware that in some parts of the country, housing authorities share a common allocation policy with their neighbours and may wish to adopt a broader residency test which would be met if an applicant lives in any of the partners' districts. Such an approach might be particularly appropriate where an established housing market area spans a number of local authority districts, and could help promote labour mobility within a wider geographical area.
15. Housing authorities may wish to consider whether there is a need to adopt other qualification criteria alongside a residency requirement to enable and ensure that applicants who are not currently resident in the district who can still demonstrate a strong association to the local area are able to qualify. Examples of such criteria might include:
    - family association – for example, where the applicant has close family who live in the district and who have done so for a minimum period of time
    - employment in the district – for example, where the applicant or member of their household is currently employed in the district and has worked there for a certain number of years
16. Whatever qualification criteria for social housing authorities adopt, they will need to have regard to their duties under the Equality Act 2010, as well as their duties under other relevant legislation such as section 225 of the Housing Act 2004.
17. Housing authorities are reminded of the desirability of operating a housing

options approach (see paragraph 3.19 of the 2012 guidance) as part of a move to a managed waiting list. In this way, people who have not lived in the area long enough to qualify for social housing can be provided with advice and any necessary support to help them find appropriate alternative solutions.

Providing for exceptions

18. Housing authorities should consider the need to provide for exceptions from their residency requirement; and must make an exception for certain members of the regular and reserve Armed Forces – see further at paragraph 23 below. Providing for appropriate exceptions when framing residency requirements would be in line with paragraphs 3.22 and 3.24 of the 2012 guidance.
19. It is important that housing authorities retain the flexibility to take proper account of special circumstances. This can include providing protection to people who need to move away from another area, to escape violence or harm; as well as enabling those who need to return, such as homeless families and care leavers whom the authority have housed outside their district, and those who need support to rehabilitate and integrate back into the community.
20. There may also be sound policy reasons not to apply a residency test to existing social tenants seeking to move between local authorities. Housing authorities should assist in tackling under-occupation, for example allowing tenants to move if they wish to downsize to a smaller social home. There may also be sound housing management reasons to disapply a residency test for hard to let stock.
21. These examples are not intended to be exhaustive and housing authorities may wish to consider providing for other appropriate exceptions in the light of local circumstances. In addition, authorities retain a discretion to deal with individual cases where there are exceptional circumstances.
22. The Government wants to increase opportunities for hardworking households. That is why we have announced an intention to introduce a Right to Move for social tenants seeking to move to take up a job or be closer to their work, whether within the local authority district or across local authority boundaries. We will consult on options for implementing this policy in Spring 2014. In the meantime, we expect housing authorities to make appropriate exceptions to their residency test for social tenants so as not to impede labour market mobility.

Members of the Armed Forces

23. The Government is committed to ensuring that Service personnel and their families have access to appropriate accommodation when they leave the Armed Forces. The Allocation of Housing (Qualification Criteria for Armed Forces) (England) Regulations 2012 SI No 1869 ensure that, where housing authorities decide to use a local connection[1] requirement as a qualification criterion, they must not apply that criterion to the following persons so as to disqualify them from an allocation of social housing:

1 As defined by s199 of the 1996 Act. A person has a local connection with the district of a housing authority if he has a connection because of normal residence there (either current or previous) of his own choice, employment there, family connections or special circumstances.

- those who are currently serving in the regular forces or who were serving in the regular forces at any time in the five years preceding their application for an allocation of social housing
- bereaved spouses or civil partners of those serving in the regular forces where (i) the bereaved spouse or civil partner has recently ceased, or will cease to be entitled, to reside in Ministry of Defence accommodation following the death of their service spouse or civil partner, and (ii) the death was wholly or partly attributable to their service
- existing or former members of the reserve forces who are suffering from a serious injury, illness, or disability which is wholly or partly attributable to their service

24. The Regulations give effect to the Government's commitment that those who serve in the regular and reserve Armed Forces are not disadvantaged in their access to social housing by the requirements of their service.
25. When adopting a residency test, we expect housing authorities to also consider the wider needs of the Armed Forces community, and to be sympathetic to changing family circumstances, recognising, for example, that the spouses and partners of Service personnel can also be disadvantaged by the need to move from base to base.

Prioritising local connection

26. Housing authorities have the ability to take account of any local connection between the applicant and their district when determining relative priorities between households who are on the waiting list (s166A(5)). For these purposes, local connection is defined by reference to s199 of the 1996 Act.
27. Housing authorities should consider whether, in the light of local circumstances, there is a need to take advantage of this flexibility, in addition to applying a residency requirement as part of their qualification criteria. Examples of circumstances in which the power might be useful would include:
    - dealing sensitively with lettings in rural villages by giving priority to those with a local connection to the parish, as part of a local lettings policy (section 166A(6)(b) – see paragraph 4.21 of the 2012 guidance)
    - where a group of housing authorities apply a wider residency qualification test, to give greater priority to people who live or work (or have close family) in any of the partner authorities' own district

Information about allocations

28. It is important that applicants and the wider community understand how social housing is allocated in their area, and that they know who is getting that social housing, so that they can see that the allocation system is fair and the authority is complying with its allocation scheme. We would encourage housing authorities to consider how accurate and anonymised information on waiting list applicants and lettings outcomes could be routinely published, to strengthen public confidence in the fairness of their allocation scheme.

Supplementary Guidance on the homelessness changes in the Localism Act 2011 and on the Homelessness (Suitability of Accommodation) (England) Order 2012 (November 2012)

Introduction

1. This supplementary guidance explains the changes sections 148 and 149 of the Localism Act make to the homelessness legislation. It explains in practice how the new power, that allows private rented sector offers to be made to end the main homelessness duty, should work and what local authorities should do as a consequence of the new power's introduction.
2. This guidance also explains the requirements of the Homelessness (Suitability of Accommodation) (England) Order 2012. The Order requires local authorities to put in place arrangements to ensure that private rented sector offer accommodation is suitable. The location requirements of the Order also extend to any accommodation secured under Part VII of the Housing Act 1996 (including temporary accommodation).
3. Sections 148 and 149 of the Localism Act 2011 amend Part 7 of the Housing Act 1996 ('the 1996 Act'). These sections as well as the Homelessness (Suitability of Accommodation) (England) Order 2012 come into force on 9th November 2012.
4. This guidance is issued by the Secretary of State under section 182 of the the 1996 Act. Under section 182(1) of the 1996 Act, local housing authorities are required to have regard to this guidance in exercising their functions under Part 7 of the 1996 Act, as amended.
5. This statutory guidance supplements the relevant sections of the Homelessness Code of Guidance for Local Authorities issued in July 2006 ('the 2006 Code'), which deal with qualifying offers and reasonable to accept an offer. This guidance should be read in conjunction with the Homelessness Code of Guidance.

Overview

Localism Act 2011

6. The principal effect of the legislative changes is to amend the way in which the duty on authorities to secure accommodation under section 193(2) of the 1996 Act can be brought to an end with an offer of suitable accommodation in the private rented sector.
7. These changes will allow local authorities to end the main homelessness duty with a private rented sector offer, without the applicant's consent. The duty can only be ended in the private rented sector in this way with a minimum 12 month assured shorthold tenancy. If the household becomes unintentionally homeless within two years of taking the tenancy then the reapplication duty (section 195A(1)) applies.

The Homelessness (Suitability of Accommodation) (England) Order 2012

8. When ending the duty using the Localism Act power, local authorities are also subject to the provisions of the Homelessness (Suitability of Accommodation)

(England) Order 2012. The order consists of two parts. The first part deals with the suitability of location of accommodation and applies to all accommodation secured under Part 7 of the 1996 Act (including temporary accommodation). The second part is concerned with those circumstances in which accommodation is not to be regarded as suitable for a person for the purposes of a private rented sector offer under section 193(7F) of the Housing Act 1996 only.

The changes

9. Under the legislation as it stood prior to the amendments made by the Localism Act 2011, the authority could arrange an offer of a fixed term assured shorthold tenancy, which was a 'qualifying offer', and the section 193(2) main homelessness duty would have ended only if the offer was accepted, but not if refused – this is discussed in more detail below.
10. In a restricted case, local housing authorities were required to end the section 193(2) duty with a *private accommodation offer*, so far as reasonably practicable. A *private accommodation offer* must be a fixed term assured shorthold tenancy for a period of at least 12 months.
11. The provisions on *qualifying offers* (s193(7B) to (7E)) are repealed. This means a local authority will no longer be able to end the section 193(2) duty with a qualifying offer of 6 months by consent for new applicants.
12. The provisions on *private accommodation offers* are amended so that they are now referred to as *private rented sector offers* and authorities can consider bringing the duty to an end in this way for all cases, not just in a restricted case. However, in a restricted case, authorities **must** bring the section 193(2) main homelessness duty to an end with a *private rented sector offer*, so far as reasonably possible; in any other case it is at the authority's discretion whether to arrange a *private rented sector offer*.

Transitional arrangements

13. The amendments made by sections 148 and 149 of the Localism Act 2011 do not apply to a case where:
    (a) a person ('the applicant') has applied to a local housing authority for accommodation, or for assistance in obtaining accommodation, under Part 7 of the 1996 Act; and
    (b) a duty of the local housing authority to secure that accommodation is available for the applicant's occupation under Part 7 of the 1996 Act (including on an interim or temporary basis) has arisen and not ceased,

    before the commencement date of 9th November 2012.

Power not a duty

14. Authorities are reminded that the discretion to arrange a private rented sector offer is a power, not a duty, and as such, authorities should not seek to rely on the power in all cases. Authorities should consider whether to arrange a private rented sector based on the individual circumstances of the household and undertake to develop clear policies around its use.

Detailed changes to section 193 of the 1996 Act

15. Section 148 of the Localism Act 2011 makes a number of other changes to section 193 of the 1996 Act.

Statement of policy on offering choice to people under Part 6

16. Section 193(3A) is repealed. This means that authorities will no longer be required to give applicants owed the section 193(2) main homelessness duty a copy of their statement about their policy on offering choice to people allocated housing accommodation under Part 6 of the 1996 Act. This recognises that there will no longer be a presumption that most applicants owed the section 193 duty will have the duty ended with an offer of accommodation under Part 6.

17. The requirement to provide a copy of the statement (about the policy on offering choice under Part 6) to applicants owed the section 195(2) duty (eligible applicants in priority need threatened with homelessness) is similarly repealed.

Refusal of offer of suitable temporary accommodation

18. Section 148 of the Localism Act 2011 also substitutes a new section 193(5). This clarifies the position where an applicant is offered 'temporary accommodation' (ie offers of accommodation that, when accepted, do not have the effect of bringing the section 193(2) duty to an end).

19. Under the revised section 193(5), where an offer of accommodation is made which is neither a *Part 6 offer* nor a *private rented sector offer* (i.e. what is being offered is 'temporary accommodation' that would not otherwise bring the duty to an end if accepted), the section 193(2) duty may end if the applicant refuses the offer, but only if:
    (a) the applicant has been notified **in writing** of the possible consequences of refusal or acceptance,
    (b) the applicant has been notified in writing of the right to request a review of the suitability of the accommodation,
    (c) the authority are satisfied that the accommodation is suitable, and
    (d) the authority notify in writing the applicant that they regard themselves as ceasing to be subject to the section 193(2) duty.

Obligations in respect of existing accommodation

20. Sections 193(7F) and (8) of the 1996 Act are amended, such that local housing authorities shall not make a final offer of accommodation under Part 6 or approve a *private rented sector offer* unless they are satisfied that:
    (a) the accommodation is suitable for the applicant, and that
    (b) if the applicant is under contractual or other obligations in respect of the applicant's existing accommodation, the applicant is able to bring those obligations to an end before being required to take up the offer.

21. The previous requirement (in section 193(7F)) that authorities must be satisfied that it is reasonable for the applicant to accept the offer has been amended so that no factors, other than contractual or other obligations in respect of existing accommodation, are to be taken into account in determining whether it is reasonable to accept the offer. Where an applicant has contractual or other obligations in respect of their existing accommodation (eg a tenancy agreement or lease), the housing authority can reasonably expect the offer to be taken up only if the applicant is able to bring those obligations to an end before he is required to take up the offer.

22. This change **does not mean** that those subjective suitability issues which have become associated with 'reasonable to accept', such as those discussed in

Ravichandranand another v Lewisham LBC[1] or *Slater v Lewisham LBC*[2] are not to be taken into account. The intention is that these factors as already highlighted in paragraph 17.6 of the Homelessness Code of Guidance for Local Authorities (for example, fear of racial harassment; risk of violence from ex-partner's associates) continue to be part of those factors/elements an authority consider in determining suitability of accommodation.

Power to amend minimum fixed term for private rented sector offers

23. Section 148 of the Localism Act 2011 inserts new sections 193(10), (11) and (12) into the 1996 Act. Section 193(10) provides a power for the appropriate authority to amend by regulations the minimum fixed term period for private rented sector offers specified in section 193(7AC)(c). Section 193(12) provides that the appropriate authority in England is the Secretary of State.

24. However, section 193(11) provides that regulations made under section 193(10) may not:
    (a) specify a period of less than 12 months, or
    (b) apply to restricted cases.

25. The Secretary of State recommends that a local private rented sector offer policy should take account of individual household circumstances, and be developed with regard to prevailing housing demand and supply pressures in the local area in order to support the best use of available housing stock locally.

Ending the duty using the new power

26. Under section 193(7AA)[3] (duties to persons with priority need and who are not homeless intentionally) a local authority shall cease to be subject to the main homelessness duty, if the applicant, having been informed of the matters mentioned in section 193(7AB), accepts or refuses a private rented sector offer.

27. A *private rented sector offer* is defined by section 193(7AC) as an offer of an assured shorthold tenancy made by a private landlord to an applicant in relation to any accommodation which:
    (a) has been made available for the applicant's occupation by arrangements made by the local authority with a private landlord or
    (b) is made with the approval of the authority, in pursuance of arrangements made by the authority with the landlord with a view to bringing the section 193(2) duty to an end, and
    (c) is a fixed term Assured Shorthold Tenancy for a period of at least 12 months.

28. The applicant must be informed in writing of the following matters (as mentioned in section 193(7AB)):
    (a) the possible consequence of refusal or acceptance of the offer,
    (b) that the applicant has the right to request a review of the suitability of the accommodation, and
    (c) the effect under new section 195A of a further application to the authority within two years of acceptance of the offer (the 'reapplication duty').

1 [2010] EWCA Civ 755.

2 [2006] EWCA Civ 394.

3 This paragraph was amended in January 2014 to correct a typographical error. The previous text mistakenly read 193(7A).

29. Applicants can continue to request a review of the housing authority's decision that the accommodation offered to them is suitable under section 202(1)(f).

Re-application within two years of acceptance of a private rented sector offer

30. Under new section 195A(1) (re-application after private rented sector offer), the section 193(2) duty will apply regardless of whether the applicant has a priority need where:
    (a) a person makes a re-application for assistance within two years of accepting a private rented sector offer, and
    (b) the applicant is eligible for assistance and has become homeless unintentionally.
31. Similarly under section 195A(3), the section 195(2) duty (owed to eligible applicants in priority need and threatened with homelessness) will apply regardless of whether the applicant has a priority need where:
    (a) a person makes a re-application for assistance within two years of accepting a private rented sector offer, and
    (b) the applicant is eligible for assistance and is threatened with homelessness unintentionally.
32. Authorities should be aware that if, following the expiry of the initial 12 month assured shorthold tenancy, an applicant secures their own accommodation and then subsequently becomes homeless within two years of the original private rented sector offer then the re-application duty will still apply.
33. Given the two year re-application duty, authorities are advised to keep the household circumstances under review as they approach the expiry of the 12 month tenancy so they can help actively manage cases where the tenancy may end unnecessarily. Please see the section below referring to section 21 notices.

Referrals to another local housing authority

34. Authorities should note that the section 193(2) duty on re-application will apply regardless of whether or not the housing authority receiving the reapplication is the same authority that arranged the *private rented sector offer*. This means that the authority receiving the re-application cannot simply refer the applicant to the authority which made the private rented sector offer but must first carry out investigations to determine whether the applicant is homeless through no fault of their own, under section 195A. It is for the receiving authority to establish whether the applicant has become homeless unintentionally. Once established, this matter cannot be reopened.
35. Once the receiving authority has established that the applicant is unintentionally homeless and eligible for assistance, the receiving authority may refer the applicant to the authority that made the private rented sector offer (provided the conditions of section 198 which refer to the referral of a case to another local housing authority are met – explored further in the 'Referrals to another local housing authority' section below). The conditions for referral of the case to the other authority are met once it has been established that the re-application has been made within two years. The authority which made the private rented sector offer will owe the reapplication duty and it will be their responsibility to secure accommodation is available for occupation by the applicant.

We would expect authorities to respond quickly to referrals. Here section 200 (which refers to referral and notification) continue to apply. This is supported by paragraphs 18.26 – 18.37 of the Homelessness Code of Guidance.

36. Similarly, authorities should note that the section 195(2) duty owed to those threatened with homelessness will apply regardless of whether the housing authority receiving the re-application is the same authority that arranged the *private rented sector offer*. (Under section 195(2), a local housing authority must take reasonable steps to secure that accommodation does not cease to be available for occupation by eligible applicants who have priority need and are threatened with homelessness.).

Section 21 Notices

37. As a consequence of the introduction of the re-application duty, an authority is required to treat section 21 notices differently.
38. Section 195(4) provides that, for the purpose of section 195A(3), where an applicant has been given a notice under section 21 of the *Housing Act 1988*, the applicant **must be treated as threatened with homelessness** from the date the notice is issued. This means that the authority must take reasonable steps to secure that accommodation does not cease to be available for their occupancy.
39. Section 195A(2) provides that, for the purpose of section 195A(1), where an applicant has been given a notice under section 21 of the Housing Act 1988, the applicant must be treated as homeless from the date the notice expires. It is not necessary for a possession order to have been sought by the landlord for the applicant to be considered homeless.

Referrals to another authority and risk of violence

40. Section 149 of the Localism Act 2011 also amends section 198 of the 1996 Act *(referrals to another local housing authority)*. Section 149 (6) inserts new section 198(2ZA). Under section 198(2ZA), the conditions for referral of a case to another local housing authority are met if:
    (a) the application is made within 2 years of the date they applicant takes the tenancy of a private rented sector offer made by the other authority, and
    (b there would be no risk of domestic violence to either the applicant, or anyone who might reasonably be expected to reside with the applicant, in the district of the other authority.
41. Section 149(7) and (8) make further amendments to section198 which mean that the new conditions for referral in section 198(2ZA) are not met if the applicant, or anyone who might reasonably be expected to reside with the applicant, has suffered violence (not limited to domestic violence) in the district of the other authority and it is probable that return to that district would lead to further violence against them.
42. Referrals regarding re-applications are not subject to any consideration of local connection. Section 200 on referrals continues to apply to these cases. Annex 18 of the Homelessness Code of Guidance for Local Authorities sets out the procedures for referrals of homeless applicants on the grounds of local connection with another local authority as well as guidelines for invoking the

disputes procedure. The LGA have recently updated this guidance and it is available on their website.[4]

When re-application does not apply

43. The provisions in section 195A(1) to (4), which apply to the re-application duty, do not apply in a restricted case. Additionally, these provisions do not apply in a case where the applicant has previously made a re-application which resulted in their being owed the duty under section 193(2) or 195(2) by virtue of section 195A(1) or (3). This effectively means that an applicant can only be owed the re-application duty once following each private rented sector offer. If an applicant becomes become unintentionally homeless again within the two year limit and have already been assisted under the re-application duty, then they must make a fresh homelessness application.

Interim duty to accommodate

44. Section 149 of the Localism Act 2011 inserts a new section 188(1A) in the 1996 Act. Under section 188(1A), any local housing authority in England that the applicant has applied to must secure accommodation for them (pending a decision as to what duty, if any, is owed to the applicant under Part 7) regardless of whether the applicant has priority need, if the authority have reason to believe that the duty under section 193(2) may apply in the circumstances mentioned in section 195A(1) (that is a reapplication within 2 years of acceptance of a *private rented sector offer*).

45. Authorities should note that the duty under section 188(1A) will apply regardless of whether the housing authority receiving the re-application is the same authority that arranged the *private rented sector offer*.

Homelessness (Suitability of Accommodation) (England) Order 2012

46. The Homelessness (Suitability of Accommodation) (England) Order 2012 consists of two parts. The first deals with the suitability of location of accommodation and applies to **all accommodation secured under Part VII** of the Housing Act 1996 (including temporary accommodation). The second deals with those circumstances in which accommodation is not to be regarded as suitable for a person for the purposes of a private rented sector offer under section 193(7F) of the Housing Act 1996 only.

Location

47. Location of accommodation is relevant to suitability. Existing guidance on this aspect is set out at paragraph 17.41 of the Homelessness Code of Guidance offers. The suitability of the location for all the members of the household must be considered by the authority. Section 208(1) of the 1996 Act requires that authorities shall, in discharging their housing functions under Part 7 of the 1996 Act, in so far as is reasonably practicable, secure accommodation within the authority's own district.

48. Where it is not possible to secure accommodation within district and an authority has secured accommodation outside their district, the authority is required to take into account the distance of that accommodation from the

4 http://www.local.gov.uk/web/guest/housing/-/journal_content/56/10171/3479463/ARTICLE-TEMPLATE

district of the authority. Where accommodation which is otherwise suitable and affordable is available nearer to the authority's district than the accommodation which it has secured, the accommodation which it has secured is not likely to be suitable unless the authority has a justifiable reason or the applicant has specified a preference.

49. Generally, where possible, authorities should try to secure accommodation that is as close as possible to where an applicant was previously living. Securing accommodation for an applicant in a different location can cause difficulties for some applicants. Local authorities are required to take into account the significance of any disruption with specific regard to employment, caring responsibilities or education of the applicant or members of their household. Where possible the authority should seek to retain established links with schools, doctors, social workers and other key services and support.

50. In assessing the significance of disruption to **employment**, account will need to be taken of their need to reach their normal workplace from the accommodation secured.

51. In assessing the significance of disruption to **caring responsibilities**, account should be taken of the type and importance of the care household members provide and the likely impact the withdrawal would cause. Authorities may want to consider the cost implications of providing care where an existing care arrangement becomes unsustainable due to a change of location.

52. Authorities should also take into account the need to minimise disruption to the **education** of young people, particularly at critical points in time such as leading up to taking GCSE (or their equivalent) examinations.

53. Account should also be taken of medical facilities and other support currently provided for the applicant and their household. Housing authorities should consider the potential impact on the health and well being of an applicant or any person reasonably expected to reside with them, were such support removed or medical facilities were no longer accessible. They should also consider whether similar facilities are accessible and available near the accommodation being offered and whether there would be any specific difficulties in the applicant or person residing with them using those essential facilities, compared to the support they are currently receiving. Examples of other support might include support from particular individuals, groups or organisations located in the area where the applicant currently resides: for example essential support from relatives or support groups which would be difficult to replicate in another location

54. Housing authorities should avoid placing applicants in isolated accommodation away from public transport, shops and other facilities, where possible.

55. Whilst authorities should, as far as is practicable, aim to secure accommodation within their own district, they should also recognise that there can be clear benefits for some applicants to be accommodated outside of the district. This could occur, for example, where the applicant, and/or a member of his or her household, would be at risk of domestic or other violence in the district and need to be accommodated elsewhere to reduce the risk of further contact with the perpetrator(s) or where exoffenders or drug/alcohol users would benefit from being accommodated outside the district to help break links with previous contacts which could exert a negative influence. Any risk of violence or racial harassment in a particular locality must also be taken into

account. Where domestic violence is involved and the applicant is not able to stay in the current home, housing authorities may need to consider the need for alternative accommodation whose location can be kept a secret and which has security measures and staffing to protect the occupants.

56. Similarly there may also be advantages in enabling some applicants to access employment opportunities outside of their current district. The availability, or otherwise, of employment opportunities in the new area may help to determine if that area is suitable for the applicant.

57. Where it is not reasonably practicable for the applicant to be placed in accommodation within the housing authority's district, and the housing authority places the applicant in accommodation in another district, section 208(2) **requires the housing authority to notify in writing within 14 days of the accommodation being made available to the applicant the housing authority in whose district the accommodation is situated.**

58. Local authorities are reminded that in determining the suitability of accommodation, affordability must be taken into account. This aspect of suitability must continue to form part of your assessment when considering the location of accommodation.

Circumstances in which accommodation secured under section 193(7F) is not to be regarded as suitable for a person

59. This part of the Order sets out those circumstances in which accommodation is not to be regarded as suitable for a person. It applies only to accommodation secured under s193(7F). The requirements can be grouped under five broad headings.

Physical condition of the property

60. Local housing authorities are obliged under section 3 of the Housing Act 2004 to keep the housing conditions in their area under review with a view to identifying any action that may need to be taken by them under the Household Health and Safety Ratings System legislation. The local housing authority is also required to keep the housing conditions in their area under review in relation to other powers/duties such as licensing of HMOs.

61. Section 4 of the 2004 Act provides that an authority must arrange for an inspection of residential premises in its district with a view to determining whether any category 1 or 2 hazard exists on those premises. Such an inspection is only required if the authority considers that it would be appropriate for them to be inspected, as a result of any matters of which they have become aware in carrying out their duty under section 3, or for any other reason.

62. Authorities should secure accommodation that is in reasonable physical condition. Authorities should ensure that the property has been visited by either a local authority officer or someone acting on their behalf to determine its suitability before an applicant moves in. Existing aspects of suitability such as space and arrangement set out in statutory guidance will continue to apply.

63. In determining whether the property is in reasonable physical condition attentions should be paid to signs of damp, mould, indications that the property would be cold, for example cracked windows, and any other physical signs that would indicate the property is not in good physical condition.

Health and safety matters

64. Landlords are by law required to ensure that all electrical equipment in a property is safe. The local authority are required to satisfy themselves that any electrical equipment provided in the property meets the requirements of regulations 5 and 7 of the Electrical Equipment (Safety) Regulations 1994. Generally speaking, it is likely that a visual inspection of the property, by a person authorised to act on behalf of the local authority, that checks for obvious signs of loose wiring, cracked or broken electrical sockets, light switches that do not work and evidence of Portable Appliance Testing will be indicative that the specific regulations have been applied.

65. The Fire Safety Order[5] applies to the common or shared parts of multi-occupied residential buildings. As such landlords, owners or managing agents will need to carry out a fire risk assessment of the common parts and implement and maintain appropriate and adequate fire safety measures. As part of their responsibilities, landlords should put in place appropriate management and maintenance systems to ensure any fire safety equipment or equipment which may represent a fire hazard, is maintained in good working order, and in accordance with the manufacturers instructions. Landlords are also required to ensure that furniture and furnishings supplied must comply with the Furniture and Furnishings (Fire) (Safety) Regulations 1988 (as amended).

66. Local authorities and fire and rescue authorities should work together to ensure the safety of domestic premises including the provision of fire safety advice to households (such as the benefits of a working smoke alarm). Local authorities will need to satisfy themselves that these regulations have been adhered to.

67. Local authorities are asked to satisfy themselves that the landlord has taken reasonable precautions to prevent the possibility of carbon monoxide poisoning in the accommodation, where such a risk exists. Taken together with a valid gas Safety Record, the installation of a carbon monoxide alarm would constitute reasonable precaution to prevent the possibility of carbon monoxide poisoning, where such a risk exists.

68. If the accommodation is or forms part of residential property which does not have a valid energy performance certificate as required by the Energy Performance of Buildings (Certificates and Inspections) (England and Wales) Regulations 2007, then it will not be regarded as suitable. Local authorities should ensure they have had sight of a current certificate to ensure that this requirement has been met.

69. Housing authorities should satisfy themselves that accommodation that is or forms part of relevant premises in accordance with regulation 36 of the Gas Safety (Installation and Use) Regulations 1994 has a current gas safety certificate. A local authority can do this by requesting sight of the valid Gas Safety certificate.

Licensing for Houses in Multiple Occupation

70. Accommodation that is in a house of multiple occupation which is subject to licensing under section 55 of the Housing Act 2004 and is not licensed is

5 Regulatory Reform (Fire Safety) Order 2005.

unsuitable. Accommodation in a house of multiple occupation that is subject to additional licensing under section 56 of the Housing Act 2004 and is not licensed is unsuitable.

Landlord behaviour

71. Authorities should satisfy themselves that landlords of accommodation secured under s 193(7F) are fit and proper persons to act in the capacity of a landlord. Local authorities are required to consider any convictions in relation to landlord and tenant law, fraud or other dishonesty, violence or drugs as well as any discrimination and/or sexual offences as set out in the legislation. Most local authorities currently do this for Houses in Multiple Occupancy and they can also check their own records for any prosecutions for offences of harassment and illegal eviction brought by the local authority. If their record checking does not satisfy them that the landlord is a fit and proper person to act in the capacity of a landlord then the local authority can require the landlord to carry out a Criminal Records Bureau check, but they are not required to do this in every case. The Secretary of State recommends that when placing households outside of their district that the authority liaise with the receiving district to check whether that authority has taken any enforcement activity against the landlord.

Elements of good management

72. The local authority should ensure that the landlord has provided to them a written tenancy agreement which they propose to use for the purposes of a private rented sector offer and which the local authority considers to be adequate. It is expected that the local authority should review the tenancy agreement to ensure that it sets out, ideally in a clear and comprehensible way, the tenant's obligations, for example a clear statement of the rent and other charges, and the responsibilities of the landlord, but does not contain unfair or unreasonable terms, such as call-out charges for repairs or professional cleaning at the end of the tenancy.

Tenancy Deposit Scheme

73. Whilst a local authority will not be able to check that a tenant's deposit has been placed in a tenancy deposit protection scheme prior to them taking the tenancy we recommend that local authorities remind prospective landlords and tenants of their responsibilities in this area.

74. Tenancy deposit protection schemes guarantee that tenants will get their deposits back at the end of the tenancy, if they meet the terms of the tenancy agreement and do not damage the property. Landlords must protect their tenants' deposits using a TDP scheme if they have let the property on an assured shorthold tenancy (AST) which started on or after 6 April 2007.

Allocation of accommodation: guidance for local housing authorities in England (June 2012)

CONTENTS

Chapter 1	Scope of guidance and definition of an allocation
Chapter 2	Overview of the amendments to Part 6 made by the Localism Act 2011
Chapter 3	Eligibility and qualification
Chapter 4	Framing an allocation scheme
Chapter 5	Allocation scheme management
Chapter 6	Private Registered Providers and contracting out
Annex 1	Indicators of criteria in reasonable preference categories (c) and (d)
Annex 2	Rights to reside in the UK derived from EU Law
Annex 3	Worker authorisation scheme
Annex 4	Habitual residence

Chapter 1
Scope of guidance and definition of an allocation

1.1 This guidance is issued to local housing authorities ('housing authorities') in England under s.169 of the Housing Act 1996 ('the 1996 Act'). Housing authorities are required to have regard to it in exercising their functions under Part 6 of the 1996 Act ('Part 6'). In so far as this guidance comments on the law, it can only reflect the Department's understanding at the time of issue.

1.2 This guidance replaces all previous guidance on social housing allocations.

Definition of an 'allocation'

1.3 For the purposes of Part 6, a housing authority allocates accommodation when it:

- selects a person to be a secure or introductory tenant of accommodation held by that authority
- nominates a person to be a secure or introductory tenant of accommodation held by another housing authority
- nominates a person to be an assured tenant of accommodation held by a Private Registered Provider (or Registered Social Landlord in Wales) (s.159(2))

1.4 The term 'assured tenant' includes a person with an assured shorthold tenancy, including of an Affordable Rent property.[1] 'Secure tenant' includes a person with a flexible tenancy granted under s.107A of the Housing Act 1985.[2]

Allocations to existing tenants

1.5 Provisions in relation to existing tenants are contained in s.159(4A) and (4B). These provide that Part 6 does not apply to an allocation of accommodation by a housing authority to a tenant of a local authority or Private Registered Provider unless:

- the allocation involves a transfer made at the tenant's request, and
- the authority is satisfied that the tenant has reasonable preference.

Accordingly, social tenants applying to the housing authority for a transfer who are considered to have reasonable preference for an allocation must be treated on the same basis as new applicants in accordance with the requirements of s.166A(3).

1.6 Transfers at the tenant's request, where the authority is satisfied the tenant does not have reasonable preference, do not fall within Part 6 and housing authorities may set their own transfer policies in relation to these tenants. Authorities should consider how to make the best use of this flexibility. Providing tenants with greater opportunities to move within the social sector can help promote social and economic mobility and make the best use of social housing stock.

1.7 Authorities should consider the importance of giving social tenants who under-occupy their accommodation appropriate priority for a transfer. This

1 Affordable Rent is not subject to the national rent regime but is subject to other rent controls that require a rent (including service charges, where applicable) of no more than 80% of the local market rent.

2 Inserted by s.154 of the Localism Act 2011.

will be important in light of the measure in the Welfare Reform Act 2012 which will reduce Housing Benefit entitlement for working age social sector tenants who under-occupy their property (measured in accordance with the Local Housing Allowance size criteria) from April 2013.[3] Authorities should also consider whether there are other provisions that might make it more difficult for under-occupiers to move, such as a prohibition against tenants with minor rent arrears transferring, and the scope for removing or revising these in relation to under-occupiers.

1.8 Housing authorities may decide to operate a separate allocation system for transferring tenants who are not in the reasonable preference categories (with a separate waiting list and lettings policy) or to continue with a single allocation system which covers all applicants but which, for example, rewards transferring tenants with a good tenancy record, or gives a degree of priority to those who want to move for work.

1.9 Transfers that the housing authority initiates for management purposes do not fall within Part 6. These would include a temporary decant to allow repairs to a property to be carried out. The renewal of a flexible tenancy in the same property also does not fall within Part 6; neither do mutual exchanges between existing tenants, including exchanges between secure and assured tenants and those with flexible tenancies (under s.107A of the Housing Act 1985). Other specific exemptions from the provisions of Part 6 are set out in s.160 of the 1996 Act and the Allocation of Housing (England) Regulations 2002 (SI 2002/3264).

Chapter 2
Overview of the amendments to Part 6 made by the Localism Act 2011

2.1 The Localism Act 2011 introduces significant amendments to Part 6. The main policy objectives behind these amendments are to:

- enable housing authorities to better manage their housing waiting list by giving them the power to determine which applicants do or do not qualify for an allocation of social housing. Authorities will be able to operate a more focused list which better reflects local circumstances and can be understood more readily by local people. It will also be easier for authorities to manage unrealistic expectations by excluding people who have little or no prospect of being allocated accommodation
- make it easier for existing social tenants to move by removing the constraints of Part 6 from those social tenants who apply to the housing authority for a transfer, unless they have reasonable preference. Housing authorities will be able to strike a balance between meeting the needs of existing tenants and new applicants for social housing, while making best use of their stock. Part 6 continues to apply to transferring tenants with

3 The LHA size criteria allow one bedroom for each: adult couple; any other adult (aged 16 or over); two children of the same sex aged 10 or over; two children under 10 regardless of sex; any other child.

reasonable preference, ensuring they continue to receive priority under the authority's allocation scheme

- maintain the protection provided by the statutory reasonable preference criteria – ensuring that priority for social housing goes to those in the greatest need

2.2 The detailed changes to Part 6 contained in the Localism Act 2011 are set out in the following paragraphs.

2.3 By virtue of new s.159(4B) the term 'allocation' continues to apply to a transfer at the request of an existing secure, introductory or assured tenant where the authority is satisfied that he or she has 'reasonable preference' for an allocation. Existing secure, introductory and assured tenants seeking a transfer who are not considered to have reasonable preference are now outside the scope of Part 6 (s.159(4A).

2.4 New s.160ZA replaces s.160A in relation to allocations by housing authorities in England. Social housing may only be allocated to 'qualifying persons' and housing authorities are given the power to determine what classes of persons are or are not qualified to be allocated housing (s.160ZA(6) and (7)). These requirements are in addition to the provisions on eligibility in respect of persons from abroad (s.160ZA(2) and (4)) which continue to be set centrally. The power for a housing authority to decide that an applicant is to be treated as ineligible by reason of unacceptable behaviour serious enough to make him unsuitable to be a tenant is redundant and has therefore been repealed.

2.5 New s.166A requires housing authorities in England to allocate accommodation in accordance with a scheme which must be framed to ensure that certain categories of applicants are given reasonable preference. With certain exceptions, s.166A replicates the provisions in s.167 which continues to apply to allocations by housing authorities in Wales. Section 166A(9) includes a new requirement for an allocation scheme to give a right to review a decision on qualification in s.160AZ(9), and to be informed of the decision on the review and the grounds for it. This is in addition to the existing right to review a decision on eligibility. Section 166A(12) is new and provides that authorities must have regard to their homelessness and tenancy strategies when framing their allocation scheme.

2.6 The provisions in s.167 which allow for no preference to be given to a person guilty of serious unacceptable behaviour (s.167(2B) – (2D)) are not reproduced in s.166A. However, the power to take behaviour – whether good or poor - into account in determining priorities between people in the reasonable preference categories remains (new s.166A(5)(b)).

2.7 The requirement for an allocation scheme to contain a statement of the authority's policy on offering a choice of accommodation or the opportunity to express preferences about their accommodation is retained (s.166A(2)). However, the requirement to provide a copy of this statement to people to whom they owe a homelessness duty (under s.193(3A) or s.195(3A) of the 1996 Act) is repealed.[4]

4 Section 148(2) and s.149(3) of the Localism Act 2011.

Chapter 3
Eligibility and qualification

3.1 Housing authorities must consider all applications made in accordance with the procedural requirements of the authority's allocation scheme (s.166(3)). In considering applications, authorities must ascertain:

- if an applicant is eligible for an allocation of accommodation, and
- if he or she qualifies for an allocation of accommodation

Eligibility

3.2 An applicant may be ineligible for an allocation of accommodation under s.160ZA(2) or (4). Authorities are advised to consider applicants' eligibility at the time of the initial application and again when considering making an allocation to them, particularly where a substantial amount of time has elapsed since the original application.

Joint Tenancies

3.3 Under s.160ZA(1)(b), a housing authority must not grant a joint tenancy to two or more people if any one of them is a person from abroad who is ineligible. However, where two or more people apply and one of them is eligible, the authority may grant a tenancy to the person who is eligible. In addition, while ineligible family members must not be granted a tenancy, they may be taken into account in determining the size of accommodation which is to be allocated.

Existing Tenants

3.4 The eligibility provisions do not apply to applicants who are already secure or introductory tenants or assured tenants of a Private Registered Provider. Most transferring tenants fall outside the scope of the allocation legislation (s.159(4A)); while those who are considered to have reasonable preference for an allocation are specifically exempted from the eligibility provisions by virtue of s.160ZA(5).

Persons from abroad

3.5 A person may not be allocated accommodation under Part 6 if he or she is a person from abroad who is ineligible for an allocation under s.160ZA of the 1996 Act. There are two categories for the purposes of s.160ZA:

(i) *a person subject to immigration control* – such a person is not eligible for an allocation of accommodation unless he or she comes within a class prescribed in regulations made by the Secretary of State (s.160ZA(2)), and

(ii) *a person from abroad other than a person subject to immigration control* – regulations may provide for other descriptions of persons from abroad who, although not subject to immigration control, are to be treated as ineligible for an allocation of accommodation (s.160ZA(4)).

3.6 The regulations setting out which classes of persons from abroad are eligible or ineligible for an allocation are the Allocation of Housing and Homelessness (Eligibility) (England) Regulations 2006 (SI 2006 No.1294) ('the Eligibility Regulations').

Persons subject to immigration control

3.7 The term 'person subject to immigration control' is defined in s.13(2) of the Asylum and Immigration Act 1996 as a person who under the Immigration Act 1971 requires leave to enter or remain in the United Kingdom (whether or not such leave has been given).

3.8 The following categories of persons do not require leave to enter or remain in the UK:

(i) British citizens

(ii) certain Commonwealth citizens with a right of abode in the UK

(iii) Irish citizens, who are not subject to immigration control in the UK because the Republic of Ireland forms part of the Common Travel Area (see paragraph 3.11 (iii) below) with the UK which allows free movement

(iv) EEA nationals,[5] and their family members, who have a right to reside in the UK that derives from EU law. Whether an EEA national (or family member) has a particular right to reside in the UK (or another Member State) will depend on the circumstances, particularly their economic status (e.g. whether he or she is a worker, self-employed, a student, or economically inactive)

(v) persons who are exempt from immigration control under the Immigration Acts, including diplomats and their family members based in the UK, and some military personnel.

3.9 Any person who does not fall within one of the four categories in paragraph 3.11 will be a person subject to immigration control and will be ineligible for an allocation of accommodation unless they fall within a class of persons prescribed by regulation 3 of the Eligibility Regulations (see further below).

3.10 If there is any uncertainty about an applicant's immigration status, housing authorities are recommended to contact the UK Border Agency (UKBA). UKBA provides a service to housing authorities to confirm the immigration status of an applicant from abroad (non asylum seekers) by email at LA@UKBA.gsi.gov.uk. Where UKBA indicates the applicant may be an asylum seeker, enquiries of their status can be made to the Immigration Enquiry Bureau helpline on 0870 606 7766.

3.11 Regulation 3 of the Eligibility Regulations provides that the following classes of persons subject to immigration control are eligible for an allocation of accommodation:

i) *a person granted refugee status*: granted 5 years' limited leave to remain in the UK

ii) *a person granted exceptional leave to enter or remain in the UK without condition that they and any dependants should make no recourse to public funds*: granted for a limited period where there are compelling humanitarian or compassionate circumstances for allowing them to stay. However, if leave is granted on condition that the applicant and any dependants are not a charge on public funds, the applicant will not be eligible for an allocation of accommodation. Exceptional leave to remain (granted at the Secretary

5 European Economic Area nationals are nationals of any EU member state (except the UK), and nationals of Iceland, Norway, Liechtenstein and Switzerland.

of State's discretion outside the Immigration Rules) now takes the form of 'discretionary leave'.

iii) *a person with current leave to enter or remain in the UK with no condition or limitation, and who is habitually resident in the UK, the Channel Islands, the Isle of Man or the Republic of Ireland (the Common Travel Area)*: such a person will have indefinite leave to enter (ILE) or remain (ILR) and is regarded as having settled status. However, where ILE or ILR status is granted as a result of an undertaking that a sponsor will be responsible for the applicant's maintenance and accommodation, the person must have been resident in the Common Travel Area for five years since the date of entry - or the date of the sponsorship undertaking, whichever is later - to be eligible. Where all sponsors have died within the first five years, the applicant will be eligible for an allocation of accommodation.

iv) *a person who has humanitarian protection granted under the Immigration Rules*:[6] a form of leave granted to persons who do not qualify for refugee status but would face a real risk of suffering serious harm if returned to their state of origin (see paragraphs 339C-344C of the Immigration Rules (HC 395))

Other persons from abroad who may be ineligible for an allocation

3.12 By virtue of regulation 4 of the Eligibility Regulations, a person who is not subject to immigration control and who falls within one of the following descriptions is to be treated as a person from abroad who is ineligible for an allocation of accommodation:

(i) a person who is not habitually resident in the Common Travel Area (subject to certain exceptions - see paragraph 3.14 below)

(ii) a person whose only right to reside in the UK is derived from his status as a jobseeker (or his status as the family member of a jobseeker). 'Jobseeker' has the same meaning as in regulation 6(1) of the Immigration (European Economic Area) Regulations 2006 (SI 2006/1003) ('the EEA Regulations').

(iii) a person whose only right to reside in the UK is an initial right to reside for a period not exceeding three months under regulation 13 of the EEA Regulations

(iv) a person whose only right to reside in the Common Travel Area is a right equivalent to one of the rights mentioned in (ii) or (iii) above and which is derived from EU Treaty rights

3.13 See annex 2 for guidance on rights to reside in the UK derived from EU law.

3.14 The following persons from abroad are eligible for an allocation of accommodation even if they are not habitually resident in the Common Travel Area:

a) an EEA national who is in the UK as a worker (which has the same meaning as in regulation 6(1) of the EEA Regulations)

b) an EEA national who is in the UK as a self-employed person (which has the same meaning as in regulation 6(1) of the EEA Regulations)

c) a person who is treated as a worker for the purposes of regulation 6(1) of the EEA Regulations, pursuant to the Accession (Immigration and

6 Inserted by the Allocation of Housing and Homelessness (Miscellaneous Provisions) (England) Regulations 2006.

Worker Authorisation) Regulations 2006 (ie nationals of Bulgaria and Romania required to be authorised by the Home Office to work until they have accrued 12 months uninterrupted authorised work)[7]

d) a person who is a family member of a person referred to in (a) to (c) above

e) a person with a right to reside permanently in the UK by virtue of regulation 15(c), (d) or (e) of the EEA Regulations

f) a person who left Montserrat after 1 November 1995 because of the effect of volcanic activity there

g) a person who is in the UK as a result of his deportation, expulsion or other removal by compulsion of law from another country to the UK. This could include EEA nationals, if the person was settled in the UK and exercising EU Treaty rights prior to deportation from the third country. Where deportation occurs, most countries will signal this in the person's passport.

3.15 A person who is no longer working or no longer in self-employment will retain his or her status as a worker or self-employed person in certain circumstances. However, accession state workers requiring authorisation will generally only be treated as a worker when they are actually working as authorised and will not retain 'worker' status between jobs until they have accrued 12 months continuous authorised employment. 'Family member' does not include a person who is an extended family member who is treated as a family member by virtue of regulation 7(3) of the EEA Regulations (see annexes 2 and 3 for further guidance).

3.16 The term 'habitual residence' is intended to convey a degree of permanence in the person's residence in the Common Travel Area; it implies an association between the individual and the place of residence and relies substantially on fact.

3.17 Applicants who have been resident in the Common Travel Area continuously during the two year period prior to their housing application are likely to be habitually resident (periods of temporary absence, e.g. visits abroad for holidays or to visit relatives may be disregarded). Where two years' continuous residency has not been established, housing authorities will need to conduct further enquiries to determine whether the applicant is habitually resident (see annex 4 for further guidance).

Qualification

3.18 Housing authorities may only allocate accommodation to people who are defined as 'qualifying persons' (s.160ZA(6)(a)). Subject to the requirement not to allocate to persons from abroad who are ineligible and the exception for members of the Armed and Reserve Forces in paragraph 3.27 below, a housing authority may decide the classes of people who are, or are not, qualifying persons.

3.19 Housing authorities are encouraged to adopt a housing options approach

7 As of 1 May 2011, nationals of the 8 Eastern European countries (A8 nationals) which acceded to the EU in 2004 are no longer required to register with the Workers Registration Scheme in order to work in the UK. Regulation 4(2)(c) of the Eligibility Regulations no longer applies to applications from A8 workers as of that date. Rather applications from A8 workers should be considered on the same basis as those from other EU workers under regulation 4(2)(a).

as part of a move to a managed waiting list. A strong and pro-active housing options approach brings several benefits: people are offered support to access the housing solution which best meets their needs (which might be private rented housing, low cost home ownership or help to stay put); expectations about accessing social housing are properly managed; and social housing is focused on those who need it most. A lower waiting list can also be a by-product.

3.20 In framing their qualification criteria, authorities will need to have regard to their duties under the equalities legislation, as well as the requirement in s.166A(3) to give overall priority for an allocation to people in the reasonable preference categories.

3.21 Housing authorities should avoid setting criteria which disqualify groups of people whose members are likely to be accorded reasonable preference for social housing, for example on medical or welfare grounds. However, authorities may wish to adopt criteria which would disqualify individuals who satisfy the reasonable preference requirements. This could be the case, for example, if applicants are disqualified on a ground of anti-social behaviour.

3.22 When deciding what classes of people do not qualify for an allocation, authorities should consider the implications of excluding all members of such groups. For instance, when framing residency criteria, authorities may wish to consider the position of people who are moving into the district to take up work or to escape violence, or homeless applicants or children in care who are placed out of borough.

3.23 The Government believes that authorities should avoid allocating social housing to people who already own their own homes. Where they do so, this should only be in exceptional circumstances; for example, for elderly owner occupiers who cannot stay in their own home and need to move into sheltered accommodation.

3.24 There may be sound policy reasons for applying different qualification criteria in relation to existing tenants from those which apply to new applicants. For example, where residency requirements are imposed, authorities may wish to ensure they do not restrict the ability of existing social tenants to move to take up work or to downsize to a smaller home. Authorities may decide to apply different qualification criteria in relation to particular types of stock, for example properties which might otherwise be hard to let.

3.25 Whatever general criteria housing authorities use to define the classes of persons who do not qualify for social housing, there may be exceptional circumstances where it is necessary to disapply these criteria in the case of individual applicants. An example might be an intimidated witness[8] who needs to move quickly to another local authority district. Authorities are encouraged to make explicit provision for dealing with exceptional cases within their qualification rules.

3.26 As with eligibility, authorities are advised to consider whether an applicant qualifies for an allocation at the time of the initial application and when considering making an allocation, particularly where a long time has elapsed since the original application.

8 'Intimidated witnesses include Protected Persons as specified in Section 82 and schedule 5 of the Serious Organised Crime and Police Act 2005.'

Members of the Armed Forces and the Reserve Forces

3.27 Subject to Parliamentary scrutiny, we will regulate to provide that authorities must not disqualify the following applicants on the grounds that they do not have a local connection[9] with the authority's district:

(a) members of the Armed Forces and former Service personnel, where the application is made within five[10] years of discharge

(b) bereaved spouses and civil partners of members of the Armed Forces leaving Services Family Accommodation following the death of their spouse or partner

(c) serving or former members of the Reserve Forces who need to move because of a serious injury, medical condition or disability sustained as a result of their service

3.28 These provisions recognise the special position of members of the Armed Forces (and their families) whose employment requires them to be mobile and who are likely therefore to be particularly disadvantaged by local connection requirements; as well as those injured reservists who may need to move to another local authority district to access treatment, care or support.

Joint tenants

3.29 In the case of an allocation to two or more persons jointly, at least one of the persons must be a qualifying person (s.160ZA(6)(b)) and all of them must be eligible.

Fresh applications

3.30 Applicants who have previously been deemed not to qualify may make a fresh application if they consider they should now be treated as qualifying, but it will be for the applicant to show that his or her circumstances have changed (s.160ZA(11)).

Reviews of decisions on eligibility and qualification

3.31 For guidance on decisions and reviews see chapter 5.

Chapter 4
Framing an allocation scheme

4.1 Housing authorities are required by s.166A(1) to have an allocation scheme for determining priorities, and for defining the procedures to be followed in allocating housing accommodation; and they must allocate in accordance with that scheme (s.166A(14)). All aspects of the allocation process must be covered in the scheme, including the people by whom decisions are taken. In the Secretary of State's view, qualification criteria form part of an allocation scheme.

4.2 All housing authorities must have an allocation scheme, regardless of whether

9 As defined by s.199 of the 1996 Act.

10 5 years reflects guidelines issued by the local authorities associations which propose a working definition of normal residence for the purposes of establishing a local connection (see paragraph 4.1(i) to Annex 18 of the Homelessness Code of Guidance 2006).

they own housing stock and whether they contract out the delivery of any of their allocation functions (see further chapter 6). When framing or modifying their scheme, authorities must have regard to their current tenancy and homelessness strategies (s.166A(12)).

Choice and preference options

4.3 An allocation scheme must include a statement as to the housing authority's policy on offering people a choice of accommodation or the opportunity to express preferences about the accommodation to be allocated to them (s.166A). It is for housing authorities to determine their policy on providing choice or the ability to express preferences.

Reasonable preference

4.4 In framing their allocation scheme to determine allocation priorities, housing authorities must ensure that reasonable preference is given to the following categories of people (s.166A(3):

(a) people who are homeless within the meaning of Part 7 of the 1996 Act (including those who are intentionally homeless and those not in priority need)

(b) people who are owed a duty by any housing authority under section 190(2), 193(2) or 195(2) of the 1996 Act (or under section 65(2) or 68(2) of the Housing Act 1985) or who are occupying accommodation secured by any housing authority under s.192(3)

(c) people occupying insanitary or overcrowded housing or otherwise living in unsatisfactory housing conditions

(d) people who need to move on medical or welfare grounds, including grounds relating to a disability,[11] and

(e) people who need to move to a particular locality in the district of the housing authority, where failure to meet that need would cause hardship (to themselves or others)

4.5 In framing their allocation scheme to give effect to s.166A(3), housing authorities should have regard to the following considerations:

- the scheme must be framed so as to give reasonable preference to applicants who fall within the categories set out in s.166A(3), over those who do not
- although there is no requirement to give equal weight to each of the reasonable preference categories, authorities will need to demonstrate that, overall, reasonable preference has been given to all of them
- there is no requirement for housing authorities to frame their scheme to afford greater priority to applicants who fall within more than one reasonable preference category (cumulative preference) over those who have reasonable preference on a single, non-urgent basis.[12]

Otherwise, it is for housing authorities to decide how to give effect to the provisions of s.166A(3) in their allocation scheme.

11 The words 'including grounds relating to a disability were added by the Housing Act 2004.

12 *R (on application of Ahmad) v London Borough of Newham* [2009] UKHL 14, [2009] HLR 31.

Restricted persons

4.6 Applicants should not be given reasonable preference under paragraph (a) or (b) of s.166A(3) if they would only qualify for reasonable preference by taking into account a 'restricted person' within the meaning of Part 7 (s.166A(4)). A restricted person is a person subject to immigration control who is not eligible for homelessness assistance because he or she does not have leave to enter or remain in the UK or has leave which is subject to a 'no recourse to public funds' condition (s.184(7) of the 1996 Act).

Homeless or owed a homelessness duty

4.7 The requirement for housing authorities to frame their allocation scheme to give reasonable preference to people who are owed certain homeless duties remains the case, notwithstanding the amendments to Part 7 made by the Localism Act which give authorities the power to end the main homelessness duty with an offer of private rented accommodation, without requiring the applicant's consent.

Overcrowding

4.8 The Secretary of State takes the view that the bedroom standard is an appropriate measure of overcrowding for allocation purposes, and recommends that all housing authorities should adopt this as a minimum. The bedroom standard allocates a separate bedroom to each:

- married or cohabiting couple
- adult aged 21 years or more
- pair of adolescents aged 10–20 years of the same sex
- pair of children aged under 10 years regardless of sex

Medical and welfare grounds

4.9 The medical and welfare reasonable preference category includes people who need to move because of their disability or access needs, and this includes people with a learning disability as well as those with a physical disability.

4.10 'Welfare grounds' would encompass a wide range of needs, including, but not limited to, the need to:

- provide a secure base from which a care leaver, or a person who is moving on from a drug or alcohol recovery programme, can build a stable life
- provide accommodation, with appropriate care and support, for those who could not be expected to find their own accommodation, such as young adults with learning disabilities who wish to live independently in the community
- provide or receive care or support. This would include foster carers, those approved to adopt, or those being assessed for approval to foster or adopt, who need to move to a larger home in order to accommodate a looked after child or a child who was previously looked after by a local authority. It would also include special guardians, holders of a residence order and family and friends carers who are not foster carers but who have taken on the care of a child because the parents are unable to provide care

Hardship grounds

4.11 This would include, for example, a person who needs to move to a different locality in order to give or receive care, to access specialised medical treatment, or to take up a particular employment, education or training opportunity.

4.12 Possible indicators of the criteria which apply to reasonable preference categories (c) and (d) are given in annex1.

Additional preference

4.13 Section 166A(3) gives housing authorities the power to frame their allocation scheme to give additional preference to particular descriptions of people who fall within the statutory reasonable preference categories and have urgent housing needs. All housing authorities must consider, in the light of local circumstances, the need to give effect to this provision. Examples of people with urgent housing needs to whom housing authorities should consider giving additional preference within their allocation scheme include:

- those who need to move urgently because of a life threatening illness or sudden disability
- families in severe overcrowding which poses a serious health hazard
- those who are homeless and require urgent re-housing as a result of violence or threats of violence, including intimidated witnesses, and those escaping serious anti-social behaviour or domestic violence

Members of the Armed and Reserve Forces

4.14 Subject to parliamentary approval, we will regulate to require authorities to frame their allocation scheme to give additional preference to the following categories of people who fall within one or more of the reasonable preference categories and who have urgent housing needs:

(a) former members of the Armed Forces

(b) serving members of the Armed Forces who need to move because of a serious injury, medical condition or disability sustained as a result of their service

(c) bereaved spouses and civil partners of members of the Armed Forces leaving Services Family Accommodation following the death of their spouse or partner

(d) serving or former members of the Reserve Forces who need to move because of a serious injury, medical condition or disability sustained as a result of their service

Determining priorities between households with a similar level of need

4.15 Authorities may frame their allocation scheme to take into account factors in determining relative priorities between applicants in the reasonable (or additional) preference categories (s.166A(5)). Examples of such factors are given in the legislation: financial resources, behaviour and local connection. However, these examples are not exclusive and authorities may take into account other factors instead or as well as these.

Financial resources available to a person to meet his housing costs

4.16 This would enable a housing authority, for example, to give less priority to owner occupiers (wherever the property is situated).

Behaviour

4.17 This would allow for greater priority to be given to applicants who have been model tenants or have benefited the community, for example.

Local connection

4.18 Local connection is defined by s.199 of the 1996 Act. A person has a local connection because of normal residence (current or previous) of their own choice, employment, family associations, or special circumstances. Residence is not of a person's choice if it is the consequence of being detained in prison or in hospital under the Mental Health Act. As a result of changes to s.199 introduced in 2008[13] a person serving in the Armed Forces can establish a local connection with a local authority district through residence or employment there, in the same way as a civilian.

Including local priorities alongside the statutory reasonable preference categories

4.19 As the House of Lords made clear in the case of *R (on application of Ahmad) v. Newham LBC,*[14] s.166A(3)[15] only requires that the people encompassed within that section are given 'reasonable preference'. It 'does not require that they should be given absolute priority over everyone else'.[16] This means that an allocation scheme may provide for other factors than those set out in s.166A(3) to be taken into account in determining which applicants are to be given preference under a scheme, provided that:

- they do not dominate the scheme, and
- overall, the scheme operates to give reasonable preference to those in the statutory reasonable preference categories over those who are not

The Secretary of State would encourage authorities to consider the scope to take advantage of this flexibility to meet local needs and local priorities.

4.20 The House of Lords also made clear that, where an allocation scheme complies with the reasonable preference requirements and any other statutory requirements, the courts should be very slow to interfere on the ground of alleged irrationality.[17]

Local lettings policies

4.21 Section 166A(6)(b) of the 1996 Act enables housing authorities to allocate particular accommodation to people of a particular description, whether or not they fall within the reasonable preference categories, provided that overall the authority is able to demonstrate compliance with the requirements of s.166A(3). This is the statutory basis for so-called 'local lettings policies' which may be used to achieve a wide variety of housing management and policy objectives.

Households affected by the under-occupation measure

4.22 When framing the rules which determine the size of property to allocate to different households and in different circumstances, housing authorities are

13 Amendment to s.199 of the 1996 Act made by s.315 of the Housing and Regeneration Act 2008.

14 [2009] UKHL 14.

15 Previously s.167(2), which continues to apply to allocations by housing authorities in Wales.

16 Baroness Hale at para [18].

17 Lord Neuberger at para [55].

free to set their own criteria, provided they do not result in a household being statutorily overcrowded. However, in setting these criteria, authorities will want to take account of the provision in the Welfare Reform Act 2012 which will reduce Housing Benefit to under-occupiers.

4.23 Social tenants affected by the under-occupation measure may choose to move to more suitably sized accommodation in the private rented sector. One way to encourage tenants to consider this option might be to ensure they are given some degree of preference for an allocation if they apply for a new social tenancy at a later date.

Members of the Armed Forces

4.24 Authorities are also strongly encouraged to take into account the needs of all serving or former Service personnel when framing their allocation schemes, and to give sympathetic consideration to the housing needs of family members of serving or former Service personnel who may themselves have been disadvantaged by the requirements of military service and, in particular, the need to move from base to base. This would be in line with terms of the Government's Armed Forces Covenant published in May 2011.

4.25 Examples of ways in which authorities can ensure that Service personnel and their families are given appropriate priority, include:

- using the flexibility within the allocation legislation to set local priorities alongside the statutory reasonable preference categories so as to give preference, for example, to those who have recently left, or are close to leaving, the Armed Forces[18] (see paragraph 4.19 above)
- using the power to determine priorities between applicants in the reasonable preference categories, so that applicants in housing need who have served in the Armed Forces are given greater priority for social housing over those who have not (see paragraph 4.15 above)
- if taking into account an applicant's financial resources in determining priorities between households with a similar level of need (see paragraph 4.16 above), disregarding any lump sum received by a member of the Armed Forces as compensation for an injury or disability sustained on active service
- setting aside a proportion of properties for former members of the Armed Forces under a local lettings policy (see paragraph 4.21 above)

4.26 A number of organisations provide specialist housing and support for veterans, such as the Royal British Legion, Stoll, Haig Homes, Alabare and Norcare, and housing authorities are encouraged to liaise with them to ensure that former Service personnel are able to access the housing option which best suits their needs.

Households in work or seeking work

4.27 Local authorities are urged to consider how they can use their allocation policies to support those households who want to work, as well as those who – while unable to engage in paid employment - are contributing to their community in other ways, for example, through voluntary work. The flexibilities

18 MoD issues a Certificate of Cessation of Entitlement to Occupy Service Living Accommodation 6 months before discharge.

which authorities are encouraged to make use of to meet the needs of Service personnel would apply equally here. This might involve, for example, framing an allocation scheme to give some preference to households who are in low paid work or employment-related training, even where they are not in the reasonable preference categories; or to give greater priority to those households in the reasonable preference categories who are also in work or who can demonstrate that they are actively seeking work. Alternatively, it might involve using local lettings policies to ensure that specific properties, or a specified proportion of properties, are allocated to households in particular types of employment where, for example, skills are in short supply.

4.28 Authorities should also consider how best they can make use of the new power to offer flexible tenancies to support households who are in low paid work, and incentivise others to take up employment opportunities.

Carers

4.29 In making accommodation offers to applicants who receive support from carers who do not reside with them but may need to stay overnight, housing authorities should, wherever possible, take account of the applicant's need for a spare bedroom.

Prospective adopters and foster carers

4.30 When considering housing applications from prospective foster carers or adopters who would require an extra bedroom to accommodate a foster or adoptive child, authorities will wish to weigh up the risk that the application to foster or adopt may be unsuccessful (leading to the property being under-occupied), against the wider benefits which would be realised if the placement was successful.

4.31 Children's services have a duty under s.22G of the Children Act 1989 to ensure sufficient accommodation to meet the needs of the looked after children in their area. Authorities should work together with children's services to best meet the needs of prospective and approved foster carers and adopters, so that children's services can meet their s.22G duty. One way to strike an appropriate balance would be to set aside a quota of properties each year for people who need to move to larger accommodation in order to foster or adopt a child on the recommendation of children's services.

4.32 The advice in paragraph 4.22 is particularly relevant in relation to prospective foster carers, as foster children are not taken into account in determining the household size for the purposes of the under-occupation measure in the Welfare Reform Act. However, current and prospective foster carers affected by the measure may be eligible to apply for a Discretionary Housing Payment.

General information about particular applications

4.33 Under s166A(9), allocation schemes must be framed so as to give applicants the right to request from housing authorities general information that will enable them to assess:

(a) how their application is likely to be treated under the scheme and, in particular, whether they are likely to have reasonable preference

(b) whether accommodation appropriate to their needs is likely to be made available and, if so, how long it is likely to be before such accommodation becomes available

Notification about decisions and the right to a review of a decision

4.34 An allocation scheme must be framed so as to give applicants the right to be informed of certain decisions and the right to review certain decisions (s.166A(9)). For further advice on decisions and reviews, see chapter 5.

Chapter 5
Allocation scheme management

Publishing and consulting on allocation schemes

5.1 Housing authorities must publish a summary of their allocation scheme and, if requested, provide a free copy of it (s.168(1)). They must also make the full scheme available for inspection at their principal office and, if requested, provide a copy of it on payment of a reasonable fee (s.168(2)).

5.2 When an alteration is made to a scheme reflecting a major change of policy, an authority must ensure within a reasonable time that those likely to be affected by the change have the effect brought to their attention, taking such steps as the housing authority considers reasonable (s.168(3)). A major policy change would include, for example, any amendment affecting the relative priority of a large number of applicants or a significant alteration to procedures. Housing authorities should be aware that they still have certain duties under s.106 of the Housing Act 1985.

5.3 Section 166A(13) requires authorities, before adopting an allocation scheme, or altering a scheme to reflect a major change of policy, to:

- send a copy of the draft scheme, or proposed alteration, to every Private Registered Provider[19] with which they have nomination arrangements, and
- ensure they have a reasonable opportunity to comment on the proposals
-

Advice and information

5.4 Housing authorities must ensure that advice and information is available free of charge to everyone in their district about the right to apply for an allocation of accommodation (s.166(1)(a)). This would include general information about application procedures; as well as information about qualification and prioritisation criteria.

5.5 If a person is likely to have difficulty making an application without assistance, the authority must secure that any necessary assistance is available free of charge (s.166(1)(b)).

5.6 Housing authorities must inform applicants that they have the right to the following general information (s.166(1A)):

- information that will enable them to assess how their application is likely to be treated under the authority's allocation scheme, and, in particular,

19 And, where relevant, every Registered Social Landlord in Wales with which they have nomination arrangements.

whether they are likely to fall within the reasonable preference categories, and
- information about whether accommodation appropriate to their needs is likely to be made available to them and, if so, how long it is likely to be before such accommodation becomes available. Maintaining a database of housing suitable for applicants with access needs would assist with this.

5.7 Section 166(4) prohibits housing authorities from divulging to other members of the public that a person is an applicant for social housing, unless they have the applicant's consent. Furthermore, authorities should process any personal data they hold about applicants consistently with the Data Protection Act 1998. If authorities are unclear about their obligations and responsibilities under the Data Protection Act they should contact the Information Commissioner.

Elected Members' Involvement in Allocation Decisions

5.8 The Allocation of Housing (Procedure) Regulations 1997 (SI 1997/483) prevent an elected Member from being part of a decision-making body at the time an allocation decision is made, when either:
- the accommodation concerned is situated in their division or electoral ward, or
- the person subject to the decision has their sole or main residence there

5.9 The regulations do not prevent an elected Member from representing their constituents in front of the decision making body, or from participating in the decision making body's deliberations prior to its decision. The regulations also do not prevent elected Members' involvement in policy decisions that affect the generality of housing accommodation in their division or electoral ward rather than individual allocations; for example, a decision that certain types of property should be prioritised for older people.

Offences related to information given or withheld by applicants

5.10 Section 171 makes it an offence for anyone, in connection with the exercise by a housing authority of its functions under Part 6, to:
- knowingly or recklessly give false information
- knowingly withhold information which the housing authority has reasonably required the applicant to give in connection with the exercise of those functions

5.11 The circumstances in which an offence is committed could include providing false information:
- on an application form for social housing
- in response to a request for further information in support of the application
- during review proceedings

5.12 Ground 5 in Schedule 2 to the Housing Act 1985 (as amended by s.146 of the 1996 Act) enables a housing authority to seek possession of a tenancy granted as a result of a false statement by the tenant or a person acting at the tenant's instigation.

Fraudulent or incorrect allocations

5.13 Authorities may also wish to take action to minimise the risk of staff allocating incorrectly or even fraudulently, for example to applicants who do not have sufficient priority under the allocation scheme or do not meet the authority's qualification criteria. Appropriate steps might include vetting staff who take allocation decisions or providing for decisions to be validated by employing senior staff to undertake random checks.

Decisions and reviews

Information about decisions and reviews

5.14 Housing authorities must inform applicants that they have the right to information about certain decisions which are taken in respect of their application and the right to review those decisions (s.166(1A)).

5.15 By virtue of s.160ZA (9) and (10) housing authorities must notify an applicant in writing of any decision that he or she:

- is ineligible for an allocation of accommodation under s.160ZA(2) or (4), or
- is not a qualifying person under s.160ZA(7).

5.16 The notification must give clear grounds for the decision based on the relevant facts of the case. Section 160ZA(10) provides that, where a notification is not received by an applicant, it can be treated as having been given to him or her, if it is made available at the housing authority's office for a reasonable period. Where an authority considers that an applicant may have difficulty in understanding the implications of a decision on ineligibility or disqualification, it would be good practice to make arrangements for the information to be explained verbally in addition to providing a written notice.

5.17 Applicants also have the right, on request, to be informed of any decision about the facts of their case which has been, or is likely to be, taken into account in considering whether to make an allocation to them (s.166A(9)(b)).

5.18 Under s.166A(9)(c) applicants have the right to request a review of any of the decisions mentioned in paragraphs 5.15 and 5.17 above and to be informed of the decision on the review and the grounds for it.

Procedures on review

5.19 Review procedures should be clearly set out, including timescales for each stage of the process, and must accord with the principles of transparency and fairness. Failure to put in place a fair procedure for reviews, which allows for all relevant factors to be considered, could result in a judicial review of any decision reached. The following are general principles of good administrative practice:

i. Applicants should be notified of the timescale within which they must request a review. 21 days from the date the applicant is notified of the decision is well-established as a reasonable timescale. A housing authority should retain the discretion to extend this time limit in exceptional circumstances.

ii. Applicants should be notified that the request for review should be made in writing, and that it would also be acceptable for the request to be submitted by a representative on their behalf. Applicants should also be advised of the information which should accompany the request.

iii. Authorities should consider whether to advise that provision can be made for verbal representations, as well as written submissions, to be made.
iv. The review should be carried out by an officer who is senior to the person who made the original decision. Alternatively, authorities may wish to appoint a panel to consider the review. If so, it should not include any person involved in the original decision.
v. The review should be considered on the basis of the authority's allocation scheme, any legal requirements and all relevant information. This should include information provided by the applicant on any relevant developments since the original decision was made – for instance, the settlement of arrears or establishment of a repayment plan, or departure of a member of the household responsible for anti-social behaviour
vi. Reviews should be completed wherever practicable within a set deadline. Eight weeks is suggested as a reasonable timescale. The applicant should be notified of any extension to this deadline and the reasons for this
viii. Applicants must be notified in writing of the outcome of the review. The notification must set out the reasons for the decision. This will assist the applicant and the authority if, for example, the applicant is not satisfied with the outcome and decides to seek a judicial review or to take their case to the Local Government Ombudsman.

Chapter 6
Private Registered Providers and contracting out

Working with Private Registered Providers

6.1 Private Registered Providers have a duty under s.170 to cooperate with housing authorities – where the authority requests it - to such extent as is reasonable in the circumstances in offering accommodation to people with priority under the authority's allocation scheme. Similarly, s.213 provides that, where a Private Registered Provider has been requested by a housing authority to assist them in the discharge of their homelessness functions under Part 7, it must cooperate to the same extent.

6.2 Housing authorities must comply with the requirements of Part 6 when they nominate an applicant to be the tenant of a Private Registered Provider. A housing authority nominates for these purposes when it does so 'in pursuance of any arrangements (whether legally enforceable or not) to require that housing accommodation, or a specified amount of housing accommodation, is made available to a person or one of a number of persons nominated by the authority' (s.159(4)).

6.3 Nomination agreements should set out the proportion of lettings that will be made available; any criteria which the Private Registered Provider has adopted for accepting or rejecting nominees; and how any disputes will be resolved. Housing authorities will want to put in place arrangements to monitor effective delivery of the nomination agreement so they can demonstrate they are meeting their obligations under Part 6.

6.4 The Secretary of State expects that Affordable Rent homes will be allocated in the same way as social rent properties and that existing lettings arrangements operated by housing authorities and Private Registered Providers will continue to apply. The statutory and regulatory framework for allocations provides scope for local flexibility, and authorities and Private Registered Providers may wish to exercise this discretion in relation to Affordable Rent in order to meet local needs and priorities effectively.

Contracting Out

6.5 The Local Authorities (Contracting Out of Allocation of Housing and Homelessness Functions) Order 1996 (SI 1996/3205) – made under s.70 of the Deregulation and Contracting Out Act 1994 ('the 1994 Act') – enables housing authorities to contract out certain functions under Part 6. In essence, it allows the contracting out of administrative functions, leaving the responsibility for strategic decisions with the housing authority.

6.6 Schedule 1 to the Order lists allocation functions which may not be contracted out:

- adopting or altering the allocation scheme, including the principles on which the scheme is framed, and consulting Private Registered Providers,
- making the allocation scheme available at the authority's principal office

6.7 The Order therefore provides that the majority of functions under Part 6 may be contracted out. These include:

i) making enquiries about and deciding a person's eligibility for an allocation
ii) carrying out reviews of decisions
iii) securing that advice and information is available free of charge on how to apply for housing
iv) securing that assistance is available free of charge to people likely to have difficulty in making a housing application without such assistance, and
v) making individual allocations in accordance with the allocation scheme

6.8 The 1994 Act provides that a contract:

i) may authorise a contractor to carry out only part of the function concerned
ii) may specify that the contractor is authorised to carry out functions only in certain cases or areas specified in the contract
iii) may include conditions relating to the carrying out of the functions, for example prescribing standards of performance
iv) shall be for a period not exceeding 10 years and may be revoked at any time by the Minister or the housing authority. Any subsisting contract is to be treated as having been repudiated in these circumstances
v) shall not prevent the authority from exercising the functions to which the contract relates

6.9 The 1994 Act also provides that the authority is responsible for any act or omission of the contractor in exercising functions under the contract, except where:

- the contractor fails to fulfil conditions specified in the contract relating to the exercise of the function
- criminal proceedings are brought in respect of the contractor's act or omission

6.10 Where a housing authority has delegated or contracted out the operation of its allocation functions to an external contractor, the contractor must be made aware of the provisions of Part 6 and advised how the legislation and this guidance apply to them.

6.11 Where there is an arrangement in force under s.101 of the Local Government Act 1972 by virtue of which one authority exercises the functions of another, the 1994 Act provides that the authority exercising the function is not allowed to contract it out without the principal authority's consent.

ANNEX 1
Indicators of criteria in reasonable preference categories (c) & (d)

Housing authorities may devise their own indicators of the criteria in the reasonable preference categories. The following list is included for illustrative purposes and to assist housing authorities in this task. It is by no means comprehensive or exhaustive, and housing authorities may have other, local factors to consider and include as indicators of the categories.

Insanitary, overcrowded and unsatisfactory housing conditions

Lacking bathroom or kitchen
Lacking inside WC
Lacking cold or hot water supplies, electricity, gas, or adequate heating
Lack of access to a garden for young children
Sharing living room, kitchen, bathroom/WC
Property in disrepair
Poor internal or external arrangements
Young children in flats above ground floor

People who need to move on medical or welfare grounds (criteria may apply to any member of the household)

A mental illness or disorder
A physical or learning disability
Chronic or progressive medical conditions (e.g. MS, HIV/AIDS)
Infirmity due to old age
The need to give or receive care
The need to recover from the effects of violence or threats of violence, or physical, emotional or sexual abuse
Ability to fend for self restricted for other reasons
Young people at risk
People with behavioural difficulties
Need for adapted housing and/or extra facilities, bedroom or bathroom
Need for improved heating (on medical grounds)
Need for sheltered housing (on medical grounds)
Need for ground floor accommodation (on medical grounds)
Need to be near friends/relatives or medical facility on medical grounds
Need to move following hospitalisation or long term care

ANNEX 2
Rights to reside in the UK derived from EU Law

1. EEA nationals and their family members who have a right to reside in the UK that derives from EU law are not persons subject to immigration control. This means that they will be eligible for an allocation of accommodation under Part 6 unless they fall within one of the categories of persons to be treated as a person from abroad who is ineligible for an allocation of accommodation by virtue of regulation 4 of the Eligibility Regulations.

GENERAL
Nationals of EU countries

2. Nationals of EU countries enjoy a number of different rights to reside in other Member States, including the UK. These rights derive from the EU Treaties, EU secondary legislation (in particular Directive 2004/38), and the case law of the European Court of Justice.
3. Whether an individual EU national has a right to reside in the UK will depend on his or her circumstances, particularly his or her economic status (e.g. whether employed, self-employed, seeking work, a student, or economically inactive etc).

Nationals of Bulgaria and Romania _ the A2 accession states

4. A slightly different regime applies to EU nationals who are nationals of Bulgaria and Romania which acceded to the EU on 1 January 2007. Bulgaria and Romania are referred to in this guidance as the A2 accession states.

The Immigration (European Economic Area) Regulations 2006

5. The Immigration (European Economic Area) Regulations 2006 ('the EEA Regulations' – SI 2006/1003) implement into UK domestic law Directive 2004/38. Broadly, the EEA Regulations provide that EU nationals have the right to reside in the UK without the requirement for leave to remain under the Immigration Act 1971 for the first 3 months of their residence, and for longer, if they are a 'qualified person' or they have acquired a permanent right of residence.

Nationals of Iceland, Liechtenstein and Norway, and Switzerland

6. The EEA Regulations extend the same rights to reside in the UK to nationals of Iceland, Liechtenstein and Norway as those afforded to EU nationals. (The EU countries plus Iceland, Liechtenstein and Norway together comprise the EEA.) The EEA Regulations also extend the same rights to reside in the UK to nationals of Switzerland. For the purposes of this guidance, 'EEA nationals' means nationals of any of the EU member states (excluding the UK), and nationals of Iceland, Norway, Liechtenstein and Switzerland.

Initial 3 months residence

7. Regulation 13 of the EEA Regulations provides that EEA nationals have the right to reside in the UK for a period of up to 3 months without any conditions or formalities other than holding a valid identity card or passport. Therefore, during their first 3 months of residence in the UK, EEA nationals will not be subject to immigration control (unless the right to reside is lost following a

decision by an immigration officer in accordance with regulation 13(3) of the EEA Regulations).

8. However, regulations 4(1)(b)(ii) and (c) of the Eligibility Regulations provide that a person who is not subject to immigration control is not eligible for an allocation of accommodation if:
   (i) his or her **only** right to reside in the UK is an initial right to reside for a period not exceeding 3 months under regulation 13 of the EEA Regulations, or
   (ii) his or her **only** right to reside in the Channel Islands, the Isle of Man or the Republic of Ireland (the Common Travel Area) is a right equivalent to the right mentioned in (i) above which is derived from the EU Treaty

Rights of residence for 'qualified persons'

9. Regulation 14 of the EEA Regulations provides that 'qualified persons' have the right to reside in the UK so long as they remain a qualified person. Under regulation 6 of the EEA Regulations, 'qualified person' means:
   a) a jobseeker
   b) a worker
   c) a self-employed person
   d) a self-sufficient person
   e) a student

Jobseekers

10. For the purposes of regulation 6(1)(a) of the EEA Regulations, 'jobseeker' means a person who enters the UK in order to seek employment and can provide evidence that he or she is seeking employment and has a genuine chance of being employed.
11. Nationals of Bulgaria and Romania who need to be authorised to work do not have a right to reside in the UK as a jobseeker.[20] However, they may have a right to reside by virtue of another status, e.g. as a self-sufficient person.
12. Although a person who is a jobseeker is not subject to immigration control, regulation 4 of the Eligibility Regulations provides that a person is not eligible for an allocation of accommodation if:
   (i) his or her only right to reside in the UK is derived from his or her status as a jobseeker or the family member of a jobseeker, or
   (ii) his or her only right to reside in the Channel Islands, the Common Travel Area is a right equivalent to the right mentioned in (i) above which is derived from the Treaty establishing the European Community

Workers

13. In order to be a worker for the purposes of the EEA Regulations, a person must be employed. That is to say, he or she is obliged to provide services for another person in return for monetary reward and is subject to the control of that other person as regards the way in which the work is to be done.
14. Activity as an employed person may include part time work, seasonal work and cross-border work (ie. where a worker is established in another Member

20 Regulation 6(2) of the Accession (Immigration and Worker Authorisation) Regulations 2006 (SI 2006/3317).

State and travels to work in the UK). However, case law provides that the employment must be effective and genuine economic activity, and not on such a small scale as to be regarded as purely marginal and ancillary.

15. Provided the employment is effective and genuine economic activity, the fact that a person's level of remuneration may be below the level of subsistence or below the national minimum wage, or the fact that a person may be receiving financial assistance from public benefits, would not exclude that person from being a 'worker'.
16. A person who is a worker is not subject to immigration control, and is eligible for an allocation of accommodation whether or not he or she is habitually resident in the Common Travel Area.

Retention of worker status

17. A person who is no longer working does not cease to be treated as a 'worker' for the purpose of regulation 6(1)(b) of the EEA Regulations, if he or she:
    (a) is temporarily unable to work as the result of an illness or accident; or
    (b) is recorded as involuntarily unemployed after having being employed in the UK, provided that he or she has registered as a jobseeker with the relevant employment office, and:
        (i) was employed for one year or more before becoming unemployed, or
        (ii) has been unemployed for no more than 6 months, or
        (iii) can provide evidence that he or she is seeking employment in the UK and has a genuine chance of being engaged; or
    (c) is involuntarily unemployed and has embarked on vocational training; or
    (d) has voluntarily ceased working and embarked on vocational training that is related to his or her previous employment.

A2 state workers requiring authorisation who are treated as workers

18. By virtue of the Accession (Immigration and Worker Authorisation) Regulations 2006 ('the Accession Regulations'), nationals of the A2 states (with certain exceptions) must obtain authorisation to work in the UK until they have accrued a period of 12 months continuous employment.
19. An A2 national requiring authorisation is only treated as a worker if he or she is actually working and:
    (i) holds an accession worker authorisation document, and
    (ii) is working in accordance with the conditions set out in that document (regulation 9(1) of the Accession Regulations)
20. Authorities may need to contact the employer named in the authorisation document, to confirm that the applicant continues to be employed.

Self-employed persons

21. 'Self-employed person' means a person who establishes himself in the UK in order to pursue activity as a self-employed person in accordance with Article 49 of the Treaty on the Functioning of the European Union.
22. A self-employed person should be able to confirm that he or she is pursuing activity as a self-employed person by providing documents relating to their business. A person who is no longer in self-employment does not cease to be treated as a self-employed person for the purposes of regulation 6(1)(c) of the

EEA regulations, if he or she is temporarily unable to pursue his or her activity as a self-employed person as the result of an illness or accident.

23. A2 nationals are not required to be authorised in order to establish themselves in the UK as a self-employed person.
24. A person who is a self-employed is not subject to immigration control and is eligible for an allocation of accommodation whether or not he or she is habitually resident in the Common Travel Area.

Self-sufficient persons

25. Regulation 4(1)(c) of the EEA regulations defines 'self-sufficient person' as a person who has:
    (i) sufficient resources not to become a burden on the social assistance system of the UK during his or her period of residence, and
    (ii) comprehensive sickness insurance cover in the UK
26. By regulation 4(4) of the EEA Regulations, the resources of a person who is a self-sufficient person (or a student – see below) and, where applicable, any family members, are to be regarded as sufficient if (a) they exceed the maximum level of resources which a UK national and his or her family members may possess if he or she is to become eligible for social assistance under the UK benefit system or, if (a) does not apply, (b) taking into account the personal situation of the person concerned and, where applicable, any family members, it appears to the decision maker that the resources of the person or persons concerned should be regarded as sufficient.
27. Where an EEA national applies for an allocation of accommodation as a self-sufficient person and does not appear to meet the conditions of regulation 4(1)(c) of the EEA regulations, the housing authority will need to consider whether he or she may have some other right to reside in the UK.
28. Where the applicant does not meet the conditions of regulation 4(1)(c) but has previously done so during his or her residence in the UK, the case should be referred to the Home Office for clarification of their status.
29. A person who is a self-sufficient person is not subject to immigration control, but must be habitually resident in the Common Travel Area to be eligible for an allocation of accommodation.

Students

30. Regulation 4(1)(d) of the EEA regulations defines 'student' as a person who: (a) is enrolled at a private or public establishment included on the Register of Education and Training Providers,[21] or is financed from public funds, for the principal purpose of following a course of study, including vocational training, and (b) has comprehensive sickness insurance cover in the UK, and (c) assures the Secretary of State, by means of a declaration or such equivalent means as the person may choose, that he or she (and if applicable his or her family members) has sufficient resources not to become a burden on the social assistance system of the UK during his or her period of residence.
31. A person who is a student is not subject to immigration control but must be habitually resident in the Common Travel Area to be eligible for an allocation of accommodation.

21 Now known as the Register of Sponsors and held by UKBA.

Permanent right of residence

32. Regulation 15 of the EEA Regulations provides that the following persons shall acquire the right to reside in the UK permanently : (a) an EEA national who has resided in the UK in accordance with the EEA regulations for a continuous period of 5 years (b) a non-EEA national who is a family member of an EEA national and who has resided in the UK with the EEA national in accordance with the EEA regulations for a continuous period of 5 years (c) a worker or self-employed person who has ceased activity (see regulation 5 of the EEA Regulations for the definition of worker or self-employed person who has ceased activity) (d) the family member of a worker or self-employed person who has ceased activity (e) a person who was the family member of a worker or self-employed person who has died, where the family member resided with the worker or self-employed person immediately before the death and the worker or self-employed person had resided continuously in the UK for at least 2 years before the death (or the death was the result of an accident at work or an occupational disease) (f) a person who has resided in the UK in accordance with the EEA regulations for a continuous period of 5 years, and at the end of that period was a family member who has retained the right of residence (see regulation 10 of the EEA Regulations for the definition of a family member who has retained the right of residence). Once acquired, the right of permanent residence can be lost through absence from the UK for a period exceeding two consecutive years.
33. A person with a right to reside permanently in the UK arising from (c), (d) or (e) above is eligible for an allocation of accommodation whether or not he or she is habitually resident in the Common Travel Area. Persons with a permanent right to reside by virtue of (a), (b), or (f) must be habitually resident to be eligible.

RIGHTS OF RESIDENCE FOR CERTAIN FAMILY MEMBERS

The right to reside

34. Regulation 14 of the EEA Regulations provides that the following family members are entitled to reside in the UK:
    (i) a family member of a qualified person residing in the UK
    (ii) a family member of an EEA national with a permanent right of residence under regulation 15
    (iii) a family member who has retained the right of residence (see regulation 10 of the EEA Regulations for the definition)
35. A person who has a right to reside in the UK as the family member of an EEA national under the EEA Regulations will not be subject to immigration control. The eligibility of such a person for an allocation of accommodation should therefore be considered in accordance with regulation 4 of the Eligibility Regulations.
36. When considering the eligibility of a family member, housing authorities should consider whether the person has acquired a right to reside in their own right, for example a permanent right to reside under regulation 15 of the EEA Regulations.

Who is a 'family member'?

37. Regulation 7 of the EEA regulations provides that the following persons are treated as the family members of another person (with certain exceptions for students – see below):
(a) the spouse of the person
(b) the civil partner of the person
(c) a direct descendant of the person, or of the person's spouse or civil partner, who is under the age of 21
(d) a direct descendant of the person, or of the person's spouse or civil partner, who is over 21 and dependent on the person, or the spouse or civil partner
(e) an ascendant relative of the person, or of the person's spouse or civil partner, who is dependent on the person or the spouse or civil partner
(f) a person who is an extended family member and is treated as a family member by virtue of regulation 7(3) of the EEA regulations (see below)

Family members of students

38. Regulation 7(2) of the EEA regulations provides that a person who falls within (c), (d) or (e) above shall not be treated as a family member of a student residing in the UK after the period of 3 months beginning on the date the student is admitted to the UK unless:
(i) in the case of paragraph 37(c) and (d) above, the person is the dependant child of the student, or of the spouse or civil partner, or
(ii) the student is also a qualified person (for the purposes of regulation 6(1) of the EEA regulations) other than as a student

Extended family members

39. Broadly, extended family members will be persons who:
(a) do not fall within any of the categories (a) to (e) in paragraph 37 above, and
(b) are either a relative of an EEA national (or of the EEA national's spouse or civil partner) or the partner of an EEA national, and
(c) have been issued with an EEA family permit, a registration certificate or a residence card which is valid and has not been revoked

Family members' eligibility for an allocation of accommodation

Relationship with other rights to reside

40. This section concerns the eligibility of an applicant for an allocation of accommodation whose right to reside is derived from his or her status as the family member of an EEA national with a right to reside. In some cases, a family member will have acquired a right to reside in his or her own right. In particular, a person who arrived in the UK as the family member of an EEA national may have subsequently acquired a permanent right of residence under regulation 15 of the EEA Regulations, as outlined in paragraph 32 (a) – (f) above. The eligibility for an allocation of accommodation of those with a permanent right of residence is discussed at paragraphs 32 and 33.

Family members who must be habitually resident

41. For family members with a right to reside under regulation 14 of the EEA Regulations, the following categories of persons must be habitually resident

in the UK, the Channel Islands, the Isle of Man or the Republic of Ireland in order to be eligible for an allocation of accommodation:

a) a person whose right to reside derives from their status as a family member of an EEA national who is a self-sufficient person for the purposes of regulation 6(1)(d) of the EEA regulations
b) a person whose right to reside derives from their status as a family member of an EEA national who is a student for the purposes of regulation 6(1)(e) of the EEA regulations
c) a person whose right to reside is dependent on their status as a family member of an EEA national with a permanent right to reside
d) a person whose right to reside is dependent on their status as a family member who has retained the right of residence

Family members who are exempt from the habitual residence requirement

42. A person with a right to reside under regulation 14 as a family member of an EEA national who is a worker or a self-employed person for the purposes of regulation 6(1) of the EEA regulations is exempted from the requirement to be habitually resident by regulation 4(2)(d) of the Eligibility Regulations. However, authorities should note that an extended family member (see above) is not counted as a family member for the purposes of regulation 4(2)(d) of the Eligibility Regulations (see regulation 2(3) of the Eligibility Regulations).

Family members of UK nationals exercising rights under the EU Treaty

43. There are some limited cases in which the non-EEA family member of a UK national may have a right to reside under EU law. Under regulation 9 of the EEA Regulations, the family member of a UK national should be treated as an EEA family member where the following conditions are met:
(i) the UK national is residing in an EEA State as a worker or self-employed person, or was so residing before returning to the UK, and
(ii) if the family member of the UK national is his spouse or civil partner, the parties are living together in the EEA State, or had entered into a marriage or civil partnership and were living together in that State before the UK national returned to the UK

44. Where the family member of a UK national is to be treated as an EEA family member by virtue of regulation 9 of the EEA Regulations, that person is not subject to immigration control, and his or her eligibility for an allocation of accommodation should therefore be determined in accordance with regulation 4 of the Eligibility Regulations.

ANNEX 3
Worker authorisation scheme

1. Bulgaria and Romania ('the A2') acceded to the European Union on 1 January 2007. A2 nationals have the right to move freely among all EU Member States. However, under the EU Accession Treaty for Bulgaria and Romania existing Member States can impose limitations on the rights of A2 nationals to access their labour markets (and the associated rights of residence) for a transitional period.

The Accession (Immigration and Worker Authorisation) Regulations 2006

2. Under the Accession (Immigration and Worker Authorisation) Regulations 2006 (SI 2006/3317) ('the Accession Regulations'), nationals of the A2 States (with certain exceptions set out in paragraph 9 below) are required to be authorised to work by the Home Office if they work in the UK during the transitional period. While looking for work (or between jobs) their right to reside will be conditional on them being self-sufficient and not imposing an unreasonable burden on the UK social assistance system. These conditions cease to apply once they have worked in the UK continuously and legally for 12 months.

3. The Accession Regulations also give workers from the A2 states the right to reside in the UK. This means that workers from the A2 states have the same right to equal treatment as other EEA workers while they are working in accordance with work authorisation requirements or are exempt from those requirements.

The worker authorisation scheme

4. Nationals of A2 states who wish to work in the UK (except those who are exempt from the requirement) must have an accession worker authorisation document and must be working in accordance with the conditions set out in that document.

5. Nationals of the A2 states who are self-employed are not required to be authorised if they are working that capacity.

6. The following constitute worker authorisation documents:
   i. a passport or other travel document endorsed to show that the person was given leave to enter or remain in the UK before 1 January 2007, subject to a condition restricting his or her employment in the UK to a particular employer or category of employment
   If the leave to enter or remain expires before the person qualifies to be exempt from the work authorisation requirements, or they wish to engage in employment other than the job for which the leave was granted, they will need to obtain an accession worker card
   ii. a seasonal agricultural work card issued by the Home Office under the Seasonal Agricultural Workers Scheme. The card is valid for 6 months from the date the person starts work for the agricultural employer specified in the card
   iii. an accession worker card issued by the Home Office

7. The accession worker card is valid for as long as the person continues to work for the employer specified in the card. If the person changes employer, he or she must apply for a new accession worker card.

8. The worker authorisation scheme is a transitional measure. The Accession Regulations provide for the scheme to operate for up to five years from 1 January 2007 (i.e. until 31 December 2011). However, there is provision for the scheme to be extended for a further two years in the event of a serious disturbance to the labour market. The decision was taken on 23 November 2011 to maintain transitional controls on Romanian and Bulgarian workers until the end of 2013.

A2 nationals exempt from worker authorisation

9. The following are the categories of A2 nationals who are not required to obtain authorisation to work:
   - those who are classified as highly skilled persons and hold a registration certificate allowing them unconditional access to the UK labour market
   - those working legally, and without interruption, in the UK for a period of 12 months or more ending on 31 December 2006 (for example, they may have been already present in the UK as a work permit holder before accession)
   - those who had leave to enter the UK under the Immigration Act 1971 on 31 December 2006 and that leave does not place any restrictions on taking employment in the United Kingdom (for example, a person may have been given leave to remain as the spouse of a British citizen or as the dependant of a work permit holder)
   - those who are providing services in the UK on behalf of an employer established elsewhere in the EEA
   - those who are also a national of the UK or another EEA state (other than an A2 state)
   - those who are a spouse or civil partner of a national of the UK or a person settled in the UK
   - those who are the spouse, civil partner or child under 18 of a person who has limited leave to enter or remain in the UK and that leave allows that person to work in the UK
   - those who are a family member (spouse, civil partner or dependant child) of an EEA national who has a right to reside in the UK under the EEA Regulations, including those who are the family member (spouse, civil partner or descendant (under 21 or dependant)) of an A2 national who is working in accordance with worker authorisation requirements
   - those who have a permanent right to reside in the UK under regulation 15 of the EEA Regulations
   - those who are in the UK as a student and are permitted to work for 20 hours a week, provided they are in possession of a registration certificate confirming that they are exercising a Treaty right as a student
10. In addition, where a person has worked legally in the UK without interruption for a 12 month period falling wholly or partly after 31 December 2006, they will be free from the requirement to seek authorisation. At that stage, they will be able to apply to the Home Office for an EEA residence permit to confirm their right to equal treatment on the same basis as other EEA nationals.

12 months' uninterrupted work

11. In order to establish '12 months' uninterrupted work' an A2 worker must have been working legally in the UK at the beginning and end of the 12 month period. The 12 month period does not have to run continuously. However, any intervening period in which an A2 national is not legally working must not exceed 30 days in total. If more than 30 days between periods of employment occur before a 12-month period of uninterrupted employment is established, a fresh period of 12 months' uninterrupted employment would need to commence from that point.

12. There is no restriction on the number of different authorised jobs (or employers) that a worker can have during a 12-month period of continuous employment.

Highly skilled workers

13. A national of an A2 state is not required to be authorised under the worker authorisation scheme, if he is a highly skilled worker who has been given a registration certificate by the Home Office which includes a statement that he or she has unconditional access to the UK labour market.

ANNEX 4
Habitual residence

1. In practice, when considering housing applications from persons subject to the habitual residence test, it is only necessary to investigate habitual residence if the applicant has arrived or returned to live in the UK during the two year period prior to making the application.

Definition of habitual residence

2. The term 'habitual residence' is not defined in legislation. Housing authorities should always consider the overall circumstances of a case to determine whether someone is habitually resident in the Common Travel Area.

General principles

3. When deciding whether a person is habitually resident, consideration must be given to all the facts of each case in a common sense way. It should be remembered that:
   - the test focuses on the fact and nature of residence
   - a person who is not resident somewhere cannot be habitually resident there
   - residence is a more settled state than mere physical presence in a country. To be resident a person must be seen to be making a home. It need not be the only home or a permanent home but it must be a genuine home for the time being. For example, a short stay visitor or person receiving short term medical treatment is not resident
   - the most important factors for habitual residence are length, continuity and general nature of actual residence rather than intention
   - the practicality of a person's arrangements for residence is a necessary part of determining whether it can be described as settled and habitual
   - established habitual residents who have periods of temporary or occasional absence of long or short duration may still be habitually resident during such absences

Action on receipt of an application

Applicant came to live in the UK during the previous two years

4. If it appears that the applicant came to live in the UK during the previous two years, authorities should make further enquiries to decide if the applicant is habitually resident, or can be treated as such.

Factors to consider

5. The applicant's stated reasons and intentions for coming to the UK will be relevant to the question of whether he or she is habitually resident. If the applicant's stated intention is to live in the UK, and not return to the country from which they came, that intention must be consistent with their actions.
6. To decide whether an applicant is habitually resident in the UK, authorities should consider the factors set out below. However, these do not provide an exhaustive check list of the questions or factors that need to be considered. Further enquiries may be needed. The circumstances of each case will dictate what information is needed, and all relevant factors should be taken into account.

Why has the applicant come to the UK?

7. If the applicant is returning to the UK after a period spent abroad, and it can be established that the applicant was previously habitually resident in the UK and is returning to resume his or her former period of habitual residence, he or she will be immediately habitually resident.
8. In determining whether an applicant is returning to resume a former period of habitual residence authorities should consider:
   - when the applicant left the UK
   - how long the applicant lived in the UK before leaving
   - why the applicant left the UK
   - how long the applicant intended to remain abroad
   - why the applicant returned
   - whether the applicant's partner and children, if any, also left the UK
   - whether the applicant kept accommodation in the UK
   - if the applicant owned property, whether it was let, and whether the lease was timed to coincide with the applicant's return to the UK
   - what links the applicant kept with the UK
   - whether there have been other brief absences
   - why the applicant has come back to the UK
9. If the applicant has arrived in the UK within the previous two years and is not resuming a period of habitual residence, consideration should be given to his or her reasons for coming to the UK, and in particular to the factors set out below.

Applicant is joining family or friends

10. If the applicant has come to the UK to join or rejoin family or friends, authorities should consider:
    - whether the applicant has sold or given up any property abroad
    - whether the applicant has bought or rented accommodation or is staying with friends
    - whether the move to the UK is intended to be permanent

Applicant's plans

11. Authorities should consider the applicant's plans, e.g:
    - if the applicant plans to remain in the UK, whether their stated plan is consistent with their actions
    - whether any arrangements were made for employment and accommodation (even if unsuccessful) before the applicant arrived in the UK

- whether the applicant bought a one-way ticket
- whether the applicant brought all their belongings
- whether there is evidence of links with the UK, e.g. membership of clubs

12. The fact that a person may intend to live in the UK for the foreseeable future does not, of itself, mean that habitual residence has been established. However, the applicant's intentions along with other factors, for example the disposal of property abroad, may indicate that the applicant is habitually resident in the UK.
13. An applicant who intends to reside in the UK for only a short period, for example for a holiday or to visit friends is unlikely to be habitually resident in the UK.

Length of residence in another country

14. Authorities should consider the length and continuity of an applicant's residence in another country:
    - whether the applicant has any remaining ties with his or her former country of residence
    - whether the applicant stayed in different countries outside the UK
15. It is possible that a person may own a property abroad but still be habitually resident in the UK. A person who has a home or close family in another country would normally retain habitual residence in that country. A person who has previously lived in several different countries but has now moved permanently to the UK may be habitually resident here.

Centre of interest

16. An applicant is likely to be habitually resident in the Common Travel Area despite spending time abroad, if his or her centre of interest is located in one of these places.
17. People who maintain their centre of interest in the Common Travel Area for example a home, a job, friends, membership of clubs, are likely to be habitually resident there. People who have retained their centre of interest in another country and have no particular ties with the Common Travel Area are unlikely to be habitually resident.
18. Authorities should take the following into account when deciding the centre of interest:
    - home
    - family ties
    - club memberships
    - finance accounts
19. If the centre of interest appears to be in the Common Travel Area but the applicant has a home somewhere else, authorities should consider the applicant's intentions regarding the property.
20. It is not uncommon for a person to live in one country but have property abroad that they do not intend to sell. Where such a person has lived in the Common Travel Area for many years, the fact that they have property elsewhere does not necessarily mean that they intend to leave, or that the applicant's centre of interest is elsewhere.

Provision of Accommodation for 16 and 17 year old young people who may be homeless and/or require accommodation

Guidance to children's services authorities and local housing authorities about their duties under Part 3 of the Children Act 1989 and Part 7 of the Housing Act 1996 to secure or provide accommodation for homeless 16 and 17 year old young people. (April 2010)

For the purposes of this guidance the term 'homeless' should be taken to mean 'homeless and/or requiring accommodation' The term 'young people' should be taken to mean 16- and 17-year-old children.

1 Introduction

1.1 In recent years a number of judgments have been handed down by the House of Lords in cases concerning the interrelationship between the duty under section 20 of the *Children Act 1989* ('the 1989 Act') and duties under Part 7 of the *Housing Act 1996* ('the 1996 Act') in the case of young people aged 16 or 17 who require accommodation. The most recent of these has been *R (G) v Southwark* [2009] UKHL 26, but these have also included *R (M) v Hammersmith and Fulham* [2008] UKHL 14. These judgments have restated and clarified the established legal position that the duty under section 20 of the 1989 Act takes precedence over the duties in the 1996 Act in providing for children in need who require accommodation, and that the specific duty owed under section 20 of the 1989 Act takes precedence over the general duty owed to children in need and their families under section 17 of the 1989 Act.

1.2 This guidance does not address the wider responsibilities of local authority children's services and their partners to identify and support families where children and young people may be at risk of negative outcomes, including homelessness in the future, by delivering integrated and targeted services in their area. This guidance is solely concerned with the functions of children's services and housing services when young people seek help from, or are referred to, local authorities because of homelessness.

1.3 This guidance is issued jointly by the Secretary of State for Children, Schools and Families and the Secretary of State for Communities and Local Government under section 7 of the *Local Authority Social Services 1970* and section 182 of the *Housing Act 1996*. Section 7 of the 1970 Act requires local authorities in exercising their social services functions to act under the general guidance of the Secretary of State; unless there are exceptional reasons in individual cases authorities are expected to comply with this guidance. Section 182 of the 1996 Act requires housing authorities and social services authorities, in the exercise of their functions relating to homelessness and the prevention of homelessness, to have regard to such guidance as may from time to time be given by the Secretary of State.

1.4 This guidance replaces the paragraphs in Circular LAC (2003) 13 Guidance *on Accommodating Children in Need and the Families,* issued by the Department of Health, which refer to how lone 16 and 17 year olds should be accommodated under the Children Act 1989 Act.

Structure of the guidance

1.5 **Part 2** of this guidance addresses children's services' and housing services' initial responses to 16 and 17 year olds seeking help because of homelessness. **Part 3** gives guidance on the provision of suitable accommodation for 16 and 17 year olds. In many cases, both children's services and housing services will need to have contact with, and provide services for, homeless 16 and 17 year olds. **Part 4** gives guidance on the provision of suitable accommodation for 16 and 17 year olds who are not owed a duty under section 20 or who refuse section 20 accommodation. **Part 5** provides guidance on joint working between children's and housing services at strategic and operational level.

2 Responding to 16 and 17 year old young people seeking help because of homelessness

Supporting families to stay together and re-unification

2.1 It is in the best interests of most young people aged 16 or 17 to live in the family home, or, where this is not safe or appropriate, with responsible adults in their wider family and friends network. Local authority responses to 16 and 17 year olds seeking help because of homelessness should explicitly recognise this and work pro-actively with young people and their families to identify and resolve the issues which have led to the homelessness crisis. This could involve family support such as family mediation or family group conferences.

2.2. It may be possible for children's services to prevent a young person from having to leave home at all, or it may take much longer to work through significant family tensions and problems while the young person is accommodated by the local authority. It is therefore important that services are designed to enable this family focus to begin on day one and continue throughout the processes of assessment and, where necessary, the provision of accommodation.

2.3. This preventative work should be undertaken alongside the statutory assessment processes outlined in this guidance and should not delay assessment or the delivery of statutory services to 16 and 17 year olds who may be homeless or at risk of homelessness.

2.4. If key issues affecting the young person's welfare and/or the sustainability of their living at home remain unresolved, post-reunification support should be provided to the family after the young person returns home.

16 and 17 year olds who may require accommodation with children and/or partners

2.5 By the age of 16 or 17 most young people are forming relationships and a few may themselves have children. Assessment, support and accommodation services should take into account young peoples' relationships as well as any dependent children and, where appropriate, support them to build a positive family life.

2.6 The needs of 16 and 17 year olds' for accommodation should be assessed in the context of their relationship with any 'partner'. In some cases it may be appropriate for a 16 or 17 year old to be accommodated in a situation where where they can live with their partner. This should not prevent local authorities from accommodating a 16 or 17 year old under section 20 where the young person is owed a duty under this section. Specific consideration should be given to placement options for young people accommodated under section 20 whilst living with a partner. For example, placement in an alternative arrangement such as a self contained property with visiting support may be appropriate. It will also be important to have contingency plans in place in case relationships break down.

2.7 Where young parents are provided with accommodation by children's services and become looked after, it does not follow that their child will also be looked after. This is an issue for an entirely separate assessment based on the needs of the infant.

Accessing services

2.8 16 and 17 year olds who seek assistance from a local authority because they are homeless or at risk of homelessness may either seek help initially from the local housing authority or from the children's services authority. Within unitary authorities, the initial approach for help may be made to either housing services or children's services. 16 and 17 year olds may also seek help from multi-disciplinary teams including co-located children's and housing services staff where local authorities have established such arrangements (these arrangements may be made in both unitary and two tier areas and will be referred to as **integrated services** for the purposes of this guidance).

Initial approaches to housing services

2.9 Where the initial approach or referral for housing assistance is made to housing services, the authority should treat the approach/referral as an application for assistance under Part 7 of the 1996 Act. The authority will therefore need to decide whether there is reason to believe the young person may be homeless or likely to become homeless within 28 days (section 184 of the1996 Act) and, if so, the authority will need to make inquiries to determine whether any duty is owed under Part 7 of the 1996 Act.

2.10 If there is reason to believe the young person may be eligible for assistance, may be homeless and may be 16 or 17 years of age, the authority will have an immediate duty to secure interim accommodation (section 188(1) of the 1996 Act) pending a decision whether any substantive duty is owed under Part 7. Such accommodation must be suitable for a 16 & 17 year old and, in considering suitability, authorities should bear in mind that 16 and 17 year olds who are homeless and estranged from their family will be particularly vulnerable and in need of support. The Secretary of State considers that Bed and Breakfast accommodation is unsuitable for 16 and 17 year olds.

2.11 If the young person may be homeless or may be likely to become homeless within 28 days, housing services should make an immediate referral to children's services for an assessment. This applies to all 16 and 17 year old applicants without exception, for example including those who are pregnant and/or a parent. The question whether any substantive duty is owed under Part 7 of the 1996 Act will depend in part on the outcome of the assessment by children's services, and whether any duty is owed under section 20 of the 1989 Act. Housing services should continue to secure accommodation under section 188 (1) until they have notified the young person whether any substantive duty is owed under Part 7 of the 1996 Act. Children's services should undertake and complete an initial assessment as soon as possible and no later than the ten days set out in the Framework for the Assessment of Children in Need and their Families. (See paragraphs 2.36–2.40). Where children's services have accepted that they have a duty under section 20 duty to provide accommodation and the 16 or 17 year old has accepted the accommodation, the young person will not be homeless and no further duty will be owed under Part 7 of the 1996 Act.

Young people from one district who seek assistance from housing services in another district

2.12 Housing services are reminded that they must consider all applications for accommodation or assistance in obtaining accommodation. Authorities cannot refuse to assist an applicant on the basis that the applicant may not (or does not) have a local connection with the district. Authorities can refer an applicant to another authority only if they have accepted that the applicant is eligible for assistance, unintentionally homeless and in priority need but consider that the applicant does not have a local connection with their district and does have one elsewhere in Great Britain. For further guidance about local connection and referrals, authorities should refer to Chapter 18 of the *Homelessness Code of Guidance for Local Authorities.*[1]

Initial approaches and referrals to integrated services

2.13 Integrated services can assist in the delivery of a seamless, child-centred response to the needs of 16 and 17 year olds who are homeless or threatened with homelessness. Given that the 1989 Act takes precedence over the 1996 Act, and given their responsibilities for children in need in their areas, children's services should be the lead agency with regard to assessing and meeting the needs of 16 and 17 year olds who seek help because of homelessness. The Secretary of State for Children, Schools and Families and the Secretary of State for Communities and Local Government consider that an initial approach or referral to integrated services should be treated in the same way as an initial approach or referral to children's services (see below).

2.14 The involvement of housing staff in this process can have a number of benefits, for example:

- improvement of joint working through better understanding and communication between children's services and housing services;
- giving 16 and 17 year olds, and their families, access to information directly from both services regarding the support and, if necessary, accommodation options that may be available both now and in the future;
- removal of the need for a referral to housing services for a fresh assessment under the homelessness legislation if the young person is not accommodated under section 20, eg following the initial assessment and consideration of their wishes and feelings in the context of their needs.

Approaches and referrals to children's services

2.15 Where a 16 or 17 year old seeks help from local authority children's services or is referred to children's services by some other person or agency (including housing services) as appearing to be homeless or at risk of homelessness, or they are an unaccompanied asylum seeker without a parent or guardian with responsibility for their care, then children's services must assess whether the

1 www.communities.gov.uk/publications/housing/homelessnesscode/.

young person is a child in need, and determine whether any duty is owed under section 20 of the 1989 Act to provide the young person with accommodation.

2.16 Where a 16 or 17 year old seeks help or is referred, and it appears he or she has nowhere safe to stay that night, then children's services must secure suitable emergency accommodation for them. This will mean that the young person will become looked after (under section 20 (1)) whilst their needs, including their need for continuing accommodation and support, are further assessed. Bed and breakfast accommodation is not considered suitable for 16 and 17 year olds even on an emergency accommodation basis. Where the young person is accommodated under section 20 they will not be eligible for welfare benefits, including housing benefit[2] and children's services will have a duty to maintain them (including meeting the cost of accommodation).

2.17 Section 17 of the 1989 Act sets out the responsibilities of local authorities to provide services for children in need and their families. It is the general duty of every local authority–

- to safeguard and promote the welfare of children within their area who are in need; and
- so far as is consistent with that duty, to promote the upbringing of such children by their families by providing a range and level of services appropriate to those children's needs.

2.18 Section 17(10) of the 1989 Act defines a child as being in need if–

(a) he is unlikely to achieve or maintain, or to have the opportunity of achieving or maintaining, a reasonable standard of health or development without the provision for him of services by a local authority under this Part;
(b) his health or development is likely to be significantly impaired, or further impaired, without the provision for him of such services; or
(c) he is disabled,

The duties described in section 17 apply to all children in need in the area of the local authority.

A child is any person under the age of 18. (see section 105(1) of the 1989 Act.)

2.19 Section 20(1) requires that:

Every local authority shall provide accommodation for any child in need within their area who appears to them to require accommodation as a result of–

(a) there being no person who has parental responsibility for him;
(b) his being lost or having been abandoned; or
(c) the person who has been caring for him being prevented (whether or not permanently, and for whatever reason) from providing him with suitable accommodation or care.

2.20 In addition, even if the criteria in section 20(1) do not apply, section 20(3) requires that: Every local authority shall provide accommodation for any child in need within their area who has reached the age of sixteen and whose welfare the authority consider is likely to be seriously prejudiced if they do not provide him with accommodation.

2.21 In addition, section 20(4), provides that: a local authority may provide accommodation for any child within their area (even though a person who has

2 There are exceptions for lone parents and for disabled young people who may have established entitlement to non-means tested benefits.

parental responsibility for him is able to provide him with accommodation) if they consider that to do so would safeguard or promote the child's welfare.

2.22 Local authority duties for accommodating young people under this section are not simply a matter for local policy. The duty is engaged whenever any authority has determined that the young person is in fact in need and requires accommodation as a result of one of the factors set out in section 20(1)(a) to (c) or in section 20(3).

2.23 There can be no doubt that where a young person requires accommodation as a result of one of the factors set out in section 20(1)(a) to (c) or section 20(3) then that young person will be in need and must be provided with accommodation. As a result of being accommodated the young person will become looked after and the local authority will owe them the duties that are owed to all looked after children, set out in sections 22 and 23 and once they cease to be looked after, the duties that are owed to care leavers under that Act.

2.24 Identifying the needs of the young person and the best response to these needs will be the function of each assessment. The critical factors to be taken into account in assessing whether a young person is in need under the 1989 Act are what will happen to the young person's health and development without services being provided or secured by children's services and the likely effect of the provision of services will have on the young person's health and development. Where a young person is excluded from home, is sofa surfing among friends, or is sleeping in a car, it is extremely likely that they will be a child in need. Similarly, where a 16 and 17 year old teenage parent is homeless they are also likely to have significant needs and require accommodation and support as a child in need. Determining who is in need and the extent of any needs requires professional judgment by children's services staff, informed by consultation with other professionals familiar with the circumstances of the individual young person and their family. The young person's and their family's wishes and feelings must be taken into account (see paragraphs 2.44–2.53 below).

2.25 At the point when the need for a children's services assessment is identified, it will be necessary for the professional undertaking the assessment to agree an assessment plan with the young person and with their family. (For a 16 or 17 year old who may be homeless, this will be the point at which they first seek help from, or are referred to, children's services). This assessment plan will make clear from the outset who is doing what, within what timescales, and what the possible outcomes of the assessment might be. These could range from the young person becoming, or continuing to be (if children's services has provided or secured emergency accommodation) accommodated by children's services to no services being provided.

2.26 Young people seeking help because of actual or threatened homelessness are likely to have a range of concurrent needs[3] and these should be assessed fully in accordance with the assessment process set out in the *Framework for the Assessment of Children in Need and their Families*. The most crucial issue to be determined through the assessment process will be whether the young

3 Statutory Homelessness in England: The Experiences of Homeless Families and 16 and 17 year olds' – CLG 2008: www.communities.gov.uk/publications/housing/experienceoffamilies/.

person is actually homeless and therefore requires accommodation. However, assessment will need to take into account every dimension of the young person's needs and, as well as the need for accommodation, it will be necessary to assess what further support the young person needs. A homeless young person not participating in education or training would in the first place need suitable accommodation but this should be arranged in conjunction with plans to re-engage them with education or training.

2.27 The majority of young people seeking help because of homelessness cite the breakdown of relationships with parents or other carers as the reason for their homelessness. The assessment will need to determine whether or not the young person can return home, with support for them and their family if necessary, or whether this is not a possible or safe option.

Undertaking assessments

2.28 An initial assessment should be carried out involving interviewing the young person and family members and making enquiries with other agencies. Where a young person seeks help because of homelessness it is good practice for an assessment of the young person's needs to be conducted jointly by both children's and housing services. Alternatively, assessment and referral processes should be underpinned by appropriate information-sharing so that young people do not have to repeat their stories each time and navigate between offices which may be some way apart. The lead agency will be children's services, given their responsibilities for children in need in their areas.

2.29 It will be essential to establish very close contact and rapport with the young person throughout the assessment process, in order to make sure their wishes and feelings are properly understood and to take their views into account (see paragraphs under 2.44 below). Similarly, it will also be important to maintain contact with the adults who retain parental responsibility for the young person and with any other family members in the young person's network. It will generally be necessary to visit the family home or other accommodation where the young person has been living as part of the assessment process.

2.30 The assessment will need to establish whether the factors set out in sections 20(1), 20(3) or 20(4) of the 1989 Act are applicable to the young person's circumstances.

2.31 Careful account will need to be taken of the factors which will promote the welfare of the young person, including the significance of the young person's relationship with their parents, or other adults in their life responsible for their care up until the point that they seek help, or are referred, as homeless. The assessment should identify the young person's and their family's, strengths as well as any difficulties and should build on strengths to attempt to develop sustainable solutions so that the young person's needs, including the need for suitable accommodation, are met for the future.

2.32 At the conclusion of the initial assessment, staff should have reached a provisional assessment of the young person's needs and the services that they are likely to require to support them in making a positive transition into adulthood. The Annex to this guidance sets out the issues that should generally be considered during the assessment process. The *Framework for the Assessment of Children in Need and their Families* (2000)[4] provides comprehensive information about the factors that the assessment must take into account.

2.33 Where a young person seeks help because of homelessness, the assessment must necessarily reach a decision as to whether or not the young person is a child in need and requires accommodation as a result of one the scenarios set out in section 20(1)(a) to (c) or section 20(3).

2.34 In some cases, it may not be necessary for the young person to be accommodated by children's services because the young person's needs can be met by providing other services - for example, support to enable the young person to return to the care of their family or other responsible adults in the young person's network. If children's services conclude that the young person does not require accommodation for this reason, they should consider whether they should provide services under section 17 of the 1989 Act, which could include financial support under section 17(6)) to sustain any plan for the young person to live with members of their family. Children's services will also need to put in place a strategy to try to avoid the young person being threatened with homelessness in the future. Where the young person is a child in need, children's services should use their powers under section 17 of the 1989 Act to provide these services.

2.35 However, if the young person requires accommodation, then this must be provided by children's services and the young person concerned will become or continue to be (if children's services has provided or secured emergency accommodation) looked after under section 20 of the 1989 Act, with the authority having the responsibilities towards them set out in sections 22 and 23 and once they cease to be looked after, the duties that are owed to care leavers under that Act.[5] The child becomes looked after at the point that the local authority determines the young person needs accommodation (including emergency accommodation) under section 20.

Timescales

2.36 *The Framework for Assessment of Children in Need and their Families* sets out the timescales that should, except in exceptional circumstances involving difficulty in obtaining relevant information or children with very complex needs, be followed when assessing whether a not a child is in need and whether, as a result, services should be provided.

2.37 Within one working day a decision must be taken about whether to carry out an initial assessment . Where a young person refers themselves, or is referred by housing services or another agency as appearing to be homeless, children's services should proceed with an assessment unless they are able to determine very quickly that the young person is not homeless and does not require support.

2.38 A decision to gather more information constitutes an initial assessment. This should be completed within ten working days.

4 www.archive.official-documents.co.uk/document/doh/facn/fw-00.htm/.

5 A looked after child who is aged 16 or 17 and has been looked after for a total of at least 13 weeks (which began after they reached the age of 14 and ends after they reach the age of 16) is an 'eligible child', and will be entitled to care leaving support under the 1989 Act. A 16 or 17 year old who was an eligible child but has ceased to be looked after, is a 'relevant child', and will also be entitled to support as a care leaver.

2.39 Where housing services have been providing interim accommodation pending assessment of the young person, once the initial assessment by children services is complete and it has been determined whether the young person will be accommodated by children's services under section 20, children's services should notify housing services immediately. Where accommodation is to be provided under section 20 arrangements for the move to a new placement should be made as quickly as possible.

2.40 An assessment is not complete until children's services have decided what action is necessary to respond to the young person's needs and this has been communicated to the young person, the adults responsible for their care, housing services and any other relevant agencies.

16 and 17 year olds from one local authority area who seek assistance from children's services in another local authority area

2.41 Where a 16 or 17 year old who was living in one local authority area and moves to another local authority area and seeks assistance from children's services in that local authority, the duty to assess falls on the authority from which they seek assistance. The authority cannot refuse to consider the young person's immediate needs and expect them to return to the authority in the area presumed to be their 'home' district.

2.42 An initial interview, perhaps combined with enquiries in the area where the young person came from, should be sufficient to establish their connection with the area where they have sought help and their reasons for seeking help there rather than in their 'home' district. These enquiries may be able to establish whether it may be possible it for the young person to return to the area where they may be presumed to have a stronger local connection. For example, it might be possible for the authority where the young person seeks help to negotiate with their 'home' authority to take over the assessment of the young person's needs, so that the young person is assessed in a familiar setting close to their family and friends.

2.43 It is essential that disputes about responsibility for the young person in the medium term should not get in the way of the authority that received the young person's request for assistance responding to the young person's immediate needs. The young person concerned must not be passed from pillar to post while the authorities determine where he or she comes from.

Young person's wishes and feelings

2.44 Section 20(6) of the Children Act requires that: Before providing accommodation under this section, a local authority shall, so far as is reasonably practicable and consistent with the child's welfare;

(a) ascertain the child's wishes and feelings regarding the provision of accommodation; and

(b) give due consideration (having regard to his age and understanding) to such wishes and feelings of the child as they have been able to ascertain.

2.45 This will include assessing their emotional and behavioral development and their capacity to make use of wider resources to manage independent living.

2.46 However, where a young person says they do not wish to be accommodated, a local authority should reach the conclusion that the young person's wishes are decisive only as part of an overall judgment of their assessed welfare needs and the type and location of accommodation that will meet those needs.

2.47 The approach to assessment must be child-centred. It will be very important that children's services staff responsible for the assessment are able to communicate the assessment plan to the young person so that he or she is provided with information about the enquiries that need to be made and the timescales involved. A key aspect of the assessment will involve reaching an understanding about how the young person views their needs.

2.48 It will be essential that the young person is fully consulted about and understands the implications of being accommodated by children's services and becoming looked after. The staff conducting the assessment must provide realistic and full information about the support that the young person can expect as a looked after child and, subsequently, as a care leaver. Children's services should also ensure that the young person receives accurate information about what assistance may be available to them, including from housing services under Part 7 of the 1996 Act, if they do not become looked after, and how any entitlement for assistance under Part 7 will be determined. In particular, the possible risk of becoming homeless intentionally in future, and the implications of this for further assistance with accommodation, should be made clear to the young person. This information should be provided in a 'child friendly' format at the start of the assessment process and be available for the young person to take away for full consideration and to help them seek advice.

2.49 Where there is any doubt about a 16 or 17 year old's capacity to judge what may be in his or her best interests, eg whether they should become looked after or seek alternative assistance, there will need to be further discussion involving children's services, housing services, the young person concerned and their family, to reach agreement on the way forward.

2.50 Young people should have access to independent advocacy and support to assist them in weighing up the advantages and disadvantages and coming to a balanced decision.[6]

2.51 Some 16 and 17 year olds may decide that they do not wish to be provided with accommodation by children's services, for example, because they do not wish to be supported as a looked after child. However, in these circumstances, it is important that children's services are clear that the young person's decision is properly informed, and has been reached after careful consideration of all the relevant information.

2.52 The fact that a young person may be reluctant to engage with the assessment process outlined above is not in itself a basis for assuming that the young person has rejected any children's services' intervention to provide them with accommodation. Lack of co-operation is no reason for the local authority not to attempt to carry out its duties under the 1989 Act. In these circumstances, the assessment will need to involve careful recording of how the authority has attempted to engage with the young person to assess their needs in order to determine and provide appropriate services. Ultimately, however, it is not

6 Children and young people who have received services under the 1989 Act are able to be supported to make complaints and representation with the help of an independent advocate. Children's services should provide information about access to advocacy services when they explain the assessment process to 16 and 17 year olds seeking help because of homelessness.

possible to force services on young people who persistently continue to refuse them.

2.53 Where a 16 or 17 year old child in need wishes to refuse accommodation offered under section 20 of the 1989 Act, children's services must be satisfied that the young person:

- has been provided with all relevant information
- is competent to make such a decision

Provision of accommodation under section 17 of the 1989 Act

2.54 Children's services authorities have powers to accommodate children under section 17(6) of the 1989 Act. A young person provided with accommodation under this section would not be looked after and the local authority would not have the corresponding duties set out at in sections 22, 23 and 24 of the 1989 Act. However, the provision of accommodation under section 17 will almost always concern children needing to be accommodated with their families.

2.55 The powers of local authorities to provide accommodation under section 17 cannot be used to substitute for their duty to provide accommodation under section 20(1) of the 1989 Act to homeless 16 and 17 year olds who are assessed as being children in need following the process described in Part 2, above. Children's services do not have the option of choosing under which provision they should provide accommodation for homeless 16 and 17 year olds. Section 20 involves an evaluative judgment on some matters but not a discretion.[7]

3 Provision of suitable supported accommodation under section 20 of the 1989 Act by children's services

3.1 Children's services must only provide children with supported accommodation which is suitable and of high quality. A range of different types of accommodation may provide suitable accommodation for 16 and 17 year olds who cannot live with their families, carers or guardians. These include foster care, children's homes, supported lodgings, foyers, properties with visiting support tailored to the young person's needs and other types of supported accommodation. In order for services to work well it is important that children's services work closely with housing services to ensure that a range of suitable supported accommodation placements are available for young people in their area, whether or not they are looked after children. Bed and breakfast accommodation is not suitable for 16 and 17 year olds. For teenage parents it is particularly important that they are provided with accommodation which gives them the holistic support they require to meet their individual needs and improve their outcomes. This should include support around parenting and independent living skills; their health and well-being; access to education and training; and their readiness for future independent living.

3.2 The choice of placement for any individual young person will be informed by the assessment of their needs.

3.3 Section 23(2) of the 1989 Act sets out the range of placement options in which a young person who is looked after by the local authority may be accommodated. These will include placements in foster care or in children's homes.

3.4 Some 16 and 17 year olds who require accommodation may be reluctant to

7 *R (G) v Southwark* [2009] UKHL 26, para 31: www.publications.pariament.uk/pa/ld200809/ldjudgmt/jd090520/appg-2.htm/.

take up these kinds of accommodation options and the assessment of their emotional and behavioural development will indicate that they do not require the level or kind of supervision and support that foster or children's home care provides.

3.5 Section 23(2)(f)(i) of the 1989 Act permits local authorities to make *such other arrangements* as seem appropriate when they place a looked after child. This provision offers scope for children's services to ensure that they are able to make appropriate provision with support tailored to the needs of the young person for those homeless 16 and 17 year olds who they accommodate, and are looked after, but for whom fostering or a children's home placement would not be the most suitable option.

3.6 From the point at which children's services accommodate a 16 or 17 year old child, they should look forward to the support that the young person will need to make a positive transition to greater independence. This might include, for example, the provision of supported accommodation (perhaps jointly funded) where young people can remain beyond the age of 18 and develop the skills they will need to manage the transition to adulthood. This kind of accommodation might be jointly commissioned by children's services and housing services and will enable children's services to meet their forthcoming duties to secure sufficient accommodation for looked after children and care leavers in their area.[8] For example, a formerly homeless young person may be placed in 'supported lodgings' to offer them opportunities to take on more responsibility for their own care in order to prepare them for the tranition to adulthood.

3.7 The primary issue to be addressed in making each and every placement in 'other arrangements', just as in any other placement setting, will be: how will making this placement meet the assessed needs of the individual young person?

3.8 Where a young person is placed in *other arrangements* then the local authority must prepare a placement plan which is agreed between the young person and the person responsible for supporting the young person in the accommodation. This should be the person who will have the most day to day contact with the young person, for example their 'key worker' or supported lodgings host/carer. Any support plan setting out how the supported accommodation service will support the young person should be integral to the placement plan and avoid duplication.

3.9 The placement planning process should involve an exchange of appropriate information included as part of the core assessment process which informed the development of the looked after young person's care plan, so that the accommodation provider has a full understanding of the young person's needs and their role in meeting these needs. It will be essential that the provider appreciates the arrangements that the local authority proposes to put in place to make sure that the young person is adequately supported. The placement plan must be explicit about the respective roles and responsibilities of the placement provider and the young person's social worker, their Independent Reviewing Officer and of other staff employed or commissioned by the authority to contribute to the plan for the young person's care.

8 Section 22G of the 1989 Act inserted by section 9 of the Children and Young Persons Act 2008.

3.10 The plan must set out:

- the respective safeguarding responsibilities of the provider and local authority - the frequency of visits the young person can expect from their responsible authority
- communication arrangements between the provider and the local authority
- the provider's responsibilities for notifying the young person's social worker and accountable staff of the authority of any significant change in the young person's circumstances
- arrangements for giving notice of intention to terminate the placement (along with the authority's responsibilities for convening a review of the young person's care plan where there is a risk of the placement being terminated).

4 Provision of accommodation for 16 and 17 year olds to whom a section 20 duty is not owed or who refuse section 20 accommodation

4.1 If children's services decide that they do not have a duty to provide accommodation for a homeless 16 or 17 year old or the young person has refused provision of accommodation, children's services must consider what other support and services should be provided for the young person to meet their needs in conjunction with housing services.

Securing accommodation under Part 7 of the 1996 Act (housing services)

4.2 Under Part 7 of the 1996 Act, and the *Homelessness (Priority Need for Accommodation) (England) Order 2002*,[9] applicants aged 16 or 17 have a priority need for accommodation if they are not owed a duty under section 20 of the 1989 Act. Where such applicants are also eligible for assistance and unintentionally homeless, the local housing authority will owe them a duty under section193 (2) of the 1996 Act to secure that accommodation is available for their occupation. Authorities should refer to the *Homelessness Code of Guidance for Local Authorities* for general guidance on discharging their homelessness functions under Part 7 of the 1996 Act.

4.3 Where children's services have decided that a section 20 duty is not owed for one of the reasons above, and the young person applies to housing services for accommodation or assistance in obtaining accommodation, housing services will need to consider whether any duty is owed under Part 7 of the 1996 Act (section 184).

4.4 In any case where housing services provide accommodation for a child in need, children's services will need to consider the provision of services under section 17 of the 1989 Act to meet the young person's other needs.

4.5 Where an application for housing assistance is already under consideration (for example, because the young person's initial approach for help was made to housing services and the young person had been referred to children's services for an assessment of need), the notification by children's services that a section 20 duty is not owed will enable housing services to complete their inquiries under section 184 of the 1996 Act and decide whether any duty is owed under Part 7.

9 www.opsi.gov.uk/SI/si2002/20022051.htm/.

4.6 In considering whether a duty under Part 7 is owed to a 16 or 17 year old who has refused section 20 accommodation, it is for the housing authority to satisfy themselves in each individual case whether the applicant is homeless or threatened with homelessness. Authorities should not adopt general policies which seek to pre-define circumstances that do or do not amount to intentional homelessness or threat of homelessness.

4.7 Where a 16 or 17 year old is secured accommodation under Part 7 of the 1996 Act, children's services should work closely with housing services to ensure that the young person is provided with sufficient support to ensure he or she does not become homeless intentionally in the future, for example, as a result of accruing rent arrears or being evicted due to bad behaviour.

4.8 Where children's services hold open the offer of accommodation on a temporary basis to ensure that a 16 or 17 year old has accommodation available to meet his or her immediate needs, housing services should not necessarily consider that the young person is not homeless. Housing services will need to consider whether, in the circumstances, it would be reasonable for the applicant to continue to occupy the accommodation indefinitely, if they did not intervene and secure alternative accommodation.

4.9 In order to help facilitate the provision of accommodation by housing services to meet the young person's accommodation needs in the longer term, children's and housing services will need to agree a procedure for children's services to inform housing services that their provision of temporary accommodation will come to an end. This process should aim to minimise anxiety for the young person associated with concerns that they may again find themselves without anywhere to live. Children's services and housing services will need to work together closely to ensure that the young person's ongoing housing needs can be met in the most practical and timely way possible.

4.10 Housing services are reminded that applicants cannot be considered to have become homeless intentionally because of failing to take up an offer of accommodation; homelessness is only capable of being 'intentional' where the applicant has ceased to occupy accommodation that it would have been reasonable for him or her to continue to occupy.

4.11 Case law has established that in some circumstances a person does not do, or fail to do, something 'deliberately' for the purpose of Part 7 of the 1996 Act if he makes a considered choice between two courses of action or inaction, either of which he or she is able to take. Thus, the Secretary of State considers that where a 16 or 17 year old is required to leave accommodation as a result of his or her decision to refuse section 20 accommodation (for example, where children's services bring to an end interim accommodation provided pending assessment of the young person's needs), that decision should not be treated as deliberate action or inaction that contributed to intentional homelessness, subject to it being an informed and considered decision.

4.12 If, for whatever reason, a 16 or 17 year old is found to have become homeless intentionally, housing services should inform children's services immediately (see section on joint protocols below). For further guidance about intentional homelessness, authorities should refer to Chapter 11 of the *Homelessness Code of Guidance for Local Authorities*.[10]

10 www.communities.gov.uk/publications/housing/homelessnesscode/.

5 Joint working to tackle youth homelessness

5.1 There is a clear legal framework for co-operation between children's services and housing services to meet the needs of children and young people. Section 27 of the 1989 Act empowers a children's services authority to ask other authorities, including any local housing authority, for 'help in the exercise of any of their functions' under Part 3; the requested authority must provide that help if it is compatible with their own statutory or other duties and does not unduly prejudice the discharge of any of their own functions. The *Children Act 2004* broadened and strengthened the statutory framework requiring co-operation between relevant statutory services to improve outcomes for children and young people as part of developing an area's Children's Trust's arrangements.[11]

Operational joint working - joint protocols

5.2 It follows from the guidance above that the particular services a 16 or 17 year old should be provided with by children's services and housing services will depend on a range of factors in each case, including which service they initially seek help from; the outcomes of assessments and enquiries; and the wishes and feelings of the young person and the young person's family. It is therefore essential that services for homeless 16 and 17 year olds are underpinned by written joint protocols which set out clear, practical arrangements for providing services that are centred on young people and their families and prevent young people from being passed from pillar to post.

5.3 An effective joint protocol will set out a mutually agreed vision, objectives, systems and processes to ensure effective action to prevent youth homelessness and the provision of sufficient accommodation to meet the range of needs of homeless young people. In formulating a joint protocol, due regard should be had to the fact that the 1989 Act takes precedence over the 1996 Act in providing for children in need.

5.4 A joint protocol might cover the following:

1) Inter-agency arrangements to prevent youth homelessness and provide support to young people to remain living with their families.
2) Information for agencies, for example Connexions services and Youth Offending Teams who may refer young people about where they should refer young people for help with homelessness.
3) Arrangements for integrated or joint assessment processes where 16 and 17 year olds seek help because they are homeless, including information-sharing procedures.
4) Agreed timescales (in line with the *Framework for the Assessment of Children in Need and their Families)* for assessing whether or not a homeless young person is a child in need and will be provided with accommodation by children's services.
5) Arrangements for timely assessment and placement provision for young people who require accommodation on release from custody
6) Arrangements for access to suitable emergency accommodation when needed.

11 See *Statutory guidance on co-operation arrangements, including the Children's Trust Board and the Children and Young People's Plan (March 2010): www.dcsf.gov.uk/everychildmatters/about/aims/childrenstrusts/childrenstrusts/.*

7) Arrangements for access to longer term accommodation with support for young people (including looked after children and care leavers) who need this service.
8) Agreed standards as to how the suitability of accommodation that is not formally regulated or inspected will be assured. These might make reference to the Quality Assessment Framework (QAF) or to the Foyer Federation's Accreditation Scheme.[12]
9) Arrangements for the provision of accommodation and other services to any 16 and 17 year olds who are neither being accommodated by children's services under section 20 nor have found to be owed the main homelessness duty by housing services (for example, because they do not wish to be accommodated under section 20 and are considered by housing services to have become homeless intentionally).
10) Integrated monitoring arrangements to provide management information regarding outcomes for young people including through reconciliation with parents or carers.
11) Processes for resolving any disputes arising between staff from children's services and staff from housing services (for example, where expectations for completing assessments within specified timescales have not been met).

5.5 The effectiveness and continuing relevance of joint protocols should be reviewed at least annually. Local authorities may find it helpful to establish multi-agency arrangements to monitor the effectiveness of protocols and the performance of local services in responding to homeless young people. Local authorities will need to consider at the outset, what data will be required for monitoring purposes and how the agencies involved in providing services to homeless young people will collect and analyse this. These monitoring arrangements will contribute to wider monitoring of the overall effectiveness of the children's trust in safeguarding children and young people and promoting their welfare.

5.6 It would be good practice for young people who have been provided with services to be consulted about the quality of services and contribute to service reviews.

Strategic joint working

5.7 Children's services will need to work with housing services (which will be within district councils in two-tier areas), registered social landlords; housing related support services and with other partners to secure a range of suitable housing and support options for young people and their families. This will include options for the provision of accommodation with support for 16 and 17 year olds who seek help because they are homeless, and for care leavers.

5.8 Children's services should be linked to housing authorities' strategic housing function, and housing authorities should be represented on the Children's Trust Board.

12 See www.sitra.org.uk/index.php?id=1019 and http://www.foyer.net/level3.asp?level3id=184 13 In this situation, where a young person remains homeless housing services should make a fresh referral to children's services - and children's services should undertake a further assessment of the young person's needs in the light of the change of circumstances. This will give the young person the opportunity to reconsider the option of being assisted under section 20.

5.9 The anticipated accommodation and support needs of vulnerable young people, including homeless 16 and 17 year olds and care leavers, should be represented in the following strategies and plans:

- The Children and Young People's Plan
- Housing and Homelessness Strategies
- Supporting People or Housing Related Support Strategies

5.10 Consideration should be given to developing collaboration between children's services and commissioners of housing and support services to meet the housing needs of young people in the area including providing suitable accommodation placements for looked after children aged 16 and 17. Services jointly planned and secured might include supported accommodation projects, floating support services, foyers, supported lodgings, and more specialist housing provision for particularly vulnerable young people.

Annex: Factors to be considered by children's services when assessing 16/17 year olds who may be homeless children in need,

	Dimensions of need	Issues to consider in assessing child's future needs
1	**Accommodation**	• Does the child have access to stable accommodation? • How far is this suitable to the full range of the child's needs?
2	**Family and Social Relationships**	• Assessment of the child's relationship with their parents and wider family. • What is the capacity of the child's family and social network to provide stable and secure accommodation and meet the child's practical, emotional and social needs.
3	**Emotional and Behavioural Development**	• Does the child show self esteem, resilience and confidence? • Assessment of their attachments and the quality of their relationships. Does the child show self control and appropriate self awareness?
4	**Education, Training and Employment**	• Information about the child's education experience and background • Assessment as to whether support may be required to enable the child to access education, training or employment.
5	**Financial Capability and independent living skills**	• Assessment of the child's financial competence and how they will secure financial support in future • Information about the support the child might need to develop self-management and independent living skills.
6	**Health and Development**	• Assessment of child's physical, emotional and mental health needs.
7	**Identity**	• Assessment of the child's needs as a result of their ethnicity, preferred langrage, cultural background, religion or sexual identity.

Homelessness Code of Guidance for Local Authorities: Supplementary Guidance on Intentional Homelessness (August 2009)

Applicants who face homelessness following difficulties in meeting mortgage commitments

In response to the current economic climate, and the robust framework of financial support the Government has put in place to help homeowners in financial difficulty,[1] this note provides guidance on how local housing authorities should exercise their homelessness functions, and apply the various statutory criteria, when considering whether applicants who are homeless having lost their home because of difficulties in meeting mortgage commitments are intentionally or unintentionally homeless.

Introduction

1. This guidance is issued by the Secretary of State under section 182 of the *Housing Act* 1996 ('the 1996 Act'). Under section 182(1) of the 1996 Act, housing authorities are required to have regard to this guidance in exercising their functions under Part 7 of the 1996 Act.
2. This statutory guidance supplements chapter 11 of the *Homelessness Code of Guidance for Local Authorities* issued in July 2006 ('the 2006 Code'), and should be read in conjunction with that chapter.

Homelessness following mortgage difficulties

3. Homeowners may be at risk of homelessness if they experience difficulties in meeting their mortgage commitments, for example, because a member of the household loses their employment or suffers an income shock. Individual homeowners may respond in different ways when faced with such difficult circumstances.
4. Some homeowners may voluntarily give up possession of the property (hand back the keys to the lender). Some homeowners may decide to sell the property. Others may seek help to remain in their home, including help under the Mortgage Rescue Scheme (MRS) or Homeowner Mortgage Support (HMS), but decide – if found eligible for the scheme – not to accept an offer because they consider that continuing with home ownership would be unsustainable or would entail unacceptable financial risk. Where homeowners who have experienced such circumstances become homeless or threatened with homelessness and apply to a local housing authority for assistance, the authority will need to give careful consideration to the substantive cause(s) of homelessness before coming to a decision on intentionality.

Definition of intentional homelessness

5. Authorities are reminded that by sections 191(1) and 196(1) of the 1996 Act, a person becomes homeless intentionally or threatened with homelessness intentionally, if:

1 The Mortgage Rescue Scheme and Homeowner Mortgage Support.

i) the person deliberately does or fails to do anything in consequence of which the person ceases to occupy accommodation (or the likely result of which is that the person will be forced to leave accommodation);
ii) the accommodation is available for the person's occupation; and
iii) it would have been reasonable for the person to continue to occupy the accommodation.

However, an act or omission made in good faith by someone who was unaware of any relevant fact must not be treated as deliberate.

6. Authorities are also reminded that they must not adopt general policies that seek to pre-define circumstances that do or do not amount to intentional homelessness or threatened homelessness (see paragraph 11.5 of the *Homelessness Code of Guidance for Local Authorities*).

Principles established by case law

7. The broad thrust of section 191 is to ascribe intentional homelessness to a person who on the facts is responsible for his homelessness by virtue of his own act or omission. Whilst it is not part of the purpose of the legislation to require local authorities to house people whose homelessness is brought upon them by their own fault, equally, it is not part of the legislation that authorities should refuse to accommodate people whose homelessness has been brought upon them without fault on their part, for example, by an inability to make ends meet.
8. Nobody may be presumed to be intentionally homeless; the local housing authority must be satisfied of intentionality and must ask and answer the questions set out in the legislation. The decision maker in the local authority must look for the substantive cause of the homelessness and the effective cause will not always be the most immediate proximate cause.
9. Intentionality does not depend on whether applicants have behaved wisely or prudently or reasonably. Where an applicant's failure to seek help may have been foolish, imprudent or even unreasonable, this would not necessarily mean his or her conduct was not in good faith.

Some possible scenarios

10. As mentioned above, some former homeowners may seek housing assistance from a local housing authority having lost their home in one of the following circumstances:
    i) having voluntarily surrendered the property (handed the keys back);
    ii) having sold the property;
    iii) where the property was repossessed after the applicant refused an offer under the MRS;
    iv) where the property was repossessed after the applicant refused an offer of HMS;
    v) where the property was repossessed and the applicant had not sought help.

    There should be no general presumption that a homeowner will have brought homelessness on him or herself in any of the above scenarios. A person cannot be found to have become intentionally homeless from a property where he or she was already statutorily homeless: eg because it was not reasonable for him to continue to occupy the property (see paragraph 8.18 et seq of the

Homelessness Code of Guidance for Local Authorities). Consequently, where someone was already homeless before surrendering or selling their home or refusing an offer under MRS or HMS, the 'acts' of surrender or sale, and the 'omission' of refusing an offer of MRS or HMS cannot be treated as the cause of homelessness.

11. In particular, authorities will need to satisfy themselves on two questions as applied at the point in time immediately before the applicant ceased to occupy accommodation (i.e. prior to the surrender, sale or refusal of help). First, was the applicant's home available as accommodation for the applicant, any other person who normally resides with him as a member of his family and any person who might reasonably be expected to reside with him? Second, did the applicant's home constitute accommodation that it would have been reasonable for him or her to continue to occupy? It would not have been reasonable for the applicant to continue to occupy his or her home, for example, if the home was not affordable, for example, because the applicant could not meet the cost of his or her mortgage commitments.

12. If the answer to either of the two questions above is in the negative, the applicant will have been homeless prior to the surrender or sale of the property or refusal of an offer of assistance under the MRS or HMS. In such a case, the authority may still consider whether the applicant's homelessness was intentional but will need to look at the substantive causes of that homelessness prior to surrender or sale of the property or refusal of an offer of assistance under the MRS or HMS.

Homelessness Code of Guidance for Local Authorities (July 2006)

CONTENTS

Chapters

1. Homelessness reviews and strategies
2. Preventing homelessness
3. Ensuring a sufficient supply of accommodation
4. Securing support services
5. Working with others
6. Applications, inquiries, decisions and notifications
7. Interim duty to accommodate
8. Homeless or threatened with homelessness
9. Eligibility for assistance
10. Priority need
11. Intentional homelessness
12. 16 & 17 year olds
13. Co-operation in certain cases involving children
14. Main duties owed to applicants on completion of inquiries
15. Discretionary powers to secure accommodation
16. Securing accommodation
17. Suitability of accommodation
18. Local connection and referrals to another housing authority
19. Review of decisions and appeals to the county court
20. Protection of personal property
21. Contracting out homelessness functions

Annexes

1. Good practice/guidance publications
2. Other strategies and programmes that may address homelessness
3. Other authorities, organisations and persons whose activities may contribute to preventing/tackling homelessness
4. Specific objectives and actions for local authorities that might be included in a homelessness strategy
5. Co-operation between registered social landlords and housing authorities
6. Homelessness strategy: specific action that might be expected to be taken by others
7. Tackling common causes of homelessness
8. How to contact the Home Office Immigration and Nationality Directorate
9. Asylum seekers

10. The habitual residence test
11. European groupings (EU, A8, EEA, Switzerland)
12. Rights to reside in the UK derived from EC law
13. Worker registration scheme
14. MOD Certificate: Certificate of cessation of entitlement for single personnel to occupy service living accommodation
15. MOD Certificate: Certificate of cessation of entitlement to occupy service families accommodation or substitute service families accommodation (SFA/SSFA)
16. Definition of overcrowding
17. Recommended minimum standards for bed and breakfast accommodation
18. Procedures for referrals of homeless applicants on the grounds of local connection with another local authority

CHAPTER 1
Homelessness reviews & strategies

This chapter provides guidance on housing authorities' duties to carry out a homelessness review and to formulate and publish a strategy based on the results of that review.

DUTY TO FORMULATE A HOMELESSNESS STRATEGY

1.1 Section 1(1) of the Homelessness Act 2002 ('the 2002 Act') gives housing authorities the power to carry out a homelessness review for their district and formulate and publish a homelessness strategy based on the results of the review. This power can be exercised from time to time, however section 1(3) required housing authorities to publish their first homelessness strategy by 31 July 2003. Section 1(4) requires housing authorities to publish a new homelessness strategy, based on the results of a further homelessness review, within the period of five years beginning with the day on which their last homelessness strategy was published (there is an exemption from this requirement for local authorities categorised as an 'excellent authority', see paragraph 1.42). However, it is open to a housing authority to conduct homelessness reviews and strategies more frequently, if they wish.

1.2 For a homelessness strategy to be effective housing authorities need to ensure that it is consistent with other local plans and strategies and takes into account any wider relevant sub-regional or regional plans and strategies. There will be a lot of common ground between an authority's housing strategy (whether its own or a sub-regional one produced with neighbouring authorities) and its homelessness strategy. It is open to authorities to produce either separate housing and homelessness strategies or combine these in a single document where it is consistent to do so. It is also open to authorities, again where it would be consistent to do so, to consider producing a wider composite plan that includes not only the housing and homelessness strategies but also their Housing Revenue Account Business Plans and Home Energy Conservation Act report. The homelessness strategy should also link with other strategies and programmes that address the wide range of problems that can cause homelessness (see indicative list at Annex 2). It will be important to consider how these strategies and programmes can help achieve the objectives of the homelessness strategy and vice-versa.

1.3 Housing authorities are encouraged to take a broad view and consider the benefits of cross-boundary, sub-regional and regional co-operation. A county-wide approach will be particularly important in non-unitary authorities, where housing and homelessness services are provided by the district authority whilst other key services, such as social services and Supporting People, are delivered at the county level. Housing authorities should ensure that the homelessness strategy for their district forms part of a coherent approach to tackling homelessness with neighbouring authorities. Authorities may wish to collaborate with neighbouring housing authorities to produce a joint homelessness strategy covering a sub-regional area. London boroughs are encouraged to work closely with the Greater London Authority when formulating their homelessness strategies.

1.4 When carrying out a review and formulating a strategy, housing authorities are encouraged to refer to *Homelessness Strategies: A good practice handbook, Local Authorities' Homelessness Strategies: Evaluation and Good Practice* and other relevant good practice documents published by the Office of the Deputy Prime Minister (see list of publications at Annex 1).

1.5 Housing authorities are reminded that when drawing up their strategies for preventing and tackling homelessness, they must consider the needs of all groups of people in their district who are homeless or likely to become homeless, including Gypsies and Travellers. Under section 225 of the *Housing Act 2004*, which supplements section 8 of the *Housing Act 1985*, when undertaking a review of housing needs in their district, local authorities are required to carry out an assessment of the accommodation needs of Gypsies and Travellers residing in or resorting to their district. Draft guidance on accommodation needs assessment for Gypsies and Travellers is available on the DCLG website, and will be finalised after further consultation in 2006.

Assistance from social services

1.6 In non-unitary districts, where the social services authority and the housing authority are different authorities, section 1(2) of the 2002 Act requires the social services authority to give the housing authority such assistance as may be reasonably required in carrying out a homelessness review and formulating and publishing a homelessness strategy. **Since a number of people who are homeless or at risk of homelessness will require social services support, it is unlikely that it would be possible for a housing authority to formulate an effective homelessness strategy without assistance from the social services authority. It will be necessary therefore in all cases for housing authorities to seek assistance from the social services authority.** In unitary authorities the authority will need to ensure that the social services department assists the housing department in carrying out a homelessness review and formulating and publishing a homelessness strategy.

1.7 The social services authority must comply with all requests for assistance from housing authorities within their district which are reasonable. Examples of the type of assistance that a housing authority may reasonably require from the social services authority when carrying out a review and formulating a strategy may include:

- information about current and likely future numbers of social services client groups who are likely to be homeless or at risk of homelessness e.g. young people in need, care leavers and those with community care needs;
- details of social services' current programme of activity, and the resources available to them, for meeting the accommodation needs of these groups;
- details of social services' current programme of activity, and the resources available to them, for providing support for vulnerable people who are homeless or likely to become homeless (and who may not currently be social services clients).

1.8 Effective co-operation will benefit both housing and social services authorities. See Chapter 5 for guidance on joint working with other agencies and Chapter 13 for guidance on co-operation in cases involving children.

Taking the strategy into account

1.9 Sections 1(5) and (6) of the 2002 Act require housing and social services authorities to take the homelessness strategy into account when exercising their functions.

1.10 For a homelessness strategy to be effective it will need to be based on realistic assumptions about how it will be delivered in practice. Whilst this will apply in respect of all the agencies and organisations involved, the key players will be the housing authority and the social services authority. Both authorities will therefore need to ensure that, on the one hand, the assumptions in the strategy about their future activities are realistic and, on the other, that in practice these activities are actually delivered through the operation of their statutory functions. When the strategy is formulated, the social services authority (or social services department within a unitary authority) will need to work closely with the housing authority (or department) to ensure that this can be achieved. All contributors will need to take ownership of the strategy if it is to be effective. Again, because of its crucial role in delivering the strategy, this will be particularly important in the case of the social services authority (or department).

HOMELESSNESS REVIEWS

1.11 Under section 2(1) of the 2002 Act a homelessness review means a review by a housing authority of:

a) the levels, and likely future levels, of homelessness in their district;
b) the activities which are carried out for any the following purposes (or which contribute to achieving any of them):
   i) preventing homelessness in the housing authority's district;
   ii) securing that accommodation is or will be available for people in the district who are or may become homeless; and
   iii) providing support for people in the district:
      – who are or may become homeless; or
      – who have been homeless and need support to prevent them becoming homeless again;
c) the resources available to the housing authority, the social services authority for the district, other public authorities, voluntary organisations and other persons for the activities outlined in (b) above.

1.12 The purpose of the review is to establish the extent of homelessness in the district, assess its likely extent in the future, and identify what is currently being done, and by whom, and what level of resources are available, to prevent and tackle homelessness.

a) Current levels, and likely future levels, of homelessness

1.13 Homelessness is defined by sections 175 to 178 of the 1996 Act (see Chapter 8 for guidance). The review must take account of **all** forms of homelessness within the meaning of the 1996 Act, not just people who are unintentionally homeless and have a priority need for accommodation under Part 7. The review should therefore consider a wide population of households who are homeless or at risk of homelessness, including those who might be more difficult to identify, including people sleeping rough, or those whose accommodation circumstances make them more likely than others to become homeless or to resort to sleeping rough.

1.14 The housing authority's own records of its activity under the homelessness legislation (Part 7 of the 1996 Act) will provide a baseline for assessing the number of people who are likely to become homeless and seek help directly from the housing authority. These records should give some indication as to why those accepted as statutorily homeless became homeless. Other useful sources of data on potential homelessness in the district may include:

- records on rough sleeping;
- estimates of people staying with friends/family on an insecure basis;
- court records on possession orders;
- records of evictions by the local authority and registered social landlords (RSLs);
- local advice service records on homelessness cases;
- hospital records of people homeless on discharge;
- armed forces records of those homeless on discharge;
- prison/probation service records of ex-prisoners homeless on discharge;
- social services records of homeless families with children;
- social services records of young people leaving care and children in need requiring accommodation;
- records of Supporting People clients;
- records available from hostels and refuges;
- voluntary sector records, e.g. day centres, advice services;
- records of asylum seekers being accommodated in the district by the National Asylum Support Service;
- data from the national population census and housing authorities' own household surveys.

1.15 Some groups of people are likely to be more at risk of homelessness than others. These may include:

- young people who have become estranged from their family; have been in care; have a history of abuse, running away or school exclusions; or whose parents have had mental health, alcohol or drug problems; (see chapter 12)
- people from ethnic minority groups;
- people with an institutionalised background, for example where they have spent time in prison or the armed forces;
- former asylum seekers who have been given permission to stay in the UK and are no longer being accommodated by the National Asylum Support Service;
- people who have experienced other problems that may increase the risk of homelessness including family/relationship breakdowns; domestic, racial or other violence; poor mental or physical health; drug and alcohol abuse; age-related problems and debt.

1.16 As part of the process of mapping and understanding the extent of current homelessness in the district, housing authorities may wish to develop a profile of those who have experienced homelessness. Elements within a profile may include:

- location of homelessness;
- reason(s) for homelessness;
- housing history including previous tenures and length of homelessness;
- ethnic background;

- other background (e.g. care provided by the local authority or other institution);
- age;
- gender and sexuality;
- disabilities;
- levels and types of debts;
- employment/benefits history;
- composition of household;
- vulnerability of applicant (or household members);
- support needs (housing-related or other);
- health/drug problems;
- immigration status;
- trends in any of these elements.

1.17 Housing authorities will also need to consider the range of factors which could affect future levels of homelessness in their district. Many of these will be similar to factors taken into account for the purpose of assessing housing needs in the district (e.g. as part of a broader housing strategy). Relevant factors in the district may include:

- the availability of affordable accommodation including housing provided by the housing authority and by RSLs;
- housing market analyses, including property prices and rent levels;
- the supply of accommodation in the private rented sector;
- the provision and effectiveness of housing advice;
- local voluntary and community sector services;
- the allocation policy of the housing authority;
- the lettings policies of RSLs;
- the effectiveness of nomination agreements between the housing authority and RSLs;
- the policy of the housing authority and RSLs on management of tenants' rent arrears and on seeking repossession;
- the efficiency of the housing authority's administration of housing benefit;
- the provision and effectiveness of housing-related support services;
- redevelopment and regeneration activity;
- unemployment;
- strength of the local economy;
- the local population (and demographic trends);
- the level of overcrowding;
- the rate of new household formation in the district;
- the level of inward migration (both national and international);
- the flow of itinerant population (i.e. Gypsies and Travellers) and availability of authorised sites;
- the number of people likely to be in housing need on leaving:
  - the armed forces,
  - residential care,
  - local authority care,
  - prison,
  - hospital or
  - accommodation provided by the National Asylum Support Service.

1.18 Individual cases of homelessness are often the result of a complex matrix of problems that may develop over time. In many cases homelessness may be triggered by individual circumstances (for example, relationship breakdown or unemployment) but it can also be the result of a failure in the housing market (for example, high rents in the private sector and a shortage of accommodation in the social sector) or a failure of the administrative system (for example, delays in the payment of housing benefit). In districts where the housing market and administrative systems are functioning well, the levels of homelessness are likely to be lower. All these factors will need to be taken into account when assessing the likely future levels of homelessness in the district.

b) Activities which are carried out

1.19 The public, private and voluntary sectors can all contribute, directly or indirectly, to the prevention of homelessness, the provision of accommodation and the provision of support for homeless people. When reviewing the activities which are being carried out for these purposes, the housing authority should consider the activities of **all** the various agencies and organisations, across all sectors, which are providing, or contributing to the provision of accommodation, support or relevant services in the district (Annex 3 provides an indicative list).

1.20 Having mapped all the current activities, the housing authority should consider whether these are appropriate and adequate to meet the aims of the strategy, and whether any changes or additional provision are needed.

Preventing homelessness

1.21 Gaining a good understanding of the causes of homelessness during the homelessness review process will help to inform the range of preventative measures that need to be put in place. Many statutory and non-statutory services can contribute to preventing homelessness. Housing authorities should adopt an open approach and recognise that there will be a broad range of organisations operating in fields other than housing, including, for example, health, education and employment, whose activities may help to prevent homelessness. Activities that contribute to preventing homelessness may include:

- advice services;
- mediation and reconciliation services;
- tenancy support schemes;
- proactive liaison with private sector landlords;
- rent deposit/guarantee schemes;
- management of social housing by the housing authority and by RSLs;
- debt counselling;
- Supporting People programme;
- social services support for vulnerable people;
- housing benefit administration;
- benefit liaison to young people delivered through Connexions;
- 'Sanctuary Schemes' to enable victims of domestic violence to stay in their homes;
- planning for the housing needs of people leaving institutions – e.g. local authority care, prison and the armed services.

Further guidance on preventing homelessness is provided in Chapter 2.

Securing accommodation

1.22 Housing authorities need to consider that a range of accommodation is likely to be required for people who are, or may become, homeless. Landlords, accommodation providers and housing developers across all sectors can contribute to the provision of accommodation in the district. Activities that contribute to securing that accommodation will be available for people who are homeless, or at risk of becoming homeless, may include:

- initiatives to increase the supply of new affordable accommodation in the district (e.g.: affordable housing secured through the planning system);
- provision of new housing for owner occupation;
- initiatives to increase the supply of specialist and/or supported accommodation;
- provision of accommodation from the housing authority's own stock;
- the proportion of lettings RSLs make available to the housing authority and to homeless people generally;
- programmes for the provision of hostel, foyer and refuge spaces;
- initiatives for maximising use of the private rented sector (e.g. rent deposit guarantee schemes and landlord/tenant mediation services);
- schemes for maximising access to affordable accommodation (e.g. rent guarantee schemes);
- local, regional and national mobility schemes (e.g. to assist tenants or homeless households to move to other areas, incentives to reduce under-occupation, and assistance to move into home ownership).

Further guidance on ensuring a sufficient supply of accommodation is provided in Chapter 3.

Providing support

1.23 As part of the review housing authorities should consider all the current activities which contribute to the provision of support for people in the district who are, or may become, homeless and people in the district who have been homeless and need support to prevent them becoming homeless again. The range of providers whose activities will be making a contribution to this area are likely to embrace the public, private and voluntary sectors.

1.24 As a starting point, the housing authority may wish to consider the level of services being provided under the Supporting People programme. Other activities which may be relevant are:

- social services support under the community care programme;
- social services support for children in need who require accommodation;
- social services support for young people at risk;
- housing advice services;
- tenancy support services;
- schemes which offer practical support for formerly homeless people (e.g. furniture schemes);
- day centres for homeless people;
- supported hostel provision;
- women's refuges;
- support for people to access health care services (e.g. registration with a GP practice);
- support for people with problems of alcohol or substance abuse;

- support for people with mental health problems;
- support for people with learning disabilities;
- support for people seeking employment, e.g. personal adviser through Connexions, Jobcentre Plus, voluntary sector organisations dealing with homelessness and worklessness;
- advocacy support.

Further guidance on securing support services is provided in Chapter 4.

c) Resources available for activities

1.25 As part of the homelessness review, the housing authority should consider the resources available for the activities set out in paragraph 1.11. The housing authority should consider not only its own resources (i.e. housing funding whether provided by central government or from authorities' own sources) but also those available for these purposes to the social services authority for their district, other public authorities, voluntary organisations and other persons. Annex 3 provides an indicative list of other authorities, organisations and persons whose activities may contribute to preventing and tackling homelessness.

Preventing homelessness

1.26 Housing authorities should invest their own resources in prevention services and measures since these are likely to produce direct net savings for the authority, for example through reduced processing of repeat homelessness applications, lower use of temporary accommodation and fewer social services interventions. Resources allocated to preventing homelessness will also help to reduce pressures on wider services, such as housing, health and employment, in the longer-term.

1.27 Resources available for the prevention of homelessness may include:
- staff or administrative budgets and resources available to the housing authority (e.g. related to the homeless persons unit, the housing advice service, the Supporting People programme, tenancy support etc.);
- the resources allocated within the housing authority for rent guarantee schemes and other preventative measures;
- the availability and quality of housing and homelessness advice in the district (e.g. number and location of advice centres);
- staff or administrative budgets and resources within other public bodies (e.g. social services authority, Primary Care Trust, local education authority) dedicated to activities that help prevent/tackle homelessness; and
- staff or administrative budgets and resources available to other agencies working to prevent homelessness in the district (e.g. housing advice services in the voluntary sector and agencies working with young people).

Securing accommodation

1.28 Resources available for securing that accommodation is, or will be, available may include:
- initiatives to increase the supply of new affordable accommodation in the district (e.g. bids for resources through the Regional Housing Strategy and Housing Corporation Approved Development Programme, cash incentive schemes, affordable housing secured through the planning system, other RSL developments, Private Finance Initiative or regeneration

developments, self-funded developments, self build schemes, shared ownership schemes, Homebuy);
- initiatives to increase the supply of specialist and/or supported accommodation;
- staff or administrative budgets and resources to make better use of the existing social housing stock (e.g. working with RSLs, managing own housing stock, mobility schemes);
- staff or administrative budgets and resources for maximising use of the private rented sector (e.g. landlord fora and accreditation schemes, rent deposit/guarantee schemes);
- initiatives to enable people to remain in their homes (e.g. through housing renewal assistance and disabled facilities grants).

Providing support

1.29 Resources available for providing support may include:
- staff or administrative budgets and resources available through the Supporting People programme;
- other staff or administrative budgets and resources available to the housing authority, for example through general fund expenditure or the Housing Revenue Account;
- staff or administrative budgets and resources available to the social services authority (e.g. personnel working to meet the support needs of homeless people);
- staff or administrative budgets and resources available to other public authorities and voluntary and community sector agencies (e.g. Primary Care Trusts, Drug Action Teams, Sure Start, Connexions and others listed at Annex 3); and
- availability of supported accommodation units and floating support for homeless people.

Results of the review

1.30 Having completed a homelessness review, housing authorities must arrange for a copy of the results of the review to be made available at their principal office; these must be available to the public for inspection at all reasonable hours without charge. A copy of the results must also be made available to any member of the public, on request (for which a reasonable charge can be made).

HOMELESSNESS STRATEGIES

1.31 Having carried out a homelessness review the housing authority will be in a position to formulate its homelessness strategy based on the results of that review as required by s.1(1)(b) of the 2002 Act. In formulating its strategy a housing authority will need to consider the necessary levels of activity required to achieve the aims set out in the paragraph below and the sufficiency of the resources available to them as revealed by the review.

1.32 Under s.3(1) of the 2002 Act a homelessness strategy means a strategy for:

i) preventing homelessness in the district (see Chapter 2 for further guidance);

ii) securing that sufficient accommodation is and will be available for people in the district who are or may become homeless (see Chapter 3 for further guidance);

iii) securing the satisfactory provision of support for people in the district who are or may become homeless or who have been homeless and need support to prevent them becoming homeless again (see Chapter 4 for further guidance).

Specific objectives and actions for housing and social services authorities

1.33 A homelessness strategy may include specific objectives to be achieved and actions planned to be taken in the course of the exercise of the functions of the housing authority and the social services authority. This will apply equally in areas where the social services authority is not also the housing authority (for example, in district councils in county areas). Examples of specific objectives and actions for housing and social services authorities that might be included in a strategy are set out in Annex 4.

Specific action by others

1.34 A homelessness strategy can also include specific action which the housing authority expects to be taken by:
i) other public authorities;
ii) voluntary organisations; and
iii) other persons whose activities could contribute to achieving the strategy's objectives.

1.35 In all housing authority districts there will be a significant number of agencies whose activities address the wide range of needs and problems that can be linked to homelessness. These will be found across all sectors: public, private and voluntary. Housing authorities will need to seek the participation of all relevant agencies in the district in order to assist them in formulating and delivering an effective homelessness strategy that includes specific action that the housing authority expects to be taken by others.

1.36 In particular, housing authorities should enter into constructive partnerships with RSLs operating in their district. See Annex 5 for guidance on co-operation between housing authorities and RSLs.

1.37 An indicative list of the other public authorities, voluntary organisations and persons whose activities could contribute to achieving the strategy's objectives is at Annex 3. However, s.3(4) provides that a housing authority cannot include in a homelessness strategy any specific action expected to be taken by another body or organisation without their approval.

1.38 Examples of specific action that the housing authority might expect to be taken by others are provided at Annex 6.

Joint action

1.39 Section 3(5) of the 2002 Act requires housing authorities, when formulating a homelessness strategy, to consider (among other things) the extent to which any of the strategy's objectives could be achieved through joint action involving two or more of the persons or other bodies tackling homelessness in the district. This could include the housing authority, the social services authority, neighbouring housing authorities and any other public bodies working to alleviate homelessness within the district, for example, the National Offender Management Service. It might also include any other organisation or person whose activities could contribute to achieving the objectives of the homelessness strategy, for example, voluntary sector organisations working with homeless people, registered social landlords, and private landlords. The most effective strategies will be those which harness the potential of all the organisations and persons working to prevent and alleviate homelessness in the district, and which ensure that all the activities concerned are consistent and complementary. It will be important for all such organisations to take ownership of the strategy if they strive to help meet its objectives. See Chapter 5 for guidance on joint working with other agencies.

Action plans

1.40 As part of the homelessness strategy housing authorities should develop effective action plans, to help ensure that the objectives set out in the homelessness strategy are achieved. Action plans could include, for example, targets, milestones and arrangements for monitoring and evaluation. Good practice guidance on developing action plans is provided in the ODPM publication *'Local Authorities' Homelessness Strategies: Evaluation and Good Practice (2004)'*.

Need to consult on a strategy

1.41 Housing authorities must consult such public or local authorities, voluntary organisations or other persons as they consider appropriate before adopting or modifying a homelessness strategy. For a strategy to be effective it will need to involve every organisation and partnership whose activities contribute, or could contribute, in some way to achieving its objectives. As a minimum, therefore, it will be appropriate for all such organisations to be consulted on the strategy before it is adopted. It will be important to consult service users and homeless people themselves, or organisations representing their interests. Consultation with ethnic minority and faith-based groups will also be important in addressing the disproportionate representation of people from ethnic minority communities amongst homeless households. Annex 3 provides an indicative list of the types of authorities, organisations and people that the housing authority may wish to consult about a strategy.

Publishing a strategy

1.42 Under s.1(3) of the 2002 Act, housing authorities were required to publish their first homelessness strategy by 31 July 2003. Section 1(4) requires housing authorities to publish a new homelessness strategy, based on the results of a further homelessness review, within the period of five years beginning with the day on which their last homelessness strategy was published. However, those authorities which are categorised as an 'excellent authority' by the Secretary of State by virtue of the *Local Authorities' Plans and Strategies (Disapplication) (England) Order 2005* are exempt from this requirement. Housing authorities must make a copy of the strategy available to the public at their principal office, and this is to be available for inspection at all reasonable hours without charge. A copy must also be made available to any member of the public, on request (for which a reasonable charge can be made).

Keeping a strategy under review and modifying it

1.43 Housing authorities must keep their homelessness strategy under review and may modify it from time to time. Before modifying the strategy, they must consult on the same basis as required before adopting a strategy (see paragraph 1.41). If a strategy is modified, the housing authority must publish the modifications or the modified strategy and make copies available to the public on the same basis as required when adopting a strategy (see paragraph 1.42).

1.44 Circumstances that might prompt modification of a homelessness strategy include: transfer of the housing authority's housing stock to an RSL; the setting up of an Arms Length Management Organisation; a review of other, relevant local plans or strategies; new data sources on homelessness becoming available; a significant change in the levels or causes of homelessness; changes in either housing/homelessness/social security policy or legislation, or new factors that could contribute to a change in the levels or nature of homelessness in the district such as significant changes to the local economy (e.g. housing markets or levels of employment).

CHAPTER 2
Preventing homelessness

2.1 **This chapter provides guidance on housing authorities' duties to have a strategy to prevent homelessness in their district and to ensure that advice and information about homelessness, and the prevention of homelessness, are available free of charge to anyone in their district. The chapter also provides some examples of the action housing authorities and their partners can take to tackle the more common causes of homelessness and to prevent homelessness recurring.**

2.2 Preventing homelessness means providing people with the ways and means to meet their housing, and any housing-related support, needs in order to avoid experiencing homelessness. Effective prevention will enable a person to remain in their current home, where appropriate, to delay a need to move out of current accommodation so that a move into alternative accommodation can be planned in a timely way; to find alternative accommodation, or to sustain independent living.

2.3 The prevention of homelessness should be a key strategic aim which housing authorities and other partners pursue through the homelessness strategy. It is vital that individuals are encouraged to seek assistance at the earliest possible time when experiencing difficulties which may lead to homelessness. In many cases early, effective intervention can prevent homelessness occurring. Housing authorities are reminded that they must not avoid their obligations under Part 7 of the 1996 Act (including the duty to make inquiries under s.184, if they have reason to believe that an applicant may be homeless or threatened with homelessness), but it is open to them to suggest alternative solutions in cases of potential homelessness where these would be appropriate and acceptable to the applicant.

2.4 The Secretary of State considers that housing authorities should take steps to prevent homelessness wherever possible, offering a broad range of advice and assistance for those in housing need. It is also important that, where homelessness does occur and is being tackled, consideration is given to the factors which may cause repeat homelessness and action taken to prevent homelessness recurring.

2.5 Homelessness can have significant negative consequences for the people who experience it. At a personal level, homelessness can have a profound impact on health, education and employment prospects. At a social level, homelessness can impact on social cohesion and economic participation. Early intervention to prevent homelessness can therefore bring benefits for those concerned, including being engaged with essential services and increasing the likelihood that children will live in a more secure environment. Investment in prevention services can also produce direct cost savings for local authorities, for example through lower use of temporary accommodation and fewer social services interventions. Furthermore, measures to prevent homelessness will also help to reduce longer-term pressures on wider services, such as health and employment.

2.6 There are three stages where intervention can prevent homelessness:

early identification – by identifying categories of people who are at risk of homelessness and ensuring that accommodation and any necessary support are available to them in time to prevent homelessness. Early identification can target people who fall within known indicator groups (e.g. those leaving local authority care, prison, secure accommodation or the armed forces, or people at known or observed risk due to mental or physical health problems) even though they may not currently have a need for housing but for whom timely intervention can avoid homelessness when they leave their institutional environment and before they reach a crisis point;

pre-crisis intervention – this can take the form of: advice services and proactive intervention such as negotiation with landlords to enable people to retain their current tenancies. Such intervention is important even if it only delays the date when a person has to leave their home, as this may allow time to plan and manage a move to alternative accommodation;

preventing recurring homelessness – ensuring tenancy sustainment can be central to preventing repeat homelessness where there is an underlying need for support and the provision of accommodation by itself is insufficient to prevent homelessness.

STRATEGY TO PREVENT HOMELESSNESS

2.7 Under s.1 of the 2002 Act, local housing authorities must formulate and publish a homelessness strategy based on a review of homelessness for their district, and they must take the strategy into account when exercising their functions. (See Chapter 1 for guidance.) Under section 3(1)(a) of the 2002 Act a homelessness strategy must include, among other things, a strategy for preventing homelessness in the district. Gaining a thorough understanding of the causes of homelessness in a local area through the review process will help to inform the range of measures required to prevent homelessness. As part of the review, housing authorities must consider all the current activities in their area that contribute to the prevention of homelessness. They must also consider the resources available. Both activities and resources are likely to involve a wide range of providers working in the public, private and voluntary sectors.

2.8 In developing their homelessness strategies, housing authorities should consider the range of measures that need to be put in place to prevent homelessness. These will depend on local circumstances. Housing authorities are advised to adopt an open approach and recognise that there will be a broad range of organisations operating in fields other than housing, for example, in education, health and employment, whose activities may help to prevent homelessness. (See Chapter 1 for further guidance on carrying out a homelessness review and formulating a homelessness strategy).

ADVICE AND INFORMATION ABOUT HOMELESSNESS AND THE PREVENTION OF HOMELESSNESS

2.9 Under s.179(1) of the 1996 Act, housing authorities have a duty to secure that advice and information about homelessness, and the prevention of homelessness, are available free of charge to **any person** in their district. The provision of comprehensive advice will play an important part in delivering the housing authority's strategy for preventing homelessness in their district.

2.10 There is an enormous variety of reasons why people become homeless or find themselves threatened with homelessness. And, in many cases, there can be multiple reasons, and a complex chain of circumstances, that lead to homelessness. Some of these may relate to the housing market, for example, high rents and a shortage of affordable accommodation in the area, or to administrative systems, for example delays in the payment of benefits. Others may relate to personal circumstances, for example, relationship breakdown, a bereavement, long-term or acute ill health or loss of employment. The provision of advice and information to those at risk of homelessness will need to reflect this. It will need to be wide-ranging and comprehensive in its coverage and may require a full multi-disciplinary assessment.

2.11 Many people who face the potential loss of their current home will be seeking practical advice and assistance to help them remain in their accommodation or secure alternative accommodation. Some may be seeking to apply for assistance under the homelessness legislation without being aware of other options that could help them to secure accommodation. Advice services should provide information on the range of housing options that are available in the district. This might include options to enable people to stay in their existing accommodation, delay homelessness for long enough to allow a planned move, or access alternative accommodation in the private or social sectors. This 'housing options' approach is central to addressing housing need as a means of preventing homelessness.

2.12 Advice on the following issues may help to prevent homelessness:

- tenants' rights and rights of occupation;
- leaseholders' rights and service charges;
- what to do about harassment and illegal eviction;
- how to deal with possession proceedings;
- rights to benefits (e.g. housing benefit) including assistance with making claims as required;
- current rent levels;
- how to retrieve rent deposits;
- rent and mortgage arrears;
- how to manage debt;

- grants available for housing repair and/or adaptation;
- how to obtain accommodation in the private rented sector – e.g. details of landlords and letting agents within the district, including any accreditation schemes, and information on rent guarantee and deposit schemes;
- how to apply for an allocation of accommodation through the social housing waiting list or choice-based lettings scheme;
- how to apply to other social landlords for accommodation.

The advisory service might also include an advocacy service, which may include providing legal representation for people facing the loss of their home.

2.13 Housing authorities will need to ensure that the implications and likely outcomes of the available housing options are made clear to all applicants, including the distinction between having priority need for accommodation under Part 7 and having priority for an allocation of social housing under Part 6.

2.14 Advice services will need to be effectively linked to other relevant statutory and non-statutory service providers. As noted in paragraph 2.10 above, it is often a combination of factors that lead to homelessness, and housing authorities are advised to ensure that people who require advice of a wider or more specialist nature, for example, to address family and relationship breakdown, mental or physical health problems, drug and alcohol abuse, or worklessness are directed to other agencies who can provide the service they need. In situations where there is a history of child abuse or where there are child protection concerns, homelessness and housing organisations will need to work closely with the Local Safeguarding Children Board (LSCB).

2.15 The effectiveness of authorities' housing advice in preventing homelessness or the threat of homelessness is measured by Best Value Performance Indicator BVPI 213. Guidance on BVPI 213 is available at www.communities.gov.uk.

Accessibility

2.16 It is recommended that advisory services are well published and accessible to everyone in the district. Appropriate provision will need to be made to ensure accessibility for people with particular needs, including those with mobility difficulties, sight or hearing loss and learning difficulties, as well as those for whom English is not their first language.

Who provides the advice and information?

2.17 The legislation does not specify how housing authorities should ensure that advice and information on homelessness and the prevention of homelessness are made available. They could do this in a number of ways, for example:

i) provide the service themselves;
ii) ensure that it is provided by another organisation; or
iii) ensure that it is provided in partnership with another organisation.

2.18 The housing authority must ensure that the service is free of charge and available and accessible to everyone in their district. Securing the provision of an independent advisory service may help to avoid conflicts of interest. Private sector tenants may not naturally look to the housing authority for advice. Some young people may be reluctant to approach a statutory authority for advice, but they may feel more at ease in dealing with a more informal advisory service provided by the voluntary sector. People from different ethnic minority groups might also find advice more accessible if it is delivered through community or faith organisations. (See Chapter 21 for guidance on contracting out homelessness functions).

2.19 Under s.179(2), housing authorities may give grants or loans to other persons who are providing advice and information about homelessness and the prevention of homelessness on behalf of the housing authority. Under s.179(3), housing authorities may also assist such persons (e.g. voluntary organisations) by:

i) allowing them to use premises belonging to the housing authority,
ii) making available furniture or other goods, by way of gift, loan or some other arrangement, and
iii) making available the services of staff employed by the housing authority.

Standards of advice

2.20 Housing authorities should ensure that information provided is current, accurate and appropriate to the individual's circumstances. To ensure they are providing an effective service to a high standard, housing authorities may wish to refer to the quality assurance systems applied by the National Association of Citizens Advice Bureaux, the Shelter network of housing advice centres, the National Disabled Housing Services Ltd (HoDis) accreditation scheme and the Community Legal Service Quality Mark. Housing authorities are also advised to monitor the provision of advisory services to ensure they continue to meet the needs of all sections of the community and help deliver the aims of their homelessness strategy.

PREVENTING HOMELESSNESS IN SPECIFIC CIRCUMSTANCES

2.21 Some groups of people are likely to be more at risk of homelessness than others. These may include:

- young people who have become estranged from their family; have been in care and/or secure accommodation; have a history of abuse, running away or school exclusions; or whose parents have had mental health, alcohol or drug problems (see Chapter 12 for further guidance on 16 and 17 year olds);
- people from ethnic minority groups;
- people with an institutionalised background, for example where they have spent time in care, in prison or in the armed forces;
- former asylum seekers who have been given permission to stay in the UK and are no longer being accommodated by the National Asylum Support Service;
- people who have experienced other problems that may increase the risk of homelessness including family/relationship breakdowns; domestic, racial or other violence; poor mental or physical health; drug and alcohol misuse; age-related problems and debt.

2.22 In many cases homelessness can be prevented by identifying people who are in circumstances which put them at risk of homelessness, and by providing services which can enable them to remain in their current home. Homelessness can also be prevented by ensuring assistance is available at known risk points such as discharge from prison or hospital. Table 2.1 below gives examples of some of the measures that may help tackle some of the more common causes of homelessness. More detailed guidance is provided in Annex 7.

Table 2.1: Tackling common causes of homelessness

Cause	**Action**
Parents, relatives or friends not being able or willing to provide accommodation	Mediation services, usually contracted out by local authority to, for example, Relate, Youth Crime prevention and parenting programmes.
Relationship breakdown, including domestic violence	'Sanctuary' schemes, which allow domestic violence victims to remain in their homes where they choose to do so once security measures are in place.
Discharge from an institutional situation e.g. hospital, custody, residential treatment/care	Early planning for discharge between institutional staff and local housing providers, including assessing support needs. Proactive provision of advice by local housing authority on housing options (prior to discharge).
End of assured shorthold tenancy	Housing advice. Rent deposit or bond schemes to encourage landlords to let to potentially homeless people. Landlord-tenant mediation services, to resolve disputes about behaviour or repairs.
Mortgage and rent arrears	Debt counselling. Advocacy services in county court. Fast tracking housing benefit claims.
Person ill-equipped to sustain a tenancy	Advice and support under the Supporting People programme for vulnerable people at risk of homelessness, for example improving budgeting and 'life' skills.
Lack of information	Early and proactive intervention from local authority homelessness services to discuss options and offer assistance and advice.

2.23 Housing authorities should also work with housing providers to encourage them to seek to maintain and sustain tenancies by employing effective strategies for the prevention and management of rent arrears. Landlords should be encouraged to make early and personal contact with tenants in arrears and to assess whether there are any additional support needs and, where relevant, to establish that all benefits to which tenants are entitled are being claimed. Landlords should offer assistance and advice on welfare benefits and in making a claim, debt counselling and money advice either in-house or through a referral to an external agency and implement ways for recovering the money such as debt management plans or attachment to benefits or earnings orders.

Possession action should only be taken as a last resort. See Annex 1 for ODPM guidance on *Improving the Effectiveness of Rent Arrears Management*.

PREVENTING HOMELESSNESS RECURRING

2.24 The underlying problems which led to homelessness in the first place have to be addressed in order to provide long-term solutions. Failure to address these root causes can lead to repeated episodes of homelessness. Recurring homelessness may be indicative of problems that are not being resolved by the provision of accommodation alone.

2.25 An effective approach to tackling recurring homelessness is likely to be based on:

- effective monitoring that identifies housing applicants who are homeless or threatened with homelessness and who have previously been secured accommodation under the homelessness legislation (either by the same authority or another authority in a different area);
- an analysis of the main causes of homelessness among housing applicants who have experienced homelessness more than once; and
- the existence of support services (and, in particular, strong links with the local Supporting People strategy and services) for housing applicants who have experienced homelessness more than once, which tackle these causes and help the applicants to sustain tenancies or other forms of settled accommodation in the longer term.

2.26 Tenancy sustainment is central to preventing repeat homelessness and can include a range of interventions. It is closely linked with good housing management and the Supporting People programme. See Chapter 4 for further guidance on securing support services and the housing-related support services that can be funded through Supporting People.

2.27 Whilst tenancy sustainment is the eventual objective, there are some individuals who may not be able to sustain accommodation due to personal circumstances, for example mental health or substance misuse difficulties. Support will need to be provided to progress towards the time when they are able to maintain accommodation.

CHAPTER 3
Ensuring a sufficient supply of accommodation

3.1 **This chapter provides guidance on options available to housing authorities to help increase the supply of new housing and maximise the use of the housing stock in their district.**

3.2 Section 3(1)(b) of the *Homelessness Act 2002* provides that a homelessness strategy is a strategy for, amongst other things, securing that sufficient accommodation is and will be available for people who are or may become homeless. Chapter 16 provides guidance on the different ways in which housing authorities can ensure that suitable accommodation is available for applicants, for example by providing the accommodation themselves or by securing it from a private landlord or a registered social landlord.

3.3 Homelessness is significantly influenced by the availability of housing, and in particular affordable housing. A shortage of affordable housing can lead to increasing numbers of people being accommodated in temporary accommodation whilst waiting for settled housing to bring the main homelessness duty to an end. 'Settled housing' in this context will primarily be social housing and good quality private sector accommodation (see chapter 14 for further guidance on bringing the main homelessness (s. 193(2)) duty to an end.)

3.4 Although, in 2005, over 80% of people living in temporary accommodation were in self-contained homes they often lack certainty over how long they will live there. This can cause disruption to their lives, make it hard for them to put roots down in the community or to access important services. For example, they may face real difficulties in gaining access to a local GP or in enrolling their children in a local school. Many may already have faced disruption and become disconnected or moved away from existing services and support networks as a result of homelessness.

3.5 The Government's current target is to halve the number of households living in temporary accommodation by 2010. Increasing the supply of new affordable housing and making better use of existing social and private rented stock to provide settled homes will be critical for achieving this target, as will measures to prevent homelessness.

INCREASE SUPPLY OF NEW HOUSING

3.6 The *Sustainable Communities Plan* and *Sustainable Communities: Homes for All* set out how the Government is creating new communities and expanding existing communities in four areas in the wider South East. Taken together, these areas are expected to deliver an extra 200,000 homes above current planning totals.

3.7 At a regional level, local authorities have a key role to play to identify the priorities for housing in their region, to ensure these are reflected in regional housing strategies and to secure funding for their plans. Housing authorities will also need to ensure that housing strategies are aligned with regional economic and planning strategies.

3.8 There are a number of ways housing authorities can increase the supply of new housing. The main source of funding for the provision of affordable housing is the Housing Corporation's national Affordable Housing Programme (AHP), known formerly as the Approved Development Programme (ADP). From the 2006–2008 biannual bidding round, the AHP is open to both registered social landlords and non-registered bodies (e.g. developers). Bids continue to be assessed against a range of criteria including housing quality and value for money, and against regional and local priorities. Housing authorities will need to work closely with RSLs and others to make best use of this funding.

3.9 Another important means of providing affordable housing is through planning obligations, which are usually negotiated in the context of granting planning permission for new housing development. Planning obligations are generally secured by agreements made between a local authority and a developer under s.106 of the *Town and Country Planning Act 1990* and they are commonly referred to as 's.106 agreements'. Obligations may be appropriate where, for example, a planning objection to a proposed development cannot be overcome by the imposition of a condition. More detailed guidance on the use of s.106 agreements is contained in ODPM Circular 05/2005: Planning Obligations.

3.10 National guidance on planning and affordable housing is currently contained in Planning Policy Guidance Note 3 (PPG3): Housing, as supplemented by Circular 06/98. These documents provide advice to planning authorities about securing the provision of affordable housing either in kind or by financial contribution. They also remind local authorities when formulating local policy or determining planning applications to take account of the need to cater for a range of housing needs and to encourage the development of mixed and balanced communities in order to avoid areas of social exclusion.

3.11 PPG3 and Circular 06/98 are presently under review and a draft Planning Policy Statement 3 (PPS3): Housing was issued for consultation in December 2005. Following the publication of final PPS3, local planning authorities will be expected to ensure that policies in their Local Development Frameworks take into account the updated national planning policy framework for delivering the Government's housing objectives.

3.12 Planning authorities will need to ensure that their affordable housing policies are evidence-based, kept up to date over time, and applied consistently across developments to ensure that affordable housing is effectively and fairly delivered through this route.

MAXIMISING THE USE OF EXISTING HOUSING STOCK

3.13 A number of options are discussed below for how housing authorities might maximise the use of current housing stock.

The private rented sector

3.14 Some people living in the private rented sector can experience homelessness, but this sector can also provide solutions to homelessness. Homelessness statistics routinely show that the end of an assured shorthold tenancy (AST) is one of the top three reasons for loss of a settled home. Authorities are encouraged to work with landlords in their area to see how this can be addressed, for example, by offering mediation between landlord and tenant where relations have broken down, and negotiating to extend or renew ASTs where appropriate.

3.15 For many, renting in the private sector may offer a practical solution to their housing need (for example, it may offer more choice over location and type of property). Authorities are therefore encouraged to consider providing rent deposits, guarantees or rent in advance, to help households access this sector. They may also consider establishing Accreditation Schemes, whereby landlords voluntarily agree to a set of standards relating to the management or physical condition of privately rented accommodation to help increase the supply of private rented accommodation.

3.16 Many local authorities have used the private rented sector as a source of good quality, self-contained temporary accommodation. However, the private rented sector can also provide a source of settled accommodation, where qualifying offers of ASTs are accepted by households who are owed the main homelessness duty.

3.17 There is scope to make greater use of the private rented sector, either to help households avoid homelessness or to provide more settled homes for people living in temporary accommodation. Authorities are recommended to establish and maintain good relations with private sector landlords, for example through landlord fora. This can be effective in securing an improved supply of properties in the private rented sector for homeless, or potentially homeless, households.

3.18 It is also recommended that authorities review the extent to which qualifying offers of ASTs are being made to households in temporary accommodation in their area; whether there are any barriers to such offers being made or accepted and, if so, what additional steps would need to be taken to address those barriers.

Social housing

3.19 The Secretary of State considers that, generally, it is inappropriate for general needs social housing to be used as temporary accommodation for long periods, especially where such properties are able to be let as settled homes.

3.20 It is important that housing authorities work effectively with RSLs to help them prevent and tackle homelessness in the district. RSLs have a key role to play in sustaining tenancies, reducing evictions and abandonment, and preventing homelessness through their housing management functions. To ensure effective collaboration between themselves and partner RSLs operating in their district housing authorities are advised to consider establishing a nominations agreement. This would include the proportion of lettings that will be made available, any conditions that will apply, and how any disputes about suitability or eligibility will be resolved. Housing authorities are also advised to aim for any exclusion criteria (that may be applied to nominees by the RSL) to be kept to a minimum. Further guidance on co-operation between RSLs and housing authorities is at Annex 5.

3.21 There are a number of schemes and policies that social housing providers can implement to facilitate the effective management and use of the existing housing stock and to keep voids and re-let times to a minimum.

- **Mobility:** 'move UK' (formerly Housing Employment and Mobility Services) has been developed to offer social housing tenants and jobseekers more choice about where they live and work around the UK. Its services will open up new opportunities for people who wish to move. 'move UK' will have three main service components:
  - (i) facilitated mobility services to social landlords and their tenants and applicants to help tenants and applicants to find new homes. This will continue and enhance the provision of the grant funded mobility previously provided by Housing Mobility and Exchange Services (HOMES) and LAWN (the Association of London Government scheme that helps tenants who want to, move out of London to areas of low demand);
  - (ii) 'one stop shop' web-based information about available housing, neighbourhoods and job vacancies;
  - (iii) web access to information on vacancies in social housing.
- **Cash Incentive Scheme** (CIS): although there is no obligation for a housing authority to provide a scheme, the main objectives of the Cash Incentive Scheme (CIS) are to release local authority accommodation required for letting to those in housing need, and to encourage sustainable home

ownership. This is achieved by the payment of a grant to a local authority tenant to assist them in buying a property in the private sector.

– **The new HomeBuy scheme**: this scheme, which commenced on 1st April 2006, provides people with the opportunity to own a home based on equity sharing, whilst protecting the supply of social housing. Existing social tenants are one of the priority groups helped under the scheme, and any rented housing association/local authority home vacated by them will then be made available to others in priority housing need. The Social HomeBuy option, which allows housing association and local authority tenants to purchase a share in their rented home, will be voluntary. Landlords will be able to reinvest the proceeds in replacement social homes.

3.22 The Secretary of State also considers that where local authority or RSL stock is provided as temporary accommodation to discharge a main homelessness duty (owed under section 193(2)) the housing authority should give very careful consideration to the scope for allocating the accommodation as a secure or assured tenancy, as appropriate, especially where a household has been living in a particular property for anything other than a short-term emergency stay.

Choice-based lettings schemes

3.23 The expansion of choice-based lettings policy aims to achieve nationwide coverage by 2010. Local authorities are encouraged to work together, and with RSL partners, to develop sub-regional and regional choice-based lettings schemes which provide maximum choice and flexibility. Local authorities are encouraged to offer choice to homeless households, while ensuring that their schemes are designed so as not to provide a perverse incentive to applicants to make a homelessness application in order to increase their priority for housing. Housing authorities should also consider involving the private rented sector in their choice-based lettings schemes in order to maximise the housing options available.

Empty homes

3.24 Housing authorities are encouraged to adopt positive strategies for minimising empty homes, and other buildings that could provide residential accommodation, across all housing sectors and tenures within their district. A strategy for minimising empty homes might include schemes for tackling low demand social housing, bringing empty private sector properties back into use and bringing flats over shops into residential use.

3.25 Under the *Housing Act 2004* new provisions on Empty Dwelling Management Orders (EDMOs) are expected to be brought into force. EDMOs are a discretionary power for local authorities to use as part of their empty homes strategy. The new powers will allow local authorities to apply to a residential property tribunal for approval to make an interim EDMO lasting for up to 12 months. During this interim period, the authority may only place tenants in the house with the consent of the owner.

3.26 Local authorities also have the discretion to set the council tax discount on long term empty properties at any point between 50% and 0%, as well as at any point between 50% and 10% on second homes, taking into account local conditions.

Housing renewal

3.27 Housing renewal assistance can also assist in meeting the aims of the homelessness strategy. Under the *Regulatory Reform (Housing Assistance) (England and Wales) Order 2002*, local authorities have power to promote housing renewal assistance to landlords, private homeowners and others to increase the supply of a particular type of accommodation through converting underutilised accommodation to meet identified housing need within the district. Empty homes, vacant accommodation above shops or commercial buildings can be targeted for assistance. Housing renewal assistance can also enable private homeowners to carry out essential repairs or improvements, and remain in their home.

Disabled facilities grant

3.28 Uptake of the Disabled Facilities Grant – a mandatory entitlement administered by housing authorities for eligible disabled people in all housing tenures – can enable homeowners to remain living an independent life at home, and should be considered as part of an effective homelessness strategy. Authorities are required to give a decision within six months of receiving an application. The grant is subject to a maximum limit and is means tested to ensure that funding goes to those most in need.

CHAPTER 4
Securing support services

4.1 **This chapter provides guidance on the importance of support services in preventing and tackling homelessness and outlines the types of housing-related and other support services that might be required.**

4.2 A homelessness strategy is defined in section 3(1)(c) of the 2002 Act as (among other things) a strategy for securing the satisfactory provision of support for people in their district:

i) who are or may become homeless; or
ii) who have been homeless and need support to prevent them from becoming homeless again.

4.3 In formulating their homelessness strategies, housing authorities need to recognise that for some households, homelessness cannot be tackled, or prevented, solely through the provision of accommodation. Some households will require a range of support services, which may include housing-related support to help them sustain their accommodation, as well as personal support relating to factors such as relationship breakdown, domestic violence, mental health problems, drug and alcohol addiction, poverty, debt and unemployment.

4.4 Support can help to prevent people who are at risk of homelessness from becoming homeless at all. In other cases, where people have experienced homelessness and been placed in temporary accommodation, the provision of support may be essential to ensure that they are able to continue to enjoy a reasonable quality of life and access the range of services they need to rebuild their lives. The provision of support can also be important in helping formerly homeless households to sustain settled housing and prevent homelessness from recurring.

4.5 Solutions to homelessness should be based on a thorough assessment of the household's needs, including support needs. Housing authorities will need to establish effective links with the Supporting People team, the social services authority and other agencies (for example, Primary Care Trusts, the Criminal Justice Service, and voluntary and community organisations) to ensure that a joint assessment of an applicant's housing and support needs can be made where necessary. Such assessments should inform decisions on intervention to enable a household to remain in their home, placements in temporary accommodation and options for the provision of more settled accommodation that will bring the main homelessness duty to an end.

4.6 Where children and young people are involved, it is important that any solutions to homelessness address the issues they are facing and do not undermine any support they may already be receiving. In particular, housing authorities will need to establish effective links with children's services authorities and establish whether a Common Assessment Framework has been undertaken, and, if so, which agency will have relevant information about the child's or young person's needs.

STRATEGY TO SECURE PROVISION OF SUPPORT SERVICES

4.7 Section 1 of the 2002 Act requires housing authorities to carry out a homelessness review for their district. Gaining a thorough understanding of the causes of homelessness through the review process will help to inform the range of support provision required. As part of the review, housing authorities must consider all the current activities in their area which contribute to the provision of support for households who are, or may become, homeless, as well as people in the district who have been homeless and need support to prevent them becoming homeless again. They must also consider the resources available. Both activities and resources are likely to involve a range of providers working in the public, private and voluntary sectors. (See Chapter 1 for further guidance on carrying out a homelessness review and formulating a homelessness strategy).

4.8 In formulating their homelessness strategies housing authorities will need to consider the different types and level of support that households may require. Households who have experienced homelessness or who are at risk of homelessness may have diverse needs. Some households may only need information and advice in order to avoid experiencing homelessness, or becoming homeless again. Others, however, will need greater assistance including housing-related support and in some cases may require intensive support from a range of services.

INDIVIDUALS AT RISK OF HOMELESSNESS

4.9 Housing authorities should be aware that some individuals may be at particular risk of homelessness, for example young people leaving care, ex-offenders, former members of the armed forces, refugees, people with mental health problems or individuals leaving hospital, and may require a broader package of resettlement support. When developing their homelessness strategies, housing authorities should consider carefully how to work effectively to prevent homelessness amongst these groups and ensure that appropriate support is available. Early identification of people at risk will be crucial to preventing homelessness. Housing authorities should consider agreeing protocols for joint action with local agencies in order to assist with early identification and prevention measures.

4.10 Individuals at risk of homelessness may also include those who have never experienced homelessness in the past and for whom, with the appropriate support, homelessness can be avoided. These individuals may be at risk of homelessness due to specific problems such as managing debt or accessing benefits and require specialist advice which may be delivered through partner agencies such as Citizens Advice Bureaux or Jobcentre Plus. See Chapter 2 for guidance on preventing homelessness.

YOUNG PEOPLE

4.11 Many young people who have experienced homelessness may lack skills in managing their affairs and require help with managing a tenancy and operating a household budget. Those estranged from their family, particularly care leavers, may lack the advice and support normally available to young people from family, friends and other mentors. 16 and 17 year olds who are homeless and estranged from their family will be particularly vulnerable and in need of support. See Chapter 12 for further guidance on 16 and 17 years olds.

HOUSING-RELATED SUPPORT SERVICES

4.12 Housing-related support services have a key role in preventing homelessness occurring or recurring. The types of housing-related support that households who have experienced homelessness may need include:

- *support in establishing a suitable home* – help, advice and support in finding and maintaining suitable accommodation for independent living in the community;
- *support with daily living skills* – help, advice and training in the day-to-day skills needed for living independently, such as budgeting and cooking;
- *support in accessing benefits, health and community care services* – information, advice and help in claiming benefits or accessing community care or health services;
- *help in establishing and maintaining social support* – help in rebuilding or establishing social networks that can help counter isolation and help support independent living.

4.13 Services might be delivered through:

- **floating support services** – using support workers who travel to clients' accommodation in order to provide support. These services can operate across all tenures and generally provide time-limited and low intensity support;
- **short and medium stay housing with support** – including direct access schemes, night shelters, hostels, transitional housing and supported lodgings. Some of these services may specialise in supporting particular groups of individuals at risk of homelessness, such as vulnerable young people;
- **long-stay supported housing services** – to provide ongoing support to those who are unable to live independently in the community.

4.14 Housing-related support can be funded through the Supporting People programme, and close co-operation between housing authorities and the

Supporting People team will be essential for ensuring effective support for households who have experienced homelessness, particularly through the local Commissioning Body and Core Strategy Group. Further information on housing-related support services is provided in separate guidance, *Supporting People – Guide to Accommodation and Support Options for Homeless Households* (ODPM, 2003).

OTHER SUPPORT SERVICES

4.15 Households who have experienced homelessness may need additional support services which are not directly housing-related and fall outside the scope of the Supporting People programme funding. Housing authorities will need to co-operate and work collaboratively with other departments within the authority and a wide range of statutory, voluntary and private sector agencies in order to ensure that the support which is required is provided. Joint working with commissioners/planners and providers of the following services will be particularly important:

- health services;
- drug/alcohol services including Drug Action Teams;
- social services;
- children's and young persons' services (e.g. Connexions, Sure Start children's centres, child care services);
- voluntary and community sector service providers;
- National Offender Management Service (incorporating the Prison Service and the Probation Service);
- Youth Offending Teams;
- Crime and Disorder Reduction Partnerships;
- the Police;
- education and training services;
- the Employment Service (Jobcentre Plus);
- grant making charities and trusts;
- local strategic partnerships.

SUPPORT FOR HOUSEHOLDS IN TEMPORARY ACCOMMODATION

4.16 The provision of support to households placed in temporary accommodation is essential to ensure that they are able to continue to enjoy a reasonable quality of life and access the range of services they need. In formulating their homelessness strategies, housing authorities should consider what arrangements need to be in place to ensure that households placed in temporary accommodation, within their district or outside, are able to access relevant support services. In particular households will need to be able to access:

- primary care services such as health visitors and GPs;
- appropriate education services;
- relevant social services; and
- employment and training services.

4.17 Housing authorities will need to liaise and work collaboratively with the relevant service providers to ensure that appropriate arrangements are put in place and monitored. When households are placed in temporary accommodation, it is recommended that housing authorities offer to liaise with the relevant health, education and social services departments in the area in which the households are temporarily housed. Liaison will be particularly important in cases where households have to be accommodated in the district of another housing authority.

4.18 The Secretary of State recommends that housing authorities offer to liaise with the appropriate Primary Care Trust of all families with babies or young children who are placed in temporary accommodation, to ensure that they have the opportunity to receive health and developmental checks from health visitors and/or other primary health care professionals and can participate in vaccination programmes. It would be insufficient for an authority simply to provide such a family with details of health centres and GP practices in the area.

Notify

4.19 Authorities are encouraged to participate in any regional or sub-regional arrangements which facilitate the notification of other authorities and agencies about the location and support needs of households in temporary accommodation. When considering procedures for notifying the relevant agencies of placements in temporary accommodation, housing authorities may wish to have regard to NOTIFY – a web-based notification and information system administered by the Greater London Authority (GLA).

4.20 NOTIFY is designed to improve access to services for households placed in temporary accommodation. Its primary role is to notify relevant services of the placement or movement of households placed in temporary accommodation by London boroughs under the homelessness legislation. The system uses information provided by London borough housing departments to notify housing, education, social services and Primary Care Trusts about households placed in, moving between or leaving temporary accommodation. Information is contained in a database and updated weekly. Authorised users of the NOTIFY notifications website can view information held on NOTIFY at any time, by accessing that website. Relevant services receive a weekly email alert from NOTIFY, informing them of any unviewed notifications and reminding them to access the website. NOTIFY will also shortly provide access for each borough to its own operational management data. The system also has the capacity to analyse aggregated data both at borough and London level. For further information on NOTIFY see notifylondon.gov.uk or contact notify@london.gov.uk.

CHAPTER 5
Working with others

5.1 **This chapter provides guidance to housing authorities on working in partnership with other agencies to deliver co-ordinated and effective services to tackle homelessness. It considers the range of organisations and people that contribute to preventing and tackling homelessness and provides examples of types of joint working. It also sets out the statutory provisions that require co-operation between various authorities.**

5.2 Under s.3(5) of the 2002 Act, when formulating a homelessness strategy the housing authority must consider, among other things, the extent to which any of the strategy's objectives could be achieved through joint action involving two or more of the organisations tackling homelessness in the district. Whilst housing authorities are best placed to take the strategic lead in tackling homelessness, it is vital that as part of their homelessness strategies effective partnerships are developed with other organisations to deliver co-ordinated and more effective approaches to tackling homelessness locally that address not only housing need but all aspects of social need.

WHY JOINT WORKING?

5.3 At its best, joint working can result in higher quality and more efficient and cost-effective services. Joint working can:

- expand the knowledge and expertise of partner agencies;
- help to provide higher quality integrated services to clients with multiple needs;
- help to ensure people who are homeless or at risk of homelessness do not fall through the net because no one agency can meet all their needs;
- reduce wasteful referrals and duplicated work between agencies. For example, common procedures for assessing clients and exchanging information mean homeless people do not have to be repeatedly assessed by different agencies.

ORGANISATIONS/PEOPLE WORKING TO PREVENT AND TACKLE HOMELESSNESS

5.4 The most effective homelessness strategies will be those which harness the potential of all the organisations and persons working to prevent and tackle homelessness in the district, and which ensure that all the activities concerned are consistent and complementary. Joint working could involve the social services authority, the Primary Care Trust, other public bodies such as the National Offender Management Service, voluntary and community sector organisations, registered social landlords, private landlords, and any other relevant organisations. Housing authorities should also consider joint working with other agencies, for example, the Police and voluntary and community sector organisations, to tackle issues related to homelessness such as street drinking, begging, drug misuse and anti-social behaviour. Such collaborative working can help reduce the numbers of people sleeping rough and provide effective services targeted at those who are homeless or at risk of becoming homeless. Annex 3 provides an indicative list of other authorities, organisations and persons whose activities may contribute to preventing and tackling homelessness. Chapter 2 provides guidance on the range of activities that housing authorities might undertake in conjunction with other bodies in order to prevent homelessness.

5.5 Housing authorities should also consider developing cross-boundary partnerships to help tackle homelessness, for example with neighbouring local authorities and local strategic partnerships. Initiatives at regional, cross-regional and sub-regional level that address issues which cut across administrative boundaries may also be relevant – for example regional strategies for refugee integration or reducing re-offending.

TYPES OF JOINT WORKING

5.6 Joint working can take many forms. Examples of types of collaborative working that could help to achieve the objectives of a homelessness strategy might include:

- establishment of a multi-agency forum for key practitioners and providers to share knowledge, information, ideas and complementary practices;
- clear links between the homelessness strategy and other key strategies such as Supporting People, and the NHS Local Delivery Plan;
- protocols for the referral of clients between services and sharing information between services – for example a joint protocol between hospital-based social workers and housing officers to address the housing needs of patients to be discharged from hospital;
- joint consideration of the needs of homeless people by housing and social services authorities under Part 7, the *Children Act 1989* and community care legislation;
- establishment of formal links with other services – for example with those provided by voluntary and community sector organisations;
- joint planning and commissioning of services;
- joint training;
- funding of joint posts, for example with the social services authority;
- senior housing representation on key corporate groups such as the Local Strategic Partnership (LSP) and the Crime and Disorder Reduction Partnership (CDRP);
- senior commitment from all stakeholders to joined-up working to ensure the homelessness strategy action plan is carried out;
- appropriate user involvement and consultation.

5.7 When offering housing advice and assistance, housing authorities should consider devising screening procedures that identify at an early stage those cases where there is a need for case-specific joint working. Authorities may also wish to encourage their partner agencies to develop similar procedures. Where there is a need for such an approach, authorities are encouraged to adopt agreed protocols to ensure that appropriate action can be quickly initiated. Early appraisal of all clients who may require multiple assessments, by whichever authority is first approached, with agreed triggers and procedures for further action, may help to prevent duplication of enquiries.

5.8 *Homelessness Strategies – A good practice handbook* (DTLR, March 2002) provides advice on successful joint working and the establishment of good links between different agencies and programmes that can prevent and alleviate homelessness. The handbook also signposts to other sources of guidance, for example, on joint protocols, joint commissioning and joint assessments.

THE STATUTORY FRAMEWORK

5.9 The need for co-operation between statutory authorities is recognised in legislation:

- s.213, s.213A and s.170 of the *Housing Act 1996;*
- s.1 of the *Homelessness Act 2002;*
- s.2 of the *Local Government Act 2000;*
- s.27 of the *Children Act 1989;*
- s.10, s.11 and s.13 of the *Children Act 2004;*

- s.47 of the *National Health Service* and *Community Care Act 1990;*
- s.27 and s.31 of the *Health Act 1999.*

These provisions are outlined in more detail below. However, the absence of a formal legal duty should not act as a barrier to joint working. Rather this should be predicated on meeting local needs and effectively implementing the homelessness strategy.

Housing Act 1996

Section 213

5.10 Where housing or inquiry duties arise under the 1996 Act a housing authority may seek co-operation from another relevant housing authority or body or a social services authority in England, Scotland or Wales. The authority or body to whom the request is made must co-operate to the extent that is reasonable in the circumstances. For this purpose, 'relevant housing authority or body' will include:

in England and Wales:
- another housing authority,
- a registered social landlord,
- a housing action trust, and

in Scotland:
- a local authority,
- a registered social landlord, and
- Scottish Homes.

5.11 The duty on the housing authority, body or social services authority receiving such a request to co-operate will depend on their other commitments and responsibilities. However, they cannot adopt a general policy of refusing such requests, and each case will need to be considered in the circumstances at the time.

5.12 Section 170 of the 1996 Act also provides that where a registered social landlord (RSL) has been requested by a housing authority to offer accommodation to people with priority under its allocation scheme, the RSL must co-operate to such extent as is reasonable in the circumstances. RSLs have a key role to play in preventing and tackling homelessness. See Annex 5 for guidance on co-operation between RSLs and housing authorities.

Section 213A

5.13 Section 213A applies where the housing authority has reason to believe than an applicant with whom a person under the age of 18 resides, or might normally be expected to reside, may be ineligible for assistance, or homeless, or threatened with homelessness, intentionally. Housing authorities are required to have arrangements in place to ensure that all such applicants are invited to agree to the housing authority notifying the social services authority of the essential facts of their case. This will give social services the opportunity to consider the circumstances of the child(ren) and family and plan any response that may be deemed by them to be appropriate. See Chapter 13 for further guidance on s.213A.

Local government acts

5.14 The promotion of well-being power contained in s.2 of the *Local Government Act 2000* gives local authorities substantial capacity for cross-boundary partnership working with other authorities and partners, such as the health and social services sectors. In particular, the power provides local authorities with increased scope to improve the social, economic and environmental well-being of their communities. Section 2(5) of the *Local Government Act 2000* makes it clear that local authorities may act in relation to and for the benefit of any person or area outside their own area if they consider that to do so is likely to promote or improve the social, economic or environmental well-being of their own area. This, therefore, provides scope for:

- co-operation between neighbouring local authorities and local strategic partnerships; and
- initiatives at regional, cross-regional and sub-regional level that address issues which cut across administrative boundaries.

It should be noted, however, that the s.2 power cannot be used by authorities to delegate, or contract out their functions. In order to do this, authorities will need to make use of specific powers such as those in s.101 of the *Local Government Act 1972* which provides for the joint exercise of functions between local authorities.

Children Act 1989

5.15 Under s.27 of the *Children Act 1989* ('the 1989 Act'), a local authority can ask a range of other statutory authorities, including a housing authority, to help them in delivering services for children and families, under their functions in Part 3 of the 1989 Act. Authorities must comply with such a request to the extent that it is compatible with their own statutory duties and other obligations, and does not unduly prejudice the discharge of any of their own functions. They cannot adopt a general policy of refusing such requests, and each case will need to be considered according to the circumstances at the time.

5.16 Children and young people should not be sent to and fro between different authorities (or between different departments within authorities). To provide an effective safety net for vulnerable young people who are homeless or at risk of homelessness, housing and social services will need to work together. Effective collaborative working will require clear corporate policies and departmental procedures agreed between the relevant departments. These should make provision for speedy resolution of any dispute as to which department should take responsibility for a particular case. Joint agreements should cover not only the assessment of clients, but should also reflect the strategic planning and delivery of provision to be set out in the local Children and Young People's Plan. Local Safeguarding Children Boards, which will co-ordinate and ensure the effectiveness of local work to safeguard and promote the welfare of children, may also be involved in drawing up policies and procedures to ensure effective inter-agency co-operation (see also paragraphs 5.17–5.20 below) and Chapter 13.

5.17 Under the 1989 Act, young people leaving care and 16/17 year old children assessed as in need are owed duties which may extend to the provision of accommodation. Where social services approach a housing authority for assistance in housing a young person, the housing authority must co-operate subject to the conditions referred to above in para 5.16. Whether a young person is accommodated under the auspices of the social services authority or the housing authority is a matter for individual authorities to determine in each case. Ideally the relationship of the two authorities should be symbiotic, with jointly agreed protocols in place in respect of the assessment of needs. In many cases the social services authority will have a continuing responsibility for the welfare of vulnerable young people and for assisting them in the transition to adulthood and independent living. Under the 1989 Act, these responsibilities can extend until the young person is aged 18 and in the case of care leavers until the age of 21 (or beyond that age if they are in an agreed programme of education and training). Thus, social services authorities can request assistance from housing authorities in meeting their obligations to provide accommodation for a young person and housing authorities can look to social services authorities to provide the support that young homeless applicants may require. In some cases, housing and social services authorities will both have responsibilities towards young people and will need to work together in order to ensure that an appropriate combination of housing and support is arranged to help the young person to live independently successfully.

Children Act 2004

5.18 The *Children Act 2004* ('the 2004 Act') provides the legislative support for the *Every Child Matters: Change for Children* programme which sets out a national framework for local change programmes to build services around the needs of children and young people. Improved outcomes for children will be driven by an analysis of local priorities and secured through more integrated front-line delivery such as multi-agency working, integrated processes such as the Common Assessment Framework, integrated strategy with joint planning and commissioning, and governance arrangements such as the creation of a Director of Children's Services and lead member for children's services.

5.19 To support the integration of systems to improve outcomes for children and young people by the creation of children's trusts, s.10 of the 2004 Act establishes a duty on county level and unitary authorities to make arrangements to promote co-operation between the authority, relevant partners (including district councils) and other persons or bodies engaged in activities in relation to children, to improve the well-being of children and young people in the authority's area. Relevant partners are required to co-operate with the authority. Section 11 of the 2004 Act requires a range of agencies – including county level and unitary authorities and district authorities where there are two tiers of local government – to make arrangements for ensuring that their functions are discharged having regard to the need to safeguard and promote the welfare of children. Section 13 of the 2004 Act requires county level and unitary authorities to set up a Local Safeguarding Children Board (LSCB) incorporating key organisations including district councils where relevant. As set out in s.14, the objective of the LSCB is to co-ordinate and ensure the effectiveness of what is done by each person or body represented on the board to safeguard and promote the welfare of children in that area.

5.20 The 2004 Act also makes provision for indexes containing basic information about children and young people to enable better sharing of information. In addition, each local authority is required to draw up a Children and Young

People's Plan (CYPP) by April 2006. The CYPP will be a single, strategic, over-arching plan for all services affecting children and young people. The CYPP and the process of joint planning should support local authorities and their partners as they work together. An integrated inspection framework is also being created with Joint Area Reviews assessing local areas' progress in improving outcomes.

The Department for Education and Skills has produced statutory guidance on the *Children Act 2004* which is available from **www.everychildmatters.gov.uk.**

National Health Service and Community Care Act 1990

5.21 Under the National Health Service (NHS) and Community Care Act 1990 ('the 1990 Act'), social services authorities are required to carry out an assessment of any person who may have a need for community care services. The purpose of the legislation is to ensure that the planning and assessment processes identify a person's full range of needs, including housing needs. Section 47 of the 1990 Act requires social service authorities to notify the housing authority if there appears to be a housing need when the assessment is carried out. The 'housing need', for example, may be for renovation or adaptation of the person's current accommodation or for alternative accommodation.

5.22 An assessment of vulnerability under the homelessness legislation will not necessarily mean that a client is eligible for social care services. Policy guidance on fair access to care services (FACS) was published on 2 June 2002 under guidance of local authority circular (LAC) (2002) 13. The guidance provides authorities with an eligibility framework for adult social care for them to use when setting and applying their eligibility criteria.

Health Act 1999

5.23 Section 27 of the *Health Act 1999* ('the 1999 Act') requires NHS bodies and local authorities to co-operate with one another in exercising their respective functions in order to secure and advance the health and welfare of the people of England and Wales.

5.24 Under s.31 of the 1999 Act, partnership arrangements can be designed to help break down the barriers between NHS and local authority services by removing existing constraints in the system and increasing flexibility in the provision and commissioning of services. The legislation introduces three flexibilities: pooled budgets, lead commissioning and integrated provision. Any health-related local authority function can be included in these partnerships, for example, housing, social services, education and leisure services.

National standards, local action: health and social care standards and planning framework 2005/06–2007/08

5.25 This document sets out the framework for all NHS organisations and social services authorities to use in planning over the financial years 2005/06–2007/08. It looks to Primary Care Trusts (PCTs) and local authorities to lead community partnership by even closer joint working to take forward the NHS Improvement Plan. Building on joint work on Local Strategic Partnerships (LSPs), they will need to work in partnership with other NHS organisations in preparing Local Delivery Plans (LDPs) for the period 2005/06 to 2007/08.

Mental health

5.26 The Mental Health National Service Framework (NSF 30/09/1999) addresses the mental health needs of working age adults up to 65. It sets out national standards; national service models; local action and national underpinning programmes for implementation; and a series of national milestones to assure progress, with performance indicators to support effective performance management. An organisational framework for providing integrated services and for commissioning services across the spectrum is also included.

5.27 The Government wants to ensure that people suffering from mental illness receive appropriate care and assistance, particularly those whose illness is severe and enduring. Research has shown that provision of suitable, settled housing is essential to the well-being of this vulnerable group. A key element in the spectrum of care and support is the development of a care plan under the Care Programme Approach (CPA). The initial assessment and ongoing reviews under the CPA must include an assessment of an individual's housing needs. It is essential that housing authorities liaise closely with social services authorities so that any provision of housing is appropriate to the needs of the individual, and meshes with the social and health care support that may be an essential part of the person's care programme.

5.28 This is equally important for young people up to the age of 18. Chapter 9 of the National Service Framework for Children, Young People and Maternity Services published in 2004 makes clear that use of the CPA is also a key marker of good practice for child and adolescent mental health services working with young people with high levels of mental health need.

CHAPTER 6
Applications, inquiries, decisions and notifications

6.1 **This chapter provides guidance on dealing with applications for accommodation or assistance in obtaining accommodation; a housing authority's duty to carry out inquiries (where it has reason to believe an applicant may be homeless or threatened with homelessness); and, following inquiries, an authority's duty to notify an applicant of its decision.**

APPLICATIONS FOR ASSISTANCE

6.2 Under s.184 of the 1996 Act, if a housing authority has reason to believe that a person applying to the authority for accommodation or assistance in obtaining accommodation may be homeless or threatened with homelessness, the authority must make such inquiries as are necessary to satisfy itself whether the applicant is eligible for assistance and if so, whether any duty, and if so what duty, is owed to that person under Part 7 of the 1996 Act. The definitions of 'homeless' and 'threatened with homelessness' are discussed in Chapter 8.

Preventing homelessness

6.3 Under s.179, housing authorities have a duty to ensure that advice and information about homelessness and the prevention of homelessness are available free of charge to anyone in their district (see Chapter 2 for further guidance on providing advice and information to prevent homelessness). In many cases early, effective intervention can prevent homelessness occurring. Many people who face the potential loss of their current home will be seeking practical advice and assistance to help them remain in their accommodation or secure alternative accommodation. Some may be seeking to apply for assistance under the homelessness legislation without being aware of other options that could help them to secure accommodation. Authorities should explain the various housing options that are available. These might include:

- advice and assistance (e.g. legal advice or mediation with a landlord) to enable them to remain in their current home;
- assistance (e.g. rent deposit or guarantee) to obtain accommodation in the private rented sector;
- an application for an allocation of long term social housing accommodation through a social housing waiting list or choice-based lettings scheme; or
- advice on how to apply to another social landlord for accommodation.

6.4 Housing authorities should ensure that the implications and likely outcomes of the available housing options are made clear to all applicants, including the distinction between having a priority need for accommodation under Part 7 and being in a 'reasonable preference' category for an allocation of housing under Part 6. Authorities must not avoid their obligations under Part 7 (especially the duty to make inquiries under s.184), but it is open to them to suggest alternative solutions in cases of potential homelessness where these would be appropriate and acceptable to the applicant.

Interim duty to accommodate

6.5 If a housing authority has reason to believe that an applicant may be eligible for assistance, homeless and have a priority need, the authority will have **an immediate duty under s.188 to ensure that suitable accommodation is available for the applicant** (and his or her household) pending the completion of the authority's inquiries and its decision as to what duty, if any, is owed to the applicant under Part 7 of the Act. Chapter 7 provides guidance on the interim duty to accommodate. Authorities are reminded that 'having reason to believe' is a lower test than 'being satisfied'.

Form of the application

6.6 Applications can be made by any adult to any department of the local authority and expressed in any particular form; they need not be expressed as explicitly seeking assistance under Part 7. Applications may also be made by a person acting on behalf of the applicant, for example, by a social worker or solicitor acting in a professional capacity, or by a relative or friend in circumstances where the applicant is unable to make an application themselves.

Applications to more than one housing authority

6.7 In some cases applicants may apply to more than one housing authority simultaneously and housing authorities will need to be alert to cases where an applicant is doing this. In such cases, where a housing authority has reason to believe that the applicant may be homeless or threatened with homelessness, it may wish to contact the other housing authorities involved, to agree which housing authority will take responsibility for conducting inquiries.

Where another housing authority has previously made decisions about an applicant's circumstances, a housing authority considering a fresh application may wish to have regard to those decisions. However, housing authorities should not rely solely on decisions made by another housing authority and will need to make their own inquiries in order to reach an independent decision on whether any duty, and if so which duty, is owed under Part 7. Any arrangements for the discharge of any of their functions by another housing authority must comply with s.101 of the *Local Government Act 1972.*

Service provision

6.8 A need for accommodation or assistance in obtaining accommodation can arise at anytime. Housing authorities will therefore need to provide access to advice and assistance at all times during normal office hours, and have arrangements in place for 24-hour emergency cover, e.g. by enabling telephone access to an appropriate duty officer. The police and other relevant services should be provided with details of how to access the service outside normal office hours.

6.9 In the interests of good administration, it is recommended that housing authorities should give proper consideration to the location of, and accessibility to, advice and information about homelessness and the prevention of homelessness, including the need to ensure privacy during interviews. Details of the service including the opening hours, address, telephone numbers and the 24-hour emergency contact should be well publicised within the housing authority's district.

6.10 Housing authorities should provide applicants with a clear and simple explanation of their procedures for handling applications and making decisions. It is recommended that this is provided in written form, for example as a leaflet, as well as orally. In order to ensure advice and assistance are accessible to everyone in the district, it is recommended that information is made available in the main languages spoken in the area, and that for languages less frequently spoken there is access to interpreters. Applicants should be kept informed of the progress of their application and the timescales involved for making a decision on their case. They should also be given a realistic expectation of the assistance to which they may be entitled.

6.11 Under s.214, it is an offence for a person, knowingly or recklessly to make a false statement, or knowingly to withhold information, with intent to induce the authority to believe that he or she, or another person, is entitled to accommodation under Part 7. If, before the applicant receives notification of a decision, there is any change of facts material to his or her case, he or she must inform the housing authority of this as soon as possible. Housing authorities must ensure that all applicants are made aware of these obligations and that they are explained in ordinary language. Housing authorities are advised to ensure that the obligations are conveyed sensitively to avoid intimidating applicants.

INQUIRIES

6.12 Under s.184, where a housing authority has reason to believe that an applicant may be homeless or threatened with homelessness, it must make inquiries to satisfy itself whether the applicant is eligible for assistance (see Chapter 9) and, if so, whether any duty and if so what duty is owed to him or her under Part 7. In order to determine this, the authority will need to establish whether the applicant is homeless or threatened with homelessness (see Chapter 8), whether he or she became homeless, or threatened with homelessness, intentionally (see Chapter 11) and whether he or she has a priority need for accommodation (see Chapter 10).

6.13 In addition to determining whether an applicant is owed any duty under Part 7, housing authorities are reminded that they have a **power** to provide further assistance to applicants who are eligible for assistance, homeless (or threatened with homelessness) unintentionally and do not have a priority need. Under s.192(3), housing authorities may secure that accommodation is available for applicants who are eligible, unintentionally homeless and do not have a priority need (see Chapter 15 for further guidance). Under s.195(9), housing authorities may take reasonable steps to secure that accommodation does not cease to be available for applicants who are eligible for assistance, unintentionally threatened with homelessness and do not have a priority need for accommodation (see paragraph 14.7 for guidance on steps to secure that accommodation does not cease to be available).

6.14 Under s.184(2), housing authorities may also make inquiries to decide whether the applicant has a local connection with another housing authority district in England, Wales or Scotland, but they are not required to do so. The possibility of a referral of an applicant to another housing authority can only arise where the applicant has been accepted as eligible for assistance, unintentionally homeless and having a priority need for accommodation (see Chapter 18 for guidance on local connection and referrals).

6.15 The obligation to make inquiries, and satisfy itself whether a duty is owed, rests with the housing authority and it is not for applicants to 'prove their case'. Applicants should always be given the opportunity to explain their circumstances fully, particularly on matters that could lead to a decision against their interests, for example, a decision that an applicant is intentionally homeless.

6.16 Housing authorities should deal with inquiries as quickly as possible, whilst ensuring that they are thorough and, in any particular case, sufficient to enable the housing authority to satisfy itself what duty, if any, is owed or what other assistance can be offered. Housing authorities are obliged to begin inquiries as soon as they have reason to believe that an applicant may be homeless or threatened with homelessness and should aim to carry out an initial interview and preliminary assessment on the day an application is received. An early assessment will be vital to determine whether the housing authority has an immediate duty to secure accommodation under s.188 (see Chapter 7 for guidance on the interim duty to accommodate). Wherever possible, it is recommended that housing authorities aim to complete their inquiries and notify the applicant of their decision within 33 working days of accepting a duty to make inquiries under s.184. In many cases it should be possible for authorities to complete the inquiries significantly earlier.

Violence

6.17 Under s.177, it is not reasonable for a person to continue to occupy accommodation if it is probable that this will lead to domestic or other violence against him or her, or against a person who normally resides with him or her as a member of his or her family, or any other person who might reasonably be expected to reside with him or her. Violence includes threats of violence from another person which are likely to be carried out. Inquiries into cases where violence is alleged will need careful handling. It is essential that inquiries do not provoke further violence. It is not advisable for the housing authority to approach the alleged perpetrator, since this could generate further violence, and may delay the assessment. Housing authorities may, however, wish to seek information from friends and relatives of the applicant, social services and the police, as appropriate. In some cases, corroborative evidence of actual or threatened violence may not be available, for example, because there were no adult witnesses and/or the applicant was too frightened or ashamed to report incidents to family, friends or the police. In many cases involving violence, the applicant may be in considerable distress and an officer trained in dealing with the particular circumstances should conduct the interview. Applicants should be given the option of being interviewed by an officer of the same sex if they so wish.

6.18 In cases where violence is a feature and the applicant may have a local connection elsewhere, the housing authority, in considering whether to notify another housing authority about a possible referral of the case, must be aware that s.198 provides that an applicant cannot be referred to another housing authority if he or she, or any person who might reasonably be expected to reside with him or her, would be at risk of violence in the district of the other housing authority (see Chapter 18 for guidance on referrals to another housing authority).

Support needs

6.19 16 and 17 year olds (including lone parents) who apply for housing assistance may also have care and support needs that need to be assessed. The Secretary of State recommends that housing authorities and social services authorities (and the relevant departments within unitary authorities) have arrangements in place for joint consideration of such young people's needs, whether the application is made initially to the housing department or social services department. See Chapter 12 for further guidance on 16 and 17 year olds.

Assistance from another authority or body

6.20 Under s. 213, a housing authority may request another relevant housing authority or body to assist them in the discharge of their functions under Part 7. In such cases the authority or body must co-operate in rendering such assistance in the discharge of the functions to which the request relates as is reasonable in the circumstances. For example, a housing authority may request another housing authority to co-operate in providing information about a previous application. See paragraph 5.10 for further guidance on s.213.

DECISIONS/NOTIFICATIONS

6.21 When a housing authority has completed its inquiries under s.184 it must notify the applicant in writing of its decision on the case. Where the decision is against the applicant's interests, e.g. a decision that he or she is ineligible for assistance, not homeless, not in priority need or homeless intentionally, the notification must explain clearly and fully the reasons for the decision. If the housing authority has decided that the conditions for referring the applicant's homelessness case to another housing authority have been met, they must notify the applicant of this and give their reasons for doing so.

6.22 All notifications must inform applicants of their right to request a review of the housing authority's decision and the time within which such a request must be made. At this stage, it is also recommended that housing authorities explain the review procedures. (See Chapter 19 for guidance on reviews of decisions and appeals to the county court).

6.23 It will be important to ensure that the applicant fully understands the decision and the nature of any housing duty that is owed. In cases where the applicant may have difficulty understanding the implications of the decision, it is recommended that housing authorities consider arranging for a member of staff to provide and explain the notification in person.

6.24 Under s.193(3A), where the housing authority accepts a duty to secure accommodation for an applicant under s.193(2), they must give the applicant a copy of the statement included in their allocation scheme of the housing authority's policy on offering people a choice of housing or the opportunity to express their preferences about the accommodation to be allocated to them. This statement is required to be included in the allocation scheme under s.167(1A).

6.25 Section 184(6) provides that where a notification is not received by an applicant, it can be treated as having been given to him or her, if it is made available at the housing authority's office for a reasonable period that would allow it to be collected by the applicant or by someone acting on his or her behalf.

WITHDRAWN APPLICATIONS

6.26 It is recommended that housing authorities have procedures in place for dealing with applications that are withdrawn or where someone fails to maintain contact with the housing authority after making an application. The Secretary of State considers that it would be reasonable to consider an application closed where there has been no contact with the applicant for three months or longer. Any further approach from the applicant after this time may need to be considered as a fresh application. Where an applicant renews contact within three months the housing authority will need to consider any change of circumstances that may affect the application.

FURTHER APPLICATIONS

6.27 There is no period of disqualification if someone wants to make a fresh application. Where a person whose application has been previously considered and determined under Part 7 makes a fresh application, the authority will need to decide whether there are any new facts in the fresh application which render it different from the earlier application. If no new facts are revealed, or any new facts are of a trivial nature, the authority would not be required to consider the new application. However, where the fresh application does reveal substantive new facts, the authority must treat the fresh application in the same way as it would any other application for accommodation or assistance in obtaining accommodation. Therefore, if the authority has reason to believe that the person is homeless, or threatened with homelessness, the authority should make inquiries under s.184 and decide whether any duty is owed under s.188(1).

CHAPTER 7
Interim duty to accommodate

7.1 **This chapter provides guidance on housing authorities' interim duty to secure that accommodation is available for an applicant if they have reason to believe that the applicant may be homeless, eligible for assistance and has a priority need.**

7.2 Section 188(1) imposes an interim duty on housing authorities to secure that accommodation is available for an applicant (and his or her household) pending their decision as to what duty, if any, is owed to the applicant under Part 7 of the Act if they have reason to believe that the applicant may:

a) be homeless,
b) be eligible for assistance, and
c) have a priority need.

7.3 The threshold for the duty is low as the local authority only has to have a reason to believe that the applicant **may** be homeless, eligible for assistance and have a priority need. (See paragraph 6.5 for guidance on the 'reason to believe' test.)

7.4 The s.188(1) duty applies even where the authority considers the applicant may not have a local connection with their district and may have one with the district of another housing authority (s.188(2)). Applicants cannot be referred to another housing authority unless the housing authority dealing with the application is satisfied that s.193 applies (i.e. the applicant is eligible for assistance, unintentionally homeless and has a priority need). (See Chapter 18 for guidance on referrals to other housing authorities.)

SUITABILITY OF ACCOMMODATION

7.5 The accommodation provided under s.188(1) must be suitable for the applicant and his or her household and the suitability requirements under s.206(1) and s.210(1) apply (see Chapter 17 for guidance on the suitability of accommodation). The applicant does not have the right to ask for a review of the housing authority's decision as to the suitability of accommodation secured under the interim duty, but housing authorities are reminded that such decisions could be subject to judicial review.

7.6 Housing authorities should avoid using Bed & Breakfast (B&B) accommodation wherever possible. Where B&B accommodation has been used in an emergency situation, applicants should be moved to more suitable accommodation as soon as possible. The *Homelessness (Suitability of Accommodation) (England) Order 2003* provides that B&B accommodation is not suitable accommodation for families with children and households that include a pregnant woman unless there is no alternative accommodation available and then only for a maximum of six weeks.

DISCHARGING THE INTERIM DUTY

7.7 Where the s.188(1) interim duty is being discharged, inquiries should be completed as quickly as possible to minimise uncertainty for the applicant and the period for which accommodation needs to be secured by the housing authority. (See Chapter 6 for guidance on inquiries).

7.8 Housing authorities can discharge their interim duty to secure accommodation by providing their own accommodation or by arranging that it is provided by some other person, or by providing advice and assistance so that it will be provided by some other person. (See Chapter 16 for more information on discharging the duty to secure accommodation).

ENDING THE INTERIM DUTY

7.9 The s.188(1) interim duty ends once the housing authority has notified the applicant of its decision as to what duty, if any, is owed to him or her under Part 7, even if the applicant requests a review of the decision.

7.10 Where, having completed their inquiries, the housing authority is satisfied that they are under no further duty to secure accommodation, they should give the applicant a reasonable period of notice to vacate the accommodation to enable him or her to make alternative accommodation arrangements for him/herself. The time allowed should be reasonable when judged against the circumstances of the applicant. Housing authorities should give the applicant time to consider whether to request a review of their decision and, if a review is requested, will need to consider whether to exercise their discretionary power under s.188(3) to secure that accommodation is available (see paragraph 7.13 below).

7.11 It has been established that, as a general rule, accommodation provided pending inquiries under s.184 does not create a tenancy or a licence under the *Protection from Eviction Act 1977*. The courts have applied this principle in cases where the accommodation provided was B&B accommodation in a hotel and where it was a self-contained flat. Consequently, where this general rule applies, housing authorities are required only to provide an applicant with reasonable notice to vacate accommodation provided under the interim duty, and do not need to apply for a possession order from the court. Authorities should note, however, that this general rule may be displaced by an agreement between the housing authority and the applicant, or if the occupation of the accommodation is allowed to continue on more than a transient basis.

7.12 In cases involving applicants who have children under 18 where the housing authority are satisfied that the applicant is ineligible for assistance, the housing authority must alert the social services authority, or social services department, as appropriate, to the case (see Chapter 13 for further guidance on co-operation with social services). Applicants should be invited to consent to social services being notified of the case, but in certain circumstances, for example where the housing authority are concerned about the welfare of the child, they should disclose information about the case even where consent has not been given.

ACCOMMODATION PENDING A REVIEW

7.13 Where a review of a decision of a housing authority is requested under s.202, although there is no duty under s.188(1), under s.188(3) the housing authority has a discretionary power to provide accommodation pending the outcome of the review. Failure to consider exercising this discretionary power could be the subject of challenge by judicial review proceedings. Housing authorities are reminded that applicants have 21 days in which to request a review of a decision. (See Chapter 19 for guidance on review of decisions and Chapter 15 for guidance on powers to accommodate pending a review).

CHAPTER 8
Homeless or threatened with Homelessness

8.1 **This chapter provides guidance on how to determine whether a person is 'homeless' or 'threatened with homelessness' for the purposes of Part 7.**

8.2 Under s.184 of the 1996 Act, if a housing authority has reason to believe that a person applying to the housing authority for accommodation, or assistance in obtaining accommodation, may be homeless or threatened with homelessness, the housing authority must make inquiries to satisfy itself whether the applicant is eligible for assistance and if so, whether a duty is owed to that person under Part 7 of the 1996 Act (see Chapter 6 for guidance on applications for assistance).

THREATENED WITH HOMELESSNESS

8.3 Under s.175(4), a person is 'threatened with homelessness' if he or she is likely to become homeless within 28 days. In many cases, effective intervention can enable homelessness to be prevented or the loss of the current home to be delayed sufficiently to allow for a planned move. The Secretary of State considers that housing authorities should take steps to prevent homelessness wherever possible, offering a broad range of advice and assistance for those in housing need. Authorities should not wait until homelessness is a likelihood or is imminent before providing advice and assistance. (See Chapter 2 for guidance on preventing homelessness).

HOMELESS

8.4 There are a number of different factors that determine whether a person is homeless. Under s.175, a person is homeless if he or she has no accommodation in the UK or elsewhere which is available for his or her occupation and which that person has a legal right to occupy. A person is also homeless if he or she has accommodation but cannot secure entry to it, or the accommodation is a moveable structure, vehicle or vessel designed or adapted for human habitation (such as a caravan or house boat) and there is no place where it can be placed in order to provide accommodation. A person who has accommodation is to be treated as homeless where it would not be reasonable for him or her to continue to occupy that accommodation.

Available for occupation

8.5 Section 176 provides that accommodation shall be treated as available for a person's occupation only if it is available for occupation by him or her together with:

i) any other person who normally resides with him or her as a member of the family, or

ii) any other person who might reasonably be expected to reside with him or her.

The first group covers those members of the family who normally reside with the applicant. The phrase 'as a member of the family' although not defined, will include those with close blood or marital relationships and cohabiting partners (including same sex partners), and, where such a person is an established member of the household, the accommodation must provide for him or her as well. The second group relates to any other person, and includes those who may not have been living as part of the household at the time of the application, but whom it would be reasonable to expect to live with the applicant as part of his or her household. Persons in the second group might include a companion for an elderly or disabled person, or children who are being fostered by the applicant or a member of his or her family. The second group will also include those members of the family who were not living as part of the household at the time of the application but who nonetheless might reasonably be expected to form part of it.

8.6 It is for the housing authority to assess whether any other person might reasonably be expected to live with the applicant and there will be a range of situations that the authority will need to consider. Persons who would normally live with the applicant but who are unable to do so because there is no accommodation in which they can all live together should be included in the assessment. When dealing with a family which has split up, housing authorities will need to take a decision as to which members of the family normally reside, or might be expected to reside, with the applicant. A court may have made a residence order indicating with whom the children are to live, but in many cases it will be a matter of agreement between the parents and a court will not have been involved.

Legal right to occupy accommodation

8.7 Under s.175(1), a person is homeless if he or she has no accommodation which he or she can legally occupy by virtue of:

i) an interest in it (e.g. as an owner, lessee or tenant) or by virtue of a court order;
ii) an express or implied licence to occupy it (e.g. as a lodger, as an employee with a service occupancy, or when living with a relative); or
iii) any enactment or rule of law giving him or her the right to remain in occupation or restricting the right of another person to recover possession (e.g. a person retaining possession as a statutory tenant under the Rent Acts where that person's contractual rights to occupy have expired or been terminated).

8.8 A person who has been occupying accommodation as a licencee whose licence has been terminated (and who does not have any other accommodation available for his or her occupation) is homeless because he or she no longer has a legal right to continue to occupy, despite the fact that that person may continue to occupy but as a trespasser. This may include, for example:

i) those required to leave hostels or hospitals; or
ii) former employees occupying premises under a service occupancy which is dependent upon contracts of employment which have ended.

People asked to leave accommodation by family or friends

8.9 Some applicants may have been asked to leave their current accommodation by family or friends with whom they have been living. In such cases, the housing authority will need to consider carefully whether the applicant's licence to occupy the accommodation has in fact been revoked. Housing authorities may need to interview the parents or friends to establish whether they are genuinely revoking the licence to occupy and rendering the applicants homeless. Authorities are encouraged to be sensitive to situations where parents or carers may have been providing a home for a family member with support needs (for example a person with learning difficulties) for a number of years and who are genuinely finding it difficult to continue with that arrangement, but are reluctant to revoke their licence to occupy formally until alternative accommodation can be secured.

8.10 In some cases the applicant may be unable to stay in his or her accommodation and in others there may be scope for preventing or postponing homelessness, and providing the applicant with an opportunity to plan their future accommodation and pursue various housing options with assistance from the housing authority. However, housing authorities will need to be sensitive to the possibility that for some applicants it may not be safe for them to remain in, or return to, their home because of a risk of violence or abuse.

8.11 In areas of high demand for affordable housing, people living with family and friends may have genuine difficulties in finding alternative accommodation that can lead to friction and disputes within their current home, culminating in a threat of homelessness. In some cases external support, or the promise of assistance with alternative housing, may help to reduce tension and prevent homelessness. The use of family mediation services may assist here.

8.12 Housing authorities will also need to be alert to the possibility of collusion where family or friends agree to revoke a licence to occupy accommodation as part of an arrangement whose purpose is to enable the applicant to be entitled to assistance under Part 7. Some parents and children, for example, may seek to take advantage of the fact that 16 and 17 year old applicants have a priority need for accommodation (see also Chapter 11 on intentional homelessness).

16 and 17 year olds

8.13 The Secretary of State considers that, generally, it will be in the best interests of 16 and 17 year olds to live in the family home, unless it would be unsafe or unsuitable for them to do so because they would be at risk of violence or abuse. See Chapter 12 for further guidance on 16 and 17 year olds.

Tenant given notice

8.14 With certain exceptions, a person who has been occupying accommodation as a tenant and who has received a valid notice to quit, or notice that the landlord requires possession of the accommodation, would have the right to remain in occupation until a warrant for possession was executed (following the granting of an order for possession by the court). The exceptions are tenants with resident landlords and certain other tenants who do not benefit from the *Protection from Eviction Act 1977*. **However, authorities should note that the fact that a tenant has a right to remain in occupation does not necessarily mean that he or she is not homeless.** In assessing whether an applicant is homeless in cases where he or she is a tenant who has a right to remain in occupation pending execution of a warrant for possession, the housing authority will also need to consider whether it would be reasonable for him or her to continue to occupy the accommodation in the circumstances (see paragraphs 8.30–8.32 below).

8.15 Some tenants may face having to leave their accommodation because their landlord has defaulted on the mortgage of the property they rent. Where a mortgage lender starts possession proceedings, the lender is obliged to give written notice of the proceedings to the occupiers of the property before an order for possession is granted. The notice must be given after issue of the possession summons and at least 14 days before the court hearing. As for tenants given notice that the landlord requires possession of the accommodation (see paragraph 8.14 above), authorities will need to consider whether it would be reasonable for a tenant to continue to occupy the accommodation after receiving notice of possession proceedings from the lender.

Inability to secure entry to accommodation

8.16 Under s.175(2), a person is homeless if he or she has a legal entitlement to accommodation, but is unable to secure entry to it, for example:

- those who have been evicted illegally, or
- those whose accommodation is being occupied illegally by squatters.

Although legal remedies may be available to the applicant to regain possession of the accommodation, housing authorities cannot refuse to assist while he or she is actually homeless.

Accommodation consisting of a moveable structure

8.17 Section 175(2)(b) provides that a person is homeless if he or she has accommodation available for his or her occupation which is a moveable structure, vehicle or vessel designed or adapted for human habitation (e.g. a caravan or houseboat), and there is nowhere that he or she is entitled or permitted to place it and reside in it. The site or mooring for the moveable structure need not be permanent in order to avoid homelessness. In many cases the nature of the structure may reflect the itinerant lifestyle of the applicant, who may not be looking for a permanent site but somewhere to park or moor on a temporary basis.

Reasonable to continue to occupy

8.18 Section 175(3) provides that a person shall not be treated as having accommodation unless it is accommodation which it would be reasonable for him or her to continue to occupy. There are a number of provisions relating to whether or not it is reasonable for someone to continue to occupy accommodation and these are discussed below. There is no simple test of reasonableness. It is for the housing authority to make a judgement on the facts of each case, taking into account the circumstances of the applicant.

Domestic violence or other violence

8.19 Section 177(1) provides that it is not reasonable for a person to continue to occupy accommodation if it is probable that this will lead to domestic violence or other violence against:

i) the applicant;
ii) a person who normally resides as a member of the applicant's family; or

iii) any other person who might reasonably be expected to reside with the applicant.

Section 177(1A) provides that violence means violence from another person or threats of violence from another person which are likely to be carried out. Domestic violence is violence from a person who is associated with the victim and also includes threats of violence which are likely to be carried out. Domestic violence is not confined to instances within the home but extends to violence outside the home.

8.20 Section 178 provides that, for the purposes of defining domestic violence, a person is associated with another if:

(a) they are, or have been, married to each other;
(b) they are or have been civil partners of each other;
(c) they are, or have been, cohabitants (including same sex partners);
(d) they live, or have lived, in the same household;
(e) they are relatives, i.e. father, mother, stepfather, stepmother, son, daughter, stepson, stepdaughter, grandmother, grandfather, grandson, granddaughter, brother, sister, uncle, aunt, niece or nephew (whether of full blood, half blood or by affinity) of that person or of that person's spouse or former spouse. A person is also included if he or she would fall into any of these categories in relation to cohabitees or former cohabitees if they were married to each other;
(f) they have agreed to marry each other whether or not that agreement has been terminated;
(g) they have entered into a civil partnership agreement between them whether or not that agreement has been terminated;
(h) in relation to a child, each of them is a parent of the child or has, or has had, parental responsibility for the child (within the meaning of the Children Act 1989). A child is a person under 18 years of age;
(i) if a child has been adopted or freed for adoption (s.16(1) *Adoption Act 1976*), two persons are also associated if one is the natural parent or grandparent of the child and the other is the child of a person who has become the parent by virtue of an adoption order (s.72(1) *Adoption Act 1976*) or has applied for an adoption order or someone with whom the child has been placed for adoption.

8.21 The Secretary of State considers that the term 'violence' should not be given a restrictive meaning, and that 'domestic violence' should be understood to include threatening behaviour, violence or abuse (psychological, physical, sexual, financial or emotional) between persons who are, or have been, intimate partners, family members or members of the same household, regardless of gender or sexuality.

8.22 An assessment of the likelihood of a threat of violence being carried out should not be based on whether there has been actual violence in the past. An assessment must be based on the facts of the case and devoid of any value judgements about what an applicant should or should not do, or should or should not have done, to mitigate the risk of any violence (e.g. seek police help or apply for an injunction against the perpetrator). Inquiries into cases where violence is alleged will need careful handling. See Chapter 6 for further guidance.

8.23 In cases involving violence, housing authorities may wish to inform applicants of the option of seeking an injunction, but should make clear that there is no obligation on the applicant to do so. Where applicants wish to pursue this option, it is advisable that they obtain independent advice as an injunction may be ill-advised in some circumstances. Housing authorities should recognise that injunctions ordering a person not to molest, or enter the home of, an applicant may not be effective in deterring perpetrators from carrying out further violence or incursions, and applicants may not have confidence in their effectiveness. Consequently, applicants should not be expected to return home on the strength of an injunction. To ensure applicants who have experienced actual or threatened violence get the support they need, authorities should inform them of appropriate organisations in the area such as agencies offering counselling and support as well as specialist advice.

8.24 When dealing with cases involving violence, or threat of violence, from outside the home, housing authorities should consider the option of improving the security of the applicant's home to enable him or her to continue to live there safely, where that is an option that the applicant wishes to pursue. In some cases, immediate action to improve security within the victim's home may prevent homelessness. A fast response combined with support from the housing authority, police and the voluntary sector may provide a victim with the confidence to remain in their home. When dealing with domestic violence within the home, where the authority is the landlord, housing authorities should consider the scope for evicting the perpetrator and allowing the victim to remain in their home. **However, where there would be a probability of violence if the applicant continued to occupy his or her present accommodation, the housing authority must treat the applicant as homeless and should not expect him or her to remain in, or return to, the accommodation. In all cases involving violence the safety of the applicant and his or her household should be the primary consideration at all stages of decision making as to whether or not the applicant remains in their own home.**

8.25 The effectiveness of housing authorities' services to assist victims of domestic violence and prevent further domestic violence is measured by Best Value Performance Indicator BVP1 225. Guidance on BVP1 225 is available at www.communities.gov.uk.

General housing circumstances in the district

8.26 Section 177(2) provides that, in determining whether it is reasonable for a person to continue to occupy accommodation, housing authorities may have regard to the general housing circumstances prevailing in the housing authority's district.

8.27 This would apply, for example, where it was suggested that an applicant was homeless because of poor physical conditions in his or her current home. In such cases it would be open to the authority to consider whether the condition of the property was so bad in comparison with other accommodation in the district that it would not be reasonable to expect someone to continue to live there.

8.28 Circumstances where an applicant may be homeless as a result of his or her accommodation being overcrowded should also be considered in relation to the general housing circumstances in the district. Statutory overcrowding, within the meaning of Part 10 of the *Housing Act 1985*, may not by itself be sufficient to determine reasonableness, but it can be a contributory factor if there are other factors which suggest unreasonableness.

Affordability

8.29 One factor that **must** be considered in all cases is affordability. The *Homelessness (Suitability of Accommodation) Order 1996* (SI 1996 No.3204) requires the housing authority to consider the affordability of the accommodation for the applicant. The Order specifies, among other things, that in determining whether it would be (or would have been) reasonable for a person to continue to occupy accommodation, a housing authority must take into account whether the accommodation is affordable for him or her and must, in particular, take account of:

(a) the financial resources available to him or her;
(b) the costs in respect of the accommodation;
(c) maintenance payments (to a spouse, former spouse or in respect of a child); and
(d) his or her reasonable living expenses.

Tenant given notice of intention to recover possession

8.30 In cases where the applicant has been occupying accommodation as a tenant and has received a valid notice to quit, or a notice that the landlord intends to recover possession, housing authorities should consider the scope for preventing homelessness through consulting the landlord at an early stage to explore the possibility of the tenancy being allowed to continue or the tenant being allowed to remain for a reasonable period to provide an opportunity for alternative accommodation to be found. If the landlord is not persuaded to agree, the authority will need to consider whether it would be reasonable for the applicant to continue to occupy the accommodation once the valid notice has expired.

8.31 In determining whether it would be reasonable for an applicant to continue to occupy accommodation, the housing authority will need to consider all the factors relevant to the case and decide the weight that individual factors should attract. As well as the factors set out elsewhere in this chapter, other factors which may be relevant include the general cost to the housing authority, the position of the tenant, the position of the landlord, the likelihood that the landlord will actually proceed with possession proceedings, and the burden on the courts of unnecessary proceedings where there is no defence to a possession claim (see paragraphs 8.14 and 8.15 above for guidance on the right to occupy where notice of possession proceedings has been given).

8.32 Each case must be decided on its facts, so **housing authorities should not adopt a general policy of accepting – or refusing to accept – applicants as homeless or threatened with homelessness when they are threatened with eviction but a court has not yet made an order for possession or issued a warrant of execution.** In any case where a housing authority decides that it would be reasonable for an applicant to continue to occupy their accommodation after a valid notice has expired – and therefore decides that he or she is not yet homeless or threatened with homelessness – that decision will need to be based on sound reasons which should be made clear to the applicant in writing (see Chapter 6 for guidance on housing authorities' duties to inform applicants of their decisions). **The Secretary of State considers that where a person applies for accommodation or assistance in obtaining accommodation, and:**

(a) the person is an assured shorthold tenant who has received proper notice in accordance with s.21 of the *Housing Act 1988*;
(b) the housing authority is satisfied that the landlord intends to seek possession; and
(c) there would be no defence to an application for a possession order;
then it is unlikely to be reasonable for the applicant to continue to occupy the accommodation beyond the date given in the s.21 notice, unless the housing authority is taking steps to persuade the landlord to withdraw the notice or allow the tenant to continue to occupy the accommodation for a reasonable period to provide an opportunity for alternative accommodation to be found.

8.32a Authorities are reminded that an applicant cannot be treated as intentionally homeless unless it would have been reasonable for him or her to have continued to occupy the accommodation. Guidance on 'intentional homelessness' is provided in Chapter 11.

Former armed forces personnel required to leave service accommodation

8.33 The Ministry of Defence recognises that housing authorities will need to be satisfied that entitlement to occupy service accommodation will end on a certain date, in order to determine whether applicants who are service personnel and who are approaching their date of discharge may be homeless or threatened with homelessness. For this purpose, the MOD issues a *Certificate of Cessation of Entitlement to Occupy Service Living Accommodation* six months before discharge (see examples at Annexes 14 and 15). These certificates indicate the date on which entitlement to occupy service accommodation ends, and the Secretary of State considers that housing authorities should not insist upon a court order for possession to establish that entitlement to occupy has ended. Authorities should take advantage of the six-month period of notice of discharge to ensure that service personnel receive timely and comprehensive advice on the housing options available to them when they leave the armed forces.

Other relevant factors

8.34 Other factors which may be relevant in determining whether it would be reasonable for an applicant to continue to occupy accommodation include:
physical characteristics: it would not be reasonable for an applicant to continue to occupy accommodation if the physical characteristics of the accommodation were unsuitable for the applicant because, for example, he or she was a wheelchair user and access was limited.
type of accommodation: some types of accommodation, for example women's refuges, direct access hostels, and night shelters are intended to provide very short-term, temporary accommodation in a crisis and it should not be regarded as reasonable to continue to occupy such accommodation in the medium and longer-term.
people fleeing harassment: in some cases severe harassment may fall short of actual violence or threats of violence likely to be carried out. Housing authorities should consider carefully whether it would be, or would have been, reasonable for an applicant to continue to occupy accommodation in circumstances where they have fled, or are seeking to leave, their home because of

non-violent forms of harassment, for example verbal abuse or damage to property. Careful consideration should be given to applicants who may be at risk of witness intimidation. In some criminal cases the police may provide alternative accommodation for witnesses, but usually this will apply for the duration of the trial only. Witnesses may have had to give up their home or may feel unable to return to it when the trial has finished.
This is not an exhaustive list and authorities will need to take account of all relevant factors when considering whether it is reasonable for an applicant to continue to occupy accommodation.

CHAPTER 9
Eligibility for assistance

GENERAL

9.1 Part 7 of the 1996 Act includes provisions that make certain persons from abroad ineligible for housing assistance. Housing authorities will therefore need to satisfy themselves that applicants are eligible before providing housing assistance. The provisions on eligibility are complex and housing authorities will need to ensure that they have procedures in place to carry out appropriate checks on housing applicants.

9.2 Housing authorities should ensure that staff who are required to screen housing applicants about eligibility for assistance are given training in the complexities of the housing provisions, the housing authority's duties and responsibilities under the race relations legislation and how to deal with applicants in a sensitive manner.

9.3 Local authorities are reminded that Schedule 3 to the *Nationality, Immigration and Asylum Act 2002* provides that certain persons shall not be eligible for support or assistance provided through the exercise of local housing authorities' powers to secure accommodation pending a review (s.188(3)) or pending an appeal to the county court (s.204(4)). See paragraph 9.22 below.

PERSONS FROM ABROAD

9.4 A person will not be eligible for assistance under Part 7 if he or she is a person from abroad who is ineligible for housing assistance under s.185 of the 1996 Act. There are two categories of 'person from abroad' for the purposes s.185:

(i) *a person subject to immigration control* – such a person is not eligible for housing assistance unless he or she comes within a class prescribed in regulations made by the Secretary of State, and

(ii) *a person from abroad other than a person subject to immigration control* – the Secretary of State can make regulations to provide for other descriptions of person from abroad who, although they are not subject to immigration control, are to be treated as ineligible for housing assistance.

9.5 The regulations that set out which classes of persons from abroad are eligible or ineligible for housing assistance are the *Allocation of Housing and Homelessness (Eligibility) (England) Regulations 2006* (SI 2006 No.1294) ('the Eligibility Regulations'). Persons subject to immigration control are not eligible for housing assistance unless they fall within a class of persons prescribed in **regulation 5** of the Eligibility Regulations. Persons who are not subject to immigration control will be eligible for housing assistance unless they fall within a description of persons who are to be treated as persons from abroad who are ineligible for assistance by virtue of **regulation 6** of the Eligibility Regulations.

PERSONS SUBJECT TO IMMIGRATION CONTROL

9.6 The term 'person subject to immigration control' is defined in s.13(2) of the *Asylum and Immigration Act 1996* as a person who requires leave to enter or remain in the United Kingdom (whether or not such leave has been given).

9.7 Only the following categories of person do **not** require leave to enter or remain in the UK:

(i) British citizens;

(ii) certain Commonwealth citizens with a right of abode in the UK;

(iii) citizens of an EEA country, ('EEA nationals') and their family members, who have a right to reside in the UK that derives from EC law. The question of whether an EEA national (or family member) has a particular right to reside in the UK (or in another Member State e.g. the Republic of Ireland) will depend on the circumstances, particularly the economic status of the EEA national (e.g. whether he or she is a worker, self-employed, a student, or economically inactive etc.). See Annex 12 for further guidance on rights to reside;

(iv) persons who are exempt from immigration control under the Immigration Acts, including diplomats and their family members based in the United Kingdom, and some military personnel.

For the purposes of this guidance, 'EEA nationals' means nationals of any of the EU member states (excluding the UK), and nationals of Iceland, Norway, Liechtenstein and Switzerland.

9.8 Any person who **does not** fall within one of the 4 categories in paragraph 9.7 above will be a person subject to immigration control and will be ineligible for housing assistance unless they fall within a class of persons prescribed by regulation 5 of the Eligibility Regulations (see paragraph 9.10 below).

9.9 If there is any uncertainty about an applicant's immigration status, it is recommended that authorities contact the Home Office Immigration and Nationality Directorate, using the procedures set out in Annex 8. In some circumstances, local authorities may be under a duty to contact the Immigration and Nationality Directorate (see paragraph 9.24).

Persons subject to immigration control who are eligible for housing assistance

9.10 Generally, persons subject to immigration control are not eligible for housing assistance. However, by virtue of regulation 5 of the Eligibility Regulations, the following classes of person subject to immigration control are eligible for housing assistance:

(i) *a person granted refugee status*: a person is granted refugee status when his or her request for asylum is accepted. Persons granted refugee status are granted 5 years' limited leave to remain in the UK. (Prior to 30 August 2005, it was the policy to provide immediate settlement (indefinite leave to remain) for persons granted refugee status.)

(ii) *a person granted exceptional leave to enter or remain in the UK without condition that they and any dependants should make no recourse to public funds*: this status is granted to persons, including some persons whose claim for asylum has been refused, for a limited period where there are compelling humanitarian and/or compassionate circumstances for allowing them to stay. However, if leave was granted on condition that the applicant and any dependants should not be a charge on public funds, the applicant will not be eligible for homelessness assistance. Since April 2003, exceptional leave to remain (which is granted at the Secretary of State's discretion outside the Immigration Rules) has taken the form of either humanitarian protection or discretionary leave.

(iii) *a person with current leave to enter or remain in the UK with no condition or limitation, and who is habitually resident in the UK, the Channel Islands, the Isle of Man or the Republic of Ireland*: such a person will have indefinite leave to enter (ILE) or remain (ILR) and will be regarded as having settled status. However, where ILE or ILR status was granted as a result of an undertaking that a sponsor would be responsible for the applicant's maintenance and accommodation, the person must have been resident in the UK, the Channel Islands, the Isle of Man or the Republic of Ireland for five years since the date of entry – or the date of the sponsorship undertaking, whichever is later – for the applicant to be eligible. Where a sponsor has (or, if there was more than one sponsor, all of the sponsors have) died within the first five years, the applicant will be eligible for housing assistance;

(iv) *a person who left the territory of Montserrat after 1 November 1995 because of the effect on that territory of a volcanic eruption.* (See paragraph 9.19 below.)

Asylum seekers

9.11 Asylum seekers will almost always be persons subject to immigration control. **Asylum seekers who are persons subject to immigration control and whose claim for asylum was made after 2 April 2000 are** *not* eligible for assistance under Part 7 of the 1996 Act. Some asylum seekers whose claim for asylum was made before 3 April 2000 would be eligible for assistance under Part 7 in certain limited circumstances, but the number of persons who fall in these classes is likely to be very small (if any). Annex 9 provides guidance on the limited categories of asylum seekers eligible for assistance under Part 7 of the 1996 Act.

9.12 Under s.186 of the 1996 Act, an asylum seeker who would otherwise be eligible for assistance under the Eligibility Regulations, will be ineligible, if he or she has any accommodation available in the UK for his or her occupation, however temporary.

OTHER PERSONS FROM ABROAD WHO MAY BE INELIGIBLE FOR ASSISTANCE

9.13 By virtue of regulation 6 of the Eligibility Regulations, a person who is not subject to immigration control and who falls within one of the following descriptions of persons is to be treated as a person from abroad who is ineligible for housing assistance:

(i) a person who is not habitually resident in the UK, the Channel Islands, the Isle of Man or the Republic of Ireland (subject to certain exceptions – see paragraph 9.14 below);
(ii) a person whose only right to reside in the UK is derived from his status as a jobseeker (or his status as the family member of a jobseeker). For this purpose, 'jobseeker' has the same meaning as for the purpose of regulation 6(1)(a) of the *Immigration (European Economic Area) Regulations 2006* (SI 2006 No. 1003) ('the EEA Regulations');
(iii) a person whose only right to reside in the UK is an initial right to reside for a period not exceeding three months under regulation 13 of the EEA Regulations;
(iv) a person whose only right to reside in the Channel Islands, the Isle of Man or the Republic of Ireland is a right equivalent to one of the rights mentioned in (ii) or (iii) above and which is derived from the Treaty establishing the European Community ('the EC Treaty').

See Annex 12 for guidance on rights to reside in the UK derived from EC law.

Persons exempted from the requirement to be habitually resident

9.14 Certain persons from abroad (not being persons subject to immigration control) will be eligible for housing assistance even though they are not habitually resident in the UK, the Channel Islands, the Isle of Man or the Republic of Ireland. Such a person will be eligible for assistance even if not habitually resident, if he or she is:

(a) an EEA national who is in the UK as a worker (which has the same meaning as it does for the purposes of regulation 6(1) of the EEA Regulations);
(b) an EEA national who is in the UK as a self-employed person (which has the same meaning as it does for the purposes of regulation 6(1) of the EEA Regulations);
(c) a person who is an accession state worker requiring registration who is treated as a worker for the purposes of regulation 6(1) of the EEA Regulations, pursuant to the *Accession (Immigration and Worker Registration) Regulations 2004*, as amended;
(d) a person who is a family member of a person referred to in (a) to (c) above;
(e) a person with a right to reside permanently in the UK by virtue of regulation 15(c), (d) or (e) of the EEA Regulations (see Annex 12);
(f) a person who left Montserrat after 1 November 1995 because of the effect of volcanic activity there (see paragraph 9.19 below);
(g) a person who is in the UK as a result of his or her deportation, expulsion or other removal by compulsion of law from another country to the UK (see paragraph 9.21 below).

On (a) and (b), authorities should note that a person who is no longer working or no longer in self-employment will retain his or her status as a worker or self-employed person in certain circumstances. (See Annex 12 for further guidance.) On (c), authorities should note that accession state workers requiring registration will generally only be treated as a worker when they are actually working and will not retain 'worker' status in the circumstances referred to above. (See annexes 12 and 13 for further guidance.) On (d), authorities should note that 'family member' does not include a person who is an extended family member who is treated as a family member by virtue of regulation 7(3) of the EEA Regulations (see Annex 12 for further guidance).

The habitual residence test

9.15 The term 'habitual residence' is intended to convey a degree of permanence in the person's residence in the UK, the Channel Islands, the Isle of Man or the Republic of Ireland; it implies an association between the individual and the place of residence and relies substantially on fact.

9.16 The Secretary of State considers that it is likely that applicants who have been resident in the UK, Channel Islands, the Isle of Man or the Republic of Ireland continuously during the 2-year period prior to their housing application will be habitually resident. In such cases, therefore, housing authorities may consider it unnecessary to make further enquiries to determine whether the person is habitually resident, unless there are other circumstances that need to be taken into account. A period of continuous residence in the UK, Channel Islands, the Isle of Man or the Republic of Ireland might include periods of temporary absence, e.g. visits abroad for holidays or to visit relatives. Where two years' continuous residency has not been established, housing authorities will need to conduct further enquiries to determine whether the applicant is habitually resident.

9.17 A person will not generally be habitually resident anywhere unless he or she has taken up residence and lived there for a period. There will be cases where the person concerned is not coming to the UK for the first time, and is resuming a previous period of habitual residence.

9.18 Annex 10 provides guidance on the factors that a housing authority should consider in determining whether an applicant is habitually resident.

Persons from Montserrat

9.19 The classes of persons (not being persons subject to immigration control) who are not required to be habitually resident in order to be eligible for assistance under Part 7 include a person who left Montserrat after 1 November 1995 because of the effect of volcanic activity there.

9.20 On 21 May 2002 most British overseas territories citizens, including those from Montserrat, became British Citizens. Since their new EU-style passport will not identify that they are from Montserrat, it has been recommended that they should also retain their old British Overseas Citizen passport, to help them demonstrate eligibility for, among other things, housing assistance in the UK.

Persons deported, expelled or removed to the UK from another country

9.21 Persons who are in the UK as a result of their deportation, expulsion or other removal by compulsion of law from another country to the UK will generally be UK nationals. (However, such persons could include EEA nationals, where the UK immigration authorities were satisfied that the person was settled in the UK and exercising EC Treaty rights prior to deportation from the third country.) Where deportation occurs, most countries will signal this in the person's passport and provide them with reasons for their removal. This should enable such persons to identify their circumstances when making an application for housing assistance.

PERSONS INELIGIBLE UNDER CERTAIN PROVISIONS BY VIRTUE OF SCHEDULE 3 TO THE NATIONALITY, IMMIGRATION AND ASYLUM ACT 2002

9.22 Section 54 of, and Schedule 3 to, the *Nationality, Immigration and Asylum Act 2002* have the effect of making certain applicants for housing assistance ineligible for accommodation under s.188(3) (*power to accommodate pending a review*) or s.204(4) (*power to accommodate pending an appeal to the county court*) of the 1996 Act. The following classes of person will be ineligible for assistance under those powers:

(i) *a person who has refugee status abroad*, i.e. a person:
  - who does not have the nationality of an EEA State, and
  - who the government of an EEA State other than the UK has determined is entitled to protection as a refugee under the Refugee Convention;

(ii) *a person who has the nationality of an EEA State other than the UK* (but see paragraph 9.23 below);

(iii) *a person who was (but is no longer) an asylum seeker and who fails to cooperate with removal directions* issued in respect of him or her;

(iv) *a person who is in the UK in breach of the immigration laws* (within the meaning of s.11 of the *Nationality, Immigration and Asylum Act 2002) and is not an asylum seeker;*

(v) *certain persons who are failed asylum seekers with dependent children*, where the Secretary of State has certified that, in his opinion, such a person has failed without reasonable excuse to take reasonable steps to leave the UK voluntarily or place himself or herself in a position where he or she is able to leave the UK voluntarily, and that person has received the Secretary of State's certificate more than 14 days previously;

(vi) *a person who is the dependant of a person who falls within class (i), (ii), (iii) or (v) above.*

9.23 **However, s.54 and Schedule 3 do not prevent the exercise of an authority's powers under s.188(3) and s.204(4) of the 1996 Act to the extent that such exercise is necessary for the purpose of avoiding a breach of a person's rights under the European Convention of Human Rights or rights under the EC Treaties.** Among other things, this means that a local authority can exercise these powers to accommodate an EEA national who has a right to reside in the UK under EC law (see Annex 12).

9.24 Paragraph 14 of Schedule 3 provides, among other things, that authorities must inform the Secretary of State where the powers under s.188(3) or s.204(4) apply, or may apply, to a person who is, or may come, within classes (iii), (iv) or (v) in paragraph 9.22 (by contacting the Home Office Immigration and Nationality Directorate).

9.25 For further guidance, local authorities should refer to Guidance to Local Authorities and Housing Authorities about the *Nationality, Immigration and Asylum Act*, Section 54 and Schedule 3, and the *Withholding and Withdrawal of Support (Travel Assistance and Temporary Accommodation) Regulations 2002*, issued by the Home Office.

ELIGIBILITY – LIST OF RELATED ANNEXES:

8 – How to contact the home Office Immigration and Nationality Directorate
9 – Asylum seekers

10 – The habitual residence test
11 – European groupings (EU, A8, EEA, Switzerland)
12 – Rights to reside in the UK derived from EC law
13 – Worker registration scheme

CHAPTER 10
Priority need

This chapter provides guidance on the categories of applicant who have a priority need for accommodation under the homelessness legislation.

10.1 Under the homelessness legislation, housing authorities must have a strategy for preventing homelessness and ensuring that accommodation and support are available to **anyone** in their district who is homeless or at risk of homelessness. They must also provide advice and assistance on housing and homelessness prevention to anyone in their district, free of charge. Stronger duties to secure accommodation exist for households who have a priority need for accommodation. Since 2002, the priority need categories have embraced a wider range of people whose age or background puts them at greater risk when homeless, including more single people.

10.2 The main homelessness duties in s.193(2) and s.195(2) of the 1996 Act (to secure accommodation or take reasonable steps to prevent the loss of accommodation) apply only to applicants who have a priority need for accommodation. Section 189(1) and the *Homelessness (Priority Need for Accommodation) (England) Order 2002* provide that the following categories of applicant have a priority need for accommodation:

i) a pregnant woman or a person with whom she resides or might reasonably be expected to reside (see paragraph 10.5);

ii) a person with whom dependent children reside or might reasonably be expected to reside (see paragraphs 10.6–10.11);

iii) a person who is vulnerable as a result of old age, mental illness or handicap or physical disability or other special reason, or with whom such a person resides or might reasonably be expected to reside (see paragraphs 10.12–10.18);

iv) a person aged 16 or 17 who is not a 'relevant child' or a child in need to whom a local authority owes a duty under section 20 of the *Children Act 1989* (see paragraphs 10.36–10.39);

v) a person under 21 who was (but is no longer) looked after, accommodated or fostered between the ages of 16 and 18 (except a person who is a 'relevant student') (see paragraphs 10.40–10.41);

vi) a person aged 21 or more who is vulnerable as a result of having been looked after, accommodated or fostered (except a person who is a 'relevant student') (see paragraphs 10.19–10.20);

vii) a person who is vulnerable as a result of having been a member of Her Majesty's regular naval, military or air forces (see paragraphs 10.21–10.23);

viii) a person who is vulnerable as a result of:

(a) having served a custodial sentence,

(b) having been committed for contempt of court or any other kindred offence, or

(c) having been remanded in custody; (see paragraphs 10.24–10.27)

ix) a person who is vulnerable as a result of ceasing to occupy accommodation because of violence from another person or threats of violence from another person which are likely to be carried out (see paragraphs 10.28–10.29);

x) a person who is vulnerable for any other special reason, or with whom such a person resides or might reasonably be expected to reside (see paragraphs 10.30–10.35);

xi) a person who is homeless, or threatened with homelessness, as a result of an emergency such as flood, fire or other disaster (see paragraph 10.42).

10.3 Inquiries as to whether an applicant has a priority need must be carried out in all cases where the housing authority has reason to believe that an applicant may be homeless or threatened with homelessness, and is eligible for assistance (s.184). Moreover, where the housing authority has reason to believe that the applicant is homeless, eligible for assistance and in priority need, they will have an immediate duty to secure interim accommodation, pending a decision on the case (see Chapter 7).

10.4 Once a housing authority has notified an applicant that he or she has a priority need and has been accepted as owed the main homelessness duty (s.193(2)) it cannot – unless the decision is subject to a request for a review – change the decision if the applicant subsequently ceases to have a priority need (e.g. because a dependent child leaves home). Any change of circumstance prior to the decision on the homelessness application should be taken into account. However, once all the relevant inquiries are completed, the housing authority should not defer making a decision on the case in anticipation of a possible change of circumstance. (See Chapter 19 for guidance on reviews.)

PREGNANT WOMEN

10.5 A pregnant woman, and anyone with whom she lives or might reasonably be expected to live, has a priority need for accommodation. This is regardless of the length of time that the woman has been pregnant. Housing authorities should seek normal confirmation of pregnancy, e.g. a letter from a medical professional, such as a midwife, should be adequate evidence of pregnancy. If a pregnant woman suffers a miscarriage or terminates her pregnancy during the assessment process the housing authority should consider whether she continues to have a priority need as a result of some other factor (e.g. she may be vulnerable as a result of an other special reason – see paragraph 10.30).

DEPENDENT CHILDREN

10.6 Applicants have a priority need if they have one or more dependent children who normally live with them or who might reasonably be expected to live with them. There must be actual dependence on the applicant, although the child need not be wholly and exclusively dependent on him or her. There must also be actual residence (or a reasonable expectation of residence) with some degree of permanence or regularity, rather than a temporary arrangement whereby the children are merely staying with the applicant for a limited period (see paragraphs 10.9 and 10.10). Similarly, the child need not be wholly and exclusively resident (or expected to reside wholly and exclusively) with the applicant.

10.7 The 1996 Act does not define dependent children, but housing authorities may wish to treat as dependent all children under 16, and all children aged 16–18 who are in, or are about to begin, full-time education or training or who for other reasons are unable to support themselves and who live at home. The meaning of dependency is not, however, limited to financial dependency. Thus, while children aged 16 and over who are in full-time employment and are financially independent of their parents would not normally be considered to be dependants, housing authorities should remember that such children may not be sufficiently mature to live independently of their parents, and there may be sound reasons for considering them to be dependent. Each case will need to be carefully considered according to the circumstances.

10.8 Dependent children need not necessarily be the applicant's own children but could, for example, be related to the applicant or his or her partner or be adopted or fostered by the applicant. There must, however, be some form of parent/child relationship.

10.9 Housing authorities may receive applications from a parent who is separated from his or her former spouse or partner. In some cases where parents separate, the court may make a residence order indicating with which parent the child normally resides. In such cases, the child may be considered to reside with the parent named in the order, and would not normally be expected to reside with the other parent. However, in many cases the parents come to an agreement themselves as to how the child is to be cared for, and a court order will not be made or required.

10.10 Residence does not have to be full-time and a child can be considered to reside with either parent even where he or she divides his or her time between both parents. However, as mentioned above, there must be some regularity to the arrangement. If the child is not currently residing with the applicant, the housing authority will need to decide whether, in the circumstances, it would be reasonable for the child to do so. An agreement between a child's parents, or a joint residence order by a court, may not automatically lead to a conclusion that it would be reasonable for the child to reside with the parent making the application, and housing authorities will need to consider each case individually. However, housing authorities should remember that where parents separate, it will often be in the best interests of the child to maintain a relationship with both parents.

10.11 Where the applicant's children are being looked after by a social services authority – for example, they are subject to a care order or are being accommodated under a voluntary agreement – and they are not currently living with the applicant, liaison with the social services authority will be essential. Joint consideration with social services will ensure that the best interests of the applicant and the children are served. This may, for example, enable a family to be reunited subject to suitable accommodation being available.

VULNERABILITY

10.12 A person has a priority need for accommodation if he or she is vulnerable as a result of:

i) old age;
ii) mental illness or learning disability (mental handicap) or physical disability;
iii) having been looked after, accommodated or fostered and is aged 21 or more;
iv) having been a member of Her Majesty's regular naval, military or air forces;
v) having been in custody or detention;
vi) ceasing to occupy accommodation because of violence from another person or threats of violence from another person which are likely to be carried out; or
vii) any other special reason.

In the case of i), ii) and vii) only, a person with whom a vulnerable person lives or might reasonably be expected to live also has a priority need for accommodation and can therefore make an application on behalf of themselves and that vulnerable person.

10.13 **It is a matter of judgement whether the applicant's circumstances make him or her vulnerable. When determining whether an applicant in any of the categories set out in paragraph 10.12 is vulnerable, the local authority should consider whether, when homeless, the applicant would be less able to fend for him/herself than an ordinary homeless person so that he or she would suffer injury or detriment, in circumstances where a less vulnerable person would be able to cope without harmful effects.**

10.14 **Some of the factors which may be relevant to determining whether a particular category of applicant is vulnerable are set out below. The assessment of an applicant's ability to cope is a composite one taking into account all of the circumstances. The applicant's vulnerability must be assessed on the basis that he or she is or will become homeless, and not on his or her ability to fend for him or herself while still housed.**

Old age

10.15 Old age alone is not sufficient for the applicant to be deemed vulnerable. However, it may be that as a result of old age the applicant would be less able to fend for him or herself as provided in paragraph 10.13 above. All applications from people aged over 60 need to be considered carefully, particularly where the applicant is leaving tied accommodation. However, housing authorities should not use 60 (or any other age) as a fixed age beyond which vulnerability occurs automatically (or below which it can be ruled out); each case will need to be considered in the light of the individual circumstances.

Mental illness or learning disability or physical disability

10.16 Housing authorities should have regard to any advice from medical professionals, social services or current providers of care and support. In cases where there is doubt as to the extent of any vulnerability authorities may also consider seeking a clinical opinion. However, the final decision on the question of vulnerability will rest with the housing authority. In considering whether such applicants are vulnerable, authorities will need to take account of all relevant factors including:

i) the nature and extent of the illness and/or disability which may render the applicant vulnerable;
ii) the relationship between the illness and/or disability and the individual's housing difficulties; and
iii) the relationship between the illness and/or disability and other factors such as drug/alcohol misuse, offending behaviour, challenging behaviours, age and personality disorder.

10.17 Assessment of vulnerability due to mental health will require close co-operation between housing authorities, social services authorities and mental health agencies. Housing authorities should consider carrying out joint assessments or using a trained mental health practitioner as part of an assessment team. Mental Health NHS Trusts and local authorities have an express duty to implement a specifically tailored care programme (the Care Programme Approach – CPA) for all patients considered for discharge from psychiatric hospitals and all new patients accepted by the specialist psychiatric services (see *Effective care co-ordination in mental health services: modernising the care programme approach*, DH, 1999). **People discharged from psychiatric hospitals and local authority hostels for people with mental health problems are likely to be vulnerable.** Effective, timely, liaison between housing, social services and NHS Trusts will be essential in such cases but authorities will also need to be sensitive to direct approaches from former patients who have been discharged and may be homeless.

10.18 Learning or physical disabilities or long-term acute illnesses, such as those defined by the *Disability Discrimination Act 1995*, which impinge on the applicant's housing situation and give rise to vulnerability may be readily discernible, but advice from health or social services staff should be sought, wherever necessary.

Having been looked after, accommodated or fostered and aged 21 or over

10.19 A person aged 21 or over who is vulnerable as a result of having been looked after, accommodated or fostered has a priority need (other than a person who is a 'relevant student'). The terms 'looked after, accommodated or fostered' are set out in the *Children Act 1989* (s.24) and include any person who has been:

i) looked after by a local authority (i.e. has been subject to a care order or accommodated under a voluntary agreement);
ii) accommodated by or on behalf of a voluntary organisation;
iii) accommodated in a private children's home;
iv) accommodated for a consecutive period of at least three months:
   - by a health authority, special health authority, primary care trust or local education authority, or
   - in any care home or independent hospital or in any accommodation provided by a National Health Service trust; or
v) privately fostered.

A 'relevant student' means a care leaver under 24 to whom section 24B(3) of the *Children Act 1989* applies, and who is in full-time further or higher education and whose term-time accommodation is not available during a vacation. Under s.24B(5), where a social services authority is satisfied that a person is someone to whom section 24B(3) applies and needs accommodation during a vacation they must provide accommodation or the means to enable it to be secured.

10.20 Housing authorities will need to make enquiries into an applicant's childhood history to establish whether he or she has been looked after, accommodated or fostered in any of these ways. If so, they will need to consider whether he or she is vulnerable as a result. In determining whether there is vulnerability (as set out in paragraph 10.13 above), factors that a housing authority may wish to consider are:

i) the length of time that the applicant was looked after, accommodated or fostered;
ii) the reasons why the applicant was looked after, accommodated or fostered;
iii) the length of time since the applicant was looked after, accommodated or fostered, and whether the applicant had been able to obtain and/or maintain accommodation during any of that period;
iv) whether the applicant has any existing support networks, particularly including family, friends or mentor.

Having been a member of the armed forces

10.21 A person who is vulnerable as a result of having been a member of Her Majesty's regular armed forces has a priority need for accommodation. Former members of the armed forces will include a person who was previously a member of the regular naval, military or air forces, including a person who has been released following detention in a military corrective training centre.

10.22 The principal responsibility for providing housing information and advice to Service personnel lies with the armed forces up to the point of discharge and these services are delivered through the Joint Service Housing Advice Office (telephone: 01722 436575). Some people, who have served in the armed forces for a long period, and those who are medically discharged, may be offered assistance with resettlement by Ministry of Defence (MOD) resettlement staff. The MOD issues a *Certificate of Cessation of Entitlement to Occupy Service Living Accommodation* (see examples at Annexes 14 and 15) six months before discharge. Applications from former members of the armed forces will need to be considered carefully to assess whether the applicant is vulnerable as a result of having served in the armed forces.

10.23 In considering whether former members of the armed forces are vulnerable (as set out in paragraph 10.13 above) as a result of their time spent in the forces, a housing authority may wish to take into account the following factors:

i) the length of time the applicant spent in the armed forces (although authorities should not assume that vulnerability could not occur as a result of a short period of service);
ii) the type of service the applicant was engaged in (those on active service may find it more difficult to cope with civilian life);
iii) whether the applicant spent any time in a military hospital (this could be an indicator of a serious health problem or of post-traumatic stress);
iv) whether HM Forces' medical and welfare advisers have judged an individual to be particularly vulnerable in their view and have issued a Medical History Release Form (F Med 133) giving a summary of the circumstances

causing that vulnerability;

v) the length of time since the applicant left the armed forces, and whether he or she had been able to obtain and/or maintain accommodation during that time;

vi) whether the applicant has any existing support networks, particularly by way of family or friends.

Having been in custody or detention

10.24 A person who is vulnerable as a result of having served a custodial sentence, been committed for contempt of court or remanded in custody has a priority need for accommodation. This category applies to applicants who are vulnerable as a result of having:

i) served a custodial sentence within the meaning of the *Powers of Criminal Courts (Sentences) Act 2000*, s.76. (This includes sentences of imprisonment for those aged 21 or over and detention for those aged under 21, including children.);

ii) been committed for contempt of court or any other kindred offence (kindred offence refers to statutory provisions for contempt as opposed to the inherent jurisdiction of the court, e.g. under the *Contempt of Court Act 1981*, s.12 (magistrates' court) and *County Court Act 1984*, s.118 (county court)). (Committal may arise, e.g. where an applicant has breached a civil injunction.);

iii) been remanded in custody within the meaning of the *Powers of Criminal Courts (Sentencing) Act 2000*, s.88(1)(b), (c) or (d), i.e. remanded in or committed to custody by an order of a court; remanded or committed to housing authority accommodation under the *Children and Young Persons Act 1969* and placed and kept in secure accommodation; or, remanded, admitted or removed to hospital under the *Mental Health Act 1983*, ss.35, 36, 38 or 48.

10.25 Applicants have a priority need for accommodation only if they are vulnerable (see paragraph 10.13 above) as a result of having been in custody or detention. In determining whether applicants who fall within one of the descriptions in paragraph 10.24 are vulnerable as a result of their period in custody or detention, a housing authority may wish to take into account the following factors:

i) the length of time the applicant served in custody or detention (although authorities should not assume that vulnerability could not occur as a result of a short period in custody or detention);

ii) whether the applicant is receiving supervision from a criminal justice agency e.g. the Probation Service, Youth Offending Team or Drug Intervention Programme. Housing authorities should have regard to any advice from criminal justice agency staff regarding their view of the applicant's general vulnerability, but the final decision on the question of vulnerability for the purposes of the homelessness legislation will rest with the housing authority;

iii) the length of time since the applicant was released from custody or detention, and the extent to which the applicant had been able to obtain and/or maintain accommodation during that time;

iv) whether the applicant has any existing support networks, for example family or friends, and how much of a positive influence these networks are likely to be in the applicant's life.

10.26 In many cases a housing needs assessment may have been completed in respect of offenders by the Probation Service, Prison Services, Youth Offending Team, Criminal Justice Intervention Team or a voluntary organisation acting on behalf of one of these agencies. Where such an assessment identifies an individual as needing help in finding accommodation and judges the individual to be particularly vulnerable and the applicant makes an application for housing assistance, this information will be made available to the relevant housing authority.

10.27 In addition to the question of priority need, when assessing applicants in this client group difficult issues may arise as to whether the applicant has become homeless intentionally. Housing authorities must consider each case in the light of all the facts and circumstances. **Housing authorities are reminded that they cannot adopt a blanket policy of assuming that homelessness will be intentional or unintentional in any given circumstances** (see Chapter 11 for guidance on intentional homelessness).

Having left accommodation because of violence

10.28 A person has a priority need if he or she is vulnerable (as set out in paragraph 10.13 above) as a result of having to leave accommodation because of violence from another person, or threats of violence from another person that are likely to be carried out. It will usually be apparent from the assessment of the reason for homelessness whether the applicant has had to leave accommodation because of violence or threats of violence (see Chapter 8 for further guidance on whether it is reasonable to continue to occupy accommodation). **In cases involving violence, the safety of the applicant and ensuring confidentiality must be of paramount concern.** It is not only domestic violence that is relevant, but all forms of violence, including racially motivated violence or threats of violence likely to be carried out. Inquiries of the perpetrators of violence should not be made. In assessing whether it is likely that threats of violence are likely to be carried out, a housing authority should only take into account the probability of violence, and not actions which the applicant could take (such as injunctions against the perpetrators). See Chapter 6 for further guidance on dealing with cases involving violence.

10.29 In considering whether applicants are vulnerable as a result of leaving accommodation because of violence or threats of violence likely to be carried out, a housing authority may wish to take into account the following factors:

i) the nature of the violence or threats of violence (there may have been a single but significant incident or a number of incidents over an extended period of time which have had a cumulative effect);
ii) the impact and likely effects of the violence or threats of violence on the applicant's current and future well being;
iii) whether the applicant has any existing support networks, particularly by way of family or friends.

Other special reason

10.30 Section 189(1)(c) provides that a person has a priority need for accommodation if he or she is vulnerable for any 'other special reason'. A person with whom such a vulnerable person normally lives or might reasonably be expected to live also has a priority need. The legislation envisages that vulnerability can arise because of factors that are not expressly provided for in statute. Each application must be considered in the light of the facts and circumstances of the case. Moreover, other special reasons giving rise to vulnerability are not restricted to the physical or mental characteristics of a person. Where applicants have a need for support but have no family or friends on whom they can depend they may be vulnerable as a result of another special reason.

10.31 **Housing authorities must keep an open mind and should avoid blanket policies that assume that particular groups of applicants will, or will not, be vulnerable for any 'other special reason'.** Where a housing authority considers that an applicant may be vulnerable, it will be important to make an in-depth assessment of the circumstances of the case. Guidance on certain categories of applicants who may be vulnerable as a result of any 'other special reason' is given below. The list below is not exhaustive and housing authorities must ensure that they give proper consideration to every application on the basis of the individual circumstances. In addition, housing authorities will need to be aware that an applicant may be considered vulnerable for any 'other special reason' because of a combination of factors which taken alone may not necessarily lead to a decision that they are vulnerable (e.g. drug and alcohol problems, common mental health problems, a history of sleeping rough, no previous experience of managing a tenancy).

10.32 *Chronically sick people, including people with AIDS and HIV-related illnesses.* People in this group may be vulnerable not only because their illness has progressed to the point of physical or mental disability (when they are likely to fall within one of the specified categories of priority need) but also because the manifestations or effects of their illness, or common attitudes to it, make it very difficult for them to find and maintain stable or suitable accommodation. Whilst this may be particularly true of people with AIDS, it could also apply in the case of people infected with HIV (who may not have any overt signs or symptoms) if the nature of their infection is known.

10.33 *Young people.* The 2002 Order makes specific provision for certain categories of young homeless people (see paragraph 10.2). However, there are many other young people who fall outside these categories but who could become homeless and be vulnerable in certain circumstances. When assessing applications from young people under 25 who do not fall within any of the specific categories of priority need, housing authorities should give careful consideration to the possibility of vulnerability. Most young people can expect a degree of support from families, friends or an institution (e.g. a college or university) with the practicalities and costs of finding, establishing, and managing a home for the first time. But some young people, particularly those who are forced to leave the parental home or who cannot remain there because they are being subjected to violence or sexual abuse, may lack this back-up network and be less able than others to establish and maintain a home for themselves. Moreover, a young person on the streets without adequate financial resources to live independently may be at risk of abuse or prostitution. See Chapter 12 for further guidance on 16 and 17 year olds.

10.34 *People fleeing harassment.* Authorities should consider whether harassment falls under the general definition of domestic violence (see definition in Chapter 8 and paragraphs 10.28–10.29 above which give guidance on vulnerability as a result of violence). In some cases, however, severe harassment may fall short of actual violence or threats of violence likely to be carried out. Housing authorities should consider carefully whether applicants who have fled their home because of non-violent forms of harassment, for example verbal abuse or damage to property, are vulnerable as a result. Careful consideration should be given to applicants who may be at risk of witness intimidation. In some criminal cases the police may provide alternative accommodation for witnesses, but usually this will apply for the duration of the trial only. Witnesses may have had to give up their home or may feel unable to return to it when the trial has finished.

10.35 *Former asylum seekers.* Former asylum seekers who have been granted refugee status or exceptional leave to remain, humanitarian protection, or discretionary leave will be eligible for homelessness assistance and may be at risk of homelessness as a result of having to leave accommodation that had been provided for them (e.g. by the National Asylum Support Service) in the period before a decision was reached on their asylum claim. They may well have experienced persecution or trauma in their country of origin or severe hardship in their efforts to reach the UK and may be vulnerable as a result. In assessing applications from this client group, housing authorities should give careful consideration to the possibility that they may be vulnerable as a result of another special reason. Authorities should be sensitive to the fact that former asylum seekers may be reluctant to discuss, or have difficulty discussing, their potential vulnerability, if, for example, they have experienced humiliating, painful or traumatic circumstances such as torture, rape or the killing of a family member.

16 AND 17 YEAR OLDS

10.36 All 16 and 17 year old homeless applicants have a priority need for accommodation except those who are:

i) a relevant child, or
ii) a child in need who is owed a duty under s.20 of the *Children Act 1989.*

Relevant child or child in need owed a duty under s.20 of the 1989 Act

10.37 A relevant child is a child aged 16 or 17 who has been looked after by a local authority for at least 13 weeks since the age of 14 and has been looked after at some time while 16 or 17 and who is not currently being looked after (i.e. an 'eligible child' for the purposes of paragraph 19B of Schedule 2 to the *Children Act 1989*). In addition, a child is also a relevant child if he or she would have been looked after by the local authority as an eligible child but for the fact that on his or her 16th birthday he or she was detained through the criminal justice system, or in hospital, or if he or she has returned home on family placement and that has broken down (see the *Children Act 1989*, s.23A and the *Children (Leaving Care) Regulations 2001* regulation 4).

10.38 The *Children Act 1989* (s.20(3)) places a duty on children's services authorities to provide accommodation for a child in need aged 16 or over whose welfare is otherwise likely to be seriously prejudiced if they do not provide accommodation; and s.20(1) places a duty on children's services authorities to provide accommodation for children in need in certain other circumstances.

10.39 Responsibility for providing suitable accommodation for a relevant child or a child in need to whom a local authority owes a duty under s.20 of the *Children*

Act 1989 rests with the children's services authority. In cases where a housing authority considers that a section 20 duty is owed, they should verify this with the relevant children's services authority. In all cases of uncertainty as to whether a 16 or 17 year old applicant may be a relevant child or a child in need, the housing authority should contact the relevant children's services authority and, where necessary, should provide interim accommodation under s.188, pending clarification. A framework for joint assessment of 16 and 17 year olds will need to be established by housing and children's services authorities (and housing and children's services departments within unitary authorities) to facilitate the seamless discharge of duties and appropriate services to this client group.

See Chapter 12 for more detailed guidance on 16 and 17 year olds.

HAVING BEEN LOOKED AFTER, ACCOMMODATED OR FOSTERED AND AGED UNDER 21

10.40 A person under 21 who was (but is no longer) looked after, accommodated or fostered between the ages of 16 and 18 has a priority need for accommodation (other than a person who is a 'relevant student'). The terms 'looked after', 'accommodated' or 'fostered' are set out in the *Children Act 1989* (s.24) and include any person who has been:

i) looked after by a local authority (i.e. has been subject to a care order or accommodated under a voluntary agreement);
ii) accommodated by or on behalf of a voluntary organisation;
iii) accommodated in a private children's home;
iv) accommodated for a consecutive period of at least three months:
   - by a health authority, special health authority, primary care trust or local education authority, or
   - in any care home or independent hospital or in any accommodation provided by a National Health Service trust; or
v) privately fostered.

A 'relevant student' means a care leaver under 24 to whom section 24B(3) of the *Children Act 1989* applies, and who is in full-time further or higher education and whose term-time accommodation is not available during a vacation. Under s.24B(5), where a social services authority is satisfied that a person is someone to whom s.24B(3) applies and needs accommodation during a vacation they must provide accommodation or the means to enable it to be secured.

10.41 Housing authorities will need to liaise with the social services authority when dealing with homeless applicants who may fall within this category of priority need.

HOMELESS AS A RESULT OF AN EMERGENCY

10.42 Applicants have a priority need for accommodation if they are homeless or threatened with homelessness as a result of an emergency such as fire, flood or other disaster. To qualify as an 'other disaster' the disaster must be in the nature of a flood or fire, and involve some form of physical damage or threat of damage. Applicants have a priority need by reason of such an emergency whether or not they have dependent children or are vulnerable for any reason.

CHAPTER 11
Intentional homelessness

11.1 **This chapter provides guidance on determining whether an applicant became homeless, or threatened with homelessness,** *intentionally* or *unintentionally*.

11.2 The duty owed towards those who are homeless, or threatened with homelessness, and who have a priority need for accommodation will depend upon whether they became homeless, or threatened with homelessness, intentionally or unintentionally. Section 191 defines the circumstances in which an applicant is to be regarded as having become homeless intentionally. Section 196 frames the same definitions in regard to someone who is threatened with homelessness.

11.3 The duty owed to applicants who have a priority need for accommodation but have become homeless, or threatened with homelessness, intentionally is less than the duty owed to those who have a priority need for accommodation and have become homeless, or threatened with homelessness, unintentionally. This recognises the general expectation that, wherever possible, people should take responsibility for their own accommodation needs and ensure that they do not behave in a way which might lead to the loss of their accommodation.

11.4 Where a housing authority finds an applicant to be homeless, or threatened with homelessness, intentionally they have a duty to provide the applicant (or secure that the applicant is provided) with advice and assistance in any attempts he or she may make to secure that accommodation becomes available (or does not cease to be available) for his or her occupation. Before this advice and assistance is given, the authority must assess the applicant's housing needs. The advice and assistance must include information about the likely availability in the authority's district of types of accommodation appropriate to the applicant's housing needs (including, in particular, the location and sources of such types of accommodation). Authorities should consider what best advice and assistance the authority could provide, for example, providing information about applying for social housing, local lettings in the private rented sector, rent deposit schemes or housing benefit eligibility – to help the applicant avoid homelessness or secure accommodation (see Chapter 2 for further guidance on preventing homelessness). Where such an applicant also has a priority need for accommodation the authority will also have a duty to secure accommodation for such period as will give the applicant a reasonable opportunity of securing accommodation for his or her occupation. See Chapter 14 for guidance on the main duties owed to applicants on completion of inquiries.

11.5 It is for housing authorities to satisfy themselves in each individual case whether an applicant is homeless or threatened with homelessness intentionally. Generally, it is not for applicants to 'prove their case'. The exception is where an applicant seeks to establish that, as a member of a household previously found to be homeless intentionally, he or she did not acquiesce in the behaviour that led to homelessness. In such cases, the applicant will need to demonstrate that he or she was not involved in the acts or omissions that led to homelessness, and did not have control over them.

11.6 **Housing authorities must not adopt general policies which seek to predefine circumstances that do or do not amount to intentional homelessness**

or threatened homelessness (for example, intentional homelessness should not be assumed in cases where an application is made following a period in custody – see paragraph 11.14). In each case, housing authorities must form a view in the light of all their inquiries about that particular case. Where the original incident of homelessness occurred some years earlier and the facts are unclear, it may not be possible for the housing authority to satisfy themselves that the applicant became homeless intentionally. In such cases, the applicant should be considered to be unintentionally homeless.

DEFINITIONS OF INTENTIONAL HOMELESSNESS

11.7 Sections 191(1) and 196(1) provide that a person becomes homeless, or threatened with homelessness, intentionally if:

i) he or she deliberately does or fails to do anything in consequence of which he or she ceases to occupy accommodation (or the likely result of which is that he or she will be forced to leave accommodation),
ii) the accommodation is available for his or her occupation, and
iii) it would have been reasonable for him or her to continue to occupy the accommodation.

However, for this purpose, an act or omission made in good faith by someone who was unaware of any relevant fact must not be treated as deliberate (see paragraph 11.20).

11.8 Sections 191(3) and 196(3) provide that a person must be treated as homeless, or threatened with homelessness, intentionally if:

i) the person enters into an arrangement under which he or she is required to cease to occupy accommodation which it would have been reasonable for the person to continue to occupy,
ii) the purpose of the arrangement is to enable the person to become entitled to assistance under Part 7, and
iii) there is no other good reason why the person is homeless or threatened with homelessness.

WHOSE CONDUCT RESULTS IN INTENTIONAL HOMELESSNESS?

11.9 Every applicant is entitled to individual consideration of his or her application. This includes applicants where another member of their family or household has made, or is making, a separate application. It is the **applicant** who must deliberately have done or failed to do something which resulted in homelessness or threatened homelessness. Where a housing authority has found an applicant to be homeless intentionally, nothing in the 1996 Act prevents another member of his or her household from making a separate application. Situations may arise where one or more members of a household found to be intentionally homeless were not responsible for the actions or omissions that led to the homelessness. For example, a person may have deliberately failed to pay the rent or defaulted on the mortgage payments, which resulted in homelessness or threatened homelessness, against the wishes or without the knowledge of his or her partner. However, where applicants were not directly responsible for the act or omission which led to their family or household becoming homeless, but they acquiesced in that behaviour, then they may be treated as having become homeless intentionally themselves. In considering whether an applicant has acquiesced in certain behaviour, the Secretary of

State recommends that the housing authority take into account whether the applicant could reasonably be expected to have taken that position through a fear of actual or probable violence.

CESSATION OF OCCUPATION

11.10 For intentional homelessness to be established there must have been actual occupation of accommodation which has ceased. However, occupation need not necessarily involve continuous occupation at all times, provided the accommodation was at the disposal of the applicant and available for his or her occupation. The accommodation which has been lost can be outside the UK.

CONSEQUENCE OF A DELIBERATE ACT OR OMISSION

11.11 For homelessness, or threatened homelessness, to be intentional it must be a consequence of a deliberate act or omission. Having established that there was a deliberate act or omission, the housing authority will need to decide whether the loss of the applicant's home, or the likelihood of its loss, is the reasonable result of that act or omission. This is a matter of cause and effect. An example would be where a person voluntarily gave up settled accommodation that it would have been reasonable for them to continue to occupy, moved into alternative accommodation of a temporary or unsettled nature and subsequently became homeless when required to leave the alternative accommodation. Housing authorities will, therefore, need to look back to the last period of settled accommodation and the reasons why the applicant left that accommodation, to determine whether the current incidence of homelessness is the result of a deliberate act or omission.

11.12 Where a person becomes homeless intentionally, that condition may persist until the link between the causal act or omission and the intentional homelessness has been broken. It could be broken, for example, by a period in settled accommodation which follows the intentional homelessness. Whether accommodation is settled will depend on the circumstances of the particular case. Factors such as security of tenure and length of residence will be relevant. It has been established that a period in settled accommodation after an incidence of intentional homelessness would make the deliberate act or omission which led to that homelessness irrelevant in the event of a subsequent application for housing assistance. Conversely, occupation of accommodation that was merely temporary rather than settled, for example, staying with friends on an insecure basis, may not be sufficient to break the link with the earlier intentional homelessness. However, a period in settled accommodation is not necessarily the only way in which a link with the earlier intentional homelessness may be broken: some other event, such as the break-up of a marriage, may be sufficient.

Probability of violence

11.13 In cases where there is a probability of violence against an applicant if they continue, or had continued, to occupy their accommodation, and the applicant was aware of measures that could have been taken to prevent or mitigate the risk of violence but decided not to take them, their decision cannot be taken as having caused the probability of violence, and thus, indirectly, having caused the homelessness. Authorities must not assume that measures which could have been taken to prevent actual or threatened violence would necessarily have been effective.

Ex-offenders

11.14 Some ex-offenders may apply for accommodation or assistance in obtaining accommodation following a period in custody or detention because they have been unable to retain their previous accommodation, due to that period in custody or detention. In considering whether such an applicant is homeless intentionally, the housing authority will have to decide whether, taking into account all the circumstances, there was a likelihood that ceasing to occupy the accommodation could reasonably have been regarded at the time as a likely consequence of committing the offence.

Former members of the armed forces

11.15 Where service personnel are required to vacate service quarters as a result of taking up an option to give notice to leave the service, and in so doing are acting in compliance with their contractual engagement, the Secretary of State considers that they should not be considered to have become homeless intentionally.

DELIBERATE ACT OR OMISSION

11.16 For homelessness to be intentional, the act or omission that led to homelessness must have been deliberate, and applicants must always be given the opportunity to explain such behaviour. An act or omission should not generally be treated as deliberate, even where deliberately carried out, if it is forced upon the applicant through no fault of their own. Moreover, an act or omission made in good faith where someone is genuinely ignorant of a relevant fact must not be treated as deliberate (see paragraph 11.24).

11.17 Generally, an act or omission should not be considered deliberate where:

i) the act or omission was non-payment of rent which was the result of housing benefit delays, or financial difficulties which were beyond the applicant's control;
ii) the housing authority has reason to believe the applicant is incapable of managing his or her affairs, for example, by reason of age, mental illness or disability;
iii) the act or omission was the result of limited mental capacity; or a temporary aberration or aberrations caused by mental illness, frailty, or an assessed substance abuse problem;
iv) the act or omission was made when the applicant was under duress;
v) imprudence or lack of foresight on the part of an applicant led to homelessness but the act or omission was in good faith.

11.18 An applicant's actions would not amount to intentional homelessness where he or she has lost his or her home, or was obliged to sell it, because of rent or mortgage arrears resulting from significant financial difficulties, and the applicant was genuinely unable to keep up the rent or mortgage payments even after claiming benefits, and no further financial help was available.

11.19 Where an applicant has lost a former home due to rent arrears, the reasons why the arrears accrued should be fully explored. Similarly, in cases which involve mortgagors, housing authorities will need to look at the reasons for mortgage arrears together with the applicant's ability to pay the mortgage commitment when it was taken on, given the applicant's financial circumstances at the time.

11.20 Examples of acts or omissions which may be regarded as deliberate (unless any of the circumstances set out in paragraph 11.17 apply) include the following, where someone:

i) chooses to sell his or her home in circumstances where he or she is under no risk of losing it;
ii) has lost his or her home because of wilful and persistent refusal to pay rent or mortgage payments;
iii) could be said to have significantly neglected his or her affairs having disregarded sound advice from qualified persons;
iv) voluntarily surrenders adequate accommodation in this country or abroad which it would have been reasonable for the applicant to continue to occupy;
v) is evicted because of his or her anti-social behaviour, for example by nuisance to neighbours, harassment etc.;
vi) is evicted because of violence or threats of violence by them towards another person;
vii) leaves a job with tied accommodation and the circumstances indicate that it would have been reasonable for him or her to continue in the employment and reasonable to continue to occupy the accommodation (but note paragraph 11.15).

AVAILABLE FOR OCCUPATION

11.21 For homelessness to be intentional the accommodation must have been available for the applicant and anyone reasonably expected to live with him or her. Further guidance on 'availability for occupation' is provided in Chapter 8.

REASONABLE TO CONTINUE TO OCCUPY THE ACCOMMODATION

11.22 An applicant cannot be treated as intentionally homeless unless it would have been reasonable for him or her to have continued to occupy the accommodation. Guidance on 'reasonable to continue to occupy' is provided in Chapter 8. It will be necessary for the housing authority to give careful consideration to the circumstances of the applicant and the household, in each case, and with particular care in cases where violence has been alleged.

11.23 Authorities are reminded that, where the applicant has fled his or her home because of violence or threats of violence likely to be carried out, and has failed to pursue legal remedies against the perpetrator(s) which might have prevented the violence or threat of violence, although these decisions (to leave the home and not pursue legal remedies) may be deliberate, the homelessness would not be intentional if it would not have been reasonable for the applicant to continue to occupy the home.

ACTS OR OMISSIONS IN GOOD FAITH

11.24 Acts or omissions made in good faith where someone was genuinely unaware of a relevant fact must not be regarded as deliberate. Provided that the applicant has acted in good faith, there is no requirement that ignorance of the relevant fact be reasonable.

11.25 A general example of an act made in good faith would be a situation where someone gave up possession of accommodation in the belief that they had no legal right to continue to occupy the accommodation and, therefore, it would not be reasonable for them to continue to occupy it. This could apply where someone leaves rented accommodation in the private sector having received a valid notice to quit or notice that the assured shorthold tenancy has come to an end and the landlord requires possession of the property, and the former tenant was genuinely unaware that he or she had a right to remain until the court granted an order and warrant for possession.

11.26 Where there was dishonesty there could be no question of an act or omission having been made in good faith.

11.27 Other examples of acts or omissions that could be made in good faith might include situations where:

i) a person gets into rent arrears, being unaware that he or she may be entitled to housing benefit or other social security benefits;

ii) an owner-occupier faced with foreclosure or possession proceedings to which there is no defence, sells before the mortgagee recovers possession through the courts or surrenders the property to the lender; or

iii) a tenant, faced with possession proceedings to which there would be no defence, and where the granting of a possession order would be mandatory, surrenders the property to the landlord.

In (iii) although the housing authority may consider that it would have been reasonable for the tenant to continue to occupy the accommodation, the act should not be regarded as deliberate if the tenant made the decision to leave the accommodation in ignorance of material facts, e.g. the general pressure on the authority for housing assistance.

APPLICANT ENTERS INTO AN ARRANGEMENT

11.28 Housing authorities will need to be alert to the possibility of collusion by which a person may claim that he or she is obliged to leave accommodation in order to take advantage of the homelessness legislation. Some parents and children, for example, may seek to take advantage of the fact that 16 and 17 year old applicants have a priority need for accommodation. Collusion is not confined to those staying with friends or relatives but can also occur between landlords and tenants. Housing authorities, while relying on experience, nonetheless need to be satisfied that collusion exists, and must not rely on hearsay or unfounded suspicions. For collusion to amount to intentional homelessness, s.191(3) specifies that there should be no other good reason for the applicant's homelessness. Examples of other good reasons include overcrowding or an obvious breakdown in relations between the applicant and his or her host or landlord. In some cases involving collusion the applicant may not actually be homeless, if there is no genuine need for the applicant to leave the accommodation. See paragraphs 8.9–8.12 for further guidance on applicants asked to leave by family or friends.

FAMILIES WITH CHILDREN UNDER 18

11.29 It is important that social services are alerted as quickly as possible to cases where the applicant has children under 18 and the housing authority considers the applicant may be homeless, or threatened with homelessness, intentionally. Section 213A(2) therefore requires housing authorities to have arrangements in place to ensure that all such applicants are invited to agree to the housing authority notifying the social services authority of the essential facts of their case. The arrangements must also provide that, where consent is given, the social services authority are made aware of the essential facts and, in due course, of the subsequent decision on the homelessness case. See Chapter 13 for further guidance on section 213A.

FURTHER APPLICATIONS FOR ASSISTANCE

11.30 There is no period of disqualification if someone wants to make a fresh application after being found intentionally homeless. Where a person whose application has just been decided makes a fresh application, the authority will need to decide whether there are any new facts in the fresh application which render it different from the earlier application. If no new facts are revealed, or any new facts are of a trivial nature, the authority would not be required to consider the new application. However, where the fresh application does reveal substantive new facts, the authority must treat the fresh application in the same way as it would any other application for accommodation or assistance in obtaining accommodation. Therefore, if the authority have reason to believe that the person is homeless or threatened with homelessness, the authority must make inquiries under s.184 and decide whether any interim duty is owed under s.188(1). See Chapter 6 for guidance on inquiries and Chapter 7 for guidance on the interim duty.

CHAPTER 12
16 & 17 Year olds

12.1 **This chapter provides guidance on specific duties towards 16 and 17 year old applicants.**

Priority need

12.2 All 16 and 17 year old homeless applicants have a priority need for accommodation except those who are:

i) a relevant child, or

ii) a child in need who is owed a duty under s.20 of the *Children Act 1989*.

See Chapter 10 for more detailed guidance on priority need.

Relevant child or child in need owed a duty under s.20 of the 1989 Act

12.3 A relevant child is a child aged 16 or 17 who has been looked after by a local authority for at least 13 weeks since the age of 14 and has been looked after at some time while 16 or 17 and who is not currently being looked after (i.e. an 'eligible child' for the purposes of paragraph 19B of Schedule 2 to the *Children Act 1989*). In addition, a child is also a relevant child if he or she would have been looked after by the local authority as an eligible child but for the fact that on his or her 16th birthday he or she was detained through the criminal justice system, or in hospital, or if he or she has returned home on family placement and that has broken down (see the *Children Act 1989*, s.23A and the *Children (Leaving Care) Regulations 2001*, Regulation 4).

12.4 The *Children Act 1989* (s.20(3)) places a duty on children's services authorities to provide accommodation for a child in need aged 16 or over whose welfare is otherwise likely to be seriously prejudiced if they do not provide accommodation; and s.20(1) places a duty on children's services authorities to provide accommodation for children in need in certain other circumstances.

12.5 Responsibility for providing suitable accommodation for a relevant child or a child in need to whom a local authority owes a duty under s.20 of the *Children Act 1989* rests with the children's services authority. In cases where a housing authority considers that a s.20 duty is owed, they should verify this with the relevant children's services authority.

12.6 In all cases of uncertainty as to whether a 16 or 17 year old applicant may be a relevant child or a child in need, the housing authority should contact the relevant children's services authority and, where necessary, should provide interim accommodation under s.188, pending clarification. A framework for joint assessment of 16 and 17 year olds will need to be established by housing and children's services authorities (and housing and children's services departments within unitary authorities) to facilitate the seamless discharge of duties and appropriate services to this client group.

Family relationships

12.7 The Secretary of State considers that, generally, it will be in the best interests of 16 and 17 year olds to live in the family home, unless it would be unsafe or unsuitable for them to do so because they would be at risk of violence or abuse. It is not unusual for 16 and 17 year olds to have a turbulent relationship with their family and this can lead to temporary disagreements and even temporary estrangement. Where such disagreements look likely to lead to actual or threatened homelessness the housing authority should consider the possibility of reconciliation with the applicant's immediate family, where appropriate, or the possibility of him or her residing with another member of the wider family.

Reconciliation

12.8 In all cases involving applicants who are 16 or 17 years of age a careful assessment of the young person's circumstances and any risk to them of remaining at home should be made at the first response. Some 16 and 17 year olds may be at risk of leaving home because of a temporary breakdown in their relationship with their family. In such cases, the housing authority may be able to effect a reconciliation with the family. In some cases, however, relationships may have broken down irretrievably, and in others it may not be safe or desirable for the applicant to remain in the family home, for example, in cases involving violence or abuse.

12.9 Therefore, any mediation or reconciliation will need careful brokering and housing authorities may wish to seek the assistance of social services in all such cases.

Collusion

12.10 Where homelessness can not be avoided, local authorities should work with 16 and 17 year olds, and their families where appropriate, to explore alternative housing options. Where the main homelessness duty is owed young people need to be given the chance to consider a range of housing options including but not limited to any accommodation to be offered under s.193. Clear and accurate information is essential to allow young people to identify the right housing solution for them.

12.11 Some parents and children may seek to take advantage of the fact that 16 and 17 year old applicants have a priority need for accommodation. Housing authorities will therefore need to be alive to the possibility of collusion when assessing applications from this client group. Section 191(3) (intentional homelessness) will apply in cases where there is no genuine basis for homelessness and parents have colluded with a child and fabricated an arrangement under which the child has been asked to leave the family home (see Chapter 11 for guidance on intentional homelessness).

Care and support needs

12.12 Where young people actually become homeless and are provided with accommodation, local authorities should consider whether they have any care or support needs. Many young people who have experienced homelessness may lack skills in managing their affairs and require help with managing a tenancy and operating a household budget. Those estranged from their family, particularly care leavers, may lack the advice and support normally available to young people from family, friends and other mentors. 16 and 17 year olds who are homeless and estranged from their family will be particularly vulnerable and in need of support.

12.13 Housing authorities will need to recognise that accommodation solutions for this client group are likely to be unsuccessful if the necessary support is not provided. Close liaison with social services, the Supporting People team and agencies working with young people will be essential. Most 16 and 17 year old applicants are likely to benefit from a period in supported accommodation before moving on to a tenancy of their own, but housing authorities should consider the circumstances of each case.

12.14 **Housing authorities are reminded that Bed and Breakfast (B&B) accommodation is unlikely to be suitable for 16 and 17 year olds who are in need of support. Where B&B accommodation is used for this group it ought to be as a last resort for the shortest time possible and housing authorities will need to ensure that appropriate support is provided where necessary**. See Chapter 17 on the suitability of accommodation for further guidance on the use of B&B accommodation.

12.15 16 and 17 year olds (including lone parents) who apply for housing assistance may also have care and support needs that need to be assessed. **The Secretary of State recommends that housing authorities and social services authorities (and the relevant departments within unitary authorities) have arrangements in place for joint assessments of such young people's needs, whether the application is made initially to the housing department or social services department.** In all cases where an applicant may have care, health or other support needs, it is recommended that the housing authority liaise with the social services authority, the Supporting People team and other agencies (for example, the Primary Care Trust, Criminal Justice Services, and voluntary and community organisations), as appropriate, as part of their inquiries. A joint consideration of an applicant's housing and support needs may be crucial to assist the authority in establishing whether the applicant has a priority need for accommodation and any non-housing support needs (see Chapter 4 for guidance on securing support services and Chapter 5 for guidance on joint working).

Lone teenage parents under 18

12.16 The provision of suitable accommodation with support for lone parents under 18 is a key part of the Government's Teenage Pregnancy Strategy. Providing accommodation with support for 16 and 17 year old lone parents is important for a very vulnerable group at risk of social isolation. It increases the likelihood of them making a successful transition to an independent tenancy and reduces the risk of subsequent homelessness.

12.17 The Government's objective is that all 16 and 17 year old lone parents who cannot live with their parents or partner should be offered accommodation with support. Housing authorities should work with social services, RSLs, the local teenage pregnancy co-ordinator and relevant voluntary organisations in their district to ensure that the Government's objective is met. The allocation of appropriate housing and support should be based on consideration of the young person's housing and support needs, their individual circumstances and their views and preferences. Young parents under the age of 16 must always be referred to social services so that their social care needs may be assessed. Housing authorities may find it helpful to refer to *Guidelines for Good Practice in Supported Accommodation for Young Parents,* separate guidance published jointly by DTLR and the Teenage Pregnancy Unit in September 2001 (available from **www.teenagepregnancyunit.gov.uk**).

CHAPTER 13
Co-operation in certain cases involving children

13.1 **This chapter provides guidance on the duty housing authorities and social services authorities have to co-operate in certain cases involving children.**

13.2 Section 10 of the *Children Act 2004* establishes a duty on county level and unitary authorities to make arrangements to promote co-operation between the authority, relevant partners (including district authorities) and other persons or bodies engaged in activities in relation to children, to improve the well-being of children and young people in the authority's area. Relevant partners are required to co-operate with the authority. Section 11 of the 2004 Act requires a range of agencies – including county level and unitary authorities and district authorities where there are two tiers of local government – to make arrangements for ensuring that their functions are discharged having regard to the need to safeguard and promote the welfare of children. See Chapter 5 for guidance on joint working.

13.3 Where an applicant is eligible for assistance and unintentionally homeless, and has a priority need because there is one or more dependent child in his or her household, the housing authority will owe a main homelessness duty to secure that accommodation is available to them. However, not all applicants with dependent children will be owed a main homelessness duty. Applicants who are found to be ineligible for assistance are not entitled to homelessness assistance under Part 7 of the 1996 Act. Where an applicant with a priority need is found to be eligible but homeless intentionally, s.190(2) requires the housing authority to secure accommodation for such period as will give the applicant a reasonable opportunity to secure accommodation for him/herself and to ensure that the applicant is provided with advice and assistance in any attempts he or she may make to secure accommodation for his or her occupation. Where an applicant with a priority need is found to be eligible but threatened with homelessness intentionally, s.195(5) requires the housing authority to ensure that the applicant is provided with advice and assistance in any attempts he or she may make to secure that accommodation does not cease to be available for his or her occupation. See Chapter 14 for guidance on the main duties owed to applicants on completion of inquiries, including the duty to provide advice and assistance.

13.4 In each of the above cases, there is a possibility that situations could arise where families may find themselves without accommodation and any prospect of further assistance from the housing authority. This could give rise to a situation in which the children of such families might become children in need, within the meaning of the term as set out in s.17 of the *Children Act 1989.*

13.5 In such cases, it is important that local authority children's services are alerted as quickly as possible because the family may wish to seek assistance under Part 3 of the *Children Act 1989*, in circumstances in which they are owed no, or only limited, assistance under the homelessness legislation. This will give local authority children's services the opportunity to consider the circumstances of the child(ren) and family, and plan any response that may be deemed by them to be appropriate.

13.6 Section 213A of the 1996 Act applies where a housing authority has reason to believe that an applicant for assistance under Part 7 with whom a person under the age of 18 normally resides, or might reasonably be expected to reside:

a) may be ineligible for assistance;
b) may be homeless and may have become so intentionally; or
c) may be threatened with homelessness intentionally.

In these circumstances, a housing authority is required to have arrangements in place to ensure that the applicant is invited to consent to the referral of the essential facts of his or her case to the social services authority for the district (or, in the case of a unitary authority, the social services department of the authority). The arrangements must also provide that, where consent is given, the social services authority or department is made aware of the essential facts and, in due course, of the subsequent decision in relation to the homelessness case.

13.7 The requirement to obtain the applicant's consent to the referral of the essential facts of his or her case under section 213A(2) or (3) does not affect any other power for the housing authority to disclose information about a homelessness case to the social services authority or department. For example, even where consent is withheld, the housing authority should disclose information about a homelessness case to the social services authority, if they have reason to believe that a child is, or may be, at risk of significant harm, as laid out in Chapter 5 of *Working Together to Safeguard Children: A guide to* *inter-agency working to safeguard and promote the welfare of children* (2006). *Working Together* was recently revised to reflect developments in legislation, policy and practice. It was published in April 2006 and can be found on the *Every Child Matters* website at http://www.everychildmatters.gov.uk/socialcare/safeguarding/workingtogether/

13.8 Where a family with one or more children has been found ineligible for assistance under Part 7 or homeless, or threatened with homelessness, intentionally and approaches the social services authority, that authority will need to decide whether the child is a 'child in need' under the terms of the *Children Act 1989*, by carrying out an assessment of their needs in accordance with the *Framework for the Assessment of Children in Need and their Families* (2000), Department of Health. The findings of the assessment should provide the basis for the decision as to whether the child is a 'child in need' and what, if any, services should be offered to the child in order to safeguard and promote his/her welfare. Section 17 of the *Children Act 1989* requires a local authority to promote the upbringing of children within their family, in so far as this is consistent with their general duty to safeguard and promote their welfare. The social services authority might wish to consider, for example, whether the best way of meeting the child's needs would be by assisting the family to obtain accommodation, for example by providing temporary accommodation or a rent deposit, as part of the exercise of its duty set out in s.17 of the Children Act 1989. *Local Authority Circular 2003(13): Guidance on accommodating children in need and their families* provides further guidance to social services authorities on the effect of s.17.

13.9 Where a social services authority has been made aware of a family found to be ineligible for assistance or homeless, or threatened with homelessness, intentionally by the housing authority, and they consider the needs of a child or children could best be met by helping the family to obtain accommodation, they can request the housing authority to provide them with such advice and assistance as is reasonable in the circumstances. Under s.213A(5), the housing authority must comply with such a request. Advice and assistance as is reasonable in the circumstances might include, for example, help with locating suitable accommodation and making an inspection of the property to ensure that it meets adequate standards of fitness and safety. However, the housing authority is not under a duty to provide accommodation for the family in these circumstances.

13.10 Section 213A(6) requires unitary authorities to have similar arrangements in place so that the housing department provide the social services department with such advice and assistance as they may reasonably request.

13.11 Housing authorities may also wish to consider alerting social services authorities to cases where an applicant whose household includes a child has refused an offer of accommodation which the authority is satisfied is suitable, and the authority has made a decision that it has discharged its homelessness duty under Part 7. In such cases the household could find itself without accommodation and any prospect of further assistance from the housing authority. The applicant would, however, need to consent to the housing authority notifying the social services authority of the essential facts of his or her case (unless the housing authority has any other powers to disclose the information without consent).

CHAPTER 14
Main duties owed to applicants on completion of inquiries

14.1 **This chapter provides guidance on the main duties owed to applicants where the housing authority has completed its inquiries and is satisfied that an applicant is eligible for assistance and homeless or threatened with homelessness. The chapter also provides guidance on the circumstances that will bring the s.193(2) duty ('the main homelessness duty') to an end.**

14.2 In many cases early, effective intervention can prevent homelessness occurring. The Secretary of State considers that housing authorities should take steps to prevent homelessness wherever possible, and offer a broad range of advice and assistance to those who face the prospect of losing their current home. However, where a housing authority has completed inquiries made under s.184 (see Chapter 6 for guidance on applications) and is satisfied that an applicant is eligible for assistance and homeless or threatened with homelessness, then one or more of the duties outlined in this chapter will apply under Part 7.

14.3 No duty is owed under Part 7 to applicants who are ineligible for assistance or not homeless or threatened with homelessness. However, homelessness strategies should aim to prevent homelessness amongst all households in the district and under s.179 advice and information about homelessness and the prevention of homelessness must be available free of charge to any person in the district, including these applicants. Housing authorities may also choose to offer other assistance to help them obtain accommodation, such as a rent deposit.

DUTIES TO PROVIDE ADVICE AND ASSISTANCE

14.4 Housing authorities have a duty to ensure that the applicant is provided with advice and assistance in a number of different circumstances, and these are dealt with below. These duties require an assessment to be made of the housing needs of the applicant before advice and assistance is provided. This assessment may need to range wider than the housing authority's inquiries into the applicant's homelessness carried out for the purpose of s.184, and should inform the provision of appropriate advice and assistance for that particular applicant. Among other things, the Secretary of State considers the assessment should identify any factors that may make it difficult for the applicant to secure accommodation for him or herself, for example, poverty, outstanding debt, health problems, disabilities and whether English is not a first language. In particular, housing authorities are advised to take account of the circumstances that led to the applicant's homelessness, or threatened homelessness, since these may impact on his or her ability to secure and maintain accommodation and may indicate what types of accommodation would be appropriate.

DUTIES OWED TO APPLICANTS WHO ARE THREATENED WITH HOMELESSNESS

14.5 Under s.175(4), a person is 'threatened with homelessness' if he or she is likely to become homeless within 28 days. However, the Secretary of State considers that housing authorities should not wait until homelessness is a likelihood or is imminent before providing advice and assistance. Early intervention may enable homelessness to be prevented, or delayed sufficiently to allow for a planned move to be arranged. However, where a housing authority has completed its inquiries under s.184 and is satisfied that an applicant is eligible for assistance and threatened with homelessness, then the specific duties outlined in paragraphs 14.6–14.9 below will apply.

Unintentionally threatened with homelessness and has priority need (s.195(2))

14.6 Where the authority are satisfied that an applicant is threatened with homelessness unintentionally, eligible for assistance and has a priority need for accommodation, it has a **duty** under s.195(2) *to take reasonable steps to secure that accommodation does not cease to be available for the applicant's occupation.*

14.7 Such reasonable steps may include for example, negotiation with the applicant's landlord or, in cases where the applicant has been asked to leave by family and friends, by exploring the scope for mediation and the provision of support to the household in order to ease any pressures that may have led to the applicant being asked to leave. Where a housing authority is able to identify the precise reasons why the applicant is being required to leave his or her current accommodation – for example, by interviewing the applicant and visiting his or her landlord or family or friends (as appropriate) – there may be specific actions that the housing authority or other organisations can take, for example, addressing rent arrears due to delays in housing benefit payments or providing mediation services through the voluntary sector, that can prevent the threat of homelessness being realised. See Chapter 2 for further guidance on preventing homelessness.

14.8 Under s.195(3A), as soon as an authority has become subject to a duty under s.195(2), the authority must give the applicant a copy of the statement included in their allocation scheme about their policy on offering choice to people allocated housing accommodation under Part 6. Authorities are required to include such a statement in their allocation scheme by virtue of s.167(1A) of the 1996 Act.

14.9 Where the housing authority is under a duty under s.195(2) and they are unable to prevent the applicant losing his or her current accommodation, the authority will need to secure alternative suitable accommodation for the applicant. Authorities should not delay; arrangements to secure alternative accommodation should begin as soon as it becomes clear that it will not be possible to prevent the applicant from losing their current home. Section 195(4) provides that, where alternative suitable accommodation is secured, the provisions of s.193(3) to (9) will apply in relation to the duty under s.195(2) as they apply in relation to the duty under s.193(2) (see paragraphs 14.17 to 14.24 below).

Unintentionally threatened with homelessness, no priority need (s.195(5) and s.195(9))

14.10 Where the housing authority are satisfied that an applicant is threatened with homelessness, eligible for assistance and does not have a priority need for accommodation, it has a **duty** under s.195(5) *to ensure that the applicant is pro-*

vided with advice and assistance in any attempts he or she may make to secure that accommodation does not cease to be available for his or her occupation.

14.11 In addition, where the housing authority are satisfied that an applicant is threatened with homelessness unintentionally, it has a **power** under s.195(9) *to take reasonable steps to secure that accommodation does not cease to be available for the applicant's occupation.* See Chapter 2 for guidance on preventing homelessness and paragraph 14.7 above.

Intentionally threatened with homelessness and has priority need (s.195(5))

14.12 Where the authority are satisfied that an applicant is threatened with homelessness intentionally, eligible for assistance and has a priority need for accommodation, the housing authority has a **duty** under s.195(5) *to ensure that the applicant is provided with advice and assistance in any attempts he or she may make to secure that accommodation does not cease to be available for his or her occupation.* See Chapter 2 for guidance on preventing homelessness.

DUTIES OWED TO APPLICANTS WHO ARE HOMELESS

14.13 Under s.175 a person is 'homeless' if he or she has no accommodation in the UK or elsewhere which is available for his or her occupation and which that person has a legal right to occupy. Where a housing authority has completed its inquiries under s.184 and is satisfied that an applicant is eligible for assistance and homeless then the specific duties outlined below will apply.

Unintentionally homeless and has priority need (s.193(2))

14.14 Where an applicant is unintentionally homeless, eligible for assistance and has a priority need for accommodation, the housing authority has a **duty** under s.193(2) *to secure that accommodation is available for occupation by the applicant* (unless it refers the application to another housing authority under s.198). This is commonly known as 'the main homelessness duty'. In all cases, the accommodation secured must be available for occupation by the applicant together with any other person who normally resides with him or her as a member of his or her family, or any other person who might reasonably be expected to reside, with him or her, and must be suitable for their occupation. See Chapter 16 for guidance on discharging the duty to secure accommodation and Chapter 17 for guidance on suitability of accommodation.

14.15 Acceptance of a duty under s.193(2) does not prevent an immediate allocation of accommodation under Part 6 of the 1996 Act if the applicant has the necessary priority under the housing authority's allocation scheme. Under s.193(3A), as soon as an authority has become subject to a duty under s.193(2), the authority must give the applicant a copy of the statement included in their allocation scheme about their policy on offering choice to people allocated housing accommodation under Part 6. Authorities are required to include such a statement in their allocation scheme by virtue of s.167(1A) of the 1996 Act.

14.16 If the housing authority has notified the applicant that it proposes to refer the case to another housing authority, the authority has a duty under s.200(1) to secure that accommodation is available for the applicant until he or she is notified of the decision whether the conditions for referral of his case are met.

The duty under s.200(1) is therefore an interim duty only. Once it has been established whether or not the conditions for referral are met, a duty under s.193(2) will be owed by either the notified housing authority or the notifying housing authority. See Chapter 18 for guidance on referrals to another housing authority.

How the s.193(2) duty ends (this also applies where alternative accommodation has been secured under s.195(2))

14.17 The housing authority will cease to be subject to the duty under s.193(2) (the main homelessness duty) in the following circumstances:

i) *the applicant accepts an offer of accommodation under Part 6 (an allocation of long term social housing)* (s.193(6)(c)): this would include an offer of an assured tenancy of a registered social landlord property via the housing authority's allocation scheme (see current guidance on the allocation of accommodation issued under s.169 of the 1996 Act);

ii) *the applicant accepts an offer of an assured tenancy (other than an assured shorthold tenancy) from a private landlord* (s.193(6)(cc): this could include an offer of an assured tenancy made by a registered social landlord;

iii) *the applicant accepts a qualifying offer of an assured shorthold tenancy from a private landlord* (s.193(7B)). The local authority must not approve an offer of an assured shorthold tenancy for the purposes of s.193(7B), unless they are satisfied that the accommodation is suitable and that it would be reasonable for the applicant to accept it (s.193(7F)) (see paragraph 14.25 below);

iv) *the applicant refuses a final offer of accommodation under Part 6 (an allocation of long term social housing)*: the duty does not end unless the applicant is informed of the possible consequences of refusal and of his or her right to ask for a review of the suitability of the accommodation (s.193(7)), the offer is made in writing and states that it is a final offer (s.193(7A)), and the housing authority is satisfied that the accommodation is suitable and that it would be reasonable for the applicant to accept it (s.193(7F)) (see paragraph 14.25 below);

v) *the applicant refuses an offer of accommodation to discharge the duty which the housing authority is satisfied is suitable for the applicant* (s.193(5)): the duty does not end unless the applicant is informed of the possible consequences of refusal and of his or her right to ask for a review of the suitability of the accommodation. The housing authority must also notify the applicant that it regards itself as having discharged its duty, before it can end;

vi) *the applicant ceases to be eligible for assistance as defined in s.185 of the 1996 Act*;

vii) *the applicant becomes homeless intentionally from accommodation made available to him or her under s.193 or s.195*; see Chapter 11 for guidance on determining whether an applicant became homeless intentionally;

viii) *the applicant otherwise voluntarily ceases to occupy as his or her principal home accommodation made available under s.193 or s.195.*

14.18 The Secretary of State recommends that applicants are given the chance to view accommodation before being required to decide whether they accept or refuse an offer, and before being required to sign any written agreement relating to the accommodation (e.g. a tenancy agreement). Under s.202(1A), an applicant who is offered accommodation can request a review of its suitability whether or not he or she has accepted the offer. See Chapter 17 for guidance on suitability and Chapter 19 for guidance on reviews.

Qualifying offer of an assured shorthold tenancy

14.19 An offer of an assured shorthold tenancy is a qualifying offer if:

i) it is made, with the approval of the authority, in pursuance of arrangements made by the authority with the landlord with a view to bringing the authority's duty under s.193 to an end;
ii) it is for a fixed term within the meaning of Part 1 of the *Housing Act 1988* (i.e. not a periodic tenancy) and
iii) it is accompanied by a written statement that states the term of the tenancy being offered and explains in ordinary language that there is no obligation on the applicant to accept the offer, but if the offer is accepted the housing authority will cease to be subject to the s.193 duty.

14.20 The s.193 duty will not end with acceptance of an offer of a qualifying tenancy unless the applicant signs a statement acknowledging that he or she has understood the written statement accompanying the offer.

Reasonable to accept an offer

14.21 Housing authorities must not make a final offer under Part 6 or approve a qualifying offer of an assured shorthold tenancy unless they are satisfied that the accommodation is suitable for the applicant and that it is reasonable for him or her to accept the offer (s.193(7F)) (see Chapter 17 for guidance on suitability). Where an applicant has contractual or other obligations in respect of his or her existing accommodation (e.g. a tenancy agreement or lease), the housing authority can reasonably expect the offer to be taken up only if the applicant is able to bring those obligations to an end before he is required to take up the offer (s.193(8)).

14.22 Housing authorities must allow applicants a reasonable period for considering offers of accommodation made under Part 6 that will bring the homelessness duty to an end whether accepted or refused. There is no set reasonable period; some applicants may require longer than others depending on their circumstances, whether they wish to seek advice in making their decision and whether they are already familiar with the property in question. Longer periods may be required where the applicant is in hospital or temporarily absent from the district. In deciding what is a reasonable period, housing authorities must take into account the applicant's circumstances in each case.

Other circumstances that bring the s.193(2) duty to an end

14.23 Under s.193(6) the housing authority will also cease to be subject to the duty under s.193 in the following circumstances:

i) *the applicant ceases to be eligible for assistance as defined in s.185 of the 1996 Act;*
ii) *the applicant becomes homeless intentionally from accommodation made available to him or her under s.193 or s.195:* see Chapter 11 for guidance on determining whether an applicant became homeless intentionally;
iii) *the applicant otherwise voluntarily ceases to occupy as his or her only or principal home accommodation made available under s.193 or s.195.*

Further applications

14.24 Under s.193(9) a person who ceases to be owed a duty under s.193(2) can make a fresh application for accommodation or assistance in obtaining accommodation (see Chapter 6 for guidance on applications).

Unintentionally homeless and has no priority need (s.192(2) and s.192(3))

14.25 Where an applicant is unintentionally homeless, eligible for assistance and does not have a priority need for accommodation, the housing authority has a **duty** under s.192(2) *to ensure that the applicant is provided with advice and assistance in any attempts he or she may make to secure that accommodation becomes available for his or her occupation.* The housing authority might, for example, provide assistance with a rent deposit or guarantee to help the applicant to obtain accommodation in the private rented sector, or advice on applying for an allocation of accommodation through the social housing waiting list or through another social landlord (see Chapter 2 for guidance on advisory services).

14.26 In addition, housing authorities have a **power** under s.192(3) *to secure that accommodation is available for occupation by the applicant.* Authorities should consider whether to use this power in all relevant cases.

Intentionally homeless and has priority need (s.190(2))

14.27 Where an applicant is intentionally homeless, eligible for assistance and has a priority need for accommodation, the housing authority has a **duty** under s.190(2) to:

a) *secure that accommodation is available for the applicant's occupation for such period as it considers will give him or her a reasonable opportunity of securing accommodation for his or her occupation (s.190(2)(a)); and*

b) *provide the applicant, or secure that the applicant is provided with, advice and assistance in any attempts he or she may make to secure that accommodation becomes available for his or her occupation (s.190(2)(b)).*

14.28 The accommodation secured must be suitable. Housing authorities must consider each case on its merits when determining the period for which accommodation will be secured. A few weeks may provide the applicant with a reasonable opportunity to secure accommodation for him or herself. However, some applicants might require longer, and others, particularly where the housing authority provides pro-active and effective advice and assistance, might require less time. In particular, housing authorities will need to take account of the housing circumstances in the local area, including how readily other accommodation is available in the district, and have regard to the particular circumstances of the applicant, including the resources available to him or her to provide rent in advance or a rent deposit where this may be required by private landlords.

14.29 In addition to securing accommodation, the housing authority must ensure the applicant is provided with advice and assistance to help him or her secure accommodation for him/herself. This might include, for example, assistance with a rent deposit or guarantee to help the applicant to obtain accommodation in the private rented sector, or advice on applying for an allocation of long term social housing or accommodation through another social landlord. See Chapter 2 for guidance on advisory services.

Intentionally homeless and has no priority need (s.190(3))

14.30 Where an applicant is intentionally homeless, eligible for assistance and does not have a priority need for accommodation, the housing authority has a **duty** under s.190(3) *to ensure that the applicant is provided with advice and assistance in any attempts he or she may make to secure that accommodation becomes available for his or her occupation.* This might include, for example, assistance with a rent deposit or guarantee to help the applicant to obtain accommodation in the private rented sector, or advice on applying for an allocation of long term social housing accommodation or through another social landlord. See Chapter 2 for guidance on advisory services.

CHAPTER 15
Discretionary powers to secure accommodation

15.1 **This chapter provides guidance on the discretionary *powers* housing authorities have to secure accommodation for a household where they do not have a *duty* to secure accommodation for that household (see Chapter 16 for guidance on discharge of duties to secure accommodation).**

15.2 Housing authorities have powers to secure accommodation for:

i) applicants who are eligible for assistance, unintentionally homeless and do not have a priority need for accommodation;
ii) applicants who request a review of the housing authority's decision on their case and who satisfy the relevant conditions, pending a decision on the review; and
iii) applicants who appeal to the county court against the housing authority's decision and who satisfy the relevant conditions, pending the determination of the appeal.

15.3 The fact that a housing authority has decided that an applicant is ineligible for housing assistance under Part 7 does not preclude it from exercising its powers to secure accommodation pending a review or appeal. However, housing authorities should note that s.54 of, and Schedule 3 to, the *Nationality, Immigration and Asylum Act 2002* prevent them from exercising their powers to accommodate an applicant pending a review or appeal to the county court, where the applicant is a person who falls within one of a number of classes of person specified in Schedule 3. See paragraphs 9.20–9.23 in Chapter 9 on eligibility for assistance for further details.

WAYS OF SECURING ACCOMMODATION

15.4 A housing authority may only discharge its housing functions under Part 7 in the following ways:

a) by securing that suitable accommodation provided by them is available for the applicant (s.206(1)(a));
b) by securing that the applicant obtains suitable accommodation from some other person (s.206(1)(b)); or

c) by giving the applicant such advice and assistance as will secure that suitable accommodation is available from some other person (s.206(1)(c)).

See Chapter 17 for guidance on the suitability of accommodation and Chapter 8 for guidance on when accommodation is available for occupation. In so far as is reasonably practicable, accommodation should be secured within the authority's own district (s.208(1)).

POWER TO SECURE ACCOMMODATION FOR APPLICANTS WHO ARE UNINTENTIONALLY HOMELESS AND DO NOT HAVE PRIORITY NEED

15.5 Under s.192(3), housing authorities may secure that accommodation is made available for applicants who are eligible for assistance, unintentionally homeless and do not have a priority need for accommodation. Where a housing authority decides to exercise this power it will still have a duty under s.192(2) to provide advice and assistance to the applicant in any attempts that he or she may make to secure accommodation for him/herself. See Chapter 14 for guidance on this duty.

15.6 By virtue of paragraph 4 of Schedule 1 to the *Housing Act 1985*, a tenancy granted under the power in s.192(3) will not be a secure tenancy. Housing authorities are reminded that all secure and introductory tenancies must be allocated in accordance with their allocation scheme, as framed under Part 6.

15.7 Housing authorities should consider using this power in all relevant cases. Any exercise of, or decision not to exercise, a power may be open to challenge by way of judicial review. In considering the use of this power, housing authorities must have regard to the legitimate expectations of others in housing need who have applied for an allocation of housing under Part 6, and to any need for accommodation to meet their obligations under Part 7.

15.8 Housing authorities should, in particular, consider exercising the s.192(3) power in circumstances where to do so would enable compliance with the obligations imposed on them by virtue of s.6 of the *Human Rights Act 1998* and where not doing so would mean acting in a way that may be incompatible with the applicant's Convention rights. The same is true of the power in s.195(8) (see paragraph 15.17 below).

15.9 Housing authorities may also wish to consider exercising the s.192(3) power to provide accommodation for a limited period to applicants such as key workers who are unintentionally homeless but do not have priority need under Part 7, or priority for an allocation under Part 6. This would be particularly appropriate where it would be in the interests of the local community for such persons to be accommodated in the district.

15.10 Non-secure tenancies will generally be suitable for a limited period only. They should be provided as part of a managed programme of accommodation to give the applicant an opportunity to secure a more settled housing solution in due course. This should be explained to the applicant from the outset and the housing authority should assist him or her to secure alternative accommodation. Reasonable notice should be given of a decision to stop exercising the power.

15.11 Housing authorities should not provide accommodation under s.192(3) as an alternative to allocating accommodation under Part 6 and should not allow non-secure tenancies to continue over the long-term.

POWERS TO ACCOMMODATE PENDING A REVIEW

15.12 Under s.202, applicants have the right to ask for a review of a housing authority's decision on a number of issues relating to their case (see Chapter 19 for guidance on reviews). Housing authorities have three powers to accommodate applicants pending a decision on the review. The relevant powers are found in s.188(3), s.195(8)(b) and s.200(5).

15.13 Under s.188(1), housing authorities must secure that accommodation is available for occupation by an applicant who they have reason to believe is:

(a) homeless,

(b) eligible for assistance, and

(c) in priority need,

pending their decision as to what duty, if any, is owed to that applicant under Part 7. See Chapter 7 for further guidance on this interim duty. Under s.188(3), if the applicant requests a review of the housing authority's decision on the duty owed to them under Part 7, the authority has the power to secure that accommodation is available for the applicant's occupation pending a decision on the review.

15.14 Section 188(3) includes a power to secure that accommodation is available where the applicant was found to be intentionally homeless and in priority need and:

(a) a duty was owed under s.190(2)(a);

(b) the s.190(2)(a) duty has been fully discharged; and

(c) the applicant is awaiting a decision on a review.

15.15 In considering whether to exercise their s.188(3) power, housing authorities will need to balance the objective of maintaining fairness between homeless persons in circumstances where they have decided that no duty is owed to them against proper consideration of the possibility that the applicant might be right. The Secretary of State is of the view that housing authorities should consider the following, although other factors may also be relevant:

(a) the merits of the applicant's case that the original decision was flawed and the extent to which it can properly be said that the decision was one which was either contrary to the apparent merits or was one which involved a very fine balance of judgment;

(b) whether any new material, information or argument has been put to them which could alter the original decision; and

(c) the personal circumstances of the applicant and the consequences to him or her of a decision not to exercise the discretion to accommodate.

The Secretary of State considers that when determining the merits of the applicant's case that the original decision was flawed, housing authorities should take account of whether there may have been procedural irregularities in making the original decision which could have affected the decision taken.

15.16 Housing authorities should give applicants reasonable notice to vacate accommodation provided under s.188(3) following an unsuccessful s.202 review. The Secretary of State considers that reasonableness should be judged against the particular applicant's circumstances. The applicant will require time to enable him or her to make alternative accommodation arrangements and housing authorities should take account of the fact that this may be easier for some applicants than others. Housing authorities may also require time to consider whether they should exercise their discretion under s.204(4) where the applicant appeals to the county court under s.204(1) (see paragraph 15.21).

15.17 Under s.195(5)(b), where a housing authority is satisfied that an applicant is:

(a) threatened with homelessness,
(b) eligible for assistance, and
(c) has a priority need, but
(d) became threatened with homelessness intentionally,

the authority is under a duty to provide the applicant (or secure that he or she is provided with) advice and assistance so that accommodation does not cease to be available for his or her occupation. Under s.195(8)(b), if the applicant requests a review of the housing authority's decision and, pending a decision on the review, becomes homeless, the housing authority may secure that accommodation is available for his or her occupation.

15.18 Under s.200(1), where a housing authority notifies another authority of its opinion that the conditions for the referral of an applicant's case to that authority are met, the authority has a duty to secure that accommodation is available for occupation by the applicant until a decision on the referral is reached. See Chapter 18 for guidance on local connection and referrals. If the applicant subsequently requests a review of the decision reached on the referral of his or her case, the notifying authority has the power under s.200(5) to secure that accommodation is available for the applicant's occupation pending the decision on that review.

15.19 Where, generally, only a small proportion of requests for a review are successful, it may be open to housing authorities to adopt a policy of deciding to exercise their powers to accommodate pending a review only in exceptional circumstances. However, such a policy would need to be applied flexibly and each case would need to be considered on its particular facts. In deciding whether there were exceptional circumstances, the housing authority would need to take account of all material considerations and disregard all those which were immaterial.

15.20 Where an applicant is refused accommodation pending a review, he or she may seek to challenge the decision by way of judicial review.

POWER TO ACCOMMODATE PENDING AN APPEAL TO THE COUNTY COURT

15.21 Applicants have the right to appeal to the county court on a point of law against a housing authority's decision on a review or, if they are not notified of the review decision, against the original homelessness decision (see Chapter 19 for guidance on appeals). Under s.204(4), housing authorities have the power to accommodate certain applicants:

(a) during the period for making an appeal against their decision, and
(b) if an appeal is brought, until it and any subsequent appeals are finally determined.

This power may be exercised where the housing authority was previously under a duty to secure accommodation for the applicant's occupation under s.188 (interim duty pending initial inquiries), s.190 (duty owed to applicants intentionally homeless and in priority need), or s.200 (interim duty owed pending decision on a referral). The power may also be exercised in a case where the applicant was owed a duty under s.195(5)(b) (intentionally threatened with homelessness and in priority need), the applicant requested a review and subsequently become homeless, and, in consequence, the housing authority had a power under s.195(8)(b) to secure accommodation pending the decision on the review.

15.22 The power under s.204(4) may be exercised whether or not the housing authority has exercised its powers to accommodate the applicant pending a review.

15.23 In deciding whether to exercise this power, housing authorities will need to adopt the same approach, and consider the same factors, as for a decision whether to exercise their power to accommodate pending a review (see paragraph 15.12).

15.24 Under s.204A, applicants have a right to appeal to the county court against a decision not to secure accommodation for them pending their main appeal. In deciding a s.204A appeal, the court must apply the principles that would be applied by the High Court on an application for judicial review. The county court cannot substitute its own decision as such. However, where the court quashes the decision of the housing authority, it may order the housing authority to accommodate the applicant, but only where it is satisfied that failure to do so would substantially prejudice the applicant's ability to pursue the main appeal on the homelessness decision.

CHAPTER 16
Securing accommodation

16.1 **This chapter provides guidance on the different ways in which housing authorities can ensure that suitable accommodation is available for applicants. In the case of the main homelessness duty the obligation to secure such accommodation will continue until such time as the duty ends in accordance with s.193.**

WAYS OF SECURING ACCOMMODATION

16.2 Section 206(1) provides that a housing authority may only discharge its housing functions under Part 7 in the following ways:

(a) by securing that suitable accommodation provided by them is available for the applicant (s.206(1)(a));
(b) by securing that the applicant obtains suitable accommodation from some other person (s.206(1)(b)); or
(c) by giving the applicant such advice and assistance as will secure that suitable accommodation is available from some other person (s.206(1)(c)).

16.3 Accommodation secured must be available for occupation by the applicant and any other person who normally resides with them as a member of their family, or might reasonably be expected to reside with them. The accommodation must also be suitable for their occupation. See Chapter 8 for guidance on when accommodation is available for occupation and Chapter 17 for guidance on the suitability of accommodation.

16.4 In deciding what accommodation needs to be secured housing authorities will need to consider whether the applicant has any support needs. Housing authorities will therefore need to make arrangements for effective links with the Supporting People team, the social services authority or other bodies (for example, Primary Care Trusts, Criminal Justice Services, RSLs and voluntary and community organisations) to ensure that a joint assessment of an applicant's housing and support needs can be made where necessary. See Chapter 4 for guidance on securing support services.

16.5 Where a housing authority has a duty under s.193(2) to secure accommodation for an applicant ('the main homelessness duty'), the Secretary of State recommends that the authority considers, where availability of suitable housing allows, securing settled (rather than temporary) accommodation that will bring the duty to an end in the immediate or short term. For example, an offer of accommodation under the housing authority's allocation scheme or a qualifying offer of an assured shorthold tenancy from a private landlord. See Chapter 14 for guidance on bringing the s.193(2) duty to an end.

16.6 The Secretary of State considers that, generally, it is inappropriate for social housing to be used as temporary accommodation for applicants other than for short periods (see paragraph 16.18 below). Except in limited circumstances where social housing is only going to be available for use for a short period, where an authority has placed a household in social housing as a temporary arrangement to fulfil a duty under s.193(2), the Secretary of State recommends that the authority considers offering the household a settled home under the terms of its allocation scheme as soon as possible.

ACCOMMODATION SECURED OUT OF DISTRICT

16.7 Section 208(1) requires housing authorities to secure accommodation within their district, in so far as is reasonably practicable. Housing authorities should, therefore, aim to secure accommodation within their own district wherever possible, except where there are clear benefits for the applicant of being accommodated outside of the district. This could occur, for example, where the applicant, and/or a member of his or her household, would be at risk of domestic or other violence in the district and need to be accommodated elsewhere to reduce the risk of further contact with the perpetrator(s) or where ex-offenders or drug/alcohol users would benefit from being accommodated outside the district to help break links with previous contacts which could exert a negative influence.

16.8 Where it is not reasonably practicable for the applicant to be placed in accommodation within the housing authority's district, and the housing authority places the applicant in accommodation elsewhere, s.208(2) requires the housing authority to notify the housing authority in whose district the accommodation is situated of the following:

i) the name of the applicant;
ii) the number and description of other persons who normally reside with the applicant as a member of his or her family or might reasonably be expected to do so;
iii) the address of the accommodation;
iv) the date on which the accommodation was made available;
v) which function the housing authority is discharging in securing the accommodation.

The notice must be given in writing within 14 days of the accommodation being made available to the applicant.

16.9 The Secretary of State considers that applicants whose household has a need for social services support or a need to maintain links with other essential services within the borough, for example specialist medical services or special schools, should be given priority for accommodation within the housing authority's own district. In particular, careful consideration should be given to applicants with a mental illness or learning disability who may have a particular need to remain in a specific area, for example to maintain links with health service professionals and/or a reliance on existing informal support networks and community links. Such applicants may be less able than others to adapt to any disruption caused by being placed in accommodation in another district.

ACCESS TO SUPPORT SERVICES

16.10 The Secretary of State recommends that housing authorities consider what arrangements need to be in place to ensure that households placed in temporary accommodation, within their district or outside, are able to access relevant support services, including health, education and social services. The Secretary of State considers that all babies and young children placed in temporary accommodation, for example, should have the opportunity to receive health and developmental checks from health visitors and/or other primary health care professionals. See Chapter 4 for further guidance on securing support services.

ACCOMMODATION PROVIDED BY THE HOUSING AUTHORITY

16.11 Housing authorities may secure accommodation by providing suitable accommodation for the applicant themselves (s.206(1)(a)), in which case the housing authority will be the immediate landlord of the applicant, for example, where the housing authority place the applicant in:

i) a house or flat from its own stock (i.e. held under Part 2 of the *Housing Act 1985*);
ii) a hostel owned by the housing authority; or
iii) accommodation leased by the housing authority from another landlord (e.g. under a private sector leasing agreement) and sub-let to the applicant.

Housing authority's own stock

16.12 In considering whether to provide accommodation from their own stock, housing authorities will need to balance the requirements of applicants owed a duty under Part 7 against the need to provide accommodation for others who have priority for an allocation under Part 6 of the 1996 Act. **The Secretary of State considers that, generally, it is inappropriate for social housing to be used as temporary accommodation for applicants other than for short periods.**

16.13 Paragraph 4 of Schedule 1 to the *Housing Act 1985* provides that a tenancy granted by a housing authority in pursuance of any function under Part 7 is not a secure tenancy unless the housing authority notifies the tenant that it is such. Housing authorities are reminded that the allocation of secure and introductory tenancies must be made in accordance with their allocation scheme framed under the provisions of Part 6.

Housing authority hostels

16.14 Some housing authorities operate their own hostels and may wish to use these to accommodate certain applicants, particularly where they consider an applicant would benefit from a supported environment. See paragraphs 16.25 and 16.26 for further guidance on the use of hostel accommodation.

Accommodation leased from a private landlord

16.15 Accommodation leased from a private landlord can provide housing authorities with a source of good quality, self-contained accommodation which can be let to applicants. Where there is a need for temporary accommodation, housing authorities are encouraged to maximise their use of this type of leasing, in so far as they can secure cost-effective arrangements with landlords.

16.16 Under the prudential capital finance system (introduced by the *Local Government Act 2003* on 1 April 2004) local authorities are free to borrow without Government consent, provided that they can service the debts without extra Government support. The authority must determine how much it can afford to borrow. The new system ended the former financial disincentives to use leasing (and other forms of credit). Consequently, there is no longer any need for special concessions relating to leases of property owned by private landlords where that property is used to accommodate households owed a duty under Part 7. When entering into leases, as when borrowing, the capital finance rules simply require authorities to be satisfied that the associated liabilities are affordable.

ACCOMMODATION SECURED FROM ANOTHER PERSON

16.17 Housing authorities may secure that the applicant obtains suitable accommodation from some other person (s.206(1)(b)). Housing authorities can make use of a wide range of accommodation, including housing in the private rented sector and accommodation held by RSLs. The following paragraphs outline a number of options for securing accommodation from another landlord, which are available to housing authorities.

Registered social landlords

16.18 As the proportion of housing stock in the social sector held by RSLs increases, housing authorities should ensure that they maximise the opportunities for securing housing from RSLs. Under s.213 of the 1996 Act, where requested by a housing authority, an RSL must assist the housing authority in carrying out their duties under the homelessness legislation by co-operating with them as far as is reasonable in the circumstances. Housing Corporation regulatory guidance, issued with the consent of the Secretary of State under s.36 of the 1996 Act, requires RSLs, on request, to provide a proportion of their stock for nominations and as temporary accommodation for people owed a homelessness duty under Part 7 of the 1996 Act – to such extent as is reasonable in the circumstances. **The Secretary of State considers that, generally, it is inappropriate for social housing to be used as temporary accommodation other than for short periods** (see paragraph 16.6 above). Where a longer-term stay occurs or seems likely, the authority and RSL should consider offering an assured tenancy to bring the main homelessness duty to an end. See Annex 5 for further guidance on RSL co-operation with housing authorities.

16.19 Housing authorities may wish to consider contracting with RSLs for assistance in discharging their housing functions under arrangements whereby the RSL lease and/or manage accommodation owned by private landlords, which can be let to households owed a homelessness duty and nominated by the housing authority. A general consent under s.25 of the *Local Government Act 1988 (The General Consent under Section 25 of the Local Government Act 1988 for Financial Assistance to Registered Social Landlords or to Private Landlords to Relieve or Prevent Homelessness 2005*) allows housing authorities to provide RSLs with financial assistance in connection with such arrangements. Housing authorities must reserve the right to terminate such agreements, without penalty, after 3 years.

Private lettings

16.20 Housing authorities may seek the assistance of private sector landlords in providing suitable accommodation direct to applicants. A general consent under s.25 of the *Local Government Act 1988 (The General Consent under Section 25 of the Local Government Act 1988 for Financial Assistance to Registered Social Landlords or to Private Landlords to Relieve or Prevent Homelessness 2005*) allows housing authorities to provide financial assistance to private landlords in order to secure accommodation for people who are homeless or at risk of homelessness. This could involve, for example, the authority paying the costs of leases; making small one-off grants ('finders' fees') to landlords to encourage them to let dwellings to households owed a homelessness duty; paying rent deposits or indemnities to ensure accommodation is secured for such households; and making one-off grant payments which would prevent an eviction. There is no limit set on the amount of financial assistance that can be provided, however authorities are obliged to act reasonably and in accordance with their fiduciary duty to local tax and rent payers. Housing authorities may also make Discretionary Housing Payments (DHP) to a private landlord to meet a shortfall between the rent and the amount of housing benefit payable to a person who is homeless or at risk of homelessness. DHPs are intended to provide extra financial assistance where there is a shortfall in a person's eligible rent and the housing authority consider that the claimant is in need of further financial assistance. They are governed by the *Discretionary Housing Payment (Grant) Order 2001*. Housing authorities should also consider working with private landlords to arrange qualifying offers of assured shorthold tenancies which would bring the main homelessness duty to an end if accepted by the applicant. See paragraph 14.19 for guidance on qualifying offers.

Tenancies granted by private landlords and registered social landlords to assist with interim duties

16.21 Section 209 governs security of tenure where a private landlord provides accommodation to assist a housing authority discharge an **interim** duty, for example, a duty under s.188(1), s.190(2), s.200(1) or 204(4). Any such accommodation is exempt from statutory security of tenure until 12 months from the date on which the applicant is notified of the authority's decision under s.184(3) or s.198(5) or from the date on which the applicant is notified of the decision of any review under s.202 or an appeal under s.204, unless the landlord notifies the applicant that the tenancy is an assured or assured shorthold tenancy.

16.22 Where a private landlord or RSL lets accommodation directly to an applicant to assist a housing authority discharge any other homelessness duty, the tenancy granted will be an assured shorthold tenancy unless the tenant is notified that it is to be regarded as an assured tenancy.

Other social landlords

16.23 Under s.213 other social landlords, i.e. new town corporations and housing action trusts, have a duty to co-operate, as far as is reasonable in the circumstances, with a housing authority in carrying out their housing functions under Part 7 of the 1996 Act, if asked to do so.

Lodgings

16.24 Lodgings provided by householders may be suitable for some young and/or vulnerable single applicants. Housing authorities may wish to establish a network of such landlords in their district, and to liaise with social services who may operate supported lodgings schemes for people with support needs.

Hostels

16.25 Some applicants may benefit from the supportive environment which managed hostels can provide. Hostels can offer short-term support to people who are experiencing a temporary crisis, and provide an opportunity for them to regain their equilibrium and subsequently move on to live independently. Where an applicant appears to need support, particularly on-going support, and there is no social worker or support worker familiar with their case, the housing authority should request a community care assessment by the social services authority. However, housing authorities should not assume that a hostel will automatically be the most appropriate form of accommodation for vulnerable people, particularly in relation to young people, people with mental health problems and those who have experienced violence and/or abuse. In addition, where hostel accommodation is used to accommodate vulnerable young people or families with children, the Secretary of State considers that it would be inappropriate to accommodate these groups alongside adults with chaotic behavioural problems.

16.26 Housing authorities will need to take into account that some hostels are designed to meet short-term needs only. In addition to the question of whether the hostel accommodation would be suitable for the applicant for other than a short period, housing authorities should have regard to the need to ensure that bed spaces continue to be available in hostels for others who need them.

Women's refuges

16.27 Housing authorities should develop close links with women's refuges within their district, and neighbouring districts, to ensure they have access to emergency accommodation for women applicants who are fleeing domestic or other violence or who are at risk of such violence. However, housing authorities should recognise that placing an applicant in a refuge will generally be a temporary expedient only, and a prolonged stay could block a bed space that was urgently needed by someone else at risk. Refuges should be used to provide accommodation for the minimum period necessary before alternative suitable accommodation is secured elsewhere. Housing authorities should not delay in securing alternative accommodation in the hope that the applicant might return to her partner.

Bed and breakfast accommodation

16.28 Bed and Breakfast (B&B) accommodation caters for very short-term stays only and generally will afford residents only limited privacy and may lack certain important amenities, such as cooking and laundry facilities. Consequently, where possible, housing authorities should avoid using B&B hotels to discharge a duty to secure accommodation for applicants, unless, in the very limited circumstances where it is likely to be the case, it is the most appropriate option for an applicant. The Secretary of State considers B&B hotels as particularly unsuitable for accommodating applicants with family commitments and applicants aged 16 or 17 years who need support. See paragraphs 17.23 *et seq* in Chapter 17 for guidance on suitability and Chapter 12 for more detailed guidance on 16 and 17 year olds.

Accommodation provided by other housing authorities

16.29 Other housing authorities experiencing less demand for housing may be able to assist a housing authority by providing temporary or settled accommodation for homeless applicants. This could be particularly appropriate in the case of applicants who would be at risk of violence or serious harassment in the district of the housing authority to whom they have applied for assistance. Other housing authorities may also be able to provide accommodation in cases where the applicant has special housing needs and the other housing authority has accommodation available which is appropriate to those needs. Under s.213(1), where one housing authority requests another to help them discharge a function under Part 7, the other housing authority must co-operate in providing such assistance as is reasonable in the circumstances. Housing authorities are encouraged to consider entering into reciprocal and co-operative arrangements under these provisions. See Chapter 5 for guidance on the statutory provisions on co-operation between authorities.

Mobile homes

16.30 Although mobile homes may sometimes provide emergency or short-term accommodation, e.g. to discharge an interim duty, housing authorities will need to be satisfied that the accommodation is suitable for the applicant and his or her household, paying particular regard to their needs, requirements and circumstances and the conditions and facilities on the site. Caravans designed primarily for short-term holiday use should not be regarded as suitable as temporary accommodation for applicants.

Tenancies for minors

16.31 There are legal complications associated with the grant of a tenancy to a minor because a minor cannot hold a legal estate in land. However, if a tenancy is granted it is likely to be enforceable as a contract for necessaries (ie. the basic necessities of life) under common law. In some circumstances, social services authorities may consider it appropriate to underwrite a tenancy agreement for a homeless applicant who is under 18.

ADVICE AND ASSISTANCE THAT WILL SECURE ACCOMMODATION FROM ANOTHER PERSON

16.32 Housing authorities may secure accommodation by giving advice and assistance to an applicant that will secure that accommodation becomes available for him or her from another person (s.206(1)(c)). However, where an authority has a duty to secure accommodation, they will need to ensure that the advice and assistance provided results in suitable accommodation actually being secured. Merely assisting the applicant in any efforts that he or she might make to find accommodation would not be sufficient if suitable accommodation did not actually become available.

16.33 One example of securing accommodation in this way is where house purchase is a possibility for the applicant. Advice on all options for financing house purchase should be made available, especially those financial packages which may be suited to people on lower incomes.

16.34 One option to help people into home ownership is shared equity schemes (e.g. part buy/part rent or equity loans to assist with purchase). These schemes are mainly funded by the Housing Corporation and generally offered by RSLs. The Housing Corporation publishes booklets (available from their publication section) giving further details of the existing shared ownership and Homebuy schemes. A new HomeBuy scheme offering further opportunities for home ownership and building on the current schemes commenced on 1st April 2006.

16.35 In other cases, applicants may have identified suitable accommodation but need practical advice and assistance to enable them to secure it, for example the applicant may require help with understanding a tenancy agreement or financial assistance with paying a rent deposit.

16.36 Housing authorities should bear in mind that the advice and assistance must result in suitable accommodation being secured, and that applicants who wish to pursue this option may need alternative accommodation until this result is achieved.

APPLICANTS WHO NORMALLY OCCUPY MOVEABLE ACCOMMODATION (E.G. CARAVANS, HOUSEBOATS)

16.37 Under s.175(2) applicants are homeless if the accommodation available for their occupation is a caravan, houseboat, or other movable structure and they do not have a place where they are entitled, or permitted, to put it and live in it. If a duty to secure accommodation arises in such cases, the housing authority is not required to make equivalent accommodation available (or provide a site or berth for the applicant's own accommodation). However, the authority must consider whether such options are reasonably available, particularly where this would provide the most suitable solution to the applicant's accommodation needs.

Gypsies and Travellers

16.38 The circumstances described in paragraph 16.37 will be particularly relevant in the case of Gypsies and Travellers. Where a duty to secure accommodation arises but an appropriate site is not immediately available, the housing authority may need to provide an alternative temporary solution until a suitable site, or some other suitable option, becomes available. Some Gypsies and Travellers may have a cultural aversion to the prospect of 'bricks and mortar' accommodation. In such cases, the authority should seek to provide an alternative solution. However, where the authority is satisfied that there is no prospect of a suitable site for the time being, there may be no alternative solution. Authorities must give consideration to the needs and lifestyle of applicants who are Gypsies and Travellers when considering their application and how best to discharge a duty to secure suitable accommodation, in line with their obligations to act consistently with the *Human Rights Act 1998*, and in particular the right to respect for private life, family and the home.

Temporary to settled accommodation

16.39 Housing authorities are encouraged to test new approaches that would enable temporary accommodation to become settled accommodation. This would reduce the uncertainty and lack of security that households in temporary accommodation can face, and provide them with a settled home more quickly. Such approaches could be developed with housing associations through a range of 'temporary to settled' housing initiatives.

16.40 Each year approximately a quarter to a third of all leases of private sector accommodation held by social landlords expire. This presents an opportunity for the leased accommodation to be converted from use as temporary accommodation to the provision of settled housing, through negotiation with the landlord and the tenant during the final months of the lease. Where the household would be content to remain in the accommodation when the lease ends if it could be provided on a more settled basis, and the landlord would be prepared to let directly to the household, the local authority may wish to arrange for the landlord to make a 'qualifying offer' of an assured shorthold tenancy, for the purposes of s.193(7B). See paragraph 14.19 for guidance on 'qualifying offer'.

16.41 Where scope for conversion of temporary accommodation to settled accommodation is explored, the interests of the household must take priority, and the household should not be pressured to accept offers of accommodation that would bring the homelessness duty to an end.

16.42 There may also be limited potential for converting temporary accommodation leased from the private sector to a qualifying offer of an assured shorthold tenancy at the beginning or mid-point of a lease. However, this would probably require the lease to include a break clause to facilitate early termination.

16.43 While the local authority holds the lease of accommodation owned by a private sector landlord, the accommodation would not be capable of being offered to a household as a qualifying offer of an assured shorthold tenancy under s.193(7B). However, where a registered social landlord held such a lease, the accommodation may be capable of being offered to a household as a qualifying offer of an assured shorthold tenancy under s.193(7B) during the period of the lease, if all the parties agreed and the qualifying offer met the terms of s.193(7D).

CHAPTER 17
Suitability of accommodation

17.1 **This chapter provides guidance on the factors to be taken into account when determining the suitability of temporary accommodation secured under the homelessness legislation. Key factors include: the needs, requirements and circumstances of each household; space and arrangement; health and safety considerations; affordability, and location. Annex 16 sets out the statutory definition of overcrowding and Annex 17 sets out the minimum recommended standards for Bed and Breakfast accommodation.**

17.2 Section 206 provides that where a housing authority discharges its functions to secure that accommodation is available for an applicant the accommodation must be suitable. This applies in respect of all powers and duties to secure accommodation under Part 7, including interim duties such as those under s.188(1) and s.200(1). The accommodation must be suitable in relation to the applicant and to all members of his or her household who normally reside with him or her, or who might reasonably be expected to reside with him or her.

17.3 Suitability of accommodation is governed by s.210. Section 210(2) provides for the Secretary of State to specify by order the circumstances in which accommodation is or is not to be regarded as suitable for someone, and matters to be taken into account or disregarded in determining whether accommodation is suitable for someone.

17.4 Space and arrangement will be key factors in determining the suitability of accommodation. However, consideration of whether accommodation is suitable will require an assessment of all aspects of the accommodation in the light of the relevant needs, requirements and circumstances of the homeless person and his or her family. The location of the accommodation will always be a relevant factor (see paragraph 17.41).

17.5 Housing authorities will need to consider carefully the suitability of accommodation for applicants whose household has particular medical and/or physical needs. The Secretary of State recommends that physical access to and around the home, space, bathroom and kitchen facilities, access to a garden and modifications to assist sensory loss as well as mobility need are all taken into account. These factors will be especially relevant where a member of the household is disabled.

17.6 Account will need to be taken of any social considerations relating to the applicant and his or her household that might affect the suitability of accommodation. Any risk of violence or racial harassment in a particular locality must also be taken into account. Where domestic violence is involved and the applicant is not able to stay in the current home, housing authorities may need to consider the need for alternative accommodation whose location can be kept a secret and which has security measures and staffing to protect the occupants. For applicants who have suffered domestic violence who are accommodated temporarily in hostels or bed and breakfast accommodation, the accommodation may need to be gender-specific as well as have security measures.

17.7 Accommodation that is suitable for a short period, for example bed and breakfast or hostel accommodation used to discharge an interim duty pending inquiries under s.188, may not necessarily be suitable for a longer period, for example to discharge a duty under s.193(2).

17.8 As the duty to provide suitable accommodation is a continuing obligation, housing authorities must keep the issue of suitability of accommodation under review. If there is a change of circumstances of substance the authority is obliged to reconsider suitability in a specific case.

STANDARDS OF ACCOMMODATION

17.9 Section 210(1) requires a housing authority to have regard to the following provisions when assessing the suitability of accommodation for an applicant:

- Parts 9 and 10 of the *Housing Act 1985* (the '1985 Act') (slum clearance and overcrowding), and
- Parts 1 to 4 of the *Housing Act 2004* (the '2004 Act') (housing conditions, licensing of houses in multiple occupation, selective licensing of other residential accommodation and additional control provisions in relation to residential accommodation.)

Fitness for habitation

17.10 Part 1 of the *Housing Act 2004* (the '2004 Act') contains provisions that replace the housing fitness regime in s.604 of the 1985 Act. From 6th April 2006, the fitness standard in the 1985 Act is replaced by a new evidence-based assessment of risks to health and safety in all residential premises (including HMOs), carried out using the Housing Health and Safety Rating System (HHSRS). Part 9 of the 1985 Act is retained, with amendments, to deal with hazards for which demolition or area clearance is the most appropriate option.

Housing Health and Safety Rating System (HHSRS)

17.11 Action by local authorities is based on a three-stage consideration: (a) the hazard rating determined under HHSRS; (b) whether the authority has a duty or power to act, determined by the presence of a hazard above or below a threshold prescribed by Regulations (Category 1 and Category 2 hazards); and (c) the authority's judgment as to the most appropriate course of action to deal with the hazard.

17.12 The purpose of the HHSRS assessment is to generate objective information in order to determine and inform enforcement decisions. HHSRS allows for the assessment of twenty nine categories of housing hazard and provides a method for rating each hazard. It does *not* provide a single rating for the dwelling as a whole or, in the case of HMOs, for the building as a whole. A hazard rating is expressed through a numerical score which falls within a band, ranging from Band A to J. Scores in Bands A to C are Category 1 hazards. Scores in Bands D to J are Category 2 hazards. If a housing authority considers that a Category 1 hazard exists on any residential premises, they have a duty under the 2004 Act to take appropriate enforcement action in relation to the hazard. They also have a power to take particular kinds of enforcement action in cases where they consider that a Category 2 hazard exists.

17.13 The HHSRS assessment is based on the risk to the *potential occupant who is most vulnerable to that hazard.* For example, stairs constitute a greater risk to the elderly, so for assessing hazards relating to stairs they are considered the most vulnerable group. The very young as well as the elderly are susceptible to low temperatures. A dwelling that is safe for those most vulnerable to a hazard is safe for all.

17.14 Housing authorities should be familiar with the principles of the HHSRS and with the operational guidance issued under s.9 of the 2004 Act.

17.15 **The Secretary of State recommends that when determining the suitability of accommodation secured under the homelessness legislation, local authorities should, as a minimum, ensure that all accommodation is free of Category 1 hazards.** In the case of an out of district placement it is the responsibility of the placing authority to ensure that accommodation is free of Category 1 hazards.

Overcrowding

17.16 Part 10 of the 1985 Act is intended to tackle the problems of overcrowding in dwellings. Section 324 provides a definition of overcrowding which in turn relies on the room standard specified in s.325 and the space standard in s.326 (the standards are set out in Annex 17).

17.17 A room provided within an HMO may be defined as a 'dwelling' under Part 10 of the 1985 Act and the room and space standards will therefore apply. Housing authorities should also note that 'crowding and space' is one of the hazards assessed by the HHSRS. Any breach of the room and space standards under Part 10 is likely to constitute a Category 1 hazard.

Houses in Multiple Occupation (HMOs)

17.18 Parts 2, 3 and 4 of the 2004 Act – which came into force on 6 April 2006 – contain provisions to replace Part 11 of the 1985 Act which relates to HMOs.

17.19 The 2004 Act introduces a new definition of an HMO. A property is an HMO if it satisfies the conditions set out in sections 254(2) to (4), has been declared an HMO under s.255 or is a converted block of flats to which s.257 applies.

17.20 Privately owned Bed and Breakfast or hostel accommodation that is used to accommodate a household pursuant to a homelessness function, and which is the household's main residence, will fall within this definition of an HMO. Buildings managed or owned by a public body (such as the police or the NHS), local housing authority, registered social landlord or buildings which are already regulated under other legislation (such as care homes or bail hostels) will be exempt from the HMO definition. Buildings which are occupied entirely by freeholders or long leaseholders, those occupied by only two people, or by a resident landlord with up to two tenants will also be exempt. Most student accommodation (housing students undertaking a course in higher or further education) will also be exempt if it is managed and controlled by the establishment in accordance with a code of management practice.

17.21 From 6 April 2006, local authorities have been required to undertake the mandatory licensing of all privately rented HMOs (except converted blocks of flats to which s.257 applies) of three or more storeys and occupied by five or more people who form two or more households. Local authorities will also have discretionary powers to introduce additional licensing schemes covering smaller HMOs. In order to be a licence holder, a landlord will have to be a 'fit and proper' person, as defined in s.89 of the Act and demonstrate that suitable management arrangements are in place in their properties.

17.22 In addition a local authority will have to be satisfied that the HMO is suitable for the number of occupants it is licensed for and meets statutory standards relating to shared amenities and facilities, e.g. that it has an adequate number, type and quality of shared bathrooms, toilets and cooking facilities. These standards are set out in Schedule 3 to the *Licensing and Management of Houses in Multiple Occupation and Other Houses (Miscellaneous Provisions) (England) Regulations 2006* (SI No 2006/373). These 'amenity standards' will run alongside the consideration of health and safety issues under HHSRS. *The Housing (Management of Houses in Multiple Occupation) Regulations 1990* are to be replaced by the *Management of Houses in Multiple Occupation (England) Regulations 2006* (SI 2006/372). Neither the amenity standards nor the new management regulations apply to HMOs that are converted blocks of flats to which s.257 applies. It is intended that separate regulations will be made by July 6th to modify Part 2 of the 2004 Act (which deals with mandatory licensing) in so far as it relates to these types of HMO, and to extend, with modifications, the application of the new amenity standards and management regulations to these types of HMO. Until then they will continue to be subject to the registration schemes made under Part 11 of the 1985 Act. Transitional arrangements have been in place since April 2006 so that most HMOs that are registered in a 1985 scheme will automatically be licensed under the 2004 Act.

17.23 Local authorities also have discretion to extend licensing to privately rented properties in all, or part of, their area to address particular problems, such as low housing demand or significant incidence of anti-social behaviour. However, licensing in these selective circumstances is concerned only with property management and not the condition of the property.

BED AND BREAKFAST ACCOMMODATION

17.24 Bed and Breakfast (B&B) accommodation caters for very short-term stays only and generally will afford residents only limited privacy and may lack certain important amenities, such as cooking and laundry facilities. Consequently, where possible, housing authorities should avoid using B&B hotels to discharge a duty to secure accommodation for homeless applicants, unless, in the very limited circumstances where it is likely to be the case, it is the most appropriate option for the applicant.

17.25 Living in B&B accommodation can be particularly detrimental to the health and development of children. Under s.210(2), the Secretary of State has made the *Homelessness (Suitability of Accommodation) (England) Order 2003* (SI 2003 No. 3326) ('the Order'). The Order specifies that when accommodation is made available for occupation under certain functions in Part 7, B&B accommodation is not to be regarded as suitable for applicants with family commitments.

17.26 Housing authorities should, therefore, use B&B hotels to discharge a duty to secure accommodation for applicants with family commitments only as a last resort. Applicants with family commitments means an applicant –

(a) who is pregnant;
(b) with whom a pregnant woman resides or might reasonably be expected to reside; or
(c) with whom dependent children reside or might reasonably be expected to reside.

17.27 For the purpose of the Order, B&B accommodation means accommodation (whether or not breakfast is included):

(a) which is not separate and self-contained premises; and
(b) in which any of the following amenities is shared by more than one household:
(i) a toilet;
(ii) personal washing facilities;
(iii) cooking facilities.

B&B accommodation does not include accommodation which is owned or managed by a local housing authority, a registered social landlord or a voluntary organisation as defined in section 180(3) of the *Housing Act 1996*.

17.28 B&B accommodation is not to be regarded as suitable for applicants with family commitments (except as specified in paragraph 17.29 below) for the purpose of discharging a duty under the following duties:
- section 188(1) (interim duty to accommodate in case of apparent priority need);
- section 190(2)(a) (duties to persons becoming homeless intentionally);
- section 193(2) (duty to persons with priority need who are not homeless intentionally);
- section 200(1) (duty to applicant whose case is considered for referral or referred); and
- section 195(2) (duties in case of threatened homelessness) where the accommodation is other than that occupied by the applicant at the time of making his or her application.

17.29 The Order provides that if no alternative accommodation is available for the applicant the housing authority may accommodate the family in B&B for a period, or periods, not exceeding six weeks in result of a single homelessness application. **Where B&B accommodation is secured for an applicant with family commitments, the Secretary of State considers that the authority should notify the applicant of the effect of the Order, and, in particular, that the authority will be unable to continue to secure B&B accommodation for such applicants any longer than 6 weeks, after which they must secure alternative, suitable accommodation.**

17.30 When determining whether accommodation other than B&B accommodation is available for use, housing authorities will need to take into account, among other things, the cost to the authority of securing the accommodation, the affordability of the accommodation for the applicant and the location of the accommodation. An authority is under no obligation to include in its considerations accommodation which is to be allocated in accordance with its allocation scheme, published under s.167 of the 1996 Act.

17.31 If there is a significant change in an applicant's circumstances that would bring the applicant within the scope of the Order (e.g. a new pregnancy), the six week period should start from the date the authority was informed of the change of circumstances not the date the applicant was originally placed in B&B accommodation.

17.32 If the conditions for referring a case are met and another housing authority accepts responsibility for an applicant under s.200(4), any time spent in B&B accommodation before this acceptance should be disregarded in calculating the six week period.

17.33 B&B accommodation is also unlikely to be suitable for 16 and 17 year olds who are in need of support. Where B&B accommodation is used for this group it ought to be as a last resort for the shortest time possible and housing authorities will need to ensure that appropriate support is provided where necessary. See Chapter 12 for guidance on the use of B&B for 16 and 17 year olds.

17.34 The Secretary of State considers that the limited circumstances in which B&B hotels may provide suitable accommodation could include those where:

(a) emergency accommodation is required at very short notice (for example to discharge the interim duty to accommodate under s.188); or

(b) there is simply no better alternative accommodation available and the use of B&B accommodation is necessary as a last resort.

17.35 The Secretary of State considers that where housing authorities are unable to avoid using B&B hotels to accommodate applicants, they should ensure that such accommodation is of a good standard (see paragraphs 17.36–17.38 below) and is used for the shortest period possible. The Secretary of State considers that where a lengthy stay seems likely, the authority should consider other accommodation more appropriate to the applicant's needs.

Standards of B&B accommodation

17.36 Where housing authorities are unable to avoid using B&B hotels to accommodate applicants they should ensure that such accommodation is of a suitable standard. Where a B&B hotel is used to accommodate an applicant and is their main residence, it falls within the definition of an HMO. Paragraphs 17.18–17.23 above explain the legislation that applies to HMOs with regard to health and safety and overcrowing. Since April 2006, local authorities have a power under the 2004 Act to issue an HMO Declaration confirming HMO status where there is uncertainty about the status of a property.

17.37 The Government recognises that living conditions in HMOs should not only be healthy and safe but should also provide acceptable, decent standards for people who may be unrelated to each other and who are sharing basic facilities. As noted at paragraph 17.22 above, the Government has set out in regulation the minimum 'amenity standards' required for a property to be granted an HMO licence. These standards will only apply to 'high-risk' HMOs covered by mandatory licensing or those HMOs that will be subject to additional licensing, and will not apply to the majority of HMOs. However, housing authorities (or groups of authorities) can adopt their own local classification, amenity specification or minimum standards for B&B and other shared accommodation provided as temporary accommodation under Part 7. In London, for example, boroughs have, since 1988, had a code of practice on the use of B&B and other shared temporary accommodation used to accommodate households under Part 7. This establishes clear benchmarks for standards across the Capital. Under the code of practice, properties are graded from A to E, with the grading dependent upon a wide range of considerations and factors relating to the facilities and services provided by an establishment. Placements are expected to be made only in those properties that meet the required standard. Setting the Standard (STS), a new automated system administered by the Greater London Authority (GLA), assists boroughs to comply with the code of practice. It collects and collates information from environmental health officers' annual inspections of properties and then makes this easily accessible to relevant borough officers across London. For further information on STS contact STS@london.gov.uk. The Secretary of State welcomes these arrangements and encourages other housing authorities to consider adopting similar systems to support the exchange of information and improve standards of temporary accommodation.

17.38 The Government considers that the size and occupancy levels of rooms, the provision and location of cooking, toilet and bathing facilities, and management standards are particularly important factors for determining whether B&B accommodation is suitable for accommodating households under Part 7. The Secretary of State therefore recommends that housing authorities have regard to the recommended minimum standards set out in Annex 17 when assessing whether B&B accommodation is suitable.

AFFORDABILITY

17.39 Under s.210(2), the Secretary of State has made the *Homelessness (Suitability of Accommodation) Order 1996* (SI 1996 No. 3204). The 1996 Order specifies that in determining whether it would be, or would have been, reasonable for a person to occupy accommodation that is considered suitable, a housing authority must take into account whether the accommodation is affordable by him or her, and in particular must take account of:

(a) the financial resources available to him or her (*i.e. all forms of income*), including, but not limited to:

- i) salary, fees and other remuneration (*from such sources as investments, grants, pensions, tax credits etc.*);
- ii) social security benefits (*such as housing benefit, income support, income-based Jobseekers Allowances or Council Tax benefit etc.*);
- iii) payments due under a court order for the making of periodical payments to a spouse or a former spouse, or to, or for the benefit of, a child;
- iv) payments of child support maintenance due under the *Child Support Act 1991*;
- v) pensions;
- vi) contributions to the costs in respect of the accommodation which are or were made or which might reasonably be expected to be, or have been, made by other members of his or her household (*most members can be assumed to contribute, but the amount depends on various factors including their age and income. Other influencing factors can be drawn from the parallels of their entitlement to housing benefit and income support in relation to housing costs. Current rates should be available from housing authority benefit sections*);
- vii) financial assistance towards the costs in respect of the accommodation, including loans, provided by a local authority, voluntary organisation or other body;
- viii) benefits derived from a policy of insurance (*such as cover against unemployment or sickness*);
- ix) savings and other capital sums (*which may be a source of income or might be available to meet accommodation expenses. However, it should be borne in mind that, again drawing from the parallel social securities assistance, capital savings below a threshold amount are disregarded for the purpose of assessing a claim*);

(b) the costs in respect of the accommodation, including, but not limited to:

i) payments of, or by way of, rent *(including rent default/property damage deposits)*;
ii) payments in respect of a licence or permission to occupy the accommodation;
iii) mortgage costs *(including an assessment of entitlement to Income Support Mortgage Interest (ISMI))*;
iv) payments of, or by way of, service charges *(e.g. maintenance or other costs required as a condition of occupation of the accommodation)*;
v) mooring charges payable for a houseboat;
vi) where the accommodation is a caravan or a mobile home, payments in respect of the site on which it stands;
vii) the amount of council tax payable in respect of the accommodation;
viii) payments by way of deposit or security in respect of the accommodation;
ix) payments required by an accommodation agency;

(c) payments which that person is required to make under a court order for the making of periodical payments to a spouse or former spouse, or to, or for the benefit of, a child and payments of child support maintenance required to be made under the *Child Support Act 1991*; and
(d) his or her other reasonable living expenses.

17.40 In considering an applicant's residual income after meeting the costs of the accommodation, the Secretary of State recommends that housing authorities regard accommodation as not being affordable if the applicant would be left with a residual income which would be less than the level of income support or income-based jobseekers allowance that is applicable in respect of the applicant, or would be applicable if he or she was entitled to claim such benefit. This amount will vary from case to case, according to the circumstances and composition of the applicant's household. A current tariff of applicable amounts in respect of such benefits should be available within the authority's housing benefit section. Housing authorities will need to consider whether the applicant can afford the housing costs without being deprived of basic essentials such as food, clothing, heating, transport and other essentials. The Secretary of State recommends that housing authorities avoid placing applicants who are in low paid employment in accommodation where they would need to resort to claiming benefit to meet the costs of that accommodation, and to consider opportunities to secure accommodation at affordable rent levels where this is likely to reduce perceived or actual disincentives to work.

LOCATION OF ACCOMMODATION

17.41 The location of the accommodation will be relevant to suitability and the suitability of the location for all the members of the household will have to be considered. Where, for example, applicants are in paid employment account will need to be taken of their need to reach their normal workplace from the accommodation secured. The Secretary of State recommends that local authorities take into account the need to minimise disruption to the education of young people, particularly at critical points in time such as close to taking GCSE examinations. Housing authorities should avoid placing applicants in isolated accommodation away from public transport, shops and other facilities, and, wherever possible, secure accommodation that is as close as possible to where they were previously living, so they can retain established links with schools, doctors, social workers and other key services and support essential to the well-being of the household.

HOUSEHOLDS WITH PETS

17.42 Housing authorities will need to be sensitive to the importance of pets to some applicants, particularly elderly people and rough sleepers who may rely on pets for companionship. Although it will not always be possible to make provision for pets, the Secretary of State recommends that housing authorities give careful consideration to this aspect when making provision for applicants who wish to retain their pet.

ASYLUM SEEKERS

17.43 Since April 2000 the National Asylum Support Service (NASS) has had responsibility for providing support, including accommodation, to asylum seekers who would otherwise be destitute, whilst their claims and appeals are being considered. Some local authorities may still be providing accommodation to asylum seekers who applied for asylum prior to April 2000 and whose cases have not yet been resolved. However, the number of these cases, if any, will be small and declining.

17.44 Section 210(1A) provides that, in considering whether accommodation is suitable for an applicant who is an asylum seeker, housing authorities:

(a) shall also have regard to the fact that the accommodation is to be temporary pending the determination of the applicant's claim for asylum; and

(b) shall not have regard to any preference that the applicant, or any person who might reasonably be expected to reside with him or her, may have as to the locality of the accommodation secured.

RIGHT TO REQUEST A REVIEW OF SUITABILITY

17.45 Applicants may ask for a review on request of the housing authority's decision that the accommodation offered to them is suitable under s.202(1)(f), although this right does not apply in the case of accommodation secured under s.188, the interim duty to accommodate pending inquiries, or s.200(1), the interim duty pending the decision on a referral. Under s.202(1A) an applicant may request a review as to suitability regardless of whether or not he or she accepts the accommodation. This applies equally to offers of accommodation made under s.193(5) to discharge the s.193(2) duty and to offers of an allocation of accommodation made under s.193(7) that would bring the s.193(2) duty to an end. This means that the applicant is able to ask for a review of suitability without inadvertently bringing the housing duty to an end (see Chapter 19 for guidance on reviews). Housing authorities should note that although there is no right of review of a decision on the suitability of accommodation secured under s.188 or s.200(1), such decisions could nevertheless be subject to judicial review in the High Court.

CHAPTER 18
Local connection and referrals to another housing authority

18.1 **This chapter provides guidance on the provisions relating to an applicant's 'local connection' with an area and explains the conditions and procedures for referring an applicant to another housing authority.**

18.2 Where a housing authority ('the notifying authority') decide that s.193 applies to an applicant (i.e. the applicant is eligible for assistance, unintentionally homeless and has a priority need) but it considers that the conditions for referral of the case to another housing authority are met, they may notify the other housing authority ('the notified authority') of their opinion.

18.3 Notwithstanding that the conditions for a referral are apparently met, it is the responsibility of the notifying authority to determine whether s.193 applies before making a reference. **Applicants can only be referred to another authority if the notifying authority is satisfied that the applicant is unintentionally homeless, eligible for assistance and has a priority need.** Applicants cannot be referred while they are owed only the interim duty under s.188, or any duty other than the s.193 duty (e.g. where they are threatened with homelessness or found to be homeless intentionally).

18.4 **Referrals are discretionary only: housing authorities are not required to refer applicants to other authorities. Nor are they, generally, required to make any inquiries as to whether an applicant has a local connection with an area.** However, by virtue of s.11 of the *Asylum and Immigration (Treatment of Claimants, etc.) Act 2004*, housing authorities will need to consider local connection in cases where the applicant is a former asylum seeker:

i) who was provided with accommodation in Scotland under s.95 of the *Immigration and Asylum Act 1999*, and

ii) whose accommodation was not provided in an accommodation centre by virtue of s.22 of the *Nationality, Immigration and Asylum Act 2002.*

In such cases, by virtue of s.11(2)(d) and (3) of the *Asylum and Immigration (Treatment of Claimants, etc) Act 2004*, local connection to a district in England, Wales or Scotland will be relevant to what duty is owed under s.193. (See paragraph 18.21 below.)

18.5 Housing authorities may have a policy about how they may exercise their discretion to refer a case. This must not, however, extend to deciding in advance that in all cases where there is a local connection to another district the case should be referred.

18.6 The Local Government Association (LGA) has issued guidelines for housing authorities about procedures for referring a case. These include guidance on issues such as local connection and invoking the disputes procedure when two housing authorities are unable to agree whether the conditions for referral are met. (A copy of the LGA guidelines is at Annex 18 for information).

CONDITIONS FOR REFERRAL

18.7 Sections 198(2) and (2A) describe the conditions which must be satisfied before a referral may be made. A notifying authority may refer an applicant to whom s.193 applies to another housing authority if all of the following are met:

i) neither the applicant nor any person who might reasonably be expected to live with him or her has a local connection with its district; and

ii) at least one member of the applicant's household has a local connection with the district of the authority to be notified; and
iii) none of them will be at risk of domestic or non-domestic violence, or threat of domestic or non-domestic violence which is likely to be carried out, in the district of the authority to be notified.

LOCAL CONNECTION

18.8 When a housing authority makes inquiries to determine whether an applicant is eligible for assistance and owed a duty under Part 7, it may also make inquiries under s.184(2) to decide whether the applicant has a local connection with the district of another housing authority in England, Wales or Scotland.

18.9 Section 199(1) provides that a person has a local connection with the district of a housing authority if he or she has a connection with it:
i) because he or she is, or was in the past, normally resident there, and that residence was of his or her own choice; or
ii) because he or she is employed there; or
iii) because of family associations there; or
iv) because of any special circumstances.

18.10 For the purposes of (i), above, residence in temporary accommodation provided by a housing authority under s.188 can constitute normal residence of choice and therefore contribute towards a local connection. With regard to (ii) the applicant should actually work in the district: it would not be sufficient that his or her employers' head office was located there. For the purposes of (iii), where the applicant raises family associations, the Secretary of State considers that this may extend beyond parents, adult children or siblings. They may include associations with other family members such as step-parents, grandparents, grandchildren, aunts or uncles provided there are sufficiently close links in the form of frequent contact, commitment or dependency. Family associations may also extend to unmarried couples, provided that the relationship is sufficiently enduring, and to same sex couples. With regard to (iv), special circumstances might include the need to be near special medical or support services which are available only in a particular district.

18.11 The grounds in s.199(1) should be applied in order to establish whether the applicant has the required local connection. However, the fact that an applicant may satisfy one of these grounds will not necessarily mean that he or she has been able to establish a local connection. For example, an applicant may be 'normally resident' in an area even though he or she does not intend to settle there permanently or indefinitely, and the local authority could therefore determine that he or she does not have a local connection. The overriding consideration should always be whether the applicant has a real local connection with an area – the specified grounds are subsidiary to that overriding consideration.

18.12 In assessing whether an applicant's household has a local connection with either its district or a district to which the case might be referred, a housing authority should also consider whether any person who might reasonably be expected to live with the applicant has such a connection.

18.13 A housing authority may not seek to transfer responsibility to another housing authority where the applicant has a local connection with their district but they consider there is a stronger local connection elsewhere. However, in such a case, it would be open to a housing authority to seek assistance from the other housing authority in securing accommodation, under s.213.

18.14 Where a person has a local connection with the districts of more than one other housing authority, the referring housing authority will wish to take account of the applicant's preference in deciding which housing authority to notify.

Ex-service personnel

18.15 Under s.199(2) and (3), serving members of the armed forces, and other persons who normally live with them as part of their household, do not establish a local connection with a district by virtue of serving, or having served, there while in the forces.

Ex-prisoners and detainees under the Mental Health Act 1983

18.16 Similarly, detention in prison (whether convicted or not) does not establish a local connection with the district the prison is in. However, any period of residence in accommodation prior to imprisonment may give rise to a local connection under s.199(1)(a). The same is true of those detained under the *Mental Health Act 1983.*

Former asylum seekers

18.17 Sections 199(6) and (7) were inserted by section 11 of the *Asylum and Immigration (Treatment of Claimants, etc.) Act 2004.* Section 199(6) provides that a person has a local connection with the district of a housing authority if he or she was (at any time) provided with accommodation there under s.95 of the *Immigration and Asylum Act 1999* ('s.95 accommodation').

18.18 Under s.199(7), however, a person does not have a local connection by virtue of s.199(6):

(a) if he or she has been subsequently provided with s.95 accommodation in a different area. Where a former asylum seeker has been provided with s.95 accommodation in more than one area, the local connection is with the area where such accommodation was last provided; or

(b) if they have been provided with s.95 accommodation in an accommodation centre in the district by virtue of s.22 of the *Nationality, Immigration and Asylum Act 2002.*

18.19 A local connection with a district by virtue of s.199(6) does not override a local connection by virtue of s.199(1). Thus, a former asylum seeker who has a local connection with a district because he or she was provided with accommodation there under s.95 may also have a local connection elsewhere for some other reason, for example, because of employment or family associations.

Former asylum seekers provided with s.95 accommodation in Scotland

18.20 Under Scottish legislation, a person does not establish a local connection with a district in Scotland if he or she is resident there in s.95 accommodation. Consequently, if such a person made a homelessness application to a housing authority in England, and he or she did not have a local connection with the district of that authority, the fact that he or she had been provided with s.95 accommodation in Scotland would not establish conditions for referral to the relevant local authority in Scotland.

18.21 Sections 11(2) and (3) of the *Asylum and Immigration (Treatment of Claimants, etc) Act 2004* provides that where a housing authority in England or Wales is satisfied that an applicant is eligible for assistance, unintentionally homeless and in priority need and:

i) the applicant has been provided with s.95 accommodation in Scotland at any time;

ii) the s.95 accommodation was not provided in an accommodation centre by virtue of s.22 of the *Nationality, Immigration and Asylum Act 2002*;

iii) the applicant does not have a local connection anywhere in England and Wales (within the meaning of s.199 of the 1996 Act); and

iv) the applicant does not have a local connection anywhere in Scotland (within the meaning of s.27 of the *Housing (Scotland) Act 1987*);

then the duty to the applicant under s.193 (the main homelessness duty) shall not apply. However, the authority:

(a) may secure that accommodation is available for occupation by the applicant for a period giving him or her a reasonable opportunity of securing accommodation for his or her occupation; and

(b) may provide the applicant (or secure that he or she is provided with) advice and assistance in any attempts he or she may make to secure accommodation for his or her occupation.

When dealing with an applicant in these circumstances, authorities will need to take into account the wishes of the applicant but should consider providing such advice and assistance as would enable the applicant to make an application for housing to the Scottish authority in the district where the s.95 accommodation was last provided, or to another Scottish authority of the applicant's choice. If such a person was unintentionally homeless and in priority need, it would be open to them to apply to any Scottish housing authority and a main homelessness duty would be owed to them.

No local connection anywhere

18.22 If an applicant, or any person who might reasonably be expected to live with the applicant, has no local connection with any district in Great Britain, the duty to secure accommodation will rest with the housing authority that has received the application.

RISK OF VIOLENCE

18.23 A housing authority cannot refer an applicant to another housing authority if that person or any person who might reasonably be expected to reside with him or her would be at risk of violence. The housing authority is under a positive duty to enquire whether the applicant would be at such a risk and, if he or she would, it should not be assumed that the applicant will take steps to deal with the threat.

18.24 Section 198(3) defines violence as violence from another person or threats of violence from another person which are likely to be carried out. This is the same definition as appears in s.177 in relation to whether it is reasonable to continue to occupy accommodation and the circumstances to be considered as to whether a person runs a risk of violence are the same.

18.25 Housing authorities should be alert to the deliberate distinction which is made in s.198(3) between actual violence and threatened violence. A high standard of proof of actual violence in the past should not be imposed. The threshold is that there must be:

(a) no risk of domestic violence (actual or threatened) in the other district; and

(b) no risk of non-domestic violence (actual or threatened) in the other district.

Nor should 'domestic violence' be interpreted restrictively (see definitions in the introduction to this Code).

DUTIES WHERE CASE REFERRED TO ANOTHER HOUSING AUTHORITY

18.26 If a housing authority decide to refer a case to another housing authority, they will need to notify the other housing authority that they believe the conditions for referral are met (s.198(1)). They must also notify the applicant that they have notified, or intend to notify, another housing authority that they consider that the conditions for referral are met (s.184(4)). At that point, the notifying authority would cease to be subject to the interim duty to accommodate under s.188(1) but will owe a duty under s.200(1) to secure that accommodation is available for the applicant until the question of whether the conditions for referral are met is decided.

18.27 Under s.200(4), if the referral is accepted by the notified authority they will be under a duty to secure accommodation for the applicant under s.193(2). Regardless of whether the notified authority had reached a different decision on a previous application, it is not open to it to re-assess the notifying authority's decision that the applicant is eligible, unintentionally homeless and in priority need. Nor may the notified authority rely on an offer of accommodation which was refused having been made in pursuance of a previous application to it.

18.28 Under s.200(3), if it is decided that the conditions for referral are not met, the notifying authority will be under a duty to secure accommodation for the applicant under s.193(2).

18.29 When the question of whether the conditions for referral to the notified authority are met has been decided, the notifying housing authority must notify the applicant of the decision and the reasons for it (s.200(2)). The notification must also advise the applicant of his or her right to request a review of the decision, and the timescale within which such a request must be made. The interim duty to accommodate under s.200(1) ends regardless of whether the applicant requests a review of the decision. However, where the applicant does request a review the notifying authority has a power under s.200(5) to secure that accommodation is available pending the review decision. (See Chapter 15 for guidance on powers to secure accommodation).

18.30 Notifications to the applicant must be provided in writing and copies made available at the housing authority's office for collection by the applicant, or his or her representative, for a reasonable period.

DISPUTES

18.31 Applicants have the right to request a review of various decisions relating to local connection and referrals (see Chapter 19 for further guidance). There is not a right to request a review of a housing authority's decision not to refer a case, although a failure by a housing authority to consider whether it has the discretion to refer an applicant may be amenable to challenge by way of judicial review. The same is true of an unreasonable use of the discretion.

18.32 The question of whether the conditions for referral are met in a particular case should be decided by agreement between the housing authorities concerned. If they cannot agree, the decision should be made in accordance with such arrangements as may be directed by order of the Secretary of State (s.198(5)).

18.33 The *Homelessness (Decisions on Referrals) Order 1998* (SI 1998 No. 1578) directs that the arrangements to be followed in such a dispute are the arrangements agreed between the local authority associations (i.e. the Local Government Association, the Convention of Scottish Local Authorities, the Welsh Local Government Association and the Association of London Government).

18.34 The arrangements are set out in the Schedule to the Order. Broadly speaking, they provide that in the event of two housing authorities being unable to agree whether the conditions for referral are met, they must agree on a person to be appointed to make the decision for them. If unable to agree on that, they should agree to request the LGA to appoint someone. In default of this, the notifying housing authority must make such a request of the LGA. In all cases the appointed person must be drawn from a panel established by the LGA for the purpose. The Local Government Association has issued guidelines for housing authorities on invoking the disputes procedure (a copy is at Annex 18 for information).

18.35 The arrangements set out in the Schedule to SI 1998 NO. 1578 apply where a housing authority in England, Wales or Scotland seek to refer a homelessness case to another housing authority in England or Wales, and they are unable to agree whether the conditions for referral are met. A similar Order, the *Homelessness (Decisions on Referrals) (Scotland) Order 1998*, SI 1998 No. 1603 applies under the Scottish homelessness legislation. The arrangements in the latter apply in cases where a housing authority in England, Wales or Scotland refer a homelessness case to a housing authority in Scotland, and they are unable to agree whether the conditions for referral are met.

18.36 Where an English or Welsh housing authority seek to refer a case to a Scottish housing authority, a request to the local authority association to appoint an arbitrator should be made to the Convention of Scottish Local Authorities.

18.37 A notified authority which wishes to refuse a referral because it disagrees on a finding as to the application of s.193 to the applicant must challenge the notifying authority's finding (for example as to intentionality) by way of judicial review.

CHAPTER 19
Review of decisions and appeals to the county court

19.1 **This chapter provides guidance on the procedures to be followed when an applicant requests the housing authority to review their decision on the homelessness case.**

RIGHT TO REQUEST A REVIEW

19.2 Applicants have the right to request the housing authority to review their decisions on homelessness cases in some circumstances. If the request is made in accordance with s.202 the housing authority must review the relevant decision.

19.3 When a housing authority have completed their inquiries into the applicant's homelessness case they must notify the applicant of:

(a) their decision and, if any decision is against the applicant's interest, the reasons for it;

(b) the applicant's right to request a review; and

(c) the time within which such a request must be made.

Housing authorities should also advise the applicant of his or her right to request a review of the suitability of any accommodation offered as a discharge of a homelessness duty, whether or not the offer is accepted. Authorities should also advise the applicant of the review procedures.

19.4 Under s.202 an applicant has the right to request a review of:

(a) any decision of a housing authority about his or her eligibility for assistance (i.e. whether he or she is considered to be a person from abroad who is ineligible for assistance under Part 7);

(b) any decision of a housing authority as to what duty (if any) is owned to him or her under s.190, s.191, s.192, s.193, s.195 and s.196 (duties owed to applicants who are homeless or threatened with homelessness);

(c) any decision of a housing authority to notify another housing authority under s.198(1) (i.e. a decision to refer the applicant to another housing authority because they appear to have a local connection with that housing authority's district and not with the district where they have made the application);

(d) any decision under s.198(5) whether the conditions are met for the referral of the applicant's case (including a decision taken by a person appointed under the *Homelessness (Decisions on Referrals) Order 1998* (SI 1998 No. 1578));

(e) any decision under s.200(3) or (4) (i.e. a decision as to whether the notified housing authority or the notifying housing authority owe the duty to secure accommodation in a case considered for referral or referred);

(f) any decision of a housing authority as to the suitability of accommodation offered to the applicant under any of the provisions in (b) or (e) above or the suitability of accommodation offered under s.193(7) (allocation under Part 6). Under s.202(1A), applicants can request a review of the suitability of accommodation whether or not they have accepted the offer.

19.5 An applicant must request a review before the end of the period of 21 days beginning with the day on which he or she is notified of the housing authority's decision. The housing authority may specify, in writing, a longer period during which a review may be requested. Applicants do not have a right to request a review of a decision made on an earlier review.

19.6 In reviewing a decision, housing authorities will need to have regard to any information relevant to the period before the decision (even if only obtained afterwards) as well as any new relevant information obtained since the decision.

THE REVIEW REGULATIONS

19.7 The *Allocation of Housing and Homelessness (Review Procedures) Regulations 1999* (SI 1999 No.71) set out the procedures to be followed by housing authorities in carrying out reviews under Part 7.

Who may carry out the review

19.8 A review may be carried out by the housing authority itself or by someone acting as an agent of the housing authority (see Chapter 21 on contracting out homelessness functions). Where the review is to be carried out by an officer of the housing authority, the officer must not have been involved in the original decision, and he or she must be senior to the officer (or officers) who took that decision. Seniority for these purposes means seniority in rank or grade within the housing authority's organisational structure. The seniority provision does not apply where a committee or sub-committee of elected members took the original decision.

19.9 Where the decision under review is a joint decision by the notifying housing authority and the notified housing authority as to whether the conditions of referral of the case are satisfied, s.202(4) requires that the review should be carried out jointly by the two housing authorities. Where the decision under review was taken by a person appointed pursuant to the arrangements set out in the Schedule to the *Homelessness (Decisions on Referrals) Order 1998* (SI 1998 No. 1578), the review must be carried out by another person appointed under those arrangements (see paragraph 19.15).

Written representations

19.10 The applicant should be invited to make representations in writing in connection with his or her request for a review. The relevant provisions in Part 7 give a person an unfettered right to request a review of a decision, so he or she is not required to provide grounds for challenging the housing authority's decision. The purpose of the requirement is to invite the applicant to state his or her grounds for requesting a review (if he or she has not already done so) and to elicit any new information that the applicant may have in relation to his or her request for a review.

19.11 Regulation 6 requires the housing authority to notify the applicant that he or she, or someone acting on his or her behalf, may make written representations in connection with the request for a review. The notice should also advise the applicant of the procedure to be followed in connection with the review (if this information has not been provided earlier). Regulation 6 also provides that:

i) where the original decision was made jointly by the notifying and notified housing authorities under s.198(5), the notification should be made by the notifying housing authority; and

ii) where the original decision was made by a person appointed pursuant to the *Homelessness (Decisions on Referrals) Order 1998* (SI 1998 No. 1578), the notification should be made by the person appointed to carry out the review.

Oral hearings

19.12 Regulation 8 provides that in cases where a review has been requested, if the housing authority, authorities or person carrying out the review consider that there is a deficiency or irregularity in the original decision, or in the manner in which it was made, but they are minded nonetheless to make a decision that is against the applicant's interests on one or more issues, they should notify the applicant:

(a) that they are so minded and the reasons why; and,
(b) that the applicant, or someone acting on his or her behalf, may, within a reasonable period, make oral representations, further written representations, or both oral and written representations.

19.13 Such deficiencies or irregularities would include:

i) failure to take into account relevant considerations and to ignore irrelevant ones;
ii) failure to base the decision on the facts;
iii) bad faith or dishonesty;
iv) mistake of law;
v) decisions that run contrary to the policy of the 1996 Act;
vi) irrationality or unreasonableness;
vii) procedural unfairness, e.g. where an applicant has not been given a chance to comment on matters relevant to a decision.

19.14 The reviewer must consider whether there is 'something lacking' in the decision, i.e. were any significant issues not addressed or addressed inadequately, which could have led to unfairness.

Period during which review must be completed

19.15 Regulation 9 provides that the period within which the applicant must be notified of the decision on review is:

i) eight weeks from the day of the request for a review, where the original decision was made by the housing authority;
ii) ten weeks, where the decision was made jointly by two housing authorities under s.198(5) (a decision whether the conditions for referral are met);
iii) twelve weeks, where the decision is taken by a person appointed pursuant to the Schedule to the *Homelessness (Decisions on Referrals) Order* (SI 1998 No.1578).

The regulations provide that in all of these cases it is open to the reviewer to seek the applicant's agreement to an extension of the prescribed period; any such agreement must be given in writing.

Late representations

19.16 The regulations require the reviewer(s) to consider any written representations received subject to compliance with the requirement to notify the applicant of the decision on review within the period of the review, i.e. the period prescribed in the regulations or any extended period agreed in writing by the applicant. It may in some circumstances be necessary to make further enquiries of the applicant about information he or she has provided. The reviewer(s) should be flexible about allowing such further exchanges, having regard to the time limits for reviews prescribed in the regulations. If this leads to significant delays, the applicant may be approached to agree an extension in the period for the review. Similarly, if an applicant has been invited to make oral representations and this requires additional time to arrange, the applicant should be asked to agree an appropriate extension.

PROCEDURES FOR REVIEW OF DECISIONS MADE UNDER THE DECISIONS ON REFERRALS ORDER

19.17 Where the original decision under s.198(5) was made by a person appointed pursuant to the Schedule to the *Homelessness (Decisions on Referrals) Order 1998* (SI 1998 No.1578), regulation 7 provides that a review should be carried out by another person appointed by the notifying housing authority and the notified housing authority. This requirement applies even where the original decision was carried out by a person appointed from the panel by the chairman of the Local Government Association, or his or her nominee. If, however, the two housing authorities fail to appoint a person to carry out the review within five working days of the date of the request for a review, the notifying housing authority must request the chairman of the Local Government Association to appoint a person from the panel. The chairman, in turn, must within seven working days of that request appoint a person from the panel to undertake the review. The housing authorities are required to provide the reviewer with the reasons for the original decision, and the information on which that decision is based, within five working days of his or her appointment.

19.18 Any person thus appointed must comply with the procedures set out in regulations 6, 7, 8 and 9. Specifically, he or she must invite written representations from the applicant and send copies of these to the two housing authorities, inviting them to respond. The reviewer is also required to notify in writing the two housing authorities of his or her decision on review and the reasons for it at least a week before the end of the prescribed period of twelve weeks (or of any extended period agreed by the applicant). This allows the housing authorities adequate time to notify the applicant of the decision before expiry of the period.

NOTIFICATION OF DECISION ON REVIEW

19.19 Section 203 requires a housing authority to notify the applicant in writing of their decision on the review. The authority must also notify the applicant of the reasons for their decision where it:

i) confirms the original decision on any issue against the interests of the applicant;
ii) confirms a previous decision to notify another housing authority under s.198; or,
iii) confirms a previous decision that the conditions for referral in s.198 are met in the applicant's case.

Where the review is carried out jointly by two housing authorities under s.198(5), or by a person appointed pursuant to the *Homelessness (Decisions on Referrals) Order 1998* (SI 1998 No.1578), the notification may be made by either of the two housing authorities concerned.

At this stage, the authority making the notification should advise the applicant of his or her right to appeal to the County Court against a review decision under s.204 and of the period in which to appeal.

POWERS TO ACCOMMODATE PENDING A REVIEW

19.20 Sections 188(3) and 200(5) give housing authorities powers to secure accommodation for certain applicants pending the decision on a review. See Chapter 15 for guidance on powers to secure accommodation.

APPEALS TO THE COUNTY COURT

19.21 Section 204 provides an applicant with the right of appeal on a point of law to the County Court if:

(a) he or she is dissatisfied with the decision on a review; or

(b) he or she is not notified of the decision on the review within the time prescribed in regulations made under s.203.

In the latter case, an applicant will be entitled to appeal against the original decision.

19.22 An appeal must be brought by an applicant within 21 days of:

(a) the date on which he or she is notified of the decision on review; or

(b) the date on which he or she should have been notified (i.e. the date marking the end of the period for the review prescribed in the regulations, or any extended period agreed in writing by the applicant).

19.23 The court may give permission for an appeal to be brought after 21 days, but only where it is satisfied that:

(a) (where permission is sought within the 21-day period), there is good reason for the applicant to be unable to bring the appeal in time; or

(b) (where permission is sought after the 21-day period has expired), there was a good reason for the applicant's failure to bring the appeal in time and for any delay in applying for permission.

19.24 On an appeal, the County Court is empowered to make an order confirming, quashing or varying the housing authority's decision as it thinks fit. It is important, therefore, that housing authorities have in place review procedures that are robust, fair, and transparent.

POWER TO ACCOMMODATE PENDING AN APPEAL TO THE COUNTY COURT

19.25 Section 204(4) gives housing authorities the power to accommodate certain applicants during the period for making an appeal, and pending the appeal and any subsequent appeal. Applicants have a right to appeal against a housing authority's decision not to secure accommodation for them pending an appeal to the County Court (s.204A). Applicants can also appeal against a housing authority's decision to secure accommodation for them for only a limited period which ends before final determination of the appeal. See Chapter 15 for guidance on powers to secure accommodation.

LOCAL GOVERNMENT OMBUDSMAN

19.26 Applicants may complain to a Local Government Ombudsman if they consider that they have been caused injustice as a result of maladministration by a housing authority. The Ombudsman may investigate the way a decision has been made, but may not question the merits of a decision properly reached. For example, maladministration would occur where a housing authority:

i) took too long to do something;

ii) did not follow their own rules or the law;
iii) broke their promises;
iv) treated the applicant unfairly;
v) gave the applicant the wrong information.

19.27 There are some matters an Ombudsman cannot investigate. These include:
i) matters the applicant knew about more than twelve months before he or she wrote to the Ombudsman or to a councillor, unless the Ombudsman considers it reasonable to investigate despite the delay;
ii) matters about which the applicant has already taken court action against the housing authority, for example, an appeal to the County Court under s.204;
iii) matters about which the applicant could go to court, unless the Ombudsman considers there are good reasons why the applicant could not reasonably be expected to do so.

19.28 Where there is a right of review the Ombudsman would expect an applicant to pursue the right before making a complaint. If there is any doubt about whether the Ombudsman can look into a complaint, the applicant should seek advice from the Ombudsman's office.

CHAPTER 20
Protection of personal property

20.1 **This chapter provides guidance on the duty and powers housing authorities have to protect the personal property of an applicant.**

20.2 Under s.211(1) and (2), where a housing authority has become subject to a duty to an applicant under specified provisions of Part 7 and it has reason to believe that:
i) there is a danger of loss of, or damage to, the applicant's personal property because the applicant is unable to protect it or deal with it, and
ii) no other suitable arrangements have been, or are being, made,

then, whether or not the housing authority is still subject to such a duty, it must take reasonable steps to prevent the loss of, or to prevent or mitigate damage to, any personal property of the applicant.

20.3 The specified provisions are:
- s.188 (interim duty to accommodate);
- s.190, s.193 or s.195 (duties to persons found to be homeless or threatened with homelessness); or
- s.200 (duties to applicant whose case is considered for referral or referred).

20.4 In all other circumstances, housing authorities have a power to take any steps they consider reasonable to protect in the same ways an applicant's personal property (s.211(3)).

20.5 Section 212 makes provisions supplementing s.211. For the purposes of both s.211 and s.212, the personal property of an applicant includes the personal property of any person who might reasonably be expected to reside with him or her (s.211(5) and s.212(6)).

20.6 A danger of loss or damage to personal property means that there is a likelihood of harm, not just that harm is a possibility. Applicants may be unable to protect their property if, for example, they are ill or are unable to afford to have it stored themselves.

20.7 Under s.212(1), in order to protect an applicant's personal property, a housing authority can enter, at all reasonable times, the applicant's current or former home, and deal with the property in any way which seems reasonably necessary. In particular, it may store the property or arrange for it to be stored; this may be particularly appropriate where the applicant is accommodated by the housing authority in furnished accommodation for a period. In some cases, where the applicant's previous home is not to be occupied immediately, it may be possible for the property to remain there, if it can be adequately protected.

20.8 Where a housing authority does take steps to protect personal property, whether by storing it or otherwise, it must take reasonable care of it and deliver it to the owner when reasonably requested to do so.

20.9 The applicant can request the housing authority to move his or her property to a particular location. If the housing authority considers that the request is reasonable, they may discharge their responsibilities under s.211 by doing as the applicant asks. Where such a request is met, the housing authority will have no further duty or power to protect the applicant's property, and it must inform the applicant of this consequence before complying with the request (s.212(2)).

20.10 Housing authorities may impose conditions on the assistance they provide where they consider these appropriate to the particular case. Conditions may include making a reasonable charge for storage of property and reserving the right to dispose of property in certain circumstances specified by the housing authority – e.g. if the applicant loses touch with them and cannot be traced after a certain period (s.211(4)).

20.11 Where a request to move personal property to another location is either not made or not carried out, the duty or power to take any action under s.211 ends when the housing authority believes there is no longer any danger of loss or damage to the property because of the applicant's inability to deal with or protect it (s.212(3)). This may be the case, for example, where an applicant recovers from illness or finds accommodation where he or she is able to place his or her possessions, or becomes able to afford the storage costs him/herself. However, where the housing authority has discharged the duty under s.211 by placing property in storage, it has a discretionary power to continue to keep the property in storage. Where it does so, any conditions imposed by the housing authority continue to apply and may be modified as necessary.

20.12 Where the housing authority ceases to be under a duty, or ceases to have a power, to protect an applicant's personal property under s.211, it must notify the applicant of this and give the reasons for it. The notification must be delivered to the applicant or sent to his or her last known address (s.212(5)).

CHAPTER 21
Contracting out homelessness functions

21.1 **This chapter provides guidance on contracting out homelessness functions and housing authorities' statutory obligations with regard to the discharge of those functions.**

21.2 The *Local Authorities (Contracting Out of Allocation of Housing and Homelessness Functions) Order 1996* (SI 1996 No. 3215) ('the Order') enables housing authorities to contract out certain functions under Parts 6 and 7 of the 1996 Act. The Order is made under s.70 of the *Deregulation and Contracting Out Act 1994* ('the 1994 Act'). In essence, the Order allows the contracting out of executive functions while leaving the responsibility for making strategic decisions with the housing authority.

21.3 The Order provides that the majority of functions under Part 7 can be contracted out. These include:

- making arrangements to secure that advice and information about homelessness, and the prevention of homelessness, is available free of charge within the housing authority's district;
- making inquiries about and deciding a person's eligibility for assistance;
- making inquiries about and deciding whether any duty, and, if so, what duty is owed to a person under Part 7;
- making referrals to another housing authority;
- carrying out reviews of decisions;
- securing accommodation to discharge homelessness duties.

21.4 Where decision-making in homelessness cases is contracted out, authorities may wish to consider retaining the review function under s.202 of the 1996 Act. This may provide an additional degree of independence between the initial decision and the decision on review.

21.5 The 1994 Act provides that a contract made:

i) may authorise a contractor to carry out only part of the function concerned;
ii) may specify that the contractor is authorised to carry out functions only in certain cases or areas specified in the contract;
iii) may include conditions relating to the carrying out of the functions, e.g. prescribing standards of performance;
iv) shall be for a period not exceeding 10 years and may be revoked at any time by the Minister or the housing authority. Any subsisting contract is to be treated as having been repudiated in these circumstances;
v) shall not prevent the housing authority from exercising themselves the functions to which the contract relates.

21.6 Schedule 2 to the Order lists the homelessness functions in Part 7 that may **not** be contracted out. These are:

- s.179(2) and (3): the provision of various forms of assistance to anyone providing advice and information about homelessness and the prevention of homelessness to people in the district, on behalf of the housing authority;
- s.180: the provision of assistance to voluntary organisations concerned with homelessness; and
- s.213: co-operation with relevant housing authorities and bodies by rendering assistance in the discharge of their homelessness functions.

21.7 Local authorities also **cannot** contract out their functions under the *Homelessness Act 2002* which relate to homelessness reviews and strategies. Chapter 1 provides guidance on homelessness reviews and strategies and outlines the main functions. These include:

- s.1(1): carry out a homelessness review for the district, and formulate and publish a homelessness strategy based on the results of that review;

- s.1(4): publish a new homelessness strategy within 5 years from the day on which their last homelessness strategy was published; and
- 3(6): keep their homelessness strategy under review and modify it from time to time.

Reviews and the formulation of strategies can, however, be informed by research commissioned from external organisations.

21.8 The 1994 Act also provides that the housing authority is responsible for any act or omission of the contractor in exercising functions under the contract, except:

i) where the contractor fails to fulfil conditions specified in the contract relating to the exercise of the function; or,
ii) where criminal proceedings are brought in respect of the contractor's act or omission.

21.9 Where there is an arrangement in force under s.101 of the *Local Government Act 1972* by virtue of which one local authority exercises the functions of another, the 1994 Act provides that the authority exercising the function is not allowed to contract it out without the principal authority's consent.

21.10 **Where a housing authority has contracted out the operation of any homelessness functions the authority remains statutorily responsible and accountable for the discharge of those functions**. This is the case whether a housing authority contracts with a Large Scale Voluntary Transfer registered social landlord, an Arms Length Management Organisation or any other organisation. The authority will therefore need to ensure that the contract provides for delivery of the homelessness functions in accordance with both the statutory obligations and the authority's own policies on tackling and preventing homelessness. The performance of a housing authority's homeless functions will continue to be part of its Comprehensive Performance Assessment and will need to be covered by Best Value reviews, whether or not it discharges the homelessness functions directly.

21.11 When contracting out homelessness functions, housing authorities will need to ensure that:

- proposed arrangements are consistent with their obligations under the 2002 Act to have a strategy for preventing homelessness and ensuring that accommodation and any necessary support will be available to everyone in their district who is homeless or at risk of homelessness;
- a high quality homelessness service will be provided, in particular the assessment of applicants and the provision of advice and assistance; and
- both short-term and settled accommodation services will be available for offer to all applicants owed the main homelessness duty.

21.12 Housing authorities should also ensure they have adequate contractual, monitoring and quality assurance mechanisms in place to ensure their statutory duties are being fully discharged.

21.13 In deciding whether to contract out homelessness functions, housing authorities are encouraged to undertake an options appraisal of each function to decide whether it would best be provided in-house or by another organisation. *Housing Allocation, Homelessness and Stock Transfer – A guide to key issues (ODPM 2004)* provides guidance on the key issues that housing authorities need to consider when deciding whether to retain or contract out the delivery of their homelessness functions.

ANNEX 1
Good Practice/Guidance Publications

DEPARTMENT FOR COMMUNITIES AND LOCAL GOVERNMENT

Homelessness prevention: a guide to good practice (2006)

OFFICE OF THE DEPUTY PRIME MINISTER

Homelessness publications

www.communities.gov.uk/index.asp?id=1162505

Sustainable Communities: settled homes, changing lives. A strategy for tackling homelessness (2005)

Tackling homelessness amongst ethnic minority households – a development guide (2005)

Resources for homeless ex-service personnel in London (2004)

Effective Co-operation in Tackling Homelessness: Nomination Agreements and Exclusions (2004)

Achieving Positive Shared Outcomes in Health and Homelessness (2004)

Local Authorities' Homelessness Strategies: Evaluation and Good Practice (2004)

Reducing B&B use and tackling homelessness – What's working: A Good Practice Handbook (2003)

Housing Associations and Homelessness Briefing (2003)

Achieving Positive Outcomes on Homelessness – A Homelessness Directorate Advice Note to Local Authorities (2003)

Addressing the health needs of rough sleepers (2002)

Care leaving strategies – a good practice handbook (2002)

Drugs services for homeless people – a good practice handbook (2002)

Homelessness Strategies: A Good Practice Handbook (2002)

More than a roof: a report into tackling homelessness *(2002*)

Helping rough sleepers off the streets: A report to the Homelessness Directorate – Randall, G and Brown, S. (2002)

Preventing tomorrow's rough sleepers – Rough Sleepers Unit (2001)

Blocking the fast track from prison to rough sleeping – Rough Sleepers Unit (2000)

Homelessness and housing support directorate policy briefings

Briefing 15: Summary of Homelessness Good Practice Guidance (June 2006)

Briefing 14: Sustainable Communities: settled homes; changing lives – one year on (March 2006)

Briefing 13: Survey of English local authorities about homelessness (December 2005)

Briefing 12: Hostels Capital Improvement Programme (HCIP) (September 2005)

Briefing 11: Providing More Settled Homes (June 2005)

Briefing 10: Delivering on the Positive Outcomes (December 2004)

Briefing 9: Homelessness Strategies: Moving Forward (November 2004)

Briefing 8: Improving the Quality of Hostels and Other Forms of Temporary Accommodation (June 2004)
Briefing 7: Addressing the Health Needs of Homeless People Policy (April 2004)
Briefing 6: Repeat Homelessness Policy (January 2004)
Briefing 5: Improving Employment Options for Homeless People (September 2003)
Briefing 4: Prevention of Homelessness Policy (June 2003)
Briefing 3: Bed and Breakfast Policy (March 2003)
Briefing 2: Domestic Violence Policy (December 2002)
Briefing 1: Ethnicity and Homelessness Policy (September 2002)

Supporting people publications
www.spkweb.org.uk
Supporting People: Guide to Accommodation and Support Options for People with Mental Health Problems (2005)
Guide to Housing and Housing Related Support Options for Offenders and People at Risk of Offending (2005)
Supporting People: Guide to Accommodation and Support Options for Homeless Households (2003)
Supporting People: The Support Needs of Homeless Households (2003)
Supporting People: Guide to Accommodation and Support Options for Households Experiencing Domestic Violence (2002)
Reflecting the Needs and Concerns of Black and Minority Ethnic Communities in Supporting People (2002)

Other ODPM publications
www.communities.gov.uk
Sustainable Communities: Homes for All. A Five Year Plan (2005)
Improving the Effectiveness of Rent Arrears Management (2005)
Housing Allocation, Homelessness and Stock Transfer – A guide to key issues (2004)
Guidance on Arms Length Management of Local Authority Housing (2004)
Allocation of Accommodation – Code of Guidance for local housing authorities (2002)
Working together, Connexions and youth homelessness agencies, London, Department for Transport, Local Government and the Regions (DTLR) and Connexions (2001)

Other government publications

Audit commission
www.audit-commission.gov.uk
Homelessness: Responding to the New Agenda (2003)
ALMO Inspections. The Delivery of Excellent Housing Management Services (2003)
Housing Services After Stock Transfer (2002)

Department for education and skills
www.dfes.gov.uk
Safeguarding Children, The second joint Chief Inspectors' Report on arrangements to Safeguard Children, Commission for Social Care Inspection (2005)

Every Child Matters: Change for Children (2004)
Working with Voluntary and Community Organisations to Deliver Change for Children and Young People (2004)

Department of Health
www.dh.gov.uk/Home/fs/en
Our health, our care, our say: a new direction for community (2006)
Working together to safeguard children (2005)
Government response to Hidden Harm: the Report of an inquiry by the Advisory Council on the Misuse of Drugs (2005)
Making a Difference: Reducing Bureaucracy in Children, Young People and Family Services (2005)
Independence, well-being and choice: Our vision for the future of social care for adults in England (2005)
Commissioning a patient-led NHS (2005)
Health reform in England: update and next steps (2005)
National service framework for mental health: modern standards and service models (1999)
National service framework for children, young people and maternity services (2004)
From Vision to Reality: Transforming Outcomes for Children and Families (2004)
What to do if you're worried a child is being abused (2003)
Tackling Health Inequalities: a programme for action (2003)
Guidance on accommodating children in need and their families – Local Authority Circular 13 (2003)
Children Missing from Care and Home – a guide for good practice published in tandem with the Social Exclusion Unit's report *Young Runaways* (2002)
Getting it Right: good practice in leaving care resource pack (2000)
The framework for assessment of children in need and their families (2000)
Valuing People: A New Strategy for Learning Disability for the 21st Century (2000)
Working Together to Safeguard Children: a guide to interagency working to safeguard and promote the welfare of children (1999) Department of Health, Home Office and Department for Education and Employment

Home Office
www.homeoffice.gov.uk
Advice note on accommodation for vulnerable young people (2001)

Housing Corporation
www.housingcorp.gov.uk
Tenancy management: eligibility and evictions (2004)
Local Authority Nominations. Circular 02/03/Regulation (2003)

Non-Government publications

Centrepoint
www.centrepoint.org.uk
Joint protocols between housing and social services departments: a good practice guide for the assessment and assistance of homeless young people aged 16 and

17 years, Bellerby, N. London (2000)

Chartered institute of housing
www.cih.org
The Housing Manual (2005)
Housing and Support Services for asylum seekers and refugees: a good practice guide. John Perry (2005)
Strategic Approaches to Homelessness; Good Practice Briefing 24 (2002)

Commission For Racial Equality
www.cre.gov.uk
CRE Code of Practice on Racial Equality in Housing (2006)

Disability Rights Commission
www.dre-gb.org/
The Duty to Promote Disability Equality: Statutory Code of Practice (2005)

National housing federation
www.housing.org.uk
Level threshold: towards equality in housing for disabled people: good practice guide (2005)
Flexible allocation and local letting schemes (2000)

Homeless link
www.homeless.org.uk
Hospital admission and discharge: Guidelines for writing a protocol for the hospital admission and discharge of people who are homeless (2006)

Shelter
http://england.shelter.org.uk/home/index.cfm
Sexual exclusion: issues and best practice in lesbian, gay and bisexual housing and homelessness (2005)
Youth housing: a good practice guide (2004)
Local authorities and registered social landlords – best practice on joint working (2002)

ANNEX 2
Other Strategies and Programmes that may Address Homelessness

- Local and Regional Housing Strategy
- Regional Homelessness Strategy
- Regional Economic Development Plan
- Local Strategic Partnership and Community Strategy
- Local Area Agreements
- Supporting People Strategy
- Children and Young People's Plan
- Sure Start
- Connexions

- Education and Employment programmes (e.g. The Princes Trust, New Deal, The Careers Service)
- Progress2work, for drug misusers, and where available, Progress2work-Link Up for alcohol misusers, offenders and homeless people
- Local health schools programme
- Quality Protects
- NHS Local Delivery Plan
- Teenage Pregnancy Strategy
- Drug Action Team Plan
- Crime and Disorder Strategy
- Regional Reducing Reoffending Strategy
- Domestic Violence Strategy
- Anti-Social Behaviour Strategy
- Anti-Poverty Strategy
- Social Inclusion Strategy
- Valuing People Plan
- Town Centre Management Strategy
- Voluntary and community sector plans
- Gypsy and Traveller Accommodation Strategy (where required by s. 225 *Housing Act 2004*)

ANNEX 3
Other Authorities, Organisations and Persons whose Activities may contribute to Preventing/Tackling Homelessness

- Registered social landlords
- Private landlords
- Lettings agencies
- Self build groups
- Housing Co-operatives
- Housing Corporation
- Supported housing providers
- Home improvement agencies
- Primary Care Trusts, health centres and GP practices
- NHS Trusts – Acute and Mental Health
- Local mental health organisations (e.g. Mind)
- Local disability groups
- Care Services Improvement Partnership Regional Development Centres
- Learning Disability Partnership Boards
- Children's Trusts
- Youth Services and youth advice groups
- Education Welfare Services
- LEA Pupil Referral Units
- Schools
- Sure Start

- Connexions
- Youth Offending Team
- Police
- Crime and Disorder Reduction Partnerships
- Drug Action Teams
- National Offender Management Service (incorporating The Prison and Probation Services)
- Victim support groups
- Anti-Social Behaviour Team
- Street Wardens
- Jobcentre Plus
- Learning and Skills Councils
- Environmental Health Team
- Housing Management Team
- Housing Benefits Team
- Armed Forces resettlement services
- National Asylum Support Service
- Refugee Community Organisations
- Law Centres
- Advice/advocacy services (e.g. Citizens Advice Bureaux and Shelter)
- Local voluntary sector infrastructure bodies (e.g. CVS)
- Faith groups
- Women's groups
- Local domestic violence fora
- Ethnic minority groups
- Age groups (e.g. Age Concern, Help the Aged)
- Lesbian, gay and bisexual groups
- Emergency accommodation providers (such as the Salvation Army)
- Day centres for homeless people
- Refuges
- The Samaritans
- Mediation Services
- Local Strategic Partnerships
- Local businesses/Chambers of Commerce
- Regional Housing Board
- Regional planning bodies
- People living in insecure accommodation (and their representative bodies)
- Rough sleepers (and their representative bodies)
- Residents/tenants organisations
- Self help/user groups
- Services supporting sex workers

ANNEX 4
Specific Objectives and Actions for Local Authorities that might be included in a Homelessness Strategy

This Annex provides suggestions for objectives and actions that local authorities may wish to consider including in their homelessness strategies.

HOUSING AUTHORITY

- **Facilitate the effective co-ordination of all service providers, across all sectors in the district, whose activities contribute to preventing homelessness and/or meeting the accommodation and support needs of people who are homeless or at risk of homelessness (objective).**
- establish a homelessness forum to co-ordinate the activities of all the key players, across all sectors, who are contributing to meeting the aims of the homelessness strategy.
- ensure the homelessness strategy is consistent with other relevant local plans and strategies and that all relevant stakeholders are aware of how they work together.
- **Ensure that people who are at risk of homelessness are aware of, and have access to, the services they may need to help them prevent homelessness (objective).**
- provide comprehensive advice and information about homelessness and the prevention of homelessness, free to everyone in the district.
- provide mediation and reconciliation services (e.g. to tackle neighbour disputes and family relationship breakdown).
- implement an effective tenancy relations service (and good liaison with private landlords).
- **Ensure that the supply of accommodation, including affordable accommodation, in the district reflects estimated housing need (objective).**
- in conjunction with RSLs operating in the district, maximise the number of social lettings available for people who have experienced homelessness or at risk of homelessness, consistent with the need to meet the reasonable aspirations of other groups in housing need.
- ensure that provision of specialised and supported accommodation for people who have experienced homelessness or at risk of homelessness (e.g. refuges and wet hostels) reflects estimated need.
- maximise the provision of affordable housing through planning requirements for new private developments.
- **Work with the social services authority to ensure that the needs of clients who have both housing and social services support needs are fully assessed and taken into account (objective)**
- develop a framework for effective joint working with the social services authority, including screening procedures to identify at an early stage where there is a need for case specific joint working.
- put in place arrangements for carrying out joint assessments of people with support needs who are homeless or have experienced homelessness.
- establish a protocol for the referral of clients and the sharing information between services.

SOCIAL SERVICES AUTHORITY

- **Work with the housing authority to ensure that the needs of clients who have both housing and social services support needs are fully assessed and taken into account (objective)**
- develop a framework for effective joint working with the housing authority, including screening procedures, to identify at an early stage where there is a need for case specific joint working.
- put in place arrangements for carrying out joint assessments of people with support needs who are homeless or have experienced homelessness.
- establish a protocol for the referral of clients and the sharing information between services.
- **Ensure that, subject to relevant eligibility criteria, vulnerable people who are homeless, or at risk of homelessness, receive the support they need to help them sustain a home and prevent homelessness recurring (objective).**
- provide a reconciliation service for young people estranged from their families.
- exercise powers under the *Children Act 1989* to make payments to assist young people who are homeless or at risk of homelessness to sustain/find accommodation.
- operate a supported lodgings scheme for homeless 16 and 17 year olds who need a supportive environment.
- provide assistance to enable families with children who have become homeless intentionally (or are ineligible for housing assistance) to secure accommodation for themselves (e.g. financial assistance with rent deposit/guarantees).

ANNEX 5
Co-operation between Registered Social Landlords and Housing Authorities

HOUSING: THE STRATEGIC CONTEXT

1 Housing authorities have a statutory obligation to consider the housing needs of their district (s.8 *Housing Act 1985*). Under the *Homelessness Act 2002* ('the 2002 Act'), they also have a statutory duty to formulate a strategy for preventing homelessness and ensuring that accommodation and support are available for people who are homeless or at risk of homelessness in their district. A homelessness strategy may include actions which the authority expects to be taken by various other organisations, with their agreement.

2 Most social housing is provided by housing authorities and by Registered Social Landlords (RSLs). Virtually all provision of new social housing is delivered through RSLs and, under the transfer programme, ownership of a significant proportion of housing authority stock is being transferred from housing authorities to RSLs, subject to tenants' agreement. This means that, increasingly, RSLs will become the main providers of social housing. Consequently, it is essential that housing authorities work closely with RSLs, as well as all other housing providers, in order to meet the housing needs in their district

and ensure that the aims and objectives of their homelessness strategy are achieved.

STATUTORY FRAMEWORK FOR CO-OPERATION

3 Section 170 of the *Housing Act 1996* ('the 1996 Act') provides that where an RSL has been requested by a housing authority to offer accommodation to people with priority under its allocation scheme, the RSL must co-operate to such extent as is reasonable in the circumstances. Similarly, s.213 provides that where an RSL has been requested by a housing authority to assist them in the discharge of their homelessness functions under Part 7, it must also co-operate to the same extent. Section 3 of the 2002 Act requires housing authorities to consult appropriate bodies and organisations before publishing a homelessness strategy, and this will inevitably need to include RSLs.

HOUSING CORPORATION REGULATORY GUIDANCE

4 RSLs are regulated by the Housing Corporation which, under s.36 of the 1996 Act, and with the approval of the Secretary of State, has issued guidance to RSLs with respect to their management of housing accommodation. The Housing Corporation's Regulatory Code and guidance requires housing associations to work with local authorities to enable them to fulfil their statutory duties to, among others, homeless people and people who have priority for an allocation of housing. In particular, RSLs must ensure that:

- their lettings policies are flexible, non-discriminatory and responsive to demand while contributing to inclusivity and sustainable communities;
- they can demonstrate their co-operation with local authorities on homelessness reviews, homelessness strategies and the delivery of authorities' homelessness functions;
- when requested, and to such extent as is reasonable in the circumstances, they provide a proportion of their stock (at least 50% – see paragraph 9 below) to housing authority nominations and as temporary accommodation for people owed a homelessness duty;
- following consultation with local authorities, criteria are adopted for accepting or rejecting nominees and other applicants for housing;
- applicants are excluded from consideration for housing only if their unacceptable behaviour is serious enough to make them unsuitable to be a tenant; and
- their lettings policies are responsive to authorities' housing duties, take account of the need to give reasonable priority to transfer applicants, are responsive to national, regional and local mobility and exchange schemes, and are demonstrably fair and effectively controlled.

5 Therefore, the overriding requirement for RSLs in relation to homelessness is to demonstrate that they are co-operating with local authorities to enable them to fulfil their statutory duties.

CO-OPERATION AND PARTNERSHIPS

6 Housing authorities need to draw on these regulatory requirements to form constructive partnerships with RSLs. It is also recommended that authorities refer to the strategic document 'A Framework for Partnership' published jointly by the Local Government Association, the National Housing Federation

and the Housing Corporation and available at www.lga.gov.uk/Documents/Briefing/framework.pdf

7 Where RSLs participate in choice-based lettings schemes, the Corporation will expect any protocols for joint working with housing authorities to make proper provision to meet the needs of vulnerable groups, and ensure that support is available to enable tenants and applicants to exercise choice. Housing authorities should involve RSLs in the implementation of choice-based lettings schemes at an early stage.

NOMINATION AGREEMENTS

8 Whilst legislation provides the framework for co-operation between housing authorities and RSLs, nomination agreements set out the way in which this co-operation is given effect. It is crucial that a housing authority has a comprehensive nomination agreement with each of its partner RSLs to ensure that both sides know what is expected of them. The need for a robust nomination agreement applies in all circumstances, but will be particularly important where the housing authority has transferred ownership of its housing stock and is reliant on the transfer RSL (and any other partner RSLs) to provide housing for their applicants. ODPM guidance on *Housing Allocation, Homelessness and Stock Transfer – A Guide to Key Issues (2004)* sets out the policy and operational matters which the nomination agreement between the housing authority and their transfer RSL should cover.

9 RSLs are required to offer at least 50% of vacancies in their stock (net of internal transfers) to housing authority nominations, unless some lower figure is agreed between the two bodies. In some circumstances, they may agree a substantially higher figure. However, housing authorities should bear in mind that RSLs are required to retain their independence. They must honour their constitutional obligations under their diverse governing instruments, and will make the final decision on the allocation of their housing, within their regulatory framework.

10 Where requested by a housing authority, RSLs should consider the possible use of a proportion of their own stock to provide temporary accommodation for people owed a homelessness duty under Part 7 of the 1996 Act. This may be necessary in some areas, particularly those where demand for housing is very high and there is a significant number of homeless families with children who need to be placed in temporary accommodation. RSLs and housing authorities will have joint responsibility for determining the appropriate use of settled housing stock for temporary lettings, taking into account that such use will reduce the volume of RSL housing stock available for nominations into long-term tenancies. Housing authorities should ensure that their partnerships take maximum advantage of the flexibility that such arrangements can provide. The Secretary of State expects that, wherever possible, social housing should be allocated on a settled basis rather than used to provide temporary accommodation in the medium to long term. Where medium to long term accommodation is required, the authority and RSL should consider whether it is possible to offer a secure or an assured tenancy under the terms of the authority's allocations scheme.

11 Housing authorities should ensure that the details of nominated households given to RSLs are accurate and comprehensive. Details should include

information about the applicant's priority status under the housing authority's policy, as well as indications of vulnerability, support needs and arrangements for support.

12 The Corporation expects that RSLs' approach to exclusions and evictions will generally reflect the principles to which housing authorities work. Housing Corporation Circular 07/04 *Tenancy management: eligibility and evictions* sets out the Corporation's expectations of RSLs when assessing the eligibility of applicants and when working to prevent or respond to breaches of tenancy.

EFFECTIVE COLLABORATION

13 It is important that housing authorities foster good partnership working with RSLs, to help them prevent and tackle homelessness in the district. The housing management and care and support approaches undertaken by RSLs are key to sustaining tenancies, reducing evictions and abandonment, and preventing homelessness. To ensure effective collaboration between themselves and partner RSLs operating in their district, housing authorities should consider the following:

nominations agreements: housing authorities should ensure that they have a formal nominations agreement with all partner RSLs and that there are robust arrangements in place to monitor effective delivery of the terms of the agreement. These should be clearly set out, and should include the proportion of lettings that will be made available, any conditions that will apply, and how any disputes about suitability or eligibility will be resolved. Housing authorities should negotiate for the maximum number of lettings that will be required to enable them to discharge their housing functions and which would be reasonable for the RSL to deliver.

exclusion criteria: when negotiating nominations agreements housing authorities should aim for any exclusion criteria (that may be applied to nominees by the RSL) to be kept to a minimum. To prevent new tenancies from failing and to minimise the likelihood of exclusion, housing authorities should also ensure that adequate support packages are in place for vulnerable applicants before a nominee is expected to take up their tenancy.

eviction policies: to help prevent homelessness, housing authorities should encourage RSLs to seek to minimise any need for eviction of their tenants by employing preventative strategies and taking early positive action where breaches of tenancy agreement have occurred. Associations should act to support and sustain, rather than terminate, a tenancy.

In cases involving anti-social behaviour eviction should, where possible, be used as a last resort, although in particularly serious cases or where perpetrators refuse to co-operate it may be necessary. A number of measures have been introduced which may be used to tackle anti-social behaviour without removing the perpetrator from their home and moving the problem to somewhere else. These include Acceptable Behaviour Contracts, Anti-Social Behaviour Orders, housing injunctions and demotion. Further information on the tools and powers available to tackle anti-social behaviour can be found on the TOGETHER website, a resource for practitioners working to tackle anti-social behaviour (www.together.gov.uk).

Similarly, in cases involving rent arrears eviction should, where possible, be used as a last resort. RSLs should employ strategies to maximise their income and to prevent and manage rent arrears. Where arrears have accrued they should seek early intervention through personal contact with the tenant(s) offering support and advice. They should offer practical ways for recovering the arrears through debt management plans, referrals to debt advice agencies and ensuring that tenants are claiming all the benefits to which they are entitled. ODPM published guidance for local authorities and RSLs on *Improving the Effectiveness of Rent Arrears Management* (June 2005).

Supporting People programme: housing authorities should ensure they work closely with RSLs in implementing the Supporting People programme to ensure that housing-related support can be delivered, where appropriate, for people who would be at risk of homelessness without such support.

mobility: housing authorities should work with RSLs in considering the scope for mobility – including moves to other areas, moves to other tenures, and joint action to reduce under-occupation and over-crowding – in meeting housing need and reducing homelessness. Larger RSLs, which operate in a number of different areas, may be uniquely placed to facilitate cross-boundary moves, including voluntary moves from high demand areas to areas of lower demand. ODPM, in conjunction with the Housing Corporation, National Housing Federation and Local Government Association, published a good practice guide for local authorities and housing associations on *Effective Co-operation in Tackling Homelessness: Nomination Agreements and Exclusions (2004)*.

ANNEX 6
Homelessness Strategy: Specific Action that might be expected to be taken by Others

PUBLIC SECTOR
Registered social landlords

- ensure allocation policies meet the needs of people accepted as homeless including specialist provision for vulnerable groups, e.g. drug misusers;
- ensure allocation policies are inclusive, defensible and do not operate 'blanket bans' for particular groups;
- ensure arrears policies take into account the aims of the homelessness strategy (and facilitate early access to money and housing advice).

Primary care trusts

- develop health services for homeless people, (e.g. Personal Medical Service pilots, walk-in centres, GP service that visits hostels and day centres);
- ensure access to primary health care for all homeless people including rough sleepers and those using emergency access accommodation;
- liaise with social services and special needs housing providers to ensure access to dependency and multiple needs services where needed;
- ensure that hospital discharge policies and protocols are developed and put in place for those leaving hospital who are in housing need;
- ensure access to mental health services, including counselling and therapy where needed.

Children's trusts
- ensure children's services and housing strategies are integrated to achieve better outcomes for children.

Youth and community services
- develop peer support schemes;
- raise awareness of homelessness issues with young people at risk.

National offender management service
- complete a basic housing needs assessment on entry to custody in all local establishments;
- share information with other agencies on risk of harm, potential homelessness and vulnerability;
- develop local protocols regarding dealing with potentially homeless offenders and information sharing;
- as part of the local Supporting People Commissioning bodies, provide specialist knowledge to help commission new services for vulnerable offender and victim groups.

Regional offender managers
- ensure regional strategic representation of the needs of offenders in custody and the community.

Community safety team/anti-social behaviour team
- develop steps/interventions to reduce anti-social behaviour and therefore reduce the risk of evictions.

Youth offending team
- work with children and young people to prevent their offending, effectively integrate them and their families within the community and ultimately prevent evictions.

Drug action team
- consider the need to commission treatment for homeless people, or whether mainstream services can be extended to meet their needs;
- develop accommodation options for substance misusers including such provision as Rent Deposit Schemes;
- develop, in collaboration with Supporting People teams, specialist housing provision for substance misusers;
- ensure that the children of adults with substance misuse problems are taken into account when planning services.

Jobcentre plus
- ensure that clients are helped to find and keep a job;
- ensure that clients claim and receive the benefits they are entitled to.

Connexions service
- provide advice and information on housing and related benefits (or referral to other agencies where appropriate) to all 13 to 19 year olds who need it;
- ensure vulnerable young people have access to a personal adviser with the aim of preventing those young people becoming homeless.

National asylum support service (NASS)

- ensure NASS accommodation providers notify local authorities of the planned withdrawal of NASS accommodation within two days of a positive asylum decision;
- encourage NASS accommodation providers to help prevent homelessness amongst new refugees (e.g. via tenancy conversion or delaying evictions);
- ensure that homelessness and housing pressures are taken into account by Regional Strategic Co-ordination Meetings when decisions are taken on future asylum seeker dispersal areas.

VOLUNTARY SECTOR

- Provision of a range of services including:
  - Rent in advance/deposit bond schemes;
  - Night stop schemes;
  - Supported lodgings schemes;
  - Homelessness awareness/preventative input to schools;
  - Advice services (housing/debt/benefits etc.);
  - Counselling, mediation, reconciliation services;
  - Provision of floating support;
  - Lay advocacy services;
  - Dependency services;
  - Hospital discharge services;
  - Women's refuges;
  - Day Centres;
  - Outreach to those sleeping rough;
  - Provision of emergency accommodation (e.g. night shelters);
  - Hostels;
  - Foyers;
  - Resettlement services (including pre-tenancy, move-on accommodation and tenancy sustainment);
  - Mental health services;
  - Peer support, self-help and user groups;
  - Meaningful occupation/personal development work/job training/skills for employment/ work placements;
  - Support for parents of young people at risk of homelessness;
  - Support for victims of crime.

PRIVATE SECTOR

- provision of hostels;
- making lettings available to people who are homeless or at risk of homelessness (e.g. through landlord accreditation schemes);
- working with tenants to address rent arrears.

ANNEX 7
Tackling Common Causes of Homelessness

1 This annex provides guidance on how authorities might tackle some of the more common causes of homelessness at an early stage.

Parents, relatives or friends not being able to provide accommodation

2 Housing authorities are advised to consider a range of approaches aimed at avoiding the crisis of homelessness, resolving problems in the long-term or providing respite and time for a planned, and often more sustainable move. Home visits and mediation services can play an important role in delaying or preventing homelessness by helping people find solutions and resolve difficulties.

3 Family tensions can make living conditions intolerable for young people and their parents. Housing authorities are advised to work closely with children's trusts at strategic level to ensure that housing need and homelessness prevention are included in the strategic planning process through the Children and Young People's Plan. They are also advised to work closely with children's trusts at delivery level as part of local multi-agency teams that provide joined up services focusing on improving outcomes for children and young people. As part of this work, they may consider developing partnerships with key agencies in the voluntary sector who work with young people at risk of homelessness. Trained staff and peer mentors can often help young people in difficult relationships restore some links to their families or supporters, resolve family conflict or facilitate planned moves into alternative accommodation.

Relationship breakdown

4 Relationships may often be strained or break down due to periods of separation, e.g. long-term hospital or drug treatment or because of the behaviour of family members, e.g. offending or violence. Local authorities should develop systems for assessing appropriate forms of intervention and the assessment of risks to vulnerable family members to inform decisions about intervention, e.g. where domestic violence or child safety is involved.

5 Local authorities should consider the use of home visits, mediation and counselling services to help couples and families reconcile their differences or facilitate planned moves to alternative accommodation.

6 Housing authorities are advised to consider the provision of specialist advice targeted at young people at risk of homelessness. Local Connexions services, for example, can play a key role in reaching vulnerable young people; helping them access information and advice, providing one-to-one support or brokering appropriate specialist support from key services such as welfare, health, substance and/or alcohol misuse services, education and employment. Housing authorities might also consider working with local schools in order to provide young people with information about the implications of leaving home and the housing choices available to them.

Domestic violence

7 As well as being a direct and underlying cause of homelessness, it is becoming increasingly apparent that domestic violence is a major factor among people who experience 'repeat' homelessness. In many cases, the provision of advice and outreach services to support people who experience domestic violence before they reach crisis point, for example on ex-partner rent arrears, tenancy agreements and property rights, can help to prevent homelessness.

8 Housing authorities are encouraged to offer people who have experienced domestic violence a range of accommodation and support options. For some, escaping domestic violence will involve leaving their home, often as a last resort,

and those who have experienced domestic violence may be placed in a refuge or another form of appropriate temporary accommodation where necessary. Many people who have experienced domestic violence would, however, prefer to remain in their own homes with their social and support networks around them. From 1 April 2005 local authorities have been strongly encouraged to develop, launch and promote a sanctuary type scheme in order to meet part of the revised domestic violence Best Value Performance Indicator 225. The scheme provides security measures to allow those experiencing domestic violence to remain in their own homes where they choose to do so, where safety can be assured and where the perpetrator no longer lives within the accommodation.

9 It is important that when developing policies, strategies and practice-based interventions, housing authorities work with all relevant bodies. For example, when considering the safety, security and confidentiality of people who have experienced domestic violence and their children, especially those children who may be vulnerable and/or at risk, housing authorities will need to work with Crime and Disorder Reduction Partnerships, the Local Domestic Violence Fora and with the Local Safeguarding Children Board. BVPI 225 encourages further work in this area.

End of an assured shorthold tenancy

10 The use of home visits, landlord-tenant mediation services and tenancy sustainment services may enable tenants who have been asked to leave their home to remain with their existing private landlords, through negotiation, mediation and the offer of practical solutions, such as clearing a debt, providing the tenant with advice on managing budgets or fast-tracking a Housing Benefit claim.

11 Housing authorities should also establish services to provide tenants in housing difficulties with advice and information about available housing options and, where necessary, assistance to help them access alternative accommodation. Advice might include, for example, advice about private landlords and letting agents, including any accreditation schemes, within the district; the availability of rent guarantee or rent deposit schemes; or how to apply for social housing through the local authority housing waiting list or from other social landlords).

Rent and mortgage arrears

12 Early intervention by the housing authority could help prevent difficulties with rent or mortgage arrears from triggering a homelessness crisis for tenants or home owners.

Options might include:

- personal contact with tenants or homeowners to offer support and advice:;
- mediation with private landlords;
- welfare benefits advice and assistance with making claims;
- debt counselling and money advice (either in-house or through referrals to specialist advice agencies);
- advice on practical ways of recovering rent arrears through debt management plans, attachment to earnings or benefits orders or by referrals to a debt advice agencies.

13 Many approaches to the prevention and management of rent arrears among tenants can apply equally whether the landlord is a social sector or a private sector landlord. ODPM published guidance for local authorities and RSLs on *Improving the Effectiveness of Rent Arrears Management (June 2005).*

14 In some cases rent arrears may be the result of an underlying problem such as alcohol or drug misuse, death of a partner, relationship breakdown, change in employment status, or physical or mental health problems. In such cases the housing authority may wish to contact the appropriate health and social services departments and other relevant agencies for advice, assistance and specialist support. The Secretary of State considers that housing authorities should always consult the Children's Trust before considering the eviction of a family with children. Vital work helping vulnerable children can be affected if families with children are forced to move out of the local area. Effective, ongoing liaison arrangements and collaborative working will be important in such instances.

Housing Benefit administration

15 Rent arrears can arise from delays in the calculation and payment of housing benefit. It is therefore in housing authorities' interests to develop prompt and efficient systems for the payment of benefit in order to avoid a risk of homelessness arising as a result of such delays. Where the administration of housing benefit and the provision of housing assistance are dealt with by different departments of the local authority, it will be necessary for the authority to ensure that effective liaison arrangements are in place. Efficient housing benefit payments systems can also help to increase the confidence of private sector landlords in letting accommodation to tenants who may rely on benefits to meet their rent costs.

Anti-social behaviour and offending

16 Tenants may be at risk of becoming homeless as a result of their own or others' anti-social or offending behaviour. Housing authorities are urged to contact tenants in these circumstances at the earliest possible stage where they have received a complaint or where it has been brought to their attention that a tenant is causing a nuisance or annoyance. This will enable them to inform such tenants of the possible consequences of continuing with the reported behaviour and may prevent homelessness resulting in some instances. Authorities will need to be aware of the need for discretion about the source of any complaint, particularly where there is concern about threatening or aggressive behaviour.

17 In cases where a housing authority is satisfied that there is a substantive complaint of anti-social behaviour they will need to consider a range of options to address the problem with the tenant before embarking on action to terminate the tenancy. Housing authorities are advised, where possible, to use eviction as a last resort, although in particularly serious cases or where perpetrators refuse to co-operate it may be necessary.

18 Mediation services may help to resolve neighbour disputes which have led to complaints of anti-social behaviour. A number of measures have been introduced which may be used to tackle anti-social behaviour without removing the perpetrator from their home and simply moving the problem somewhere else. These include: Acceptable Behaviour Contracts, Anti-Social Behaviour

Orders, housing injunctions and demotion. Further information can be found on the TOGETHER website, a resource for practitioners working to tackle anti-social behaviour (www.together.gov.uk).

19 Where local authority tenants are at risk of homelessness as a result of other tenants' anti-social behaviour, authorities should be aware of the powers they have to take action against the perpetrators and make urgent housing transfers to protect victims of violence or harassment, where requested.

20 Housing authorities will need to work closely with the National Offender Management Service (NOMS) and their partners in the voluntary and community sector to manage the housing arrangements of offenders in the community, and ensure they receive any support necessary to avoid a risk of homelessness. Where an authority may be considering the eviction of an offender, it will need to consult closely with NOMS to ensure this can be avoided wherever possible. This will also help reduce re-offending and promote community safety.

Leaving an institutional environment

21 People leaving an institutional environment can be particularly at risk of homelessness and may seek assistance from the housing authority to obtain accommodation when they move on. Authorities should have systems in place to ensure that they have advance notice of such people's needs for accommodation in such circumstances to allow them to take steps well in advance to ensure that arrangements are in place to enable a planned and timely move.

Young people leaving care

22 It is important that, wherever possible, the housing needs of care leavers are addressed before they leave care. All care leavers must have a pathway plan prepared by appropriate staff of the authority responsible for their care; setting out the support they will be provided with to enable them make a successful transition to a more independent lifestyle. Making arrangements for accommodation and ensuring that, where necessary, care leavers are provided with suitable housing support will be an essential aspect of the pathway plan. Where care leavers may require social housing, their housing and related support needs should be discussed with the appropriate agencies. Where necessary, arrangements will need to be made for joint assessment between social services and housing authorities, as part of a multi-agency assessment necessary to inform the pathway plan of individual young people.

23 Consideration of an individual care leaver's housing needs should take account of their need for support and reasonable access to places of education, employment, training and health care. As far as possible, pathway plans should include contingency plans in the event of any breakdown in the young person's accommodation arrangements. It is recommended that housing and social services authorities (and relevant departments within unitary authorities) develop joint protocols for meeting the needs of care leavers to ensure that each agency (or department) plays a full role in providing support to – and building trust with – this client group.

Custody or detention

24 Around a third of prisoners lose their housing on imprisonment, so it is important that prisoners receive effective advice and assistance about housing options, either prior to or when being remanded or sentenced to custody. Assessing an offender's housing needs at this point will help to identify those prisoners who may require assistance to bring to an end, sustain or transfer an existing tenancy, make a claim for Housing Benefit to meet rent costs while in prison, or to help a prisoner transfer or close down an existing tenancy appropriately. Local authorities are advised to assist the Prison Service in providing advice to prisoners and taking action to ensure they can sustain their accommodation while in custody.

25 It is recommended that housing advice be made available to offender throughout the period of custody or detention to ensure that any housing needs are addressed. It is important that early planning takes place between prison staff and housing providers to identify housing options on release, to prevent homelessness and enable them to make a smooth transition from prison, or remand, to independent living.

26 All prisoners in local prisons and Category C prisons have access to housing advice. And, from April 2005 all local prisons have been required to carry out a housing needs assessment for every new prisoner, including those serving short sentences. Local authorities are advised to assist the Prison Service in delivering these services.

27 All Youth Offending Teams (YOTs) now have named accommodation officers. YOTs can offer both practical support to children, young people and their families and can increasingly play a key strategic role in ensuring that young offenders are effectively resettled through accessing mainstream provision and services.

28 Joint working between the National Offender Management Service/Youth Offending Teams and their local housing authorities is essential to help prevent homelessness amongst offenders, ex-offenders and others who have experience of the criminal justice system. Options might include:

- having a single contact point within the housing authority to provide housing advice and assistance for those who have experience of the criminal justice system;
- Probation staff offering information on securing or terminating tenancies prior to custody;
- running housing advice sessions in local prisons to further enable prisoners to access advice on housing options prior to their release;
- prisons granting prisoners Release On Temporary Licence to attend housing interviews with landlords;
- developing tenancy support services for those who have experienced the criminal justice system.

Armed forces

29 Members of Her Majesty's regular naval, military and air forces are generally provided with accommodation by the Ministry of Defence (MOD), but are required to leave this when they are discharged from the service. The principal responsibility for providing housing information and advice to Service personnel lies with the armed forces up to the point of discharge and these services are delivered through the Joint Service Housing Advice Office (telephone: 01722 436575). Some people, who have served in the armed forces for a long period, and those who are medically discharged, may be offered assistance with resettlement by Ministry of Defence (MOD) resettlement staff. The MOD issues a *Certificate of Cessation of Entitlement to Occupy Service Living Accommodation* (see examples at Annexes 14 and 15) six months before discharge.

30 Housing authorities that have a significant number of service personnel stationed in their area will need to work closely with relevant partners, such as the Joint Service Housing Advice Office and MOD's resettlement services, to ascertain likely levels of need for housing assistance amongst people leaving the forces and plan their services accordingly. In particular, housing authorities are advised to take advantage of the six-month period of notice of discharge to ensure that service personnel receive timely and comprehensive advice on the housing options available to them when they leave the armed forces. Authorities may also wish to consider creating links with the employment and business communities to assist people leaving the armed forces to find work or meaningful occupation, enabling them further to make a successful transition to independent living in the community.

31 The Veterans Agency should be the first point of contact for all former armed forces personnel who require information about housing issues. The agency provide a free help line (telephone: 0800 169 2277) which offers former armed forces personnel advice and signposting to ex-Service benevolent organisations who may be able to offer assistance with housing matters.

Hospital

32 Some people who are admitted to hospital – even for a short time – may be in housing need or at risk of homelessness. And some people who may not be in housing need when they are admitted may become at risk of losing their home during a protracted stay in hospital, for example, if they are unable to maintain their rent or mortgage payments. This can apply, in particular, to people admitted to hospital for mental health reasons and for whom family, tenancy or mortgage breakdown is an accompanying factor to the admission to hospital.

33 Housing authorities are advised to work closely with social services and NHS Trusts in order to establish good procedures for the discharge of patients, and to ensure that former patients are not homeless or at risk of homelessness on leaving hospital. This could involve agreeing joint protocols for hospital admissions and discharge of patients to ensure that the housing and support needs of inpatients are identified as early as possible after admission, and that arrangements are put in place to meet the needs of patients in good time prior to discharge. Measures might include, for example, setting up a multi-agency discharge team as part of the homelessness strategy action plan or funding a dedicated post to support patients who may be at risk of homelessness when discharged from hospital.

34 Further guidance is provided in Department of Health publications on *Achieving timely simple discharge from hospital: A toolkit for the multi-disciplinary team (2004)* and *Discharge from hospital: pathway, process and practice (2003).*

Accommodation provided by National Asylum Support Service (NASS)

35 Asylum seekers who receive leave to remain in the UK must move on from their NASS accommodation within 28 days of the decision on their case. Former asylum seekers will therefore have little time to find alternative accommodation and are unlikely to have had any experience of renting or buying accommodation in the UK, or experience of related matters such as claiming benefits or arranging essential services such as gas, water and electricity. These difficulties are likely to be compounded by the fact that many former asylum seekers may face cultural barriers such as language.

36 In order to prevent these factors leading to homelessness amongst former asylum seekers, housing authorities are advised to develop protocols with NASS accommodation providers, refugee support services and NASS regional managers to ensure that, where possible, a planned and timely move to alternative accommodation or the sustainment of existing accommodation can take place. Housing benefit, rent deposits, homeless prevention loans and discretionary housing benefit payments can all help to fund temporary extensions of the NASS notice period or longer-term tenancy conversion through the establishment of assured shorthold tenancies.

37 Former asylum seekers will need effective and timely advice on the range of housing options available. It is vital that housing authorities ensure that this advice and information can be readily translated into community languages and delivered in locations accessible to asylum seekers and refugees. Authorities are also advised to consider whether there may be a need for ongoing resettlement support in order to maximise the chances of tenancy sustainment. As standard, authorities are advised to ensure that new refugees are made fully aware of the steps that they need to take to maintain a UK tenancy.

38 Authorities may wish to refer to *Housing and Support Services for asylum seekers and refugees: a good practice guide (2005)* published by the Chartered Institute of Housing.

Ethnic minority populations

39 Statistics provided by local authorities show that people from ethnic minority backgrounds are around three times more likely to be accepted as owed a main homelessness duty than their White counterparts. This pattern is found across all regions in England and the reasons are varied and complex. It is therefore critical that housing authorities and their partner agencies develop comprehensive strategies to better prevent and respond to homelessness among people from ethnic minority communities.

40 ODPM published *Tackling homelessness amongst ethnic minority households – a development guide (2005)* to assist local authorities and their partner agencies in the development of inclusive, evidence-based and cost-effective homelessness services for their local ethnic minority populations.

Drug users

41 Drug use can both precede and occur as a result of homelessness. Between half and three quarters of single homeless people have in the past been problematic drug misusers. Many have a wide range of support needs, which reinforce each other and heighten the risk of drug use and homelessness. For those who are engaging in drug treatment, or have stabilised their use, homelessness increases their chances of relapse and continued problematic drug use. Housing authorities are advised to work closely with Drug Action Teams (multi-agency partnerships who co-ordinate the drug strategy at the local level) to ensure that housing and homelessness strategies are aligned with DAT treatment plans and Supporting People strategies help address the needs of homeless drug users as a shared client group.

ANNEX 8
How to Contact the Home Office Immigration and Nationality Directorate

1 The Home Office's Immigration and Nationality Directorate (IND) will exchange information with housing authorities subject to relevant data protection and disclosure policy requirements being met and properly managed, provided that the information is required to assist with the carrying out of statutory functions or prevention and detection of fraud.

2 The Evidence and Enquiries Unit (EEU) will provide a service to housing authorities to confirm the immigration status of an applicant from abroad (Non-Asylum Seekers). In order to take advantage of the service, housing authorities first need to register with the Evidence and Enquiries Unit, Immigration and Nationality Directorate, 12th Floor Lunar House, Croydon, CR9 2BY either by letter or **Fax: 020 8196 3049**

3 Registration details required by the EEU's Local Authorities' Team are:
   (a) Name of enquiring housing authority on headed paper;
   (b) Job title/status of officer registering on behalf of the local housing authority; and
   (c) Names of housing authority staff and their respective job titles/status who will be making enquiries on behalf of the housing authority.

4 Once the housing authority is registered with the EEU, and this has been confirmed, then the authorised personnel can make individual enquiries by letter or fax, but replies will be returned by post.

5 The EEU will not usually indicate that someone is an asylum seeker unless the applicant has signed a disclaimer and it is attached to the enquiry or if the enquirer has specifically asked about asylum.

6 If a response indicates that the applicant has an outstanding asylum claim, or there are any queries regarding an ongoing asylum case, enquiries should be made to NASS LA Comms on 020 8760 4527. Local authorities will also need to be registered with this team before any information can be provided.

7 The Home Office (IND) can only advise whether an EEA/foreign national has a right of residence in the United Kingdom. IND does not decide whether an EEA/Foreign national qualifies for benefits or for local authority housing.

ANNEX 9
Asylum Seekers

OVERVIEW

1 Generally, asylum seekers can be expected to be *persons subject to immigration control* who have been given *temporary admission* but have not been granted leave to enter or remain in the UK.

2 **Asylum seekers who are** *persons subject to immigration control* **and whose claim for asylum was made** *after 2 April 2000* **are not eligible for assistance under Part 7.** However, some asylum seekers who are *persons subject to immigration control* and whose claim for asylum was made before 3 April 2000 may be eligible (see below).

3 Broadly speaking, an asylum seeker is a person claiming to have a well-founded

fear of being persecuted for reasons of race, religion, nationality, membership of a particular social group, or political opinion, and who is unable or unwilling to avail him or her self of the protection of the authorities in his or her own country.

4 A person only becomes an asylum seeker when his or her claim for asylum has been recorded by the Home Secretary, and he or she remains an asylum seeker until such time as that application has been finally resolved (including the resolution of any appeal). The recording, consideration and resolution of such claims is a matter for the Home Office Immigration and Nationality Directorate (IND).

5 If there is any uncertainty about an applicant's immigration or asylum status, housing authorities should contact the Home Office Immigration and Nationality Directorate, using the procedures set out in Annex 8. Before doing so, the applicant should be advised that an inquiry will be made: if at this stage the applicant prefers to withdraw his or her application, no further action will be required

ASYLUM SEEKERS WHO ARE ELIGIBLE FOR PART 7 ASSISTANCE

6 The *Allocation of Housing and Homelessness (Eligibility) (England) Regulations 2006* (SI 2006 No.1294) ('the Eligibility Regulations') provide that asylum seekers who are *persons subject to immigration control* and who claimed asylum before 3 April 2000 are eligible for assistance under Part 7 in certain circumstances (set out below). However, by virtue of s.186(1), an asylum seeker is not eligible for Part 7 assistance if he or she has any accommodation in the UK – however temporary – available for his or her occupation. This would include a place in a hostel or bed and breakfast hotel.

7 Subject to s.186(1), such asylum seekers are eligible for assistance under Part 7, if they claimed asylum *before 3 April 2000*, and:

i) the claim for asylum was made at the port on initial arrival in the UK (but not on re-entry) from a country outside the United Kingdom, the Channel Islands, the Isle of Man or the Republic of Ireland; **or**

ii) the claim for asylum was made within 3 months of a declaration by the Secretary of State that he would not normally order the return of a person to the country of which he or she is a national because of a fundamental change of circumstances in that country, and the asylum seeker was present in Great Britain on the date the declaration was made; **or**

iii) the claim for asylum was made on or before 4 February 1996 and the applicant was entitled to housing benefit on 4 February 1996 under regulation 7A of the *Housing Benefit (General) Regulations 1987.*

8 Generally, a person ceases to be an asylum seeker for the purposes of the Eligibility Regulations when his claim for asylum is recorded by the Secretary of State as having been decided (other than on appeal) or abandoned. However, a person does not cease to be an asylum seeker in these circumstances for the purposes of paragraph 7(iii) if he continues to be eligible for housing benefit by virtue of:

- regulation 10(6) of the *Housing Benefit Regulations 2006* (SI 2006 No. 213), or
- regulation 10(6) of the *Housing Benefit (persons who have attained the qualifying age for state pension credit) Regulations 2006* (SI 2006 No. 214).

as amended by the *Housing Benefit and Council Tax Benefit (Consequential Provisions) Regulations 2006* (SI 2006 No.217).

FORMER ASYLUM SEEKERS

9 Where an asylum claim is successful – either initially or following an appeal – the claimant will normally be granted refugee status. If a claim is unsuccessful, leave to remain in the UK may still be granted, in accordance with published policies on Humanitarian Protection and Discretionary Leave. Former asylum seekers granted refugee status, or those granted Humanitarian Protection or Discretionary Leave which is not subject to a condition requiring him to maintain and accommodate himself without recourse to public funds will be eligible for homelessness assistance.

10 Prior to April 2003, Exceptional Leave to Remain was granted rather than Humanitarian Protection or Discretionary Leave. Those with Exceptional Leave to Remain which is not subject to a condition requiring him to maintain and accommodate himself without recourse to public funds will also be eligible for homelessness assistance.

INFORMATION

11 Under s.187 of the *Housing Act 1996*, the Home Office Immigration and Nationality Directorate (IND) will, on request, provide local housing authorities with the information necessary to determine whether a particular housing applicant is an asylum seeker, or a dependant of an asylum seeker, and whether he or she is eligible for assistance under Part 7. In cases where it is confirmed that a housing applicant is an asylum seeker, or the dependant of an asylum seeker, any subsequent change in circumstances which affect the applicant's housing status (eg. a decision on the asylum claim) will be notified to the authority by the IND. The procedures for contacting the IND are set out in Annex 8.

ANNEX 10
The Habitual Residence Test

1 In practice, when considering housing applications from persons who are subject to the habitual residence test, it is only necessary to investigate habitual residence if the applicant has arrived or returned to live in the UK during the two year period prior to making the application.

DEFINITION OF HABITUALLY RESIDENT

2 The term 'habitually resident' is not defined in legislation. Local authorities should always consider the overall circumstances of a case to determine whether someone is habitually resident in the UK, the Channel Islands, the Isle of Man or the Republic of Ireland.

GENERAL PRINCIPLES

3 When deciding whether a person is habitually resident in a place, consideration must be given to all the facts of each case in a common sense way. It should be remembered that:–

- the test focuses on the fact and nature of residence;
- a person who is not resident somewhere cannot be habitually resident there. Residence is a more settled state than mere physical presence in a country. To be resident a person must be seen to be making a home. It need not be the only home or a permanent home but it must be a genuine home for the time being. For example, a short stay visitor or a person receiving short term medical treatment is not resident;
- the most important factors for habitual residence are the length, continuity and general nature of actual residence rather than intention;
- the practicality of a person's arrangements for residence is a necessary part of determining whether it can be described as settled and habitual;
- established habitual residents who have periods of temporary or occasional absence of long or short duration may still be habitually resident during such absences.

ACTION ON RECEIPT OF AN APPLICATION

Applicant came to live in the UK during the previous two years

4 If it appears that the applicant came to live in the UK during the previous two years, authorities should make further enquiries to decide if the applicant is habitually resident, or can be treated as such.

Factors to consider

5 The applicant's stated reasons and intentions for coming to the UK will be relevant to the question of whether he or she is habitually resident. If the applicant's stated intention is to live in the UK, and not return to the country from which they came, that intention must be consistent with their actions.

6 To decide whether an applicant is habitually resident in the UK, authorities should consider the factors set out below. However, these do not provide an exhaustive check list of the questions or factors that need to be considered. Further enquiries may be needed. The circumstances of each case will dictate what information is needed, and all relevant factors should be taken into account.

Why has the applicant come to the UK?

7 If the applicant is returning to the UK after a period spent abroad, and it can be established that the applicant was previously habitually resident in the UK and is returning to resume his or her former period of habitual residence, **he or she will be immediately habitually resident.**

8 In determining whether an applicant is returning to resume a former period of habitual residence authorities should consider:

- when did the applicant leave the UK?
- how long did the applicant live in the UK before leaving?
- why did the applicant leave the UK?
- how long did the applicant intend to remain abroad?
- why did the applicant return?
- did the applicant's partner and children, if any, also leave the UK?
- did the applicant keep accommodation in the UK?
- if the applicant owned property, was it let, and was the lease timed to coincide with the applicant's return to the UK?
- what links did the applicant keep with the UK?

- have there been other brief absences? If yes, obtain details
- why has the applicant come to the UK?

9 If the applicant has arrived in the UK within the previous two years and is not resuming a period of habitual residence, consideration should be given to his or her reasons for coming to the UK, and in particular to the factors set out below.

Applicant is joining family or friends

10 If the applicant has come to the UK to join or rejoin family or friends, authorities should consider:

- has the applicant sold or given up any property abroad?
- has the applicant bought or rented accommodation or is he or she staying with friends?
- is the move to the UK intended to be permanent?

Applicant's plans

11 Authorities should consider the applicant's plans, e.g.:

- if the applicant plans to remain in the UK, is the applicant's stated plan consistent with his or her actions?
- were any arrangements made for employment and accommodation (even if unsuccessful) before the applicant arrived in the UK?
- did the applicant buy a one-way ticket?
- did the applicant bring all his or her belongings?
- is there any evidence of links with the UK, eg membership of clubs?

12 The fact that a person may intend to live in the UK for the foreseeable future does not, of itself, mean that habitual residence has been established. However, the applicant's intentions along with other factors, for example the disposal of property abroad, may indicate that the applicant is habitually resident in the UK.

13 An applicant who intends to reside in the UK for only a short period, for example for a holiday or to visit friends is unlikely to be habitually resident in the UK.

Length of residence in another country

14 Authorities should consider the length and continuity of an applicant's residence in another country:

- how long did the applicant live in the previous country?
- does the applicant have any remaining ties with his or her former country of residence?
- has the applicant stayed in different countries outside the UK?

15 It is possible that a person may own a property abroad but still be habitually resident in the UK. A person who has a home or close family in another country would normally retain habitual residence in that country. A person who has previously lived in several different countries but has now moved permanently to the UK may be habitually resident here.

Centre of interest

16 An applicant is likely to be habitually resident in the UK, the Channel Islands, the Isle of Man or the Republic of Ireland, despite spending time abroad, if his or her centre of interest is located in one of these places.

17 People who maintain their centre of interest in the UK, the Channel Islands, the Isle of Man or the Republic of Ireland, for example a home, a job, friends, membership of clubs, are likely to be habitually resident there. People who have retained their centre of interest in another country and have no particular ties with the UK, the Channel Islands, the Isle of Man or the Republic of Ireland, are unlikely to be habitually resident in the UK, the Channel Islands, the Isle of Man or the Republic of Ireland.

18 Authorities should take the following into account when deciding the centre of interest:

- home;
- family ties;
- club memberships;
- finance accounts

19 If the centre of interest appears to be in the UK, the Channel Islands, the Isle of Man or the Republic of Ireland but the applicant has a home somewhere else, authorities should consider the applicant's intentions regarding the property.

20 In certain cultures, e.g. the Asian culture, it is quite common for a person to live in one country but have property abroad that they do not intend to sell. Where such a person has lived in the UK, the Channel Islands, the Isle of Man or the Republic of Ireland for many years, the fact that they have property elsewhere does not necessarily mean that they intend to leave, or that the applicant's centre of interest is elsewhere.

ANNEX 11
European Groupings (EU, A8, EEA, Switzerland)

THE EUROPEAN UNION (EU)

Austria, Belgium, Cyprus, the Czech Republic, Denmark, Estonia, Finland, France, Germany, Greece, Hungary, Ireland, Italy, Latvia, Lithuania, Luxembourg, Malta, the Netherlands, Poland, Portugal, Slovakia, Slovenia, Spain, Sweden, the United Kingdom and the A8 or Accession States.

THE 'A8' OR 'ACCESSION STATES'

The 8 eastern European States that acceded to the EU in 2004 (and whose nationals may be subject to the UK Worker Registration Scheme for a transitional period):
the Czech Republic, Estonia, Hungary, Latvia, Lithuania, Poland, Slovakia and Slovenia.

THE EUROPEAN ECONOMIC AREA (EEA)

All EU countries, plus: Iceland, Norway and Liechtenstein

SWITZERLAND

Note: Although not an EEA State, Switzerland should be treated as an EEA State for the purpose of this guidance. (See the *Immigration (European Economic Area) Regulations 2006* (S.I. 2006 No. 1003), regulation 2(1))

ANNEX 12
Rights to Reside in the UK Derived from EC Law

1 EEA nationals and their family members who have a right to reside in the UK that derives from EC law are not persons subject to immigration control. This means that they will be eligible for assistance under Part 7 of the *Housing Act 1996* ('housing assistance') unless they fall within one of the categories of persons to be treated as a person from abroad who is ineligible for assistance by virtue of regulation 6 of the *Allocation of Housing and Homelessness (Eligibility) (England) Regulations 2006* ('the Eligibility Regulations').

GENERAL

Nationals of EU countries

2 Nationals of EU countries enjoy a number of different rights to reside in other Member States, including the UK. These rights derive from the EC Treaty, EC secondary legislation (in particular *Directive 2004/38/EC*), and the case law of the European Court of Justice.

3 Whether an individual EU national has a right to reside in the UK will depend on his or her circumstances, particularly his or her economic status (e.g. whether employed, self-employed, seeking work, a student, or economically inactive etc.).

The accession states

4 A slightly different regime applies to EU nationals who are nationals of the accession states. For the purposes of this guidance, 'the accession states' are the 8 eastern European countries that acceded to the EU on 1 May 2004: Poland, Lithuania, Estonia, Latvia, Slovenia, Slovakia, Hungary and the Czech Republic.

The Immigration (European Economic Area) Regulations 2006

5 The Immigration (European Economic Area) Regulations 2006 ('the EEA Regulations') implement into UK domestic law EC legislation conferring rights of residence on EU nationals. Broadly, the EEA Regulations provide that EU nationals have the right to reside in the UK without the requirement for leave to remain under the *Immigration Act 1971* for the first 3 months of their residence, and for longer, if they are a 'qualified person' or they have acquired a permanent right of residence.

Nationals of Iceland, Liechtenstein and Norway.

6 The EEA Regulations extend the same rights to reside in the UK to nationals of Iceland, Liechtenstein and Norway as those afforded to EU nationals (The EU countries plus Iceland, Liechtenstein and Norway together comprise the EEA.)

Nationals of Switzerland

7 The EEA Regulations also extend the same rights to reside in the UK to nationals of Switzerland.

8 For the purposes of this guidance, 'EEA nationals' means nationals of any of the EU member states (excluding the UK), and nationals of Iceland, Norway, Liechtenstein and Switzerland.

INITIAL 3 MONTHS OF RESIDENCE

9 Regulation 13 of the EEA Regulations provides that EEA nationals have the right to reside in the UK for a period of up to 3 months without any conditions or formalities other than holding a valid identity card or passport. Therefore, during their first 3 months of residence in the UK, EEA nationals will not be subject to immigration control (unless the right to reside is lost following a decision by an immigration officer in accordance with regulation 13(3) of the EEA Regulations).

10 However, regulations 6(1)(b)(i) and (c) of the Eligibility Regulations provide that a person who is not subject to immigration control is not eligible for housing assistance if:

i) his or her **only** right to reside in the UK is an initial right to reside for a period not exceeding 3 months under regulation 13 of the EEA Regulations, or
ii) his or her **only** right to reside in the Channel Islands, the Isle of Man or the Republic of Ireland is a right equivalent to the right mentioned in (i) above which is derived from the Treaty establishing the European Community.

On (ii), article 6 of *Directive 2004/38/EC* provides that EU citizens have the right of residence in the territory of another Member State (e.g. the Republic of Ireland) for a period of up to 3 months without any conditions or formalities other than holding a valid identity card or passport.

RIGHTS OF RESIDENCE FOR 'QUALIFIED PERSONS'

11 Regulation 14 of the EEA Regulations provides that 'qualified persons' have the right to reside in the UK so long as they remain a qualified person. Under regulation 6 of the EEA Regulations, 'qualified person' means:

a) a jobseeker,
b) a worker,
c) a self-employed person,
d) a self-sufficient person,
e) a student.

Jobseekers

12 For the purposes of regulation 6(1)(a) of the EEA Regulations, 'jobseeker' means a person who enters the UK in order to seek employment and can provide evidence that he or she is seeking employment and has a genuine chance of being employed.

13 Accession state nationals who need to register to work (see paragraph 20 below) do not have a right to reside in the UK as a jobseeker (see regulation 5(2) of the Accession Regulations, as amended). However, accession state nationals seeking work may have a right to reside by virtue of another status, e.g. as a self-sufficient person.

14 Although a person who is a jobseeker for the purposes of the definition of 'qualified person' in regulation 6(1)(a) of the EEA Regulations is not subject to immigration control, regulation 6 of the Eligibility Regulations provides that a person is not eligible for housing assistance if:

(i) his or her only right to reside in the UK is derived from his status as a jobseeker or the family member of a jobseeker, or

(ii) his or her only right to reside in the Channel Islands, the Isle of Man or the Republic of Ireland is a right equivalent to the right mentioned in (i) above which is derived from the Treaty establishing the European Community.

Workers

15 In order to be a worker for the purposes of the EEA Regulations, a person must be employed, that is, the person is obliged to provide services for another person in return for monetary reward and who is subject to the control of that other person as regards the way in which the work is to be done.

16 Activity as an employed person may include part-time work, seasonal work and cross-border work (i.e. where a worker is established in another Member State and travels to work in the UK). However, the case law provides that the employment must be effective and genuine economic activity, and not on such a small scale as to be regarded as purely marginal and ancillary.

17 Provided the employment is effective and genuine economic activity, the fact that a person's level of remuneration may be below the level of subsistence or below the national minimum wage, or the fact that a person may be receiving financial assistance from public benefits, would not exclude that person from being a 'worker'. Housing authorities should note that surprisingly small amounts of work can be regarded as effective and genuine economic activity.

18 Applicants in the labour market should be able to confirm that they are, or have been, working in the UK by providing, for example:

- payslips,
- a contract of employment, or
- a letter of employment.

Retention of worker status

19 A person who is no longer working does not cease to be treated as a 'worker' for the purpose of regulation 6(1)(b) of the EEA Regulations, if he or she:

(a) is temporarily unable to work as the result of an illness or accident; or

(b) is recorded as involuntarily unemployed after having being employed in the UK, provided that he or she has registered as a jobseeker with the relevant employment office, and:

  (i) was employed for one year or more before becoming unemployed, or

  (ii) has been unemployed for no more than 6 months, or

  (iii) can provide evidence that he or she is seeking employment in the UK and has a genuine chance of being engaged; or

(c) is involuntarily unemployed and has embarked on vocational training; or

(d) has voluntarily ceased working and embarked on vocational training that is related to his or her previous employment.

Accession state workers requiring registration who are treated as workers

20 By virtue of the *Accession (Immigration and Worker Registration) Regulations 2004* (SI 2004/1219) ('the Accession Regulations'), accession state nationals (with certain exceptions) are required to register their employment in the UK until they have accrued a period of 12 months' continuous employment. The exceptions are set out in Annex 13.

21 An accession state national requiring registration is only treated as a worker if he or she is actually working and:

(a) has registered his or her employment and is working in the UK for an authorised employer (see regulation 5(2) of the Accession Regulations, as amended), or
(b) is not registered for employment, but has been working for an employer for less than one month (regulation 7(3) of the Accession Regulations), or
(c) has applied to register under the Worker Registration Scheme and is working for the employer with whom he or she has applied to register (regulation 7(2)(b) of the Accession Regulations).

22 To demonstrate eligibility for housing assistance, accession state workers requiring registration should be able to:
(a) provide a valid worker registration card, and a valid worker registration certificate showing their current employer (see Annex 13 for specimens of these documents), or
(b) (where the accession state worker has applied to register but not yet received the registration certificate) provide a copy of their application to register, or
(c) show they have been working for their current employer for less than one month.

23 Authorities may need to contact the employer named in the registration certificate, to confirm that the applicant continues to be employed.

24 See Annex 13 for guidance on the Worker Registration Scheme.

25 A person who is a 'worker' for the purposes of the definition of a qualified person in regulation 6(1) of the EEA Regulations is not subject to immigration control, and is eligible for housing assistance whether or not he or she is habitually resident in the UK, the Channel Islands, the Isle of Man or the Republic of Ireland.

Self-employed persons

26 'Self-employed person' means a person who establishes himself in the UK in order to pursue activity as a self-employed person in accordance with Article 43 of the Treaty establishing the European Union.

27 A self-employed person should be able to confirm that he or she is pursuing activity as a self-employed person by providing documents relating to their business such as:
a) invoices,
b) tax accounts, or
c) utility bills.

28 A person who is no longer in self-employment does not cease to be treated as a self-employed person for the purposes of regulation 6(1)(c) of the EEA regulations, if he or she is temporarily unable to pursue his or her activity as a self-employed person as the result of an illness or accident.

29 Accession state nationals are not required to register in order to establish themselves in the UK as a self-employed person.

30 A person who is a self-employed person for the purposes of the definition of a qualified person in regulation 6(1) of the EEA Regulations is not subject to immigration control, and is eligible for housing assistance whether or not he or she is habitually resident in the UK, the Channel Islands, the Isle of Man or the Republic of Ireland.

Self-sufficient persons

31 Regulation 4(1)(c) of the EEA regulations defines 'self-sufficient person' as a person who has:

(i) sufficient resources not to become a burden on the social assistance system of the UK during his or her period of residence, and

(ii) comprehensive sickness insurance cover in the UK.

32 By regulation 4(4) of the EEA Regulations, the resources of a person who is a self-sufficient person or a student (see below), and where applicable, any family members, are to be regarded as sufficient if they exceed the maximum level of resources which a UK national and his or her family members may possess if he or she is to become eligible for social assistance under the UK benefit system.

33 Where an EEA national applies for housing assistance as a self-sufficient person and does not appear to meet the conditions of regulation 4(1)(c), the housing authority will need to consider whether he or she may have some other right to reside in the UK.

34 Where the applicant does not meet the conditions of regulation 4(1)(c) but has previously done so during his or her residence in the UK, the case should be referred to the Home Office for clarification of their status.

35 A person who is a self-sufficient person for the purposes of the definition of a qualified person in regulation 6(1) of the EEA Regulations is not subject to immigration control, but must be habitually resident in the UK, the Channel Islands, the Isle of Man or the Republic of Ireland to be eligible for housing assistance.

Students

36 Regulation 4(1)(d) of the EEA regulations defines 'student' as a person who:

(a) is enrolled at a private or public establishment included on the Department of Education and Skills' Register of Education and Training Providers, or is financed from public funds, for the principal purpose of following a course of study, including vocational training, and

(b) has comprehensive sickness insurance cover in the UK, and

(c) assures the Secretary of State, by means of a declaration or such equivalent means as the person may choose, that he or she (and if applicable his or her family members) has sufficient resources not to become a burden on the social assistance system of the UK during his or her period of residence.

37 A person who is a student for the purposes of the definition of a qualified person in regulation 6(1) of the EEA Regulations is not subject to immigration control. The eligibility of such a person for housing assistance should therefore be considered in accordance with regulation 6 of the Eligibility Regulations.

PERMANENT RIGHT OF RESIDENCE

38 Regulation 15 of the EEA Regulations provides that the following persons shall acquire the right to reside in the UK permanently:

(a) an EEA national who has resided in the UK in accordance with the EEA regulations for a continuous period of 5 years;

(b) a non-EEA national who is a family member of an EEA national and who has resided in the UK with the EEA national in accordance with the EEA regulations for a continuous period of 5 years;

(c) a worker or self-employed person who has ceased activity (see regulation 5 of the EEA Regulations for the definition of worker or self-employed person who has ceased activity);
(d) the family member of a worker or self-employed person who has ceased activity;
(e) a person who was the family member of a worker or self-employed person who has died, where the family member resided with the worker or self-employed person immediately before the death and the worker or self-employed person had resided continuously in the UK for at least 2 years before the death (or the death was the result of an accident at work or an occupational disease);
(f) a person who has resided in the UK in accordance with the EEA regulations for a continuous period of 5 years, and at the end of that period was a family member who has retained the right of residence (see regulation 10 of the EEA Regulations for the definition of a family member who has retained the right of residence).

Once acquired, the right of permanent residence can be lost through absence from the UK for a period exceeding two consecutive years.

39 A person with a right to reside permanently in the UK arising from (c), (d) or (e) above is eligible for housing assistance whether or not he or she is habitually resident in the UK, the Channel Islands, the Isle of Man or the Republic of Ireland. Persons with a permanent right to reside by virtue of (a),(b), or (f) must be habitually resident to be eligible.

RIGHTS OF RESIDENCE FOR CERTAIN FAMILY MEMBERS

The right to reside

40 Regulation 14 of the EEA Regulations provides that the following family members are entitled to reside in the UK:
(i) a family member of a qualified person residing in the UK;
(ii) a family member of an EEA national with a permanent right of residence under regulation 15; and
(iii) a family member who has retained the right of residence (see regulation 10 of the EEA Regulations for the definition).

41 A person who has a right to reside in the UK as the family member of an EEA national under the EEA Regulations will not be subject to immigration control. The eligibility of such a person for housing assistance should therefore be considered in accordance with regulation 6 of the Eligibility Regulations.

42 When considering the eligibility of a family member, local authorities should consider whether the person has acquired a right to reside in their own right, for example a permanent right to reside under regulation 15 of the EEA Regulations (see paragraph 38 above).

Who is a 'family member'?

43 Regulation 7 of the EEA regulations provides that the following persons are treated as the family members of another person (with certain exceptions for students – see below):
(a) the spouse of the person;
(b) the civil partner of the person (part of a registered partnership equivalent to marriage);

(c) a direct descendant of the person, or of the person's spouse or civil partner, who is under the age of 21;
(d) a direct descendant of the person, or of the person's spouse or civil partner, who is over 21 and dependent on the person, or the spouse or civil partner;
(e) an ascendant relative of the person, or of the person's spouse or civil partner, who is dependent on the person or the spouse or civil partner.
(f) a person who is an extended family member and is treated as a family member by virtue of regulation 7(3) of the EEA regulations (see below).

Family members of students

44 Regulation 7(2) of the EEA regulations provides that a person who falls within (c), (d) or (e) above shall not be treated as a family member of a student residing in the UK after the period of 3 months beginning on the date the student is admitted to the UK unless:
(i) in the case of paragraph 43 (c) and (d) above, the person is the dependent child of the student, or of the spouse or civil partner, or
(ii) the student is also a qualified person (for the purposes of regulation 6(1) of the EEA regulations) other than as a student.

Extended family members

45 Broadly, extended family members will be persons who:
(a) do not fall within any of the categories (a) to (e) in paragraph 43 above, and
(b) are either a relative of an EEA national (or of the EEA national's spouse or civil partner) or the partner of an EEA national, and
(c) have been issued with an EEA family permit, a registration certificate or a residence card which is valid and has not been revoked.

Family members' eligibility for housing assistance

Relationship with other rights to reside

46 This section concerns the eligibility of an applicant for housing assistance whose right to reside is derived from his or her status as the family member of an EEA national with a right to reside. In some cases, a family member will have acquired a right to reside in his or her own right. In particular, a person who arrived in the UK as the family member of an EEA national may have subsequently acquired a permanent right of residence under regulation 15 of the EEA Regulations, as outlined in paragraph 38(a)–(f) above. The eligibility for housing assistance of those with a permanent right of residence is discussed at paragraph 39.

Family members who must be habitually resident

47 For family members with a right to reside under regulation 14 of the EEA Regulations, the following categories of persons must be habitually resident in the UK, the Channel Islands, the Isle of Man or the Republic of Ireland in order to be eligible for housing assistance:
a) a person whose right to reside derives from their status as a family member of an EEA national who is a self-sufficient person for the purposes of regulation 6(1)(d) of the EEA regulations;
b) a person whose right to reside derives from their status as a family member of an EEA national who is a student for the purposes of regulation 6(1)(e) of the EEA regulations;

c) a person whose right to reside is dependent on their status as a family member of an EEA national with a permanent right to reside;
d) a person whose right to reside is dependent on their status as a family member who has retained the right of residence.

Family members who are exempt from the habitual residence requirement

48 A person with a right to reside under regulation 14 as a family member of an EEA national who is a worker or a self-employed person for the purposes of regulation 6(1) of the EEA regulations is exempted from the requirement to be habitually resident by regulation 6(2)(d) of the Eligibility Regulations. However, authorities should note that an extended family member (see above) is not counted as a family member for the purposes of regulation 6(2)(d) of the Eligibility Regulations (see regulation 2(3) of the Eligibility Regulations).

Family members of UK nationals exercising rights under the EC Treaty

49 There are some limited cases in which the non-EEA family member of a UK national may have a right to reside under EU law. Under regulation 9 of the EEA Regulations, the family member of a UK national should be treated as an EEA family member where the following conditions are met:
(i) the UK national is residing in an EEA State as a worker or self-employed person, or was so residing before returning to the UK; and
(ii) if the family member of the UK national is his spouse or civil partner, the parties are living together in the EEA State, or had entered into a marriage or civil partnership and were living together in that State before the UK national returned to the UK.

50 Where the family member of a UK national is to be treated as an EEA family member by virtue of regulation 9 of the EEA Regulations, that person is not subject to immigration control, and his or her eligibility for housing assistance should therefore be determined in accordance with regulation 6 of the Eligibility Regulations.

ANNEX 13
Worker Registration Scheme

Introduction

1 On 1 May 2004, 10 new countries acceded to the European Union: Cyprus, Malta, Poland, Lithuania, Estonia, Latvia, Slovenia, Slovakia, Hungary and the Czech Republic.

2 Nationals of all of these countries have the right to move freely among all member states. Nationals of 2 of the Accession countries – Malta and Cyprus – enjoyed full EU Treaty rights from 1 May 2004. These include the right to seek work and take up employment in another Member State.

3 However, under the EU Accession Treaties that apply to the other 8 Accession states ('the A8 Member States'), existing Member States can impose limitations on the rights of nationals of the A8 Member States to access their labour markets (and the associated rights of residence), for a transitional period. (The EU Accession Treaties do not allow existing Member States to restrict access to their labour markets by nationals of Malta or Cyprus.)

4 Under the *Accession (Immigration and Worker Registration) Regulations 2004* (SI 2004/1219) as amended ('the Accession Regulations'), nationals of the A8 Member States (with certain exceptions) are required to register with the Home Office if they work in the UK during the transitional period. While looking for work (or between jobs) their right to reside will be conditional on them being self-sufficient and not imposing an unreasonable burden on the UK social assistance system. These conditions cease to apply once they have worked in the UK continuously for 12 months.

The Accession (Immigration and Worker Registration) Regulations 2004

5 The *Accession (Immigration and Worker Registration) Regulations 2004* provide that, from 1 May 2004, nationals of the A8 Member States can take up employment in the UK provided they are authorised to work for their employer under the Worker Registration scheme.

6 The Accession Regulations also give workers from the A8 Member States the right to reside in the UK. Workers from the A8 Member States who are working lawfully have the same right to equal treatment as other EEA workers while they are working.

The Worker Registration scheme

7 The Worker Registration scheme applies only to nationals of: Poland, Lithuania, Estonia, Latvia, Slovenia, Slovakia, Hungary and the Czech Republic (the A8 Member States). It is a transitional scheme under which the UK Government allows nationals of the A8 Member States access to the UK labour market provided they comply with the registration scheme.

8 The derogation from EC law allowed by the Treaties of Accession does not apply to nationals of existing EEA states. Workers from those states, therefore, have an EC right to work and reside in the UK.

9 The Worker Registration scheme is a transitional measure. The *Accession (Immigration and Worker Registration) Regulations 2004* provide for the registration scheme to operate for up to five years from 1 May 2004 (i.e. until 30 April 2009). The Government reviewed the scheme within its first two years of operation and decided that the scheme will continue beyond 1 May 2006, and may continue throughout the second phase of the transitional arrangements. However, the need to retain the scheme during the whole of the second phase will be kept under review.

10 Nationals of A8 Member States who are self-employed are not required to register. (Under the Accession Treaties, there is no derogation from the right of EU citizens to establish themselves in another Member State (including the UK) as self-employed persons.) However, nationals of A8 Member States who are self-employed cannot take paid employment unless they register (unless they are exempt from registration, see below).

Registration under the scheme

11 Nationals of A8 Member States (except those who are exempt from the scheme, see below) must apply to register with the Home Office as soon as they start work in the UK, and within one month of taking up employment at the very latest. They will be issued with a **worker registration card** and a **worker registration certificate**, authorising them to work for the employer concerned.

12 If they change employers they will have to apply to for a new **registration certificate** authorising them to work for their new employer. They will then be provided with a new certificate for that employer. If they change employer or have a break in employment and resume working for the same employer, they must apply for a new registration certificate.

13 Workers from the A8 Member States have the same right to equal treatment as other EEA workers while they are working.

14 After 12 months' uninterrupted work in the UK, a worker from an A8 Member State will acquire full EU Treaty rights, and will be free from the requirement to register to work. At that stage, they will be able to apply to the Home Office for an EEA residence permit to confirm their right to equal treatment on the same basis as other EEA nationals.

15 The Worker Registration Team issues applicants with a secure **worker registration card** containing:

- Name;
- Date of Birth;
- Nationality;
- Date of issue;
- Unique identification number;
- A facial identifier (photograph);

and

a **certificate** (on secure paper) which states:

- Worker's name;
- Worker's Date of Birth;
- Nationality;
- Worker's unique identification number;
- Name and address (head or main office) of employer;
- Job title;
- Start date;
- Date of issue.

16 The **registration card** is a secure document that provides applicants with a unique identification reference number. This is valid for as long as the applicant requires registration under the scheme.

17 The **registration certificate** is specific to a particular employer. The certificate expires as soon as the person stops working for that employer. If the person changes employers or has a break in employment and resumes working for the same employer, he or she must apply for a new registration certificate.

18 Specimen copies of the registration card and registration certificate are provided at the end of this annex.

12 months' uninterrupted work

19 A worker from an A8 Member State (who is subject to the registration scheme) must not be out of wormore than a total of 30 days in a 12-month period, in order to establish '12 months' uninterrupted work'.

20 If a national of an A8 Member State has worked for a period of less than 12 months when the employment comes to an end, he or she will need to find another job within 30 days to be able to count the first period of work towards accruing a period of 12 months' uninterrupted employment.

21 If the worker's second (or subsequent) employment comes to an end before he or she has accrued a period of 12 months' uninterrupted employment, he or she must ensure that there has been no more than a total of 30 days between all of the periods of employment. If more than 30 days between periods of employment occur before a 12-month period of uninterrupted employment is established, a fresh period of 12 months' uninterrupted employment would need to commence from that point.

22 The Worker Registration scheme is based on continuity of employment – there is no restriction on the number of different jobs (or employers) that a worker can have during a 12-month period of continuous employment.

23 When an A8 Member State worker has worked for 12 months without interruption he or she can apply to the Home Office for an EEA residence permit. Evidence of 12 months' uninterrupted employment would include the worker registration card, registration certificates for each of the jobs they have undertaken, letters from employers and pay slips.

A8 nationals who must register

24 The Worker Registration Scheme applies to nationals of the following accession states: Poland; Lithuania; Estonia; Latvia; Slovenia; Slovakia; Hungary; and the Czech Republic.

25 Nationals of A8 Member States need to apply for a registration certificate under the Worker Registration Scheme, if they are a citizen of one of the countries listed above and they:

- start a new job on or after 1 May 2004;
- have been working in the UK before 1 May 2004 without authorisation or in breach of their immigration conditions;
- are working on a short-term or temporary basis; or
- are a student who is also working.

A8 nationals exempt from registration

26 The following are the categories of nationals of an A8 Member State who are not required to register under the Worker Registration Scheme:

- those working in a self-employed capacity;
- those who have been working with permission in the UK for 12 months or more without interruption;
- those who have been working with permission in the UK for their current employer since before 1 May 2004;
- those who have leave to enter the UK under the *Immigration Act 1971* on 30 April 2004 and their leave was not subject to any condition restricting their employment;
- those who are providing services in the UK on behalf of an employer who is not established in the UK;
- those who are a citizen of the UK, another EEA state (other than an A8 state) or Switzerland;
- those who are a family member (spouse, civil partner, or child under the age of 21 or dependant) of a Swiss or EEA national (other than an A8 national) who is working in the UK;
- those who are a family member (spouse, civil partner or dependant child) of a Swiss or EEA national who is in the UK and is a student, self-employed, retired, or self-sufficient.

Home Office
BUILDING A SAFE, JUST AND TOLERANT SOCIETY

[First Name] [Surname]
[House Number] [Street Name]
[Town]
[County]
[Post Code]

DATE OF ISSUE	:	[Issue Date]
REFERENCE No	:	[URN]
WORK CARD SERIAL No	:	[redacted]
TELEPHONE	:	0114 207 6022

Accession State Worker Registration Scheme

Thank you for your application to register on the Accession State Worker Registration scheme. I am pleased to inform you that we have approved your application and that you are now registered.

Your worker registration card is attached below. If you have any queries about this document, then please contact Work Permits (UK) on the telephone number above.

Accession State Worker Registration Scheme
Registration Card

SURNAME	:	[Surname]
FORENAME(S)	:	[First Name]
DATE OF BIRTH	:	[Date of Birth]
NATIONALITY	:	[Nationality]
REFERENCE No	:	[URN]
DATE OF ISSUE	:	[Issue Date]

Photo Here

This worker registration card should be retained as evidence of your registration with the Accession State Worker Registration Scheme.

PLEASE DO NOT LOSE - REPLACEMENTS MAY NOT BE ISSUED

WORK CARD SERIAL No [redacted]

Home Office
BUILDING A SAFE, JUST AND TOLERANT SOCIETY

Managed Migration
Home Office
PO Box 3468
Sheffield S3 8WA

www.workingintheuk.gov.uk

[First Name] [Surname]
[House Number] [Street]
[Town]
[County]
[Post Code]

Date of Issue: [Issue Date]

ACCESSION STATE WORKER REGISTRATION SCHEME
REGISTRATION CERTIFICATE

Thank you for your application to register on the Accession State Worker Registration Scheme. I am pleased to inform you that we have approved your application.

This is your worker registration certificate. It authorises you to work for the employer specified in this certificate.

This certificate ceases to be valid if you are no longer working for the employer specified in this certificate on the date on which it is issued.

This certificate expires on the date you cease working for the specified employer.

This certificate should be retained with your worker registration card.

Name	: [First Name] [Surname]
Date of Birth	: [Date of Birth]
Nationality	: [Nationality]
Unique Reference Number	: [URN]
Job start date	: [Date Started Employment]
Employer's Name	: [Employer Name]
Employer's Address	: [Unit Number] [Street Name] [Town] [County] [Post Code]

ANNEX 14
MOD Certificate: Certificate of Cessation of Entitlement for Single Personnel to Occupy Service Living Accommodation

	MINISTRY OF DEFENCE	MOD Form 1166 *Introduced 5/97* *Revised 4/03*

CERTIFICATE OF CESSATION OF ENTITLEMENT FOR SINGLE PERSONNEL TO OCCUPY SERVICE LIVING ACCOMMODATION

I certify that	(Name)	
	(Rank & Number)	
Of	(Unit)	
Will cease to be entitled to occupy Service Living Accommodation	(Address)	
From	(Date)	
By reason of		

An application for housing was made to ………………………………Housing

Authority/Housing Association on …………………………… (copy of letter attached)

The person has the following special circumstances ……………………………………

…………………………………………………………………………………………………

Signed	UNIT STAMP
Name	
Position	
Date	

1. This certificate provides evidence of cessation of entitlement to occupy Service Living Accommodation.
2. The certificate should be completed by the unit admin authority and sent at the earliest possible date to the Housing Authority/Association to which application for accommodation has been made, preferably as soon as it is known that entitlement to occupy Service Living Accommodation will cease.
3. Copies of this form are published in the Homelessness Code of Guidance For Local Authorities issued by DCLG, and in guidance issued by the Welsh Assembly and Scottish Executive.

ANNEX 15
Certificate of Cessation of Entitlement to Occupy Service Families Accommodation or Substitute Service Families Accommodate (SFA/SSFA)

MINISTRY OF DEFENCE

MOD Form
Introduced 4/03

CERTIFICATE OF CESSATION OF ENTITLEMENT TO OCCUPY SERVICE FAMILIES ACCOMMODATION OR SUBSTITUTE SERVICE FAMILIES ACCOMMODATION(SFA/SSFA)

I certify that	(Name)	
	(Rank & Number) #	
Of (# Omit if only family involved)	(Unit) #	
Will cease to be entitled to occupy	(Address of SFA or SSFA)	
From	(Date)	

By reason of loss of entitlement to occupy Service Families Accommodation.

An application for housing was made to ....Housing Authority/ Housing Association on .... (copy of letter attached)

The following special circumstances apply ....

....

The household is as follows ....

....

....

Signed	DHE STAMP
Name	
Designation	
Date	

1. **This certificate provides evidence of cessation of entitlement to occupy Service Families Accommodation or Substitute Service Families Accommodation. Authorities should not insist on a Court Order for possession to establish a threat of homelessness.**
2. The certificate should be completed by the Licences Officer of the Defence Housing Executive and sent at the earliest possible date to the Housing Authority/Association to which application for accommodation has been made, preferably as soon as it is known that entitlement to occupy Service Families Accommodation will cease.
3. A period of at least six months notice should normally be allowed so that the appropriate arrangements can be made.
4. Copies of this form are published in the Homelessness Code of Guidance For Local Authorities issued by DCLG, and in guidance issued by the Welsh Assembly and Scottish Executive.

ANNEX 16
Definition of Overcrowding

Under s.324 of the *Housing Act 1985* a dwelling is overcrowded when the number of persons sleeping in the dwelling is such as to contravene –
(a) the standard specified in s.325 (the room standard), or
(b) the standard specified in s.326 (the space standard).

a) The room standard

(1) The room standard is contravened when the number of persons sleeping in a dwelling and the number of rooms available as sleeping accommodation is such that two persons of opposite sexes who are not living together as husband and wife must sleep in the same room.
(2) For this purpose –
  (a) children under the age of ten shall be left out of account, and
  (b) a room is available as sleeping accommodation if it is of a type normally used in the locality either as a bedroom or as a living room.

b) The space standard

(1) The space standard is contravened when the number of persons sleeping in a dwelling is in excess of the permitted number, having regard to the number and floor area of the rooms of the dwelling available as sleeping accommodation.
(2) For this purpose –
  (a) no account shall be taken of a child under the age of one and a child aged one or over but under ten shall be reckoned as one-half of a unit, and
  (b) a room is available as sleeping accommodation if it is of a type normally used in the locality either as a living room or as a bedroom.
(3) The permitted number of persons in relation to a dwelling is whichever is the less of –
  (a) the number specified in Table I in relation to the number of rooms in the dwelling available as sleeping accommodation, and

Table I

Number of rooms	Number of persons
1	2
2	3
3	5
4	7½
5 or more	2 for each room

  (b) the aggregate for all such rooms in the dwelling of the numbers specified in column 2 of Table II in relation to each room of the floor area specified in column 1.

Table II

Floor area of room	Number of persons
110 sq ft or more 90 sq ft or more but less than 110 sq ft 70 sq ft or more but less than 90 sq ft 50 sq ft or more but less than 70 sq ft	2 1½ 1 ½

No account shall be taken for the purposes of either Table of a room having a floor area of less than 50 square feet.

(4) The Secretary of State may by regulations prescribe the manner in which the floor area of a room is to be ascertained for the purposes of this section; and the regulations may provide for the exclusion from computation, or the bringing into computation at a reduced figure, of floor space in a part of the room which is of less than a specified height not exceeding eight feet.

(5) Regulations under subsection (4) shall be made by statutory instrument which shall be subject to annulment in pursuance of a resolution of either House of Parliament.

(6) A certificate of the local housing authority stating the number and floor areas of the rooms in dwelling, and that the floor areas have been ascertained in the prescribed manner, is prima facie evidence for the purposes of legal proceedings of the facts stated in it.

ANNEX 17
Recommended Minimum Standards for Bed and Breakfast Accommodation

The Secretary of State recommends that housing authorities apply the standards set out below as minimum standards in deciding whether Bed and Breakfast accommodation is suitable for an applicant for the purposes of Part 7 of the Housing Act 1996 ('the homelessness leglislation') in the very limited circumstances where an authority may use such accommodation for this purpose.

Space standards for sleeping accommodation

1 *Room sizes where cooking facilities provided in a separate room/kitchen*

Floor Area of Room	*Maximum No of Persons*
Less than 70 sq ft (6.5 m^2)	Nil persons
Not less than 70 sq ft (6.5 m^2)	1 person
Not less than 110 sq ft (10.2 m^2)	2 persons
Not less than 160 sq ft (14.9 m^2)	3 persons
Not less than 210 sq ft (19.6 m^2)	4 persons
Not less than 260 sq ft (24.2 m^2)	5 persons

Room sizes where cooking facilities provided within the room

Floor Area of Room	*Maximum No of Persons*
Less than 110 sq ft (10.2 m^2)	Nil persons
Not less than 110 sq ft (10.2 m^2)	1 persons
Not less than 150 sq ft (13.9 m^2)	2 persons
Not less than 200 sq ft (18.6 m^2)	3 persons
Not less than 250 sq ft (23.2 m^2)	4 persons
Not less than 300 sq ft (27.9 m^2)	5 persons

2 In no case should a room be occupied by more than 5 persons. The standard is to be applied irrespective of the age of the occupants. The sharing of rooms in bed and breakfast accommodation is not desirable, but it is accepted that where accommodation is not self-contained families may find it preferable to share.

3 No persons of the opposite sex who are aged 12 and over should have to share a room unless they are living together as partners and both are above the age of consent or are lawfully married.

4 All rooms must have a minimum floor to ceiling height of at least 7 feet (2.14 metres) over not less than 75% of the room area. Any floor area where the ceiling height is less than 5 feet (1.53 metres) should be disregarded.

5 Separate kitchens, bathrooms, toilets, shower rooms, communal rooms and en-suite rooms are deemed unsuitable for sleeping accommodation.

Installation for heating

6 The premises should have adequate provision for heating. All habitable rooms and baths or shower rooms should be provided with a fixed space-heating appliance. The appliance must be capable of efficiently maintaining the room at a minimum temperature of 18°C when the outside temperature is –1°C. 'Fixed space heating appliance' means fixed gas appliance, fixed electrical appliance or an adequate system of central heating, operable at all times.

Facilities for the storage, preparation and cooking of food and disposal of waste water

7 Wherever practicable, each household should have exclusive use of a full set of kitchen facilities including:

- cooking facilities – a gas or electric cooker with a four-burner hob, oven and grill. In single person lettings, a cooker with a minimum of two burners, oven and grill is permissible. Where the establishment caters for fewer than 6 persons, a small guest house for example, a microwave may be substituted for a gas or electric cooker for periods of stay not exceeding 6 weeks for any homeless household;
- sink and integral drainer – with a constant supply of hot and cold water and properly connected to the drainage system;
- storage cupboard, minimum capacity 0.4 m^3 (400 litres/15 ft^3). This provision is in addition to any base unit cupboards provided below the sink/drainer;
- refrigerator – minimum capacity 0.14 m^3 (140 litres/5 ft^3);
- electrical power sockets – minimum of two double 13 amp sockets situated at worktop height. These are in addition to electrical power sockets provided elsewhere in the letting;
- worktop – minimum surface area 1000 mm x 600 mm.

8 There may be circumstances where the housing authority is satisfied that the provision of kitchen facilities for exclusive use is not practicable or appropriate. These circumstances could, for example, include where a property is very small, no more than two or three letting rooms, or where the overall standard of the property is considered reasonable in all other respects and the costs of provision of exclusive use kitchens would be prohibitive or detrimentally affect the remaining amenity space. In circumstances such as these, the following standards for communal kitchens may be applied.

9 Kitchen facilities may be provided in the ratio of no less than one set for every 10 persons, irrespective of age. Such kitchen facilities should comprise a minimum of shared:

- gas or electric cooker with four burners, oven and grill. Where the establishment caters for fewer than 6 persons, a small guest house for example, a microwave may be substituted for a gas or electric cooker for periods of stay not exceeding 6 weeks for any homeless household;
- sink and integral drainer – with a constant supply of hot and cold water and properly connected to the drainage system;
- storage cupboard, minimum capacity 0.4 m^3 (400 litres/15 ft^3). This provision is in addition to any base unit cupboards provided below the sink/drainer;
- electrical power sockets – minimum of two double 13 amp sockets situated at worktop height. These are in addition to electrical power sockets provided elsewhere in the letting;
- worktop – minimum surface area 1000 mm 600 mm;
- lockable storage cupboards, minimum capacity 0.14 m^3 (140 litres/5 ft^3) for each bedroom whose occupants use the kitchen. In calculating the required provision of storage cupboards, base unit cupboards below sinks/drainers should be discounted.

10 In addition, the following facilities should be provided within each bedroom, or within the total accommodation occupied exclusively by each household:

- worktop – minimum surface area 1000 mm 600 mm;
- refrigerator – minimum capacity 0.14 m^3 (140 litres/5 ft^3);
- storage cupboard – minimum capacity 0.4 m^3 (400 litres/15 ft^3).

11 The kitchen used by management to provide breakfast may be included when calculating the one in ten ratio, unless it is not available, does not meet the conditions above or is deemed unsuitable for use by residents because:

- of the size of the kitchen and the equipment provided in it. In a commercial kitchen some equipment may be dangerous or unsatisfactory for use by residents; or
- the unsatisfactory location of the kitchen in relation to the accommodation it is supposed to serve.

12 In schemes providing a mix of kitchens for shared and exclusive use, one set of kitchen facilities should be provided for every 10 persons sharing. The number of persons who have kitchen facilities provided for their exclusive use should not be included in the calculations. Again, the kitchen used by management to provide breakfast may be included in the one in ten calculation subject to the above conditions.

13 Cooking facilities which are provided should be reasonably located in relation to the room(s) occupied by the person(s) for whom they are provided and in any event not more than one floor distant from these rooms. Please note the exception for smaller establishments described below.

14 In smaller establishments of not more than three storeys and not more than 30 bed spaces, communal cooking facilities may be provided in one area of the premises more than one floor distant from some bedrooms. In such cases, these kitchens must be provided in association with a suitable dining room or dining rooms of adequate size calculated on the basis of 1 m^2 per bed space. This should include one area of at least 15 m^2. Only effective usable space will be considered when calculating the areas for the purpose of this requirement. Dining room facilities should be provided with adequate seating provision.

15 Kitchen facilities should be made available for use 24 hours per day, subject to any representation from the owner/manager, which must be agreed by the receiving and placing authorities.

Toilet and personal washing facilities

16 One internal water closet should be provided for every five persons irrespective of age. The water closet must be within a reasonable distance from its users and not more than one floor distant and, where practicable, a water closet should not be situated within a bathroom. At least 50% of the water closets that are required to be provided should be situated in separate accommodation. The number of persons occupying a bedroom where this facility is provided for their exclusive use should not be included in the calculations.

17 A suitable wash hand basin (minimum dimensions 500 mm 400 mm) with constant hot and cold water supplies, should be provided in every bedroom, except where an en suite bathroom is available, when the wash hand basin may be provided in that bathroom.

18 Each separate water closet compartment and bathroom should be provided with a suitable wash hand basin (minimum dimensions 500 mm x 400 mm), together with constant supplies of hot and cold running water. A tiled splashback (minimum 300 mm high) is to be provided to each wash hand basin.

19 One bath (minimum dimensions 1700 mm 700 mm) or one shower (minimum dimensions 800 mm 800 mm) should be provided for every eight persons, irrespective of age. These facilities must be within a reasonable distance of each user and not more than one floor distant. The number of persons having the exclusive use of a bath or shower should not be included in the calculations.

20 Where the operator chooses to provide showers for the exclusive use of each separate household or the majority of households, a minimum provision of baths, rather than showers will always be required. In such circumstances a minimum of one communal bath should be provided for every 20 persons, irrespective of age, with a minimum of one bath per property. These facilities must be within a reasonable distance of each user and ideally no more than one floor distant.

Other facilities

21 In the case of families with young children, the facilities should include a safe play area(s) that is located away from sleeping accommodation and cooking areas.

Management standards

22 In any B&B accommodation, suitability for the purposes of Part 7 will depend upon the management standards operated within an establishment as well as the adequate provision of basic amenities. The minimum management standards set out below should apply and it is the responsibility of the housing authority to monitor the management of the property.

- Operators are required to ensure the property complies with all relevant statutory and regulatory requirements especially in relation to fire, gas and electrical safety. The supply of gas or electricity to any resident should never be interfered with.
- A clear emergency evacuation plan should be in place setting out action upon hearing the fire alarm, escape routes and safe assembly points. The manager must ensure that each person newly arriving at the premises is told what to do in the event of a fire and about the fire precautions provided.
- Residents should have access to their rooms at all times except when rooms are being cleaned. Provision should be made to accommodate residents at these times.
- Refuse and litter should be cleared from the property and not allowed to accumulate in, or in the curtilage, of the property, except in adequately sized and suitable bulk refuse container(s).
- All communal areas (including, hallways, kitchens, bathrooms/showers, WCs, dining areas, lounges if provided) should be regularly cleaned.
- Appropriate officers of the authority in whose area the premises are situated should have access to inspect the premises as and when they consider necessary, to ensure that the requirements are being complied with. The manager should allow such inspections to take place, if necessary without notice.
- Officers of the health authority, local authority and authorised community workers for the area in which the premises are situated should have access to visit the occupiers of the premises and interview them in private in the room(s) they occupy.
- A manager with adequate day to day responsibility to ensure the good management of the property should be contactable at all times. A notice giving the name, address and telephone number of the manager should be displayed in a readily visible position in the property.
- Procedures should be in place to deal with any complaints relating to harassment on racial, sexual or other discriminatory grounds by either residents or staff.
- There should be a clear complaints procedure for the resolution of disputes between residents and/or staff.
- There should be available within the premises a working telephone available for use by the occupiers and a notice should be displayed by the telephone with information on the address and telephone numbers of: the local Environmental Health Department, Fire Brigade, Gas Company, Electricity Company, Police Station and local doctors.

ANNEX 18

This is not guidance issued by the Secretaries of State.

Procedures for Referrals of Homeless Applicants on the Grounds of Local Connection with Another Local Authority

Guidelines for Local Authorities and Referees

AGREED BY

ASSOCIATION OF LONDON GOVERNMENT (ALG)
CONVENTION OF SCOTTISH LOCAL AUTHORITIES (CoSLA)
LOCAL GOVERNMENT ASSOCIATION (LGA)
WELSH LOCAL GOVERNMENT ASSOCIATION (WLGA)
(*'the local authority associations'*)

INDEX

Guidelines for Local Authorities on Procedures for Referral

1. PURPOSE OF THE GUIDELINES
2. DEFINITIONS
3. CRITERIA FOR NOTIFICATION
4. LOCAL CONNECTION
5. PROCEDURES PRIOR TO MAKING A REFERRAL
6. MAKING THE NOTIFICATION
7. ARRANGEMENTS FOR SECURING ACCOMMODATION
8. RIGHT OF REVIEW
9. PROCEDURE ON REVIEW
10. DISPUTES BETWEEN AUTHORITIES

Guidelines for Invoking the Disputes Procedure

11. DETERMINING DISPUTES
12. ARRANGEMENTS FOR APPOINTING REFEREES
13. PROCEDURES FOR DETERMINING THE DISPUTE
14. ORAL HEARINGS
15. NOTIFICATION OF DETERMINATION
16. COSTS OF DETERMINATION
17. CIRCULATION OF DETERMINATION
18. PAYMENT OF FEES AND COSTS
19. REOPENING A DISPUTE
20. RIGHT OF REVIEW OF REFEREE'S DECISION
21. PROCEDURE ON A REVIEW

Standard Notification Form

Procedures for Referrals of Homeless Applicants on the Grounds of Local Connection with Another Local Authority

Guidelines for Local Authorities on Procedures for Referral

AGREED BY

ASSOCIATION OF LONDON GOVERNMENT (ALG)
CONVENTION OF SCOTTISH LOCAL AUTHORITIES (CoSLA)
LOCAL GOVERNMENT ASSOCIATION (LGA)
WELSH LOCAL GOVERNMENT ASSOCIATION (WLGA)
(*'the local authority associations'*)

This procedure concerns the situation where, under Part 7 of the *Housing Act 1996*, a housing authority is satisfied that a housing applicant is eligible for assistance, homeless and has a priority need for accommodation, is not satisfied that the applicant is homeless intentionally and the authority consider that the conditions for referral of the case to another housing authority are met, and notifies the other housing authority of its opinion. Referrals are discretionary only. Housing authorities are not required to make inquiries as to whether an applicant has a local connection with another district, and where they decide to do so, there is no requirement to refer applicants to another authority, if the conditions for referral are met. Authorities may have a policy about how they may exercise their discretion. However, they cannot decide in advance that a referral will be made in all cases where an applicant who is eligible for assistance, unintentionally homeless and in priority need may have a local connection with another district.

1 PURPOSE OF THE GUIDELINES

1.1 For English and Welsh authorities s.198 of the *Housing Act 1996* provides that:

'(5) The question whether the conditions for referral of a case are satisfied shall be determined by agreement between the notifying authority and the notified authority or, in default of agreement, in accordance with such arrangements as the Secretary of State may direct by order.

(6) An order may direct that the arrangements shall be:

(a) those agreed by any relevant authorities or associations of relevant authorities, or

(b) in default of such agreement, such arrangements as appear to the Secretary of State to be suitable, after consultation with such associations representing relevant authorities, and such other persons, as he thinks appropriate.'

1.2 Subsections 33(4) and (5) of the *Housing (Scotland) Act 1987* make the same provision for Scotland. However, s.8 of the *Homelessness (Scotland) Act 2003* gives Scottish ministers the power to suspend or vary the circumstnaces under which a homeless applicant may be referred by a Scottish local authority to another authority in Scotland. Please note any future orders made will need to be taken into account.

1.3 The ALG, CoSLA, LGA and the WLGA, the local authority associations in England, Scotland and Wales, have agreed guidelines for referrals which they recommend to local housing authorities. Section 198 *Housing Act 1996* and s.33 *Housing (Scotland) Act 1987* lay down the general procedures to be followed where it appears that s.192(2) (England and Wales) or s.31 (Scotland) applies to the applicant and the applicant does not have a local connection with the area of the authority receiving the housing application but does have one with another area in England, Scotland or Wales. There are, however, considerable areas of possible disagreement and dispute in determining whether the conditions of referral are met in any particular case. Although, in the last resort, disagreements can only be resolved by the courts, the associations are anxious to avoid, as far as possible, legal disputes between local authorities. The associations therefore issue these agreed guidelines on the procedures and criteria to be followed, and recommend them for general adoption by all their members. **These Guidelines are without prejudice to the duty of local authorities to treat each case on its merits and to take into account existing and future case law.** Furthermore, these Guidelines only apply to the issues of local connection and whether the conditions for referral are met for the purposes of Part 7 of the *Housing Act 1996* (England and Wales) and s.33 of the *Housing (Scotland) Act 1987.*

1.4 *In Re Betts (1983) the House of Lords considered the application of the referral arrangements agreed between the local authority associations. Their Lordships decided that a rigid application of the arrangements would constitute a fetter on an authority's discretion. The agreement could be taken into account, and applied as a guideline, provided its application to each case is given individual consideration.*

2 DEFINITIONS

2.1 All references in this agreement to an 'applicant' are to be taken as references to a housing applicant to whom s.193 of the *Housing Act 1996* (England and Wales) or s.28 *Housing (Scotland) Act 1987* or s.31 *Housing (Scotland) Act 1987* would apply but for the decision to refer the case to another authority. For the purposes of this agreement the 1996 Act and 1987 (Scotland) Act definitions apply.

2.2 The authority to whom the applicant applies for accommodation or assistance (for the purposes of s.183 *Housing Act 1996* or s.28 *Housing (Scotland) Act 1987*) and which decides to refer the case to another authority is the '*notifying authority*'.

2.3 Where the notifying authority consider that neither the applicant nor any person who might reasonably reside with the applicant, has a local connection with its district but does have one with another local authority district and notifies the other local authority of its opinion, the authority which they notify is known as the '*notified authority*'.

2.4 Section 199 *Housing Act 1996* and s.27 *Housing (Scotland) Act 1987* set out the circumstances when a person may have a 'local connection' with a district. These guidelines provide a framework within which the local connection referral procedures may be applied.

3 CRITERIA FOR NOTIFICATION

3.1 Before a local authority can consider referring an applicant to another local authority it must first be satisfied that the applicant is:

(i) eligible for assistance

(ii) homeless, and
(iii) in priority need,
(iv) not homeless intentionally.

3.2 Before making a referral the notifying authority must be satisfied that the conditions of referral are met. Broadly, the conditions for referral will be met if:

(a) neither the applicant nor any person who might reasonably be expected to reside with the applicant has a local connection with the district of the authority receiving the application,
(b) either the applicant or any person who might reasonably be expected to reside with the applicant has a local connection with the district of another authority in England, Scotland or Wales
(c) neither the applicant nor any person who might reasonably be expected to reside with the applicant would run the risk of domestic violence/domestic abuse (Scotland) or face a probability of other violence in the district of the other authority (Refer to s.198 of the 1996 Act as amended by s.10 subsection (2&3) *Homelessness Act 2002* (England and Wales)). However, there are exceptions to these conditions, for example, where an applicant applies to an English or Welsh authority for assistance and has been provided with NASS support in Scotland
(d) **For Welsh authorities only**, the conditions for referral to another authority will also be met if the applicant was placed in accommodation in the district of the notifying authority by the other authority as a discharge of a duty to secure accommodation under Part 7 of the 1996 Act following an application to the other authority made within the last five years. The period of 5 years is prescribed by the *Homelessness (Wales) Regulations 2000 SI 2000 No.1079.*)

3.3 3.2(a)(b) and (c) above apply to Scottish authorities. 3.2(d) above does not apply in Scotland.

3.4 In deciding whether or not to make a referral authorities should also consider the court judgment in the case of *R v LB Newham ex parte LB Tower Hamlets* (1990). The notifying authority should have regard to any decisions made by the notified authority that may have a bearing on the case in question (e.g. a previous decision that the applicant was intentionally homeless) as well as any other material considerations, which should include the general housing circumstances prevailing in the district of the notifying authority and in the district of the notified authority. The notifying authority should also consider whether it is in the public interest to accept a duty to secure accommodation under s.193(2) (England and Wales)

3.5 Should a local authority wish to accept a duty to secure accommodation for an applicant who does not have a local connection with its district, nothing in this agreement shall prevent the authority from providing such assistance. The decision to make a referral is discretionary and could be challenged if the discretion was considered to have been exercised unreasonably.

3.6 Under s.202 of the 1996 Act, housing applicants in England and Wales have the right to request a review of certain decisions made by the local authority about their application, including a decision to notify another authority under s.198 and a decision that the conditions are met for referral of the case. The equivalent right to review in Scotland is set out in s.4 of the *Housing (Scotland) Act 2001.*

4 LOCAL CONNECTION

4.1 The relevant date for deciding whether or not a local connection has been established is not the date when the application for housing assistance was made but the date of the decision or, if there is a review, the date of the review decision (cf. House of Lords' judgment in *Mohamed v Hammersmith and Fulham London Borough Council 2001*). Moreover, if inquiries prior to a decision have been prolonged, the notifying authority should also consider whether there may have been any material change in circumstances that might affect the question of whether a local connection has been established. A local connection may be established where the following grounds apply, subject to the exceptions outlined in paragraph 4.2:

(i) the applicant or a person who might reasonably be expected to reside with the applicant is, or in the past was, normally resident in the district. It is suggested that a working definition of 'normal residence' should be residence for at least 6 months in the area during the previous 12 months, or for not less than 3 years during the previous 5 year period. The period taken into account should be up to the date of the authority's decision. This should include any periods living in temporary accommodation secured by the authority under s.188 (interim duty pending inquiries);

(ii) the applicant or a person who might reasonably be expected to reside with the applicant is at present employed in the district. The local authority should obtain confirmation from the employer that the person is in employment and that the employment is not of a casual nature;

(iii) the applicant or a person who might reasonably be expected to reside with the applicant has family associations in the district. Family associations normally arise where an applicant or a person who might reasonably be expected to reside with the applicant has parents, adult children or brothers or sisters who have been resident in the district for a period of at least 5 years at the date of the decision, and the applicant indicates a wish to be near them. Only in exceptional circumstances would the residence of relatives other than those listed above be taken to establish a local connection. The residence of dependent children in a different district from their parents would not be residence of their own choice and therefore would not establish a local connection with that district. However, a referral should not be made to another local authority on the grounds of a local connection because of family associations if the applicant objects to those grounds. **NB**: A Scottish authority, when considering the application of this clause, is advised to bear in mind the definition of 'family' in s.83 of the *Housing (Scotland) Act 1987* as amended.

(iv) there are special circumstances which the authority considers establish a local connection with the district. This may be particularly relevant where the applicant has been in prison or hospital and his or her circumstances do not conform to the criteria in (i) – (iii) above. Where, for example, an applicant seeks to return to a district where he or she was brought up or lived for a considerable length of time in the past, there may be grounds for considering that the applicant has a local connection with that district because of special circumstances. An authority must exercise its discretion when considering whether special circumstances apply.

4.2 A notifying authority should not refer an applicant to another authority on grounds of a local connection because of special circumstances without the prior consent of the notified authority. Alternatively, authorities may come to an informal arrangement in such cases on a reciprocal basis, subject to the agreement of the applicants.

4.3 There are certain circumstances where a local connection is not established because of residence or employment in a district. For these purposes:

(i) a person is not employed in a district if he or she is serving in the Regular Armed Forces of the Crown; and

(ii) residence in a district is not of a person's own choice if he or she (or anyone who might reasonably be expected to reside with them) becomes resident there because he or she is serving in the Regular Armed Forces of the Crown or is detained under the authority of any Act of Parliament (e.g. held in prison, or a secure hospital).

4.4 **For Welsh authorities only** the conditions for referral to another authority are met if the applicant was placed in accommodation in the district of the notifying authority by the other authority as a discharge of a duty to secure accommodation under Part 7 of the 1996 Act following an application to the other authority made within the last five years. This is without prejudice to whether or not the applicant may have established a local connection with a particular district.

4.5 **Former asylum seekers (England and Wales).** Broadly, s.199(6) of the 1996 Act (inserted by s.11 of the *Asylum and Immigration (Treatment of Claimants, etc.) Act 2004* ('the 2004 Act')) (England and Wales) provides that a person has a local connection with the district of a local housing authority if that person was provided with accommodation there under s.95 of the *Immigration and Asylum Act 1999* (NASS accommodation). Where a person has been provided with NASS accommodation in more than one area, the local connection is with the area where accommodation was last provided. A local connection with a district by virtue of s.199(6) does not override a local connection by virtue of s.199(1). So, a former asylum seeker who has a local connection with a district because he or she was provided with NASS accommodation there could also have a local connection elsewhere for some other reason, for example, because of employment or family associations.

4.6 **Former asylum seekers (Scotland).** Under s.27(2)(a)(iii) of the *Housing (Scotland) Act 2001*, as inserted by s.7 of the *Homelessness etc (Scotland) Act 2003*, residence in accommodation provided in pursuance of s.95 of the *Immigration and Asylum Act 1999* does not constitute a local connection as it is deemed to be residence which is not of the applicant's own choice. A local connection could be formed for other reasons, such as family association.

4.7 **Former asylum seekers (cross-border arrangements).** If a former asylum seeker who was provided with asylum support in England or Wales seeks homelessness assistance in Scotland the Scottish local authority could refer the application to another area where a local connection is established, if there was no local connection with the authority applied to. However under Scottish legislation, a local connection would not be formed by virtue of residence in accommodation provided in pursuance of s.95 of the *Immigration and Asylum Act 1999.*

4.8 This paragraph explains the position where a former asylum seeker who was provided with asylum support in Scotland seeks homelessness assistance in England or Wales. The provisions of s.11(2) and (3) of the 2004 Act provide that where a local housing authority in England or Wales are satisfied that an applicant is eligible for assistance, unintentionally homeless and in priority need, the s.193 duty to secure accommodation does not apply if the authority are satisfied that the applicant: has been provided with s.95 accommodation in Scotland at any time and does not have a local connection anywhere in England and Wales (within the meaning of s.199(1) of the 1996 Act) or anywhere in Scotland (within the meaning of s.27 of the *Housing (Scotland) Act 1987*). However, the authority may secure that accommodation is available for the applicant for a period giving him a reasonable opportunity of securing accommodation for himself, and provide the applicant (or secure that he is provided with) advice and assistance in any attempts he may make to secure accommodation for himself.

4.9 Subject to paragraphs 4.6 to 4.9 above (former asylum seekers), once the local authority is satisfied that the applicant is eligible, unintentionally homeless, falls within a priority need category, and does not have a local connection with the district, the authority may notify another authority under s.198 *Housing Act 1996* or s.33 *Housing (Scotland) Act 1987*, provided it is satisfied that all the conditions for referral set out in paragraph 3.3 above are met.

4.10 Once the local authority has established that the applicant is eligible, homeless, in a priority need category, not intentionally homeless and does not have any local connection in its own area it may notify another authority under s.198 *Housing Act 1996* or s.33 *Housing (Scotland) Act 1987*, provided it has satisfied itself that a local connection with the notified authority exists and that no member of the household would be at risk of domestic violence or threat of domestic violence in returning to that area. In determining whether or not there is such a risk authorities should have regard, where relevant, to the advice in the Homelessness Code of Guidance.

4.11 The notifying authority must consider that neither the applicant nor any person who might reasonably be expected to reside with the applicant has **any** local connection with its own district but **does** have a local connection with another local authority district in England, Scotland or Wales, in accordance with the criteria and exceptions listed above. The strength of local connection is irrelevant except where an applicant has no local connection with the notifying authority's district but has a local connection with more than one other local authority district. In such a scenario, the notifying authority must weigh up all the relevant factors in deciding to which authority it would be appropriate to refer the applicant.

4.12 Any relevant changes in an applicant's circumstances, e.g. obtaining employment, will need to be taken into account in determining whether the applicant has a local connection. Authorities should always consider whether special circumstances may apply.

5 PROCEDURES PRIOR TO MAKING A REFERRAL

5.1 If an authority considers that the conditions for referral s.198 *Housing Act 1996* or s.33 *Housing (Scotland) Act 1987* are likely to be met in a particular case it should make any necessary enquiries in the area/s where there may be a local connection. This should be undertaken as soon as possible. An authority that is considering making a referral must investigate all the circumstances of the case with the same thoroughness as if it were not considering a referral.

5.2 The notifying authority has a duty under s.200(1)(England and Wales) or s.34 *Housing (Scotland) Act 1987* to ensure that suitable accommodation is available for occupation by the applicant until the question of whether the conditions for referral are met have been decided.

5.3 Under section 184(4) *Housing Act 1996* or s.34 *Housing (Scotland) Act 1987*, if a housing authority notify, or intend to notify another authority that they consider that the conditions for referral of a case are met, the authority must notify the applicant of this decision, and the reasons for it, at the same time. For English and Welsh authorities, under s.184(5) of the 1996 Act, the notice must also inform the applicant of his right, under s.202, to request a review of the decision and that any request must be made within 21 days (or such longer period as the authority allows in writing). Regulations made under s.203 of the 1996 Act set out the procedure to be followed when making a review and the period within which a request for review must be carried out and the decision made. The *Allocation of Housing and Homelessness (Review Procedures) Regulations 1999 (SI 1999 No. 71)* establishes for England and Wales the period within which the review must be carried out and the decision made. For England and Wales s.204 of the 1996 Act gives applicants the right to appeal to the county court on a point of law if dissatisfied with the decision on the review (or the initial decision, if a review decision is not made within the prescribed time limit).

5.4 Scottish local authorities have a duty to review homelessness decisions under s. 35A of the *Housing (Scotland) Act 1987* as amended by s. 4 of the *Housing (Scotland) Act 2001*. This process does not affect the rights of a homeless applicant to seek judicial review or to seek the redress of the Scottish Public Services Ombudsman.

5.5 Once the notifying authority is has decided that the applicant is eligible, unintentionally homeless, and in priority need, there is no provision for the notified authority to challenge the decision other than judicial review in the High Court. The local authority associations' disputes procedure should be used only where there is a disagreement over the question of whether the conditions for referral are met and not for resolving disagreement on any other matter.

6 MAKING THE NOTIFICATION

6.1 All notifications and arrangements concerning an applicant should be made by telephone and then confirmed in writing. A specimen standard notification form is attached, which authorities are advised to use. If telephone contact cannot be made a fax or e-mail should be sent. Where the notified authority accepts the conditions for referral are met, it should not wait for the receipt of written confirmation of notification before making appropriate arrangements to secure accommodation for the applicant and his or her household.

6.2 Each authority should nominate an officer responsible for making decisions about applications notified by another authority. Appropriate arrangements should also be put in place to ensure cover during any absences of the designated officer.

6.3 The notified authority should normally accept the facts of the case relating to residence, employment, family associations etc., as stated by the notifying authority, unless they have clear evidence to the contrary. It is the notifying authority's duty to make inquiries into the circumstances of homelessness with the same degree of care and thoroughness before referring a case to another authority as it would for any other case.

6.4 Local authorities should try to avoid causing undue disruption to the applicant which could arise from the operation of the criteria and procedures set out above. For instance, where it is agreed that the conditions for referral are met two authorities involved could agree, subject to the applicants' consent, to enter into a reciprocal arrangement so as to avoid having to move a household which may already have made arrangements within the notifying authority's area for schooling, medical treatment etc. Such arrangements could involve provision via nominations to other social housing providers such as registered social landlords. Authorities are reminded that there is no requirement to refer applicants to another authority even where it is agreed that the conditions for referral are met.

6.5 Once written confirmation of notification has been received the notified authority should, within 10 days, reply to the notifying authority. If, despite reminders, there is an unreasonable delay by the notified authority in formally responding to the notification, the notifying authority may ask its local authority association to intercede on its behalf.

7 ARRANGEMENTS FOR SECURING ACCOMMODATION

7.1 As soon as the notifying authority has advised the applicant that it intends to notify, or has already notified, another authority that it considers that the conditions for referral are met, the notifying authority has a duty (under s.200 (1) of the 1996 Act) (England and Wales) and s.34 *Housing (Scotland) Act 1987* to secure accommodation until the applicant is informed of the decision whether the conditions for referral are met. During this period, the notifying authority also has a duty (under s.211) (England and Wales) and s.36 of the *Housing (Scotland) Act 1987* to take reasonable steps for the protection of property belonging to the applicant or anyone who might reasonably be expected to reside with the applicant.

7.2.1 When it has been decided whether the conditions for referral are met the notifying authority must inform the applicant of the decision and the reason for it (s.200(2), England and Wales or s.34 of the *Housing (Scotland) Act 1987*). The applicant must also be informed of his right to ask for a review of the decision and that any request must be made within 21 days or such longer period as the authority may allow in writing

7.2.2 If it is decided that the conditions for referral are not met, under s.200(3) England and Wales or s.34(2) of the *Housing (Scotland) Act 1987* the notifying authority will be subject to the s.193 duty (England and Wales) or s.31 of the *Housing (Scotland) Act 1987* and must ensure that suitable accommodation is available for the applicant.

7.2.3 If it is decided that the conditions for referral are met, under s.200(4) or s.34(2) of the *Housing (Scotland) Act 1987*), the notified authority will be subject to the s.193 duty (England and Wales) s.31 of the *Housing (Scotland) Act 1987* and must ensure that suitable accommodation is available for the applicant.

7.3 The local authority associations recommend that once a notified authority has accepted that the conditions of referral are met it shall reimburse the notifying authority for any expenses which may reasonably have been incurred in providing temporary accommodation, including protection of property. If the notifying authority unduly delays advising an authority of its intention to refer an applicant then the notified authority shall only be responsible for expenses incurred after the receipt of notification. In normal circumstances a period of more than 30 working days, commencing from the date when the notifying authority had reason to believe that the applicant may be homeless or threatened with homelessness and commenced inquiries under s.184, (England & Wales), s.28 of the *Housing (Scotland) Act 1987*, should be considered as constituting undue delay.

8 RIGHT OF REVIEW OF REFERRAL DECISIONS (England and Wales)

8.1 Under s.202(1)(c) *Housing Act 1996*, applicants in England and Wales have the right to request a review of any decision by the authority to notify another authority of its opinion that the conditions for referral are met. And, under s.202(1)(d), applicants in England and Wales have the right to request a review of any decision whether the conditions for referral are met. In Scotland (under s.34(3A) and s.35A(2)(b) of the *Housing (Scotland) Act 1987*) as inserted by s.4 of the *Housing Scotland Act 2001* the applicant must be notified that they can request a review of any decision to refer their case to another authority, any determination reached following referral and the time within which this request should be made – the authority should also notify the applicant of advice and assistance available to him in connection with this review. In both cases the request for review will be made to the notifying authority.

9 STATUTORY PROCEDURE ON REVIEW

9.1 **Review procedure for England** – The procedural requirements for a review are set out in the *Allocation of Housing and Homelessness (Review Procedures) Regulations 1999* (SI 1999 No. 71).

9.2 The notifying authority shall notify the applicant:
- (i) that the applicant, or someone acting on the applicant's behalf, may make written representations,
- (ii) of the review procedures

9.3 If the reviewer acting for the notifying authority considers that there is an irregularity in the original decision, or in the manner in which it was made, but is nevertheless minded to make a decision which is against the interests of the applicant, the reviewer shall notify the applicant:
- (i) that the reviewer is so minded, and the reasons why
- (ii) that the applicant, or someone acting on the applicant's behalf, may make further written or oral representations.

9.4 In carrying out a review the reviewer shall:
- (i) consider any representations made by, or on behalf of, the applicant,
- (ii) consider any further written or oral representations made by, or on behalf of, the applicant in response to a notification referred to in paragraph 9.2 (b) above
- (iii) make a decision on the basis of the facts known at the date of the review.

9.5 The applicant should be notified of the decision on a review within: eight weeks from the date on which a request for review was made under s.202(1)(c), ten weeks from the date on which a request for review was made under s.202(1)(d), or such longer period as the applicant may agree in writing.

9.6 **Review procedure for Scotland** – Procedures are set out in s.35A and s.35B of the *Housing (Scotland) Act 1987*. Good practice guidance on the procedures is set out in Chapter 11 of the Code of Guidance on Homelessness.

9.7 **Review Procedure for Wales.** The procedures are set out in *The Allocation of Housing and Homelessness (Review Procedures) Regulations 1999* (SI 1999 No 71).

9.8 Where the decision under review is a joint decision by the notifying housing authority and the notified housing authority s202 (4) requires that the review should be carried out jointly by the two housing authorities.

9.9 The notifying authority shall notify the applicant:
(i) that the applicant, or someone acting on the applicant's behalf, may make written representations,
(ii) of the review procedures

9.10 If the reviewer acting for the notifying authority considers that there is an irregularity in the original decision, or in the manner in which it was made, but is nevertheless minded to make a decision which is against the interests of the applicant, the reviewer shall notify the applicant:
(i) that the reviewer is so minded, and the reasons why
(ii) that the applicant, or someone acting on the applicant's behalf, may make further written and/or oral representations.

9.11 In carrying out a review the reviewer shall:
(i) consider any representations made by, or on behalf of, the applicant,
(ii) consider any further written or oral representations made by, or on behalf of, the applicant in response to a notification referred to in paragraph 9.9 (ii) above
(iii) make a decision on the basis of the facts known at the date of the review.

9.12 The applicant should be notified of the decision on a review within:
(i) eight weeks from the date on which a request for review, where the original decision was made by the housing authority,
(ii) ten weeks from the date on which a request for review was made where the decision was made jointly by two housing authorities
(iii) twelve weeks, where the decision is taken by a person appointed pursuant to the Schedule to the *Homelessness (Decisions on Referrals) Order 1998* (SI 1998 No. 1578).

In all these cases it is open to the reviewer to seek the applicant's agreement to an extension of the proscribed period; any such agreement must be given in writing.

10 DISPUTES BETWEEN AUTHORITIES

10.1 *The Homelessness (Decisions on Referrals (Scotland) Order 1998* and the *Homelessness (Decisions on Referrals) Order 1998* (SI 1998 No.1578) (England and Wales) set out the arrangements for determining whether the conditions for referral are met, should the notifying and the notified authority fail to agree. These arrangements allow the question to be decided either by a person agreed between the two authorities concerned or, in default of such agreement, by a person appointed from a panel established by the LGA.

10.2 Where a notified authority considers the conditions for referral are not met it should write to the notifying authority giving its reasons in full, within 10 days. The letter should contain all the reasons for its opinion, to avoid delaying the appointment of a referee and to minimise any inconvenience for the applicant.

10.3 Where two authorities cannot reach agreement on whether the conditions for referral are met they must seek to agree on a referee who will make the decision. CoSLA and the LGA have jointly established an independent panel of referees for this purpose. A referee should be appointed within 21 days of the notified authority receiving the notification.

10.4 Authorities invoking the disputes procedure should, having first agreed on the proposed referee, establish that he or she is available and willing to accept the case. Each authority is then responsible for providing the referee with such information as he or she requires to reach a decision, making copies of the submission available to the applicant and ensuring prompt payment of fees and expenses. Sections 10–19 (Guidelines for Invoking the Disputes Procedure) set out in greater detail the requirements and timescale for the disputes procedure.

10.5 Authorities invoking the disputes procedure should be bound by the decision of the referee, including the apportionment of fees and expenses, subject to a further decision by a referee where the applicant asks for a review of the initial decision.

10.6 If the authorities are unable to agree on the choice of a referee, they must jointly request that CoSLA (for Scottish authorities) or the LGA (for English or Welsh authorities) appoint a referee on their behalf as outlined in paragraph 10.8 below.

10.7 If a referee has not been appointed within six weeks of the notified authority receiving the referral the notifying authority may request CoSLA or the LGA, as appropriate, to appoint a referee as outlined in paragraph 10.8 below.

10.8 Where two authorities fail to agree on the appointment of a referee CoSLA (if the dispute is between Scottish authorities) or the LGA (if the dispute is between English or Welsh authorities) may appoint a referee from the panel. Where the **notified** authority is Scottish then the local authority association responsible for appointing a referee will be CoSLA, even if the notifying authority is in England or Wales. The LGA will be the responsible association if the notified authority is English or Welsh.

10.9 The local authority associations should only be involved in the direct appointment of referees as a last resort. Under normal circumstances authorities should jointly agree the arrangements between themselves in accordance with the Guidelines for Invoking the Disputes Procedure.

Procedures for Referrals of Homeless Applicants on the Grounds of Local Connection with Another Local Authority Guidelines for Invoking the Disputes Procedure

AGREED BY

ASSOCIATION OF LONDON GOVERNMENT (ALG)
CONVENTION OF SCOTTISH LOCAL AUTHORITIES (CoSLA)
LOCAL GOVERNMENT ASSOCIATION (LGA)
WELSH LOCAL GOVERNMENT ASSOCIATION (WLGA)
(*'the local authority associations'*)

11 DETERMINING DISPUTES

11.1 The local authority associations have been concerned to establish an inexpensive, simple, speedy, fair and consistent way of resolving disputes between authorities arising from the referral of homeless applicants under s.198 *Housing Act 1996* (England and Wales). In Scotland the provisions of s.33 *Housing (Scotland) Act 1987* apply.

11.2 For the purpose of this Disputes procedure, arbitrators are referred to as 'referees'. Referees will not normally be entitled to apply the criteria set out in this agreed procedure without the consent of the local authorities involved in the dispute. Where the issues in the case are evenly balanced, referees may have regard to the wishes of the applicant.

11.3 In determining disputes referees will need to have regard to:

a) for English and Welsh authorities
- Part 7 *Housing Act 1996*
- regulation 6 of the *Homelessness Regulations 1996* (SI 1996 No. 2754) for Wales
- the *Homelessness (Decisions on Referrals) Order 1998* (SI 1998 No. 1578)
- the *Allocation of Housing and Homelessness (Review Procedures) Regulations 1999* (SI 1999 No. 71)
- *Code of Guidance for Local Authorities on Allocation of Accommodation and Homelessness 2003 (Wales)* – currently under review
- *Homelessness Code of Guidance for Local Authorities 2006 (England)*

b) for Scottish authorities
- *Housing (Scotland) Act 1987*
- the *Homelessness (Decisions on Referrals) (Scotland) Order 1998*
- the *Persons subject to Immigration Control (Housing Authority Accommodation and Homelessness) Order 2000* (SI 2000 706)
- *Homelessness etc (Scotland) Act 2003*
- *Code of Guidance on Homelessness: Guidance on legislation, policies and practices to prevent and resolve homelessness 2005 (Scotland)*

c) for all authorities
- the *Procedures for s.198 (Local Connection) Homeless Referrals: Guidelines for Local Authorities and Referees* produced by the local authority associations
- *Asylum and Immigration (Treatment of Claimants, etc.) Act 2004*

11.4 Where there is a cross border dispute between a Scottish authority and an English or Welsh authority then the legislation relevant to the location of the *notified* authority should be applied in determining whether the conditions for referral are met.

11.5 Scottish authorities need to be aware of any orders exercised by s.8 of the *Homelessness (Scotland) Act 2003* that may effect referrals between Scottish authorities in the future.

12 ARRANGEMENTS FOR APPOINTING REFEREES

12.1 Referees will be approached by the authorities in dispute, both of which must agree that the referee should be invited to accept the appointment, to establish whether they are willing and able to act in a particular dispute. The referee should be appointed within 21 days of the notified authority receiving the referral. If the local authorities are unable to agree on the choice of referee they should contact CoSLA or the LGA, as appropriate, in accordance with section 10 of the Guidelines for Local Authorities on Procedures for Referral.

12.2 A referee will be given an initial indication of the reason for the dispute by the relevant authorities or the local authority association. The referee's jurisdiction is limited to the issue of whether the conditions for referral are met.

12.3 A referee must not have any personal interest in the outcome of the dispute and should not accept the appointment if he or she is, or was, employed by, or is a council tax payer in, one of the disputing local authorities, or if he or she has any connection with the applicant.

13 PROCEDURES FOR DETERMINING THE DISPUTE

13.1 The general procedures to be followed by a referee in determining a dispute are outlined in the Schedule to the *Homelessness (Decisions on Referrals) Order 1998* (SI 1998 No. 1578). (England and Wales) and SI 1998 No. 1603 *(Scotland)*. It is recommended that the following, more detailed, procedures are applied to *all* cases.

13.2 Following appointment, the referee shall invite the notifying and notified authorities to submit written representations within a period of *fourteen* working days, specifying the closing date, and requiring them to send copies of their submission to the applicant and to the other authority involved in the dispute. Authorities must have the opportunity to see each other's written statements, and should be allowed a further period of *ten* working days to comment thereon before the referee proceeds to determine the issue. The referee may also invite further written representations from the authorities, if considered necessary.

13.3 The homeless applicant to whom the dispute relates is not a direct party to the dispute but the referee may invite written or oral representations from the applicant, or any other person, which is proper and relevant to the issue. Where the referee invites representations from a person they may be made by another person acting on the person's behalf, whether or not the other person is legally qualified.

13.4 The disputing authorities should make copies of their submissions available to the applicant. The authorities should have the opportunity to comment on any information from the applicant (or any other source) upon which the referee intends to rely in reaching his/her decision.

13.5 Since the applicant's place of abode is in question, and temporary accommodation and property storage charges may be involved, it is important that a decision should be reached as quickly as possible – normally within *a month* of the receipt of the written representations and comments from the notifying and notified authority. This period will commence at the end of the process described in point 13.2. In the last resort, a referee may determine a dispute on the facts before him/her if one authority has, after reminders, failed to present its case without reasonable cause.

14 ORAL HEARINGS

14.1 Where an oral hearing is necessary or more convenient (e.g. where the applicant is illiterate, English is not his/her first language or further information is necessary to resolve issues in dispute), it is suggested that the notifying authority should be invited to present its case first, followed by the notified authority and any other persons whom the referee wishes to hear. The applicant may be invited to provide information on relevant matters. The authorities should then be given a right to reply to earlier submissions.

14.2 The referee's determination must be in writing even when there is an oral hearing. The referee will have to arrange the venue for the hearing and it is suggested that the offices of the notifying authority would often be the most convenient location.

14.3 Where a person has made oral representations the referee may direct either or both authorities to pay reasonable travelling expenses. The notifying and notified authorities will pay their own costs.

15 NOTIFICATION OF DETERMINATION

15.1 The written decision of the referee should set out:

(a) the issue(s) which he has been asked to determine
(b) the findings of fact which are relevant to the question(s) in issue
(c) the decision
(d) the reasons for the decision.

The referee's determination is binding upon the participating local authorities, subject to the applicant's right to ask for a review of the decision under s.202 of the 1996 Act (and possible right of appeal to the county court on a point of law under s.204). The statutory right to review does not apply to Scottish legislation.

16 COSTS OF DETERMINATION

16.1 Referees will be expected to provide their own secretarial services and to obtain their own advice on points of law. The cost of so doing, however, will be costs of the determination and recoverable as such.

17 CIRCULATION OF DETERMINATION

17.1 Referees should send copies of the determination to both disputing authorities and to the LGA. The LGA will circulate copies to other members of the Panel of Referees as an aid to settling future disputes and promoting consistency in decisions.

17.2 The notifying authority should inform the applicant of the outcome promptly.

18 PAYMENT OF FEES AND COSTS[2]

18.1 The local authority associations recommend a flat rate fee of **£500** per determination (including determinations made on a review) which should be paid in full and as speedily as possible after the determination has been received. However, in exceptional cases where a dispute takes a disproportionate time to resolve, a referee may negotiate a higher fee. In addition, the referee may claim the actual cost of any travelling, secretarial or other incidental expenses which s/he has incurred, including any additional costs arising from the right of review or the right of appeal to a county court on a point of law.

18.2 The LGA will determine such additional fees as may be appropriate for any additional work which may subsequently arise should there be a further dispute or appeal after the initial determination has been made or should a referee be party to an appeal, under s.204 *Housing Act 1996*, to the county court on a point of law.

18.3 The referee's fees and expenses, and any third party costs, would normally be recovered from the unsuccessful party to the dispute, although a referee may choose to apportion expenses between the disputing authorities if he considers it warranted. Referees are advised, when issuing invoices to local authorities, to stipulate that payment be made within **28 days**.

19 REOPENING A DISPUTE

19.1 Once a determination on a dispute is made, a referee is not permitted to reopen the case, even though new facts may be presented to him or her, unless a fresh determination is required to rectify an error arising from a mistake or omission.

20 RIGHT OF REVIEW OF REFEREE'S DECISION

20.1 Section 202(1)(d) *Housing Act 1996* gives an applicant the right to request a review of any decision made under these procedures. The right to review does not apply to Scottish legislation.

20.2 If an applicant asks for a review of a referee's decision the notifying and notified authority must, within five working days, appoint another referee ('the reviewer') from the panel. This applies even if the original referee was appointed by the LGA. The reviewer must be a different referee from the referee who made the initial decision. If the two authorities fail to appoint a reviewer within this period then the notifying authority must, within five working days, request the LGA to appoint a reviewer and the LGA must do so within seven days of the request.

20.3 The authorities are required to provide the reviewer with the reasons for the initial decision, and the information on which the decision is based, within five working days of his or her appointment. The two authorities should decide between them who will be responsible for notifying the applicant of the reviewer's decision, once received.

2 This has recently been raised to £1,000.

21 STATUTORY PROCEDURE ON REVIEW

21.1 The procedural requirements for a review are set out in the *Allocation of Housing and Homelessness (Review Procedures) Regulations 1999* (SI 1999 No 71).

21.2 The reviewer is required to:
- (i) notify the applicant that he or she, or someone acting on his or her behalf, may make written representations,
- (ii) notify the applicant of the review procedures, and
- (iii) send copies of the applicant's representations to the two authorities and invite them to respond.

21.3 If the reviewer considers that there is an irregularity in the original decision, or in the manner in which it was made, but is nevertheless minded to make a decision which is against the interests of the applicant, the reviewer shall notify the applicant:
- (a) that the reviewer is so minded and the reasons why, and
- (b) that the applicant, or someone acting on his behalf, may make further written or oral representations.

21.4 In carrying out a review, the reviewer is required to:
- (i) consider any representations made by, or on behalf of, the applicant,
- (ii) consider any responses to (i) above,
- (iii) consider any further written or oral representations made by, or on behalf of, the applicant in response to a notification referred to in paragraph 21.3 (b), and
- (iv) make a decision on the basis of the facts known at the date of the review.

21.5 The applicant should be notified of the decision on a review within twelve weeks from the date on which the request for the review was made, or such longer period as the applicant may agree in writing. The two authorities should be advised in writing of the decision on the review, and the reasons for it, **at least a week before the end of the period** in order to allow them adequate time to notify the applicant. Copies of the decision should also be sent to the LGA.

Procedures for Referrals of Homeless Applicants on the Grounds of Local Connection with Another Local Authority

Standard Notification Form

AGREED BY

ASSOCIATION OF LONDON GOVERNMENT (ALG)
CONVENTION OF SCOTTISH LOCAL AUTHORITIES (CoSLA)
LOCAL GOVERNMENT ASSOCIATION (LGA)
WELSH LOCAL GOVERNMENT ASSOCIATION (WLGA)
(*'the local authority associations'*)

A NOTIFYING AUTHORITY DETAILS

Contact Name ____________________

Authority ____________________

Telephone Number Fax Number ____________

E-mail ____________________

Address for Correspondence ____________________

____

B APPLICANT DETAILS

Name of Main Applicant Date of Birth ____________

Current Address ____________________

____

____

____

____

C FAMILY MEMBERS

Name	Relationship	Date of Birth

D ADDRESS IN LAST 5 YEARS (include dates and type of tenure)

E PRESENT/PREVIOUS EMPLOYMENT DETAILS

Employer Tel No ________________

Address ________________

Contact name Job Title ________________

Previous Employer ________________

Date from Date to ________________

Address ________________

F REASONS FOR HOMELESSNESS

H PRIORITY NEED CATEGORY

I LOCAL CONNECTION DETAILS

J WISHES OF THE APPLICANT(S) (in the context of the referral)

K THE NOTIFYING AUTHORITY CONSIDER THE CONDITIONS FOR REFERRAL ARE MET BECAUSE:

L ANY SUPPLEMENTARY INFORMATION (attach supporting documentation if relevant)

I confirm that, in accordance with s.198 Housing Act 1996, this authority considers that neither the applicant nor any person who might reasonably be expected to reside with the applicant would run the risk of domestic violence or face a probability of other violence in the district of your authority, if this referral is made.

Signed Date ____________________

Index

A2 nationals 3.6–3.71
accession worker card 3.71
worker authorisation 3.68–3.69
A8 nationals 3.60–3.65
derogation 3.61
Worker Registration Scheme, and 3.63–3.65
Accommodation 4.4–4.15
location 4.4, 4.5
meaning 1.63–1.65
nature 4.6–4.15
non-qualifying accommodation 4.10–4.15
settled 4.7–4.9
Accommodation available for accommodation 4.16–4.38
family 4.25–4.33
for whom 4.20
immigration 4.21–4.24
preconditions 4.16–4.19
who is reasonably expected to reside with applicant 4.34–4.38
Accommodation pending decision 10.8–10.28
action on part of authority 10.14
area 10.23
priority need, and 10.10
quality 10.19–10.22
'reason to believe' 10.11
reasonable charges 10.15
security 10.16–10.18
termination 10.24–10.28
Accommodation pending review 10.29–10.42
balancing exercise 10.35, 10.36
fairness, and 10.35
merits of the case 10.37
Administrative law 12.5–12.11
CCSU 12.22
general principles 12.20–12.22
Wednesbury 12.20, 12.21
Advice and assistance 10.85–10.89
duty care of authority, and 10.88
Homelessness Reduction Act 2017 14.31–14.33
Wales 10.89
Advice and information 2.138–2.144, 14.23–14.33
Advisory services 14.23–14.33
Allocation scheme 11.59–11.94
adopters 11.89
anti-social behaviour 11.69–11.72
armed forces 11.90
carers 11.89
categories of reasonable preference 11.62–11.67, 11.74–11.87
children 11.88
choice-based and local lettings 11.93, 11.94
choice-based housing 11.60
considerations 11.68
consultation 11.73
fosterers 11.89
households in or seeking work 11.91
under-occupation 11.92
unlawful allocations 11.61
Allocations 2.168–2.203, 11.1–11.130
applications 2.181, 11.106–11.109
change 2.197
choice policy 2.188
Code of Guidance 2.198

Allocations *continued*
consultation 2.197
co-operation 2.199
criminal offences 2.202
disqualification in England 11.39–11.45
discrimination, and 11.40
reasonable preference, and 11.42
eligibility 2.173–2.177, 11.23–11.53
existing applicants 11.52, 11.53
notification 11.46
re-applications 11.47–11.51
enquiries 11.98–11.102
excluded 2.170–2.172
exemptions 11.19–11.22
information 2.200, 2.201, 11.103–11.105
scheme 11.103–11.105
internal review and challenge 11.110–11.114
meaning 2.169, 11.10–11.22
nominations 11.14–11.18
notification 2.195
persons from abroad 2.174, 2.175
priority 2.189–2.191
priority for homeless peoples 11.5
private registered providers of social housing 11.115–11.130
procedure 2.186, 11.95–11.109
qualification 11.23–11.53
re-application 2.178–2.180
Localism Act 2011 2.180
notification 2.179
registered social landlords 11.115–11.130
regulations 2.187, 2.193
review 2.196
selecting person to be secure or introductory tenant 11.11–11.13
serious unacceptable behaviour in Wales 11.28–11.38
transfer applicants 11.27
unacceptable behaviour 2.176, 2.177, 2.192
Anti-social behaviour
allocations, and 11.69–11.72
Appeal 2.154–2.159
accommodation pending 2.158, 2.159
county court, to *see* County Court, appeals to
Court of Appeal, to 12.188–12.195
powers of court 2.157
time for 2.156
Applications 9.9–9.47
applicant, meaning 9.10, 9.11
capacity 9.19
dependent children 9.17, 9.18
how to apply 9.45
immigrants 9.13–9.16
other authorities, to 9.38–9.44
other family members, by 9.36, 9.37
provision of accommodation on 9.46, 9.47
qualifications 9.13–9.44
renewed 9.22
repeat 9.23–9.35
change of circumstances, and 9.26–9.35
'identical' application 9.28–9.35
who may make 9.25
transfers 9.20, 9.21
who can apply 9.9–9.44
Applications for housing 11.54–11.58
advice and information 11.56, 11.57
consideration of applications 11.55
disclosure of information 11.58
housing register 11.54
Arbitration
local connection, and 7.82–7.88
local connection provisions, and 2.98, 2.99
Article 6, ECHR 12.96–12.99
Article 8, ECHR 12.100–12.102
Article 14, ECHR 12.103–12.105
Associated people
definition 2.27
Asylum and Immigration Appeals Act 1993 1.59–1.61
Asylum seekers 1.82
suitability of accommodation 10.150

Available accommodation
definition 2.22

Bed and breakfast accommodation 10.156, 10.157, 10.161, 10.162
reduction in use 1.108
Bias 12.61–12.63
British citizenship 3.21

Care Act 2014/Social Services and Well-being (Wales) Act 2014 13.7–13.26
assessment of need 13.14
asylum-seekers 13.15–13.21
discharge of duty 13.26
duty to meet needs for care and support 13.9–13.11
eligibility criteria 13.9–13.11
immigrants 13.15–13.21
'ordinary resident' 13.10
power to meet needs 13.12
provision of housing accommodation 13.22–13.25
Central government
definition 2.11
Cessation of occupation *see* Intentional homelessness
Child Abduction and Custody Act 1985 13.97, 13.98
Children Act 1989 13.41–13.65
age of person 13.55, 13.56
assessment of need 13.45
child in need 13.58
children leaving care 13.74–13.80
see also Children leaving care
co-operation between social services and housing authorities 13.66–13.73
DCLG Guidance 13.52, 13.53
general policy 13.44
'looked after child' 13.62
notice to social services authority 13.59
provision of services 13.43
s17 13.41–13.49
s20 13.50–13.65
withdrawal of accommodation 13.47–13.49
Children in social services care 5.30, 5.31
Children leaving care 13.74–13.80
eligible child 13.75
former relevant child 13.77–13.79
relevant child 13.76
Code of Guidance 2.145
Code of Practice 2.146, 14.20–14.22
Collusive arrangements 2.38
intentional homelessness, and 6.149–6.154
Commonwealth citizens with right of abode in UK 3.22
Co-operation between authorities 2.163–2.167
referral 2.166, 2.167
Costs
appeal to county court 12.177–12.180
judicial review 12.138–12.143
County court, appeals to 12.159–12.219
agreement to further review 12.169
ancillary relief 12.218
confidentiality 12.217
costs 12.177–12.180
damages 12.215, 12.216
district judges 12.175, 12.176
extension of time 12.167, 12.168
from what decision 12.162–12.164
further appeal 12.188–12.195
interim relief 12.196–12.202
letter before action 12.170
point of law 12.159–12.161
powers on appeal 12.203–12.214
varying decision 12.203–12.214
procedure 12.159–12.195
reconsideration 12.165
refusal of relief 12.219
response 12.173, 12.174
review 12.165
specimen documents 12.234
supporting documents 12.171–12.172
time for 12.166
Court of Appeal 12.188–12.195

Criminal offences 2.160–2.162, 15.1–15.15
Croatians 3.72–3.78
  worker authorisation 3.74–3.78

Damages
  county court 12.215, 12.216
Definitions 2.11–2.43
Dependency
  meaning 3.53
Dependent children 5.13–5.31
  alternative tests 5.15–5.17
  children in social services care 5.30, 5.31
  dependence on applicant 5.18–5.21, 5.23–5.24
  priority need 5.13–5.31
  reasonably expected to reside 5.27–5.29
  residing with applicant 5.25, 5.26
  separated parents 5.22–5.29
Disability 5.39–5.49
  enquiries, and 9.69, 9.70
Discharge of homelessness duties 10.1–10.225
  accommodation pending decision *see* Accommodation pending decision
  accommodation pending review *see* Accommodation pending review
  advice and assistance 10.85–10.89 *see also* Advice and assistance
  assessment and plan 10.43–10.51
    agreement 10.44, 10.45
    review 10.46
    Wales 10.49–10.51
  contracting out of functions 10.4
  co-operation 10.5–10.7
  duties without priority need 10.79–10.89
  Homelessness Act 2002 10.80–10.83
  initial help duty *see* Initial help duty
  Localism Act 2011 10.84
  threat of homelessness, and 10.52–10.65
    notice bringing duty to end 10.59, 10.60
    reasonable steps 10.56, 10.58
    restricted cases 10.57
    Wales 10.62–10.65
Discrimination
  allocations, and 11.40
Domestic violence/abuse 2.26, 4.89–4.91
Duties to intentionally homeless 2.87–2.90, 10.90–10.107
  acquiescence or participation in act resulting in finding of intentionality 10.100
  local connection referral 10.108
  policies 10.107
  priority need 10.90, 10.91, 10.93
  reasonable opportunity 10.102
  time 10.95–10.106
    circumstances of applicant 10.105
    local circumstances 10.104
  unintentionally homeless in priority need 10.109–10.225 *see also* Duties towards unintentionally homeless in priority need
  Wales 10.92
Duties to those threatened with homelessness 2.64–2.68
Duties towards unintentionally homeless in priority need 10.109–10.225
  added considerations 10.151
  advice and assistance 10.126
  cessation 10.181–10.184
    eligibility 10.182
    loss of accommodation 10.183
    offers 10.184
  discharge by authority 10.135
  discharge through another 10.127–10.134
  England 10.152–10.157
  gypsies 10.176
  Homelessness Reduction Act 2017 ñ England 10.220–10.225
    section 193C 10.221–10.225

Housing Act 1996 s193 10.111–10.219
Housing (Wales) Act 2014 s75 10.111
keeping offers open 10.215–10.217
means of discharge 10.121–10.135
out-of-area placements 10.136–10.144
Part 6 offer 10.189–10.198
'auto-bid', and 10.195
consequences of acceptance 10.197, 10.198
consequences of refusal 10.190
England post- LA 2011 and Wales post H (W) A 2014 10.196
notification 10.192
postponement 10.114–10.120
degrees of suitability 10.119
rent arrears 10.114
private sector accommodation offers 10.199–10.204
assured tenancy 10.200
cessation of duty 10.202
qualifying conditions 10.203
rejection 10.201
restricted cases 10.205–10.219
reasonable refusals 10.212–10.214
re-application 10.219
refusal of suitable offers 10.185–10.188
resources 10.124, 10.125
restricted cases 10.205–10.219
review 10.218
suitability of accommodation 10.145–10.180
adaptations 10.174
asylum-seekers 10.150
bed and breakfast accommodation 10.156, 10.157, 10.161, 10.162
challenges to 10.180
England 10.152–10.157
enquiries 10.178
family 10.170
location 10.173
material considerations 10.163
personal circumstances 10.164–10.169
private rented sector 10.155, 10.160
racial harassment 10.171
security 10.175
separation 10.172
viewing property 10.179
Wales 10.158–10.162
Duties without priority need 2.84–2.86

EEA nationals with right to reside in UK 3.23–3.99
A2 nationals *see* A2 nationals
A8 nationals 3.60–3.65 *see also* A8 nationals
extended right to reside 3.30–3.43
family members 3.52–3.59
dependency 3.53
extended 3.56–3.57
not EEA nationals 3.59
retention of right 3.58
initial right to reside 3.27–3.29
social assistance 3.29
jobseeker 3.31
permanent right to reside 3.44–3.50
length of residence, and 3.47–3.50
workers and self-employed persons who have stopped working 3.45, 3.46
residence documentation 3.51
right to reside 3.24–3.26
self-employer person 3.37–3.39
self-sufficient person 3.40–3.42
student 3.43
TFEU, and 3.23
worker 3.32–3.36
pregnancy, and 3.36
Emergency 5.56–5.61
'other disaster' 5.59
priority need, and 5.56–5.61
Employment
definition 2.42
local connection, and 7.23–7.25

Enforcement 12.1–12.234
administrative law 12.5–12.11
challenge, nature of 12.12–12.15
grounds for challenge
practical classification 12.31–12.94
High Court 12.111, 12.112
Human Rights Act 1998 12.95–12.105 *see also* Human Rights Act 1998
proportionality, and 12.23–12.30
procedural law 12.106–12.233
substantive law 12.5–12.105
ultra vires 12.16–12.19
which court 12.107–12.115
Enquiries 9.48–9.131
accuracy of agreed facts 9.69
adequacy 9.81–9.94
all relevant matters 9.96–9.100
allocations, and 11.98–11.102
ambit of 9.66–9.111
blanket policies 9.109, 9.110
burden of making 9.66
burden of proof 9.75–9.80
conduct of 9.62–9.65
disability, and 9.69, 9.70
doubt 9.122
duty to make 9.49–9.57
failure to make 9.51
fairness 9.112–9.121
financial issues 9.83, 9.84
further 9.123–9.129
interpreters 9.64, 9.65
interview 9.62, 9.63
limits of duty 9.67
local connection 9.56, 9.57
loss of employment 9.111
matters to be put to applicant 9.118, 9.119
medical evidence 9.101–9.108
disclosure 9.102
vulnerability 9.105–9.108
other departments within authority 9.68
preliminary 9.55
reconsideration 9.123–9.129
relevant matters 9.76–9.80
reliance on particular circumstances 9.95–9.100
right to review, and 9.92
size and nature of accommodation 9.78–9.80
successful challenge 9.88–9.94
time-scales 9.130, 9.131
unsuccessful challenge 9.83–9.87
who must make 9.58–9.61
whose circumstances 9.71–9.74
Ex p Awua 1.62–1.65
accommodation, meaning 1.63–1.65

Failure to notify changes 15.11–15.15
False statement 15.3–15.6
allocations 15.6
homelessness 15.5
Family associations
local connection, and 7.26–7.29
Family members
meaning 3.52
Former asylum-seekers
definition 2.43
local connection, and 7.33–7.36

General housing circumstances of area 4.93–4.140
employment 4.130, 4.131
financial conditions 4.121–4.129
legal conditions 4.114–4.120
location 4.101
overcrowding 4.111–4.113
permanence 4.102
physical conditions 4.103–4.110
reasonableness 4.100
type of accommodation 4.132
Gypsies and Travellers
suitability of accommodation 10.176

Habitual residence 3.100–3.105
definition 3.105
question of fact 3.102
requirements 3.101–3.104
Homelessness 2.21–2.29, 4.1–4.146

accommodation *see* Accommodation
accommodation available for occupation *see* Accommodation available for occupation
definition 1.27–1.31, 2.21–2.29, 4.2
general housing circumstance of area 4.93–4.140 *see also* General housing circumstances of area
reasonable to continue to occupy 4.69–4.140 *see also* Reasonable to continue to occupy
restriction on entry or use *see* Restriction on entry or use
rights of occupation *see* Rights of occupation
threatened with 4.141–4.146
Homelessness Act 2002 1.92–1.106
allocations 1.100–1.106
duties 1.94, 1.95
non-priority need applicants 1.96
strategies 1.92, 1.93
Homelessness decisions 9.1–9.198
applications *see* Applications
changes in law 9.3
decision-making 9.4
decisions 9.132–9.148
enquiries *see* Enquiries
gatekeeping 9.135
material to be taken into account 9.136–9.139
notification 9.142–9.148
local connection 9.143
oral explanation 9.148
reasons 9.142
relationship with substantive duty 9.145
restricted cases 9.147
review 9.144
written 9.146
own decision 9.140, 9.141
postponement 9.132–9.134
relationship between decision and review 9.6–9.8
review 9.149–9.161
duties 9.152, 9.153
eligibility 9.151
further 9.160, 9.161
local connection 9.154–9.156
suitability and availability of offers 9.157–9.159
review procedure 9.162–9.198
change of circumstances 9.182
deficiency 9.180
fairness 9.187, 9.188
Human Rights Act 1998 9.174
identity of reviewer 9.165–9.173
irregularity 9.180
local connection reviews 9.172, 9.173
notification of decision 9.194–9.196
reasons 9.198
representations in writing 9.175–9.179
time 9.191–9.193
Homelessness Reduction Act 2017 1.123–1.125
Homelessness review 2.131, 2.132
Homelessness strategies 2.128–2.137, 14.3–14.22
authorities 2.130
functions 14.12
guidance 14.15–14.17
homelessness review 2.131, 2.132
meaning 14.9
partnership 14.13, 14.14
publication 14.19
review of strategy 14.18
reviews 14.6–14.8
guidance 14.7
publication 14.8
strategy 2.133–2.137
Housing Act 1985 Part 3 1.21–1.54
Housing Act 1996 Parts 6 and 7 1.66–1.79
Allocation of housing accommodation by local authorities, and 1.73, 1.74
allocations 1.77, 1.78
ancillary provisions 1.79
Our future homes, and 1.72
policy 1.66–1.75
principal homelessness changes 1.76

Housing and Planning Act 1986 1.55–1.58
Housing authorities
co-operation with social services 13.66–13.73
Housing (Homeless Persons) Act 1977 1.21–1.54
aims 1.22, 1.23
discharge of local authority duty 1.43–1.46
homelessness 1.27–1.31
intentional homelessness 1.35–1.42
judge-made law, and 1.47–1.54
local connection provisions 1.24
national criterion 1.25
priority need 1.32–1.34
Re Puhlhofer 1.47–1.54
Housing (Wales) Act 2014 1.119–1.122
Human Rights Act 1998 12.95–12.105
Article 6, ECHR 12.96–12.99
Article 8, ECHR 12.100–12.102
Article 14, ECHR 12.103–12.105
proportionality, and 12.23–12.30
review procedure, and 9.174

Illegality 12.34–12.51
authority's decision must be reached properly 12.48–12.51
decisions must be based on facts 12.35–12.37
disproportionate weight for relevant considerations 12.40
failure to take into account relevant considerations 12.41, 12.42
fettering discretion 12.44
misdirection of law 12.34
promoting object of legislation 12.43
taking into account irrelevant considerations 12.38, 12.39
unlawful delegation or dictation 12.46, 1247
Immigration 3.1–3.174
applications 9.13–9.16
Asylum and Immigration Appeals Act 1993 3.7
CJEU, and 3.13, 3.14
disqualification, and 3.3–3.5
illegal entrant 3.6
priority need, and 5.8–5.11
right to reside test 3.11–3.13
secondary legislation 3.10
Immigration and asylum
changes since Housing Act 2002 1.109, 1.110
Immigration and Asylum Act 1999 13.27–13.39
asylum support 13.27–13.29
destitution 13.31
exclusions 13.30
facilities for accommodation 13.38
'hard cases' support 13.36, 13.37
residuary power 13.39
temporary support 13.33
Immigration control 3.136–3.109
British citizens and their families 3.90–3.99
British citizenship 3.21
Commonwealth citizens with right of abode in UK 3.22
Croatians *see* Croatians
EEA nationals with right to reside in UK 3.23–3.99 *see also* EEA nationals with right to reside in UK
eligibility-allocations 3.161–3.174
persons not subject to immigration control 3.171, 3.174
persons subject to immigration control 3.170, 3.173
eligibility-homelessness 3.110–3.160
homelessness assistance 3.120–3.150
other members of the household 3.113–3.119
habitual residence 3.100–3.105
homelessness assistance 3.120–3.150
class A 3.122–3.127
class B 3.128–3.130
class C 3.131–3.133
class D 3.134–3.137

class E 3.138–3.142
class F 3.143
class G 3.144
persons not subject to immigration control 3.145, 3.150
Wales 3.148–3.150
interim accommodation 3.151–3.160
exceptions to ineligibility 3.154–3.160
ineligibility 3.151–3.153
persons not subject to 3.17, 3.18–3.99
persons subject to 3.17
primary carers of children in education 3.81–3.89
provision of information 3.106–3.109
self-sufficient families 3.79–3.80
Immigration status
meaning 2.16–2.18
Initial assessment and plan – England 2.61–2.63
Initial help duty 2.69–2.73, 10.66–10.78
additional circumstances 10.70
coming to an end 10.68–10.70
deliberate and unreasonable refusal to co-operate 10.72–10.74
reasonable steps 10.67
refusal of final offer 10.71
Wales 10.75–10.78
duty coming to end 10.77, 10.78
unreasonable failure to co-operate 10.78
Information
definition 2.19, 2.20
Intentional homelessness 1.35–1.42, 2.34–2.38, 6.1–6.154
act causing loss of accommodation 6.47–6.52
act or omission in good faith 2.37
bad faith 6.53, 6.54
breaking chain of causation 6.101–6133
means other than settled accommodation 6.120–6.133
'but for' test 6.90
carelessness v deliberate conduct 6.39–6.46
cause and effect 6.85–6.100
departure from earlier accommodation 6.95, 6.96
cessation of occupation 6.134–6.141
accommodation abroad 6.134, 6.135
notional occupation 6.138–6.141
short-term accommodation 6.136, 6.137
collusive arrangements 2.38, 6.149–6.154
commission of criminal act 6.48–6.50
definition 2.34–2.38
deliberate act or omission 6.26–6.82
good faith 6.27–6.54
ignorance of facts 6.29–6.38
mistake of fact 6.33
elements 2.36
failure to use other remedies 6.64–6.66
findings of acquiescence 6.18–6.20
genuine misapprehension 6.45
in consequence of deliberate act or omission 6.83–6.133
loss of tied accommodation 6.67–6.75
mortgage arrears 6.51
non-acquiescent applicants 6.14–6.17
non-cohabitants 6.23–6.25
nuisance and annoyance 6.60–6.62
original cause 6.86
preconditions 1.41
pregnancy 6.63
pregnant woman, and 1.38, 1.39
principal definition 6.4–6.25
'reasonable to continue to occupy' 6.78–6.82, 6.143–6.148
rent arrears 6.21, 6.22
rent/mortgage arrears 6.56–6.59

Intentional homelessness *continued*
sale of jointly owned home 6.76–6.77
settled accommodation 6.103–6.119 *see also* Settled accommodation
whose conduct 6.10–6.25
burden 6.13
Interpreters
enquiries, and 9,64, 9.65
Irrationality 12.52–12.55
bad faith 12.53–12.55
improper purposes or motives 12.53–12.55
Wednesbury 12.52

Jobseeker
meaning 3.31
Joint Circular 1.17–1.19
aims 1.18
'priority groups' 1.19
Judicial review 12.2, 12.12–12.15, 12.107–12.110, 12.113–12.115, 12.116–12.158
attendance of respondent 12.130
burden of proof 12.137
confidentiality 12.154–12.158
minors 12.158
costs 12.138–12.143
disclosure 12.133, 12.134
duty of care 12.125
form of application 12.122
further appeal 12.135
further stages 12.132
hearing 12.136
illegality 12.22
interim applications 12.129
interim relief 12.144–12.149
orders granted without notice 12.149
irrationality 12.22
letter before claim 12.117
letter of response 12.118
paper applications 12.128
permission 12.119
post-permission response 12.127, 12.131
procedural impropriety 12.22
procedure 12.116–12.143
refusal of relief 12.153
remedies
substantive hearing 12.150
service 12.126
specimen documents 12.234
supporting documents 12.123, 12.124
time 12.120, 12.121

Local Authority Agreement
local connection, and 7.75–7.81
Local connection 2.39–2.43, 7.1–7.92
application of provisions 7.37–7.58
arbitration 7.82–7.88
conditions 7.4–7.6, 7.40–7.52
definition 2.39–2.43
discretion to make enquiries 7.46
dispute between authorities 7.7
duty to make preliminary enquiries 7.59
employment 7.23–7.25
England: additional application of provisions 7.53–7.58
enquiries 9.56, 9.57
erroneous reference 7.62
family associations 7.26–7.29
former asylum-seekers 7.33–7.36
initial help duty 7.68–7.72
Local Authority Agreement 7.75–7.81
meaning 7.9–7.36
membership of evangelical church 7.31
normal residence 7.12–7.15
operation of provisions 7.3–7.7
'other special circumstances' 7.30–7.32
post-resolution procedure 7.89–7.92
private sector offer of accommodation 7.56
procedure on prospective reference 7.59–7.72
relevant time for determining 7.16
residence 7.17–7.22
interim accommodation 7.19
service in armed forces 7.18

resolution of disputes 7.73–7.88
temporary accommodation, and 7.65
threatened homelessness, and 7.38, 7.39
transfer of applicant 7.67
violence, and 7.42, 7.43, 7.48–7.50
Local connection provisions 2.91–2.102
arbitration 2.98, 2.99
charges 2.105
discharge of duty 2.110–2.113
domestic violence 2.94
full duties 2.100–2.102
Homeless Reduction Act 2017 2.115–2.117
interim accommodation 2.96
notification 2.96
out-of-area accommodation 2.106–2.108
passing and retaining responsibility 2.95
restricted cases 2.114
securing accommodation 2.103–2.104
security 2.109
violence 2.94
Local government
definition 2.12–2.15
Local Government Act 2000/ Localism Act 2011 13.87–13.96
specified public authorities 13.94–13.96
'well-being' 13.87–13.93
Local Government Ombudsman 12.220–12.333
enforcement of decisions 12.230
maladministration 12.220–12.223
procedure 12.225–12.233
report 12.227, 12.231
time for complaint 12.225
Local housing authority
definition 2.13
Localism Act 2011 1.113–1.118
allocations 1.118
consultation paper preceding 1.114–1.116
flexible tenancy 1.113
private sector, use of 1.117
Loss of employment
enquiries, and 9.111

Medical evidence
enquiries, and 9.101–9.108
Mental or physical illness 5.39–5.49
Mortgage arrears
intentional homelessness, and 6.51, 6.56–6.59

National Assistance Act 1948 1.7–1.20
division of responsibilities 1.13
duty of local authorities 1.7–1.13
emergencies 1.11
ordinary residence 1.12
Nominations 11.14–11.18
Nuisance and annoyance
intentional homelessness, and 6.60–6.62

Old age 5.38

Policy of provisions 1.1–1.125
Pregnancy
intentional homelessness, and 6.63
priority need 5.12
Preliminary duties 2.44–2.59
accommodation pending decision 2.55–2.59
assessment 2.47–2.50
enquiries 2.47–2.50
notification of decision 2.51–2.54
Principal duties 2.60–2.117
Priority need 1.32–1.34, 2.30–2.33, 5.1–5.81
16 and 17 year olds 5.65–5.70
18 to 30 year old care leavers 5.71, 5.72
additional categories 5.62–5.81
additional classes 2.32
categories 5.2–5.6
definition 2.30–2.33
dependent children 5.13–5.31 *see also* Dependent children
emergency 5.56–5.61
former members of armed forces 5.75, 5.76

Priority need *continued*
immigration 5.8–5.11
persons fleeing violence 5.79, 5.80
pregnancy 5.12
priority groups 5.3
review, and 5.7
vulnerable care leavers 5.73, 5.74
vulnerable former prisoners 5.77, 5.78
vulnerability 5.32–5.55 *see also* Vulnerability
Wales 2.33
young person at risk of exploitation 5.81
Priority need categories 1.89–1.91
Private registered providers of social housing
allocations by 11.115–11.130
Procedural impropriety 12.56–12.94
bias 12.61–12.63
fairness and Article 6 of ECHR 12.56–12.60
legitimate expectation 12.92–12.94
reasons 12.65–12.91 *see also* Reasons
right to be heard 12.64
Protection of property 2.118–2.127, 8.1–8.20
charges and terms 2.122
choice of storage 2.124
danger of loss or damage 8.5–8.8
duty 2.118–2.120
notifications of cessation of responsibility 8.20
personal property 8.11
power 2.121, 8.19
power of entry 2.123, 8.10
review 2.127
scope of duty 8.10–8.18
storage 8.12–8.18
termination 2.125, 2.126
to whom duty owed 8.3, 8.4
when duty owed 8.5–8.9
Public Services Ombudsman for Wales 12.233

Quality and choice: a decent home for all 1.83–1.91
aims 1.84, 1.85
reform proposals 1.86

Racial harassment
suitability of accommodation, and 10.17
Re Puhlhofer 1.47–1.54
Reasons 12.65–12.91
detail 12.70
failure to state 12.80–12.83
proper, intelligible and adequate 12.67
simple 12.71–12.74, 12.77
supplementary 12.86
Reasonable to continue to occupy 2.23–2.27, 4.69–4.140
definition 2.23–2.27
domestic violence/ abuse 2.26, 4.89–4.91
entitlement 4.73
'other violence' 4.92
subjective test 4.78
suitability, and 4.71
threats 4.87
violence 4.83–4.86
residing with applicant 4.88
violence/abuse 2.24, 2.25
violence and abuse 4.82–4.92
Reasonable preference 11.62–11.67, 11.74–11.87
allocations, and 11.62–11.67, 11.74–11.87
judicial intervention 11.84
overcrowding, and 11.86
power to choose 11.75
Registered social landlords
allocations by 11.115–11.130
Relevant authority
meaning 2.14
Rent arrears
intentional homelessness, and 6.21, 6.22, 6.56–6.59
Residence
local connection, and 7.17–7.22
Residence of choice
definition 2.41
Restoration of priority to homeless people 1.80, 1.81
Restriction on entry or use 4.62–4.68

entry prevented 4.62–4.65
moveable structures 4.66–4.68
Review 2.147–2.153
accommodation pending 2.150
notification 2.153
procedure 2.152
request for 2.151
Rights of occupation 4.39–4.61
actual occupation v right to occupy 4.49
civil partners 4.56
cohabitants 4.56
former long leaseholders 4.54
former unprotected tenants and licensees 4.55
non-qualifying persons 4.57–4.59
occupation by enactment or restriction 4.48–4.61
occupation under express or implied licence 4.44–4.47
occupation under interest or order 4.41–4.43
Protection from Eviction Act 1977 4.50
Rent Act protection 4.51
secure/assured protection 4.52
spouses 4.56
tied accommodation 4.46, 4.47, 4.53
timing 4.60, 4.61
use of judicial review, and 1.53

Sale of jointly owned home
intentional homelessness, and 6.76–6.77
Self-employed person
meaning 3.37–3.39
Self-sufficient person
meaning 3.40–3.42
Serious unacceptable behaviour in Wales 11.28–11.38
criminal convictions 11.33
outright order 11.35
suspended or postponed order 11.35–11.37
unacceptable behaviour, meaning 11.30–11.32
Settled accommodation 6.103–6.119
applicant's view 6.112
combination of factors 6.118
fact and degree, question of 6.115–6.117
intentional homelessness, and 6.103–6.119
length of time 6.114
physical conditions 6.106
security 6.107–6.117
temporal conditions 6.107–6.117
Social assistance
meaning 3.29
Social services
co-operation with housing authorities 13.66–13.73
Social services authority
meaning 2.15
Social Services and Well-being (Wales) Act 2014 13.81–13.88
need for care and support 13.82–13.86
Student
meaning 3.43

Temporary accommodation
local connection, and 7.62
Threatened homelessness
local connection, and 7.38, 7.39
Threatened with homelessness 2.64–2.68, 2.74–2.83, 4.141–4.146
definition 2.29
England 2.74–2.80
Wales 2.81–2.83
Tied accommodation 4.46, 4.47, 4.53
loss of
intentional homelessness, and 6.67–6.75

Ultra vires 12.16–12.19
Unacceptable behaviour
meaning 2.177, 11.30–11.32
Unusable accommodation
definition 2.28

Violence
definition 2.25
local connection, and 7.42, 7.43, 7.48–7.50
meaning 4.83–4.86
Violence/abuse 2.24, 2.25

Violence and abuse 4.82–4.92
Voluntary organisations 2.138–2.144
advice and information 2.138–2.144
aid to 14.34–14.40
Vulnerability 5.32–5.55
disability 5.39–5.49
meaning 5.32–5.37
mental or physical illness 5.39–5.49
multiple causes 5.55
old age 5.38
other special reason 5.50–5.54
particular circumstances 5.35
stated reasons, and 5.36

Wasted costs 12.181–12.187
Wednesbury 12.20, 12.21, 12.52
Withholding information 15.7–15.10
allocations 15.10
homelessness 15.9
Worker
meaning 3.32–3.36
Worker authorisation 3.68–3.69, 3.74–3.78
Worker Registration Scheme 3.63–3.65